Personnel

A diagnostic approach

William F. Glueck
The University of Georgia

Personnel

A diagnostic approach

1978   Revised Edition

BUSINESS PUBLICATIONS, INC.   Dallas, Texas   75243
Irwin-Dorsey Limited   Georgetown, Ontario   L7G 4B3

ISBN 0-256-01951-7

Library of Congress Catalog Card No. 77–90482

Printed in the United States of America

1 2 3 4 5 6 7 8 9 0 K 5 4 3 2 1 0 9 8

To the Grandparents I knew
Estelle, Nell, and John

Preface

The first edition of *Personnel: A Diagnostic Approach* was well received. For that, I am most grateful to all the professors who adopted it and students and managers who purchased it.

This book, as was the first edition, is about managing people at work. Experienced managers tell us constantly that their most significant problems at work are "people" problems. These problems are increasing because of a significant influence of government regulation and legislation.

First the book deals with factors in the individual and in the work environment that influence people at work. This portion draws heavily on the most recent and relevant findings of the behavioral sciences and other disciplines. Then the challenges of personnel management are discussed—planning for employment, recruitment, selection, and so on.

This revised edition retains the basic structure and approach of the first edition. But the book has been completely rewritten to improve its readability. Of course, the revision updates all the material in the book.

Each chapter begins with a diagnostic model and an analysis of how the individual and environmental factors affecting the personnel function influence the topic of the chapter. The revision discusses the diagnostic factors more fully, and the organization of the chapter is more directly tied to the model. As in the first edition, the model provides a mechanism for continuity for the book.

We know that the personnel function is not performed the same way in all organizations. Each chapter concludes with recommendations for the most effective way to use personnel in different organizations. The mechanism used to do this is seven model organizations. These seven differ systematically by size (number of employees), complexity of products or services, and volatility of organization (degree to which the products/services change over time). Examples of the model organizations are given from business, government, and hospitals. The reader is invited to focus on the organization where she or he has worked or wants to work. Thus the reader can get an idea of how personnel management is practiced.

This book is based on a larger number of research references. No footnotes clutter the pages however, as the references are listed at the end of each chapter. Where it is possible to summarize these findings, these summaries take the form of propositions in the conclusions and recommendations section.

A new emphasis in this edition is to contrast personnel practices in different sectors of the economy. Whenever personnel practices differ significantly among the private (business), public (government), and third (education, health, nonprofit) sectors, the differences are described. Important differences exist, for example, in labor relations, equal employment opportunities, health and safety, selection, compensation, and other areas.

Another new emphasis in this edition is how various types of managers perform parts of the personnel function. For example, early in each chapter, the roles the personnel manager or personnel specialist and the operating managers play are described, as are the strategic decisions top managers make to lead to personnel effectiveness. This ties in with the new emphasis in Chapter 1 on how personnel relates to top managers' strategic decisions.

The organization of each chapter has been refined so that it is more systematic and, it is hoped, more interesting and easier to follow. Each chapter (and major subparts of longer chapters) begins with vignettes or practical examples of the kinds of problems the chapter is designed to solve. The introduction defines the subject area, explains its purpose, and gives the diagnostic analysis applicable to the chapter.

The chapter summary, conclusions, and recommendations include a summary of the major points, often in the form of propositions and recommendations for use in the seven model organizations.

Another emphasis of this book is cost/benefits analysis of the personnel function. In each personnel area, an attempt has been made to try to evaluate its usefulness in terms of cost and benefits to the employer. Since personnel must compete for resources against requests for new machinery, more advertising, and new buildings, the expenditures and investments in the organization's people must be justified.

It is important to remember that the *way Americans deal* with personnel problems is not the only way. We have important economic, cultural, and social relations around the world. The realization that there are other ways comes when the American way is contrasted with other relevant examples. Throughout this book, this contrast is made primarily with one country, Canada. This country was chosen for several reasons: Canada is our neighbor and shares many things with us; but there are differences as well; and Canada is our largest trading partner. In 1976, we exported about $27 billion to each other. Yet the typical U.S. resident knows less about Canadian ways than German ways. We can learn from each other's laws and practices, I believe, since in some ways, Canadian personnel practices are more advanced than those in the United States, though in other ways the opposite is true.

I have tried very hard to put emphasis on the most significant and relevant topics in personnel today, including equal employment opportunity, health and safety, compensation and benefits (including pensions), and career development.

Some new topics include: personnel specialization and professionalization, including ASPA's Accreditation Program (Chapter 1); better integration of the organizational behavior and environmental materials into the diagnostic personnel model (Chapter 2); and improved discussion of the labor force data (Chapter 3). Employment planning has been divided into two chapters (4 and 5); the section on job analysis and job specifications has been enlarged and improved (Chapter 4), and the section on working conditions including 4-day weeks and flexitime has been significantly increased (Chapter 5).

An appendix to the recruiting chapter (Chapter 6) develops a strategy for the reader on how to find a job, and one to the selection chapter (Chapter 7) describes effective interviewing techniques. The latter chapter combines selection techniques for all employees, including managerial and professional. The performance evaluation chapter (Chapter 10) integrates evaluation of all employees, including managers, and has been reorganized with the positive and negative research of formal evaluation carefully reviewed. Chapters 11 and 12 have a greatly enlarged section on evaluation of training and development.

New topics or topics significantly increased in the management development chapter include organizational development, transactional analysis, and behavioral modeling training.

Compensation has been split into two chapters and completely reorganized. The coverage is more thorough on all aspects, especially pay surveys and compensation issues such as salaries for everyone, pay secrecy, security in pay, and size of pay raises (Chapters 13 and 14). The pension chapter is heavily revised to include current questions such as the solvency of social security, ERISA, and ERISA's impact (Chapter 16). The health and safety chapter has been completely rewritten and careful attention has been given to the current problems in Workers' Compensation and OSHA (Chapter 17). The EEO-Human Rights chapter (18) has been completely redone. This chapter provides a complete summary of the legal status of EEO-HR, as well as effective programs to deal with EEO problems. The labor chapter (Chapter 19) now includes current changes in the law and regulations of collective bargaining in all three sectors in the United States and Canada.

In sum, the book has undergone a significant revision, keeping the structure and approach of the first edition, but thoroughly updating all the material and selectively increasing the coverage of the most crucial issues in personnel today. In addition, more pages are devoted to cases and exercises to provide a simulated laboratory experience in which the constructs discussed can be applied. Most of the cases in the text are new. A new feature is the addition of incident cases, role playing exercises, and field exercises.

Another book published by Business Publications, Inc., that can expand your understanding of personnel is William F. Glueck, *Cases and Exercises in Personnel,* rev. ed. (1978). This book is composed entirely of cases, incident cases, role playing exercises, in-basket exercises, and experimental and field exercises.

This book has been written with the purpose of informing and exciting you about the importance and challenges of personnel. I hope it has achieved its purpose.

ACKNOWLEDGMENTS

A book is always the product of many people. As the dedication page indicates, I want to acknowledge the love and learning I received from the grandparents I knew.

But there are several additional people I wish to thank for their help on the book. A number of persons helped revise this book. The reviewers were helpful. They included Thomas H. Stone, University of Iowa; Ken Van Voorhis, University of South Florida; M. Gene Newport, University of Alabama–Birmingham; James L. Gibson, University of Kentucky; John A. Belt, Wichita State University; Cary D. Thorp, Jr., University of Nebraska; Herbert Heneman, Jr., University of Minnesota; David W. Belcher, San Diego State University; Walter Newsom, Mississippi State University; Jerry Wall, Western Illinois University; Jerry Geisler, Eastern Illinois University; and Harish Jain, McMaster University.

Others who were helpful include many who have adopted and used the first edition. They are too many to mention and they know who they are. Several who were especially helpful include Thomas Patten, Michigan State University, and Thomas Guteridge, SUNY–Buffalo.

I also wish to thank those giving me the permission to reprint their cases and exercises in this book: Richard Calhoon, University of North Carolina–Chapel Hill; Danny Worsell, University of Southwestern Louisiana; Donald White, University of Arkansas; William Vroman, University of Baltimore; Ernest Gurmar and Roland Cousins, University of Southwestern Louisiana; and Thomas Wheeler, University of Virginia.

My colleagues at the University of Georgia contributed ideas and useful criticism. Especially helpful were James Ledvinka, who helped greatly in the EEO area; James Lahiff, who helped in selection; and Robert Finn and Robert Gatewood who helped in a number of areas. I also wish to thank Cynthia Martin, my graduate assistant during the period of the revision, and my administrative assistant, Jean Miller.

I am most grateful for the very supportive climate at The University of Georgia. This is due to the efforts of Richard Huseman, Head, Department of Management and Dean William Flewellen. They have helped me in more ways than they realize.

Finally, I wish to thank my wife Nancy and children: Melissa, David, Lisa, and Bill for their patience, understanding and motivation.

January 1978   William F. Glueck

Contents

taining inventory systems. Problems with skills inventories. Work schedules and supply of employees: *Shift work. Compressed work weeks. Flexible hours (flexitime).* Action decisions in employment planning: *Analyzing the composition of the work force. Action decisions with no variance in supply and demand. Action decisions with a shortage of employees. Action decisions in surplus conditions.* Computers and cost/benefit analysis in employment planning. *Employment planning systems for model organizations.*

A diagnostic approach to attraction and recruitment: *External influences.* Interactions of the applicant / recruit and the organization: *The organization's view of recruiting. The potential employee's view of recruiting.* Who does the recruiting? Sources of recruits. Methods of recruiting: *Media advertisements. Use of recruiters. Computer matching services. Special-event recruiting. Summer internships.* College recruiting: *The college recruiting process. The decision to sign up for an interview. The job-choice decision. The effective recruiter.* Cost / benefit analysis of recruiting. Appendix: How to get a job.

A diagnostic approach to the selection process: *Environmental circumstances influencing selection.* Selection criteria: *Formal education. Experience. Physical characteristics. Personal characteristics and personality type. Whom you know.* The selection process: *Step 1: Preliminary screening interview. Step 2: Completion of application blank/ biodata form. Step 3: Employment interview. Step 4: Employment tests. Step 5: Reference checks and recommendation letters. Step 6: Physical examinations.* Selection of managers: *Assessment centers.* The selection decision. Cost / benefit analysis for the selection decision. Appendix: How to conduct effective interviews.

A diagnostic approach to orientation. The purposes of orientation. Who orients employees? How orientation programs work. Orienting management trainees: *Formal management training programs.* Assignment, placement, and orientation follow-up. Cost / benefit analysis of orientation programs.

Careers and career development defined. A diagnostic approach to career development. Career development: Pro and con. Who is involved in career planning and development? Career planning by individuals: *Phases in career planning. Preparation for one's own business. Midlife career change.* Career development by organizations. Career development counseling.

Executive perks. Bonuses. Stock options, performance shares, and book-value devices. Executive compensation in Canada. Executive compensation policy. Compensation administration issues: *Pay secrecy or openness. Security in pay. Pay raises.*

PART SIX
SAFETY, EQUAL EMPLOYMENT OPPORTUNITY, AND
LABOR RELATIONS 549

rights programs. Mandated actions in EEO–affirmative action programs. Cost / benefit analysis of EEO–affirmative action programs.

19. LABOR RELATIONS AND GROUP REPRESENTATION 635

A diagnostic approach to labor relations and collective bargaining. Conceptual frameworks for labor relations. The psychology of labor-management relations: *Unionized employees. Employees not presently unionized. Union officials and labor relations executives. A managers' union? Government officials and others.* Unions in the United States: *The local union and labor relations.* Unions and labor relations in Canada. U.S. labor laws and regulations: *The private sector: Union organizing law. Other private-sector labor relations laws. The third sector. The public sector. State labor relations laws.* Labor relations law in Canada. Union organizing: *The organizing campaign.* Negotiating contracts with unions: *Preparations for contract negotiations. Contract issues. The structure of negotiations. Negotiating and bargaining approaches. Agreeing upon, ratifying, and formalizing the contract.* Impasses in collective bargaining: *Conciliation and mediation. Strikes and lockouts. Arbitration.* Group representation and grievances: *The grievance-processing system. Grievances in the public and third sectors. Grievances in nonunionized enterprises. Reducing grievances and improving the process.*

PART SEVEN
DISCIPLINE, CONTROL, AND EVALUATION 697

20. DISCIPLINE AND THE DIFFICULT EMPLOYEE 699

A diagnostic approach to discipline. Categories of difficult employees: *Category 1: The ineffective employee. Category 2: Alcoholic and addicted employees. Category 3: Participants in theft, crime, and illegal acts. Category 4: The rule violators. Are certain types of employees likely to be difficult?* The discipline process. Philosophies of discipline. Disciplinary methods. Administration of discipline: *Hierarchical discipline systems. Other discipline and appeal systems.*

21. EVALUATION OF THE PERSONNEL FUNCTION AND PERSONNEL'S FUTURE. 731

A diagnostic approach to evaluation. Personnel reports and records. Personnel research. Approaches to evaluation of the personnel process. Evaluation by checklist or copying. Statistical approaches to evaluation: *Evaluation of turnover. Evaluation of absenteeism. Evaluation of complaints and grievances. Evaluation of other indicators. Evaluation using attitude and opinion surveys. Statistical analyses of personnel department operations.* Compliance methods of evaluation: *Evaluation of personnel using management by objectives.* The new personnel manager and personnel's future.

CASES AND EXERCISES 759

I. Cases 761

Introduction

Personnel is that aspect of management which is concerned with the effective management of people at work. Personnel examines what is, can be, or should be done to make people both more productive and more satisfied with their working lives.

This book has been written for all those interested in personnel: employees, supervisors, managers, and other administrators. Its goal is to help develop more effective managers and staff specialists who work directly in people management functions. Their function is called personnel, employee relations, or human resources management.

Part One consists of three chapters. Chapter 1 is an introduction to personnel. The diagnostic approach to personnel is introduced in Chapter 2, which also reviews what is generally known about people and how this knowledge affects their effectiveness at work. The ways managers use knowledge of environmental factors such as the work setting, government regulations, and union restrictions to influence the performance of people at work are discussed in Chapter 3.

An introduction to personnel

CHAPTER OBJECTIVES

■ To indicate what personnel is and why it is worth studying.

■ To show that personnel work is performed by operating managers, personnel specialists, and sometimes both working together.

■ To introduce the world of the personnel specialist and the personnel department.

■ To detail how this book approaches personnel management.

CHAPTER OUTLINE

For any enterprise to operate effectively, it must have money, materials, supplies, equipment, ideas about the services or products to offer those who might use its outputs, and people (the human resource) to run the enterprise. The effective management of people at work—the function of personnel—is the subject of this book.

The human resource is the most important resource in the enterprise, since people make the decisions concerning all other organizational resources. People operate the machines, borrow the money, and come up with the ideas which give the enterprise its purpose.

In spite of its importance, however, the personnel function has been misunderstood, undermanaged, or mismanaged in many enterprises. The material in this book, supplemented with practical experience, should make the task of managing people at work easier and should produce better results.

In this book, "personnel" is the term used for the personnel or people function of an organization. Some enterprises call this function manpower management, human resources management, or employee relations or use other terms which are virtually the same as personnel. For simplicity's sake, only the term "personnel" will be used here.

> DEFINITION
> Personnel is that function of all enterprises which provides for effective utilization of human resources to achieve both the objectives of the enterprise and the satisfaction and development of the employees.

Personnel consists of numerous activities, including:

- Employee planning.
- Employee recruitment, selection, and orientation.
- Career development and counseling, performance evaluation, and training and development.
- Compensation and protection.
- Labor relations.
- Equal employment opportunity programs.
- Discipline, control, and evaluation of the personnel function.

These activities are the subjects of the various chapters in the book and appear as factors in the diagnostic model of the personnel function which is employed throughout. (This model is described in Chapters 2 and 3.)

Three things should be stressed about personnel at the outset. One is that effective personnel management is *future* oriented. It is concerned with helping an enterprise achieve its objectives in the future by providing for competent, well-motivated employees. A second is that effective personnel management is *action* oriented. Personnel is not focused on record keeping, written procedures, or rules; rather, it emphasizes the solution of employment problems to help achieve organizational objectives and facilitate employee development and satisfaction. Third, whenever possible personnel treats each employee as an *individual* and offers the services and programs to meet his or her needs. McDonald's, the fast-food chain, has gone so far as to give its chief personnel executive the title Vice President of Individuality.

PERSONNEL AND ORGANIZATIONAL EFFECTIVENESS

Personnel activities can help in many ways to ensure that the enterprise will survive and prosper. The following case example illustrates how oversight of the personnel function can detract from the effectiveness of the enterprise.

John Byers is the president of a firm with 225 employees, called Services Unlimited, which offers maintenance and repair services to enterprises in its area on a contract or fee basis. The firm is reasonably successful.

John, who is mechanically inclined, is a registered professional engineer in the state of Illinois. He graduated with honors in mechanical engineering from Purdue University ten years ago. He worked for a similar firm in Chicago, then started his own service company there.

Helen Brooks is in charge of financial and accounting activities, and Ed Webber contacts the accounts and sells SU's services. John handles purchasing and oversees the operations of the equipment himself, but whenever he is working on an important mechanical problem or bidding a job he is likely to be interrupted. It may be a dispute between supervisor and worker; or someone quits; or an employee wants a raise or is dissatisfied with the holiday schedule.

It should be fairly obvious that John has organized to take care of his money, marketing, and machinery problems, but he is disinclined to deal with people problems. Yet a closer analysis of his firm would show that these problems are limiting his growth and his satisfaction with SU. What John needs is some help on personnel management.

Successful firms recognize that the human resource deserves attention because it is a significant factor in top management's strategic decisions, which guide the organization in its future operations. The human resource does the work and creates the ideas that allow the enterprise to survive. Even the most capital-intensive enterprises need people to run them.

Managers analyze the objectives, examine the environment for opportunities and threats, evaluate the strengths and weaknesses of the organization, and make strategic decisions based on these analyses.[1] Personnel considerations are a significant part of these decisions in several ways. For one thing, the people resource limits or enhances the strengths and weaknesses of the enterprise: A construction firm with too few engineers could not get the contract it seeks, for example. Current changes in the environment often are related to human resources, such as shifts in the composition, education, and work attitudes of employees; demands for more liberalized work organizations; and increased expectations of what the personnel function should provide.[2]

One problem top management has in making strategic planning decisions regarding people is that all other resources are evaluated in terms of money. At present, people are not. There has been a movement toward human resource accounting which would place dollar values on the human assets of the enterprise. Until now, however, it has been talked about by professors but rarely implemented.[3]

The contributions of the personnel function to organizational effectiveness are reflected in the objectives pursued by personnel specialists and departments:

- To provide the enterprise with well-trained and well-motivated employees.[4]
- To use the work force efficiently and effectively.[5]
- To increase to the fullest the employee's job satisfaction and self-actualization.
- To develop and maintain a quality of work life which makes employment in the enterprise a desirable personal and social situation.[6]

The impact of personnel on organizational effectiveness can be illustrated further by three more examples:

Managers in the coal mining business must deal with the United Mine Workers. Internal union problems in 1977, when the union split over election of its president, spilled over into the workplace. This limited management's ability to increase coal output.

Eaton Corporation had a problem with its productivity rate which made it less competitive. One way it solved this problem was by placing all employees on salaries.

To be competitive and survive in a labor-intensive industry, the enterprise must find the lowest cost labor it can. For example, recently Zenith Corporation laid off 25 percent of its employees to move part of its production to Taiwan and Mexico. Zenith's management claimed they had to do this to survive.

Thus it can be said that personnel activities are essential for the survival of an organization. All enterprises engage in personnel work because it provides the necessary human resources. In addition, however, organizations will survive and prosper to the extent that they include personnel inputs in their strategic decisions and implement these decisions with effective personnel policies and programs.

WHO PERFORMS PERSONNEL ACTIVITIES?

In most organizations two groups perform personnel activities: personnel managers and specialists, and operating managers. The pattern performing in personnel duties has changed over time. In all organizations, operating managers (supervisors, department heads, vice presidents) are involved in personnel, since they are responsible for effective utilization of *all* the resources at their disposal. The human resource is a very special kind of resource; if improperly managed, its effectiveness declines more quickly than with other resources. And in all but the most capital-intensive enterprises, the people investment has more effect on organizational effectiveness than other resources, such as money, materials, and equipment.

Therefore, operating managers must spend some of their time as managers of people. In the same way an operating manager is personally responsible if a machine breaks down and production drops, he or she must see to the training, performance, and satisfaction of employees. Studies of how managers use their time indicate that they spend much of their day with other people. Supervisors spend a majority of their time with subordinates.[7] Middle managers spend most of their time with people but less time with employees than supervisors do,[8] and top managers spend less time with employees (about 20 percent) than middle managers do.[9]

In smaller organizations, only operating managers are involved in personnel work. They have many responsibilities: scheduling work, supervising equipment maintenance, and doing personnel work such as hiring and paying people. As the organization increases in size, the operating manager's work is divided up and some of it becomes specialized. Personnel is one such function. Usually the manager of a unit first assigns an assistant to coordinate certain personnel matters. Personnel specialists are employed in enterprises with about 100–150 employees, and a personnel department is created when the number of employees reaches 200–500, depending on the nature of the enterprise.[10]

The interaction of operating and personnel managers

With two managers—operating managers and personnel specialists—making personnel decisions, there is frequent conflict. This is partly because operating and personnel managers differ on who has authority for what decisions." Exhibit 1–1 indicates how one survey group of 1,400 personnel executives saw their relationships with their superiors, some of whom are in personnel, others in operating positions.

In addition to role conflict, there may be systemic differences between operating and personnel managers. They have different orientations, called line and staff, which have different objectives.[12]

John and Mary Miner argue that operating and personnel managers also have different motivations, if not personalities. They sent questionnaires to about 425 personnel and operating managers. Measured by the Miner sentence completion test, personnel managers are less assertive, less competitive, less interested in administrative detail, and have less positive attitudes toward authority than operating managers do.[13]

The conflict between personnel people and operating managers is most manifest where the decisions must be joint efforts, as on such issues as discipline, physical working conditions, termination, transfer, promotion,

EXHIBIT 1–1
Working relationships of personnel executives with superiors

Industry	Good	Neutral (superiors let them do their jobs)	Minor conflict	Major Problem
Manufacturing (under 500 employees)	70.8%	17.7%	8.6%	2.9%
Manufacturing (500–999)	78.5	12.3	8.5	0.7
Manufacturing (1,000–4,999)	65.9	19.3	11.9	2.9
Manufacturing (over 5,000)	65.2	17.4	13.0	4.4
Research and development	69.2	30.8	—	—
Public utilities	74.2	9.7	9.7	6.4
Hospitals	82.2	11.9	2.0	3.9
Retail stores	63.6	18.2	13.6	4.6
Banks	70.6	20.6	4.9	3.9
Insurance companies	65.3	21.8	11.9	1.0
Transportation and distribution	87.4	4.2	4.2	4.2
Government agencies	67.5	20.0	7.5	5.0
Education	70.6	17.6	11.8	—
Nonprofit organizations	63.0	18.5	11.1	7.4
Other.......................................	69.7	18.9	8.8	2.6

Source: *The Personnel Executive's Job* (Englewood Cliffs, N.J.: Prentice-Hall/ASPA, 1977).

and employment planning. Research by H. White and R. Boynton indicates which activities operating and personnel managers thought personnel departments should handle. Both groups tended to agree on the amount of advice, policy, service, and control personnel should offer. They differed on how much authority personnel should have over job design, labor relations, organization planning, and certain rewards, such as bonuses and promotions.[14] (See Exhibit 1–2).

One way to work out actual or potential conflict so that the employee is not caught in the middle is to try to assign the responsibility for some personnel decisions exclusively to operating managers and for others exclusively to personnel specialists. Some observers feel that this is what is happening, and personnel is gaining more power at the expense of the operating managers.[15] Others feel the trend is dysfunctional. Herbert Heneman put it bluntly when he described how to ease this problem in a speech at the American Society of Personnel Administrators (ASPA) 25th anniversary meeting:

We [personnel executives] need to push more of the personnel function back into operating management where it belongs, because

That's the most important part of *his* job whether he knows it or not—the key to his success or failure—and the success or failure of his organization.

We, as *professionals*, need to have the guts to *tell* operating management how they *must* accept this challenge. It's like the doctor-patient relationship—we're the doctor, and the boss is our patient in personnel.[16]

Another approach is to train both sets of managers in how to get along together and how to make joint decisions better. This training is more effec-

EXHIBIT 1–2

Personnel activities wanted in personnel departments by 27 personnel executives (E) and 55 operating managers (M)

| | Activities | | | | | | | | | | | |
| | Policy | | Advice | | Service | | Control | | None | | Rank | |
Functions	E	M	E	M	E	M	E	M	E	M	E	M
Collective bargaining	30	44	30	29	22	35	11	25	44	25	26	26
Civil rights	56	60	52	60	22	38	30	36	4	2	12	6
Complaints and grievances	37	51	68	69	52	51	26	27	4	0	9	5
Counseling	37	40	37	69	48	55	19	27	4	0	23	9
Discipline	41	49	57	71	33	27	4	29	11	6	24	15
Employee communications	37	44	52	51	59	60	19	27	7	2	11	14
Fringe benefits	52	71	44	44	67	66	56	44	0	2	1	1
Health and safety	41	60	52	56	44	58	22	40	7	2	10	2
Hiring decisions	30	44	59	69	30	47	30	33	4	6	16	7
Incentive programs	41	31	44	40	30	24	33	18	19	20	20	28
Job descriptions	48	42	30	54	48	38	63	31	0	9	5	21
Job design	15	25	37	38	19	24	19	15	19	24	27	29
Layoffs and discharges	48	42	41	66	37	35	22	29	11	6	21	17
Organizational planning	22	27	55	64	19	31	19	11	7	11	15	25
Orientation of new employees	59	58	37	44	63	62	48	38	0	2	3	3
Pay raises	37	58	56	62	33	31	22	40	0	10	19	10
Performance appraisal	52	46	56	58	22	24	30	42	0	7	13	19
Personnel planning	41	33	56	66	33	40	21	25	7	9	18	22
Personnel research	41	55	26	33	59	47	26	36	4	2	17	18
Personnel surveys	56	67	26	26	56	53	33	42	4	2	8	12
Promotions	37	42	67	62	7	25	11	31	7	9	25	23
Public relations	22	44	37	29	19	40	7	26	30	16	28	24
Recruiting	59	69	37	31	59	44	44	44	4	0	4	11
Selection	41	71	52	55	41	31	37	29	0	0	7	13
Selection testing	48	60	41	29	56	51	56	33	0	2	2	16
Setting wages and salaries	41	62	56	58	30	38	30	42	0	2	14	4
Training	48	47	59	49	37	57	33	40	7	6	6	8
Transfers	44	44	56	55	19	36	26	31	0	6	22	20
Union contract administration	30	40	15	27	22	33	11	16	44	24	29	27
Average responses	41.0	49.6	43.9	50.8	37.6	40.9	28.0	31.3				

Source: H. White and R. Boynton, "The Role of Personnel: A Management View," *Arizona Business* 21 (1974).

tive if the enterprise has a career pattern that rotates its managers through both operating and staff positions such as those in personnel. This rotation helps each group understand the other's problems.

To summarize, both personnel specialists and operating managers perform personnel work, and personnel decisions may involve both types of managers. Beginning with Chapter 4, these interrelationships are explained for each chapter's topic.

The role of the personnel manager or specialist

Certain facts are known about the professional personnel person. In 1977, there were about 235,000 people employed in personnel work in the United States and about 34,000 in Canada. About 60 percent of these work in the private sector, 30 percent in the public sector, and the remaining 10 percent in the third sector (health, education, the arts, libraries, voluntary organizations, and so on). There has been about a 5 percent growth in personnel positions per year since 1970. Most personnel managers are men (75 percent in the United States and Canada), and their experience is primarily in personnel work, especially the younger managers. Women managers are usually found in medium- and small-sized organizations. In the United States, most personnel managers have college degrees; in Canada, most do not. Those who have attended college in recent years have usually majored in business, economics, psychology, or engineering.[17]

Personnel specialists have been moving toward greater specialization, if not actual professionalism. College training includes courses such as personnel management, compensation administration, personnel problems, labor law and legislation, and collective bargaining.[18] Those who want to become more specialized may join an association (like the American Society for Personnel Administrators or one of the Council of Canadian Personnel Asso-

EXHIBIT 1–3
How personnel executives rate their salary/benefit packages

Industry	Too low	About average	Better than average for job background
Manufacturing (under 500 employees)	26.8%	49.8%	23.4%
Manufacturing (500–999)	22.4	50.7	26.9
Manufacturing (1,000–4,999)	12.9	49.6	37.5
Manufacturing (over 5,000)	12.0	52.0	36.0
Research and development	—	40.0	60.0
Public utilities	10.0	63.3	26.7
Hospitals	18.4	57.3	24.3
Retail stores	21.7	50.0	28.3
Banks	14.9	48.5	36.3
Insurance companies	21.8	46.5	31.7
Transportation and distribution	8.4	45.8	45.8
Government agencies	30.0	55.0	15.0
Education	35.3	35.3	29.4
Nonprofit organizations	17.2	62.1	20.7
Other	20.1	48.5	31.4

Source: *The Personnel Executive's Job* (Englewood Cliffs, N.J.: Prentice-Hall/ASPA, 1977).

ciations), attend meetings, read professional journals (see Appendix B) or seek ASPA accreditation (see Appendix B).[19]

Personnel specialists generally are paid similarly to other graduates of business schools at the supervisory and middle management levels. At top management levels, they sometimes are paid slightly less than operating vice presidents. Current salaries of personnel specialists and executives are published yearly by the ASPA in its *Salary Survey*. Exhibit 1–3 shows how personnel executives rate their salary and benefit packages.

A career in personnel work follows the patterns shown in Exhibit 1–4. In general, personnel executives work hard (see Exhibit 1–5) and are satisfied with some aspects of their jobs, such as the challenge and working with

EXHIBIT 1–4
Sample career patterns of personnel professionals

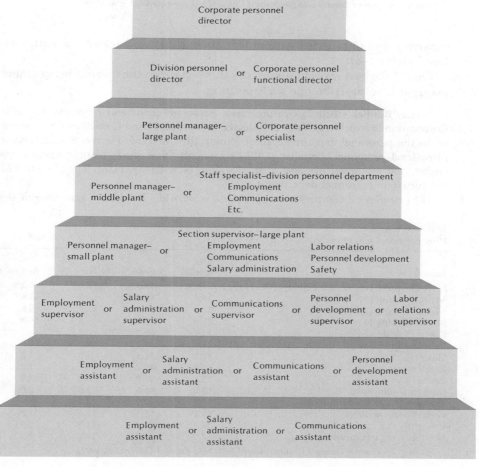

Source: H. H. Mitchell, "Selecting and Developing Personnel Professionals," *Personnel Journal* 49 (1970).

EXHIBIT 1-5
Work load of personnel executives

	Average hours worked each week				
Industry	*40 or less*	*41–45*	*46–50*	*51–60*	*Over 60*
Manufacturing (under 500 employees)	7.4%	21.4%	32.1%	30.7%	8.4%
Manufacturing (500–999)	2.9	11.8	35.3	39.7	10.3
Manufacturing (1,000–4,999)	2.1	12.1	29.8	47.5	8.5
Manufacturing (over 5,000)	—	17.4	21.7	47.8	13.1
Research and development	7.1	21.4	57.1	14.4	—
Public utilities	11.5	17.2	31.0	33.3	7.0
Hospitals	10.3	13.1	43.9	29.9	2.8
Retail stores	2.2	20.0	35.6	33.3	8.9
Banks	5.0	27.7	31.7	30.7	4.9
Insurance companies	7.3	22.5	37.1	31.1	2.0
Transportation and distribution	4.2	16.7	37.5	37.5	4.1
Government agencies	9.8	39.0	26.8	24.4	—
Education	18.2	12.1	48.5	21.2	—
Nonprofit organizations	17.6	25.0	50.0	7.4	—
Other	9.7	20.4	42.0	21.3	6.6

Source: *The Personnel Executive's Job* (Englewood Cliffs, N.J.: Prentice-Hall/ASPA, 1977).

superiors, and unsatisifed with others, such as pay and amount of authority
(see Exhibit 1–6).

One of the best ways to summarize this section on the role of the personnel
manager is to describe one such position.

Walter Burdick's title is vice president, personnel plans and programs, for IBM
Corporation. Burdick received a B.S. degree in personnel from Cornell and has moved
up in the personnel department since joining IBM in 1955. He was successively a
plant-level personnel specialist at IBM's Endicott, New York, plant; corporate recruiter; and personnel manager at the Dayton, New Jersey, plant. Then he entered
the corporate personnel department.

IBM employs 2,880 personnel specialists worldwide. Burdick is a member of the

EXHIBIT 1-6
How personnel executives rate their job satisfaction

Industry	*Very satisfied*	*Good*	*Fair*	*Poor; dissatisfied*
Manufacturing (under 500 employees)	34.0%	43.9%	18.9%	3.2%
Manufacturing (500–999)	36.6	48.9	13.7	0.8
Manufacturing (1,000–4,999)	32.9	53.6	12.9	0.6
Manufacturing (over 5,000)	25.0	50.0	8.3	16.7
Research & development	23.1	69.2	7.7	—
Public utilities	22.9	57.1	14.3	5.7
Hospitals	37.1	52.4	9.5	1.0
Retail stores	38.6	47.7	9.1	4.6
Banks	31.4	57.8	6.9	3.9
Insurance companies	35.6	48.5	13.9	2.0
Transportation & distribution	37.5	50.0	12.5	—
Government agencies	21.1	55.3	15.8	7.8
Education	32.4	52.9	11.8	2.9
Nonprofit organizations	37.9	34.5	17.2	4.2

Source: *The Personnel Executive's Job* (Englewood Cliffs, N.J.: Prentice-Hall/ASPA, 1977).

Advisory Council of Management and Personnel for the Conference Board, a director of the National Merit Scholarship Corporation, a director of Junior Achievement (New York), and a trustee of the National Manpower Institute, and he holds other honors. This is how he sees the job of personnel: "Personnel staffs exist to add value to the organization, to add to management's knowledge, to improve their decision making, to increase the individual dignity and efficiency of the human resources, and to add a dimension that is the human factor. Our achievements must be measured against how well we contribute toward meeting our organization's goals. . . ."

With regard to how personnel relates to operating managers at IBM, Burdick says: "Personnel is purely a staff role. Our major objectives, such as educating managers to potential change, preparing them to address the change by developing the right policies, and helping to communicate these policies are pure staff. We must keep our personnel professionals from attempting to manage the business."

When asked to describe the kind of people doing personnel work at IBM, Burdick said: "It is desirable to have a mix of people who have experience in personnel and other functional areas. By design, about half of our senior personnel people have come from nonpersonnel areas of business. To implement this mix, we have a program through which high-potential people from personnel and other functions in the company come to the corporate personnel staff to work for two years. About a third of my staff is comprised of these people."

What of the future personnel executive? Burdick says: "The future will require the further professionalization of the personnel function: the right people, the right training, a complete understanding of corporate principles and business objectives, and a thorough understanding of the role of personnel in the organization. The last quarter of the 20th century is going to be one of primary emphasis on human resource management. The time is right for professional personnel people to make the most significant contribution of their careers."[20]

PERSONNEL DEPARTMENT OPERATIONS

The makeup of personnel departments and how they operate have both changed since the concepts were introduced about 1900 (see Appendix A). Personnel units vary by size and sector; but most enterprises keep them small. A recent Bureau of National Affairs study found that in the largest headquarters unit there were 150 people.[21]

The number of personnel specialists in relation to the number of operating employees, or the personnel ratio, varies in different industries. The national average, according to the BNA, is one personnel specialist per 200 employees. Some industries, such as construction, agriculture, retail and wholesale trade, and services, have fewer personnel specialists than the average. Others, such as public utilities, durable goods manufacturing, banking, insurance, and government, have an above-average ratio.[22]

In the largest recent study of the personnel function, Prentice-Hall surveyed 1,400 personnel executives and found both personnel staffs and budgets to be growing. Based on this study, Exhibit 1–7 indicates current size and personnel ratio variations, and Exhibit 1–8 gives some interesting personnel budget data.

EXHIBIT 1–7
Size of personnel staff

Industry—number reporting	Personnel staff ratio*	Number on personnel staff †
Manufacturing (under 500 persons)—217	1 : 96	1–12 (300)
Manufacturing (500–999)—136	1 : 116	1–20 (800)
Manufacturing (1,000–4,999)—142	1 : 130	2–90 (4,900)
Manufacturing (over 5,000)—26	1 : 352	7–126 (22,000)
Research and development—15	1 : 102	1–60 (5,000)
Public utilities—30	1 : 154	1–110 (22,339)
Hospitals—108	1 : 180	1–28 (4,000)
Retail stores—47	1 : 228	1–31 (5,800)
Banks—104	1 : 98	1–72 (9,000)
Insurance companies—101	1 : 101	1–142 (30,000)
Transportation and distribution—24	1 : 272	1–75 (26,000)
Government agencies—41	1 : 272	2–104 (68,000)
Education—34	1 : 161	1–46 (11,300)
Nonprofit organizations—28	1 : 76	1–12 (1,955)
Other firms—328	1 : 194	1–120 (35,000)

    * Average number of employees on payroll for each person on personnel staff.
    † Smallest and largest personnel staff reported for each industry; numbers in parentheses refer to number of employees on payroll for firms reporting largest personnel staffs. (Firms represented here do not necessarily have the lowest or highest *ratio* of personnel staffers, relative to total work force.)
    Source: *The Personnel Executive's Job* (Englewood Cliffs, N.J.: Prentice-Hall/ASPA, 1977).

How personnel specialists spend their time will be demonstrated by the chapters to follow on the various personnel activities. An idea of what proportions are devoted to types of activities can be given here, however. The greatest amount of time (33 percent) is spent on staffing (recruiting, selection, orientation, evaluation, discipline). Next comes compensation and benefits (28.5 percent); and then training and development (11 percent) and labor relations (10 percent.) The other activities take 5 percent or less of a personnel specialist's time.[23]

EXHIBIT 1–8
The personnel budget

Industry	Personnel executive has definite budget	Average budget as % of total payroll	Personnel executive has complete financial responsibility
Manufacturing (under 500 employees)	31.9%	4.2%	86.8%
Manufacturing (500–999)	63.2	3.9	79.5
Manufacturing (1,000–4,999)	77.4	3.9	80.3
Manufacturing (over 5,000)	80.0	1.6	66.7
Research and development	71.4	3.0	76.9
Public utilities	65.4	1.8	66.7
Hospitals	73.3	2.8	81.8
Retail stores	44.7	1.0	85.7
Banks	53.5	4.2	90.6
Insurance companies	63.3	5.6	82.1
Transportation and distribution	47.8	5.4	63.6
Government agencies	77.5	1.0	65.5
Education	73.5	1.2	76.0
Nonprofit organizations	46.2	5.6	84.6
Other	64.9	3.0	74.2

    Source: *The Personnel Executive's Job* (Englewood Cliffs, N.J.: Prentice-Hall/ASPA, 1977).

Organizational arrangements

The chief personnel executive reports to the top manager of most enterprises or, in the larger ones, he or she may report to an executive vice president. As personnel increases in importance, more personnel executives are becoming members of boards of directors, as in such firms as RCA and United Parcel Service.

Exhibit 1–9 shows one way personnel could be organized in a large business. In some larger firms, personnel is divided into two departments, personnel and labor relations. In medium-sized and smaller enterprises, however, personnel and other functions, such as public relations, may be located within a single department.

Of all personnel administrators, 30 percent work for local, state, and federal governments. Exhibit 1–10 is an example of personnel organization in a "typical" state government. The legislature and the governor set policy for departments, subject to review by the courts, and appoint a personnel commission which headed by a personnel officer. This central personnel unit is a policy-making body which serves a policy, advisory, and regulatory purpose which is similar to that of the home office personnel unit of a business. At the federal government level, this personnel commission is called the Civil Service Commission.

In the third sector, such as hospitals and universities, personnel typically is a unit in the business office, as shown in Exhibit 1–11. More will be said about differences in personnel work in these three settings in Chapter 3.

Personnel specialists are usually located at the headquarters of an enterprise, but larger organizations may divide their assignments. Usually the

EXHIBIT 1–9
Personnel department in a large business

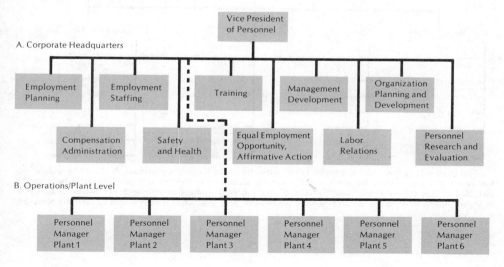

EXHIBIT 1–10
Personnel organization in a U.S. state government

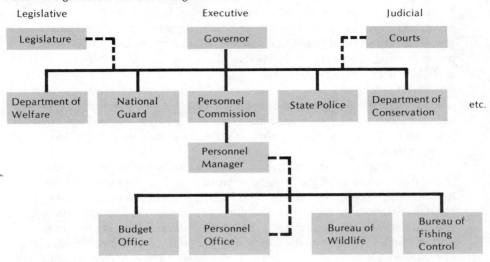

EXHIBIT 1–11
Organization of a county hospital

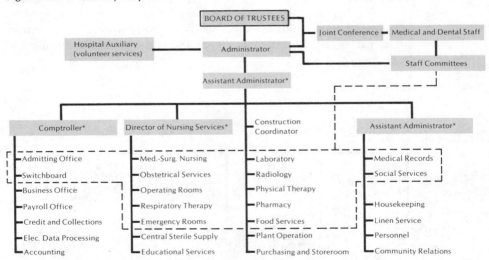

This chart reflects the "line" responsibility and authority in the hospital organization. It should be understood, however, that a great part of the work of the hospital is accomplished through informal interaction between the identified services and functions. These "functional" working relationships are encouraged. Where there is difference in understanding or when changes in procedure are required, the "line" organization should be carefully observed.
    * Area directors.

largest group is at headquarters, but personnel advisors are also stationed at unit levels (for example, a plant) and divisional levels. In this case, the headquarters unit consists of specialists or experts on certain topics and advisers to top management, while the unit-level personnel people are generalists who serve as advisers to operating managers at that level.

Personnel and computerization[24]

To perform personnel functions effectively today, the computer is an essential tool. Accounting and operations were the earliest users of comput-

EXHIBIT 1–12
Computer-generated graph reports

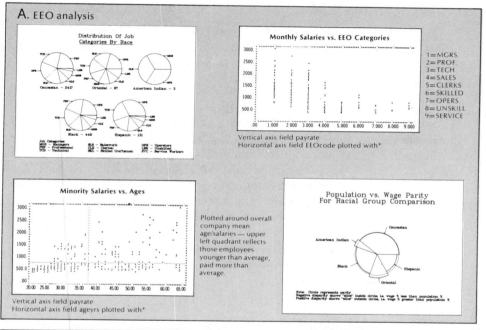

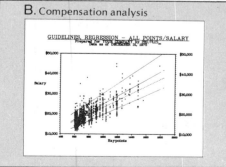

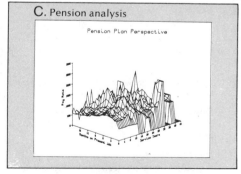

Source: Carlton Dukes, "Use of Graphic Techniques in Human Resource Management," *The Personnel Administrator,* January 1970.

ers, but many organizations began to use it for aspects of personnel work when the payroll was computerized, followed by computerization of compensation and benefits administration.

The output provided by computers has progressed from simple printouts of data to sophisticated computer graphics such as those shown in Exhibit 1–12. Such graphic-printouts make it much easier to analyze equal employment opportunities, compensation, pensions, and other personnel aspects.

The computer's use in nearly all facets of personnel work will be seen in later chapters. When the amount of routine detail work is reduced by means such as computerization, personnel people can concentrate on the more meaningful aspects of their jobs.

PLAN OF THE BOOK

The material on the personnel function presented in this book is organized to suggest solutions to real-life problems. Beginning with Part Two, the chapters (and many of the sections) begin with a case study from a real organization which describes a personnel problem being faced today. The method suggested to solve the problem is a personnel activity, which is defined precisely. Then who performs this activity is discussed. The interrelationship between operating and personnel managers and the role of top management in the activity are described and analyzed.

In each chapter (or group of chapters, where an activity is described in more than one), the extent to which the activity has been developed is analyzed. Some personnel activities (or functions) are quite well established, while others are just emerging. The activity being considered is assigned to one of four stages through which personnel activities seem to evolve. The stage at which an activity is currently located can be assessed by examining the literature on the topic—articles, books, and speeches presented at association meetings—and plotting how far along the activity has come, as shown in Exhibit 1–13.

EXHIBIT 1–13
Stages of development of a personnel activity

Almost
Unknown

Stage I: New, New
In this stage the experts or originators are exhorting specialists to adopt the function. Panaceas are promised.

Stage II: Early Development
In this stage, articles describe how companies perform the function and how happy they are with the results.

Stage III: Conflict
The doubts begin. The articles warn: it didn't work for us. Multiple organization studies are undertaken.

Stage IV: Maturity
A great deal of empirical data has been gathered, and theories and explanations for the conflict in Stage III are established.

Well Known

Currently it is most likely that included in Stage I would be career development and overall organization and management development schemes. In Stage II would be systematic evaluation of the total personnel function and formal orientation. Typical activities in Stage III would be performance evaluation and informal management development. Stage IV functions would include many employment and compensation activities. It appears that the personnel function begins by focusing on blue-collar employees and then adds white collar and clerical workers. Only fully developed personnel departments focus on management and professional employees as well.

The chapters also include a diagnostic analysis of the activity being discussed. The book's subtitle, *A Diagnostic Approach,* indicates my view that personnel activities are affected by many different factors, such as the types of people employed, organized labor, and government, and the solution of personnel problems depends on consideration of all these factors. This idea will be thoroughly examined in Chapters 2 and 3.

For each personnel activity, suggestions are given for the techniques, tools, and approaches available to solve the problem, with an evaluation of when each tool is most useful and tips on how to use them well.

References to Canadian personnel practices throughout provide one perspective on the activity in other countries. (The environmental differences affecting personnel are described in Chapter 3). U.S.–based enterprises located in many other countries must adapt their personnel practices to accommodate local expectations. Canada was chosen as the primary basis of comparison because, as a neighbor, it shares many practices with the United States, but there are differences as well. Canada and the United States are each other's largest trading partners. We can learn much from each other's laws and personnel practices.

The various personnel activities are evaluated with a cost/benefit approach. Since personnel must compete with requests for other resources, such as machinery, advertising, and buildings, the expenditures and investments in the organization's people must be justifiable in cost benefit terms.[25]

The chapter summary, conclusion, and recommendation sections review the major points in each chapter and list them in proposition form. For example, in Chapter 5:

> *PROPOSITION 5.1.* The larger the organization's work force, the more likely is the effective organization to use more sophisticated and computerized skills inventories.

The recommendations for application of the activity are in the form of suggestions for its use in various types of organizations. Since personnel functions are not performed the same way in all organizations, recommendations are given for the most effective way to handle each problem in seven model organizations which differ systematically by size (number of employees), complexity of products or services, and stability or volatility (degree to which the organization's products or services change over time). If you place your focal organization (where you have worked or want to work) on this scale, you can get an idea of how the personnel challenge would best be handled there. The seven model organizations are defined in Exhibit 1–14.

EXHIBIT 1–14
Seven model organizations in which various personnel practices might be used

1. Large size, low complexity, high stability.
   Examples: Social security agencies, copper smelter, tuberculosis hospital in the 1930s.

2. Medium size, low complexity, high stability.
   Examples: gym shoe manufacturer, Department of Commerce, state of Indiana.

3. Small size, low complexity, high stability.
   Examples: wooden pencil manufacturer, small exterminator.

4. Medium size, moderate complexity, moderate stability.
   Examples: food manufacturer, Memphis city welfare agency.

5. Large size, high complexity, low stability.
   Examples: Mattel Toy Corporation, innovative community general hospital.

6. Medium size, high complexity, low stability.
   Examples: U.S. Office of Economic Opportunity agencies in 1968, fashion clothing manufacturer, innovative multiple-purpose hospital.

7. Small size, high complexity, low stability.
   Examples: Peace Corps, 1961, early OEO agencies, elite psychiatric hospital, small media conglomerate.

SUMMARY

In introducing you to the field of personnel, this chapter defined personnel as that function of all enterprises which provides for effective utilization of human resources to achieve both the objectives of the enterprise and the satisfaction and development of the employees. Personnel is future and action oriented and focuses on satisfying the needs of individuals at work. Personnel is a necessary function; effectively performed, it can make the crucial difference between successful and unsuccessful enterprises.

One of the challenges faced in personnel is that many decisions require inputs from both operating managers and personnel specialists. This can lead to conflict, or it can result in more effective personnel decisions.

The chapter described some of the characteristics of today's personnel managers and a number of approaches to the organization and operation of personnel units. It concluded with a brief description of how the material in this book is organized and the devices we have used to present it. The appendixes to the chapter describe the history of personnel in the United States and two aspects of personnel professionalism: the literature on the topic, and accreditation procedures.

Personnel is one of the most challenging and exciting functions in organizations today, and this book has been written to help you face these challenges more effectively. Chapter 2 introduces an important variable in personnel effectiveness: people.

APPENDIX A: A BRIEF HISTORY OF PERSONNEL IN THE UNITED STATES

The history of personnel can be traced back to ancient and medieval times, as Cyril Ling has done.[26] First-line supervisors handled personnel prior to 1900, when a few firms began to turn over the employment and clerical aspects of personnel to employment specialists.[27] A parallel development was the industrial welfare movement, which was intended to improve the lot of the worker. This movement had much in common with the values of early industrialists such as Robert Owen and received the support of numerous churchmen.

Historians attribute the development of personnel departments to multiple causes, mostly practical. Some observers point out that personnel has risen and fallen in prestige as the power of trade unions has fluctuated. Others note that its importance increased as managers became aware of the costs of turnover of personnel and in time of worker shortages. The prevalence of personnel departments grew during World War I, dropped off slightly in the depression of 1921, and rose in the twenties, as fear of unions and labor shortages increased. They decreased during the depression of the late twenties and early thirties and became important again with the new union strength of the late thirties and the labor shortages in the World War II years.

Various disciplines and groups have contributed to the development of the personnel function. Scientific management pointed out the inefficiency of the foremen-personnel system. The industrial welfare–social secretaries movement was an early means to fight unions and satisfy workers. Industrial psychologists provided several new personnel tools, particularly in selecting employees. The work of Hugo Munsterberg and Walter Scott in the development of employee tests during World Wars I and II was especially noteworthy.[28] More sophisticated tests and better training methods were developed by psychologists in World War II. Studies and experiments in leadership and supervisory behavior increased interest in personnel both in the practical sense (better leaders = better productivity) and the welfare sense (better leaders = more satisfied workers).

In the public sector, the Civil Service Commission was set up in 1883 to professionalize public employment in this country. The system was modeled on the British Civil Servants system.[29] Civil Service Commission activities in testing, job criteria, employment, promotion, and other areas of personnel work have done much to advance the field.

With the growth of collective bargaining in the late forties and early fifties, more complex and more expensive benefits have added to the complexity of the programs to be administered by personnel departments.

Personnel has come a long way—from a few employment departments in 1912 at such companies as National Cash Register and B. F. Goodrich, to the formation of personnel associations during World War I, to college courses in the field of study by 1920, to the employment of over 235,000 personnel specialists in 1977. Although there have been many changes in the personnel function, however, its focus and purpose have not changed much. Personnel still seeks to provide the right employee for the right job. This gives the employee satisfaction and helps the enterprise achieve its goals.[30]

APPENDIX B: PERSONNEL SPECIALIZATION AND PROFESSIONALIZATION

The personnel specialist can advance his or her knowledge of the field by reading professional journals. These include:

1. Journals for the American personnel executive:
   American Federationist
   Administrative Management
   Employment Benefit Plan Review
   Labor Law Journal
   Monthly Labor Review
   The Personnel Administrator
   Personnel
   Personnel Journal
   Public Personnel Management

2. Journals for the Canadian personnel executive:
   Canadian Personnel and Industrial Relations Review
   Labour Gazette
   Relations Industrielles/Industrial Relations

3. Scholarly journals. The following is a list of publications written for scholars and executives interested in personnel. Reading these requires more technical training than the journals listed above.
   Human Relations
   Human Organization
   Human Resources Management
   Industrial Relations
   Industrial and Labor Relations Review
   Journal of Applied Psychology
   Organizational Behavior and Human Performance
   Personnel Psychology

4. Abstracts and services.
   For those wishing to study specialized parts of literature or to get a total overview, *Personnel Management Abstracts* lists most articles in the field and abstracts many of them. *Psychological Abstracts,* especially the "Industrial and Organizational Psychology" section, can suggest leads. And

the *Annual Review of Psychology* often has chapters summarizing the latest trends in personnel.

In addition, several companies offer personnel information services. The best known of these are the Bureau of National Affairs (BNA), Commerce Clearing House (CCH), and Prentice-Hall Services.

Accreditation

One move to increase the professionalism of personnel executives is the American Society of Personnel Administrators Accreditation Program. ASPA has set up the ASPA Accreditation Institute (AAI) to offer personnel executives the opportunity to be accredited as a specialist (in a functional area such as employment, placement and personnel planning, or training and development) or a generalist (multiple specialities). Specialists can qualify as accredited personnel specialists or the more advanced accredited personnel diplomates. For generalists, the basic accreditation is accredited personnel manager and the advanced level is accredited executive in personnel. Accreditation requires passing three-hour examinations developed by the Psychological Corporation of New York. It is difficult to predict the potential impact of accreditation on personnel work at this time. A survey of 1,400 personnel executives published in 1977 found that 4.6 percent had applied for ASPA accreditation and 20 percent planned to apply. Ten percent said they would not apply, and the rest were unsure.[31]

QUESTIONS

1. What is personnel? What activities make up the personnel function?
2. Why do all enterprises engage in personnel work?
3. How do top management's strategic decisions interact with personnel?
4. Personnel is a means to help achieve the enterprise's objectives. Comment.
5. In what ways do operating managers make personnel decisions and do personnel work?
6. What personnel activities do personnel specialists perform?
7. Describe the interaction of personnel and operating managers in making personnel decisions.
8. What are personnel managers like? Is personnel a growth career path?
9. What industries and sectors employ the most personnel specialists? The least?
10. Describe typical organizational arrangements for personnel units.
11. What are the four stages of development of a personnel activity? How does this concept help you understand personnel work?
12. Describe the seven model organizations in which personnel practices might be used. How does this help you understand personnel work?
13. Briefly outline how personnel has developed as a field, indicating the most significant factors in this development.

14. If you decide to become a personnel professional, what journals would you read to keep up to date?

15. If you decide to become a personnel professional, how would you go about becoming accredited? Would you want to do so?

NOTES AND REFERENCES

1. Tamara Gilman, "Managing the Human Resource System as a Strategic Function," Harvard Business School, 1977, mimeographed; William F. Glueck, *Business Policy* (New York: McGraw-Hill Book Co., 1976); A. M. Wurr, "Developing Personnel Strategy," in Charles Margerison and David Ashton, *Planning for Human Resources* (London: Longman, 1974).

2. J. H. Foegen, "The Community Service Subsidy," *Human Resource Management,* Spring, 1973, pp. 17–20; Thelma Hunt, "Critical Issues Facing Personnel Administrators Today," *Public Personnel Management,* November–December 1974, pp. 464–72; Thomas Patten, Jr., "Personnel Management in the 1970's," *Human Resource Management,* Fall 1973, pp. 7–19.

3. James Craft and Jacob Bernberg, "Human Resource Accounting: Perspective and Prospects," *Industrial Relations* February 1976, pp. 2–12; Jackson Gillespie et al., "A Human Resource Planning and Valuation Model," *Academy of Management Journal* December 1976, pp. 650–56; Phillip Mirvis and Edward Lawler, III, "Measuring the Financial Impact of Employee Attitudes," *Journal of Applied Psychology* 62, 1 (1977), pp. 1–8; Jacob Paperman and Desmond Martin, "Human Resource Accounting: A Managerial Tool?" *Personnel,* March–April 1977, pp. 41–50. Joseph Puett and Daniel Roman, "Human Resource Valuation," *Academy of Management Journal* December 1976, pp. 656–62; John Rhode et al., "Human Resource Accounting: A Critical Assessment," *Industrial Relations* February 1976, pp. 13–25; Richard Savich and Keith Ehrenreich, "Cost Benefit Analysis of Human Resource Accounting Alternatives," *Human Resource Management,* Spring 1976, pp. 7–18.

4. Herbert Heneman, Jr., "The Changing Role of the Personnel Function," Industrial Relations Center, The University of Minnesota, 1973, mimeographed.

5. Carl Driessnack, "Financial Impact of Effective Human Resources Management," *The Personnel Administrator,* January 1976, pp. 22–25; Marshall Howes and Bennie Yates, "How to Control Personnel Costs in Overhead Functions," *Personnel,* July–August 1976, pp. 22–29.

6. J. Lloyd Suttle, "Improving Life at Work—Problems and Prospects," in *Improving Life at Work,* ed. J. Richard Hackman, and J. Lloyd Suttle (Santa Monica, Calif.: Goodyear Publishing Co., 1977), pp. 1–29.

7. Robert Guest, "Of Time and the Foreman," *Personnel* 32 (1955–56), pp. 478–86; Frank Jasinski, "Foremen Relationships Outside the Work Group," *Personnel* 33 (1956–57), pp. 130–36; D. L. Marples, "Studies of Managers: A Fresh Start?" *Journal of Management Studies* 4, 3 (1967), pp. 282–99.

8. Tom Burns, "Management in Action," *Operational Research Quarterly* 8 (1957), pp. 46–60; J. H. Horne and Tom Lupton, "The Work Activities of Middle Managers," *Journal of Management Studies* 2 (1965), pp. 14–33.

9. Sune Carlson, *Executive Behavior* (Stockholm: Stromberts, 1951); G. Copeman et al., *How the Executive Spends His Time* (London: Business Publications, 1963); Thomas Mahoney, et al., "The Job(s) of Management," *Industrial Relations,* February 1964, pp. 97–110.

10. Bruce De Spelder, *Ratios of Staff to Line Personnel* (Columbus: Bureau of Business Research, Ohio State University, 1962); Roland Simonds, "Human Resources Administration," in *Human Resources Administration* ed. William Wasmuth et al., (Boston: Houghton Mifflin Co., 1970); William Wasmuth, "Human Resources Administration: Dilemmas of Growth," in Wasmuth et al., *Human Resources Administration.*

11. Wendell French and Dale Henning, "The Authority Influence Role of the Functional Specialist in Management," *Academy of Management Journal* 9, 2 (1966), pp. 187–203; Dale Henning and R. Moseley, "Authority Role of a Functional Manager," *Administrative Science Quarterly* 15, 4 (1970), pp. 482–89; H. White and R. Boynton, "The Role of Personnel: A Management View," *Arizona Business* 21, 8 (1974), pp. 17–21.

12. Melville Dalton, "Changing Staff-Line Relationships," *Personnel Administration,* March 1966, pp. 4–5; 40–49; Geert Hofstede, "Frustrations of Personnel Managers," *Management International Review,* 4, 5 (1973), pp. 127–32; Charles Myers and John Turnbull, "Line and Staff in Industrial Relations," *Harvard Business Review,* October–November, 1969, pp. 1–12; Leonard Sayles, *Managerial Behavior* (New York: McGraw-Hill Book Co., 1964).

13. John Miner and Mary Miner, "Managerial Characteristics of Personnel Managers," *Industrial Relations* May 1976, pp. 225–34; John Miner, "Levels of Motivation to Manage among Personnel and Industrial Relations Managers," *Journal of Applied Psychology* 61, 4 (1976), pp. 419–27.

14. White and Boynton, "Role of Personnel."

15. "Personnel: Fast Track to the Top," *Duns Review,* April 1975, pp. 74–77.

16. Heneman, "Changing Role of Personnel Function."

17. John Belt and James Richardson, "Academic Preparation for Personnel Management," *Personnel Journal,* May 1973, pp. 373–80; Jeff Harris, "Personnel Administrators: The Truth About Their Background," *MSU Business Topics,* Summer 1969, pp. 22–29; M. Jane Kay, "What Do Women in Personnel Do?" *Personnel Journal,* October 1969, pp. 810–12; Pradip Kumar, "Personnel Management in Canada: A Manpower Profile," *Canadian Personnel and Industrial Relations Journal,* January 1976, pp. 32–34; "Canada's Personnel People," *Labour Gazette,* December 1975, pp. 892–94; Dalton E. McFarland, *Company Officers Assess the Personnel Function,* AMA Research Study 79 (New York: American Management Association, 1967); George Ritzer and Harrison Trice, *An Occupation in Conflict* (Ithaca, N.Y.: Cornell University Press, 1969); J. P. Siegel et al., "Education and Development of Employee Relations Staff," *Canadian Personnel and Industrial Relations Journal,* March 1974, pp. 25–31; Charles Ramser, "The Personnel Executive," *North Texas State University Business Studies,* Fall 1968, pp. 59–62.

18. D. L. Howell et al., "College Courses and Their Respective Values: 10 Years After," *The Personnel Administrator,* February 1976, pp. 34–37.

19. George Ritzer, "The Professionals," *The Personnel Administrator* 16, 3 (1971), pp. 34–36.

20. "Walter Burdick: A Look at Corporate and Personnel Philosophy," *The Personnel Administrator,* July 1976, pp. 21–26.

21. Bureau of National Affairs, "Planning and Budgeting the Personnel Program," ASPA–BNA Survey no. 23, 1974.

22. Robert Boynton, "Where Can We Find a Good Personnel Man?" *The Personnel Administrator* 15, 5 (1970), pp. 34–36; "Canada's Personnel People"; Dale Yoder, "Personnel Ratios 1970," *The Personnel Administrator* 15, 6 (1970), pp. 36–37.

23. Yoder, "Personnel Ratios 1970."

24. Roland Lenniger, "Personnel Management and the Computer," *The Personnel Administrator,* January 1975, pp. 54–55; Rolf E. Rogers, "An Integrated Personnel System," *Personnel Administration,* March–April 1970, pp. 22–28; Frank Tetz, "Evaluating Computer Based Human Resource Information Systems: Costs vs. Benefits," *Personnel Journal,* June 1973, pp. 451–55; Edward Tomeski and Harold Lazarus, "Computerized Information Systems in Personnel," *Academy of Management Journal,* March 1974, pp. 168–72.

25. Ray Killian, *Human Resource Management: An ROI Approach* (New York: Amacon, 1976), Appendix 1.

26. Cyril Ling, *The Management of Personnel Relations: History and Origins* (Homewood, Ill.: Richard D. Irwin, Inc., 1965).

27. Henry Eilbirt, "The Development of Personnel Management in the United States," *Business History Review* 33 (1959), pp. 345–64; Homer J. Hagedorn, "A Note on the Motivation of Personnel Management: Industrial Welfare 1895–1910," *Explorations in Entrepreneural History* 10 (1958), pp. 134–39.

28. Hugo Munsterberg, *Psychology and Industrial Efficiency* (Boston: Houghton Mifflin Co., 1913); Walter Scott, *Influencing Human Efficiency* (New York: Macmillan Co., 1911).

29. Paul Van Riper, *History of the U.S. Civil Service* (Evanston, Ill.: Row Peterson, 1958).

30. For a more thorough history of personnel and labor relations see Alan Nash and John Miner, *Personnel and Labor Relations: An Evolutionary Approach* (New York: Macmillan Co., 1973).

31. *The Personnel Executive's Job* (Englewood Cliffs, N.J.: Prentice-Hall/ASPA, 1977).

A diagnostic approach to personnel

CHAPTER OBJECTIVES

■ To introduce the concept of a diagnostic approach to personnel and management.

■ To show how managers use their knowledge of human behavior to make better personnel decisions.

■ To demonstrate how the task to be performed, the work group, and the leader influence personnel decisions.

■ To help you be a more effective manager of personnel activities.

CHAPTER OUTLINE

In today's world, there is the possibility that things have become too specialized; so that we are taught how to do things without understanding why we do them. Thus we fail to discern the big picture behind the little picture of our own job and our own world.

This can happen in a lot of jobs. A tailor could be very efficient at cutting and sewing cloth, but if he did not take into account variations in physique, his suits would not look attractive on most people. An architect who is skilled in mechanical drawing, creative in design work, and aware of the importance of meeting clients preferences must also be knowledgeable about the stress capabilities of various building materials. A landscape architect must understand soil science and botany as well as aesthetics.

Many operating managers and personnel managers have been too narrowly trained. They know that personnel includes such activities as compensation and performance evaluation, and they may know about such compensation methods as incentive pay and profit sharing and such performance evaluation approaches as rating scales and management by objectives. But if they do not link this technical knowledge with an understanding of people and the environment in which the personnel function takes place, they are as likely to be as ineffective as an architect who does not know how much stress the joints could take or a physician who does not know that insulin helps a diabetic.

Even people who are trained in the social sciences can neglect to use them when it is appropriate to do so. The mechanism used here to remind you to apply the right technique to the work situation, given the kind of people working in the situation, is called *the diagnostic approach.* This chapter describes the people, the operating manager—leader, the work group, and the tasks to be performed as aspects of the total personnel situation. Chapter 3 completes this big picture by describing how the organizational and environmental aspects of the personnel setting influence the personnel function. Then this framework is used to help analyze how each personnel activity (such as employee selection) can be performed more effectively.

THE DIAGNOSTIC APPROACH TO PERSONNEL DECISIONS

Simply put, the diagnostic approach means that, in making personnel decisions, the decision maker considers the people who are working (as individuals and groups), the task leader, the task they are performing, and the organizational and external environmental settings. The manager who uses this approach makes the best possible decision, considering the diagnostic factors. Since human behavior is so complex, however, in the preliminary decision the factors may have been weighted incorrectly. If the first decision does not lead to the desired results, the decision maker reexamines the factors and makes another decision.

The term "diagnostic" is used because the model decision maker on which it is based is the physician. An effective physician examines all the evidence bearing on a case. He gets as much objective data as he can from laboratory tests, observes the patient's medical history, and asks what the symptoms are. Then he makes a judgment of the most probable cause of the symptoms and prescribes the treatment most likely to alleviate the pain and eliminate the cause. If his treatment does not work, he assumes that the next most probable cause is at work and attempts to treat it, and so on.

Managers concerned with personnel should follow a similar model. First they need to analyze the personnel problem—or the person with a problem— by looking at all the data at hand. Then they decide which causes are operating and how the problem can be alleviated. They do not give up if the most probable cause does not seem to be operating, but proceed down the list of causes until the underlying source of the problem is found.

Suppose a manager had noticed from the weekly production reports that productivity in the department had been declining over the past few weeks. There could be a number of causes or reasons for this decline. Perhaps the equipment in the department has become defective and is not working properly, or the materials and supplies have been of a comparatively lower quality. Or the cause might be the workers: Perhaps some of the more highly skilled employees have been promoted, transferred to other departments, or quit, and their replacements lack the necessary skills and experience to perform the work effectively. Or, perhaps the problem is one of poor employee morale.

In investigating the problem, the diagnostic manager may have found that turnover in the department has been quite high, that absenteeism has been increasing, and that there have been more complaints and grievances. All of these are symptoms of low morale. If the manager concludes that the most likely cause of poor production in the department is the low morale of employees, a solution for this problem will be sought. The manager may consider such prescriptions as providing better working conditions, increasing pay and other financial benefits, improving communication between supervisor and employees, redesigning the jobs to make them more interesting and challenging, or modifying the manager's own leadership style.

If, after treating the morale problem, productivity is still low, the manager will turn to the next most probable cause of this production problem and continue down the list of causes until the right one is found and corrected.

The diagnostic model

Once it is accepted that effective managers of people should consider the big picture in trying to solve personnel problems, the next issue is what factors in this picture are relevant. Of all the factors that could be considered, the most important are given in the diagnostic model shown in Exhibit 2–1, which is used throughout this book. The model is rather complex because understanding what goes on at work is a complicated process. The model is divided into three sectors which influence personnel practices and therefore affect organizational effectiveness and personal satisfaction and productivity.

EXHIBIT 2–1
The diagnostic model: Factors affecting personnel activities and organizational effectiveness

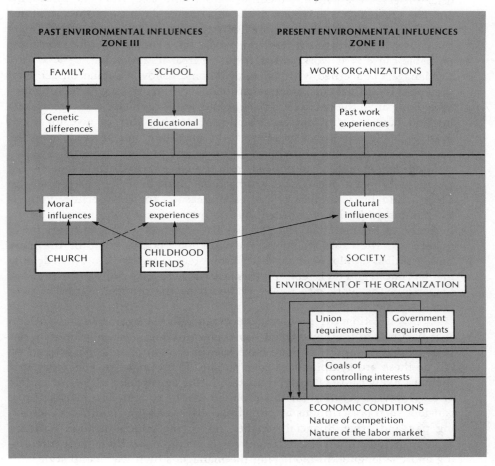

The most important sector is the immediate environment in which personnel activities take place (Zone I). The main factors in the immediate environment include:

The nature of the employee.   The employee is an individual with abilities and attitudes he or she was born with or learned. The origin of these influences is shown in Zones II and III.

The nature of the task.   This is the job done by the individual and the work group.

The work group.   This is the set of people with whom the individual interacts to accomplish the task.

The leader.   This is the person responsible for the productivity of the employee and the work group.

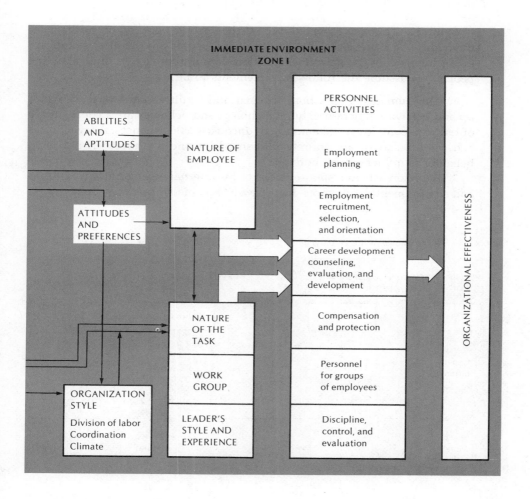

These factors and how they affect the personnel function will be discussed in this chapter.

The other major influence on personnel decisions in the immediate environment is the organization style. The work organization is restricted in the way it arranges the work by forces in its environment (Zone II). These forces include government, labor unions (if any), the economic environment, and the style of the organization. These will be discussed in Chapter 3.

In examining the parts of the diagnostic model, we will begin by considering how the nature of the employee affects the personnel process. Since this is not a book on psychology or human behavior in organizations, this section will simply summarize some basic concepts from these areas of knowledge and relate them to personnel management.

PEOPLE AND THE PERSONNEL FUNCTION

Exhibit 2–2 extracts from Exhibit 2–1 the "people" portion of the diagnostic model. We believe that in all enterprises, people are the most significant factor influencing the personnel function. In our approach to understanding people, we assume the following statements to be true:

1. The human being is both rational and intuitive-emotional in make-up and behavior. Therefore, human choices and behavior are a consequence of rational (conscious) and emotional (unconscious) influences. A few choices and some behavior are entirely influenced by one or the other, but most behavior is influenced by both.

2. A person acts in response to her or his internal inclinations and choices and environmental influences. Kurt Lewin explained it this way: Behavior = *f*

EXHIBIT 2–2
Factors affecting the nature of the employee

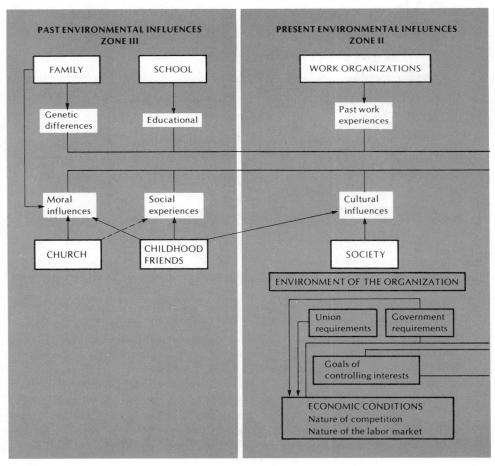

(P,E), or Behavior is a function of the person and the environment. At times one or the other predominates, but most behavior is influenced by both.[1]

3. Each individual is unique. He or she acts and thinks in a certain way because of

- The personality the person develops.
- The aptitudes and abilities the person has or learns.
- The attitudes and preferences the person has or develops.
- The motives the person has or develops.

Exhibit 2–2 indicates how abilities, attitudes, motives, and personality are developed in the individual. The family, school, church, society, friends,

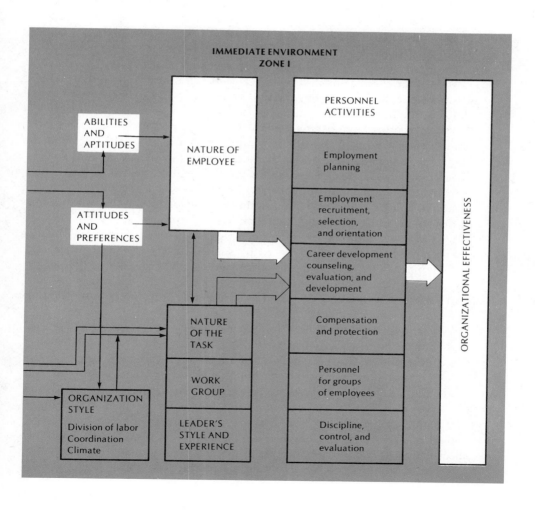

and work organizations all influence these attributes, which in turn affect personnel activities and organizational effectiveness.

The employee's personality

To the average person, the word "personality" has a special meaning. When you hear someone described as having "a great personality," you probably picture the subject as very outgoing, witty, and interesting to be with. When the description is applied to a prospective date, you might conclude the subject was not too attractive physically.

Social scientists use the term in a different way.

DEFINITION

Personality is the characteristic way a person thinks and behaves in adjusting to his or her environment. It includes the person's traits, values, motives, genetic blueprint, attitudes, emotional reactivity, abilities, self-image, and intelligence. It also includes the person's visible behavior patterns.[2]

We will discuss personality first because it is the summary concept which describes people as they are experienced by others. The other three factors affecting the nature of the employee are in fact parts of the personality.

Three theories have been advanced to explain personality development. One gives as a primary explanation human biology, or what the diagnostic model labels genetic differences. Sigmund Freud's explanation tends to emphasis biological factors in personality development; he described the human personality in terms of an animal struggling to become a psychic individual.[3] A second approach to understanding human personality is the intrapsychic or private mental-functioning approach, whose strongest spokesman is Carl Jung. Jung saw humans as primarily spiritual beings.[4] The third theory, the social-behavioral, was advanced by such theorists as Alfred Adler, and B. F. Skinner, who believe the personality develops primarily as the person interacts with the environment.[5] More modern theorists such as Erik Erikson, Carl Rogers, Abraham Maslow, and others see the personality as developing as a consequence of several of these forces.[6]

Why should managers know about personality—or care about it? Because they can be more effective in personnel management if they understand the differences in the personalities of their employees. We can be more specific about how managers use their knowledge of personality in their work. Suppose you are trying to understand an employee (Sam) so you can explain his lack of productivity and help improve it. You determine that Sam is extroverted, to use Jung's term. At present he does not receive enough social interaction, and he is bored. You might suggest, as a personnel specialist, moving Sam's job location physically, redesigning his job, transferring him to another job, or accepting his productivity level. If you were a supervisor, you would try to increase your social interaction with Sam, once you knew the problem.

A key point to remember is that each person's personality is unique, and it is highly unlikely that a single set of leadership approaches or personnel activities would be successful for all employees.

Abilities and aptitudes

All humans have abilities and aptitudes, which vary with the individual. Abilities (skills) and aptitudes (potential skills) are classified as mechanical, motor coordination, mental, or creative. Some studies report differences in abilities according to sex or race, but it has not been proven that these are due to either genetic or learning factors.[7]

> DEFINITION
> Abilities are skills which humans possess.
> Aptitudes are inclinations and potential skills.

According to many psychologists, some of these differences in ability are caused by genetic factors which are rarely subject to change through training. Examples of these differences are finger dexterity and response time. Other aptitudes and abilities, such as interpersonal skills and leadership, are much more easily subject to change. (More will be said about these factors in Chapter 7.)

A major personnel activity is to train employees or facilitate their learning and acquisition of skills and knowledge. They learn at home, at school, and at work, and their present inventories of abilities are at least partly a consequence of past learning.

Because people differ in abilities and aptitudes, the extent to which employees can be trained in a specific skill varies. In most cases, an aptitude can be developed into an ability by training and experience, but in others it makes more sense to match people who have certain abilities to jobs requiring these abilities. Everyone will not have all the abilities necessary to do these jobs, and a manager does not always have the time or money needed to train people who do not not have them.

Managers always seek high levels of performance from employees. Performance can be improved by application of the following formula: Performance = Ability × Motivation. Usually, managers overemphasize the ability side of the equation; that is, they are too quick to attribute failure to lack of ability. More frequently, the problem is one of motivation. A person somewhat lacking in ability can make up for it with greater motivation which leads to harder work.

To see what the manager can do with knowledge of employee ability and aptitude differences, consider the example of Julie, an employee who seems to be working hard yet fails to accomplish the expected output. Could she lack the abilities to do the job?

If it appears that Julie's problem is in fact ability, the manager would have at least two options: training, whereby Julie's aptitudes would be developed into the ability needed for the job, or matching, whereby she would be matched with a job requiring her present abilities. Then someone who has the needed abilities would be selected for Julie's former job.

Recognizing the differences in people's ability to learn, the manager can stimulate the desire to acquire skills with rewards such as pay and promotion. There are also differences in phases of learning, so that at various times the willingness to learn is greater or less, and the present life phase of the employee affects the amount of learning that will occur. Another factor affecting learning is who imparts it; the manager's skills as a teacher are important in this respect.

Attitudes and values

In addition to aptitudes and abilities, attitudes and values also affect the nature of the employee, as Exhibit 2–2 shows. Just as employees differ in such abilities as lifting heavy objects or creating advertising campaigns, so do they differ in their attitudes towards work and how they value it.

> DEFINITIONS
> An attitude is a characteristic and usually long-lasting way of thinking, feeling, and behaving toward an object, idea, person, or group of persons. A value is a type of attitude which evaluates an object, idea, or person in a positive or negative way.

Attitudes and values develop as a consequence of past experiences in the home, school, and at work.[8] Some psychologists believe that cognitive concepts and attitudes also can be transmitted genetically.

For the personnel function, the most relevant attitude is the person's attitude toward work and the place of work in his or her life. People are motivated by powerful emotional forces, and work provides an opportunity for the expression of both aggressive and libidinal (pleasure-seeking) drives. Freud said that a person with the most successful personality development knows how to heighten his or her capacity for obtaining pleasure from mental and intellectual work.

Besides offering a way to channel energy, work also provides the person with income, a justification for existence, and the opportunity to achieve self-esteem and self-worth. How much energy is directed into work is related to how much is directed to family, interpersonal relations, and recreation;

and this is partly a consequence of a person's attitudes toward the value or worth of work in life.

Historically, cultures and individuals have had two fundamentally opposed attitudes towards work:

Instrumental attitude. Work is a means to another end, and usually an unpleasant means. We work so we can reach the goals we seek and to pay our bills.

Work ethic attitude. Work is a satisfying end in itself. By performing work, we can find satisfying, even pleasurable, results and self-fulfillment.

The first view has been the predominant one for most workers throughout history. It even prevailed in the United States in the 1800s, when some historians believe the work ethic was strongest. In most early societies, such as ancient Greece, Egypt, Rome, or Israel, work was regarded as degrading and fit only for the masses whose lot was to be born to work. The Old Testament view that work was a consequence of original sin and therefore a means of expiating it is typical of these early beliefs. Later Protestant Christianity put forth the view that work was not only the means to earn one's way in life but provided wealth whereby less fortunate people could be served through charity.

Attitudes toward work evolve from the culture and one's family, school, and work experiences.[9] Today, perhaps the most predominant attitude is the instrumental one, but individuals in the work force have varying views of work. Although these attitudes probably differ with age, sex, race, education, and experience, there is some tendency for blue-collar and clerical employees to hold instrumental attitudes and for professional, technical, and managerial employees to hold work ethic attitudes. Most people move back and forth along the continuum between these attitudes over their lifetimes, however.

The Wall Street Journal has reported on several cases in which work attitudes have changed. Chuck Robichaux had been an auto worker with instrumental attitudes and a low motivation to work. Then he was laid off. When he was called back, his work attitudes moved toward the work ethic, as his motivation improved. In contrast, Tony Rousellot was a successful stockbroker with work ethic attitudes and a strong work motivation. His attitude changed to the extent that he now raises tropical plants to make only an adequate living so he can ski a lot.[10]

How does understanding attitudes and values help managers understand people at work and thus improve their effectiveness? Whether a worker holds instrumental or work ethic attitudes toward work should affect the way in which he or she is treated. Job design, or enlarging the job and assigning it more responsibility, is more likely to be successful if work is seen as a satisfying end in itself than if it is viewed only as a means to another end. Such instrumental attitudes are more likely to call for closer supervision and control systems. Many personnel management programs (job enlargement, compensation, leadership, and participation programs) are designed to shift employees from instrumental to work ethic attitudes, with the assumption the behavior changes will result in better quality and higher production.

Because attitudes influence behavior, they also affect performance. But performance is also influenced by learning, perception, motivation, and abilities. Many studies indicate that the results are mixed or tests of the relationship which equates good attitudes with good performance. In general, employees with "good" work attitudes (satisfaction with work) are absent less often, quit less often, have fewer accidents. But in some cases, employees with good attitudes are only average in performances; perhaps they lack the necessary abilities.

Motivation

In applying the formula which sees effective human performance as the product of ability and motivation, many managers seem to believe that abilities are fixed, and the variable is motivation. A lot of money is made selling books and executive development programs which claim to provide the key to the treasured knowledge about motivation. Sometimes they imply that you can push a motivation button and your problem will be solved. If it were only so simple!

Work motivation is concerned with those attitudes that channel the person's behavior toward work and away from recreation or other life activity areas. The motivation to work probably changes as other life activities change.

> DEFINITION
> Motivation is that set of attitudes which predispose a person to act in a specific, goal-directed way. Motivation is thus an inner state which energizes, channels, and sustains human behavior to achieve goals.

A number of theories which attempt to explain work motivation are shown on the continuum in Exhibit 2–3. The theories differ in their assumptions about how rational the human is and how much behavior is directed by the conscious and the unconscious mind. (It should be noted that Exhibit 2–3 tends to oversimplify these theories somewhat.)

At the left side are those who explain the motivation of behavior as responses to external stimuli (behaviorism) or to unconscious (and possibly unknown) motives. Psychoanalytic theory deemphasizes the rationality of the person, and behaviorism treats the person as easily programmable. At the other extreme is expectancy theory, which sees the person as a rational, hedonistic, but also predictable being. In between is a set of theories which, intentionally or not, portray the person as a quasirational, quasiemotional being. These theories, or some variation of them, are likely to provide a

EXHIBIT 2–3
Views of the nature of the human being and motivation theories

The human acts instinctively (*the unconscious*)	*The human is a mix of instinctual and rational*	*The human acts rationally* (*the conscious*)
Psychoanalytic theory	Maslow's hierarchy of needs theory	Consistency theory
Behaviorism theory	McClelland/Atkinson's needs theory	Equity theory
Behavior modification theory	Herzberg's two-factor theory	Expectancy theory

fuller explanation of human motivation at work than the extreme positions do.

Behaviorism tries to explain the motivation to work with instinctual drives to satisfy deprivation of basic needs. John B. Watson and Clark Hull gave this explanation.[11] Most researchers regard this as an oversimplified view of behavior. Behavior modification (B. F. Skinner) sees motivation to work as resulting from the pairing of prior stimuli to operant behavior. Past positive consequences lead to future positively desired behavior. This approach is more realistic than behaviorism, but it is oversimplified.[12]

Psychoanalytic theory, as developed by Sigmund Freud and Carl Jung, argues that humans do not fully understand why they act; and they act in response to conflicting, often unknown and unconscious, motives. This theory rejects rational, conscious motives as "causes" of work behavior. But the evidence from studies of the rational or conscious theories indicate that, at least some of the time, people do act in response to conscious, rational motives.

There are a number of mixed instinctual-rational theories of motivation. Frederick Herzberg argues that a set of motives called hygiene must be present in the workplace, but this does not affect performance; another set of motives called motivators (or satisfiers) motivate work behavior.[13] Maslow explains how various motives become activated and influence work behavior. His hierarchy of needs theory contends that innate needs predominate, and ego and self-fulfillment needs are actuated only after the innate needs are satisfied. Maslow's theory has recently been reformulated by Clayton Alderfer.[14] David McClelland and J. W. Atkinson's achievement need theory, using a different set of needs than Maslow's, provides useful insights into when employees are well motivated to success.[15]

The right side of the continuum lists the more rational theories. Consistency theory, as described by Abraham Korman, contends that people are motivated to keep themselves in balance with their self-image.[16] Equity theory contends that employees are motivated to work to the extent that they are treated equitably (and especially rewarded) for their contributions at work.[17] Expectancy theory posits that people work harder (or better) if

EXHIBIT 2–4
The employee as a crucial variable in the personnel function

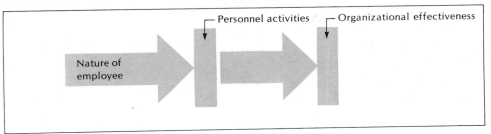

they can calculate how their work will contribute to the achievement of the ends they seek.[18]

All of these theories have received some research support, but none has been overwhelmingly substantiated. The extreme theories are not likely to achieve full acceptance. There is no comprehensive theory of motivation which weighs both the rational and the emotional/instinctual motives.[19]

What will a knowledge of motivation do to help a manager be a more effective manager of people? As with work attitudes, a manager who can determine what the work motivations of the employees are will make more effective personnel decisions. For employees who appear to be work oriented and well motivated toward work, incentive compensation systems will likely lead to more production and better quality work. For those who are consciously motivated to do a better job at work, performance evaluation techniques like management by objectives make sense. Managers who can determine which employees are motivated to work harder can select the employees they want. If they know (or can find out) that present employees would respond to security motives (in Maslow's terms), personnel policies like promotion from within, seniority-based personnel systems, and only extremely rare terminations make sense.

This section has refreshed your memory on some relevant concepts from the behavioral sciences, to show that the nature of the employee has a great influence on some personnel decisions. This concept is summarized in Exhibit 2–4; the effective manager realizes that the employee's nature is a crucial variable in personnel activities and organizational effectiveness. The implications of this knowledge of human behavior for the various personnel activities to be considered in this book will be described in chapters to come.

THE LEADER, THE WORK GROUP, AND THE TASK

In addition to the nature of the employee, three other variables in the immediate environment (Zone I) directly influence the personnel process: the nature of the task, the work group, and the leader's experience and

EXHIBIT 2–5
Other variables in the immediate environment

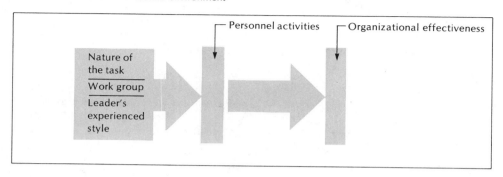

style. Exhibit 2–5 extracts the part of the diagnostic model (Exhibit 2–1) that applies to this section.

The operating manager–leader

The experience and leadership style of the operating manager directly affect personnel activities because many, if not most, personnel programs must be implemented at the work-unit level. Thus the operating manager is a crucial link in the personnel function.

To illustrate how the experience and style of operating management influences the personnel function, consider the following case situation I analyzed recently.

The Acme Manufacturing Company has just completed its evaluation of personnel procedures (see Chapter 21). At Acme, this process includes sending the supervisors reports on the previous period's personnel indicators, accident rates, turnover (number of persons quitting), amount of absenteeism from the job, and quality reports (number of items that had to be remanufactured because of poor quality). Supervisors were also provided with results of the company attitude survey. Each supervisor was given the average response for all employees in the company for each item on the survey, and the average response for the employees in the supervisor's unit. Those items that differed significantly from the company response were circled.

In unit 1 the supervisor is Jenny Argo, who has been a supervisor for less than a year. Her unit's absenteeism, turnover, accident rate, and quality were more than 10 percent worse than the company average. The attitude survey indicated that Jenny's employees were significantly more dissatisfied with Jenny's leadership style, style of communicating, amount of communication, and willingness to discuss work problems with employees.

In unit 2 the supervisor is Claudia Wagner. Claudia has been supervisor for five years. Her unit's absenteeism, turnover, accident rate and quality were 3 percent worse than the company average. The attitude survey indicated about average evaluations of Claudia's supervisory skills.

The day the reports came out, Jenny and Claudia had lunch together and discussed the reports.

Claudia: I'm really upset. Those results tell me I'm doing something wrong. I plan to invite Mary Jane Uvalde from Personnel down. I must be doing something wrong. Maybe my weekly employee meetings are being conducted wrong.

Jenny: What weekly meeting?

Claudia: I have a meeting on Friday afternoon about coffee break time and we kick around suggestions on how to get the job done better. My gang tells me when I'm leaning too hard on them and about their problems.

Jenny: What a waste of time! You're the supervisor. Why do you give up your authority to the girls like that?

Claudia: I don't give up anything. We help each other. Besides, my results are three times better than yours. Why should I listen to your advice?

Jenny: Don't worry about results. Mine aren't bad. And if it gets any worse, I plan to knock some heads and kick some butts around. That'll shape them up.

This case example is designed to point out that the way supervisory and personnel decisions are made varies with the leadership style of the managers. Jenny's attitude indicates she follows a conservative leadership style, and Claudia pursues a middle-of-the-road style. (The leadership styles are described in Chapter 3.) Jenny is also inexperienced as a leader. She is not concerned about some rather poor personnel indicators and seems to assume that tough disciplinary measures will solve whatever is causing the problems. Claudia, more experienced, is seeking all the help she can get from the personnel specialist and her employees to get at the causes of her problem, which is much less severe. But Claudia sees the problem as serious—Jenny does not.

Of course leadership style is a complicated topic. Many management experts believe that most styles can be effective, given the right match of leader, employees, and task situation.[20] In any case, the experience and preferred leadership style of the operating manager–leader will influence how personnel decisions are made and how personnel programs are communicated and implemented.

The work group

Managers and personnel specialists deal with the personnel problems of individual employees and groups of employees. Examples of the latter are problems in labor relations and equal employment opportunity regulations.

A group which is effective as a work unit will help achieve the goals of the enterprise. Thus it is in the manager's interest to make the groups effective. This also is in the interests of workers, because effective groups serve their members' social needs.

> DEFINITION
>
> A work group is a set of two or more people who see themselves as a group, who are interdependent with one another for the accomplishment of a purpose, and who communicate and interact with one another on a more or less continuous basis. In many cases (but not always), they work closely together physically.

An effective group is one whose:

- Members function and act as a team.
- Members participate fully in group discussions.
- Group goals are clearly developed.
- Resources are adequate to accomplish group goals.
- Members furnish many useful suggestions toward goal achievement.

Most effective work groups are small (research indicates that 7 to 14 members is a good range), and their members have eye contact and work closely together. Effective groups also generally have stability of membership, and their members are similar in backgrounds.

While the effective group generally supports management and the organization's goals, it also can work against them. This usually is so when the group perceives the organization's goals as being in conflict with its own. If the work group is effective and works with management, the manager's job is easier and objectives are more likely to be achieved. If the group is working against the manager, an effort must be made to change the group's norms and behavior by use of the manager's leadership, discipline, and reward powers, or by the transfer of some group members.[21]

Work groups are directly related to the success of personnel activities. If they oppose personnel programs, they can ruin them. Examples of programs which can be successes or failures depending on work-group support or resistance include incentive compensation, profit sharing, safety, and orientation. Operational and personnel managers who desire success in such programs should build work-group participation into the design and implementation of personnel activities.

The task to be performed

The nature of the task is one of the two most important factors affecting personnel success. In fact, many would summarize the personnel function this way:

$$\text{Nature of the employee} \longleftrightarrow \text{Nature of the task}$$

They contend that to get maximum performance and employee satisfaction, the key is get the right person on the right job. It is arguable that the major cause of employee turnover in the first five years of work is a bad match between these two variables. This mismatch often is due to the employee's lacking skills in the tasks to be performed and having an ego which is not fully developed. (Some psychoanalysts believe that the ego is not fully developed until age 40.)

Many people have stereotyped attitudes toward various jobs. They watch Perry Mason reruns on television and therefore think lawyers' lives are spent in court defending wronged clients. In fact, most lawyers never present a case in court, and when they do, this takes only a small part of their time. Students in a school of education may dream of thirsting minds awaiting refreshment from their teaching talents, and then they get assigned to teach algebra in a ghetto school and find out differently. I was a salesman before becoming a professor; a salesman's job is a good one and can be very lucrative, but it was the wrong job for me.

You must work out your occupational identity. This section will make you aware of the different dimensions of various tasks, and we suggest that you work out a profile of your own preferences. In Chapter 6, "Recruiting and Job Search," there is a mechanism for completion of an instrument to help you formulate a job choice strategy which will increase your success and satisfaction. The task is not a universally measurable quantity, such as a liter of water or 100 meters of ground. People perceive the same jobs differently.[22]

There is perhaps an unlimited number of similarities and differences among jobs which will attract or repel possible workers and influence the meaning of work for them. Only a few will be discussed here. These are intended to provide the data by which the diagnostic manager can assess the job situations with which he or she must deal. The manager who understands the human dimensions of the workplace and why some people behave the way they do regarding their jobs will make better personnel decisions.

In general, the less pleasant the workers perceive the work to be, the more rewards (financial and otherwise) will be necessary to attract employees and reduce turnover in good times. In bad times, dissatisfied workers may be unable to quit, but they find ways to work less and thus increase their relative rewards. In such ways, the task affects personnel activities and decisions directly.

Some dimensions of the task

Dimensions of the task to be discussed are: the physical exertion required, the degree of environmental pleasantness, the physical location of the work, the time of work, human interaction on the job, the amount of specialization in the job, and psychological aspects of work.

Degree of physical exertion required.   Consider a series of jobs: bookkeeper, mail carrier, automobile assembler, ditchdigger. Each job in the list requires a greater expenditure of physical energy than the preceding one. Since individuals differ in their physical abilities (compare a healthy 18-year-old youth and a 64-year-old man with heart trouble for the ditchdigger job) and in their preference for physical work, their valuation of the desirability of these jobs will differ. In general, work involving relatively heavy physical exertion is less preferred than lighter work is today.

Degree of environmental pleasantness.   Some working conditions are perceived as unpleasant; when these conditions are absent, it is pleasant. Examples are excessive heat, particles in the air, noise, darkness, and unpleasant smells. The more of these conditions present, the less pleasant most workers will find the work. Another condition is how safe it is at the workplace. Miners and food inspectors face more hazards than typists or accountants.

Physical location of work.   Work location includes such aspects as whether the work is performed outside or inside and in one place or many. Many prefer to work outdoors but may change this preference at times; for example, construction work is not attractive in frigid temperatures. Others prefer protected inside work. Examples of work in one location include assembly-line worker, bank teller, medical technologist in a laboratory. Others prefer to move about, such as outside salesmen, a weights and measures supervisor for a city, union business agents, and entertainers.

The time dimension of work.   Some jobs call for long hours of less taxing work, others for shorter periods of intense effort. In some jobs the work is continuous, in others intermittent. There has been much experimentation recently on hours of work. Some firms have shifted to a four-day week, or four 10-hour days and a three-day weekend. Others have shifted to more flexible hours. These programs will be discussed more in Chapter 5.

Human interaction on the job.   Another technical characteristic of a job is the degree of human interaction possible and whether or not the employee finds this desirable. A person who was an only child who had been reared on a farm and often worked alone might prefer a position which required working on one's own, such as a keeper of a lighthouse. The same job would probably be ill suited for an extrovert from a large family who prefers frequent contact with others.

Closely related to these interaction characteristics is the degree of interpersonal conflict likely to be present in a position. Conflict seems less likely when working by oneself, but an additional dimension of the job can be required interactions which could lead to conflict. Most jobs have some built-in conflict, but some have much more than others. Labor negotiators are a good example of conflict-laden positions, as are troubleshooters, product managers, external auditors, quality control inspectors, disciplinary deans in universities, game wardens, internal revenue agents, and equal employment opportunity investigators. Less conflict would be expected in jobs such as placement officers in universities, lab technicians in hospitals, statisticians in a state highway department, and market researchers in business.

Degree of specialization of work. As will be discussed in Chapter 4, some jobs involve lots of different functions, others only a few. In an engineering sense, the number of functions can be measured and the number of physical motions expended can be counted. The worker who puts nut 42 on bolt 84 so many times a day (as Charlie Chaplin stereotyped all industrial work in *Modern Times*) has a very narrow, routine job. A troubleshooter for the President of the United States, in contrast, would have a variety of assignments.

Psychological aspects of work. Various psychological dimensions influence jobs and therefore the meaning of work in a person's life. Important psychological dimensions and characteristics by which tasks can be described include:

- Degree of freedom to do the job.
- Degree of risk-taking necessary on the job.
- Degree of responsibility in the job.

Some positions are structured to provide a great deal of freedom on the job. For example, many college professors are not closely supervised in teaching their courses and may be quite free in the choice of their other activities: research and writing, counseling, committee work, and so on. Some "missionary" salesmen are free to do their jobs independently, as long as they meet a goal of so many new orders or items sold. Other jobs involve very little freedom of choice of what, when, and how the work is to be done. Assembly-line workers are good examples of these jobs, as are licensed practical nurses in hospitals, garrison infantrymen, fee clerks in college bursar's offices, and route salesmen for bread companies. Some firms try to reduce this control by eliminating time clocks, as Motorola has.

Other psychological dimensions involve the degree of risk and responsibility required in decision making on the job. Hedging decisions for agricultural concerns involves risk, as do the jobs of a purchasing agent for a top discount store or the vice president of programming for a TV network. So do certain police positions, emergency room staff positions in hospitals, and the work of military combat officers. Less risk is present for a cost accountant, a ticket manager for state university football games, a supervisor of highway operations, or a laundry manager at a convalescent hospital.

Job design

The aspect of personnel or industrial engineering that directly affects the degree of specialization of the job and the psychological dimensions of the task is called job design.

Human factors engineering (ergonomics) and industrial psychology are concerned with whatever affects job design. They also study how human limitations affect efficiency. Researchers in these fields have found, for exam-

> DEFINITION
>
> Job design is the personnel or engineering activity of specifying the contents of the job, the tools and techniques to be used, the surroundings of the work, and the relationship of one job to other jobs.

ple, that there is an efficient and an inefficient way to provide information input to employees. They also have learned that fatigue can affect output: work speed and accuracy decrease as the work period increases. Another finding is that mental fatigue, which affects performance, is a result of certain kinds of work being performed at length. These are the types of factors studied by engineers in their design or redesign of jobs.

Personnel and operating managers are involved in other kinds of job design. For example, they help determine the amount of variety in the job, as well as the amount of responsibility and autonomy. Both theory and research indicate that this aspect of job design has an impact on motivation and performance.[23]

There are four approaches to those aspects of job design that affect the degree of specialization and the psychological dimensions of work. The first is called *work simplification;* this job design leads to very specialized jobs. In the work simplification approach, the complete job (such as making a car) is broken down into small subparts, usually consisting of a few operations. This is done because:

Less well-trained and less well-paid employees can do these jobs.

More workers are available for hire, since there are more unskilled than skilled workers.

By repeating the same operations over and over, the employee gets better at it.

Many small jobs can be performed simultaneously, so that the complete operation can be done more quickly.

The second approach to job design is *job rotation.* In job rotation, the employees take turns at several work-simplified jobs. Job rotation provides more flexible work assignments, makes it easier to staff the more unpleasant jobs (or heavier jobs), and reduces the boredom and monotony of the work-simplified jobs.

The third approach is *job enlargement,* the opposite of work simplification. If the work-simplified job consisted of three operations, the job enlargement approach expands this until a meaningful subunit (or subprocess) is completed by one person. The theory is that "whole" jobs reduce boredom (through more variety) and give more meaning to work.

The fourth approach is *job enrichment.* Job enrichment increases the responsibility of the workers and gives them more autonomy and freedom of control. Job enrichment is said to provide more meaning to work for many employees.

Obviously, there can be a combination of several of these strategies. For example, a likely combination is job enrichment and job enlargement.

There have been few studies of the effectiveness of job rotation,[24] but, in general, employees prefer job rotation to work-simplified jobs, and their productivity is greater with this plan. Most of the research has contrasted work-simplified jobs with jobs that have been enlarged. The research is vast on this comparison, and there are studies favoring both approaches. Probably the best criterion for choosing between the two is that employees who hold work ethic attitudes prefer job enlargement and job enrichment, and those who hold instrumental attitudes do not respond positively to either of these approaches as a matter of course. J. Richard Hackman, who favors job enlargement and job enrichment, contends that the negative findings on these two approaches are due to their being poorly implemented. Many managements are not sold on them, and some unions are opposed. In any case, only about 20 percent of all enterprises have tried job enrichment or job enlargement.[25] Much less research has been done on contrasting job-simplified with enriched jobs. Some studies are positive;[26] others are neutral or negative.[27]

In the best summary of job design at present, Hackman indicates that the relationship between job design and effective performance is complex. He shows that effective job design *can contribute* to performance and employee satisfaction, but there *is no universally good design of work.* Individual differences, interpersonal relationships, organizational climate, and style and technology affect the relative effectiveness of the four job design models.[28]

What does this job design research mean to the operating or personnel manager? To the extent that the research done thus far is accurate, job enlargement and job enrichment may help improve the satisfaction of some workers (generally those who are more educated, and especially those holding work ethic values). Otherwise, the 80 percent of the jobs that have been simplified, perhaps combined with job rotation, can be effective.

Exhibit 2–6 profiles two jobs along the task dimensions discussed above. Note the significant differences between the two jobs. A job-seeker could match his preferences in regard to these factors against the task dimensions of a particular position. No one would get all his or her preferences, but those that are most strongly held could be satisfied.

How do these task factors affect personnel decisions? They obviously affect recruiting and selection, since the employee will probably be more satisfied and productive if his or her preferences on physical exertion, environmental pleasantries, location, time patterns, specialization, interaction, conflict, freedom, risk, and responsibility are met. Few jobs match these preferences exactly; these are too many preferences. For jobs that few people prefer because the work is difficult, dirty, or in smoky or hot environments, the manager must provide additional incentives such as more pay, shorter hours, or priority in vacations. Or the manager may try to find employees who can handle the conditions better; for example, hire a deaf person to work in a noisy environment, or a mentally retarded person to do routine,

EXHIBIT 2–6
A profile of task dimension differences for stock clerks and carpenter's assistants

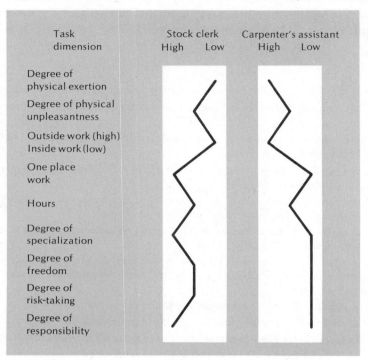

repetitive work which a person with a higher IQ might find boring. For each personnel decision discussed in the chapters to follow, the task factors that are most salient to each activity will be described.

SUMMARY

One objective of this chapter was to introduce you to the diagnostic model. As a beginning in discussing this model, the employee's nature and three factors in the immediate environment—the task, the work group, and the leader—were discussed.

This book has been written with the assumption that effective personnel management will result if the manager or specialist follows the diagnostic approach. Good personnel relations contribute to organizational effectiveness, along with such functions as financial management, operations management, and marketing and client relations activities.

The diagnostic approach suggests that before you choose a personnel program you examine the kind of employees you have, the tasks they do, and the work groups and their leaders. Personnel decisions are made with these factors as the independent variables, and the personnel activities flow from them. Chapter 2 briefly reviewed some applicable findings from the social sciences to show you how they apply to personnel decisions.

Chapter 3 completes the introductory portion of the book by describing how organizational and environmental variables affect personnel decisions.

QUESTIONS

1. What is the diagnostic approach to personnel functions? Why is it important?
2. What are the major factors in the immediate environment of the personnel function?
3. What is personality? How does an understanding of personality help a manager make better personnel decisions?
4. What are abilities? How does an understanding of abilities help a manager make better personnel decisions?
5. What are attitudes and values? How does an understanding of attitudes and values help a manager make better personnel decisions?
6. What is motivation? How does an understanding of motivation help a manager make better personnel decisions?
7. Discuss briefly why employees differ in personality, abilities, attitude, values, and motivation. Of what significance are these differences to personnel decisions?
8. How do leadership styles and leader experience affect personnel?
9. What is an effective group? How does it affect personnel activities?
10. How do tasks differ? How does this affect the manager interested in personnel?
11. How can jobs be designed? How does job design affect employee performance and satisfaction, or does it?

NOTES AND REFERENCES

1. Kurt Lewin, *Dynamic Theory of Personality* (New York: McGraw-Hill Book Co., 1935).
2. James McConnell, *Understanding Human Behavior* (New York: Holt, Rinehart, & Winston, 1974).
3. Sigmund Freud, *The Basic Writings of S. Freud,* trans. A. Brill (New York: Modern Library, 1938).
4. Carl Jung, *Personality Types* (New York: Harcourt Brace, 1923).
5. Alfred Adler, *The Individual Psychology of Alfred Adler,* ed. H. and R. Ansbacher (New York: Basic Books, 1956); B. F. Skinner, *Science and Behavior* (New York: Macmillan Co., 1953).
6. Erik Erikson, *Childhood and Society* (New York: W. W. Norton & Co., 1963); Carl Rogers, *On Becoming A Person* (Boston: Houghton Mifflin Co., 1961); Abraham Maslow, *Motivation and Personality* (New York: Harper & Row, 1954).
7. Anne Anastasi, *Differential Psychology* (New York: Macmillan Co., 1970).
8. For a psychoanalytical analysis of this, see Walter W. Menninger, "The Power of Emotions, The Role of Feelings," in *Man and Work in Society,* ed. Eugene Case and Frederick Zimmer (New York: Van Nostrand Reinhold, 1975).
9. Cultural differences also influence people within a country. For example, French and English Canadians appear to hold different work attitudes and motivations. See for exam-

ple: Rabindra Kanungo et al., "Motivational Orientations of Canadian Anglophone and Francophone Managers," in H. C. Jain, and R. N. Kanungo, *Behavioral Issues in Management: The Canadian Context* (Toronto: McGraw-Hill Ryerson, 1977); L. W. Slivinski, "Attitudes of Managers in the Canadian Public Service," *Studies in Personnel Psychology I* (1969) pp. 71–92; M. Bunstein et al., *Canadian Work Values* (Information Canada, 1975).

10. John Emshwiller, "Change in Attitudes," *Wall Street Journal,* February 3, 1977; Eric Morgenthaler, "Dropouts Revisited," *Wall Street Journal,* December 27, 1976.

11. J. B. Watson, *Psychology from the Standpoint of a Behaviorist* (Philadelphia: Lippincott, 1924); Clark Hull, *Principles of Behavior* (New York: Appleton-Century-Crofts, 1943).

12. Craig Schneier, "Behavior Modification in Management: A Review and Critique," *Academy of Management Journal,* September 1974, pp. 528–48.

13. Frederick Herzberg, Bernard Mausner, and Barbara Snyderman, *The Motivation to Work* (New York: John Wiley & Sons, 1959).

14. Maslow, *Motivation and Personality;* Clayton Alderfer, *Existence, Relatedness, and Growth* (New York: Free Press, 1972).

15. David McClelland, *The Personality* (New York: Dryden Press, 1951); J. W. Atkinson, *An Introduction to Motivation* (New York: American Book Co., 1964).

16. Abraham Korman, *The Psychology of Motivation* (Englewood Cliffs, N.J.: Prentice-Hall, Inc., 1974).

17. J. Stacey Adams, "Inequity in Social Exchange," in *Advances in Experimental Social Psychology,* ed. Leonard Berkowitz (New York: Academic Press, 1965); J. Stacey Adams, "Toward an Understanding of Inequity," *Journal of Abnormal and Social Psychology* 67 (1963), pp. 422–36; Elliot Jaques, *Equitable Payment* (New York: John Wiley & Sons, 1961); Karl Weick, "The Concept of Equity in the Perception of Pay," *Administrative Science Quarterly,* 11 (1966), pp. 414–439.

18. Victor Vroom, *Work and Motivation* (New York: John Wiley & Sons, 1964).

19. John Campbell, and Robert Pritchard, "Motivation Theory in Industrial and Organizational Psychology," in Marvin Dunnette, *Handbook of Industrial and Organizational Psychology* (Chicago: Rand-McNally & Co., 1976).

20. For further understanding of leadership style, see Fred E. Fiedler, *A Theory of Leadership Effectiveness* (New York: McGraw-Hill Book Co., 1967); Fred Fiedler, and Martin Chemers, *Leadership and Effective Management* (Glenview, Ill.: Scott, Foresman & Co., 1974); Robert House, "A Path Goal Theory of Leadership Effectiveness," *Administrative Science Quarterly* 16 (1970), pp. 321–38; Ralph Stogdill, *Handbook of Leadership* (New York: Free Press, 1974); Victor Vroom and Phillip Yetton, *Leadership and Decision Making* (Pittsburgh: University of Pittsburgh Press, 1973).

21. James David, *Group Performance* (Reading, Mass.: Addison-Wesley Publishing, Co., 1969).

22. Robert Dubin et al., "Implications of Differential Job Perceptions," *Industrial Relations,* October 1974, pp. 265–73.

23. Donald Schwab and L. L. Cummings, "A Theoretical Analysis of the Impact of Task Scope on Employee Performance," *Academy of Management Review,* April 1976, pp. 23–25.

24. J. R. P. French, "Field Experiments Changing Group Productivity," in *Experiments in Social Psychology,* ed. J. G. Miller (New York: McGraw-Hill Book Co. 1950); Floyd Mann et al., *Automation and the Worker* (New York: Holt, Rinehart, & Winston, 1960); F. G. Miller, et al., "Job Rotation Raises Productivity," *Industrial Engineering* 5 (1973).

25. M. Blood and C. Hulin, "Alienation, Environmental Characteristics, and Worker Responses," *Journal of Applied Psychology,* 51 (1967), pp. 284–90; Donald Collins and Robert Raubolt, "A Study of Employee Resistance to Job Enrichment," *Personnel Journal,* April 1975, pp. 232–48. J. Richard Hackman, "Is Job Enrichment Just a Fad?" *Harvard Business Review,*

September–October 1975, pp. 129–38; J. Richard Hackman, et al., "A New Strategy for Job Enrichment," *California Management Review,* Summer 1975, pp. 57–71; Charles Hulin, "Individual Differences and Job Enrichment: The Case Against General Treatments," in *New Perspectives in Job Enrichment,* ed. John Mahler (New York: Van Nostrand Reinhold, 1971).

26. Edwin Locke, et al., "An Experimental Case Study of the Success and Failures of Job Enrichment in a Government Agency," *Journal of Applied Psychology* 61, 6 (1976), pp. 701–11; Greg Oldham, et al., "Conditions under Which Employees Respond Positively to Enriched Work," *Journal of Applied Psychology* 61, 4 (1976), pp. 395–403; D. A. Ondrack, "Emerging Occupational Values," *Academy of Management Journal,* September 1973, pp. 423–32; William Paul, et al., "Job Enrichment Pays Off," *Harvard Business Review,* March–April, 1969, pp. 61–78; Rollin Simonds and John Orife "Work Behavior versus Enrichment Theory," *Administrative Science Quarterly,* December 1975, pp. 606–12; David Whitsett and Erik K. Winslow "An Analysis of Studies Critical of the Motivation Hygiene Theory," *Personnel Psychology* 20 (1967), pp. 391–415.

27. Elliot Carlson, "Job Enrichment: Sometimes it Works," *Wall Street Journal,* December 13, 1971; Louis Davis et al., *Supervisory Job Design,* University of California, Institute of Engineering Research Report IE–64–5 (Berkeley, Calif., 1964); Louis Davis and E. Valfer, "Intervening Responses to Changes in Supervisor Job Design," *Occupational Psychology* 39 (1965), pp. 171–90; Linda Frank and Richard J. Hackman, "A Failure of Job Enrichment," *Journal of Applied Behavioral Science* 2, 4 (1975), pp. 413–36; "Rushton: An Experiment with Miners Regulating Their Own Work Activities," in *Recent Initiatives in Labor Management Cooperation* (Washington, D.C.: U.S. National Center for Productivity and Quality of Working Life, 1976), pp. 51–57; Howard Schwartz and Leopold Gruenfeld, "Psychological Assumptions and Utopian Asperations: A Critique of *Work in America,*" *Administrative Science Quarterly,* March 1975, pp. 126–130; Dennis Umstol et al., "Effects of Job Enrichment and Task Goals on Satisfaction and Productivity," *Journal of Applied Psychology* 61, 4 (1976), pp. 379–94.

28. J. Richard Hackman, "Work Design," in J. Richard Hackman and J. Lloyd Suttle, *Improving Life at Work* (Santa Monica, Calif.: Goodyear Publishing Co., Inc., 1977).

Organizational and other environmental factors affecting personnel

CHAPTER OBJECTIVES

■ To complete the presentations of the diagnostic personnel model.

■ To show how managers use their knowledge of environmental and organizational factors to improve their personnel decisions.

CHAPTER OUTLINE

John Searcy is a political consultant. His job is to help his candidate get elected. To do this, he uses many tools and techniques. He knows about the impact of various communications media, such as TV, radio, and newspapers, and how they work. He knows how to time a press release to make the morning newspaper or the early evening TV news and how to poll voters on their preferences. He can raise money, organize precinct workers, and coach his candidate on body language, speaking ability, hair style, clothing, and interpersonal relations.

How successful would John be in electing candidates if he tried to use *exactly* the same advertising appeals, speeches, and broadsides for a conservative Republican candidate running in Cincinnati's solid Republican district *and* a liberal Democrat running in a solid liberal district in Massachusetts? Before he applies the tools he uses, he studies the district, its political organization, past voting records, and winning appeals in the past. He gets to know the local political leaders, and so on. In sum, he would adapt the tools of the trade to the environment and the organization he is working in.

Personnel decisions are similar. A personnel manager may know his tools of the trade: what a performance share is, how to use a behaviorally anchored rating scale, what to do with a form EEO–1, how to conduct a legal and valid employment interview, and so on. But whether he would use the tools, and how, would depend on what kind of enterprise it is, government regulations, whether there is a local union or not, and similar environmental conditions. These are the external factors that affect personnel decisions.

THE ENVIRONMENT OF THE PERSONNEL FUNCTION

Exhibit 3–1 is essentially the bottom half of Zones I and II in the diagnostic model (Exhibit 2.1 in the preceding chapter). This chapter has essentially the same purpose as Chapter 2; that is, to help you understand how personnel activities vary with the environmental factors that surround the function. In Chapter 2 the factors discussed were the employee's nature, the task factors, and group and leadership variables. This chapter illustrates how some major environmental and organization factors influence the employee and the task, and thereby affect the personnel function. The first factor to be discussed is the physical location of the enterprise in which the personnel job is located.

Physical location of the enterprise

The location of the enterprise influences the kinds of people it hires and the personnel activities conducted in it. If a hospital, plant, university, or government bureau is located in a rural area, certain conditions are more likely than if it is located in an urban area. For example, the work force in a rural area might be more willing to accept conservative organization practices.[1] Recruiting and selection in rural areas will be different in that there may be fewer applicants. It also may be harder to schedule overtime if workers are supplementing farm incomes with an eight-hour shift at a factory. There may be fewer minority problems, but it also may be difficult to recruit professional/technical personnel, who have shown a preference to work near continuing education and cultural opportunities. While wages may be lower in rural areas, so are costs of living.

An urban location might be advantageous for recruiting and holding professional workers; urban locations provide a bigger labor force and call for higher wages. The late shifts may be a problem here, too, but for different reasons. Workers may not feel safe late at night in the parking lots or going home.

Thus geographic location influences the kinds of workers available to staff the enterprise. The location or setting is extremely significant for companies operating in other countries. The employees may speak a different language, abide by the Napoleonic legal code, practice different religions, have different work attitudes and so on. The major differences between home-based and other-country enterprises are:

Educational factors. Examples include the number of skilled employees available, attitudes toward education, and literacy level. Educational deficiencies in some countries can lead to a scarcity of qualified employees, as well as a lack of educational facilities to upgrade potential employees.

Behavioral factors. Societies differ in factors such as attitudes toward wealth, the desirability of profits, managerial role, and authority.

Legal-political factors. Laws and political structures differ and can encourage or discourage private enterprise. Nations also differ in degree of political stability. Some countries are very nationalistic (even xenophobic). Such countries can require local ownership of enterprises or, if they are so inclined, expropriate foreign concerns.

Economic factors. Economics differ in basic structure, inflation rate, ownership constraints, and the like.

The nations of the world can be divided into three economic categories: fully developed, developing, and less developed. The fully developed nations include the United States and Canada, Australia, Israel, Japan, South Africa, and most European countries (the United Kingdom, West Germany, France, the U.S.S.R., Belgium, Luxembourg, the Netherlands, Switzerland, Italy, Sweden, Denmark, Norway, Finland). In these countries American and Canadian managers will find fewer differences in educational, behavioral, economic, and legal-political factors than they are likely to encounter in developing or less developed countries.

The developing nations are those that are well along in economic development but cannot yet be said to be fully developed. Examples include Brazil, Mexico, Argentina, Venezuela, Chile, Spain, Portugal, Nigeria, Saudi Arabia, Iran, Libya, India, Singapore, Taiwan, eastern Europe (Yugoslavia, Romania, East Germany, Czechoslovakia), Korea, and possibly China. These countries provide more constraints in all four factors than developed countries do.

Third-World nations—the less developed countries—are the most difficult

EXHIBIT 3–1
Organizational factors in the environment which affect personnel

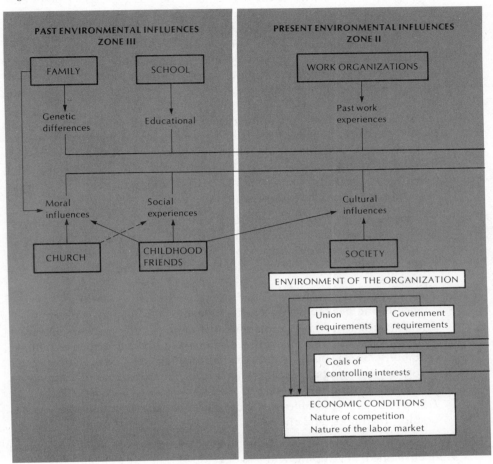

to work in because of significant constraints in all four factors. The remaining 90 or so countries in the world are in this group. A sample list would include Egypt, Pakistan, Bolivia, Paraguay, Upper Volta, and Sudan.

To be successful abroad, personnel managers must learn all they can about the countries in which they will be working. There are many sources of this kind of information. Mason Haire et al., for example, describes managerial attitudes around the world. Frederick Harbeson and Charles Myers, though their book dates back to 1959, provide a description of what it is like to manage in ten countries around the world; Joseph Massie and Jan Luytjes give advice on effective management in 12 countries.[2]

Knowledge of differences among nations in educational, behavioral, legal-political and economic factors is essential for managerial success abroad. It is equally important (and more difficult) for the enterprise to obtain managers

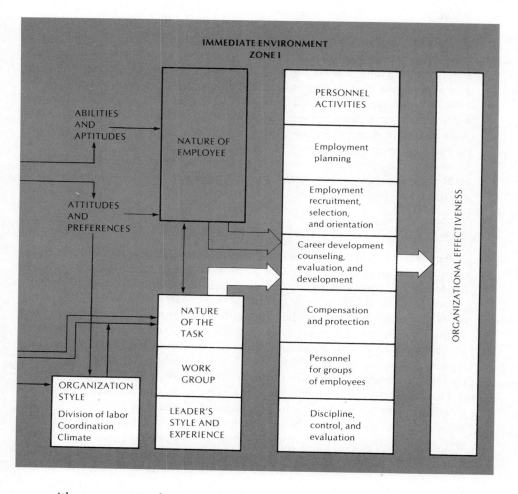

with proper attitudes toward other countries and their cultures. U.S. and Canadian managers working abroad may develop a mind set which compares the home country to the host nation abroad as follows:

U.S./Canada	Characteristic	Host nation
Strong	Strength	Weak
Wealthy	Wealth	Poor
Advanced	Managerial practice	Primitive
Important	Culture	Insignificant

A manager with this set of attitudes may try to transfer North American ways of doing things directly to the host country without considering the constraints in these four factors. The more significant the differences, the more likely they are to cause problems for the unperceptive manager.

Effective managers who work abroad must adapt their personnel practices to conditions in the host country and learn to understand the new culture. There are resources available to acquaint the manager with Canadian values that affect personnel,[3] European and Asian differences,[4] and so on. A whole new field is developing for human resource planning in multinational enterprises.[5] There are significant challenges in such personnel activities. Just as the tools of management science do not work on very unstable problems, so leadership styles and personnel activities that work for educated, achievement-oriented employees may not do so for uneducated nonachievers A liberal-style manager in the United States may have to become a middle-of-the-road manager in Egypt, for example.

In sum, the physical location of the enterprise (rural or urban, or at home or abroad, for example) can have significant impact on how personnel tools are used and which activities are conducted.

Private-, public-, and third-sector settings

About 60 percent of professional personnel specialists work for businesses; or in the private sector. The public sector is that part of the economy which is owned and operated by a government; in the United States, 30 percent of personnel specialists work in this sector. Many economists define the other institutions in society that are neither government nor profit oriented as the third sector. Examples of these institutions are museums, symphony orchestras, private schools and colleges, not-for-profit hospitals and nursing homes, voluntary organizations like churches, and social clubs. About 10 percent of personnel specialists operate in the third sector.

How does the sector or setting of the personnel function affect personnel activities? One factor shown in the diagnostic model in Exhibit 3–1 is the goals of the controlling interests, which can differ significantly in the three sectors. All sectors probably include enterprises that have the goals of employee satisfaction, survival, and adaptability to change. They differ on effectiveness goals: the extent to which surplus revenue (called profit in the private sector) is seen as desirable and the extent to which efficiency and cost-oriented goals are important.

To illustrate some of the potential differences in personnel settings, consider first a third-sector example. A museum is people oriented and offers art to be enjoyed as a service. Some people would find this work setting desirable, because museums are relaxed and intellectually stimulating. But museums normally have little money, so if people chose to work there they would have to expect less pay, fewer benefits, and little opportunity for advancement. Hospitals, too, might attract dedicated persons who would work for lower wages because they value the work.

In general, private- and third-sector personnel work is structured similarly. Hospitals have different conflicts than most businesses, though. The presence of three hierarchies—the physicians, the administrators, and the board of trustees (representing the public)—can lead to conflicts. Pressures put on by third-party payees such as Blue Cross or Medicare can lead to internal conflicts. Hospitals also employ professional groups that zealously guard their "rights," and this leads to conflict. There are specialized sources which consider personnel in the third sector, such as hospitals[6] and colleges and universities.[7] Structurally, personnel work in these two sectors is similar although organizational differences make personnel jobs vary.

Personnel in the public sector is fundamentally different from the other two sectors because it varies structurally, and the public manager faces a different world. In fact, a manager who moved from the private or third sector to the public sector would find the personnel role much more complicated. The diagnostic model was developed primarily for the private and third sectors. Exhibit 3–2 adjusts the basic model for the public sector.

People management in the public sector generally is much more laden with conflict. Politicians, the general public, pressure groups, and reporters look over the shoulders of the public manager and public personnel manager much more than in a private business.

Like all managers, the one in the public sector must seek resources from a hierarchy. But the public hierarchy can include a split between the executive branch (president, governor, city manager, prime minister) and the legislative branch (Congress or parliament, the state legislature, the city council). These forces may choose to have a political fight over any program. Then there is the press or the communications media, whose business it is to expose "useless, inefficient bureaucrats"; they are helped by out-of-power politicians who feed them information to discredit those in office.[8] In addition to these complications, the legal and regulatory restrictions are much greater in the public sector, so there is less flexibility and less room for initiative in that setting.[9] Also, public employee unions often lobby for their demands directly with politicians. The unions can muscle more votes than the public personnel managers.

In addition to these complications, most public managers must also deal with a central personnel bureau such as the Civil Service Commission. A special problem faced by public managers has always been the appointment to public positions of persons because of political reasons. Formerly, politicians always saw to it that their party workers were employed between elections in government jobs; this is usually called the spoils system. In an attempt to assure that public jobs are assigned on the basis of merit, not political pull, civil service or equivalent central personnel bureaus were established which set personnel policies to govern public employment. Civil Service standardized examinations are now required as part of the selection process for many public-sector jobs. This system was intended to establish merit as the criterion for public employment, but it also increases the system's rigidity and entrenches bureaucracy.[10]

There are reference sources specifically designed to help you prepare for public personnel management.[11] But the differences among public, private, and third-sector personnel activities are largely in the structure of the personnel function and the environment of the public manager's job.

EXHIBIT 3–2
The environment of personnel in the public sector

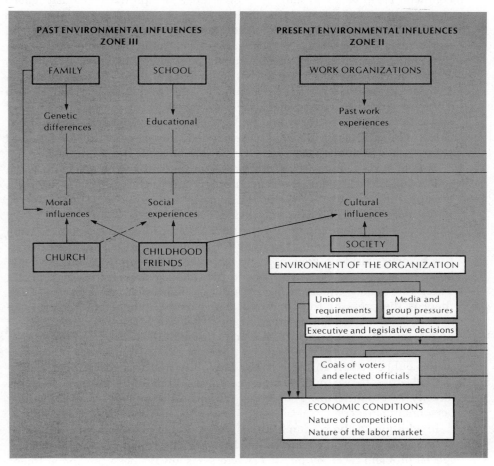

ENVIRONMENTAL INFLUENCES

Besides the physical location of the enterprise and the sector in which it operates, other factors in the environment also influence personnel activities. These factors are unions, governmental regulations and laws, and the economy, which involves the labor market and direct competition.

Labor unions

Mary Agular had been a supervisor at the John Madison Life Insurance Company. At that firm, she could hire her employees, usually with only slight coordination with the personnel department. She could hire them on the basis of merit and promote the best ones when they were ready.

When Mary took a new job with Consolidated Electronics, she found that promo-

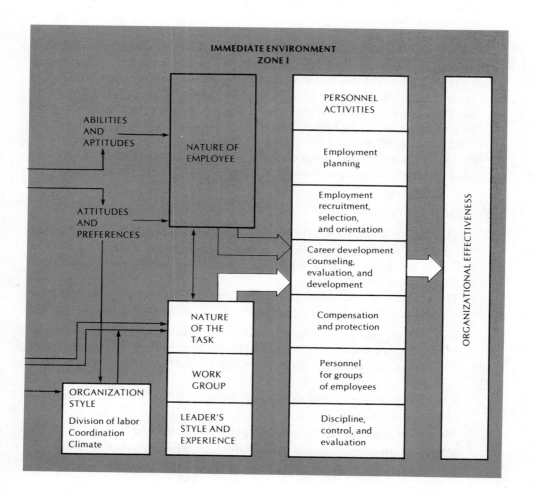

IMMEDIATE ENVIRONMENT
ZONE I

ABILITIES AND APTITUDES

NATURE OF EMPLOYEE

PERSONNEL ACTIVITIES

Employment planning

ATTITUDES AND PREFERENCES

Employment recruitment, selection, and orientation

Career development counseling, evaluation, and development

NATURE OF THE TASK

Compensation and protection

WORK GROUP

Personnel for groups of employees

ORGANIZATION STYLE

Division of labor
Coordination
Climate

LEADER'S STYLE AND EXPERIENCE

Discipline, control, and evaluation

ORGANIZATIONAL EFFECTIVENESS

tion was determined by seniority and that her employees griped about having to pay union dues. She was warned to watch her step by fellow supervisors—to live by the rules, or a grievance would be filed. Pay raises were to follow a schedule, and everyone in a senority group was to get the same raise. A number of other working conditions were spelled out in the union contract, and there was a steward in her unit who was, in effect, a countervailing force to her leadership. All these conditions existed because CE's employees belonged to the union. (Chapter 19 discusses unions and their impact and considers ways to deal with them in more depth.)

At one time, unions were concentrated in a few sectors of the economy, such as mining and manufacturing, and were influential in only a few sections of the United States and Canada, primarily the highly industrialized areas. But the fastest growing sector for unions in the United States today is in the third and public sectors. No longer is it useful to think of the unionized employee as a blue-collar factory worker. Today engineers, nurses, teachers, secretaries, salesmen, college professors, and even physicians belong to unions.

Unions differ as people differ. There are cooperative unions and combative unions. Those familiar with union history are aware of the kind of toughness a James Hoffa or John L. Lewis can bring to the employment scene. The union leadership of the Air Line Pilots Association, State, Local and Municipal Workers, and others is not so well known, because they have different bargaining styles and philosophies.

In sum, most aspects of personnel—recruiting, selection, performance evaluation, promotion, compensation, and benefits, among others—are directly affected by the presence of a union.

Government regulations

The second environmental influence is government law and regulations. These affect the private and third sectors directly. Many federal regulations limit the flexibility of other jurisdictions such as cities, states, provinces, and territories.

The government regulates and influences some aspects of personnel more directly than others. The major areas of legislation and regulation include:

Equal employment opportunity and human rights legislation affects recruiting, selection, evaluation, and promotion directly, and employment planning, orientation, career planning, training and development indirectly.

Compensation regulation affects pay, hours of work, unemployment, and similar conditions.

Benefits regulation affects pension plans and retirement.

Workers compensation and safety laws affect health and safety.

Labor relations laws and regulations affect the conduct of collective bargaining.

A Carter administration proposal would give tax incentives to enterprises to hire more workers.

In fact, there are almost no personnel decisions today that are unaffected by the government. In what ways and to what degree they affect the personnel function will be discussed in each chapter, beginning in Chapter 4, to help you take a diagnostic approach to personnel.

To cope with increasing governmental control, management has tried to influence the passage of relevant legislation and the way it is administered. Managements have sued to determine the constitutionality of many of the laws. When efforts fail to influence the process in the ways it prefers, management has learned to adapt its personnel policies.

The seriousness of the increase in governmental regulation is indicated by the fact that the U.S. Department of Labor in 1940 administered 18 regulatory programs; by 1975, it administered 134.[12] And that's just *one* government agency affecting the manager and the personnel process.

John Dunlop lists a number of the problems government regulation imposes on management, all of which make the operating and personnel manager's jobs more difficult.[13]

> Regulation encourages simplistic thinking on complicated issues. Small enterprises are treated like large ones. Different industries are regulated the same.
>
> Designing and administering regulations is an incredibly complex task. This leads to very slow decision making.
>
> Regulation does not encourage mutual accommodation but rather leads to complicated legal manuevering.
>
> Many regulations are out of date and serve little social purpose, yet they are not eliminated.
>
> There is increasing evidence of regulatory overlap and contradictions between different regulatory agencies.

The economy

Two aspects of the economy particularly affect the personnel function. One is the degree of competition in a sector. The other is the status of the labor market.

Degree of competition. The degree of competition affects all three personnel sectors. In industry, competition is considered high when there are many producers competing for the customers' business; the result usually is price pressures. A similar condition can exist in the third sector. When there are more college classrooms and dormitory rooms than there are students, competitive pressures operate on tuition charges, extra services offered, and so on. This can happen in hospitals too. In the public sector, competition for budget increases for an agency when the total budget (in real dollars) is stable or declining is fierce. This is happening at federal, state-provincial-territory, and local levels.

The greater the economic or competitive pressure, the less able the organization is to offer additional inducements to employees (higher pay, tangible benefits, etc.). Effective organizations under economic pressure can compete for good employees by offering nonmonetary rewards. For example, they can provide greater job satisfaction through more socializing opportunities, better recognition systems for ego needs, or job matching, which can facilitate personal fulfillment or self-actualization. Sometimes the pressure to produce acts against these possibilities, however.

If there is less competitive pressure, the enterprise has greater flexibility in the variety of personnel programs it can offer. For example, as director of the MBA program at Michigan State University, I interviewed two engineers from a defense contractor in Detroit, 90 miles away, who wanted to enter the program. When it was pointed out there was no night program, they said they could come during the day. This was astonishing. In pressing further, it was found that they had done nothing for the company for two years except to bring in the coffee and do odds and ends. The company was on a cost-plus contract; thus it could "stockpile" them *in case* they were needed and could still recoup their salaries *plus* their built-in profit percentage. Obviously there was no economic or competitive pressure there, and the company could afford to be very generous. Contrast this with the competitive food industry, in which five cents on a $5 case of vegetables could lose the order. These firms had to watch their pennies. Thus competitive pressures directly and indirectly affect personnel.

The state of the labor market.   The labor market directly affects the personnel function. When there are more workers than jobs, employers find recruiting costs minimal. Employees apply readily, and selection is less difficult; the employer may be able to choose from five or more qualified applicants for each position. Work attitudes tend to be work ethic oriented (see Chapter 2). When the work ethic predominates in employee attitudes, output rises and performance evaluation can be a motivating experience. A surplus of labor also can reduce employee pressures for compensation and benefit increases. Disciplinary problems, absenteeism, and turnover are likely to decrease, and equal employment opportunity goals may be easier to fill.

The employer must be aware of several labor markets. The primary concern is with the local labor market, from which most blue- and white-collar employees are drawn. Managerial, professional, and technical employees may be recruited from a regional or even national market.

It is quite possible that the local labor market is different from the regional or national markets. For example, in 1976, there was about 7 percent unemployment nationwide but in Detroit 14 percent of workers were unemployed. Recruiting blue-collar workers in Detroit was twice or three times as easy as in Dallas that year.

If the national and local labor markets differ significantly, there will be some exchange between them. Thus, if Detroit's unemployment rate consistently stays high, those among the unemployed who are younger, have the knowledge of jobs elsewhere, and have the money and motivation to move will do so.[14] This movement tends to increase the labor supply in areas with shortages. There also are international labor markets; when illegal aliens come to the United States and Canada to seek work, this changes the labor market balance. It was estimated that there were over 8,000,000 illegal aliens working in the United States in 1975.[15] Currently, British executives are trying to emigrate to the United States and Canada to leave an economy they feel has little future.

In addition to geographic differences in labor markets, there are markets organized by skills and age cohorts. If you are seeking an accountant, it is not much help if the labor market as a whole has a surplus but accountants are scarce.[16] The supply of labor with a particular skill is related to many factors: the number of persons of work age; the attractiveness of the job in pay, benefits, and psychological rewards; the availability of training institutes, and so on. With regard to age, for example, in 1976 the U.S. Department of Labor predicted that by 1990, workers aged 25–54 will rise by 22.4 million, while those in the teen-age years will decline by almost 2,000,000.[17]

In sum, the personnel function is affected fundamentally by the state of the labor market in the enterprise's location, in the region, nation, and world, and for the kinds of employees the enterprise seeks. The labor force is so significant we will examine it by major subcategories: sex, age, race, and so on. These data are especially important in understanding equal employment opportunity and human rights programs in the United States and Canada.

THE LABOR FORCE IN THE UNITED STATES

In 1977, the U.S. population was approximately 217,000,000 and the labor force about 88,000,000. 1977 figures indicated that about 62 percent of all males 16 years and over were employed. This ranges from about 47 percent for males 16–17 to 25 percent for males over 65; and the largest percentage of employed males was about 96 percent of all males 25–44 years of age. Female employment participation was 47 percent, but this is growing. About 34 percent of girls 16–17 were employed; the highest proportion was about 54 percent of women 45–54; only 9 percent of women over 65 were employed. From 1947 to 1975, female population increased 52 percent, but the percentage of women working increased 123 percent. The U.S. labor force is becoming composed of more single and fewer married persons; 33 percent is now single and 90 percent of recent growth in the labor force is single workers. Projections for future labor force participation through 1990 are given in Exhibit 3–3.

More participation in the labor force has become possible with the greater life-span of the population. In the United States, the typical man now lives about 67 years, and the typical woman about 72 years. Until recently this level has been increasing, but a slight decline in male life-span has been recorded.

In general, the contribution of the U.S. labor force has beein growing as productivity has increased. The most productive workers are in (and are expected to be in) the agriculture, forestry, and fishing industries, followed by transportation, communication, public utilities, mining, finance, insurance, and real estate. In the lower productivity category are merchandising, manufacturing, and construction. The least productive category is services.

The percentage of the labor force employed by manufacturing, construction, mining, and agriculture has stabilized or declined. It is estimated that by 1980 two times as many persons (60,000,000) will be employed in service industries such as transportation, utilities, trade, financial, general services, and government as in the stabilized industries (30,000,000). As far as types of workers are concerned, by 1980 it is predicted that farm workers will represent about 2 to 3 percent; service workers, about 12 percent; blue-collar workers, 33 percent; and the rest—over 50 percent—will be white-

EXHIBIT 3-3
Total population, total labor force, and labor force participation rates, by age and sex (actual 1960 and 1970 and projected 1980, 1985, and 1990 figures; numbers in thousands)

Sex and age group	Total population, July 1 — Actual 1960	1970	Projected 1980	1985	1990	Total labor force, annual averages — Actual 1960	1970	Projected 1980	1985	1990	Labor force participation rates, annual averages (percent of population in labor force) — Actual 1960	1970	1980	Projected 1985	1990
Both sexes:															
Total, 16 years and over	121,817	142,366	167,339	175,722	183,078	72,104	85,903	101,809	107,716	112,576	59.2	60.3	60.8	61.3	61.5
16 to 24 years	21,773	32,257	37,463	34,405	31,643	12,720	19,916	23,781	22,184	20,319	58.4	61.7	63.5	64.5	64.2
25 to 54 years	67,764	71,777	84,740	94,028	103,309	46,596	51,487	61,944	69,202	76,421	68.8	71.7	73.1	73.6	74.0
55 years and over	32,279	38,333	45,136	47,289	48,126	12,788	14,500	16,084	16,330	15,836	39.6	37.8	35.6	34.5	32.9
Men:															
Total, 16 years and over	59,420	68,641	80,261	84,285	87,911	48,933	54,343	62,590	66,017	68,907	82.4	79.2	78.0	78.3	78.4
16 to 19 years	5,398	7,649	8,339	7,141	7,045	3,162	4,395	4,668	3,962	3,901	58.6	57.5	56.0	55.5	55.4
16 and 17 years	2,880	3,937	4,111	3,515	3,373	1,322	1,840	1,887	1,603	1,530	45.9	46.7	45.9	45.6	45.4
18 and 19 years	2,518	3,712	4,228	3,626	3,672	1,840	2,555	2,781	2,359	2,371	73.1	68.8	65.8	65.1	64.6
20 to 24 years	5,553	8,668	10,666	10,305	9,021	4,939	7,378	8,852	8,496	7,404	88.9	85.1	83.0	82.5	82.1
25 to 34 years	11,347	12,601	18,521	20,540	21,040	10,940	11,974	17,523	19,400	19,853	96.4	95.0	94.6	94.4	94.4
35 to 44 years	11,878	11,303	12,468	15,409	18,378	11,454	10,818	11,851	14,617	17,398	96.4	95.7	95.1	94.9	94.7
45 to 54 years	10,148	11,283	10,781	10,630	11,922	9,568	10,487	9,908	9,744	10,909	94.3	92.9	91.9	91.7	91.5
55 to 64 years	7,564	8,742	9,776	9,874	9,424	6,445	7,127	7,730	7,716	7,307	85.2	81.5	79.1	78.1	77.5
55 to 59 years	4,144	4,794	5,263	5,129	4,787	3,727	4,221	4,558	4,421	4,112	89.9	88.0	86.6	86.2	85.9
60 to 64 years	3,420	3,948	4,513	4,745	4,637	2,718	2,906	3,172	3,295	3,195	79.5	73.6	70.3	69.4	68.9
65 years and over	7,530	8,395	9,710	10,386	11,081	2,425	2,164	2,058	2,082	2,135	32.2	25.8	21.2	20.0	19.3
65 to 69 years	2,941	3,139	3,633	3,852	4,065	1,348	1,278	1,289	1,322	1,365	45.8	40.7	35.5	34.3	33.6
70 years and over	4,590	5,256	6,077	6,534	7,016	1,077	886	769	760	770	23.5	16.9	12.7	11.6	11.0
Women:															
Total, 16 years and over	62,397	73,725	87,078	91,437	95,167	23,171	31,560	39,219	41,699	43,669	37.1	42.8	45.0	45.6	45.9
16 to 19 years	5,275	7,432	8,057	6,910	6,776	2,061	3,250	3,669	3,203	3,188	39.1	43.7	45.5	46.4	47.0
16 and 17 years	2,803	3,828	3,969	3,397	3,243	801	1,324	1,427	1,247	1,205	28.6	34.6	36.0	36.7	37.2
18 and 19 years	2,472	3,604	4,088	3,513	3,533	1,260	1,926	2,242	1,956	1,983	51.0	53.4	54.8	55.7	56.1
20 to 24 years	5,547	8,508	10,401	10,049	8,801	2,558	4,893	6,592	6,523	5,826	46.1	57.5	63.4	64.9	66.2
25 to 34 years	11,605	12,743	18,442	20,301	20,750	4,159	5,704	9,256	10,339	10,678	35.8	44.8	50.2	50.9	51.5
35 to 44 years	12,348	11,741	12,903	15,741	18,524	5,325	5,971	6,869	8,560	10,219	43.1	50.9	53.2	54.4	55.2
45 to 54 years	10,438	12,106	11,625	11,407	12,695	5,150	6,533	6,537	6,542	7,364	49.3	54.0	56.2	57.4	58.0
55 to 64 years	8,070	9,763	11,307	11,492	10,934	2,964	4,153	5,057	5,213	5,003	36.7	42.5	44.7	45.4	45.8
55 to 59 years	4,321	5,257	5,966	5,804	5,396	1,803	2,547	3,055	3,033	2,853	41.7	48.4	51.2	52.3	52.9
60 to 64 years	3,749	4,506	5,341	5,688	5,538	1,161	1,606	2,002	2,180	2,150	31.0	35.6	37.5	38.3	38.8
65 years and over	9,115	11,433	14,343	15,537	16,687	954	1,056	1,239	1,319	1,391	10.5	9.2	8.6	8.5	8.3
65 to 69 years	3,347	3,780	4,595	4,942	5,267	579	644	758	814	864	17.3	17.0	16.5	16.5	16.4
70 years and over	5,768	7,653	9,748	10,595	11,420	375	412	481	505	527	6.5	5.4	4.9	4.8	4.6

Source: Population and labor force data for 1960 are from Special Labor Force Report 119 and differ slightly from later estimates. Corresponding 1970 data are from Current Population Survey estimates. Projected population data are from *Current Population Reports*, Series P-25, No. 493, Series E.

collar workers (professional and technical, clerical, sales, and managers). Blue-collar workers, especially unskilled workers, are declining in relative importance. One of the fastest growing segments of employment is state and local government workers. From 1950 to 1975, total employment was up 44 percent, while state and local government employment increased by 193 percent.

Exhibit 3–4 provides data on the current occupations of employees in the United States. This exhibit not only gives specific relationships among occupations, it also categorizes the occupations by age and sex—two of the categories that are important for equal employment opportunity purposes. Some of the groups protected by EEO and other human rights legislation are examined below.

A closer look at some groups of employees in the labor force

The recent emphasis on affirmative action programs makes analysis of subgroups in the population of special interest, so we will look at some statistics on them. Then we will examine the case of temporary and part-time employees, many of whom come from these groups.

Women in the labor force.[18]   In recent years, about 40 percent of the full-time U.S. work force has been women. The number of married women in the labor force has increased 205 percent since 1947, at the same time that the number of male married employees has increased by 27 percent. In the midseventies, 52 percent of married women with children aged 6–17 held full-time jobs, and 35 percent of married women with children aged six or under worked. The percentage of married black women working (60 percent) was greater than for white women. Put another way, 51 percent of black children and 37 percent of white children 18 and under had mothers who are in the labor force.

Exhibit 3–5 compares female with male employment. Although it is alleged that everyone has equal job opportunities, it is difficult to argue with the facts of discrimination against women in the workplace. Typically women hold the lower status, low-pay jobs. For example, one recent study of 163 companies found that 31 percent of companies had 50 percent or more women employees, and 82 percent of companies employed at least 19 percent women. If discrimination were not practiced, at least half of the companies with 50 percent women workers should have a majority of women in higher status, higher paying jobs. This study found that less than 10 percent of the high-pay, high-status jobs were held by women.[19]

So there is discrimination against women in business; surely it's different in universities! No, it isn't. Since 1949 the percentage of college professors who are women has dropped from 35 to 22 percent; only 5 percent hold the highest rank (professor) and 7 percent the intermediate rank (associate professor). What about the government? In the federal government, less

EXHIBIT 3–4

Employed persons by occupational group, sex, and age (in thousands)

Occupation	Total		Males, 20 years and over		Females, 20 years and over		Males, 16–19 years		Females, 16–19 years	
	April 1975	April 1976	April 1975	April 1976	April 1975	April 1976	April 1975	April 1976	April 1975	April 1976
Total	83,549	86,584	46,901	48,129	30,145	31,625	3,506	3,682	2,996	3,147
White-collar workers	42,092	43,360	20,438	20,753	19,487	20,466	627	597	1,540	1,543
Professional and technical	12,780	13,134	7,360	7,558	5,276	5,443	81	54	63	79
Health workers	2,148	2,262	805	808	1,340	1,437	—	2	4	15
Teachers, except college	3,180	3,171	918	958	2,236	2,188	8	3	19	22
Other professional and technical	7,452	7,701	5,638	5,792	1,700	1,818	74	49	40	42
Managers and administrators, except farm	8,612	9,237	6,963	7,284	1,583	1,883	43	58	22	12
Salaried workers	6,924	7,523	5,616	5,926	1,249	1,532	39	53	20	13
Self-employed workers in retail trade	894	853	660	606	230	247	2	1	3	—
Self-employed workers, except retail trade	793	860	687	752	103	103	3	5	—	—
Sales workers	5,515	5,483	2,965	2,921	1,949	1,967	240	244	362	350
Retail trade	3,092	2,940	1,009	890	1,549	1,561	190	186	343	303
Other industries	2,423	2,542	1,955	2,031	399	405	50	58	19	47
Clerical workers	15,185	15,507	3,150	2,990	10,679	11,174	263	241	1,092	1,102
Stenographers, typists, and secretaries	4,363	4,641	71	63	3,948	4,246	8	9	335	323
Other clerical workers	10,822	10,866	3,079	2,927	6,731	6,928	255	232	757	779
Blue-collar workers	27,216	28,470	20,756	21,508	4,342	4,724	1,834	1,893	284	345
Craft and kindred workers	10,716	10,982	9,866	10,131	498	501	330	324	21	26
Carpenters	927	983	880	935	6	7	40	39	2	2
Construction craft, except carpenters	2,069	2,179	1,971	2,092	25	12	67	71	6	3
Mechanics and repairers	2,827	2,880	2,663	2,718	24	29	139	133	1	2
Metal craft	1,181	1,141	1,119	1,093	21	26	39	20	3	2
Blue-collar worker supervisors, not else-where classified	1,394	1,455	1,260	1,334	130	114	4	6	—	1
All other	2,318	2,345	1,973	1,959	292	313	43	55	10	17

Operatives, except transport	9,451	10,006	5,334	5,530	3,409	3,688	532	537	177	251
Durable goods manufacturing	4,100	4,482	2,697	2,861	1,213	1,411	145	138	46	74
Nondurable goods manufacturing	3,012	3,232	1,210	1,296	1,637	1,727	79	93	86	121
Other industries	2,340	2,292	1,427	1,374	558	550	307	306	45	56
Transport equipment operatives	3,185	3,259	2,844	2,896	173	192	161	161	7	10
Drivers, motor vehicles	2,712	2,762	2,406	2,434	166	183	133	136	7	9
All other	473	497	438	461	7	8	28	26	—	1
Nonfarm laborers	3,864	4,223	2,712	2,951	263	344	811	871	79	57
Construction	620	678	506	571	5	10	106	96	3	1
Manufacturing	936	980	746	780	79	112	105	86	6	3
Other industries	2,309	2,565	1,460	1,601	178	221	599	689	71	54
Service workers	11,493	11,923	3,581	3,772	5,998	6,048	786	891	1,129	1,212
Private household workers	1,159	1,098	25	15	875	812	7	8	251	263
Service workers, except private household	10,335	10,826	3,555	3,757	5,123	5,237	778	883	878	948
Food service workers	3,581	3,926	663	689	1,896	2,081	454	533	568	624
Protective service workers	1,292	1,345	1,190	1,228	80	88	22	23	—	6
All other	5,462	5,555	1,702	1,840	3,147	3,068	302	327	310	318
Farm workers	2,747	2,830	2,126	2,096	318	386	260	301	43	47
Farmers and farm managers	1,589	1,512	1,499	1,423	72	70	18	15	—	4
Farm laborers and supervisors	1,157	1,318	627	673	246	316	242	286	42	43
Paid workers	836	974	579	639	83	95	147	214	27	27
Unpaid family workers	321	344	48	34	163	221	95	72	16	16

Source: *Employment and Earnings*, U.S. Government publication, May 1976.

EXHIBIT 3–5
Occupation distribution of men and women workers (in percent)

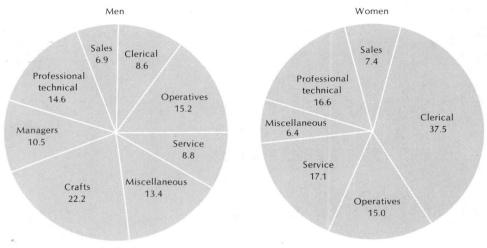

Men

Women

Source: Bureau of the Census.

than 2 percent of the top jobs are held by women, according to the Civil Service Commission.

Surely things are getting better in the professions for women! No again. Some women entered the medical, dental, legal and other professions after the feminist movement which followed World War I. There actually was a greater percentage of women in these professions then than in 1960. In the late 1970s, women comprised the following percentages of professional school enrollment: engineering, 6 percent; architecture, 10 percent; dentistry, 11 percent; optometry, 13 percent; medicine, 22 percent; law, 23 percent; veterinary medicine, 25 percent; and pharmacy, 32 percent. Some of these women will not complete the program and enter the professions, and it will be many decades before women can have a major impact on any profession. In 1960, only 1 percent of optometry students were women; now the percentage is 13 percent, but in a profession dominated by men for generations it will be many years before major female representation in its ranks is realized.

Minorities in the labor force. The situation in women's employment also prevails for racial and ethnic minorities in the United States. Large numbers of minority peoples, such as Hispanic Americans, blacks, and American Indians, are employed in low-skill, low-pay jobs, and few in high-status, high-pay jobs[20] (see Exhibit 3–6).

Historically, the most recent immigrant group took the lowest level jobs offered. This was true of the Irish, Polish, Yugoslavs, and Jews. One difference between the immigrant groups and other minorities is that most of the minority groups were residents of the United States long before the immigrants arrived; the Indians from the beginning, as were many of the

EXHIBIT 3–6
Occupational distribution of minority workers and all workers

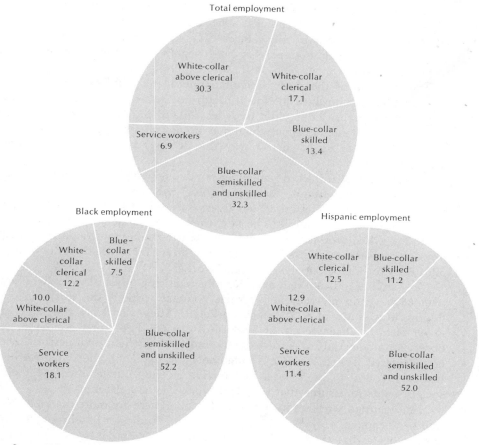

Total employment

White-collar above clerical 30.3
White-collar clerical 17.1
Service workers 6.9
Blue-collar skilled 13.4
Blue-collar semiskilled and unskilled 32.3

Black employment

White-collar clerical 12.2
Blue-collar skilled 7.5
10.0 White-collar above clerical
Service workers 18.1
Blue-collar semiskilled and unskilled 52.2

Hispanic employment

White-collar clerical 12.5
Blue-collar skilled 11.2
12.9 White-collar above clerical
Service workers 11.4
Blue-collar semiskilled and unskilled 52.0

Source: U.S. Government statistics.

Hispanics in the Southwest, and the blacks since the mid 1700s. They have not advanced to the degree that the immigrants have, however. The Indians were kept on reservations, and the Hispanics remained in the areas that belonged to the Mexican Republic (except for the Cuban and Puerto Rican immigrants, who came much later). Most blacks remained in Southern agriculture until relatively recently. These minorities represent 11 to 12 percent of the U.S. population. They have been less well educated than the majority, although recent programs have attempted to improve this situation.

Mobility into better jobs has been a problem for these groups. For example, in 1966 in New York City, there were 2,500,000 white-collar positions, and a population that was 19 percent black and 10 percent Hispanic. Of 4,200 organizations studied, 43 percent had no minorities in white-collar positions.[21] Somewhat similar conditions are said to exist in Canada insofar as minorities such as Indians are concerned.

The older employee.   The age discrimination legislation defines an older employee as one between the ages of 40 and 65; about 21 percent of the labor force currently is in this category. This portion of the labor force is protected because some employers hold negative stereotypes about older workers.

Probably one of the most difficult employment problems today is the older employee who loses his job through no fault of his own. Employers assume that because he is older he is less qualified and less able to adapt. And personnel benefits plans (which may amount to one third of base compensation) are set up in such a way that it costs more to employ older people.

One of the first things to remember about the aging process is that each of us ages at a different rate. As we grow older, we lose some of our faculties. But this process is going on all our lives. Rarely is a swimmer better than in his midteens, for example. The key, then, is the matching of employees with jobs. Older workers may be less efficient on some jobs requiring quick physical response rates, but this is more important for a race driver or airline pilot than for a stock analyst or social worker.

Most studies indicate that even for jobs requiring physical work, workers over 45 have no more accidents than younger workers do; this was the finding in a study of 9,000 steel workers.[22] They also have the same or lower rates of absenteeism, at least until age 55. The worst accident rate observed in one study was for workers under 35.[23] When total performance is considered (speed, accuracy, judgment, loyalty, etc.), the older worker has been found to be at least as effective as the younger one.[24] Yet our society tends to assume that the older worker is less effective.

Handicapped workers in the labor force.   There are more than 6.5 million handicapped workers in the United States. Studies of handicapped persons indicate that they are of all age groups, of both sexes, and in many occupations. About 56 percent have been disabled by disease, 30 percent by accident, and 14 percent by congenital diseases. In the latter category, the largest group of people have lost the use of arms, legs, or back. The next largest number are amputees and blind (or partially blind) workers.

Many handicapped persons have had difficulty finding employment of any kind because employers and fellow workers believe that they could not do the job or would cause an excessive number of accidents. Recently, the government, social welfare agencies, and employer groups such as the Chamber of Commerce and the National Association of Manufacturers have studied the situation and have been encouraging the employment of the handicapped.

Few people use all their faculties on a job, and there are many jobs for those who do not have all their faculties. As far as my "abilities" at carpentry are concerned, a builder is probably better off with a one-legged carpenter.

When the handicapped are properly matched to jobs, studies show that two thirds of the physically handicapped produce at the same rate as able-bodied workers, 24 percent perform at higher levels, and only 10 percent at a lower rate. Absenteeism and turnover are normally lower for the handicapped, for two reasons: the handicapped have had their abilities matched to their jobs better, and most handicapped workers seem better adjusted to working, with more favorable attitudes toward work, and thus are better motivated to do a good job.

As far as accidents are concerned, the Pennsylvania State Bureau of Rehabilitation found that less than 1 percent of handicapped workers had auto accidents, compared to 4.5 percent of able-bodied workers.[25] Western Electric found that handicapped workers had one third fewer accidents on the job than able-bodied workers, and they resigned 7 percent less often, were discharged 5 percent less often, and had 7 percent fewer absences.[26]

Of course, some handicapped people are physically or psychologically unable to work. Some who are marginally employable can work in training jobs at sheltered workshops and organizations such as Goodwill Industries. But for those able to work, it is most important that the handicapped be treated as normally as other workers. They will respond better to fair treatment than to paternalism. They want a chance.

It is in the interest of the nation's economy that the handicapped be transferred from liabilities to assets. It is even more important to the individuals to be able to attain employment and thus economic and psychological independence. Some states such as Illinois now have programs which legally encourage hiring the handicapped. Other legal requirements are discussed in Chapter 18.

Veterans in the labor force. Veterans are former servicemen released from active duty by the military. They are not easily recognized as special employees by employers, but they do have a readjustment to make to civilian life. The government has attempted to ease reentry to civilian life of Vietnam veterans with several programs.

About one fourth of all returning veterans resumed their interrupted educational careers. But the great majority entered the civilian labor market, many seeking their first full-time jobs. As of January 1, 1977, there were 558,000 Vietnam veterans aged 20–34 unemployed in this country. The unemployment rate for veterans was 8.6 percent, at the same time the average unemployment rate was 7.8 percent. In the 20–24 age bracket, veterans' unemployment was 18 percent.

Congress has provided specific reentry adjustments for veterans, usually referred to as reemployment rights. Excerpts from laws giving veterans certain preferences at the time of reemployment are as follows:

Eligibility—(1) Private employment: Veteran must have left other than temporary employment to enter military service; must have served not more than 5 years after August 1, 1961, after leaving the employment to which he claims restoration, provided that any service over four years was at the request and for the convenience of the Government; must have been separated honorably or under honorable conditions; and must be qualified to perform the duties of the job or, if disabled while in military service, some other job in employer's organization of comparable seniority, status, and pay. (2) Federal employment: Generally the same as for private employment.

Nature of Benefit—Restoration in the position the veteran would have attained had he not been absent, or in another position of like seniority, status, and pay, including all benefits falling due after reemployment which would have accrued by his seniority. Protection against discharge without cause for one year, six months in the case of a Reservist or Guardsman returning from initial active duty for training.

Applying for Reemployment—A veteran must apply to his preservice employer within 90 days after separation from active duty or release from hospitalization continuing for not more than a year immediately after active duty. For Reservists and National Guardsmen returning from initial active duty for training of three consecutive months or more, the application period is 31 days instead of 90. Reservists and National Guardsmen returning from other types of military training duty must report back to their employer for the next regularly scheduled work period after their return home, allowing for hospitalization and necessary travel time.

In addition to reemployment, Congress has enacted laws making it easier for veterans to enter the federal career service. These include a preference system of points added to test scores for veterans, the Veterans Readjustment Appointment, waivers of physical requirements, the restriction of certain jobs to veterans, preference for retention in case of reduction of force, and similar procedures. The Veterans' Administration also assists veterans who are seeking employment through job marts and apprenticeship training programs. Priority for referral to appropriate training programs and job openings is given to eligible veterans, with first consideration to the disabled veteran. Other federal benefits have also become available to veterans operating their own businesses through the Small Business Administration. Similarly, unemployment compensation for veterans provides a weekly income for a limited period of time, varying with state laws. And in 1977, the Carter administration proposed a $1.3 billion program of economic stimuli designed to get the Vietnam era veterans back to work.

Full-time and part-time employees

The labor force members considered so far have been full-time employees: those who regularly work about 40 hours weekly. But the labor market includes another group the part-time employees, those who regularly (and usually voluntarily) are employed for less than the normal work week. A person who is working part-time because she or he cannot get a full-time job is involuntarily a part-time employee. The focus in this section is on the *voluntary* part-time employee.

One of the more neglected areas of labor force analysis is that of the part-time worker.[27] In the United States, the government lists 10,500,000 part-time employees, of whom 3,500,000 classified themselves as involuntary in 1976. But there are many more part-time employees who, because of the nature of their employment, never are listed in these statistics. Daniel Bell estimated in 1975 that there actually were about 15,000,000 part-time employees in the United States.[28] Part-time employment, in fact, is growing faster than full-time employment.

A related type of worker works full-time but at various locations. These employees usually are employed by temporary help employment services. There are both similarities and differences between part-time workers and temporary workers.

The major types of part-time workers are discussed below.

Women.   About 25 percent of employed women work at part-time jobs. Some experts have found that more husbands would rather have their wives work part-time than full-time.[29] Richard Schonberger estimates some 10,-000,000 more women would work part-time if better child care centers were available.[30]

Students.   About 40 percent of students aged 18–24 and enrolled in educational institutions work part-time. On the average, students work 26 hours a week.[31]

Retired and older persons.   A number of older citizens work part-time to keep active and to supplement their social security payments up to the limit of $3,000 per year (1977 limit; this is adjusted annually). The Louisville State Employment Office has set up a Retired Workers Job Service Center which places about 4,000 persons a year. These employees often are quite skilled. It has been estimated that the senior citizen labor pool throughout the country equals 17,200,000 persons.[32]

The physically and mentally handicapped.   Part-time work is often the best kind for handicapped persons. This enables them to work without aggravating their disabilities.[33]

Moonlighters.   There are about 4,000,000 moonlighters, most of whom are married men between the ages of 25 and 42. Often they are teachers below the college level and police and fire personnel. More than one third of all moonlighters are self-employed, often in farming.

Most part time work is in the service industries, especially education, health care, personal services (for example, beauty shops), business services such as advertising, and entertainment and recreation. The second most frequent location of part-time industry is in retail and wholesale trade, and next is manufacturing. Very few part-time jobs exist in mining, construction, transportation, public utilities, finance, and insurance.

In addition, many enterprises lease employees from service companies for custodial, security, maintenance and food service jobs. The advantages of leasing these employees are small recruiting and selection costs, less compensation (because benefits are fewer), and lower turnover and training costs. Leasing employees may be prohibited by the union contract, however, and the enterprise has less control over the quality of work.

There are many advantages in part-time work for employers. These include flexibility in scheduling, lower total compensation costs (direct and indirect), and stabilization of employment. Some plants have been set up entirely for part-timers.[34]

Employees like part-time work because it fits their hours, or they want to work less than full time. Some women work out job sharing plans; for example, one woman works mornings while the other does housework and cares for the children; in the afternoons, the roles are reversed.

There are disadvantages, too. Part-time work may require additional training and record-keeping expenses and can increase supervisory burdens. Some studies indicate that the performance levels of part-timers (especially student part-timers) are lower.[35] Unions sometimes oppose the use of part-timers, viewing them as substitutes for additional full-time employees.

Little research has been done on the use of temporary help agencies for part-time workers.[36] Martin Gannon contends that there are about 3,000,000 persons working for these firms, usually in clerical jobs, usually young women. Often these workers are not fully satisfied with their jobs because they lack the usual fringe benefits.[37]

The implications of part-time employees for the personnel function will be discussed in the chapters on selection, orientation, training, compensation, benefits, and pensions.

THE LABOR FORCE IN CANADA

The Canadian labor force is composed of about 10,000,000 full-time and 2,500,000 part-time employees. Employment in Canada has increased 50 percent in the past 15 years, at a much higher rate than for any other developed country. Still, its unemployment rate is over 7 percent. The productivity of Canadian labor is lower than in all other countries in the Organization for Economic Cooperation and Development (OECD), except the United States. This partly reflects job seasonality and very high turnover. Quits and layoffs are 20 percent higher than in the United States, 50 percent higher than in France, and triple the rate in Germany.

The rate of increase in employment reflects immigration and major growth in female and youth employment. In the past 15 years, women's employment increased 81 percent, and that for youth increased 91 percent. Today about one third of all females are employed, and 60 percent of these are married women. With the increase of females in the labor force, there has been more pressure for affirmative action programs such as those in the United States.[38]

Unemployment is high in Canada because of the increase in youth and female employment and the heavy turnover rate. The typical adult Canadian male changes jobs every three to four years, and adult females do so every two to three years. Among young people, the typical male changes jobs at least yearly, and the typical female, every 18 months. Studies of Canadian work values indicate that the majority of Canadians want to work and enjoy it.[39]

ORGANIZATION STYLE AND THE PERSONNEL FUNCTION

The seven model organizations described in Chapter 1 vary by degrees of size, simplicity, and stability. It makes sense that all these various types of enterprises could not equally effectively follow exactly the same personnel procedures. Large enterprises can do their employment planning on computers, use an elaborate set of tests for hiring, offer a wide variety of training programs, and provide numerous fringe benefits. Some small enterprises cannot do all these things, yet they also need to be effective in their personnel programs.

The diagnostic model (Exhibit 2–1) shows that organization style (division of labor, coordination, and climate) influences the task to be performed and thus personnel activities and organizational effectiveness. Organization style, as in the seven model organizations, is affected by the organization's size and complexity and the volatility of the environment. These factors affect how the work setting of an enterprise is organized. The way employees are related to one another and grouped into work units is called organization structure.

Modern organization theory has suggested many ways to organize. The two most extreme forms of organization, the liberal and the conservative, are described in Exhibit 3–7. Obviously there are many ways to organize which fall *between* these extreme styles. The two extremes are reflections of fundamentally different managerial philosophies about the nature of the person, the role of work in life, and the most effective ways to supervise people at work.

These basic beliefs about how workers are to be treated translate into the kinds of personnel programs that should be made available to employees. Exhibit 3–8 shows how personnel programs can vary with the two extreme organization styles.

Most work organizations will fall between these two extremes. However, as the exhibit shows, conservative organizations, for example, are likely to prefer more formalized personnel policies, tighter controls on personnel, more directly job-related training, compensation policies tied to stimulus-response motivation theories, and so on. It seems reasonable to hypothesize that truly liberal and truly conservative organizations would have different personnel policies, along the lines shown in Exhibit 3–8. Of course, most organizations are made up of some units that are liberal and some that are conservative, so their personnel policies would also vary along these dimensions.

SUMMARY

The purpose of Chapters 2 and 3 was to make you aware that personnel tools vary in their applicability. They should or should not be used, or

EXHIBIT 3–7
Three managerial styles

LIBERAL— Participative management (informal; distant)	MIDDLE OF THE ROAD— Leadership (careful delegation)	CONSERVATIVE— Boss-centered leadership (close; formal)
	COMMUNICATIONS	
Informal, multichannel communications "system"	General description of communications	Well-defined chain of command
Much communication encouraged in all directions (up, down, and lateral)	Amount and direction of communication	Little communication encouraged; mostly downward
Adequate; mostly accurate	Quality of communication	Needs supplementary system; somewhat inaccurate
	PLANNING	
Manager helped by employees	General description	Performed by the manager
Work group sets the objectives in conjunction with the manager	Setting objectives	A manager's job
Multiple overlapping objectives	Nature of objectives	Clearly defined for the enterprise and for each subunit
	DECISION MAKING	
Decentralized	General decision description	Centralized
Wherever the knowledge necessary for good decisions is located	Location of most critical decisions	Toward the top of the hierarchy
Responsibility for decisions given to doers	Attitude toward decision-making responsibility	Responsibility for decisions is administrator's
Encourages employees to take reasonable risks	Risk taking	Discourages risk taking by employees
Encourages creative decisions by experimentation, cross-fertilization, and rewards	Creativity (in decisions and tasks)	Expects creativity to come from administrators and filter down from there
	DESIGN OF JOBS	
Enlarged and enriched		Specialized and simplified
Broadly defined		Narrowly defined
Either not used or very general	Job descriptions	Used; clear and specific
	ORGANIZATION	
	Horizontal division of labor	
Used, extensive	Formalization (degree to which documents and forms are used)	Nonexistent or not used
Departmentation by process; not too specialized	Departmentation	Departmentation by function; grouping by function; much specialization
Nonexistent or not used	Standardization of policies, procedures, and rules	Used, extensive
Flat organization, few levels	Vertical division of labor (chain of command)	Tall organization, many levels
	COORDINATION	
Informal, unprogrammed; performed by work groups	General description	Programmed by use of SOPs, individual coordinators, or managers
	CONTROL	
Large	Span of control	Small
Decentralized	Centralization	Centralized
Few things controlled; general controls	Degrees of control (some general, some specific)	Many things controlled; specific controls

EXHIBIT 3–8
Hypothesized personnel policies of liberal-style and conservative-style organizations

Liberal organizations		Conservative organizations
Vague or not used	Job descriptions	Present, detailed use
Emphasis on output, not process of output	Working conditions	Time clocks, close check on hours and times
Worked out by work groups	Employment planning	Worked out by management
Human-asset accounting	Human assets accounting	Traditional accounting
By work groups and management	Recruiting activities	By management
Some risky candidates recruited	Recruiting standards	Only safe candidates recruited
Informal procedure: Primary interviews, some by the work group	Selection	Extensive use of formal procedures, tests, interviews by management
Relaxed, social as well as technical	Orientation	Stressful, sink or swim
Planned by employee and management	Career development	Unplanned or planned by management
Voluntary by employees after management announces openings	Transfers	Transfer by management with no rewards for those refusing transfers
None	Employment contracts	For key positions
Planned by management and work group	Technical training	Planned by management
Integrated on-the-job and off-job experiences, with work-group input in planning	Management development	Not stressed or tenuously related to job
Jointly by superior(s), subordinates, and peers	Performance evaluation	By superiors, sometimes announced to subordinates
Management announces that positions are open, interviews all interested in the positions	Promotion systems	Management initiates and decides
Multiple compensation systems, including group incentives	Compensation	Individual incentive, oriented
Employees have a voice in how benefit money is spent	Benefits	Management "giveth"
Used	Productivity schemes	Management refuses to use
Supervisor separated from discipline—independent channel	Discipline	Management both boss and judge
Cooperative fair play to both sides	Labor relations	Competitive zero-sum games

should be used in one way or another, depending on a set of factors. The diagnostic model described these factors.

Chapter 2 showed how human factors, leadership style, the work group, and task variables influence personnel effectiveness. Chapter 3 examined two other aspects of the environment of the personnel function: the physical location of the enterprise and the sector in which it is located. Public-sector personnel work is more complicated and bureaucratic than private or third-sector work, and rural locations provide quite different problems and opportunities from urban locations. U.S. locations are different from Canadian,

European from Venezuelan. Thus personnel must adapt to the cultural environments of work.

Three environmental influences in zone II of the diagnostic model were described in terms of how they affect personnel activities: union and government requirements and economic conditions. Unionized enterprises operate with many more contractual constraints on the personnel function. Governmental regulations and laws regulate many personnel activities these days, especially labor relations, safety, benefits, compensation, and ensuring equal employment opportunity and human rights. In the economy, competitive pressures can restrict management's ability to offer the personnel program it would like. The status of the labor market also can facilitate or be detrimental to a company's personnel efforts.

Organization style, or how the organization structures itself and develops its organizational climate, is another environmental influence on the personnel process. Conservative organizations perform personnel activities differently than liberal organizations do.

We are ready now to begin to apply the diagnostic model to the personnel decision-making process. This begins in Part II with Chapter 4, "Employment Planning."

QUESTIONS

1. In what ways does the environment in which the personnel function is located affect personnel activities?
2. What factors in the diagnostic model make up the organizational and other environmental factors affecting personnel discussed in this chapter?
3. There should be no significant differences in personnel activities between a firm's rural and urban settings. Comment.
4. In what ways could personnel activities be different for a firm's plants in Bangladesh and Buffalo, New York?
5. The personnel function is essentially the same in the private, public, and third sectors. Comment.
6. Personnel activities are not much affected by a union. Do you agree or disagree? If you disagree, *how* does the union make a difference?
7. How have governmental regulations and laws affected personnel activities in the past 15 years?
8. Does the degree of competition affect the personnel function? How?
9. How does the state of the labor market affect the personnel function? Please be specific!
10. Discuss specific labor market trends and their effect on personnel.
11. In what ways does an organization's style affect personnel?

NOTES AND REFERENCES

1. Arthur Turner and Paul Lawrence, *Industrial Jobs and the Worker* (Cambridge, Mass.: Harvard Business School, 1965).

2. George England et al., *The Manager and the Man* (Kent, Ohio: Kent State University Press, 1974); Mason Haire et al., *Managerial Thinking* (New York: John Wiley & Sons, 1966); Frederick Harbison and Charles Myers, *Management in the Industrial World; An International Analysis* (New York: McGraw-Hill Book Co., 1959); Joseph Massie and Jan Luytjes, *Management in an International Context* (New York: Harper & Row, 1972).

3. V. V. Murray, "Canadian Cultural Values and Personnel Administration," *Contemporary Issues in Canadian Personnel Administration,* ed. Harish Jain (Scarborough, Ontario: Prentice-Hall of Canada, 1974).

4. Herbert Chruden and Arthur Sherman, Jr., *Personnel Practices of American Companies in Europe* (New York: American Management Association, 1972).

5. David Heenan and Calvin Reynolds "RPO's: A Step toward Global Human Resource Management," *California Management Review,* Fall 1976, pp. 5–9; David Heenan, *Multinational Management of Human Resources* (Austin: University of Texas Press, 1976); Cecil Howard, "Overseas Compensation Policies of U.S. Multinationals," *The Personnel Administrator,* November 1975, pp. 50–55; Edwin Miller, "The International Selection Decision," *Academy of Management Journal,* June 1973, pp. 239–52; J. Alex Murray, "International Personnel Repatriations," *MSU Business Topics,* Summer 1973, pp. 59–66; David Noer, *Multinational People Management* (Washington, D.C.: Bureau of National Affairs, 1975); John Shearer, "The External and Internal Manpower Resources of MNC's," *Columbia Journal of World Business,* Summer 1974, pp. 9–17; Derek Thomas, "International Transfers and Compensation," *The Canadian Business Review,* Spring 1976, pp. 27–29; Yoram Zeira, "Overworked Personnel Problems of Multinational Corporations," *Columbia Journal of World Business,* Summer 1975, pp. 96–103; Harish Jain, Neil Hood, and Steve Young, "Crosscultural Aspects of Personnel in Multinationals: A Case Study of Chrysler UK," Working Paper no. 134, McMaster University, June 1977.

6. Richard Dubin and Herbert Springall, *Organization and Administration of Health Care* (St. Louis, Mo.: C. V. Mosby Co., 1969); Norma Metzger, *Personnel Administration in the Health Services Industry* (New York: Wiley Halstead, 1975); George Wren, "Personnel Administration in Hospitals," *Personnel Journal,* January 1973, pp. 54–56.

7. E. F. Ricketts, "Universities and City Personnel Needs," *Public Personnel Review,* April 1971, pp. 106–9.

8. R. H. Dowdell, "Personnel Administration in the Federal Public Service," in *Public Administration in Canada,* ed. A. M. Williams (Toronto: WDK Kernaghan, 1968); Jay Shafritz, "Political Culture—The Determinant of Merit System Viability," *Public Personnel Management,* January–February 1974; Max Wortman and Dale Meyer, "The Impact of Centralized Personnel Functions in State Government," *Academy of Management Journal,* March 1969, pp. 21–31.

9. Jean Couturier, "The Quiet Revolution in Public Personnel Laws," *Public Personnel Management,* May–June 1976, pp. 150–67; David Rosenbloom, "Public Personnel Administration and the Constitution," *Public Administration Review,* January–February 1975, pp. 52–54.

10. Enid Beaumont, "A Pivotal Point for the Merit Concept," *Public Administration Review,* September–October 1974, pp. 426–30; Jerry Wurf, "Merit: A Union View," *Public Administration Review,* September–October 1974, pp. 431–34; Karen House, "Balky Bureaus," *Wall Street Journal,* September 26, 1977.

11. Joseph N. Cayer, *Public Personnel Administration in the United States* (New York: St. Martin's Press, 1975); Charles Messick, *An Adventure in Public Personnel Administration* (Newark: University of Delaware Press, 1973); Glenn O. Stahl, *The Personnel Job of Government Managers* (Chicago: International Personnel Management Association, 1971).

12. John Dunlop, "The Limits of Legal Compulsion," *Labor Law Journal,* February 1976, pp. 67–74.

13. Ibid.

14.   Duane Leigh, "The Occupational Mobility of Young Men," *Industrial and Labor Relations Review,* October 1976, pp. 68–78.

15.   "How Illegal Aliens Rob Jobs from Unemployed Americans," *Nation's Business,* May 1975, pp. 18–24.

16.   Arch Patton, "The Coming Flood of Young Executives," *Harvard Business Review,* September–October 1976, pp. 20–22 ff.

17.   "Labor Force Study to 1990 Shows Jump in Prime Age Group," *Wall Street Journal,* December 29, 1976.

18.   *Digest of Educational Statistics* (Washington, D.C.: U.S. Government Printing Office, 1970); Stuart Garfinkle, "Occupations of Women and Black Workers, 1962–1974," *Monthly Labor Review,* November 1975, pp. 25–35; Allyson Grossman, "Women in the Labor Force," *Monthly Labor Review,* November 1975, pp. 3–16; Howard Hayghe, "Marital and Family Characteristics of the Labor Force," *Monthly Labor Review,* Nov. 1975, pp. 52–61; John Parrish, "Women in Professional Training," *Monthly Labor Review* November 1975, pp. 49–51; Kathleen Ritter, and Lowell Hargens, "Occupational Position and Class Identifications of Married Working Women," *American Journal of Sociology* 80, 4 (1975) pp. 934–48.

19.. U.S. Department of Labor, Employment Standards Administration, Women's Bureau, *The Myth and the Reality* (Washington, D.C.: U.S. Government Printing Office, 1971).

20.   Clifford Alexander, Jr. "White Collar Help Wanted: Or Is It?" *Personnel Administration,* March–April 1969, pp. 4–9; Garfinkle, "Women and Black Workers"; Robert Quinn et al., *The Chosen Few: A Study of Discrimination in Executive Selection* (Ann Arbor, Mich.: Institute of Social Research, 1968).

21.   Alexander, "White Collar Help Wanted."

22.   Joseph Tiffin, *Industrial Psychology* (Englewood Cliffs, N.J.: Prentice-Hall, Inc., 1941).

23.   H. Kahne et al., "Don't Take the Older Workers for Granted," *Harvard Business Review* 35 (1957), pp. 90–94.

24.   B. Gilmer, "Handicapped, Unemployed and Aging Persons," in *Industrial Psychology* (New York: McGraw-Hill Book Co., 1966); Beverly McEaddy, "Women in the Labor Force: The Later Years," *Monthly Labor Review,* November 1975, pp. 17–24.

25.   Pennsylvania State Bureau of Rehabilitation, *Report of Handicapped Workers* (Harrisburg, 1955).

26.   William Form and Delbert Miller, *Industrial Sociology* (New York: Harper & Row, 1970).

27.   Robert Bednarzik, "Involuntary Part Time Work," *Monthly Labor Review,* September 1975, pp. 12–18; Daniel Bell, "The Clock Watchers," *Time,* September 8, 1975.

28.   Bell, "Clock Watchers."

29.   Mark Moore, *The Role of Temporary Help Services in the Clerical Labor Market,* unpublished Ph.D. thesis, University of Wisconsin, 1963; Elmer Winter, *Cutting Costs through Effective Use of Temporary and Part Time Help* (Waterford, Conn.: National Sales Development Institute, 1965).

30.   Richard Schonberger, "Ten Million U.S. Housewives Want to Work." *Labor Law Journal,* June 1970; also see Richard Schonberger, "Private Lives vs. Job Demands," *Human Resource Management,* Summer 1975, pp. 27–32; Richard Morgenstern, and William Hamovitch, "Labor Supply of Married Women in Part Time and Full Time Occupations," *Industrial and Labor Relations Review* October 1976, pp. 59–67.

31.   Felix Rehman, "College Trainees Make the Best Help in Part Time Lower Jobs," *The Office,* April 1969, pp. 58–59.

32. Emil Ann, "Not the Retiring Kind," *Manpower,* August 1974, pp. 9–13; "Senior Citizens Enjoy Part Time Work," *Burroughs Clearing House,* March 1970, p. 6.

33. Carl Rosenfeld and Elizabeth Waldman, "Work Limitations and Chronic Health Problems," *Monthly Labor Review,* January 1967, pp. 38–41.

34. "A Plant for Part Timers," *Business Week,* November 29, 1969.

35. Marc Wallace and Lynn Spruill, "How to Minimize Labor Costs During Peak Demand Periods," *Personnel,* July–August 1975, pp. 61–67; William Werther, Jr., "Part Timers: Overlooked and Undervalued," *Business Horizons,* February 1975, pp. 13–20.

36. Kathie Graham, "Part Time Employment," *Canadian Personnel and Industrial Relations Journal,* January 1974, pp. 35–38.

37. Martin Gannon, "A Profile of the Temporary Help Industry and Its Workers," *Monthly Labor Review,* May 1974, pp. 44–49.

38. Sharleen Bannon, "Women in the Workplace," *The Labour Gazette,* February 1976, pp. 69–74; Jane Burton, "Studies on the Status of Canadian Women," *The Labour Gazette,* July 1976, pp. 377–80; *Women in the Labour Force: Facts and Figures* (Ottawa: Labour Canada Women's Bureau, 1973).

39. Economic Council of Canada, *People and Jobs* (Ottawa: Information Canada, 1976); Stephen Peitchinis, *The Canadian Labour Market* (Toronto: Oxford University Press, 1975); J. Tait Montague, *Labour Markets in Canada* (Scarborough, Ont.: Prentice-Hall of Canada, 1970).

Determining
personnel needs

Part Two begins the discussion of personnel activities performed formally or informally to meet the organization's
needs. Chapters 4 and 5 describe formal employment planning. These chapters investigate the processes management
uses to provide for the human resources through which
the organization's goals can be met. Important factors affecting employment planning, such as job analysis and the employment of women, minorities, the handicapped, and veterans are discussed, as are such new working conditions
as scheduling by flexitime and the four-day week.

Employment planning: Forecasting needs

CHAPTER OBJECTIVES

■ To show what employment planning is and why effective enterprises perform it.

■ To help you become competent in using the tools and techniques of forecasting demand for employees.

■ To indicate how job analysis affects employment planning.

CHAPTER OUTLINE

"What do you mean we're going to lose the government contract?" asked the company president, Ted Sloane.

"We're going to lose it," said the personnel vice president, Anne Wilson. "We don't have trained personnel to meet the contract specifications. We have to furnish records to show that we have an adequate number of employees with the right technical qualifications who meet the government's equal employment opportunity goals. I don't have those kinds of records available at a moment's notice. You know I asked you to let me set up an employment planning information system, and we never got around to it."

"John, should I schedule a trip to visit State University next month, like last year?" asked Maggie Smith, the company's employee recruiter. John, the personnel manager, agreed she should. When Maggie asked "How many people should I recruit, and what types?" John said, "I guess like last year. Let's see how many good ones you turn up. Then we'll decide if we have enough slots for them."

Experiences like these, which are common, are evidence that many managers fail to plan for human resource needs. They never know what their needs are because they neglect employment planning (called manpower planning by some).

> ### DEFINITION
> Employment planning is the personnel process which attempts to provide adequate human resources to achieve future organizational objectives. It includes forecasting future needs for employees of various types; comparing these needs with the present work force; and determining the numbers and types of employees to be recruited or phased out of the organization's employment group.

INTRODUCTION TO EMPLOYMENT PLANNING

Exhibit 4–1 models the employment planning process. As the model indicates, top management examines the environment, analyzes the strategic advantages of the enterprise, and sets its objectives for the coming period. Then it makes strategic and operating decisions to achieve the objectives of the enterprise. The personnel capabilities of the enterprise are among the factors analyzed in the strategic management process.[1] The strategic decisions thus are interactive, as Exhibit 4–2 indicates.

Once the strategy is set, personnel does its part to assure the success of the strategy and achieve the enterprise's objectives. It does this by comparing the present supply of human resources with projected demand for them. This comparison leads to action decisions: add employees, cut employees, or reallocate employees internally. This chapter focuses on the demand side. Chapter 5 completes the employment planning topic by analyzing the supply side and action decisions.

EXHIBIT 4–1
The employment planning process

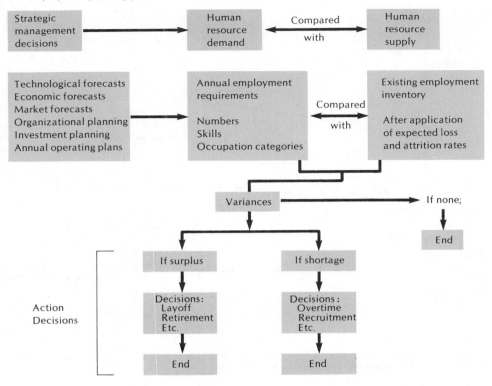

Thus effective employment planning requires strategic decisions by operating managers to set the thrust of the demand. Operating managers also furnish the data for analysis of the supply side. The personnel function compares demand and supply and, in conjunction with operating managers, makes the employment planning action decisions.[2]

Reasons for employment planning

All organizations perform employment planning, informally or formally. The formal employment techniques are described in this chapter because the informal methods are increasingly unsatisfactory for organizations requiring skilled labor in a fast-changing labor market. It is important to point out that most enterprises do more talking about formal employment planning than performing it.

The major reasons for formal employment planning are to achieve:

• More effective and efficient use of human resources.
• More satisfied and more developed employees.
• More effective equal employment opportunity planning.

EXHIBIT 4–2
The interaction between strategic management decisions and employment planning

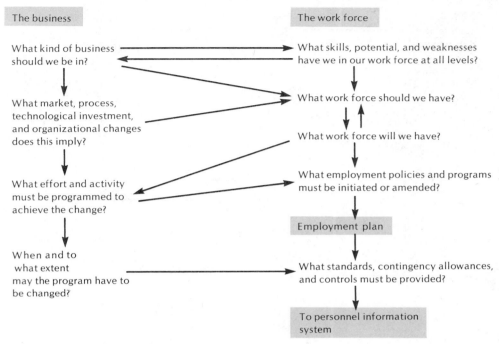

Source: B. L. Donald, "Manpower and a Planned Future," in *Planning for Human Resources,* ed. Charles Margerison and David Ashton (Londin: Longmans, Green & Co., 1974).

More effective and efficient use of people at work.   Employment planning should precede all other personnel activities. How could you schedule recruiting if you did not know how many people you needed? How could you select effectively if you do not know the kinds of persons needed for job openings? How large an orientation program should you schedule? When? How large a training program should you schedule, and when and on what topics? Careful analysis of all personnel activities shows that their effectiveness and efficiency depend on employment planning. There is some empirical support to reinforce this reasoning too.[3]

More effective employee development and greater employee satisfaction.   Employees who work for enterprises that use good employment planning systems have a better chance to participate in planning their own careers and to share in training and development experiences. Thus they are likely to feel their talents are important to the employer, and they have a better chance to use their talents in the kinds of job that use these talents. This often leads to greater employer satisfaction and its consequences: lower absenteeism, lower turnover, fewer accidents, and higher quality of work.

More effective EEO planning.   As will be pointed out frequently in this book, the government has increased its demands for equal employment opportunity. To complete the government reports and satisfactorily respond to EEO demands, enterprises must develop personnel information systems and use them to formally plan their employment distribution.

In sum, effective employment planning assures that the rest of the personnel process will be built on a foundation of good planning.

Stages of development of employment planning

With all these good reasons, you might expect almost every enterprise to carry out formal employment planning. In fact, employment planning is now only a Stage II activity: early development (the stages of development are listed in Exhibit 1–13, Chapter 1.) The government, especially the military, has used sophisticated employment planning for many years, especially during World War II, but the military methods and approaches have not been widely disseminated. Studies in the United States and Canada and in Europe show that only a minority of enterprises do a systematic job. There is more lip service than action.[4]

Why, you may ask, are two chapters necessary for a topic which receives more lip service than action? Because employment planning is a *key* to personnel and organizational effectiveness, more enterprises have begun to use it. This book must be *future oriented* if it is to achieve one of its goals: to train better managers of people and personnel managers for tomorrow's organizations.

A DIAGNOSTIC APPROACH TO EMPLOYMENT PLANNING

Exhibit 4–3 highlights the factors in the diagnostic model that are most important to employment planning. One of the most significant factors affecting employment planning is the goals of the controlling interests. If planning and effective utilization of human resources is not a significant goal for the enterprise, employment planning will not be performed formally, or it will be done in a slipshod way. If the goals of top management include stable growth, employment planning will be less important than if the goals include rapid expansion, diversification, or other factors with a significant impact on future employment needs.

Government policies are another important factor in employment planning. Requirements for equal employment opportunity and promotion call for more employment planning for women and other employees in minority groups and special categories.

The conditions in the labor market also have a significant impact on the amount and type of employment planning done in an enterprise: When there is 14 percent unemployment an employer has more hiring flexibility than when there is 2 percent unemployment in the relevant sector.

The types of persons employed and the tasks they do also determine the kind of planning necessary. Unskilled employees need not be planned

EXHIBIT 4–3
Factors affecting employment planning and organizational effectiveness

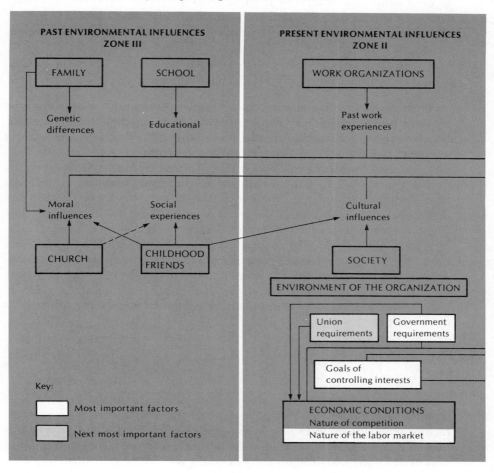

for two years ahead; but computer salesmen, for example, need years of training before coming on track.

To a lesser extent than the government, unions may restrict the ability to hire and promote employees, so they are a factor in employment planning. The sections on methods of employment planning show how these factors affect whether employment planning takes place, and if it does, how often, how far ahead, and in what ways.

FORECASTING FUTURE DEMAND FOR EMPLOYEES

Scene: Board meeting at the Acme Publishing Company.

George Slone (chairman and chief executive): Exhibit A is our planned budget and our objectives for next year. I'd appreciate your comments.

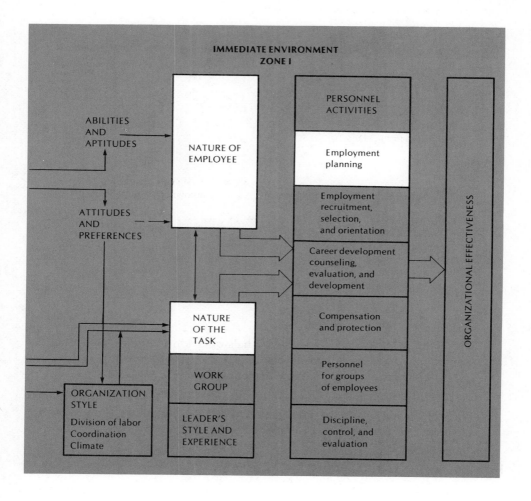

IMMEDIATE ENVIRONMENT
ZONE I

ABILITIES AND APTITUDES

NATURE OF EMPLOYEE

ATTITUDES AND PREFERENCES

ORGANIZATION STYLE
Division of labor
Coordination
Climate

NATURE OF THE TASK

WORK GROUP

LEADER'S STYLE AND EXPERIENCE

PERSONNEL ACTIVITIES

Employment planning

Employment recruitment, selection, and orientation

Career development counseling, evaluation, and development

Compensation and protection

Personnel for groups of employees

Discipline, control, and evaluation

ORGANIZATIONAL EFFECTIVENESS

Martha Kemp (outside director): George, I note that overall, you are projecting a modest growth trend for next year. You also have had a series of increased worker productivity projects going to cut employee costs. Just how many people will you employ next year to reach your sales and profit objectives?"

George: That's a good question, Martha. I don't know exactly. John, what's the answer?

John Arturo (vice president, personnel): That's hard to say. It depends on lots of factors.

Martha: Frankly, John, that's not much of an answer. I can look at the figures in this exhibit and see how much money we need. The marketing people tell me how many units they are going to sell. Why can't you tell me how many people we'll need to get the job done—our people-cost figure?

EXHIBIT 4–4
Forecasting employee demand for employment planning

A. Business

Strategic management decisions   Annual employment requirements

| Economic forecasts |
| Market forecasts |
| Technological forecasts |
| Investment planning |
| Organizational planning |
| Annual operating plans |

Numbers

Skills

Occupational categories

B. Nonbusiness

Strategic management decisions

U.S. Military annual
employment requirements

| Political forecasts |
| Military forecasts |
| Technological forecasts |
| Congressional requirements |
| Presidential requirements |
| Annual operating plans |

Numbers

Skills

Occupational categories

John could have answered Martha's question if Acme's personnel department had developed an effective employee forecasting system; the first element of the employment planning system.

The employment requirements of an enterprise flow from the strategic decisions made by its top managers. Exhibit 4–4 illustrates the process for business and nonbusiness examples.

Employment forecasting techniques

Essentially there are three organizational approaches to employment forecasting. The headquarters can forecast the total demand (top-down approach); the units can forecast their own demand (bottom-up approach), or there can be a combination of the other two.

Sophisticated forecasting techniques are seldom developed in enterprises which have not forecast employment in the past. The techniques used tend to evolve over time from less formal, simpler methods toward the more sophisticated approaches, as Exhibit 4–5 indicates.

Four forecasting techniques will be described here: three top-down techniques—expert estimate, trend projection, and modeling—and the bottom-up unit-forecasting technique.

The expert-estimate technique. The least sophisticated approach to employment planning is for an "expert" to forecast the employment needs based on her or his own experience and intuition. The personnel manager

EXHIBIT 4–5
Evolution of employment forecasting over time

Stage I	Stage II	Stage III	Stage IV
Managers discuss goals, plans, and thus types and numbers of people needed in the short term	Annual planning and budgeting process includes manpower needs	Using computer-generated analyses, causes of problems and future trends regarding supply and demand (the flow of talent) are examined	On-line modeling and simulation of talent needs, flows, and costs aid in a continuing process of updating and projecting needs, staffing plans, career opportunities, and thus program plans
Highly informal and subjective	Quantity and quality of talent needs are specified as far out in time as possible	Computer is used to relieve managers of routine forecasting tasks (such as vacancies or turnover)	Best possible current information for managerial decision is provided
	Problems requiring action, individual or general, are identified	Career paths and career progress are analyzed, using computer data files	Data are exchanged with other companies and with government (such as economic, employment, and social data)
	Management succession and readiness of successors are analyzed		

Source: James Walker, "Evaluating the Practical Effectiveness of Human Resource Planning Applications," *Human Resource Management*, Spring 1974.

may do this by thinking about past employment levels and questioning future needs, which is a quite informal system. The expert-estimate technique can be more effective if the experts use the Delphi technique.[5]

The Delphi technique is a set of procedures originally developed by the Rand Corporation in the late 1940s with the purpose of obtaining the most reliable consensus of opinion of a group of experts. Basically, the Delphi consists of a series of intensive interrogations of each individual expert, through a series of questionnaires, to get the data desired. The procedures, which are designed to avoid direct meetings between the experts, were described in a working paper of the Industrial Relations Center of the University of Minnesota as follows:

> The interaction among the experts is accomplished through an intermediary who gathers the data requests of the experts and summarizes them, along with the experts' answers to the primary question. This mode of controlled interaction among the experts is a deliberate attempt to avoid the disadvantages associated with more conventional uses of experts such as in round table discussions or direct confrontation of opposing views. The developers of the Delphi argue the procedures are more conducive to independent thought and allow more gradual formulation to a considered opinion. In addition to an answer to the problem, the interrogation of the experts is designed to cull out the parameters each expert considers relevant to the problem, and the kinds of information he feels would enable him to arrive at a confident answer to the question.[6]

Typically, the answer to the primary question is a numerical quantity. Originators of the technique expect that individual experts' estimates will tend to converge as the experiment continues, even if initially they are widely divergent. The most crucial shortcomings of the technique were summarized in the working paper as follows:

> *Role of the intermediary.* Standard feedback takes the form of answers to an expert's inquiry for data, summaries of all inquiries and interquartile ranges of the estimates. The summaries of all inquiries are brief and do not include the richness of interpretation each expert brings to bear on the problem. This is the price paid for not allowing the experts to directly interact.
>
> *Independent expert responses.* Experts are initially instructed not to discuss the experiment with others; however, in practice, it is difficult to isolate managers' discussion of these issues.
>
> *Number of rounds.* Five rounds seemed to be the typical number used in reported experiments. However, most of the convergence and most of the data requests occurred in the early rounds, leaving the usefulness of latter rounds open to question.
>
> *Changes in estimates.* Five out of the seven experts changed their estimate only once, while one didn't change his initial estimate at all. From the reports of experiments in nonlaboratory settings, this is a low frequency of change. It may be attributed to the short range (one year) of the forecast, and more changes in successively approximating the "true" answer would occur in a long-range problem with greater uncertainty.[7]

The trend-projection technique. The second technique is to develop a forecast based on a past relationship between a factor related to employment and employment itself. For example, in many businesses, sales levels are related to employment needs, so the personnel planner can develop a table or graph showing past relationships between sales and employment.[8] Exhibit 4–6 gives an example for a hypothetical company, Rugby Sporting Goods Company. Note that as Rugby's sales increased, so did the firms employment needs, but the increases are not linear. In late 1975 Rugby instituted a productivity plan which led to 3 percent increased productivity per year. As Rugby forecasted employee needs it adjusted them for expected productivity gains for 1978, 1979, and 1980.

Modeling and multiple-predictive techniques. The third top-down approach to prediction of demand uses the most sophisticated forecasting and modeling techniques. Trend projections are based on relating a single factor (such as sales) to employment. The more advanced approaches relate many factors, such as sales, gross national product, and discretionary income, to employment. Or they mathematically model the enterprise and simulate, using such methods as Markov models and analytical formulations. Only larger enterprises with corporate staff capacities can use this approach.[9]

The unit demand forecasting technique. The unit forecast is a bottom-up approach to forecasting demands. Headquarters sums these unit forecasts, and the result becomes the employment forecast. The unit manager analyzes the units person-by-person, job-by-job needs in the present as well as the future.

By analyzing present and future requirements on the job, and the skills of the incumbents, this method focuses on quality of workers. Often it is initiated by a letter or a phone call, such as:

Vice president, personnel: John, Bill Foster here. We're trying to get our forecast for employment needs together for next year so that we can get it into the budget. Will you get your net needs for next budget year to me by the end of the week? Use Form EP–1—it has a place for present employees in each of your units, less retirements, plus new employees needed for new business. Thanks!

Manager, division 1: "Bill, I'll get right on it."

EXHIBIT 4–6
Sample trend-projection employment forecast for Rugby Sporting Goods Company

Year	Sales	Employee census	Employee forecast adjusted for annual productivity rate of 3 percent
Actual data			
1975	100,000,000	5,000	5,000
1976	120,000,000	6,000	5,825
1977	140,000,000	7,000	6,598
	Sales forecast	*Employee forecast*	
Forecast			
1978	160,000,000	8,000	7,321
1979	180,000,000	9,000	7,996
1980	200,000,000	10,000	8,626

EXHIBIT 4-7
Excerpt from a manning table

MANNING TABLE
PART III
REPLACEMENT SUMMARY
(for selective service)

SHEET ____ OF ____ SHEETS

LINE NUMBER	PLANT JOB TITLE	DICTIONARY CODE (OPTIONAL)	TOTAL NUMBER OF WORKERS	NUMBER OF WOMEN	MALE WORKERS 38 AND OVER OR UNDER 18			MALE WORKERS 18 THROUGH 37			
					45 AND OVER	38 THROUGH 44	UNDER 18	PHYSICAL- LY DIS- QUALIFIED	WITH CHILDREN	MARRIED WITHOUT CHILDREN	SINGLE
	28	29	30	31	32	33	34	35	36	37	38

Usually the manager would start with a present census of people compiled on a list called a manning table, an example of which is given in Exhibit 4–7. Manning tables list the jobs in an organization by name and number and record the number of jobholders for each entry.

The resulting tables must be evaluated in terms of both numbers and skills of the present personnel. Consideration must be given to the effects of expected losses through retirement, promotion, or other reasons. Whether those losses will require replacement and what the projected growth needs, if any, will be are questions the planner must answer and project into his calculations in determining net employment needs.

The use of a table such as Exhibit 4–8 has been suggested for observing the flow of employees through the system. The manager could assign probabilities to each of these contingencies and use these data to analyze the need for replacements. If the positions in question are important enough, he may have already prepared replacement charts like the one in Exhibit 4–9.

Thus the manager knows the status of the employees. But this knowledge has two assumptions built into it: that she or he has made the best use of the available personnel, and that demand for the product or service of the unit will be the same for next year as this. With regard to the first assumption, the manager can examine the job design and work load of each employee, using such techniques as time and motion studies. The manager may also attempt to judge the productivity of the employees in his unit by comparing the cost per product or service produced by his unit with those of similar

EXHIBIT 4–8
Personnel flow table form

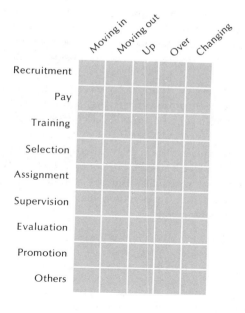

EXHIBIT 4–9
Employee replacement chart

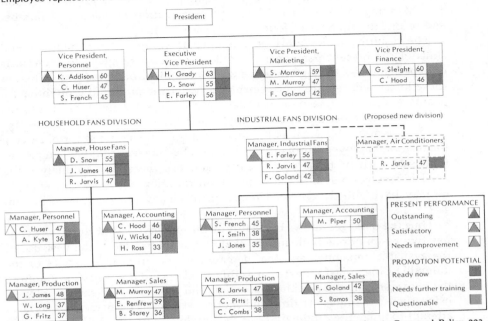

Source: National Industrial Conference Board, *The Expanded Personnel Function,* Studies in Personnel Policy 203 (New York, 1966).

units in the organization and others. Past productivity rates can be compared with present ones, after adjusting for changes in the job, or subjective evaluations can be made of the productivity of certain employees compared to others. In addition, it may be necessary to base employment needs on work-force analysis, with adjustments for current data on absenteeism and turnover.

The unit analyzes its product or service demand by extrapolating trends. Using methods similar to the trend technique for the organization, the unit determines if it may need more employees because of a change in product or service demand.

Finally, the unit manager prepares an estimate of total employment needs and plans for how the unit can fulfill these needs. He could prepare a series of detailed requisitions or replacement cards like the one shown in Exhibit 4–10. In considering when to replace certain persons, learning curves (see Chapter 11) are helpful in forward planning.

Using forecasting techniques

The first issue in forecasting employee demand in the future is that, although formal employment forecasting is increasing in use and sophistica-

EXHIBIT 4–10
Detailed position replacement chart

Position			
MANAGER, SALES (House Fans Division)			
Performance Incumbent		Salary	May Move
Outstanding Mel Murray		$32,000	1 year
Replacement		Salary	Age
Earl Renfraw		$17,000	39
Present Position		Employed:	
		Present Job	Company
Field Sales Manager, House Fans		3 years	10 years
Training Needed		When Ready	
Special assignment to study market potential for air conditioners to provide forecasting experience.		Now	
Replacement 2		Salary	Age
Bernard Storey		$16,500	36
Present Position		Employed:	
		Present Job	Company
Promotion Manager, House Fans		4 years	7 years
Training Needed		When Ready	
Rotation to field sales Marketing conference in fall		2 years	

Source: National Industrial Conference Board, *The Expanded Personnel Function,* Studies in Personnel Policy 203 (New York, 1966).

tion, many more enterprises use unit-level planning and expert estimates than trend projection, and many more use trend projection than modeling and multiple-predictive techniques.[10] The latter are used only by very large and very sophisticated enterprises like the U.S. military, the U.S. and Canadian federal governments, and a few large businesses like Exxon.

How good are the various forecasting techniques? Are the more sophisticated ones better than expert estimate? Not necessarily. One study showed that expert estimates using the Delphi method were more accurate and useful than the more "sophisticated methods."[11]

One attempt to evaluate the four techniques (as correlated with our categories) is given in Exhibit 4–11. Don Bryant and his associates rate the

EXHIBIT 4-11
Employment planning models and techniques

Problem areas	Supervisor estimates*	Replacements charts§	Delphi technique*	Management MPP matrix§	Matrix model for executive development§	Time series analysis†	Stochastic statistical analysis‡	Goal programming model‡	Naval shore activity model‡	Minimum risk manpower scheduling‡	Network flow model‡	PERSYM‡	U.S. Army Reserve simulation model‡	Weber model‡
Forecasting	G–F	G–F	G	F	G–F	G–F	G	G	G–F	G	G	G	G	G
Scheduling	G–F	P	P	P	F	P	G–F	G	G–F	G	G–F	G–F	G–F	F
Allocation	G–F	F	P	F–P	F	P	F	G	G	G–F	G–F	G–F	G–F	G
Uncertainty	F	P	G	F–P	F–P	F–P	G	G–F	F	G	F	G	G	G
Costing ability	F	F	F–P	P	P	P	G–F	G	G	G	F–P	G–F	G	G
Time horizon L	P	F	G–F	F–P	F	F–P	P	F	P	P	F–P	F–P	G–F	G
Time horizon M	F	F	G	G	G	G	G	G	F	G–F	G	G	G	G
Time horizon S	G	G	G	F	G	G–F	G	G	G	G	G	G	G	G
Aggregate	F	F	G	F	F	G	G	G	F	G	G	G–F	G	G
Individual	G–F	G–F	F	F	F	P	P	F–P	F–P	F–P	F	F	P	F
Test policy changes	F	P	F	F	F–P	P	F–P	G	F	F–P	F	G–F	G–F	G
Hierarchy level U	P	F	G–F	F	F	P	P	F	P	P	P	G–F	F	G
Hierarchy level M	F	G	G	G	F	G	G	G	F	G	F	G	F	G
Hierarchy level L	G	P	G	G	G	G	G	G	G	G	G	G	G	G
Static versus dynamic	G–F	G	G	G–F	G–F	F	F	G	G–F	G–F	G	F	G–F	G
	F–P	P	G	G–F	F	F	F	G	G–F	G–F	G	G	G–F	G

Key: G = good; F = fair; G–F = good to fair; F–P = fair to poor; P = poor.
* Expert Estimate
† Trend Projection
‡ Modeling and multiple-predictive technique
§ Unit estimates
Source: Don Bryant et al., "Manpower Planning Models and Techniques," *Business Horizons*, April 1973, p. 76.

techniques as good (G), fair (F), good to fair (G–F), fair to poor (F–P), or poor (P) in their ability to forecast and other characteristics. This exhibit reemphasizes that each technique has certain strengths and weaknesses. The effective manager matches the forecasting requirements with the capabilities of the technique. The relative cost of each technique is such a factor. The most expensive is the modeling and multiple-predictive technique and the least is expert estimates, with the other two in between.[12]

The technique to be used varies first with the length of the time period the manager is trying to predict (Exhibit 4–12).

The technique used also must fit the nature of the enterprise and its environment—size, complexity, volatility, geographic dispersion, and so on. Obviously, the simplest demand forecast will be possible for the small, uncomplicated organization located in one place. If the organization is large but not complex and in a slow-changing environment, headquarters can do the planning. It should be decentralized to the unit level when the opposite conditions prevail and the organization is volatile, complex, or dispersed. For organizations between these extremes, employment planning can use both approaches: top down and bottom up, and the techniques that fit it best. Bruce Coleman notes the need for varying demand forecast methods:

> For sales and manufacturing manpower, a method employing correlation analysis may be a highly effective first approximation of manpower requirements, particularly where products, territories, and production operations are not changing rapidly. In other organizations, however, where new and more complex products are marketed, new skills may be needed in the sales force. The qualitative aspects of the problem then become significant. . . . Skills obsolescence among operative workers is a real danger.

EXHIBIT 4–12

Three ranges of employment forecasting

Range / Forecast	Short range (0–2 years)	Intermediate range (2–5 years)	Long range (beyond 5 years)
Demand	Authorized employment (including growth, changes, and turnover)	Operating needs from budgets and plans	In some organizations the same as "intermediate"; in others, an increased awareness of changes in environment and technology—essentially judgmental
Supply	Employee census less expected losses plus expected promotions from subordinate groups	Manpower vacancies expected from individual promotability data derived from development plans	Management expectations of changing characteristics of employees and future available manpower
Net needs	Numbers and kinds of employees needed	Numbers, kinds, dates, and levels of needs	Management expectations of future conditions affecting immediate decisions

Source: James Walker, "Forecasting Manpower Needs," in *Manpower Planning and Programming,* ed. Elmer H. Burack and James W. Walker (Boston: Allyn & Bacon, Inc., 1972), p. 94.

Some types of manpower activities are more amenable to a method based on the function of mission of an organizational unit. For service functions such as a maintenance department, where heterogeneous groups of skills are utilized, manpower requirements can be based on work functions and work load factors. This method permits tradeoffs among skill levels and types of skills.[13]

The role of employment demand forecasting in employment planning

A personnel executive at headquarters who is responsible for employment demand forecast will improve the estimates by checking with personnel and operating executives in the field. If the units forecast their own needs, the personnel executive sums their estimates, and this becomes the forecast. What happens if both the bottom-up and top-down approaches are used and the forecasts conflict? In all probability, the manager reconciles the two totals by averaging them or examining more closely the major variances between the two. The Delphi technique could be used to do this. One or several forecasts can be used to produce a single employment forecast.

EMPLOYMENT PLANNING AND THE JOB

In the employment demand forecasting aspect of employment planning, the bottom-up or unit-forecasting method calls for each unit to determine the number of people needed to accomplish the unit's objectives. The basic building block of this forecast is the number of jobs to be filled.

Some dimensions of job design were introduced in Chapter 2. The rest of this chapter will focus on the formalization of jobs through the job analysis process. It will show how the job analysis aspect of employment planning interacts with the rest of the employment planning process and many other personnel activities.

Job analysis

> **DEFINITION**
> Job analysis is the aspect of employment planning which is concerned with study of the jobs in an enterprise. In particular, job analysis and the resultant job specifications clarify these aspects of each job: the work activities; the tools, equipment, and work aids used; job-related tangibles and intangibles (such as materials used, products made, services rendered); work performance; job context (working conditions); and requirements necessary to do the job (such as knowledge, skills, experience, and personal attributes).[14]

Job analysis is performed for many reasons: to provide information for the preparation of job descriptions and specifications; to help in the hiring, orientation, and training of employees; as an aid in job evaluation for pay purposes; for collective bargaining reasons; for safety purposes; and as a requirement in equal employment opportunity planning and analysis.[15] Exhibit 4–13 indicates how this process cascades through the personnel function.

EXHIBIT 4–13
Impact of job analysis on personnel activities

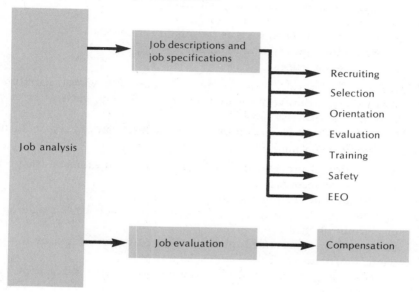

In job analysis, the following information is gathered:

1. Work activities.
   a. Work activities and processes.
   b. Activity records (in film form, for example).
   c. Procedures used.
   d. Personal responsibility.
2. Worker-oriented activities.
   a. Human behaviors such as physical actions and communicating on the job.
   b. Elemental motions for methods analysis.
   c. Personal job demands, such as energy expenditure.
3. Machines, tools, equipment and work aids used.
4. Job-related tangibles and intangibles.
   a. Knowledge dealt with or applied (as in accounting).
   b. Materials processed.
   c. Products made or services performed.

5. Work performance. (Note: All job analysis systems do not develop the work performance aspects.)
   a. Error analysis.
   b. Work standards.
   c. Work measurements, such as time taken for a task.
6. Job context.
   a. Work schedule.
   b. Financial and nonfinancial incentives.
   c. Physical working conditions.
   d. Organizational and social contexts.
7. Personnel requirements for the job.
   a. Personal attributes such as personality, interests.
   b. Education and training required.
   c. Work experience.

This information can be in the form of qualitative, verbal, narrative descriptions or quantitative measurements of each item, such as error rates per unit of time or noise level.[16]

How job analysis is carried out. Job analysis can use one or many of the following seven methods:

1. Examination of previous job analyses or job descriptions on the position and/or other records.
2. Observation of the job and the job occupant.
3. Interviewing the job occupant and/or supervision by a single analyst or a group of them.
4. Structured or open-ended questionnaires to be completed by job occupants and/or supervisors.
5. Self-recording of data and observations, in a log or diary kept by the job occupant.
6. Recording of job activities on film or with audio means.
7. Analyzing equipment design information from blueprints and design data.

Methods 1, 4, and 7 are the quickest but may develop less reliable data than other methods. Methods 2, 3, 5, and 6 are more accurate but more costly. As far as observation and other data gathering techniques are concerned, it has been found that proper work-sampling techniques add to the quality of the data's reliability and validity.[17]

The most advanced job analysis work is being done by the U.S. Training and Employment Service,[18] and the Personnel Division of the Air Force Human Resources Lab.[19]

The information gathered in this form of job analysis is recorded on a form called a job analysis schedule, which describes work performed, skills involved, and conditions of work, as well as giving the job title and location and a job summary. The form also lists the relationships of this job to other jobs. An example of a job analysis schedule is excerpted in Exhibit 4–14.

EXHIBIT 4–14
Excerpts from U.S. Training and Employment Service job analysis schedule for a dough mixer

Job: Dough Mixer (Bakery Products Industry)

4. Job Summary:

   Operates mixing machine to mix ingredients for straight and sponge (yeast) doughs according to established formulas, directs other workers in fermentation of dough, and cuts dough into pieces with hand cutter.

15. Description of Tasks:

    1. Dumps ingredients into mixing machine: Examines production schedule to determine type of bread to be produced, such as rye, whole wheat, or white. Refers to formula card for quantities and types of ingredients required, such as flour, water, milk, vitamin solutions, and shortening. Weighs out, measures, and dumps ingredients into mixing machine.

    2. Operates mixing machine: Turns valves and other hand controls to set mixing time according to type of dough being mixed. Presses button to start agitator blades in machine. Observes gauges and dials on equipment continuously to verify temperature of dough and mixing time. Feels dough for desired consistency. Adds water or flour to mix measuring vessels and adjusts mixing time and controls to obtain desired elasticity in mix.

    3. Directs other workers in fermentation of dough: Perpares fermentation schedule according to type of dough being raised. Sprays portable dough *trough* with lubricant to prevent adherence of mixed dough to trough. Directs *dough-mixer helper* in positioning trough beneath door of mixer to catch dough when mixing cycle is complete. Pushes, or directs other workers to push, troughs of dough into fermentation room.

    4. Cuts dough: Dumps fermentated dough onto worktable. Manually kneads dough to eliminate gases formed by yeast. Cuts dough into pieces with hand cutter. Places cut dough on proofing rack and covers with cloth.

    5. Performs miscellaneous duties: Records on work sheet number of batches mixed during work shift. Informs *bake shop foreman* when repairs or major adjustments are required for machines and equipment.

Other advanced techniques include the Position Analysis Questionnaire[20] and the functional occupational classification approach.[21] Two other comprehensive job analysis systems have been developed by the U.S. Department of Labor and by Ernest McCormick and Joseph Tiffin. The Department of Labor's *Handbook for Analyzing Jobs* has guidelines for analyzing jobs and 298 work fields as related to the *Dictionary of Occupational Titles*. This approach emphasizes systematic verbal description of the functions performed on the job.

Tiffin has a more quantitative approach which uses factor analysis to group various aspects of jobs.[22] In this system, the analyst rates the job on 194 elements of work (such as use of keyboard devices). From job analysis, the jobs are grouped into sets of jobs called job families; these are homogeneous job types, and one or several characteristics can be used to group them. McCormick lists some of the dimensions for grouping one job: mental and educational development v. adaptability to routine; adaptability to precision operations; body agility; artistic ability and aesthetic appreciation; manual adaptability; personal contact v. adaptability to routine, heavy manual work v. clerical ability.[23] The job families are used for career planning and development (see Chapter 9).

Job descriptions and job specifications

When a manager advertises to hire employees, where does he get the information to describe the openings? How does she or he instruct an interviewer to select the best person from those who apply? The answer to these questions is with job descriptions and job specifications.

From the data gathered in job analysis, organizations (particularly larger ones) prepare records of what jobs are being performed in the organization (job descriptions) and the qualifications necessary to perform them (job specifications). These are used when replacement becomes necessary. A combined job description and job specifications for a personnel officer is given in Exhibit 4–15.

EXHIBIT 4–15
Job description and specifications for a personnel officer

Job Description

General description

Performs responsible administrative work managing personnel activities of a large state agency or institution. Work involves responsibility for the planning and administration of a personnel program which includes recruitment, examination, selection, evaluation, appointment, promotion, transfer, and recommended change of status of agency employees, and a system of communication for disseminating necessary information to workers. Works under general supervision, exercising initiative and independent judgment in the performance of assigned tasks.

Examples of work performed

Participates in overall planning and policy making to provide effective and uniform personnel services.

Communicates policy through organization levels by bulletin, meetings, and personal contact.

Interviews applicants, evaluates qualifications, classifies applications.

Recruits and screens applicants to fill vacancies and reviews applications of qualified persons.

Confers with supervisors on personnel matters, including placement problems, retention or release of probationary employees, transfers, demotions, and dismissals of permanent employees.

Supervises administration of tests.

Initiates personnel training activities and coordinates these activities with work of officials and supervisors.

Establishes effective service rating system, trains unit supervisors in making employee evaluations.

Maintains employee personnel files.

Supervises a group of employees directly and through subordinates.

Performs related work as assigned.

Job Specification

General qualification requirements

Experience and training

Should have considerable experience in personnel administration.

Education

Graduation from a four-year college or university, with major work in education and personnel administration.

Knowledge, skills, and abilities

Considerable knowledge of principles and practices of personnel administration; selection and assignment of personnel; job evaluation.

A great deal of time and energy can go into preparing these forms. Their value depends on how up to date and accurate they are, how often they are used, and in which ways. Most personnel and operating managers are quite critical of typical job descriptions and how they are used. Many organizations prepare them only for lower level jobs and do not update them for long periods. Or the data in them are incomplete because inappropriate or inadequate methods were used to compile them. If there is an antagonistic work climate in the organization, employees can use job descriptions to avoid work: "It's not in my job description." And for most non–assembly-line jobs, it is impossible to list all aspects of the jobs.

One source of help on job analysis, job specifications, and job description is *The Dictionary of Occupational Titles,* mentioned above. In its latest form, it contains almost 40,000 titles and almost 25,000 actual job descriptions. More than half of these are in production and transportation, followed by professional, technical, managerial, and unclassified positions.

Craig Schneier makes the point that many job descriptions are almost useless and may not meet the requirements of EEO guidelines.[24] To be useful and to meet the guidelines, the job description must be behaviorally based. At present, this is not a part of job analysis and job descriptions, but it makes sense to enlarge the process to include Schneier's ideas. Schneier lists a series of steps necessary to develop behavioral job objectives:

1. Decide upon job objectives and state them in the form of terminal behaviors (what the job occupant actually does).
2. List the tasks required for desired performance.

EXHIBIT 4–16
Ambiguous and behaviorally defined objectives in a job description

Comparison of ambiguous and terminal behavior job objectives	
Ambiguous job objectives	*Terminal behavior job objectives*
1. To demonstrate satisfactory ability on the job and perform at required standards.	1. To operate the press such that a minimum of 120 pieces are produced correctly each hour, with no more than 1 incorrect (defective) piece produced in any hour.
2. To develop a positive attitude toward the work and to be dependable.	2. To give evidence of willingness to perform the job by not being absent from work except for those reasons and on those days specified by the union agreement; and by being at the proper work place when the shift bell sounds.
3. To be able to communicate effectively with subordinates.	3. To notify each division head of all changes in the budget by written memo to each no later than one day after notification of such change reaches your desk.

Source: Craig Schneier, "Content Validity: The Necessity of a Behavioral Job Description," *The Personnel Administrator,* February 1976.

3. Differentiate between routine and critical task performance.
4. List alternative methods of performing tasks.
5. Specify criteria used to determine if terminal behavior has been evidenced and thus if the job has been performed successfully.
6. Specify favorable and unfavorable conditions for the attainment of objectives and performance criteria.
7. Specify other general information regarding the job (for example, title, salary, supervisor).
8. List work qualifications, education, and/or experience levels required.

When this approach is used, job descriptions with vague parts like the job objectives on the left of Exhibit 4–16 (on page 109) are converted into behaviorally based items like those on the right.

SUMMARY, CONCLUSIONS, AND RECOMMENDATIONS

This chapter, the first of two on employment planning, defined employment planning, explained how it is tied in to the diagnostic model, and gave reasons for performing it. The methods of forecasting organizational and unit-level employee demand were described, and the role of job analysis, job descriptions, and job specifications in the personnel function was discussed. Some methods used for these aspects of employment planning were also described.

It should be clear that both operating managers and personnel managers have a part to play in employment planning. Personnel summarizes and analyzes the forecasts of needs by operating managers and prepares the formal employment plans for the enterprise.

This chapter introduces the use of summary propositions to highlight some of the major points that have been made about the various personnel activities. They serve as recommendations as well as a concise form of summary. The following propositions summarize the aspects of employment planning presented in Chapter 4.

The first topic discussed was formal planning of employment demand, as summarized in propositions 4.1–4.5.

Proposition 4.1. The larger the organization's work force, the more likely is the effective organization to forecast the demand for labor formally and to forecast it centrally at organization headquarters.

Proposition 4.2. The more volatile the organization's environment, the more likely is the effective organization to forecast the demand for labor formally at each unit and to sum the demand at headquarters.

Proposition 4.3. The more complex the product and services offered by the organization, the more likely is the effective organization to forecast the demand for labor formally at each unit level and to sum the demand at headquarters.

Proposition 4.4   The more geographically dispersed the organization's members to subdivisions, the more likely is the effective organization to forecast the demand for labor formally at each unit and to sum the demand at headquarters.

Proposition 4.5.   The larger the organization, the more stable its environment, and the less complex its product-service line, the more likely is the effective organization to use modeling or multiple-predictive techniques to forecast its employment demand.

The next topics discussed were job analysis, job descriptions, and job specifications and how they affect employment planning. The propositions on these topics are Propositions 4.6 and 4.7.

Proposition 4.6.   The larger the organization, the more likely are formal job analysis, description, and specification systems to be efficient.

Proposition 4.7.   The more volatile the organization's environment, the less likely are detailed formal job analysis, description, and specification systems to be efficient.

A more complete summary of employment planning will be given at the end of Chapter 5, after the total process has been described. Chapter 5 completes the discussion of employment planning by analyzing its supply side.

QUESTIONS

1. What is employment planning? How does it relate to other personnel activities?
2. Why do some employers perform formal employment planning? Why don't others?
3. In what ways does employment planning interact with the strategic management decisions of top managers?
4. What factors in the diagnostic model are most significant to employment planning? Why?
5. What techniques are used for forecasting future employment needs?
6. Which types of enterprises can use the various forecasting technique effectively? Why? Describe each technique briefly.
7. Describe how you would choose a forecasting technique for several kinds of enterprises, such as: a small manufacturer of ashtrays; a large steel company; a moderate-sized general hospital.
8. What is job analysis? Why is it performed?
9. Describe several methods of performing job analysis.
10. How does job analysis relate to other personnel activities?
11. Contrast job descriptions, job specifications, and job analysis.
12. Describe how to prepare a behaviorally oriented job description.

NOTES AND REFERENCES

1. B. L. Donald, "Manpower and a Planned Future," in *Planning for Human Resources,* ed. Charles Margerison and David Ashton (London: Longmans Green & Co., 1974), chap. 3; A. N. Navas, Kendrich Rowland, and Edward Williams, *Managerial Manpower Forecasting and Planning Research Project Report* (Berea, Ohio: American Society for Personnel Administration, 1965); D. Newton, "Manpower Planning," in Margerison and Ashton, *Planning for Human Resources.*

2. Some general references on employment planning include: David Bell, *Planning Corporate Manpower* (London: Longmans Green & Co., 1974); Elmer Burack, and James Walker, *Manpower Planning and Programming* (Boston: Allyn & Bacon, 1972); Bruce Coleman, "An Integrated System for Manpower Planning," *Business Horizons,* October 1970, pp. 89–95; Conference Board in Canada, *Corporate Manpower Planning in Canada* (Scarborough, Ontario, 1976); B. A. Keys et al., *Meeting Managerial Manpower Needs* (Ottawa: Economic Council of Canada, 1971); J. R. Levesque, "Manpower Planning in Canada: Trends and Prospects," *The Canadian Business Review,* Spring 1976, pp. 30–33; Gary Lilien and Ambar G. Ras, "Model for Manpower Management," *Management Science,* August 1975, pp. 1447–57; Magerison and Ashton, *Planning for Human Resources;* Malcolm Salter, "Manpower Planning Priorities in Emerging Multinationals," ICH 4–375–286, Intercollegiate Case Clearing House, Harvard Business School, 1975; Gilbert Siegel, "A Conceptual Framework for Manpower Planning and Forecasting in Governmental Organizations," in *Human Resource Management in Public Organizations* ed. Gilbert Siegel (Los Angeles: University Publishers, 1973); Eric Vetter, *Manpower Planning for High Talent Personnel* (Ann Arbor: University of Michigan, Bureau of Industrial Relations, 1967); Ian Watson, "Identifying and Reducing Manpower Inbalances in the Public Service of Canada," *Public Personnel Management,* July–August 1974, pp. 258–64; Klaus Weiermair, "A Note on Manpower Forecasting," *Relations Industrielles* 30, 2 (1974) pp. 228–38; A. M. Wurr, "Developing Personnel Strategy," in Margerison and Ashton, *Planning for Human Resources,* chap. 2; Douglas Reid, "Human Resource Planning: A Tool for People Development," (March–April, 1977), pp. 15–25.

3. D. Conrath, and W. Hamilton, "The Economics of Manpower Pooling," *Management Science,* October 1971; Vetter, *Planning for High Talent Personnel.*

4. Conference Board in Canada, *Corporate Manpower Planning;* Levesque, "Manpower Planning in Canada"; Navas et al., *Managerial Manpower Forecasting.*

5. G. Milkovich, A. J. Annoni, and T. A. Mahoney, *The Use of the Delphi Procedures in Manpower Forecasting.* Working Paper 71–07, Industrial Relations Center, University of Minnesota, 1971; Harold Sackman, *Delphi Technique (1975).*

6. Milkovich et al., *Use of Delphi Procedures.*

7. Ibid.

8. Milton Drandell, "A Composite Forecasting Method for Manpower Planning, Utility Objective and Subjective Criteria," *Academy of Management Journal,* September 1975, pp. 510–19; Vetter, *Planning for High Talent Personnel.*

9. T. W. Bonham, et al., "A GERT Model to Meet Future Organizational Manpower Needs," *Personnel Journal,* July 1975, pp. 402–6; Don Bryant et al., "Manpower Planning Models and Techniques," *Business Horizons,* April 1973, pp. 69–78; Norbert Elbert and William Kehoe, "How to Bridge Fact and Theory in Manpower Planning," *Personnel,* November–December 1976, pp. 31–39; Thomas Mahoney and George Milkovich, "Computer Simulation: A Training Tool for Manpower Managers," *Personnel Journal,* December 1975, pp. 609–12 ff.; Myles Vogel, "Manpower Forecasting with Linear Programming," *Industrial Engineering,* January 1976, pp. 43–45.

10. J. G. Heneman, Jr., and George Seltzer, *Manpower Planning and Forecasting in the Firm: An Exploratory Probe* (Minneapolis: University of Minnesota, 1968); Levesque "Manpower Planning in Canada"; Navas et al., *Managerial Manpower Forecasting;* Thomas Patten, *Manpower*

Planning and the Development of Human Resources (New York: Wiley Interscience, 1971), pp. 63–119; F. James Staszak and Nicholas J. Mathys, "Organization Gap: Implications for Manpower Planning," *California Management Review,* Spring 1975, pp. 32–39.

11. Milkovich et al., *Use of Delphi Procedures.*

12. Robert Dacey, "Manpower Management," in *Army Command and Management,* ed. Raymond Cook (Carlisle, Pa.: Army War College, 1976); Robert Sylvia, "TOSS: An Aerospace System That's Go for Manpower Planning," *Personnel,* January–February 1977, pp. 56–64.

13. Coleman, "Integrated System for Manpower Planning."

14. This definition is adapted from Ernest McCormick, "Job and Task Analysis," in *Handbook of Industrial and Organizational Psychology,* ed. Marvin Dunnette (Chicago: Rand McNally & Co., 1976).

15. E. Rouleau, and B. Krain, "Using Job Analyses to Design Selection Procedures," *Public Personnel Management* 4 (1975), pp. 300–304; R. Deckman, *Handbook for Supporting Staff, Job Analyses and Job Evaluation* (Baltimore: Johns Hopkins University Press, 1971); Sidney Fine and Wretha Wiley, *An Introduction to Functional Job Analysis* (Kalamazoo, Mich.; Upjohn Institute, 1971); Sidney Fine, "Functional Job Analysis: An Approach to a Technology for Manpower Planning," *Personnel Journal,* November 1974, pp. 813–18; J. E. Morsh, *Handbook for Analyzing Jobs,* U.S. Department of Labor (Washington, D.C.: U.S. Government Printing Office, 1972).

16. McCormick, "Job and Task Analysis."

17. J. E. Morsh, "Collecting, Analyzing and Reporting Information Describing Jobs in the U.S. Air Force," in *Proceedings,* American Psychological Association, 1969.

18. L. Lewis, "Job Analysis in the U.S. Training and Employment Service," *Proceedings,* American Psychological Association, 1969.

19. R. E. Christal, "Comments by the Chairman," *Proceedings,* American Psychological Association, 1969; Morsh, "Jobs in the U.S. Air Force."

20. Ernest McCormick, et al., *A Study of Job Characteristics and Job Dimensions as Based on PAQ,* Report no. 6, Occupational Research Center, Purdue University, 1969.

21. Lewis, "Job Analysis."

22. Joseph Tiffin, *Industrial Psychology* (Englewood Cliffs, N.J.: Prentice-Hall, Inc., 1941).

23. McCormick, "Job and Task Analysis."

24. Craig Schreier, "Content Validity: The Necessity of a Behavioral Job Description," *The Personnel Administrator* 21 (February 1976), pp. 38–44; See also David Austin, "A New Approach to Position Descriptions," *Personnel Journal,* (July 1977), pp. 354–55, 363–66 ff; George Wendt, "Should Courts Write Your Job Descriptions?" *Personnel Journal* (September 1976), pp. 442–50.

Employment planning: Analysis of supply and action decisions

CHAPTER OBJECTIVES

■ To demonstrate how managers analyze the supply of employees in the enterprise.

■ To show how various work schedules, such as shift work, flexitime, and compressed work weeks, affect the supply of employees and their satisfaction and effectiveness.

■ To indicate how to analyze the supply of employees for EEO implications and action decisions such as layoffs, demotions, and terminations.

CHAPTER OUTLINE

I. Analysis of the Supply of Present Employees
   A. Skills Inventories
   B. Designing Skills Inventory Systems
   C. Some Examples of Skills Inventory Systems
   D. Management Inventories
   E. Maintaining Inventory Systems
   F. Problems with Skills Inventories

II. Work Schedules and Supply of Employees
   A. Shift Work
   B. Compressed Work Weeks
   C. Flexitime (flexible hours)

III. Action Decisions in Employment Planning
   A. Analyzing the Composition of the Work Force
   B. Action Decisions with No Variance in Supply and Demand
   C. Action Decisions with a Shortage of Workers
   D. Action Decisions in Surplus Conditions

IV. Computers and Cost/Benefit Analysis in Employment Planning

V. Summary, Conclusions, and Recommendations
   A. Employment Planning Systems for Model Organization

After a manager has projected the employment needs of the enterprise, the next step in employment planning is to determine the availability of those presently at work in it. The employment planning process was modeled in Exhibit 4–1 in the preceding chapter, and the relevant part for this chapter is highlighted in Exhibit 5–1.

On the basis of strategic management decisions, the personnel manager compares the demand for people needed to achieve the enterprise's objectives with the present supply of people to determine the need to hire, lay off, promote, or train. These are the action decisions. The major tool of analysis used to analyze employment supply is the skills inventory.

ANALYSIS OF THE SUPPLY OF PRESENT EMPLOYEES

For a small organization, it is relatively easy to know how many employees there are, what they do, and what they can do. A "mom-and-pop" grocery store may employ only the owners and have two part-time helpers to "plan" for. When they see that one part-time employee is going to graduate in June, they know they need to replace him. Sources of supply could include their own children, converting their other part-time helper into a full-time assistant, or calling the school's employment office for candidates.

It is quite a different situation with a school system employing hundreds at numerous locations, or such mammoth organizations as the Royal Canadian Air Force or IBM. One writer discussed the problem of "keeping tabs" on 7,500 middle managers at Canadian National Railways.[1] These kinds of organizations must know how many full-time and peripheral workers they have working for them, and where. They must know what skills prospective employees would need to replace people who quit, retire, or are fired or to add them for new functions or more work.

The methods for handling such a challenge range from simple records on 3 × 5 cards to sophisticated statistical and mathematical techniques such as simulation and Markov chain analysis.[2] But the basic tool for assessing the supply of people and talents available within the organization is the

EXHIBIT 5–1
Employment planning relationships for supply analysis and action decisions

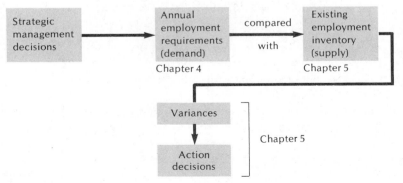

skills inventory. When separate inventories are kept for managerial employees they are called management inventories.

The systems for recording and analyzing employee skills range from informal to sophisticated. The simplest form for keeping track of the numbers of various jobs or persons with the required skills or experience is the manning table (see Exhibit 4–7 in preceding chapter). Skills inventory tools can range from simple pieces of paper and forms to sophisticated computer information systems. The degree of sophistication necessary is related to the size, complexity, and volatility of the organization.

Skills inventories

Marjorie Lancer is vice president, personnel, of a medium-sized firm. One of the division vice presidents, Howard Cantobello, calls her on the phone and says, after some small talk, "Marge, we've decided to enter the Latin American market and we need a person who has 10 years' experience, and a degree in industrial engineering and who can speak Spanish. Before I go outside, why not check to see if we have a person like that who might be interested in a job in our division. We can make it worthwhile financially, and the sky's the limit on promotions." Marjorie agrees to see what she can do.

This is one example of the uses to which a skills inventory can be put in the enterprise; there are many others. If the firm has a computerized skills inventory, Marjorie can give Howard an answer quickly. If there is no such inventory, she will have to call or write a lot of people and ask about many prospects.

A skills inventory in its simplest form is a list of the names, certain characteristics, and skills of the people working for the organization. It provides a way to acquire these data and makes them available where needed in an efficient manner.

The National Industrial Conference Board found that many organizations introduced skills inventories when computer time became available for this purpose.[3] Most organizations do have the information in one form or another, but frequently it is buried in personnel folders, and time and effort are needed to get at it. Good skills inventories enable organizations to determine quickly and expeditiously what kinds of people with specific skills are presently available, whenever they decide to expand to accept new contracts or change their strategies. It is also useful in planning for training, management development, promotion, transfer, and related personnel activities.

Designing skills inventory systems

Once the decision is made to have a skills inventory system, the challenge is what data the system should contain. This is the "parameters problem." An organization can only retrieve what is designed into the system.

The list of data coded into skills inventories is almost endless, and it must be tailored to the needs of each organization. Some of the more common

items include: name, employee number, present location, date of birth, date
of employment, job classification or code, prior experience, history of work
experience in the organization, specific skills and knowledge, education, field
of education (formal education and courses taken since leaving school),
knowledge of a foreign language, health, professional qualifications, publications, licenses, patents, hobbies, a supervisory evaluation of the employee's
capabilities, and salary/salary range. Items often omitted, but becoming increasingly important, are the employee's own stated career goals and objectives, including geographical preferences and intended retirement date.

Skills inventory data serve to identify employees for specific assignments
which will fulfill not only organizational objectives but individual ones as
well. Exhibit 5–2 is an example of the summarization of data from the
forms used on a skills inventory, either computerized or manual. These
summary cards provide the data that are used in assessing and analyzing
the supply of people working for the organization.

EXHIBIT 5–2
Skills inventory summary card

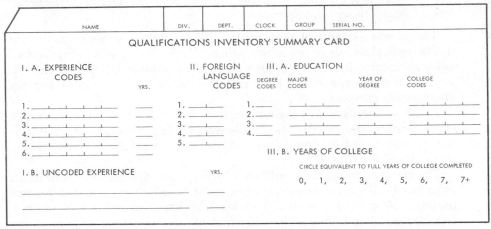

Source: W. Barnes, *Identifying Manpower Potential* (New York: American Management Association, 1963).

Some examples of skills inventory systems

In smaller manual systems of skills inventories, the data are entered on
cards, the more advanced having notches or loops which can be "pulled"
by the use of long metal bars (Keydex). Thus, if a Canadian organization
wants to get a list of workers speaking French fluently, it pulls all the cards
notched at a particular place or with loop 15 on the card. If there are multiple
criteria, this subset is then checked for the next characteristic. This can
also be done with summary overlays: All those with certain characteristics
are punched onto cards, several of these summary cards are laid atop one

another, and only those still visible on the last overlay fit the criteria for selection.

Several studies have indicated the many personnel and nonpersonnel uses of sophisticated computerized skills inventories. IBM's system contains information on such data as career plans, family needs, and educational goals for over 100,000 of its employees. One of the main problems in designing such a system is developing a standard data format, with records stored in an easily accessible form for all units. This system allows IBM to project five-year engineering and other personnel needs for various rates of corporate growth, and a monthly personnel transaction report is developed for all divisions which can be used to pinpoint possible imbalances within the total organizational system.[4] The RCA Service Company uses its skill inventories to help management define what businesses it could be in.[5]

Robert Smith examined the skill inventory system of the U.S. Civil Service Commission for all individuals above GS–14 (middle management), which included about 25,000 executives. The data in the base allowed the U.S. government to examine age distributions by such factors as occupation, educational attainment, mobility, and reasons for entering and leaving, and to make these data available in a usable form for analysis. Smith points out several uses of such a system:

A carefully prepared skills inventory can be used as a basis for long-range personnel planning and development by providing precise definitions of the aptitudes and abilities available and needed by the organization. It can be used to assist in the evaluation of growth potential of the present executive work force and help to identify group strengths and weaknesses for future recruiting strategies. It may uncover interdivisional imbalances (e.g., understaffing) which could lead to future overall corporate personnel problems. Most importantly, it will serve as a motivating device by demonstrating through written feedback that the organization has a systematic approach to personal data utilization and that it is eager to develop each man to his full potential.[6]

Other enterprises with well-known skills inventory systems include Grumnar Data Systems,[7] the Canadian Public Service,[8] and the U.S. Army.[9]

Management inventories

Some enterprises use separate skills inventory systems for managerial employees, since different information may be required for managers than for workers. Management inventories become inputs to management personnel analysis.

A management inventory system can be designed on the basis of individual managers or the management positions to be filled. If the former approach is taken, detailed information is compiled about the incumbent in a position, such as age (which would indicate retirement date as well as maturity), date of employment, present position and length of service. The summary also indicates a brief appraisal of present performance and notes strengths, weaknesses, and potential for promotion (Exhibit 5–3). If the system is main-

EXHIBIT 5–3
Management inventory card

Name	Age	Employed
Murray, Mel	47	1945

Present position	On job
Manager, Sales (House Fans Division)	6 yrs.

Present performance
Outstanding — exceeded sales goal in spite of stiffer competition.

Strengths
Good planner — motivates subordinates very well — excellent communication.

Weaknesses
Still does not always delegate as much as situation requires. Sometimes does not understand production's problems.

Efforts to improve
Has greatly improved in delegating in last 2 years; also has organized more effectively after taking a management course on own time and initiative.

Could move to	When
Vice President–Marketing	1963

Training needed
More exposure to problems of other divisions (attend top staff conference?). Perhaps university program stressing staff role of corporate marketing vs. line sales.

Could move to	When
Manager — House or Industrial Fans Division	1964/5

Training needed
Course in production management; same project working with production people; perhaps a good business game somewhere.

Source: National Industrial Conference Board, *The Expanded Personnel Function,* Studies in Personnel Policy 203 (New York, 1966).

tained on the basis of jobs rather than individuals, little about the incumbent manager is included, but a great deal about several of his possible replacements is indicated, such as their present positions, duration of employment, salary, and the nature and amount of additional training necessary before promotion. (See the positions replacement chart, Exhibit 4–10, in Chapter 4.)

Regardless of which data collection system is used, the important element is the synthesis of the data for presentation to top management in the form of a management personnel replacement chart. By indicating the age, present performance evaluation, and promotion potential of each job's incumbent and replacements, such a chart provides management with the information that makes it possible to evaluate the present and future managerial employment status of the company. This type of information provides a valuable tool for preparing long-range plans, formulating management development programs, and providing guidelines for managerial recruiting.

Maintaining inventory systems

While designing the system is the most difficult part of developing a skills inventory, planning for the gathering, maintaining, handling, and updating of data is also important. The two principal methods for gathering data are the interview and the questionnaire. Each method has unique costs and benefits. The questionnaire is faster and less expensive when many employees are involved, but inaccuracies are usually greater; people often do not spend enough time on a questionnaire. There are those who contend, therefore, that the trained interviewer can complete the reports more quickly and accurately, and this in the long run more than offsets the costs of the interviewer.

A procedure for keeping the files updated also must be planned. The method used depends upon the frequency of change and the uses of the data. For some organizations, an annual update is adequate. In others, where changes are made often and use is frequent, shorter update periods may be necessary. Some organizations make provisions for monthly updating of changeable data and annual checks for less changeable data. One way to do this is to include updating forms in payroll envelopes.

The data can be stored on manual cardex cards or on a computer. The key differential involves costs and the need for speed in retrieval. A few days may be an adequate time period if the system is used primarily to fill vacancies; in that case, one of the slower manual card systems may suffice. If immediate answers are required or if the organization is quite large, a computerized system may be needed. Other determinants include such factors as frequency of searches and number of personnel included in the inventory. If either is large, a computerized system would again be indicated. Another factor is the availability of computer time and its costs.

Computerized systems have the advantage of providing more effective turnover studies. The data can generate reports which can project employee

turnover to determine the work force required to maximize the capital investment. Comparative analysis of employment on a time series basis can also
be generated on the computer; observing the changes in promotable personnel over time may provide insights into the effectiveness of recruiting and
development activities. Computerized systems also provide the interaction
capacity to utilize such systematic planning methods as program evaluation
review technique (PERT) and the critical path method (CPM). By providing
for an analysis of all the sequential events necessary in a production process,
with an estimation of their associated time and cost factors, these systems
can enhance accuracy of planning by defining all the necessary work activities, suggesting the latest allowable starting date for each activity, and identifying the potential costs of various courses of action.[10]

Problems with skills inventories

Skills inventories will probably not succeed without the full and continuing support of top management. Certain types of organizational structures,
especially those that are functionally based, are not conducive to effective
implementation of skills retrieval systems. A company philosophy which
endorses participative management might unfavorably affect the operation
of a skills inventory system.[11]

Several specific problems have been identified by Robert Murphy, who
made a study of personalized skills inventories at North American Rockwell.
Murphy notes that:

Contrary to what some managers might think, skills inventories are not self-
sustaining "push-button" tools. Computers make skills inventories possible, but they
don't make them work. Skills inventories require constant refinement and change
to keep them responsive to changing business needs requirements. They also require
a high degree of personal judgment in assuring proper use. Some of the problems
encountered are:

Provincialism. Before the advent of computer-aided personnel systems, many selections were made based upon whom a manager knew. Some managers still want to
operate in this fashion and do not feel a need for help from this management tool.
However, there have been quite a few instances where managers have been quite
surprised to find that the Skills Inventory helped turn up qualified candidates of
whom they were *not* aware.

Reasonability. It is one thing to identify good people but quite another to get
them released. In an initial six-month review of the Skills Inventory's performance,
too many requests for availability for interview and subsequent transfer were met
with a flat NO answer. As a result, a company directive was published setting
forth certain guidelines for managers—guidelines which balance the best interests
of the two managers, the employee, and the company. As a result of the policy
and positive management support, the problem has been greatly improved.

Managerial data. The Skills Inventory is much better in serving up technical and
educational specialties than it is in locating and evaluating managerial capabilities.
Part of this problem is because managers' jobs are more difficult to describe, and
because performance on them is more difficult to evaluate than for the individual
engineer or accountant. . . .

System abuse and nonuse.   There are two types of abuse:

1.   Managers making requests simply on the basis that "it would be nice to know," and

2.   Requests for searches which are not backed up by bona fide requisitions that have been budgeted for and approved by an organization planning function. There has been no evidence of the kind of abuse some managers were initially concerned about—that of managers using the system to "pirate away" people to other parts of the company.[12]

A problem that arises when a manager is not used to the system is that he tends to search for too many characteristics and thus eliminates the possibility of finding any job candidate. For example, consider the following:

Wanted—A person with the following qualifications: BS in business, experience in finance and marketing, with at least two years with the company and making less than $14,000 per year.

Assume 1,000 employees. The chance of finding a person with all these characteristics is the product of the percent of probability in each category. Thus if 20 percent of the 1,000 have a BS in business; 10 percent, experience in finance; 10 percent, experience in marketing; 70 percent, two years or more seniority; and 50 percent make more than $14,000, the chance of finding such a person is .02 × .10 × .10 × .70 × .50, or .0007, or less than one chance in a thousand. Those who set requirements must recognize that being overly specific reduces the chance of finding any suitable employee.[13]

WORK SCHEDULES AND SUPPLY OF EMPLOYEES

When people work and how long they work affects the analysis of employee needs and the supply of employees. For example, eight hours of work can be performed by one full-time employee or two part-time employees; ten hours of work can be performed by one employee on overtime or one full-time and one part-time employee.

Hours of work also affect the facilities the employer must provide. When schools are used for two shifts a day, this reduces the need for added buildings. Factories can run two regular-time shifts per week if one shift works four 10-hour days and the other works three 12-hour days.

Of course, the hours employees work is not entirely up to the discretion of employers; the government limits the number of working hours. It also requires overtime to be paid beyond the normal working hours (see Chapter 13). The full-time work week has not changed much since 1940: on average, it is 40 hours.[14]

Several trends in employment and working hours have the potential for significant impact on the personnel function in the future. One is the use of more part-time workers employed on a regular basis. This practice will be explored in Chapter 6, and the impact of part-time employment will be discussed in subsequent chapters. Another is the management of shift work, moonlighting, and overtime. And one of the most innovative of these trends involves experiments in daytime working hours other than 8:00 to 4:00 or 9:00 to 5:00 five days a week. The two major experiments of this type are compressed work weeks and flexitime.

Shift work

One way to increase output is to schedule a second shift or minishift, in addition to the regular day shift.[15] An enterprise might also add a night shift, if power costs are cheaper then.

When shift work is used, there are two approaches to scheduling it: to assign people to shifts, or to rotate them through shifts. Most employees prefer not to rotate their work schedules, but if rotation is used, they would rather have changes every several days rather than at week-long or month-long intervals.[16]

Second and third shift work generally affects employees adversely. It interferes with time-oriented bodily functions, such as digestion, sleeping, and elimination. Rotating shift work particularly affects personal and family lives and social participation, adversely.[17]

There are some advantages to second and third shift work for employees. Usually the pay is better. There are free daytime hours, and often there is less responsibility and supervision. Studies have found that shift workers take such shifts because they provide the only jobs available, and they afford higher pay. About one-third of shift workers prefer shift work, and younger men and women with prior shift-work experience adjust most easily to it.[18]

Enterprises adopt second and third shifts to use their equipment and facilities more efficiently and to get the work out. Are these shifts really efficient, from a human resource point of view? One study found that the day shift was 3 percent more productive than second shifts overall, but there were marked individual productivity differences between employees on the two shifts.[19]

Compressed work weeks

Terry and Vicki Shea and their two sons are walking down Padre Island's beach on a Friday morning. Why isn't Terry working? Because United Services Auto Insurance, where Terry is employed as director of research, operates on a four-day week, Monday through Thursday. The company works four ten-hour days, with a half hour off for lunch. In fact, Terry tends to work a half day on two of the four Fridays each month to catch up on his work.

Ralph and Cindee Hurlburt also work four-day weeks. Ralph works for Armour in a meat-packing plant as blue-collar worker. He works from 6:30 A.M. to 5 P.M., with a 30-minute lunch hour. He shovels five tons of ground beef a day from a machine to a metal hopper. Ralph says he's ready to drop when the day is over, goes to bed each night at 8:00 and has developed a bad arm from the strain. He's paid $4.06 per hour. Cindee stands for ten hours per day carrying trays of meat and loading them in a 50-degree plant. She earns $3.73 per hour. And what do Ralph and Cindee do on their extra day off? They moonlight to earn extra money.[20]

The Norgen Company in Denver, a capital intensive manufacturer of accessory equipment for pneumatic machinery, adopted the four-day week seven years ago. It did so to compete for skilled labor when it could not compete on the basis of pay, and to keep a union out. Initially, employees and customers were unhappy with the change; working mothers particularly do not like the schedule. But over the long run, absenteeism and turnover were reduced. Productivity did not decline because losses from fatigue were offset by savings from fewer clean-up and start-up periods, fewer breaks, and three fewer holidays each year. Accidents did not increase. The management believes the experiment is a success partly because the job is boring, in a noisy atmosphere and employees like an extra day away from the job, especially in an area like Denver.[21]

DEFINITION

A compressed work week is the scheduling of the normal 40 hours of weekly work in less than five days. The typical compressed work week follows a four-day, 40-hour schedule. Less frequently a three-day, 36-hour weekly schedule is used. Usually, in a four-day week, the work days are Tuesday through Friday or Monday through Thursday.

Is a four-day work week of 36 or 40 hours, or even a three-day work week, a new idea, or is it simply the latest move in a long-term trend to shorter work weeks? In 1822, Philadelphia carpenters demanded that their work day be cut to 12 hours, from a sunup to sundown schedule. By 1835, craft workers had secured ten-hour days and six- or seven-day weeks, and in 1915 the eight-hour day was supported by President Woodrow Wilson. In the Great Depression, federal government action (the National Industrial Recovery Act of 1933, Public Contracts Act of 1936, and Fair Labor Standards Act of 1938) helped standardize the five-day, 40-hour week. Thus it appears the compressed work week could be a continuation of a trend.

How could people work such long hours and long weeks? Herbert Gutman examined historical records of 19th-century work hours and found that employees may have been *present* for long hours, but they did not work during all of them; they alternated intense periods of work with periods of idleness.[22] This work pattern reflected their prior experience as farmers or craftsmen. In the 1840s, workers in cabinet factories worked, then stopped for food, wine, and song. In New York shipyards at that time, the workers took regular breaks. In 1877, a boss said of his cigar markers: "The difficulty with my workers is this: they come down to the shop in the morning; roll a few cigars and then go to a beer saloon and play pinochle or some other game . . . working probably only two or three hours a day."

One of the best examples Gutman gives is of barrel makers in the mid-1800s. On Monday, they spent their time sharpening tools, carrying in stock, and discussing current events and their weekends. Tuesday through Friday they worked hard. On Saturday, a barrel of beer was delivered and they would play poker and drink beer until they were paid. In addition, the workers celebrated many religious holidays. One Chicago manufacturer moaned, "My Greek workers are never here, it seems. The Greek Orthodox Church has 80 festival days per year and they never fall on Sunday."

So proposals for four-day weeks may not be as new as they seem— they may be a return to preindustrial times or the reality of the 19th century. Of course, the four-day week is not the ultimate solution. In a series on the four-day week, *The Wall Street Journal* pointed out that riverboat pilots work 30 days and are off 30, and there are proposals for working six months and being off six.

Is compressed work-week scheduling a widespread practice? In the United States, about 10,000 enterprises, involving about 744,000 employees, use it.[23] In fact, the number of employees on compressed work weeks declined by 35,000 from 1975 to 1976, and many more employees (1,115,000) work seven-day weeks than compressed work weeks.[24] In most cases, the management initiates the plan, but some unions, such as the UAW, seem to favor it.[25]

Advantages and disadvantages of compressed work weeks. Various analysts of the compressed work week have contended that it should be instituted because:

It increases employee leisure.

It decreases employee commuting costs.

It lowers setup and clean-up costs.

It decreases absenteeism, partly because employees take less time off to keep personal appointments.

Scheduling problems caused by greater product demand are eased because more shifts can be added.

It increases employee satisfaction and lowers turnover.

It increases the quality of work and production output.

Accidents are decreased.

Those opposed to the compressed week are against it because:

It increases employee fatigue, which leads to poorer output quality.

Working mothers, and unmarried and older employees do not like it.

It increases the difficulties of scheduling work.

It lowers the usage of equipment and facilities if only one shift is used.

It curtails customer's service.

It increases opportunities for moonlighting, and therefore fatigue on the job.

It will lead to pressure for a 36-hour week for 40 hours' pay.

Is the compressed work week a good idea? There is case study research to support both sides.[26] One pattern in the negative studies indicates that positive results are realized early in the experiment, and then they decline. Although it is too early to say for sure, it appears that individual and job differences explain many of the contradictions in the research findings. In general, older employees find a compressed work week where the work is physically or mentally taxing undesirable, and many younger single employees find it interferes with their social life. Working mothers with younger children also tend to be unhappy with it. Thus middle-aged people may be most likely to accept compressed work weeks. Another factor is the task involved. In general, heavy physical or taxing mental work probably is not suitable for a compressed work-week schedule. Long ago, researchers studied what happened when hours were increased to help the World War II military effort. Heavy work or machine-paced work was not too efficient beyond the eight-hour day, as fatigue set in.[27] Recent work tends to support these early studies.[28]

It appears that the compressed work week has limited applicability. Work loads which result in fatigue, preferences of many employees, and customer demands limit its usefulness. It tends to lead to more moonlighting; those who are most likely to moonlight currently are those who are working compressed work weeks.[29] Statistics now indicate a decline in its use. Flexitime is likely to be the more popular scheduling system in the future.

Flexible hours (flexitime)

The State Street Bank in Boston is typical of enterprises who have recently installed flexitime. Flexitime gives each employee some freedom in selecting the hours they choose to work. At SSB, the employees work a five-day week but can vary their starting times, as long as they work their full hours over the week. The plan for State Street's typical work week is shown in Exhibit 5–4.

All employees work from 11:00 to 2:00, since these are the hours with peak work loads and communications. This is also the time meetings take place and employees work together. A survey of the results of SSB's introduction of flexitime indicated that;

63 percent of employees felt more satisfied with their jobs.

59 percent experienced shorter commuting time.

70 percent indicated more time for leisure or family activities.

42 percent had received additional cross-training since flexitime.

47 percent felt they were more productive with flexitime.

The majority were extremely satisfied with flexitime in this typical application of the flexitime concept.[30]

EXHIBIT 5–4
Typical work schedule at State Street Bank

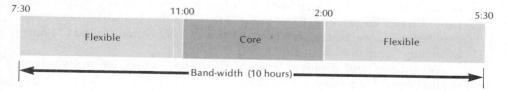

> **DEFINITION**
>
> Flexitime is an arrangement of working hours which provides for all work-
> ers to be present for a specified period in the morning and afternoon
> (core time), but the rest of the required hours may be completed at
> their discretion within a specified period.

Douglas Fleuter describes four typical approaches to flexitime:

1. *Daily flexible with fixed lunch period, core time, and two flexible periods.* In this plan, the person must work the full hours (usually eight) each day.
2. *Daily flexible with flexible lunch period.* The same as in no. 1, except the enterprise is more flexible regarding lunch periods.
3. *Weekly flexible.* Employees must work core times each day, but as long as they get in their weekly total hours, it does not matter if they work more hours on any one day than another. This is SSB's plan.
4. *Monthly flexible.* This plan works like no. 3, except that each employee's hours are checked for completeness monthly instead of weekly. For example, an employee who works a total of 160 hours per month can work 40 hours one week, 30 the next, 50 the following week, and 40 the last week, since they total to 160 hours.[31]

Sometimes the late afternoon is designated "quiet time," during which phone calls and meetings are not scheduled.

How widespread is flexitime?   In Europe, flexitime is quite widespread and is increasing as use of the compressed work week declines. About 5,000,000 Europeans work on flexitime schedules; this involves the following percentages of the work force in various countries; Switzerland, 30 percent; Germany 10 percent overall and 50 percent of white-collar employees; and Austria, 25 percent. In France, there are 30,000 employees on such schedules. Italy, Spain, Britain, and other European countries are following Germany's example.[32]

In the United States more employees are now on flexitime than in compressed work-week plans.[33] About 1,000,000 workers *officially* have flexitime. Most management and professional employees have unofficial flexitime, of course. Enterprises using flexitime in the United States and Canada include General Motors, Control Data, Wards, NCR, Nestlé, American Airlines, First National Bank of Boston, Blue Cross–Blue Shield of California, Exxon, Pacific Gas and Electric, Hewlett Packard, Smith Kline, John Hancock Life, Continental Telephone, the Social Security Administration, Defense Supply Company, City of Englewood, Bank of Canada, Canadian Industries Ltd., Canadian Federal Government, Sun Life Insurance Co. Ltd., and United Provinces Insurance Company Ltd.

Advantages and disadvantages of flexitime.   There are many advantages claimed for flexitime, including:

The employee saves on commuting time. In Germany, flexitime reduced this factor by 20 to 30 percent.

There is more leisure time, if the employee desires it.

It is easier to schedule personal appointments and personal time for employees.

It lowers the stress of getting to work on time.

It has the motivational effect of job enrichment, since employees schedule their time. Flexitime allows employees the same freedom of time most managers, professionals, and salespersons have.

It lowers employee absenteeism and turnover and makes recruiting easier.

It allows employees to fit work to their body's "clock," or biorhythm. Many psychologists and physiologists believe there are individual differences in the optimal time for performance.

Employees can make better use of their time; they can "sleep in" some mornings and quit early on other days if they desire.

It increases employee satisfaction and leads to better quality of work by employees.

It increases employee performance. It makes better use of work time, less killing time until "quitting time."

It provides improved handling of fluctuating work loads.

It allows for increased customer service because the enterprise is open longer.

The major disadvantages which may come with flexitime include:

Utility costs are increased by longer hours of operation.

All employees are not present when others want them; so some problems cannot be solved as easily as with the regular work week.

There may be difficulty in keeping records of hours worked for pay purposes, and this can increase costs.

Middle management and unions may oppose it. The former may perceive loss of control, and the latter desire fewer hours, not rearranged hours.

There can be conflicts between flexitime and the present wage and hours laws, especially over overtime pay and lunch breaks.

Flexitime may be hard to implement in interdependent jobs. Manufacturing buffer stocks are costly, and, in service industries, coordination may be inefficient.

Supervision can become a problem. In some cases various employees may be on the job from 6:00 A.M. to 7:00 P.M., and the supervisor cannot be there 13 hours a day.

Does flexitime make sense?   There has been less research on flexitime than the compressed work week because it is newer, and the research that has been done is less scientific and sophisticated. In a summary of the research, I found that there are no studies showing negative results.[34] This can be because flexitime is still in Stage 1 of development or because it is a useful method. Its future appears bright, as Jo Hartley points out, because it has fewer serious disadvantages and because it is easier to implement than the compressed work week.[35]

Flexitime affects the supply of labor to the extent that it can lead to more productivity and can lower the need for workers. Because it provides for longer operating hours, there is a possibility of using minishifts with part-time or temporary employees.

ACTION DECISIONS IN EMPLOYMENT PLANNING

There are several managerial decisions to be made once demand for people has been forecast and compared to supply. Exhibit 5–5 presents a more

EXHIBIT 5–5
Employment planning action decisions

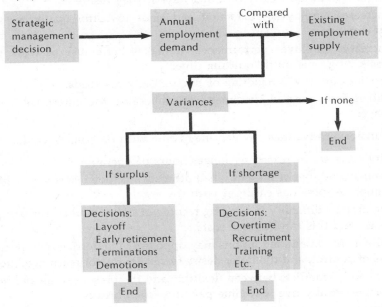

detailed schema of the action decisions.[36] Another action decision which is not shown in the figure is increasingly important today: analyzing the work force to comply with government equal employment opportunity programs. We will discuss this problem first.

Analyzing the composition of the work force

The extent to which the work force of an enterprise approximates the composition of the total work force for the area is an essential consideration in programs enacted by the federal, state, and provincial governments of the United States and Canada to protect members of certain groups from being discriminated against in employment opportunities. Government agencies enforce these laws. In the United States, these agencies are the Equal Employment Opportunities Commission and the Office of Federal Contract Compliance, at the federal level, and state fair employment practices commissions. In Canada, human rights commissions are the government bodies enforcing antidiscrimination regulations.

The makeup of the present labor force in the United States and some discrepancies between the ideal of equal employment opportunity and the reality of these opportunities for certain groups was described in Chapter 3, and Chapter 18 will discuss the affirmative action programs set up by employers to make the ideal more of a reality. Briefly, Title VII of the Civil Rights Act of 1964, as amended in 1972, says that an employer cannot discriminate on the basis of race, color, religion, sex, or national origin. Presidential Executive Orders 11246 and 11141 supplement this law with respect to doing business with the government. These acts cover the entire private sector in interstate commerce, the public sector, and the educational part of the third sector. Governmental and other funding of a large portion of the rest of the third sector, especially health care, means that almost all employers are covered.

The enterprise must keep records of the distribution of employees by categories, levels (top management, professional, operatives, etc.), and pay groups. If the statistics show that the enterprise's employment patterns are substantially different from the overall population and by employment category, the employer is vulnerable to EEO legal action, with the threat of back-pay liability, mandatory hiring goals for women and minorities, and the like. Many socially responsible employers have voluntarily tried to improve the employment opportunities of these groups.

The U.S. federal government classifies citizens by race as follows:

- Whites (not of Hispanic origin).
- Hispanic (mostly Mexican Americans, Cuban Americans, and Puerto Rican Americans).
- Asian or Pacific islanders (mostly Chinese, Japanese, Filipinos, native Hawaiians, Guamanians, etc.).
- Blacks (not of Hispanic origin).
- American Indians.
- Alaskan natives.

Most suits for discrimination against racial (or color) groups have been filed by the EEOC in behalf of blacks or Hispanic Americans. Patterns of settlement by these groups reflect where the suits are filed. Most Hispanic Americans live in South Florida, the Southwest, California, Colorado, New York City, and Chicago, for example. Few blacks live in Minnesota but many live in Georgia.

In sexual discrimination cases, the primary emphasis thus far has been to prevent employers from discriminating against hiring women for upper level jobs, or not promoting from within for these jobs. Homosexuals are lobbying for protection against discrimination in hiring based on personal sexual preferences.

Discrimination based on religion, national origin, or age has not received the same attention as race or color and sexual discrimination have from the EEOC. Other groups receiving protection in one form or another in employment are handicapped persons and veterans of the military service. Some employers have developed their own programs to hire and thus help rehabilitate ex-convicts.

Antidiscriminatory programs enforced by government or promoted by popular opinion make it essential for the employer to examine the distribution of employees in protected categories (race, sex, etc.) at all levels to see if the enterprise has *in fact* discriminated against any group in its hiring and promotion practices. The enterprise cannot discriminate against any group (including, of course, white males, who are not ordinarily considered a minority group) solely on the basis of their personal characteristics. The purpose of this analysis is to assure that all potential employees of equal ability have an equal chance at hiring and promotion and other rewards. The specific programs used for analysis of these items will be discussed throughout the book.

Action decisions with no variance in supply and demand

It is possible for the enterprise, after matching the demand for employees with the supply at hand, to find that previous planning has been so excellent that the demand is matched exactly with the supply. In this case employment planning has served its purpose well in helping the enterprise to meet its objectives.

An exact match is rare. More frequently the total supply is correct, but there are variances in subgroups. These data become inputs to facilitate decisions about training, promotion, demotion, and similar decisions. Thus Exhibit 5–5 shows "end" if there are no variances, but the process may not end; it may require additional personnel decisions.

Action decisions with a shortage of employees

When employment specialists comparing demand to supply find the supply of workers is less than the demand, several possibilities are open to the enterprise. If the shortage is small and employees are willing to work overtime, it can be filled with present employees. If the shortage is of higher skilled employees, training and promotions of present employees, together with recruitment of lower skilled workers, is a possibility. This decision can also include recalling previously laid-off employees. Outside the enter-

EXHIBIT 5–6
Manpower projection plan for a division

Division	Current on roll 9/15/70 (1)	Anticipate on roll 9/15/71 (2)	Net change (1) – (2) (3)	Total employees required (4)	Total employees made available (5)	Promoted from within (6)	Transferred from inside the organization (7)	To be recruited (8)
A. Production 　Managers 　Supervisors 　Professional (exempt nonsupervisory)								
B. Finance 　Managers 　Supervisors 　Professional (exempt nonsupervisory)								
C. Marketing 　Managers 　Supervisors 　Professional (exempt nonsupervisory)								
D. Engineering 　Managers 　Supervisors 　Professional (exempt nonsupervisory)								
E. Total management (A + B + C + D)								
F. Other salaried—nonexempt, nonsupervisory technical and clerical employees								
G. Hourly employees 　(skilled trades) 　(semiskilled and unskilled)								
H. Total (A + B + C + D + F + G)								

Source: Thomas Patten, *Manpower Planning and the Development of Human Resources* (New York: Wiley Interscience, 1971), p. 34.

prise, additional employees, either part time or full time, can be hired, or some of the work can be contracted out to other enterprises.

One way to plan for employment shortages is shown in Exhibit 5–6.

Action decisions in surplus conditions

When comparison of employee demand and supply indicates a surplus, the alternative solutions include attrition, early retirements, demotions, lay-offs, and terminations. Surplus employee decisions are some of the most difficult managers must make, because the employees who are considered surplus are seldom responsible for the conditions leading to the surplus. A shortage of a raw material such as fuel, or a poorly designed or marketed product can cause an enterprise to have a surplus of employees.

As a first approach to deal with a surplus most enterprises avoid layoffs and terminations by such means as attrition, early retirement, work creation, and work sharing.[37] Many enterprises can reduce their work force simply by not replacing those who retire or quit (attrition). Sometimes this approach is accelerated by encouraging employees close to retirement to leave early (see Chapter 16), but this can amount to layoffs of older employees if the enterprise is not careful. Another approach is for the enterprise to give surplus employees jobs such as painting the plant or extra maintenance chores to keep them on the payroll. In the mid-seventies recessions, firms such as Kimberly Clark, Toyo Kogyo, Dow Chemical, Lockheed, American Shipbuilding, Aerojet General, and Raytheon used this approach.

Another variation of this approach is work sharing. Instead of attempting to decide whom to layoff, the enterprise asks all employees to work less than normal hours and thus share the work. Many unions favor this approach. In recent recessions, many firms have given the employees a voice in how to deal with surplus conditions, and some groups of workers have elected work sharing.

If there is a surplus of employees at higher levels, demotion may be used to reduce the work force. After World War II, as the Army reduced its size it had too many higher level officers to staff the number of positions left, and many officers were demoted to their "permanent" rank, not the rank they held in 1945. Among the numerous ways demotion can be handled, Douglas More suggests: lowered job status with the same salary or lowered salary; the same status with lower compensation; being bypassed in seniority for promotion; changing the person to a less desirable job; the same formal status, but with decreased span of control; being excluded from a general salary increase; insertion of positions above the person in the hierarchy; moving to a staff position; elimination of the position and reassignment; and transfer out of direct line for promotion.[38] Demotions are very difficult for employees to accept, and valued employees may leave because of them.

In managing a surplus through layoffs, employers take the surplus employees off the payroll "temporarily" to reduce the surplus. Some employers may feel more willing to accept this method because unemployment compensation plans are now available (see Chapter 13). If the layoff is likely to be semipermanent or permanent, it is in effect a termination and results usually in the payment of severance pay as well as unemployment compensation.

When the enterprise is getting close to the point where layoffs are necessary, employees know business is down, and the workplace buzzes with rumors. Managers should make layoff decisions as early as possible to give employees ample notice. This is especially important when there will be mass layoffs, as in the auto industry in the midseventies. Charles Watson has given some helpful suggestions on how to ease the pain of mass layoffs.[39]

EXHIBIT 5–7
Employees' reply to layoffs

To: All Employees
From: Personnel Department

As a result of new "effective management programming" and a declining work load, management must of necessity take steps to reduce our work force.

Arrangements have been developed which appear to be the most equitable under the circumstances.

Under the plan, older employees will be placed on early retirement, thus permitting the retention of employees who represent the future of the company.

Therefore a program to phase out older personnel by the end of the year via early retirement will be placed in effect immediately. The program will be known as "RAPE" (Retire Aged Personnel Early).

Employees who are raped will be given an opportunity to seek other jobs within the company, provided that while being raped they request a review of their employment records before actual retirement takes place. This phase of the operation is called "SCREW" (Survey of Capabilities of Retired Early Workers).

All employees who have been raped and screwed may also apply for a final review. This will be called "SHAFT" (Study of Higher Authority Following Termination).

"Effective Management Programming" dictates that employees may be raped once and screwed twice, but may get the shaft as many times as the company deems appropriate.

Employees can get bitter at layoff time.[40] For example, Ford Motor Company experienced sabotage in the midst of the layoffs in the midseventies, and communications like Exhibit 5–7 began to circulate. Fear affects productivity and employee satisfaction, and most employers will try to avoid layoffs if at all possible.

How does a manager decide whom to lay off? Two criteria have been used: merit and seniority. In the past the most senior employee was laid off last; a second approach now is to lay off those with lower merit ratings (see Chapter 10). If merit ratings are not precise, unions may fight their exclusive use as a reason for laying off particular workers. For example, the United Professors of California (AFL–CIO) is suing California State Universities and Colleges over the decision of that board to lay off professors on the basis of merit alone.

Using seniority as the only criterion may mean that recently hired minorities and women are laid off first. This pits minority rights against seniority rights, and the courts have been hard pressed to resolve the conflict.[41] In a case with important implications for seniority systems, the U.S. Supreme Court decided that minority applicants who are discriminatorily rejected by an employer and later hired must be given seniority credit from the date of that rejection.[42] Such seniority credits represent a breach in the tradition of seniority rights, but they do not apply to most minorities and women hired under affirmative action plans, for by and large they never were discriminately rejected. In short, federal EEO policies have not endangered seniority very much. While seniority has lost some judicial skirmishes to EEO, it remains the principal criterion of employment rights for hourly employees.

The final approach used to reduce employment surpluses is termination. Most employers use it as a last resort. Anyone who has watched Willy Loman in *Death of a Salesman* or the star of Neil Simon's *Prisoner of Second Avenue* knows why. Termination is usually very painful to both the employer and the employee. EEO requirements apply to terminations as well as layoffs.

When termination must take place, some good suggestions for psychological support and help for the terminated employee can be found in the reported experiences of a firm which had to terminate 200 managers and professionals recently.[43] Jack Mendelson suggests that the enterprise engage in "outplacement"—conscious attempts to help the employee select and find useful employment.[44]

How does management decide which of these approaches to use in order to deal with a surplus of workers? Richard Traum has shown how the human resource accounting approach can help make this decision.[45] Termination costs include reparation pay, benefits costs to stock vesting, early retirement, unemployment insurance, accrued vacation pay, miscellaneous costs, plus replacing those additional workers who would leave to protest the terminations. Traum compares these costs to the costs of attrition, which include paying surplus people who are not needed.

Exhibit 5–8 is a tradeoff table which shows the cost of alternatives varying from all terminations to all attrition for professional workers.

In his calculation, Traum considered that termination cost $21,000 per professional, and attrition cost $1,500 per month per professional. To construct the table he used the formula:

$$\text{Total cost} = \text{Termination costs} + \text{attrition costs.}$$

The table indicates that the least costly approach is to terminate 50 and lose 50 professionals through attrition ($1,557,000). This kind of analysis can be of help in the often painful termination decision.

EXHIBIT 5–8
Attrition/termination alternatives

Termination	Attrition	Termination cost	+	Attrition cost	=	Total cost
100	0	$2,100,000		$ 0		$2,100,000
90	10	1,890,000		27,000		1,917,000
80	20	1,680,000		90,000		1,770,000
70	30	1,470,000		192,000		1,662,000
60	40	1,260,000		330,000		1,590,000
50	50	1,050,000		507,000		1,557,000
40	60	840,000		720,000		1,560,000
30	70	630,000		972,000		1,602,000
20	80	420,000		1,260,000		1,680,000
10	90	210,000		1,587,000		1,797,000
0	100	0		1,950,000		1,950,000

Source: Richard Traum, "Reducing Headcount through Attrition and/or Termination," *Personnel*, January–February 1975, p. 22.

COMPUTERS AND COST/BENEFIT ANALYSIS IN EMPLOYMENT PLANNING

For larger organizations especially, computers are an essential tool in effective employment planning. A number of experts have described computer programs which demonstrate that the computer is the most effective way to update employment demand forecasts and scheduling frequently.[46] This permits an employer to head off possible layoffs and avoid shortages. The system can be tied directly to the sales forecast and the scheduling of operations units. The computer can also be used to simulate the two sides of employment planning simultaneously. A series of "what ifs" can be run to give managers data on the best and worse cases so that contingency plans can be made for employment planning.

Employment planning is so new that few cost/benefits studies have been made of it, and such studies are difficult at the present stage of development of this function. Estimating the cost side may be the easier of the two. The costs of employment planning include the cost of hiring employment planners, the materials and computer time used by them, and the cost of the time given to this function by line managers.[47]

The benefits to be derived from employment planning include cost savings resulting from more efficient planning of such programs as recruitment and training, an improved work environment, and increased demand for products or services as a result of utilizing the capabilities developed by such programs. But these benefits are difficult to estimate. It can be shown that employee capability is only part of the firm's ability to get an order, and one on which it is difficult to put a dollar figure. Most people would rather work in an organization that cares enough about them to provide for their department's needs. How much of the workers' job satisfaction is attributable to this factor? And how many of the turnover dollars saved can be allocated to employment planning? Careful employment planning obviously will lower recruiting surpluses, reduce excess training costs, and provide efficiencies by assuring that the right people will be in the right place at the right time. But how many dollars of benefits can be attributed to this factor?

Most organizations must begin employment planning in the faith that such savings will result. Post hoc studies may follow of attitudes toward its possible benefits: more business, more employee satisfaction, and dollar reductions in personnel costs per amount of sales. At the beginning stage of development (Stage II), few organizations could do a realistic cost/benefits analysis for employment planning. Nevertheless, James Walker has developed a preliminary framework for cost/benefit analysis of employment planning.[48]

SUMMARY, CONCLUSIONS, AND RECOMMENDATIONS

Chapters 4 and 5 have pointed out the significant factors in the diagnostic model that affect employment planning: the nature of the labor market, the goals of the controlling interests, the nature of the task and of the employee, government requirements, and to a lesser extent, union requirements. Throughout these chapters, their impact was analyzed to help you become a more effective manager by taking the diagnostic approach to personnel activities.

This two-chapter unit on employment planning began by emphasizing that this personnel activity is an integral aspect of strategic planning by top management. Once management chooses its strategy for assessing and maintaining the personnel capacities of the enterprise, the personnel function assures its success by comparing the present supply of human resources with the projected demand for them. This comparison leads to the action decisions: add employees, terminate employees, or reallocate employees internally.

Top management must make the decision to set up and support the employment planning process. On occasion it must also decide whether to terminate employees immediately or to decrease the work force through attrition, accelerated early retirement programs, or in other ways.

The employment planning action decision system is modeled in Exhibit 5–9.

Employment planning systems have not been used widely or long enough to demonstrate their contribution to organizational effectiveness as a personnel activity. Nevertheless, there exists, as all experienced administrators and managers know, a condition which Herbert Simon called Gresham's law of planning. According to this whimsical "law," which is nonetheless fact, immediate problems drive out time for planning. The hospital administrator knows that in September he should be planning for employment needs for next year, but when he plans only informally, a crisis in the emergency room or a human relations problem with the nursing staff can fill up his time, and he "never gets around to it."

When a formal employment planning system is set up, with the personnel manager to prod the operating manager into providing certain data, the

EXHIBIT 5–9
Model of employment planning action decisions

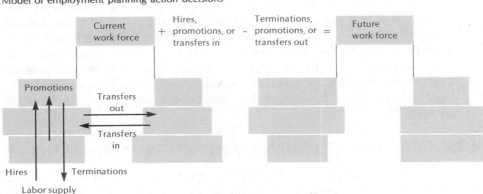

planning *will* get done. The manager might have come up with the plans using an informal system if she ever got around to it, but she seldom does. The personnel specialist who does the planning works with the operating manager—hospital administrator, school superintendent, division manager, bureau chief; he or she alone cannot do the job.

This chapter examined the methods used to formally analyze the supply of workers for the enterprise and discussed the action decisions in the employment planning process. The methods used to analyze supply are summarized in Propositions 5.1–5.4.

> *Proposition 5.1.* The larger the organization's work force, the more likely is the effective organization to use more sophisticated and computerized skills inventories.

> *Proposition 5.2.* The more volatile the organization's environment, the more likely is the effective organization to use more sophisticated and computerized skills inventories.

> *Proposition 5.3.* The more complex the products and services offered by the organization, the more likely is the effective organization to use more sophisticated and computerized skills inventories.

> *Proposition 5.4.* The more geographically dispersed the organization's members, the more likely is the effective organization to use more sophisticated and computerized skills inventories.

Then we examined how enterprises can affect employment supply by adjusting work schedules. Propositions 5.5–5.7 apply here.

> *Proposition 5.5.* Compressed work weeks are likely to be preferred by employees with instrumental work values whose jobs do not require heavy physical or taxing mental work and who are middle aged.

> *Proposition 5.6.* Flexitime systems are likely to be successful in work that does not require significant interdependence, with supportive middle management and unions, and where significant outlays for buffer stocks and utility costs are not required.

> *Proposition 5.7.* If shift work is required, it is more likely to be successful if the employees are assigned to a shift permanently with the right to bid for better shifts, and if there are reasonable shift differentials in pay and other rewards.

Finally, Proposition 5.8 concerns action decisions on supply/demand relationships:

> *Proposition 5.8.* Effective enterprises will analyze the supply/demand match of employees in advance so as to take necessary steps to reschedule, recruit, or lay off employees, and will analyze the work force composition for legal constraints on it.

It can be seen that many of these propositions are related to size of work force, volatility of the environment, complexity of products or services, and geographical dispersion. If the work force is larger than a certain number, it is almost impossible for management to keep track of all the skills available

EXHIBIT 5–10
Recommendations on employment planning for model organizations

Type of organization	Analysis of supply (skills inventory)		Method of demand analysis				Level where employment is analyzed		
	Manual	Computerized	Expert	Trend	Model/multiple	Unit	HQ	Unit	Both
1. Large size, low complexity, high stability		X			X	X	X		
2. Medium size, low complexity, high stability	X				X	X	X		
3. Small size, low complexity, high stability	X			X			X		
4. Medium size, moderate complexity, moderate stability	X			X		X		X	
5. Large size, high complexity, low stability		X		X		X			X
6. Medium size, high complexity, low stability	X			X		X		X	
7. Small size, high complexity, low stability	X		X					X	

in the organization. The limit may be 50 to 75 employees or even fewer, depending on the complexity of the organization. This problem is compounded if several schools, factories, or other units must be supervised. If the environment changes quickly or the product or service requires a variety of skills, it is harder to assess supply informally, and formal employment planning systems are more important.

Employment planning systems for model organizations

Another feature of this text which is introduced in this chapter is a summary of the possible uses of each personnel activity in the seven model organizations identified in Chapter 1 (Exhibit 1–14). The recommendations for employment planning in these model organizations are given in Exhibit 5–10. The exhibit outlines the major activities of employment planning that are most useful for various types of enterprises.

As far as skills inventories are concerned, smaller and medium-sized organizations probably will have manual systems, at most. They may provide these only for subgroups of employees (management, professional, or technical) that they feel are critical. Probably only larger organizations have computerized inventories.

On the demand side, it would appear reasonable that the larger the organization, the more sophisticated are the techniques, as modified by the amount of change in the system. As regards where employment planning is done, it seems advantageous to formulate plans for larger, more stable organizations at headquarters, for smaller and medium-sized, volatile ones at the unit level, and for large, volatile organizations on both levels.

Employment planning can be an integral part of the personnel process. It is most directly related to recruitment, selection, training, promotion, and career development. By matching employment supply and demand, the organization can know how many persons of what type it needs to fill positions from within (by promotion or training) and how many it must acquire from outside (by recruitment and selection). Part Three, to follow, is devoted to recruitment and selection—filling employment needs from outside the organization when employment planning decisions show this need.

QUESTIONS

1. How is analysis of employment supply related to demand analysis?
2. What is a skills inventory? A management inventory?
3. Discuss how to design an effective skills inventory.
4. How does a skills inventory differ from a management inventory?
5. What are the major problems in operating skills inventories?
6. Compressed work weeks are the wave of the future—the way most of us will have our work scheduled. Comment.
7. What are the advantages and disadvantages of compressed work weeks?

8. What is flexitime? What is good and bad about flexitime?

9. Discuss the probable future of flexitime.

10. Why should an enterprise analyze the composition of its work force? How?

11. How does employment planning help a firm with no employment variance?

12. What action decisions can be made when there is a worker shortage? Which is best?

13. What action decision can be made when there is a worker surplus? Which is best?

14. Can employment planning be analyzed using cost/benefit analysis? How?

15. What are the major summary propositions on employment planning of demand? Of supply? Comment on which ones make sense to you and which do not.

16. In examining recommended systems for the model organizations, which should use manual skills inventories? Which should expect to use demand analysis? Which should do the analysis at headquarters; at the unit; or on both levels?

NOTES AND REFERENCES

1. A. Matthews, "Keeping Tabs on 7500 Middle Managers," *Personnel*, May–June 1966, pp. 24–29.

2. Kendrith Rowland and Michael Sovereign, "Markov-Chain Analysis of Internal Manpower Supply," *Industrial Relations*, October 1969, pp. 88–99.

3. National Industrial Conference Board, *The Expanded Personnel Function*, Studies in Personnel Policy 203 (New York, 1966).

4. William J. Pedicord, "Advanced Data Systems for Personnel Planning and Placement," in *Computers and Automation* (Newtonville, Mass.: Berkley Enterprises, 1966).

5. T. I. Bradshaw, "Computerized Employee Search Program," *Data Processing Magazine*, November 1965, pp. 48–50.

6. Robert Smith, "Information Systems for More Effective Use of Executive Resources," *Personnel Journal*, June 1969, pp. 452–65.

7. James Grey and Robert Waas, "A Mini Human Resources Inventory System," *Personnel*, November–December 1974, pp. 59–64.

8. T. F. Hercus, "Management Inventory Systems," *Canadian Personnel and Industrial Relations Journal*, January 1973, pp. 22–29.

9. Robert Dacey, "Manpower Management," in Raymond Cook (ed.), *Army Command and Management: Theory and Practice* (Carlisle, Pa.: Army War College, 1976); George Milkovich and Thomas Mahoney, "Human Resources Planning and PAIR Policy," in *PAIR Handbook*, vol. 4, ed. Dale Yoder and Herbert Heneman (Berea, Ohio: American Society of Personnel Administrators, 1976).

10. Richard Bueschel, "How EDP Is Improving the Personnel Function," *Personnel*, September–October 1964, pp. 59–64.

11. Robert Martin, "Skills Inventories," *Personnel Journal*, January 1967, pp. 28–30.

12. Robert Murphy, "A Personalized Skills Inventory: The North American Rockwell Story," *Manpower Planning and Programming*, ed. Elmer H. Burack and James W. Walker (Boston: Allyn & Bacon, 1972).

13. Lyman Seamans, Jr., "What's Lacking in Most Skills Inventories?" *Personnel Journal*, February 1973, pp. 101–5.

14. Thomas Kniesner, "The Fulltime Work Week in the United States—1900–1970," *Industrial and Labor Relations Review,* October 1976, pp. 3–15; Derek Leslie, "Hours and Overtime in British and United States Manufacturing Industries: A Comparison," *British Journal of Industrial Relations* 14, 2 (1975) pp. 194–201.

15. William Werther, "Mini Shifts: An Alternative to Overtime," *Personnel Journal,* March 1976, pp. 130–33.

16. A. A. Wedderburn, "Social Factors in Satisfaction with Swiftly Rotating Shifts," *Occupational Psychology,* 41, 243(1967), pp. 85–107.

17. Paul Mott et al. *Shift Work* (Ann Arbor: University of Michigan, 1965); Wedderburn, "Swiftly Rotating Shifts."

18. Eileen Phillip and Stephen Griew, *One Hundred Shift Workers* (New Zealand Institute of Economic Research, 1920); Thomas Zimmerer, "Who are Our Nightpeople in Business?" *Human Resource Management,* Winter 1976, pp. 18–20.

19. Pratibha Malavuja and K. Ganesh, "Shift Work and Individual Differences in the Productivity of Weavers in an Indian Textile Mill," *Journal of Applied Psychology* 61, 6 (1976), pp. 774–76.

20. Joann Lublin, "The Four Day Week," *The Wall Street Journal,* February 16, 1977.

21. Victor Zonana, "The Four Day Week," *The Wall Street Journal,* February 17, 1977.

22. Herbert Gutman, *Work, Culture, and Society in Industrializing America* (New York: Alfred A. Knopf, Inc., 1975).

23. Lublin, "Four Day Week."

24. Department of Labor Analysis of work patterns for year ending May 1976, as reported in *The Wall Street Journal,* March 18, 1977, p. 27.

25. Kenneth Wheeler et al., *The Four Day Week* (New York: American Management Association, 1972).

26. The research is summarized in William Glueck, "Changing Hours of Work: A Review of the Literature," *Proceedings,* Academy of Management, 1977. Some of the better studies include B. W. Balch, "The Four Day Week and the Older Workers," *Personnel Journal,* December 1974, pp. 894–96; Eugene Calvasina and Randy Boxx, "Efficiency of Workers on the Four Day Work Week," *Academy of Management Journal,* September, 1975, pp. 604–10; David Herbert et al., "A Quantitative Decision Making Guide to Four-Day Work Week Conversion, *The Personnel Administrator,* February 1976, pp. 45–50; B. J. Hodge and Richard Tellier, "Employer Reactions to the Four Day Week," *California Management Review,* Fall 1975, pp. 25–30; John Ivancevitch, "Effects of the Shorter Workweek on Selected Satisfaction and Performance Measures," *Journal of Applied Psychology* 59, 6 (1974), pp. 717–21; Martin Kenny, "Public Employer Attitudes Toward the Four Day Workweek," *Public Personnel Management,* March–April 1974, pp. 159–61; Thomas Mahoney et al., "Working Perceptions of the Four Day Week," *California Management Review,* Fall 1975, pp. 31–35; Walter Nord and Robert Costigan, "Worker Adjustment to the Four Day Week," *Journal of Applied Psychology* 58, 1 (1973), pp. 60–66; Riva Poor, *4 Days, 40 Hours* (New York: New American Library, 1973).

27. M. D. Kossoris et al., *Hours of Work and Output,* Bureau of Labor Statistics, Bulletin no. 917 (Washington, D.C.: U.S. Department of Labor, 1947).

28. Earl Alluisi and Ben Morgan, Jr., "Engineering Psychology and Human Performance," *Annual Review of Psychology* (Palo Alto: Annual Reviews, Inc., 1976).

29. Allyson Grossman, "Multiple Jobholding in May 1974," *Monthly Labor Review,* February 1975, pp. 60–64; Glenn Miller and Mark Sniderman, "Multijobholdings of Wichita Public School Teachers," *Public Personnel Management,* September–October 1974, pp. 392–402.

30. Warren Magoon and Larry Schnicker, "Flexible Hours at State Street Bank of Boston," *The Personnel Administrator,* October 1976, pp. 34–37.

31. Douglas Fleuter, *The Workweek Revolution* (Reading, Mass.: Addison-Wesley Publishing Co., 1975).

32. Jo Hartley, "Experience with Flexible Hours of Work," *Monthly Labor Review,* May 1976, pp. 41–44.

33. Virginia Martin, *Hours of Work When Workers Can Choose* (Washington, D.C.: Washington's Business and Professional Women's Foundation, 1975).

34. Glueck, "Changing Hours of Work: A Review of the Literature." Some of the better research pieces on flexitime include: Edgar Busch, "Flexitime in the Mid Seventies," *Proceedings,* Academy of Management, 1975, pp. 100–102; Cynthia Fields, "Variable Work Hours: The Mony Experience," *Personnel Journal,* September 1974, pp. 675–78; Robert Golembiewski et al., "Factor Analysis of Some Flexitime Effects," *Academy of Management Journal,* September 1975, pp. 500–509; Robert Golembiewski et al., "A Longitudinal Study of Flexitime Effects," *Journal of Applied Behavioral Sciences,* 10, 4 (1974) pp. 503–32; William Holley, Jr., et al., "Employee Reactions to a Flexitime Program: A Longitudinal Study," *Human Resource Management,* Winter 1976; Frank Morgan, "Your (Flex) Time May Come," *Personnel Journal,* February 1977, pp. 82–85, 96 ff; B. E. Partridge, "Notes on the Impact of Flexitime in a Large Insurance Company," *Occupational Psychology,* 47(1973), pp. 241–42.

35. Hartley, "Experience with Flexible Hours of Work."

36. Exhibit 5–5 is partially modeled on the analysis in Robert Gutherie, "Personnel's Emerging Role," *Personnel Journal,* September 1974, pp. 657–61.

37. Barry Hughes, "Redundancy: Some Insights from Overseas Experience," *Journal of Industrial Relations,* December 1975, pp. 356–68; Richard Traum, "Reducing Headcount through Attrition and/or Termination," *Personnel,* January–February 1975, pp. 19–25.

38. Douglas More, "Demotion," *Social Problems,* Winter 1962, pp. 213–21.

39. Charles Watson, "A Sensible Approach to Mass Layoffs," *Public Personnel Management,* May–June 1974, pp. 233–37.

40. Maurice Blounder, *Organizational Repercussions of Personnel Cutback: Impact of Layoffs on Retained Employees,* unpublished Ph.D. thesis, City University of New York, 1977.

41. James Ledvinka, "EEO, Seniority, and Layoffs," *Personnel,* January–February, 1976, pp. 61–67; William Torrence, "Manpower Planning and Reductions in Force: Competitive Status Seniority and EEOC Compliance," *Personnel Journal,* May 1975, pp. 287–89; William Walter and Anthony Obadal, "Layoffs: The Judicial View," *The Personnel Administrator,* May 1975, pp. 13–16.

42. *Franks v. Bowman Transportation Co.,* 423 U.S. 814 (U.S. Supreme Court, 1976).

43. Basil Cuddihy, "How to Give Phased Out Managers a New Start," *Harvard Business Review,* July–August 1976, pp. 61–69.

44. Jack Mendelson, "Does Your Company Need Outplacement?" *SAM Advanced Management Journal,* Winter 1975, pp. 4–12; Jack Mendelson, "What's Fair Treatment for Terminated Employees?" *Supervisory Management,* November 1974, pp. 25–34.

45. Traum, "Reducing Headcount."

46. See M. Lynn Sprull et al., "A Planning Model for Short Run Staffing Decisions," *Proceedings,* Academy of Management, 1976; Thomas Mahoney and George Milkovich, "Computer Simulation: A Training Tool for Manpower Managers," *Personnel Journal,* December 1975, pp. 609–12, 637 ff; Thomas O'Neill and Mahendra Nath, "Computer Aided Manpower Planning Using On-Line Terminals," *Industrial Management,* March 1973, pp. 1–6; Pedicord, "Advanced Data Systems"; Smith, "Information Systems for Executive Resources."

47. Glenn Bassett, "Elements of Manpower Forecasting and Scheduling," *Human Resource Management,* Fall 1973, pp. 35–43; Richard Bueschal, *EDP and Personnel,* AMA Management Bulletin 86. New York: American Management Association, 1966; R. H. Fulton, "A Company Technique for Estimating Future Manpower Requirements," in *Manpower and Planning,* ed. R. A. Beaumont (New York: Industrial Relations Counselors, 1970).

48. James Walker, "Evaluating The Practical Effectiveness of Human Resource Planning Applications," *Human Resource Management,* Spring 1974, pp. 19–27.

Recruiting, selecting, and orienting personnel

PART THREE

Part Three is concerned with recruitment, selection, and orientation of employees. Given the data provided by employment planning—how many people are needed, of what type, and when and where—the organization sets out to acquire the persons needed in the most effective way. Chapter 6 discusses recruiting, or attracting good personnel to the organization. Recruitment results in a list of potential employees for each position, from which the organization selects the most qualified people available. This chapter also includes an appendix on effective ways to find a job. Chapter 7 shows how organizations select the best recruits from among those who apply for open positions. The final chapter of this part, Chapter 8, is concerned with orienting new employees to their jobs.

Recruiting and job search

CHAPTER OBJECTIVES

■ To show that the recruiting process is a mutual matching of the expectations of recruits and the organization, and a compromise between them.

■ To describe the recruiting process: who does it, how they do it, and where they seek recruits.

■ To show you how to find a job for yourself.

CHAPTER OUTLINE

The mission of the military is to defend the country against its enemies. In performing this duty, the military's "employees" may be injured, perhaps incapacitated for life; many also may die. The military's "executives" expect unquestioning obedience, and military personnel must live in the same area where they work, in communities that may consist almost entirely of military staff. The "employer" provides for many of their social and off-work facilities—recreational, religious, social, shopping.

Everyone does not find this way of life appealing; each year, thousands of military personnel retire or leave the service. But Congress has mandated a volunteer military force. (In Canada, other than during the two world wars, the military has always been all volunteer.) If the economy provides many positions with more attractive rewards, how does the military attract enough applicants to offer them jobs?

Mary Buggins is about to graduate from pharmacy school. She wants to work in or around the Los Angeles area because its an exciting place to live, and she believes it will offer her a secure future in her chosen profession. Now she needs a job, but how does she find one? The college has a placement office, and there are the help-wanted ads to check. Or she could walk into pharmacies that appeal to her and ask for a job, or run an ad in the situations-wanted column, or go to an employment agency. How does she find her job?

These two examples illustrate problems faced by organizations and individuals which the recruiting process can help solve. This chapter describes effective ways to recruit the people needed to offset shortages in human resources which become apparent as a result of employment planning.

> DEFINITIONS
>
> Recruiting is that set of activities an enterprise uses to attract job candidates who have the abilities and attitudes needed to help the enterprise achieve its objectives.
>
> Job search is the set of activities a person undertakes to seek and find a position which will provide him or her with sustenance and other rewards.

Recruiting is related directly to a number of other personnel activities, as shown in Exhibit 6–1.

Employment planning determines the number of employees needed, and all subsequent personnel activities (such as selection, orientation, development, compensation) cannot be effective unless good employees have been recruited. The Prentice-Hall/ASPA survey of 1,400 personnel executives found that they rated recruiting/selection as their most important function in a nonunionized firm.[1] Recruiting can be costly. For example, it has been

EXHIBIT 6–1
Recruiting and other personnel activities

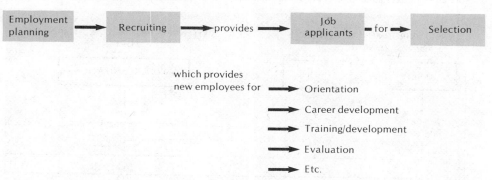

estimated[2] that recruiting cost the following percentages of the first-year salary of various specialists and managers:

Senior engineer 68%
Accountant 61
Secretary 51
Supervisor 40
Middle manager 33
Top manager 25

Thus for a $60,000-a-year executive, recruiting can cost $15,000; recruiting engineers can cost $11,900. Yet recruiting is not a well-developed personnel function; it is at Stage II or possibly Stage III (see Exhibit 1–13 in Chapter 1).

A DIAGNOSTIC APPROACH TO ATTRACTION AND RECRUITMENT

Exhibit 6–2 examines how the recruiting process is affected by various factors in the environment. The recruiting process begins with an attempt to find employees with the abilities and attitudes desired by the enterprise and to match them with the tasks to be performed. Whether potential employees will respond to the recruiting effort depends on the attitudes they have developed toward those tasks and the enterprise, on the basis of their past social and working experiences. Their perception of the task will also be affected by the work climate in the enterprise.

How difficult the recruiting job is depends on a number of factors: external influences such as government and union restrictions and the labor market, plus the employer's requirements and candidates' preferences. External factors are discussed in this section, and the important interaction of the organization as a recruiter and the employee as a recruit is examined in the next section.

EXHIBIT 6–2
Factors affecting recruitment, selections and orientation of employees and organizational effectiveness

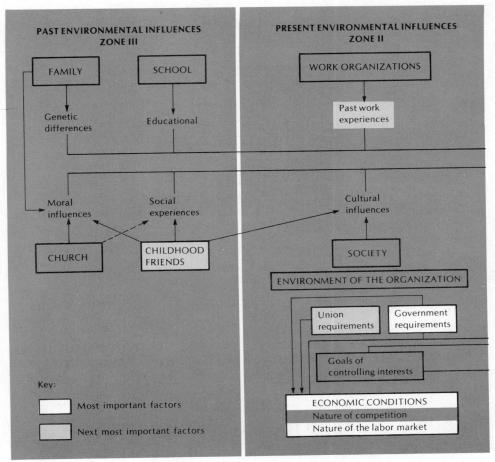

External influences

Government and union restrictions.   Government regulations prohibiting discrimination in hiring and employment have a direct impact on recruiting practices. As will be described in more detail in Chapter 18, government agencies can and do review the following information about recruiting to see if an enterprise has violated the law:

- The list of recruitment sources (such as employment agencies, civic organizations, schools) for each job category.
- Recruiting advertising.[3]
- Estimates of the firm's employment needs for the coming year.

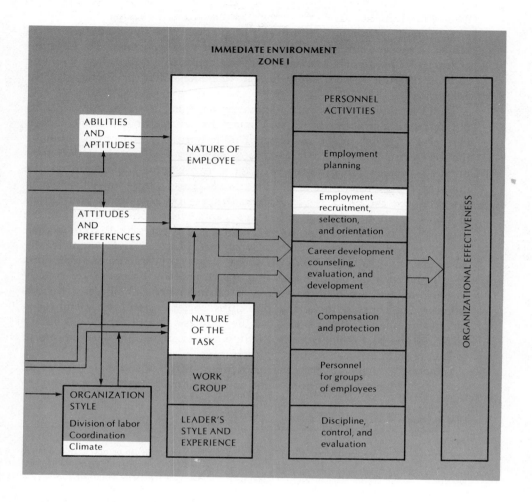

- Statistics on the number of applicants processed by category (sex, race, etc.) and by job category or level.

Of course job descriptions and job specifications cannot be drawn up so that the jobs are sex stereotyped; that is, if the job can be done by both sexes, the descriptions should not suggest one sex or the other. Recruiters need to be aware of perhaps unconscious sex stereotypes which would cause them to screen out a candidate on the sole basis of sex.[4]

The government requires reports of recruiting and hiring practices and may require statistics on the number of recruits accepted and rejected by job and employee categories. Thus recruiters should keep records showing which candidates they have interviewed belong to certain minorities. Agencies also review a firm's employment advertising for legality—it must have no reference to preferences for sex, race, and other protected categories unless these characteristics are bona fide occupational qualifications.

Affirmative action programs to recruit qualified employees not well represented in present employees may be required by government. For example, a firm with no female managers may be required to recruit at women's colleges offering degrees likely to lead to management positions with the enterprise.

Paul Wernimont points out that government agencies can examine recruiting and hiring procedures on two somewhat contradictory basis. One is percentage "goals" in the recruitment of minorities and women, whereby the enterprise is asked to hire enough minority employees so that their numbers in each job category (managers, for example) approximates the minority population in the area. The other basis is adverse impact; whereby the enterprise can be judged as discriminating if it rejects higher proportions of minority applicants than other applicants.[5] The conflict is that if the firm recruits more minorities, its rejection rate of them is likely to be higher.

Exhibit 6–3 provides a guide to what recruiters can and cannot legally do or ask in recruiting interviews. Other personal characteristics recruiters need to be wary of, because they may discriminate or do not relate directly to performance, are birthplace, use of second names or aliases, religious affiliation, citizenship, membership in clubs, societies, and lodges, and social security numbers. In some states, it is illegal to ask about the type of military discharge and past police records. Many public organizations must be careful to follow state or local statutes on recruiting.

Obviously, these government restrictions affect who can be recruited, how, and where. In addition, some union contracts restrict recruiting to

EXHIBIT 6–3
Dos and don'ts in recruiting interviews

Subject	Can do or ask	Cannot do or ask
Sex	Notice appearance.	Make comments or notes unless sex is a bona fide occupational qualification.
Marital status	Ask status after hiring, for insurance purposes.	Are you married? Single? Divorced? Engaged? Are you living with anyone? Do you see your ex-spouse?
Children	Ask numbers and ages of children after hiring, for insurance purposes.	Do you have children at home? How old? Who cares for them? Do you plan more children?
Physical data	Explain manual labor, lifting, other requirements of the job. Show how it is performed. Require physical exam.	How tall are you? How heavy?
Criminal record	If security clearance is necessary, can be done prior to employment.	Have you ever been arrested, convicted, or spent time in jail?
Military status	Are you a veteran? Why not? Any job-related experience?	What type of discharge do you have? What branch did you serve in?
Age	Age after hiring. Are you over 18?	How old are you? Estimate age.
Housing	If you have no phone, how can we reach you?	Do you own your home? Do you rent? Do you live in an apartment or a house?

Source: *Business Week*, May 26, 1975, p. 77.

union hiring halls (as will be discussed in Chapter 19). This restriction does not apply for many employers, but where it does the recruiting function is turned over to the union, or at least for those employees who are unionized.

Labor market conditions. The second external environmental factor affecting recruiting is labor market conditions (these were described in some detail in Chapter 3). The labor market affects recruiting in this way: If there is a surplus of labor at recruiting time, even informal attempts at recruiting will probably attract more than enough applicants. But when full employment is approximated, skillful and prolonged recruiting may be necessary to attract any applicants that fulfill the expectations of the enterprise.

The employer can find out about the current employment picture in several ways. The federal Department of Labor issues employment reports, and state or provincial divisions of employment security and labor usually can provide information on local employment conditions. There are also sources of information about specific types of employees. Craft unions and profession associations keep track of employment conditions as they affect their members. Current college recruiting efforts are analyzed by the Conference Board, A. C. Nielsen, and the Endicott Report, which appears in *The Journal of College Placement*. Various personnel journals and *The Wall Street Journal* also regularly report on employment conditions.

Other sources provide summary data such as indexes of employment. One of the most interesting indexes is that of the Conference Board, which keeps track of help-wanted advertising in 52 major newspapers across the nation, using 1967 as a base year of 100. Local conditions are more important than national conditions, unless the employer is recruiting nationwide.

INTERACTIONS OF THE APPLICANT/RECRUIT AND THE ORGANIZATION

After considering how external factors such as government, unions, and labor market conditions restrict the options of an enterprise to recruit (and an applicant to be recruited), the next step in understanding the recruiting process is to consider the interaction of the applicants and the enterprise in recruiting.

In Exhibit 6–2 (the diagnostic model for recruitment and selection), the nature of the organization and the goals of the managers are highlighted, as is the nature of the task; the techniques used and sources of recruits vary with the job. As far as the applicants are concerned, their abilities, attitudes, past work experience and friends' attitudes affect how they go about seeking a job.

Before discussing the enterprise and the job-seeker separately, it is useful to consider the recruitment process from both the employer's and the employee's viewpoint. Exhibit 6–4 shows how effective recruiting takes place: The employer offers a job with associated rewards; he is looking for certain characteristics in a potential employee. The recruit has abilities and attitudes

EXHIBIT 6–4
A model of the recruiting/attraction process

Organizational expectations			*Potential employee expectations*
Requirements:			Characteristics:
Abilities	From education	←- →	Abilities
	From work experience	←- →	Experience
Attitudes	From prior experience	←- - - - - - - - - - - - - - - - - - - →	Attitudes
Personality		←- →	Personality
Job offering:			Job expectations:
Job characteristics (for example, variety and responsibility)		←- →	Minimum expectations of job characteristics
Job rewards:			
Pay		←- →	Minimum expectations of pay, benefits, promotion
Benefits			
Promotions			
Intrinsic rewards			

to offer and is looking for a kind of job that meets his minimum expectations. A match is made when sufficient overlap exists between these two sets of expectations. The recruiting process usually requires some modifications and compromises on both sides.

The organization's view of recruiting

Three aspects affect recruiting from the organization's viewpoint: the recruiting requirements set, organization policies and procedures, and the organizational image.

Requirements for recruits.   Organizations specify the requirements they consider ideal in applicants for positions. The employer easily can have unrealistic expectations of potential employees: They might expect applicants who stand first in their class, are president of all extracurricular activities, have worked their way through school, have Johnny Carson's ability to charm, are good looking, have ten years' experience (at age 21), and are willing to work long hours for almost no money. Or, to meet federal requirements, they might specify a black woman, but one who is in the upper 10 percent of her graduating class and has an undergraduate degree in engineering and an MBA.

As contrasted with this unrealistic approach, the effective enterprise examines the specifications that are absolutely necessary for the job and uses these as its beginning expectations (see the section on job analysis, job description, and job specifications in Chapter 4). Effective job specifications have been carefully examined to make sure that all the specifications are directly necessary for performance. For example, if specifications for a job such as, school custodian call for a high school diploma, it must be shown that when custodians without diplomas were hired in the past they could not perform effectively. If they could, this requirement does not make sense, and it is not legal.

Organization policies and practices. In some organizations personnel policies and practices affect recruiting and who is recruited. One of the most important of these is promotion from within. For all practical purposes, this policy means that many organizations only recruit from outside the organization at the initial hiring level. They feel this is fair to present loyal employees and assures them a secure future and a fair chance at promotion, and most employees favor this approach. Some employers also feel this practice helps protect trade secrets. Charles Hughes calls this "Help Wanted: Present Employees Please Apply."[6] The techniques used for internal recruiting will be discussed below.

Is promotion from within always a good policy? No. Organizations may grow so stable that they are set in its ways: The business does not compete effectively, or the government bureau will not adjust to legislative requirements. In such cases, promotion from within may be detrimental, and new employees from outside might be helpful.

Other recruiting policies can also affect recruiting. Certain organizations have always hired more than their fair share of the handicapped, or veterans, or ex-convicts, for example, and they may look to these sources first. Others may be involved in nepotism to favor relatives. All these policies affect who is recruited.

Organizational image. The image of the employer generally held by the public also affects recruitment. There are differences in attracting engineers, systems analysts, tool and die makers, marketing researchers and cost accountants, or employment specialists, for such diverse organizations and situations as:

- NASA at the height of the space program, when men were walking on the moon.
- The U.S. Army attempting to recruit volunteers just after Vietnam was completely taken over by Hanoi.
- St. John's hospital—the best known, best equipped hospital in town.
- Harvard University trying to recruit faculty members to teach and students to attend its MBA program.
- A small soap company trying to hire salespersons who is competing with Procter and Gamble for recruits.
- IBM trying to recruit research scientists for its lab.

As you can imagine the good or bad, well known or unknown images of these organizations will affect how they are viewed by the public and job recruits.

The organization's image is complex, but it probably is based on what the organization does and whether it is perceived as providing a good place to work. The larger the organization, the more likely it is to have a well-developed image. The organization that produces a product or service the potential employee knows about or uses is also more likely to have an image for the applicant. The probability is that a potential employee will have a clearer image of a chewing gum company than a manufacturer of subassemblies for a cyclotron.

How does this image affect recruiting? Job applicants seldom can have interviews with all the organizations that have job openings of interest to them. Because there are time and energy limits to the job search, they do some preliminary screening. One of these screens is the image the applicants have of the organization, which can attract or repel them.[7] For example, the image of the banking industry is such that it attracts persons who are deferential to authority and well suited to the autocratic, regimented, and highly structured bank environment.[8] The industry has tried to change this image, however.

One study attempted to determine what industries have positive images in society by asking 400 respondents about the prestige of various industries.[9] Their composite ranking is given in Exhibit 6–5. If people are indeed influenced by prestige in their choices, this study indicates it should be much easier to recruit employees for atomic energy plants than coal mines.

Studies of college students' positive and negative images of industries[10] found they had these reactions:

- Positive: Computers, space, oil, steel, banking, drugs, chemicals, automobiles, pharmaceuticals, and rubber.
- Negative: Insurance, tobacco, soap and detergents, toiletries, utilities, and government.

These images can change, however; the ecology movement may have changed formerly positive attitudes toward atomic energy and petroleum,

EXHIBIT 6–5
Perceived prestige of various industries

1.	Atomic energy plants	16.	Telephone companies
2.	Medical services	17.	Rubber products manufacturing
3.	Research laboratories	18.	Weapons manufacturing
4.	Commercial airlines	19.	Ship and boat building
5.	Colleges and universities	20.	Iron and steel mills
6.	Banking	21.	Railroads
7.	Aircraft manufacturing	22.	Labor organizations
8.	Chemical products manufacturing	23.	Department stores
9.	Motion pictures	24.	Clothing manufacturing
10.	Publishing companies	25.	Furniture manufacturing
11.	Electric power and light	26.	Hotels
12.	Petroleum refining	27.	Tobacco companies
13.	Automobile manufacturing	28.	Farming
14.	Building construction	29.	Meat packing
15.	Federal government	30.	Coal mining

Source: C. R. Tatro and A. P. Garbin, "Industrial Prestige Hierarchy," *Journal of Vocational Behavior*, 3 (1973), pp. 383–91.

for example. Organizations with poor images may find that attempts to change these perceptions will help them attract more or better qualified potential employees. Extraordinary recruiting efforts may help overcome these images for some enterprises. Thus the image of the organization generally held by potential employees is another limiting factor on the ideal requirements it can stipulate.

Recruiting in the public sector.   Recruiting in the public sector has some similarities to and differences from recruiting in the private and third sectors. Municipal and state governments in the United States are subject to federal regulations on hiring requirements; in Canada, the federal government exerts less pressure on the provinces and municipalities. In the United States, public personnel often must abide by local legislation which requires them to live within the municipality's limits. This, of course, limits who can be recruited. A big difference in recruiting in the public sector is that applicants often must take competitive tests (like the civil service examinations) prior to screening for hiring, and placement on the tests determines who can be considered for the openings.

The recruiting efforts of public managers must cope with labor market problems, just as other managers do. As the public sector becomes more unionized, public managers may also face as many union restrictions as the private sector.

Public managers set up specifications and policies for personnel procurement. Promotion from within is quite prevalent in the public sector; in Washington, federal agencies must prove that government employees declared surplus are not capable of doing any open position before they can recruit from outside the government.

The government too has image problems, but recent federal pay raises have alleviated them. Public managers also may face the reality of pressures from politicians and interest-group leaders to hire specific persons. Some recent reform efforts toward model public personnel administration laws in the states and cities may help counter this practice.[11]

In sum, the ideal job specifications preferred by the organization may have to be adjusted to meet the realities of the labor market, government or union restrictions, the limitations of organization policies and practices, and the organization's image. If an inadequate number of quality personnel apply, the organization may have to either adjust the job to fit the best applicant or increase its recruiting efforts.

The potential employee's view of recruiting

Exhibit 6–2 highlighted several factors relevant to how the recruit looks for a job: The applicant has abilities and aptitudes and attitudes and preferences based on past work experiences, friends' attitudes, and influences by parents, teachers, and others. These factors affect the recruit two ways: how he sets his job preferences and how he goes about seeking a job. Understanding both of these is vital to effective recruiting by the organization, but only the first is discussed here. Job search is the subject of the appendix to this chapter.

Preferences of recruits for organizations and jobs. Just as enterprises have ideal specifications for recruits, so the recruits have a set of preferences they have for a job. A student leaving college may want a job in San Diego because of its climate, paying $25,000 a year and with little or no responsibility or supervision. This recruit is as unlikely to get *all* his expectations fulfilled as the enterprise is. The recruit also faces the limits of the labor market (good or bad from the recruit's point of view, which is usually the opposite of the enterprise's), government and union restrictions, and the limits of organizational policies and practices. The recruit must anticipate compromises just as the enterprise does.

From the individual's point of view, organization choice is a two-step process. First, the individual makes an occupational choice—probably in high school or just after. Then she or he makes a choice of the organization to work for within the occupation chosen.

Occupational choice. This part of the process has been analyzed from a number of perspectives; the three most notable are psychological, economic, and sociological. Occupational choice is influenced by the person's preferences and images (psychological), the realities of the labor market and the person's calculation of his net advantage (economic) and the structural limitations of the world of work and the individual's socialization to it (sociological).

Psychologists analyze how occupational choice is part of the person's emotional and intellectual growth. They also show how occupational choice is influenced by the person's needs, desires, hopes, and aspirations.[12] Economists see the occupational choice process as the way people seek to receive the greatest future flow of income with the smallest expenditures of time and money.[13] Sociologists regard occupational choice as a form of socialization and part of the allocation of occupational roles. They emphasize how the family, educational system, the peer group, and guidance agencies influence and constrain the choice.[14]

Timperley points out that all three approaches to understanding occupational choice are interrelated. To talk about an individuals' aspirations without reference to the structural limitations on them, or to talk about maximizing net advantages without discussing a persons' motivations, makes little sense.[15] In my opinion, it seems reasonable to view occupational choice as a decision which reacts to personal motivation and aspirations (including economic motivations), given the restrictions of the labor market and the "conditioning" of the social structure in which the person lives.

Organizational choice. We have implied that everyone make an occupational choice, and then an organizational choice within that occupation. This is true for many persons, especially those that stay in school through high school and beyond.

But some do not even go to high school. In an excellent study of 1,600 men, Michael Ornstein found that 25 percent of American blacks and 15 percent of whites enter the job market without high school educations.[16] For these persons, chances are the occupational choice is quite limited, and they would make a job-organization choice, without considering occupational choice. Ornstein also found that 50 percent of whites and 33 percent of blacks completed high school before entering the labor market full-time, and 10 percent of whites and 3 percent of blacks completed college before doing so.

Many persons had work experience prior to entering the labor market full-time. According to Ornstein, one third of whites and one seventh of blacks held full-time jobs while in school (in summers or between school years). Before entering the labor market for good, 90 percent of white and 44 percent of black college graduates, and 38 percent of white and 19 percent of black high school graduates had some full-time work experience.

When they left school, two thirds of the men surveyed got a job within a month. Blacks actually experienced less unemployment than whites did. The typical job seeker was single: less than 3 percent of blacks and 4.6 percent of whites were married before entering the labor force full-time. Ten percent moved ten miles or more to find their first jobs.

What factors affect the organization-choice decision? A number of researchers have found that more educated persons know the labor market better, have higher expectations of work, and find organizations that pay more and more stable employment.[17] Although much of the research suggests that this decision is fairly rational, the more careful studies indicate that the decision is also influenced by unconscious processes, chance, and luck.[18] Whether one seeks a job at all or how hard one looks depends partly on the availability of unemployment insurance (see Chapter 13).

Some studies have indicated that the organizational choice tends to be correlated with single factors. One study found blue-collar workers took the highest paying jobs;[19] another found workers trying to match multiple needs with multiple job characteristics;[20] and a third found the approach varied by personality differences.[21]

A number of studies have examined the job-choice patterns of college and graduate students, often focusing solely on the rational aspects of the choice. One stream of research sees the students consciously trying to match their need satisfactions in the job choice.[22] Peer Soelberg found a pattern among students of matching needs but always getting a comparative final offer before accepting their preferred job.[23] In separate studies I found that decision makers use a variety of choice patterns, and the recruiter is a crucial influencer in the process.[24] Another study found that differences in job-choice patterns vary with personality differences.[25] Obviously, organizational image affects this choice too.

In sum, enterprises need to seek additional workers to meet their people resource shortages, while people are looking for jobs to satisfy their wants and needs. How you yourself should seek a job is described in the appendix to this chapter. The rest of the chapter is concerned with how an enterprise actively seeks to attract job-seekers. This personnel activity is called recruiting.

WHO DOES THE RECRUITING?

Assume that employment planning has been completed. The enterprise has decided that a certain number of outsiders must be recruited, and the specifications for the jobs to be filled are understood. In larger enterprises, sometimes this process is formalized by authorizations; that is, a budget is prepared showing the maximum number of people to be recruited and the maximum salary that can be paid.

Who does the recruiting? In larger enterprises, the personnel department; the branch of the department with this responsibility is called the employment office or department. It is staffed by recruiters, interviewers, and clerical persons. This group also does the preliminary selection, as will be described in Chapter 7. Employment offices are specialized units which provide a place to which applicants can apply. It conducts the recruiting both at the work site and away from it.

In smaller enterprises, multipurpose personnel people do the recruiting, along with their other duties, or operating managers may take time to recruit and interview applicants. Sometimes, the enterprise puts together a recruiting committee of operating and personnel managers.

The role of recruiter is very important. The recruiter is usually the first person from the enterprise that an applicant away from the work site meets. Applicants' impressions about the enterprise are based to a large degree on their encounter with the recruiter; effective recruiter behavior is described later in the chapter as an aspect of college recruiting.

If the applicant applies in person at the work site, those in the employment office serve a similar purpose. This initial meeting might be called the reception phase of employment. The applicant is greeted, supplied with an application blank, and perhaps given some information on present hiring conditions and the enterprise as a place to work. If the applicant is treated indifferently or rudely at this phase, he or she can form a lasting poor impression of the workplace. The reception phase is a great deal like the initial contact a salesperson makes to a prospective customer. All applicants are potential employees, as well as clients for the enterprise's services or products. Therefore, it is vital that those who greet and process applicants (in person or by phone) be well trained in communication techniques and interpersonal skills. They should enjoy meeting the public and helping people in stressful conditions, for job-seeking can be a difficult experience for many applicants.

SOURCES OF RECRUITS

Once the enterprise has decided it needs additional employees, it is faced with two recruiting decisions: where to search (sources) and how to notify applicants of the positions (methods).

Two sources of applicants could be used: internal (present employees), and external (those not presently affiliated with the enterprise).

Exhibit 6–6 illustrates many of the sources of recruits. If the shortage is for higher level employees, and assuming the enterprise approves of promoting from within, it will use the skills inventories to search for candidates (see Chapter 5). But personnel managers may not be aware of all employees who want to be considered for promotion, so they use an approach called job posting and bidding.[26] In the job-posting system, the enterprise notifies its present employees of openings, using bulletin boards, company publications and so on. About 25 percent of white-collar firms surveyed used the system, as did most large Minnesota firms. Most firms found the system useful; for example, the Bank of Virginia filled 18 percent of its openings as a result of job posting.[27]

Dave Dahl and Patrick Pinto provide a useful set of guidelines[28] for effective job-posting systems:

Post all permanent promotion and transfer opportunities.

Post the jobs for about one week prior to recruiting outside the enterprise.

Eligibility rules should be clarified. For example, minimum service in the present position might be specified as six months. And seniority may be the decision rule used to choose between several equally qualified applicants.

Job specifications should be listed. Application forms should be available.

All applicant should find out what happened in the choice.

If the labor shortage is short term or a great amount of additional work is not necessary, the organization can use inside moonlighting. It could offer

EXHIBIT 6–6
Sources for recruiting various types of employees

Sources	Blue-collar	Gray-collar	White-collar	Managerial, technical, professional
Internal				
Job posting and bidding	X	X	X	
Friends of present employees	X	X	X	
Skills inventories	X	X	X	X
External				
Walk-ins	X	X	X	
Agencies				
Temporary help			X	
Private employment agencies			X	
Public employment agencies	X	X	X	
Executive search firms				X
Schools				
High school	X	X	X	
Vocational/technical	X	X	X	X
College and universities				X
Other				
Unions	X			
Professional associations				X
Military services	X			X
Former employees	X	X	X	X

to pay bonuses of various types to people not on a time payroll; overtime procedures are already developed for those on time payrolls.

Before going outside to recruit, many organizations ask present employees to encourage friends or relatives to apply. Some equal employment opportunities programs prohibit this, however. In his study of the job-search behavior of 1,500 men, Ornstein found that 23 percent of white and 29 percent of black men found their first jobs through friends, and 31 percent of both whites and blacks found their jobs through help of the family.[29] These are *first* jobs; there presently are no data on what percentage of applicants for later jobs use these sources. These data indicate how powerful this source of recruits could be for enterprises, should they use it wisely.

Exhibit 6–6 also indicates a number of external sources of recruits and which sources supply applicants for various types of jobs. When an enterprise has exhausted internal sources, these sources are used. Studies indicating when each external source is used are not extensive.

The most fruitful of the outside sources is walk-ins; Ornstein found that one third of his sample found their first jobs that way. Private employment agencies place some white-collar employees and serve as a source of recruits for many employers.[30] Counselors in schools and teachers can also help, usually for managerial, professional, technical, and white-collar employees.[31] The state employment security offices, partially using federal funds, have tried to serve more applicants and enterprise needs, but these agencies still provide primarily blue-collar, gray-collar, and only a few white-collar applicants. They try to tie into school counseling services, too. Still most studies, including a recent one of state employment services by the General Accounting Office, are very critical of the costs and benefits of the state agencies.[32] They just do not help employees or applicants much.

Thus, even though there appear to be many sources from which employees can be recruited, employers use only a few to recruit each type of employee. Much more research is needed to explain why these patterns of sources prevail.

METHODS OF RECRUITING

A number of methods can be used to recruit external applicants; advertising, personal recruiting, computerized matching services, special-event recruiting, and summer internships are discussed here. There is also a separate section on college recruitment of potential managers and professionals.

To decide which method to use, the organization should know which are most likely to attract potential employees. Relatively few studies of the job-seeking helps used by applicants have been made.[33]

Media advertisements

Organizations advertise to sell their products or services—the outputs of the organization. They also advertise to acquire human inputs. Various media are used, the most common of which are the daily newspaper help-wanted ads. Organizations also advertise for people in trade and professional publications. Other media used are billboards, subway and bus cards, radio, telephone, and television. Some job-seekers do a reverse twist; they advertise for a situation wanted and reward anyone who tips them off about a job.

An example of an innovative recruiting ad is one used to staff Halls Crown Shopping Center, in Kansas City, a full-page ad in the Sunday *Kansas City Star.* This ad is reproduced in the accompanying box. Note how it disassociates the center from seeking clerks and attempts to recruit persons whose interests are likely to affect performance.

THIS IS A WANT AD

What we want is a show of hands from you out there who would be interested in pursuing your personal pastimes . . . and getting paid for it.

For instance: are you a sports nut, a music buff, an antique collector, a candle-dipper, a Canoe Clubber, a shutterbug, a rock hound or a stargazer? If so, a very satisfying career awaits you on our Leisure-Lifestyle Level.

Or, do you have a personal passion for fabrics, jewels, furs, fine art, furniture, designer fashions? We think you could find happiness working on our Gracious-Lifestyle Level.

Or, are you a here-and-now type who loves the passing parade of things that are fun and topical, whether that means horoscopes or exciting new fashions? Then you'd never tire of your job on our New-Lifestyle Level.

Mind you, we're not looking for sales clerks. (If we were, we'd advertise in the Classified Section.) What we're seeking is people with a deep personal interest in all the exciting lifestyle concepts we'll be introducing at Halls Crown Center. The way we have it figured, nobody is better qualified to sell telescopes all day than the guy or gal who spends evenings stargazing. And nobody will be happier with the job.

Even if dealing with customers isn't your thing, come see us if you're interested in quality merchandising and all that goes with it. We need attendants, markers, receivers, packers wrappers, handlers, finishers, fitters. In short, you can find an especially rewarding career at Halls Crown Center, whether or not you're interested in selling.

Make sense to you? Then come tell us your dream . . . and we'll show you ours.

Apply Now to Our Interviewing Office
Open 8:30 to 5:30, Monday through Friday

The major considerations in the use of media other than want ads are cost, the number of employees needed, and the time available to recruit them. Newspapers tend to be the cheapest method, followed by telephone, radio, billboards, and television. But cost is a relative thing. A small electronics firm tried an innovative method of recruiting in Southern California a few years ago, as reported by the American Management Association:

President W. E. Trantham, Jr., explains that the company's budget didn't permit it to make a big splash in the newspapers, where its ads would be lost among the multiple-page spreads of the large companies. "I checked with my agency," says Trantham. "We compared notes, and we agreed that the competition hadn't used radio effectively. I told them to prepare an effective radio campaign and to select the best stations to reach men in their cars during the peak traffic hours."

The real hook was the "Tasker Instant Interviewer": A direct telephone line to the engineering manager's office was installed, and engineers were invited in the radio spots to call in and talk directly to a Tasker engineer to learn more about the company and the opportunities offered. About half of the engineers who called passed the initial screening, and the company was able to fill its quota of specialists at salaries up to $23,000 per year. They saved on average $1,800 per engineer in recruiting costs this way.

Additional benefits from the campaign: Production and clerical workers appeared seeking jobs because they had "heard of Tasker on the radio," and recruitment costs of 305 production and administrative personnel during 1967 averaged slightly over seven dollars per worker. Businessmen and suppliers also remember the company's name from the radio spots—and workers are pleased that they no longer have to explain to friends who, what, or where Tasker is.

The Wall Street Journal recently reported:

Recorded want ads will be used by 40 companies recruiting engineers and scientists at a New York City convention next week. At a special recruiting center, job-hunters will be able to pick up a telephone and hear a three-minute taped recruiting message covering job description and company contract.

Each of these methods can be evaluated in the way advertising is evaluated in marketing and media research cost/benefit terms. The ads must be carefully prepared, media chosen, coded for media study, and impact analyzed afterwards. If the organization name is not used and a box number is substituted, the impact may not be as great, but if the name is used too many applicants may appear, and screening procedures for too many people can be costly. This is a difficult decision to make in preparing recruitment advertisements.[34]

In addition, the ad must not violate EEO requirements by indicating preferences in the ad for a particular racial, religious, national origin, or sex group. Researchers who designed an experiment to see if recruiting advertising encouraged discrimination in employment found that sex-based ads did discourage members of the other sex from applying for a job designed to be performed by members of a particular sex.[35]

Use of recruiters

Some organizations use recruiters or scouts who search the schools (like the ball diamonds) for new talent. Recruiters can be ineffective as screeners of good applicants if they use stereotypes in screening or are more influenced by recent interviews than earlier ones.[36] This will be made more clear in the discussion of college recruiters in this chapter and the problems of interviewing in Chapter 7.

Computer matching services

Systems similar to the computer dating services that flourished a few years ago have been developed to match people desiring jobs and organizations needing people. These amount to extraorganizational skills inventories, and they are a natural use of the computer.[37] The U.S. Employment Service's Job Bank is attempting to fill the need for a nationwide job-matching network to reduce unemployment. In addition to this government service, there are several private-sector systems (GRAD, IRIS, PICS) and the Department of Labor's LINCS.

Little is known about these systems in practice, but they seem to have potential use for specifically qualified jobs. I doubt they will be effective at managerial levels, however.

Special-event recruiting

When the supply of employees available is not large or when the organization is new or not well known, some organizations have successfully used special events to attract potential employees. They may stage open houses, schedule headquarters visits, provide literature, and advertise these events in appropriate media. To attract professionals, organizations they may have hospitality suites at professional meetings. Executives also make speeches at association meetings or schools to get the organization's image across. Ford Motor Company conducted symposia on college campuses and sponsored cultural events to attract attention to its qualifications as a good employer.

One of the most interesting approaches is to promote job fairs and native daughter and son days. A group of firms sponsors a meeting or exhibition at which each has a booth to publicize jobs available. Some experts claim recruiting costs have been cut 80 percent using these methods. They may be scheduled on holidays to reach college students home at that time or to give the presently employed a chance to look around. This technique is especially useful for smaller, less well-known employers. It appeals to jobseekers who wish to locate in a particular area and those wanting to minimize travel and interview time.

Summer internships

Another approach to recruiting and getting specialized work done that has been tried by many organizations is to hire college students during the summer as interns. These have been used by businesses (Sherwin-Williams Company, Chase Manhattan Bank, Standard Oil Company of Ohio, Kaiser Aluminum, First National City Bank), government agencies (City of New York), and hospitals. Students in accredited graduate hospital programs, for example, serve a summer period called a preceptorship. Pay is from $100 per week up.

There are a number of purposes for these programs. They allow organizations to get specific projects done, expose them to talented potential employees who may become their ambassadors on campus, and provide trial-run employment to determine if they want to hire particular people full-time. The *Wall Street Journal* has reported that some firms are using this technique to help recruit women and blacks.

From the college student's point of view, the summer internship means a job with pay, some experience in the world of work, a possible future job, and a chance to use the talents he has in a realistic environment. In a way, it is a short form of some co-op college work and study programs.

The organization usually provides supervision and a choice of projects to be done. Some of the projects the City of New York's interns worked on during one summer were snow emergency planning, complaint handling, attitude survey of lower level employees, and information dissemination.[38]

There are costs to these programs, of course. Sometimes the interns take up a lot of supervisory time, and the work done is not always the best. But the major problem some organizations have encountered concerns the expectations of students. Some college students expect everything to be perfect at work. When it is not, they get down on the organization they worked for, assuming that it is more messed up than others in the field. Such disillusioned students become reverse ambassadors. This effect has caused some organizations to drop the programs, and others did so when they found they were not able to recruit many interns.

There is no reason these programs could not be used for noncollege students as well, but there is little or nothing about this approach in the literature. In my opinion, the programs are costly in salaries and supervisory costs and provide rather illusory benefits to the organization, but they are of real value to the students. Socially responsible firms may wish to try them on a small-scale, experimental basis.

COLLEGE RECRUITING

Many of you reading this section will be interested in learning how to improve your chances at getting a job; that's why an appendix to this chapter is provided on this subject. This section looks at college recruiting from the point of view of the enterprise. You will learn a lot about the job situation by knowing what goes on on the recruiter's side of the desk. Mary Kale, a recruiter for Bethlehem Steel,[39] has a recruiting day like this:

Mary Kale is 28 and has been with Bethlehem for 7 years. She was a metallurgist for two years and has been a recruiter for five. In 1976, she recruited 26 of the 106 persons Bethlehem hired and has a high acceptance rate among her recruits. She is one of the 3,500 full-time recruiters in the United States today.

Two recent weeks are typical of her work life. One week she interviewed for five days at Cornell; she had to drive three hours through a snow squall to get there. The next week, she flew and drove on Sunday to Grove City to interview there Monday. She drove to Youngstown, Ohio, and interviewed there Tuesday, then drove back to Pittsburgh. Wednesday and Thursday she interviewed at Carnegie Mellon and other Pittsburgh schools. Friday was spent in a hotel interviewing.

What's her day like? She eats an early breakfast and begins interviewing at 9 A.M. She interviews candidates for 30 minutes each, takes a 30-minute walk instead of lunch, and resumes interviews until 5:30 P.M. In brief open periods she tries to line up other candidates, but typically she interviews 54 people a week. After a quick supper, she spends the evening in her hotel room writing reports on the day's recruits, calling recruit prospects for later interviews, and reading the resumés of the next day's prospects.

In each interview, she begins by putting the recruit at ease, then asks the recruit about himself or herself. Next she discusses the job requirements and what the company has to offer, and asks for questions. She sees herself as much as a job counselor as recruiter. She wants to help recruits find a direction for their lives, and also to acquire the best employees for Bethlehem.

So if, when you are interviewed, you suspect the recruiter is tired, usually he or she is. Recruiters do not want prospects to have a stressful experience; rather they see a mutually satisfactory interview as a first step in your organizational choice.

The college recruiting process

The college recruiting process is modeled in Exhibit 6–7. The process is similar in some ways to other recruiting, but in college recruiting the organization sends an employee, usually called a recruiter, to the campus to interview candidates and describe the organization to them. Coinciding with the visit, brochures and other literature about the organization are often distributed. This literature is customarily expensively designed and produced, but much of it is poorly written and includes the wrong materials for recruiting purposes.[40] Organizations may also run ads to attract students or conduct seminars at which company executives talk about various facets of the organization.

In the typical procedure, those seeking employment register at the college placement service. The placement service is a labor market exchange providing opportunities for students and employers to meet and discuss potential hiring. During the recruiting season (from about mid-October to mid-March), candidates are advised through student newspapers, mailings, bulletin boards, and so forth of scheduled visits. At the placement service, they book preliminary interviews with employers they want to see and are given brochures and other literature about the firms. After the preliminary interviews and before leaving the campus, each recruiter invites the chosen candidates to make a site visit at a later date. Those lower on the list are told they are being considered and are called upon if students chosen first decide not to accept employment with the firm.

Students who are invited to the site are given more job information and meet appropriate potential supervisors and other executives. They are entertained and may be given a series of psychological tests as well. The organization bears all expenses. If the organization desires to hire an individual,

EXHIBIT 6–7
The college recruiting process

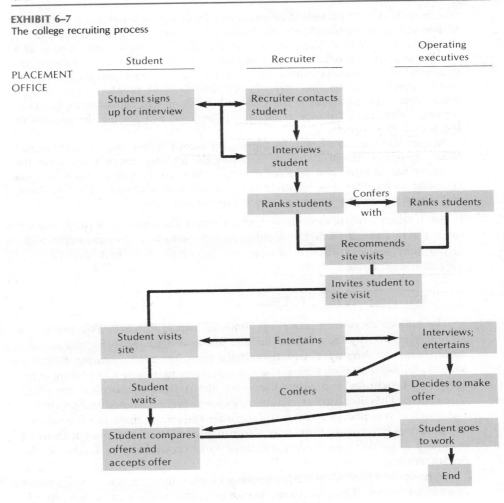

he or she is given an offer prior to leaving the site or shortly thereafter by mail or phone. Some bargaining may take place on salary and benefits, depending on the current labor market. The candidate then decides whether to accept or reject the offer.

Data have been gathered by various services to improve the operation of this specialized labor market. The former placement director of Northwestern University, Dr. Frank Endicott, gathers data about the job market each year for publication in general business journals. Information is collected on the number of job vacancies by various categories and the number of students seeking employment by category. Endicott also compiles data on current average salary and benefits offers and their range for different types of students, including comparisons with prior years. A. C. Nielsen, an advertising and market research firm, has surveyed job applicants by questionnaires to be completed after job interviews which indicate applicants' evaluations of the various companies and details of what the applicants regard as desirable job characteristics.

The decision to sign up for an interview

Several studies have been made of why college students choose to have interviews with organizations. Nancy Ingram and Donald Hunt examined choice as related to organization climate or image over ten years for several thousand students at the University of Detroit. Students were asked what influenced them to take an interview with a particular company. Frequently mentioned influences were: placement office notices, company literature, contact with company employees, and other students.[41] Another study by Orlando Behling and Henry Rodkin analyzed the questionnaires filled out by 17,000 students in 1968 in the A. C. Nielsen survey described above, using methods similar to those used by Ingram and Hunt.[42] Quite different results were found, but the times and questions considered also differed. These researchers found that the most important reasons for interviewing a company were type of work done by company (60–75 percent) and company reputation (30–50 percent), and these additional reasons were also cited: possibilities of avoiding the draft, size of company, opportunity for travel, fringe benefits, and location. Results differed by college major and level of degree. Behling and Rodkin drew these conclusions from a number of studies they surveyed on the topic:

> The nature of work done by the organization is important in the choice of which firms to interview.
>
> Some organizations could do a better recruiting job if their names (and therefore images) accurately reflected what they do.

It has always seemed to me that meaningless names like ABC Incorporated and dull-sounding names like Podunk Septic Tank and Sludge Pump, Inc., turn students off. I studied how 50 graduating seniors made their choices over a semester's period.[43] It was assumed that there would be wide differences in what each preferred; some would be more money oriented, others would prefer certain locations or types of company. My interest was: How do students actually make the decision to interview certain firms, and who influences them? I found three approaches were followed:

1. *Maximizers.* These students assumed there was a big, wide, differentiated world out there. They almost all had had some work experience. So they took as many job interviews as they could, got as many offers as they could, and rationally chose the best one, based on what they were looking for.

2. *Satisficers.* These students had no choice or did not feel a choice was important. They got one offer and took the first one. They tended to be inexperienced and to believe that one company was about the same as any other.

3. *Validators.* These students were in between. They would get an offer (their favorite), get one more just to see if their favorite was a good one, and then take the favorite one.

The sample was roughly equally divided among the three approaches. Students studied were business and engineering students, however. My guess is that in other majors (arts and science) there would be more satisficers. Thomas Gutteridge and Joseph Ullman studied MBA job-search behavior and found that those who followed the maximizer choice pattern got higher salary offers, held their first jobs longer, and had more job satisfaction.[44]

The job-choice decision

It is also of interest to determine who or what (if anyone or anything) influences an applicant to accept one rather than another job offer. Knowledge of this would help recruiters know how to influence a student to accept the jobs they offer.

Various persons are said to influence the student as a job decision maker, including peers, family, and wife or husband or campanion. Some studies conclude that the father is a very strong influence, as are executives and professors the student knows. Companies hope their recruiters, executives met on site visits, literature, and advertisements will affect the decision favorably.

My studies also analyzed the sources students said would influence them prior to their interviews and the interview data during and after the interview. I concluded that the recruiter and company employees met on the site visit and company literature given at the time of interview are the major influences on this decision. The spouse may be consulted about the location, and if the father is considered knowledgeable, he may be asked to validate but not to make the decision.

The effective recruiter

In recruiting, generally three elements are involved: the organization, the applicant, and the intervening variable—the recruiter. The recruiter is the filter and the matcher, the one who is actually seen by the applicants and is studied as a representative of the company. The recruiter is not just an employee but is viewed as an example of the kind of person the organization employs and wants in the future.

One study indicates that recruiters have a tough job: Accounting students tended not to believe company advertising or recruiter's statements, but trusted the statements of their professors and present and past company employees.[45]

Certain personal characteristics are preferred in recruiters by students. The students I studied tended to prefer recruiters who are middle-aged (between 35 and 55 years old). Most students felt that persons over 55 do not understand them, but those under 30 were not well regarded. Often they considered it a ploy of the organization to send a 23-year-old alumnus as an interviewer because it seemed obvious that the recruiter did not have the experience to answer their questions. They also liked it if the recruiter had had work experience in their specialities and some personal knowledge of the university they were visiting.[46]

The students also had preferences for behavior during the recruiting interview. Characteristics in the recruiter the students wanted most were friendliness, knowledge, personal interest in the applicant, and truthfulness. Secondarily, some applicants (usually average students) preferred enthusiastic and convincing communicators.

Major flaws students found in typical recruiters were:

1. *Lack of interest in the applicant.* They inferred this if the recruiter was mechanical in his presentation—bureaucratic—programmed. One student said, "The company might just as well have sent a tape recorder as him." A study of 112 students also found that recruits accepted offers from recruiters who showed interest and concern for them as individuals.[47]

2. *Lack of enthusiasm.* If the recruiter seemed bored the students inferred it was a dull and uninteresting company.

3. *Stress or too-personal interviews.* The students resented too many personal questions about their social class, their parents, and so forth. They wanted to be evaluated for their own accomplishments. They also unanimously rejected stress or sarcastic interviewing styles.

4. *Time allocation by recruiters.* The final criticism of recruiters had to do with how much time they talked and how much they let the applicant talk or ask questions. From the point of view of the applicant, much of the recruiter's time was wasted with a long canned history of the company, number of employees, branches, products, assets, pension plans, and so forth. Many of the questions the recruiter asked the applicant were answered on the application blank, anyway.

These findings reemphasize the need for organizations engaged in college recruiting to train effective recruiters and to have a well-planned visitation schedule. Too many organizations do not plan the recruiting interview as well as they do their product sales presentations. The recruiter normally has 30 minutes per interview; he should use them well. The applicant should receive printed material describing the less interesting aspects of information (such as organization history and details of organization operations). The interview period should be divided about equally between the recruiter and the applicant. Students want to hear about the job itself, the work climate, and the kind of person the organization is trying to hire for the job. Then they would like to be able to discuss how they might fit in and to ask a few questions. Too often, the recruiter talks for 25 minutes and almost as an afterthought asks if there are any questions.

It is also important for recruiters to provide realistic expectations of the job. When they do so, there is significantly lower turnover of new employees,[48] and the same number of people apply. Researchers have found that most recruiters give general, glowing descriptions of the company rather than balanced or truthful presentations.[49]

Methods for training recruiters have been devised. The College Placement Council, the American Management Association, regional college placement associations, university placement directors, personnel consulting firms, and others have available good short but intensive courses on recruiting and interviewing for both inexperienced and experienced interviewers. Recently, programmed learning courses, which are relatively inexpensive and can be effective if they are followed by practice sessions, have also become available.

A new approach to training both effective recruiters and students being recruited is reported by T. Higham, who claims that the number of applicants increased, turnover dropped 50 percent, and there was an acceptance rate of 65 percent of applicants after his training program began.[50] It is a reciprocal approach in which:

> The applicants see videotapes of prior recruit interviews, some of which were prepared for and others with recruits who "wing" the interview.
>
> Recruits are given forms to help them do a self-analysis of their skills, interests, temperament, and so on.
>
> Recruits are told what the interviewer will want to know, what to wear to the interview, and how to cope with nervousness.
>
> Recruits are told to form impressions of the company which they can check out later.
>
> The company issues statements to recruits about work. These statements are supplemented by an account of a typical day or week.

Companies that wish to influence applicants should also review their recruiting literature to make sure it appeals to the most successful students. This literature, plus advertisements and articles in trade publications, is the main nonhuman influence on the organization-choice decision.

COST/BENEFIT ANALYSIS OF RECRUITING

Many aspects of recruitment, such as the effectiveness of recruiters, can be evaluated. Enterprises assign goals to recruiting by types of employees. For example, a goal for a recruiter might be to hire 350 unskilled and semis-killed employees, or 100 technicians, or 100 managerial employees per year. Then the organization can decide who are the best recruiters, perhaps those who meet or exceed quotas and those whose recruits stay with the organization and are evaluated well by their superiors.

Sources of recruits also can be evaluated. In college recruiting, the organization can divide the number of job acceptances by the number of campus interviews to compute the cost per hire at each college. Then it drops from the list campuses that are not productive.

The methods of recruiting can be evaluated by various means; Exhibit 6–8 compares the results of a number of them. The enterprise can calculate

EXHIBIT 6–8
Yields of recruiting methods by various calculations

Source of recruit	Yield	Total yield (percent)	Ratio of acceptance to receipt of resumé	Ratio of acceptance to offer
Write-ins	2,127	34.77%	6.40	58.37
Advertising	1,979	32.35	1.16	38.98
Agencies	856	14.00	1.99	32.07
Direct college placement	465	7.60	1.50	13.21
Internal company	447	7.30	10.07	65.22
Walk-ins	134	2.19	5.97	57.14
Employee referrals	109	1.78	8.26	81.82

Source: Roger Hawk, *The Recruitment Function* (New York: American Management Association, 1967).

the cost of each method (such as advertising) and divide it by the benefits it yields (acceptances of offers).[51]

SUMMARY, CONCLUSIONS, AND RECOMMENDATIONS

This chapter has demonstrated the process whereby enterprises recruit additional employees, suggested the importance of recruiting, and shown who recruits, where, and how. A series of propositions about recruiting can be specified as a form of summary.

Proposition 6.1. The lower the unemployment in the relevant sector of the labor market, the more likely effective organizations are to use formal recruiting methods and multiple sources.

Proposition 6.2. The less known the organization is to relevant applicants, the harder it must work to recruit in times of lower unemployment.

Proposition 6.3. The worse the job or organizational image, the harder the organization must work to recruit added employees.

Proposition 6.4 The higher the level of the job, the larger the geographic area from which the organization must recruit.

Proposition 6.5. The worse the job or organizational image and the lower the unemployment, the harder the organization must work to recruit and the more of its preferences it must relax or the more it must improve the employment conditions offered.

Proposition 6.6. The better the job of recruiting and matching employee to job, the lower will be employee turnover and the greater will be employee satisfaction and organizational effectiveness.

Proposition 6.7 The larger the organization, the more extensively planned and evaluated will be its recruiting functions.

Harder work at recruiting means the use of more sources of supply, more media, and larger expenditures for each medium. If times are bad (high

EXHIBIT 6–9
Recommendation on recruiting practices for model organizations

Type of organization	Employment conditions affect recruiting		Importance of image		Methods of recruiting								
	Greatly	Little	Crucial	Not too important	Employment agencies	Newspaper ads	Ratio commercials	Television commercials	Present employees	Computer matching	Special events	College recruiting	Summer internships
1. Large size, low complexity, high stability	X			X	X	X				X		X	X
2. Medium size, low complexity, high stability		X		X	X	X			X	X		X	
3. Small size, low complexity, high stability	X		X		X	X	X		X		X		
4. Medium size, moderate complexity, moderate stability		X	X		X	X	X		X	X	X	X	
5. Large size, high complexity, low stability		X		X	X	X		X		X		X	X
6. Medium size, high complexity, low stability		X	X		X	X	X		X		X	X	
7. Small size, high complexity, low stability	X		X		X	X	X		X		X		X

unemployment), the reverse of Propositions 6.3 and 6.5 will be true. Chapter 18 describes recruiting methods most appropriate for disadvantaged employees, in response to EEO pressures.

Likely approaches used by the seven model organizations specified in Exhibit 1–14 (Chapter 1) are summarized in Exhibit 6–9. It should be noted that several of the model organizations employ different categories of employees. For example, a small, volatile hospital and a small, volatile toy company employ different kinds of employees, and the sources of recruits used would vary in such organizations. Only a few of the aspects of recruitment have been summarized in this table.

Top management's policy decisions can affect the success of the recruiting. These include:

The establishment and maintenance of an organizational image to attract good recruits.

The establishment of policies which deal with the issue of recruitment only at entry level. Is promotion *always* from within, or is that simply the predominant policy?

Top management must decide whether it wishes to adjust job offers to market conditions or to consider only internal conditions.

The setting of these policies by top management, in consultation with the personnel department, will make recruiting more effective.

Recruiting part-timers is much more informal than recruiting full-time employees. Either the enterprise uses temporary help agencies or it relies on walk-ins or possibly runs want ads for them.

There are some significant ethical issues in recruiting, for both the enterprise and the applicant. For the enterprise, it is ethical (and effective) to tell the truth about the job and its characteristics, rewards, and problems. It is ethical to keep the applicant informed on his status and potential chances for employment. The employer must actually recruit minorities and other protected groups; it is unethical (and illegal) to just go through the motions with no intention of hiring them. If the employer has a policy to recruit from within first, they should actually do so, or change the policy.

For the applicant, it is unethical to be dishonest with employers about the seriousness of intentions to work for the enterprise. Accepting trips to sites just to travel, with little or no intention of working there, is unethical.

The appendix to this chapter is aimed at helping you be more skillful in finding a job. Chapter 7 describes how enterprises select "the best" of the recruits for the job.

APPENDIX: HOW TO GET A JOB

This appendix is designed to help you extract some information from Chapters 6 and 8 and other material which will give you some advice on how to go about seeking employment as a manager, professional, or technician. It analyses your job preferences and needs; briefly mentions the factors in the personnel environment, makes some comments on job sources; and shows how to plan your job campaign.

You: Career planning and job preferences

Before you can be effective as a job-seeker and job occupant, you must know what you are looking for. This helps you seek a job effectively and to answer recruiter questions honestly.

B. Greco has modeled the process of looking for a job[52] (see Exhibit 6–10). Your first job choice is part of your career objectives. Do you see this job as the first of a chain of jobs with this company? Or is this just a job to get experience before you start your own business? More is said about this and Steps 5 and 6 in Chapter 8.

As far as Step 4 is concerned, there are several questions you need to answer. I believe these questions are:

Questions about Me

1. How hard do I like to work?
2. Do I like to be my own boss, or would I rather work for someone else?
3. Do I like to work alone, with a few others, or with large groups?
4. Do I like work at an even pace or in bursts of energy?
5. Does location matter? Do I want to work near home? In warmer climates? In ski country? Am I willing to be mobile?
6. How much money do I want? Am I willing to work for less money but in a more interesting job?

EXHIBIT 6–10
Career decision strategy

STEP 1. Realize that you're looking for a career objective and the sequence of jobs you'll use to achieve it

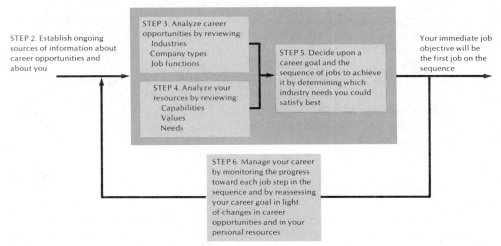

STEP 2. Establish ongoing sources of information about career opportunities and about you

STEP 3. Analyze career opportunities by reviewing:
Industries
Company types
Job functions

STEP 4. Analyze your resources by reviewing:
Capabilities
Values
Needs

STEP 5. Decide upon a career goal and the sequence of jobs to achieve it by determining which industry needs you could satisfy best

Your immediate job objective will be the first job on the sequence

STEP 6. Manage your career by monitoring the progress toward each job step in the sequence and by reassessing your career goal in light of changes in career opportunities and in your personal resources

Source: B. Greco, *How to Get a Job That's Right for You* (Homewood, Ill.: Dow Jones–Irwin, 1975).

7. Do I like to work in one place or many, indoors or outdoors?
8. How much variety do I want in work?

Questions of this type are almost unlimited. What you must do first is rank them in importance so you know the tradeoffs between them. You *will not* find a job with *all* the characteristics you choose.

Now here is a set of questions about the potential employers (Step 3):

1. Do I have a size preference: small, medium, or large, or no size preference?
2. Do I have a sector preference (private, not for profit, public sector)?
3. What kinds of industries interest me? This is usually based on interests in company products or services. Do I prefer mechanical objects or counseling people? This is a crucial question.
4. Have I checked to make sure that the sector or product or service has a good future and will lead to growth in opportunity?

At this point, you may have determined, for example, that what you really want is a job near home, in a small firm in the toy industry, that you can buy out some day.

Answers to these questions will help you narrow the list of potential employers to a reasonable size.

Step 4 involves preparing a list of your comparative advantages to help sell yourself to the employers you have chosen. A sample list is:

My advantages are as follows:

Education
 Grades
 Kind of courses
 Skills developed

Experience
 Variety
 Relevance to company
 Amount
 Skills developed

Personality and personal characteritics
 Interpersonal skills
 Conscientious, ambitious
 Leadership skill

Contacts with company
 Businessmen
 Bankers
 Professors

Recognizing the factors in the environment

As discussed in Chapter 6, four factors in the personnel environment affect your job-seeking behavior. The first is the labor market. If jobs are scarce, you will have to start looking earlier and look harder (take more interviews, etc.). You must be willing to compromise on your expectations if you do not want to get in the unemployment line.

If you are not in a protected discrimination category, government restrictions may not help you. If you recognize that the organizational image limits some employers' lists of applicants, in tight times, you can apply to enterprises with bad images first (see Chapter 6 for clues).

Realize that in an enterprise where the policy is to promote from within, you can only get an entry-level job. If the firm or group has an open employment policy, you can apply at any level.

Your job sources

Next, you want to use as many sources of jobs and job information as you can. And you want to use the right sources. You are unlikely to get a job at the public employment service, for example. Some of the sources you should use include:

Newspapers and professional publications. Read the media ads for the type of job you want, and read the professional publications and newspapers in the area you have selected. *The Wall Street Journal* and *The New York Times* are examples of where to look. Respond to ads that sound interesting.

College placement offices. These offices have some job information, and they are the place where recruiters offer job interviews. Get to know the placement office people and sign up for all interviews that sound interesting and can work into your schedule.

Professional associations. Many professional associations provide job placement services. Get your name in the placement application file. Job ads are run in there publications, too.

Private employment agencies and executive search firms. Another source of jobs is the private employment agency. Generally, you should visit with them and bring a resumé. They charge a fee, often payable by the employer, but sometimes payable by you. The fee can be as much as 15 percent of the first year's salary. Executive search firms tend to recruit middle managers and up (salaries in the $17,500 + range).

Some firms also offer resumé preparation and testing services and career counseling. They often charge up to $1,500, whether you get a job or not.

Personal contacts. One of the best sources of jobs is to contact people working for the enterprise or who have worked there in the past. Develop your contacts from as many sources as you can: parents, relatives, friends, fraternity brothers or sorority sisters, and so on. Some experts estimate that 80 percent of jobs is never advertized. Contacts get these jobs.

Direct mail. It is probably useless to mail unsolicited resumés to personnel offices without a personal approach. One way that works is to write a personalized letter to the personnel manager of the enterprise explaining why you are applying to them. Find out the manager's name. Specify your preferences and advantages in the letter and tell the manager you will call in ten days to two weeks for a job interview. Sitting back and waiting for an enterprise to come to you is not fruitful. Personalized, honest approaches like this work if the enterprise has a job that fits you.

Other less frequently used sources include job-finding clubs (for out-of-work, experienced persons) and computerized matching services. Other methods you can use are taking part in special recruiting events, applying for internships, and reading employment guides.

Your job search

Preparing a resumé. One of the first things you should do in initiating your job campaign is to prepare a resumé. A sample resumé by Thomas Sutteridge and Jerry Newman[53] is included as Exhibit 6–11.

Gutteridge and Newman provide these explanations of points on the resumé:

Personal: Only date of birth is really essential in this section. Marital status can be left off if you have strong feelings about this. Statements about health, weight, height, etc., are not necessary and should not be included.

Education: List most recent education first. Include educational experiences for which no degree was received (e.g., transfer), but don't include individual courses taken sporadically *unless* they are particularly relevant to a job opening. *Do not* include list of courses at MBA level or elsewhere because this consumes too much space. If you have completed an internship, include it here along with a description of the activities you pursued during the internship.

Work experience: Most recent first—reverse chronology. Don't include summer jobs unless: (1) they involved supervisory experience, HRM experience, self motivated suggestions which were adopted, or self employment of a responsible nature; (2) you have no other job experiences and you want to fill out a one page resumé by showing diversity of experience. In this case, stress experience which would indicate exposure to diverse environments and occupational groups. If you paid for your educational expenses through part-time and/or summer employment say so, e.g., earned x percent of educational expenses through part-time and summer jobs.

Special comments:
1. You want to include material which will help sell *you!* This is the most important criterion to use in deciding what to include on your resumé. If possible, the resumé should be restricted to one page, but if this requires that you delete important information, expand the resumé to two pages.
2. It is preferable to get copies offset or printed. Xerox and mimeographed copies look sloppy.
3. A special color page may catch an employer's eye. Its up to you. But don't use a loud color (e.g., purple, fluorescent orange, etc.)
4. Including a picture in one corner may help personalize the process and assist employers in remembering you; however, this is also optional. Your choice depends on whether you think a picture will be a positive factor in influencing an employer's decision to interview you.

Interview preparation. You need to prepare for interviews, as Higham suggested.[54] Go to your college media center and practice interviewing with

EXHIBIT 6–11
Sample resumé

John Q. Student
127 Quixmire Street
City, State Zip Code
(716) xxx–xxxx

PERSONAL DATA
    Date of birth—August 11, 19xx
    Marital status—Married, no children

CAREER OBJECTIVES
    If you have definite objectives include them here. If your objectives are, however,
    rather general or cover several areas, delete this section and, in a cover letter, tailor
    the discussion of your career objectives to the specific position you are applying for.

EDUCATION

19xx–19xx   School of Management
                                   State University of New York at Buffalo
                                   MBA (expected June 19xx)

                                   —Major area: Human Resources Management
                                   —Minor area: (if any)
                                   —Grade point average: (If you are proud of it, include
                                     it; otherwise delete.)
                                   —Honors: (cum laude, etc.)
                                   —Completed six credit internship in human resource man-
                                     agement-personnel area with the Carborundum Corpo-
                                     ration during Spring, 19xx. Internship activities included
                                     (list projects you worked on, subject of final paper and
                                     other relevant information).

19xx–19xx   Hartford College for Girls
                                   Hartford, Michigan
                                   BA in Sociology—June, 19xx

                                   —GPA (If included above, include here and vice versa.)
                                   —Honors

WORK EXPERIENCE

June 19xx—   Completed paid employment traineeship in personnel area
August 19xx   with Xerox Corporation, Rochester, New York. Duties in-
                                   cluded: stress projects you were involved in, topic of final
                                   paper and other relevant information.

June 19xx—   Jane Doe Manufacturing Company, Columbus, Ohio. Key
March 19xx   Press Operator. Duties included: Here you should stress
(if still on   supervision of others, involvement in HRM related activi-
job, put June   ties and any changes in operating procedures recom-
19xx—present)   mended by you and adopted by the company.

xxxx–xxxx   Repeat, same format as above.

EXTRACURRICULAR ACTIVITIES
    Should include non-paid positions which can not reasonably be "sold" as relevant
    work experience. Example: student body president, offices in any post—high school
    organization, memberships in professional organizations such as American Society of
    Personnel Administration.

HOBBIES
    Optional, of minor importance except to fill out a one-page resumé.

REFERENCES
    Furnished upon request.
    (Be sure you have individual's approval before giving name as reference. References
    should be secured before sending out first resumé.)

friends. Take turns as recruiter and applicant. Videotape the result, examine you responses, and work toward improvement. The recruiter can use some of the questions which Rosemary Gaymer suggests should be asked.[55]

Appearance is *very important.* Recruiters expect neat, clean appearances; men should wear a suit and tie, and women should show comparable formality. First impressions are vital. Researchers have found that recruiters do make negative decisions during the interview,[56] so you will want to present yourself confidently and competently.

Interview follow-up. Gutteridge gives this advice about interview follow-ups: Be sure to keep a record of your contacts. Immediately upon leaving the interview make the following notations:

- The name of the interviewer.
- The type of opportunity for which you were considered.
- Location of work.
- Your reaction and possible interest.
- *Your next action.*

Answers to invitations for visits. If you receive an invitation for a plant visit, Gutteridge suggests you acknowledge it in one of three ways:

1. Accept and set the date when you will be there.
2. Indicate your desire to accept at a later date if you need more time to consider.
3. Decline for whatever honest reason you have.

Follow-up to site visit. If you make a site visit, as soon as you return send a letter of thanks to the individual who issued the invitation, as well as to any others you believe should receive a special note of appreciation.

Replying to an offer. Offers of employment may be made verbally, by telegram, or by letter, the last two being the most usual means. If by telegram that indicates "reply collect," then do so by straight wire if answer is brief, or by night letter if answer is rather lengthy.

Again, there are innumerable ways of handling an offer. The quickest, naturally, is to accept. However, for every acceptance today, there are many rejections, and those involve some details. Most companies do not expect an immediate acceptance or rejection, but they do expect an acknowledgment. *Therefore, be sure to reply within three days* after receiving the offer, thanking them and stating a time when you will send definite word, provided they have not already specified a deadline date. If they have, send a letter of acknowledgment and indicate your final answer will be forthcoming by the specific time.

Delaying a final answer. The occasion might arise when you want a further extension of time from one previously agreed to. If so, send another letter and state quite frankly your reasons and request their indulgence. Remember always to keep in mind the employer's position as well as your own.

Accepting an offer. It is probably unnecessary to go into detail on how to accept an offer beyond the fact that an enthusiastic note of appreciation should be sent, together with an indication of when you will report for work. This latter point, of course, will be developed by mutual agreement.

Rejecting an offer. Letters of rejection should be sent just as soon as you realize you are definitely not interested in accepting. It is not necessary to state your exact reasons for turning down an offer, or to say where you expect to go, but it is courteous to express your sincere thanks for having been favorably considered. It is helpful for the organization to know what your true feelings are regarding them, such as preference for a different location, another type of product, or different initial training.[57]

QUESTIONS

1. What is recruiting? Job search?
2. How does recruiting relate to other personnel activities?
3. What are the most significant factors in the diagnostic model affecting recruiting?
4. Give some dos and dont's in recruiting interviews as far as legality is concerned.
5. Describe a model of the recruiting/attraction process. How do enterprise requirements, organizational policies, and organizational pay affect the process?
6. How might recruiting differ between the public and private sectors?
7. Discuss the relationship between organizational-choice and occupational-choice decisions. How are they similar and different?
8. Who is responsible for recruiting?
9. What sources of recruits do enterprises use for: blue-collar, white-collar, and managerial recruits?
10. Compare and contrast the effectiveness of the methods of recruiting, such as advertising, special events, internships, and others.
11. How do enterprises recruit college students for jobs? What are effective and ineffective recruiters like?
12. How do career planning and job preferences relate to effective job finding? Outline an approach to specify the job characteristics you want prior to job search.
13. Describe how you plan to get your job when you leave college.

NOTES AND REFERENCES

1. American Society of Personnel Administrators, *The Personnel Executive's Job* (Englewood Cliffs, N.J.: Prentice-Hall ASPA, 1977).

2. Robert Sibson, "The High Cost of Hiring," *Nation's Business,* February 1975, pp. 85–88.

3. Sandra Bem and Daryl Bem, "Does Sex Biased Job Advertising 'Aid and Abet' Sex Discrimination?" *Journal of Applied Psychology,* 1 (1973), pp. 6–18.

4. Stephen Cohen, "The Basis of Sex Bias in the Job Recruitment Situation," *Human Resource Management,* Fall 1976, pp. 8–10.

5. Paul Wernimont, "Recruitment Policies and Practices," in *Staffing Policies and Strategies,* vol. 1, ASPA Handbook of Personnel and Industrial Relations, ed. Dale Yoder and Herbert Heneman, Jr. (Washington, D.C.: Bureau of National Affairs, 1974).

6. Charles Hughes, "Help Wanted: Present Employees Please Apply," *Personnel,* July–August 1974, pp. 36–45.

7. G. R. Pieters et al., "Predicting Organizational Choice: A Post Hoc Analysis," *Proceedings,* 76th Annual Convention, American Psychological Association, pp. 573–74.

8. Robert N. McMurray, "Recruitment, Dependency, and Morale in the Banking Industry," *Administrative Science Quarterly,* June 1958, pp. 87–106.

9. C. R. Tatro and A. P. Garbin, "Industrial Prestige Hierarchy," *Journal of Vocational Behavior,* 3 (1973), pp. 383–91.

10. Anthony Avirgan, "Report on College Recruiting Problems," *Conference Board Record,* May 1967, pp. 272–81; Richard R. Hise and John K. Ryans, Jr., "Industry Image: Its Role in MBA Recruitment," *Personnel Journal,* May 1976, pp. 359–68; John Morgan, *Managing the Young Adult* (New York: American Management Association, 1967).

11. Jean J. Couturier, "The Model Public Personnel Administration Law: Two Views," *Public Personnel Review,* October 1971, pp. 202–9.

12. Anne Roe, *The Psychology of Occupations* (New York: John Wiley & Sons, 1956); John Holland, "Vocational Preferences," in Marvin Dunnette, *Handbook on Industrial and Organizational Psychology* (Chicago: Rand McNally & Co., 1976); Donald Super, "The Future of Vocational Development Theory," in *Perspectives in Vocational Development,* ed. J. M. Whitely (Washington, D.C.: American Personnel and Guidance Association, 1972); D. V. Tiedeman and R. P. O'Hara, *Career Development: Choice and Adjustment* (New York: College Entrance Examination Board, 1963).

13. S. Rottenberg, "On Choice in the Labor Markets," *Industrial and Labor Relations Review* 9, 2 (1965), pp. 183–99; Clark Kerr, "Labor Markets: Their Character and Consequences," *American Economic Review,* May 1950; Eli Ginzberg, et al., *Occupational Choice* (New York: Columbia University Press, 1951).

14. L. T. Keil et al., "Youth and Work: Problems and Perspectives," *Sociological Review* 14 (1966), pp. 117–37; Delbert Miller and William Form, *Industrial Sociology* (New York: Harper & Row, 1973); K. Robert, "The Entry into Employment," *Sociological Review* 2 (1968), pp. 165–84; M. Rosenberg, *Occupations and Values* (New York: Free Press, 1957).

15. Stuart Timperley, *Personnel Planning and Occupational Choice* (London: George Allen & Univin Ltd., 1974).

16. Micheal Ornstein, *Entry into the American Labor Force* (New York: Academic Press, 1976).

17. A. A. Kohen and H. S. Parnes, *Career Thresholds: A Longitudinal Study of the Educational and Labor Market Experiences of Male Youth,* vol. 3. (Columbus: Ohio State Center for Human Resources Research, 1971); A. S. Kohen and P. Andrisani, *Career Thresholds,* vol 4 (Columbus: Ohio State Center for Human Resources Research, 1973); H. S. Parnes et al., *Career Thresholds,* vol. 1 (Columbus: Ohio State Center for the Study of Human Resources, 1970); F. A. Zeller et al., *Career Thresholds,* vol. 2. (Columbus: Ohio State Center for the Study of Human Resources, 1970).

18. P. E. Davidson and H. D. Anderson, *Occupational Mobility in an American Community* (Palo Alto, Calif.: Stanford University Press, 1937); Christopher Jencks et al., *Inequality* (New York: Basic Books, 1972).

19. Dale Yoder, *Job Seeking Behavior of Workers* (New York: Organization for Economic Cooperation Development, 1965).

20. Joseph Champagne, "Job Recruitment of the Unskilled," *Personnel Journal,* April 1969, pp. 259–68.

21. John Morse, "Person-Job Consequence and Individual Adjustment and Development," *Human Relations,* December 1975, pp. 841–61.

22. Victor H. Vroom, *Work and Motivation.* New York: John Wiley & Sons, 1964; Victor Vroom

and Edward Deci, "The Stability of Post Decision Dissonance; A Follow-Up Study of Job Attitudes of Business School Graduates," *Organizational Behavior and Human Performance,* January 1971, pp. 36–49; O. Jeff. Harris, "The Expectations of Young College Graduates," *Proceedings,* Academy of Management, 1975, pp. 88–90; Edward Lawler et al., "Job Choice and Post Decision Dissonance," *Organizational Behavior and Human Performance,* February 1975, pp. 133–45; John Wanous, "Individual Differences and Reactions to Job Characteristics," *Journal of Applied Psychology* 59 (1974), pp. 16–22; John Wanous, "Organizational Entry: The Individual's Viewpoint," working paper, Graduate School of Business, New York University, 1974; James L. Sheard, "College Student Preferences for Types of Work Organizations," *Personnel Journal,* April 1970, pp. 299–304; Robert Swinth, "A Decision Process Model for Predicting Job Preferences," *Journal of Applied Psychology* 61, 2 (1976), pp. 242–45; Pieters et al., "Predicting Occupational Choice."

23. Peer Soelberg, "Structure of Individual Goals: Implications for Organization Theory," in *The Psychology of Management Decision,* ed. George Fish (Lund, Sweden: CWK Gleerup Publishers, 1967); Peer Soelberg, "Unprogrammed Decision Making: Job Choice," *Industrial Management Review,* Spring 1967.

24. William Glueck, "Decision Making: Organization Choice," *Personnel Psychology,* Spring 1974, pp. 77–93; William F. Glueck, "How Recruiters Influence Job Choices on Campus," *Personnel,* March–April 1971, pp. 46–52.

25. V. R. Tom, "The Role of Personality and Organizational Images in the Recruiting Process," *Organizational Behavior and Human Performance* 6 (1971), pp. 573–92.

26. Sheila Connelly, "Job Posting," *Personnel Journal,* May 1975, pp. 295–97; Dave Dahl and Patrick Pinto, "Job Posting: An Industry Survey," *Personnel Journal,* January 1977, pp. 40–42; Hughes, "Help Wanted"; H. Nathaniel Taylor, "Job Posting Update," *The Personnel Administrator,* January 1977, pp. 45–46.

27. Taylor, "Job Posting Update."

28. Dahl and Pinto, "Job Posting."

29. Ornstein, *Entry into American Labor Force,* pp. 53–56.

30. Max S. Wortman, Jr., "The Role of the Private Employment Agency in a Growing Economy," in *Creative Personnel Management,* ed. Max Wortman (Boston: Allyn & Bacon, 1967).

31. "The Role of the Employment Counselor," *Journal of Employment Counseling,* December, 1975; Gay Miller, "Hunting for Work," *The Wall Street Journal,* May 11, 1976; Thomas H. Patten, Jr., *Manpower Planning and the Development of Human Resources* (New York: John Wiley & Sons, 1971).

32. Harvey Kahalas and David Groves, "A Historical and Factor Analytic view of the Employment Service," *Labor Law Journal,* September 1974, pp. 550–61; Vernon Louviere, "How Texas Brings Jobs and Jobless Together," *Nations Business,* November 1975, pp. 51–52; F. T. Malm, "Recruiting Patterns and the Functioning of Labor Markets," *Industrial and Labor Relations Review,* July 1954, pp. 502–25; U.S. Government Accounting Office, *The Operation of the Federal State Employment Service System* (Washington, D.C.: U.S. Government Printing Office), May 24, 1976.

33. One exception is Harold Sheppard and A. Harvey Belitsky, *The Job Hunt* (Baltimore: John Hopkins Press, 1966).

34. Joan Bishop, "ECPO Picks the Best in Recruiting Literature," *Journal of College Placement,* December 1960, pp. 23–25; James Farr and Michael Young, "Amount of Information and Privacy, Recency Effects in Recruitment Decisions," *Personnel Psychology,* Summer 1975, pp. 233–38.

35. Bem and Bem, "Sex Job Advertising."

36. Edward Shaw, "Commonality of Applicant Stereotypes among Recruiters," *Personnel Psychol-*

ogy, Autumn 1972, pp. 421–32; Farr and Young, "Recency Effects in Recruitment Decisions."

37. Gordon K. Davies, "Needed: A National Job Matching Network," *Harvard Business Review*, September–October 1969, pp. 63–72; Joseph Ullman, "Manpower Policies and Job Market Information," in *Public-Private Manpower Policies*, ed. Arnold Weber et al. (Madison, Wis.: Industrial Relations Research Association, 1969).

38. Sigmund G. Ginsburgh, "Summer Intern Programs: A Case History," *Personnel*, May–June 1970, pp. 35–41.

39. Robert Simison, "Sifting Seniors," *The Wall Street Journal*, March 30, 1977.

40. Robert Dickinson, "Making the Recruiting Brochure a Useful Tool," *Personnel Administration*, Summer 1965, pp. 40–44; J. L. Johnson, "A Placement Officer Looks at Company Literature," *Journal of College Placement*, April 1960, pp. 43–44, 72–73.

41. Nancy Ingram and Donald Hunt, *Their First Jobs after College, 1951–1960*. (Detroit, Mich.: University of Detroit, 1960).

42. Orlando Behling and Henry Rodkin, "How College Students Find Jobs," *Personnel Administration*, September–October 1969, pp. 35–42.

43. Glueck, "Decision Making."

44. Thomas Gutteridge and Joseph Ullman, "On the Return to Job Search," *Proceedings*, Academy of Management, 1973, pp. 366–72.

45. James E. Sorensen, et al., "Professional and Bureaucratic Organization in the Public Accounting Firm," *The Accounting Review* 42 (1967), pp. 553–65.

46. Glueck, "Decision Making."

47. Clayton Alderfer and C. G. McCord, "Personnel and Situational Factors in Recruitment Interview," *Journal of Applied Psychology* 54 (1970), pp. 377–85.

48. Wanous, "Organizational Entry."

49. Daniel Ilgen and William Seely, "Realistic Expectations as an Aid in Reducing Voluntary Resignations," *Journal of Applied Psychology* 59, 4 (1974), pp. 452–55; Benjamin Schneider, "Organization Climate: Individual Preferences and Organizational Realities Revisited," *Journal of Applied Psychology* 59 (1975), pp. 459–65; Lewis Ward and Anthony Athos, *Student Expectations of Corporate Life* (Cambridge, Mass.: Harvard Business School, 1972); Larry Drake, et al., "Organizational Performance: A Function of Recruitment Criteria and Effectiveness," *Personnel Journal*, October 1973, pp. 885–91.

50. T. Higham, "Graduate Selection: A New Approach," *Occupational Psychology* 45 (1971), pp. 209–16.

51. William Sands, "A Method for Evaluating Alternative Recruiting—Selection Strategies," *Journal of Applied Psychology* 57 (1973), pp. 222–27; Leon Teach and John Thompson, "Simulation in Recruitment Planning," *Personnel Journal* 48 (April 1969), pp. 286–99; Carlton W. Dukes, "Effective Measurement of a Professional Recruiting Effort—A Systems Approach," *Personnel Journal* 44 (January 1965), pp. 12–17.

52. B. Greco, *How to Get a Job That's Right for You* (Chicago: Dow Jones–Irwin, 1975).

53. This material is based on Thomas Gutteridge, "Job Search: Guidelines for the Prospective Business School Graduate, unpublished paper, State University of New York, Buffalo. The resumé is by Gutteridge and Jerry Newman.

54. Higham, "Graduate Selections."

55. Rosemary Gaymer, "Preparing Students to Apply to You for a Position," *Canadian Personnel and Industrial Relations*, November 1975.

56. Jon Huegli and Harvey Tschirgi, "An Investigation of the Relationship of Time to Recruit-

ment Interview Decision Making," *Proceedings,* Academy of Management, 1972, pp. 234–36; Charles Coleman et al., "Who Wants What From the Interview?" *Journal of College Placement,* Winter 1977, pp. 53–56; "What Recruiters Watch for in College Graduates," *Nation's Business,* March 1976, pp. 34–35.

57. Other references for job finding include: Sam Adams, "How to Charm the Campus Recruiter," *MBA,* November 1974, pp. 47–50; *MBA's Employment Guide,* Association of MBA Executives, yearly; Lee Dyer, "Job Search Success of Middle Aged Managers and Engineers," *Industrial and Labor Relations Review,* January 1973, pp. 969–79; Arthur Pell, *The College Graduate's Guide to Job Finding* (New York: Simon & Schuster, 1973); Lee Smith, "Notes From the Job Underground," *Dun's Review,* August 1975; James Stern et al., "The Influence of Social Psychological Traits and Job Search Patterns on the Earnings of Workers Affected by a Plant Closure," *Industrial and Labor Relations Review,* October 1973, pp. 103–21.

Selection of personnel

CHAPTER OBJECTIVES

■ To show how the selection process is affected by the environment of the organization, the labor market, government and union requirements, managerial preferences, the task, and employee abilities and attitudes.

■ To demonstrate what selection criteria are available and how they can be used to make selection more effective.

■ To help you understand the selection process and how to use selection tools such as interviews and biodata more effectively.

CHAPTER OUTLINE

If employee planning leads the enterprise to believe additional people are needed to get the work done, recruiting takes place. Recruiting provides a list of potential employees (recruits). Selection is the decision that makes the choice of who should be chosen from that list.

> DEFINITION
> Selection is the process by which an enterprise chooses from a list of applicants the person or persons who best meet the selection criteria for the position available, considering current environmental conditions.

This definition emphasizes the effectiveness aspect of selection, but selection decisions must also be efficient. The second purpose of selection is to improve the proportion of successful employees chosen at the least cost from the applicant list. Selection costs can be high. In 1975, it was estimated that it costs enterprises $4,000 to select a top-level executive, $1,500 to select a middle manager, $1,000 for a supervisor, $1,925 for an engineer, $2,250 for an accountant, and $1,800 for a secretary.[1] An illustration of how to compute the relative costs of selection, using various selection methods, is given in a later section.

How do enterprises select their employees? There are various approaches, such as if the recruiting list contains 24 names and the firm needs to hire eight persons, it could pick every third name on the list. Or it could choose eight names randomly. Few enterprises use these chance approaches, however. This chapter discusses the techniques used to make the selection decision more effective and efficient.

Practices vary as to who actually makes the selection decision. In many larger organizations, personnel specialists screen the applicants, and the operating manager involved makes the choice. In smaller organizations, the operating manager does the screening and selecting.

Many enterprises also give co-workers a voice in the selection choice. Applicants are interviewed by their co-workers and the workers express their preferences. This procedure is used in university departments where the faculty expresses its preferences on applicants, and at the Lincoln Electric Company in Cleveland, in which the work group recruits and selects replacements or additions.

Generally, more effective selection decisions are made when many people are involved in the decision and when adequate information is furnished to those selecting the candidates. The operating manager and the work group should have more to say about the selection decision than the personnel specialist.

The selection activity is in Stage IV of development or maturity (see Exhibit 1–13, Chapter 1). It is well developed, and many studies have analyzed the use of the various selection methods.

A DIAGNOSTIC APPROACH TO THE SELECTION PROCESS

Argoyne Enterprises wants to hire some additional clerk-typists because of an increase in business. Whether the enterprise will actually be able to hire the typists depends on a number of factors, including the following:

1. The circumstances at the time, such as:
   a. How much time there is to make the choice.
   b. The number of typists presently available.
   c. Restrictions of the union and the government.
2. The characteristics the enterprise lists as desirable for the typists (the criteria).
3. The decision approach to be used. This can include:
   a. Systematic comparison of the applicants.
   b. Random choice.
   c. Gut feelings or emotional response to the applicants.

Chapter 7 analyzes these three factors in selection as a personnel activity. The objective of this activity is to make the best match between the employee and the task. The selection process varies with the nature of the task, and the techniques of selection vary as well.

Four factors in Zone 2 of the diagnostic model (Exhibit 7–1) comprise the circumstances affecting the selection process: the environment of the organization, the nature of the labor market, union requirements, and government regulations. Exhibit 7–1 also highlights the relevant factors which affect the criteria for selection: the nature of the employee, the task, and managerial goals and preferences. The circumstances or environmental factors influencing selection are discussed in this section, and the next section considers the many variables in selection criteria.

Environmental circumstances influencing selection

The environment of the organization. The nature of the organization doing the selecting affects the process it uses. The private and third sectors use similar methods, but the public sector is in another category. Traditionally, in the public sector selection has been made on the basis of either political patronage or merit. The patronage system rewards with jobs those who have worked to elect public officials. This was the only method used in the public sector until the civil service reforms of the late 1800s. Patronage is still practiced, and civil service has been criticized as too inflexible.[2] In the private and third sectors friendship with managers or employees can become a factor in the choice, but this is not the same thing as patronage. Pure "merit" selection (choice based only on the employee's excellence in abilities and experience) is an idea which systematic personnel selection tries to achieve but seldom does.

Other aspects of the enterprise affecting selection are its size, complexity, and technological volatility. Systematic, reliable, and valid personnel selec-

EXHIBIT 7–1
Factors affecting selection of personnel and organizational effectiveness

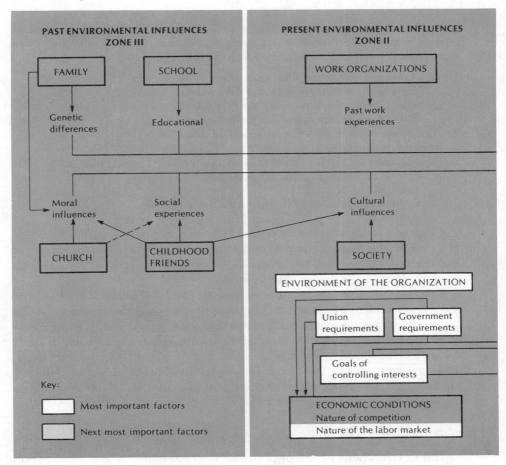

tion techniques are sometimes costly to develop and use; when this is so, only large enterprises can afford to use them. To justify the development of these techniques, there must be stability in the technology and thus the jobs. If the enterprise is complex and has a large number of jobs with only a few occupants, sophisticated techniques to select these jobholders are not cost effective. The extent to which size dictates how many employees there are in each work group also affects the usefulness of the techniques. (Specific recommendations about these factors will be given in the propositions at the end of the chapter). In sum, the size, complexity, technological volatility, and nature of the enterprise will influence the selection techniques that are cost effective for the enterprise.

Nature of the labor market. The second circumstance affecting the selection decision is the labor market with which the enterprise must deal.

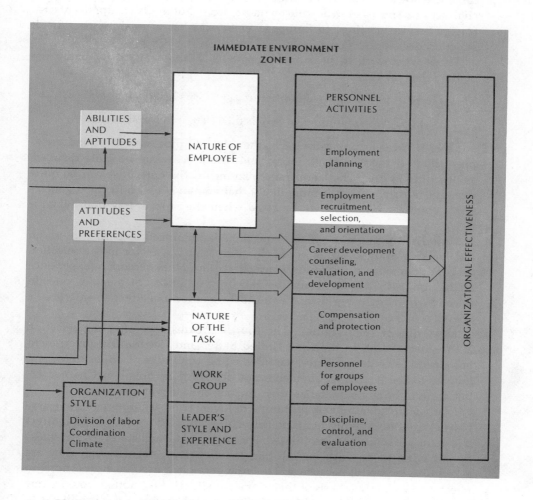

If there are many applicants, the selection decision can be complicated; if there is only one applicant, it is relatively easy. The labor market for the enterprise is affected by the labor market in the country as a whole, the region, or the city in which the enterprise is located. It is further affected by the working conditions the organization offers, the job itself, and the organization's image. (These were discussed earlier in the book and will be covered in Chapters 13–16, on compensation and benefits.) For example hospital dieticians trying to hire dishwashers or food preparation helpers do not have much of a selection decision to worry about. The job can be unpleasant, and it is performed at unpopular hours (the breakfast crew might have to arrive at 5:30 A.M.). The work day can be long, the pay is not good, and frequently there are no possibilities for promotion. For such jobs, an applicant who can walk in the door and be found not to have a communicable disease will usually be hired. Rarely are there enough applicants. A civil service specialist who must choose from hundreds of applicants for foreign service postings to European embassies has a much more difficult selection decision to make.

Those who work in personnel analyze this labor market factor by use of the selection ratio:

$$\text{Selection ratio} = \frac{\text{Number of applicants selected}}{\text{Number of applicants available for selection}}$$

Thus, if the selection ratio is 1:1, the selection process is short and unsophisticated; if the selection ratio is 1:44, the process can be quite detailed, as described below. The larger ratio also means the enterprise can be quite selective in its choice. It is more likely that employees who fit the organization's criteria for success will be hired when the ratio is 1:44 than when it is 1:1.

Union requirements. If the enterprise is unionized or partly so, union membership prior to hiring or shortly thereafter is a factor in the selection decision. Sometimes the union contract requires that seniority (experience at the job with the company) be the only criterion, or a major one, in selection. In many ways, openly and subtly, a union can affect an enterprise's selection process.

Government regulations. The fourth circumstance affecting selection is the government. In both the United States and Canada the government has passed laws designed to guarantee equal employment opportunity and human rights. These requirements are described in detail in Chapter 18, but we will briefly summarize their impact on selection decisions.

Many state governments prohibit employers from asking prospective employees questions about race, sex, national origin, and the like. Even indirect questions are sometimes prohibited. For example, several states restrict questions having to do with marital and family status, even though they are asked of everybody, because some employers have used such questions to reject women on their basis of their domestic situations. Another troublesome area is credit: the logic is that various minority groups are more likely to have encountered credit problems, so such questions tend to have an adverse impact on members of those groups.

In the United States, the federal government also regulates selection practices. Generally, the important question is whether a practice is likely to have an adverse impact on a prospect because of her or his age, race, sex, religion, or national origin. Members of racial and ethnic groups are less likely to meet educational requirements or to score high on certain standardized ability and aptitude tests. Women are generally less likely to pass weight-lifting tests, and women, Asian Americans, and Hispanic Americans are less likely to meet minimum height requirements.[3]

If selection procedures have unequal impact on prospective employees, they must conform to U.S. regulations such as the Guidelines for Employee

Selection Procedures issued by the U.S. Equal Employment Opportunity Commission (EEOC). These guidelines must be followed by virtually all employers with 15 or more employees. Recently a second set of guidelines (known as the Federal Executive Agency Guidelines) was jointly issued by three other agencies. These are applicable to most employers who have federal contracts or receive federal funds (who must also follow the first set of guidelines issued by EEOC). For the most part these guidelines are quite similar, but there are some differences, and the EEOC guidelines are generally the more demanding.

Much has been said about how stringent, complex, and unreasonable the federal selection guidelines are. While there is some truth in those complaints, the selection guidelines call for little more than adequate development and validation of selection procedures—the same sort of procedures that have been called for by industrial psychologists for decades. Technically competent test validation is costly and complex, however, so it is advisable to seek expert advice from those who specialize in the validation of selection procedures.

The Canadian federal government and other jurisdictions (the provinces and territories) have similar restrictions affecting the selection process. Canadians call the appropriate agencies human rights agencies. Specific Canadian restrictions are given in more detail in Chapter 18.

SELECTION CRITERIA

If a selection program is to be successful, the personal characteristics believed necessary for effective performance on the job should be specified at the unit level. Only then can those selecting from the applicants do so with any reasonable chance of hiring people who will perform well. Vague descriptions such as "Get me a good man (or woman)" do not help much, for each person has strengths and weaknesses. One may be long on education but short on experience; another is creative but not efficient at detailed work. Selection techniques sometimes can detect the characteristics desired in an employee, provided they have been specified. The requirements should come from the job specifications developed as part of the job analysis process (see Chapter 4).

The criteria usually can be summarized in several categories: education, experience, physical characteristics, and personal characteristics. Basically, the selection criteria should list the characteristics of present employees who have performed well in the position to be filled. As in employment planning, however, if the list of characteristics desired is too long, it may not be possible to select anyone; with no list of criteria, the wrong prospects are likely to be selected.

Before the organization can specify the characteristics to be sought in selection, it must have the success criteria defined. One example of success criteria is to achieve x level of performance in output terms, y level of quality, and z level of absenteeism and turnover. These also can be derived from the job analysis process.

The next step is to determine ways of predicting which of the applicants can reach these levels of expectation. Sometimes direct success indicators are available; other times proxies such as levels of intelligence, the presence of specified abilities, or certain amounts and types of experience are used.

These predictors of success, particularly the more formal mechanisms such as items on a paper-and-pencil test, have two characteristics: reliability and validity. The *reliability* of a selection instrument such as a test is the extent to which the instrument is a *consistent* measure of something. An intelligence test is said to be reliable if the same person's scores do not vary greatly when the test is taken several times. The higher the reliability, the more confidence can be placed in the measurement method. Usually, the instrument is more reliable if it is longer. The instrument used must also be internally consistent to be considered reliable.

Validity in a personnel measurement instrument is the extent to which it is a good indicator or predictor of success for the job performance in question. Laurence Siegel contrasts reliability and validity in this way. He points out that the yardstick is a *reliable* measure of space; no matter how many times you carefully measure a basketball player, he will be the same number of feet and inches. But a yardstick has no *validity* as a measure of muscular coordination.[4] Thus a selection device such as a test may be reliable without being valid.

Personnel specialists can compute the validity of a selection instrument several ways. One is to look at presently successful employees, find a factor that is common to them, and designate it as a predictor. This is called *concurrent validity*. A second way is to use an instrument such as a test during the hiring process, then wait until the successful employees are identified and correlate the test or test measures with the successful and unsuccessful employees. This is called *predictive validity*. A third method used sometimes by smaller organizations, because the numbers of persons in similar jobs is too small to use concurrent or predictive methods, is called *synthetic validity*. In this case, elements of several jobs that are similar, rather than whole job, are used to validate the selection instrument. This method is newer than the other two and is used less frequently.

It should be noted that the criterion used to predict performance or success is a proxy for actual performance. Since good job performance is usually a combination of many things (quality of work, quantity of work, etc.), a criterion such as a supervisor's rating is a proxy for the real measure: job success or performance.

The criteria for selection are affected in the diagnostic model (Exhibit 7–1) by the nature of the employee, the task, and managerial goals and preferences. Employee attitudes and preferences, abilities and aptitudes comprise the criteria, which vary with the focal task. For example, one would expect more emphasis on physical strength and abilities for heavy construction workers and more emphasis on formal education for a cost accountant.

The managerial goals and preferences are the filters which affect the choice of the criteria and the tradeoff weights among conflicting criteria, even when formal performance studies are used.

Formal education

An employer selecting among applicants for a job wants to find the person who has the right abilities and attitudes to be successful in the job. These cognitive, motor, physical, and interpersonal attributes[5] are present because of genetic predisposition and because they were learned in the home, at school, on the job, and so on. Most employers attempt to screen for abilities by specifying educational and experiential criteria. They may seek to achieve their preferences for attitudes similarly.

Employers tend to specify as a criterion the completion of certain amounts of formal education and types of education. For the job of accountant, the employer may list as an educational criterion a bachelor's degree in accounting. The employer may prefer that the degree is from certain institutions, that the grade point average is higher than some minimum, and that certain honors have been achieved. To be legal, such criteria must relate to past performance of successful accountants at the firm.

Formal education can indicate ability or skills present, and level of accomplishment may indicate the degree of work motivation and intelligence of the applicant. In general, other things being equal, employers tend to prefer more to less education, higher to lower grades, and graduates of more to lesser prestigious schools. But these characteristics must be correlated with job success if the criterion is to be an effective predictor. For example, a group of studies found that two-year nursing programs produce more of the kind of nurses many hospital administrators prefer than four-year programs do.[6] Insurance companies have found the most effective insurance salespersons come from lower prestige schools. And Leonard Nadler points out that nonschool experience is an important factor in prediction.[7] While one study found higher grades predicted better earnings for Stanford MBAs,[8] another found that grades and school "quality" were an insignificant predictor of earnings (success?).[9]

Thus the educational criteria must be validated against job performance. The employer must examine the amount and type of education that correlates with job effectiveness at the enterprise and use it as the selection criterion.[10] This is more effective than relying on preferences, and it is the legal and ethical way to set an educational criterion.

Experience

A second criterion for selection is experience. In general, employers prefer relatively more experience to less and relevant experience to less relevant, and significant to insignificant. Their first choice for a jobholder would probably be someone who has done the same job successfully for some time for an employer known to be demanding of its employees. They equate experience with ability as well as with attitude, reasoning that a prospect who has performed the job before and is applying for a similar job likes the work and will do it well. As a part of this attitude is loyalty to the job and the organization, most employers prefer to hire from within, as discussed in Chapter 6.

One way to measure experience within the enterprise is to provide each employee with a seniority rating, which indicates the length of time an employee has been employed. In the military, the date of rank is an equivalent seniority measure. Seniority is measured in various ways: as total time worked for the firm or time worked for the firm on a particular job or in a certain unit. Because some enterprises in the past did not allow certain groups to hold certain jobs, the courts and the EEOC are assigning retroactive and compensatory seniority to some employees.[11]

Physical characteristics

In the past, many employers consciously or unconsciously used physical characteristics (including how an applicant looked) as a selection criterion. Many times this discriminated against ethnic groups and females, and the practice is now illegal unless it can be shown that a physical characteristic is directly related to work effectiveness. Studies show that employers were more likely to hire and pay more to taller men, airlines chose stewardesses on the basis of beauty (or their definition of it), and receptionists were often chosen on the same basis. I found one employer who used an "elbow test" as his method of hiring secretaries: He mentally calculated whether, if the woman clasped her hands behind her head, her elbows or her breasts would protrude further. Only those where the elbows lost out were hired, which was hardly relevant to competence for secretarial tasks.

There are some tasks which require certain physical characteristics, usually stamina and strength, which can be tested. Candidates cannot legally be screened out by arbitrary height, weight, and similar requirements.[12] The enterprise should determine the physical characteristics of present successful employees and use an attribute as a criterion *only* when all or most of them have it.

Personal characteristics and personality type

The final criterion category is a catchall called personal characteristics and personality types. One personal characteristic is marital status. Some employers have preferred "stable" married employees, assuming this would lead to lower turnover and higher performance.[13] Discrimination in selection based on marital status is illegal in Canada, and unless an organization has data to support the relation of this criterion to performance, it makes little sense. Since more than one third of all marriages end in divorce today and many people prefer to stay single, good potential employees can be overlooked if they are screened out because they are single.

A second personal characteristic is age. It is illegal to discriminate against persons over 40 in the United States and Canada. It is not illegal to discriminate against young people, although protecting this group also has been proposed. Any age criterion should be examined by seeing how it relates to present successful employees.

Employers may prefer certain "personality" types for jobs. For example, to use Carl Jung's classification, they may prefer extroverts to introverts: This can be an important characteristic for employees who deal with the public, such as receptionists, salespersons, and caseworkers, but it may not be useful for other jobs, such as actuaries, lab technicians, or keypunch operators. The personality type specified should be based on past experience or be weighted lower than other, more directly relevant criteria.

Whom you know

It must be pointed out that an informal selection process runs parallel to the formal selection process being described here. For many selection decisions, the formal criteria must be met, but who is selected for the job depends on whom the applicant knows. If the applicant has connections and can get introduced to those doing the hiring, this can have greater impact than somewhat better test scores or references. This informal selection factor is very important in getting hired, as was noted in Chapter 6.

The rest of this chapter will focus on how to make a systematic decision so the activity is more effective. It should be remembered that the decision is affected by environmental circumstances and the criteria by which prospective employees for specific tasks are judged.

THE SELECTION PROCESS

All organizations make selection decisions, and most make them at least in part informally. The smaller the organization, the more likely it is to take an informal approach to selection decisions. Formal or systematic selection decisions were developed first during World Wars I and II, when employee shortages brought tremendous placement problems and the military had to select and place large numbers of men in many different jobs very quickly and efficiently.

Selection is often thought to be an easy decision. The boss interviews applicants, sizes them up, and lets his or her gut reaction guide the choice. The boss likes one man or woman for the job, and that's it. Selection tools are designed to aid this gut reaction. For most selection decisions, that is all the tools are intended to do; they are designed to increase the proportion of successful employees selected.

The selection decision usually is perceived as a series of steps through which applicants pass. At each step, a few more applicants are screened

EXHIBIT 7–2
Typical selection decision when all possible steps are used (private and third sectors)

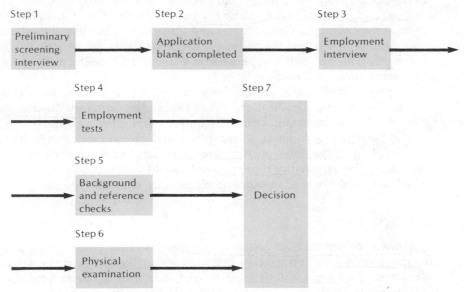

out by the enterprise, or more applicants accept other job offers and drop from the applicant list. Exhibit 7–2 illustrates a typical series of steps for the selection process.

This list is not universally used; for example, government employers test at Step 3 instead of Step 4, as do some private and third-sector employers.[14] Few organizations use all steps, for they can be time-consuming and expensive, and several steps such as 4, 5, and 6 may be performed concurrently or at about the same time. Generally speaking, the more important the job, the more each step is likely to be used formally. Almost all employers in the United States and Canada use the screening interview, application blank, and interview. Tests are used by a relatively small (and declining) number of employers. Background and reference checks and physical exams are used for some jobs and not others.[15]

Step 1: Preliminary screening interview

Jamie Meadows has just graduated from Martin Luther King High School. She is trying to decide which company to work for. She goes first to James Metal Works and enters the personnel office. John Walker, a personnel specialist, looks up after about ten minutes. He stays seated.

John: Yes?

Jamie: I've just graduated from high school and am wondering if. . . .

John: (interrupting) Can't you see the sign? Walker goes back to his paper work.

Over in the corner, Jamie notices a small sign that says: We are not hiring now. Jamie leaves James Metal Works without a word.

Next she goes to Arnold Office Supplies, where she is met by Tom Trovers. After her first experience, she approaches Tom somewhat reluctantly.

Jamie: Hello, I'm Jamie Meadows. I just graduated from Martin Luther King High School and I'm looking for a job.

Tom: Nice to meet you Jamie. Let's sit down over here and talk about you and the jobs we have open right now.

Different enterprises can handle Step 1 in various ways: ineffectively, or effectively.

For some types of jobs, applicants are likely to walk in to the employment office or job location. In these cases, a personnel specialist or line manager usually spends a few moments with applicants in what is called the preliminary screening. The organization develops some rough guidelines to be applied in order to reduce the time and expense of actual selection. These guidelines could specify, for example, minimum education or the number of words typed per minute. Only those who meet these criteria are deemed potential employees and are interviewed.

If general appearance and personal characteristics are deemed important, preliminary screening is often done through a brief personal interview in which the personnel specialist or the manager determines key information and forms a general impression of the applicant. On this basis, the successful applicant then moves to the next step in selection, perhaps with the knowledge that lack of an essential characteristic has lessened the chances of being seriously considered for the job. In smaller organizations, if the applicant appears to be a likely candidate for the position the preliminary screening can proceed as an employment interview (Step 3).

The employer must be sure that the criteria used in this first step do not violate government antidiscrimination requirements. The EEOC has a publication, *Affirmative Action and Equal Employment: A Guidebook for Employers,* which provides help on this issue (vol. 1, pp. 40–44).

Step 1 is part of the reception portion of recruiting (see Chapter 6). The enterprise has the opportunity to make a good or bad impression on the applicant in this step. James Metal Works made one kind of impression, Arnold Office Supplies another.

Step 2: Completion of application blank/biodata form

If Jamie appears roughly qualified for the jobs available at Arnold's Office Supplies, the next step is to have her complete an application blank or other biodata form. One of the oldest instruments in personnel selection is the application blank. Surveys show that all but the tiniest enterprises have applicants complete an application form or other biodata instrument (such as a biographical data form, biographical information blanks, an individual background survey, or an interview guide).[16] William Owens has shown that biodata forms are useful in selection, career planning and counseling, and performance evaluation, and biodata approaches are most likely to meet the EEOC's criticisms of other selection techniques.[17] Of course, application blanks and biodata forms could be illegal if they include items not relevant to job content.[18]

Essentially, those advocating the biodata approach argue that past behavior patterns are the best predictor of future behavior patterns. Thus data should be gathered on a person's demographic, experiential and attitudinal characteristics in a form that lends itself to psychometric evaluation and intrepretation. In constructing the biodata form, a variety of approaches is possible. According to Owens, the form should be brief; the items should be stated in neutral or pleasant terms; the items should offer all possible answers or categories plus an "escape clause"; and numbered items should add to a scale. Owens argues that continuum items are preferable to noncontinuum items, and choose-one option items are better than multiple-choice items.[19]

An important biodata substitute or supplement for the application blank is the *biographical information blank* (BIB). The BIB usually has more items than an application blank and includes different kinds of items, relating to such things as attitudes, health, and early life experiences. It uses the multiple-choice answer system. Instead of asking just about education, it might ask:

How old were you when you graduated from the 6th grade?
1. Younger than 10
2. 10–12
3. 13–14
4. 15–16

It also asks opinion questions such as:

How do you feel about being transferred from this city by this company?
1. Would thoroughly enjoy a transfer
2. Would like to experience a transfer
3. Would accept a transfer
4. Would reject a transfer

To use the BIB as a selection tool, the personnel specialist correlates each item on the form with the selection criteria for job success. Those criteria that predict the best for a position are used to help select applicants for that position.

Another variety of biodata form is the *weighted application blank,* an application form designed to be scored as a systematic selection device. The purpose of a weighted application blank is to relate the characteristics of applicants to success on the job. It has been estimated that to develop a weighted blank for a job takes about 100 hours, so it makes sense to develop such blanks only for positions with many jobholders.

The typical approach is to divide present jobholders into two or three categories (in half, high or low; or in thirds, high, middle, or low), based on some success criterion such as performance as measured by production records or supervisor's evaluation, or high versus low turnover. Then the characteristics of high and low performers are examined. On many characteristics for a particular organization and job, there may be no difference by age or education level, but there may be differences on where applicants live and years of experience, for example. A weight is assigned to the degree of differences: for no difference, 0; for some difference, ±1; for a big difference, ±2. Then these weights are totaled for all applicants, and the one with the highest positive score is hired.

Studies indicate that these predictive characteristics vary by job and occupation. For example, sometimes the age of the applicant is a good predictor; other times it is not. They may also change over time, so weights need to be recomputed every several years or so.[20] Therefore the weighted application blank must be validated for each job and organization.[21]

Studies suggest confidence regarding the validity of biodata. Many of these studies are longitudinal.[22] Ghiselli's studies led him to believe that the biodata form has the highest validity of any selection approach,[23] and Owens shows the validity exists for this approach across cultures, age, race, sex, and companies. The reliability of the biodata approach is also strong,[24] although one study found negative results.[25]

A properly designed and well-analyzed application blank or similar biodata instrument can be a useful selection device. Studies indicate, however, that although most organizations use application blanks, fewer than a third of the *larger* organizations have utilized weighted application blanks or other biodata approaches. Given the problems with tests, references, and other selection techniques, the percentage of enterprises using biodata approaches is likely to increase.

Step 3: Employment interview[26]

Employment interviews are part of almost all selection procedures. For many positions, biodata, interviews, and reference checks are the pattern followed in making selection decisions. In government organizations and some others that use tests, tests may precede the interview, but in most the tests are given after interviews.

The employment interview is one of the most widely used tools in the selection process. One study found that 98 percent of the companies surveyed used interviewing, although it did not document the importance of the interview in the selection process.[27] The personnel survey by the Bureau of National Affairs in 1976 reported that 56 percent of the participating companies stated that interviews are *the most important aspect* of the selection procedure, and 90 percent revealed that of all possible sources of information, they had the most confidence in the interview.[28] There seems little question that as the use of tests declines, the employment interview will continue to grow in significance.

Types of interviews. There are three general types of employment interview: structured, semistructured, and unstructured. While all employment interviews are alike in certain respects, each type is also unique in some way. All three include interaction between two or more parties, an applicant and one or more representatives of the potential employer, for a predetermined purpose: consideration for employment. Information is exchanged, usually through questions and answers. The main differencess in employment interviews lie in the interviewer's approach to the process, and the type used depends both on the kind of information desired and the nature of the situation.

In the structured type of employment interview the interviewer prepares a list of questions in advance and does not deviate from it. In many organizations a standard form is used on which the interviewer notes the applicant's responses to the predetermined questions. Many of the questions asked in a structured interview are forced choice in nature, and the interviewer need only indicate the applicant's response with a check mark on the form.

If the approach is highly structured, the interviewer may also follow a prearranged sequence of questions. In such an interview the interviewer is often little more than a recorder of the interviewee's responses, and little training is required to conduct it. The structured approach is very restrictive, however, for the information elicited is narrow and there is little opportunity to adapt to the individual applicant. This approach is equally constraining to the applicant, who is unable to qualify or elaborate on answers to the questions. The Bureau of National Affairs survey found that 19 percent of the companies used a written interview form, while 26 percent employed a standard format for employment interviews.[29]

In the semistructured interview only the major questions to be asked are prepared in advance, though the interviewer may also prepare some probing questions in areas of inquiry. While this approach calls for greater interviewer preparation, it also allows for more flexibility than the structured approach. The interviewer is free to probe into those areas that seem to merit further investigation. With less structure, however, it is more difficult to replicate these interviews. This approach combines enough structure to facilitate the exchange of factual information with adequate freedom to develop insights.

The unstructured interview involves little preparation. The interviewer prepares a list of possible topics to be covered, and sometimes does not even do that. The overriding advantage of the unstructured type is the freedom it allows the interviewer to adapt to the situation and to the changing stream of applicants. Spontaneity characterizes this approach, but under the control of an untrained interviewer digressions, discontinuity, and eventual frustration for both parties may result.

While this approach lends itself to the counseling of individuals with problems, it is not limited to guidance. Students frequently encounter personnel recruiters whose sole contribution, other than the opening and closing pleasantries, is "Tell me about yourself." When used by a highly skilled interviewer, the unstructured interview can lead to significant insights which might enable the interviewer to make fine distinctions among applicants. As used by most employment interviewers, however, that is not the case, and it is seldom appropriate for an employment interviewer to relinquish control to such an extent.

The stress interview. The idea of using the interview format to determine an applicant's ability to cope with stress is fascinating but of dubious value. Fortunately it appears to be talked about more than it is actually employed. While stories are legion about interviewers who misrepresent themselves or cast aspersions on applicants or in some other way try to disorient them, few interviewers say they use such an approach.

The suggested approach to interviewing as described in Appendix A to this chapter emphasizes the reduction of the stress that is naturally present in any employment interview. Stress, whether natural or contrived, creates defensiveness in the applicant and inhibits communication.

An attempt is sometimes made to justify the use of stress interviews when the position for which the applicant is applying is a stressful one. Rarely is the stress created in an interview similar to that found on a job, however, and rare also is a position for which the ability to cope with stress is a primary characteristic. Another dysfunctional aspect of such an approach is the effect it might have on the relationship between the interviewer and the applicant, should the applicant be hired.

Reliability of the interview. Despite the widespread use of the employment interview, it continues to be a source of controversy. The question of its reliability and validity is a frequent subject of analysis. There have been two major reviews of the literature on the employment interview and numerous investigations on a smaller scale. Most research shows that structured interviews are more reliable than those that are less structured,[30] but other studies question these findings.[31] Most of the research substantiates the link between structure and reliability, however. It is possible to conduct interviews that avoid discrimination problems,[32] but various firms, such as Western Electric Company, have been questioned by the EEOC about the use of unstructured interviewing methods in selection.

There is no doubt that problems of reliability can develop in the use of interviews when they are less structured or conducted by relatively untrained interviewers.[33] In this regard, there are some excellent studies which question the reliability of the interview,[34] but with proper training and structuring, these criticisms can be overcome.[35] For example, in a study of the reliability of selecting police officers with interview methods, one researcher found that using averages of interview factor scores was more reliable and valid than using averaged recommendations of the interviewers.[36]

Besides the desirability of structuring interviews, these generalizations about interviews are also supported by research:

The attitudes of the interviewer and the interviewee influence the reliability of the interview, as does the form of questions and answers.[37]

Unfavorable relevant information influences interviewers more than favorable information, and the earlier in the interview negative information is introduced, the greater is the negative effect.[38]

The interviewer's decision may be affected as much by the characteristics of a previous applicant as by the current applicant.

There is greater agreement between the interviewers on unsatisfactory applicants than on satisfactory ones.

In unstructured interviews, interviewers talk more than interviewees, and they make their decision earlier.

Such research findings suggest some of the pitfalls faced by the employment interviewer. But as more personnel specialists are trained in interviewing, the tool's reliability and usefulness should increase correspondingly. The Bureau of National Affairs reported that 61 percent of the companies polled provided special training for their interviewers.[39]

Some concluding comments on effective interviewing.   It was once thought that almost anyone who could carry on a conversation could conduct an interview. Now, following decades of questionable selection decisions and ineffective counseling practices, interviewing techniques are finally being recognized as behavior to be learned rather than acquired at birth. The appendix to this chapter describes how to conduct an effective employment interview, and five guidelines for becoming a more effective employment interviewer are given below:

1. Work at listening to what and how the applicant communicates to you. Unlike hearing, listening is an active process and requires concentration. Many interviewers plan their next question when they should be listening to the applicant's present response.

2. Be aware of the applicant's nonverbal cues as well as the verbal message. In attempting to get as complete a picture of the applicant as possible, you must not ignore what some consider the most meaningful type of communication, body language.

3. Remain aware of the job requirements throughout the interview. No one is immune to the halo effect, which gives undue weight to one characteristic. You must constantly keep the requirements of the job in mind. Sometimes an applicant possesses some personal mannerism or trait that so attracts or repels the interviewer that the decision is made mostly on the strength of that characteristic, which may be completely irrelevant to the requirements of the job in question.

4. Maintain a balance between open and overly structured questions. Too many of the former, and the interview becomes a meandering conversation; while too many of the latter turn the interview into an interrogation.

5. Wait until you have all of the necessary information before making a decision. Some interviewees start more slowly than others, and what may appear to be disinterest may later prove to have been an initial reserve which dissipates after a few minutes. *Don't evaluate on the basis of a first impression.*

Step 4: Employment tests

A technique some enterprises use to aid their selection decisions is the employment test. Such a test is a mechanism (either a paper-and-pencil test or a simulation exercise) which attempts to measure certain characteristics of individuals, such as manual dexterity. Psychologists or personnel specialists develop these tests with a procedure that is similar to that described for the weighted application blank. First those most knowledgeable about the job are asked to rank (in order of importance) the abilities and attitudes essential for effective performance in a job. Thus for a secretarial position, the rank might be (A) ability to type, (B) ability to take shorthand, and (c) positive work attitudes. The psychologist prepares items or simulations which it is thought will measure these required characteristics. These are tried out to see if they can in fact separate the qualified from less qualified (on A and B) and easygoing from less easygoing. On such items, psychologists prefer those that about half the applicants will answer with "right" answers and half with the opposite.

The terms or simulations that distinguish the best from the worst are combined into tests. A measure of effectiveness (criterion) is developed, such as typing x words per minute with y percent errors. All new applicants are given the test. After about two years, those items that prove to have been the best predictors of high performance are kept in the test used for selection, and those found not to be predictive are dropped.

Few organizations have the personnel, time, or money to develop their own tests. Instead, they often purchase and use tests developed elsewhere. The test organization provides a key (or notation) of the typical performance of good and bad employees of past users. This is not enough, however; the test must be validated in each organization and for minority and nonminority employee groups before it can be useful. Therefore it must be given to all applicants. More information on validation and selection of tests will be given at the end of this section.

There are various kinds of tests. The following will be discussed here: performance tests, simulations of performance, paper-and-pencil tests, personality and temperament inventories, and others.

Performance tests. A performance test is an experience that involves actually doing a sample of the work the job involves in a controlled situation. Examples of performance tests include:

Employees running a miniature punch press at a Philadelphia quartermaster depot.

A standardized driving course as performance test for forklift operators at the same location.[40]

The auditions used by symphony orchestras for hiring purposes. For example, when symphony orchestras select new musicians, the selection panel listens to them play the same piece of music with the same instrument. The applicants are hidden behind a screen at the time.

Standardized typing tests. The applications are asked to type some work. The speed and accuracy are then computed.

Variations of these performance tests exist in many enterprises. The applicants are asked to run the machines they would run if they got the job, and quality and quantity of output are recorded.

Performance tests tend to have the highest validities and reliabilities of all tests because they systematically measure behavior directly related to the job. This is not surprising. Imagine that you are an artist who is applying for graduate work in art. You typically must take the Graduate Record Exam; a paper-and-pencil test designed to measure verbal and mathematical "ability." You also must present 12 paintings, drawings, and watercolors (a portfolio) to the Art Department. Which of these selection devices appears likely to be the most reliable and valid measure of your painting ability? Or recall that when you took your driving test, you took two: a paper-and-pencil test, and, when you drove the car, a performance test. Which better tested your driving ability: the paper-and-pencil test, or that tension-filled drive including the thrilling attempt at parallel parking?

A similar principle applies to job selection. Which would be a better predictor of the forklift operator's job performance: the standardized test in which the applicant drives the truck down and around piles of goods, or a paper-and-pencil test of driving knowledge, intelligence, or whatever?

Reliability and validity figures for all the standardized tests discussed here are available from the test developers. Many are reviewed in regular summaries.[41]

Performance simulations. A performance simulation is a non-paper-and-pencil experience designed to determine abilities related to job performance. For example, suppose job analysis indicates that successful job occupants of a specific job require highly developed mechanical or clerical abilities. A number of simulations are available to measure these abilities. The simulation is not direct performance of part of the job, but it comes close to that through simulation. You may have learned to drive by performing first on simulation machines; it was not the same as on the street driving, but it was closer than reading about it or observing other drivers.

There are many of these simulation tests; here are some:

Revised Minnesota Paper Form Board Test. Exhibit 7–3 is an excerpt from the MPFB, which is a test of space visualization. It is used for various jobs; for example, to be a draftsman requires the ability to see things in their relation to space. The applicant must select the item (A–E) which best represents what a group of shapes will look like when assembled.

Psychomotor ability simulations. Two of the tests which measure such psychomotor abilities as choice reaction time, speed of limb movement, and finger dexterity are the O'Connor Finger and Tweezer Dexterity Test and the Purdue Pegboard. Exhibit 7–4 is a picture of the O'Connor test. The person being tested picks up pins with the tweezer and row by row inserts them in the holes across the board, or inserts the pins with the hand normally used. These tests are used for positions with high manual requirements for success, such as assemblers of radio or TV components and watches.

Excerpt from Revised Minnesota Paper Form Board Test

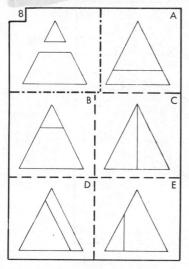

O'Connor Finger and Tweezer Dexterity Test equipment

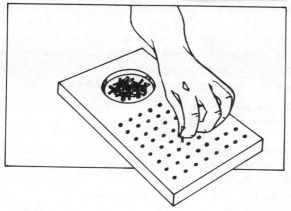

Exhibit 7–5 shows the Purdue Pegboard, a simulation designed to measure ability to do routine manual jobs. The pegboard has two rows of 25 holes. The applicant must place pins in the holes within 30 seconds for first the right hand, then the left, then alternating both. Then the applicant actually assembles washers, pins, and collars, using right and left hands. The test measures arm, hand, and finger dexterity.

EXHIBIT 7–5
Purdue Pegboard

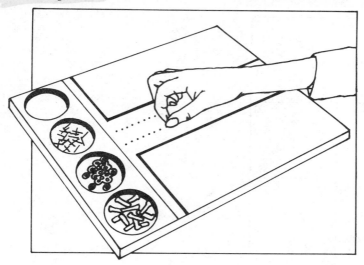

Clerical abilities.   Exhibit 7–6 is the first page of the Minnesota Clerical Test. This simulation requires the applicants to check numbers and names, skills frequently used in clerical tasks.

Paper-and-pencil tests.   The third group of tests are designed to measure general intelligence and aptitudes on paper-and-pencil tests. Many employers assume that mental abilities are an important component of performance for many jobs. Intelligence and mental ability tests attempt to sample intellectual mental development or skills. Some examples are given below,

Otis Quick Scoring Mental Ability Test.   This test samples several intellectual functions, including vocabulary, arithmetic skills, reasoning, and perception, totaling them to one score. It includes items such as the following:

(a)   Which one of the five things below is soft?
     (1) glass (2) stone (3) cotton (4) iron (5) ice
(b)   A robin is a kind of:
     (6) plant (7) bird (8) worm (9) fish (10) flower
(c)   Which one of the five numbers below is larger than 55?
     (11) 53 (12) 48 (13) 29 (14) 57 (15) 16

Wechsler Adult Intelligence Scale.   The Wechsler is a comprehensive paper-and-pencil test of 14 sections grouped into two scores. The verbal score includes general information, arithmetic, similarities, vocabulary, and other items. The performance score includes picture completion, picture arrangement, object assembly, and similar items.

Wonderlic Personnel Test.   The Wonderlic is a shortened form of the Otis

EXHIBIT 7–6

MINNESOTA CLERICAL TEST

(formerly the Minnesota Vocational Test for Clerical Workers)
by Dorothy M. Andrew, Donald G. Patterson, and Howard P. Longstaff

Name _____   Date _____

TEST 1—Number Comparison	TEST 2—Name Comparison
Number Right _____	Number Right _____
Number Wrong _____	Number Wrong _____
Score = R — W _____	Score = R — W _____
Percentile Rating _____	Percentile Rating _____
Norms Used _____	Norms Used _____

INSTRUCTIONS

On the inside pages there are two tests. One of the tests consists of pairs of names and the other of pairs of numbers. If the two names or the two numbers of a pair are exactly the same make a check mark (√) on the line between them: if they are different, make no mark on that line. When the examiner says "Stop!" draw a line under the last pair at which you have looked.

SAMPLES done correctly of pairs of NUMBERS

79542____79524
1234567_√_1234567

SAMPLES done correctly of pairs of NAMES

John C. Linder____John C. Lender
Investors Syndicate_√_Investors Syndicate

This is a test for speed and accuracy. Work as fast as you can without making mistakes. Do not turn this page until you are told to begin.

test using a variety of perceptual, verbal and arithmetical items which provide a total score. Other well-known tests include the Differential Aptitude Test, the SRA Primary Mental Abilities Test, and multiple aptitude tests.

The above three tests are administered to individuals and are paper-and-pencil tests similar to those taken in school. There are also tests of mental ability designed to be administered to groups, including the following example:

California Test of Mental Maturity (*adult level*). This test is administered to groups and scored by machine. Scores are developed from a series of short tests on spatial relationships, verbal concepts, logic and reasoning, numerical reasoning, memory, and others. These scores are converted to IQ equivalents, and profiles are developed for analyzing performance.

The reliability and validity of paper-and-pencil tests have been studied extensively[42]. In general, they are not as reliable as performance tests or other selection devices such as biodata forms or structured interviews.

Personality inventories and temperament tests. The least reliable of the employment tests are those instruments that attempt to measure a person's personality or temperament. The most frequently used inventory is the Minnesota Multiphasic Personality Inventory. Other paper-and-pencil inventories are the California Psychological Inventory, the Minnesota Counseling Inventory, the Manifest Anxiety Scale, and the Edwards Personal Preference Schedule.

A different approach, not as direct as the self-reporting inventory, utilizes projective techniques to present vague stimuli, the reactions to which provide data on which psychologists base their assessment and interpretation of a personality. The stimuli are purposely vague in order to reach the unconscious aspects of the personality. Many techniques are used; the most common are the Rorschach Inkblot Test, the Thematic Apperception Test, and others.

Most of these instruments were developed for use by psychiatrists and psychologists in counseling and mental health work, rather than in selection. Because of employee resistance, ethical problems in some questions, and lower reliability and validities, use of the inventories is likely to continue to decline in the future.[43]

Other methods.   Two other methods currently used by some employers to test employees will be briefly noted. These are the polygraph and graphology.

The polygraph.   This device is sometimes erroneously called a lie detector. Developed in the 1920s, it is an instrument that records changes in breathing, blood pressure, pulse, and skin response associated with sweating of palms, and plots these reactions on paper. The person being questioned with a polygraph attached is asked a series of questions. Some are neutral, to achieve a normal response, others stressful, to indicate a response made under pressure. Thus the applicant may be asked: "Is your name Pajanowski?" Then, "Have you ever stolen from an employer?"[44]

Although originally developed for police work, the great majority of polygraph tests today are used to check data during personnel selection. One survey of the literature indicated that over 300,000 polygraph tests are administered yearly.[45] It is understandable why organizations need to determine certain facts about potential employees. On-the-job crime has increased tremendously, and it is estimated that dishonest employees cost employers about $5 billion per year.[46] A good reference check may cost $100; a polygraph test only $25. Some employers offer applicants a choice: Take a polygraph test now, making it possible to make an immediate selection decision, or await the results of a reference check and run the risk of losing the job. Local, state, and federal agencies have begun to use the polygraph, especially for security, police, fire, and health positions.

There are many objections to the use of the polygraph in personnel selection. One is that this device is an invasion of the applicants' privacy and thus a violation of the Fourth Amendment to the Constitution. Second, it is believed that its use could lead to self-incrimination, a violation of the Fifth Amendment. A third objection is that it insults the dignity of the applicant. One study cites cases of applicants being asked questions about their sex lives, for example.[47]

As severe as these objections are, the most serious question is whether the polygraph is reliable and can get the truth. The fact is that the polygraph records *physiological* changes in response to stress, not lying or even the conditions necessarily accompanying lying. Many cases have come to light in which persons who lie easily have beaten the polygraph, and it has been shown that the polygraph brands as liars people who respond emotionally to questions.[48] There is significant evidence that polygraphs are neither reliable nor valid; this is the conclusion reached following recent studies by a congressional committee and the Pentagon which made a thorough analysis of all the available data. Compounding this deficiency, one expert, Fred Inbau, has estimated that 80 percent of the 1,500 polygraph practitioners are not sufficiently trained to interpret the results of the tests, even if they were reliable and valid.[49]

Such criticisms have led to the banning of the polygraph for employee selection in many jurisdictions. Arbitrators have held against forcing employees to take such tests, and polygraph evidence is not admissible in court unless both sides agree. As a result of congressional hearings, the federal government has severely reduced the use of polygraphs. In spite of these criticisms, however, it appears that the use of the polygraph in selection is increasing.

Graphology. Graphology, or handwriting analysis, has also been proposed as a possible tool in personnel selection, with the claim that this technique can provide insights into the personality of the applicant.[50] There are said to be about 30,000 graphologists in the United States, only a few of whom are called upon for such interpretation in the personnel process.

Basically, the graphologist interprets the handwriting of the applicant. He infers certain personality traits from the shapes of letters, location of words, use of words, and so forth. This is not a great deal different from some of the personality inventory instruments like the Draw a Picture Test. There are no reliability and validity data on graphology. In the case of the fake Howard Hughes biography by Clifford Irving, for example, expert graphologists were unable to detect falsification of Howard Hughes's signature by Mrs. Irving.

Selection, validation, and uses of tests. Suggestions on the effective selection and use of tests[51] include the following by W. Wilson:

Test results should be weighed in the context of the applicant's employment history.

Make sure the test is right for the job in question.

Be aware of the differences in what the various tests try to measure.

Use tests that have both general and specific norms.

Have as high a selection ratio as possible.

Try the test on present employees before adopting it.

Seek advice of consultants in test selection.

Organizations which need to process rather large numbers of applicants for jobs have developed job tests or groups of tests called test batteries which allow them to keep records on the usefulness of these tests in hiring.

A well-known example is the civil service examinations given by U.S. governmental agencies for many positions.

A beginning point for compiling such test batteries is to refer to a text on texts. C. H. Lawsche and Michael Balma, for example, describe test batteries or specific tests for blue-collar jobs such as assemblers and inspectors, white-collar positions such as routine clerical work and office management, and professional and managerial positions.[52] Suggested tests or batteries of tests would have to be validated for each organization, however.

For the test to be used in a way that meets legal and EEOC requirements and to make sure the enterprise is testing what it wants to, the test or test battery must be validated in the organization. The best way of doing this is: for the personnel specialist, after a period such as 18 months or two years, to find the scores on the test for the items which are the best predictors for successful performance in the jobs in the organization. This can be done by running correlations between the items and success on the job or by plotting regressions, such as between test scores on finger dexterity and job performance criteria for assemblers, as shown in Exhibit 7–7.

It is not easy to validate a test. In a recent study of 2,500 ASPA members, it was found that, on average, a validation study costs $5,000 per job, and some studies cost as much as $20,000.[53] The eight most frequent validation "headaches" ASPA members listed were:

There's no way we could get enough data for validation.

We'd like to validate, but the cost would be prohibitive. (66 percent of the personnel directors used this reason for not performing validation studies.)

We'll validate if we can find a way that doesn't require getting outside consultants.

EXHIBIT 7–7
Relationship between dexterity scores and employee performance

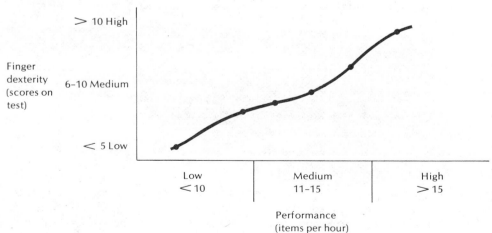

No one on our staff knows enough about validation to conduct a study, and we can't find anyone who does.

Supervisors can't or won't cooperate with validation studies.

We couldn't get top management go-ahead to conduct joint validation studies with other employers.

Union resistance has prevented us from validating.

We wanted to conduct joint validation studies with other employers, but couldn't find other companies willing to cooperate.

Those selecting and using tests tend to systematically overestimate their validity.[54] In the light of criticisms from the courts and practitioners that tests discriminate against minority applicants, it is useful to consider whether this is so. J. Kirkpatrick et al. examined studies of the use of tests on 1,200 employees, one third of them minority applicants, and concluded that it is not possible to make general statements about the fairness or unfairness of tests. Nevertheless they contend that separate validity studies need to be done for minority or disadvantaged groups if tests are to be useful.[55] B. O'Leary et al. examined results of tests on 1,700 employees, one third of whom were minority members; they strongly argue for the necessity of separate validity studies for minority employees.[56] This has not generally been done, and many employers have abandoned the use of tests for disadvantaged applicants.

The Prentice-Hall ASPA study found the use of tests is declining, and they are used most frequently for clerical jobs.[57] As Exhibit 7–8 indicates, about half of the surveyed employers use tests in selection. Middle-sized

EXHIBIT 7–8
Test usage in the United States in 1975

A. INCIDENCE OF TESTING FOR HIRING AND PROMOTION (BY EMPLOYER CATEGORY)*

	Manufac- turers	Public utilities	Hospitals	Banks	Insurance	Other offices	Retail stores	Transpor- tation and communi- cations	Other	All re- spondents
Test for hiring	41.2%	59.1%	41.8%	47.5%	67.9%	69.2%	44.2%	75.5%	55.1%	49.1%
Test for promotion	24.9	49.2	17.4	16.0	25.5	19.7	22.5	42.2	19.7	24.0
Don't test	42.3	22.4	46.6	36.5	21.8	25.0	42.5	18.3	33.8	36.5

B. INCIDENCE OF TESTING FOR HIRING AND PROMOTION (BY SIZE OF EMPLOYER)*

	Fewer than 100 employees	100–499 employees	500–999 employees	1,000– 4,999 employees	5,000– 9,999 employees	10,000– 25,000 employees	More than 25,000 employees	All re- spondents
Test for hiring	30.4%	43.4%	46.8%	55.4%	62.7%	54.9%	57.1%	49.1%
Test for promotion	17.9	17.3	24.0	29.3	27.4	32.7	32.4	24.0
Don't test	61.0	49.2	45.1	40.4	32.9	38.4	39.6	36.5

* Percentages total more than 100 percent because some respondents test for both hiring and promotion.
Source: *The Personnel Executive's Job* (Englewood Cliffs, N.J.: Prentice-Hall/ASPA, 1977).

firms are most likely to use them, followed by larger firms; the smaller firms are least likely to use them. Some industries (transportation and communications, offices, insurance) are more likely to use tests than manufacturers, hospitals, and retailers.

Of the 2,500 personnel managers consulted in this survey, 37.9 percent considered tests "about the same in importance" and 36.5 percent considered them less important than other selection techniques such as the interview and biodata. Less than 20 percent said they disqualified applicants on the basis of test scores alone.[58]

Step 5: Reference checks and recommendation letters

If you have ever applied for a job, at some point you were asked to provide a list of references of past supervisors and others. In general, you picked people who could evaluate you effectively and fairly for your new employer—people who know and express your good and bad points equally, like your mother, lover, best friend, and other objective references, right?

For years, as part of the selection process, applicants have been required to submit references or recommendation letters. These indicate past behavior and how well the applicant did at her or his last job. Studies indicate that this has been a common practice for white-collar jobs.[59]

For a letter of recommendation to be useful, it must meet certain conditions:

The writer must have known the applicant's performance level and be competent to assess it.

The writer must communicate the evaluation effectively to the potential employer.

The writer must be truthful.

If the applicant chooses the references, the first two conditions may not be met. With regard to the third, many people are reluctant to put in writing what they really think of the applicant, since he or she may see it. As a result, the person writing the reference either glosses over shortcomings or overemphasizes the applicant's good points. Because of these and other shortcomings, studies of the validity of written references have not been comforting to those using them in selection.[60]

Clemm Kessler and Georgia Gibbs propose a method for potentially improving the validity of letters of reference as a selection tool.[61] In their approach, letters of reference are required only for jobs which have had job analysis performed to develop job specifications (see Chapter 4). A panel of judges (three to six persons) familiar with the job ranks the specifications for relative importance. Then a reference letter is drafted asking the respondent to rate the applicant on the job specifications, which are listed randomly. A sample reference letter for the position of employment interviewer is given as Exhibit 7–9. The references must be familiar with the applicant's past employment. The rankings of the panel and the references are correlated,

EXHIBIT 7–9
Sample reference letter for applicant for employment interviewer positions

Dear _____

Mr. _____ is applying for a position with our company and has supplied your name as a reference. We would appreciate it if you would take a few moments to give us your opinions about him.

Listed below is a series of items that may describe skills, abilities, knowledge, or personal characteristics of the applicant to a greater or lesser degree. Will you please look at this list and rank them from most to least like the applicant by placing the appropriate letter in the space below. If you do not have an opinion about a specific item, skip it and rank what you can, beginning with Space 1.

    A.   Has the ability to develop scheduled and nonscheduled interview formats for various jobs.
    B.   Can conduct an interview using the nondirective approach
    C.   Has a neat appearance (clothes clean, in good condition)
    D.   Makes checks to see if people understand his meaning when he speaks to them.
    E.   Makes checks to see if he understands people when they speak to him.

    1.   _____ (Most characteristic of the applicant)
    2.   _____
    3.   _____
    4.   _____
    5.   _____ (Least characteristic of the applicant)

Now, on the rating scale below, please indicate with a check in the appropriate space the degree to which the applicant possesses the last ranked skill, ability, knowledge or personal characteristic. If he is very high in the characteristic, give a rating of 5; if he is very low, give him a rating of 1. Place your check in between the two extremes if you consider that a more appropriate rating.

    Very low |___|___|___|___|___| Very high
            1   2   3   4   5

Comments about the applicant:

Source: Clemm C. Kessler, III, and Georgia J. Gibbs, "Getting the Most from Application Blanks and References," *Personnel,* January–February 1975.

and the greater the correlation, the more likely is the applicant to be hired.

In addition to validity, there is another problem with written references. In 1974 the U.S. Congress passed the Privacy Act of 1974 (Public Law 93–579), and since then legislation and judicial rulings have had a major effect on reference letters. Under the act, persons have a legal right to examine letters of reference concerning them unless they waive their right to do so. The EEOC sued the National Academy of Sciences over letters of recommendation which it contends discriminates against minorities. One applicant who lost a job because of a bad reference letter sued the letter writer and won damages. As a result, objective reference letters are now hard to come by. Many prior employers will verify in writing only the last job title, salary, and date of employment.[62]

One way to get around the privacy law is for the applicant to sign a release form stating that he or she waives the right to examine the letter(s). Whether the courts will allow this is yet to be determined. David Shaffer et al. found that applicants who waived this right were favored by employers because their credentials seemed more creditable.[63]

When there is need to verify biodata, a more acceptable alternative for a letter might be a phone call to the applicant's previous supervisors. The organization can contact certain persons in order to cross-check opinions or to probe further on doubtful points. Of the firms studied by the National Industrial Conference Board, only 13 percent of manufacturers, 19 percent of insurance companies, 44 percent of banks, 15 percent of utilities, 40 percent of retailers, and 8 percent of wholesale companies felt written reference checks alone were the most reliable method of checking references.[64]

One study investigated how 122 companies conducted checks on biodata and references.[65] Almost 85 percent of the checks were done by employment interviewers or other personnel specialists; less than 17 percent used outside agencies. Telephone checks alone were used in 12 percent of the cases; the other 88 percent used a combination of telephone, personal interviews, and letters of reference, primarily to check previous employment records. Employment with several previous employers was checked by 79 percent, and only the most recent employer by 10 percent. Education was the next most frequently checked item; 16 percent did not check it, but almost 64 percent tried to get education transcripts. Less frequently checked and investigated were military discharge and police records.

Although little data for reliability exists, it appears to be very useful to find out how the applicant performed on previous jobs. This can be the most relevant information for predicting future work behavior. Reference checks would seem in order for the most crucial jobs at any time. Costs of these checks vary from a few cents for a few quick telephone calls to several hundred dollars for a thorough field investigation. It is not known whether privacy legislation is affecting telephone reference checks in the way it has written letters of reference.

Step 6: Physical examinations

Some organizations require that those most likely to be selected for a position complete a medical questionnaire or take a physical examination. The reasons for such a requirement include the following:

In case of later worker's compensation claims, physical condition at the time of hiring should be known.

It is important to prevent the hiring of those with serious communicable diseases. This is especially so in hospitals, but it applies in other organizations as well.

It may be necessary to determine whether the applicant is physically capable of performing the job in question.

These purposes can be served by the completion of a medical question-naire, a physical examination, or a work physiology analysis. Richard Chase has discussed the latter technique,[66] which is neither a physical examination to determine whether or not the applicant is in good health nor a psychomo-tor test. Commonly used for selection of manual workers who will be doing hard labor, it attempts to determine, by physiological indices (heart rate and oxygen consumption), the true fatigue engendered by the work. This is analyzed through simulated job performance. First, the analyst measures applicants and obtains baseline information on these indices while they are seated. Then data are gathered while they are working. The data are analyzed and the workers are ranked; those with the lowest heart rate and oxygen consumption should be hired (all other factors being equal).

Physical examinations have *not* been shown to be very reliable as a predica-tor of future medical problems.[67] This is at least partially so because of the state of the art of medicine; different physicians emphasize different factors in the exam, based on their training and specialties. There is some evidence that correlating the presence of certain past medical problems (as learned from the completion of a medical questionnaire) can be as reliable as a physical exam performed by a physician and is probably less costly.[68]

SELECTION OF MANAGERS

The selection process and the tools used vary with the type of employee being hired. The preceding section focused on blue-, gray-, and white-collar employees, but the general process is similar for the managerial employee.[69]

Before a manager is hired, the job is studied. Then the criteria are selected, based on the characteristics of effective managers in the organization at present and likely future needs. *Each enterprise* must do this, since the manage-rial task differs by level, function, industry, and in other ways. Studies of successful managers across these groups have concluded that many (not all) successful executives have intelligence, drive, good judgment, and mana-gerial skills.[70] Most of the studies avoid the real-world problem of asymmet-rical choices. Candidate A scores high on intelligence and motivation, low on verbal skills, and moderate on hard work. Candidate B scores moderate on intelligence, high on motivation, moderate on verbal skills, and high on hard work. Both have good success records. Which one would you choose? The tradeoffs must be assessed for particular jobs and particular organi-zations.

One recruiter told me this:

I've read the studies about high intelligence, test scores, and so on in managerial selection. But I've found I've got to look at the job. For example, our most successful sales managers are those who grew up on a farm where they learned to work hard on their own. They went to the nearest state college (all they could afford) and majored in business. They got good to better than average grades. They might have done better gradewise if they hadn't had to work their way through school. Our best accounting managers *did not* have that background.

Again the message: these studies can indicate the likely predictors of success *in general,* but executive success must be analyzed in each organization. Each of the factors mentioned must be correlated with success measured several ways, to see which works for the organization. However, the focus of selection must be on *behavior,* not just on scores on tests or general impressions.

Once the criteria of managerial success are known, the selection tools to be used are chosen. In general, tests are not frequently used in managerial selection. Reference checks have been a major source of data on managerial applicants, but the legal problems with this tool also apply at this level. Biodata and curriculum vitae analysis is a major tool used for managerial selection. As John Campbell et al. put it, "Very often, a carefully developed typical behavior inventory based on biographical information has proved to be the single best predictor of future job behavior . . . biographic information has proved particularly useful for assessing managerial effectiveness."[71]

The most frequently used selection tool for managers is the interview. More often than not, it is used in conjunction with the other methods. But if only one method is used by an organization, it is likely to be the personal interview.

One study found more successful managers are hired using judgments derived in employment interviews than decisions based on test scores.[72] This is no doubt so because these judgments can be based on factorially complex behavior, and typical executive performance is behaviorally complex. The interview is likely to continue to be the most used selection method because organizations want to hire managers they feel they can trust and feel comfortable with.

Assessment centers

One very promising method used for managerial selection that is not used for employee selection is the assessment center. It uses multiple selection methods and has many purposes, but the major one is managerial selection and evaluation. They have been used by Sears, J. C. Penney, General Electric, IBM, AT&T, and Sohio, among other companies. Originated by Henry Murray, they were used by the OSS and the British War Office to select spies in World War II.

There are, of course, a variety of approaches to any technique, including the assessment center. Essentially, it is a multiple peer-superior rating method using many inputs of data (it is described in some detail in Chapter 10). This is an expensive mechanism. Although it is new, evaluation studies so far strongly support the use of assessment center procedures as the most effective method of managerial selection.[73]

THE SELECTION DECISION

These are three types of approaches to the selection decision:

Random choice or chance approaches. Examples are choosing the third applicant interviewed or putting names in a hat and drawing one out.[74]

Emotional-clinical approach. The manager unconsciously picks the applicant who was most likeable in the interviews.

Systematic-quasirational. The chapter has focused on a systemic approach using various selection techniques, while recognizing that unconscious emotional choices are likely to enter into the decision.

Some studies have been done to contrast and evaluate the various selection techniques.[75] Lawrence Jauch proposes an interesting combination of the systematic and clinical approaches to the selection decision which is inexpensive and realistic enough for the average manager to use.[76] He calls it the paired-comparison method, in which a matrix of the candidates and the criteria is developed, as shown in Exhibit 7–10.

EXHIBIT 7–10
Selection decision matrix for paired-comparison technique

Criteria \ Candidates	A–Mr. Black	B–Mr. White	C–Ms. Neutral	D–Mrs. Other
I. Education	College grad.	High school grad.	High school grad.	Two years college
II. Test scores	130	110	115	120
III. Experience	None	5 years	8 years	2 years
IV. Job knowledge	Above average	Excellent	Excellent	Average
V. Past performance	Excellent	Average	Above average	Above average
VI. Desire	Above average	Average	High	Above average
VII. Stability	Low	Average	High	Below average
VIII. Interviewer 1	1	3.5	2	3.5
IX. Interviewer 2	2	3	1	4
X. Interviewer 3	2	4	3	1

Then each interviewer compares each candidate to the others on each criterion (I–VII) and ranks them relative to each other (VIII–X). These ranks then are summed or weighted according to the decision makers' evaluation of the opinion of each interviewer.

A method similar to Jauch's might be used to try to reconcile differences of opinion on selection between personnel specialists and operating managers. If that does not work it appears reasonable that the operating manager who will supervise the applicant should prevail, since this is the manager who must deal with an unsuitable or ineffective employee.

COST/BENEFIT ANALYSIS FOR THE SELECTION DECISION

One way to evaluate which selection techniques should be used is to consider the probabilities that particular methods will select successful candidates and the costs of these methods. The seven steps in the selection procedure and their probable costs are:

Method	Cost
1. Preliminary screening interview	Negligible
2. Application blank/biodata	Negligible
3. Employment interview	Time used X cost per hour
4. Employment tests	$5–$1,000
5. Background and reference checks	$100
6. Physical examination	$25
7. Decision	

Each of these steps can be regarded as a hurdle which will select out the least qualified candidates. Steps 1, 2, and 3 probably will be used in most cases. The questionable ones are 4, 5, and 6 for many persons, and step 6 may not be appropriate. As for Step 5, the checks need not be used for many jobs which do not involve much responsibility. Each selection technique can be evaluated in terms of costs and benefits, as in the following example which evaluates the use of tests.

Costs of training and selecting personnel may have tradeoff features which can be calculated. In a hypothetical company, there is a current need for hiring 25 new employees. It is known from prior experience with these positions that for every satisfactory employee you have selected, an unsatisfactory employee has also been chosen. Consequently, if this present method is continued, you will have hired and trained 50 people in order to satisfy the need for 25 satisfactory employees.

In the past, the training cost for one selectee has been $150. Thus it costs $7,500 ($150 X 50) to ultimately obtain 25 satisfactory people. On the basis of unit-training cost per satisfactory employee, the cost of the present method is $300 ($7,500/25).

It might be possible to reduce total personnel costs by using some additional selection device, such as a test. Tests cost $2.50 per applicant for the instrument and administration. The experience with such a test for the types of positions to be filled is shown in Exhibit 7–11. Now the question is: Would the use of this device decrease overall costs?

First, if a score of 30 is used as a cutoff point, the cost of selecting and training 25 employees can be calculated as follows. Fifty applicants out of 100 will be satisfactory trainees at the 30 cutoff point. Fifty applicants must be tested if you want the end result of 25 satisfactory people (25 X 100/50). (Note that the distributions shown in Exhibit 7–12 follow a "normal distribution," and all distributions do not have this quality.)

So the cost of testing, which was not encountered in the previous selection method, adds $125 ($2.50 X 50) to the selection cost. But what happens to training costs? The number of people to be trained will be reduced by screen-

EXHIBIT 7–11
Employee selection and personnel costs using tests

```
                                              20
                 20                            X
                 19                            X
                 18                            X
                 17                    16      X      16
                 16                    X       X      X
                 15                    X       X      X
                 14                    X       X      X
                 13             12     X       X      X      12
                 12             X      X       X      X      X
                 11             X      X       X      X      X
Frequency        10            X      X       X      X      X
                  9             X      X       X      X      X
                  8             X      X       X      X      X
                  7       6     X      X       X      X      X      6
                  6       X     X      X       X      X      X      X
                  5    4  X     X      X       X      X      X      X      4
                  4    X  X     X      X       X      X      X      X      X
                  3    X  X     X      X       X      X      X      X      X      2
                  2 2  X  X     X      X       X      X      X      X      X      X
                  1 X  X  X     X      X       X      X      X      X      X      X
Score             10 20 30    40     50      60     70     80     90    100    110

Percent            2  6  12   24     40      60     76     88     94     98    100
```

```
                                                  16     12     6      4      2
                                                  X      X      X      X      X
High                                       20     X      X      X      X      X
                                           X      X      X      X      X
                                           X      X      X      X      X
                                           X      X      X      X
                                           X      X      X      X
                                           X      X      X      X
                                    16     X      X      X
                                    X      X      X      X
                                    X      X      X      X
                                    X      X      X      X
Criterion                    12     X      X      X      X              (50) Successful
Measure                      X      X      X      X
                             X      X      X      X
                             X      X      X      X
                             X      X      X      X                     (50) Unsuccessful
                       6     X      X      X      X
                       X     X      X      X
                       X     X      X      X
                   4   X     X      X      X
                   X   X     X      X      X
                   X   X     X      X
                 2 X         X      X
Low              X   X       X      X
                 X
Score            10 20 30   40     50     60     70     80     90    100    110

Percent           2  6  12  24     40     60     76     88     94     98    100

                                  Predictor
```

ing out some unsatisfactory people. Exhibit 7–11 shows that 88 applicants in 100 will score above 30, but of these 38 still will end up being unsatisfactory. To select the 25 satisfactory people, then, 50 will have to be tested. Six will be eliminated immediately, and another 19 will go through training unsatisfactorily. The total number of trainees is thus 44 (25 + 19). Since the training costs are $6,600 ($150 × 44) the total costs are $6,725 (selection and training). The unit cost per satisfactory employee has now become $269 ($6,725/25). By using the test with a cutoff score of 30, the total cost has been reduced by $31 per satisfactory employee ($300—$269) under the previous method.

It might now be asked whether you can do better: You still have had to train 19 unsatisfactory employees. You can try the method used above with a cutoff point of 60 on the test. This time, however, more than 50 people will have to be tested. Again looking at Exhibit 7–11 it can be seen that 36 out of 100 applicants will be "satisfactory" at a cutoff point of 60. To reach 25 satisfactory people, about 70 applicants must be tested (25 × 100/36); 28 of these will score above 60, and 25 of these will be satisfactory, while 3 will be unsatisfactory. Now the costs are as follows: testing = $175 ($2.50 × 70); training = $4,200 (28 × $150); total cost = $4,375 ($175 + $4,200); unit cost per satisfactory employee = $177 ($4,375/25). This is $125 per unit less than the initial method without the test, and $94 per unit less than the cost of using the test with a cutoff score of 30.

There are still three trained individuals who will not be satisfactory. What would happen if you eliminated all unsatisfactory applicants by moving the cutoff score to 100? Compute this on your own to see what the answer is. You might find some interesting tradeoffs which go into costs of selecting and training satisfactory employees.

One final comment about the selection decision. The greater the number of scources of data into the decision, the more probable it is that it will be a good decision. Tests alone will not suffice. Interviews supplemented by background checks and some test results are better. Costs and time constraints, however, are obviously crucial.

SUMMARY, CONCLUSIONS, AND RECOMMENDATIONS

This chapter has been designed to help you make more effective selection decisions. These decisions are influenced by a number of environmental characteristics: whether the enterprise is public or private, labor market conditions and the selection ratio, union requirements, and legal restrictions on selection. In addition reasonable criteria for employees must be set prior to choice. The selection process can include up to six steps which involve various techniques. How many and which ones are used depends on the environment, the criteria for selection, and the cost of bad selection decisions. These costs can be high in training and orientation needed, court challenges, and so on. The costs and benefits of the techniques used can be assessed according to the method just described.

Exhibit 7–12 summarizes the recommendations for use of the various selection methods in the model organizations. While selection appears to be universally used as a personnel activitity, the techniques adopted are likely to be based on the types of personnel selected rather than the type of organization doing the selection.

EXHIBIT 7–12
Recommendations on selection methods for model organizations

Type of organization	Screening interview	Application blank, biodata	Employ-ment interview	Performance and ability tests*	Telephoned background reference check †	Physical exam
1. Large size, low complexity, high stability	X	X	X	X	X	Hospital
2. Medium size, low complexity, high stability	X	X	X	X	X	
3. Small size, low complexity, high stability	X	X				
4. Medium size, moderate complexity, moderate stability	X	X	X	X	X	
5. Large size, high complexity, low stability	X	X	X	X	X	Hospital
6. Medium size, high complexity, low stability	X	X	X			
7. Small size, high complexity, low stability	X	X	X			Hospital

* Usually for blue- and white-collar positions.
† Usually for white-collar and managerial positions.

The following propositions summarize the conclusions of this chapter.

Proposition 7.1 The larger the organization, the more likely is it for selection decisions to follow a systematic-quasirational procedure involving most selection steps or techniques.

Proposition 7.2 The more important the position (measured by higher pay and responsibility), the more likely is the selection decision to be formalized and to use more selection techniques.

Proposition 7.3 Other things being equal, the effective organization prefers to select persons already in the organization over outside candidates, except in time of major upheaval or change.

Proposition 7.4 More effective selection decisions are made if both personnel managers and the future supervisors of potential employees are involved in the selection decision.

Proposition 7.5 The greater the number of accepted methods used to gather data for selection decisions, the greater the number of successful candidates that will be selected.

Proposition 7.6 The larger the organization, the more likely is it to use the more sophisticated selection techniques.

Proposition 7.7 The more complex and volatile the organization, the less likely is it to use effectively techniques of selection which do not require extensive validation (such as interviews).

Proposition 7.8 The more measurable the job, the more effectively can tests be used in the selection decision.

Proposition 7.9 The lower the job is in the hierarchy, the more likely is it that tests can be used effectively in the selection decision.

It is not likely that all six steps in selection will be used to select part-time employees. The screening and employment interview and the application blank are most likely to be used for this selection decision.

Communication is important in the interview and reference-check aspects of selection. The employer or the employer's representative must communicate effectively in describing the job and in trying to induce a desirable applicant to come to work for the employer. It is also very important for the employer to communicate with those not selected in such a way as to enhance their self-esteem, despite failing to be hired for a particular position.

One final point about selection should be made. We began this chapter with a description of the purpose of formal selection techniques: to aid the manager in selection activities. It should be noted that even if, as a result of the selection process, the most able applicant is chosen, this is no guarantee of successful performance on the job. Other factors, such as the employee's motivation and needs, the supervisor's skills, and nonwork factors, may cause an employee to fail to use his or her abilities to enhance the effectiveness of the organization.

Top managers can influence the selection process by setting the climate for the selection decision and helping to decide on the techniques to be used. More importantly, they set the policy for whether informal or formal methods will predominate in selection decisions in the organization.

Chapter 8 describes orientation programs: the next personnel activity to affect the employee after selection.

APPENDIX: HOW TO CONDUCT EFFECTIVE INTERVIEWS*

Purposes of selection interviews

Many employment interviewers perceive their only task as being to screen and select those individuals best suited for employment. While this is unquestionably the *main* function of the employment interview, it is not the only one. In one study of an oil company in 1969 it was found that for every 37 collegians interviewed, one was hired. A ratio of 53 interviews

---

* This appendix was written by James Lahiff, The University of Georgia. References used to develop the appendix are given in References 26–39 for the chapter.

for each hire was reported in the study of another company in 1971. When you consider the tremendous number of employment interviews conducted, the potential for effective public relations in the employment interview becomes obvious.

In addition to the selection and public relations roles, the employment interviewer also must function as an educator. It is the interviewer's responsibility to "educate" the applicants concerning those details of the job in question which are not immediately apparent. The interviewer must be able to answer the applicant's questions with honesty and candor and, to be effective, must remain aware of all three of these functions while conducting the employment interview.

Phases of interviews

There are five distinct phases into which the employment interview may be divided. The fact that the interview is divided into five phases does not mean that each phase is separate and distinct from what precedes it and from what follows it, for the interview is a continuous process. The phases of the interview simply suggest the changing nature of the interviewer's strategy as the interview progresses. The sequence of steps followed in the employment interview is described below.

Phase 1: Preplanning.   The more informed the interviewer is both on the job in question and on the individual applicant, the more appropriate the interviewer's eventual decision should be. The interviewer should be aware of the duties of the job to be filled. If the job description is unclear or incomplete, the interviewer should get this information from someone presently holding the job or from the person whose job it is to supervise that position.

Many employment interviewers perceive their job as being to get to know the applicant and to make an educated guess on the likelihood of the applicant's possible effectiveness. Instead, the interviewer should determine the most critical requirements for the job. That is, what characteristics or traits are most necessary in performing the duties of the job? If a person could succeed on the job without a certain factor, it is not truly a critical requirement. For example, one researcher found these factors to be critical requirements for the job of airline reservation clerk: pleasant appearance and manner, interest in serving people, adaptability, willingness to accept shift work, and an interest in a career in the industry.

Thus the interviewer's task is more complex than just getting to know the applicant. The interaction will be directed toward the critical requirements, and the interviewer's biases should be less influential than if the task were more general. These critical requirements can usually be limited to four to six; it is such limitation that makes the interviewer's job manageable in a relatively short period of time. By introducing these specifics, the interviewer will be freed from the uncertainties surrounding the global judgments which still characterize many employment interviews.

In addition to becoming familiar with the job, the interviewer must also be acquainted in advance with the applicant. In general, an application blank is available, and in some cases a resumé and test scores. These should be read in advance. Sometimes the applicant has already been interviewed by another interviewer, and a report of that interview may be available. In order to maintain objectivity, however, the interviewer should avoid reading the interview report prior to the interview.

By becoming familiar with the applicant's background in advance, the interviewer avoids the temptation of using the application blank as an outline for the interview. When an interview is tied directly to the application blank, the information elicited usually duplicates what is already a matter of record. Such an approach, in addition to being tedious, is extremely limiting to both participants. The interviewer learns little new information, and the applicant has scant opportunity to elaborate.

When analyzing the application and resumé in advance, the interviewer should look for such things as discrepancies in the information, unexplained gaps in the time periods covered, and other items which raise questions. When planned properly the interview will provide answers to these questions, and it will reveal additional information on the applicant.

The interviewer should know the time frame within which the interview must be conducted and plan accordingly, deciding on the topics to be covered and the time to be budgeted to each of them. Most employment interviewers attempt to cover work experience, education, and outside interests. Planning should also include how to terminate the interview and what to tell the applicant about the selection process. Enough time also should be budgeted to allow for writing whatever notes and comments are necessary immediately following the interview.

There has been ample research to show that the arrangement of furniture in a setting can either enhance or inhibit communication. A desk may constitute a barrier to communication when placed between interviewer and applicant. Many interviewers who have heeded such findings and restructured their offices accordingly have been pleased with the results. More important than the physical environment, however, is the climate created by the interviewer. The interviewer who provides privacy for the interview and who actively preplans the employment interview is taking a giant step to providing a climate conducive to effective interviewing.

Phase 2: Clarify purpose and enhance relaxation.   No survey has ever shown the number of employment interviews conducted in which one or both parties were mistaken as to the job being discussed. Such a survey would probably reveal a high rate of such misunderstandings. In order to avoid such occurrences, even at the risk of belaboring the obvious, the interviewer should ascertain that both parties are discussing the same job.

Having accomplished this, the interviewer should establish rapport with the applicant and thereby reduce the tension level. Many interviewers appear to believe that several minutes of chatting about some innocuous topic is a prerequisite for rapport to be established. If the total number of hours devoted annually in interviews to talking about the weather were instead applied to interview preparation, much more information would be exchanged, and better selection decisions would result.

Rather than forcing artificial conversation, the interviewer should allow the applicant a minute or two to become familiar with the surroundings. This can be accomplished by taking a quick reappraisal of the application blank before commencing, thus providing a brief respite for the applicant to relax. If this review of the application blank reveals a topic of possible mutual interest to interviewer and applicant, the interviewer can use it to help put the applicant at ease. In the absence of such a topic of mutual interest, however, it is better to launch right into the interview after allowing adequate time to get comfortably settled. When an interviewer begins an interview by straining to make small talk, the applicant recognizes the artificiality of the attempt and what had originally been intended to reduce tension actually heightens it.

Phase 3: Preview the topics. After clarifying the purpose of the interview and attempting to put the applicant at ease, the interviewer can do much to reduce the uncertainty in the interviewer's mind by briefly previewing the topics to be covered in the interview. By simply stating the categories of information of interest and the sequence in which the categories will be covered, the interviewer will be adding some structure which will result in a more confident and trusting applicant and usually in a more productive interview. When the interviewer tells a job-seeker that they will be discussing the applicant's background, work experience, formal education, and outside interests, the interviewer is helping the applicant to get organized.

Phase 4: Elicit and give information. Most of the time budgeted for the interview is devoted to this phase. After previewing the topics to be covered, the interviewer should return to the first topic and cover it in as much detail as is deemed necessary. The interviewer implements the strategy determined in the preplanning stage, and the amount of structure becomes obvious. The more structured the interviewer's approach, the more closed questions will be employed and the more directive will be the techniques of the interviewer.

In most employment interviews, which are of the semistructured type, the interviewer begins each topic with an open-ended question and then proceeds toward a more specific question. This pattern is usually repeated for each topic, while the interviewer is aware of the constraints in the situation.

Although employment interviews are generally perceived as question-and-answer sessions, with the interviewer asking the questions, the interviewer must also encourage questions from the interviewee and be prepared to tell the applicant about the job and the enterprise. It should be the interviewer's task to provide those facts that will help the applicant to make the employment decision.

Phase 5: Close the interview. When approximately 90 percent of the interview has been completed, the interviewer must begin to close the interview. In the remaining minutes the interviewer seeks to answer any remaining questions, to summarize what has been discussed, and to point to the future, indicating what lies ahead for the applicant. The applicant has the right to know whether the interviewer has made a decision and, if so, what it is. It is unethical to allow an applicant to leave an interview not knowing that an adverse decision has already been made. If the applicant is being favorably considered, this also should be made clear and the remainder of the selection procedure should be explained.

QUESTIONS

1. What is personnel selection? Who makes these decisions?
2. What circumstances influence personnel selection? How?
3. What government regulations affect personnel selection?
4. What is a selection ratio? How does it apply to personnel selection?
5. Who sets selection criteria? How are they developed? Why are they used?
6. What is reliability? Validity? How does one compute these two?
7. Which selection criteria are most important? When?
8. Describe a typical selection process for a manual laborer; top executive; typist.
9. What is a preliminary screening interview? How is it effectively performed?
10. How are biodata forms used in selection? How effective are they? Are they reliable and valid? How frequently are they used?
11. What is an employment interview? How often is it used? What are three types of interview styles? Which are the most reliable?
12. Describe some guidelines to effective interviewing.
13. What is a test? A performance test? A simulation? A paper-and-pencil test?
14. Tests are increasing in use in the United States. Comment.
15. Which tests are most reliable and valid?
16. How do you validate a test? Is it an easy task? Why or why not?
17. When would you use reference checks? For which jobs? How would you do the checks?
18. All applicants should undergo a physical exam. Comment.
19. How does the process of selecting a manager differ from selecting a typist? How is it similar?
20. The systematic-quasirational selection decision is best. Comment.
21. In the propositions, which factors in the environment least affect selection?
22. In the propositions, which factors affect the selection process the most?
23. Which of the model organizations are not likely to use performance and ability tests?
24. Which of the model organizations need to use physical exams?
25. How many phases are there to effective employment interviews? Briefly describe each.
26. Can we compute the costs and benefits of selection decisions? How?

NOTES AND REFERENCES

1. Robert Sibson, "The High Cost of Hiring," *Nation's Business,* February, 1975, pp. 85–88.

2. Associated Press, "Civil Service Favoritism Probed," February 17, 1976, Matthew Coffey, "A Death at the White House: The Short Life of the New Patronage," *Public Administration Review,* September–October 1974, pp. 440–44; Jonathan Laing, "Fighting the System: Civil Service Set Up, Born as a Reform Idea, Now Hit by Reformers," *The Wall Street Journal,* December 22, 1975.

3. James Levinka and Robert Gatewood, "EEO Issues with Preemployment Inquiries," *The Personnel Administrator,* February 1977, pp. 22–26.

4. Laurence Siegel, *Industrial Psychology* (Homewood, Ill.: Richard D. Irwin, Inc., 1969).

5. Marvin Dunnette, "Basic Attributes of Individuals in Relation to Behavior in Organizations," in *Handbook of Industrial and Organizational Psychology,* ed. Marvin Dunnette (Chicago: Rand McNally & Co., 1976).

6. Nicholas Di Marco and Mildred Hilliard, "Comparisons of Quality of Patient Care and Competency between Baccalaureate and Technical Degree Nurses," *Proceedings,* Academy of Management, 1976; Nicholas di Marco and Mildred Hilliard, "Comparisons of Associate, Diploma, and Baccalaureate Degree Nurses' State Board, Quality of Patient Care, Competency Rating, Supervisor Rating, Subordinates' Satisfaction with Supervisor, and Self-Report Job Satisfaction Scores," *Proceedings,* Southern Management Association, 1976.

7. Leonard Nadler, "Recognition of Non-Collegiate Learning Experiences," *Training and Development Journal,* July 1975, pp. 8–11.

8. Thomas Harrell, and Margaret Harrell, "Relation of Second Year MBA Grades to Business Earnings," *Personnel Psychology* 27 (1974), pp. 487–91.

9. Charles Link, "Graduate Education, School Quality, Experience, Student Ability, and Earnings," *Journal of Business,* October 1975, pp. 477–91.

10. Georgia Psacharopoulos, "College Quality as a Screening Device," *The Journal of Human Resources,* Fall 1974, pp. 556–58.

11. For example, see Sara Behman, "The Affirmative Action Position (on Seniority)" *Labor Law Journal,* August 1976, pp. 490–96; Charles Burck, "A Group Profile of the Fortune 500 Chief Executive," *Fortune,* May 1976, pp. 173–77 ff.; Sheila Connelly, "Job Posting," *Personnel Journal,* May 1975, pp. 295–97; James Craft, "Equal Opportunity and Seniority," *Labor Law Journal,* December 1975, pp. 750–58; Ben Fischer, "Seniority Is Health," *Labor Law Journal,* August 1976, pp. 497–503; Wayne Green, "Justices Uphold Giving Seniority Retroactively," *The Wall Street Journal,* March 25, 1976; George Leonard, "Practical Applications of Superseniority," *Labor Law Journal,* January 1975, pp. 44–48; Robert Lund et al., "Inverse Seniority: Timely Answer to the Layoff Dilemma," *Harvard Business Review,* September–October 1975, pp. 65–72; Richard Sibbernsen, "A Review of Job and Seniority Structures in Light of EEO Liability," *Labor Law Journal,* October 1975; Norman Wood, "EEO and Seniority: Rights in Conflict," *Labor Law Journal,* June, 1975, pp. 345–49; David Ziskind, "Retroactive Seniority: A Remedy for Hiring Discrimination," *Labor Law Journal,* August 1976, pp. 480–89.

12. Phillip Callis, "Minimum Height and Weight Requirements as a Form of Sex Discrimination," *Labor Law Journal,* December 1974, pp. 736–45.

13. John Kriegsmann and David Hardin, "Does Divorce Hamper Job Performance?" *The Personnel Administrators,* March–April 1974, pp. 26–29.

14. C. O. Neidt, "Applicant Flow Data Analysis," *The Personnel Administrator,* June 1974.

15. Harish Jain, "Managerial Recruitment and Selection in the Canadian Manufacturing Industry," *Public Personnel Management,* May–June 1974, pp. 207–15.

16. National Industrial Conference Board, *Personnel Practices for Factory and Office: Manufacturing,* Studies in Personnel Policy 194 (New York, 1964); National Industrial Conference Board, *Personnel Practices in the Office: Non-Manufacturing,* Studies in Personnel Policy 197 (New York, 1965).

17. William Owens, "Background Data," in *Handbook of Industrial and Organizational Psychology,* ed. Marvin Dunnette.

18. Clemm C. Kessler, III, and Georgia J. Gibbs, "Getting the Most from Application Blanks and References," *Personnel,* January–February 1975, pp. 53–62.

19. Owens, "Background Data."

20. Allen Schuh, "Application Blank and Intelligence as Predictors of Turnover," *Personnel Psychology,* Spring 1967, pp. 59–63; Allen Schuh, The Predictability of Employer Tenure: A Review of the Literature," *Personnel Psychology,* Spring 1967, pp. 133–52.

21. George W. England, *Development and Use of Weighted Application Blanks,* Bulletin 55, Industrial Relations Center, University of Minnesota, rev. ed. (Minneapolis, 1971); David Weiss, "Multivariate Procedures," in *Handbook of Industrial and Organizational Psychology,* ed. Marvin Dunnette, pp. 344–54.

22. J. P. Guilford, and J. I. Lacey, (eds), AAF Aviation Psychology Research Program, Report no. 5 (Washington, D.C.: U.S. Government Printing Office, 1947); J. A. Parish, and A. J. Drucher, "Personnel Research for OCS," VAATAGO Personnel Branch, Technical Research Report no. 117, 1957; H. Roy et al., "Selection of Army and Air Force ROTC Students," *USA Personnel Research Branch Notes* no. 28 (1954), Standard Oil Co. (N.J.), Social Science Research Reports; vol. 1, *Selection and Placement* (New York: 1962), vol 3, *Performance Review and Evaluation;* Patrick Pinto, *Subgrouping in Prediction* unpublished Ph.D. thesis, University of Georgia, 1970; E. S. Ruda, *The Effect of Interpersonal Simularity on Management Performance,* unpublished Ph.D. thesis, Purdue University, 1970.

23. Edwin Ghiselli, *The Validity of Occupational Aptitude Tests* (New York: John Wiley & Sons, 1966).

24. J. L. Mosel and L. W. Cozan, "The Accuracy of Application Work Histories," *Journal of Applied Psychology* 36 (1952), pp. 365–69; E. Keating, et al.; "Validity of Work Histories Obtained by Interview," *Journal of Applied Psychology* 34 (1950), pp. 1–5; Melany Baehr, and Glen Williams, "Prediction of Sales Success from Factorally Determined Dimensions of Personal Background Data," *Journal of Applied Psychology,* 52 (April 1968), pp. 98–103; Institute for Behavioral Research in Creativity (IBRIC), *Manual for Alpha Biographical Inventory* (Greensboro, N.C.: Predictions Press, 1968).

25. D. I. Weiss, and R. V. Davis, "An Objective Validation of Factual Interview Data," *Journal of Applied Psychology* 44 (1968), pp. 381–85.

26. The author wishes to thank James Lahiff, of the University of Georgia, for his contributions to Step 3 and for writing the appendix on interviews.

27. W. R. Spriegel et al., *Personnel Practices in Industry* (Austin: University of Texas, Bureau of Business Research, 1958).

28. Bureau of National Affairs, *Personnel Policies Forum,* Survey no. 114, September 1976.

29. Ibid.

30. Eugene Mayfield, "The Selection Interview—A Re-Evaluation of Published Research," *Personnel Psychology,* Autumn 1964, pp. 239–60; Lynn Ulrich, and Don Trumbo, "The Selection Interview Since 1949," *Psychological Bulletin* 63 (February 1965), pp. 110–16; Donald P. Schwab, and Herbert Heneman, III, "Relationship between Interview Structure and Interinterviewer Reliability in an Employment Situation," *Journal of Applied Psychology* 53 (1969), 214–17; James J. Asher, "Reliability of a Novel Format for the Selection Interview," *Psychological Reports* 26 (1970), pp. 451–56.

31. Micheal M. Burgess, Virginia Calkins, and James M. Richards, "The Structured Interview: A Selection Device," *Psychological Reports* 31 (1972), pp. 867–77; Herbert Heneman, III, et al., "Interviewer Validity as a Function of Interview Structure, Biographical Data, and Interviewee Order," *Journal of Applied Psychology* 60 (1975), pp. 748–53.

32. Executive Enterprises Publications *Conducting the Lawful Employment Interview* (New York, 1974).

33. Herbert Heneman, III, "The Impact of Interviewer Training and Interview Structure on the Reliability and Validity of the Selection Interview," *Proceedings,* Academy of Management, 1975; R. C. Carlson et al; "Improvements in the Selection Interview," *Personnel Journal* 50 (1971), pp. 268–74.

34. Mayfield, "The Selection Interview"; E. C. Webster, *Decision Making in the Employment Interview* (Montreal: Eagle Press, 1964).

35. Benjamin Schneider, *Staffing Organizations* (Pacific Palisades, Cal.: Goodyear Publishing Co., 1976), ch. 4.

36. Frank Landy, "The Validity of the Interview in Police Officer Selection," *Journal of Applied Psychology* 61, 2 (1976), pp. 193–98.

37. Marvin Okanes, and Harvey Tschirgi, "Impact of the Face to Face Interview on Prior Judgments of a Candidate," *Proceedings,* Midwest Academy of Management, April 1977.

38. S. W. Constantin, "An Investigation of Information Favorability in the Employment Interview," *Journal of Applied Psychology* 61, 6 (1976), pp. 743–49.

39. BNA, *Personnel Policies Forum.*

40. Joseph McCormick, and Ernest Tiffin, *Industrial Psychology* (Englewood Cliffs, Prentice-Hall, Inc. 1975); Arthur Siegel and Brian Bergman, "A Job Learning Approach to Performance Predictions," *Personnel Psychology* 28 (1975), pp. 325–39.

41. The following is a list of some of the summaries. They are updated regularly. Phillip Ash, and Leonard Krocker, "Personnel Selection, Classification, and Placement," *Annual Review of Psychology* (Palo Alto, Cal.; Annual Reviews, Inc., 1975); Douglas Jackson, and Samuel Messick, *Problems in Human Assessment* (New York: McGraw-Hill Book Co., 1966); Lewis Goldberg, "Objective Diagnostic Tests and Measures," *Annual Review of Psychology* (Palo Alto, Cal.; Annual Reviews, Inc., 1974). John Horn, "Human Abilities," *Annual Review of Psychology* (Palo Alto, Cal.; Annual Reviews, Inc., 1976). Marvin Dunnette, "Attitudes, Abilities, and Skills," in *Handbook of Industrial and Organizational Psychology*, ed. Marvin Dunnette; Oscar K. Buros, *The Sixth Mental Measurements Year Book,* Highland Park, N.J.: Gryphon Press, 1965).

42. Edwin Ghiselli, "The Validity of Aptitude Tests in Personnel Selection," *Personnel Psychology,* Winter 1973, pp. 461–78.

43. Harrison Gough, "Personality and Personality Assessment," in *Handbook of Industrial and Organizational Psychology,* ed. Marvin Dunnette; Phillip Holzman, "Personality," in *Annual Review of Psychology* (Palo Alto, Cal.; Annual Reviews, Inc., 1974); Walter Klopfer and Earl Taulbee, "Projective Tests," *Annual Review of Psychology* (Palo Alto, Cal.: Annual Reviews, Inc., 1976).

44. John E. Reid, and Fred E. Inbau, *Truth and Deception: the Polygraph Technique* (Baltimore, Md.: Williams & Wilkins Co., 1966).

45. Robert J. Ferguson, Jr. *The Polygraph in Private Industry* (Springfield, Ill.: Charles C Thomas, Publisher, 1966); Mary Ann Coghill, *The Lie Detector in Employment,* Industrial and Labor Relations Library, Key Issues Series no. 2, 1970.

46. Bruce Gunn, "The Polygraph and Personnel," *Personnel Administration,* May 1970, pp. 32–37.

47. Ibid.

48. Burke M. Smith, "The Polygraph," *Scientific American,* January 1967, pp. 25–31.

49. Reid and Inbau, *Truth and Deception.*

50. S. Zdep, and H. Weaver, "The Graphoanalytic Approach to Selecting Life Insurance Sales-men," *Journal of Applied Psychology,* June 1967, pp. 295–99.

51. R. S. Barrett, "Gray Areas in Black and White Testing," *Harvard Business Review* 46 (1968), pp. 92–95; W. Wilson, "Toward Better Use of Psychological Testing," *Personnel,* May–June, 1962, pp. 55–62.

52. C. H. Lawshe, and J. Michael Balma, *Principles of Personnel Testing* (New York: McGraw-Hill Book Co., 1966), pp. 135–66; James Lumsden, "Test Theory," *Annual Review of Psychology* (Palo Alto, Cal.: Annual Reviews, Inc., 1976).

53. American Society of Personnel Administrators, *The Personnel Executive's Job* (Englewood Cliffs, N.J.: Prentice-Hall, ASPA, 1977).

54. M. Parry, "Ability of Psychologists to Estimate the Validities of Personnel Tests," *Personnel Psychology* 21 (1968), pp. 139–47; Erwin Taylor, and Thomas Griess, "The Missing Middle in Validation Research," *Personnel Psychology* 29 (1976), pp. 5–11; Robert Wherry, "Under-prediction from Overfitting: 45 Years of Shrinkage," *Personnel Psychology* 28 (1973), pp. 1–18.

55. J. Kirkpatrick et al., *Testing and Fair Employment* (New York: New York University Press, 1968).

56. B. O'Leary et al. *Ethnic Group Membership as a Moderator of Job Performance* (Washington, D.C.: Institute of Research, 1970).

57. American Society of Personnel Administrators, *The Personnel Executive's Job.*

58. Ibid. Other references on the use of tests include Hal Lancaster, "Failing System: Job Tests Are Dropped by Many Companies," *The Wall Street Journal,* September 3, 1975; David Rosenbloom and Carloe Obuchowski, "Public Personal Examinations and the Constitu-tion," *Public Administration Review* January–February 1977, pp. 9–18; James Mosel and Howard Goheen, "Validity of Employment Recommendation Questionnaire in Personnel Selec-tion," *Personnel Psychology,* Winter 1958, pp. 481–90; R. C. Browning, "Validity of Reference Rating from Previous Employers," *Personnel Psychology* 21, 3 (1968), pp. 389–93.

59. National Industrial Conference Board, *Personnel Practices for Factory and Office;* National Indus-trial Conference Board, *Personnel Practices in the Office.*

60. James Mosel and Howard Goheen, "Validity of the Employment Recommendation Ques-tionnaire in Personnel Selection," *Personnel Psychology;* R. C. Browning, "Validity of Reference Ratings from Previous Employers."

61. Kessler and Gibbs, "Application Blanks and References."

62. Lawrence Wangler, "Employee Reference Request Revisited," *The Personnel Administrator,* November 1975, pp. 60–62; Liz Gallese, "Campus Concern: Student Job Referrals By Teachers Hit Snags Due to a Privacy Law," *The Wall Street Journal,* January 14, 1977; *The Wall Street Journal* "References Dry Up," January 6, 1976, p. 1.

63. David Shaffer et al., "Who Shall be Hired: A Biasing Effect of the Buckley Amendment on Employment Practices," *Journal of Applied Psychology* 61, 5 (1976), pp. 571–75.

64. NICB, Personnel Practices for Factory and Office; Personnel Practices in the Office.

65. George Beason, and John Belt, "Verifying Job Applicants' Backgrounds," *The Personnel Administrator,* November–December 1974, pp. 29–32.

66. Richard Chase, "Working Physiology," *Personnel Administration,* November 1969, pp. 47–53.

67. E. P. Luongo, "The Preplacement Physical Examination in Industry—Its Values," *Archives of Environmental Health* 5 (1962), pp. 358–64; *Time,* January 10, 1977.

68. A. J., Erdmann, et al., "Health Questionnaire Use in Industrial Medical Department," *Industrial Medicine and Surgery* 22 (1953).

69. J. Hemphill, *Dimensions of Executive Positions,* Ohio State University, Bureau of Business Research Research Monograph #98. (Columbus, 1960); Henry Mintzberg, "Managerial Work: Analysis from Observation," *Management Science,* October 1971, pp. 97–110; Leonard Sayles, *Managerial Behavior* (New York: McGraw-Hill Book Co., 1964), Rosemary Stewart, *Managers and Their Jobs* (London: Macmillan & Co., 1967).

70. John P., Campbell et al., *Managerial Behavior, Performances, and Effectiveness* (New York: McGraw-Hill Book Co., 1970); Joseph Stegner, "Early Identification of Management Talent," Report no. 36–72–R1, May 1972, Rensselaer Polytechnic Institute, Troy, N.J.

71. Campbell et al., *Managerial Behavior.*

72. Korman, Abraham, "The Prediction of Managerial Performance: A Review." *Personnel Psychology,* Autumn 1968, pp. 295–322.

73. Harold Alexander et al., "Usefulness of the Assessment Center Process for Selection to Upward Mobility Programs," *Human Resource Management,* Spring 1975, pp. 10–13; Allen Kraut, "Management Assessment in International Organizations," *Industrial Relations,* 1976, pp. 172–82; James Huck and Douglas Bray, "Management Assessment Center Evaluations and Subsequent Job Performance of White and Black Females," *Personnel Psychology* 29 (1976), pp. 13–30; G. M. Worbois, "Validation of Externally Developed Assessment Procedures for Identification of Supervisory Potential," *Personnel Psychology,* Spring 1975, pp. 77–91.

74. James Tschechtelin, "Picking College Administrators Out of A Hat," *The Chronicle of Higher Education,* March, 14, 1977, p. 17.

75. William Sands, "A Method for Evaluating Alternative Recruiting and Selection Strategies," *Journal of Applied Psychology* 57, 3 (1973), pp. 222–27.

76. Lawrence Jauch, "Systemizing the Selection Decision," *Personnel Journal,* November, 1976, pp. 564–66.

Orientation
of personnel

CHAPTER OBJECTIVES

■ To demonstrate the importance of effective orientation for employee satisfaction and performance.

■ To show how new employees can be oriented effectively.

■ To illustrate the effective assignment of new employees.

CHAPTER OUTLINE

Art Johnson was so glad when he got the job at the Coca-Cola bottling works. Art really needed the job; he had been out of work six weeks now, and his wife, Betty, was busy with their two-month-old daughter. Art wanted to do a good job; he wanted to keep the job and get ahead with the company. He certainly hoped they explained how to do the job and what he was expected to get done in a good day's work.

Gigi Martinez reported to her first day's job at the department store. She didn't know whether to go back to personnel or where, but she went to the personnel department. She told the receptionist she was hired as a new sales associate. The receptionist told Gigi to sit down and they'd get to her in a while. She sat there an hour. Finally, the personnel interviewer noticed her and said, "Gigi, what are you doing here? You're supposed to be in Men's Clothing."

Mumbling that no one told her, she rushed out and eventually found Men's Clothing. She approached several sales associates and finally found the department manager. He began: "So you're the new one. A bad start—late your first day. Well, get to work. If you need any help, ask for it."

Sam Lavalle reported to Personnel as the notice of employment said to do. After about six of the new employees were there, orientation began. Miss Wentworth welcomed them to the company and then the "paper blitz" took place. In the next 30 minutes, she gave them a lot of paper—work rules, benefits booklets, pay forms to fill out, and so on. His head was swimming. Then Sam got a slip telling him to report to his new supervisor, Andrew Villanueva in Room 810. Andrew took him around the facility for three minutes and then pointed out Sam's new workbench and wished him good luck.

Art is an example of the attitude of many if not most new employees— ready to go to work and wanting so much to succeed. Art's case described the orientation challenge. Gigi is an example of what happens to too many new employees: no help at all. Sam is an example of what most employees encounter: a formal orientation program that is adequate but not all it could be.

> ## DEFINITION
> Orientation is the personnel activity which introduces new employees to the enterprise and to their tasks, superiors, and work groups.

Orientation has not been studied a great deal, and little scientific research has been done on whether the programs are adequate. In terms of the stages of development of personnel functions discussed earlier and shown in Exhibit 1–13 (Chapter 1), it is a Stage II function.

A DIAGNOSTIC APPROACH TO ORIENTATION

Exhibit 8–1 highlights the environmental factors in the diagnostic model that are most important to effective orientation programs: the nature of the employee, and the nature of the task, the work group, and the leadership. The nature of the employee and the task are critical factors; for example, managers are given more detailed orientation programs than other employees. The orientation program focuses on introducing the new employee to the task, the work group, and the supervisor-leader. During orientation the work policies of the organization, the job conditions, and the people the employee will work with to get the job done are discussed.

The style the enterprise uses to orient new employees is affected by the organization and its climate. What I called conservative organizations in Chapter 2 will orient employees quite differently than liberal organizations will. The diagnostic manager adapts the orientation program to the individual and gives it a different emphasis for a person with 20 years' experience in the industry than for a new employee who is just out of high school and from a disadvantaged background.

THE PURPOSES OF ORIENTATION

Effectively done, orientation serves a number of purposes. In general, the orientation process is similar to what sociologists call socialization.[1] The principal purposes of orientation are as follows:

Reduces the start-up costs for a new employee.[2] The new employee does not know the job, how the organization works, or whom to see to get the job done. This means that for a while, the new employee is less efficient than the experienced employee, and additional costs are involved in getting the new employee started. These start-up costs have been estimated for various positions as follows: top manager, to $2,000; middle manager, $1,000; supervisor, $1,000; senior engineer, $900; accountant, $750; and secretary, $400.[3] Effective orientation reduces these start-up costs and enables the new employee to reach standards sooner.

Reduces the amount of anxiety and hazing a new employee experiences. Anxiety in this case means fear of failure on the job. Hazing takes place when experienced employees "kid" the new employee. For example, experienced employees may ask the new worker, "How many toys are you producing per hour?" When she answers, she is told, "You'll never last. The last one who did that few was no longer here after two days."

When I was in the service I was an artilleryman, and one of our initiation rites was the "orienting line" caper. An orienting line is an imaginary line on the ground measured by a device like a compass and used to point the cannons in the right direction. The new recruit was told: "Private (or Lieutenant) Lumbago, we need 100 yards of orienting line. Please get it from the supply sergeant for me." The recruit dutifully proceeds to ask for it. The sergeant goes to the back of the room (knowing the caper) and comes back a few moments later, saying, "Gee, I'm all out. Try B Battery Supply—three-quarters mile down the road." This variation of the snipe hunt continues until the recruit is exhausted or catches on.

EXHIBIT 8–1
Factors affecting orientation and organizational effectiveness

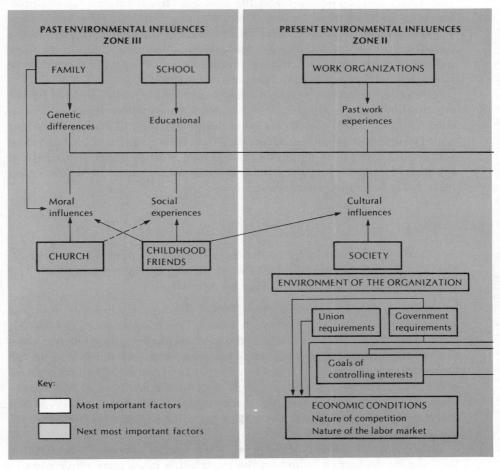

Such hazing serves several purposes. It lets the recruit know he has a lot to learn and thus is dependent on the others for his job, and it is "fun" for the old-timers. But it can cause great anxiety for the recruit. Effective orientation alerts the new person to hazing and reduces anxiety.

Reduces employee turnover.[4]   If employees perceive themselves to be ineffective, unwanted, or unneeded and have similar negative feelings, they may seek to deal with them by quitting. Turnover is high during the break-in period, and effective orientation can reduce this costly practice.

Saves time for supervisor and coworkers.[5]   Improperly oriented employees must still get the job done, and to do so they need help. The most likely people to provide this help are the co-workers and supervisors, who will have to spend time breaking in new employees. Good orientation programs save everyone time.

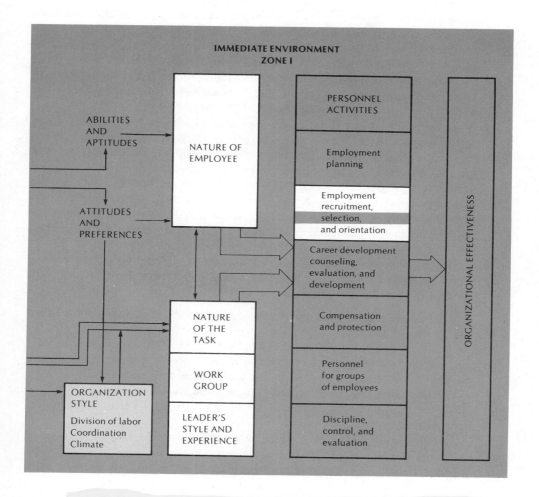

Develops realistic job expectations, positive attitudes toward the employer, and job satisfaction.[7]   In what sociologists call the older professions (law, medicine) or total institutions (the church, prison, the army), the job expectations are clear because they have been developed over long years of training and education. Society has built up a set of attitudes and behaviors that are considered proper for these jobs. For most of the world of work, however, this does not hold true. New employees must learn realistically what the organization expects of them, and their own expectations of the job must be neither too low nor too high. Each worker must incorporate the job and its work values into his or her self-image.

John Van Maanen does a masterful job of explaining the psychological and sociological processes that take place in orientation.[7] Probably the best way to explain them, however, is to describe the classic research study in the area: the Texas Instruments experiment.[8] Texas Instruments found that anxieties existing in the early period of work reduced competence and led to dissatisfaction and turnover. The anxiety resulted from awareness on the part of the female assemblers that they must reach the competence level they observed in the experienced employees around them. Many times they did not understand their supervisors' instructions but were afraid to ask further questions and appear stupid. Sometimes this anxiety was compounded by initiation rites or "hazing."

Anxiety turned out to be a very important factor in the study at Texas Instruments, which investigated whether an orientation program designed to reduce anxiety would increase competence, heighten satisfaction, and lower turnover. The control group of new recruits was given the traditional orientation program: a typical two-hour briefing on the first day by the personnel department. This included the topics normally covered in orientation (these will be described shortly) and the usual description of the minimum level of performance desired. Then they were introduced to the supervisor, who gave them a short job introduction, and they were off.

The experimental group was given the two-hour orientation the control group received and then six hours of social orientation. Four factors were stressed in the social orientation:

1. They were told that their opportunity to succeed was good. Those being oriented were given facts showing that over 99 percent of the employees achieved company standards. They were shown learning curves of how long it took to achieve various levels of competence. Five or six times during the day it was stressed that all in the group would be successful.

2. They were told to disregard "hall talk." New employees were tipped off about typical hazing. It was suggested that they take it in good humor but ignore it.

3. They were told to take the initiative in communication. It was explained that supervisors were busy and not likely to ask the new worker if she "needed help." Supervisors would be glad to help, but the worker must ask for it, and she would not appear stupid if she did so.

4. They were told to get to know their supervisor. The supervisor was described in important details—what she liked as hobbies, whether she was strict or not, quiet or boisterous, and so forth.

This social orientation had dramatic results. The experimental group had 50 percent less tardiness and absenteeism, and waste was reduced by 80 percent, product costs were cut 15 to 30 percent, training time was cut 50 percent, and training costs cut 66⅔ percent.

WHO ORIENTS EMPLOYEES?

Normally, orientation is a joint effort of operating managers and employees of the personnel department. The personnel department or technician usually introduces new employees to the enterprise, handles the paper work of getting them enrolled in the enterprise, puts them on the payroll, and explains personnel policies regarding pay, benefits, and work rules. It also may develop an orientation checklist and brief employees on their supervisor's expectations.

The operating manager or supervisor explains the task to the new employees. He or she shows them around the workplace and introduces them to other employees. The supervisor also explains what is expected in the way of job performance and work rules. Better supervisors usually alert present employees about the hiring of new employees and encourage them to help the recruits and welcome them to the work group.

In some unionized organizations, trade union officials also take part in orienting new employees.

HOW ORIENTATION PROGRAMS WORK

Orientation programs vary from quite informal, primarily verbal efforts to formal schedules which supplement verbal presentations with written handouts. Formal orientations often include a tour of the facilities or slides, charts, and pictures of them. Usually, they are used when a large number of employees must be oriented.

The formal program usually covers such items as:

• History and general policies of the enteprise.
• Descriptions of the enterprise's services or products.
• Organization of the enterprise.
• Safety measures and regulations.
• Personnel policies and practices.
• Compensation, benefits, and employee services provided.
• Daily routine and regulations.

The material can be presented in a variety of forms. For example, in an experiment at Union Electric Company in St. Louis it was found that programmed learning approaches were efficient and effective.[9] The written material may be in the form of handouts and booklets or combined into a single employee handbook.[10] The literature and handouts should be examined to see that the reading level is right for the employees in question. Frequently they are too technical or are written at too high a reading level for the employee. A study of the orientations of disadvantaged employees found that initial presentations should be in oral form, followed by written materials, to avoid a feeling of communication overload. The oral, then written, communication pattern should be followed by both personnel people and supervisors.

Here are five guidelines[12] for conducting an employee orientation:

1. Orientation should begin with the most relevant and immediate kinds of information and then proceed to more general company policies.

2. The most significant part of orientation is the human side giving new employees knowledge of what supervisors and co-workers are like, telling them how long it should take to reach standards of effective work, and encouraging them to seek help and advice when needed.

3. New employees should be "sponsored" or directed by an experienced worker or supervisor in the immediate environment who can respond to questions and keep in close touch during the early induction period.

4. New employees should be gradually introduced to the people with whom they will work rather than given a superficial introduction to all of them on the first day. The object should be to help them get to know their co-workers and supervisors.

5. New employees should be allowed sufficient time to get their feet on the ground before demands on them are increased.

To make sure that the orientation program is complete and works well, larger enterprises prepare checklists of what should be covered. One example of a complete set of checklists is the one compiled for American Airlines, which is given in Exhibit 8–2. To make sure the supervisor covers all the important points, some enterprises also prepare an orientation checklist to be filled out for each employee. An example is given in Exhibit 8–3.

ORIENTING MANAGEMENT TRAINEES

Management trainees are in a special orientation category. Most of these recruits must adjust from college life to work life. Many organizations have prepared rather elaborate orientation programs for potential managers called management training programs.

There is little doubt that initial experiences with an organization are important predictors of future managerial performance.[13] Hall and Patten contend that if the employee-manager comes to the organization with blank "life space," the first impressions received are very important to career and employee development.[14] J. Sterling Livingston cites case research evidence which indicates that success is at least partially a function of the expectations of the trainee's superior and refers to this phenomenon as the Pygmalion effect. Therefore, he argues, the first superiors management trainees encounter should be the best in the organization, for they will serve as models and will perpetuate the expectations of new managers for some time to come.[15] This will not be so forever, since learning does not cease after one or two years with an organization.

There is no doubt that the selection of trainers of the future leaders of the organization is crucial. Too often they are trained by roadblock executives who see themelves as failures because they have not been promoted beyond a certain point. They are likely to haze recruits and give them tough experiences, always supposedly for their own good. Instead, recruits need a good supervisor who understands their problems and wants to get them off to a good start.

EXHIBIT 8–2
Orientation checklist for American Airlines

Source: National Industrial Conference Board, *Personnel Practices in Factory and Office: Manufacturing,* Studies in Personnel Policy 194 (New York, 1964), and *Office Personnel Practices: Non-Manufacturing,* Studies in Personnel Policy 197 (New York, 1965).

When I was in the food business, I observed one of the best "trainers" in the business. Ray Scheid was also one of the most effective purchasing agents in the food business, the head grocery buyer at the Cincinnati branch of the Kroger Company. Because he was very good at his job, earlier in his career he had been offered many promotions. As is often the case with such promotions, each would have involved a geographic transfer. He liked

EXHIBIT 8–3
Supervisor's orientation checklist

Employee's Name:		Discussion completed (please check *each* individual item)
I.	Word of welcome	
II.	Explain overall departmental organization and its relationship to other activities of the company	
III.	Explain employee's individual contribution to the objectives of the department and his starting assignment in broad terms	
IV.	Discuss job content with employee and give him a copy of job description (if available)	
V.	Explain departmental training program(s) and salary increase practices and procedures	
VI.	Discuss where the employee lives and transportation facilities	
VII.	Explain working conditions: a. Hours of work, time sheets b. Use of employee entrance and elevators c. Lunch hours d. Coffee breaks, rest periods e. Personal telephone calls and mail f. Overtime policy and requirements g. Paydays and procedure for being paid h. Lockers i. Other_____	
VIII.	Requirements for continuance of employment—explain company standards as to: a. Performance of duties b. Attendance and punctuality c. Handling confidential information d. Behavior e. General appearance f. Wearing of uniforms	
IX.	Introduce new staff member to manager(s) and other supervisors. Special attention should be paid to the person to whom the new employee will be assigned.	
X.	Release employee to immediate supervisor who will: a. Introduce new staff member to fellow workers b. Familiarize the employee with his work place c. Begin on-the-job training	

If not applicable, insert N/A in space provided.

_____   _____
Employee's Signature   Supervisor's Signature

_____   _____
Date   Division

Form examined for filing: _____   _____
                                                   Date   Personnel Department

Source: Joan Holland and Theodore Curtis, "Orientation of New Employees," in *Handbook of Modern Personnel Administration,* ed. Joseph Famularo (New York: McGraw-Hill Book Co., 1972), ch. 23.

Cincinnati, and for this and other reasons he preferred to stay in his position there. He liked his job and found it rewarding, but one of his most important rewards was training new managers for Kroger. He often told me of the men he had trained—some of whom later became his bosses. He was as proud of them as if they were his sons. His joy was to teach them all he knew so they could be promoted elsewhere and advance in their careers. He showed no jealousy or desire to be in their shoes. He had had his chances and had chosen a different life. His career was satisfying to him and he lived theirs vicariously. He had all that was needed: technical expertise, a sincere desire to help people learn, and reward when they had learned all he had to teach.

Instead of encountering people like Ray Scheid, too many managerial trainees have unpleasant experiences. Thomas Patten attributes the tremendous turnover of those in management training programs to "bad" initial supervisors and poorly designed management training programs.[16] Some of the unbelievable strategies adopted by a sample of companies that actually *increased* the anxiety of new employees were reported by Edgar Schein.[17] Such programs no doubt partially account for turnover rates of up to 50 percent in the first year or two of employment. In a way, these experiences are like the initiation rites of primitive tribes. Instead of making trainees run a gauntlet and get beaten with sticks for a few minutes, these companies might use the sink or swim approach, whereby trainees are given responsibility but little training or support, and only the "fittest" survive. They also might give recruits deliberately menial tasks or set them up for elaborate hazing, in the belief that such upending experiences will teach them their proper place. Supervisors like Ray Scheid do not just happen; they require training for their job.[18]

Anthony Athos points out that it is difficult enough to adjust from college life to job life without such experiences.[19] Work differs from school in various ways:

There are no regular "promotions" each year or semester.

The work is narrow—school was usually broadening.

Unlike professors (the former "bosses"), who could either be talked to or avoided, some work bosses can be neither talked to nor avoided.

Thus expectations can be a problem for managers as well as other employees.[20]

Schein also discussed the positive way to develop future managers through socialization. Organizations socialize their members, including new management recruits, by teaching them new values or norms or by forming peer groups of novice management trainees. These norms are reinforced by the official literature of the organization; the example set by key leaders; the trainees' supervisors and slightly older peers, who can serve as "big brothers"; and the reward systems of the organization.[21]

Effective methods of socialization and orientation to management positions include (1) a formal training program in management, (2) training while working, and (3) working while training. Items 2 and 3 are the same approach with different emphasis. Item 1 is quite different. All of these exist, however, because as has been pointed out, "They don't start in the mailroom any more."[22] A brief discussion of item 1 will argue for the use of items 2 or 3.

Formal management training programs

After recruits have been selected to become managers, there are two distinct approaches to their orientation and placement. The first is to orient them briefly and let them go to work; this is the approach most organizations take with nonmanagerial employees. The second is to orient and train them in a management training program and then assign them to specific positions.

Some organizations use a combination of both approaches. The National Industrial Conference Board has examined these programs in two studies. The 1956 study considered the various methods used in management training programs.[23] Trainees of the 240 companies studied rank-ordered preferences for possible methods as follows:

Informal, learn while doing	40%
Formal on-the-job training	33
Classroom training	12
Trainee observes others working	10
"Assistant to" positions	4
Written assignments	1
	100%

Most companies felt that 16 years of formal schooling was enough for trainees, and the best method was to provide actual learning experiences, with much less emphasis on classroom methods and written assignments.

Eight years later, the NICB again studied management training programs, this time considering 26 highly rated programs. The study was based on questionnaires from 1,074 male college graduates who had completed the programs. One third of the trainees had been awarded liberal arts degrees and two thirds, business administration or technical degrees.[24]

This study focused first on those who had quit the companies and the training programs. It found those who quit did so because:

Training was not active enough for trainees.

The trainee's progress was not checked often enough.

Training was too slow-moving and not tough enough.

The trainers were weak instructors.

The programs examined lasted from 4 to 24 months, and trainees felt the objectives of the programs were satisfactory. They strongly preferred on-the-job training, which gave them an opportunity to show what they could do and to learn what the business was all about. The best program, as evaluated by the trainees, was relatively short (five months), well planned (detailed course outlines and exams if classroom oriented), with feedback (receiving ratings from being closely supervised), and emphasis on real problems and practice. The worst program was longer (one year), poorly planned, emphasized "background material" (history of company, detailed product list), was too classroom oriented (many lectures, tests), and offered infrequent ratings.

Generally, these evaluations are congruent for both companies and trainees. Both prefer a minimum of formal classroom work and a maximum of actual work so the company gets productivity sooner and the individual receives rewards sooner. Most of the trainees want to test themselves against the challenge of the real world to see if they can do the job. Training programs that do not allow this and emphasize lectures or mere observation of how departments work will satisfy neither of these objectives.

ASSIGNMENT, PLACEMENT, AND ORIENTATION FOLLOW-UP

The final phase of the orientation program is the assignment of the new employee to the job. At this point, the supervisor is supposed to take over and continue the orientation program. But as the Texas Instrument study demonstrated, supervisors are busy people, and even though they might be well intentioned, they can overlook some of the facts needed by the new employee to do a good job.

One way to assure adequate orientation is to design a feedback system to control the program, or use the management by objectives techique.[25] A form that could be used for this feedback from the trainee is the job information form shown in Exhibit 8–4. The new employee is instructed: "Complete this checklist as well as you can; then take it to your supervisor, who will go over it with you and give you any additional information you may need." The job information form is signed by employee and supervisor. An appointment set up with the orientation group in the first month on the job provides a follow-up opportunity to determine how well the employee is adjusting and permits evaluation of the orientation program (as discussed in the summary section). The form is designed not as a test of knowledge but to help improve the process of orientation.

In general, the placement process is direct: the person is assigned to the job she or he was selected for, often with the supervisor participating in selection. When selection is separated from assignment, various methods of assignment are used: assign the newest recruit to the highest priority position, use a multiple priority system, and or adopt a linear programming method. Researchers who studied these three approaches found that the straight priority method was the least effective, linear programming best, and differential priorities about as effective as linear programming.[27] In the civil service, the personnel unit supervises the recruiting and selection, but the operating agencies decide on which system of assignment to use and which of the hired persons will be assigned to which jobs.[28]

COST/BENEFIT ANALYSIS OF ORIENTATION PROGRAMS

Evaluating the costs and benefits of orientation programs can follow several approaches. One is to compute the cost per new employee for the orientation program. This is done as follows:

EXHIBIT 8–4
Orientation follow-up form

JOB INFORMATION

1. The job of my department is to _____

   My assigned area is_____

   The most important part of my job is _____
   _____

2. My department head's name is _____
   His/her office is located _____
3. I receive my time card from_____
   Time cards must be turned in on (day)_____
   to (person)_____ . Pay day for our
   department is _____
   If I am out of the hospital on pay day, I can get my
   pay from _____ The cashier's
   office is (where)_____
4. If I feel ill while at work, I should_____
   _____
   If I become ill while at home, I should notify my
   supervisor by calling (hosp. phone no.) _____
   (dept. ext.)_____at least one hour before I am
   expected at work
5. My locker or checkroom is located_____
6. The hours I am scheduled to work are assigned by_____
   _____
   Any change in my work schedule (days off etc.) is
   arranged in advance by_____
   My lunch hour and relief are assigned by_____
7. Work assignments are given to me by_____
   I can get help on the job from_____
8. Some of the things I do on my job are:
   A. _____
   B. _____
   C. _____
   D. _____
   E. _____
9. In doing my work I handle the following (check the boxes)

   PAPER   [   ]   EQUIPMENT   [   ]

   SUPPLIES   [   ]   FOOD   [   ]

   PRODUCTS   [   ]   PATIENTS   [   ]

10. If I work with papers:
    Papers I handle   They come   When I finish
    daily include   from   they are used by
    _____
    _____
11. If I use equipment, I use _____
    _____

To keep the equipment in good working order I must
_____
_____

12. If I work with supplies, products or food – the way
    I handle them is important because_____
    _____

13. My work helps Lenox Hill Hospital give better patient
    care by_____
    _____
    _____

14. When I need supplies, I get them from
    (person)_____ (place)_____
    (time)_____ (day)_____
15. To keep things running smoothly, I should bring to my
    supervisor's attention such things as:_____
    _____
    _____
    _____

16. How well I do my work can be measured by_____
    _____

17. 2 Safety rules that apply in my job are:
    1. _____
    _____
    2. _____
    _____

18. I have had the most difficulty with_____
    _____
    _____

19. Things I'd like to know more about are_____
    _____
    _____

20. Things I like best about my job are:_____
    _____
    _____

SUGGESTIONS I HAVE _____
_____
_____
_____

Source: Joan Holland and Theodore Curtis, "Orientation of New Employees," in *Handbook of Modern Personnel Administration,* ed. Joseph Famularo (New York: McGraw-Hill Book Co., 1972), ch. 23.

Direct costs
    Cost of trainers or orientation specialists
+Cost of materials provided
+Cost of space used (if applicable)

Indirect costs
> Cost of time to supervise trainers/orientation specialists
> +Cost of supervisors of new employees on the job
> =Orientation costs

After computing these costs, the organization should compare its costs per employee to the costs for comparable organizations. The organization also can compare the costs of running its own program versus contracting it with outside vendors. This is not done often at present.

Trainees can be asked to evaluate the benefits, using an attitude questionnaire such as is given in Exhibit 8–5. Companies can also experiment (as Texas Instruments did) and measure the differential retention rate and the output rate for a specific orientation program versus no program.[29] The results of two different orientation programs can be compared, and results of attitude surveys and retention rates can be compared with those of other organizations. In all cases, it is easier to compute costs than benefits.

SUMMARY, CONCLUSIONS, AND RECOMMENDATIONS

Orientation programs are an important part of the employment process. One way to summarize the conclusions of this chapter is to provide appropriate propositions. Although these statements require substantially more proof before they can be accepted as fact, it seems reasonable to state:

Proposition 8.1.   The more a person's first job fits his preferences, the more will he continue to be positively motivated for commitment and performance.

Proposition 8.2.   The larger the organization, the more effectively will it use a formal orientation and assignment program.

Proposition 8.3.   The more stable the organization, the more will the effective organization use a formal orientation and assignment program.

Proposition 8.4.   The more the orientation program includes minimum technical information and emphasizes the social dimensions of the new job (organization and supervisory expectations, encouragement, etc.), the more effective will it be.

Proposition 8.5.   The shorter the management training and orientation program, and the closer to actual work experience it is, the more effective will it be.

It is relatively easy to design an orientation program for supervisors of assembly-line operators who do routine work, and more difficult to design one for supervisors of computer maintenance personnel. The technical content of the latter job takes much longer to get across.

EXHIBIT 8–5
Evalution of orientation program using attitude questionnaire

PROGRAM EVALUATION

1. Which section of the orientation program do you feel is most important for meeting the needs of your job: (check one)
   - a. History of company_____
   - b. Job opportunities_____
   - c. Human relations_____
   - d. Benefits _____
   - e. Practices, office_____
   - f. Techniques for learning _____
   - g. Skill training _____

2. What were your thoughts on the company after viewing the history of the company?
   _____
   _____

3. After seeing "job opportunities," what job do you think you would like to do:
   1 year from now _____
   5 years from now_____
   If you are undecided on a future job, could you please suggest a way we could help you _____
   _____

4. Having participated in the orientation, do you feel you are better able to:

	Yes	No
a. Handle situations or problems at work		
b. Handle situations or problems outside work		
c. Understand problems of a supervisor		
d. Realize that help is available for solving problems		

5. Which benefits that the company offers are most important to you: (number the best 5 from 1st best to 5th best).
   - a. Pay _____
   - b. Medical _____
   - c. Insurance _____
   - d. Training _____
   - e. Employee activities _____
   - f. Tuition refund _____
   - g. Holiday _____
   - h. Vacation _____
   - i. Cafeteria _____
   - j. Loan service _____
   - k. Security _____
   - l. Sick leave _____

6. Did your session of office practices prepare you for your job?
   Yes_____
   No_____
   Please explain _____

7. Was there enough time for each part of your orientation?
   Yes_____
   No _____
   Please explain _____

8. How would you rate your orientation leader: (check one)
   Excellent _____
   Good _____
   Fair _____
   Poor _____
   Please explain your answer_____
   _____

9. To what extent were you involved in the session: (check one)
   Deeply involved _____
   Interested _____
   Slightly involved _____
   Not much interest _____
   Can you explain your answer _____

10. What suggestions would you have for improving the sessions?
    _____
    _____

11. Would you refer friends for positions here?
    Yes_____
    No_____

Source: Joan Holland and Theodore Curtis, "Orientation of New Employees," in *Handbook of Modern Personnel Administration,* ed. Joseph Famularo (New York: McGraw-Hill Book Co., 1972), ch. 23 (modified).

Assignment to and evaluation of orientation programs are likely to be more crucial in larger organizations with more turnover. In stable, smaller work groups it soon becomes obvious which of the new employees are "making it" and which need additional help. Recommendations for use of orientation programs by model organizations are given in Exhibit 8–6.

EXHIBIT 8–6
Recommendations on orientation programs for model organizations

Type of organization	Informal orientation programs	Formal orientation programs	Informal placement follow-up	Formal placement follow-up
1. Large size, low complexity, high stability		X		X
2. Medium size, low complexity, high stability		X		X
3. Small size, low complexity, high stability	X		X	
4. Medium size, moderate complexity, moderate stability	X		X	
5. Large size, high complexity, low stability		X		X
6. Medium size, high complexity, low stability		X		X
7. Small size, high complexity, low stability	X		X	

Part-time employees are likely to receive much shorter and less elaborate orientations; it is probably that orientation will be done by the personnel specialist, who will get them on the payroll, explain pay and hours, and turn them over to a supervisor. The supervisor is likely to explain her or his expectations for work, introduce new employees around, show them the job, and encourage them to ask for help.

The diagnostic manager will recognize that the amount and emphasis of orientation varies by the complexity of the task, the experience of the employee, and the climate in the work group and will adjust the orientation program accordingly. Top managers should involve themselves in orientation programs to the extent that they set policies to keep the management training program short and on-the-job oriented, and to make sure the program is humanistic and considers behavioral aspects, as Texas Instruments did.

This chapter completes Part Three of the book; Part Four opens with Chapter 9, which examines career development and counseling of employees once they are on the job working.

QUESTIONS

1. At what stage of development is the orientation function?
2. What are the main purposes of orientation programs?

3. What aspects of orientation seem to be the most neglected?

4. Describe the study of Texas Instruments' orientation program. What does it indicate to you about how to operate an orientation program?

5. Describe a typical orientation program. Which parts of it would you describe as important, very important, or less important: To the employee? To the employer?

6. How important is it to involve the employee's supervisor in the orientation program? Will forms signed by the employee assure the supervisor's participation?

7. How important is an employee's first supervisor to the employee's future success at work?

8. Have you had one of Edgar Schein's experiences with a first supervisor (for example, sink or swim)? Have you experienced a Ray Scheid?

9. Why is adjustment from college to a job so hard? Is it equally hard for those who worked their way through school and those who did not?

10. How can an organization provide for an effective transition from college to job?

11. How much classroom teaching should there be in management training programs?

12. How can you compute costs and benefits of orientation? Is this an easy process?

13. What effect does the employing organization's size and complexity have on orientation programs?

NOTES AND REFERENCES

1. John Van Maanen, "Breaking In: Socialization to Work," in *Handbook of Work, Organization, and Society,* ed. Robert Dubin. (Chicago: Rand McNally & Co., 1976).

2. Earl R. Gomersall and M. Scott Myers, "Breakthrough in On-the-Job Training," *Harvard Business Review,* July–August 1966, pp. 62–71; B. W. Marion and S. E. Trieb, "Job Orientation: A Factor in Employee Performance and Turnover," *Personnel Journal,* October 1969, pp. 799–804; Richard D. James, "Learning to Work, " *The Wall Street Journal,* May 21, 1968, pp. 1, 11.

3. Robert Sibson, "The High Cost of Hiring," *Nation's Business,* February 1975, pp. 85–86.

4. John Wanous, "Effects of a Realistic Job Preview on Job Acceptance, Job Attitudes and Job Survival," *Journal of Applied Psychology* 58, 3 (1973), pp. 327–32; Marion and Trieb, "Job Orientation"; Daniel Ilgen and William Seeley, "Realistic Expectations as an Aid in Reducing Voluntary Resignations," *Journal of Applied Psychology* 59, 4 (1974), pp. 452–55; J. Weitz, "Job Expectancy and Survival," *Journal of Applied Psychology* 40 (1956), pp. 245–47; Max Wortman and Leland Forst, "Role of the Personnel Manager in Manpower Follow-up Services," *Personnel Journal,* February 1974, pp. 98–103; R. M. Macedonia, *Expectations: Press and Survival,* unpublished Ph.D. Thesis, New York University, 1959; C. F. Youngberg, *An Experimental Study of Job Satisfaction and Turnover in Relation to Job Expectations and Self-Expectations,* unpublished Ph.D. thesis, New York University, 1963; Michael Ornstein, *Entry into the American Labor Force* (New York: Academic Press, 1976); R. D. Scott, "Job Expectancy: An Important Factor in Labor Turnover," *Personnel Journal,* May 1972, pp. 360–63.

5. Richard Schubert, "We Need A Rite of Passage Between School and Work," *Occupational Outlook Quarterly,* Summer 1975, pp. 31–34; Gomersall and Myers, "Breakthrough in On-the-Job Training."

6. Russell Thornton and Peter Nardi, "The Dynamics of Role Acquisition," *American Journal of Sociology* 80, 4 (1975), pp. 870–85; Dale Seiler and William Williams, "Assessing Engineers' Early Job Adjustment: A Longitudinal Approach," *Personnel Psychology* 25 (1972), pp. 687–96; Marion and Trieb, "Job Orientation"; Schubert, "Rite of Passage"; Gomersall and Myers, "Breakthrough in On-the-Job Training"; Youngberg, "Job Satisfaction and Turnover"; Wanous, "Realistic Job Preview"; Van Maanen, "Breaking In."

7. Van Maanen, "Breaking In."

8. Gomersall and Myers, "Breakthrough in On-the-Job Training."

9. Marian McClintock, et al., "Orienting the New Employee with Programmed Instruction," *Training and Development Journal,* May 1967, pp. 18–22.

10. Don Jones, "The Employee Handbook," *Personnel Journal,* February 1973, pp. 136–41.

11. M. M. Petty, "Relative Effectiveness of Four Combinations of Oral and Written Presentations of Job Related Information to Disadvantaged Employees," *Journal of Applied Psychology* 39 (1973), pp. 105–6.

12. This list is heavily dependent on a list compiled by Dr. Cary Thorp, Jr., University of Nebraska.

13. David Berlew and Douglas Hall, "The Socialization of Managers: Effects of Expectations on Performance," *Administrative Science Quarterly,* September 1966, pp. 207–23; Thomas Patten, Jr., "The College Graduate Trainee: Behavioral Science Perspectives on Management's Prime Personnel Problem," *Personnel Journal,* August 1969, pp. 581–92; John Kotter, "The Psychological Contract: Managing the Joining Up Process," *California Management Review* 15, 3 (1973), pp. 91–99.

14. Ibid.

15. J. Sterling Livingston, "Pygamalion in Management," *Harvard Business Review,* July–August 1969, pp. 81–89; also see Charles Vaver, "The Right Way to Straighten Out a Young Manager," *Nation's Business,* December 1975, pp. 62–64.

16. Thomas Patten, *Manpower Planning and the Development of Human Resources* (New York: Wiley Interscience, 1971), ch. 11.

17. Edgar H. Schein, "How to Break in the College Graduate," *Harvard Business Review,* November–December 1964, pp. 68–76; Thomas Gutteridge, "MBA Recruitment and Utilization," *Personnel Journal,* April 1973, pp. 293–303.

18. Schein, "How to Break in the College Graduate."

19. Anthony Athos, "From Campus to Company to Company," *Journal of College Placement,* December 1963, pp. 20–25.

20. John Wanous, "Organizational Entry: From Naive Expectations to Realistic Belief," *Journal of Applied Psychology* February 1976, pp. 22–29.

21. Schein, "How to Break in the College Graduate."

22. Lawrence Stressin, "They Don't Start in the Mail Room Anymore," in *Management Research and Practice,* ed. William Frey, proceedings of the seventh Eastern Academy of Management, 1970.

23. Stephen Habbe, *Employment of the College Graduate,* Studies in Personnel Policy 152 (New York: National Industrial Conference Board, 1956).

24. Stephen Habbe, *College Graduates Assess Their Company Training,* Studies in Personnel Policy 188 (New York: National Industrial Conference Board, 1963).

25. Ronald Pilengo, "Placement by Objectives," *Personnel Journal,* September 1973, pp. 804–10.

26. Joan Holland and Theodore Curtis, "Orientation of New Employees," in *Handbook of Modern Personnel Administration,* ed. Joseph Famularo (New York: McGraw-Hill Book Co., 1972), ch. 23.

27. Warren Boe and Thomas Stone, "A Comparison of Three Placement Methods," *Proceedings,* Academy of Management 1973, pp. 372–77.

28. U.S. Civil Service Commission, "How Federal Jobs are Filled: Commission Agency Roles," in *People in the Public Service,* ed. Robert Golembiewski and Michael Cohen (Itasca, Ill.: F. E. Peacock, Publishers, 1970).

29. Gommersall and Myers, "Breakthrough in On-the-Job Training"; Holland and Curtis, "Orientation of New Employees."

Career development, performance evaluation, and development of personnel

Part Four is concerned with one of the most vital activities in the personnel function: career development, or how employers can help managers and employees develop meaningful and useful careers for themselves in the organization. Chapter 9 describes what a career is or can be and the counseling and interaction which aid in its development. Chapter 10 focuses on performance evaluation, the most frequently used career counseling aid, which employees can either endure or profit from. Chapters 11 and 12 discuss how the enterprises can improve the abilities and attitudes of employees at work through training and development activities.

PART FOUR

Careers, career development, and counseling

CHAPTER

9

CHAPTER OBJECTIVES

■ To show what career planning is and why individuals perform it.

■ To show what career development is and why some organizations help employees develop careers.

■ To help you understand the techniques used to make career planning, career development, and career counseling effective.

CHAPTER OUTLINE

Mary Hall and Jim Thomsen are having a few drinks after work at The Golden Bough, a bar in their office building. Mary is having a down day. She shares her feelings with Jim.

Mary: Well another Friday and the week is over. But something's missing.

Jim: What do you mean, Mary?

Mary: I go to work on Monday, Tuesday, every day, and what do I accomplish?

Jim: Mary, you've got a good job. You make good money. You make a contribution to your company. What else do you want?

Mary: I'm not sure. I've been with RIC for four years. After a training program, I started on my first job and now I'm on my second. But what does it lead to? Where am I going? And why am I going there? The first job didn't have much to do with the second; I get the feeling I got it because it opened up, not because I was needed or that it built anything for me. My brother is a career army officer. He pretty much knows how his life will be spent. I don't.

Jim: My company has a career development plan to help me with that. Doesn't yours?

Mary: No.

Jim: Well, you could develop a career plan for yourself. Would that help?

Mary: Sure, but how do I do that? And besides would it mean anything if my company isn't involved?

Jim: I'm not sure.

Mary: I've got to get some control of my life so I can see some purpose to it—some sort of plan.

Jim: Yea. Bartender, I'll have another piña colada.

Do you have a career plan? Do you know now what you'll be doing 5, 10, or 20 years later? If you were in a theology or medical school you would probably know; these older professions have evolved a typical career pattern for ministers or priests and doctors. For most nonprofessional jobs, the career paths are not that clear.

This chapter begins Part Four which is designed to show how a person can plan his or her career, or how a person in conjunction with an enterprise can develop a specific career. Career development takes the employee from the orientation period up to retirement. The activity involves developing careers and the related activities of evaluation and training and development. This chapter focuses on the first step: career development and career counseling. This is a Stage I function, a personnel activity that is advocated more than practiced but has promise of becoming a significant personnel activity.

CAREERS AND CAREER DEVELOPMENT DEFINED

A career evolves through at least four stages: exploration, early career, maintenance, and decline.[1] Exhibit 9–1 describes these stages. Stage 1 takes place prior to work. Stage 2a is recruitment (Chapter 6), and 2b and 2c are

EXHIBIT 9–1
Major stages and processes of the career

External stages and individual processes	*Internal stages and processes*
1. *Exploration Stage*	*Exploration*

Occupational images from mass media, books, movies.
Advice and example of parents, siblings, teachers, and other models.
Actual success/failure in school, sports, hobbies, and self-tests.
Stated constraints or opportunities based on family circumstances—economic, historical, etc.: "We can't afford to send you to college," or "Every boy of mine must try the law."
Actual choice of educational path—vocational school, college major, professional school.
Counseling, letter of recommendation, and other external influences.
Test results of manual and intellectual aptitude and achievement tests.

Exploration

Development of self-image of what one "might be," what sort of work would be fun.
Self-assessment of own talents and limitations—"things I could never be."
Development of ambitions, goals, motives.
Tentative choices and commitments.
Enlarged self-image based on integration of personality, social and educational accomplishments.
Growing need for real test of ability to work and accomplish real-life vocational tasks.
Anticipatory socialization based on role models, teachers, and images of the occupation.

2. *Establishment Stage (early career)*

   a. Mutual recruitment

Organization is looking for talent, individual is looking for a good job.
Constrained by labor market and pool of available talent.
Selection, testing, screening.

Getting Started Finding a Job

Reality shock.
Insecurity around new task of interviews, applying, being tested, facing being turned down.
Developing image of occupation/organization based on recruitment/selection process

   b. Acceptance and Entry

Induction and orientation.
Assignment to further training or first job.
Informal or formal initiation rites and conferring of organizational status (identity cards, parking sticker, uniform, company manual).

Making a *"real"* choice, take job or not, which job, first commitment.
Maximum need for self-test and fear of failure.
Exhilaration at being accepted or despair at being turned down; readjustment of self-image.
Beginning development of themes.

   c. First Job Assignment

Meeting the boss and co-workers.
Learning period, indoctrination.
Period of full performance "doing the job."
Leveling off and/or becoming obsolete.
Preparing for a new assignment.

Expectation of being tested for the first time under *real* conditions.
Feeling of playing for keeps.
Socialization by boss, peers, and subordinates—"learning the ropes."
Reality shock—what the work is really like, doing "the dirty work."
Testing the commitment to occupation/organization, developing the theme.

EXHIBIT 9–1 (*continued*)

External stages and individual processes	Internal stages and processes
d. *Leveling Off, Transfer, and/or Promotion* Feedback on meaning of the move or lack of move, performance review, career counseling, salary action (usually more frequent but has special meaning here). If transferred or promoted, repeat of the five steps under 2c. (If individual fails, "does not fit in," or has to be laid off, the process goes back to 2a.) (If individual is succeeding, he is probably developing a speciality or special areas of competence leading to a period of real contribution in that area of competence. If that area of competence is needed in the organization, the individual is given actual or de facto tenure.)	Feeling of success or failure. Reassessment of self-image and how it matches perceived opportunities in occupation/organization—"Is there a career here?" Sorting out family/work issues and finding a comfortable level of accommodation. Forming a career strategy, how "to make it"—working hard, finding mentors, conforming to organization, making a contribution. Decision to leave organization if things do not look positive. Adjusting to failure, reassessment of self, occupation and organization—effort to avoid losing self-esteem, elaboration or revision of theme. Turning to unions or other sources of strength if feeling unfairly treated or threatened. Growing feeling of success and competence, commitment to organization and occupation. Period of maximum insecurity if organization has formal tenure review—"Will I make it or not?"
e. *Granting of Tenure* (If tenure is *not* granted, individual will be moved *out* or *over* in a less central role.)	Feeling of being accepted fully by organization, "having made it." Crisis of reassessment, trying to determine the "meaning" of not getting tenure, possible loss of work involvement, or casting about for new career options, period of high learning about self, testing of one's assumptions about self, occupation, and organization.
3. *Maintenance Stage* a. *Midcareer* Person is given more crucial, important work of the organization and expected to enter his period of maximum productivity. Occupation and organization secrets are shared. Person is expected to become more of a teacher/mentor than learner. Problem of how to deal with the plateaued person—remotivation.	New sense of growth and realistic assessment of one's ambition and potential (timetable revision). Period of settling in or new ambitions based on self-assessment. More feeling of security, relaxation, but danger of leveling off and stagnating. Threat from younger, better trained, more energetic and ambitious persons. Possible thoughts of "new pastures" second careers, new challenges, etc., in relation to biosocial "mid-life" crisis.

EXHIBIT 9–1 (*concluded*)

External stages and individual processes	Internal stages and processes
b. *Late career* Jobs assigned and responsibilities draw primarily on wisdom and perspective and maturity of judgment. More commuity and society-oriented jobs. More jobs involving teaching others less likely to be on the "firing line" unless contacts and experience dictate.	Working through of midlife crisis toward greater acceptance of oneself and others. More concern with teaching others, passing on one's wisdom both at home and at work. Psychological preparation for retirement. Deceleration in momentum. Finding new sources of self-improvement off the job.
4. *Decline Stage* Formal preparation for retirement. Retirement rituals. Continued association on new basis if contribution is still possible.	Learning to accept a reduced role and less responsibility. Learning to manage a less structured life. New accommodations to family and community.

Source: John Van Maanen and Edgar Schein, "Career Development," in *Improving Life at Work,* ed. J. Richard Hackman and J. Lloyd Suttle (Santa Monica, Cal.: Goodyear Publishing Co., 1977).

orientation and placement (Chapter 7). Stages 2*d* and 2*e* will be discussed in Chapter 10, and Stage 4 in Chapter 16. Stage 3 is the subject of this chapter.

A career is an individual concept; an employee can have a career with one enterprise or many. In career development, the enterprise helps a person plan the employee's future career in the enterprise. Obviously, many persons plan their careers for themselves. The focus of the chapter is how the planning can be done jointly.

Exhibit 9–2 shows how career development fits into the personnel function. From employment planning (Chapter 4 and 5) is derived employee demand, and job analysis, which determines the kinds of persons needed and arranges jobs into job families. In recruiting, selection, and orientation of employees, their biodata and career preferences are gathered (Chapters 6, 7, and 8). In career development, evaluations (Chapter 10) provide feedback

DEFINITIONS

A career is a sequence of work-related experiences in which a person participates during the span of his or her work life.[2]

Career development is the personnel activity which helps individuals plan their future careers within the enterprise, in order to help the enterprise achieve its objectives and the employee achieve maximum self-development.

EXHIBIT 9–2
Career development and the personnel function

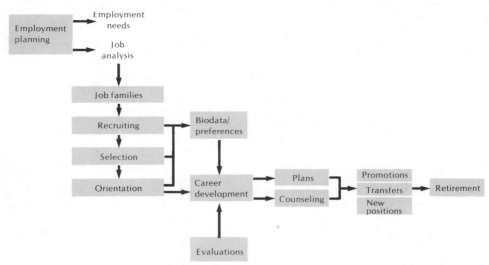

for planning and counseling the employee through a series of training and development activities (Chapters 11 and 12) leading to promotions, transfers, and new positions (Chapter 10) and finally to retirement (Chapter 16).

A DIAGNOSTIC APPROACH TO CAREER DEVELOPMENT

The crucial factors in the environment of the personnel function which influence the career development process are shown in Exhibit 9–3. The first factor is the nature of the task. At present, the tendency is for career development to take place primarily for professional, technical, and managerial employees, and only for those individuals who are interested in it.

Thus the nature of the employee is a second factor. Since career development is new and voluntary, those most interested in work and in their own careers get involved in it. Career development is more effective if the employee is interested in a career and if the supervisor is a willing and able counselor. The natures of the task and the employee are the two most crucial factors.

Other factors in the diagnostic model that affect the organization's interest in career development are government requirements and goals of the controlling interests. Career development plans are likely to be formulated in order to assure compliance with affirmative action programs to assure proportionate representation of minorities. If the controlling interests of the organization are personnel oriented, career development is more likely to be adopted.

CAREER DEVELOPMENT: PRO AND CON

As with many personnel activities, the reasons given for pursuing career development reflect a mix of individual and organizational purposes which are served when the activity is effectively carried out. Five reasons are generally given:

1. *Helps achieve employee and organizational goals.*   The primary purpose of career development is to design programs to "grow" employees who will be effective in achieving the goals of the enterprise. One way the organization can help assure that its goals will be reached is to make sure that, by achieving organizational goals, the individual employee can attain her or his own.

A goal of most talented employees is to control their own careers. When this goal is achieved, the employee is more satisfied and productive and has more personal dignity.[3]

2. *Reduces the hoarding of people.*   Lawrence Ferguson argues that inadequate career development leads to hoarding of people, to the detriment of both the employee and the organization.[4] Some supervisors build a work team, then never want to break it up. This is convenient for their work experience but holds people back from useful promotional and developmental experience. Some employees may become overqualified; they should be promoted and moved on after a few years. When the supervisor holds onto these employees, they may become frustrated, to their own detriment and that of the organization as well. The hoarding of people by organization units has probably been reduced somewhat by recent cost pressures.

3. *Reduces obsolescence.*   Chapter 12 will discuss the serious problem of managerial obsolescence. Many employees who become obsolete stay on the payroll. Perhaps this is due to lack of training, but more often it is lack of motivation to keep up to date, which can result from inadequate career planning and development by employee and employer.[5] Often obsolescence coincides with the midcareer crisis discussed in Chapter 2. Career development is designed to prevent or alleviate obsolescence and midcareer crises.[6]

4. *Aids EEO programs.*   Career development can help solve problems for an enterprise that result when its workforce is found to represent protected groups like women and racial and ethnic minorities inadequately. In the state of Washington, the Civil Service Commission started a career development program in 1973 which is designed to help 1,000 women employees with their career planning.[7] This should help Washington meet its equal employment opportunity goals, too.

5. *Reduces turnover and personal costs.*   Studies by personnel experts have found that when the enterprise makes a conscious effort to help its employees plan their careers, it benefits through lower turnover and personnel costs.[8] This is the best kind of reason why management should institute programs such as career development.

Everyone does not see career development positively, or as useful for all employees. For example, if the employees have instrumental work attitudes (see Chapter 2), it is unlikely that career development is for them.[9] Other employees may develop their own career plans but plan to job hop or start their own business, so career development may not be too useful for them.[10] Most likely to benefit are those who hold work ethic attitudes and plan to seek work fulfillment within one enterprise.[11]

Even for these employees, career development is not easy to do. First,

EXHIBIT 9–3
Factors affecting career development and organizational effectiveness

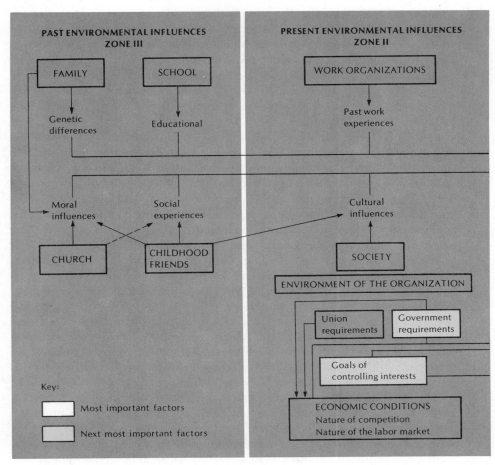

there are differences in the individual's desires for career development.[12] Then, too, careers differ widely within organizations, so it is not possible to set up a standardized career path all enterprises can follow. Each must develop plans for the groups of employees it has, and in conjunction with the individuals concerned.

Finally, career development tools are new. Some experts question whether the enterprises are capable of career development at all.[13] Still, it seems useful to try.

WHO IS INVOLVED IN CAREER PLANNING AND DEVELOPMENT?

Three persons are necessary to have effective career planning and development. The most important is the employee; only the individual worker can

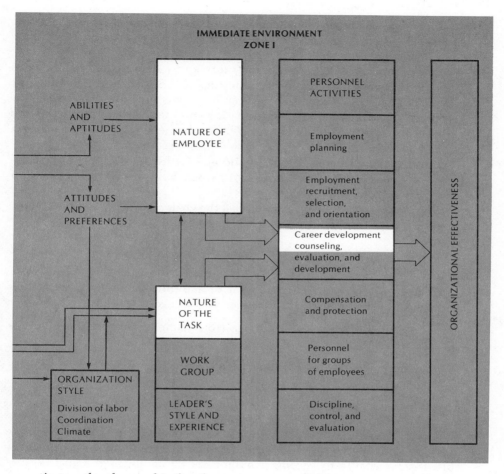

tie together her or his family stages, personal life stages, and career stages in order to develop a whole life plan.

There must also be a personnel specialist to help guide and advise the employees whose career is being developed; and the employee's operating supervisor can be very helpful in terms of advice, counseling, and sponsorship. This is normally an informal process between the supervisor and the employee, however.

CAREER PLANNING BY INDIVIDUALS[14]

A career can lend order and meaning to events and provide a relationship, including work, in which a person is involved. And a career is central to the complete development of an individual's identity.[15] Thus it is important for the employee to plan a career, even if the employer provides little guidance or encouragement.

Phases in career planning

Individual career planning normally involves a number of phases: self-appraisal, information gathering on occupations, goal selection, and planning and implementation.

Self-appraisal.   First, the person must know himself. He is helped to do this by counseling, guidance, and testing. The Strong Vocational Interest Blank and Kuder Preference Record can help determine interests, and counseling can interpret the results in relation to other aspects of the person's life. Feedback from parents and supervisors also helps, and simulations such as Self-Directed Search[16] can help the person become more self-aware.

Information gathering on occupations.   Gathering information on current job opportunities (see Chapter 6) helps employees in their choices of careers, jobs, and employers.

Goal selection.   The person must set the goals sought in his career. These goals can be set in quantitative terms, such as:

- Number of persons to be supervised by a specific age (for example, 8,000 by age 30).

- Target salary for numbers of year or age (for example, to make one's age in salary by age 35: $35,00 per year at age 35).

- To attain a title by a certain age (for example, vice president by age 40).

- Colleague goal: to be working with at least four compatible colleagues by age 25.

- Whether or not to own one's own business.

Due to individual differences, people's objectives will vary. What is important is setting goals precisely. But the individual should not become inflexible. If your goal is to become a millionaire by 35 and if the goal is close at that age, you should be willing to wait until you are 36.

The success of this career planning depends on how good the employee is at assessing his comparative advantages and in knowing how the industry he works in typically moves people along.

The goals listed above were oriented towards men. When women set career goals, some may choose to have several phases, to include a period for child bearing and care. In this case, women's goals may be different from men's. When women seek only work careers, the goals could be very similar.[17] In a family where both husband and wife have careers, the career goals of the two must be developed together so the tradeoffs are clear. Whose career suffers if one is transferred? Or do they both refuse transfers? These potential career goal conflicts must be planned.[18]

Planning and implementation.   The next phase is planning the career to achieve the goals. Regular checkpoints are used to make sure that the goals are achieved on time. Real career success often requires playing "success chess."[19] By the rules for this game, a successful manager:

- Maintains the largest number of job options possible.
- Does not waste time working for an immobile manager.
- Becomes a crucial subordinate to a mobile superior.
- Always favors increased exposure and visibility.
- Is prepared to nominate himself or herself for jobs that come open. This manager defines the corporation as a market of jobs.
- Leaves a company when the career has slowed too much.
- Is ready to quit if necessary.
- Does not let success in a present job preempt the career plan; this could reduce upward mobility.

Preparation for one's own business

The career suggestions above apply to a person who is employed by someone else. What about career plans for those who want to be employed for a short time only and then start their own businesses or enter a family business?

It is a good idea for future executives in family firms to acquire experience in at least one other firm before entering the family business. Preferably, this should be a successful firm in a similar business in another location. This allows the executive to achieve a success story independent of the family first (very important psychologically) and provides perspective for the family experience. A good career plan for a future family business executive is shown below:

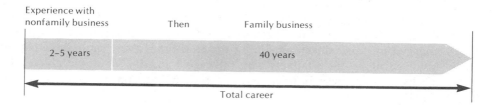

An entrepreneur follows two patterns in starting her or his own business: direct entry and postponed entry.

The most frequent pattern is postponed entry:

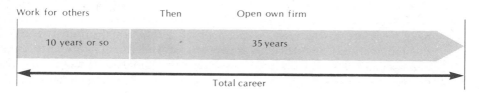

In this pattern, the potential entrepreneur learns the business and develops his capital and entrepreneurial plan while at work for a firm in the business he is interested in. This experience can take place in any successful firm or in one with which he is interested in competing. The entrepreneur builds capital by saving his salary and builds a believable case with a bank or friends so it will be possible to borrow the needed cash later. Often, an entrepreneur fails several times before succeeding. If he did not save enough capital, failure of his enterprise means returning to work for someone else. Then the process begins again.

In the direct entry pattern, the entrepreneur borrows from relatives, friends, or businessmen to start the business directly. This is a much less frequent pattern. But if he is lucky, the entrepreneur can succeed more quickly through direct entry.

Midlife career change

In another career pattern, the employee expects to totally change careers at midlife. Most military officers and those in stressful occupations, such as air traffic controllers do this. This is an increasingly popular career pattern; the first career may be necessarily short, opportunities may be limited, or stress or boredom may be too great.[20]

While career planning is the primary responsibility of the individual, others help, as noted above. Examples of enterprises that leave the *primary* planning to the individual but offer professional help and guidance include the General Electric Company, the U.S. federal government, and the U.S. Naval Weapons Center.[21]

CAREER DEVELOPMENT BY ORGANIZATIONS

Many other organizations actively help employees build careers for themselves. A U.S. Army study in 1968 found only 12 large private-sector firms engaged in career development;[22] since that time, many more have become involved. It is still relatively rare (a Stage I activity, as noted above), but it is likely to increase in the future, and it can have an impact on the personnel function as a whole.

Several recent books and studies can be of great help to enterprises considering career development. Walter Mahler and William Wrightnour suggest that the most effective way to build a career development program is around central career crossroads[23] (Exhibit 9–4).

In this analysis, it is clear that future managers normally are hired to perform a specific job (such as salesperson or accountant). If they succeed at this job they reach Crossroad 1; this usually takes several years. The next steps are to become a supervisor of a functional group (usually for the job worked) and then to move out of functional work into general management. This is Crossroad 2, a sharp turn to managing a business which has more than one function. After this, at Crossroad 3, the manager is asked to manager several businesses. Finally, he or she becomes a top manager

EXHIBIT 9–4
Critical career crossroads in a large business organization

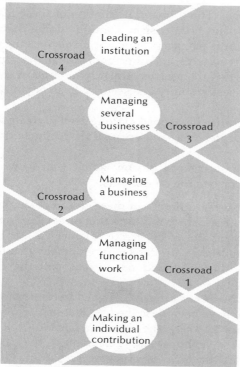

Source: Walter Mahler and Willian Wrightnour, *Executive Continuity* (Homewood, Ill.: Dow Jones-Irwin, Inc., 1973).

and passes Crossroad 4. Based on a study of six large companies, the authors found that the average age for each of these crossroads is as follows:

	Average age	*Range*
Crossroads 1	31	29–34
Crossroads 2	43	41–46
Crossroads 3	48	46–50
Crossroads 4	52	50–53

Edgar Schein analyzed the careers of 44 MIT masters graduates for 15 years. He concluded that the most sensible way to approach career development is to base it on the individual's career "anchor"—or major career need.[24] Schein found five career pattern orientations (anchors):

1. *Managerial competence.* The primary career goal for this group is to develop managerial abilities such as interpersonal and analytical competence

and emotional stability. The kinds of positions these persons held or aspired to included director of corporate plans administration, director of administration, or president.

2. *Technical/functional competence.* The primary orientation of these managers is the actual work they do, and they wish to continue doing that kind of work. Examples of titles of these managers are plant manufacturing engineer, manager of market support systems, and director of cost analysis group.

3. *Security.* These managers saw themselves primarily in terms of serving a particular organization. They seek stability and security in an organization. Their career titles varied.

4. *Creativity.* These managers had developed a strong need to create something and intended to be entrepreneurs, and creators of products or new ventures.

5. *Autonomy/independence.* These persons did not adapt well to working in organization life and left it or became consultants.

Schein found differences in the backgrounds of these groups of employees. His research reinforces that of others which indicates that career development work requires a number of career paths to be effective. James Walker points out, however, that creating multiple-path career development is difficult. The paths must be realistic, that is, based on current patterns in the enterprise.[25]

Although only a few enterprises are seriously involved in career development, the experiences of some have been described.[26] These enterprises include the U.S. Internal Revenue Service,[27] the Canadian Federal Civil Service,[28] Union Oil,[29] American Telephone and Telegraph,[30] the state of Washington,[31] G. D. Searle,[32] and the U.S. Government Accounting Office.[33]

Two more detailed examples of career development plans for enterprises will illustrate the process more fully. One example is from the career develop-

EXHIBIT 9–5
Typical career path for general manager in telephone company

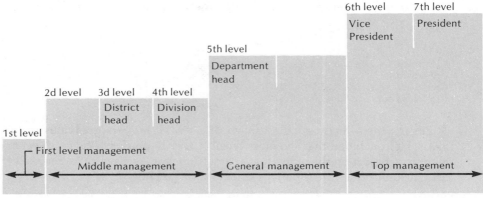

0 1 2 3 4 5 6 7 8 9 10 11 12 13 14 15 16 17 18 19 20 21 22 23 24 25 26 27 28 29 30 31 32 33 34 35 36

EXHIBIT 9–6
Career path of a general manager in telephone company

Level	Job title	Location	Department	Years in position
1st	Staff assistant	Home office	Commercial	2½ years
1st	Manager	District office, small city	Commercial	1½ years
2d	Unit manager	Home office	Commercial	1 year
2d	Data sales manager	Home office	Commercial	2½ years
2d	Rate engineer	District office	Commercial	1½ years
3d	District manager	District office	Commercial	1½ years
3d	College employment representative	Home office	Personnel	1 year
3d	Corporate head-quarters	New York	Human resource development	2 years
4th	College relations director	Home office	Personnel	1 year
4th	Division manager	Division office	Commercial	3½ years
5th	Assistant vice president, personnel	Home office	Personnel	5 years

ment planning of a large telephone company. The typical career path it uses to develop a general manager is given in Exhibit 9–5. Exhibit 9–6 lists the steps in an actual career for a general manager with this company. In addition to position rotation and on-the-job training, the company provides one- and two-week training programs at the manager's current location. It also offers a college tuition reimbursement plan if the managers choose to further their formal educations.

A second case study illustrating career development is the program in the U.S. Air Force.[34] The Air Force, a large organization, employs hundreds of thousands of employees. It has a very sophisticated employment planning system based on determination of needs and a personnel planning system for determining assignments. In conjunction with these systems, the Air Force has developed a complex career development plan for its cadre of officers. The purpose of career development for the Air Force is to assure that enough highly qualified officers are available and that these officers are promoted to responsible positions.

Specific career plans which specify the different kinds of experience and education desirable for each career specialty are also developed. The service develops career progression guides to help in career development (the guide for a manpower planning officer is given in Exhibit 9–7). Each career specialty has career management positional experience and on- and off-the-job training. Individuals hired will experience assignments that develop them personally and use their particular talents. While in these positions they serve as understudies and are counseled and coached by a superior.[35]

CAREER DEVELOPMENT COUNSELING

One of the essential parts of a supervisor's role is to help subordinates develop as persons and reach their goals. The employee frequently produces

EXHIBIT 9-7
Career progression guide, manpower management, U.S. Air Force

PHASE	GRADE	PME	TRAINING	EDUCATION	ASSIGNMENTS	OPTIMUM PHASE DUTIES
Executive/Leader	(PROJECTED) (AUTHORIZA-TION THRU) FY 1/72	Refer to AFM 53-1	Refer to AFM 50-5 for complete list.	FY /1 Graduate Degree Requirements.	— Officers in this phase will occupy key managerial positions at all echelons of command. — Officers entering the career field should attend appropriate AFIT (SEC) short courses.	
	COLONEL (10.8% of Auth)			PhD - 4 Masters - 345		
Staff	LT COLONEL (18.% of Auth)	Selected Officers attend Senior Service Schools such as: National War College, Industrial College of Armed Forces, Air War College	Executive Engineering (5 Wks); DOD Courses; Army Courses; Navy Courses; Protective Coating (2 Wks); Photo Terrain Analysis (2 Wks); Sonic Boom (1 Wk)	Preferable graduate degrees are: Architectural Engineering; Civil Engineering; Electrical Engineering; Industrial Engineering; Mechanical Engineering; Space Facilities Engrg; Engineering Management	**Career Specialists:** — Officers hold staff assignment, heavy emphasis on broad managerial responsibilities. Assignments include duties as programs officer or Base Civil Engineer, base level, duties with "R&D DOBER" Squadron, Management of important programs or projects, duties involving staff planning and policy formulation at MAJCOM or higher level. — Selected rated officers returned to operations area for single tour. — Career C.E. officers may be selected for management positions in other functional areas. — Attendance at AFIT (SEC) short courses desirable. — Officers entering the field should attend appropriate AFIT (SEC) short courses. — Officers complete at least one tour at Hq USAF between eighth and twenty second year service. — Assignments above wing level - officers completing assignment at MAJCOM or higher should be assigned to lower level or given opportunity to broaden outside career area.	Limited number of Rated Officers will Return to Operations Area.
Advanced Development	MAJOR (25.% of Auth)	Selected Officers will attend Intermediate Service Schools such as: Air Command & Staff College or Armed Forces Staff College	Executive Engineering (5 Wks); Corrosion Control (2 Wks); Cold Regions Engrg; Applied Engrg (2 Wks); Network Planning (2 Wks); Beams Course (2 Wks); Air Conditioning Engineer (6 Wks)		**Career Specialists:** — Greater number of officers quality and selected for special category assignments above wing level. Officers completing critical assignment at MAJCOM level or higher normally assigned at a lower organizational level. Duty as chief of: Operation and Maintenance, Programs, Engineering and Construction branches at base level. — Career officers encouraged to evaluate AFIT opportunities at the Masters & PhD levels. Officers completing AFIT graduate and EWI programs assigned positions which utilize training to maximum advantage. **Non-Specialists:** — Officers entering the field as potential career Civil Engineering Officers assigned initially at wing or base level. — Officers entering the field attend the CEC - BCE course and appropriate short courses.	A few highly selected officers enter AFIT at PhD level. Broadening Assignments Between Utilization Fields Occur During 6 - 11 Phase. Rated Officers Desiring to Progress in the Operations Area Return to Rated Duties.
Intermediate Development	CAPTAIN (30.9% of Auth)		Appropriate ECI Courses: Firefighting; Fireprotection;	All New Accessions Must Possess A Baccalaureate Degree Preferably in an Engineering discipline, Architecture, Astronomy or Forestry or Professional registration in an Engineering discipline or Architecture.	**Career Specialists:** — Assignment to MAJCOM, base or special activities. — Qualified officers attend AFIT graduate program in appropriate disciplines. — AFIT graduates and EWI returnees assigned to positions utilizing their training to maximum advantage. Normally, assigned above base level. — Selected officers transitioned to other utilization fields for broadening. Officers returning from broadening assignments normally assigned above wing level. — Career officers attend appropriate AFIT (SEC) short courses. — Obtain professional registration. **Non-Specialists:** — Officers entering the field by AFIT training and/or AFIT-CE BCE course. — Officers broadening assigned to basic Civil Engineering organization. — Potential career civil engineers will normally be assigned at group or wing level and rotated through various functions first two years. — Officers entering the field attend AFIT-CE BCE course prior to assignment.	Rated Officers Transition to Field via AFIT/Tech Training.
Initial	LIEUTENANT (14.7% of Auth)	Base Civil Engineer Course (6 Wks)	All career officers attend squadron officer school - residence or correspondence		— Bases, Squadron, Group or Wing duty, Obtain EIT or AIT certificates, attain fully qualified AFS. — Interested officers apply for admission to AFIT. — Complete Base Civil Engineer course in first 12 months. — Officers rotated through as many positions as practicable in Base C.E. organization. — Highly qualified officers selected for duty above wing level.	Selected Officers Enter AFIT Masters Level Programs and EWI Programs.

BROADENING ASSIGNMENTS

Source: *Air Force Manual, 36-23.*

more because of such programs. However, work organizations are not schools; their primary purpose is to serve their owners and clients. The human relations movement probably overstressed personal counseling of employees. Still, the technical skills of the employee cannot be separated from the rest of the person. One does not hire just a pair of hands.

Counseling of employees is discussed a number of times in this book. The interview methods used are described in Chapter 7. Chapter 10 discusses work-related counseling as part of the evaluation interview. Chapter 16 discusses financial counseling, and Chapter 20 discusses counseling of employees on personnel or emotional problems. This chapter focuses on career counseling.

Various experts have described effective career development counseling.[36] One of the best descriptions is by M. Gould, who gives an interesting example of an interview between a career counselor and a junior manager.[37] (It could have been between a superior and a subordinate.) He describes how the counselor tried to gather hard data on the employee prior to the interview: how many courses and seminars he had attended, his reading habits (extent and kinds of books), and his civic and professional activities. Gould maintains that this information is an indication of the importance the individual attaches to the need for continuing development. Then the counselor asks about the employee's career goals and tries to work realism into the discussion of goals. The following is Gould's report on an abbreviated conversation with a junior employee who requested a transfer:

Employee: Goal? I guess I'd like to hold an important position in the company.

Counselor: What level in the organization do you have in mind when you refer to an important position?

Employee: Well, chairman of the board or president, I guess.

Counselor: Those are certainly important positions. Suppose we determine, if we can, whether that's a realistic goal for you.

Employee: How do we do that?

Counselor: We could try to set down all the skills and experience we feel the president should have and evaluate just how much you'd need to do to get to that level of expertise. You could then decide whether you'd commit yourself to that kind of effort and try to estimate how successful you might be in carrying it off. But we'd also have to take a look at your competition, so let's examine that angle first. Assuming the next president will come from within the company, how many people do you figure you'd be competing with?

Employee: I'm not sure.

Counselor: What thoughts do you have about the kind of person who would be more likely to be promoted? Do you feel that the next president could be someone upgraded from the wage ranks?

Employee: Oh no, the job will require a professional background.

Counselor: Then your competition will number, say, some 400 or more people. What we have to do now is to identify what you have, that they don't have, which gives you an edge in achieving the presidency of the company.

Employee: (no response)

Counselor: In view of our type of operations, how significant do you feel the level of technical or professional proficiency, broadly speaking, would be in the selection?

Employee: I'd say that it would be very important.

Counselor: Well, then, how do you see yourself in this regard as compared to the 400 people we're looking at?

Employee: Smarter than some, not as capable as others.

Counselor: About in the middle?

Employee: Yes.

Counselor: If this kind of proficiency were the prime consideration, then we might say that the competition has been narrowed to 200. Now what advantage do you see yourself as having over these 200?

Employee: (no response)

Counselor: Well, to what extent would you work harder than they would, to get there?

Employee: I don't think I could say I'd work harder. I'm sure they'd all make as much effort.

Counselor: How about desire? How much more do you feel you want the position than they do?

Employee: I couldn't truly say that I'd want it more. I really hadn't thought out very carefully what I said about the presidency. I guess that the goal isn't a realistic one for me at this stage of the game. Perhaps an intermediate goal is what I should establish.

The interview continued, directed toward a lesser, more attainable goal for that individual. Another test for realism is the individual's discussion of what he sees as his strong point (characteristics or factors which will help him achieve his goal) and soft spots (those that may impede his progress). Difficulties and successes the individual is experiencing with subordinates, peers, and superiors are also a part of this phase of the conversations.

Careful listening has frequently helped to expand this information most usefully. For example, one individual in Gould's study stated, "I think I'm pretty fair in the field of labor relations." In feeding back what he had heard, the counselor was careful to include this comment. The conversation at that point went like this:

Counselor: And you see yourself as only pretty fair in labor relations, right?

Employee: No, that's not right.

Counselor: You see yourself as better than fair?

Employee: I sure do.

Counselor: Good?

Employee: Darned good.

There then followed a fruitful discussion of the risks of understatement—you might be believed! The point was also made that due concern should be shown about image so that what others see and hear is compatible with the individual's true worth.

This is one example of the kind of career counseling possible in a career development program. There are many other possibilities, including midlife career crisis counseling.[38]

SUMMARY, CONCLUSIONS, AND RECOMMENDATIONS

This chapter is designed to introduce you to the process of career development. Career planning and development is a relatively new personnel activity and is performed more often by individuals than enterprises.

One way to determine if career development is effective is to consider the alternatives. The consequences of lack of attention to career development by either the employee or the organization have been described by David Moment and Salwar Fisher, who call this dysfunction *career drift:* Employees drift along with no goals or plans for self-development, while the job and environment may be demanding new talents or approaches. The organization winds up with a good deal of deadwood, or obsolete employees. This is costly to both the person and the organization.[39]

It is hard to describe cost/benefit analysis for a developing activity such as career development. In general, the less developed the function, the "softer" must be the analysis. Organizations using the plans can do attitude surveys to determine if the employees find career development helpful, useful, rewarding, and so forth, but there tends to be a positive bias to these surveys. Who wants to tell an organization it is wasting its money trying to help him develop himself? Analysis can determine if the organization has reduced the turnover rate, but turnover is affected by many factors: pay, opportunity elsewhere, job interest, current supervisor, and organization personnel benefits, for example.

Cost measures could be developed for the amount of time supervisors spend with employees on career development multiplied by their hourly rate of pay. Similar costs could be computed for personnel specialists.

Career development is likely to be more effective with some employees than with others. My expectation would be that those who are involved with the work ethic, who feel work is important to their self-identity, would respond well to it. To an instrumental worker, it may not make a dent, but it is not likely to hurt, either. This leads to the first proposition for this chapter:

> *Proposition 9.1.* The more employees identify with the work ethic, the more likely are they to find career development satisfying, and the more likely is it to affect their performance positively.

Some propositions suggesting when career development will be practiced include:

Proposition 9.2. The larger the organization, the more likely is it that the effective organization will engage in career development and counseling.

Proposition 9.3. The more complex the organization's product or service offering, the more complex are its needs for varying types of personnel, and thus the more likely is it that the effective organization will engage in career development.

Proposition 9.4. The more volatile the organization's environment, the more difficult is it to pursue detailed career development plans, and thus the less likely is the function to be found.

Proposition 9.5. The higher the percentage of educated and well-trained employees in the organization, the more likely is it that the effective organization will offer career development and counseling.

Career planning can be practiced by the employee without much help from the employer. The following proposition applies here:

Proposition 9.6. The more the employee holds work ethic values and is upwardly mobile, the more likely is he to do his own career planning seriously.

Besides the personnel specialist and the employee, the third party who can be involved in career development is the employee's supervisor or manager. Two propositions are appropriate here:

Proposition 9.7. The more the organization rewards its managers for developing human resources, the more likely is the organization to offer career development and counseling.

Proposition 9.8. The more the supervisor identifies with the participation model of leadership, the more likely he or she is to perform effective career development and counseling.

Unlike the other chapters, Chapter 9 will not have a chart indicating recommendations on career development for model organizations. It is too new a function to make this prediction. It is to be expected, however, that large and medium-sized and more stable organizations will develop formal career development programs if top management chooses to support them as part of its personnel strategy. This is likely if management wants to develop employees fully. Personnel specialists should be trained to aid supervisors in this work.

Other types of organizations should develop informal methods as part of the personnel process, probably in conjunction with a performance evaluation program. In a small organization, the conscientious administrator tries to get to know the employees and encourages them to discuss their career aspirations. From this information, the administrator helps develop a career plan with the employee. When I was in the food business, I encouraged salesmen to talk about their aspirations. One salesman indicated he longed to become a sales supervisor over several salesmen. When such a job became vacant, the salesman was called in, his prior discussions were mentioned, and he was asked to think about whether he wanted to be considered for the vacancy. When confronted with an actual opportunity for his career aspiration, he chose not to be considered. He had decided he was satisfied as a salesman, and he was more productive after he had been given a chance at his imagined career ideal.

Often career development takes place in a small organization in conjunction with performance evaluation, the subject of Chapter 10.

QUESTIONS

1. What is a career? What is career development?
2. How is career development related to a person's life stages, according to Schein?
3. How does career development interact with other personnel functions?
4. What factors in the diagnostic model significantly influence career development?
5. Why does a business undertake career development? Why should you do career planning?
6. Describe the interrelationships between the employee, her or his supervisor, and the personnel specialist in career development.
7. Briefly outline the stages of career planning by individuals.
8. How might a career plan differ for an unmarried person? A person who wishes a work life with two careers to it?
9. How widespread is career development? Give some examples of how career development plans work.
10. How does a person's career anchor affect the career developed?
11. How does career counseling take place?
12. Which types of enterprises are most likely to have career development? Which individuals do career planning?

NOTES AND REFERENCES

1. John Van Maanen and Edgar Schein, "Career Development," in *Improving Life at Work,* ed. J. Richard Hackman and J. Lloyd Suttle (Santa Monica, Cal.: Goodyear Publishing Co., 1977).

2. The definition is a synthesis of the following sources: John Crites, "Work and Careers," in *Handbook of Work, Organization and Society,* ed. Robert Dubin (Chicago: Rand McNally & Co., 1977); William F. Glueck, "Career Management of Managerial, Professional and Technical Personnel," in *Manpower Planning and Programming,* ed. Elmer Buarack and James Walker (Boston: Allyn & Bacon, 1972); Douglas Hall, *Careers in Organizations* (Santa Monica, Ca.: Goodyear Publishing Co., 1976).

3. Edward Gross, *Work and Society* (New York: Thomas Y. Crowell Co., 1958), esp. ch. 1, 5; Everett Hughes, *Men and Their Work.* (Glencoe, Ill.: Free Press, 1958), esp. ch. 3, 7; Herbert Kaufman, *The Forest Ranger,* Resources for the Future series (Baltimore, Md.: Johns Hopkins Press, 1967); Alan Schoonmaker, "Individualism in Management," *California Management Review,* Winter 1968, pp. 9–22. Howard Becker and Anselm Strauss, "Careers, Personality, and Adult Socialization," *Journal of Sociology,* November 1956, pp. 253–63.

4. Lawrence L. Ferguson, "Better Management of Manager's Careers," *Harvard Business Review,* March–April 1966, pp. 139–52.

5. Herbert Kaufman, *Obsolescence and Professional Career Development* (New York: Amacon, 1974).

6. Richard Leiden, "Mid-Career Renewal," *Training and Development Journal,* May 1976, pp. 16–20.

7. Janice Kay, "Career Development for Women: An Affirmative Action First," *Training and Development Journal,* May 1976, pp. 22–24.

8. Wayne A. Dressel, "Coping with Executive Mobility," *Business Horizons,* August 1970, pp. 53–58; Oscar Grusky, "Career Mobility and Organizational Commitment," *Administrative Science Quarterly,* March 1966, pp. 488–503; William Papier, "Push Pull and Brain Train," *Personnel Administration,* November–December 1968, pp. 43–49; Edmond Rosenthal, "Greener Pastures: Why Employees Change Jobs," *Personnel,* January–February 1969, pp. 22–30; Hall, *Careers in Organizations;* Douglas Hall and Franice Hall, "What's New in Career Development," *Organizational Dynamics,* Summer 1976, pp. 17–33.

9. J. H. Goldthorpe et al., *The Affluent Worker* (Cambridge, Mass.: Cambridge University Press, 1968); Robert Dubin, "Industrial Workers Worlds," *Social Problems* 3 (1956), pp. 131–42.

10. Eugene Jennings, "Mobicentric Man," *Psychology Today,* July 1970, pp. 34–36; Christopher Sofer, *Men in Mid Career* (Cambridge: Cambridge University Press, 1970).

11. Kaufman, *Obsolescence and Career Development;* Lyman Porter et al., "Organizational Commitment and Managerial Turnover," technical report no. 13, University of California–Irvine, 1972.

12. Michael Moore et al., "Predictions of Managerial Career Expectations," *Journal of Applied Psychology* 59, 1 (1974), pp. 90–92.

13. Leonard Ackerman, "Career Development: Preparing Round Pegs for Square Holes," *Training and Development Journal,* February 1976, pp. 12–14.

14. This section draws heavily on Hall, *Careers in Organizations,* ch. 7. See also Walter Slocum, *Occupational Careers* (Chicago: Aldine-Atherton, 1974) pp. 304–40; Verne Walter, "Self-Motivated Personnel Career Planning," *Personnel Journal,* April 1976, pp. 162–67.

15. Van Maanen and Schein, "Career Development."

16. John Holland, *Making Vocational Choices: A Theory of Careers* (Englewood Cliffs, N.J.: Prentice-Hall, Inc., 1973).

17. Anne Harlan, "Career Differences among Male and Female Managers," *Proceedings,* Academy of Management, 1976; Margaret Henny and Anne Jardin, "Women Executives in the Old Boy Network," *Psychology Today,* January 1977, pp. 76–81; John Verga, "Female Career Myopia," *Human Resource Management,* Winter 1976, pp. 24–27; Deborah Yaeger, "The Balany Act," *The MBA,* February 1977, pp. 37–40.

18. "When Career Couples Have Conflicts of Interest," *Business Week,* December 13, 1976; "Marriage and the Corporation," *Nation's Business,* March 1975; Alan Otten, "Two Career Couples," *Wall Street Journal,* July 20, 1976; Carl Ridley, "Exploring the Impact of Work Satisfaction Involvement on Marital Interaction When Both Partners Are Employed," *Journal of Marriage and the Family,* May 1973, pp. 229–237.

19. Eugene Jennings, "Success Chess," *Management of Personnel Quarterly,* Fall 1970, pp. 2–8. A similar approach is given in "Plotting A Route to the Top," *Business Week,* October 12, 1974.

20. See, for example, Thomas Driskell and Dean Dauw, "Executive Mid Career Change," *Personnel Journal,* November 1975; B. B. Dunning, and A. Biderman, "The Case of Military Retirement," *Industrial Gerontology,* Spring 1973, pp. 18–37; J. M. Kim, "Unemployment and Mid-Career Change," *Industrial Gerontology,* Spring 1973, pp. 18–37; Nina Laserson, "Profiles of Five Second Careerists," *Personnel,* (January–Feburary 1973), pp. 36–46; Michael Mann, *Workers on the Move* (Cambridge, Mass.: Cambridge University Press, 1973); Robert Pearse and Purdy Pelzer, *Self-Directed Change for the Mid-Career Manager* (New York: Amacon, 1975); C. H. Rittenhouse, *The Transferability and Retraining of Defense Engineers* (Palo Alto, Ca.: Stanford Research Institute, 1967).

21. Walter Storey, "Self-Directed Career Planning at the General Electric Company," *Proceedings,* Academy of Management, 1976; Merle Junker and Donald Crane, "The Federal Personnel Administration Career Program: A Case Study," *Proceedings,* Academy of Management, 1976; Allen Hard and Clara Erickson, "Career Development at the Naval Weapons Center: A Case Study," *Proceedings,* Academy of Management, 1976.

22. U.S. Army, *Special Study of Career Programs in Industry* (Washington, D.C.: Department of the Army, Deputy Chief of Staff for Personnel, May–June, 1968).

23. Walter Mahler and William Wrightnour, *Executive Continuity* (Homewood, Ill.: Dow Jones–Irwin, Inc., 1973).

24. Edgar Schein, "How 'Career Anchors' Hold Executives to their Career Paths," *Personnel,* May–June 1975, pp. 11–24. See also David Thomsen, "Keeping Track of Managers in a Large Corporation," *Personnel,* November–December 1976, pp. 23–30.

25. James Walker, "Let's Get Realistic about Career Paths," *Human Resource Management,* Fall 1976, pp. 2–7.

26. Joseph Yeager and Richard Leider, "Career Planning: Personnel in the Third Party Role," *Human Resource Management,* Spring 1975, pp. 31–35; W. P. Fisher and P. L. Gaurmier, *A Study of Career Ladders and Manpower Development for Non-Management Personnel in the Food Service Industry* (Ithaca, N.Y.: School of Hotel Administration, Cornell University, June 1970); Jack Epstein, "Career Management Programs," *Personnel Journal,* March 1974, pp. 191–95; Elmer Burack, "The First City Bank," *Proceedings,* Academy of Management, 1976; Douglas Hall, and Roger Mansfield, "Relationships of Age and Seniority with Career Variables of Engineers and Scientists," *Journal of Applied Psychology* 60, 2 (1975), pp. 201–10.

27. Carl Bellas, "The Dual Track Career System within the Internal Revenue Service," *Personnel Administration and Public Personnel Review* 1, 2 (1972), pp. 4–8.

28. P. J. Chartrand, and K. L. Pond, *A Study of Executive Career Paths in the Public Service of Canada* (Chicago: Public Personnel Associations, 1968).

29. William Bright, "How One company Manages Its Human Resources," *Harvard Business Review,* January–February 1976, pp. 81–92.

30. Douglas Bray et al., *Formative Years in Business* (New York: Wiley Interscience, 1974).

31. Kay, "Career Development for Women."

32. Matt Starcevich, "Career Management at G. D. Searle and Company," *Proceedings,* Academy of Management, 1976.

33. William Kushnick and Leo Herbert, "Career and Professional Development in the United States General Accounting Office," in *Human Resource Management in Public Organizations,* ed. Gilbert Siegel (Los Angeles: University Publishers, 1973); Lloyd Musolf, "Separate Career Executive Systems," in Siegel, *Human Resource Management.*

34. U.S. Air Force, *Air Force Manual,* 36–23.

35. Thomas Morris, "Merit Principles in Military Officer Personnel Administration," *Public Administration Review,* September–October 1974, pp. 445–50.

36. Marion Kellogg, *Career Management* (New York: American Management Association, 1972), ch. 11; J. D. Henry, "Are You Good at Career Counseling?" *Supervisory Management,* March 1974; F. Holloway, et al., "How to Foster the Continuing Development of Professional People," *Research Management,* July 1970, pp. 281–84.

37. M. Gould, "Counseling for Self-Development," *Personnel Journal,* March 1970, pp. 226–34.

38. Alan Entive, "Mid-Life Counseling: Prognosis and Potential," *Personnel and Guidance Journal,* November 1976, pp. 112–14.

39. David Moment and Galmar Fisher, "Managerial Career Development and Generational Confrontation," *California Management Review,* Spring 1973, pp. 46–55.

Performance evaluation and promotion

CHAPTER OBJECTIVES

- ■ To show why evaluation performance takes place.
- ■ To indicate how often evaluation takes place and who conducts evaluations.
- ■ To help you understand the criteria and tools to use to conduct effective performance evaluations.
- ■ To demonstrate how to evaluate employees effectively.
- ■ To understand enterprise promotion systems.

CHAPTER OUTLINE

Mary has been oriented as a production helper and has been on the job a while. Now her employer faces some decisions that affect her a great deal.

One is: Should Mary be kept on the payroll now that the budget has been cut, or should someone else be laid off?

A second is: Now that Joe has quit, who should get his job, which is better than Mary's—Mary or someone else?

A third is: We don't have enough money to give everyone a big raise this year. Should Mary get a raise?

Mary is a dedicated worker. She often gets criticism from her supervisor, but rarely receives praise. The supervisor doesn't mean to be so negative; when it comes to encouragement, she just "never gets around to it."

These and similar situations give rise to formal evaluation and promotion systems, the subject of this chapter. Performance evaluation is called by many names, such as performance review, personnel rating, merit rating, performance appraisal, employee appraisal, or employee evaluation. The term used here is performance evaluation.

> DEFINITION
> Performance evaluation is the personnel activity by means of which the enterprise determines the extent to which the employee is performing the job effectively.

Normally there are the several steps in performance evaluation:

1. Establish performance evaluation policies on when and how often to evaluate, who should evaluate, the criteria for evaluation, and the evaluation tools to be used.
2. Have evaluators gather data on employee performance.
3. Have evaluators (and employees in some systems) evaluate employees' performance.
4. Discuss the evaluation with the employee.
5. Decisions are made and the evaluation is filed.

In many organizations, two evaluation (and promotion) systems exist side by side: the formal and the informal. Supervisors often think about how well employees are doing; this is the informal system. It is influenced by political and interpersonal processes so that employees who are liked better than others have an edge. Formal performance evaluation is a system set up by the enterprise to *regularly* and *systematically* evaluate employee performance. This is the main focus of this chapter.

Studies by the National Industrial Conference Board (NICB) and the Bureau of National Affairs (BNA) indicate that a majority of white-collar employees participate in regular performance evaluation plans.[1] For example, a 1974 BNA survey found that about three fourths of supervisors, office workers, and middle managers experienced formal performance evaluation,[2] and a 1975 BNA survey found that 54 percent of blue-collar employees participated in it. White-collar employees are more likely to be evaluated in manufacturing than in nonmanufacturing firms. Blue-collar employees are less likely to be evaluated in manufacturing than nonmanufacturing firms, primarily because of union pressures against formal evaluation. Specifically, 84 percent of white-collar employees (87 percent in manufacturing) are evaluated; 75 percent of blue-collar employees in nonbusiness and 53 percent in nonmanufacturing jobs are evaluated; and 47 percent of blue-collar workers in manufacturing firms participate in formal evaluation programs.[3]

Performance evaluation is another personnel activity which involves both line managers and personnel specialists. Generally speaking, the personnel specialists design the performance evaluation system, train the line managers in the use of the systems, and maintain the records. The line managers do the evaluation of the employees and, in many cases, communicate the results to their employees. For performance evaluation to be more than a yearly paper-work exercise, top management must encourage its use and use it to make reward decisions such as promotions.

Performance evaluation and promotion are personnel activities which are between Stage II and Stage III in development, as defined in Chapter 1 (Exhibit 1–13). There have been studies of evaluation and promotion, as in Stage II, but there is some conflict in the data from the studies, as is true of Stage III functions.

A DIAGNOSTIC APPROACH TO PERFORMANCE EVALUATION

Exhibit 10–1 highlights the relevant factors from the diagnostic model which have significance for performance evaluation and promotion. The first factor is the task performed. As indicated, a white-collar or supervisory task is more likely to be formally evaluated than some blue-collar tasks. In addition, the performance evaluation technique used will differ with the task being evaluated.

The second factor affecting performance evaluation is the government. Since the passage of antidiscrimination legislation, the government has investigated to determine if enterprises discriminate against protected categories of employees in promotion, pay raises, and other rewards. Performance evaluation is the critical tool used in making these rewards. By inducing enterprises to keep better records to support their decisions, government action has indirectly encouraged better performance evaluation systems. In some cases, enterprises have dropped performance evaluation and rely more strictly on seniority.

What impact has the government had on promotions? One example is the 1973 agreement of American Telephone and Telegraph with the EEOC. AT&T agreed to provide 50,000 higher paying jobs (5,000 of them managerial jobs) for women and 6,000 jobs for minorities (800 managerial jobs). New

EXHIBIT 10–1
Factors affecting performance evaluation and promotion

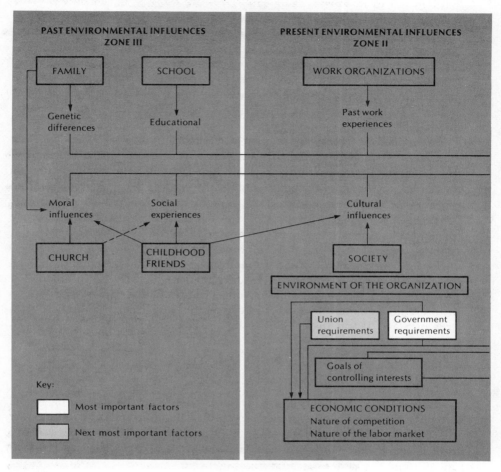

York Bell, in a response to a State of New York Human Rights Division investigation, agreed to promote women to 57 percent of its supervisory jobs, 46 percent of the middle manager jobs, and 20 percent of its top management jobs.

Recent court cases (*Rome* v. *General Motors Corporation, Baxter* v. *Savannah Sugar Refining Corporation*) have tended to require enterprises to set up formal performance evaluation systems so that promotions do not discriminate. Other recent cases (*Albemarle Paper Co.* v. *Moody, Wade* v. *Mississippi Cooperative Extension Service, Brito* v. *Zita Co.; Harper* v. *Mayor and City Council of Baltimore*) have indicated that when formal performance evaluation systems are used, they must not be administered or set up in such a way that the results discriminate against protected groups. More will be said later in the chapter on how to deal with EEO requirements.[4]

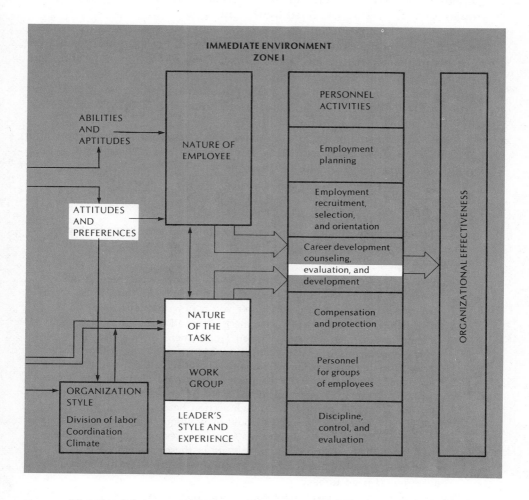

IMMEDIATE ENVIRONMENT
ZONE I

PERSONNEL ACTIVITIES

ABILITIES AND APTITUDES

NATURE OF EMPLOYEE

Employment planning

Employment recruitment, selection, and orientation

ATTITUDES AND PREFERENCES

Career development counseling, evaluation, and development

Compensation and protection

NATURE OF THE TASK

WORK GROUP

Personnel for groups of employees

ORGANIZATION STYLE

Division of labor
Coordination
Climate

LEADER'S STYLE AND EXPERIENCE

Discipline, control, and evaluation

ORGANIZATIONAL EFFECTIVENESS

The third factor influencing performance evaluation is the attitudes and preferences of employees. For many people, especially those whose values fit the work ethic, evaluations and promotions can be very important. If this process is badly handled, turnover can increase, morale decline, and productivity drop, as equity and expectancy theory would predict. For employees with instrumental attitudes toward work, performance evaluation is just another process at work; since work is not too important to them, neither are evaluations. They want a job to get money, and that is it. They might even refuse promotions that involve more responsibility.

Another factor that can affect performance evaluation is the leader's (supervisors) style. Supervisors can use the formal system in a number of ways: fairly or unfairly, in a supportive manner or punitively, positively or negatively. If the supervisor is punitive and negative with an employee who responds to positive reinforcement, performance evaluation can lead to the opposite of the results expected by the enterprise.

Finally, if there is a union present in the enterprise, performance evaluations and the promotion process might be affected. For example, promotion criteria might be written into the contract. Different unions take different positions in support of or opposition to formal performance evaluation. Most oppose the use of nonmeasurable, nonproduction-related factors in performance evaluation. They have good reason to doubt the usefulness of a factor like "initiative" in promotion.

These are the major factors affecting the performance evaluation and promotion process. Now we will briefly examine the case for and against the use of formal performance evaluation.

TO EVALUATE OR NOT TO EVALUATE

The setting: Office of the executive vice president of a medium-sized corporation. Present are the executive vice president and the vice presidents of the corporation.

Tom Smith (executive vice president): As you know, we're here to make a recommendation to John (the president) on what if anything to do about Mary's suggestion. Mary, why don't you review the issue.

Mary Hartford (vice president, personnel): You all received a copy of my memo to J. B. As you know, when I came here three years ago I felt one of our top priorities in personnel would be to get an evaluation system really running on line here. I want this because P. E. is an outstanding motivation technique. So, after much thought and planning, the results are in my memo. I recommend we institute an MBO type evaluation system from vice presidents through section heads and a graphic rating scale for below that. The MBO would be done quarterly, the rating scale semiannually, and we'd tie rewards such as raises and promotions to the results of the evaluation. The details are in these memos. We're too big and geographically dispersed now to continue using our informal system.

Tom: Sounds good to me.

Dave Artem (vice president marketing): Me too.

Will Roxer (vice president, finance): Looks fine, Mary.

Fred Fairfax (vice president, manufacturing): Well, it doesn't to me. We had one of these paper-mill forms systems here ten years ago, and it was a waste of time. It just meant more paper work for us down on the firing line. You staff people sit up here dreaming up more for us to do. We're overburdened now. Besides, I called a few buddies in big firms who have P.E. They say it involves a lot of training of evaluators and it makes half the employees mad when they don't get 100 scores on the "grade report." It gets down to a lot of politics when it's all said and done. If you recommend this I'll send J. B. a counterproposal and I'll call him to see I get my way too.

This vignette illustrates some of the reasons people give for putting in performance evaluation systems or keeping them out. The fact that there is a chapter on performance evaluation in this book implies that we think it ought to be performed, but this section looks at the pros and cons of the process. Generally speaking, the purposes of performance evaluation are to help managers make better promotions and reward decisions, to foster the individual's satisfaction and development, and to motivate more effective performance.

Larry Cummings and Donald Schwab have made a good case for utilizing performance evaluation in enterprises.[5] Overall, it serves several general purposes. From the enterprise's point of view, performance evaluation helps to maintain control and to make efficient use of human resources. It can reduce employee tension and stress by letting employees know how they are doing on the job; most employees desire this kind of feedback.[6]

Exhibit 10–2 reproduces Cummings and Schwab's model of performance evaluation. Their reference numbers will be used to explain the outcomes they suggest can be derived:

Ability–performance (1–3). In defining the performance criteria in performance evaluation, the process helps specify the abilities (and levels of abilities) necessary for effective performance. If the job changes, it helps adjust the ability definition accordingly.

Motivation–performance (2–3). In defining expected performance goals, performance evaluation helps the employee direct his or her energies toward the work-oriented goals desired by the enterprise.[7]

Performance–intrinsic outcomes (3–5; relationship 4). An intrinsic outcome or reward is an internal satisfaction perceived by the employee as desirable. An example is the good feeling experienced by a work-oriented employee who has done a good job or accomplished an important task. Properly developed, performance evaluation can give effective employees these intrinsic rewards as a consequence of achieving enterprise objectives.[8]

EXHIBIT 10–2
Model of performance determinants with evaluation applications

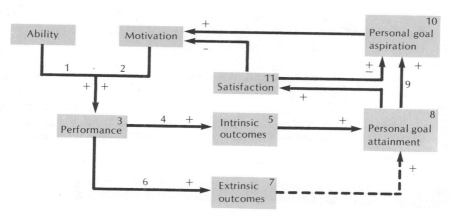

Source: Larry Cummings and Donald Schwab, *Performance in Organizations* (Glenview, Ill.: Scott, Foresman & Co., 1973).

Performance–extrinsic outcomes (*3–7; relationship 6*).   An extrinsic reward or outcome is the response an enterprise gives to employee effectiveness. These can include raises, promotions, and similar rewards. Effective performance evaluation links performance to these rewards and thus encourages (motivates) the employee to be effective.

Personal goal aspiration (*10*) *and goal attainment* (*8*).   Personal goal aspirations are those goals an employee seeks to attain for herself or himself. Personal goal attainments are the goals the employee achieves. A developmentally oriented performance evaluation approach (discussed below) can lead to some merging of personal and organizational goals, and organizational goal attainment leads to personal achievement and satisfaction.

In addition to these reasons for using performance evaluation, effective evaluation becomes an input to other important personnel activities: compensation (pay increases), promotion, training (to prepare the employee for another job or to improve deficient performance), layoff planning, and providing information for personal self-development and career planning. A case study generally supports the usefulness of developmentally oriented performance evaluation in a major U.S. airline.[9] One survey of 46 organizations using performance evaluation found most of them satisfied with its usefulness,[10] but another survey found users were usually only moderately satisfied with them.[11] Generally, they were dissatisfied because operating management did not use the results effectively.

The ultimate purpose of performance evaluation is to improve the performance of the employee, so as to increase the enterprise's goal achievement and the employees' satisfaction and fulfillment in the future. These are the broad purposes of the evaluation. But many studies show how performance evaluation results help determine other personnel decisions. For example, the BNA found that evaluations of white-collar employees were used for determining wage increases (85 percent), promotions (83 percent), training needs (62 percent), as inputs to skills inventories (27 percent), and for validating selection procedures (24 percent). For blue-collar employees, the data were used for promotion decisions (83 percent), wage increases (67 percent), training need determination (61 percent), validating selection procedures (30 percent), and skills inventories (30 percent).[12]

These purposes can be grouped into three categories: reward purposes (wage increases, promotion) developmental purposes (training, counseling) and internal personnel purposes (validation, skills inventories). There also are a number of split-purpose evaluations, whereby a person is evaluated at one time with one method for developmental purposes and at another time, and with perhaps a different method, for reward purposes.[13] More will be said on this shortly.

REASONS FOR MALFUNCTION OR FAILURE

Any system or function can fail or malfunction. Performance evaluation is no exception. Many managers are aware of this and have heeded the warning of Paul Thompson and Gene Dalton to "beware."[14] In this section we will examine some of the problems that performance evaluation can develop and ways to alleviate them. The problems are concerned with system design and operation, the evaluator, and the employee.

System design and operating problems

Performance evaluation systems can fail or malfunction because they are poorly designed. The design can be blamed if the criteria for evaluation are poor, the technique used is cumbersome, or the system is more form than substance. If the criteria used focus on activities instead of output results, or on the person rather than performance, performance evaluation will be hurt.[15] This chapter will explain how to deal with this shortly. Some evaluation techniques take a long time to do or require extensive written analysis, both of which many managers resist. If this is the problem, another technique can be chosen. Finally, some systems are not on line and running. Some supervisors use it, but others just fill out the paper work. Denis Pym calls this "the politics and ritualization of evaluation."[16] Top management support for performance evaluation can remedy this problem.

Problems with the evaluator

Even if the system is well designed, problems can arise if the evaluators (usually supervisors) are not cooperative and well trained. Supervisors may not be comfortable with the process of evaluation, or what Douglas Mc-Gregor called playing God.[17] Often this is because they have not been adequately trained or they have not participated in the design of the program. Inadequate training of evaluators can lead to a series of evaluator problems in performance, several of which are discussed below.

The halo effect. The halo effect appears in evaluation when the evaluator tends to assign the same rating or level to each factor being rated for an employee. This results from an overall assessment of the person which totally colors the evaluator's view of the employee. What can be done about this? Some who advocate rating scales argue that only a few criteria should be rated. Others argue that all employees should be rated on one criterion, then all rated on another criterion at another time. This can be cumbersome, however. It has been shown that supervisory training can reduce halo problems, which are present more in some techniques (e.g., graphic rating scales) than in others.[18] (The various performance techniques are described in the section "How to Evaluate" below.)

Standards of evaluation. Problems with evaluation standards arise because of perceptual differences in the meaning of the evaluative words. Thus *good, adequate, satisfactory,* and *excellent* may mean different things to different evaluators. Some teachers are "easy As," while others almost never give an A. They differ in their interpretation of *excellent.* If only one evaluator is used the evaluation can be distorted, and there may be a constant error between the two. This difficulty arises mostly in graphic rating scales but may also appear with essays, critical incidents, and checklists.

In many systems there is a tendency to rate persons higher than they should be, especially if negative ratings must be explained to employees.[19] This leads to overly lenient evaluations—the performance evaluation equivalent of grade inflation. For example, in a study of U.S. Army officer evaluations, it was found that in 1922, 72 percent were rated below excellent, and less than 1 percent were rated superior, the highest rating. Since then, the percentage rated below excellent has dropped each year, and by 1940 it had fallen to 8 percent, while superior ratings increased to almost 20 percent by 1939.[20] Training of the evaluators plus review of the evaluation patterns by the evaluator's superiors can reduce this problem somewhat.

Central tendency.   Studies have found that some evaluators rate all their personnel within a narrow range. No matter what the actual performance differences between individuals might be, supervisors may rate them all either average or above average. This distorts the results for promotion and compensation decisions. The problem is most likely to be found with graphic rating scales. Evaluator training probably would help this problem, too.

Recent-behavior bias.   One difficulty with many of the evaluation systems is the time frame of the behavior being evaluated. Evaluators forget more about past behavior than current behavior. Thus many persons are evaluated more on the results of the past several weeks than on six months' average behavior.

Some employees are well aware of this difficulty. If they know the dates of the evaluation, they make it their business to be visible and noticed in many positive ways for several weeks in advance. Many evaluation systems suffer from this difficulty. It can be mitigated by using a technique such as critical incident or management by objectives (MBO) or by irregularly scheduled evaluations.

Personal biases.   Various studies have indicated that evaluators' biases can influence their evaluation of employees. If evaluators like certain employees better than others, this can influence the ratings they give.[21] This problem is related to the effects of prejudices against groups of people. Pressures from governmental agencies in the United States and Canada and managerial values of fairness should lead to equal opportunity and fair performance evaluation. The result should be increased rewards, promotions, and significant careers for all employees, of both sexes and all races, religions, and nationalities. Some studies indicate that sexual and racial stereotypes can creep into evaluations and lessen the opportunities for minority males or females.[22] Others found less sex bias present[23] or indicated that effective training of evaluators removes these biases.[24] Some evaluation techniques (such as forced choice, field review, performance tests, and MBO) tend to reduce this problem.[25]

Managers should examine the patterns of evaluation and promotion to determine if there might be systematic discrimination at evaluation time and take steps such as supervisory training or discipline to reduce this bias.

The theme that many evaluator problems can be solved by training the evaluator runs through the topics discussed above. This training is of two types, how to rate effectively and how to conduct effective evaluation interviews; the latter is discussed later in this chapter. There is much research to indicate that evaluator training reduces rating errors.[26] In fact, the quality of the evaluator is more important to effective evaluation than the technique used. Training alone will not eliminate all evaluator problems, just as driver training does not eliminate speeding and accidents. But evaluator training, combined with good system design, can make performance evaluation more effective.

Employee problems with performance evaluation

For the evaluation system to work well, the employees must understand it, must feel it is fair, and must be work oriented enough to care about the results. If the system is not explained to the employees so that they understand it, they will not work well. One way to foster this understanding is for the employees to participate in system design and be trained to some extent in performance evaluation. Another is the use of self-evaluation systems.[27] With regard to fairness, performance evaluation is in some ways like grading systems in schools. If you have received grades that you thought were unfair and inequitable, that were incorrectly computed or based on the "wrong things" (like attendance alone, for example), you know what your reactions were! Students will say "I got an A" for a course in which they worked hard and were fairly rewarded. They will say *"He* (or she) gave me a D" if they feel it was unfair. Their reactions sometimes are to give up or get angry in this case. Similar responses can come from employees as well, if the performance evaluations are incompetent or unfair, they may just not listen.[28]

Performance evaluation may also be less effective than desired if the employee is not work oriented and sees work only as a means to ends sought off the job. It might be seen only as paper work, unless the evaluation is so negative that the employee fears termination.[29]

Some analysts, such as Herbert Meyer, believe those who are rated poorly will not improve their performance but will give up.[30] This is compounded if the technique used is viewed as a zero-sum game—that is, some win and some lose as a result of it. With a system like forced distribution, 90 percent of the people must be told they are not highly regarded, whether they are or not. One study found that 77 percent of General Electric's personnel rank themselves rather highly. In forced choice only 10 percent would be rated highly so 67 to 77 percent of them would find such an evaluation a deflating experience.[31] Some of the performance evaluation tools (forced distribution, ranking, paired comparisons) do not build in an explanation of why the person was ranked as he was. It might be argued that everyone cannot be tops, so the best are rewarded, and the worst will leave. Sometimes quite the contrary happens! Of those who were evaluated poorly at G.E.,

60 percent lost heart but stayed because they figured they had nowhere to go.

But Meyer's analysis is too simple. J. S. Shrauger has summarized the research on how a person's expectations of what was going to happen in the evaluation affected his or her reactions to evaluation and behavior afterwards. Reaction to positive and negative feedback varied depending on a series of variables: (1) the importance of the task and the motivation to perform it, (2) how highly the employee rates the evaluator, (3) the extent to which the employee has a positive self-image, and (4) the expectancies the employee had prior to the evaluation; for example, did the employee expect a good evaluation or a bad one?[32]

Meyer's analysis is based on one theory of the reactions to feedback (self-enhancement/esteem theory). But most research, like Shrauger's, does *not* support this position. Rather, all four conditions listed above affect the likely results of evaluation.

In sum, there are problems with performance evaluation: with the system, the evaluator, and the employee. However, following the suggestions given here can make performance evaluation a useful personnel activity.

FORMAL EVALUATION

Whether formal performance evaluation becomes a problem for the human resources of an enterprise or has a positive influence on them depends on four factors:

- When evaluation takes place—the timing.
- Who evaluates—the evaluators.
- What is evaluated—the criteria for evaluation.
- How evaluation takes place—the evaluation techniques.

The first three are discussed in this section; the fourth is the topic of the next section, which details the various techniques.

When and how often to evaluate

There are two basic decisions to be made regarding the timing of performance appraisal: one is when to do it, and the other is how often. In many enterprises performance evaluations are scheduled for arbitrary dates such as the date the person was hired (anniversary date), or every employee may be evaluated on or near a single calendar date (e.g., May 25). Although the single-day approach is convenient administratively, it probably is not a good idea. It requires managers to spend a lot of time conducting evaluation interviews and completing forms at one time, which may lead them to "get it over with" quickly. This probably encourages halo effect ratings, for example. In addition, it may not be related to the normal task cycle of the employee, which can make it difficult for the manager to evaluate performance effectively.

It makes more sense to schedule the evaluation at the completion of a task cycle. For example, tax accountants see the year as April 16 to April 15. Professors consider that the year starts at the beginning of the fall term and terminates after the spring term. For others without clear task cycles based on dates, one way to set the date is by use of the MBO technique, whereby the manager and employee agree upon a task cycle terminating in evaluation at a specific time.[33]

The second question concerns how often evaluation should be done. A BNA study found that 74 percent of white-collar and 58 percent of blue-collar employees were evaluated annually, and 25 percent of white-collar and 30 percent of blue collar employees were evaluated semiannually. About 10 percent were evaluated more often than semiannually.[34]

Psychologists have found that feedback on performance should be given frequently, and the closer the feedback to the action, the more effective it is.[35] For example, it is more effective for a professor to correct an error on a computer program the first time the error appears and show the student how to change it than to wait and flunk the student at the end of the term. Why, then, do so few firms evaluate frequently? Generally speaking, it is because managers and employees have lots of other things to do. One way to reconcile the ideal with the reality in this respect is for the manager to give frequent feedback to employees informally, and then formally summarize it at evaluation time. This, of course, is based on the assumption that employees value evaluation and feedback.

Who evaluates the employee?

The setting: Office of the vice president for personnel and industrial relations in a large manufacturing concern.

Harry Griffith (vice president, sales): John, I can't believe what my division head for Region 1 just told me. She says the regional personnel guy told her that in the future the division head doesn't evaluate the sales managers. They do it on each other. We can't have personality contests like that going on.

John Marsh (vice president, personnel): Harry, we're trying an experiment in Region 1. There is very good evidence that peers do a better job evaluating each other than the superior does. We want to try it out, and we randomly chose Region 1. Henderson (the president) approved it, and I saw that he contacted you to give you a chance to comment.

Harry: Look, I was in the field and just didn't get around to commenting on Henderson's note. But John, you can't let the people on the firing line rate each other. We'll have all 100 percent ratings for sure. That's the job of the boss, and we both know it.

This case example raises some of the issues to be discussed in this portion of the chapter: If evaluation is performed, who evaluates whom?

EXHIBIT 10–3
Possible evaluators of an employee

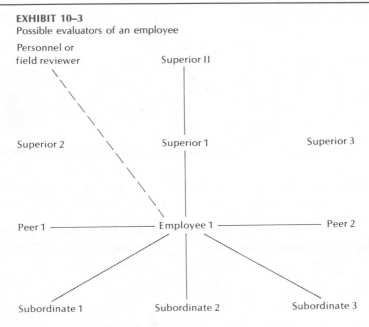

Exhibit 10–3 focuses on employee 1, the person to be evaluated, surrounded by potential evaluators—the employee's superiors and subordinates plus the personnel specialist. First, employee 1 could be evaluated by superior 1. This approach is used because it is assumed that this superior has the greatest opportunity to observe the subordinate's behavior. It is also assumed that he or she is able to interpret and analyze the subordinate's performance in light of the organization's objectives. In most organizations, the employee's supervisor is responsible for reward decisions such as pay and promotion. If the superior evaluates the subordinate, the superior can possibly link effective performance (as measured by performance evaluation) with rewards.

Another potential evaluator is a rating committee of several superiors most likely to come in contact with the employee. This could be superiors 1, 2, 3, and II, for example (superior II represents a higher level of management). This has the advantages of offsetting bias on the part of one superior alone and adding additional information to the evaluation, especially if it follows a group meeting format.

The third approach is to have the employee rated by her or his peers (for example, peers 1 and 2 in the work unit). In the work setting, a peer is a person working with and at the same level as the employee. In the peer evaluation system the co-workers must know the level of performance of the employee being evaluated. For this system to work, it is preferable for the evaluating peers to trust one another and not to be competitive for raises and promotions. This approach may be useful when the tasks of the work unit require frequent working contacts among peers.

A fourth approach is subordinate evaluation of superior; for example, subordinates 1, 2, and 3 would evaluate employee 1. It has been used by Exxon[36] and is used in some universities (students evaluate faculty). It is used more for the developmental aspects of performance evaluation than some of the other methods.

The fifth approach is the field review technique.[37] In this method, a specialized appraiser from outside the job setting, such as a personnel specialist, rates the employee. This is often costly, so it is generally used only for exceptionally important jobs, but it might be used for the entire work force if accusations of prejudice must be countered. A crucial consideration is that the outside evaluator is not likely to have as much data as evaluators in any of the other four approaches, and the data developed are from an atypical situation.

A sixth approach is self-evaluation. In this case, employee 1 evaluates herself or himself with the techniques used by other evaluators or different ones. This approach seems to be used more often for the developmental (as opposed to evaluative) aspects of performance evaluation. It is also used to evaluate an employee who works in physical isolation.

Finally, a combination of these approaches can be used. The supervisor's evaluation can be supplemented by a self-evaluation; when evaluation is done jointly, this can be an MBO exercise. The supervisor's results could also be supplemented by subordinates' or peers' evaluations.

Which of the potential evaluators most often does the evaluation? The 1975 BNA survey found that almost all enterprises use the supervisor alone to do the evaluation. The rating committee was almost never used. Cummings and Schwab found that in general the evaluation of a trained superior is as effective as that of the typical rating committee. In about one fifth of the BNA sample (mostly nonbusiness enterprises) superiors I and II were involved in evaluation. Peer evaluation and field review were used so infrequently that it was not even reported in the survey. Self-evaluation was used in 4 to 5 percent of reporting firms.[38]

Regardless of what is being done, which approach is best to use? Exhibit 10–4 summarizes many of the studies on the relative effectiveness of the various approaches; there are studies supporting and criticizing each approach.[39] The relation of the purposes of the appraisal to its means and ends is highlighted in Exhibit 10–5. There are at least two basic purposes, development, and evaluation with a view towards future rewards; the various approaches are sometimes good for one purpose and not another. Perhaps the reasons for mixed findings is that each approach to evaluation has a different kind of bias or taps different kinds of data. Or individual differences in evaluators may affect the evaluations differently in each of these approaches.[40]

Although all approaches have had positive and negative research results, Lewin and Zwany's literature search shows many more positive than negative studies for peer evaluations.[41] Yet peer evaluations are practically never used outside the military. I believe this is most likely because supervisors

EXHIBIT 10-4
Research studies supporting and criticizing evaluation by various approaches

Approach	Supporting studies	Criticizing studies
Superior	Smith (1976) Webster (1969)	Bedeian (1976) Taylor & Wilsted (1976) Thompson (1970) Heneman (1974)
Superiors (rating committee)	Bayroff et al. (1954) Whitla & Tirrell (1953)	Cummings & Schwab (1973)
Peers	Berkshire & Nelson (1958) Hollander (1954, 1956, 1957) Wherry & Fryer (1949) Gordon & Medlund (1965) Roadman (1964) Downey et al. (1976) Lewin & Zwany (1976) Schneier (1977) Fiske & Cox (1960) Booker & Miller (1966) Amir (1970) Weitz & Nuckols (1953)	Mayfield (1970) Waters & Waters (1970)
Subordinate	Maloney & Hinrichs (1959) Hegarty (1974)	
Field review Self	McMurray (1965) Bassett & Meyer (1968) Hall (1951) Kircher (1965) Heneman (1974) Lowrie (1966) Taylor & Wilsted (1976)	Thornton (1968) Nealey & Owen (1970) Parker et al. (1959)

Note: A bibliographical list of these studies is given in note 39 at the end of the chapter.

EXHIBIT 10-5
Superior, peer, self, and outside appraisal in relation to purposes and
dimensions of appraisal

Purpose of appraisal / Dimension of appraisal	Evaluation		Development	
Means (method used)	Superior Peer Self Subordinate Outsider	1	Superior Peer Self Subordinate Outsider	3
Ends (outcomes achieved)	Superior Peer Self Subordinate Outsider	2	Superior Peer Self Subordinate Outsider	4

Source: Larry Cummings and Donald Schwab, *Performance in Organizations* (Chicago.
Scott, Foresman & Co., 1973).

have the power to evaluate and reward employees, and many are reluctant to give it up. It is probable that evaluation by superiors will continue to be the principal approach used. If the primary purpose of the evaluation is developmental, then the enterprise might consider supplementing it with subordinate evaluations or self evaluation. If the purpose of the process is reward, then the enterprise might consider adding peer evaluation to superiors' ratings. The field review approach would be used only in special cases. The key to successful performance evaluation appears to be well-trained, carefully selected evaluators who are knowledgeable about the performance of those being evaluated.

What is and should be evaluated

The factors on which an employee is evaluated are called the criteria of the evaluation. Examples include quality of work, quantity of work, and how well the employee gets along with others at work. One of the major problems is that some systems become *person evaluation* rather than performance evaluation. The criteria used are critical in effective performance evaluation systems. They must be established to keep EEO agencies satisfied, too.[42]

After a thorough review of the literature, Patricia Smith gave four characteristics of effective criteria.[43] They must be:

Relevant. Reliable and valid measures of the characteristics being evaluated, and as closely related to job output as possible.

Unbiased. Based on the characteristic, not the person.

Significant. Directly related to enterprise goals.

Practical. Measurable and efficient for the enterprise in question.

The evidence is very clear that single performance measures are ineffective because success is multifaceted; most studies indicate that multiple criteria are necessary to measure performance completely.[44] The multiple criteria are added together statistically or combined into a single multifaceted measure. The criteria choice is not an easy process. One must be careful to evaluate both activities (for example, number of calls a salesperson makes) and results (for example, dollars of sales). A variation of this is to evaluate both results and how they were accomplished.

Probably a combination of results and activities is desirable for criteria. How do you weight the importance of multiple criteria? For example, if the salesperson is being evaluated on both number of calls and sales dollars and is high on one and low on the other, what is the person's overall rating? Management must weight these criteria.

'Michael Kelley studied the evaluation of persons whose job duties are not clear: research scientists. When the tasks are not clear and performance standards are hard to specify, he found the enterprise responds by asking third persons (such as employee peers and other supervisors) for their opinion of the employee's performance.[45]

Care must be taken to evaluate both activities (e.g., number of calls a salesperson makes) and results (e.g., dollars of sales). A variation is to evaluate the final outcome and how it came about. Probably a combination of results and activities is desirable.[46]

The criteria selected depend on the purpose of the evaluation. If the purpose is to improve performance on the job, they should be performance related. It social skills or personality are vital on this or future jobs, these should be stressed.

There is not much research evidence on what criteria are used. The 1965 NICB study of office personnel practices asked insurance companies, banks, utilities, retailers, and wholesalers what criteria they used in their evaluation programs, giving them these choices: (1) mostly performance; (2) about one-half performance, one-half personality; and (3) mostly personality. Banks and wholesalers seemed to place more emphasis on personality, as did smaller firms (although there were exceptions).[47]

The more recent BNA study found that for white-collar workers, performance factors such as the following were used by these percentages: quality of work (93 percent), quantity of work (90 percent), job knowledge (85 percent), and attendance (79 percent); personality factors used were: initiative (87 percent), cooperation (87 percent), dependability (86 percent), and need for supervision (67 percent). The data for blue-collar workers were parallel: performance factors included quality of work (used by 91 percent), quantity of work (91 percent), attendance (86 percent), and job knowledge (85 percent); personality factors surveyed were dependability (86 percent), initiative (83 percent), cooperation (83 percent), and need for supervision (77 percent).[48]

If these studies are comparable, it implies that hard-to-measure personality traits have increased in importance: a very surprising result. But the key issue is the weighting of the factors. NICB asked the surveyed companies to weight them; BNA did not. So perhaps they evaluate the personality factors but do not weight them equally with performance. But perhaps they do.

Whether the evaluation should be based on actual or potential performance depends, it seems to me, on the major purpose of the evaluation for the personnel function. In this respect there are three principal purposes of performance evaluation: improvement of performance, promotion consideration, and salary and wage adjustments. If the main purposes are improved performance or wage adjustment, the emphasis should be on actual performance. If the main purpose is possible promotion, a different emphasis is needed which will assess potential performance on a new job. This is similar to the selection decision, in which past performance on one job must be extrapolated to possible performance on a different one; this is easier to do if the employee has had experience that is relevant to the new job. But the emphasis is different, and assessment of future potential on a different job is more difficult than actual assessment of past performance.

HOW TO EVALUATE: EVALUATION TECHNIQUES

When it has been decided who will evaluate, on what basis, and when, the technique to be used must be selected. A number of approaches will be described here. There are several ways to classify these tools.[49] The three categories used here will be: individual evaluation methods; multiple person evaluation methods; and other methods.

Individual evaluation methods

There are five ways to evaluate the person individually. In these systems, employees are evaluated one at a time without *directly* comparing them to other employees.

Graphic rating scale.   The most widely used performance evaluation technique is a graphic rating scale. It is also one of the oldest techniques in use; Walter Dill Scott, a pioneering industrial psychologist, used the method, and it was described in some detail in an article in the early 1920s. In this technique, the evaluator is presented with a graph such as that shown in Exhibit 10–6 and asked to rate employees on each of the characteristics listed. The number of characteristics rated varies from a few to several dozen. In one study a graphic rating scale was used to study performance evaluations of 1,100 employees, evaluating 12 separate traits.[50] A factor analysis of the results indicates that only two traits were being rated: quality of performance and ability to do the present job. This brings into question whether lengthy rating scales are more useful than shorter scales or other methods of evaluation.

The ratings can be in a series of boxes as in the exhibit, or they can be on a continuous scale (0–9) or so. In the latter case, the evaluator places a check above descriptive words ranging from *none* to *maximum.* Typically, these ratings are then assigned points. For example, in Exhibit 10–5, *outstanding* may be assigned a score of 4 and *unsatisfactory* a score of 0. Total scores are then computed. In some plans, greater weights may be assigned to more important traits. Evaluators are often asked to explain each rating with a sentence or two.

Two recent modifications of the scale have been designed to make it more effective. One is Blanz and Ghiselli's mixed standard scale. Instead of just rating a trait like initiative, the evaluator is given three statements to describe the trait, such as:

1.   He is a real self-starter. He always takes the initiative and his superior never has to stimulate him (best description).
2.   While generally he shows initiative, occasionally his superior has to prod him to get his work done.
3.   He has a tendency to sit around and wait for directions (poorest description).

After each description the rater places a check mark (the employee fits the description), a plus sign (the employee is better than the statement), or a minus sign (the employee is poorer than the statement). This results in a

EXHIBIT 10–6
Typical graphic rating scale

	Out-standing	Good	Satis-factory	Fair	Unsatis-factory
Name _____ Dept. _____ Date _____					
Quantity of work Volume of acceptable work under normal conditions Comments:	☐	☐	☐	☐	☐
Quality of work Thoroughness, neatness and accuracy of work Comments:	☐	☐	☐	☐	☐
Knowledge of job Clear understanding of the facts or factors pertinent to the job Comments:	☐	☐	☐	☐	☐
Personal qualities Personality, appearance, sociability, leadership, integrity Comments:	☐	☐	☐	☐	☐
Cooperation Ability and willingness to work with associates, supervisors, and subordinates toward common goals Comments:	☐	☐	☐	☐	☐
Dependability Conscientious, thorough, accurate, reliable with respect to attendance, lunch periods, reliefs, etc. Comments:	☐	☐	☐	☐	☐
Initiative Earnestness in seeking increased responsibilities. Self-starting, unafraid to proceed alone? Comments:	☐	☐	☐	☐	☐

seven-point scale, which the authors contend is better than the graphic rating scale.[51]

The second modification is to add operational or benchmark statements to describe different levels of performance. For example, an excerpt from the U.S. Air Force's current scale is given in Exhibit 10–7. Part A shows part of the evaluation scale listing some of the factors to be evaluated. The factors are briefly described. Part B describes the standards to be used in evaluating the four factors. This approach is more likely to result in greater reliability of the evaluation.

Forced choice. The forced-choice method of evaluation was developed because other methods used at the time led to a preponderance of higher ratings, which made promotion decisions difficult. In forced choice, the evaluator must choose from a set of descriptive statements about the employee. Typical sets of these statements are given in Exhibit 10–8 and 10–9. The two-, three-, or four-statement items are grouped in a way that the evaluator cannot easily judge which statements apply to the most effective employee.

Typically, personnel specialists prepare the items for the form, and supervisors or other personnel specialists rate the items for applicability; that is, they determine which statements describe effective and ineffective behavior. The supervisor then evaluates the employee. The personnel department adds up the number of statements in each category (for example, effective behavior), and they are summed into an effectiveness index. Forced choice can be used by superiors, peers, subordinates, or a combination of these in evaluating employees.

Essay evaluation. In the essay technique of evaluation, the evaluator is asked to describe the strong and weak aspects of the employee's behavior. In some enterprises, the essay technique is the only one used; in others, the essay is combined with another form, such as a graphic rating scale. In this case, the essay summarizes the scale, elaborates on some of the ratings, or discusses added dimensions not on the scale. In both of these approaches the essay can be open ended, but in most cases there are guidelines on the topics to be covered, the purpose of the essay, and so on. The essay method can be used by evaluators who are superiors, peers, or subordinates of the employee to be evaluated.

Management by objectives. Another individual evaluation method in use today is management by objectives (MBO). In this system, the supervisor and employee to be evaluated jointly set objectives in advance for the employee to try to achieve during a specified period. The method encourages, if not requires, them to phrase these objectives primarily in quantitative terms. The evaluation consists of a joint review of the degree of achievement of the objectives. This approach combines the superior and self-evaluation systems.

Exhibit 10–10 is an example of a report developed by a salesperson to show to what extent the objectives were achieved. The employee would also be asked to explain why some were not achieved. Then the objectives for the next period would be agreed upon jointly.

EXHIBIT 10–7
Excerpts from U.S. Air Force's officer evaluation graphic rating scale

A. PERFORMANCE FACTORS *Specific example of performance required*	Not observed or not relevant	Far below standard	Below standard	Meets standard	Above standard	Well above standard
1. Job knowledge (*depth, currency, breadth*). Specific example: What has the officer done to actually demonstrate depth, currency, or breadth of job knowledge in the performance of duties? Consider both quality and quantity of work.	0				X	
2. Judgment and decisions (*consistent, accurate, effective*). Specific example: Does this officer think clearly and develop correct and logical conclusions? Report on how the officer grasps, analyzes, and presents workable solutions to problems.	0			X		
3. Plan and organize work (*timely and creative*). Specific example: Does this officer look beyond immediate job requirements? How well does he/she anticipate critical events?	0				X	
4. Management of resources (*manpower and material*). Specific example: Does this officer "manage" to achieve optimum economy through effective utilization of personnel and material? Consider the balance between minimum cost and false economy to the ultimate expense of the mission.	0			X		

B. STANDARDS PERFORMANCE FACTOR

	Far below standard	*Below standard*	*Meets standard*	*Above standard*	*Well above standard*
1.	Has serious gaps in technical/professional knowledge Knows only most rudimentary phases of job Lack of knowledge affects productivity Requires abnormal amount of checking	Technical/professional knowledge is inadequate for the job Must be assigned only routine duties and monitored regularly Requires close supervision	Demonstrates adequate technical/professional knowledge required for the job Searches out facts and arrives at sound solutions to problems Broad knowledge of related jobs and functions Conversant with significant job-related developments	Possesses keen insight and the ability to evolve it into practical solutions Keeps informed of important developments in related fields Can handle difficult situations effectively Broad knowledge of related missions Rarely requires guidance or assistance	Possesses superb technical/professional knowledge Sufficiently well versed in his job to discuss and implement improved methods resulting in savings in manpower or material Maintains and increases professional/technical knowledge Actively pursues new ideas and developments and their relation to the overall mission Recognized authority in his field
2.	Reluctant to make decisions on his own Decisions are usually not reliable Declines to accept responsibility for decisions	Usually makes sound routine decisions Tends to procrastinate on necessary decisions Reluctant to evaluate factors before arriving at decisions	Seeks out all available data before arriving at decision Consistently provides accurate decisions Accepts responsibility for decisions and learns from incorrect judgments Provides effective decisions by clear and logical thinking	An exceptionally sound, logical thinker Does not hesitate to make required decisions Decisions are consistently correct Opinions and judgment are often solicited by others	Keen, analytical thinker Makes accurate decisions under intense pressure Extremely effective in exercising logic in broad areas of responsibility
3.	Fails to plan ahead Disorganized and usually unprepared Objectives are not met on time	Scheduling and organizational efforts normally fail Encounters difficulty with tasks other than routine Finished products are usually behind schedule	Careful, effective planner Anticipates and takes action to solve problems Effectively balances resources Finished products are consistently submitted on time	Plans beyond requirements of present job Plans coincide with related activities Is flexible and able to adjust priorities Frequently called upon to organize complex tasks	Able to anticipate critical events and makes prior provisions to deal with them Plans encompass all feasible contingencies Extremely effective in utilization of resources
4.	Wastes or misuses resources No system established for accounting of material Causes delay for others by mismanagement	Accomplishes conservation of material on a sporadic basis Squanders resources to get job done	Uses minimum material with good results Establishes controls to insure that manpower and material are accounted for and conserved Develops and utilizes cost-effectiveness methods	Excellent results accomplished at minimum cost Consistently suggests methods of conserving resources Skillfully utilizes cost-effectiveness studies	Extremely effective in utilization of material Consistently seeks and projects ways of utilizing existing equipment Is often assigned to difficult and important projects where use of resources is a significant factor.

EXHIBIT 10–8
Forced-choice items used by Exxon, Inc.

MOST			1	MOST
A	Does not anticipate difficulties.			A
B	Grasps explanations quickly.			B
C	Rarely wastes time.			C
D	Easy to talk to.			D
MOST			2	MOST
A	Leader in group activities.			A
B	Wastes time on unimportant things.			B
C	Cool and calm at all times.			C
D	Hard worker.			D

Source: Richard S. Barrett, *Performance Rating* (Chicago: Science Research Associates, 1966).

EXHIBIT 10–9
Forced-choice items used for Air Force instructors

a) Aim of lesson is clearly presented
b) Refrains from spending too much time boasting of his experiences
c) May "bawl out" or ridicule a student in the presence of others
d) Doesn't get to know each student's problems

a) Patient with slow learners
b) Lectures with confidence
c) Could improve cleanliness of classroom
d) Does not put class at ease

Source: James Berkshire and Richard Highland, "Forced Choice Performance Rating," *Personnel Psychology* 6 (1953).

Critical incident technique.   In this technique, personnel specialists and operating managers prepare lists of statements of very effective and very ineffective behavior for an employee. These are the *critical incidents.* The personnel specialists combine these statements into categories, which vary with the job. For example, W. K. Kircher and Marvin Dunnette described 13 categories they used for evaluating salespersons at the 3M Company; two of the categories are calling on all accounts and initiating new sales approaches.[52] J. C. Flanagan described a set of categories for evaluating managers generally, including, for example, control of quality, control of people, and organizing activities.[53]

Once the categories are developed and statements of effective and ineffective behavior are provided, the evaluator prepares a log for each employee. During the evaluation period, the evaluator records examples of critical (outstandingly good or bad) behaviors in each of the categories, and the log is used to evaluate the employee at the end of the period. It is also *very useful* for the evaluation interview, since the evaluator can be specific in making positive and negative comments, and it avoids recency bias. The critical incident technique is more likely to be used by superiors than in peer or subordinate evaluations.

Checklists and weighted checklists.   Another type of individual evalua-

EXHIBIT 10–10
MBO evaluation report for salesperson

Objectives set	Period objective	Accomplish-ments	Variance
1. Number of sales calls	100	104	104%
2. Number of new customers contacted	20	18	90
3. Number of wholesalers stocking new product 117	30	30	100
4. Sales of product 12	10,000	9,750	92.5
5. Sales of product 17	17,000	18,700	110
6. Customer complaints/Service calls	35	11	$66^2/_3$
7. Number of sales correspondence courses successfully completed	4	2	50
8. Number of sales reports in home office within 1 day of end of month	12	10	80

tion method is the checklist. In its simplest form, the checklist is a set of adjectives or descriptive statements. If the rater believes that the employee possesses a trait listed, the rater checks the item; if not, the rater leaves it blank. A rating score from the checklist equals the number of checks.

A more recent variation is the weighted checklist. Supervisors or personnel specialists familiar with the jobs to be evaluated prepare a large list of descrip-

EXHIBIT 10–11
Weighted checklist for bakery shop managers

Item	Scale value
He occasionally buys some of his competitor's products	6.8
He never consults with his head salesgirl when making out a bake order	1.4
He belongs to a local merchants' association	4.9
He criticizes his employees unnecessarily	0.8
The window display is usually just fair	3.1
He enjoys contacting customers personally	7.4
He does not know how to figure costs of products	0.6
He lacks a long range viewpoint	3.5
His products are of uniformly high quality	8.5
He expects too much of his employees	2.2
His weekly and monthly reports are sometimes inaccurate	4.2
He does not always give enough thought to his bake orders	1.6
He occasionally runs a selling contest among his salesgirls	6.8
Baking in his shop continues until 2 P.M. or later	8.2
He keeps complaining about employees but doesn't remedy the situation	0.9
He has originated one or more workable new formulas	6.4
He sometimes has an unreasonably large inventory of certain items	3.3
Employees enjoy working for him	7.6
He does not delegate enough responsibility to others	2.8
He has accurately figured the costs of most of his products	7.8
He wishes he were just a baker	0.8
His shop is about average in cleanliness	4.4
He is tardy in making minor repairs in his sales room	1.9
He periodically samples all of his products for quality	8.1

Source: E. B. Knauft, "Construction and Use of Weighted Checklists Rating Scales for Two Industrial Situations," *Journal of Applied Psychology* 32 (1948), pp. 63–70.

tive statements about effective and ineffective behavior on jobs, similar to the critical incident process. Judges who have observed behavior on the job sort the statements into piles describing behavior that is scaled from excellent to poor (usually on a 7–11 scale). When there is reasonable agreement on an item (for example, when the standard deviation is small), it is included in the weighted checklist. The weight is the average score of the raters prior to the checklist's use. Exhibit 10–11 is an example of a weighted checklist for bakery shop managers.

The supervisors or other raters receive the checklist without the scores, and they check the items that apply, as with an unweighted checklist. The employee's evaluation is the sum of the scores (weights) on the items checked. Checklists and weighted checklists can be used by evaluators who are superiors, peers, or subordinates, or by a combination.

Behaviorly anchored rating scales. Another technique which essentially is based on the critical incident approach is the behaviorally anchored

EXHIBIT 10–12
Behaviorally anchored rating scale for evaluating judgment and knowledge of grocery clerks

Extremely good performance	7	–
	–	–By knowing the price of items, this checker would be expected to look for mismarked and unmarked items.
Good performance	6	–
	–	–You can expect this checker to be aware of items that constantly fluctuate in price.
		–You can expect this checker to know the various sizes of cans—No. 303, No. 2½.
Slightly good performance	5	–
	–	–When in doubt, this checker would ask the other clerk if the item is taxable.
	–	–This checker can be expected to verify with another checker a discrepancy between the shelf and the marked price before ringing up that item.
Neither poor nor good performance	4	–
	–	–When operating the quick check, the lights are flashing, this checker can be expected to check out a customer with 15 items.
Slightly poor performance	3	–
	–	–You could expect this checker to ask the customer the price of an item that he does not know.
	–	–In the daily course of personal relationships, may be expected to linger in long conversations with a customer or another checker.
Poor performance	2	–
	–	–In order to take a break, this checker can be expected to block off the checkstand with people in line.
Extremely poor performance	1	–

Source: L. Fogli, C. L. Hulin, and M. R. Blood, "Development of First-Level Behavioral Job Criteria," *Journal of Applied Psychology* 55 (1971), pp. 3–8.

rating scale (BARS). This technique is also called the behavioral expectation scale (BES). This is a new, relatively infrequently used technique.

Supervisors give descriptions of actually good and bad performance, and personnel specialists group these into categories (five to ten is typical). As with weighted checklists, the items are evaluated by supervisors (often other than those who submitted the items). A procedure similar to that for weighted checklists is used to verify the evaluations (outstandingly good, for example) with the smallest standard deviation, hopefully around 1.5 on a 7-point scale. These items are then used to construct the BARS.

Exhibit 10–12 is an example of a BARS for a grocery clerk's knowledge and judgment scale. As with this scale, typically the BARS is constructed of six to seven items for each behavioral category.

Recently James Goodale and Ronald Burke have developed an evaluation scale that follows the BARS approach but is not based on specific behavior for a job. The ten dimensions on which all personnel are evaluated are: interpersonal relationships, organizing and planning, reaction to problems, reliability, communicating, adaptability, growth, productivity, quality of work, and teaching.[54] In a sense, this scale is a great deal like a graphic rating scale in that it is used for all employees, but the scale is based on descriptions of behavioral incidents, as in BARS. This approach may prove to be a major step forward for usage of BARS. BARS can be used for evaluation by superiors, peers, or subordinates, or a combination of these.

Multiple-person evaluation methods

The techniques described above are used to evaluate employees one at a time. Three techniques that have been used to evaluate an employee in comparison with other employees being evaluated are discussed in this section.

Ranking. In using the ranking method, the evaluator is asked to rate employees from highest to lowest on some overall criterion. This is very difficult to do if the group of employees being compared numbers over 20. It is also easier to rank the best and worst employees than it is to evaluate the average ones. Simple ranking can be improved by alternative ranking. In this approach the evaluators pick the top and bottom employee first, then select the next highest and next lowest, and move toward the middle.

Exxon's form for this procedure is given in Exhibit 10–13. The ranking method is normally used by superiors evaluating subordinates but could be used by peers as well. It is not normally used for evaluation by subordinates.

Paired comparison. This approach makes the ranking method easier and more reliable. First, the names of the persons to be evaluated are placed on separate sheets (or cards) in a predetermined order, so that each person is compared to all others to be evaluated. The evaluator then checks the person he feels is the better of the two on a criterion for each comparison.

EXHIBIT 10–13

Exxon, Inc., employee ranking form

INSTRUCTIONS FOR ALTERNATION RANKING

Read these instructions all the way through before ranking anyone.

Alternation ranking is a technique which accomplishes the most consistent ranking of people in an order-of-merit. In order to use the technique effectively, two basic requirements must be met. 1) The ranker must know the characteristic behavior of the people to be ranked. 2) The ranker must formulate or learn the important elements which make up the subject-matter of the ranking and he must adhere strictly to these elements in making his judgments of the people to be ranked.

Alternation ranking may be used to obtain an order-of-merit within a group on very diverse characteristics or situations. Among these are present job performance, ultimate potential, promotion to the next higher job, ability to deal with people outside the immediate work group, adaptability to different jobs in the Company, priority for salary increase, or almost any other subject which can be given a basic definition and which can be observed or properly inferred by the ranker.

The subject of the ranking requested here is

On the other side of this sheet is a list of employees.

PROCEED AS FOLLOWS:

A. First, eliminate those you cannot rank:

1. Look over the list of names on the other side of this page and draw a line through the name of any person whose characteristic behavior on the point in question is not well known to you.

2. Look over the list again and draw a line through the name of any person whose situation, in your opinion, is so different from most of the others that you do not think he can be compared with them.

B. Second, proceed with your ranking:

1. Look over the list of remaining names and decide which one person you think is the best on the list. Draw a line through his name and write it in the blank space marked "1-Highest" at the top of the page.

2. Look over the remaining names and decide which one person is not as good as the others on the list. Draw a line through his name and write it in the blank space marked "1-Lowest" at the bottom of the page. Remember, you are not saying that he is unsatisfactory; you are merely saying that you consider the others better.

3. Next, select the person you think is best of those remaining on the list, draw a line through his name and write it in the blank space marked "2-Next Highest."

4. Next, select the person you think is not as good as the others remaining on the list, draw a line through his name and write it in the blank space marked "2-Next Lowest."

5. Continue this ranking procedure (selecting next highest, then next lowest) until you have drawn a line through each name on the list.

ALTERNATION RANKING REPORT

CONFIDENTIAL

IMPORTANT. Before you begin read carefully the instructions on the back of this form.   DATE:

CLASSIFICATION OF GROUP BEING RANKED

DEPARTMENT	RANKER:	
		DO NOT WRITE IN THIS SPACE
EMPLOYEES TO BE RANKED (DO NOT LIST MORE THAN 30)	1 - HIGHEST	
	2 - NEXT HIGHEST	
	3 - NEXT HIGHEST	
	4 - NEXT HIGHEST	
	5 - NEXT HIGHEST	
	6 - NEXT HIGHEST	
	7 - NEXT HIGHEST	
	8 - NEXT HIGHEST	
	9 - NEXT HIGHEST	
	10 - NEXT HIGHEST	
	11 - NEXT HIGHEST	
	12 - NEXT HIGHEST	
	13 - NEXT HIGHEST	
	14 - NEXT HIGHEST	
	15 - NEXT HIGHEST	
	15 - NEXT LOWEST	
	14 - NEXT LOWEST	
	13 - NEXT LOWEST	
	12 - NEXT LOWEST	
	11 - NEXT LOWEST	
	10 - NEXT LOWEST	
	9 - NEXT LOWEST	
	8 - NEXT LOWEST	
	7 - NEXT LOWEST	
	6 - NEXT LOWEST	
	5 - NEXT LOWEST	
	4 - NEXT LOWEST	
	3 - NEXT LOWEST	
	2 - NEXT LOWEST	
	1 - LOWEST	

Source: Richard S. Barrett, Performance Rating (Chicago: Science Research Associates, 1966).

Typically the criterion is overall ability to do the present job. The number of times a person is preferred is tallied, and this develops an index of the number of preferences compared to the number being evaluated.

These scores can be converted into standard scores by comparing the scores to the standard deviation and the average of all scores. This method can be used by superiors, peers, subordinates, or some combination of these groups.

Forced distribution. The forced-distribution system is similar to grading on a curve. The evaluator is asked to rate employees in some fixed distribution of categories, such as 10 percent in low, 20 percent in low average, 40 percent in average, 20 percent in high average, and 10 percent in high. One way to do this is to type each employee's name on a card and ask the evaluators to sort the cards into five piles corresponding to the ratings. This should be done twice for the two key criteria of job performance and promotability.[55]

Exhibit 10–14 shows the results of forced-distribution evaluation of 20 employees. One reason forced distribution was developed was to try to alleviate such problems as inflated ratings and central tendency in the graphic rating scale.

A newer variation of forced distribution is the point allocation technique (PAT). In PAT, each rater is given a number of points per employee in the group to be evaluated, and the total points for all employees evaluated cannot exceed the number of points per employee times the number of employees evaluated. The points are allocated on a criterion.[56] The forced distribution and PAT are most likely to be used by superiors but could be used by peers or subordinates.

Other methods

Performance tests. One approach to evaluation is to design a job performance test or simulation. Depending on how well the employees do on this, they are promoted or their salaries are adjusted. One such test is used for operating personnel in the Air Force.[57] The assessment center discussed later in the chapter utilizes another.

Field review technique. Unlike many of the approaches discussed above, the field review uses an "objective" outsider as evaluator. The person to be evaluated and the supervisor are questioned orally by an investigator,

EXHIBIT 10–14

Forced-distribution evaluation of employees in a marketing research unit

High 10%	Next 20%	Middle 40%	Next 20%	Low 10%
Leslie Moore	Cinde Lanyon	Max Coggins	Art Willis	Wayne Allison
Tina Little	Sharon Feltman	Tina Holmes	Debbie Salter	Sherry Gruber
	Eddie Dorsey	Julis Jimenex	Tom Booth	
	John Dyer	Lis Amendale	Lance Smith	
		Vince Gaillard		
		Missy Harrington		
		Bill King		
		Shelly Sweat		

who usually is from the personnel department. The personnel evaluator probes and questions the supervisor about the employee, and this results in an overall rating such as outstanding, satisfactory, or unsatisfactory.[58]

Which technique to use

Perhaps you now feel saturated with the large number of evaluation techniques. You should know that not all of them are used that often. Which ones are used most frequently is a difficult question to answer. Results of a BNA survey on that question are given in Exhibit 10–15. It is generally believed that the graphic rating scale is the most widely used technique (BNA called it the rating scale), but this study found the most frequently used method is the discussion or essay, which often is part of the rating scale form. Checklists are also frequently used. BNA does not specify whether these are weighted or regular, but 29 percent of office employees and 35 percent of production employees are likely to be evaluated by an unweighted checklist. Note the big drop after these three. Other methods such as forced choice, critical incident, BARS, performance tests, field review, and MBO—*combined* equal only about 5 percent. Ranking and paired comparison are used by 10 to 13 percent of the employees. MBO is most likely to be used more for managerial, professional, and technical employees, not production and office personnel.

Which technique should be used in a specific instance? The literature on the shortcomings and strengths, reliabilities, and validities of each of these techniques is vast.[59] In essence, there are studies showing that each of the techniques is sometimes good, sometimes poor. The major problems are not with the techniques themselves but *how they are used* and *by whom.* Untrained evaluators or those that have little talent or motivation to evaluate well can destroy or hamper *any* evaluation technique. Earlier in the chapter, evidence was cited to show that the evaluator is more critical than the technique in developing effective evaluation systems.

Evaluation techniques can be scaled on a series of criteria such as costs and purposes. As noted in the discussion of the approaches to evaluation above, at least two major purposes are served by evaluation; counseling and personal *development,* and evaluation for rewards, such as to aid in promotion and decisions. Some evaluation techniques serve one purpose better than others. Some systems cost more to develop and operate than others. Exhibit 10–16 scales the techniques on these criteria to help in the choice.

If the primary purpose of the evaluation is development, for example, then the effective enterprise will use BARS, essay, critical incident, MBO, and field review tools. If the primary purpose of the evaluation is rewards, the effective enterprise will use graphic rating scales, field review, performance tests, forced distribution, MBO, critical incidents, or BARS. And if the primary purpose of the evaluation is developmental and costs are not a concern currently, then field review, MBO, or critical incident methods should be chosen. If the primary purpose is development and costs are a consideration, then BARS or essay methods might be chosen.[59]

EXHIBIT 10–15
Use of evaluation techniques for production and office employees

Percentage of companies with appraisal programs

	Type of industry			Size		All companies
	Manufacturing	*Nonmanufacturing*	*Nonbusiness*	*Large*	*Small*	
A standard rating form used for						
Office employees	77%	76%	96%	80%	81%	81%
Production employees	74	40	95	76	76	76
Techniques used in rating						
Office employees						
Discussion or essay	49	45	43	41	51	47
Rating scale	46	39	39	51	37	43
Checklist	23	24	50	25	32	29
Comparison system	5	9	7	4	8	6
Ranking	5	9	—	2	7	5
Other methods	9	—	—	8	3	5
(No response)	(3)	(9)	—	(6)	(3)	(4)
Production employees						
Discussion or essay	46	50	48	45	49	47
Rating scale	49	10	33	48	30	38
Checklist	29	10	57	31	38	35
Ranking	9	20	—	7	8	8
Comparison system	6	20	5	—	14	8
Other methods	9	—	—	7	3	5
(No response)	(3)	(10)	—	(4)	(3)	(3)

Source: Bureau of National Affairs, "Employee Performance: Evaluation and Control," *Personnel Policies Forum,* no. 108, February 1975.

EXHIBIT 10–16
Criteria for choice of performance evaluation techniques

Evaluative Base	Graphic rating scale	Forced choice	MBO	Essay	Critical incidents	Weighted checklist	BARS	Ranking	Paired comparison	Forced distribution	Performance test	Field review
Developmental cost	Moderate	High	Moderate	Low	Moderate	Moderate	High	Low	Low	Low	High	Moderate
Usage costs	Low	Low	High	High supervisory costs	High	Low	Low	Low	Low	Low	High	High
Ease of use by evaluators	Easy	Moderately difficult	Moderate	Difficult	Difficult	Easy	Easy	Easy	Easy	Easy	Moderately difficult	Easy
Ease of understanding by those evaluated	Easy	Difficult	Moderate	Easy	Easy	Easy	Moderate	Easy	Easy	Easy	Easy	Easy
Useful in promotion decisions	Yes	Yes	Yes	Not easily	Yes	Yes	Yes	Yes	Yes	Yes	Yes	Yes
Useful in compensation and reward decisions	Yes	Moderate	Yes	Not easily	Yes	Moderate	Yes	Not easily	Not easily	Yes	Yes	Yes
Useful in counseling and development of employees	Moderate	Moderate	Yes	Yes	Yes	Moderate	Yes	No	No	No	Moderately	Yes

REVIEW AND USAGE OF
PERFORMANCE EVALUATIONS

Bob Woods (divisional vice president):   Dot, I'm just reviewing your suggested salary and promotions for your region. You know I try to delegate as much as I can, but I know some of the people you have in for big raises and promotions and I notice some surprising omissions. Since I'm responsible for the whole division, I'd like to review this with you. Understand, I'm not trying to undercut you.

Dot Williams (regional manager):   Oh I understand, Bob. No problem! Where do you want to start?

Bob: Let me just high spot. I note that Mo Gibbs, who's always been in our high reward group, isn't here, nor is Ed Strauss, another winner in the past. And you do have Joe Berlioz and Sandra Wagner in your high reward group. In the past, they never appeared. How did you make these recommendations?

Dot: I looked my people over and used my best judgment. That's what you pay me for, isn't it?

Bob: Sure, Dot, but what facts did you use—did you look at the quarterly sales printout, their personnel files with ratings in them, or what?

Dot: I believe I know my people best. I don't need to go through a lot of paper work and files to come up with my recommendations.

Too often, Dot is a typical manager. She knows there is a formal performance evaluation system, but she files it instead of using it.

After the evaluator has completed the evaluation, the following things should happen:

First, the evaluation is discussed with the employee by the evaluator or evaluators in an evaluation interview. Some enterprises use split evaluations to accomplish the dual purposes of evaluations. In the evaluation for developmental purposes, the ratings are communicated and appropriate counseling takes place. And in the one to determine pay, promotion, and other rewards, the ratings sometimes are not given to the employee. In the usual evaluation, however, the employee acknowledges the evaluation in some way, often by signing a receipt form.

Then, the evaluator's superior reviews the evaluation. BNA found that 80 percent of office employees and 76 percent of production employees surveyed had their evaluations reviewed in this manner.[60] Next the personnel department reviews the evaluation and places it on file.

If the employee is unhappy with the evaluation, BNA found that 68 percent of the production employees and 56 percent of office employees can appeal it through the union (if they are unionized) or to the evaluator's superior.[61] This is less common in nonbusiness enterprises than businesses. For more data on this, see Chapter 21.

In the discussion of evaluation approaches and techniques, we have implied that each person is evaluated independent of others, unless the employee is one of the few being evaluated with a multiperson evaluation technique. But this may not be strictly true; the evaluation of one employee can be affected by the evaluations of the others in the work group.

Laboratory research has indicated that when a work group included one employee with poor work attitudes who refused to obey orders, the supervisor evaluated other employees higher.[62] In a study by Ronald Grey and David Kipnis, 59 supervisors of 473 clerical employees were asked to evaluate their employees. The researchers examined how the supervisors evaluated and rewarded them with promotions and pay raises. They found that the presence of employees who were poor in ability and work attitudes (and the proportion of the work group they comprised) affected how the supervisors evaluated *all* the employees. Specifically, when there is one or a small percentage of noncompliant employees, the supervisor gave a *much lower* evaluation to the noncompliant employees and a slightly higher evaluation to the compliant employees. As the percentage of noncompliant employees increased, the supervisors raised the evaluations of the compliant employees *much, much higher.*

Case study research also indicates that some supervisors may perceive pressure not to evaluate all employees at the top of the range. They modify the ratings so they do not seem to have all "excellent" employees.

At least some of the time, therefore, evaluators are likely to be influenced in their evaluations of one employee by their evaluations of others in the work group, even when individual evaluation techniques are used.

EVALUATION INTERVIEWS

In 97 percent of the enterprises with formal performance evaluation systems, the employee receives feedback, normally in the form of an evaluation interview.[63] The evaluator and employee get together for an interview which allows the evaluator to communicate the employee's ratings and comment on them.

Three generally used approaches to these interview situations are shown in Exhibit 10–17: Tell and sell, tell and listen, and problem solving. Research on when each should be used indicates that the tell-and-sell approach is best for new and inexperienced employees,[64] and that the problem-solving approach, which encourages employee participation, is useful for more experienced employees, especially those with work ethic attitudes.[65]

I can recommend these hints to help you conduct effective evaluation interviews:

1. Superiors and subordinates should prepare for the meeting and be ready to discuss the employee's past performance against the objectives for the period.

2. The superior should put the employee at ease and stress that the interview is not a disciplinary session but a time to review past work, in order to improve the employee's future performance, satisfaction, and personal development.

EXHIBIT 10–17
Three types of evaluation interviews

Method	Tell and sell	Tell and listen	Problem solving
Role of interviewer	Judge	Judge	Helper
Objective	To communicate evaluation To persuade employee to improve	To communicate evaluation To release defensive feelings	To stimulate growth and development in employee
Assumptions	Employee desires to correct weaknesses if he knows them Any person can improve if he so chooses A superior is qualified to evaluate a subordinate	People will change if defensive feelings are removed	Growth can occur without correcting faults Discussing job problems leads to improved performance
Reactions	Defensive behavior suppressed Attempts to cover hostility	Defensive behavior expressed Employee feels accepted	Problem-solving behavior
Skills	Salesmanship Patience	Listening and reflecting feelings Summarizing	Listening and reflecting feelings Reflecting ideas Using exploratory questions Summarizing
Attitude	People profit from criticism and appreciate help	One can respect the feelings of others if one understands them	Discussion develops new ideas and mutual interests
Motivation	Use of positive or negative incentives or both (Extrinsic in that motivation is added to the job itself)	Resistance to change reduced Positive incentive (Extrinsic and some intrinsic motivation)	Increased freedom Increased responsibility (Intrinsic motivation in that interest is inherent in the task)
Gains	Success most probable when employee respects interviewer	Develops favorable attitude to superior which increases probability of success	Almost assured of improvement in some respect
Risks	Loss of loyalty Inhibition of independent judgment Face-saving problems created	Need for change may not be developed	Employee may lack ideas Change may be other than what superior had in mind
Values	Perpetuates existing practices and values	Permits interviewer to change his views in the light of employee's responses Some upward communication	Both learn, since experience and views are pooled Change is facilitated

Source: Reproduced from Norman R. F. Maier, *The Appraisal Interview: Three Basic Approaches* (La Jolla, California: University Associates, 1976). Used with permission.

3. The superior should budget the time so that the employee has approximately half the time to discuss the evaluation and his or her future behavior.

4. The superior should structure the interview as follows:

First, open with *specific positive* results. For example, if the employee's quantity of work is good, the superior might say: "John, your work output is excellent. You processed 10 percent more claims than was budgeted."

Second, sandwich performance shortcomings between two positive result discussions. Be specific, and orient the discussion to *performance* comments, *not personal* criticisms. Stress that the purpose of bringing the specific issues up is to alleviate the problems in the *future,* not to criticize the past. Probably no more than one or two important negative points should be brought up at one evaluation. It is difficult for many people to work toward improving more than two points. The handling of negative comments is critical. They should be phrased specifically and be related to *performance,* and it should be apparent to the employee that their purpose is not to criticize but to improve future performance. Many people become very defensive when criticized. Of course, the interviews should be private, between the employee and the evaluator.

Third, conclude with *positive* comments and overall evaluation results.

5. The superior should budget the time for these three aspects of the interview to match the rating. For example, if the employee is an 85 on a scale of 100, 85 percent of the time should be spent on positive comments to *reinforce* this behavior.

6. The final aspect of the interview should focus on *future* objectives and how the superior can help the employee achieve enterprise and personal goals. Properly done, the interviews contribute importantly to the purposes of performance evaluation.

MANAGERIAL PERFORMANCE EVALUATION

The evaluation approaches and techniques discussed above apply mainly to performance evaluation for nonmanagerial employees. There are some differences with regard to performance evaluations for managers.

Many if not most employees evaluate their managers. A recent BNA survey found that the groups most likely to be evaluated formally are professional/technical employees (76 percent), and supervisory managers (76 percent) and middle managers (72 percent). Top managers are formally evaluated in about 50 percent of the enterprises and informally appraised in another 25 percent.[66]

On what criteria are managers appraised and evaluated? There are many approaches that could be used. One that shows great promise is a system developed by Walter Tornow and Patrick Pinto, who used a management position description questionnaire to identify 13 managerial job factors and to systematically compare and group 433 managerial positions into ten clusters.[67] This kind of approach could lead to systematic evaluation of managerial positions. At present, however, most managers are still evaluated on general factors like managerial skills, personal traits, and capacity.

Typically, the manager is evaluated yearly. The most frequently used techniques, according to a BNA study, include the essay (52 percent), rating scales (45 percent), checklists (26 percent), ranking (13 percent), forced choice (10 percent), and critical incident (8 percent). Many of those in the "other" category (13 percent) use some variation of MBO systems. In 96 percent of the cases, the manager is evaluated by his or her immediate superior. The information is used primarily for reward decisions. In this survey, only 10 percent of the personnel executives rated their management evaluation systems as effective,[68] a discouraging statistic.

Assessment centers

There is one performance evaluation technique that is used primarily for managerial evaluation and selection: the assessment center. One study, however, describes the use of a mini assessment center for use in selecting and evaluating blue-collar employees.[69] Assessment centers were introduced in Chapter 7, on selection.

Joseph Moses et al. define an assessment center as "a standardized evaluation of behavior based on multiple inputs." Trained observers using multiple techniques make judgments about behavior, based in part on specially developed assessment simulations. These judgments are pooled at an evaluations meeting at which all relevant data are reported and discussed. The assessors agree on the evaluation of the dimensions and any overall evaluation that is made.[70]

Individuals to be assessed or selected are brought to a facility where, for periods ranging from several days to a week, they are given tests and interviews. They participate in a series of exercises such as management games, leaderless group discussions, in-basket exercises, and mock selection interviews. Assessors are managers whose judgment of people is insightful; they participate in the activities and rate the performance of those being evaluated.

It has been estimated that in 1972 over 100,000 managers passed through assessment centers of such enterprises as AT&T, Sears, J. C. Penney, General Electric, IBM, Sohio, the state of Illinois, the province of Manitoba, the Internal Revenue Service, Canadian customs, and the British civil service commission.[71]

This tool is new, but some evaluations of its usefulness have been done. Most of the research is very positive.[72] Recent literature reviews and analyses, however, have found some problems with them.[73] These problems include overemphasis on interpersonal skills in the evaluations, and examination nerves: the experience of getting nervous and doing poorly on exams. Although assessment centers are new and have shortcomings, they appear to be a very useful mechanism for the evaluation and selection of managers.[74]

PROMOTION SYSTEMS

> **DEFINITION**
>
> A promotion is an upward change of position, normally involving greater responsibility and different duties from those of the present position.

For many, promotion does not happen often; some never experience it in their lifetimes. This is why organizations design reward systems other than promotion—compensation, benefit plans, and so forth (see Part Five). Sometimes what can be called quasipromotions are created to supplement these rewards. The person's title is changed, but the work is not. The older, experienced bookkeeper is promoted to senior bookkeeper, the priest to ArchPriest, the assistant professor to associate professor. Often these are not promotions in the true sense of the word. A promotion usually involves additional or quite different sets of duties and more privileges (added security, admission to clubs, a pension plan, etc.).

The promotion decision is in many ways like the selection decision. The administrator tries to match the best person with the right job. It is different in that, in the promotion decision, the organization has the opportunity to examine performance data. The employer can examine how the employee has done in a job, rather than having to predict how she or he might perform on the job based on test scores, reactions to interviews, or reference letters. It is also different in that the decision is open to greater political pressure. Some candidates for promotion try to influence decision makers by applying their interpersonal skills.

Several criteria have traditionally been used for promotion. Formally, two are most important: merit and seniority. Informally, there is the personality of the candidates and their interpersonal influences.

Seniority, the length of time a person has served, is an important consideration in many promotion decisions. It is calculated on several bases: the organization, the job section, the function performed. Thus, an employee may have ten years' seniority with HEW, five years' seniority in X department (section seniority), and eight years' seniority as a computer programmer (job seniority). This is the required basis for employee promotion in many unionized firms; the unions argue that experience leads to expertise. Unions which take this position resemble Max Weber's bureaucratic model, in which those with the greatest expertise rise to the top. Unions also argue that seniority is a good criterion because it rewards loyalty to the company, is impartial, and is less subject to the biases and favoritism of evaluators.

Management often prefers merit alone, as measured by performance evaluation. They raise the spectre of aged incompetents getting all the good jobs if seniority is the sole criterion. The truth lies in between these positions.

Research studies on promotion decisions

There are few studies of promotion criteria and their perceived importance for nonmanagerial employees in business. One study found that managers did in fact prefer past meritorious experience as the major criterion for promotion. Unions and employees tended to prefer seniority, although the unions and employees recognized its shortcomings.[75] In a lab experiment, Ronald Taylor asked 15 line managers to choose one of three salesmen to promote and to rank the sources of information they preferred to use to make the decision. Then he observed how they did make the simulated decision. Prior to the decisions, the managers ranked very highly performance evaluation ratings and said they would use them to make the evaluation decision. When they made the simulated promotion decision, however, they did *not* use the ratings in a significant way.[76]

Several research projects have looked at promotion decisions for top managers in business. Albert Glickman et al. studied how promotion to top management was affected by management training, personal characteristics, experience, background, organization policies, and supervisory practices.[77] They interviewed 71 top managers at 13 corporations. The tentative conclusions of this exploratory study of promotion to top management are:

Informal procedures and consensual decision making are used in the selection and promotion of top managers.

Because of diverse power groups within most large complex organizations, there is a check-and-balance system that reduces personal favoritism in promotions.

Promotion and development of top managers follows a different process than at lower- and middle-management levels.

To reach the top, younger executives must be discovered early, receive broad experience, and become visible to top management by proven successes.

Other studies found that most top managers are promoted from within rather than brought in from the outside,[78] that different criteria were used to promote different functional types of executives,[79] and that the environment of the enterprise affects its promotion pattern.[80]

One other aspect of promotion in business that has received some attention recently is the legal and equal employment opportunity dimension. Studies have shown that many male executives who make promotion decisions have sex stereotypes which are likely to make it more difficult for them to promote women.[81] One analyst points out that in a number of cases the courts have ordered businesses to promote persons because it appeared they had discriminated against them in past promotion decisions.[82] Finally, it appears that managers are getting more militant in protecting themselves in promotion decisions. One account discusses a number of cases in which managers who were not promoted have sued their employers.[83]

In sum, it appears that businesses promote employees on the basis of seniority and merit, the relative weight of the criteria varying by the decision and the enterprise. The promotion decisions of managers tend to be informal and based on merit, seniority, and interpersonal attractiveness. EEO and other legal issues may influence some firms to adopt a more formal approach.

How do promotional systems in business compare to other sectors? In the third sector, a few studies have been done. A study of the promotion of Roman Catholic priests found that it was based entirely on seniority ranking, although many priests wanted to include a merit criterion too.[84] In most universities, time in grade or seniority is a prior factor in promotion. Most assistant professors must have worked at a university a certain number of years (five to six) before consideration for promotion. Merit is the other consideration, although studies indicate that professors and administrators do not agree on what is meritorious, and the decisions are not always consistent with the definition of merit.[85]

The institution which appears to make the most serious attempt to formalize promotion is the American military.[86] The essential promotion decisions are made not by individuals but by groups of individuals. Pentagon personnel officials first screen the officers to be considered for promotion into two groups: primary and secondary zones. The senior officers make policy decisions, such as the number of officers at each rank to be promoted and the portion of primary and secondary groups to be selected. The primary group is composed of those who must be reviewed because of the "up or out" policy and those whose merit ratings are highest. The secondary group includes those who are especially meritorious but whose seniority rating does not require a promotion decision at the time.

The performance evaluation files and personnel files of these groups are then sent to the decision-making body: the Promotion Board.[87] This board is formally trained to make promotion decisions by participating in Promotion Board exercises during career training, such as the Army War College.[88] The Promotion Board consists of 15 officially selected and trained officers senior to the rank of those being reviewed; it is chaired by a general. A very carefully drafted letter from the Pentagon specifies the criteria and model of selection. The board is balanced to include male and female, regular and reserve, and line and staff representatives, from different branches and different experience groups. The board is sworn in and then examines the several thousand files in a series of examinations and votes on rankings. The typical officer being reviewed is ranked *at least* nine times by nine different board members individually and can be ranked as often as 15 times. Major variances among rankings are discussed. The major criteria used for promotion are performance evaluation ratings, education, awards, and letters of recommendation. A similar process is followed for promotion of warrant officers and senior noncommissioned officers.

In sum, promotions vary from the formal, merit-based military decisions and formal seniority-based decisions in the Roman Catholic Church to formal and informal decisions in business and education. In most decisions, seniority and merit criteria are mixed, the emphasis varying by institutional climate and the preferences of the decision makers. Performance evaluation ratings are a major but hardly the only indication of merit considered in promotion decisions.

COMPUTERS AND COST/BENEFIT ANALYSIS IN EVALUATION

Some fairly sophisticated employers have begun to computerize their analysis of performance evaluation, recording on tape or cards the quantitative results of evaluation. They can then analyze to what extent departments distribute high or low ratings. They also might be able to pick up training problems where there is a larger than average percentage of low ratings, for example. These data also become part of the employment-planning process in determining the organization's ability to undertake certain projects.

It is very difficult to calculate the cost/benefit relationships of such programs. One way to calculate benefits is to administer attitude surveys both before and after the implementation of evaluation and promotion systems. Direct costs can be calculated; these would include the development cost of the system and the time tied up by supervisors and employees, multiplied by their base pay. Some indication of relative developmental and usage costs of the various evaluation techniques was given in Exhibit 10–16 above. I am not sure that at this stage of development of the performance evaluation activity a meaningful cost/benefits formula can be developed. But William Holley et al. have done a study showing how an enterprise can evaluate the strengths and weaknesses of the evaluation system presently in use.[89]

SUMMARY, CONCLUSIONS, AND RECOMMENDATIONS

Formal performance evaluation of employees is the personnel process by which the enterprise determines how effectively the employee is performing the job. It takes place primarily for white-collar, professional/technical, and managerial employees. It rarely is done for part-time employees, and only about half of all blue-collar employees experience it. Although the data are not entirely clear, it appears that, properly done, performance evaluation is useful for most enterprises and most employees.

The best way to conclude the chapter is with some summary propositions. Three that apply to performance evaluation in general are:

> *Proposition 10.1.*   The larger the enterprise, the more likely it is to have a formal performance evaluation system.

> *Proposition 10.2.*   The more the government presses equal opportunity goals, the more likely is it that formal performance evaluation and promotion systems will be developed, validated, and performance related.

Proposition 10.3. Properly performed, performance evaluation can contribute to enterprise objectives and employee development and satisfaction.

A proposition summarizing the timing of performance evaluation is:

Proposition 10.4. The more frequent the performance evaluation, the more likely is it to have a positive impact on employee performance, if the employee holds work ethic attitudes.

With regard to the evaluators, it seems reasonable to propose:

Proposition 10.5. The better trained the evaluators are in interviewing, counseling, and developmental methods, and the better the evaluation system is understood by the employees, the more effective will performance evaluation be.

With regard to evaluation criteria, three conclusions seem reasonable:

Proposition 10.6. The more carefully defined the evaluation criteria are, the more effective is performance evaluation.

Proposition 10.7. The better the employee understands the criteria of evaluation, the more effective will the evaluation process be.

Proposition 10.8. The more the evaluation criteria are related to performance, *not the person,* the more effective will the performance evaluation be.

Some propositions regarding evaluation techniques are:

Propositions 10.9. The larger the enterprise, the less volatile it is, and the less complex it is, the more sophisticated will its evaluation tools be (sophisticated tools include performance tests, forced choice, BARS, and some rating scales).

Proposition 10.10. If the primary purpose of the evaluation is development, then the effective enterprise will use the BARS, essay, critical incidents, MBO, or field review tools.

Proposition 10.11. If the primary purpose of evaluation is rewards, then the effective enterprise will use graphic ratings, field review, performance tests, forced distribution, MBO, critical incidents, or BARS.

Some propositions on performance evaluation for managers are:

Proposition 10.12. The higher the rank of the executive in the organization, the less likely is it that formal evaluation will be used.

Proposition 10.13. The more important the managerial job and the higher the job in the organization, the more evaluators will be involved, however informally.

Proposition 10.14. The larger the organization, the more likely is formal executive evaluation to take place.

Some propositions affecting the evaluation interview are:

> *Proposition 10.15.* Except for new and inexperienced employees, the more closely the evaluation interview follows the problem-solving approach, the more effective will the evaluation process be.

> *Proposition 10.16.* The more future oriented the evaluation interview, the more effective the evaluation process.

> *Proposition 10.17.* The more past positive behavior is reinforced in the interview, the more effective the evaluation process.

> *Proposition 10.18.* For most employees, promotion criteria include seniority and merit.

> *Proposition 10.19.* If the employees belong to a union, it is more likely that promotion criteria will be formalized into policies, procedures, and employment contract provisions.

> *Proposition 10.20.* Most formal promotion systems have become more developed and detailed since passage of Title VII of the Civil Rights Act.

> *Proposition 10.21.* The larger the organization, the more likely it is to have developed formal promotion systems such as promotable managers' lists and career development plans.

Formal evaluations and promotion systems are recommended for all enterprises, with the possible exception of those that are small, complex, and volatile; here the formal systems may be difficult to operate. Wherever possible, multiple-criteria evaluation systems also make sense, since few jobs are so simple they involve only a single measure of effectiveness.

Exhibit 10–18 gives recommendations on the usage of evaluation tools in terms of the ability of the model organizations to use them. Proposition 10.9 addressed this issue briefly. Essentially, only large and prosperous enterprises have the financial resources and personnel expertise to use all the techniques, should they choose to do. Only stable organizations have the incentive to develop detailed systems based on behavior, such as BARS. Volatile organizations could not get a standard set of behaviors reliable enough over time to justify the expenditure of time and energy. Note that organization 1 is capable of using most tools, and organization seven many fewer. It should also be obvious from Exhibit 10–18 that some tools are more universally applicable (essay, critical incident, graphic rating scale, MBO, ranking, paired comparison, forced distribution), others have fewer applications (performance test, field review, forced choice), and others are in the middle (assessment centers, weighted checklist).

Communication of evaluation systems and results is vital to their effectiveness. The training and communication mechanisms can make employees aware of the purposes of evaluation and the methods used in the enterprise. The evaluation interview is the primary method for communication of the results. Evaluators and employees should be trained to make these sessions

EXHIBIT 10–18

Recommendations on evaluation techniques for model organizations

Type of organization	Graphic rating scale	Forced choice	MBO	Essay	Critical incident	Weighted checklist	BARS	Ranking	Paired comparison	Forced distribution	Performance test	Field review	Assessment centers
1. Large size, low complexity, high stability	X	X	X	X	X	X	X	X	X	X	X	X	X
2. Medium size, low complexity, high stability	X		X	X	X	X	X	X	X	X			X
3. Small size, low complexity, high stability	X		X	X	X			X	X	X			
4. Medium size, moderate complexity, moderate stability	X		X	X	X	X		X	X	X			X
5. Large size, high complexity, low stability	X		X	X	X			X	X	X		X	X
6. Medium size, high complexity, low stability	X		X	X	X			X	X	X			
7. Small size, high complexity, low stability	X		X	X	X			X	X	X			

fruitful. In addition, supervisors should be rewarded for the development of employees, for it takes time, energy, and ability to perform these evaluations.

It appears to me that the use of superiors as evaluators is satisfactory for most jobs. For employees who have internalized the work ethic, a joint supervisor–self-evaluation makes good sense. Peer and subordinate evaluations may usefully supplement superior's evaluations in critical positions where coordination between persons is necessary.

For performance evaluation to have the impact it can have on an enterprise, top managers must make certain decisions and give operating and personnel managers the responsibility to make the system operate effectively. If top managers decide on a formal evaluation system, they must let everyone know that they mean the system to be more than pieces of paper put in personnel files once or twice a year. These records must be used as part of developmental and reward decisions.

Top management must also create an environment suitable to the type of evaluation system they desire: primarily developmental or reward oriented, or both. Personnel and operating people can decide who will perform the evaluation and the technique to be used, but top managers should specify the primary criteria to be used in evaluation and promotion and how often the evaluation should take place. Finally, top managers must decide whether they want to get serious about formal promotion decisions or will continue a pattern of informal decisions, using performance evaluations in part. These decisions will include many criteria and bits of information, but if performance evaluation is seen as influencing reward decisions, the ratings ought to be used in promotion, salary, raises, transfers, and similar reward decisions.

This is how the top management, personnel, and operating managers can work together to make performance evaluations an effective personnel activity for the enterprise.

QUESTIONS

1. What is performance evaluation?
2. What factors in the diagnostic model are most influential for performance evaluation?
3. "Performance evaluations cause as many problems as they are designed to solve." Comment.
4. If you agree performance evaluation should take place, explain why.
5. Describe the major problems and malfunctions which can arise for the system, the evaluator, and the employee in performance evaluation.
6. How often should formal performance evaluations take place? Informal ones? How often do they take place?
7. Who usually evaluates employees in enterprises? Who should do so? Under what circumstances?
8. What criteria should be used to evaluate employees? Which ones are used?

9. Compare and contrast the individual performance evaluation techniques. If you were to choose one to be used to evaluate you, which one would it be? Why?

10. Compare and contrast the multiple-person evaluation techniques. If you were to choose one to be used to evaluate you, which one would it be? Why?

11. What happens after the employee is evaluated? What should happen?

12. Describe how to conduct an effective evaluation interview with a new, inexperienced employee. With an experienced employee.

13. How do managerial evaluations differ from employee evaluations? How are they similar?

14. Would you like to be evaluated by the assessment center method? Why or why not?

15. How are promotion decisions made in business, the military, and the third sector? Which is the best approach?

16. What do you consider are the four most significant propositions in Chapter 10? Why are these so important?

17. Which evaluation techniques should be used by large, low-complexity, and stable enterprises?

18. What decisions must top managers make to ensure performance evaluation will be effective?

NOTES AND REFERENCES

1. National Industrial Conference Board, *Personnel Practices in Factory and Office: Manufacturing*, Studies in Personnel Policy 194 (New York, 1964); National Industrial Conference Board, *Office Personnel Practices: Non-Manufacturing*, Studies in Personnel Policy 197 (New York, 1965); Robert Lazer, *Appraising Management Performance* (New York: The Conference Board, 1976); Bureau of National Affairs, *Labor Policy and Practice—Personnel Management* (Washington, D.C., 1974); Bureau of National Affairs, "Employee Performance: Evaluation and Control," *Personnel Policies Forum* no. 108, February 1975.

2. BNA, *Labor Policy and Practice.*

3. BNA, "Employee Performance."

4. See William Holley and Hubert Field, "Performance Appraisal and the Law," *Labor Law Journal*, July 1975; Robert Lazer, "The 'Discrimination' Danger in Performance Appraisal," *The Conference Board Record*, 13, 3 (March 1976), pp. 60–64.

5. Larry Cummings and Donald Schwab, *Performance in Organizations* (Glenview, Ill.: Scott Foresman & Co., 1973), ch. 5.

6. Leon Festinger, "A Theory of Social Comparison Processes," *Human Relations*, 7 (1954), pp. 117–40; T. F. Pettigrew, "Social Evaluation Theory: Convergences and Applications," in *Nebraska Symposium on Motivation*, ed. J. D. Levine (Lincoln: University of Nebraska Press, 1967).

7. See Donald Campbell and Daniel Ilgen, "Additive Effects of Task Difficulty and Goal Setting on Subsequent Task Performance," *Journal of Applied Psychology*, 61, 3 (1976), pp. 319–324; Jay Kim and W. Clay Hamner, "Effect of Performance Feedback and Goal Setting on Productivity and Satisfaction in an Organizational Setting," *Journal of Applied Psychology* 61, 1 (1976), pp. 48–56; John Ivancevitch, "Effects of Goal Setting on Performance and Job Satisfaction," *Journal of Applied Psychology* 61, 5 (1976), pp. 605–12; Gary Latham and Gary Yukl, "Effects of Assigned and Participative Goal Setting on Performance and Job Satisfaction," *Journal of Applied Psychology* 61, 2 (1976) pp. 166–71; James Terborg, "The

Motivational Components of Goal Setting," Journal of Applied Psychology 16, 5 (1976) pp. 613–21.

8. See Hugh Arnold, "Effects of Performance Feedback and Extrinsic Reward upon High Intrinsic Motivation," *Organizational Behavior and Human Performance* 17 (1976), pp. 275–88.

9. Cal Downs and David Spohn, "Case Study of an Appraisal System in an Airline," *Proceedings,* Academy of Management, 1976.

10. Robert Zawacki and Robert Taylor, "A View of Performance Appraisal from Organizations Using It," *Personnel Journal,* June 1976, pp. 290–292; 299 ff.

11. BNA, "Employee Performance."

12. Ibid.

13. Richard Williams et al., "International Review of Staff Appraisal Practices," *Public Personnel Management,* January–February 1977, pp. 5–12.

14. Paul H. Thompson and Gene W. Dalton, "Performance Appraisal: Managers Beware." *Harvard Business Review,* January–February 1970, pp. 149–57.

15. John Campbell et al., *Managerial Behavior, Performance and Effectiveness* (New York: McGraw-Hill Book Co., 1970); Cummings and Schwab, *Performance in Organizations,* ch. 5; H. E. Anderson et al., "Relationships among Ratings of Production Efficiency, and the General Aptitude Test Battery Scales in an Industrial Setting," *Journal of Applied Psychology,* 58 (1973), pp. 77–82.

16. Denis Pym, "The Politics and Ritual of Appraisal," *Occupational Psychology,* 47 (1973), pp. 231–35.

17. Douglas McGregor, "An Uneasy Look at Performance Appraisal," *Harvard Business Review,* May–June, 1975, pp. 89–94.

18. Walter Borman, "Effects of Instruction to Avoid Halo Error on Reliability and Validity of Performance Evaluation Ratings," *Journal of Applied Psychology* 60, 5 (1975), pp. 556–60.

19. Thomas Stone, "An Examination of Sex Prevalent Assumptions Concerning Performance Appraisal," *Public Personnel Management,* November–December, 1973, pp. 408–14.

20. Robert Dilworth, "Officer Evaluation: Seven Systems," *Military Review,* May 1973, pp. 15–26.

21. Stephen Jones, "Self and Interpersonal Evaluations," *Psychological Bulletin* 79, 3 (1973), pp. 185–99; Verne Kallejian et al., "The Impact of Interpersonal Relations of Ratings of Performance," *Public Personnel Review,* October 1973, pp. 166–70.

22. Francine Hall and Douglas Hall, "Effects of Job Incumbents' Race and Sex on Evaluations of Managerial Performance," *Academy of Management Review,* September 1976 pp. 476–81; Benson Rosen and Thomas Jerdee, "The Influence of Sex Role Stereotypes on Evaluations of Male and Female Supervisory Behavior," *Journal of Applied Psychology* 57, 1 (1973), pp. 44–48; Stone, "Sex Prevalent Assumptions," William Bigoness, "Effect of Applicant's Sex, Race, and Performance on Employee's Performance Ratings," *Journal of Applied Psychology* 61, 1 (1976), pp. 80–84.

23. Arthur Brief and Marc Wallace, "The Impact of Employee Sex and Performance on the Allocation of Organizational Rewards," *Proceedings,* Academy of Management, 1976.

24. Frank Schmidt and Raymond Johnson, "Effect of Race on Peer Ratings in an Industrial Setting," *Journal of Applied Psychology* 57, 3 (1973), pp. 237–41.

25. James L. Quinn, "Bias in Performance Appraisal," *The Personnel Administrator,* January–February 1969, pp. 40–43.

26. H. John Bernardin and C. S. Walter, "Effects of Rater Training and Diary Keeping on Psychometric Error in Ratings," *Journal of Applied Psychology* 62, 5 (1977), pp. 64–69; Gary Latham et al., "Training Managers to Minimize Rating Errors in the Observation of Behav-

ior," *Journal of Applied Psychology* 60, 5 (1975), pp. 550–55; A. G. Bayroff, et al., "Validity of Ratings as Related to Rating Techniques and Conditions," *Personnel Psychology* 7 (1954), pp. 93–114; Milton Hakel, *Perceiver Differences in Interpersonal Perceptions,* unpublished Ph.D. thesis, Univeristy of Minnesota, 1966; Ronald Taft, "The Ability to Judge People," *Psychological Bulletin* 52 (January 1955), pp. 1–23; Patricia Smith, "Behaviors, Results, and Organizational Effectiveness," in *Handbook of Industrial and Organizational Psychology,* ed. Marvin Dunnette (Chicago: Rand McNally & Co., 1976); Patricia Smith and L. M. Kendall, "Retranslation of Expectations," *Journal of Applied Psychology* 47, 2 (1963), pp. 149–55; Lee Stockford and H. W. Bissell, "Factors Involved in Establishing a Merit Rating Scale," Personnel 26 (1949), pp. 94–116.

27. Downs and Spohn, "Appraisal System in an Airline."

28. McGregor, "Uneasy Look at Performance Appraisal," Herbert Meyer et al., "Split Roles in Performance Appraisal," *Harvard Business Review,* January–February, 1965, pp. 123–29.

29. Cummings and Schwab, *Performance in Organizations,* ch. 2–4.

30. Herbert Meyer, "The Pay for Performance Dilemma," *Organizational Dynamics,* Winter 1975, pp. 39–50.

31. Thompson and Dalton, "Performance Appraisal."

32. J. Sidney Shrauger, "Responses to Evaluation as a Function of Initial Self Perceptions," *Psychological Bulletin* 82, 4 (1975), pp. 581–596.

33. Thompson and Dalton, "Performance Appraisal."

34. BNA, "Employee Performance."

35. D. Cook, "The Impact on Managers of Frequency of Feedback," *Academy of Management Journal* 11, 2 (1968), pp. 263–77.

36. P. Maloney and J. Hinrichs, "A New Tool for Supervisory Self-Development," *Personnel,* July 1959, pp. 46–53.

37. Robert McMurray, "Clear Communications for Chief Executives," *Harvard Business Review,* March–April 1965, pp. 131–48.

38. BNA, "Employee Performance"; Cummings & Schwab, *Performance in Organizations.*

39. Yetal Amir, "Peer Nominations as a Predictor of Multistage Promotion," *Journal of Applied Psychology* 54 (1970), pp. 462–69; Lloyd Baird, "Self and Superior Ratings of Performance," *Academy of Management Journal* 20, 2 (1977), pp. 291–300; G. A. Bassett and Herbert Meyer, "Performance Appraisal Based on Self Review," *Personnel Psychology* 21 (1968), pp. 421–30; A. G. Bayroff, et al., "Validity of Ratings as Related to Rating Techniques and Conditions," *Personnel Psychology* 7 (1954), pp. 93–114; Arthur Bedeian, "Rater Characteristics Affecting the Validity of Performance Appraisals," *Journal of Management,* Spring 1976, pp. 37–45; J. R. Berkshire, and P. D. Nelson, "Leadership Peer Rating Related to Subsequent Proficiency in Training and in the Fleet," Naval School of Aviation Medicine, Special Report 58–20, Pensacola, Fla., 1958; G. S. Booker, and R. W. Miller, "A Closer Look at Peer Ratings," *Personnel* 43 (1966) pp. 42–47; Larry Cummings and Donald Schwab, *Performance in Organizations* (Chicago: Scott, Foresman & Co., 1973); R. G. Downey et al., "Evaluation of Peer Rating Systems for Preduty Subsequent Promotion of Senior Military Officers," *Journal of Applied Psychology* 61, 2 (1976), pp. 206–9; D. Fiske and J. Cox, "The Consistency of Ratings By Peers," *Journal of Applied Psychology,* 44 (1960), pp. 11–17. Also L. V. Gordon and F. F. Medland, "The Cross Group Stability of Peer Ratings of Leadership Potential," *Personnel Psychology* 18 (1965), pp. 173–77; William B. Hall, "Employee Self Appraisal for Improved Performance," in *Tools for Improved Personnel Relations,* American Management Association Personnel Series 140, pp. 29–34 (New York, 1951); Harvey Hegarty, "Using Subordinate Ratings to Elicit Behavioral Changes in Supervisors," *Journal of Applied Psychology* 59, 6 (1974), pp. 764–66; Herbert Heneman III, "Comparisons of Self and Superior Ratings of Managerial Performance," *Journal of Applied Psychology* 59, 5 (1974), pp. 638–42;

E. P. Hollander, "Buddy Ratings: Military Research and Industrial Implications," *Personnel Psychology* 7 (Autumn 1954), pp. 385–93; E. P. Hollander, "The Friendship Factor in Peer Nominations," *Personnel Psychology* 9 (1956), pp. 425–47; E. P. Hollander, "The Reliability of Peer Nominations under Various Conditions of Administration," *Journal of Applied Psychology* 41 (1957), pp. 85–90; Arie Lewin and Abram Zwany, "Peer Nominations: A Model, Literature Critique, and a Paradigm for Research," *Personnel Psychology* 29 (1976), pp. 423–47; W. K. Kircher, "Relationship between Supervisory and Subordinate Ratings for Technical Personnel," *Journal of Industrial Psychology* 3 (1965), pp. 57–60; J. W. Lowrie, "Convergent Job Expectations and Ratings of Industrial Foremen," *Journal of Applied Psychology* 50 (1966), pp. 97–101; P. Maloney and J. Hinricks, "A New Tool for Supervisory Self-Development," *Personnel*, July 1959, pp. 46–53; Eugene Mayfield, "Management Selection," *Personnel Psychology* 23 (1970), pp. 377–391. Also Robert McMurray, "Clear Communications for Chief Executives," *Harvard Business Review*, March–April 1965, pp. 131–48; Stanley Nealey and T. W. Owen, "Multi Trait-Multi Method Analysis of Predictors and Criteria of Nursing Performance," *Organizational Behavior and Human Performance* 5 (1970), pp. 348–65; J. W. Parker, et al., "Rating Scale Content: Relationships between Supervisory and Self Ratings," *Personnel Psychology*, Spring 1959, pp. 49–63; H. E. Roadman, "An Industrial Use of Peer Ratings," *Journal of Applied Psychology*, August 1964, pp. 211–13; Craig Schneier, "Multiple Rater Groups and Performance Appraisal," *Public Personnel Management*, January–February, 1977, pp. 13–20; Patricia Smith, "Behaviors, Results, and Organizational Effectiveness," in *Handbook of Industrial and Organizational Psychology*, ed. Marvin Dunnette (Chicago: Rand McNally & Co., 1976); Robert Taylor and William Wilsted, "Capturing Judgment Policies in Performance Rating," *Industrial Relations*, May 1976, pp. 216–24; H. Thompson, "Comparison of Predictor and Criterion Judgments of Managerial Performance," *Journal of Applied Psychology* 54 (1970), pp. 496–502; G. C. Thornton, "The Relationship between Supervisory and Self Appraisals of Executive Performance," *Personnel Psychology* 21 (1968), pp. 441–45; L. K. Waters and C. W. Waters, "Peer Nominations as Predictors of Short Term Sales Performance," *Journal of Applied Psychology* 54 (1970), pp. 42–44; M. J. Webster, "Source of Evaluations and Expectations for Performance," *Sociometry* 32 (1969), pp. 243–58; J. Weitz and R. C. Nuckols, "A Validation Study of How to Supervise," *Journal of Applied Psychology* 37 (1953), pp. 7–8; R. J. Wherry and D. H. Fryer, "Buddy Ratings," *Personnel Psychology* 2 (1949), pp. 147–59; D. K. Whitla and J. E. Tirrell, "The Validity of Ratings of Several Levels of Supervisors," *Personnel Psychology* 6 (1953), pp. 461–66.

40. Richard Klimoski and Manuel London, "Role of the Rater in Performance Appraisal," *Journal of Applied Psychology* 59, 4 (1974), pp. 445–51; Walter Borman, "The Rating of Individuals in Organizations," *Organizational Behavior and Human Performance* 12 (1974), pp. 105–24.

41. Lewin and Zwany, "Peer Nominations."

42. Terry Talbert et al., "Measuring Clerical Job Performance," *Personnel Journal*, November 1976, pp. 573–75.

43. Smith, "Behaviors, Results, and Organizational Effectiveness."

44. Ibid.; Borman, "Rating of Individuals in Organizations"; Allan Easton, "A Forward Step in Performance Evaluation," *Journal of Marketing*, July 1966, pp. 26–32; Guy Besnard and Leslie Briggs, "Measuring Job Proficiency by Means of a Performance Test," in *Comparison of Performance upon the E-4 Fire Control System Simulation and upon Operational Equipment*, Lackland Air Force Base, Texas, April 1956.

45. Michael Kelley, "Subjective Performance Evaluation and Person-Role Conflict under Conditions of Uncertainty," *Academy of Management Journal*, 20, 2 (1977), pp. 301–14.

46. Henry Tosi et al., "Setting Goals in Management by Objectives," *California Management Review* 12 (1970), pp. 70–78; Harry Levinson, "Appraisal of *What* Performance?" *Harvard Business Review*, July–August, 1976, pp. 30–34 ff.

47. NICB, *Office Personnel Practices.*

48. BNA, "Employee Performance."

49. Andrew Baggaley, "A Scheme for Classifying Rating Methods," *Personnel Psychology* (Summer 1974), pp. 139–44; Cummings and Schwab, *Performance in Organizations*.

50. E. Ewart et al., "A Factor Analysis of an Industrial Merit Rating Scale," *Journal of Applied Psychology* 25 (1941), pp. 481–86.

51. Fritz Blanz, and Edwin Ghiselli, "The Mixed Standard Scale: A New Rating System," *Personnel Psychology* 25 (1972), pp. 185–99.

52. W. K. Kircher and Marvin Dunnette, "Using Critical Incidents to Measure Job Proficiency Factors," *Personnel* 34 (1957), pp. 54–59.

53. J. C. Flanagan, "The Critical Incident Technique," *Psychological Bulletin* 51 (1954), pp. 327–58; J. C. Flanagan and R. K. Burns, "The Employee Performance Record," *Harvard Business Review* 33 (1955), pp. 95–102.

54. James Goodale and Ronald Burke, "BARS Need Not Be Job Specific," *Journal of Applied Psychology* 60, 3 (1975), pp. 389–91.

55. Joseph Tiffin and Ernest McCormick, *Industrial Psychology* (Englewood Cliffs, N.J.: Prentice-Hall, Inc., 1965).

56. Kirt Duffey and Robert Webber, "On 'Relative' Rating Systems," *Personnel Psychology* 27 (1974), pp. 307–11.

57. Guy Besnard and Leslie Brigges, "Measuring Job Proficiency by Means of a Performance Test."

58. Guy Wadsworth, "The Field Review Method of Employee Evaluation and Internal Placement," *Personnel Journal* 27 (1948), pp. 227–32.

59. Kenneth Bernardin et al., "A Recomparison of BES to Summated Scales," *Journal of Applied Psychology* 61, 5 (1976), pp. 564–70; John Bernardin et al., "BES: Effects of Developmental Procedures and Formats," *Journal of Applied Psychology* 61, 1 (1976), pp. 75–79; Walter Borman and Marvin Dunnette, "Behavior-Based vs. Trait Oriented Performance Ratings," *Journal of Applied Psychology* 60, 5 (1975), pp. 561–65; William Bruvold, "Reconciliation of Apparent Non Equivalence among Alternative Rating Methods," *Journal of Applied Psychology* 62, 1 (1977), pp. 111–15; Barry Friedman and Edwin Cornelius, "Effect of Rater Participation Scale Construction on the Psychometric Characteristics of Two Rating Scale Formats," *Journal of Applied Psychology* 61, 2 (1976), pp. 210–16; Timothy Keaveny and Anthony McGann, "A Comparison of BES and Graphic Rating Scales," *Journal of Applied Psychology* 60, 6 (1975), pp. 695–703; Frank Saal and Frank Landy, "The Mixed Standard Rating Scale: An Evaluation," *Organizational Behavior and Human Performance* 18 (1977), pp. 19–35; Sheldon Zedeck et al., "Format and Scoring Variations in BES Evaluations," *Organizational Behavior and Human Performance* 17 (1976), pp. 171–84.

60. BNA, "Employee Performance."

61. Ibid.

62. Ronald Grey and David Kipnis, "Untangling the Performance Appraisal Dilemma: The Influence of Perceived Organizational Context on Evaluative Processes," *Journal of Applied Psychology* 61, 3 (1976), pp. 329–35.

63. BNA, "Employee Performance."

64. Norman R. Maier, *The Appraisal Interview; Three Basic Approaches* (La Jolla, Cal.: University Associates, 1976); Joseph Hillery and Kenneth Wexley, "Participation Effects in Appraisal Interviews Conducted in a Training Situation," *Journal of Applied Psychology* 59, 2 (1974), pp. 168–71.

65. R. J. Burke and D. S. Wilcox, "Characteristics of Effective Performance Review and Development Interviews," *Personnel Psychology* 22, 3 (1969), pp. 291–305; Downs and Spohn, "Appraisal System in an Airline"; Cummings and Schwab, *Performance in Organizations*.

66. Bureau of National Affairs, "Management Performance Appraisal Programs," BNA Personnel Policies Forum no. 104, 1974.

67. Walter Tornow and Patrick Pinto, "The Development of a Managerial Job Taxonomy: A System for Describing, Classifying and Evaluating Executive Positions," *Journal of Applied Psychology* 61, 4 (1976), pp. 410–18.

68. BNA, "Management Performance Appraisal Programs."

69. Joseph Thoresen and Cabot Jaffee, "A Unique Assessment Center Application with Some Unexpected By-Products," *Human Resource Management,* Spring 1973, pp. 3–7.

70. Joseph Moses et al., *Standards and Ethical Considerations for Assessment Center Operations* (Quebec: Third International Congress on the Assessment Center Method, May 1975).

71. Douglas Bray and Joseph Moses, "Personnel Selection," *Annual Review of Psychology, 1972,* Palo Alto Annual Reviews, pp. 545–76.

72. Ibid.; James Huck and Douglas Bray, "Management Assessment Center Evaluation and Subsequent Job Performance of White and Black Females," *Personnel Psychology* 29 (1976), pp. 13–30; F. Carleton, "Relationships between Follow-Up Evaluations and Information Developed in a Management Assessment Center," *Proceedings of the American Psychological Association,* 1970, pp. 565–66; D. Porritt, *Research Evaluation and Development Responsibilities for the Personnel Assessment Center* (New South Wales, Australia: Publishers Service Board), 1970; James Mitchel, "Assessment Center Validity: A Longitudinal Study," *Journal of Applied Psychology* 60, 5 (1975), pp. 573–79; Allen Kraut, "Prediction of Managerial Success by Peer and Training Staff Ratings," *Journal of Applied Psychology* 60, 1 (1975), pp. 14–19; Joseph Moses and Virginia Boehm, "Relationship of Assessment Center Performance to Management Progress of Women," *Journal of Applied Psychology,* 60, 4 (1975), pp. 527–29.

73. Steven Norton, "The Empirical and Content Validity of Assessment Centers vs. Traditional Methods of Predicting Managerial Success," *Academy of Management Review,* July 1977, pp. 442–53; John Hinricks and Seppo Haapera, "Reliability of Measurement in Situational Exercises: An Assessment of the Assessment Center Method," *Personnel Psychology* 29 (1976), pp. 31–40; Douglas Bray et al., *Formative Years in Business* (New York: John Wiley & Sons, 1974).

74. Robert Finkle, "Management Assessment Centers," in *Handbook of Industrial and Organizational Psychology,* ed. Marvin Dunnette (Chicago: Rand McNally & Co., 1976), pp. 861–88; Frank Heller and Alfred Clark, "Personnel and Human Resources Development," *Annual Review of Psychology, 1976,* pp. 405–35.

75. Vinay Kothari, "The Importance and Application of Promotional Criteria as Perceived by Management, Union, and Employee," *Proceedings,* Academy of Management, 1974.

76. Ronald Taylor, "Preferences of Industrial Managers for Information Sources in Making Promotion Decisions," *Journal of Applied Psychology* 60, 2 (1975), pp. 269–72.

77. Albert Glickman et al., *Top Management Development and Succession* (New York: Macmillan–Arkville Press, 1968).

78. Newman Peery and Y. K. Shetty, "An Empirical Study of Executive Transferability and Organizational Performance," *Proceedings,* Academy of Management, 1976.

79. Ned Rosen et al., "The Emergence and Allocation of Leadership Resources Overtime in a Technical Organization," *Academy of Management Review,* June 1976, pp. 165–83.

80. Jeffery Pfeffer and Huseyin Leblebici, "Executive Recruitment and Development of Interfirm Operations," *Administrative Science Quarterly* 18 (1973), pp. 449–61.

81. Christine Hobart and Karen Harries, "Sex Role Stereotyping among Future Managers," *Proceedings,* Academy of Management, 1976.

82. Lipman Feld, "Executive Promotion by Court Order at Ford," *Industrial Management,* June 1973, pp. 3–6.

83. Terry Brown, "The Managers," *Wall Street Journal,* April 29, 1977.

84. Douglas Hall and Benjamin Schneider, *Organizational Climates and Careers: The Work Lives of Priests,* (New York: Academic Press, 1974), pp. 30–31; 98–102.

85. Marvin Jolson, "Criteria for Promotion and Tenure," *Academy of Management Journal* 17, 1 (1974), pp. 149–54; David Katz, "Faculty Salaries, Promotions, and Productivity at a Large University," *American Economic Review,* June 1973, pp. 469–77.

86. Thomas Morris, "Merit Principles in Military Officer Personnel Administration," *Public Administration Review,* September–October 1974, pp. 445–50.

87. *The Officer Promotion System,* Department of the Army Pamphlet 360–830, December 1976.

88. *Promotion Board Exercise,* Department of the Army, U.S. Army War College, Carlisle Barracks, Pa., January 1977.

89. William Holley et al., "Analyzing Performance Appraisal Systems: An Empirical Study," *Personnel Journal* (September 1976), pp. 457–63.

Employee training

CHAPTER OBJECTIVES

■ To suggest why enterprises engage in training and what effective training is.

■ To demonstrate how to manage training in an enterprise.

■ To help you understand the varieties of training programs and methods used by enterprises to improve employee effectiveness and satisfaction.

CHAPTER OUTLINE

INTRODUCTION TO EMPLOYEE TRAINING

Numerous occasions arise in the daily operations of an enterprise that point up the need for employee training or retraining. These are examples:

Employment planning determines that the new solar heating division is going to grow. At the same time, the aerosol manufacturing division in the same city is expected to decline. Top management decides to shift employees from aerosols to solar heat. The jobs are different; the employees must be prepared for their new jobs.

In recruiting in a tight labor market, the enterprise is able to attract 20 persons who will not be able to be effective without more knowledge of the jobs to be done.

In selecting employees, the skill levels of certain employees transferred to a unit were overestimated. The work is not up to standard.

Performance evaluation ratings show that some recently promoted employees are not meeting the output standards of recently retired employees.

All these occasions and many more can lead an enterprise to undertake a training program or expand one it has. Training is a major personnel activity for most employers.

DEFINITIONS

Training is systematic process of altering the behavior and/or attitudes of employees in a direction to increase organizational goal achievement.[1]

A formal training program is an effort by the employer to provide opportunities for the employee to acquire job-related skills, attitudes, and knowledge.

Learning is the act by which the individual acquires skills, knowledge, and abilities which result in a relatively permanent change in his behavior.

Since training is a form of education, some of the findings of learning theory logically might be applicable to training. These principles can be important in the design of both formal and informal training programs. A great deal of material has been accumulated on the application of learning theory to organizational training.[2] The following is a brief summary of the way learning principles can be applied to job training.[3]

All human beings can learn. Most normal human beings can choose whether they will learn at any time in their lives; people can and do learn, but there are individual differences in learning.

The individual must be motivated to learn. This motivation involves two factors: awareness of the need to learn, based on the individual's own inadequacy in this regard, and a clear understanding of what needs to be learned.

Learning is an active process. The individual learns better when more of his senses are utilized in the effort and he becomes more involved in the learning process.

Normally, the learner must have guidance. Learning is more efficient if it is not by trial and error. Guidance can speed the learning process and provide feedback as well as reinforce appropriate learning and prevent inadequate behavior patterns from developing.

Appropriate materials for sequential learning (cases, problems, discussion outlines, reading lists) must be provided. The trainer is an aid in an efficient learning process.

Learning requires time to assimilate what has been learned, to accept it, to internalize it, and to build confidence in what has been learned.

Learning methods should be as varied as possible. It is boredom that destroys learning, not fatigue. Any method—whether old-fashioned lecture or programmed learning or the jazziest computer game—will begin to bore some learners if overused.

The learner must secure satisfaction from the learning. He must see the usefulness of the material in terms of his own needs.

The learner must get reinforcement of correct behavior. As behavioral psychologists have shown, learners learn best with fairly immediate reinforcement of appropriate behavior. The learner must be rewarded for new behavior in various ways—pay, recognition, promotion.

Standards of performance should be set for the learner. Benchmarks for learning will provide goals and give a feeling of accomplishment when reached. P. Harmon has shown how to develop these performance objectives.[4]

Different levels of learning are appropriate at different times and require different methods.

Leslie This and Gordon Lippitt distinguish among four levels of learning.[5] They are:

1. The simplest level: skills of motor response, memorization, and simple conditioning.
2. The second level: adaptation to a simple environment (example: learning to operate an electric typewriter when one already knows how to use a manual typewriter).
3. The third level: complex learning, such as finding meaning in seemingly isolated parts (for example, improving interpersonal competence).
4. The fourth level: most complex (example: learning new lifestyles and new values).

Each of these types of learning requires different methods (simple to complex) and various lengths of time to learn (shortest at the first level to longest at the fourth).

In recent years, a group of researchers have tried to apply learning theory more directly through behavior modification techniques. (For more details on behavior modification, see Chapter 2).

John Campbell argues that in the future, more applications of behavior modification will be made to improve the effectiveness of training.[6] Summarizing Albert Bandura, Campbell describes how the behavior modification process can work in a training setting.[7]

> The training objectives must be carefully specified in terms of specific desired behaviors.
>
> For purposes of alteration, the existing reinforcement contingencies or stimulus pairings currently operating must be carefully described.
>
> New contingencies or pairings must be selected that will directly support the desired behavior. The new reinforcers must be powerful enough to alter behavior and to maintain it once it has been changed.
>
> Change agents must be selected to administer the reinforcement.
>
> If the desired behavior is seldom emitted or is too complex to be reinforced continuously, then subgoals must be defined and the appropriate reinforcement contingencies applied to them (i.e., behavior must be "shaped").
>
> After the behavior has been altered, provisions must be made so it is self-regulating.

You will see, as each aspect of training program design and implementation is discussed, how these learning theory and behavior modification principles are applied.

A DIAGNOSTIC APPROACH TO TRAINING

Exhibit 11–1 highlights those aspects of the diagnostic model that are especially important to employee training. The most important determinants of training are the task to be done and the employees' abilities and attitudes. If the current employees have work ethic attitudes and the skills needed to do the jobs, training may not be too important for the enterprise. More often, because of conditions in the labor market, the enterprise is losing some employees to other enterprises who provide better rewards.

It is also unlikely that the task demands are stable. More frequently, because of volatile technology and market conditions, the jobs are changing, and this requires more training so employees can meet current effectiveness standards. When computers are introduced or new production or operating techniques are instituted, employees must be retrained.

The government also is becoming a vital force in training. This has been happening in two ways. One is the pressure for equal employment opportunities and human rights (see Chapter 18). If in an enterprise minorities and women work only at its lowest paid, lowest skilled positions, pressure will be applied to upgrade the skills of those who have the potential for upward mobility. This increases the demand for training or retraining.

The second way government influences training is that it provides many training programs. These programs frequently have public policy purposes, such as reduction of unemployment, upgrading the incomes of minority groups, or increasing the competitiveness of underdeveloped regions of the country.

In the United States, the federal government, through the Comprehensive Employment and Training Act (1974) and other manpower legislation, has allocated large sums to the training of potential workers for jobs. The government reimburses training organizations (schools, businesses, unions) or trains the workers itself.[8] The Carter administration has indicated that it intends to increase these programs greatly in the next few years. The focal groups will be black teen-agers, construction workers, blue-collar workers (generally blacks), farm-wage workers, and women—the groups with the highest unemployment rates. Some of the training will be conducted by employers and paid for directly or indirectly by the U.S. government.[9]

The Canadian government operates several manpower training programs. From 1967 to 1975, Canada spent over $2 billion, three to four times the per capita spending for this purpose in the United States. By the terms of the Canadian law, the Adult Occupational Training Act of 1967, the federal government matches provincial funds. A joint federal-provincial manpower-needs committee operates the program; some of the training is done by schools, but much is now done by employers. The program operates in conjunction with the 350 Canada and Quebec Manpower Centres, whose 3,500 counselors contract for employee training. Besides job-specific training, basic training for skills development, basic job readiness training, and work adjustment training are provided for disadvantaged persons.[10]

Some unions also are involved in employee training, especially in industries such as construction where the union is larger than the employer. In these cases, the union often does most or all of the training.

PURPOSES OF TRAINING

Employee training is a major undertaking for employers. Almost all large enterprises and most medium-sized ones run their own training programs.[11] They employ 50,000 full-time trainers and spend $100 billion per year on it.[12] Why do they do this? The reasons given tend to relate to the kind of training being offered. They include:

- To improve the quantity of output.
- To improve the quality of output.
- To lower the costs of waste and equipment maintenance.
- To lower the number and costs of accidents.
- To lower turnover and absenteeism and increase job satisfaction, since training can improve the employee's self-esteem.

EXHIBIT 11–1
Factors affecting employee training and organizational effectiveness

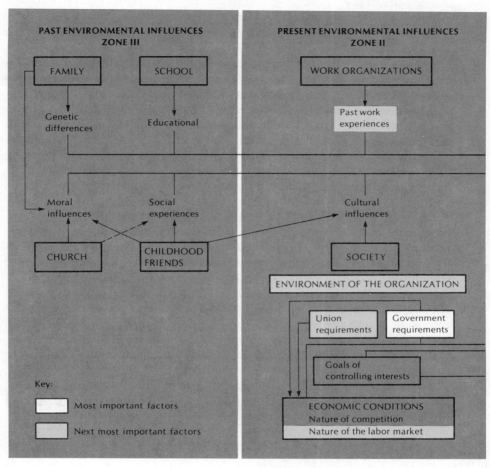

Another way to state the objectives is to ask key executives why they train employees. Edgar Speer, chairman and chief executive officer of United States Steel, put it this way:

> We support training and development activities to get results. . . . We're interested in specific things that provide greater rewards to the employee, increased return to the stockholder, and enable reinvestment needs of the business. In other words, [we're interested in] those things which affect the "bottom line." Although you cannot always evaluate training as readily as some other functions, as people improve their performance it is reflected in on-the-job results as well as all aspects of their lives.[13]

William Murray, chairman of the board and chief executive officer of Harris Bank of Chicago, says:

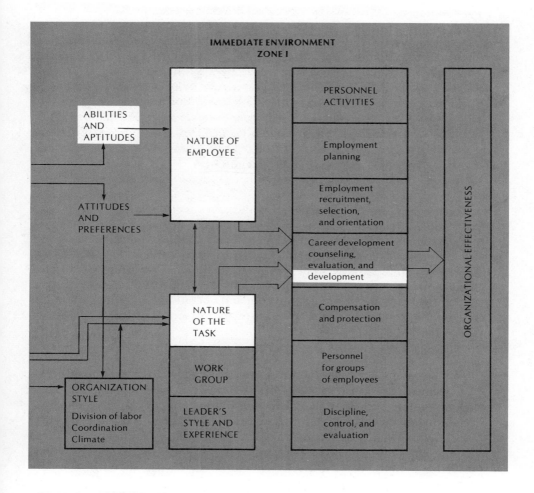

I readily relate to the fundamentals of good technical training. . . . The training function plays an integral role in the bank by helping upgrade employee performance and the from hire to retire approach provides continuity in the developing process of bank personnel. While we can't measure the absolute results of training programs, our record as an organization indicates we're doing something right.[14]

Employee training is a moderately well-developed function—a Stage III or possibly Stage IV function in personnel. Therefore, evaluation must be more possible than some seem to believe.

Who is involved in training?

For the training program to be effective, it must receive support from top management, such as Murray and Speer give it. Top managers must provide the budget for it and develop the guidelines to be emphasized. Operating managers must be encouraged to allow their employees time off for training.

Operating managers are an important part of the training team. They help select training topics and choose the participants, and they cooperate in scheduling programs. In smaller enterprises (with 500 employees or less), training will be done by the operations staff, primarily as on-the-job training. In larger enterprises, personnel people manage the training program and do at least some of the specialized training other than on-the-job programs. On-the-job training is done by operations personnel, of course. Thus effective training programs are a result of effectively coordinated efforts of the personnel and operating groups in an enterprise.

In medium-sized and smaller enterprises, the personnel manager and specialists spend some of their time doing training. In other medium-sized and most larger enterprises, a division of the personnel department is devoted to training, and specialists headed by a training manager do the planning and implementation of training. Some believe training should be separated from personnel. George Ordiorne contends that in almost half the largest companies, training is separate organizationally from personnel because of unimaginative leadership in the personnel department.[15] In any case, the job of the manager of training is to plan and operate the enterprise's training program, in conjunction with the rest of the personnel effort.

MANAGING THE TRAINING PROGRAM

Because training is important to the enterprise and costly to run, effective management is a must. Personnel runs most training programs, but some important line functions may have their own programs. For example, if marketing is an important function for a firm, there may be a separate sales training group reporting to the vice president of marketing. These staff groups must have close liason with the line departments to assure that the training fits the needs of the users of the training—the line departments.

Exhibit 11–2, a model of the training process, includes these steps: determination of training needs and objectives, selection of trainees and training methods and aids, and evaluation of training programs. This section discusses the first two steps in the efficient and effective management of training. Then a section on implementing the program describes types of programs and training methods and aids, and there is a separate section on evaluations.

Determining training needs and objectives

The first step in managing training is to determine training needs and set objectives for these needs. In effect, the trainers are preparing a training forecast (this is the assessment phase in Exhibit 11–2).

One way to analyze training needs is in a framework of three levels of analysis: organizational, operational, and individual.[16]

EXHIBIT 11–2
Training model

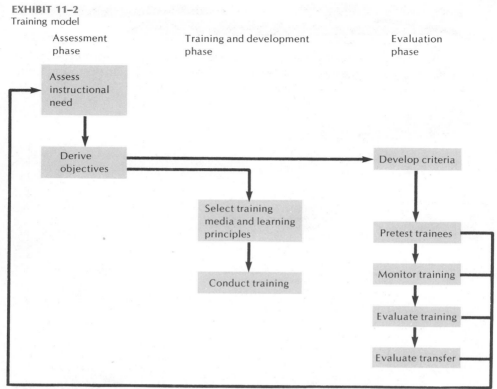

From *Training: Program Development and Evaluation* by I. L. Goldstein. Copyright © 1974 by Wadsworth Publishing Company, Inc. Reprinted by permission of the publisher, Brooks/Cole Publishing Company, Monterey, California.

Organizational analysis.   Training managers examine the strategic objectives and strategic plans to determine if there are added training needs. These usually can be derived from the results of employment planning (see Chapters 4 and 5) or past training programs that have met the enterprise's needs. Training managers also can examine the enterprise's achievement of objectives (measured by MBO results) to determine the major variances between success and failure and which ones training could help remedy. Specific training requests received from operating managers provide other inputs to training needs.

Operational analysis.   At this level, training managers analyze the specific ability needs determined by job descriptions and job specifications of the jobs in a work area or work unit. They may also observe the job performance of work groups and survey jobholders, supervisors, training committees, and others. The results of a unit's output—its efficiency and effectiveness—can also be analyzed to determine training needs.

Person analysis.   Moving to the individual employee's training needs, training managers can measure individual performance (efficiency and effectiveness) against standards. This can be done by interviews, observation, attitude surveys, or objective records of performance.

Thus at all three levels—organization, operational, and individual—gaps between expected results and actual results can suggest training needs. Active solicitation of suggestions from employees, supervisors, managers, and training committees can also provide training-needs ideas.

EXHIBIT 11–3
Needs analysis survey form

Check One: Prototype_____ Operational _____

Employee _____ Department:_____

Form Completed By: _____ Title: _____ Date:_____

INSTRUCTIONS
This form was designed to enable you to list skills and evaluate the degree of relevancy of these skills to positions in your own department. In addition you will be asked to assess the degree of proficiency in designated skill areas displayed by the employees occupying these positions. To accomplish this task, you are asked to follow the steps outlined below:

A) **Prototype Form**

1) Rank the **General Job Skills** in order of your perception of their importance to successfully performing the subject job.

2) Review the **Specific Job Skills** section — this is the preliminary listing prepared by the survey coordinator based on existing job descriptions — and add or delete skills as you feel appropriate.

3) Rank the **Specific Job Skills** in order of your perception of their importance to successfully performing the subject job and divide into five groups as the coordinator has done for the General Skills listing (this is the skill group level).

B) **Operational Form**

After the Prototype Form has been finalized (through rater consensus) with respect to both the type and degree of relevance of skill areas, you will be asked to evaluate each employee's degree of proficiency in each skill area. Please use the scale below.

NO PROFICIENCY   1   2   3   4   5   HIGH LEVEL OF PROFICIENCY

General Skills	General Skills in Ranked Order		Group	Place "x" on Employee Evaluation					
				1	2	3	4	5	*
Planning		1							
Control		2	V						
Writing Ability		3							
Oral Communications		4							
Company Credibility		5	IV						
Decision Making		6							
Creativity		7							
Initiative		8	III						
Adaptability		9							
Problem Solving		10							
People Sensitivity		11	II						
Self-Evaluation		12							
Relationship to Supervisor		13							
Work Attitude		14	I						
Organizing Ability		15							

Specific Skills	Specific Skills in Ranked Order	Group	Place "x" on Employee Evaluation					
			1	2	3	4	5	*

*Check when there is a discrepancy of more than two points (employee vs. group) or when the employee is rated below 3 in Groups III and below.

Source: Lance Berger, "A Dew Line for Training and Development: The Needs Analysis Survey," *The Personnel Administrator*, November 1976, pp. 51–55.

One recent attempt to operationalize these ideas proposed setting up an early warning system for determining training needs. This is done by active solicitation of ideas from operating managers.[17] A proposed needs analysis survey form to solicit supervisory suggestions for training needs is given as Exhibit 11–3.

From this analysis of training needs, the training manager proposes specific training programs.[18] To be truly effective, specific measurable objectives for the program should be developed. An example of a statement of objectives for Naval tasks is given as Exhibit 11–4.

To what extent do enterprises formally plan for training needs? Earlier surveys indicated that from 10 percent to about a third used some formal methods.[19] More recent studies indicate there is a trend for larger firms to plan these needs formally, but less than half do so at present.[20] It has to be assumed that still fewer middle-sized and smaller enterprises do formal assessment studies prior to implementing training programs.

Use of the learning curve. A factor important in planning the training courses is the length of time it takes to learn the material. A frequently used tool in this planning is the learning curve, which indicates the extent to which the rate of learning increases or decreases with practice. Three

EXHIBIT 11–4
Specific training objectives

Illustrative Objectives as They Appear in the Basic Curriculum Outline

1. *Shipboard Task:* Performs preliminary settings on the AN/SPA–34.

   Training Task: Given an unlabeled drawing of the front panel controls of the AN/SPA–34 the trainee labels each control and identifies its functions. Technical manual and class notes may be used.
   Standards: No errors.

   Training Task: Performs preliminary settings, from memory.
   Standards: No errors.

2. *Shipboard Task:* Serves as a combat information center watch officer (CICWO) during a normal steaming combat information center (CIC) watch on a combatant ship steaming independently.

   Shipboard Task: Monitors CIC personnel during a normal steaming CIC watch on a combatant ship steaming independently.

   Shipboard Task: Evaluates the CIC information of a ship steaming independently.

   Shipboard Task: Recommends to Bridge all maneuvers and/or other actions required of own ship steaming independently.

   Shipboard Task: Monitors the dissemination of key information to both internal and external stations.

   Training Task: In a classroom exercise, three slides will be displayed simultaneously depicting various CIC status boards, plots, and equipment accompanied by audio-taped transmissions of sound powered telephone and radiotelephone communications. The situations will present problems of a ship steaming independently. Information from the various sources is not always compatible.
   The student must (1) compare the information with displays for their compatibility; (2) detect and record plotting, display, and communications errors; (3) assess, in writing, the immediate situation as shown on the slides; and (4) state in writing what recommendation CIC should make to the bridge.
   Standards: 80% accuracy.

Source: Edward Rundquist, "Designing and Improving Job Training Courses," *Personnel Psychology,* Spring 1972, pp. 41–52.

EXHIBIT 11–5
Three typical learning curves

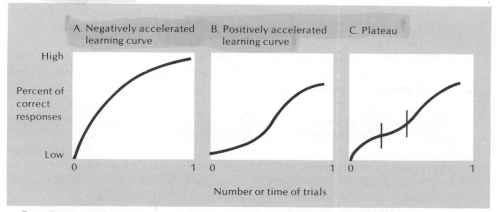

From *Training in Industry: The Management of Learning*, by B. M. Bass and J. A. Vaughan. Copyright © 1966 by Wadsworth Publishing Company, Inc. Reprinted by permission of the publisher, Brooks/Cole Publishing Company, Monterey, California.

typical learning curves as identified by B. M. Bass and J. A. Vaughn[21] are shown in Exhibit 11–5. The most frequently occurring curve is the negatively accelerated curve shown in A, where increments of learning are very large early in training and decline later. Beyond the leveling off of the curve, more practice will not contribute a great deal to learning. Bass and Vaughn suggest this curve is likely to be found in easier material and when the learner has high initial motivation.

The positively accelerated curve shown in B is the opposite of that shown in A—learning is slow at first but speeds up as the material is absorbed. This is found in learning difficult material, or when the learner's past preparation was insufficient or the initial motivation is low.

The curve shown in C represents a plateau—a period when learning seems to stop for a period. This may occur because of loss of motivation, or where new learning may not appear to be occurring but elimination of incorrect learning is taking place, among other reasons. Trainers can use learning curves effectively in planning the length and content of training programs.

In summary, training program development results from training needs analysis, studying other enterprises' programs, and reading the literature on the latest training programs.[22] Decision making in the planning of training programs is not too unique: it is incremental, satisficing, and quasirational—as Herbert Simon has described all decision making.[23] The training director adds programs as the need becomes apparent and drops them as the need is no longer present, subject to budget constraints.

Choosing trainers and trainees

Great care must be exercised in hiring or developing effective instructors or trainers.[24] To some extent, the success of the training program depends upon proper selection of the person who performs the training task. Personal characteristics (the ability to speak well, to write convincingly, to organize the work of others, to be inventive, to inspire others to greater achievements) are important factors in the selection of trainers.

Another planning factor is the selection of trainees who will participate in the programs. In some cases this is obvious; the program may have been designed to train particular new employees in certain skills. In some cases, the training program is designed to help with EEO goals;[25] in others it is to help employees find better jobs elsewhere when layoffs are necessary[26] or to retrain older employees.[27] Techniques similar to selection procedures may be used to select trainees, especially when those who attend the program may be promoted or receive higher wages or salaries as a result.[28] If formal selection techniques are not used, quotas, supervisor nominations, self-nominations, and seniority rules may develop unofficially or officially as selection mechanisms for the programs.

This discussion of trainee selection is normative, however; it implies that enterprises rationally select those employees who need the training and train them. Roger Roderick and Joseph Yaney studied selection of and participation in training programs by 1,247 young males who worked for businesses over a four-year period. Only one out of seven received any training during the period. The companies tended to select for further training those men with the best educational backgrounds and from the highest socioeconomic group. This "creaming" meant that those who needed the training the most did not get it, and the gap between the trained and untrained widened. Also because of these selection procedures, blacks received much less training than whites. The companies seemed to select trainees based on the most probable "success ratio" for the training, not those needing the training the most.[29]

IMPLEMENTING THE TRAINING PROGRAM

After needs and objectives have been determined and trainees and trainers have been selected, the program is run. This step includes scheduling and follow-up on trainees' progress. As noted above, operating executives are consulted on the best time to schedule the programs. One example of a follow-up schedule for training is given in Exhibit 11–6.

Training programs

Both training for the unskilled and retraining for the obsolete employee follow one of four approaches which combine elements of the *where* and *what* of training. The four principal types of training are: apprenticeship, vestibule, on-the-job training, and off-the-job training.

Apprentice training. Apprentice training is a combination of on-the-job and off-the-job training. It requires the cooperation of the employer,

EXHIBIT 11–6
Follow-up records for training

	Training Steps	1	2	3	4	5
Name of Trainee	Target Time					
Job Title						
Date of Entry Entry Test						
Steps Completion						
January						
February						
March						
April						
May						
June						
Etc.						

trainers at the work place and in schools (such as vocational schools), government agencies, and the skilled-trade unions.

The governments regulate apprentice training. In the United States, the major law is the Apprenticeship Act of 1937. In Canada, Ottawa and the provinces have apprenticeship acts which vary by province.[30] The Canadian federal law is the Adult Occupational Training Act.

Typically the governments also subsidize these programs. For example, in Canada, the federal government provides loans to build facilities and/or pays up to 50 percent of the costs of the province to research needs for apprenticeship programs. All provinces have apprenticeship laws providing for an organized procedure of on-the-job training and school instruction in designated skilled trades, and statutory provision is made in most provinces for issuing qualification certificates, on application, to qualified tradesmen in certain trades. In some provinces, legislation is in effect making it mandatory for certain classes of tradesmen to hold a certificate of competency. The trades covered by apprenticeship programs are always being changed to meet the needs of a changing labor market.

Research evaluating construction workers trained by the apprenticeship method versus on-the-job training indicates that apprentices are better trained, get promoted sooner, and experience less unemployment later.[31] Thus apprentice training can be effective.

In the United States, the U.S. Department of Labor funds apprenticeship programs in the building trades, mining, auto repair, oil, and other fields.

In 1976, these were funded for $18,000,000. The Department also issues standards and regulations governing these programs.[32]

The apprentice commits herself or himself to a period of training and learning that involves both formal classroom learning and practical on-the-job experience. These periods can vary from two years or so (barber, iron-worker, foundryman, baker, meat cutter, engraver) through four or five years (electrician, engraver, photoengraver, tool and die maker, plumber, job press-man), up to ten years (steel-plate engraver). During this period, the pay is less than that for the master worker.

Vestibule training. In vestibule training, the trainee learns the job in an environment that simulates the real working environment as closely as possible but is not involved in actual work. The trainee may, for example, run a machine under the supervision of a trainer until he or she learns how to use it properly, and only then be sent to the shop floor. This procedure can be quite expensive if the number of trainees supervised is not large, but it can be effective under certain circumstances.[33] Some employees trained in the vestibule method have adjustment problems when they begin full-time work, since the vestibule area is safer and less hectic.

On-the-job training. Probably the most widely used method of training (formal and informal) is on-the-job training. The employee is placed into the real work situation and shown the job and the tricks of the trade by an experienced worker or the supervisor. Although this program is apparently simple and relatively less costly, if it is not handled properly the costs can be high in damaged machinery, unsatisfied customers, misfiled forms, and poorly taught workers.

One approach to systematic on-the-job training is the job instruction training (JIT) system developed during World War II. In this system, the trainers first train the supervisors, who in turn train the employees. Exhibit 11–7 describes the steps of JIT training as given in the War Manpower Commission's bulletin, "Training within Industry Series in 1945." These are the instructions given to supervisors on how to train new or present employees. Fred Wickert has updated and improved the JIT method in many ways.[34]

Off-the-job training. Other than apprenticeship, on-the-job training, and vestibule training, all other training is off the job, whether it is done in organization classrooms, vocational schools, or elsewhere. Organizations with the biggest training programs often use off-the-job training. The majority of the 50,000 trainers in the United States and the $100 billion on training is in off-the-job training. The methods used for off-the-job training are discussed in the next section.

Training methods and aids

After deciding what programs to offer, the next step is determination of the best methods to use for the training. This choice is made on the basis of the number of trainees for each program, the relative costs per

EXHIBIT 11–7
Job instruction training (JIT) methods

First, here's what you *must do* to *get ready* to teach a job:
1. Decide what the learner must be taught in order to do the job efficiently, safely, economically, and intelligently.
2. Have the right tools, equipment, supplies, and material ready.
3. Have the workplace properly arranged, just as the worker will be expected to keep it.

Then, you should *instruct* the learner by the following *four basic steps:*

Step I—*Preparation* (of the learner)
1. Put the learner at *ease.*
2. Find out what he already knows about the job.
3. Get him interested and desirous of learning the job.

Step II—*Presentation* (of the operations and knowledge)
1. *Tell, show, illustrate,* and *question* in order to put over the new knowledge and operations.
2. Instruct slowly, clearly, completely, and patiently, one point at a time.
3. Check, question, and repeat.
4. Make sure the learner really knows.

Step III—*Performance try-out*
1. Test learner by having him perform the job.
2. Ask questions beginning with *why, how, when* or *where.*
3. Observe performance, correct errors, and repeat instructions if necessary.
4. Continue until you *know he knows.*

Step IV—*Follow-up*
1. Put him "on his own."
2. Check frequently to be sure he follows instructions.
3. Taper off extra supervision and close follow-up until he is qualified to work with normal supervision.

Remember—If the learner hasn't learned, the teacher hasn't taught.

trainee for each method, the availability of training materials in various forms (including the trainers' capabilities), and the employees' relative efficiency in learning. If there are only a few trainers, individualized programmed instruction may be considered. If none of the trainers is capable of giving certain instruction, outside trainers may be contacted, or movies or videotapes might be used. Finally, the method used should reflect the degree of active participation desired for the program as illustrated in Exhibit 11–8.

Studies have found the following training methods being used by larger companies with with advanced personnel practices: 53 percent used the lecture method; 29 percent, the conference method; and 20 percent, programmed instruction. As to the tools available, 67 percent had chalkboards; 63 percent, movies; and almost 50 percent, film clips, flip charts, and slides. More than a third used exhibits and posters, and a few had magnetic boards, closed-circuit TV, and tape recorders.[35] The use of the newer techniques has undoubtedly increased since this study.

Probably the most frequently used methods are lectures and conferences. These are useful to the extent that the trainer is skilled in communication and there are enough trainees to average out the costs per trainee. Methods that frequently supplement the lecture are movies, slides, tapes, and other audiovisual aids.

EXHIBIT 11-8
Roles of trainees effected by different training methods

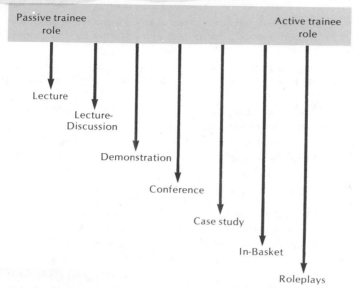

Another survey found that almost all enterprises used lectures, conferences, and services. Other techniques such as simulation, role playing, and
programmed instruction were used by about 15 percent of the companies.[36]

One of the newer methods being used in organizational training is programmed instruction.[37] Material can be presented on teaching machines or
in text form, and behaviorist learning principles are followed closely. Programmed instruction is a useful method for self-instruction when the development cost of the materials has been paid by another organization and
the materials are available. It might also be a useful method if there are
enough trainees to amortize the development cost, if the trainees are likely
to be motivated enough to move ahead with this approach, and if the material
to be presented is suitable to the method.

Leonard Silvern has described the method as follows:

Programmed instruction is a technique for instructing without the presence or
intervention of a human instructor. It is a learner-centered method of instruction,
which presents subject-matter to the trainee in small steps or increments, requiring
frequent responses from him and immediately informing him of the correctness of
his responses. The trainee's responses may be written, oral, or manipulative. A response may be constructed, as in the completion type; it may be selected from
among several alternatives, as in the multiple-choice type; or it may assume one
or more of a variety of other styles.[38]

Features of programmed instruction, according to Silvern are:

Instruction is provided without the presence or intervention of a human instructor.

The learner learns at his own rate (conventional group instruction, films, television, and other media and methods that do not allow learner control do not satisfy this criterion).

Instruction is presented in small incremental steps requiring frequent responses by the learner; step size is a function of the subject matter and the characteristics of the learner population.

There is a participative overt interaction, or two-way communication, between the learner and the instructional program.

The learner receives immediate feedback informing him of his progress.

Reinforcement is used to strengthen learning.

The sequence of lessons is carefully controlled and consistent.

The instructional program shapes and controls behavior.[39]

Programmed instruction may have wide application in organizational training programs, especially for programs whose characteristics fit those discussed above. It can also be developed in computer-assisted forms.[40]

Another new training method is the use of closed-circuit television, audio tapes, and videotape recording. One study found the use of videotape in training expanding rapidly.[41] The method allows the trainer's message to be given in many locations and to be repeated as often as needed for the benefit of the trainees. Videotape recording also allows for self-confrontation, which is especially useful in such programs as sales training and interpersonal relations. The trainee's presentation can be taped and played back for analysis.

Inevitably, the question as to how effective each form of training is must be answered. In Exhibit 11–9 Bass and Vaughn provide an evaluation of the methods discussed here and some of those discussed in Chapter 12.[42] Stephen Carroll et. al. asked training directors from 200 large firms to evaluate the effectiveness of such training methods as lectures, discussions, case studies, games, movies, programmed instruction, and television. They then compared their evaluations with those of research studies on the differentiated effectiveness of various methods. In general, the training directors underestimated the relative effectiveness of the lecture and seminar method and overestimated the effectiveness of programmed instruction.[43] There are studies to support the effectiveness of all methods;[44] if a method is appropriate for the particular program in question, it should be used.

EVALUATION OF TRAINING

Evaluation of training is the final phase of the training program. Everyone advocates it, but it is advocated more than it is performed.[45]

Cost/benefit analysis generally is more feasible for training than for many other personnel functions. Costs are relatively easy to compute: they equal direct costs of training (trainer cost, materials cost, and lost productivity,

EXHIBIT 11–9
Evaluation of usefulness of training methods

	Motivation: Active participation of learner	Reinforcement: Feedback of knowledge of results	Stimulus: Meaningful organization of materials	Responses: Practice and repetition	Stimulus-response conditions most favorable for transfer
On-the-job techniques					
Job-instruction training	Yes	Sometimes	Yes	Yes	Yes
Apprentice training	Yes	Sometimes	?	Sometimes	Yes
Internships and assistantships	Yes	Sometimes	?	Sometimes	Yes
Job rotation	Yes	No	?	Sometimes	Yes
Junior board	Yes	Sometimes	Sometimes	Sometimes	Yes
Coaching	Yes	Yes	Sometimes	Sometimes	Yes
Off-the-job techniques					
Vestibule	Yes	Sometimes	Yes	Yes	Sometimes
Lecture	No	No	Yes	No	No
Special study	Yes	No	Yes	?	No
Films	No	No	Yes	No	No
Television	No	No	Yes	No	No
Conference or discussion	Yes	Sometimes	Sometimes	Sometimes	Sometimes
Case study	Yes	Sometimes	Sometimes	Sometimes	Sometimes
Role playing	Yes	Sometimes	No	Sometimes	Sometimes
Simulation	Yes	Sometimes	Sometimes	Sometimes	Sometimes
Programmed instruction	Yes	Yes	Yes	Yes	No
Laboratory training	Yes	Yes	No	Yes	Sometimes
Programmed group exercises	Yes	Yes	Yes	Sometimes	Sometimes

From *Training in Industry: The Management of Learning*, by B. M. Bass and J. A. Vaughan. Copyright © 1966 by Wadsworth Publishing Company, Inc. Reprinted by permission of the publisher, Brooks/Cole Publishing Company, Monterey, California.

if it is done on company time) and indirect costs (a fair share of administrative overhead of the personnel department). These data can be analyzed by hand or with a computer.

Essentially, the evaluation needs to be made by comparing the results with the objectives of the training program that were set in the assessment phase. It is easier to evaluate the results of some training programs (for example, typing) than others (for example, decision making and leadership).

Harry Belman and H. H. Remmers specify the wide range of aspects of training which can be evaluated.[46] Categories that can be measured in some way are:

Purposes and goals. Achieving change in point of view, developing skills, disseminating knowledge, creating organizational atmosphere, influencing relationships, and developing individuals.

Practice, performance, and method. Trainer performance—ability to gain acceptance, understanding, and use of methods, ability to develop content; trainee performance—before and after; validity of methods—soundness of instructional procedures, applicability of instructional aids; speed or rate of learning—progress of trainees, and behavior of those with whom the trainees come in contact.

Programs. Applicability of content to a particular need; types of skills required; and kind of knowledge sought.

People. Aptitudes—learning ability; attitudes—opinions, feelings, prejudices; and behavior—reactions to situations.

Product. Quality—improvement or otherwise; quantity—increase or decrease; time—speed or rate of production; and cost—procedure for determining.

The criteria used to evaluate training depend on the objectives of the program and who sets the criteria: management, the trainers, or the trainees. For example, one study found that trainees who were asked to develop their own evaluative criteria chose standards which varied from knowledge to the amount of socializing allowed during training sessions.[47]

There are three types of criteria for evaluating training: internal, external, and participant reaction. Internal criteria are those directly associated with the content of the program. External criteria are related more to the ultimate purpose of training—for example, improving the effectiveness of the subject. Possible external criteria include job performance rating, increases in sales volume, or decrease in turnover. Participant reaction, or how the subjects feel about the benefits of a specific training or development experience, is commonly used as an internal criterion.[48]

Most experts argue that it is preferable to use multiple criteria in order to evaluate training effectively.[49] Others contend that a single criterion, such as the extent of transfer of training to on-the-job performance or other aspects of performance, is a satisfactory evaluation approach.[50]

One design for a multiple-criteria evaluation system was developed by D. L. Kirkpatrick.[51] He suggests measuring the following:

Participant reaction. Whether subjects like or dislike the program.

Learning. Extent to which the subjects have assimilated the training program.

Behavior. An external measure of changes or lack of changes in job behavior.

Results. Effect of the program upon organizational dimensions such as employee turnover or productivity.

In a survey of 110 firms, a large percentage reported assessing trainee reaction, but very few claimed to measure behavioral results.[52] It can be assumed this pattern continues, since numerous recent writers have advocated the use of behavioral results.[53] Some have suggested using the systems approach, but most studies attempting to evaluate with this approach were not too successful.[54]

A number of evaluation instruments and methods can be used to evaluate training.[55] These include:

Company records. Either existing records or those devised for the evaluation of training or development, used to measure production turnover, grievances, absenteeism, and so on.

Observational techniques. Interviewing, field observation, and so on, to evaluate skills, ability, communication, productivity, and so on.

Ratings. Judgments of ability, performance, or ratings of satisfaction with various factors.

Questionnaires. A variety of types to measure decision making, problem solving, attitudes, values, personality, perceptions, and so on.

Tests. Written examinations or performance tests to measure changes in ability or knowledge.

Data that can be used for evaluation include information on the trainee in the program; the trainee's immediate superiors and superiors above immediate supervisors; the trainee's subordinates (where applicable); nonparticipants from the work setting, including the subject's peers, company records; and nonparticipants from outside the work setting who might be affected by the program (e.g., clients).

While, as we have noted, evaluation of training is advocated more than practiced, some examples of training evaluation are worth describing.

James Cullen *et al.* evaluated training programs, with formal programs as the experimental group and on-the-job training as the control group.[56] This carefully designed and implemented study showed that formal training of blue-collar workers led to more competent workers, for less cost, in less time, with lower scrap loss and higher quality. Formally trained employees handled more of their own product problems than the control group, who tended to have more peer and superior help.

A number of other studies demonstrate the overall effectiveness of formal training of employees.[57] Other studies show that formal training is cost effective.[58]

In sum, formal training has been shown to be more effective than informal training or no training. But the results tend to be assumed rather than evaluated for most training programs.

SUMMARY, CONCLUSIONS, AND RECOMMENDATIONS

Training is a significant part of an enterprise's investment in human resources. Supervisors train new employees and retrain older ones. More experienced employees help train less experienced employees. Personnel training specialists provide technical training and coordinate the overall training effort of the enterprise.

A table of recommended training practices for the model organizations will not be given for this chapter, because each enterprise must train a variety of employee groups, each of which might require different methods and approaches. A few propositions might be useful as a form of summary, however:

> *Proposition 11.1.* The larger the organization, the more likely it is to provide formal technical training for its employees.

> *Proposition 11.2.* The greater the turnover in employment, the more important is it for the organization to provide formal technical training for employees.

> *Proposition 11.3.* The more stable the jobs are over time, the more likely is the organization to provide formal technical training for its employees.

Smaller organizations are more likely to try to hire already qualified persons or send new employees to schools or courses elsewhere. Medium-sized organizations may occasionally bring in outside trainers or send their employees to programs run by others outside. It is the larger, stable organization which will find economies of scale with organization-run training programs. If the organization is too volatile, it probably will be better off sending its employees to off-the-job programs or hiring already trained people. If it has a stable work environment, the organization can provide relevant training on its own premises economically. Thus it will develop formal training programs.

With regard to the management of training programs, these propositions seem appropriate:

> *Proposition 11.4.* Effective organizations design their training programs only after assessing the organization's and individual's training needs and setting training objectives.

Proposition 11.5.   Effective training programs carefully select and develop the trainers for the programs.

Proposition 11.6.   Effective training programs select trainees on the basis of the trainees' needs as well as organizational objectives.

Proposition 11.7.   Effective enterprises use a variety of training methods, fitting the method to the nature of the program and its objectives.

Proposition 11.8.   Effective enterprises evaluate the training programs against the program objectives (effectiveness measure) and cost benefit ratios (efficiency measures).

For training programs to be *successful,* top management must make strategic decisions to provide personnel with guidelines on its training budget and emphasis. For example, top management must indicate to personnel the strategic decisions that affect diversification or major growth or retrenchment. Personnel must react to these decisions with employment planning and training decisions. Top management must also cue personnel in on how much upgrading training it desires, to help meet EEO goals and comply with promote-from-within policies. In general, personnel and top management must cooperate to make training effective.

Chapter 12 completes the treatment of training and development by discussing management development programs.

QUESTIONS

1.   What is training?
2.   Can everyone learn or be trained?
3.   What principles of learning affect training? How?
4.   What factors in the diagnostic model affect training the most? Why?
5.   Why do enterprises perform training?
6.   Who is involved in the planning and operating of formal training in enterprises?
7.   How do training managers determine training needs and objectives? Why do they do so (or should they)?
8.   Draw the three typical learning curves. What do they mean? How do they affect training programs?
9.   What kinds of persons make good trainers?
10.   How do enterprises choose trainees? How should they?
11.   Describe the four types of training programs. When is each type effective?
12.   Describe the major training methods. Which are best?
13.   Why should enterprises evaluate training? How can they do so?
14.   What are the major propositions for Chapter 11?

NOTES AND REFERENCES

1.   This definition is based on the definition John Hinrichs gives in "Personnel Training," in *Handbook of Industrial and Organizational Psychology* ed. Marvin Dunnette (Chicago: Rand McNally & Co., 1976).

2. See, for example, Bernard Bass and James Vaughn, *Training in Industry: The Management of Learning* (Belmont, Cal.: Wadsworth Publishing Co., 1966); Irwin Goldstein, *Training: Program Development and Evaluation* (Monterey, Cal.: Brooks/Cole Publishing Co., 1974); Tom Lawson, "Gagné's Learning Theory Applied to Technical Instruction," *Training and Development Journal,* April 1974, pp. 32–39.

3. Essentially, this is my modification and elaboration on Leslie This and Gordon Lippitt, "Learning Theories and Training," *Training and Development Journal,* April 1966, pp. 2–11.

4. P. Harmon, "A Classification of Performance Objective Behaviors in Job Training Programs," *Educational Technology* 8 (1968) pp. 11–16.

5. This and Lippitt, "Learning Theories and Training."

6. John Campbell, "Personnel Training and Development," *Annual Review of Psychology* (1971), pp. 565–602.

7. Albert Bandura, *Principles of Behavior Modification* (New York: Holt, Rinehart, & Winston, 1969); also see Fred Luthans and Robert Kreitner, *Organizational Behavior Modification* (Glenview, Ill.: Scott Foresman & Co., 1975).

8. William Mirengoff and Lester Rindler, *The Comprehensive Employment and Training Act: Impact on People, Places, and Programs* (Washington, D.C.: National Academy of Sciences, 1976); "Washington Tightens Its Grasp on CETA," *Business Week,* Oct. 3, 1977.

9. "Carter's Job Policy: A Key Role for Business," *Business Week,* December 13, 1976, pp. 63–64.

10. See, for example, William Dymond, "Public Manpower Training," *The Canadian Business Review,* Winter 1974, pp. 21–25; Harish Jain and Robert Hines, "Current Objectives of Canadian Federal Manpower Programs," *Relations Industrielles* 28, 1 (1973), pp. 125–48; J. F. Lefebvre, "Canada Manpower Training Programs," *The Labour Gazette* (November 1975), pp. 822–25; Larry Truesdall, "Determinants of the Demand for Manpower Training," *Relations Industrielles* 30, 3 (1975), pp. 424–34.

11. National Industrial Conference Board, *Personnel Practices in Factory and Office: Manufacturing,* Studies in Personnel Policy 194 (New York, 1964); National Industrial Conference Board, *Office Personnel Practices: Non Manufacturing,* Studies in Personnel Policy 197 (New York, 1965); W. R. Spriegel et al., *Personnel Practices in Industry* (Austin: University of Texas, Bureau of Business Research, 1958); H. O. Holt, "Programmed Instruction," *Bell Telephone Magazine,* Spring 1963; Frederic Meyers, *Training in European Enterprises* (Los Angeles: Institute of Industrial Relations, UCLA, 1969).

12. J. S. Jenness, "Change for the Future," *Training and Development Journal* 26 (1972), pp. 2–4; Thomas Gilbert, "The High Cost of Knowledge," *Personnel,* March–April 1976, pp. 11–23. For an empirical analysis of training objectives see David Georgoff and Robert Murdick, "Learning Objectives and Business Purposes of Large Company Educational Activities (Boca Raton, Fla.: Florida Atlantic University, 1977), mimeographed.

13. Edgar Speer, "The Role of Training at United States Steel," *Training and Development Journal,* June 1976, pp. 18–21.

14. William Murray "The Role of Training at Harris Bank of Chicago," *Training and Development Journal,* December 1976, pp. 16–18.

15. George Odiorne, "Training Director–Personnel Manager: Who's in Charge Here?" *Training and Development Journal,* June 1976, pp. 3–6.

16. W. McGehee, and P. Thayer, *Training in Business and Industry* (New York: John Wiley & Sons, 1961).

17. Lance Berger, "A Dew Line for Training and Development: The Needs Analysis Survey," *The Personnel Administrator,* November 1976, pp. 51–55.

18. Edward Rundquist, "Designing and Improving Job Training Courses," *Personnel Psychology,*

Spring 1972, pp. 41–52; Robert Gallegos and Joseph Phelan, "Using Behavioral Objectives in Industrial Training," *Training and Development Journal*, April 1974, pp. 42–48; Henry Duel, "Determining Training Needs and Writing Relevant Objectives," in *Employee Training and Development in the Public Sector* ed. Kenneth Byers (Chicago: International Personnel Management Association, 1974); Richard Morano, "Determining Organizational Training Needs," *Personnel Psychology* 26 (1973), pp. 479–87; Gale Newell, "How to Plan a Training Program," *Personnel Journal*, May 1976, pp. 220–25.

19. W. Mahler and W. Monroe, *How Industry Determines the Need for and Effectiveness of Training*, Personnel Research Branch, Department of the Army, PRB Technical Research Report 929, 1952; Wendell Wood, *Identification of Management Training Needs*, unpublished Ph.D. thesis, Purdue University, 1956; Bureau of National Affairs, *Survey No. 66: Training Rank and File Employees*, Personnel Policies Forum, Survey no. 66 (Washington, 1962).

20. Bureau of National Affairs, *Survey No. 88: Training Employees*, Personnel Policies Forum, Survey no. 88 (Washington, 1969).

21. Bass and Vaughan, *Training in Industry*.

22. See, for example, current issues of the *Training and Development Journal*. Examples of the literature include: Markus Loftin, III, and Benjamin Roter, "Training Clerical Employees," in *Handbook of Modern Personnel Administration* ed. Joseph Famularo (New York: McGraw-Hill Book Co., 1972); John Gaylord, "The Development of Skills Training Courses," *Training and Development Journal*, April 1974, pp. 16–31; Calvin Otto and Rollin Glaser, *The Management of Training* (Reading, Mass.: Addison-Wesley Publishing Co., 1970), Ch. 2–4, 7, 9; Robert R. Reichenbach, "Training Professional and Technical Employees," in *Handbook of Modern Personnel Administration,* ed. Famularo; J. C. Smith, "Training Plant Employees," in *Handbook of Modern Personnel Administration,* ed. Famularo; William Tracey, *Designing Training and Development Systems* (New York: American Management Association, 1971), ch. 2, 4, 7, 12, 3.

23. Herbert Simon, *Administrative Behavior* (New York: Macmillan Co., 1946).

24. Bass and Vaughn, *Training in Industry*.

25. See, for example, Susan Christen and Frances Syptak, "Helping Women to Move Up: A Successful First Start," *Training and Development Journal*, October 1976, pp. 42–45.

26. See James Judson, "Training Continued through Plant Phase Out," *Training and Development Journal*, August 1976, pp. 22–23.

27. J. M. Smith, "Age and Retraining," *Occupational Psychology* 47 (1973), pp. 141–47.

28. Michael Gordon and Lawrence Kleiman, "The Prediction of Trainability Using a Work Sample Test and an Aptitude Test: A Direct Comparison," *Personnel Psychology* 29 (1976), pp. 243–53.

29. Roger Roderick and Joseph Yaney, "Developing Younger Workers: A Look at Who Gets Trained," *Journal of Management*, Spring 1976, pp. 19–26.

30. Cal McKerral, "Labour Legislation in 1974, Part VII: Apprenticeship and Tradesmen's Qualification," *The Labour Gazette*, October 1975, pp. 735–40.

31. William Franklin, "A Comparison of Formally and Informally Trained Journeymen in Construction," *Industrial and Labor Relations Review*, July 1973, pp. 1086–94.

32. A sample includes: *National Apprenticeship and Training Standards for the Sheet Metal Industry* (1972); *National Apprenticeship and Training Standards for Painting and Decorating and Drywall Finishing* (1976); *National Apprenticeship and Training Standards for the Graphic Arts International Union* (1975); *National Apprenticeship and Training Standards for Dental Technicians* (1975).

33. McGehee and Thayer, *Training in Business and Industry*.

34. Fred Wickert, "The Famous JIT Card: A Basic Way to Improve It," *Training and Development Journal*, February 1974, pp. 6–9.

35. NICB, *Office Personnel Practices;* NICB, *Personnel Practices in Factory and Office.*

36. S. B. Utgaard and R. V. Davis, "The Most Frequently Used Training Techniques," *Training and Development Journal* 24, 2 (1970), pp. 40–43.

37. E. H. Fox, "Programmed Learning," *Personnel Administration* 11 (1966), pp. 1–9; John Murphy, and Irving Goldberg. "Strategies for Using Programmed Instruction," *Harvard Business Review,* May–June 1964, pp. 115–32; Hinrichs, "Personnel Training."

38. Leonard Silvern, "Training: Man-Man and Man-Machine Communications," in *Systems Psychology* ed. Kenyon De Greene (New York: McGraw-Hill Book Co., 1970), pp. 383–405.

39. Ibid.

40. R. C. Atkinson and H. A. Wilson (eds.), *Computer Assisted Instruction* (New York: Academic Press, 1969); Hinrichs, "Personnel Training."

41. Thomas F. Stroh, *The Uses of Video Tape in Training and Development,* AMA Research Study 93 (New York: American Management Association, 1969).

42. Bass and Vaughn, *Training in Industry.*

43. Stephen Carroll, Jr. et al., "The Relative Effectiveness of Alternative Training Methods for Various Training Objectives," *Proceedings,* Midwest Academy of Management, 1970, pp. 298–318.

44. See, for example, Herbert Engel, *Handbook of Creative Learning Exercises;* Norman Maier, *Psychology in Industrial Organizations* (Boston: Houghton Mifflin Co., 1973), pp. 316–24.

45. For example, see, Robert S. Dvorkin, "Evaluation of Training," in *Handbook of Modern Personnel Administration* ed. Famularo; Franz Fauley, "Cost Models: A Study in Persuasion," *Training and Development Journal,* June 1975, pp. 3–8; Willard Wirtz and Harold Goldstein, "Measurement and Analysis of Work Training," *Monthly Labor Review,* September 1975, pp. 19–26.

46. Harry Belman and H. H. Remmers, "Evaluating the Results of Training," *Journal of the American Society of Training Directors* 12 (1958), pp. 28–33.

47. W. B. Eddy et al., "Organization Effects on Training," *Training and Development Journal* 21, 2 (1967), pp. 15–23.

48. Andrew J. Dubrin, *The Practice of Managerial Psychology* (New York: Pergamon Press, 1972).

49. See, for example, J. P. Campbell et al., *Managerial Behavior, Performance and Effectiveness* (New York: McGraw-Hill Book Co., 1970).

50. W. Biel, "Training Programs and Devices," in *Psychological Aspects in Systems Development* ed. Robert Gagné (New York: Holt, Rinehard & Winston, 1962); David Wood and Lawrence W. Head, Jr., "Field Evaluation of Training," *USAF Instructors Journal,* Winter 1969–70, pp. 19–23.

51. D. L. Kirkpatrick, "Techniques for Evaluating Training Programs," *Journal of the American Society for Training Directors* 13, 14 (1969–70).

52. Ralph Catalanello and D. Kirkpatrick, "Evaluating Training Programs," *Training and Development Journal* 22, 5 (1968), pp. 2–9.

53. See, for example, Gerald E. Mirsberger, "The Four Crucial Phases of Evaluation," *Training,* August 1974, pp. 34–35; Munro H. Stell, "An Organized Evaluation of Management Training," *Personnel Journal,* October 1972, pp. 723–27.

54. Yoram Zeira, "The Systems Approach to Management Development: Studies in Frustration and Failure," *Organizational Dynamics,* Fall 1974, pp. 65–80.

55. The list that follows is adapted from Robert House et al., *Management Development: Design Evaluation and Implementation* (Ann Arbor: University of Michigan, 1967).

56. James Cullen et al., "Training: What's It Worth?" *Training and Development Journal,* August 1976, pp. 12–20.

57. See, for example, F. B. Chaney and K. S. Teel, "Improving Inspector Performance through Training and Visual Aids," *Journal of Applied Psychology* 51, 4 (1967), pp. 311–15; Joel Lefkowitz, "Effect of Training on the Productivity and Tenure of Sewing Machine Operators," *Journal of Applied Psychology,* February 1970, pp. 81–86; William G. Mollenkopf, "Some Results of Three Basic Skills Training Programs in an Industrial Setting," *Journal of Applied Psychology,* October 1969, pp. 343–47.

58. See, for example, S. Gubins, *"The Impact of Age and Education on the Effectiveness of Training: A Benefit Cost Analysis"* Baltimore: Johns Hopkins Press, 1970; E. Manuel, *Final Report, Human Resources Management System: Project Evaluation,* Ozarks Regional Commission, 1970; Loren C. Scott, "The Economic Effectiveness of On-the-job Training: The Experience of the Bureau of Indian Affairs in Oklahoma," *Industrial and Labor Relations Review,* January 1970, pp. 220–36; Brinley Thomas et al., "A Cost-Benefit Analysis of Industrial Training," *British Journal of Industrial Relations,* July 1969, pp. 231–64.

Development of managers and professionals

CHAPTER OBJECTIVES

■ To demonstrate why employers try to develop the abilities and interpersonal skills of managerial and professional employees.

■ To illustrate how managerial and professional employees are developed on and off the job.

■ To help you understand the major techniques used to develop professional and managerial employees and their advantages and shortcomings.

CHAPTER OUTLINE

CHAPTER OUTLINE, CONTINUED

In the discussion of employee training in Chapter 11, the approaches and techniques for improving performance and satisfaction applied largely to operative, clerical, and service employees. This chapter extends the topic to include development programs and training for managers and professionals.

Managers and professionals are crucial in effective decision making for the enterprise, and therefore most enterprises want to be sure these personnel are all up to date and well motivated. The main focus of this chapter is management development; some reference will be made to development of professionals, but less is known about this aspect of development.

Some of the material on employee training applies to this chapter too. The diagnostic model factors are similar. For example, the major points made in the "Managing the Training Program" section also apply to management and professional development programs.

DEFINITION

Management development is the process by which managers gain the experience, skills, and attitudes to become or remain successful leaders in their enterprises.

Management and professional development is closely related to other personnel activities. A management development program may be a consequence of an employment planning forecast that the enterprise needs more managers, the career plans of employees formulated in career development, or the results of performance evaluation and promotion—ratings of an employee may indicate a high potential for development.

Effective management development requires full support and participation by top management. Supervisors and middle managers look to top management to see if this activity is valued. When management development is valued, it is more efficient and successful. Operating managers help develop other managers and professionals in on-the-job experiences. Personnel specialists and outside consultants help the process along in off-the-job programs and by coordinating the total program.

Top management makes the final decision as to the development programs to be conducted in the enterprise. Diana Pheysey and others have pointed out that development programs are based on different sets of values.[1] Some encourage rational, emotionless decision making; others seek to involve emotions in decision making and the workplace. (see Exhibit 12–1). These programs can be used to reinforce current behavior patterns or to try to change them. She points out that these programs are part of the total environment of work (Exhibit 12–2).

Pheysey's research points out why top managers must involve themselves

EXHIBIT 12–1
Typology of manager's ability and attitude training precepts

Mental precepts *Social precepts*	*Be flexible* (*innovation oriented*)	*Be systematic* (*certainty oriented*)
Be open (*risk oriented*)	Outspoken ideas man Bombastic intellectual	Candid systematizer Unsophisticated bore
Be guarded (*security oriented*)	Diplomatic ideas man Intellectual intriguer	Salt of the earth Deadwood

EXHIBIT 12–2
Context of managers' tasks and management development in the work environment

Economic, political and social structure of the environment
Planned systematically, allowing spontaneous modification

Structure of organizations
Carefully designed, allowing spontaneous modification

Structure of groups
Formally laid down, with scope for informality

Managers' activities
systematic, flexible

5 4 3 2 1   INTELLECTUAL AND EMOTIONAL
INFORMATION PROCESSING

Managers' methods of working
Open, guarded

Norms of groups
self-expressive, self-controlled

Climate of organizations
Developmental, controlling

Culture of the environment
Permissive, law-abiding

in management development decisions: so they will not wake up and find
values that conflict with their own being developed in the enterprise, or
different units reinforcing different values and climates, which could lead
to an increase in intergroup conflict. This is not to suggest that top management could or should manipulate the organization's climate without regard

to employees' preferences. The point is that management development decisions could have a significant impact on the enterprise, and they deserve strategic consideration.

PURPOSES OF MANAGEMENT DEVELOPMENT

The general purposes of management development parallel those discussed for employee training. These include:

- To increase the effectiveness of managers and professionals.
- To increase the satisfaction of the employee.
- To satisfy the requirements of EEO/human rights programs.[2]
- To reduce or prevent managerial obsolescence. This will be examined at some length.

Obsolescence

> **DEFINITION**
> Obsolescence exists when the person holding a position lacks the current skills and knowledge generally considered important by other managers and professionals to maintain effective performance in current or future work.

Obsolescence can occur because managers have not kept up with changing techniques of doing their jobs effectively, or the jobs they have been doing may no longer be needed, and the managers may fail to adjust to the needs of other available jobs.

Obsolescence varies in the degree to which it can be overcome. In the form that can be coped with most easily, the manager has become obsolete and knows it. He is not using the newest approaches, and this is hurting his performance. But he is aware that this is the case. Next in degree of difficulty is the manager who is unaware of his obsolescence. In both of these forms, when obsolescence does become recognized, retraining may be possible. The most difficult form is the manager who knows he is obsolete at the gut level but denies it at the conscious level and refuses help.

There are probably three major causes of managerial obsolescence. One is technological obsolescence: Some fields change quickly, and it is hard to keep up. A second cause is the "Peter principle," which operates when managers are promoted, often against their wishes, to jobs for which they were not qualified and which they cannot handle. Finally, there is the aging process. Some persons find it hard to stay motivated and to keep up as they get older.

Obsolescence, however, does not affect all employers equally. If the environment of the organization is volatile or the technology of the job is not stable, there will be a greater likelihood that managers presently on the job will be obsolete.[3] There will be more obsolescent managers in a managerial group comprised of older people and fewer in a group which is composed of capable and motivated managers.[4]

How extensive is obsolescence? One study estimated that obsolescence could characterize from 2 to 25 percent of all managers.[5] This study and others found that obsolescence was greatest in the over-55 age group and among engineering personnel. It has also been found that those with the most education and strongest work ethic motivations are *least likely* to be obsolete.[6]

Herbert Kaufman has summarized a vast literature on studies of obsolescence among professional and technical employees.[7] To Kaufman, obsolescence is lack of new capabilities which the employee never had. He finds that age is not *the* major explanation for obsolescence. The major factor is limited intellectual and cognitive abilities and low motivation, personal rigidity, and low self-esteem. To prevent obsolescence, Kaufman prescribes better selection, evaluation, career counseling, and flexibile personnel policies. He also prescribes job redesign to provide more challenge, in line with his conclusion that the lack of challenging jobs is the most crucial cause of obsolescence. He also believes that obsolescence will be reduced by more professional involvement in decision making and job rotation into jobs requiring new skills; here management development or additional training is crucial.

As to what can be done about managerial obsolescence, Frank Bird offers three choices: (1) change the job, which can lead to other useful work or featherbedding; (2) change the manager through management development programs; or (3) retire or fire the manager.[8] Relatively few companies use the third choice; most prefer the second. Management development as a solution to obsolescence among managers and professionals is the topic of this chapter.

USE OF MANAGEMENT AND PROFESSIONAL DEVELOPMENT PROGRAMS

Whether an enterprise has a management or professional development program depends a great deal on its size. Smaller enterprises rarely run their own formal development programs; they are informal at best. Larger enterprises have elaborate formal programs combining on-the-job with off-the-job development. Others, such as the U.S. military, Exxon, and AT&T, have established large, complex training and development centers for their managers. The Federal Executive Institute at Charlottesville, Virginia, is set up to develop federal government executives, as is the Executive Seminar Center in Berkeley, and California, the U.S. Post Office Center in Norman, Oklahoma.

Formal management development programs exist in almost all large and medium-sized institutions in the United States and Canada and many smaller enterprises as well.[9] There has been tremendous growth in this area in the last thirty years and the trend is still upward. Perhaps as many as 1,000,000 executives per year participate in off-the-job management development exercises.[10] Still, management development is a Stage II personnel function: Most people do it, but scientific evaluation of its results is slim.

MANAGEMENT AND PROFESSIONAL DEVELOPMENT TECHNIQUES

Once the organization has seen the need for management and professional development, it must determine how to develop or redevelop its managers and professionals. Some of the training techniques used in employee development (described in Chapter 11) also apply to management development. The emphasis in this section will be on effective techniques used *primarily* in management and professional development programs.

Experts have noted that effective management development requires a positive attitude toward self-development by the individual manager.[11] No elaborate management development system is of any use if the manager is not aware of the need for change and development or is not willing to expend the energy to change. The organization can try to induce this awareness in the manager and can reinforce such desires, but, essentially, effective management development springs from a personal desire for continuous self-development on the part of the manager.

Organizations can have formal or informal management development programs. There are two ways an organization can formally and consciously seek to develop its executives. One is to devise a mix of on-the-job experiences which the organization feels are optimal for its experienced executives. The second approach is formal management development experiences which take place off the job; in these, the executive or future executive leaves the job for a period to obtain additional ability or attitude training and development.

On-the-job experience

There are four thrusts to on-the-job management development:

- Coaching and counseling in the present position.
- Transition to new job experiences while staying at the old job.
- Self-improvement programs.
- Job rotation and transfer career plans.

These programs are not mutually exclusive; often they are run simultaneously.

On-the-job management development is the preferred type from many points of view. One of the major difficulties with off-the-job development is relevance and reinforcement in the job situation. For example, the literature offers many examples of managers who did well in a T group but then made no changes in their work behavior. Properly developed, on-the-job development is relevant and will be reinforced in the superior-subordinate dyad.

Coaching and counseling. One of the best methods of developing new managers is for effective managers to teach them. The coach-superior sets a good example of how to be a manager. He also answers questions and explains why things are done the way they are. It is the coach-superior's obligation to see to it that the manager-trainee makes the proper contacts so that the job can be learned easily and performed in a more adequate way. In some ways, the coach-superior–manager-trainee relationship resembles the buddy system. Many of the points made about counseling in Chapter 9 should be kept in mind here.

One technique the superior may use is to have decision-making meetings with the trainee at which procedures are agreed upon. If the trainee is to learn, the superior must give him or her enough authority to make decisions and perhaps even make mistakes. Myles Mace's studies of coaching led him to stress how important it is for the superior to develop a climate for learning.[12] This not only provides opportunities to learn, it requires effective delegation, which develops a feeling of mutual confidence. Appropriately chosen committee assignments can be used as a form of coaching and counseling.

Although most organizations use coaching and counseling as either a formal or an informal management development technique, it is not without its problems. Harry Levinson found that coaching and counseling fail when inadequate time is set aside for them, the subordinate is allowed to make no mistakes, rivalry develops, or the dependency needs of the subordinate are not recognized or accepted by the superior.[13] Chris Argyris points out that coaching reinforces or perpetuates current executive styles, which may not be desirable. He also says the system fails when the superior is not rewarded for effective coaching or the system will not allow the subordinate to make mistakes.[14]

Despite these difficulties, coaching and counseling are probably the most widely used management development techniques and often yield good results. There has been little systematic study of or evaluation of these techniques, however, so it is difficult to demonstrate their effectiveness. One exception is a study of thousands of executives which found that the major shortcoming in coaching and counseling was infrequent counseling to tell subordinates what they must do to qualify for a promotion and to offer concrete suggestions for improvement. They found that managers could be divided into two groups: Those who were skilled enough and cared enough to coach subordinates and those who were not.[15] Another expert argues that on-the-job techniques such as counseling are essential to effective development, and off-the-job approaches are only supplements.[16] In sum, many experts contend that coaching and counseling, when coupled with planned job rotation through jobs and functions, is an effective technique. It can fit the manager's background and utilizes the principle of learning by doing, which has been proven effective. Finally, the method involves the supervisors, which is essential to successful management development.[17]

Transitory, anticipatory experiences. Another approach to management development is to provide transitory experiences. Once it has been determined that a person will be promoted to a specific job, provision is made for a short period before the promotion in which he learns the new job, performing some of his new duties while still performing most of his old ones. This intermediate position is labeled differently in various organizations as assistant to, understudy, multiple management, or management apprenticeships.

The main characteristic of this type of program is that it gives a person likely to hold a position in the future partial prior experience. In some approaches, the trainee performs a part of the actual job; thus, an assistant to does some parts of the job for the incumbent. In multiple management, several decision-making bodies make decisions about the same problem and compare them—a junior board or group's decisions are compared to those of senior management groups. Another variation is to provide trainees with a series of assignments that are part of the new job in order to train them and broaden their experience.[18]

To the extent that transitory experiences simulate the future job and are challenging, and the trainees' supervisors are effective managers themselves, they seem to provide an eminently reasonable approach to management development. Little systematic study has been made of the effectiveness of this approach, however, and it appears to be used less often than coaching or counseling.

Self-improvement programs. The third approach to on-th-job experience is a self-improvement program pursued while on the job. The manager may take a correspondence course or study individually at home to improve job skills, attend local professional association meetings in the evenings or at lunchtime, and take part in *annual or quarterly* professional meetings.[19] This approach was discussed in Chapter 9; it overlaps the off-the-job approach to be discussed shortly.

Transfers and rotation. The fourth on-the-job approach, trainees are rotated through a series of jobs to broaden their managerial experience. Enterprises that develop programmed career plans which include a mix of functional and geographic transfers were described in Chapter 9.

Advocates of rotation and transfer contend that this approach broadens the manager's background, accelerates the promotion of highly competent individuals, introduces more new ideas into the organization, and increases the effectiveness of the enterprise.[20] But some research evidence questions this. Individual differences affect whether or not the results will be positive, and generalists may not be the most effective managers in many specialized positions.[21]

Geographic transfers are desirable when fundamentally different job situations exist at various places. They allow new ideas to be tried instead of meeting each situation with the comment, "We always do it that way here." As in many other types of development, trained supervisors can make this technique more effective.[22]

I have examined geographic transfers in two field studies, using field interviews and questionnaries completed by over 500 executives. These studies led to these major conclusions:

1. There appear to be about a quarter of a million executive geographic transfers yearly. These seem to be caused by (in the order of importance): a need for a particular type of executive at a location (employment need), career planning and management development, and physical relocation of facilities.[23]

2. Although there are studies indicating that some executives are frequently transferred, less than 18 percent of 500 executives I questioned had been transferred three or more times. About 50 percent had been transferred once.

3. Executives have mixed feelings about geographic transfers. In general, managers who have been transferred feel it is an excellent management development tool. They do not feel the companies consult them sufficiently before they are transferred, however. Nor do they feel they are sufficiently compensated to offset the costs of moving.[24]

There has been other negative reaction to transfers. A report by Tricor Relocation Management Company found that in 1975 42 percent of the companies reported employees refusing to be transferred. This was a huge increase from prior years. Where a person is being transferred to affects refusals. The cities most often refused are New York, Cleveland, Detroit, Chicago, and most small towns; those with few if any refusals include San Francisco, Atlanta, Los Angeles, Boston, Houston, and Dallas. Native New Yorkers frequently will not transfer from there, however.[25]

In general, because of the perceived relevance of on-the-job experience, it should be provided in management development programs. Because of individual differences in development and rewards by organizations, however, off-the-job development programs should supplement them where expertise is not readily available inside the organization. Exclusively on-the-job programs lead to a narrow perspective and the inhibition of new ideas coming into the organization.

Development off the job

The other major approach to professional and management development is off-the-job programs. In these programs, the employee participates in a series of events that are removed from the work situation. Off-the-job programs are designed to develop or increase abilities or interpersonal skills and managerial attitudes.

Development programs for professionals such as scientists and engineers usually involve their return to universities or research centers for seminars, or sabbaticals may be granted for work leading to postdoctoral programs or advanced degrees. In the development of managers, a number of approaches are used.

Many large enterprises run their own advanced management programs; examples include General Electric's Crotonville facility, IBM at Sands Point, CPC in Brussels, Motorola in Tucson, the U.S. Army War College, and the Federal Executive Institute in Charlottesville. In other enterprises, the personnel staff or consultants run programs at various work sites. Professional associations such as the American Management Association and the Conference Board also run extensive management development programs.

Another source of management development programs is the universities, especially the colleges of business administration or management. Many of them offer advanced management programs, running from a few weeks to summer-long sessions; information on these has been compiled in an annual directory.[26] In general, most managers attending these programs are quite satisfied with them.[27] Some enterprises handle management development by enrolling their managers in the nearest MBA program.

TECHNIQUES FOR DEVELOPING MANAGERIAL ABILITIES

The techniques used for developing managerial abilities attempt to simulate real managerial situations. The most frequently used techniques are discussed below.

The case method

One widely used technique is the case method. A case is a written description of a real decision-making situation. Trainees are asked to study the case to determine problems, analyze them for their significance, propose solutions, choose the best solution, and implement it. More learning takes place if there is interaction between the trainer and trainees and among trainees.

The case method lends itself more to some kinds of material (business policy) than to others (linear programming). It is not the most efficient method for presenting well-structured material, such as statistical theory. It is easier to listen to a lecture and be given a formula than to tease the formula out of a case, for example. With proper trainers and good cases, the case method is a very effective device for improving and clarifying rational decision making. Little research has been done to provide data on which it could be evaluated, however. One study found that cases presented in film form are more effective than written cases.[28]

Variations on the case method. Variations of the case method include the incident method and the demand technique.[29] In the incident method, just the bare outlines of the situation are given initially, and the students are assigned a role in which to view the incident. Additional data are available if the students ask the right questions. Each student "solves" the case, and groups based on similarity of solutions are formed. Each group then formulate a strong statement of position, and the groups debate or role play their solutions. The instructor tells what actually happened in the case and the consequences, and everyone compares their solutions with the results. The final step is for participants to try to apply this knowledge to their own job situations.

Role playing

Role playing is a cross between the case method and attitude development programs (to be described shortly). Each manager being developed is assigned a role in a training situation (such as a case) and asked to play the role and to react to other players' role playing. The player is asked to pretend he or she is a focal person in the situation and to react to the stimuli as that person would. The players are provided with background information on the situation and the other players, there are no scripts. Sometimes the role plays are videotaped and reanalyzed as part of the development situation. Often role playing is done in trainee groups of a dozen or so persons.

The success of this method depends on the ability of the players to play the assigned roles believably.[30] Evidence on role playing effectiveness is mixed.[31]

The task model

Another method is the task model. In this approach a work group is asked to make a complex object that can be constructed by following complicated instructions.[32] The task model is used to illustrate communication difficulties. There are few data evaluating this method's effectiveness.

The in-basket technique

Another method used to develop managerial decision-making abilities is the in-basket technique. This approach has been used for managerial selection (separately, or as part of an assessment center package), as well as for management development.

The trainee is given a box of material which includes typical items from a specific manager's mail and a telephone list. Important and pressing matters such as out-of-stock positions, customer complaints, or the demand for a report from a superior are mixed in with routine business matters such as a request to speak at a dinner or a decision on the date of the company picnic four weeks hence. The trainee is analyzed and critiqued on the number of decisions made in the time period allotted, the quality of decisions, and the priorities chosen for making them.[33]

Felix Lopez examined data on 3,000 executives who used in-basket exercises in company settings and 726 who participated in American Management Association exercises. He found that trainess like the method and that it is useful in predicting future effectiveness.[34] Other studies support this.[35] Lopez also showed that it is reliable in scoring. It is expensive, however.

The Kepner-Tregoe technique. A method related to in-basket management development utilizes the Kepner-Tregoe "rational manager" concept.[36] Thousands of executives have been trained using this technique, which centers around the fictional Apex Company with 400 employees. It utilizes the case, incident, in-basket, and role-playing methods.

The Kepner-Tregoe technique resembles the case method in that material about the company is provided in writing ahead of time. It involves role playing in that each trainee is assigned one of four roles for the company: production manager, sales manager, purchasing and shipping manager, or division general manager. The people playing these roles have their own offices; they talk to one another on the phone and have meetings to solve problems. They play each role for a 90-minute segment dealing with a specific problem before they switch roles, and they are evaluated on how well they do in each role. The method is similar to the incident method in that all managers do not have all the information; they must seek some of it from the most likely manager, as in real life. The data are provided in case form and in an in-basket with memos, phone calls, and letters to which the manager must attend during the exercise. Some problems are more urgent than others, and they must sort the important from the unimportant, gather the right data for good decisions, and so on. At the end of each segment there are feedback and critique sessions.

The originators, Charles Kepner and Benjamin Tregoe, claim the following results from these sessions: better awareness of the manager's decision process, better problem solving, and (if work teams take the exercise together) better understanding of the decision processes of the management team. An in-basket exercise which introduces further stress and spontaneity into the situation utilizes a film depicting a vice president demanding immediate solution of additional problems, which is shown intermittently.[37]

This method of training appears to utilize many useful constructs for learning, such as simulation of reality, multiple media, and time pressures. It stresses rational, step-by-step decision making as the only effective approach, which may not be equally useful for all decision problems. Although the Kepner-Tregoe approach appears useful, no scientific reliability or validity studies have been reported on its usefulness.

Synectics

One approach which attempts to deal with nonprogrammed decision training and to stimulate creativity in decision making is synectics, or the development of creative capacity. William Gordon defines the creative process as "the mental activity in a problem stating, problem solving situation where artistic or technical inventions are the result."[38] Creative strategic decisions can be regarded as analogous to these results. Gordon contends that intuition, deferment, play, involvement, empathy, irrelevance, and detachment are vital to creativity. They are also almost impossible to teach, however. Synectics has created mechanisms to simulate these characteristics through analogies that are direct and personal or symbolic and fantastical. It seeks to make the strange familiar and the familiar strange through creativity.

Gordon suggests that synectics can lead to greater creative efficiency in people by showing them how creativity takes place. Those supporting synectics contend that the emotional component of invention is more important than its intellectual component. They also argue that the emotional and irrational elements of problem solving, where they are properly understood, increase the probability of success.

Gordon cites a series of cases in which synectics has been used effectively in creative situations. Less is generally known about it than about the other methods discussed here.

Management games

Essentially, management games describe the operating characteristics of a company, industry, or enterprise. These descriptions take the form of equations which are manipulated after decisions have been made. The games became popular when computer usage became widespread.

Modern simulation exercises have been traced to the board war games developed by the Prussian army.[39] The first widely known business game was developed by the American Management Association in 1956 as an outgrowth of military war games. There are now literally hundreds of games.

In a typical operation, teams of players are asked to make a series of operating (or top-management) decisions. In business games, for example, the players may be asked to decide on such matters as the price of the product, purchase of materials, production scheduling, funds borrowing, marketing, and R&D expenditures. When each player on the team has made his decision, the interactions of these decisions are computed (manually or by computer) in accordance with the model. For example, if price is linearly related to volume, a decrease in price of X percent will affect the volume, subject to general price levels. Players on the team must reconcile their individual decisions with those of the other team members prior to the final decision. Then each team's decisions compete with those of the other teams. The output is how much profit, market share, and so forth each team has won in the competition. The results are given to the participants, who then make their next decisions.

Games are used to train managers in all sectors. The government uses games at the Air Force Institute of Technology, the Department of State, and the Industrial War College, for example. Business tends to use them extensively too. Some games are used to train managers in specific functions, such as Mahoney and Milkovich's game for personnel managers.[40]

Advantages of games include the integration of several interacting decisions, the ability to experiment with decisions, the provision of feedback experiences on decisions, and the requirement that decisions be made with inadequate data, which usually simulates reality. The main criticisms of most games concern their limitation of novelty or creativity in decision making, the cost of development and administration, the unreality of some of the models, and the disturbing tendency of many participants to look for the key to win the game instead of concentrating on making good decisions. Many participants seem to feel the games are rigged and a few factors or even a single factor may be the key to winning.

Are games effective training mechanisms? In a content analysis of a random sample of books and articles on the effectiveness of games, the researchers found that although games led to high participant interest and motivation and participant recognition of the interrelationships in decisions, the empirical evidence of effectiveness was mixed: "actually very little empirical support exists for their use . . . neither game effectiveness nor ineffectiveness appear to be confirmed by the available empirical evidence."[41]

Audiovisual aids

No discussion of training would be complete without mentioning that audiovisual and other training aids have an important role to play in improving the effectiveness of off-the-job development. The tools used vary from blackboards to films and videotapes. Good guides for their use are available.[42]

DEVELOPING INTERPERSONAL SKILLS AND ORGANIZATION DEVELOPMENT

Besides training individuals to make better decisions and improving specific managerial abilities, management development also involves interpersonal skills and managerial attitudes. It can be argued that effective interpersonal skills are also abilities, but these programs have as their goals the changing of attitudes as well as the development of skills.

Organizations enter into attitude-change and interpersonal skills training programs for many reasons. One is to improve the effectiveness of their employees, especially managers, in their day-to-day work or in specific programs. The latter might be designed to improve meetings and conferences or to help employees adjust their attitudes toward overseas assignments.[43] A second and very important purpose is to help the organization's managers understand themselves better and be better prepared to cope with modern living.

Some programs designed to affect managerial attitudes are oriented toward the attitudes, interpersonal skills, and organization climate of whole organizational units. These programs, which are called *organization development* (OD), generally take as the ideal what I called the liberal organization and liberal leadership style in Chapter 2.

The earliest programs designed to affect managerial attitudes, called *human relations programs,* were oriented toward individual managerial development. Human relations programs were an outgrowth of the human relations movement, which fostered consideration of the individual in the operation of industry in the 1930s to the 1950s. The rationale of the movement for enterprises was that an employee-centered, liberal supervisory style would lead to more satisfied employees. This in turn would reduce absenteeism, employee turnover, and strikes. Sometimes the style also increased performance. But, as was discussed in Chapter 2, effective performance has multiple causes, and supervisory attitudes and behavior are only one factor influencing it.

The effectiveness of these general human relations programs has been measured by direct improvement in objectively measured results, such as a reduction in turnover. They have also been called effective if they change the attitudes of the managers in the direction desired or if the managers participating say the programs were worthwhile. In reviewing the evidence in 1970, John Campbell et al. found that 80 percent of the programs evaluated had significant positive results, as measured by attitudes and opinions about these programs.[44]

There are a number of other programs that could be described. The ones that will be emphasized here are behavioral modeling–interaction management, transactional analysis, sensitivity training, and organization development.

Behavior modeling–interaction management

A relatively new approach to training supervisors and middle managers in interpersonal skills is behavior modeling, which is also called interaction management. The traditional training model could be modeled as in Exhibit 12–3. In behavior modeling, as developed by A. P. Goldstein and M. Sorcher,[45] the development model is as shown in Exhibit 12–4.

The behavior modeling–interaction management (BMIM) approach begins by identifying 19 interpersonal problems that managers face. Typical problems are: gaining acceptance as a new supervisor, handling discrimination complaints, delegating responsibility, improving attendance, effective disci-

EXHIBIT 12–3
Model of traditional training program

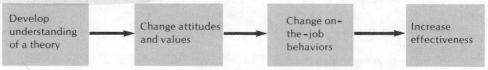

From *Training: Program Development and Evaluation* by I. L. Goldstein. Copyright © 1974 by Wadsworth Publishing Company, Inc. Reprinted by permission of the publisher, Brooks/Cole Publishing Company, Monterey, California.

EXHIBIT 12–4
Model of behavior modeling training program

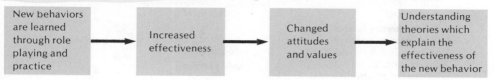

| New behaviors are learned through role playing and practice | → | Increased effectiveness | → | Changed attitudes and values | → | Understanding theories which explain the effectiveness of the new behavior |

pline, overcoming resistance to change, setting performance goals, motivating average performance, handling emotional situations, reducing tardiness, and taking corrective action.

There are four steps in the process:

1. Modeling of effective behavior—often by use of films.
2. Role playing.
3. Social reinforcement—Trainees and trainers praise effective role plays.
4. Transfer of training to the job.

A typical BMIM training module is shown in Exhibit 12–5.

In BMIM, the principles of learning described in Chapter 11 are applied to the development situation. Exhibit 12–6 shows how.

BMIM has been introduced into a number of enterprises, including AT&T, General Electric, IBM, RCA, Boise Cascade, Kaiser Corporation, Olin, B. F. Goodrich, and others. So far, the research evidence is generally positive. In a series of studies, the groups trained in BMIM have outperformed those

---

EXHIBIT 12–5
BMIM module

Administrator announces the interaction skill being considered and the supervisors read an overview of the interaction skill .... 5 minutes
Administrator describes critical steps in handling the interaction .... 5 minutes
Administrator shows a film or video tape of a supervisor effectively handling the interaction with an employee .... 10 minutes
Administrator and supervisors discuss how the supervisor depicted handled the critical steps .... 5 minutes
Three supervisors take turns in skill practice exercises by handling similar situations with employees. Background information is provided the "supervisor" and "employee" in each skill practice exercise. The handling of the situations is observed by the other supervisors and the administrator using specially prepared Observer Guides. The use of positive reinforcement by the observers helps to build confidence and skill in skill-practicing supervisors .... 60 minutes
Supervisors write their own interaction situations based on job-related problems, using forms provided in workbooks .... 10 minutes
Supervisors take turns in skill practice sessions by becoming the "employee" in the participant-written situations, while other supervisors use the interaction skills to handle these situations. These skills practice exercises are also observed and discussed .... 60 minutes
Supervisors read a summary of the skill module. Using specially designed forms, they plan on-the-job applications of the interaction skills. The administrator hands out a Critical Steps card for supervisors to utilize on the job .... 10 minutes

Source: William Byham and James Robinson, "Interaction Management: Supervisory Training that Changes Performance," *The Personnel Administrator*, February 1976.

EXHIBIT 12–6
Learning theory principles applied to BMIM (*conditions for effective learning*)

Learning principles	*BMIM method*
Principles whereby learner:	
Is motivated to improve	
Understands desired skills	Modeling
Actively participates	Role playing
Gets needed practice	
Gets feedback on performance	Social reinforcement
Is reinforced for appropriate skills	
Experiences well-organized training	
Simple to complex	Transfer of training
Easy to hard	
Undergoes training performance akin	
to job	

Source: Allen Kraut, "Developing Managerial Skills via Modeling Techniques," *Personnel Psychology* 29 (1976), pp. 325–28.

who received no training or traditional management development training.[46] BMIM appears to have a bright future.

Transactional analysis

One of the newer management and organization development programs is transactional analysis (TA). One survey found that it was rarely used in small companies and occasionally used in medium-sized, large, and very large firms.[47]

Transactional analysis was originally developed by Eric Berne to be used in psychotherapy. Since then, its application has spread to mental counseling, family counseling, and the world of work. TA uses Gestalt therapy and Berne's analysis to help people understand themselves and achieve better self-awareness, responsibility, and genuineness. It focuses on *now* as opposed to the Freudian emphasis on the past. Its goal is to make those who undergo the analysis "winners"—that is, people who respond authentically to others by being credible, genuine, responsive, and trustworthy, who understand themselves and appreciate others and who are self-reliant. "Losers" are not genuine persons and "play games" instead of communicating and behaving honestly.[48]

The analytical technique Berne uses is his description of the personality structure. According to Berne, the personality structure is composed of the Parent, the Adult, and the Child. Although Berne sees differences, I believe his analysis is an adaptation of Freud's superego, ego, and id (see Chapter 2). But the analysis of interactions, communications, and behavior is much more direct in transactional analysis than in Freudian analysis.

For purposes of transactional analysis, each person's personality has a Parent, Adult, and Child ego state. The Parent tends to be righteous, dogmatic, evaluative, and protective. The Adult is the reasoning ego state. It seeks factual discussion in decisions and interactions. The Child is dependent,

EXHIBIT 12–7
Complementary transactions in parent, adult, and child ego states

$\mathbb{P}$ = Parent; $\mathbb{A}$ = Adult; $\mathbb{C}$ = Child.

Source: Muriel James, "The OK Boss," *Psychology Today,* February 1976.

selfish, and rebellious. The child desires immediate satisfaction, is emotional, and seeks approval.

When two people interact, they face each other with one of the three ego states predominating. This leads to two possible transactions:

1. *Complementary.* The ego states match. For example, both persons operate in the adult ego state. Exhibit 12–7 exemplifies complementary transactions in a business setting.

2. *Crossed.* The two persons are operating in different ego states that do not parallel each other. Exhibit 12–8 gives examples of these relationships between business associates.

EXHIBIT 12–8
Crossed transactions in parent, adult, and child ego states

$\mathbb{P}$ = Parent; $\mathbb{A}$ = Adult; $\mathbb{C}$ = Child.

Source: Muriel James, "The OK Boss," *Psychology Today,* February 1976.

Transactional analysis points out that all interactions involve "stroking." By this, TA people mean any verbal and nonverbal signal of recognition and approval or disapproval. Positive verbal stroking is shown in Exhibit 12–7 A, B, and D; negative verbal strokes are illustrated in Exhibit 12–8 A, B, and C.

Few studies have been done on the effectiveness of the technique, but those who have used it tend to approve of its results, and those who have not are usually dubious.[49] In a study of TA at General Telephone, the researchers found significantly lower turnover in employees supervised by those trained in TA than the control group, and the benefit cost ratio is good.[50] TA should have a significant impact on management and professional development programs and OD in the future.

Sensitivity training

Probably the most controversial and most investigated form of attitude-change–interpersonal skills training is sensitivity training (ST). Sensitivity training is also called T-group training, encounter-group training, and by other terms.

The many approaches to sensitivity training vary in the degree to which the training is structured, the role of the trainer, the mix of the emotional and rational in the training, and the focus of the training: on the individual, the group, or the total organization. All tend to have these characteristics in common:

There is a permissive atmosphere to encourage free discussion.

There is an unstructured agenda; the members partially determine the subject of the meetings.

The learning takes place by nonlecture methods. Typically the members learn by the experience in the meetings.

Frustration is likely when the meeting seems to wander.

Just as the style of the training varies, so do its objectives. In some, the objectives are personal growth and self-understanding. In other, more structural approaches, some job-centered problems are introduced.

Sensitivity training has been criticized for being expensive, for invading trainees' privacy, for hastening breakdowns, and for lack of carryover into the workplace. Although it was a very popular technique in the 1960s, it seems to have declined severely by the late 1970s.

The evidence is mixed on whether sensitivity training achieves its objectives.[51] Individual differences influence its effectiveness, as George Strauss noted in a review of the literature. He believes it is most likely to be effective on persons who are open to new ideas prior to ST, have high levels of interpersonal trust, participate most during ST, change most during ST, and have the power to introduce changes at work.[52]

I participated in a ST group in the late 1960s.[53] Based on that experience and a literature review, I believe that ST could be useful to a person whose job requires frequent interaction with others, who also knows little about interpersonal skills, and whose personality is such that self-revelation is not threatening. It can be a powerful mechanism for attitude change and development, but it should be used only on *carefully chosen managers* and for positions that *require sensitive interpersonal skills* for successful execution of the job.

Organization development

One type of development which overlaps several of the methods already discussed is organization development (OD), which seeks to change attitudes, values, organization structure, and managerial practices to improve performance. There are a number of variations of organization development, but some of the more common characteristics are:

The focus of the development is the total organization, not the individual or a small group of individuals.

The methods used are group discussions, team-building exercises, confrontation meetings, and intergroup conflict experiences. Thus the primary methodology is experiential learning.

A consultant or change agent is used as a facilitator or catalyst.

Organization development frequently takes place in a series of phases.

1. *Initial diagnosis.* The consultants seek to determine the organization's problems.
2. *Data collection.* After the initial diagnosis, the consultant surveys the enterprise extensively to find out the problem and possible solutions.
3. *Feedback and confrontation.* The consultants feed their findings back to the group and set priorities for change.
4. *Planning–problem solving.* The problem-solving groups begin to solve the problems chosen for solutions.
5. *Team building.* The consultant uses role play, sensitivity training, and games to strengthen the bonds of the problem-solving groups (teams).
6. *Intergroup development.* The consultant develops bonds between teams to build larger groups.
7. *Follow-up and evaluation.* The consultant analyzes the results against the objectives of OD.

How effective is organization development? That is hard to say; Strauss notes that "as a rapidly evolving field, OD presents a moving target, making it difficult to define or criticize." Strauss has identified eight common forms of OD, for example. Most of the studies have been done by OD consultants, and most show positive results in terms of employee satisfaction. Strauss points out that since the consultants are in the business of selling OD, it is unlikely that they would report its failures.[54] There have been about five studies indicating that OD increases productivity or organizational effectiveness, although in all the studies it was only one of several changes taking place at the time.[55]

In sum, it appears plausible that organizations development can help increase productivity and satisfaction. But much more research is needed before we know what kind of OD, in which kind of organizations, and under what conditions.

Other programs

New training programs aimed at changing managerial interpersonal skills are always appearing. For example, Kepner and Tregoe now offer Telos, a program based on a leadership model which utilizes on-line computer feedback.[56] And Robert Blake and Jane Mouton, of Managerial Grid fame, now offer Critiqube.[57]

Sometimes, MBO systems and approaches are used in organization and management development. A survey of ASPA members and personnel professors found that MBO was used rather widely in medium-size and larger companies and occasionally in smaller ones. Top and middle managers were widely involved. The MBO programs were rated as moderately successful, and most felt the benefits justified their costs.[58]

It would be impossible to review all the development programs being offered today. This chapter has touched on only a few.

COST/BENEFIT ANALYSIS OF DEVELOPMENT

> Never ask of money spent
> Where the spender thinks it went.
> Nobody was ever meant
> To remember or invent
> What he did with every cent.
> —Robert Frost

To some extent, Frost is right, of course. Still, the funds and time spent on development could be used elsewhere by the enterprise, so it is worthwhile evaluating it. (Chapter 11 also discussed this subject.) Though there have been many articles and books advocating scientific analyses of development costs and benefits, most cost/benefit analyses of management development programs take the form of participant evaluation. Few participants are negative, since in many organizations participating in the program is a sign that you are a "comer" and will be promoted.

Many researchers feel that participant evaluation is a poor way to analyze the costs and benefits of a program.[59] Others feel it is quite satisfactory.[60] Some evaluation studies are quite negative on off-the-job development programs. For example, Robert Pearse studied the reactions of 2,000 managers to management development. In general, they felt that on-the-job development, self-study, and self-development were much more effective than off-the-job development programs. They were especially critical of in-house programs by company trainers and implied that better off-the-job development might be somewhat effective.[61]

A number of criteria of effectiveness of development programs could be used. One way to measure developmental effectiveness would be to measure management obsolescence. If managerial obsolescence is rather low for a particular company in a particular industry, the management development program may be a factor. Management development programs, however informal, are essential for the survival and effectiveness of an organization. How much to spend on them and what methods to use are the only significant cost/benefit questions.

SUMMARY, CONCLUSIONS, AND RECOMMENDATIONS

Chapter 11, "Employee Training" and this chapter on management development could comprise a unit on training and development. This chapter has concentrated on professional and managerial development.

Management development is the process by which managers gain the experience, skills, and attitudes to become or remain successful leaders in their enterprises. Management and professional development is designed to reduce obsolescence, to increase employee satisfaction and productivity, and to expedite EEO goal achievement.

Obsolescence exists when the jobholder lacks the skills necessary to meet current performance expectations. Three propositions about obsolescence are:

> *Proposition 12.1* The more volatile the envionment of the organization or the job, the higher will be the proportion of obsolescent managers in the job.

> *Proposition 12.2.* The older the managerial group, the higher will be the percentage of obsolescent managers.

> *Proposition 12.3.* The greater the abilities and motivation of the managers, the lower will be the obsolescence rate.

Proposition 12.4 indicates which organizations are likely to have which kinds of management development programs:

> *Proposition 12.4.* The larger the organization, the more likely it is to provide formal management development training for its managers, potential managers, and professionals.

The chapter reviewed a series of management development techniques. These include on-the-job techniques such as coaching and counseling, transition experiences, job rotation and transfers, and self-improvement programs. Proposition 12.5 summarizes the findings about on-the-job programs.

> *Proposition 12.5.* Effective management development programs emphasize on-the-job development programs and supplement them with off-the-job experiences and programs.

EXHIBIT 12–9
Recommendations on management development programs for model organizations

Type of organizations	Formal program	Informal program	On-the-job programs	Off-the-job programs
1. Large size, low complexity, high stability	X		X	X
2. Medium size, low complexity, high stability	X		X	
3. Small size, low complexity, high stability		X	X	
4. Medium size, moderate complexity, moderate stability	X		X	X
5. Large size, high complexity, low stability	X		X	X
6. Medium size, high complexity, low stability	X		X	
7. Small size, high complexity, low stability		X	X	

Next the major off-the-job programs designed to improve managers' abilities and interpersonal skills and attitudes were discussed. The major ability techniques described included the case method, role playing, the task model, in-baskets, synectics, and games. Then the major programs designed to affect managerial attitudes and improve interpersonal skills were described. The major programs currently are: behavior modeling–interaction management (BMIM); transactional analysis (TA); sensitivity training (ST); and organizational development (OD).

Two propositions appear in order here:

> Proposition 12.6. The more complex and volatile the organizational environment and set of goals, the more diverse will the content and emphasis of the management development program be.

> Proposition 12.7. If an effective leadership style has been developed and now pervades the organization, past leaders' experiences will influence the content of management development programs strongly.

The recommendations for use of management development programs in the model organization defined in Exhibit 1–14. (Chapter 1) are listed in Exhibit 12–9.

The final section of the chapter discussed evaluations of management development programs though cost/benefit analysis. To be effective, management and professional development must be fully supported and receive adequate budget support from top management. Many studies have shown that middle and supervisory managers make better use of these programs if they perceive top management's support of them.

This chapter completes Part Four. Compensation and benefits for employees is the topic of Part Five.

QUESTIONS

1.   What is management development?

2.   Why do enterprises have management and professional development programs?

3.   What is obsolescence? How does it develop? How can it be reduced?

4.   Which kinds of organizations are most likely to have management development programs? Why?

5.   What are the major on-the-job management development programs? Which are the best programs? Why?

6.   Describe the major management development programs designed to improve managerial abilities. Which do you like the best?

7.   Describe the major management development programs designed to improve interpersonal skills and affect managerial attitudes. Describe the ones you'd urge your supervisors to develop so that you could participate in them.

8.   Can you evaluate (in cost/benefit terms) today's management development programs? If so how?

9.   What are the major recommendations of this chapter? Its most crucial propositions?

NOTES AND REFERENCES

1.   Diana Pheysey, "Management Skills Training and Company Structure and Climate," *Management Education and Development* 1 (1971) pp. 137–50; Diana Pheysey, "Individual Skills and Organizational Requirements," University of Aston (England) mimeographed, 1971; Diana Pheysey, "Managers' Occupational Histories, Organizational Environments, and Climates for Management Development," *Journal of Management Studies* 14, 1 (1977), pp. 58–79.

2.   For example, Susan Christen and Frances Syptak, "Helping Women to Move Up: A Successful First Step," *Training and Development Journal,* October, 1976, pp. 42–45; Bette Stead, "Educating Women for Administration," *Business Horizons,* April 1975, pp. 51–56; Elizabeth Bolton and Luther Humphreys, "A Training Model for Women—An Androgynous Approach," *Personnel Journal,* May 1977, pp. 230–34; 255 ff.

3.   Elmer Burack and Gopal Pati, "Technology and Managerial Obsolescence," *MSU Business Topics,* Spring 1970, pp. 49–56; Steven Zelikoff, "On the Obsolescence and Retraining of Engineering Personnel," *Training and Development Journal,* May 1969, pp. 3–14.

4.   William Henry, "Conflict, Age, and the Executive," *MSU Business Topics,* Spring 1961, pp. 15–25.

5.   Frederick Haas, *Executive Obsolescence,* AMA Research Study 90 (New York: American Management Association, 1968).

6.   Ibid.; See also, Lawrence Baughler and John Lee, "Personal Obsolescence: The Employee's Perspective," *Southern Journal of Business,* November 1971, pp. 52–61; Richard Shearer and Joseph Steger, "Manpower Obsolescence," *Academy of Management Journal,* June 1975, pp. 263–75.

7.   Herbert Kaufman, *Obsolescence and Professional Career Development* (New York: Amacon, 1974).

8.   Frank Bird, "The Displaced Executive, or The Man on the Shelf," *MSU Business Topics,* Summer 1966.

9.   On Canadian programs, see Harish Jain, "Education and Training of Managers in the

Canadian Manufacturing Industry," *Canadian Personnel and Industrial Relations Journal,* January 1975, pp. 30–36.

10. John P. Campbell et al., *Managerial Behavior, Performance and Effectiveness,* (New York: McGraw-Hill Book Co., 1970). Later data include "The Big Business of Teaching Managers," *Business Week,* July 25, 1977, pp. 106–8.

11. See, for example, Harry Levinson, "A Psychologist Looks at Executive Development," *Harvard Business Review,* 40 (1962), pp. 69–75.

12. Myles Mace, "The Supervisor's Responsibility toward His Subordinates," in *Developing Executive Skills* (New York: American Management Association, 1958.

13. Levinson, "Psychologist Looks at Executive Development."

14. Chris Argyris, "Puzzle and Perplexity in Executive Development," *Personnel Journal* 39 (1969), pp. 463–65 ff.

15. Walter Mahler and William Wrightnour, *Executive Continuity* (Homewood, Ill.: Dow Jones–Irwin, 1973) ch. 6, 7.

16. Charles Bowen, Jr., "Let's Put Realism into Management Development," *Harvard Business Review,* July–August 1973, pp. 80–87.

17. See Yoram Zeira, "Introduction to Management Development," *Personnel Journal,* December 1973, pp. 1049–55; Yoram Zeira, "Job Rotation for Management Development," *Personnel,* July–August 1974, pp. 25–35.

18. Roger O'Meara, "Off the Job Assignments for Key Employees," *Manpower Planning and Programming,* ed. Elmer Burack and James Walker (Boston: Allyn & Bacon, 1972), pp. 339–46.

19. See Sidney Siegel, "The Night School MBA: Long Investment, Low Return," *The MBA,* May 1976; John Steele and Lewis Ward, "MBA's: Mobile, Well Situated, and Well Paid," *Harvard Business Review,* January–February 1974, pp. 99–110.

20. Eugene Jennings, *The Mobile Manager* (Ann Arbor: University of Michigan, 1967); John Veiga, "The Mobile Manager at Mid Career," *Harvard Business Review,* January–February 1973), pp. 115–19; Robert Pitts, "Unshackle Your 'Comers'," *Harvard Business Review,* May–June 1977, pp. 127–36; Robert Pitts, "Developing Division Level Managers; Correlates of Interdivisional Managerial Transfers," *Proceedings,* Academy of Management, 1977, pp. 43–47.

21. Eugene Jennings, "The Supermobile," *Human Resources Management* 11, 1 (1972), pp. 4–17; S. D. Saleh and V. Pasricha, "Job Orientation and Work Behavior," *Academy of Management Journal,* September 1975, pp. 638–45; Jerome Saroff, "Is Mobility Enough for the Temporary Society?" *Public Administration Review,* September–October 1974, pp. 480–86; John Costello, "Why More Managers Are Refusing Transfers," *Nation's Business,* October 1976, pp. 4–5.

22. Dwight Sargent, "The Job Rotation Method," in *Developing Executive Skills* eds. H. Merrill and E. Marting (New York: American Management Association, 1958), pp. 124–30.

23. William F. Glueck, "Management Development and Geographic Transfers," *Journal of Management Studies* 6, 2 (1969), pp. 243–51.

24. William F. Glueck, "Managers, Mobility and Morale," *Business Horizons,* January–February 1975, pp. 65–70. For other studies of transfers see Eleanor Dienstag, *Whither Thou Goest* (New York: E. P. Dutton & Co., 1976).

25. Jay Galbraith and Anders Adstrom, "Internation Transfer of Managers: Some Important Policy Considerations," *Columbia Journal of World Business,* Summer 1976, pp. 100–112; Taking the Jolts Out of Moving," *Nation's Business,* November 1975, pp. 36–38; "Moving on Loses Its Glamor for More Employees," *The Wall Street Journal,* August 3, 1976, p. 1; Michael Baer, "Employee Desires in Residential Relocation Situation," *Human Resource Management,* Fall 1974, pp. 19–22.

26.   *Bricker's Directory of University Sponsored Executive Development Programs* (South Chatham, Mass., annually).

27.   Kenneth Andrews, *The Effectiveness of University Management Development Programs* (Cambridge: Harvard Business School, 1966); "A Guide to Executive Education," *Business Week,* March 8, 1976, pp. 79–85.

28.   Tad Green and Morton Cotlar, "Do Filmed Cases Improve the Case Method?" *Training and Development Journal,* May 1973, pp. 28–31.

29.   Paul Pigors and Faith Pigors, *Case Method in Human Relations: The Incident Process* (New York: McGraw-Hill Book Co., 1961); C. Potter and G. Strachan, "Project Training Groups: A 'Demand' Technique for Middle Managers," *Training Directors Journal* 19 (1965), pp. 34–41.

30.   Norman Maier et al., *Supervisory and Executive Development* (New York: John Wiley & Sons, 1957).

31.   Michael Gold et al., "The Effect of Role Playing in a Problem Solving Situation," *Industrial Management Review* 6, 1 (Fall 1964); Melvin Sorcher and Arnold Goldstein, "A Behavior Modeling Approach in Training," *Personnel Administration,* March-April 1972, pp. 35–40; C. H. Lawshe, et al., "Studies in Management Training Evaluation," *Journal of Applied Psychology* 43 (1959), pp. 29–33; J. Maxwell Towers, *Role Playing for Managers* (Oxford: Pergamon Press, 1974).

32.   J. Keltner, "The Task Model as a Training Method," *Training Director's Journal* 19 (1965), pp. 18–21.

33.   Felix Lopez, *Evaluating Executive Decision Making: The In-Basket Technique,* AMA Research Study 75 (New York: American Management Association, 1966); L. Crooks, "Issues in the Development and Validation of In-Basket Exercises for Specific Objectives," Research memorandum 68–23 (Princeton N.J.: Educational Testing Service, 1968); Calvin Otto and Rollin Glaser, *The Management of Training* (Reading, Mass.: Addison-Wesley Publishing Co., 1970), ch. 9.

34.   Lopez, *Evaluating Executive Decision Making.*

35.   See, for example, J. Meyer, "The Validity of the In-Basket Test as a Measure of Managerial Performance," *Personnel Psychology* 23 (1970), pp. 297–307.

36.   Charles Kepner and Benjamin Tregoe, *The Rational Manager* (New York: McGraw-Hill Book Co., 1965).

37.   G. Gibson, "A New Dimension for 'In Basket' Training," *Personnel* 38 (1961), pp. 76–79.

38.   William Gordon, *Synectics: The Development of Creative Capacity* (New York: Harper & Row, 1961).

39.   Kalman Cohen and E. Rhenman, "The Role of Management Games in Education and Research," *Management Science,* January 1961, pp. B–131–66.

40.   Thomas Mahoney and George Milkovich, "The Use of a Computer Based Simulation in Manpower Management Education," *Proceedings,* Academy of Management 1975, pp. 240–42.

41.   Janet Schriesheim and Chester Shriesheim, "The Effectiveness of Business Games in Management Training," *Training and Development Journal,* May 1974, pp. 14–17.

42.   Otto and Glaser, *Management of Training,* ch. 13–18; Herbert Engel, *Handbook of Creative Learning Exercises* (Houston: Gulf Publishing Co., 1973); For several applications, see Richard Kritzer, "The Use of Videotape in Behavioral Change," *Public Personnel Management,* July–August 1974, pp. 325–31; Robert Hess, "A Supervisory Development Program: On Videotape," *Personnel Journal,* January 1977, pp. 34–36.

43. Harvey Hornstein and Noel Ticky, "Developing Organization Development for a Multi National Corporation," *Columbia Journal of World Business,* Summer 1976, pp. 124–37.

44. Campbell et al., *Managerial Behavior.*

45. A. P. Goldstein and M. Sorcher, *Changing Supervisory Behavior* (New York: Pergamon Press, 1974).

46. Robert Burnaska, "The Effects of Behavior Modeling Training upon Manager's Behaviors and Employee's Perceptions," *Personnel Psychology* 29 (1976), pp. 329–35; William Byham et al., "Transfer of Modeling Training to the Job," *Personnel Psychology* 29 (1976, pp. 345–49; William Byham and James Robinson, "Interaction Modeling: A New Concept in Supervisory Training," *Training and Development Journal,* February 1976, pp. 25–33; Joseph Moses and Richard Ritchie, "Supervisory Relationships Training: A Behavioral Evaluation of a Behavior Modeling Program," *Personnel Psychology* 29 (1976), pp. 337–43.

47. Jack Rettig and Matt Amano, "A Survey of ASPA Experience with Management by Objectives, Sensitivity Training and Transactional Analysis," *Personnel Journal,* January 1976, pp. 26–29.

48. Eric Berne, *Transactional Analysis in Psychotherapy* (New York: Ballantine 1961); Eric Berne, *Games People Play* (New York: Ballantine Books, 1964); Muriel James and Dorothy Jongeward, *Born to Win* (Reading, Mass.: Addison-Wesley Publishing Co., 1971); Dudley Bennett, "Transactional Analysis in Management," *Personnel,* January–February 1975, pp. 34–44.

49. Rettig and Amano, "Survey of ASPA Experience."

50. Donald Ely and John Morse, "TA and Reinforcement Theory," *Personnel,* March–April 1974, pp. 38–41.

51. Peter Smith, "Controlled Studies of the Outcome of Sensitivity Training," *Psychological Bulletin* 82, 4 (1975), pp. 597–622; Rolf Loeber and R. G. Weisman, "Contingencies of Therapist and Trainer Performance: A Review," *Psychological Bulletin* 82, 5 (1975), pp. 660–668; Campbell et al., *Managerial Behavior;* George Strauss, "Organization Development," in *Handbook of Work, Organization and Society* ed. Robert Dubin (Chicago: Rand McNally & Co., 1976).

52. Strauss, "Organization Development."

53. William Glueck, "Reflection on a T-Group Experience," *Personnel Journal* 47 (1968), pp. 500–504.

54. Strauss, "Organization Development."

55. H. Stanley Steelman, "Is There a Payoff to OD?" *Training and Development Journal,* April 1976, pp. 18–23.

56. Victor Vroom and Phillip Yetton, *Leadership and Decision Making* (Pittsburgh: University of Pittsburgh Press, 1973).

57. Robert Blake and Jane Mouton, *The Managerial Grid* (Houston: Gulf Publishing Co., 1964); Robert Blake and Jane Mouton, "Some Effects of Managerial Grid Seminar Training on Union and Management Attitudes towards Supervision," *Journal of Applied Behavioral Science* 2 (1966), pp. 387–400; Robert Blake et al., "Breakthrough in Organization Development," *Harvard Business Review,* November–December 1964, pp. 133–55; Robert Blake and Jane Mouton, *Critique* (Austin, Tex.: Scientific Methods, Inc., 1976).

58. Rettig and Amano, "Survey of ASPA Experience."

59. Campbell et al., *Managerial Behavior.* I. L. Goldstein, *Training: Program Development and Evaluation* (Monterey, Cal.: Brooks/Cole Publishing Co., 1974) ch. 4, 5; A. F. Jurkus et al., "An Application of Quasi-Experimental Design in the Evaluation of a University Sponsored Management Development Program," *Proceedings,* Academy of Management, 1973, pp. 16–18.

60. John Burgoyne, "The Judgment Process in Management Students' Evaluation of Their Learning Experiences," *Human Relations,* August 1975, pp. 543–69.

61. Robert Pearse, *Manager to Manager* (New York: Amacon, 1974). One exception to the statement in the text about how few good cost/benefit studies there are is, Richard Steiner and Frank Kelly, "A Key Factors Approach to Assessing Management Development," *Personnel Journal,* July 1975, pp. 344, 348 ff., 358–61.

Compensation, benefits, and services

Part Five discusses a very important set of personnel activities: compensation, benefits, and services.

Chapter 13 introduces the subject of compensation and pay. It discusses the potential impact of pay on employees and discusses pay level, pay structure, and individual pay determination. Chapter 14 completes the pay discussion by focusing on incentives and pay schemes, managerial compensation, and several significant policy issues regarding compensation.

Chapter 15 covers all benefits and services except for pensions. The potential impact of benefits and services is outlined, as are the major benefits employers provide employees in the United States and Canada.

Chapter 16, the final chapter in Part Five, focuses on retirement policies and a very important benefit: pensions. It is considered separately from the other benefits because of the legal requirements for pensions and their complex nature.

An introduction to compensation

CHAPTER OBJECTIVES

■ To show how employee preferences and motivation affect pay.

■ To show how environmental influences and internal factors affect pay levels and policy.

■ To discuss pay surveys and how they help management assess its pay status relative to comparable enterprises.

■ To discuss how internal enterprise factors influence pay levels and pay policies.

■ To show how to evaluate jobs and set up a pay structure.

■ To help you understand how individual pay determination is done.

CHAPTER OUTLINE

CHAPTER OUTLINE, CONTINUED

INTRODUCTION

In June 1977, a *Time* cover story was entitled "The Hot New Rich." In this article, the authors describe many people who have become very rich at a very young age: rock stars like Peter Frampton, writers like Coleen McCullough, sports stars like Muhammed Ali, and business persons like Alan Silverstone, the bubblegum king. The article points out that in the United States in 1976, there were 200,000 persons who had net worths of $1,000,000 or more; 1,200 make more than $1,000,000 per year. Many of them are motivated by these kinds of incomes to work harder or to be smarter.

In the same article, a perennial issue was raised: Should people like rock stars and boxers make so much money? Some typical salaries for various jobs were given: a typical Yale assistant professor makes $14,750; a New York garbage collector is paid $16,350. A minister in Chicago is paid $10,500 but a disc jockey in Detroit makes $100,000. A U.S. Senator is paid $57,500 while a pilot of a 747 is paid $80,000. A bus driver in Atlanta makes $13,500, an over-the-road truck driver makes $30,000, and a teacher is paid $8,000. A vice president of Anheuser Busch makes $115,000, and a Washington trial lawyer, $500,000.[1]

Why are these salaries so different? Should they differ so widely? Is a garbage collector or assembly-line worker really worth more than a Yale professor? This chapter will address the question: how are salaries determined? The equity question will also be discussed briefly. Basically, the major differences in pay are due to our economic system, and they exist because the alternative methods of assigning salaries are no better or have not been tried extensively.[2]

At last, then, we're going to talk about money and pay. Compensation is part of a transaction between an employee and an employer which results in an employment contract.

From the employee's point of view, pay is a necessity in life. Few people are so wealthy they do not accept financial remuneration for their work. The compensation received for work is one of the chief reasons people seek employment. Pay is the means by which they provide for their own and their family's needs. For the person with an instrumental attitude toward work (as discussed in Chapter 2), compensation may be the only (or certainly a major) reason why they work. Others find compensation a contributing factor to their efforts. Pay can do more than provide for the physiological needs of employees, however: it can also serve their recognition needs.

Compensation is one of the most important functions in the personnel functions for the employer, too. Compensation often equals 50 percent of the cash flow of an enterprise, and a larger percentage in service enterprises. It may be the major method used by an enterprise to attract the employees needed to get the work done, as well as a means to try to motivate more effective performance.

Compensation is also significant to the economy. For the past 30 years, salaries and wages have equaled about 60 percent of the gross national product of the United States and Canada.

> DEFINITION
> Compensation is the monetary reward paid by an enterprise for the work
> done by an employee.

Note that compensation or pay is only one way the employee is rewarded for work. Work also provides benefits (Chapters 15, 16), promotions and status (Chapter 11), intrinsic rewards of the job, and other rewards.[3] The relative importance of pay to the other rewards varies with the employee, as will be seen shortly.

Objectives of compensation

The objective of a compensation system is to create a system of rewards which is equitable to the employer and employee alike, so that the employee is attracted to the work and *motivated* to do a good job for the employer. Thomas Patten suggests that in compensation policy there are seven criteria for effectiveness.[4] The compensation should be:

Adequate. Minimum governmental, union, and managerial levels should be met.

Equitable. Each person is paid fairly, in line with his or her effort, abilities, training, and so on.

Balanced. Pay, benefits, and other rewards provide a reasonable total reward package.

Cost effective. Pay is not excessive, considering what the enterprise can afford to pay.

Secure. The employee's security needs relative to pay and the needs which pay satisfies

Incentive providing. Pay motivates effective and productive work.

Acceptable to the employee. The employee understands the pay system and feels it is a reasonable system for the enterprise and himself.

Compensation and other personnel activities

Exhibit 13–1 shows how compensation is related to other activities in the personnel function. Employment planning (Chapters 4, 5) affects the pay package offered to attract employees. The enterprise knows what it can afford, given the industry and the budget on profitability. This affects beginning compensation and recruiting (Chapter 6) and the number and quality of applicants. If the enterprise is unionized, the beginning pay is also affected by the collective bargaining process (Chapter 19). Once the employee for an enterprise, is working later collective bargaining negotiation

EXHIBIT 13–1
Relationship of compensation to other personnel activities

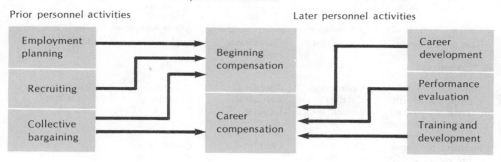

affects the pay over the life of the career. Merit, as determined by performance evaluation (Chapter 10), affects pay, as does additional training and development (Chapters 11, 12). The employee's career development plan (Chapter 9) also influences the trend of the person's pay throughout the career.

Compensation decision makers

Three groups of managers are involved in compensation decisions. The first are personnel executives; the personnel department develops the pay system and administers it. For smaller enterprises, the personnel specialist does this as part of the total job. When an enterprise has more than about 500 employees, a compensation manager (also called wage and salary administrator) may be made responsible for the compensation activity. The compensation administrator is a consultant, coordinator, catalyst, and implementer of the system, which is designed in conjunction with top managers and the chief personnel executive. A Prentice-Hall/ASPA survey of 1,400 personnel managers found that personnel executives rate compensation as their second or third most important activity.[5]

The roles of the compensation manager relative to other managers are identified in Exhibit 13–2. Operating managers make the raise decisions, for example, but a crucial factor is the policy decisions made by top management. As will be seen shortly, they determine the pay policies of the enterprise (for example, pacesetter or follower in the industry). Top managers make the decisions which determine the total amount of the budget that goes to pay, the form pay will take (time v. incentive) and other pay policies such as raise levels, secrecy and communication policies, security in pay policies, and executive compensation. Compensation decisions generally are made by operating management (as advised by personnel) and administered and implemented by personnel.

EXHIBIT 13–2
The roles of a compensation manager

Activity	Top management	Senior management	Middle management	First-line management– operative employees
Base compensation	Consultant	Coordinator	Implementer	Implementer
Job evaluation		Implementer		
Pay surveys				
Employee benefits	Coordinator	Coordinator	Coordinator	Coordinator
Employee security	Catalyst	Consultant	Consultant	Consultant
Time not worked	Consultant	Catalyst	Catalyst	Catalyst
Employee services				
Incentive programs	Consultant	Coordinator	Coordinator	Coordinator
Individual pay for	Coordinator		Implementer	Implementer
performance			Catalyst	Catalyst
Cost reduction			Consultant	Consultant
Profit sharing				
Base-pay premiums				
Dangerous-job				
premiums				

Top management: chief executive officer, president, and senior vice-president.
Senior management: regional, divisional, and functional managers and senior professionals.
Middle management: department and unit managers, superintendents, professionals, and senior paraprofessionals.
First-line management–operative employees: foremen, supervisors, paraprofessionals, skilled craftsmen, technicians, and semiskilled and unskilled laborers.

Source: Richard Henderson, "The Changing Role of the Wage and Salary Administrator," *Personnel*, November–December 1976, pp. 56–63.

Compensation is a Stage IV personnel function. It is mature in that all work organizations compensate employees, and there is a good deal of empirical data with which to analyze the relative effectiveness of various compensation methods.

Compensation decisions

Perhaps you believe that pay can be determined by a manager and employee sitting down and talking it over, or you think the government or unions determine pay. In fact, pay is influenced by a series of internal and external factors. The diagnostic approach will be used to help you understand these factors better.

Pay can be determined absolutely or relatively. Eliott Jaques and others have argued that a pay system set by a single criterion for a whole nation or the world, an absolute control of pay, is the best procedure.[6] However, in one of the few recorded attempts to use this approach, in Denmark, it was not a great success.[7] Since absolute pay systems are not used, the pay for each individual is set *relative* to the pay of others.

Allen Nash and Stephen Carroll point out that pay for a particular position is set relative to three groups.[8] These are:

• Employees working on similar jobs in other enterprises (Group A).

• Employees working on different jobs within the enterprise (Group B).

• Employees working on the same job within the enterprise (Group C).

The decision to examine pay relative to group A is called *the pay-level decision;* we will consider this first. The objective of the pay-level decision is to keep the enterprise competitive in the labor market. The major tool used in this decision is the pay survey. The pay decision relative to group B is called *the pay-structure decision* and uses an approach called job evaluation. The decision involving pay relative to group C is called *individual pay determination.*

Consider Joe Johnson, a maintenance worker at a plant. Joe's pay is affected first by the pay-level policy of his enterprise. Is it a high-pay enterprise (a pace-setter), or does it pay the going wage? Next his pay is affected by how highly ranked *his* job is relative to other jobs, such as tool and die worker. Finally, his pay depends on how good a maintenance man he is, how long he has been with the enterprise and other individual factors (individual pay determination).

Chapter 13 begins with an examination of pay levels, which are influenced by the factors shown in the diagnostic model in Exhibit 13–3. The diagnostic approach to compensation is introduced, and the impact of external and internal factors on the pay-level decision is considered. Then pay structures in the enterprise are examined, and finally individual pay determination is explained. Chapter 14 completes the discussion on pay by describing pay methods, executive pay, and compensation policies.

A DIAGNOSTIC APPROACH TO COMPENSATION

Exhibit 13–3 highlights the diagnostic factors most important to compensation as a personnel activity. The nature of the task affects compensation primarily in the method of payment for the job, such as payment for time worked or incentive compensation, which depends on the task performed. These issues, and executive compensation, which differs in many ways from other types, are discussed in Chapter 14.

One of the most significant factors in compensation is the nature of the employee. How employee attitudes and preferences directly affect performance is discussed in the section below. Employee attitudes and preferences also affect the pay structure, which is discussed later in the chapter.

There are other external and internal factors that affect compensation. The factors external to the enterprise influencing pay are the government, unions, economic conditions, and labor market conditions. Enterprise factors are managerial goals and pay structures and size and age of the enterprise. Discussion of these factors in the sections below will illustrate why people are paid the amounts they receive and which methods are used to pay people.

EXHIBIT 13–3
Factors affecting compensation and organizational effectiveness

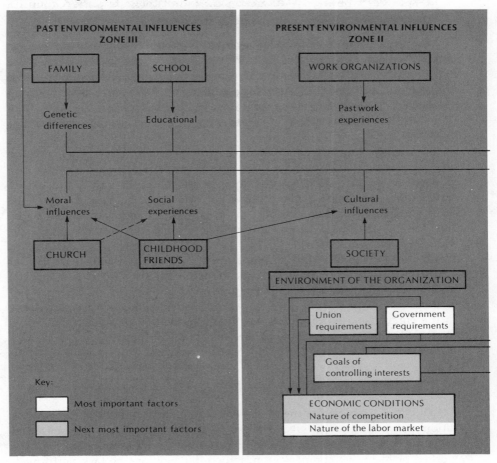

COMPENSATION AND EMPLOYEE SATISFACTION AND PERFORMANCE

Does a well-designed pay system motivate employees to greater performance, higher quality performance, or greater employee satisfaction? The answer to this question has varied from the yes of scientific management in the early 1900s to the no of human relations theorists in the 1930s. The controversy still rages, and I am not sure we can settle this age old-dispute here, but the various positions will be presented. All would agree that effective compensation administration is a desirable factor in increasing employee satisfaction. Where they differ essentially is on the desirability of incentive compensation schemes to increase production. Those saying yes favor them; those saying no do not.

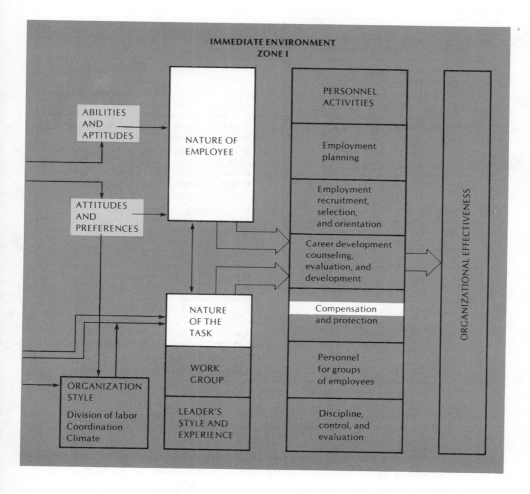

We can tie this discussion to the motivation theories described in Chapter 2. Exhibit 13–4 portrays the answers each theory would give to the question: Will incentive pay motivate greater performance?

Various scholars working in behaviorism or behavior modification have examined how money could become a generalized conditional reinforcer of behavior,[9] a conditioned incentive,[10] or an anxiety reducer.[11] In general, these theorists believe that, under the proper conditions, money can affect employee's work behavior positively.

In his studies of motivation, Frederick Herzberg found that often money is a hygiene factor—that is, it did not affect behavior. If pay could be tied more directly to performance, however, it *could* become a motivator of behavior.[12]

Applying Abraham Maslow's needs theory to pay leads to the conclusion

EXHIBIT 13–4
How motivation theories answer the question: Will incentive pay motivate greater performance?

Theories*	Answers: (yes; yes, if; no, if)
Behaviorism, behavior modification	Yes.
Herzberg's two-factor theory: motivators/hygiene	Yes, if pay can be tied to performance—money is a motivator. No, if pay is not tied to performance—money is a hygiene factor.
Maslow's hierarchy of needs	Yes, if the strongest needs are physiological, safety, or recognition. No, if the strongest needs are social or self actualization.
McClelland/Atkinson's needs theory	Yes, if pay is seen as a means to power or as a measure of achievement. No, if social needs are paramount.
Korman's consistency theory	Yes, if the self-concept includes money as a strong measure of achievement. No, if this is not so.
Equity theory	Yes, if pay is perceived to be equitable. No, if pay is perceived to be inequitable.
Expectancy theory	Yes, if pay and what it buys is a strong need (valence), and if pay is tied to performance and employees believe they will receive the added pay for added performance (expectancy). No, if these two conditions are not met.

* See Chapter 2 for details and references on these theories.

that pay can serve many needs—physiological, security, and recognition, especially—as indicated in a summary of the research by E. E. Lawler, Jr.[13] The research also concluded that pay is least likely to serve self-actualization or social needs. A similar analysis would seem to apply to the McClelland/Atkinson needs theory and Korman's consistency theory.[14]

The two most directly relevant and most frequently tested motivation theories are equity theory and expectancy theory. From the expectancy point of view, Maslow, McClelland/Atkinson, and the Korman theories concentrate on condition 1, the valence of money, and behavior modification concentrates on condition 2, the expectancy of receiving money. The other theories, therefore, can be subsumed under the expectancy theory label.

None of the motivation theories discussed in Chapter 2 answer no to the money and performance issue, although Herzberg tends to be the most negative. Other pay theorists discussed shortly do argue against using pay to motivate behavior. Thus motivation theories can lead to three answers— yes, no, or it depends—to the question: Does money motivate performance? The second part of the question is: Do effective pay systems lead to satisfaction, and thus lower absenteeism, turnover, and accidents and higher quality? Applying March and Simon's theories,[15] David Belcher points out that pay can influence two aspects of motivation: the motivation to produce, and the motivation to acquire and keep organization membership (membership motivation).[16] The latter motivation is examined by equity theory, the former by expectancy theory. We will examine the motivation to produce first.

Money and motivation to increase performance

As we have indicated a number of times, high performance requires much more than employee motivation: employee ability, adequate equipment, good physical working conditions, effective leadership and management, employee health, and other conditions all help raise employee performance levels. But employee motivation to work harder and better can be an important factor.

A number of studies indicate that when pay systems are designed to fit expectancy theory conditions, pay will lead to greater performance.[17] One researcher's studies led him to speculate that merit pay and performance are mutually reinforcing.[18]

Of course, everyone does not agree with the expectancy approach. Some question whether the first condition (valence of money) is strong enough.[19] More recently, the argument has been that organizations should not use pay to motivate.[20] Herbert Meyer argues that organizations should not try to increase the potential valence of money because doing so destroys more powerful and useful motives such as intrinsic work motivation and the recognition which flows from promotion. Meyer supports his position by citing the laboratory research of Edward Deci, who appeared to conclude that employees cannot achieve intrinsic motivation (a person is intrinsically motivated if he or she does a job to feel competent and self-determining) and extrinsic (pay) motivation at the same time. There is research to support Deci.[21] But some research indicates there are individual differences in the consequences pay has for intrinsic motivation.[22] In effect, Meyer and those opposed to the use of pay as motivators argue that other motivations are more functional for employees and enterprises. Therefore they support a standardized pay system with no incentive pay elements.

Other researchers question whether the second condition (expectancy) is present in the workplace. A series of studies has shown that although managers give lip service to merit–incentive pay approaches, they actually pay people for long service and attendance (seniority), not merit.[23] If Meyer is right, or if management pays for seniority and not merit, pay is less likely to have an effect on employee performance. Although there are problems with pay systems tied to performance, recent evidence indicates that enterprises are increasingly trying to implement them.[24]

Pay and employee satisfaction

Satisfaction with pay is important because, as the research summarized by Nash and Carroll shows, if pay satisfaction is low, job satisfaction is low.[25] As a consequence, absenteeism and turnover will be high and more costly.

Two theories have tried to explain employee's satisfaction or dissatisfaction with pay. One is the *equity theory* of Eliott Jaques and J. Stacey Adams.[26] Adams's theory has received significant laboratory research support. Equity theory contends that pay satisfaction exists when an employee's job inputs (such as education, experience, effort, seniority, and training) and outputs (such as pay, promotion, and intrinsic rewards) are equivalent to the job inputs and outputs of the other employees the employee considers comparable. If there is inequity, the employee will change his behavior (for example, decreased performance); if the behavior cannot be changed, he changes attitudes (reduced satisfaction); and finally he withdraws (absenteeism, turnover). Research and other studies tend to support the explanation offered in equity theory.[27] Charles Greene's study clearly indicates that the pay-for-performance approach increases manager's satisfaction.

EXHIBIT 13–5
Determinants of pay satisfaction

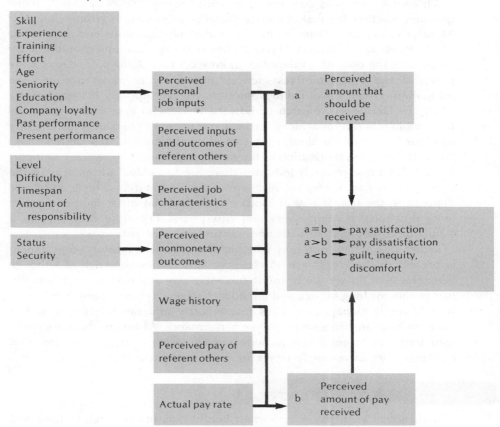

Source: E. E. Lawler, Jr., *Pay and Organizational Effectiveness* (New York: McGraw-Hill Book Co., 1971).

The second theory which can explain the effect of pay on satisfaction is *discrepancy theory,* which holds that pay satisfaction or dissatisfaction is the consequence of an employee comparing pay received with pay desired. Edward Locke has shown that this theory has much support.[28] Lawler's model of pay satisfaction and its causes is useful in explaining pay and satisfaction (Exhibit 13–5).

Nash and Carroll have summarized much of the research on pay satisfaction.[29] They point out that pay satisfaction varies with these factors:

Salary level. The higher the pay, the higher the pay satisfaction within an occupational group at each job level (For example, higher paid presidents are more satisfied than lower paid presidents).

Community cost of living. The lower the cost of living in a community, the higher the pay satisfaction.

Education. The lower the educational level, the higher the pay satisfaction.

Future expectations. The more optimistic the employee is about future job conditions, the higher the pay satisfaction.

Sex. Females are more satisfied with pay than males.

Other personal characteristics. The more intelligent, self-assured, and decisive a person is, the lower the pay satisfaction.

Pay basis. The more pay is perceived to be based on merit or performance, the greater the pay satisfaction.

In sum, most people believe it is desirable to have a pay system that leads to satisfaction with pay. Exhibit 13–6 shows Lawler's summary of

EXHIBIT 13–6
Effects of pay dissatisfaction

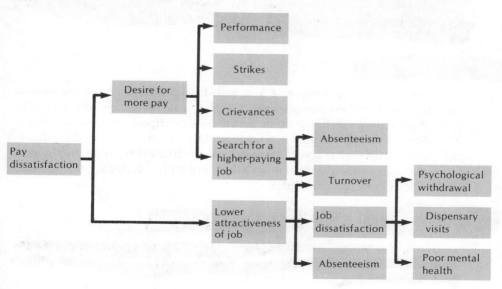

Source: E. E. Lawler, Jr., *Pay and Organizational Effectiveness* (New York: McGraw-Hill Book Co., 1971).

the research concerning the consequences when pay dissatisfaction is present. Some believe it is desirable to have pay used as a motivator, others do not. To complicate matters further, the research by Donald Schwab and his associates shows that the same pay systems which produced the most pay satisfaction (hourly pay) did not produce the highest performance (incentive pay did that). In effect, their research suggests the manager must choose either a satisfying pay system or a performance pay system.[30] This requires taking sides on the question: Will pay increase long-run enterprise effectiveness? This is what today's research tells us. Frankly, I suspect that this condition—either satisfaction or performance for pay must be chosen—is primarily true for instrumentally motivated employees. In effect, I am suggesting that Deci's research will not be fully supported and that intrinsic and extrinsic motivators are not an either-or choice in a work situation (as opposed to his laboratory setting, with college students working on puzzles) *for all employees.* It seems reasonable that for many employees a pay system which is incentive oriented can *reinforce* intrinsic motivations and that pay need not become a substitute for intrinsic motivations.

This further suggests that more flexible, cafeteria-type compensation systems, which might allow employees to pick from among several compensation approaches, are desirable.[31] The practicality of these systems administratively are problematical, however. (See Chapter 14 for more on this topic.) In sum, at present there are theorists who suggest that pay is a useful mechanism to motivate and satisfy employees. Others disagree. It seems to me that research that tries to give a yes or no answer to this question is misdirected. Because of individual differences in employees and jobs, it seems more fruitful to redirect this research to examine (a) the range of behaviors which pay may affect positively or negatively; (b) the amount of change pay can influence; (c) the kind of employee pay influences positively and negatively; and (d) the environmental conditions that are present when pay leads to positive and negative results.

Job desirability

As we indicated in Chapter 4 and will discuss more fully in the section on job evaluation, employees expect higher pay levels for less desirable jobs. If an enterprise has jobs in a bad neighborhood, in aged buildings, in a dirty, noisy environment, and low status is attached to the jobs, it will have to pay higher level compensation to attract competent employees. Of course, perceptions of what is desirable vary with individual backgrounds, expectations, and job motivations.

EXTERNAL INFLUENCES ON PAY LEVELS

Among the factors which influence pay and compensation policies are these outside the enterprise: the government, unions, the economy, and the labor market.

Government influences

If the government is the employer, it may legislate pay levels by setting statutory rates. For example, for teachers, the pay scale may be set by law or by edict of the school board, and pay depends on revenues from the current tax base. If taxes decline relative to organizations' revenue streams, no matter how much the organization may wish to pay higher wages, it cannot.

The government affects compensation through its employment-level policy too. In the United States and Canada, one of the goals of government is full employment of all citizens seeking work. The government may even create jobs for certain categories of workers, which reduces the supply of workers available and affects pay rates (see Chapter 5).

The government also directly affects compensation through wage controls and guidelines, which prohibit an increase in compensation for certain workers at certain times, and laws directed at the establishment of minimum wage rates, wage and hour regulations, and the prevention of discrimination toward certain groups. Government regulation affects pay levels in these and other ways.

Wage controls and guidelines. Several times in the past quarter century or so, the United States and Canada have established wage freezes and guidelines. Wage freezes are government orders which permit no wage increases, and wage controls limit the size of wage increases. Wage guidelines are similar to wage controls, but they are voluntary rather than legally required restrictions.

President Harry Truman imposed a wage and price freeze from January 1951 to 1953, and President Richard Nixon imposed freezes from 1971 to 1974, which came to be called Phases I–IV. Premier Pierre Trudeau imposed similar freezes in 1975. It is expected that Canada will remove controls in 1978.

Economists and compensation specialists differ on the usefulness of wage and price freezes.[32] The critics argue that the controls are an administrative nightmare, that they seriously disrupt the effective resource allocation market process and lead to frustration, strikes, and so on, as in Canada in 1976. Even the critics admit, however, that during times of perceived national emergencies and for relatively brief periods, the controls might help slow (but not indefinitely postpone) inflation. Those favoring them believe that controls reduce inflation. The important point is that employers must adjust their compensation policies to any governmental wage guidelines and controls. Considerable data gathering is necessary when such programs are in effect, and the employer must be prepared to justify any proposed wage increases. Even when the controls have been lifted (as in the United States now) frequently there are wage and price advisory groups—government or quasi-government groups which some politicians use to try to "jawbone" executives into keeping price increases lower. These bodies at times might influence prices, which in turn could limit the profits needed to give wage increases. One proposed solution is "TIP" (Tax-based Income Policy). In TIP, when employers give employees bigger raises than government standards, the employer receives a tax increase; when the raise is below standard, he receives a tax reduction.

U.S. wage and hour regulations.   The Fair Labor Standards Act of 1938 is the basic pay act in the United States. It has been amended many times, most recently in 1974. This law has a number of provisions, including the following:

Minimum wages.   All employers covered by the law (all but some small firms and with some specific exemptions, such as restaurants) must pay an employee at least a minimum wage per hour. Exempt small businesses are those whose gross sales do not exceed $275,000 (1978), $325,000 (1980), and $362,500 (1981). In 1938, the minimum wage was 25 cents per hour. In 1978, the minimum is $2.65. Present legislation calls for it to increase to $2.90 in 1979, $3.10 in 1980, and $3.35 in 1981. A number of economists question the desirability of minimum wages, arguing that this law may price the marginal worker out of a job.[34] All do not agree, however.[35] Many experts propose a lower minimum wage for trainees to help reduce the unemployment problem.

Overtime pay.   An employee covered by the law who works more than 40 hours per week must be paid one and one half times the base wage. If bonuses are also paid on a monthly or quarterly basis, the overtime pay equals one and one half the base pay and bonuses. Overtime pay tends to reduce the scheduling of longer hours of work.[36]

Child labor prohibition.   The law prohibits employing persons between 16 and 18 in hazardous jobs such as meatpacking and logging. Persons under 16 cannot be employed in jobs in interstate commerce except for nonhazardous work for a parent or guardian, this requires a temporary permit. However, there are exceptions and limitations to the law.[37] The Department of Labor caught 10,113 underaged persons in 1977 working in violation of the law.

Government agencies such as the Department of Labor's Wage and Hour Division enforce the wage and hour law. It has the right to examine employers' records and issue orders for back pay, get an injunction to prohibit future violations, and prosecute violators and send them to prison. For example, the department estimates that in 1976 U.S. employers underpaid employees by $89 million, in violation of minimum wage and overtime regulations. The department forced employers to pay $32 million to 293,000 employees for minimum wage violations, and 262,000 workers recovered $33 million from employers violating overtime regulations.

Antidiscrimination laws.   The Equal Pay Act of 1963, the Civil Rights Act of 1964, and the Age Discrimination Act of 1967 are designed to assure that all persons of similar ability, seniority, and background receive the same pay for the same work. The Equal Employment Opportunity Commission enforces the Civil Rights Act, while the Wage and Hour Division enforces the other two acts. In one recent case, AT&T had to pay women employees a settlement of $23,000,000 for past differences in pay. The evidence is clear that men and women are not paid equally, although experts disagree on why there is disparity.[38] Nor are whites and minorities paid equally.[39] In fact, some experts contend that for women, the gap has *widened* since 1970. The EEOC requires employers to keep pay records of employees by sex, race, national origin, and religion (the protected categories) for purposes of analysis. Employers are advised to examine their pay practices to see that they meet the requirements of the law.[40]

Other U.S. federal pay laws.   The Portal to Portal Act of 1947 requires some employers to start the pay period when an employee enters the company property and continue the pay until the employee leaves it. This applies primarily where employees spend considerable amounts of time getting to their work stations from the entry to company property.

The Walsh-Healey Act of 1936 requires firms doing business with the federal government to pay wages at least equal to those prevailing in the area where the firm is located. It parallels the Fair Labor Standards Act on child labor and requires time-and-a-half pay for any work performed after eight hours a day. It also has some exempted industries. The Davis Bacon Act of 1931 requires the payment of minimum wages to workers engaged in federally sponsored public works—construction jobs.

McNamara-O'Hara Service Contract Act requires employers who have contracts with the federal government of $2,500 per year or more or that provide services to federal agencies as contractors or subcontractors must pay prevailing wages and fringe benefits to their employees.

Several of these acts encourage the development of guaranteed annual wage plans by allowing organizations that will guarantee a worker at least 1,840 hours of work per year (but will not work the employees more than 1,040 hours in 20 executive weeks) an exemption from overtime pay. If the employees work more than 12 hours a day, 56 hours in a week, or 2,080 hours in a year, overtime must be paid beyond these hours.

State pay laws.   The U.S. Department of Labor reports that 39 states have minimum-wage laws covering intrastate employers and others not covered by federal law. Some of these laws have higher state minimums than the federal laws; the state law applies in such cases.

Minimum wages and local and state government employees.   In 1974 the federal government tried to make the federal minimum wages and overtime provisions of the Wages and Hour Law applicable to state and local government employees. In 1976 the U.S. Supreme Court ruled this application to be unconstitutional, so these employees are covered only by state minimum-wage laws.

Maximum-hour laws.   At one time, 40 states had laws that were designed to protect women by limiting the number of hours women could work. Many women felt this discriminated against them. Due to court rulings, only 12 states now have maximum-hour laws, and these are in greatly modified forms which permit women to accept overtime if they choose.

A parity wage?   Most of the laws discussed above affect the minimum wage an employee can be paid. These laws may appear to be desirable socially, but as minimum wages have been raised, they have had the effect of eliminating certain categories of persons from the employable work force. Younger workers and the unskilled may be unable to produce enough to make it worthwhile for employers to hire them at minimum wages. Various legislators have considered introducing more exemptions to the laws or creating different minimum wages for youth, unskilled, and skilled workers. Canada has experimented with this, for example.

Perhaps the answer is to create a parity wage. If we can do this for a bushel of wheat, why not for human labor? The minimum wage would become a parity, or guaranteed base price for labor. When certain categories of workers seeking employment cannot produce enough to justify the employer's expenditure, the government would subsidize the difference to keep such workers working and off the welfare rolls. This might be basis of the kind of a guaranteed income plan such as that proposed by Milton Friedman to eliminate welfare.

Other pay legislation: Pay deductions.   The government directly affects the amount of pay the employee takes home by requiring employers to deduct funds from employees' wages. For the federal government, this entails federal income taxes (withholding taxes) and social security taxes. The employer may also be required to deduct state and local income taxes.

The federal government also has other laws governing pay deductions. The Copeland Act (1934) and Anti-Kickback Law (1948) are designed to protect the employee from unlawful or unauthorized deductions. The Federal Wage Garnishment Act (1970) is designed to limit the amount deducted from a person's pay to reduce debts. It also prohibits the employer from firing an employee if the employee goes in debt only once and has his pay garnished. The employer may deduct as much from the paycheck as required by court orders for alimony or child support, debts due for taxes, or bankruptcy court requirements. Other than these, the maximum garnishment is 25 percent of take-home pay or 30 times the minimum wage per hour, whichever is smaller.

Canadian pay legislation.   The major pay legislation in Canada is the minimum-wage laws, which exist in all provinces and territories. Authority to establish minimum wages for employees is vested in minimum-wage boards, the governor in council or the lieutenant-governor in council. Minimum-wage rates cover all employment except farm labor and domestic service, with a few exceptions and some other excluded categories. These rates apply to members to both sexes.

Exhibit 13–7 gives the most recent minimum wage in Canadian jurisdictions. Each jurisdiction also sets lower minimum wages for younger employees. In 1976, these minimum wage rates were federal, $2.65 (under 17); Alberta, $2.60 (under 18), or $2.25 (students and part-time); British Columbia, $2.60 (under 18); Manitoba, $2.35 (under 18); Nova Scotia, $2.25 (under 18); Ontario, $2.15 (under 18 and part-time); PEI, $2.00 (under 18); Quebec,

EXHIBIT 13–7
Minimum rates for experienced adult workers

Jurisdiction	Hourly rates
Federal	$2.90
Newfoundland	$2.50
Prince Edward Island	$2.70
Nova Scotia	$2.75
New Brunswick	$2.80
Quebec	$3.15
Ontario	$2.65
Manitoba	$2.95
Saskatchewan	$3.00
Alberta	$3.00
British Columbia	$3.00
Yukon Territory*	$3.00
Northwest territories	$3.00

* Federal minimum wage plus 10 cents.

$2.60 (under 18); Northwest, $2.00. Although these wages rates are legally required, it has been said that the provinces do not enforce them strictly, and the small fines assessed for violation are not a significant deterent to violation of the law.[41] Of course, Canadians face the same debates about the desirability of minimum-wage laws as in the United States. Some contend that the rates are too low to support a family, and others say that they are so high they cause unemployment for the marginal worker.[42]

An indirect governmental influence on pay is the tax structure. In general, Canadian income tax base rates are more "progressive" than in the United States. The taxes are indexed with inflation, however. Information on Canadian pay laws is published regularly in the Canadian personnel journals.[43]

Union influences on compensation

Another important external influence on an employer's compensation program is labor unionization. Unions have an effect whether or not the enterprise's employees are unionized, if it is in an area where unionized enterprises exist, for unions have tended to be pace setters in demands for pay, benefits, and working conditions. There is reasonable evidence that unions tend to increase pay levels,[44] although this is more likely where an industry has been organized by strong unions.[45] If the enterprise elects to stay in an area where unions are strong, its compensation policies will be affected.

A series of legal cases has required employers to share compensation information with the unions if employees are unionized. For example, in *Shell Development* v. *Association of Industrial Scientists–Professional Employees,* Shell was required to provide the union with a written explanation of salary curves and the merit system, as well as copies of current salary curve guides, merit ratings, and so on. In *Time Incorporated* v. *Newspaper Guild, Time* was required to provide the union with a list of salaries of employees. In *General Electric* v. *International Union of Electrical Workers,* GE was required to provide the union with the pay survey information it had gathered to form compensation decisions. Thus employers would do well to communicate with and try to influence the union on compensation policy and levels.

Unions do try to bargain for higher pay and benefits, of course. The union is more likely to increase the compensation of its members when the enterprise is financially and competitively strong and the union is financially strong enough to support a strike; when the union has the support of other unions; and when general economic and labor market conditions are such that unemployment is low and the economy is strong.

Unions also bargain over working conditions and other policies that affect compensation. There is a tendency for unions to prefer fixed pay for each job category, or rate ranges that are administered to primarily reflect seniority rather than merit increases. This is true in the private and other sectors.

Not all authorities agree with this. David Lewin and Raymond Horton, for example, argue that unions might strengthen the merit system by helping end patronage and encouraging equitable merit pay in the public sector.[46]

Economic conditions and compensation

Also affecting compensation as an external factor are the economic conditions of the industry, especially the degree of competitiveness, which affects the organization's ability to pay high wages. Certain industries are more profitable than others at any one time, which is often related to the degree of competitiveness in the industry: the more competitive the situation, the less able is the enterprise to pay higher wages. Ability to pay is also a consequence of the relative productivity of the organization or industry or sector. If a firm is very productive, it can pay higher wages. Productivity can be increased by advanced technology, more efficient operating methods, a harder working and more talented work force, or a combination of these factors.

One productivity index that is used by many organizations as a criterion in the determination of a general level of wages is the Bureau of Labor Statistics' "Output per Man-Hour in Manufacturing." This productivity index is published in each issue of the *Monthly Labor Review*. Over the past 75 years, productivity has increased at an average annual rate of approximately 3 percent. The percentage increase in average weekly earnings in the United States is very closely related to the percentage change in productivity, plus the percentage change in the Consumer Price Index.[47]

The degree of profitability and productivity is a significant factor in determining the ability of firms in the private and third sector to pay wages. In the public sector, the limitations of the budget determine the ability to pay. If tax rates are low or the tax base is low or declining, the public-sector employer may be unable to give pay increases even if they are deserved.[48]

Nature of the labor market and compensation

The final external factor affecting compensation to be discussed is the state of the labor market. Although many feel that human labor should not be regulated by forces such as the supply and demand, in fact this happens. In times of full employment, wages and salaries may have to be higher to attract and retain enough qualified employees; in depressions, the reverse is true. Pay may be higher if few skilled employees are available in the job market; this may be because unions or accrediting associations limit the numbers certified to do the job.[49] In certain locations, due to higher birth rates or a recent loss of a major employer, more persons may be seeking work than others. These factors lead to what is called *differential pay levels.* At any one time in a particular locale, unskilled labor rates seek a single level, and minimally skilled clerical work rates seek another. Research evidence from the labor economics field provides adequate support for the impact of labor market conditions on compensation.

Besides differences in pay levels by occupations in a locale, there are also differentials between government and private employees and exempt and nonexempt employees,[50] as well as international differences. For example, there are differences in pay levels between the United States and Canada.[51]

Increases in productivity are typically passed on to employees in the form of higher pay. Studies indicate that, in general, employers do not exploit employees when market conditions do not favor the employees.

Employers use compensation surveys and general studies of the labor market in the area to serve as inputs to their pay-level compensation decision. The pay survey is the major pay-level decision tool.

PAY SURVEYS AND COMPARABLE PAY LEVELS

A unique factor in the external environment for the compensation personnel activity is pay surveys (also called wage surveys). These surveys of the compensation paid to employees by all employers in a geographic area, an industry, or an occupational group are the principal tool used in the pay-level decision, as noted above.

Pay surveys are made by large employers, professional and consulting enterprises, trade associations, and the government. Some examples of surveys conducted by professional and consulting enterprises include:

American Management Association. AMA conducts surveys of professional and managerial compensation and provides about 12 reports on U.S. executive salaries and 16 reports on foreign executive's salaries. The *Top Management Report* shows the salaries of 31,000 top executives in 75 top positions in 3,000 firms in 53 industries. The *Middle Management Report* covers 73 key exempt jobs between supervisor and top executives. The sample includes

EXHIBIT 13–8

Typical area wage survey: Weekly earnings of office workers in Chicago, May 1976

Occupation and industry division	Number of workers	Average weekly hours (standard)	Weekly earnings (standard)			$ 80 and under 90	$ 90 - 100	$ 100 - 110
			Mean	Median	Middle range			
ALL WORKERS			$	$	$ $			
SECRETARIES	23,101	38.5	196.00	190.00	168.00-217.50	-	-	10
MANUFACTURING	10,080	39.0	196.00	190.00	170.00-214.50	-	-	-
NONMANUFACTURING	13,021	38.0	196.00	190.00	167.00-220.00	-	-	10
PUBLIC UTILITIES	1,499	39.0	240.00	248.50	203.50-273.50	-	-	-
WHOLESALE TRADE	2,138	38.0	200.00	195.00	172.50-220.50	-	-	-
RETAIL TRADE	1,956	39.5	195.50	195.00	169.00-220.00	-	-	-
FINANCE	4,423	38.0	183.00	180.00	160.00-202.50	-	-	10
SERVICES	3,005	36.5	190.50	185.00	161.00-217.50	-	-	-
SECRETARIES, CLASS A	1,930	38.5	240.50	235.00	213.00-265.00	-	-	-
MANUFACTURING	834	38.5	245.50	240.00	218.50-278.50	-	-	-
NONMANUFACTURING	1,096	38.5	236.50	234.00	211.00-254.50	-	-	-
PUBLIC UTILITIES	167	39.5	271.50	264.50	242.50-305.00	-	-	-
WHOLESALE TRADE	189	38.5	237.00	235.00	220.50-252.00	-	-	-
RETAIL TRADE	247	39.0	231.50	236.00	210.00-252.00	-	-	-
FINANCE	271	38.0	225.00	219.50	208.00-242.50	-	-	-
SERVICES	222	38.0	229.50	221.00	207.00-245.00	-	-	-
SECRETARIES, CLASS B	5,749	38.5	210.00	207.00	185.00-230.00	-	-	-
MANUFACTURING	2,195	39.0	210.50	207.00	186.50-226.00	-	-	-
NONMANUFACTURING	3,554	38.0	210.00	207.00	184.00-231.00	-	-	-
PUBLIC UTILITIES	382	38.5	253.50	261.50	222.50-272.00	-	-	-
WHOLESALE TRADE	577	38.5	209.00	207.00	175.00-235.00	-	-	-
RETAIL TRADE	687	39.5	208.00	209.00	189.50-229.00	-	-	-
FINANCE	1,182	38.0	200.00	200.00	182.00-215.00	-	-	-
SERVICES	726	37.0	204.50	201.50	178.50-230.00	-	-	-
SECRETARIES, CLASS C	7,722	38.5	193.50	187.50	169.00-210.00	-	-	-
MANUFACTURING	3,763	39.0	193.00	187.50	170.00-207.00	-	-	-
NONMANUFACTURING	3,959	38.0	194.00	188.00	167.00-213.00	-	-	-
PUBLIC UTILITIES	603	39.0	244.50	249.00	218.50-275.00	-	-	-
WHOLESALE TRADE	694	38.5	201.50	197.50	184.00-217.50	-	-	-
RETAIL TRADE	214	39.5	181.00	179.50	167.00-200.00	-	-	-
FINANCE	1,721	38.0	180.00	178.50	161.50-195.50	-	-	-
SERVICES	727	37.5	181.50	173.00	157.50-203.00	-	-	-
SECRETARIES, CLASS D	6,604	38.0	175.00	172.00	153.00-190.50	-	-	10
MANUFACTURING	2,798	39.0	174.00	172.00	157.00-189.00	-	-	-
NONMANUFACTURING	3,806	37.0	175.50	171.00	150.00-194.50	-	-	10
PUBLIC UTILITIES	347	38.0	202.00	183.00	165.00-251.50	-	-	-
WHOLESALE TRADE	678	37.0	180.00	179.50	160.00-198.00	-	-	-
RETAIL TRADE	342	39.0	164.50	162.00	149.50-179.00	-	-	-
FINANCE	1,109	37.5	161.50	157.50	144.00-175.00	-	-	10
SERVICES	1,330	36.0	181.50	178.00	155.00-201.50	-	-	-
STENOGRAPHERS, GENERAL	1,816	38.5	171.50	163.00	145.00-186.00	-	-	24
MANUFACTURING	652	39.0	165.00	162.00	143.00-177.50	-	-	-
NONMANUFACTURING	1,164	38.0	175.00	163.50	145.00-198.00	-	-	24
PUBLIC UTILITIES	289	40.0	232.00	235.50	229.50-249.00	-	-	-
WHOLESALE TRADE	166	39.0	158.00	155.00	140.00-170.00	-	-	-
FINANCE	291	37.5	148.00	149.00	132.50-161.00	-	-	20
SERVICES	389	36.5	163.00	162.00	148.00-176.50	-	-	-

Number of workers receiving straight-time weekly earnings of—

$110-120	$120-130	$130-140	$140-150	$150-160	$160-170	$170-180	$180-200	$200-220	$220-240	$240-260	$260-280	$280-300	$300-320	$320-340	$340-360	$360-380	$380 and over
46	281	546	1200	1667	2311	2723	5097	3807	2213	1458	824	545	269	67	27	6	4
20	137	146	396	705	1024	1347	2466	1679	843	479	388	282	134	19	13	1	1
26	144	400	804	962	1287	1376	2631	2128	1370	979	436	263	135	48	14	5	3
-	-	9	11	50	63	72	132	168	178	259	254	158	92	40	9	2	2
-	5	33	126	41	203	265	516	380	304	114	61	50	26	7	3	3	1
3	22	54	78	158	205	135	414	395	281	155	40	10	5	1	-	-	-
23	72	175	362	453	485	569	1037	735	292	165	23	13	8	-	1	-	-
-	45	129	227	260	331	335	532	450	315	286	58	32	4	-	1	-	-
-	-	-	1	1	43	40	181	330	446	338	195	169	154	19	6	4	3
-	-	-	-	-	29	7	81	112	186	98	114	119	80	3	3	1	1
-	-	-	1	1	14	33	100	218	260	240	81	50	74	16	3	3	2
-	-	-	-	-	-	-	4	9	23	45	13	10	49	13	-	-	1
-	-	-	-	-	-	21	12	6	78	40	9	3	12	2	2	3	1
-	-	-	1	1	11	2	29	30	54	80	28	5	5	1	-	-	-
-	-	-	-	-	-	10	35	98	49	48	13	11	7	-	-	-	-
-	-	-	-	-	3	-	20	75	56	27	18	21	1	-	1	-	-
-	24	50	95	160	289	461	1299	1451	884	443	296	168	80	26	20	2	1
-	20	20	41	62	80	141	522	637	276	166	86	75	43	16	10	-	-
-	4	30	54	98	209	320	777	814	608	277	210	93	37	10	10	2	1
-	-	-	-	2	-	9	31	48	52	36	124	43	27	5	8	2	1
-	-	-	21	5	62	76	103	108	89	31	32	35	9	5	1	-	-
-	-	1	6	16	30	35	155	190	180	62	9	3	-	-	-	-	-
-	4	1	24	49	49	128	330	354	160	70	10	1	1	-	1	-	-
-	-	28	3	26	68	72	158	114	127	84	35	11	-	-	-	-	-
2	24	112	331	598	949	1059	1924	1251	581	415	245	177	31	22	1	-	-
-	-	36	145	267	460	549	1044	612	238	147	150	84	11	-	-	-	-
2	24	76	186	331	489	510	880	639	323	268	95	93	20	22	1	-	-
-	-	-	-	4	11	22	44	79	92	156	78	82	12	22	1	-	-
-	-	2	7	7	59	63	223	182	81	43	12	10	5	-	-	-	-
-	-	7	4	13	40	43	49	52	6	-	-	-	-	-	-	-	-
2	11	67	106	191	257	276	467	233	63	47	-	1	-	-	-	-	-
-	13	-	69	116	122	106	97	93	81	22	5	-	3	-	-	-	-
44	233	360	719	793	909	1036	1354	596	218	222	80	26	4	-	-	-	-
20	117	90	210	353	423	566	646	218	80	41	33	1	-	-	-	-	-
24	116	270	509	440	486	470	708	378	138	181	47	25	4	-	-	-	-
-	-	9	11	44	52	41	53	32	11	28	39	23	4	-	-	-	-
-	5	31	98	29	82	105	178	84	56	-	8	2	-	-	-	-	-
3	22	30	31	66	57	50	39	44	-	-	-	-	-	-	-	-	-
21	57	99	214	183	157	117	181	50	20	-	-	-	-	-	-	-	-
-	32	101	155	118	138	157	257	168	51	153	-	-	-	-	-	-	-
40	85	115	314	221	274	197	169	93	166	83	28	7	-	-	-	-	-
29	30	37	113	79	123	84	67	33	46	6	-	-	-	-	-	-	-
11	55	78	201	142	151	113	102	55	129	77	28	7	-	-	-	-	-
-	-	1	1	6	12	9	13	15	119	77	28	7	-	-	-	-	-
-	-	5	51	46	19	28	15	2	-	-	-	-	-	-	-	-	-
4	38	22	74	48	53	6	26	-	-	-	-	-	-	-	-	-	-
3	14	41	75	41	67	67	47	34	-	-	-	-	-	-	-	-	-

640 firms with 15,000 middle-level executives. The *Administrative and Technical Report* covers jobs below the middle management level. The sample is 568 firms. The *Supervisory Management Report* provides national and regional data on salaries of 55 categories of foremen and staff supervisors in 700 companies.

Administrative Management Society. This group compiles records on the compensation of clerical and data processing employees. AMS surveys 7,132 firms with 621,000 clerical and data processing employees in 132 cities. The data are gathered on 20 positions. A directory published every other year by cities and regions reports interquarterly ranges of salaries.

American Society for Personnel Administration. ASPA conducts salary surveys for personnel executives and others every other year.

International Personnel Management Association. This group surveys compensation practices for public personnel.

Other enterprises which do pay surveys include Pay Data Service (Chicago), Management Compensation Services, Bureau of National Affairs, and Prentice-Hall. Many journals report on compensation, including *Compensation Review, Business Week, Duns, Forbes, Fortune, Hospital Administration, Nation's Business,* and *Monthly Labor Review.*

U.S. government pay surveys include those by Federal Reserve banks, which survey private industry pay to set their employees' pay, and the Bureau of Labor Statistics. The BLS publishes three different surveys:

Area wage surveys. Annually, BLS surveys 168 areas (usually the Standard Metropolitan Statistical Areas) on the pay and benefits for white-collar, skilled blue-collar, and indirect manufacturing labor jobs (in alternate years). An example of one of these is given in Exhibit 13–8.

Industry wage surveys. The BLS surveys 50 manufacturing industries, 20 service industries and public employees. Blue- and white-collar employees are covered. The surveys are done on yearly, three- and five-year cycles. Some industries are surveyed nationally (utilities, mining, manufacturing), and others by metropolitan area (finance, service, and trade).

Professional, administrative, technical, and clerical surveys. BLS also annually surveys 80 occupational work-level positions on a nationwide basis. Although the BLS studies tend to follow the most sophisticated survey methods, they too need improvement, and BLS constantly tries to achieve this.[52]

The Canadian government also runs pay surveys. The Department of Labour's Labour Data Branch, Surveys Division, issues a series of studies on *Wage Rates, Salaries, and Hours of Labour.* Canada Labour issues the surveys for the 30 largest cities for 47 industries and covers a large number of occupations.

How are these surveys done? One method is the personal interview which develops the most accurate responses[53] but is also the most expensive one. Mailed questionnaires are probably the most frequently used method, and one of the cheapest. The jobs being surveyed by mail must be clearly defined, or the data may not be reliable. Telephone inquiries are used to follow up the mail questionnaires or to gather data. This procedure is quick, but it is also difficult to get a great deal of detailed data over the phone.

There are a number of critical issues determining the usefulness of the surveys: the jobs to be covered, the employers to be contacted, and the method to be used in gathering the data. Other employers cannot be expected to complete endless data requests for all the organization's jobs, so the jobs that are surveyed should be the 2 to 20 most crucial ones. If the point method of job evaluation is used (see the section below), the key jobs might be selected for surveying, since they cover all ranges. The jobs which most employees hold should also be on the list (clerk-typists, underwriters, and keypunch operators for an insurance company, for example).

The second issue concerns who will be surveyed. Most organizations tend to compare themselves with similar competitors in their industry; American Airlines may compare its pay rates to those of United Airlines, for example. It has been shown that employees may not compare their pay to that offered by competitors at all.[54] Their basis of comparison might be friends' employers, or employers that they worked for previously. If the survey is to be useful, employees should be involved in choosing the organizations to be surveyed. The employers to be surveyed should include the most dominant ones in the area and a small sample of those suggested by employees.

Government agencies use pay surveys of comparable private-sector jobs to set their pay levels.[55] In private-sector enterprises, the evidence suggests their own pay surveys are used more than those provided by the government or other services.[56] And they use the surveys primarily as general guidelines, as only one of several factors considered in pay-level decisions. In fact, there is some evidence that enterprises weigh job evaluation and individual pay determination more heavily than external pay comparisons.[57] This makes sense because pay surveys are not taken often (perhaps yearly); they average many differences into single numbers and are sometimes hard to interpret meaningfully.

At the start of this section, I suspect you thought that design and use of pay surveys was a simple matter. Now you understand why they can be difficult. An employer never knows if there is a pay differential between the job he offers and others, how much of the difference is due to differences in the job or other fringe benefits provided, the time of the survey, the pay level of the two areas, or other factors.

ENTERPRISE INFLUENCES ON PAY LEVELS

In addition to the external influences on compensation discussed above, several internal factors affect pay levels: enterprise size, enterprise age, and the goals of the controlling interests of the enterprise.

Enterprise size

The evidence thus far is that larger enterprises tend to have higher pay levels. This may not be true for all jobs in all enterprises, but the tendency is clear: the larger the enterprise, the higher the pay level.[58]

Enterprise age

Age of the enterprise is the second internal factor affecting compensation. This is an area where there has been more speculation than research. One researcher found that newer enterprises paid more than established ones;[59] this makes sense because the potential employee probably sees more risk in working for a new (and unknown) enterprise than for the Port of New York Authority, the Mayo Clinic, or Ford Motor Company. But does this risk decline relatively with age? Better known, older universities can pay some of the lowest salaries in the country because of their age and prestige. Does this happen in other settings? This is hard to say, but it is doubtful. Size is probably the major factor.

Goals of controlling interests and managerial pay strategies

Managers differ as much as employees do. Some believe their employees should be compensated at high pay levels because they deserve it, for example. They also accept or reject the idea that high pay or merit pay leads to greater performance or employee satisfaction. These attitudes are reflected in the pay-level strategy chosen by the managers of the enterprise. This is a major strategic choice top managers must make.

Essentially, three strategies of pay level can be chosen: high, low, or comparable.

1. The high-pay-level strategy. In this strategy, the manager choses to pay higher than average pay levels. The assumption behind this strategy is that you get what you pay for. Paying higher wages and salaries, these managers believe, will attract and hold the best employees, and this is the most effective long-range policy. This strategy is sometimes called the pace setter. It may be influenced by pay criteria such as paying a living wage or paying on the basis of productivity.

2. The low-pay-level strategy. At the opposite extreme is the low-pay strategy. In this case, the manager may choose to pay at the minimum level needed to hire enough employees. This strategy may be used because this is all the enterprise can pay—the ability to pay is restricted by other internal or external factors. (In the public or third sector, the comparable problem is a tight budget.) Or the manager may be trying to maximize short-run profits or to live with a tight budget.

3. The comparable-pay-level strategy. The most frequently used strategy is to set the pay level at the going wage level. The wage criteria are comparable wages, perhaps modified by cost of living or purchasing power adjustments. For example, the Federal Pay Comparability Act of 1970 limits federal government compensation to the comparable pay paid in the private sector at the time. This going wage is determined from pay surveys (discussed below). Thus the policy of a manager of this type is to pay the current market rate in the community or industry, ±5 percent or so.

These three strategies are usually set for the total enterprise, although the strategy might have to be modified for a few hard-to-fill jobs from time to time.

The choice of strategy in part reflects the motivation and attitude set of the manager. If the manager has a high need for recognition, the high-pay strategy might be chosen; otherwise, the low-pay strategy might be chosen.[60] Another factor is the ethical and moral attitude of the manager. If the manager is ethically oriented, then a low pay strategy is not likely to be chosen willingly. In equity, the manager tries to pay more. One study showed that even in depressions, managers tried not to cut salaries,[61] and another found a strong ethical theme in managers' pay-level decisions.[62]

THE PAY-LEVEL DECISION

The pay-level decision is made by managers in comparing the pay of persons working inside the enterprise with those outside it. This decision

EXHIBIT 13–9
Factors affecting the pay-level decision

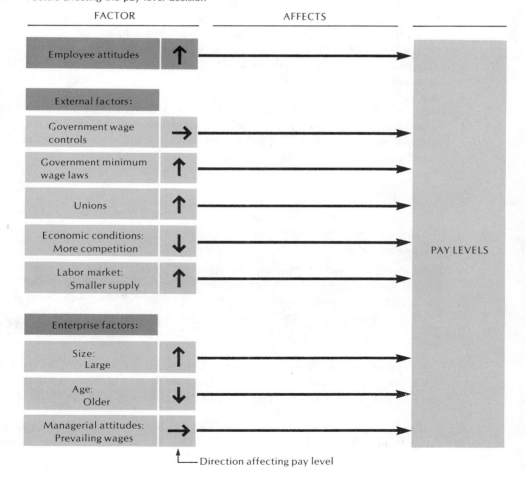

is affected by multiple factors in interaction with each other, as shown in Exhibit 13–9. Numerous factors affecting pay levels laterally, upward, or downward. Most employees' unions and minimum-wage laws push the level up. Wage controls steady the level or tend to hold it down. More competition and older enterprises hold it down. Managerial attitudes toward prevailing wages would steady the level. The size of the enterprise would tend to increase pay level, as would a smaller supply of employees in the labor market.

This is one example of how some of the factors in the compensation activity could affect the pay-level decision. When factors such as managerial attitudes, the labor market, and competition change, the pressures on pay level shift.

PAY STRUCTURES

In addition to relating pay to pay levels paid for comparable jobs in other enterprises, the enterprise must also determine pay structures for its employees having different jobs *within* the organization. Factors similar to those affecting pay levels affect these pay structures too.

Managers can cope with the attempt to provide equal pay for positions of approximately equal worth by arbitrary management decisions, collective bargaining, or job evaluation. If managers try to make these decisions without help from tools such as job evaluation, unsystematic decision making is likely to lead to perceived inequities. Bargaining alone can lead to decisions based solely on relative power. Therefore, most management experts suggest that managerial decisions be influenced both by the results of collective bargaining and job evaluation.

Job evaluation

> DEFINITION
> Job evaluation is the formal process by which the relative worth of various jobs in the organization is determined for pay purposes. Essentially, it attempts to relate the amount of the employee's pay to the extent that her or his job contributes to organizational effectiveness.

It is not always easy to evaluate the worth of all the jobs in an enterprise. It may be obvious that the effective physician will contribute more to the goals of patient care in the hospital than the nurse's aid; the point at issue is *how much* the differential is worth.

Since computing exactly how much a particular job contributes to organizational effectiveness is difficult, proxies for effectiveness are used. These proxies include skills required to do the job, amount and significance of responsibility involved, effort required, and working conditions. Compensation must vary with the differing demands of various jobs if employees are to be satisfied and if the organization is to be able to attract the personnel it wants.[63]

Effectively performed, job evaluation simplifies pay-structure decisions and makes them more rational. It makes job comparisons a more efficient operation and can be used in performance measurement, pay negotiations, selection, and promotion. It is also likely to reduce grievances about pay.

Job evaluation is widely used. At least two thirds of all jobs have been evaluated. The Bureau of National Affairs has found that 75 percent of large enterprises and 60 percent of smaller ones use it, and it is used for most clerical, professional, technical, and managerial jobs and about half of all blue-collar jobs.[64] Surveys indicate that most enterprises using it regard it as successful.

Once an enterprise decides to use job evaluation, a series of decisions must be made to ensure its effectiveness. Part of the decision to use job evaluation, or the first step in using it effectively, is for management to involve employees (and, where appropriate, the union) in the system and its implementation. Most experts emphasize that job evaluation is a difficult task which is more likely to be successful if the employees whose jobs are being evaluated are involved in the process by being allowed to express their perceptions of the relative merits of their jobs compared to others. This participation affords an opportunity to explain the fairly complicated process of job evaluation to those most directly affected by it, and it will usually lead to better communication and improved employee understanding.

The willingness or desire of unions to participate in job evaluation is not universal.[65] Some unions want to participate jointly with management; for example, the United Steel Workers Union and the steel industry run a joint union-management job evaluation program. Other unions ignore it. It makes sense for management to invite the union to participate and help implement the program, for this is likely to lead to their support for it. Even if the union does not want to participate in job evaluation, it still seems useful to keep union officials informed.

After the program is off to a cooperative start, usually a committee of about five members evaluates the jobs. Ideally, the committee includes employees, managers, and personnel specialists. All members should be familiar with the jobs to be evaluated.[66]

Job evaluation is usually performed by analyzing job descriptions and occasionally job specifications. Early in the process, it is imperative that job evaluators check the availability and accuracy of the job descriptions and specifications (see Chapter 4). It is usually suggested that job descriptions be split into several job series, such as managerial, professional and technical, clerical, and operative. It makes sense in writing job descriptions to use the words that are keyed to the job evaluation factors.

Another essential step in effective job evaluation is to select and weight the criteria used to evaluate the job.[67] Although there is not a lot of research in this area, it appears that only a few factors will do as good a job as many factors, especially if they are carefully designed and scaled. Typical of the most frequently used factors for job evaluation are education, experience, amount of responsibility, job knowledge, and work hazards and working conditions. It is important that the factors used be accepted as valid for the job by those being evaluated.

Once the method of evaluating the job (to be discussed in the next section) is chosen, the evaluators make the job evaluations. Basically, those familiar with the jobs tend to rate them higher, especially if they supervise the jobs.[68] It seems useful for each committee member to evaluate each job individually. Then the evaluators should discuss each job on which the ratings differ significantly, factor by factor, until agreement is reached.

Job evaluation methods. The four most frequently used job evaluation methods are job ranking, factor comparison, classification, and the point system. Although there is little research in the area, it appears that the four methods do about equally reliable jobs of evaluation.[69] In a recent study, David Robinson and his associates found the four roughly equal in reliability, and a fifth method—a policy capturing multiple regression weighting of numerical job analysis data—the most efficient.[70]

Ranking of jobs. The simplest system, used primarily in smaller, simpler organizations, is job ranking. Instead of analyzing the full complexity of jobs by evaluating parts of jobs, the job-ranking method has the evaluator rank order *whole* jobs, from the simplest to the most challenging.

Sometimes this is done by providing the evaluator with the information on cards. The evaluator sorts the jobs into ranks, allowing for the possibility of ties. If the list of jobs is large, the paired-comparison method, whereby each job is compared to every other job being evaluated, can be used. The evaluator counts the number of times a particular job is ranked above another, and the one with the largest number of highest rankings is the highest ranked. There is no assurance that the ranking thus provided is composed of equal-interval ranks. The differential between the highest job and next highest may not be exactly the same as that between the lowest and next lowest. If the system is used in an enterprise with many jobs to be rated, it is clumsy to use, and the reliability of the ratings is not good. Because of these problems, ranking is probably the least frequently used method of job evaluation.

Factor comparison. At the other extreme is the most complex (and the next least frequently used) system: the factor comparison method. This is probably the most costly, and it is probably slightly more reliable than the other methods. The factor comparison method requires five steps.

1. Choose the key jobs to be evaluated. These jobs are well known in the enterprise and, in the opinion of the evaluators, are properly paid at present.
2. Rank the key jobs on important factors of job evaluation. These factors

usually are mental requirements, skill requirements, physical requirements, responsibility, and working conditions.

3. Divide up the current pay among the factors. Thus, the rater is asked: If the jobs pays $2.75 per hour, how much of the $2.75 is for mental requirements? and so on.

4. Reconcile the differences in rankings found in steps 1 and 2 by the committee members.

5. Place the key jobs on a scale for each factor. This becomes the basis for evaluating nonkey jobs in the structure. An example of this is given in Exhibit 13–10.

Classification or grading system.   This system used in federal, state, and local governments, groups a set of jobs together into a grade or classification. Then these sets of jobs are ranked in levels of difficulty or sophistication. For example, the least challenging jobs in the federal service are grouped into GS–1, the next more challenging into GS–2, and so.

The classification approach is more sophisticated than ranking but less

EXHIBIT 13–10
Job comparison scale

Cents, points, or percents	Mental factor	Physical factor	Skill	Responsibility	Working conditions and hazards
$1.50					
—					Janitor
—		Janitor			
—			Mechanic		
—		Lathe operator			
1.25	Mechanic				
—				Purchasing clerk	
—					
—					
1.00					
.95					
—	Riveter		Lathe operator		
—	Lathe operator				
—	Purchasing clerk				
.75					
—					Lathe operator
—				Mechanic	
—					Mechanic
—		Mechanic	Purchasing clerk		
.50				Lathe operator	
—					
—					
—				Janitor	
—			Janitor		
.25		Purchasing clerk			
—	Janitor				
—					
—					Purchasing clerk
—					
.00					

From *The Management of Compensation,* by A. N. Nash and S. J. Carroll, Jr. Copyright © 1975 by Wadsworth Publishing Company, Inc. Reprinted by permission of the publisher, Brooks/Cole Publishing Company, Monterey, California.

so than the point system or factor comparison. It can work reasonably well if the classifications are well defined. It is the second most frequently used system. It is also used in the private and third sectors.

The point system. The greatest number of job evaluation plans use the point system.[72] It is the most frequently used because it is more sophisticated than ranking and classification systems, but it is relatively easy to use.

Essentially, the point system requires evaluators to quantify the value of the elements of a job. On the basis of the job description or interviews with job occupants, points are assigned to the degree of various factors required—for example, skill required, physical and mental effort needed, degree of dangerous or unpleasant working conditions involved, and amount of responsibility involved in the job. When these are summed, the job has been evaluated.

Most point systems evaluate about ten aspects of each job. The aspects chosen should not overlap, should distinguish real differences between jobs, should be as objectively defined as possible, and should be understood and acceptable to both management and employees. Because all aspects are not of equal importance in all jobs, different weights reflecting the differential importance of these aspects to a job must be set. These weights are assigned by summing the judgments of several independent but knowledgeable evaluators. Thus a clerical job might result in the following weightings, according to Robert Kelly: education required, 20 percent; experience required, 25 percent; complexity of job, 35 percent; responsibility for relationships with others, 15 percent; working conditions and physical requirements, 5 percent.[73]

Once the weights are agreed upon, reference to a point manual is appropriate. Experience required by jobs varies, as does education. The point manual carefully defines degrees of points from first (lowest) to sixth, for example. Experience might be defined in this way:

> First degree, up to and including three months . . . .   25 points
> Second degree, more than three months but less than six . . . .   50 points
> Third degree, more than six months to one year . . . .   75 points
> Fourth degree, more than one year and up to three years . . . .   100 points
> Fifth degree, more than three years and up to five years . . . .   125 points
> Sixth degree, over five years . . . .   150 points

These definitions must be clearly defined and measurable to ensure consistency in ratings of requirements from the job description to the job evaluation. The preliminary point manuals must be pretested prior to widespread use.

Exhibit 13–11 lists Kelly's points and factors for evaluating clerical jobs. The maximum point total for any job is often a number such as 500, although this is arbitrary. Using the point system, the evaluator compares the job description by job aspect and by degree. Points are assigned and totaled to a point score; total points up to 135 could be assigned to grade 1, 136–60 to Grade 2, 161–85 to Grade 3, and so on. The careful preparation required for the point system is one of its shortcomings; time and cost of development work against its acceptance.

EXHIBIT 13–11
Evaluation points for clerical jobs

Factor	*Degree points*					
	1st	*2d*	*3d*	*4th*	*5th*	*6th*
Education required	20	40	60	80	100	120
Experience required	25	50	75	100	125	150
Complexity of job	35	70	105	140		
Responsibility for relationships with others	15	30	45	60		
Working conditions	5	10	15	20		

Note: Weights assigned fit Kelly's weights of job aspects referred to above: e.g., education = 20 percent, experience = 25 percent, complexity = 35 percent, responsibility = 15 percent; working conditions = 5 percent.
Source: Robert Kelly, "Job Evaluation and Pay Plans: Office Personnel," in *Handbook of Modern Personnel Administration,* ed. Joseph Famularo (New York: McGraw-Hill Book Co., 1972).

Pay classes, rate ranges, and classifications

After completion of job evaluation, the pay-structure process is completed by establishing pay classes, rate ranges, and job classifications for ease of administration. If an enterprise uses the factor comparison or point system of job evaluation, this is accomplished by use of pay-class graphs or point conversion tables. An example of a pay-class graph is given in Exhibit 13–12. At intervals of say 50 points, a new pay class is marked off. The pay curve illustrated in Exhibit 13–12 is based on information obtained from wage and salary surveys and modified as necessary to reflect the enterprise's policy to pay at, above, or below prevailing rates. This exhibit shows a single-rate pay system rather than a rate-range system in that all jobs within a given labor class will receive the same rate of pay. In this example, pay classes are determined by the point value determined through a point system method of job evaluation.

Exhibit 13–13, another pay-class graph, demonstrates how wage and salary survey data are combined with job evaluation information to determine the pay structure for an organization. A compensation trend line is derived by first establishing the general pay pattern plotting the surveyed rates of key jobs against the point value of these jobs. The trend line can then be determined by a variety of methods, ranging from a simple eyeball estimate of the pay trend to a formalized statistical formulation of a regression line based on the sum of the least squares method. The appropriate pay rate for any job can then be ascertained by calculating the point value of the job and observing the pay level for that value as shown by the trend line. By taking a set percentage (e.g., 15 percent) above and below the trend line, minimum and maximum limit lines can be established. These limit lines can be used to help set the minimum and maximum rates if a pay range is used instead of a single rate for each job. The limit lines can also be used in place of the trend line for those enterprises that wish to establish

EXHIBIT 13–12
Pay Classes

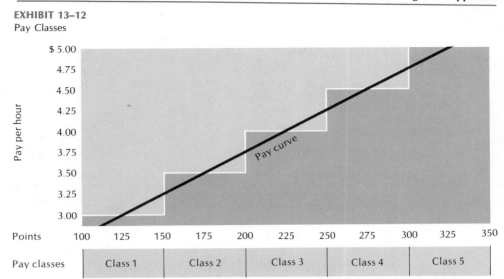

pay levels above market—the pay leaders—or those that want to pay slightly under the prevailing rates.

Although it is possible for a pay class to have a single pay rate (as in Exhibit 13–12), the more likely condition is to have a range of pays. These ranges can have the same spread or can increase the spread as the pay rate increases. An example of a pay structure with increasing rate ranges

EXHIBIT 13–13

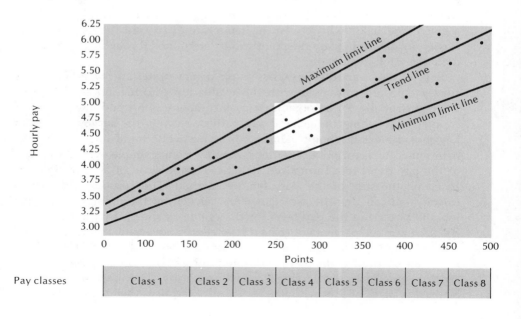

is given in Exhibit 13–13. The ranges are usually divided into a series of steps. Thus, within class 4 (250–300 points), there might be four steps:

	Pay range
Step 1	$4.20–4.40
Step 2	4.40–4.60
Step 3	4.60–4.85
Step 4	4.85–5.10

These steps in effect are money raises within a pay range to help take care of the needs of individual pay determination (to be discussed shortly).

While Exhibit 13–13 shows only the pay range for class 4, similar ranges would ordinarily be drawn for all other classes to illustrate the pay structure for all jobs in the pay plan. Within-grade increases are typically based upon seniority, merit, or a combination of both, as described in the next section. The entire pay structure should be evaluated periodically and adjusted accordingly to reflect changes in labor market conditions, level of inflation, and other factors affecting pay. Although the typical structure is shown as linear, generally a more fair structure is curvilinear, with rates increasing exponentially as pay increases.[74]

Exhibit 13–14 shows how the classification system of job evaluation leads to pay classes for U.S. federal government employees.

INDIVIDUAL PAY DETERMINATION

The final group considered in establishing pay is the employees working on the same job in an enterprise. This leads to setting the pay of each individual, within the pay ranges that have been established. This is called individual pay determination, and it is done first when the employee is hired. Then it takes place each year (or more frequently in some cases) when the employee's pay is reconsidered, often tied to performance evaluation (Chapter 10). It also is closely tied to raises (see pay administration in Chapter 14). Essentially the issue is: Given that a job can pay varying amounts within a range, which pay rate should this individual receive?

Without a doubt, in terms of equity and relative motivation, the most *crucial* aspect of setting pay is individual pay determination. The persons most employees know and can compare their own pay to are other employees doing similar jobs *within the enterprise.* This often leads employers to pursue a policy of pay secrecy (see Chapter 14).

Individual pay determination is supposed to be based on differences in performance, and most managers interpret this to mean *current* performance. Thus if welder 1 makes 10 percent more welds than welder 2, and if the quality of all the welds is similar, welder 1 ought to be paid higher in the rate range, according to most compensation specialists. Most white-collar employees, managers, professionals, and salesmen also believe this.[75] Note I did not say some other major employee groups also want the emphasis

EXHIBIT 13–14

General pay scale for employees of the U.S. federal government [pay rates of the General Schedule (5 U.S.C. 5332), as adjusted by Executive Orders 11941 (1976) and 11883 (1975)]

Grade	1	2	3	4	5	6	7	8	9	10	Amount of within-grade increase
GS-1	$5,810	$6,004	$6,198	$6,392	$6,586	$6,780	$6,974	$7,168	$7,362	$7,556	185
	5,559	5,744	5,929	6,114	6,299	6,484	6,669	6,854	7,039	7,224	
2	6,572	6,791	7,010	7,229	7,448	7,667	7,886	8,105	8,324	8,543	210
	6,296	6,506	6,716	6,926	7,136	7,346	7,556	7,766	7,976	8,186	
3	7,408	7,655	7,902	8,149	8,396	8,643	8,890	9,137	9,384	9,631	237
	7,102	7,339	7,576	7,813	8,050	8,287	8,524	8,761	8,998	9,235	
4	8,316	8,593	8,870	9,147	9,424	9,701	9,978	10,255	10,532	10,809	266
	7,976	8,242	8,508	8,774	9,040	9,306	9,572	9,838	10,104	10,370	
5	9,303	9,613	9,923	10,233	10,543	10,853	11,163	11,473	11,783	12,093	298
	8,925	9,223	9,521	9,819	10,117	10,415	10,713	11,011	11,309	11,607	
6	10,370	10,716	11,062	11,408	11,754	12,100	12,446	12,792	13,138	13,484	332
	9,946	10,278	10,610	10,942	11,274	11,606	11,938	12,270	12,602	12,934	
7	11,523	11,907	12,291	12,675	13,059	13,443	13,827	14,211	14,595	14,979	368
	11,046	11,414	11,782	12,150	12,518	12,886	13,254	13,622	13,990	14,358	
8	12,763	13,188	13,613	14,038	14,463	14,888	15,313	15,738	16,163	16,588	407
	12,222	12,629	13,036	13,443	13,850	14,257	14,664	15,071	15,478	15,885	
9	14,097	14,567	15,037	15,507	15,977	16,447	16,917	17,387	17,857	18,327	449
	13,482	13,931	14,380	14,829	15,278	15,727	16,176	16,625	17,074	17,523	
10	15,524	16,041	16,558	17,075	17,592	18,109	18,626	19,143	19,660	20,177	494
	14,824	15,318	15,812	16,306	16,800	17,294	17,788	18,282	18,776	19,270	
11	17,056	17,625	18,194	18,763	19,332	19,901	20,470	21,039	21,608	22,177	542
	16,255	16,797	17,339	17,881	18,423	18,965	19,507	20,049	20,591	21,133	
12	20,442	21,123	21,804	22,485	23,166	23,847	24,528	25,209	25,890	26,571	646
	19,386	20,032	20,678	21,324	21,970	22,616	23,262	23,908	24,554	25,200	
13	24,308	25,118	25,928	26,738	27,548	28,358	29,168	29,978	30,788	31,598	764
	22,906	23,670	24,434	25,198	25,962	26,726	27,490	28,254	29,018	29,782	
14	28,725	29,683	30,641	31,599	32,557	33,515	34,473	35,431	36,389	37,347	895
	26,861	27,756	28,651	29,546	30,441	31,336	32,231	33,126	34,021	34,916	
15	33,789	34,915	36,041	37,167	38,293	39,419	40,545 a/	41,671 a/	42,797 a/	43,923 a/	1,044
	31,309	32,353	33,397	34,441	35,485	36,529	37,573	38,617*	39,661 a/	40,705*	
16	39,629 a/	40,950 a/	42,271 a/	43,592 a/	44,913 a/	46,234 a/	47,555 a/	48,876*	50,197 a/		1,211
	36,338	37,549	38,760*	39,971*	41,182 a/	42,393*	43,604*				
17	46,423 a/	47,970 a/	49,517 a/	51,064 a/	52,611 a/						1,402
	42,066*	43,468*	44,870*	46,272*	47,674*						
18	54,410 a/										....
	48,654*										

a/ The rate of basic pay for employees at these rates is limited by section 5308 of title 5 of the United States Code to the rate for level V of the Executive Schedule (as of the effective date of this salary adjustment, $39,600).

* The rate of basic pay for employees at these rates is limited by section 5308 of title 5 of the United States Code to the rate for level V of the Executive Schedule (as of the effective date of this salary adjustment, $37,800).

Note: The top line opposite each grade number shows the rates which became effective beginning with the first pay period on or after October 1, 1976. The second line shows the on current performance. A few employees are rated higher than their current performance because their *future* performance looks good. This is normally the case for new employees of great promise; in effect, it is a recruiting device to get the person hired.

The fact is that although many employees believe employees' pay should be differentiated on the basis of current performance, many others (perhaps a majority) believe that seniority, age, and therefore *past* performance and loyalty should have equal or greater weight in individual pay determination.[76] Managers may claim they have merit or performance-based pay systems, but many studies indicate they are more accurately based on current performance plus seniority, or seniority alone.[77] This can have the effect of reducing the motivations of higher performing younger employees. And although many may believe that this should not be, it has been shown that sex, race, personal appearance, and lifestyle influence individual pay.[78] For example, tall, white males who are married and live a clean life tend to be higher paid.

Thus the final compensation decision is to place the employee within the pay range based on performance and other factors—individual pay determination.

SUMMARY, CONCLUSIONS, AND RECOMMENDATIONS

This concluding part of Chapter 13 will summarize briefly the aspects of compensation covered and present some summary propositions. But since there are two chapters on compensation, recommendations and some concluding remarks will be saved for Chapter 14.

In this chapter, the first purpose was to impress upon you the multiple meanings of pay at work. The employee can see pay as satisfying physiological and other needs. Next we discussed how pay is set relative to several groups: those outside the enterprise working similar jobs (pay level), those inside on different jobs (pay structure), and those inside on the same job (individual pay determination).

With regard to pay level, we analyzed the impact of external and internal factors on pay in general and pay level in particular. We used the diagnostic approach to weave these together.

The first topic discussed was the possible impact of pay on employees' performance and satisfaction. The following propositions seem appropriate:

> *Proposition 13.1.* If enterprise employees believe that pay is equitable, pay will increase employee satisfaction.
>
> *Proposition 13.2.* If enterprise employees desire pay to be related to performance, and if the enterprise designs its pay plan accordingly, merit pay plans will tend to improve performance.
>
> *Proposition 13.3.* If a merit pay plan is designed to improve employee performance, the pay should reflect both present and past performance contributions of the employee.

The external factors affecting pay levels—the government, unions, economic conditions, and the labor market—were discussed. Some propositions flowing from this analysis include:

> *Proposition 13.4.* The greater the government legislation in the pay area, the less flexible is the employer in pay policy, and the higher is the pay level of employees.
>
> *Proposition 13.5.* The greater the influence of unions in the geographic area of the employer, the less flexible is the employer in pay policy, and the higher is the pay level.
>
> *Proposition 13.6.* The smaller the supply of labor and the more prosperous the economy, the higher the pay level the employer must use.

The major tool used to help the employer set the pay level is the pay survey. With regard to the use of pay surveys, these propositions are suggested:

> *Proposition 13.7.* The larger the organization, the more likely it is to use pay surveys and to develop the enterprise's own pay surveys.
>
> *Proposition 13.8.* The more complex and volatile the organization and its environment, the more frequently must pay surveys be run, and the more difficult they are to use.
>
> *Proposition 13.9.* The more useful the pay survey is, the greater the likelihood that employees were involved in the choice of the jobs and enterprises to be surveyed.

Enterprise factors affecting pay level and pay in general include enterprise age, size, and managerial goals and pay strategy. Some propositions in this area include:

> *Proposition 13.10.* The larger the organization, the higher the pay levels.
>
> *Proposition 13.11.* The most significant influence on pay level is the management pay-level strategy pursued by the enterprise.

Pay structure is that aspect of pay that relates an employee's pay to the pay of others in the enterprise not performing the same job. The most frequently used tool in pay structuring is job evaluation. Several propositions apply to this area.

> *Proposition 13.12.* The more involved the employees who are to be evaluated are in the job evaluation, the more effective will formal job evaluation be.
>
> *Proposition 13.13.* The larger the organization, the more likely is a formal job evaluation system to be used.
>
> *Proposition 13.14.* If the organization is unionized, it is more likely to use formal job evaluation.

Proposition 13.15. The more complex and volatile the organization, the more likely is it to use a more sophisticated job evaluation system such as the point method.

After jobs are evaluated, rate ranges and pay classes are developed for each job category. This then becomes the basis for individual pay determination and establishing the actual pay for each person within the range.

Chapter 14 will complete the treatment of compensation.

QUESTIONS

1. Is pay important to employees, employers, society? If so, how?
2. What is compensation? How does it fit into the total reward system of the enterprise?
3. How does compensation relate to other personnel functions?
4. Who makes compensation decisions? How are the decision makers related?
5. Distinguish pay-level decisions, pay-structure decisions, and individual pay determination decisions.
6. What are the most significant diagnostic factors affecting compensation?
7. Does compensation affect employee satisfaction? How and under what circumstances?
8. What do motivation theories say about the effect of compensation on employee performance?
9. Does compensation affect employee performance? If so, how, and under what circumstances?
10. What are the external factors affecting pay-level decisions?
11. Discuss the major laws affecting compensation. How do they affect the enterprise's pay level?
12. How do unions affect the pay level?
13. How does the economy affect the pay level?
14. How does the state of the labor market affect the pay level?
15. What is a pay survey? What is the best way to run one?
16. If you are going to use pay surveys completed by outside agencies, which ones would you use for blue collar employees? For managers?
17. What are the enterprise factors affecting pay level?
18. How does management's pay strategy affect pay level? Give an example of the most typical pay strategy. Which strategy would you pursue?
19. What is a pay structure?
20. What is job evaluation? What are the techniques for performing job evaluation.
21. Why are job evaluations performed? Which technique is best? Which is most frequently used?
22. Distinguish and describe the interrelationships among pay classes, rate ranges, and pay classifications.
23. How are individual pay determination decisions made?
24. What are the most significant propositions for this chapter?

NOTES AND REFERENCES

1. "The Hot New Rich" *Time*, June 13, 1977, pp. 72–83.

2. For references that discuss compensation issues, see David Belcher and Thomas Atchison, "Compensation for Work," in *Handbook of Work, Organization, and Society* ed. Robert Dubin (Chicago: Rand McNally & Co., 1976); David Belcher, *Compensation Administration* (Englewood Cliffs, N.J.: Prentice-Hall, Inc., 1974), ch. 1, 2; Thomas Guthrie et al., "The Remuneration Riddle," *Personnel Journal*, April 1974, pp. 253–57; Allen Nash and Stephen Carroll, *The Management of Compensation* (Monterey, Cal.: Brooks/Cole Publishing Co., 1975); Thomas Patten, *Pay* (Chicago: Glencoe Press, 1977); Herbert Zollitsch and Adolph Langsner, *Wage and Salary Administration* (Cincinnati: Southwestern Co., 1970).

3. Richard Farrell, "Compensation and Benefits," *Personnel Journal*, November 1976, pp. 557–63, 567 ff.

4. Patten, *Pay*, ch. 1.

5. *The Personnel Executive's Job* (Englewood Cliffs, N.J.: Prentice-Hall/ASPA, 1977). For a current view of the role of the compensation manager see Bruce Ellig, "Compensation Management: Its Past and Its Future," *Personnel*, May–June 1977, pp. 30–40.

6. Eliott Jaques, *Equitable Payment* (New York: John Wiley & Sons, 1963).

7. E. R. Livernash, "Wages and Benefits," in *Review of Industrial Relations Research* ed. Woodrow Ginsberg et al. (Madison, Wis.: Industrial Relations Research Association, 1970), pp. 79–144.

8. Nash and Carroll, *Management of Compensation*.

9. B. F. Skinner, *Science and Human Behavior* (New York: Macmillan Co., 1953).

10. J. B. Wolfe, "Effectiveness of Token Rewards for Chimpanzees," *Comparative Psychology Monographs* 12, 5 (1936), pp. 1–72; J. Cowles, "Food Tokens as Incentives for Learning by Chimpanzees," *Comparative Psychology Monographs* 14 (1937), pp. 1–96.

11. Judson Brown. *The Nature of Behavior* (New York: McGraw-Hill Book Co., 1961).

12. Frederick Herzberg, "New Approaches in Management Organization and Job Design," in *Studies in Management Process and Organizational Behavior* ed. John Turner et al. (Glenview, Ill.: Scott Foresman & Co., 1972).

13. E. E. Lawler, Jr., *Pay and Organizational Effectiveness* (New York: McGraw-Hill Book Co., 1971).

14. For information and references on these theories, see Chapter 2.

15. James March and Herbert Simon, *Organizations* (New York: John Wiley & Sons, 1958).

16. Belcher, *Compensation Administration*.

17. See, for example, Lee Dyer et al., "Managerial Perceptions of Salary Criteria for Themselves, Their Subordinates, and Their Satisfaction with These Criteria," *Proceedings, Academy of Management*, 1976; D. O. Jorgenson et al., "Effects of the Manipulation of a Performance-Reward Contingency on Behavior in a Simulated Work Setting," *Journal of Applied Psychology* 57, 3 (1973), pp. 271–80; Donald Schwab, "The Motivational Impact of a Compensation System on Employee Performance," *Organizational Behavior and Human Performance* 9 (1973), pp. 215–25; Donald Schwab, "Impact of Alternative Compensation Systems on Pay Valence and Instrumentality Perceptions," *Journal of Applied Psychology* 58, 3 (1973), pp. 308–312; Donald Schwab and Marc Wallace, Jr., "Correlates of Employee Satisfaction with Pay," *Industrial Relations*, May 1974, pp. 78–89; E. E. Lawler, "Reward Systems," in *Improving Life at Work* ed. Richard Hackman and Lloyd Suttle (Santa Monica, Cal.: Goodyear Publishing Co., 1977).

18. Charles Greene, "Causal Correlations among Managers' Merit Pay, Job Satisfaction, and Performance," *Journal of Applied Psychology* 58, 1 (1973) pp. 95–100.

19. Herzberg, "Management Organization and Job Design.

20. Herbert Meyer, "The Pay for Performance Dilemma," *Organizational Dynamics,* Winter 1975, pp. 39–50; A. Mikalachi, "There Is No Merit in Merit Pay," *Business Quarterly,* Spring 1976, pp. 46–50; Edward Deci, *Intrinsic Motivation* (New York: Plenum Publishing Corp., 1975).

21. Robert Pritchard et al., "Effects of Extrinsic Financial Rewards on Intrinsic Motivation," *Journal of Applied Psychology* 62, 1 (1977), pp. 9–15; Craig Pinder, "Additivity vs. Nonadditivity of Intrinsic and Extrinsic Incentives," *Journal of Applied Psychology* 61, 6 (1976), pp. 693–700.

22. G. R. Salancik, "Interaction Effects of Performance and Money on Self-Perception of Intrinsic Motivation," *Organizational Behavior and Human Performance,* June 1975, pp. 339–51.

23. M. H. Brenner and H. C. Lockwood, "Salary as a Predictor of Satisfaction: A 20 Year Study," *Journal of Applied Psychology* 48 (August 1965), pp. 295–98; Mason Haire, "The Incentive Character of Pay," in *Management Compensation* ed. Robert Andrews (Ann Arbor: Foundation for Research on Human Behavior, 1965); Thomas Patten, "Merit Increases and the Facts of Organizational Life," *Management of Personnel Quarterly,* Summer 1968, pp. 30–38; E. E. Lawler, Jr., "The Multi Trait-Multi Rater Approach to Measuring Managerial Job Performance," *Journal of Applied Psychology* 50 (October 1967), pp. 369–81.

24. James Hyatt, "Merit Money," *The Wall Street Journal,* March 7, 1977.

25. Nash and Carroll, *Management of Compensation.*

26. Jaques, *Equitable Payment;* J. Stacey Adams, "Inequity in Social Exchange," in *Advances in Experimental Social Psychology,* ed. Leonard Berkowitz (New York: Academic Press, 1965); J. Stacey Adams, "Toward an Understanding of Equity," *Journal of Abnormal and Social Psychology* 67 (1963), pp. 422–36.

27. E. E. Lawler, Jr., "Equity Theory as a Predictor of Productivity and Work Quality," *Psychological Bulletin,* December 1968; pp. 596–610; Thomas Atchison and David Belcher "Equity, Rewards and Compensation Administration," *Personnel Administration,* March–April 1971, pp. 32–36; R. D. Pritchard, "Equity Theory: A Review and Critique," *Organizational Behavior and Human Performance,* May 1969, pp. 176–211; Lee Dyer and Roland Theriault, "The Determinants of Pay Satisfaction," *Journal of Applied Psychology* 61, 5 (1976), pp. 596–604; Greene, "Managers' Merit Pay, Job Satisfaction, and Performance."

28. Edward Locke, "Satisfiers and Dissatisfiers among White Collar and Blue Collar Employees," *Journal of Applied Psychology* 58, 1 (1973), pp. 67–76.

29. Nash and Carroll, *Management of Compensation.*

30. Schwab, "Motivational Impact of Compensation System"; Schwab, "Alternative Compensation Systems"; Schwab and Wallace, "Correlates of Employee Satisfaction with Pay."

31. John Todd, "Cafeteria Compensation: Making Management Motivators Meaningful," *Personnel Journal,* May 1975, pp. 275–81; Thomas Paine, "Flexible Compensation Can Work," *Financial Executive,* February 1974, pp. 56–69.

32. W. Donald Wood and Pradeep Kumar, *Canadian Perspective on Wage-Price Guidelines* (Queens University: Industrial Relations Center, 1976); Sidney Jones, "The Lessons of Wage and Price Controls," *Canadian Business Review,* Summer 1974, pp. 12–15; George Schultz and Kenneth Dam, "Reflectors on Wage and Price Controls," *Industrial and Labor Relations Review,* January 1977, pp. 139–51; Craufurd D. Goodwin, *Exhortation and Controls* (Washington, D.C.: Brookings Institution, 1975); C. Jackson Grayson, *Confessions of a Price Controller* (Homewood, Ill.: Dow Jones–Irwin, 1974); Daniel Mitchell and Ross Azevedo, "A Pay Board Assessment of Wage Controls," *Monthly Labor Review,* April 1973, pp. 21–23; John

Kraft and Blain Roberts, *Wage and Price Controls: The U.S. Experiment* (New York: Praeger Publications, Inc., 1975); Robert Lanzilotti, et al., *Phase II in Review* (Washington, D.C.: Brookings Institution, 1975); Daniel Mills, *Government, Labor and Inflation* (Chicago: University of Chicago Press, 1975).

33.   Amanda Bennett, "Trouble for Trudeau," *The Wall Street Journal*, September 27, 1976; "Half of Canada's Union Workers Strike in One-Day Protest against Wage Controls," *The Wall Street Journal*, October 15, 1976. Regarding "TIP," see "Another Weapon against Inflation: Tax Policy," *Business Week*, Oct. 3, 1977, pp. 94–96.

34.   James Kau and Mary Kau, "Social Policy Implications of the Minimum Wage Law," *Policy Sciences*, March 1973, pp. 21–27; Burton Teague, "The Minimum Wage—How Minimum Should It Be?" *Conference Board Record*, January 1974, pp. 21–26; Alfred Malabre, "The Jobless Young," *The Wall Street Journal*, February 9, 1977; Thomas Moore, "The Effect of Minimum Wages on Teenage Unemployment Rates," *Journal of Political Economy*, August 1971; Douglas Adie, "Teenage Unemployment and Real Federal Minimum Wages," *Journal of Political Economy*, March/April 1973, pp. 435–41. Martin Feldstein, *Lowering the Permanent Rate of Unemployment Report*, Joint Economic Committee, U.S. Congress, September 18, 1973.

35.   Hyman Kaitz, "Experience of the Past," in *Youth Employment and Minimum Wages*, Department of Labor, Bureau of Labor Statistics no. 1657 (Washington, D.C., 1970), pp. 30–54; Abraham Weiss, "A Look at the Minimum Wage and HR 10130," *Labor Law Journal*, March 1976, pp. 131–40.

36.   Janice Hedges, "Long Weedends and Premium Pay," *Monthly Labor Review*, April 1976, pp. 7–12; Bevars Mabry, "The Sources of Overtime: An Integrated Perspective," *Industrial Relations*, May 1976, pp. 248–51.

37.   "Young Workers and the Wage and Hour Law," *Occupational Outlook Quarterly*, Fall 1974, pp. 6–9.

38.   John Buckley, "Pay Differences between Men and Women in the Same Job," *Monthly Labor Review*, November 1971, pp. 36–39; William Hrabak, "EEO and Base Compensation: Effects Count, Not Intent," *Management Review*, September 1973, pp. 15–20; Jack Magarrell, "Faculty Women's Status Deteriorated in Year," *Chronicle of Higher Education*, June 28, 1976; Robert Frank, "Sources of Male-Female Wage Differentials," International Institute of Management, 1976, mimeographed; Marianne Ferber and Helen Lowry, "The Sex Differential in Earnings," *Industrial and Labor Relations Review* (1975–1976), pp. 377–87; Wilburn Reif, et al., "Sex as a Discriminating Variable in Organizational Reward Decisions," *Academy of Management Journal*, September 1976, pp. 469–76; Evelyne Sullerot, "Equality of Remuneration for Men and Women in the Member States of the EEC," *International Labor Review*, August–September 1975, pp. 87–108.

39.   Alan Blender, "Wage Discrimination: Reduced Form and Structural Estimates," *Journal of Human Resources*, Fall 1973, pp. 436–55; Robert Flanagan, "Racial Wage Discrimination and Employment Segregation," *Journal of Human Resources*, Fall 1973, pp. 456–71.

40.   John Burns and Catherine Burns, "An Analysis of the Equal Pay Act," *Labor Law Journal*, February 1973, pp. 92–99.

41.   Ivan Guay, "Is There a Minimum Wage?" *The Labour Gazette*, October 1975, pp. 705–6.

42.   Harry Waisglass, "Questions of Public Policy for the Consideration of Periodic Revision in the Minimum Wage," *Relations Industrielles* 28, 3 (1973), pp. 629–32; E. G. West, "Canadian Minimum Wages and the New American Debate," *The Canadian Business Review*, Winter 1975, pp. 19–21; E. G. West, "New Tests of the Efficiency of Minimum Wage Laws," *The Labour Gazette*, October 1975, pp. 707–10.

43.   S. Allan Nodwell, Labour Legislation in Canada, 1975, Part 4: Employment Standards," *The Labour Gazette*, June 1976, pp. 328–31.

44.   R. Ozanne, *Wages in Practice and Theory* (Madison: University of Wisconsin Press, 1968); R. L. Raimon and V. Stockov, "The Effect of Blue Collar Unionism on White Collar

Earnings," *Industrial and Labor Relations Review,* April 1969, pp. 358–74; Edwin Beal et al., *The Practice of Collective Bargaining* (Homewood, Ill.; Richard D. Irwin, Inc., 1976), ch. 10; Robert McKersie and L. C. Hunter, *Pay, Productivity and Collective Bargaining* (London: Macmillan & Co., 1973).

45.   Livernash, "Wages and Benefits."

46.   David Lewin and Raymond Horton, "The Impact of Collective Bargaining on the Merit System in Government," *The Arbitration Journal,* September 1975, pp. 199–211.

47.   *Handbook of Labor Statistics,* U.S. Department of Labor, Bureau of Labor Statistics (Washington, D.C.: U.S. Government Printing Office, 1975).

48.   Charles Mulcahy, "Ability to Pay: The Public Employee Dilemma," *The Arbitration Journal,* 31, 2 (1977), pp. 90–96.

49.   William Barnes, "Job Search Models, The Duration of Unemployment and the Asking Wage: Some Empirical Evidence," *Journal of Human Resources,* Spring 1975, pp. 230–40; Livernash, "Wages and Benefits"; G. L. Perry, *Unemployment, Money Wage Rates, and Inflation* (Cambridge, Mass.: MIT Press, 1966); Richard Lester, "Pay Differentials by Size of Establishment," *Industrial Relations,* October 1967, pp. 57–67. Differences may also exist because of different pay levels in different geographic regions. See "A Roundtable on Geographic Factors and Compensation," *The Personnel Administrator,* May 1977, pp. 19–25.

50.   Sharon Smith, "Pay Differentials between Federal Government and Private Sector Workers," *Industrial and Labor Relations Review* (1975–76), pp. 179–97; William Hoke, "Equity for Exempt Personnel," *The Personnel Administrator,* July 1976, pp. 41–46.

51.   Chris Jecchinis and T. D. Harris, "Factors Determining Wage Differentials in the Americas," *Relations Industrielles* 29, 1 (1974), pp. 305–18; Douglas Smith, "Wage Linkages between Canada and the United States," *Industrial and Labour Relations Review,* 2 (1975), pp. 258–68; "C. D. Howe Research Institute Study: A Change in the Canada–U.S. Wage Gap Picture," *The Labour Gazette,* June 1976, pp. 320–22; Pradeep Kumar, *Relative Wage Differentials in Canada Industries* (Kingston, Ont.: Industrial Relations Centre, Queens University, 1975).

52.   James Houff, "Improving Area Wage Survey Indexes," *Monthly Labor Review,* January 1973, pp. 52–57.

53.   Glenn Engelke, "Conducting Surveys," in *Handbook of Wage and Salary Administration,* ed. Milton Rock (New York: McGraw-Hill Book Co., 1972); H. M. Douty and T. P. Kanninen, "Community Approach to Wage Studies," *Monthly Labor Review,* October 1949, pp. 365–70; George Mellgard, "Achieving External Competitiveness Through Survey Use," in *Handbook of Wage and Salary Administration,* ed. Rock; Nash and Carroll, *Management of Compensation,* ch. 4.

54.   Martin Patchen, *The Choice of Wage Comparisons* (Englewood Cliffs, N.J.: Prentice-Hall, Inc., 1961); Bureau of National Affairs, *Personnel Policies Forum,* Survey no. 97 (1972); D. L. Norrgard, "The Public Pay Plan: Some New Approaches," *Public Personnel Review* 32 (1971), pp. 91–95.

55.   David Lewin, "Aspects of Wage Determination in Local Government Employment," *Public Administration Review,* March–April 1974, pp. 149–55; David Lewin, "Prevailing Wage Principle and Public Wage Decisions," *Public Personnel Management,* November–December 1974, pp. 473–85.

56.   Belcher, *Compensation Administration,* pp. 239–41; 474–75; BNA, *Personnel Policies Forum;* F. Elliott Avery, *Handbook of Wage and Salary Administration,* ed. Rock.

57.   R. S. Stockton, *Wages Policies and Wage Surveys* (Columbus: Ohio State University, Bureau of Business Research, 1959).

58.   G. K. Ingham, *Size of Industrial Organization and Worker Behavior* (London: Cambridge University Press, 1970); Lester, "Pay Differentials by Size of Establishment"; D. L. Peters and Ernest

McCormick, "Comparative Reliability of Numerically Anchored versus Job Task Anchored Rating Scales," *Journal of Applied Psychology* 50, 1 (1966), pp. 92–96.

59. Lloyd Reynolds, *The Structure of the Labor Market* (New York: Greenwood Press, 1951).

60. Sumner Slichter et al., *The Impact of Collective Bargaining on Management* (Washington, D.C.: Brookings Institution, 1960).

61. Allan Nash and John Minter, *Personnel and Labor Relations: An Evolutionary Approach* (New York: Macmillan Co., 1973).

62. Reynolds, *Structure of the Labor Market.*

63. Raymond Jacobson et al., "Specific Job Evaluation Systems in Action," in *Handbook of Wage and Salary Administration,* ed. Rock; Philip Oliver, "Modernizing a State Job Evaluation and Pay Plan," *Public Personnel Management,* May–June 1976, pp. 168–73; Edward Shils, "Developing a Perspective on Job Measurement," in *Handbook of Wage and Salary Administration,* ed. Rock; Richard Wing, "Achieving Internal Equity through Job Measurement," in *Handbook of Wage and Salary Administration,* ed. Rock.

64. BNA, *Personnel Policies Forum.*

65. Harold Janes, "Issues in Job Evaluation: The Union View," *Personnel Journal,* September 1972, pp. 675–79; Edward Hay, "The Attitude of the AFL on Job Evaluation," *Personnel Journal,* April–May 1947, pp. 163–69.

66. R. E. Christal and J. M. Madden, *The Effect of Degree of Familiarity in Job Evaluation,"* USAF Personnel Laboratory WADD–TN 60–257 (Dayton, 1960); J. M. Madden, *Familiarity Effects in Evaluation Judgments,* USAF Personnel Laboratory, WADD–TN 60–261 (Lockland, Tex., 1960).

67. William Scott, Jr., *The Reliability and Validity of a Six Factor Job Evaluation,* unpublished Ph.D. thesis, Purdue University, 1963; M. K. Davis and Joseph Tiffin, "Cross Validation of an Abbreviated Point Job Evaluation System," *Journal of Applied Psychology* 34, 4 (1956), pp. 225–28.

68. Clark Kerr, and L. H. Fisher, "The Effect of the Environment and Administration on Job Evaluation, *Harvard Business Review,* May 1950, pp. 77–96.

69. D. J. Chesler, "Reliability and Comparability of Different Job Evaluation Systems," *Journal of Applied Psychology* 32, 5 (1948), pp. 465–75; Robert Kelly, "Job Evaluation and Pay Plans: Office Personnel," in *Handbook of Modern Personnel Administration* ed. Joseph Famularo (New York: McGraw-Hill Book Co., 1972); Lawler, *Pay and Organizational Effectiveness;* E. C. Snyder, "Equitable Wage and Salary Structuring," *Personnel Journal,* May 1977, pp. 240–44.

70. David Robinson et al., "Comparison of Job Evaluation Methods," *Journal of Applied Psychology* 59, 5 (1974), pp. 633–37.

71. Eugene Benge, "Using Factor Methods to Measure Jobs," in *Handbook of Wage and Salary Administration,* ed. Rock.

72. Henry Sargent, "Using the Point Method to Measure Jobs," in *Handbook of Wage and Salary Administration,* ed. Rock.

73. Robert Kelly, "Job Evaluation and Pay Plans: Office Personnel," in *Handbook of Modern Personnel Administration,* ed. Famularo.

74. A. W. Charles, "Installing Single Factor Job Evaluation," *Compensation Review* 3, 3 (1971), pp. 9–24; David Van Fleet and Douglas Stone, "Progression Curves in Salary Administration for Colleges and Universities," *Journal of College and University Personnel Association* July–August 1975, pp. 20–27.

75. Lawler, *Pay and Organizational Effectiveness;* Nash and Carroll, *Management of Compensation,* pp. 148–155.

76. R. Van Zelst, and W. Kerr, "Worker Attitudes toward Merit Ratings," *Personnel Psychology* 6 (1953), pp. 159–72; Lawler, *Pay and Organizational Effectiveness.*

77. National Industrial Conference Board, *Personnel Practices in Factory and Office: Manufacturing Studies in Personnel Policy* 194 (New York, 1964); J. M. Greiner, "Employee Incentive in Local Government," Labor Management Relations Service Newsletter, National League of Cities, no. 4 (1973), pp. 4–6; Slichter, *Impact of Collective Bargaining;* Albert Rees and George Schultz, *Workers and Wages in an Urban Labor Market* (Chicago: University of Chicago Press, 1970).

78. Belcher, *Compensation Administration,* pp. 216–22.

Compensation: Methods and policy issues

CHAPTER OBJECTIVES

■ To show how to implement assumptions on pay and performance; to illustrate methods of payment.

■ To demonstrate that executive compensation is similar yet different from operative, clerical, and professional/technical compensation.

■ To help you become cognizant of current crucial pay policy issues.

CHAPTER OUTLINE

I. Methods of Payment
   A. Payment for Time Worked
   B. Incentive Plans
   C. Individual Incentives
   D. Group Incentives
   E. Enterprise Incentive Schemes

II. Executive Compensation
   A. Executive Salaries
   B. Executive Perks
   C. Bonuses
   D. Stock Options, Performance Shares, and Book Value Devices
   E. Canadian Executive Compensation
   F. Executive Compensation Policy

III. Compensation Administration Issues
   A. Pay Secrecy or Openness
   B. Security in Pay
   C. Pay Raises

IV. Summary, Conclusions, and Recommendations

This chapter will complete the discussion of the seven criteria for effective compensation introduced in Chapter 13. A compensation system which meets all these criteria will accomplish the objective of providing a system of rewards which is equitable to employer and employee alike, so that the employee's satisfaction and production are both heightened. The effective compensation system should be:

Adequate. Chapter 13 gave the legal definition of adequacy as set forth in minimum-wage and other legislation. The managerial definition of adequacy, or pay-level policies designed to pay the going wage, was also described.

Equitable. Chapter 13 discussed job evaluation as one technique to be used to attain equity. Chapter 14 will touch upon the related policy issue of whether all employees should be paid salaries.

Incentive-providing. Chapter 13 discussed the theory behind the merit or incentive pay system. This chapter will discuss how incentive pay systems are designed and how raises are used as a form of incentive.

Four of the criteria will be discussed primarily in this chapter:

Secure. The extent to which the employee's pay seems secure to him or her.

Balanced. The extent to which pay is a reasonable part of the total reward package, which includes benefits, promotions, and so on.

Control. The extent to which the pay system is cost effective for the organization.

Acceptable to the Employee. Whether employees think the pay system makes sense. Three aspects of this will be discussed in Chapter 14: whether pay should be secret; compensation communication to achieve acceptability; and employee participation in pay decision making.

Several vignettes will illustrate the compensation issues to be described in this chapter:

Johnson R. Verden has been thinking about doing something about the productivity at his plant. Recently J. R. has had an opportunity to compare his costs with his competitors'. Although his costs are in line for most aspects of operations, and base wages are similar, his labor costs are higher. J. R. pays by the hour. Some of his competitors use pay incentives, a piece rate, or group incentive plans. Productivity appears to be low, and J. R. wonders if one of these schemes would improve his workers' productivity level. Or is the problem poor supervisory skills?

Martha Lesner is president of a financial services enterprise. Recently her executive turnover has been high, and Martha wonders if her executive compensation package is a contributing factor. Those leaving have given this as the main reason, but Martha realizes that compensation is more acceptable than other reasons to give a former employer for leaving. That's why it's hard for her to figure out if pay is really the problem.

Martha pays the going rate for salaries and has a bonus system when profits allow it. But some of those leaving said their new employers had performance-share programs. Martha is wondering if she should hire a consultant to advise her on her executive compensation program.

Tom Nichols, the personnel manager at the San Francisco plant, was about to sit down to a meeting he did not want to attend, but then, did he ever go to meetings he wanted? This one in particular was going to be bad, though; the guys were never satisfied over money. Back in school, Tom had learned that one thing that never was settled in personnel was pay; people were almost always griping about it.

The knock came on the door; in they filed, and Tom found himself shaking hands and making small talk. He sat back in his chair and heard from the committee of supervisors.

Chet: Tom we're here because the troops are unhappy.

Tom: The troops are always unhappy.

Chet: Sure. But this time it sounds serious. My boys are tired of punching time clocks, being laid off regularly, and getting paid by the hour. Everyone else here—salesmen, office help, executives, R&D—they don't punch no clocks. And they get salaries—52 weeks a year. Why don't my troops?

Tom: Well, you know, it's always been that way. Besides. . . .

Chet: Don't give me that it's always been that way sh____. You can do something about it. My men want the security of a regular paycheck and the dignity of no time clock. You know the UAW's been around. This is the kind of issue that gets a union in a shop. What are you going to do about it?

The other supervisors were nodding their heads, and Tom wondered what to say.

Mary: Did you hear that Joanne makes $15.00 a week more than me? I've been here longer, too. What is this?

Sandra: Why not go to June about it? She's the boss.

Mary (to June): How come Joanne makes $15 a week more than me? I've been here longer.

June: How do you know that's true? We don't reveal salaries around here, and it's company policy not to discuss others' pay."

Mary: Never mind how I found out about it, and let's cut out that company policy stuff. Why is Joanne paid more than me?

Dick Bates is a department head. He's just been given 10 percent raise money for his 25 employees. Some deserve no raise, really; others deserve something; a few deserve a lot. How should he divide the money? Should Dick really give no money to some? With inflation what it is, that's really a pay cut. Do they really deserve a cut? And how much should the average get? The cost of living went up 7 percent. If Dick gives them much more than that, there won't be enough to give big raises to those who really deserve it. And that says nothing about people who deserve raises because their base pay is too low, or who are being promoted. How does Dick allocate the raise money?

METHODS OF PAYMENT

Employees can be paid for the time they work, the output they produce, or a combination of these two factors.

Payment for time worked

The great majority of employees are paid for time worked, in the form of wages or salaries. Paying for time worked and establishing compensation systems based on time were the compensation methods discussed in Chapter 13. Pay surveys are used to establish competitive pay for the industry, and job evaluation is the principal method for setting time-pay schedules. Then pay ranges, pay classifications, and similar tools are developed for individual pay determination, the final step in a time-based pay system.

Salaries for everyone?   Typically, most employees are paid salaries; exceptions are blue-collar and some clerical employees, who are paid hourly wages. One issue in the time-pay system is whether everyone should be paid a salary. (Remember Tom Nichols's dilemma in dealing with his supervisors?) Would you rather be paid strictly by the hour and not know your income week to week, month to month, or be paid a salary so you could plan your life? In general, most blue-collar employees are given hourly pay, but there has been a movement to place all employees on salaries and give them the same benefits and working conditions others have. Firms such as IBM, Alcan (Canada), Texas Instruments, Polaroid, Phillips (Canada), Avon, Gillette, Black and Decker, and Kinetic Dispersion have experimented with this plan.

The advantage claimed for this move is that blue-collar workers become more integrated into the enterprise, and this improves the climate of employee relations. No study claims that it improves productivity, and the reports of its effects on absenteeism are mixed. Some studies claim absenteeism decreases,[1] others that it increases but management controls and peer pressure later bring it down to acceptable levels.[2] Exhibit 14–1 lists the improvements claimed when salaries are paid to every employee.

But if everyone goes on salaries, it is possible that the long-run security of positions will be diminished. With hourly workers, if business is down it is relatively easy for an enterprise to reduce the hours worked daily or weekly, save the labor costs, and adjust to the realities of the marketplace. If everyone is on salary, management tends to look toward full layoffs or reduction in the labor force by attrition or terminations. Salaries for everyone changes labor costs from variable to fixed, and this can have serious employment security implications.

The success of a total-salaries program requires stable, mature, responsible employees, a cooperative union, willing supervisors, and a work load that allows continuous employment. Caution is urged in adopting this approach until more studies have been done on this issue.

EXHIBIT 14-1
Some positive results of salaries for everyone

Company	Union status	Date of change-over	Objective of changeover	Treatment of time clocks	Absence rate for workers affected by plan*			Employee reaction	Employer appraisal
					Before	After	Current		
Avon Products	Nonunion	1972†	Eliminate distinctions in treatment of office and factory employees	Removed	4.1%	4.4%	4.2%	Some preimplementation resistance from management; favorable postimplementation reaction, including that of supervisors	There were no specific gains, but management is satisfied that the approach is an essential part of its philosophy
Gillette	Nonunion	1955	Provide a logical alternative to improved sick leave	Retained	4.6	4.7	4.7	Generally favorable reaction, but initial minor concern about loss of status of clerical employees	Management is satisfied with the results
Black and Decker	Nonunion	1971	Improve employee relationships, with consequent benefits to operational effectiveness	Removed	1.5‡	2.3	2.0	Introduction of plan a contribution to favorable attitudes; some supervisory concern over payment decisions	Response generated by the plan has enabled continued productivity improvements.
Kinetic Dispersion	Union (UAW)	1962	Eliminate distinctions and provide security of income	Retained	§	§	§	Plan welcomed, but misused initially	Management is reasonably satisfied, although problems were far more severe than anticipated
Polaroid	Nonunion	1966	Unify hourly and salaried employees	Retained until 1972	5.0	6.0	6.0	Benefits of plan well accepted, but no fundamental change of attitude	Management is not unhappy and considers program now controlled

* Basis of measurement may vary, so figures are not comparable between companies.
† Weekly salary plan was introduced in 1972, but 1968 changes equalized treatment in most cases.
‡ This applies for sickness only.
§ Rates were not measured; substantial increase occurred after changeover.
Source: Robert Hulme and Richard Bevan, "The Blue Collar Worker Goes on Salary," *Harvard Business Review*, March–April 1975. Copyright © 1975 by the President and Fellows of Harvard College; all rights reserved.

Incentive plans

The methods for paying employees on the basis of output are usually referred to as incentive forms of compensation.[3] Incentives can be paid individually, to the work group, or on an enterprisewide basis. Incentive compensation assumes it is possible and useful to tie performance directly to pay, an issue discussed in detail in Chapter 13.

Individual incentives

Perhaps the oldest form of compensation is the individual incentive plan, in which the employee is paid for units produced. Today the individual incentive plan takes several forms: piecework, production bonus, and commissions. (Whether or not to use an incentive wage was the issue facing J. R. Verden.) These methods seek to achieve the incentive goal of compensation.

Straight piecework usually works like this: an employee is guaranteed an hourly rate (probably the minimum wage) for performing an expected minimum output (the standard). For production over the standard, the employer pays so much per piece produced. This is probably the most frequently used incentive pay plan. The standard is set through work measurement studies, as modified by collective bargaining. The base rate and piece rates may develop from pay surveys.[4]

A variation of the straight piece rate is the differential piece rate. In this plan, the employer pays a smaller piece rate up to standard and then a higher piece rate above the standard. Research indicates that the differential piece rate is a more effective incentive than the straight piece rate, although it is much less frequently used.[5]

Production bonus systems pay an employee an hourly rate, and then a bonus when the employee exceeds standard, typically 50 percent of labor savings. This system is not widely used.

Commissions are paid to sales employees. Straight commission is the equivalent of straight piecework and is typically a percentage of the price of the item. A variation of the production bonus system for sales is to pay the salesperson a small salary and commission or bonus when she or he exceeds standard (the budgeted sales goal).

Individual incentives are used more frequently in some industries (clothing, steel, textiles) than others (lumber, beverage, bakery), and more in some jobs (sales, production) than others (maintenance, clerical).

Are individual incentives effective? The research results are mixed; most studies indicate they do increase output,[6] but some question this outcome.[7] Although production increases, other aspects decline. For example, in sales, straight commission can lead to less attention being paid to servicing accounts. There is also evidence that there are individual differences in the effect of incentives on performance; some employees are more inclined to perform better than others. This should not surprise you, since equity, expectancy, and other theories of motivation indicate that people have varying motivations to work.

Incentive systems may be designed to affect outputs other than performance; for example, employers may use them to try to lower absenteeism and turnover.[8] At least for some employees, incentive pay may lower satisfaction, however; employees may be dissatisfied if they have to work harder or if they feel manipulated by the system.[9]

For incentive schemes to work, they must be well designed and administered.[10] After reviewing the incentive compensation research, Allan Nash and Stephen Carroll conclude that the incentive plan is likely to be more effective under certain circumstances.[11] These are when:

The task is liked.

The task is not boring.

The supervisor reinforces and supports the system.

The plan is acceptable to employees and managers and probably includes them in plan design.

The standards are carefully designed.

The incentive is financially sufficient to induce increased output.

Quality of work is not especially important.

Most delays in work are under the employees' control.

Group incentives

Piecework, production bonuses, commissions and other individual incentives can also be paid to groups of individuals. This might be done when it is difficult to measure individual output, when cooperation is needed to get production, and when management feels this is a more appropriate unit on which to base incentives. Group incentive plans also reduce administrative costs.

Group incentive plans are used less frequently than individual incentive plans are. The amount of research on group incentives is less than on individual or enterprisewide incentive plans. Some studies suggest that group incentives are less effective than other incentive plans but more effective than straight time wages or salaries.[12] Perhaps the group does not work well together, or less-well-motivated members decide to coast along on the work of others.

One problem incentive compensation schemes face is restriction of output. The Supreme Court recently ruled (*Scofield et al.* v. *National Labor Relations Board et al.*) that a union can discipline a member who exceeds the piecework norm. This legitimates restriction of output and makes it more difficult to install group incentive plans.

Enterprise incentive schemes

Four approaches to incentive plans are used at the enterprise level: suggestion systems; company group incentive plans; profit sharing; and stock ownership plans.

Suggestion systems.   Most large and medium-size enterprises have suggestion systems designed to encourage employee input for improvements in enterprise effectiveness. Typically, the employee submits the suggestion in writing, perhaps placing it in a suggestion box. If, after being screened by a committee, the idea is tried and proven useful, the employee receives a financial reward. If the savings due to the idea are hard to compute, the employee is given a standard reward, such as $25 or $100. If they are measurable, the employee receives a percentage of the first year's savings, typically 10 to 20 percent.[13]

The literature contains many examples of the success of suggestion systems. For example, in 1976 a General Motors factory worker in Indianapolis (Raymond Roberts) collected $30,000 for his suggestions; that raised his lifetime total from the suggestion system to over $100,000. Goodyear paid $80,000 to employees for energy conservation ideas in 1977. In 1967 the 244 companies participating in the National Association of Suggestion Systems claimed yearly savings of $407,000,000;[14] in 1973, the same companies found they received $4.46 back from every dollar they invested in the system.[15] Of course there can be problems. United Airlines is being sued by employees who contend it stole their idea and did not pay them fairly.[16]

Effective administration of the suggestion program is essential to its success. The reasons for rejecting a suggestion must be carefully explained to the submitter. If a group idea is successful it is useful to reward the whole group rather than an individual.

In general, suggestion systems seem to be useful incentive plans. One study suggests that all employees do not contribute equally; suggestion systems tap the ideas of educated, creative, well-motivated employees, regardless of the environment they work in or the job they do.[17]

Company group incentive plans.   Several companies have developed elaborate group incentive and participation schemes which generally have been quite successful. One is the Kaiser Steel Cost Savings and Sharing Plan.[18] Kaiser produces steel in one plant in California where about 40 percent of the workers were covered by individual incentives.

Kaiser and the U.S. Steel Workers Union developed a plan which provided benefits for each party. By the terms of the agreement, the employees were to receive one third of all increases in productivity attributible to cost savings resulting from technological changes or increased effort. They were to be paid in monthly bonus form, with the bonus in addition to wages and benefits equal to or better than the rest of the steel industry. The employees also were to receive protection against loss of jobs through automation. The company received the right to change work rules. It also was permitted to phase out the individual incentive plan, and it got a promise of four years during which there would be no new collective bargaining over wages and benefits or the threat of strikes.

In the first year of the plan, the approximately 7,000 workers received about $700 each in bonuses. Eight years later, the bonus was about $100 per man per year. Thus workers on the group incentive scheme were worse off than other steel workers on individual incentive plans. The workers claimed this was because of Kaiser's profit difficulties. The plan now is in a state of transition.

The most successful group incentive scheme at a single company is the Lincoln Electric Plan, initially described by its founder, James Lincoln.[19] The benefits of the plan are impressive: stable prices for customers, good employee-management relations, and large financial rewards to employees. Individual workers have received huge bonuses year in and out, into the thousands of dollars, in addition to competitive wages. From 1933 to 1951, the bonuses per worker averaged $40,000! The employee's share in the bonus is based on a merit rating three times a year.

Lincoln Electric, with $120,000,000 yearly in sales of welding and similar equipment, has multiple incentives for its workers tied to a participation scheme. An advisory board of several executives and about 30 employees reviews and makes suggestions for company improvements. The suggestion system pays 50 percent of savings in the first year. The base rate of wages is a piece rate. The firm also has a stock purchase plan in which about two thirds of the employees participate; they now own about one third of the total stock. The stock is privately traded and not sold on any exchange.

Lincoln Electric has been extraordinarily successful in mobilizing employee energies. Employees hire the replacements for the work group. The company basically subcontracts the work to the work group, using its past performance and time studies as standards. When these standards are beaten, the employees share generously. This bonus is not used as a substitute for adequate wages and benefits, either. Needless to say, workers bid to go to work for Lincoln Electric.

Scanlon Plan companies. The Scanlon Plan is a combination group incentive, suggestion, and employee participation scheme that has been adopted by about 100 smaller and medium-sized manufacturing firms and at least one large firm, Midland Ross. It is named after Joseph Scanlon, its designer. The Scanlon Plan avoids many of the problems of the other group incentive schemes. Here is how it works. Each department of the firm has a production committee composed of the foreman and employee representatives elected by the members or appointed by the union. The committee screens the suggestions for improvements made by employees and management. The number of suggestions that come from workers in these plans is about double the normal suggestion-plan rate, and about 80 percent of them are usable. If accepted, the cost savings is paid to the work group, not just to the person suggesting it.

The plan also involves a wage formula. Gains from increased productivity are paid in bonus form to all employees: operative workers, supervisors, indirect workers such as typists, and salesmen. They receive bonuses in proportional shares. Management receives its share of productivity gains in increased profits.

Scanlon Plan advocates contend that there are positive results for everyone. These include increased participation by employees, better acceptance of change on everyone's part, greater efficiency for the company, and improved union-management relations. Most of the research studies are positive,[20] although some negative research has been reported.[21]

This plan is a most promising incentive scheme. For the plan to succeed, management must be willing to encourage and work with participating workers. All workers must provide their fair shares of suggestions and work. The union must develop a new degree of cooperation. It is likely to be more successful in organizations that are less than gigantic. It also has worked well in troubled companies that provide the necessary conditions of participation, communication, and identification.

Profit-sharing plans. Essentially, profit sharing is the payment of a regular share of company profits to employees as a supplement to their normal compensation. About 100,000 enterprises do this today. The plans must be approved by the Internal Revenue Service, which issued a "model plan" in late 1976 to fit the 1976 tax revision law in the United States.

The number of plans is growing in smaller firms and declining in larger ones. Profit-sharing plans divide a set percentage of net profit among employees. The percentage varies, but 25 percent is about normal. The funds can be divided equally based on the base salary or job grade, or in several other ways. The profit share can be paid often (such as quarterly) or less frequently (such as yearly), or deferred until retirement. The latter plan has tax advantages for the recipient.

Advocates of profit sharing contend that the plans successfully motivate greater performance by employees.[22] Many firms also see profit sharing as a way to increase employee satisfaction and quality workmanship and to reduce absenteeism and turnover. Essentially, they contend that employees who have profit-sharing plans identify more closely with the company and its profit goal, and thus they reduce waste and increase productivity.

There are problems with profit sharing. First, an enterprise cannot share what it does not have; and in bad years, there are no profits to share. The employees may have cut costs and worked hard, but perhaps a recession slowed sales and thus profits, or management chose an expensive but ineffective marketing program. According to the Edward Lawler model of pay satisfaction and its causes discussed in Chapter 13, after several bad years the employee no longer links his extra efforts to increased financial rewards. Often, even in good years, it is difficult for the employee to see the significance of extra work to profit sharing a year away, or worse, at retirement 40 years later.

Profit sharing has had limited success because of the difficulty of tying individual rewards to effort and the problems raised when there are no profits to share. The plans probably are more successful in smaller firms because the employees can identify with a smaller organization more closely and can see the relation between their productivity and company profits more easily. Plans restricted to executives have been more successful, as will be discussed later in the chapter.

In the United States, the passage of the Employee Retirement Income Security Act of 1974 (ERISA; see Chapter 16) may induce more companies to set up profit-sharing plans. The payment of annual profit-sharing funds are not subject to ERISA's requirements, and some employers may choose to use the profit-sharing mechanism to avoid the financial and paper-work problems associated with ERISA.

But the Tax Reform Act of 1976 created disadvantages for profit-sharing plans. Persons with modest or high incomes must be careful not to take profit sharing in lump sums, or there are major tax costs. Ten-year averaging may be the wisest way to do it.[23]

Stock ownership plans. Many companies encourage employee purchase of company stock (often at advantageous prices), to increase employees' incentives to work, satisfaction, and work quality, and to reduce absenteeism and turnover. Purchase plans often allow for payroll deductions or company financing of the stock. Sometimes the company will agree to buy the stock back at a guaranteed rate if it appears that the employee would take a significant loss. Companies use these plans for the same reasons as they do profit-sharing plans; when employees become partners in the business, they work harder.

Some of these plans (such as Procter and Gamble's) are very successful. But in general stock purchase plans have most of the disadvantages of profit sharing. It is hard for the truck driver to identify his working harder with an increase in the value of his stock. It is more difficult when the stock drops in price. Many of these plans were terminated in the 1930s because of big drops in stock prices.

A major change in U.S. laws may have increased the usage of stock ownership plans. Recently, the U.S. Congress authorized the setting up of an employee stock ownership plan (ESOP) through the mechanism of an employee stock ownership trust (ESOT).

Firms have a number of incentives for setting up an ESOT. ERISA views an ESOT as an employee benefit plan. The Tax Reduction Act of 1975 allows firms with an ESOT to take an extra 1 percent investment tax credit in addition to the 10 percent investment tax credit. The Trade Reform Act gives a company with an ESOT preference in receiving government expansion funds for growth in areas where foreign competition has hurt. And the recent DeCouper Industries ruling by the Securities Exchange Commission (SEC) appears to allow a firm to convert a standard profit-sharing fund into an ESOT.

The ESOT has been popularized by Louis Kelso. Essentially the firm setting up an ESOT puts into the trust unissued stock or stock held by a dominant stockholder. The shares are sold to the trust, and the trust uses the stock as collateral and borrows the value of the stock from a bank.

The trust then turns the cash over to the company and pays the trust back by making tax-deductible contributions to the ESOT (a maximum of 15 percent of eligible payroll of pretax income). This allows the company to borrow at half the normal cost (it pays back principal only, not the interest) and creates a market for the shares of smaller and middle-sized firms. The retiring employee (or the family of an accidentally killed employee) is given his share of the ESOT.

It is clear that for the corporation an ESOT improves liquidity and cash flow, can help the firm acquire life insurance for key stockholders, and can be useful in effecting divestitures and mergers. Peter Hearst maintains that the ESOT is best for an enterprise that is doing well financially, is in the full corporate income tax bracket, is a domestic corporation (not a subchapter S corporation or partnership), and is labor intensive, that is, has a minimum "covered" payroll of at least $500,000 annually.[24]

Compensation specialists foresee the spread of ESOTs and ESOPs. There were about 240 in existence on January 1, 1977. For example, the founding family of Hallmark, Mr. and Mrs. Joyce Hall, plans to transfer 65 percent of the Hallmark stock to the ESOT which is replacing a standard profit-sharing plan. The employee leaving the company will receive his share of the ESOT stock. When a former employee wishes the funds, he sells the certificate to the ESOT. Other firms involved in ESOTs recently include Merrill Lynch's Lionel Edie Company, Okonite Division of Omega Alpha, Gerber Sheter Corporation of American, Armsted Industries, Bates Fabrics, South Bend Lathe, and others.

Not everyone has a positive opinion on ESOPs. Some critics feel it is a legal loophole in ERISA and can endanger employee pension funds. The problems with profit-sharing plans (stocks decline in value, and so will retirement funds)[25] could be worse for ESOPs if all the funds are invested in the company stock. ESOPs also have the effect of diluting earnings per share and thus stockholder equity.

The proponents of ESOPs usually devote 1 percent of their arguments to the probable motivational effects of ESOPs on employees, and 99 percent to their corporate financial advantages. It appears that tax and other financial advantages will encourage enterprises to convert profit-sharing plans to ESOPs. But the motivational effects of profit sharing (which are mixed) are also likely to be true of ESOPs. It is a long time until retirement for most employees, so they are not likely to work much harder for an ESOP. In the end, the ESOP is likely to have effects similar to pensions and profit sharing—slightly reduced turnover and absenteeism and increased employee satisfaction.

EXECUTIVE COMPENSATION

Executives in the public and third sectors are normally compensated by salaries. In the private sector, business executives receive salaries too, but many of them also receive incentive compensation such as bonuses, stock options, or performance shares and their variations. In addition, executives in all sectors receive benefits and special treatment which are usually called perks. (This was the problem Martha Lesner was trying to solve.)

Business executives expect their own compensation plans to provide for their physiological and security needs and their long-run security, including estate-planning.[26] Changing tax systems significantly influence the form of executive compensation.[27]

A fundamental question in executive compensation is why business executives should be paid incentives as well as salaries. A number of answers can be given. First, it is argued that these incentives improve performance, and this is good for stockholders and employees. The research on incentive compensation indicates that in general business executives are ideal employees for incentive compensation. A second reason is that incentive compensation is a way of retaining talented executives. Many have alternative employment opportunities with other corporations or as entrepreneurs. The third reason is that business executives are more likely to control their own compensation in the private sector than in the public where legislative bodies determine it, or the third sector, where boards normally from outside the enterprise have a great deal of control. For these and other reasons, the compensation of business executives tends to be lucrative and innovative enough to sidestep the ever-changing tax laws.

Executive salaries

Salaries of executives in the public sector are generally known to the public (see Chapter 13), and salaries of executives in the third sector have not been widely studied.[28] In general, the highest salaries are paid in the private sector, and there are many studies of this form of compensation. Wilbur Lewellen examined the pay of 550 executives of 50 large corporations over a 23-year period and found that executives' aggregate after-tax remuneration had doubled, and physicians, dentists, and other professionals had increased their compensation over the period even more.[29]

To give you an idea of the salaries of some top executives, the presidents or chief executive officers (CEOs) of corporations received the following salaries (and, in some cases, bonuses) in 1977: Rapid American, $916,000; IT&T, $776,000; Exxon $518,000. The total cash remuneration of others include: Halliburton $1,593,000; J. Roy McDermott Corp. $1,223,000; White Consolidated, $706,000.

Some journals publish the top salaries in industry regularly. For example, *Business Week* and *Business Management* prepare a yearly executive compensation report, and *Forbes* publishes its "Who Gets the Most Pay" yearly. (In 1976, *Forbes* listed the salaries of 822 chief executives.) Every other year, the Conference Board publishes the salaries of the top three executives in about 1,300 companies.

Some studies have been done on the relationship of size, kind of business, and business function to salary size. With regard to size, in general, as the firm increases in size, the top executive's salary increases. One study found that the CEO's pay increases 20 percent for every 100 percent increase in sales.[30] The Conference Board derives a formula relating CEO salary to company size. Most studies also find that the salaries below the CEO level fit a percentage pattern by industry grouping. For example, the second highest executive is usually paid about 71 percent of the CEO's salary in all except retail trade, where it is 84 percent. The third highest executive tends to be paid 55–60 percent of the CEO's salary.

An older study examined how well each financial executive was paid relative to others. It found that the highest paid executives are in marketing; those in manufacturing, product engineering, control, personnel, industrial engineering, and purchasing follow, in that order.[31] Several studies have examined the relative salaries of executives in different industries. For example, one study found that in companies with sales larger than $10 billion, motor vehicle companies paid the highest, followed (in order) by conglomerates and firms in office machines and oils; in the $5 billion category the order was: motor vehicles, office machines, conglomerates, and oils. In the $2.5 billion sales category, the order was: pharmaceuticals, packaged goods, forest products, chemicals, and food processors; in the $500 million sales category the order was: packaged goods, pharmaceuticals, chemicals, office machines, and forest products.[32] The highest paying companies in these industries are also listed in this study.

Various experts have tried to explain industry differences in executive compensation. Arch Patton suggested that industries that pay higher salaries are dynamic, decentralized, and result oriented. Industries that pay poorly tend to be static, centralized, seniority oriented, and monopolies with a great deal of regulation.[33] In a later study, he added that high-paying companies tend to have stock that is widely held.[34]

If top managers believe that pay is a motivator to higher performance, it follows that they well pay themselves in a way that rewards performance. And if performance is defined as more profits, pay should be correlated with profits; some studies indicate that this is done.[35] Other studies show that top executive pay is correlated with sales, a proxy for size.[36]

More sophisticated studies point out that simple correlations such as these are not likely to explain very much. The factors which influence executive pay (as seen by Marc Wallace in the most sophisticated study[37]) are ownership and market concentration. Wallace found that in closely held firms, executive pay was correlated with profitability. Patton's studies agree with this,[38] and it makes sense. In firms where the owners can put pressure, executives are likely to encourage higher profitability. In firms with no strong ownership interest, executives can set their salaries similar to those of executives in equal-size firms, regardless of profitability. Wallace also found that in firms in competitive industries, pay was correlated with profitability. In quasi-monopolistic industries, size was the predictor of pay.

K. R. Murthy and Malcolm Salter examined the relationship of executive pay to corporate strategy and found pay tied more closely to profitability in high-performing related businesses and conglomerates than in single-product firms (what they called dominant business companies). They theorize this is so because conglomerate executives tend to evaluate their divisions in this way, and it is inconsistent to reward divisional managers on profitability and themselves on size.[39]

A third intervening variable, industry, was added in another study which found that in service-oriented industries (insurance, retailing), pay was related to sales and size, but in manufacturing industries (chemicals, food, petroleum), pay was related more to profitability.[40]

Less is known about the compensation of middle managers and supervisors than that of top executives. Middle managers are paid a percentage of top executive compensation, as modified by comparable salaries in pay surveys. Supervisory pay is influenced by subordinates' pay; supervisors generally earn 15 percent more than straight time workers, 10 percent more than their highest paid subordinate, or 25 percent more than the average gross pay of all subordinates.[41]

Executive perks

All over the world and in all sectors of the economy, executives receive special perquisites and extras called perks. These tend to be larger in Europe than in the United States; the European executive can receive free housing, a chauffered Rolls Royce, and other niceties in lieu of or in addition to higher salaries. The differences can be easily explained; these perks are taxed as income in the United States and not elsewhere.

In 1975, the American Management Association studied perks in 742 companies; 34 perks were examined, but only 7 were regularly available in more than half of the companies studied. These include: better office decor; choice office location; a company car; reserved parking; a car for personal use; and first-class air tickets.[42]

Robert Sbarra's list of executive perks is given as Exhibit 14–2. Some of what he calls perks are also called benefits; these are discussed in Chapter 15 and 16, as noted in the exhibit.

Sbarra indicates that executives prefer the following perks the most: insurance (96 percent), company car (87 percent), club memberships (84 percent), financial counseling (77 percent), travel (66 percent), company airplane (56 percent), loans (57 percent).[43]

Perks have not been widely studied. In Maslow's terms, however, they are likely to fulfill the physiological and especially the recognition needs of the executive. Obviously, a big office provides for recognition needs. But a company car, club membership, financial counseling, and so on provide the executive with nontaxable income—something many of them prefer to taxable income.

EXHIBIT 14–2
Executive perquisites: A selected list

1. Insured or Internal Revenue Service qualified benefits

    Voluntary supplementary retirement benefits[a]
    Voluntary supplementary life insurance and disability insurance[b]
    Officers and directors liability insurance
    Profit sharing, thrift saving, stock purchase plans

2. Special privileges

    Financial counseling services[b]
    Company loans for stock option exercise, stock purchase, home purchase, education, personal investment, and so forth
    Company cars
    Paid memberships (initiation and dues) to country clubs, athletic clubs, luncheon clubs, dinner clubs, professional associations
    Liberal expense accounts
    Extra time off from work, sabbatical leaves
    Company housing, hotel suites
    Income deferral
    Employment or termination contracts
    Combined business and vacation trips
    Second office in-home or near-home location
    Executive medical examinations
    Executive dining room privilege
    Unique investment opportunities
    Special office decorating allowance

3. Expense assumptions

    Educational assistance (tuition, dependent scholarships or loans)
    Discounts on company products, services, or use of company facilities
    Uncovered family medical and dental expenses

[a] a benefit discussed in Chapter 16.
[b] a benefit discussed in Chapter 15.
Source: Robert Sbarra, "The New Language of Executive Compensation," *Personnel,* November–December 1975, p. 12.

Bonuses

A bonus is a compensation payment that supplements salary and can be paid in the present or in the future, in which case it is called a deferred bonus.

Exhibit 14–3 gives the salary and bonuses paid to the 15 highest paid business executives of publicly held companies. Exhibit 14–4, which shows the total compensation of the average top executive of a large U.S. corporation, indicates how this compensation is related to the size of the firm. The size of bonuses and long-term payments relative to salary clearly changes with the size of the chief executive officer's company. The larger the company, the greater is the proportion of incentive awards making up total

EXHIBIT 14–3
The 15 highest paid U.S. executives in 1976

	Salary and bonus (in thousands)	Gains from options exercised (in thousands)	Total compensa- tion (in thousands)	Sales (in millions)	Corporate profits (in millions)
1. Harry J. Gray, chairman and president, United Technologies	$650	$1,012	$1,662	$ 5,166	$ 157
2. C. B. Branch, chairman, Dow Chemical	453	1,195	1,648	5,652	613
3. David S. Lewis, chairman and president, General Dynamics	438	862	1,300	2,550	100
4. Zoltan Merszei, president, Dow Chemical	326	909	1,235	5,652	613
5. Elton H. Rule, president, American Broad- casting	649	584	1,233	1,342	72
6. Michel C. Bergerac, chairman and president, Revlon	694	469	1,163	956	82
7. Leonard H. Goldenson, chairman, American Broadcasting	747	313	1,060	1,342	72
8. Henry Ford II, chairman, Ford	970	—	970	28,840	983
9. Lee A. Iacocca, president, Ford	970	—	970	28,840	983
10. Thomas A. Murphy, chairman, General Motors	950	—	950	47,181	2,903
11. George H. Weyerhaeuser, president, Weyerhaeuser	364	580	944	2,868	306
12. J. W. McSwiney, chairman, Mead	364	528	892	1,599	89
13. Elliott M. Estes, president, General Motors	885	—	885	47,181	2,903
14. James P. McFarland, chairman, General Mills	450	414	864	2,645	101
15. Richard L. Terrell, vice-chairman, General Motors	860	—	860	47,181	2,903

Source: "A Year for Stock Options and Big Bonuses," *Business Week*, May 23, 1977, p. 48; data from Booz, Allen and Hamilton and *Business Week*, p. 48.

annual compensation.[44] Exhibit 14–5 shows how salaries and bonuses vary by the function of line or staff executives and size of the corporation.

A majority of large firms pay bonuses, on the belief that this leads to better profitability and other advantages for enterprises. Bonuses involve large expenditures of funds; they vary from 80 percent of top executive's salaries to 20 percent of the salaries of lowest levels participants. In spite of wide usuage and high costs, there is little research support for their effec- tiveness. Several unsophisticated case studies of companies found their bo- nuses effective,[45] as did one reasonably sophisticated study,[46] but a more sophisticated study of 571 companies over two years did not do so.[47] Unless more research does support bonuses, many may conclude they are an example of management's power to pay itself what it wants, passing the bill on to the public in price increases whether it performs well or not. Boards of directors are shirking their duties in such cases, and this can lead to legal problems.[48]

John Dearden suggests a more rational approach to bonuses.[49] His plan has these features:

The total bonus for top executives is based on percentage of net profits after a reasonable earnings per share for the stockholder.

EXHIBIT 14–4
Total compensation of chief executive officers (in thousands)

Salary	Bonus	Average long-term income*	Total annual income
$ 50	$ 15	$ 20	$ 85
75	26	33	134
100	38	48	186
125	53	66	244
150	71	86	307
175	91	109	375
200	116	132	448
225	144	158	527
250	170	185	605
275	195	215	685
300	225	249	774

* Includes only executives who actually realized gains from stock options or long-term bonus plans.
Source: Robert Sibson, "The Outlook for Executive Pay," *Nation's Business*, November–December 1975, pp. 26–27.

EXHIBIT 14–5

A. Salaries of line and staff executives (in thousands)*

Functional positions

Size of company (by sales volume in millions)	Mar-keting	Manu-facturing	Finance	Legal	Re-search	Per-sonnel
$ 1–$ 5	$26	$22	$25	$22	$23	$21
5– 15	31	27	33	26	28	24
15– 25	34	32	37	31	32	26
25– 35	38	36	41	34	36	27
35– 50	42	38	45	36	40	29
50– 75	46	42	49	40	44	33
75– 125	50	45	53	45	48	36
125– 250	54	48	58	49	51	40
250– 500	68	61	72	61	60	51
500– 1,000	76	69	84	70	66	56
1,000– 2,000	83	75	99	98	75	66

B. Bonus levels for line and staff executives (as a percent of salary—salary in thousands)

Functional positions

Salary	Marketing	Manu-facturing	Finance	Legal	Re-search	Per-sonnel
$ 20	10%	10%	15%	14%	22%	13%
30	13	14	20	18	25	17
40	18	18	25	22	28	21
50	22	22	30	26	30	24
60	26	25	35	29	31	27
70	30	28	40	32	33	30
80	34	32	45	35	34	33
90	38	35	49	37	36	36
100	42	38	53	40	37	39

* Note: Salary data are for bonus-paying industrial companies, projected to reflect levels of January, 1976.
Source: Robert Sibson, "The Outlook for Executive Pay," *Nation's Business*, November–December 1975, pp. 26–27.

The standard bonus per executive is based on number of bonus points assigned to the job, based on the position's potential impact on company profitability.

The actual bonus payments are spread over a three- to five-year period.

A limit (cutoff level) is put on the total of the bonus to be paid in one year. The excess funds are reserved for leaner years.

As far as bonuses for division managers are concerned, Robert Pitts suggests it makes sense to pay higher bonuses to division managers who have greater autonomy and responsibility. Pitts found systematic differences on bonus payments depending on whether the firm grew primarily internally or externally and the amount of autonomy and responsibility held by managers.[50]

Stock options, performance shares, and book-value devices

Another form of executive compensation used in the private sector is a set of devices tied to the firm's stock. The oldest form is the stock option, which gives executive the right to purchase company stock at a fixed price for a certain period of time. The option's price usually is close to the market price of the stock at the time the option is issued. The executive gains if the price rises above the option price during the option period enough to cover the capital gains tax on the stock should it be purchased.

The popularity of stock options has risen and fallen with the tax laws (especially the 1969 and 1976 bills), the level of interest rates, the state of the stock market, and the feelings of stockholders about them.[51] At present, because of tax law changes and these other factors, the use of stock options as incentive compensation is decreasing. For all practical purposes, the Tax Reform Act took the incentive out of new stock option plans after May 20, 1976, and all incentive stock options must be exercised by May 20, 1981.[52]

Is this a great loss? Probably not. There was little research to indicate that stock options led to better performance; what evidence there was tended to indicate that they did not.[53] But one implication of the research is that as management's income from ownership-related sources (dividends and capital gain) increases, these instruments can serve to improve performance.[54]

Innovative tax lawyers and tax accountants have worked up some new compensation forms to replace the stock option and still provide ownership and incentive compensation. Several variations are primarily incentive compensation oriented, others ownership oriented, and still others a mix of the two. The ownership-oriented devices are:

Market-value purchases. The company lends the executive funds at low interest rates to buy company stock at current market value. The executive repays the loan by direct payment or receives credits on the loan payments for staying with the company and/or achieving a performance level.

EXHIBIT 14–6
How business rewards executives

Form of extra compensation (other than cash bonus)	Percentage of 587 large companies using it*
Qualified stock option	78%
Nonqualified stock option	59
Nonqualified option with stock appreciation rights	16
Performance shares or bonus units	12
Restricted stock	9
Phantom shares	6
None	14

* Totals more than 100 percent because most companies offer more than one form of compensation.
Source: "Tax Reform Remodels the Pay Package," *Business Week*, February 28, 1977, p. 48. Data from McKinsey & Co.

Book-value purchases. The executive is offered a chance to buy the company stock at book value (or some similar nonmarket value measure) but can resell it to the company later, using the same formula price.

Exercise bonuses. Payment to an executive when he exercises a stock option that is equal to or proportionate to the option gain is called an exercise bonus. This helps the executive keep the stock rather than sell it to pay the taxes on the gain.

One device appears to be primarily a form of compensation that is linked to stocks. This is *performance shares and performance units,* used by such companies as General Motors, Gulf, Texaco, Pepsico and International Nickel. Performance shares grant stock units due the executive in the future (such as five years later) if performance targets are met. These units appreciate or depreciate as the stock does. Performance units are performance shares paid in cash instead of stock. The units are compensation unless they are to be used to buy stock. Both are viewed as compensation by the IRS.[55]

Another device, *stock appreciation rights,* can be either compensation or ownership oriented. This device, attached to a stock option, allows the executive to accept appreciation in value in either stock or cash.

Exhibit 14–6 shows the percentage of 587 large companies which used these incentive compensation devices and others in 1977.

Most of these devices are very new and are rarely used. All could have performance implications for the enterprise, but there is inadequate research at this stage to determine under what conditions they do so. Ralph Winter points out that the key to their success is the definition of performance. He cites evidence to show that if the definition of performance is return on assets, the willingness of executives to take the risks necessary to the long-run success of the enterprise may be reduced.[56]

Executive compensation in Canada

Generally speaking, Canadian executive compensation consists of salary, benefits, perks, bonuses, stock options, performance shares, and book-value devices. As elsewhere, the competent compensation specialist tries to make the executive's compensation competitive, equitable, balanced on short- and long-run factors, incentive oriented, and of reasonable cost to the enterprise. In Canada, these objectives have been hard to realize in the 1970s because of Canadian wage and price controls and Canadian tax laws. For example, the Anti-Inflation Act (the 1975 Controls Bill) prevents a pay increase of over 10 percent or more than $2,400, including benefits, bonuses, performance shares and so on. In addition, a surtax was imposed on incomes over $30,000 per year.

Wage and price controls have hurt middle managers the most. Middle managers have averaged less in pay increases than unionized employees, and their raises have not kept pace with inflation rates, since 1974 or so.

Compared to the United States, the Canadian tax structure hurts executives more, because: fewer deductions from income are allowed, and taxable compensation is calculated as salary plus cash value of all benefits and allowances. Also, the tax rates are much higher; for example, the tax rate for income above $60,000 per year in Canada is 60 percent. Thus if an executive is transferred from New York to Toronto, it usually takes about a 50 percent raise to make it comparable in compensation; thus a $38,000 executive in New York needs to make more than $50,000 in Toronto.

All of these reasons discourage higher compensation of Canadian executives. The tax structure and controls lead executives to try tax deferment schemes such as statutory retirement, pensions, savings, and profit-sharing plans which could shelter $9,000 per year in income. Another form is a nonstatutory plan to defer compensation until after retirement if the executive works continuously for a firm and serves as a consultant after retirement. Performance shares, stock options, phantom stock, and similar plans are less attractive taxwise in Canada, and their amount is severly restricted at present.[57]

Executive compensation policy

How does an enterprise choose the compensation package for its executives? Effective executive compensation must meet the needs of both the enterprise and the individual executive.

With regard to the enterprise, the total compensation must be competitive with that of similar enterprises. Thus it makes no sense to look at total compensation of executives, or averages. The effective enterprise determines the compensation of executives in similar-sized enterprises, in the same industry group, and with the same degree of competitiveness. Executive compensation must also be directly tied to the enterprise's strategy and objectives, so executive rewards will further achievement of the goals of the enterprise. Malcolm Salter gives recommendations on this in Exhibit 14–7.[58]

One way enterprises try to satisfy the needs and desires of their executives is to adjust compensation methods to changing tax laws, as was done in

EXHIBIT 14–7
Executive compensation and enterprise strategy

Strategic objective criteria — Policy issues	Executive compensation issues — Financial instruments	Performance measures	Degree of discretion in allocating bonus awards	Size and frequency of awards	Degree of uniformity	Funding
Short run v. long run	Mix of current bonus awards and stock options should reflect the relevant time horizon for policy-level executives. Deferred instruments are weak reinforcers of short-term performance.	Mix of quantitative measures of performance and more qualitative measures should reflect the relevant time horizon for executives. Qualitative measures usually reflect long-run considerations more effectively than quantitative measures.	Nondiscretionary, formula-based bonuses tend to encourage a short-run point of view.	Frequent bonus awards encourage concentration on short-term performance.		
Risk aversion v. risk-taking	Current bonus awards, in cash or stock, can reinforce risk-taking behavior.	Qualitative measures of performance can reinforce initiative by assuring executives that total performance will be evaluated for purposes of bonus awards.	Completely discretionary, highly personalized bonuses do not clarify the "rules of the game" and as a result can discourage risk-taking behavior.	The size of both salary and incentive awards should be commensurate with the business and personal risks involved.		
Interdivisional relationships		Bonus pools can be based on divisional performance, total corporate performance, or some mix of the two. Each arrangement sends different signals in terms of interdivisional cooperation.	Nondiscretionary, formula-based bonuses for division managers are most practical in companies where little cooperation among divisions is required. Discretionary bonuses are practical when top management wants to encourage cooperation among divisions.		Uniformity among divisions in the design of measurement and reward systems facilitates interdivisional cooperation.	The choice between divisional and corporate bonus pools should reflect the reasoning used in selecting appropriate performance measures.
Company-division relationships	Stock options can effectively link the interests of division personnel to the interests of the corporation.	Use of objective measures of performance for division managers is more meaningful where the primary role of headquarters is to allocate capital than it is in instances where the head office plays an important role in "managing the business" of the divisions.	Nondiscretionary, formula-based bonuses are most practical in companies where headquarters does not interfere in management of the profit centers. Discretionary bonuses are most useful when top management wants to exert a direct influence on decisions in the divisions.		Uniformity among divisions in the design of measurement and reward systems facilitates the resource allocation process at the corporate level. With respect to uniformity among levels of management, the more decentralized the organization, the more reason there is to differentiate the reward systems of each group.	Bonus pools funded solely from divisional profits tend to limit the ability of corporate headquarters to use financial incentives as an instrument of control. Bonus pools funded solely from corporate profits tend to increase the influence of headquarters over the divisions and other profit centers.

Source: Malcolm S. Salter, "Tailor Executive Compensation to Strategy," *Harvard Business Review*, March–April 1973, Copyright © 1973 by the President and Fellows of Harvard College; all rights reserved.

1976. This often leads to the use of more deferred compensation methods.

Another way is to study the preferences and attitudes of executives toward the various compensation approaches. However, as Chapter 2 should have made you aware, since each executive is different and has differing needs for compensation, studies of pay preferences are only partly indicative of what an enterprise should do. In one study of the pay preferences of 300 executives in seven large companies, it was found that executives' compensation preferences vary widely. One consistency was a preference for 75 percent of total compensation in cash and 25 percent in benefits and deferred items, which would mean a shift from the present 85/15 percent to more benefits.[59]

Another study examined the preferences of public-sector as compared to private-sector managers. The sample was 100 executives aged about 40, supervising about 200 research employees, with budgets of about $1,000,000, with 16 years' experience, and paid about $24,000 per year; half were public-sector and half private-sector managers. This study found that there were significant differences between managers in the two sectors along dimensions such as management performance. With regard to compensation, the study found that public managers would rather have a more secure job than higher pay; private managers had the opposite preference. Public managers preferred more pay to more responsibility and more autonomy; private managers preferred the opposite. There were other differences.[60] Thus managers probably differ in compensation preferences in the different sectors, and they do differ on preferences as individuals.

The recommendation is that compensation should vary according to these preferences, if it is believed to lead to greater executive satisfaction or performance. At present this is not possible in the public sector because of rigid pay classifications and a system of a single salary plus fixed benefits. But it is possible in the private and third sectors. The mechanism used to satisfy these requirements is the cafeteria approach to compensation, which was noted in Chapter 13. The idea is that executives should be able to determine the range of their compensation between present pay, deferred compensation, and benefits and services (this is described in more detail in the next chapter, where the cafeteria approach to benefits is considered for all employees). This does not change the total compensation (that could lead to perceived inequities), but the mix of how the compensation is received. Although there are administrative hurdles to be overcome, this approach fits compensation theories and makes sense. We await research to see if, in fact, the cafeteria approach does lead to increased satisfaction and performance.[61]

What does the future hold for executive compensation? That depends on whose crystal ball musings you accept. As Fred Meuter, Xerox's expert on this, foresees the future,[62] it will be characterized by:

Greater scrutiny of executive compensation by shareholders. That makes sense and is desirable.

Less executive mobility, if the no-growth theory comes to be.

Growing desire for second careers. If this comes to be, there will be greater emphasis on immediate cash.

Greater inflation and therefore more problems for compensation. If inflation rises rapidly, employees may in effect take pay cuts.

Greater potential for cafeteria or individually designed compensation systems.

It is very difficult, however, to try to predict future value changes, legislative tax changes, growth policies of enterprises, and other factors likely to affect executive compensation practices.

COMPENSATION ADMINISTRATION ISSUES

Managers must make policy decisions on three issues in compensation administration for employees and executives. These issues involve the extent to which (1) compensation will be secret, (2) compensation will be secure, and (3) raises will vary with performance.

Pay secrecy or openness

The first compensation issue to be discussed is the extent to which the pay of employees is known by others in the enterprise. (This is the issue Mary Markos raised in the examples in the beginning of the chapter.) How would you feel if your creditors, your ex-spouse, or your worst enemy could find out what you make? Would you care? Maybe you would be proud to let them see.

There are varieties of secretness and openness as regards pay information. In many institutions and enterprises, pay ranges and even an individual's pay are open to the public and fellow employees. Examples are public-sector salaries (federal, state, and local governments), some universities, and unionized wage employees. This is called the open system.

The opposite is the secret system, in which pay is regarded as privileged information known only to the employee, her or his superior, and such staff employees as personnel and payroll. In the most secrecy-oriented enterprises, employees are told they cannot discuss pay matters and specifically their own pay. Recently, the National Labor Relations Board ruled that this is not a legitimate policy in findings against Blue Cross–Blue Shield of Alabama and Jeannette Corporation.

In the private and third sectors, secrecy is clearly the predominant pattern. For example, a BNA study found that only 18 percent of personnel officials felt pay should be an open matter, and only a minority of enterprises provides even general pay information, such as pay rates, much less data on individual's pay.[63]

Should this be changed? Lawler found that more open policies lead to greater satisfaction with pay and possibly greater performance, but where employees with inadequate pay information overestimate the pay of peers and subordinates and underestimate the pay of superiors, this could lead to undesirable results.[64] Most of the research has not supported this position. One study found that an enterprise that provided more open information did not reduce the inaccurate estimates of pay, and those managers who had more accurate estimates had lower pay satisfaction.[65] Other studies found that better performing employees preferred secrecy,[66] that an open pay policy increased turnover and lowered satisfaction,[67] that pay openness increased pay satisfaction but did not affect performance,[68] and that many persons were neutral about pay secrecy—they neither preferred nor opposed it.[69]

Before an open system is tried, the individual's performance must be objectively measurable, and the measurable aspects of the jobs to be rewarded must be the significant ones. There should be little need for cooperation among jobs, and employees in the system should have a direct causal relationship on performance.[70] I would add that the employees must prefer the open system. Although more research needs to be done to specify the conditions under which individuals and enterprises might benefit from openness on pay, it appears that the majority of managers and enterprises oriented toward secret pay systems are not irrational in their policies.

Security in pay

Not only can current compensation be a motivator of performance, but the expectation that there will be future security in compensation may also affect it. Various schemes for providing this security have been developed: the guaranteed annual wage, supplementary unemployment benefits, severance pay, seniority rules, and the employment contract.

A few companies provide a guaranteed annual wage to employees who meet certain characteristics. For this type of plan to work, general employee management relations must be good. Demand for the product or service must be steady or developable into a stable situation. The best known such plans are those of Procter and Gamble, Hormel Meats, and the Nunn-Bush Shoe Company. In one plan, the employer guarantees the employee a certain number of weeks of work at a certain wage after the worker has passed a probation period of (say, two years). Morton Salt Company guarantees 80 percent of full-time work to all employees after one year of standard employment. Procter & Gamble has invoked its emergency clause only once since 1923—in 1933 for a brief period at three plants. In the Hormel and Spiegel plans and others, a minimum income is guaranteed.[71]

In the supplementary unemployment benefits (SUB) approach, the employer adds to unemployment compensation payments to help the employee achieve income security if not job security (as in the GAW). The auto, steel, rubber, garment, and glass industries, among others, contribute (for example, 50 cents per hour worked) to a fund from which laid-off employees are paid. In the 1973–74 recession, many of these SUB funds in the auto industry went bankrupt and thus provided less income security than was thought. Studies on plans where unemployment was less severe than in autos show the system has helped.[72]

In many enterprises, the employer provides some income bridge from employment to unemployment and back to employment. This is severance pay; typically, it amounts to one week's pay for each year of service. About 25 percent of union contracts require such severance pay. This doesn't guarantee a job, but it helps when a job is lost.

In times of layoff the basic security for most employees is their seniority standing. If an organization is unionized, the contract normally specifies how seniority is to be computed. Seniority guarantees the jobs (and thus the compensation) to the employees with the longest continuous employment in the organization or work unit. Even in nonunionized situations, a strong seniority norm prevails which gives some security to senior employees.

The employment contract guarantees that the employee will receive compensation of a minimum of $X and Y years. This form of security is rarely offered, however, and normally only to a few managerial professional employees.[73]

Pay raises

The final compensation issue to be discussed in this section concerns pay increases, or raises. The aspects to be examined are:

When should they be given and how often?

Should increases be given to meet the cost of living?

What criteria should be used to give raises?

How large an increase is meaningful? (These are some of the issues Dick faced in the vignette at the beginning of the chapter.)

The first aspect is timing. If the enterprise accepts the position that pay affects performance favorably, raises should be closely tied to performance. Employees generally prefer raises to be as frequent and as large as possible (except possibly for executives with tax problems), but there may be individual differences in timing preferences. However, administrative costs for personnel and supervisory evaluation usually limit pay raises to annual events. Annual raises can be given to everyone at the same time or tied to annual reviews dating from the date of hire.

One problem with the current timing of raises is that raises tend to get "buried." A raise usually is given on an annual basis, so it gets divided up in 12 parts and mixed up with increases in taxes and insurance deductions, and the take-home paycheck often looks the same after the raise. A new attempt to deal with this problem is the "lump-sum raise," which allows the employee to elect to spread the raise over as many as 12 paychecks as desired or to take it at one time—in a lump sum. If the employee elects the lump-sum raise for the entire year at the start of the year, the employer deducts the interest that would otherwise accrue to the sum and pays it out. If the employee leaves before the full year is over, the proportion of the raise not earned is deducted from the last paycheck.[74] Time will tell whether this system will increase pay satisfaction or performance.

The second aspect of raises is the use of the cost of living as a criterion. Most pay experts believe that an enterprise must adjust its pay scale to reflect the amount of inflation in the economy to some degree, so employees will not perceive a growing inequity as compared to those who receive cost-of-living adjustments. There are several ways to adjust for cost-of-living increases. Pay can be adjusted yearly or at regular intervals, or by automatic cost-of-living adjustment (COLA). In COLA plans, when the Bureau of Labor Statistics's Cost-of-Living Index increases by a rounded percentage, the wages and salaries are automatically increased by that percentage. COLA adjustments are not made each time an increase takes place, to help reduce the costs of administration.[75]

Typically the employer informs employees of the adjustment, how it was calculated, and how it affects employees as wages or salaries are adjusted. Unions have pressed for contracts calling for this provision, especially in high inflation times like 1973–75. Logically it also means that in the event of deflation (as in some years of the 1930s), wages or salaries will decrease. About 60 percent of employees belonging to the major unions have some form of COLA; some experts contend this has reduced the frequency of strikes.

Economists differ on the impact of COLA on the economy as a whole. A study by the Council on Wage and Price Stability concluded: "COLAs contribute to instability and exacerbate economic problems . . . by raising wages more than they would increase in response to demand conditions. But during recoveries, when the reacceleration of inflation also tends to lag, the opposite is true. COLAs become an inflation-retarding factor then because they produce smaller wage increases than might otherwise be demanded." In Holland, COLA (called indexation) led to a 40 percent rise in labor costs from 1974 to 1977. Dutch industry is fighting this trend now since it has led to a drop in economic growth and lowered their competitiveness in world markets.[76]

COLAs seem to be a trend at present, but what the ultimate economic impact of these plans will be is not known. They tend to assume that enterprises have the ability to pay the new pay rates regardless of market conditions or, for government and third sectors, budget considerations. This may be quite unrealistic. The only alternative to COLAs in bad times is for employees to take pay cuts to keep the enterprises viable. Pan American Airways engineers took pay cuts totaling $2,750,000 in 1976 to keep that airline flying, for example.

The third issue is what criteria should be used to allocate raises, other than cost-of-living factors. This takes us back to the pay-for-performance or for merit or seniority issue. It is also tied to how to give raises: with percentage or flat-amount increases? David Belcher recommends percentage increases when there are problems in recruiting skilled workers, maintaining

differentials in a a finely divided pay structure, or satisfying employee demands for greater or more equal differentials. He recommends flat increases
when the employer faces problems of recruiting beginning employees, satisfying a larger number of employees, or reducing the cost increase to a
minimum.[77]

With regard to whether or not pay should be related to performance,
the two are related in merit pay and not related in automatic increases. A
combination of these two approaches can also be applied. Automatic increases make sense if Herbert Meyer's or Edward Deci's position that pay
should not be used as a motivator, as set forth in Chapter 13, is accepted.[78]
It also makes sense if it is difficult or impossible to measure and relate
individual performance to individual pay, or if there are few significant
differences among individual performers. This approach is also the easiest
to administer.

A combination approach may be best in some situations. If new employees
need a chance to get started, they could receive automatic increases for a
trial period and then be shifted to the merit pay system.

The merit approach tries to relate pay increases to performance increases,
but the opposite is also true: If a person is performing less than desired,
the merit pay approach recommends no increase or a token increase to send
the employee "a message." One pay administrator told me he referred to
a token increase as a "disciplinary raise." Some research indicates that even
in merit pay systems, a majority automatically get increases until they are
at the top of the pay range.[79] One researcher found that in a merit pay
system performance was more related to pay changes (raises) than to pay
levels for managers at a department store.[80] The negative impact on employees who do not receive merit raises can be a problem in merit pay systems,
and many employees feel a fair pay raise system includes merit pay for
current and past performance (seniority, etc.).[81]

A study of what criteria managers use to make pay increase decisions
found that raises are given for performance, the nature of the job, effort
expended, and experience and training for the job (in that order). When
asked what criteria should be used, respondents ranked the same items and
added cost-of-living changes. They felt budgetary restrictions overly influenced raise decisions.[82]

The final issue is: How large must a raise be for it to affect satisfaction
and performance? Not much research has been done in this area.[83] Several
theories have been advanced to suggest that pay increases should be related
to current pay, past pay increases, current consumption, or some combination
of these if they are to influence the employee's satisfaction or performance.
In the most sophisticated recent study, Linda Krefting and Thomas Mahoney
found large individual differences in regard to an effective pay increase
policy. The authors studied two groups of employees: those who perceived
the increase as primarily a form of recognition for their performance, and
those who saw it as satisfying physiological needs through money. The
best predictors of a satisfactory increase for those who saw the raise in

terms of recognition were *anticipated changes in the cost of living and expected pay increases.* For those who valued the money increase itself, the best predictors were *expected changes in the cost of living, the last pay increase, and current pay satisfaction.* Either these groups were influenced by different factors, or all individuals were influenced by more than one factor. The researchers recommend against flat percentage increases in view of their findings, because current pay was not a significant factor in predicting meaningful pay increases.[84]

This research shows how preceding studies oversimplified the specification of raises. More research is needed to provide better guidelines on the size of effective pay raises, given these individual differences. Perhaps a cafeteria approach to pay and benefits, including pay raises, might help with this problem. Obviously the enterprise's ability to pay and other factors are important, in addition to the perceptions of employees of what a good raise is.

SUMMARY, CONCLUSIONS, AND RECOMMENDATIONS

Operating managers, personnel specialists, and top managers all have a part to play in making compensation as effective as possible. But you should be warned: Experienced personnel experts have found that the area of most complaints and perhaps most employee dissatisfaction is pay. In view of the multiple needs pay serves and the individual differences employees have about pay, this is not surprising.

A number of policy issues must be addressed by top management. One is the relationship between pay for full-time as compared to part-time employees. Equity is important, and managers follow widely varying policies in this regard.[85] Other matters on which top management must set policy concern pay for performance, pay secrecy, salaries for everyone, and pay security. There are good arguments on both sides of these issues. Management must make the best decisions it can, given its compensation goals of incentive, security, and equity.

Another important policy issue is the goal of acceptability by employees of the compensation system. This relates to effective communication about pay: For a pay system to be effective, it must be well designed, well administered, and *understood* by employees. Various media of communication can be used: written (handbooks, magazines, booklets, bulletin boards, computer printouts, payroll stuffers, annual reports), audiovisual (movies, filmstrips, flip charts, posters), and verbal (individual, small-group, and large-group meetings). In view of the individual differences in the perceived importance of pay, individual meetings between the employee and supervisor and/or personnel specialist are best, although group meetings can be used to discuss general pay policies.

Donald Petrie suggests that several key points about compensation should be communicated.[86] These are:

The enterprise has a planned approach to salary administration.

The enterprise spends a lot of time and effort surveying others to make sure its salaries are fair.

The enterprise has a formal approach to reviewing individual salaries.

The salary plan works for employees and not against them.

How much more detail is communicated depends on the enterprise's policy on pay secrecy.

It is vital that an employer get feedback from employees on the effectiveness of its pay system. One approach uses attitude surveys; another is to try to make sense of information employees offer when they leave (see Chapter 20). The most direct approach is for supervisors and personnel specialists to ask employees to speak up when they feel the pay system (or their own pay) needs attention. How much response is received depends on how open the organizational climate at the enterprise is.

A final top management compensation policy issue is reduction of pay costs to the minimum needed to meet the pay objective of control or cost effectiveness. Obviously, if the enterprise is to survive, it must keep its payroll costs within budget and comparable with competitors in the private sector. This requires effective cost/benefit analyses of compensation.

Various environmental and personal factors that tend to increase the costs of employment should be anticipated and analyzed. These include increased turnover, increases in minimum wages or going pay, rises in the cost of living, and some managers' desire to please their employees by increasing their pay. Other factors that make cost consciousness even more necessary are increased competition or decreasing profits or budgets.

One way an enterprise tries to control or lower employment costs is to analyze the payroll to see if the number of employees could be reduced without loss of output. A second way is to replace higher paid employees with lower paid ones. For example, universities are in a financial bind at present; as full professors retire or leave, some of the positions are eliminated and others are filled with assistant professors or instructors. This must be done without discriminating against groups of people.[87] A third way is to analyze the effectiveness of the pay systems used. Various experts have suggested ways to analyze whether incentive compensation is really worth the extra cost (direct and administrative) involved.[88] Administrative costs, of course, might be cut by the use of computers.[89]

Cost/benefit analyses of individual pay adjustments can be done too. One study provides an excellent analysis of how to provide for selective raises designed to reduce costs and increase equity, rather than using the typical across-the-board raises.[90]

We can now summarize the major points of Chapter 14 by stating them in proposition form. Chapter 14 began by examining the time versus incentive pay methods. If management believes that pay should not be tied directly to performance, then a straight wage or salary should be used. If it believes that pay should be tied to one or several of the incentive pay schemes described in the chapter could be substituted. Lawler believes in incentive

EXHIBIT 14-8
Appropriate merit pay plans for various types of organizations

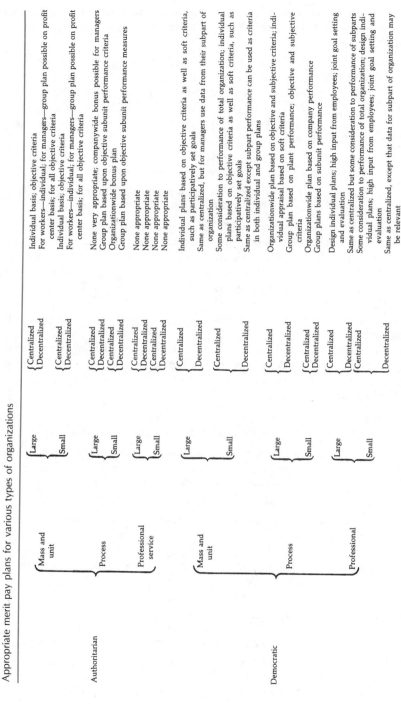

Authoritarian	Mass and unit	Large	Centralized	Individual basis; objective criteria
			Decentralized	For workers—individual; for managers—group plan possible on profit center basis; for all objective criteria
		Small	Centralized	Individual basis; objective criteria
			Decentralized	For workers—individual; for managers—group plan possible on profit center basis; for all objective criteria
	Process	Large	Centralized	None very appropriate; companywide bonus possible for managers
			Decentralized	Group plan based upon objective subunit performance criteria
		Small	Centralized	Organizationwide bonus plan
			Decentralized	Group plan based upon objective subunit performance measures
	Professional service	Large	Centralized	None appropriate
			Decentralized	None appropriate
		Small	Centralized	None appropriate
			Decentralized	None appropriate
Democratic	Mass and unit	Large	Centralized	Individual plans based on objective criteria as well as soft criteria, such as participatively set goals
			Decentralized	Same as centralized, but for managers use data from their subpart of organization
		Small	Centralized	Some consideration to performance of total organization; individual plans based on objective criteria as well as soft criteria, such as participatively set goals
			Decentralized	Same as centralized except subpart performance can be used as criteria in both individual and group plans
	Process	Large	Centralized	Organizationwide plan based on objective and subjective criteria; individual appraisal based on soft criteria
			Decentralized	Group plan based on plant performance; objective and subjective criteria
		Small	Centralized	Organizationwide plan based on company performance
			Decentralized	Group plans based on subunit performance
	Professional	Large	Centralized	Design individual plans; high input from employees; joint goal setting and evaluation
			Decentralized	Same as centralized but some consideration to performance of subparts
		Small	Centralized	Some consideration to performance of total organization; design individual plans; high input from employees; joint goal setting and evaluation
			Decentralized	Same as centralized, except that data for subpart of organization may be relevant

Source: E. E. Lawler, Jr., *Pay and Organizational Effectiveness* (New York: McGraw-Hill Book Co., 1971), p. 282.

pay schemes;[91] to the extent that the enterprise embraces this belief, the following propositions, which are modifications of Lawler's recommendations, apply:

> *Proposition 14.1.* Individual incentive plans are the most effective methods to tie pay to performance; group incentive plans are the next most effective; organizationwide schemes the least effective.

> *Proposition 14.2.* Group and enterprise incentive schemes provide more nonpay rewards (such as social acceptance, esteem) than individual incentive plans.

> *Proposition 14.3.* The least effective plans for tying pay to performance are across-the-board raises and seniority increases.

> *Proposition 14.4.* The smaller the organization, the more likely is a group incentive participation scheme to be effective.

Instead of presenting the table of recommended usages of financial compensation for model organizations, similar to those in other chapters, we will take a final look at Lawler's analysis. He observes that most organizations express dissatisfaction with their compensation systems and want to change them, and he contends that this is because many variables affect compensation. Lawler believes these include human relations and leadership style, as do the degree of centralization of an organization, and organization size and technology.

Lawler's recommendations of the best pay systems for the various types of organizations are given in Exhibit 14–8. These will serve as recommendations for model organizations if management accepts the concept that pay should be tied to performance.

Proposition 14.5 appears reasonable to me since executives are the most likely to believe that pay should be tied to performance.

> *Proposition 14.5.* The more executive compensation is tied directly to performance for executives, the greater the performance effects. The most effective performance devices are bonuses tied to specific reachable and challenging objectives, and performance shares.

Too little research is available on the various compensation issues to give propositions on salaries for everyone, pay secrecy, security, and raises.

This concludes our treatment of the pay aspect of compensation. Chapters 15 and 16 discuss benefits and pensions the final aspects of compensation to be considered in Part Five.

QUESTIONS

1. What is the most typical payment method: time based or output based? Why?
2. Should everyone be paid a salary? Why? Why not?
3. Are individual incentive pay schemes effective?
4. Which of the individual incentive pay schemes are used most frequently?
5. Are group incentive pay schemes effective? Why or why not?
6. Compare and contrast the positive and negative aspects of suggestion plans,

company group incentive plans, profit-sharing plans, the Scanlon plan, and the stock ownership plan.

7. What is an ESOP? Why is this approach to incentives growing?

8. How is executive compensation similar to (and different from) compensation for other employees?

9. Business executive compensation is excessive today. Comment.

10. Are executive salaries effective in increasing performance? Are perks? Bonuses? Stock options and performance shares?

11. How does Canadian executive compensation compare to U.S. executive compensation? Why are they different?

12. How does Salter suggest compensation policy is related to strategic objectives?

13. Should compensation be kept secret? Why or why not?

14. Should compensation be made more secure? Why or why not? How?

15. When should raises be given?

16. Should raises be given for cost-of-living changes?

17. What criteria should be used for giving raises? What criteria are used?

18. How big should raises be to have a performance impact?

19. What are the major policy issues in compensation that top management must consider in order to ensure an effective compensation system?

20. What are the major propositions of Chapter 14?

NOTES AND REFERENCES

1. P. G. Kaponya, "Salaries for All Workers," *Harvard Business Review,* May–June 1962, pp. 49–57; J. Gooding, "It Pays to Wake Up the Blue-Collar Worker," *Fortune* 82 (1970), pp. 133–35; 156 ff.

2. Robert Hulme and Richard Bevan, "The Blue Collar Worker Goes on Salary," *Harvard Business Review,* March–April 1975, pp. 104–12; David Peach, "Salaries for Production Workers: What Happens?" *The Business Quarterly,* Spring 1974, pp. 67–69.

3. Mitchell Fein, "Work Measurement and Wage Incentives," *Industrial Engineering,* September 1973, pp. 49–51; Allan Nash and Stephen Carroll, Jr., *The Management of Compensation,* Monterey, Ca.: Brooks/Cole Publishing Co., 1975, ch. 7.

4. Tino Johnson, "Computer Generated Wage Incentive Rates," *Industrial Engineering,* June 1973, pp. 10–13; Richard Pitsch, "Auditing Incentive Plans," *Industrial Engineering,* February 1976, pp. 20–23.

5. Edward Locke et al., "Goals and Intentions as Mediators of the Effects of Monetary Incentive on Behavior," *Journal of Applied Psychology* 52, 2 (1968), pp. 104–21.

6. R. E. Pritchard et al., "Effects of Equity and Inequity on Worker Performance and Satisfaction," *Journal of Applied Psychology* Monograph 56 (1972), pp. 75–94; E. E. Lawler, Jr., *Pay and Organizational Effectiveness* (New York: McGraw-Hill Book Co., 1971); Locke et al., "Goals and Intentions as Mediators of the Effects of Monetary Incentive on Behavior"; R. Marriott, *Incentive Wage System* (London: Staples Press, 1968).

7. William Whyte, *Money and Motivation* (New York: Harper & Row, 1955); David Hickson, "Motives of People Who Restrict Their Output," *Occupational Psychology* 35 (1961), pp. 479–503.

8. E. E. Lawler, Jr., and J. Hackman, "The Impact of Employee Participation in the Development of Pay Incentive Plans: A Field Experiment," *Journal of Applied Psychology* 53 (1969)

pp. 467–71; Walter Nord, "Beyond the Teaching Machine," *Organizational Behavior and Human Performance* 4 (1969), pp. 375–401.

9. Donald Schwab and Marc Wallace, Jr., "Correlates of Employee Satisfaction with Pay," *Industrial Relations,* May 1974, pp. 78–89.

10. Arch Patton, "Why Incentive Plans Fail," *Harvard Business Review,* May–June 1972, pp. 58–66; Fein, "Work Measurement and Wage Incentives"; Mervyn Watkins, "Anatomy of a Failure," *Industrial Engineering,* May 1973, pp. 29–31.

11. Nash & Carroll, *Management of Compensation.*

12. H. Campbell, "Group Incentives," *Occupational Psychology,* January 1952, pp. 15–21; R. Marriott, "Size of Working Group and Output," *Occupational Psychology,* January 1949, pp. 47–57; Keith Miller and Robert Homblin, "Interdependence, Differential Rewards and Productivity," *American Sociological Review,* October 1963, pp. 768–78; Manuel London and Gred Oldham, "A Comparison of Group and Individual Incentive Plans," *Academy of Management Journal* 20, 1 (1977), pp. 34–41.

13. Herbert Northrup, *Suggestion Systems,* National Industrial Conference Board Studies in Personnel 135. (New York, 1953).

14. Abraham Pizam, "Some Correlates of Innovation within Industrial Suggestion Systems," *Personnel Psychology* 27 (1974), pp. 63–76.

15. John Hein, "Employee Suggestion Systems Pay," *Personnel Journal,* March 1973, pp. 218–21.

16. Richard James, "Unfriendly Skies," *The Wall Street Journal,* February 23, 1976.

17. Pizam, "Correlates of Innovation."

18. Harold Stieglitz, *The Kaiser Steel Union Sharing Plan.* National Industrial Conference Board Studies in Personnel Policy 187. (New York, 1963).

19. James Lincoln, *Incentive Management* (Cleveland, Ohio: Lincoln Electric Co., 1969).

20. Fred Lesieur and Elbridge Puckett, "The Scanlon Plan Has Proved Itself," *Harvard Business Review,* September–October 1969, pp. 109–18; A. J. Geare, "Productivity from Scanlon-type Plans," *Academy of Management Review,* July 1976, pp. 99–108; George Schultz and Robert McKersie, "Participation-Achievement-Reward Systems," *Journal of Management Studies,* May 1973, pp. 141–161; Brian Moore, "The Scanlon Plant Wide Incentive Plan," *Training and Development Journal,* February 1976, pp. 50–53; Bernard Wysoocki, "Productivity Push," *The Wall Street Journal,* December 9, 1976; George Sherman, "The Scanlon Plan: Its Capabilities for Productivity Improvement," *The Personnel Administrator,* July 1976, pp. 17–20.

21. T. Gilson and M. Lefcowitz, "A Plant Wide Productivity Bonus in a Small Factory," *Industrial and Labor Relations Review* 10 (1957), pp. 284–96; Marriott, "Size of Working Group and Output."

22. Bert Metzger, "As You Were Saying: Share Profits: Don't Freeze Them," *Personnel Journal,* January 1972, Bert Metzger and Jerome Colletti, *Does Profit Sharing Pay?* (Evanston, Ill.: Profit Sharing Research Foundation, 1971). For a critical view of profit sharing see "Employee Wrath Hits Profit Sharing," *Business Week,* July 18, 1977, pp. 25–27.

23. Donald Moffitt, "How Change in Tax Law Can Take New Bite of Profit Sharing Funds Given Employees," *The Wall Street Journal,* October 25, 1976.

24. Peter Hearst, "Employee Stock Ownership Trusts and Their Uses," *Personnel Journal,* February 1975, pp. 104–6. For another discussion of ESOPs see, Paul Burke, "Total Compensation Planning under the 1976 Tax Reform Act," *Personnel Journal,* March 1977, pp. 137–39, 150 ff.

25. David Thomsen, "Calculating the Score on ESOP's: Winners and Losers," *Compensation*

Review 7, 4 (1975), pp. 47–53; Robert Reum and Sherry Reum, "Employee Stock Ownership Plans: Pluses and Minuses," *Harvard Business Review,* July–August 1976, pp. 133–43.

26. Milton Rock, "Management Executive Compensation," *Chief Executives Handbook,* in John Glover and Gerland Simon (Homewood, Ill.: Dow Jones–Irwin, Inc., 1976); Harland Fox, *Top Executive Compensation,* Report 640 (New York: Conference Board, 1974); David Belcher, *Compensation Administration* (Englewood Cliffs; N.J.: Prentice-Hall, Inc., 1974), pp. 536–44; "Who Gets the Most Pay," *Forbes,* May 15, 1976, pp. 225–51.

27. Donald Moffitt, "Executive Taxes," *The Wall Street Journal,* January 31, 1977.

28. One exception is, American Society of Association Executives, *Compensation and Benefits for Association Executive Personnel* (Washington, 1973).

29. Wilbur Lewellen, *Executive Compensation in Large Industrial Corporations* (New York: National Bureau of Economic Research, 1968).

30. Arch Patton, "Top Executive Pay," *Harvard Business Review,* September–October 1966, pp. 94–97.

31. R. Howe, "Price Tags for Executives," *Harvard Business Review,* May–June 1956, pp. 94–100.

32. Susan Goodman, "Salaries: Industry by Industry" *The MBA,* August–September 1973, pp. 9–10.

33. Arch Patton, "How Should An Executive Be Paid?" American Management Financial Management Series no. 97, 1951, pp. 16–22.

34. Arch Patton, "What Is An Executive Worth?" *Harvard Business Review,* March–April 1961, pp. 65–73.

35. Joseph McGuire, et al., "Executive Incomes, Sales and Profits," *American Economic Review,* September 1962, pp. 753–61; Wilbur Lewellen, *The Ownership Income of Management* (New York: National Bureau of Economic Research, 1971); Wilbur Lewellen and Blaine Huntsman, "Managerial Pay and Corporate Performance," *American Economic Review,* September 1970, pp. 710–20.

36. Robert Sibson, Executive Pay: The Long Term Is Where the Action Is," *Nation's Business,* November 1971, pp. 29–33.

37. Marc Wallace, "Type of Control, Industrial Concentration and Executive Pay," *Proceedings,* Academy of Management, 1976.

38. Arch Patton, *Men, Money and Motivation* (New York: McGraw-Hill Book Co., 1961); Arch Patton, "Are We Sabotaging Executive Motivation?" *The McKinsey Quarterly,* Summer 1970, pp. 52–67.

39. K. R. Murthy and Malcolm Salter, "Should CEO Pay Be Linked to Results?" *Harvard Business Review,* May–June 1975, pp. 66–73.

40. S. B. Prasad and H. Shawky, "Technology and Executive Compensation" Eastern Economic Association, Albany, N.Y., October, 1974, mimeographed.

41. Belcher, *Compensation Administration.* For a recent analysis of executive pay see, "The Tightening Squeeze on White-Collar Pay," *Business Week,* September 12, 1977, pp. 82–93.

42. "Special Privileges," *The Wall Street Journal,* September 18, 1975.

43. Robert Sbarra, "The New Language of Executive Compensation," *Personnel,* November–December 1975, p. 10. Some recent discussions of executive perks include: Robert Coffin, "Developing a Program of Executive Benefits & Perquisites, *The Personnel Administrator,* February 1977, pp. 58–62; "Persistent Perks," *Wall Street Journal,* October 14, 1977.

44. Robert Sibson, "The Outlook for Executive Pay," *Nation's Business,* November–December 1975, pp. 23–27.

45. Arch Patton, "Old Fashioned Initiative for Modern Enterprises," *Harvard Business Review,* July–August, 1954, pp. 67–73; R. Smyth, *Financial Incentives for Management* (New York: McGraw-Hill Book Co., 1971); "The Bonus Is a Real Incentive," *Business Week,* March 14, 1977, pp. 54, 58.

46. Patton, *Men, Money and Motivation.*

47. J. Perham, "What's Wrong With Bonuses?" *Duns Review,* April 1971, pp. 40–44.

48. James Cheek, *How to Compensate Executives* (Homewood, Ill.: Dow Jones–Irwin, 1974), ch. 3.

49. John Deardon, "How to Make Incentive Plans Work," *Harvard Business Review,* July–August 1972, pp. 117–24.

50. Robert Pitts, "Incentive Compensation and Organization Design," *Personnel Journal,* May 1974, pp. 338–44; 348 ff.

51. Roger Ricklefs, "Sweetening the Pot," *The Wall Street Journal,* May 27, 1975; "The Year Stock Options Came Back," *Business Week,* May 10, 1976, pp. 117–28.

52. "Tax Reform Remodels the Pay Package," *Business Week,* February 28, 1977, p.48; Donald Moffitt, "Your Money Matters," *The Wall Street Journal,* June 6, 1977; Hutchins, "Personal Business," *Business Week,* June 13, 1977; James McKinney, "The Reform Act of 1976 and Executive Stock Compensation Plans," *Personnel,* May–June 1977, pp. 50–56.

53. E. Wallace, "From the Thoughtful Businessman," *Harvard Business Review* 39 (1961), pp. 26–28; B. Bignier et al., "From the Thoughtful Businessman," *Harvard Business Review,* January–February 1977, pp. 16, 21, 22, 24.

54. Lewellen, *Ownership Income of Management.*

55. George Foote, "Performance Shares Revitalize Executive Stock Plans," *Harvard Business Review,* November–December 1973, pp. 121–30.

56. Ralph Winter, "Avoiding Risks" *The Wall Street Journal,* June 10, 1977.

57. W. T. McConnell, "Executive Compensation: The Controls That Bind," *Canadian Business Review,* Spring 1976, pp. 24–26; Benjamin Swirshy, "Executive Compensation and the Tax Structure," *Canadian Business Review,* Spring 1964, pp. 33–36; Brian Herbison and James Rockley, "Trends in Compensation in Canada," *Canadian Personnel and Industrial Relations Journal,* March 1976, pp. 27–30.

58. Malcolm Salter, "Tailor Executive Compensation to Strategy," *Harvard Business Review,* March–April 1973, pp. 94–102.

59. Wilbur Lewellen and Howard Lanser, "Executive Pay Preferences," *Harvard Business Review,* September–October 1973, pp. 115–22.

60. Jay Schuster, "Management Compensation Policy and the Public Interest," *Public Personnel Management,* November–December 1974, pp. 510–23.

61. Thomas Paine, "Flexible Compensation Can Work," *Financial Executive,* February 1974, pp. 56–59; Howard Risher and Colin Mills, "Cafeteria Compensation: Present Status and Future Potential," *Canadian Personnel and Industrial Relations Journal,* March 1974, pp. 35–39; John Todd, "Cafeteria Compensation: Making Management Motivators Meaningful," *Personnel Journal,* May 1975, pp. 275–81.

62. Fred Meuter, "Executive Compensation: A Look at the Shape of Things to Come," *Personnel,* January–February 1977, pp. 65–70.

63. Bureau of National Affairs, *Personnel Policies Forum,* Survey no. 97 (1972).

64. Edward Lawler, "Managers' Perceptions of Their Subordinates' Pay and of Their Superiors' Pay," *Personnel Psychology* 18 (1965), pp. 413–22; Edward Lawler, "The Mythology of Management Compensation," *California Management Review,* Fall 1966, pp. 11–22; Lawler, *Pay and Organizational Effectiveness.*

65. George Milkovich and Phillip Anderson, "Management Compensation and Secrecy Policies," *Personnel Psychology,* Summer 1972, pp. 293–302.

66. Jay Schuster, and Jerome Colletti, "Pay Secrecy: Who Is For and Against It?" *Academy of Management Journal,* March 1973, pp. 35–40.

67. John Pronsky, *Pay System Motivation: A Comparative Study,* unpublished DBA thesis, Harvard Business School, 1970.

68. Paul Thompson and John Pronsky, "Secrecy Disclosure in Management and Compensation," *Business Horizons,* June 1975, pp. 67–74.

69. John Fossum, "Publicity or Secrecy? Pay and Performance Feedback Effects on Satisfaction," *Proceedings,* Academy of Management, 1976.

70. Thompson and Pronsky, "Secrecy Disclosure in Management and Compensation."

71. F. Blum, *Toward A Democratic Work Process* (New York: Harper & Bros., 1953); Murray Latimer, "Guaranteed Wages," in *Unions, Management and the Public,* ed. E. W. Bakke et al., 2d ed. (New York: Harcourt, Brace & World, 1960).

72. Beverly Schaffer, "Experience with Supplementary Unemployment Benefits: A Case Study of the Atlantic Steel Company," *Industrial and Labor Relations Review,* October 1968, pp. 85–94.

73. William F. Glueck and Robert Mittelstaedt, "Protection of Trade Secrets in the 70's," *California Management Review,* Fall 1973, pp. 34–39; John Villarreal, "Employment Contracts for Managers and Professionals," *Personnel Journal,* October 1974, pp. 736–38.

74. Edward Lawler, "New Approaches to Pay: Innovations That Work," *Personnel,* September–October 1976, pp. 11–23.

75. Husain Mustafa, "Escalator Pay Plans," *Public Personnel Management,* January–February 1974, pp. 4–9.

76. "The Netherlands: Close to a Showdown over Indexation," *Business Week,* February 7, 1977.

77. Belcher, *Compensation Administration,* pp. 246–48.

78. Herbert Meyer, "The Pay for Performance Dilemma," *Organization Dynamics,* Winter 1975, pp. 39–50; Edward Deci, *'Intrinsic Motivation* (New York: Plenum Publishing Corp., 1975).

79. Sumner Slichter, et al., *The Impact of Collective Bargaining on Management* (Washington, D.C.: The Brookings Institute, 1960); W. A. Evans, "Pay for Performance: Fact or Fable?" *Personnel Journal,* 49 (1970), pp. 726–31.

80. Herbert Heneman, III, "Impact of Performance on Managerial Pay Levels and Pay Changes," *Journal of Applied Psychology* 58, 1 (1973), pp. 128–30.

81. M. Beer and G. J. Gerry, "Individual and Organizational Correlates of Pay System Preferences," in *Managerial Motivation and Compensation* ed. Henry Tosi et al. (East Lansing: Michigan State University, 1972); P. S. Goodman, "Effect of Perceived Inequity on Salary Allocation Decisions," *Journal of Applied Psychology* 60 (1975), pp. 372–75.

82. Lee Dyer et al., "Managerial Perceptions Regarding Salary Increase Criteria," *Personnel Psychology* 29 (1976), pp. 233–42.

83. For some exceptions see, Raymond Kieft, "Salary Equity Adjustment: For Whom and How Much?" *Journal of College and University Personnel Association,* July–August 1975, pp. 28–32; Sheldon Zedeck and Patricia Smith, "A Psychological Determinator of Equitable Payment," *Journal of Applied Psychology* 52 (1960), pp. 343–47; John Hinricks, "Correlates of Employees' Evaluations of Pay Increases," *Journal of Applied Psychology* 53 (1969), pp. 481–89; W. Corbett and R. Potocko, "Economic and Psychological Determinants of the Comparability of Pay," *Proceedings,* American Psychological Association, 4, 2 (1969), pp. 711–12.

84. Linda Krefting and Thomas Mahoney, "Determining the Size of a Meaningful Pay Increase," *Proceedings,* Academy of Management, 1976.

85. Robert Daski, "Area Wage Survey Test Focuses on Part Timers," *Monthly Labor Review,* April 1974, pp. 60–62; Martin Gannon, "The Management of Peripheral Employees" *Personnel Journal,* September 1975, pp. 482–86.

86. Donald Petrie, "How to Explain the Dollars and Sense of Pay Policies," *Personnel,* January–February 1970, pp. 27–32.

87. Alan Blender, "Wage Discrimination: Reduced Form and Structural Estimates," *The Journal of Human Resources,* Fall 1973, pp. 436, 455; Robert Flanagan, "Racial Wage Discrimination and Employment Segregation," *The Journal of Human Resources,* Fall 1973, pp. 456–71.

88. Peter Grinyer and Sidney Kessler, "The Systematic Evaluation of Methods of Wage Payments," *Journal of Management Studies* 4, 3 (1967), pp. 309–20; Salter, "Tailor Executive Compensation to Strategy"; George Hettenhouse, "Cost-Benefit Analysis of Executive Compensation," *Harvard Business Review,* July–August 1970, pp. 114–24; Charles Russon, "A Suggested Method of Auditing Incentive Plans and Related IE Practices," *Industrial Management,* July 1973, pp. 5–11.

89. Belcher, *Compensation Administration,* pp. 571–89.

90. George Milkovich, et al., "A Systematic Approach to University Faculty Compensation," *Compensation Review* 7, 4 (1975), pp. 38–46.

91. Lawler, *Pay and Organizational Effectiveness.*

Employee benefits and services

CHAPTER OBJECTIVES

■ To discuss employee benefits and services.

■ To suggest why they are offered, to whom, and what the results in satisfaction and performance might be

■ To show you how to manage a benefit and service program effectively.

CHAPTER OUTLINE

Recently a union negotiating for a group of police asked for pay raises; increases in two insurance programs; 17 paid holidays, including Valentine's Day and Halloween; a gymnasium and swimming pool; and free abortions for their wives. Everything except the pay increase is a benefit or service. In reporting this story, *The Wall Street Journal* asked, "Anything else?"

Howard Hyatt, president of a medium-sized insurance company, was on a business trip. On the plane, he sat next to an official of one of the major telephone companies. They talked business, and H. H. learned that the phone company in a distant city was in the process of adding dental insurance to its list of employee benefits.

When H. H. got back to the office, he called in the personnel vice president and said, "John, I just learned that the Far West Telephone Company is giving its employees dental insurance benefits. My brother is a dentist. I know that most people neglect their dental care because they have no insurance. Dental insurance sounds like a good idea to me. Let's put one in next year."

Joan Black (benefits clerk):   Yes the company does have a health insurance plan. What kind of claim do you have?

Arlene Smith: My son has to have an operation.

Joan: Does your son live with you? How old is he?

Arlene: Yes, he lives with me, although he is 20.

Joan: Are you his sole source of support? Does he have a job? Does he have insurance there?

Arlene: Yes, I support him. He has a part-time job, but I don't know if they have a medical plan.

Joan: How long have you worked here? I must determine eligibility, you see.

Arlene: Three years.

Joan: Which medical plan do you have? Plan A, Plan B, or Plan C? Do you have major medical plan? What's the deductible?

Arlene: I'm not sure. Why don't you get out my file?

Joan: But you should know that.

Arlene: I forget.

Joan (irritated):   When you go to the hospital, be sure to bring your ID card. Fill out these forms in triplicate before you file the claim and we'll process it as fast as we can.

These three case examples illustrate several significant points about benefits and services:

As with the police union, benefits and services are increasing in variety and costs. Typical benefits and services equal one third (and can be as much as 50 percent) of compensation costs. Benefits have been increasing at double the rate of pay increases. As a result, on occasion employers try to reduce benefits, often with the result that employees are unhappy or even strike. For example, the United Mine Workers threatened to strike unless their health plan was improved (1977). In Georgia (1977) the state government tried to reduce the number of paid holidays from 12 to 9.[1]

As with Arlene, most studies show that employees are frequently unaware of the details of benefits and sometimes of their existence. And benefits are complicated to administer.

As with H. H., benefits are often decided upon without significant study of costs, employee preferences, or fit with the existing benefit and services program. Worse, there is almost no evidence that employees are more productive or satisfied because of these programs, and some that show no productivity results.[2] One exception is Frederick Herzberg, who found benefits to be a hygiene factor, not a motivator.[3]

In sum, the administration of benefits and services is a perplexing, complicated, and important activity in the personnel function.

INTRODUCTION

> **DEFINITION**
> Employee benefits and services are a part of the rewards (including pay and promotion) which reinforce loyal service to the employer. Major benefits and services programs include pay for time not worked, subsidized insurance, subsidized retirement, and services.

This definition is a bit vague because the term "benefits and services" is applied to hundreds of programs, as we shall see. Benefits and services are important because of their cost, obviously. But in an ASPA/Prentice-Hall survey, 1,400 personnel executives rated benefits and services as their third (or at lowest, fourth) most significant duty.[4]

Why are benefits and services programs offered to employees? The programs offered in work organizations today are the product of efforts in this area for the past 30 years. Before World War II employers offered a few pensions and services because they had the employees' welfare at heart, or they wanted to keep out the union. But most benefit programs began in earnest during the war, when wages were strictly regulated. In the United States, unions pushed for nonwage compensation increases, and they got them. Court cases in the late forties confirmed the right of unions to bargain for benefits: *Inland Steel* v. *National Labor Relations Board* (1948), over pensions, and *W. W. Cross* v. *National Labor Relations Board,* over insurance. The growth of these programs indicates the extent to which unions have used this right: In 1929, benefits cost the employer 3 percent of total wages and salaries; by 1949, the cost was up to 16 percent; and in the seventies, it is nearly 30 percent, sometimes 50 percent or more.

Some employers provide these programs for labor market reasons; that is, to keep the enterprise competitive in recruiting and retaining employees in relation to other employers. Or they may provide them to keep a union out, or because the unions have won them. Another reason often given is that they are provided because they increase employee performance. Is this reason valid?

In the most sophisticated study of benefits, Robert Ashall and John Child found that none of these reasons explained the degree to which benefits and services were provided. They found that only *size* of enterprise explained this factor and concluded that Parkinson's law works so that as enterprises grow in size, they offer more benefits. They suggest the move to provide employee benefit and services is just another manifestation of bureaucratization.[5]

This brings us to the significance of top management decision making in the benefits and services area. Big money is involved in benefit decisions, in direct costs and indirectly in administrative costs, yet too many top executives ignore them, or they make unresearched, poorly thought-through decisions (as H. H. did). In both cases, personnel has not done the job it should. As a group, personnel managers have not explained the potential costs of benefits to top management, nor have they demonstrated or managed benefits so that the potential positive results have been demonstrated or will come about. Operating managers are not too involved in benefits and services at present, although they could help with the research that is desperately needed in the area. Benefits are still primarily a Stage I function, with many authorities arguing that all organizations should have benefits and services, but little concrete evidence that they affect employee productivity or satisfaction.

Some programs that are sometimes called benefits or services have already been discussed (e.g., stock purchase plans). One benefit is so important to most employees that a separate chapter will be devoted to it (pensions, Chapter 16).

A DIAGNOSTIC APPROACH TO BENEFITS AND SERVICES

Exhibit 15–1 highlights the most important factors in the diagnostic model of the personnel function which affect the administration of employee benefits and services. These include union and government requirements, economic and labor market conditions, the goals of controlling interest, and employees attitudes and preferences.

Unions have had a major impact on benefits. In the 1940s and 1950s, a major thrust of their bargaining was for increased or innovative benefits. Unions pressure for additional holidays is being followed by demands for such benefits as group auto insurance, dental care, and prepaid legal fees.

Experts differ on the objectives and strategies of unions in regard to benefits. One contends that unions have sought added benefits to increase their members' ties to them and to improve their members' socioeconomic status.[6] Another argues that the unions' objectives in this area have been primarily to make their members' income security the responsibility of the employer. Union leaders have varied the strategy and tactics they use to get "more" in order to achieve the long-run goal of getting employers to perceive benefits not as compensation but as part of their own social responsibility.[7]

Government requirements have affected the benefits area significantly. In the United States, three major benefits are legally required: workers' compensation, (see Chapter 17), unemployment compensation, and social security. Recently, the passage of the Employee Retirement Income Security Act of 1974 (ERISA) has regulated private pensions (Chapter 16). Progressive income taxes and the policy of the Internal Revenue Service to allow deductions of benefits costs as expenses encourage their development. In 1971, the federal government mandated four long holiday weekends. Passage of the Welfare Fund Disclosure Act requires descriptions and reports of benefits plans, and the government is considering national health insurance as a required worker benefit. The National Labor Relations Board and the courts have stringent rules on eligibility for benefits and the employer's ability to change an established benefits plan.[8]

In Canada, employer participation is required in the same three benefit programs: the Canada Pension Plan (Quebec Pension Plan), unemployment compensation, and workers' compensation. The Canadian government also has legislated holiday and vacation policies. The most costly insurance benefit in Canada, health and major medical insurance, is provided by a National Health Program jointly run by the federal and provincial/territorial governments.

Economic and labor market conditions influence benefit decisions because in tight labor markets, enterprises seeking the best employees compete by offering better benefits and services packages, which are nontaxable income in the United States. Various experts have shown how firms can determine how competitive their benefit packages are.[9]

Certain employers are apparently pacesetters who introduce the newer benefits first; one example is the American Telephone and Telegraph Company. Other leading employers follow the practice, and then enterprises who follow the leading companies set the program up. The benefits managers of the pacesetters regularly discuss benefit trends and read surveys of what the competition is offering. Therefore competition can induce an enterprise to add or adjust its benefits-services plan.

The goals of managers and controlling interests affect the benefits-services package offered. Managers or owners may aim at employee satisfaction or may oppose unions. Other goals also can influence whether a benefits program is set up and how generous it is. These goals have limits, however. For example, even if the mayor and city administrators of New York wanted to improve pay and benefits, the budget would not allow it. At American Motors in 1975, salaried employees gave up dental insurance and cost-of-

EXHIBIT 15-1
Factors affecting employee benefits and services and organizational effectiveness

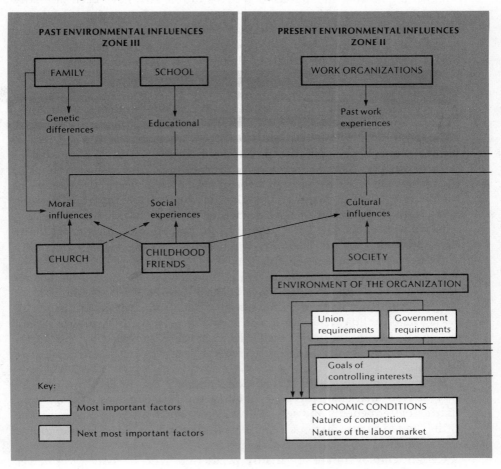

living allowances to avoid layoffs, because business was bad. Some Kentucky teachers accepted a raise of $100 instead of increased medical insurance because of budget problems. The point management must get across is that it cannot print money; the amount available for compensation is limited by profits or budget constraints and must be split among pay, benefits, and services.

The final factor affecting benefits and services is the preferences and attitudes of employees toward them. For benefits to have an effect on employee satisfaction, employees must:

• Know about their benefits.

• Prefer the enterprise's benefits to those offered by other enterprises.

• Perceive the enterprise's benefits as satisfying more of their needs than competing employers' benefits.

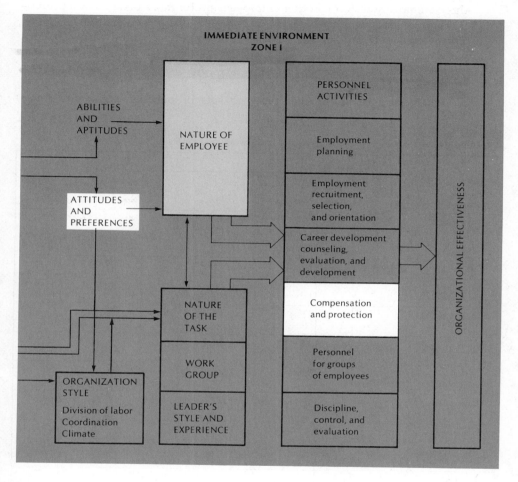

Presumably, if employees are satisfied with their benefits package, they will be absent less, be reluctant to quit, produce higher quality products, and have fewer accidents.

For benefits to affect employee performance, employees must:

• See them as a strongly preferred end.

• Perceive that by performing better they can increase their benefits.

These statements fit the beliefs of expectancy theory (see Chapter 2) and make it clear that employee preferences for benefits are a significant factor in their satisfaction and performance.

Exhibit 15–2 summarizes the studies on employee preferences for pay versus benefits, or preferences selected from a set of benefits.[10]

Note that there are many empty cells in the exhibit. We know relatively little about these preferences.

As far as preference for benefits relative to other rewards is concerned, there are no studies on whether employees prefer more benefits or a promotion; more perks or more benefits; or enlarged jobs or benefits, for example. There are a few studies on whether the employee would rather have a pay raise or more benefits. In general, more educated, older, higher status people prefer more benefits to more pay, but the majority of employees prefer pay raises.

With regard to preferences between sets of benefits, some preference

EXHIBIT 15–2
Preferences of employees for benefits, pay, and some working conditions

Employee category	Paid time off				Unemployment insurance	Profit sharing	Counseling and services
	Sick leave	Breaks	Holidays	Vacation			
Total sample	L^1, H^2, H^3	L^2	L^1, L^3, H^2, H^9, M^8	M^3, L^4, H^9, H^2, H^{10}, H^8	M^2	L^2	L^2
Male	M^2		M^2, L^{11}, H^9	H^9		L^2	
Female	H^{11}, M^2		H^9, M^2	H^{11}, H^{12}		L^2	
Under 30 years old			L^{11}	H^{11}, M^6, L^2			L^2
30–39 years old			L^{11}	H^{11}, M^6, M^2			L^2
40–49 years old			M^{11}	H^{11}, M^6, H^2			L^2
Over 50 years old			L^{11}	L^6, H^2			L^2
Blue collar	H^{11}		L^{11}, H^{13}, H^{14}	H^{11}, M^6, L^{15}			L^{14}
White collar	H^{11}		L^{11}	H^{11}, M^6, L^{15}			
Manager-professional	L^{11}		L^{11}				
Married			L^{11}, H^9	M^6, H^9			
Single			H^{11}, H^9	H^{11}, H^9, M^6			
No children				H^{11}			
Children							
High salary							
Medium salary	H^{11}		H^{11}				
Low salary	H^{11}			H^{11}			

Preference key: H = high; M = medium; L = low.

[1] Goode (1974)	[6] Nealey (1963)	[11] Schuster (1969)
[2] Geisler & Glueck (1977)	[7] Chapman & Overton (1975)	[12] Nealey & Goodale (1975)
[3] Lawler (1966)	[8] Chapman & Otteman (1975)	[13] Brosnan (1973)
[4] Wagner & Bakerman (1960)	[9] Nealey & Goodale (1967)	[14] Brosnan (1975)
[5] Chapman & Otteman (1967)	[10] Jain & Janzen (1974)	[15] Gluskinos & Kesterman (1971)

* A Canadian study: Health care is provided as government program.
Note: A bibliographical list of these studies is given at the end of the chapter in note 10.

patterns seem rather stable. For example, medical insurance is a preferred benefit in the United States and shorter hours are not; stock plans are preferred and early retirement is not. But most preferences vary widely (such as concerning holidays, vacations, and pensions), although the results may be due to differences in the research methods of the studies which reported them.[11] And preferences have changed from the 1950s and 1960s to the present.[12]

Many factors affect benefits and services: unions bargaining for more,

Insurance							
Health/medical	Life	Accident and disability	Stock plan	Early retirement	Pensions	Shorter hours	Pay/pay raise
H⁴, H², L¹⁰*, H⁹	L¹, M², L¹⁰	M¹, M², L³		L³, L⁹, M⁸	H⁵, M³, H¹, H⁴, H², M¹⁰	L⁶, L⁹, L³, L⁸	H⁷, H¹, L⁴, L⁹, H², H³, H¹⁰
H¹¹			H¹¹	L⁹	L¹¹, H⁴	M⁹	H¹¹, M⁹
H¹¹				L⁹	L¹¹, M²	M⁹	L⁹
H⁶, H¹¹			H¹¹		L¹¹, M⁴, M⁸, L⁶	L⁶, M⁸	
H¹¹, H⁶			H¹¹		M², H⁴, L¹¹, L⁶	L⁶, L⁸	H¹¹, M⁶
H¹¹, M⁶			H¹¹		H⁴, M⁸, H², L¹¹, M⁶	L⁶, L⁸	H¹¹, M⁶
H¹¹, M⁶					H², H⁴, H¹¹, H⁸, H⁶	L⁶, L⁸	L⁶
H¹¹, H⁶			H¹¹		L¹¹, H⁴, M⁶, H¹⁵	L⁶, L¹³, M¹⁴	H¹¹, H¹⁴, H¹⁵, M⁶, H¹³
H¹¹, M⁶			H¹¹		L¹¹, H⁴	L⁶	H¹¹, M⁶, L¹⁵
H¹¹	H¹¹	L¹¹	H¹¹		H¹¹		L¹¹
H¹¹, H⁶			H¹¹		L¹¹, H⁸	L⁶, M⁹	M⁶, L⁹
M⁶			L¹¹	L⁹	L¹¹, M⁸	M⁶, L⁹	M⁶, L⁹
M⁶	L¹¹		H¹¹		L¹¹, H⁶, L⁹	L⁶, L⁹	M⁶
H⁶					M⁶	L⁶, L⁹	M to H⁶
H¹¹			H¹¹		H¹¹		
					H¹¹		
			H¹¹		H¹¹		H¹¹

governments mandating and regulating them, competition and the labor market inducing increases or stability. Managerial goals vary from concern with employee satisfaction and welfare (and thus larger benefit programs) to an overriding desire to keep labor costs low. And employees' perferences vary by economic group, age, and experience.

All the while, the costs are increasing, though there is very little evidence that the employee cares about benefits, is satisfied by them, or lets his behavior be positively influenced by the program. This poses the decision problems for the chapter:

What benefits and services should the enterprise offer?

How does the enterprise cope with the apparently serious preference differences among employees?

Most decisions concerning new benefit and service programs start with what is presently offered. This chapter considers current programs, examines the relative costs of the benefits, and shows how to make competent benefit decisions.

MANDATED BENEFIT PROGRAMS

For three benefit programs, the employer has no choice but to offer the programs to employees. An employer who wishes to change these programs or to stop offering them must get involved in the political process and change the laws. These three programs, as noted above, are: unemployment compensation, pensions (social security or Canada Pension Plan), and workers' compensation.

Unemployment compensation

In the 1930s, when unemployment was very high, the governments were pressured to create programs to keep people from starving who were out of work through no fault of their own. Unemployment compensation (UC) was set up in the United States as part of the Social Security Act of 1935.

Unemployment compensation is designed to provide a subsistence payment for employees between jobs. The employer pays in to the UC fund (in Alabama, Alaska, and New Jersey so do employees). The base payment is increased if there is more than an average number of employees from an enterprise drawing from the fund (this is called the experience rating.) Unemployment compensation and allied systems for railroad and federal government and military employees covers about 65,000,000 U.S. employees. Major groups excluded are: self-employed workers, employees of small firms with less than four employees, domestics, farm employees, state and local government employees, and nonprofit employers such as hospitals.

To be eligible for compensation, the employee must have worked a minimum number of weeks, be without a job, and be willing to accept a suitable position offered through the State Unemployment Compensation Commission. Recent court decisions support an Ohio law which denies compensation to employees on strike.

To fund Unemployment Compensation the employer pays a tax to the state and federal government on total wages paid. Both the percentage of tax paid and the base wage level paid have been raised recently; for example, the federal tax was raised from 0.5% to 0.7 percent as of January 1977. State taxes vary; they used to average round 2.9 percent, in Illinois, for example, the state tax for an employer with 25 employees recently went from $1,995 to $3,565, and the base wage level is being raised to $6,000 per employee.

The employee receives compensation for a limited period. Typically the maximum is 26 weeks, although a few states extend the term beyond this in emergency situations. The payment is intended to be about 50 percent of a typical wage and varies from a few dollars up to about $88 a week in some states. The average payment nationwide in 1976 was $60 per week.

The unemployment compensation program is jointly run by the federal and state governments and is administered by the states. Each state has its own set of interpretations and payments. Payments by employers and to employees vary because the benefits paid vary, the experience ratings of enterprises vary, and some states are much more efficient in administering the program than others.[13]

At present there are serious problems with UC funding, due to increased benefits, recent high unemployment, extended length of benefits, poor administration, and cheating by claimants.[14] Exhibit 15–3 shows how much in debt the states UC funds are. The options are to reverse the effects of these factors or to increase the taxes, perhaps by as much as double.[15]

Canadian unemployment insurance. In 1940 Canada instituted a government program designed to help alleviate transition between jobs. As in

EXHIBIT 15–3
Who needs federal aid for unemployment funds

	Millions of dollars	
	Loans pending or approved, 1st quarter, 1977	Outstanding loans, Dec. 31, 1976
New York	$155.8	—
Illinois	135.2	$515.3
Pennsylvania	124.5	552.9
New Jersey	91.8	497.2
Connecticut	35.0	363.6
Alabama	14.2	30.0
District of Columbia	9.8	33.6
Montana	4.3	1.4
Vermont	3.7	37.5
Arkansas	3.0	20.0
Maryland	2.5	36.1

Data from U.S. Department of Labor.
Source: "The Hidden Crises in Jobless Pay," *Business Week,* January 24, 1977.

the United States, it is a joint federal-provincial-territorial program. The Unemployment Insurance Act of 1971 significantly changed the program.[16]

Unemployment benefits paid to claimants in 1975 exceeded $3.5 billion, compared with $2.1 billion in 1974. The maximum weekly payment was $183, significantly larger than in the United States; the payment base was up to two thirds of earnings covered by the act. The average payment for men was $95 weekly; for women, $68. Unemployment insurance (UI) was funded by employer payments of $1.40 per $100 of insured earnings in 1974, and this went up considerably in 1975. The maximum payment was $2.38 per $100, and the employer rate was 1.4 times the employee payment.

There are two kinds of payments—regular and special—under the almost universal UI coverage offered now. A worker who has worked 8 weeks out of the past 52 is eligible for regular benefits and one who has worked 20 weeks of the past 52 weeks qualifies for regular and special benefits. The maximum payment period is 52 weeks, unless the area is covered by extended benefits. Special benefits are available when the cause of unemployment is sickness, maternity leave, or early retirement.

The claimant reports to one of 351 UI centers in Canada for processing and counseling (in conjunction with the Department of Labour). The 1971 act led to many more claimants, but the number of reasons for disqualifications was also increased. In one study of 170,000 claimants, it was found 15,000 claimants had been placed in jobs, 1,045 were given training courses, 21,000 found jobs on their own or with the help of Canada Manpower Centres, 59,000 were disqualified, and the rest went on receiving compensation.[17]

Greene and Cousineau found that women over 25 receive UI benefits more frequently than any other group; the conclusion is that married women are milking the system. The more generous system instituted in 1971 has led to some increase in voluntary quits, some delay of search for jobs when workers are laid off or quit, some increased work-seeking to be eligible for UI benefits, and more money in the economy from UI payments. Needless to say, employer payments are rising in Canada too.

Issues in unemployment compensation. Higher unemployment compensation may increase quits or lengthen the time people do not work between jobs in Canada. Is this true elsewhere too? Many studies show that, in general, as unemployment insurance plus other benefits come close to wage rates, people stay unemployed longer,[18] and not all of them improve their previous wages when they go back to work. Some studies indicate the unemployed do not look for work seriously until their benefits are about to run out.[19]

This issue is related to the length of time benefits are offered. In the 1974 recession, when benefits ran out for many employees (both government and private supplementary unemployment benefits (SUB) benefits), the federal government supplemented benefits and extended payments up to 65 weeks. In 1977 the maximum payment period was again 52 weeks, and government administrators were told that the 1977 law required them to cut off benefits from those who would not accept available work, even if they did not consider it suitable. Furthermore, the claimant is now expected to show that she or he is systematically and regularly seeking employment. These provisions may be difficult to administer, however.

There are mixed evaluations of the performance of unemployment compensation programs. Some feel they have done a good job and would do better if the payments kept up with inflation.[20] Most people out of work are glad to have the funds, but one study indicates that employees have only average preferences for this benefit.[21]

Others are critical of the system. The studies cited above tend to indicate employees abuse the system, as in several examples cited and *The Wall Street Journal*.[22] A friend of mine reports a job applicant dropped in and filled out an application blank, but when told he fit the needs of the job perfectly and was hired, he replied, "Oh no, I'm not; they told me I had to apply at three places to get my unemployment, and I did! I don't want a job." Recently in Washington, D.C., a study found ten workers drawing unemployment compensation while holding full-time jobs. One best-seller, by Raymond Arvites, is called *How to Collect Unemployment Benefits.*

Many managers think the system is abused, especially as regards work requirements, and most people feel that claimants must take an available job within their competence range rather than draw unemployment pay, others find it difficult to decide whether an unemployed plumber should be required to take a job as a shoeshine person or dishwasher, for example.

Various proposals have been made to improve unemployment insurance. Congress recently proposed to extend coverage to 10,000,000 local government employees, but a Supreme Court ruling may negate this possibility. Others have proposed federalizing the benefit in order to standardize procedures and payments. This would no doubt substantially raise costs, since congress would not standardize it at the lowest rate. I believe this is the wrong way to go. What is needed is a plan that would prevent persons unemployed in economic recessions from starving yet would not encourage unemployment. One way to do this is to relate the size of benefits and length of payment (and other conditions) to the reasons for unemployment. If an area has almost full employment (as determined by the Department of Labor), low payments for short periods would be available. High unemployment areas would offer higher payments for longer periods of time, but not high enough to encourage movement to the geographic area, as happened in welfare programs. A flexible approach appears the best way to try to improve administration of this benefit.

What can the employer do about UC cost increases? Responsible employers want to pay their fair share but do not want to support abusers. They also do not want their experience ratings to increase costs. Much expert advice has been offered on how to cut costs of the program by stabilizing employment, keeping good records, challenging fraudulent claims, and issuing effective claims control procedures. Careful hiring and separation procedures, and claims verification and control can also cut costs. Effective managers try to control the costs of unemployment compensation just as much as inventory, advertising, or other costs.[23]

Government pensions

Employers have no choice in government pension participation, either. Many U.S. employers also are required to contribute to social security programs for retirement of employees. Similar requirements apply to the Canada and Quebec Pension Plans for Canadian employers. This topic will be described in more detail in Chapter 16.

Workers' compensation

U.S. and Canadian laws require the compensation of workers for death or permanent or total disabilities arising out of the employment situation. This program is discussed more fully in Chapter 17 on employee health and safety.

VOLUNTARY BENEFIT AND SERVICE PLANS

In addition to the benefits required by the law, many employers also provide three kinds of benefits voluntarily: compensation for time not worked, insurance protection, and employee services. There are many differences in employers' practices regarding these benefits, which provide examples of benefit decisions to be made by management.

Compensation for time off

Can you imagine a life in which you went to work six days a week, 12 hours a day, 52 weeks a year for life? That's what life used to be like, although, as discussed earlier, it has been shown that employees did not always work hard all that time.[24] The concepts of a paid holiday or vacation with pay did not exist, however. Now most employers compensate employees for some time that they have not worked: break time, get ready time, wash-up time, clothes change time, paid lunch and rest periods, coffee breaks, and so on. Employers also pay employees when they are not actually at work—holidays, vacations, sick leave, funeral leave, jury duty, and other personal leaves, such as to fulfill military obligations.

The preference studies reported in Exhibit 15–2 indicate that work breaks are not strongly preferred; they are just expected. Vacations are generally a highly preferred benefit. Preferences for holidays varies, and lower paid and women employees have stronger preferences for sick leave. Unions have negotiated hard for added time off to give their members more leisure and to create jobs.[25]

One variation of the sick leave or disability benefit which has received a great deal of attention lately is the maternity leave. Recent court cases and action by the EEOC and the Women's Movement have led to major changes in maternity leave. The Supreme Court ruled in 1976 that employers did *not* have to provide maternity leave as part of a disability program. But the Court in 1975 did specify some limits that could be placed on the program if it existed.[26]

With regard to sick leave, a BNA survey found that paid sick leave applies to office and managerial employees in more than 9 out of 10 companies, and to production employees in two thirds; only one third have formal policies providing for paid leave in case of family illness or for other "personal" reasons, and in one fifth there is an overall limit on the number of days of paid leave an employee can take in a year, for all reasons.[27]

Paid holidays. Probably the most frequently offered of these time-off-with-pay items is paid holidays. At one time, every employee was paid only for actual days worked. In the past 25 years, more and more employers have been giving holidays off with pay. The typical number of paid holidays has been increasing. In 1970, it appeared to be between six and seven,[28] but some recent surveys showed that this has shifted upward to about nine or more.[29] The most typical holidays are New Year's Day, Good Friday, Memorial Day, July 4, Labor Day, Thanksgiving Day, Christmas, President's Day, Friday after Thanksgiving, December 24 and January 2. The new mini-vacation dates created by Congress through the federal Monday-holiday law allow for three-day weekends in February for President's Day, in May for Memorial Day, in October for Columbus Day, and in November for Veteran's Day.

Paid holidays in Canada. Paid holidays are required by law in 14 jurisdictions in Canada, and in the other 3 (Newfoundland, Prince Edward Island, and Quebec), legislation is being considered. Where federal regulations prevail, the legal minimum number of paid holidays is ten, but in British Columbia, Saskatchewan, and the Yukon Territory, employees are entitled to nine; in Alberta and Northwest Territories they receive eight; in Ontario and Manitoba, seven (Manitoba also has special provisions for Remembrance Day), and in Nova Scotia and New Brunswick, six. Most provinces also have required sick leave and maternity leave policies.

Paid vacations. Another example of voluntary compensation offered for time not worked is paid vacations. This is the most expensive benefit for American and Canadian employers. Most organizations offer vacations with pay after a certain minimum period of service. The theory behind vacations is that they provide an opportunity for employees to rest and refresh themselves; when they return, hopefully, they will be more effective employees. Employees have pressed for more leisure to enjoy the fruit of their labors.

American government and military employers traditionally have given 30 days' vacation. Some universities give sabbatical years after six years of service.

In the United States, however, the typical vacation is one week of paid vacation for an employee of less than a year's service, and two weeks for

1–10 years' service. Three weeks of vacation are offered annually to veterans of 10–20 years, and four weeks to the over-20-year tenured. Over one fourth of the companies studied by the Conference Board now offer five- and six-week vacations, usually for 25-year employees.[30] The trend in paid vacations for unionized employees is upward, as a glance at Exhibit 15–4 shows.

Paid vacations in Canada.   Employees in Canada are legally entitled to paid annual vacations. The plan for employees covered by federal jurisdiction is two weeks' vacation after one year of service and three weeks' after six years of continuous service to one employer. In Manitoba, the employee receives three weeks after five years' service. Saskatchewan requires (July 1978) four weeks after ten years. Vacation pay equals 6 percent of annual earnings at the federal level, 4 percent in Newfoundland, Nova Scotia, Prince Edward Island, New Brunswick, Yukon and Northwest Territories, Quebec, and Ontario (though Ontario pays 2 percent for the first year). Vacation pay in Manitoba and Alberta is the same as weekly compensation. In Saskatchewan vacation pay is calculated by dividing annual compensation by the number of weeks' vacation.

In a recent symposium sponsored by the Conference Board of Canada, experts predicted the following trends for time off with pay.[31]

EXHIBIT 15–4
Trends in paid vacations granted to U.S. unionized employees

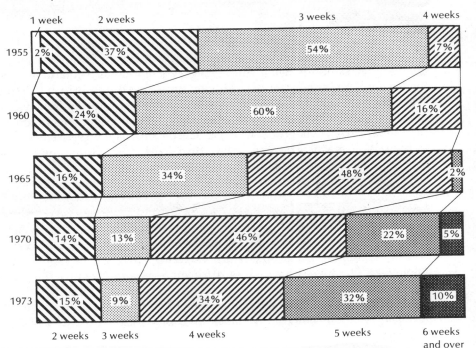

Source: Bureau of National Affairs, *Basic Patterns in Union Contracts* (Washington, D.C.: U.S. Government Printing Office, 1975).

The paid vacation standard will soon be three weeks, with longer periods for shorter periods of service.

Bonus vacations will be given to employees who take them in slack periods.

No major increase in the number of paid holidays is foreseen.

Holiday and vacation banks and other plans. Some companies offer to "bank" employees' vacation pay if they forego all or part of the permitted vacation time off; the money or time off saved can be set aside for retirement or emergency purposes. Employers such as Swedish-American Hospital combine sick leave, vacation, and paid holidays into a single package or personal-time bank. *The Wall Street Journal* cited a study which found that one employee in six skips all or part of a vacation.

Some unions are negotiating for bonuses to provide extra money prior to vacations. A few firms arrange for packaged vacations for their employees. Of course, there are problems in administering the timing of vacations so that adequate help is always available. The steel and aluminum industries experimented with extended vacations or sabbaticals for workers. These provided for 13 weeks off after five years' employment; they produced mixed results and have not caught on.[32]

Personal time off. Many employers pay employees for time off for funerals, medical/dental appointments, sickness in the family, religious observances, marriage, personal-choice holidays, and birthdays as holidays. If an enterprise uses flexitime scheduling (see Chapter 5), the need for time off is minimized. The BNA survey found that 9 out of 10 firms provide paid jury duty, 9 out of 10 provide paid leave for funerals of close relatives, and 7 out of 10 provide paid leave for military duty time. Typically, the pay is the difference between normal pay and military pays. A variety of policies apply to leaves for personal reasons, such as sickness in the family or marriage. A typical policy is to allow no more than five days per year personal time.[33]

Employer-purchased insurance

The many risks encountered throughout life—illness, accident, and early death, among others—can be spread by buying insurance. Many employers can buy insurance cheaper than their employees can, and insurance is frequently offered as a benefit. The employer may provide it free to the employee or pay part of it, and the employee "participates" by paying a share. Three major forms of insurance are involved: health, disability-accident, and life.

Health insurance. One of the most costly kinds of insurance, health or medical insurance, is financed at least partially by employers as a benefit for employees. What studies have been done indicate that employees prefer it over most other benefits (Exhibit 15–2). Health insurance includes hospitalization (room and board and hospital service charges), surgical (actual surgical fees or maximum limits) major medical (maximum benefits, typically $5,000–10,000 beyond hospitalization and surgical payments.) Recently increased coverage has been provided in major medical and comprehensive health insurance plans. Surveys report that almost all enterprises have hospitalization plans, almost all non–blue-collar workers are provided with surgical and major medical plans, and about three fourths of blue-collar employees have major medical insurance.[34]

Typically, all employees get basic coverage; beyond this, plans differ. Plans for salaried employees typically are of the major medical variety and provide "last-dollar coverage"; this means that the employee must pay the first $50 of the cost or a similar deductible. The benefits may be based on either a specified cash allowance for various procedures or a service benefit which pays the full amount of all reasonable charges.

Negotiated plans for time-pay workers generally have expanded coverage which provides specific benefits rather than comprehensive major medical coverage. This approach is preferred by union leaders because they feel individual benefits which can be clearly labeled will impress members, and these benefits can be obtained with no deductible payments by employees. Also, until recently, coverage of some desired services was not available under major medical plans. Some of the more rapidly expanding benefits of the negotiated plans are prescription drugs, vision care, mental health services, and dental care. For example, typical dental care ranges from $1,000 to $2,000 yearly. About one employer in eight provides this insurance now.[35]

Life insurance.   Group life insurance is one of the oldest and most widely available employee benefits. The employer purchases life insurance for the employee, to benefit the employee's family. Group life insurance plans provide coverage to all employees without physical examinations, with premiums based on the characteristics of the group as a whole.

As noted in Exhibit 15–2, employee preference for group life insurance is not high, being low or moderate. Surveys indicate that almost all employers offer group life insurance. In a typical program for a large company, the amount of insurance provided by the plan increases as salary increases, the typical amount being twice the salary in life insurance. But about a third of the companies surveyed have different plans for blue-collar employees, who usually get a flat amount (usually $5,000). Initially, the enterprise paid part of the premium, the employee the rest (contributory plan). The trend is to noncontributory plans in which the company pays it all but 34 percent of blue-collar, 38 percent of white-collar, and 40 percent of managerial plans are still contributory and, in view of employee preferences, probably should stay that way. Continued life insurance coverage after retirement, usually one third the coverage while working, is provided by 72 percent of large American companies.[36]

Long-term sickness and accident disability insurance.   What happens to employees who have accidents at work which leave them unable to work, temporarily or permanently? Workers' compensation pays a very small part of these costs, since it was designed primarily to take care of short-term disability problems (see Chapter 17). Employer-funded long-term disability insurance is designed to cover these cases, with payments supplementing benefits from workers' compensation, social security, and other agencies. The studies surveyed in Exhibit 15–2 indicate moderate preferences for these types of benefits.

Some disability payments are very large; recently a roofer who fell off a roof received over $5,000,000. About 75 percent of larger firms have this kind of insurance. Usually blue-collar workers are covered by flat-amount coverage (usually $5,000–10,000). For other employees, coverage is tied to salary level. Usually, there is noncontributory coverage for all employees. The goal is to provide employees with at least half pay until pension time, but the primary recipients have been non-blue-collar employees.

The majority of long-term sickness and accident disability insurance plans provide benefits for up to 26 weeks, but about 20 percent provide these benefits for a year. About 75 percent of enterprises provide such sickness and accident coverage.[37]

Recently the lower courts had ruled that pregnant women were entitled to collect disability pay, but the Supreme Court ruled in *General Electric* v. *Gilbert,* that a company need not provide pregnancy disability coverage. Congressmen have since introduced a bill to require such payments. What has been the experience of companies who paid pregnancy costs as a disability? When Xerox included pregnancy as a disability in the first year 178 salaried women made claims which cost the company $275,000, or $1,550 per employee. Administration of the program was difficult. The typical employee claimed 75 days' disability, although the range was 7 to 226 days. After taking the disability pay, 96 quit and 82 returned to work. The company reported the per-case costs for the second year increased considerably over the first year.

Employer-purchased insurance in Canada.   In Canada, the most costly insurance benefit—health and major medical insurance—is provided by National Health Insurance, jointly run by the provinces and the federal government. The Medical Care Act of 1966 became fully national in scope in April 1972 Under the program which is paid for by taxes, the care is adequate but the costs are escalating.[38] Some firms still offer major medical insurance for employees when they travel outside Canada.

Group life insurance has been offered increasingly as an employee benefit in Canada. Starting out as burial insurance, it is now on average two to four times the annual salary for executives, with smaller amounts for lower-level employees. Disability insurance is also reaching the U.S. level

The major new insurance program in Canada is dental insurance. Full coverage can cost as much as $30 a month per family. This is a high-priority item for Canadian unions in their labor negotiations.[39]

In Canada, the value of benefits becomes part of the taxable income of that employer. A few benefits which are not subject to tax are: discounts on company merchandise, subsidized meals, uniforms and special clothing, subsided schooling for children in remote areas, recreational facilities, moving expenses, premiums for private health services, and interest free loans for employees.

Employee services

Services is something of a catchall category of voluntary benefits; it includes all other benefits or services provided by employers. These are such varied programs as cafeterias; saunas and gyms, free parking lots; commuter vans; infirmaries; ability to purchase company products at a discount; and death, personal, and financial counseling. The BNA reports that almost half of the companies surveyed provide subsidized food in cafeterias on their premises, and 82 percent of companies surveyed provided free parking to their employees.[40]

Education programs. Many organizations provide for off-the-job general educational support for their employees. This varies from teaching basic skills such as reading to illiterate workers, to tuition-refund programs for managers, to scholarship and loan plans for employees' children.[41] The Internal Revenue Service has ruled that trusts to send executive's children to college were not tax free. Alexander Smith is critical of education plans as presently administered; they are costly, and the employer gains little from them.[42]

Where employers provide for tuition refunds for courses they usually place some restrictions on them; the courses must be relevant to the work being done, and a minimum grade level must be achieved. The Administrative Management Society studied 620 U.S. and Canadian firms to determine the extent and nature of educational assistance available to employees. Some form of educational assistance was reported by 96 percent of the respondents, although a large majority required the course of study to be either directly or indirectly related to the employee's present job in order to qualify for reimbursement. Among the U.S. companies, approximately half paid 100 percent of the tuition costs. A few firms based the degree of remuneration on the grade attained in the course. More than 75 percent of the firms made refunds only upon completion of the course.[43]

Comparing the data from this study with one done by the Conference Board in the late 1950s[44] indicates few changes in the nature and level of this benefit during this period. Companies often develop future executives in this way.

Financial services. Some organizations give their employees help and encouragement to save funds through employee savings plans, credit unions, and thrift plans.[45] Essentially, savings plans encourage employee thrift by matching all or part of an employee's contribution, up to, say, 5 percent of the wage or salary. Credit unions help employees avoid loan sharks and wage garnishments; BNA found that 61 percent of the firms it surveyed provided credit unions for employees.[46]

In the thrift plans, funds are often invested for distribution at retirement. One study found that two thirds of the plans fit this characteristic, and when companies have such plans, 85 percent of employees participate. Typically the company matches 50 percent of the employee contribution. In the early 1960s thrift plans cost participating companies about $167 per year per employee, plus 4 percent administration costs.[47]

As with many other services, it is difficult to tie performance or even employee satisfaction to such plans. However, they may contribute to the perception of the organization as a good place to work and thus attract better employees.

One benefit provided employees, usually executives, is financial counseling and estate planning.[48] The other benefits and perks executives receive were discussed in Chapter 14.

Social and recreational programs. Many organizations provide recreation facilities for employees, on or off the job. Some experts foresee a growing trend to release employees from work time to participate in company-sponsored sports activities, which are intended to keep employees physically fit and tie them to employers.[49] In one survey, three fourths of companies responding said they sponsored recreation programs, and half of them sponsored atheletic teams.[50] The median expenditure is $6 per employee per year.

Robert Bauer has described his experience with sports programs in his position as activities and recreation director at Armco Steel. He argues that company-run picnic groves, club activities, softball teams, and physical fitness programs are necessary for the full development of the human being.[51] Maybe so; it ties in with the practice of some companies in providing chapels and chaplains for the moral development of employees. Why not symphony orchestras and museums for their cultural development? There are no available studies of the value, if any, of such benefits to the employer. These plans could be extensions of the paternalistic antiunion activities of some employers in the 1920s and later. Studies of the preferences of employees indicate that recreational services are *the least preferred* of all benefits and services offered by enterprises.

Emerging services. Four services seem to be emerging at present: child care centers, prepaid legal services, group auto insurance, and counseling services.

About 6 percent of employers surveyed by BNA provide child care centers for children of employees.[52] Shirley Chisholm has argued that the availability of child care centers at low cost (with help provided by employers or government) would bring thousands of women off welfare and onto job rolls.[53] An excellent study by George Milkovich and Luis Gomez of one of the largest day care centers in the United States, in Minneapolis, showed that employees who used the day care center had much lower rates of absenteeism and turnover.[54] (This center was not run by the employer.) A good case can be made for the availability of well-run, efficient day care centers. Whether employers should provide their own except in geographically isolated areas is another question.

Some benefits experts believe that prepaid legal services are likely to be sought as an employee benefit in the future.[55] In the tax revision bill of 1976, prepaid legal services are tax deductible to the employer and are not counted as income to the employee. Before the passage of this law, about 175 employees were covered. The plan allows employees to use the services of lawyers at no cost. The lawyers are chosen ahead of time and paid for all services for all employees by the employer or, in some cases, the union.

Group auto insurance is the newest major benefit being offered employees. Employees want it, and it is not costly for employers. The employee typically gets a 15 percent saving on premiums, which are paid through payroll deductions. The employer pays administrative costs. What worries some employers is that auto insurance might be the next employer-paid benefit employees demand.

Employers also are providing counseling services to employees, some of it of a religious nature.[56] Other counseling includes general problem solving and help for family troubles and alcoholism, legal or financial aid, and advice in other nonwork related situations.

FUTURE TRENDS IN BENEFITS AND SERVICES

There is perhaps an unlimited number of new benefits that could be offered by employers. Teamsters Union locals in California negotiated for what *The Wall Street Journal* called the final fringe benefit: A $1,000 funeral payment.[57] Other benefits are extensions of the present benefits. To keep up, many executives read *Employee Benefit Plan Review* monthly.

A number of sources attempt to predict the future of benefit plans.[58] When 150 experts in benefits were polled,[59] they predicted the following trends in benefits:

1. Increased coverage of health insurance plans:
   a. Hospitalization for 120 days.
   b. Full surgical expense coverage, with inflation covered by use of a relative-value scale.
   c. Major medical coverage, with employees paying only 10 percent of cost of coverage.
2. Newer coverage in allied health fields:
   a. Dental coverage. Although about 60 percent of hospital bills are paid by private insurance plans, less than 5 percent of $3.5 billion dental bills are covered. No doubt this will be added to Blue Cross–type coverage.
   b. Drug insurance. Coverage of major prescription drug costs of employees by employer paid insurance.
   c. Vision care. Payment for examination and provision of glasses as needed.
   d. Preventive care. Payment for regular physical examinations.
3. Group auto insurance. Provision of liability and collision coverage by employer-provided group auto insurance. United Auto Workers union has been pressing for this.

Other researchers used the Delphi technique to attempt to determine likely employee benefits in 1985. Participating in the prediction were 100 benefits experts, who predicted the following benefits will increase greatly:

1. Longer vacations.
2. Increased flexibility in scheduling time off.
3. Elimination of all employee expenses in connection with major medical coverage.
4. Inclusion of dental coverage and yearly physical exams in medical benefits package.
5. Higher prospective pension incomes for future retirees, relative to their final pay, than current pensioners now have.
6. Periodic increases to pensioners' income during retirement to reflect cost-of-living increases.
7. Earlier vesting and pension portability.[60]

And many experts since this study was done predict that a major new benefit on the horizon is prepaid legal insurance. For example, in 1977, the UAW and Chrysler announced such a plan that will eventually cover 150,000 employees.

COSTS OF BENEFITS

Conrad Fiorello tells the story about a gunman who suddenly appeared at the paymaster's window at a large plant and demanded: "Never mind the payroll, Bud. Just hand over the welfare and pension funds, the group insurance premiums, and the withholding taxes." As indicated earlier, costs of benefits are going up twice as fast as pay. That would make a good haul.

When benefit costs increase the price of products and services, they are less competitive with other products, especially those from countries where the government pays for benefits. Higher benefits can reduce permanent employment, too, since it is cheaper to pay overtime or to hire part-time employees than to pay full-time wages and benefits.[61] It may also reduce employee mobility,[62] but most evidence thus far is that it does not affect turnover at all.

It is rational for employees in the United States to want additional benefits, since they are tax-free income. For example, in 1977, the typical United Auto Workers member received $7,000 in fringe benefits—tax free. The costs of such benefits, however, have been rising substantially, and many enterprises cannot afford to offer endless benefits and high wages too. Just what does it cost employers to provide these benefits for their employees?

Various groups, including the Department of Labor, and the U.S. Chamber of Commerce, report on the costs of benefits. Exhibits 15–5 and 15–6 present some of the latest Chamber figures, by industry and per employee. The trends by benefit area are indicated in Exhibit 15–7. These studies indicate that benefits (not including services) cost 14 to 60 percent of payroll, although

EXHIBIT 15–5
Weekly employee benefits, per employee, 1975 and 1965

	1975	1965	Percent change
Old-age, survivors, disability and health insurance taxes	$ 12.23	$ 3.13	+291%
Private pensions (nongovernment)	11.92	4.35	+174
Insurance (life, accident, hospitalization, etc.)	11.19	3.54	+216
Paid vacations	11.15	4.85	+130
Paid rest periods, lunch periods, wash-up time, etc	7.85	2.88	+173
Paid holidays	7.23	3.10	+133
Workers' compensation	2.71	0.87	+211
Paid sick leave	2.58	0.83	+211
Profit-sharing payments	2.37	1.29	+84
Unemployment compensation taxes	2.19	1.58	+39
Christmas or other special bonuses	0.90	0.52	+73
Contributions to employee thrift plans	0.60	0.12	+400
Salary continuation or long-term disability	0.44	N.A.	N.A.
Employee meals furnished free	0.40	0.33	+21
Discounts on goods and services purchased from company by employees	0.35	0.25	+40
Other employee benefits	2.51	1.24	+102
Total employee benefits	$ 76.62	$ 28.88	+165%
Average weekly earnings	$216.42	$116.94	+85%

N.A. = Data not available.
Source: *Nation's Business,* October 1976, p. 37.

EXHIBIT 15–6
Weekly employee benefits cost, by industry, 1975

	Per employee per week
All industries	$ 76.62
Manufacturers	
Petroleum industries	101.54
Chemicals and allied industries	96.31
Primary metal industries	92.00
Transportation equipment	88.12
Machinery (excluding electrical)	80.04
Rubber, leather, and plastic products	75.29
Electrical machinery, equipment, and supplies	73.73
Food, beverages, and tobacco	73.50
Fabricated metal products (excluding machinery and transportation equipment)	71.60
Stone, clay, and glass products	71.04
Printing and publishing	69.87
Instruments and miscellaneous products	69.04
Pulp, paper, lumber, and furniture	66.29
Textile products and apparel	41.98
Nonmanufacturing industries	
Public utilities	96.21
Miscellaneous nonmanufacturing industries (mining, transportation, research, hotels, etc.)	84.31
Banks, finance and trust companies	72.02
Insurance companies	71.48
Wholesale and retail trade	53.75
Hospitals	42.38
Department stores	41.17

Source: *Nation's Business,* October 1976, p. 37.

EXHIBIT 15–7
Trends in employee benefits, 1955–1975

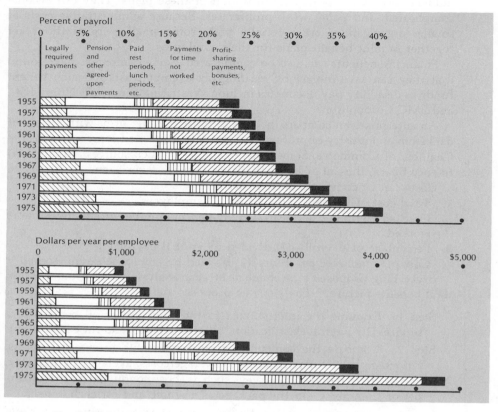

Source: Chamber of Commerce of the United States, *Employee Benefits 1975* (Washington, D.C., 1976).

they vary by size of employer and industry. The most typical figures are 20 to 30 percent. For example, retailers and textile firms offer low benefits. Petroleum and chemical and public utilities offer a high level of benefits. The most costly benefits are time off with pay (holidays, rest periods, vacations), insurance (especially health insurance), and pensions. In sum, benefits are very costly and getting more so.[63]

Cost/benefit analysis of benefits and services

That benefits and services involve large sums of money was indicated above; however, there has been little significant empirical research on the effects of benefits on productivity. In one of the few studies touching on the subject, Robert Ashall and John Child found no relationship between financial success of a sample of British firms and generous benefits and services programs.[64] There are few significant studies examining whether adding benefits tends to increase employee performance, but employers keep adding them to their personnel programs.

In addition to the direct costs of benefits, there are added burdens, or indirect costs. One is the administration of these plans. They can become complicated, and paper work proliferates. Because administrative costs at smaller organizations are especially high, some smaller organizations get together in joint benefit plans for their employees.

Financing benefits can also be complicated. Some companies have found that they can save money by creating tax-exempt trusts for such benefit funds as disability pay. Examples include Westvaco, General Electric, TRW, and FMC Corporation.

An enterprise can compare its costs to those of other firms with the aid of data from an industry or professional group or published sources such as the Chamber of Commerce. Some other examples of such sources are the Conference Board, Bureau of Labor Statistics, *Nation's Business,* and *Business Week.*

Costs can be compared on four bases:
1. Total cost of benefits annually for all employees.
2. Cost per employee per year—(1) divided by number of employee hours worked.
3. Percentage of payroll—(1) divided by annual payroll.
4. Cost per employee per hour—(2) divided by employee hours worked.[65]

Bruce Ellig proposes a mechanism of cost analysis which examines the total benefits picture.[66] The steps he proposes are:

Step 1. Examine the internal cost to the company of all benefits and services, by payroll classification, by profit center, and for each benefit.

Step 2. Compare the company's costs for benefits to external norms. For example, compare its costs to average costs, averages by industry, and so on, as reported in surveys such as those conducted by the Chamber of Commerce, for the package as a whole and for each benefit.

Step 3. Prepare a report for the decision maker contrasting steps 1 and 2 and highlighting major variances.

EXHIBIT 15–8
Brucell employee benefit costs, 1971, sample base payroll analysis by location

| | Total | Per employee | | |
Location	expended	$/year	¢/hour	% base
Atlanta	$ 937	$27.38	1.24¢	0.53%
Boston	376	18.46	1.02	0.31
Chicago	4,952	24.69	1.63	0.43
Dallas	1,833	21.83	1.57	0.44
Houston	3,489	26.18	1.72	0.57
Los Angeles	10,167	61.19	2.67	0.76
Milwaukee	473	8.43	.25	0.09
Newark	2,786	23.31	.76	0.20
New York	21,623	78.32	3.15	0.87
St. Louis	1,281	48.17	1.38	0.41
Totals (average)	$ 47,917	($40.21)	(2.13¢)	(0.64)
Totals, All Classes	172,315	($19.96)	(1.02¢)	(0.28)

Source: Bruce Ellig, "Determining the Competitiveness of Employee Benefits Systems," *Compensation Review,* 1st quarter 1974.

Step 4.   Analyze the costs of the program to employees. Determine what each employee is paying for benefits, totally and by benefit.

Step 5.   Compare the data in Step 4 with external data such as the Chamber of Commerce data.

Step 6.   Analyze how satisfied the individual is with the enterprises program and as compared to competitors' programs.

Ellig also presents a series of reports that are useful for analyzing the data supplied in each of these steps. Exhibit 15–8 is an analysis of the benefits per employee paid at each of the locations of the hypothetical Brucell Company. Note, for example, the wide variance between cents-per-hour costs in Milwaukee and New York.

Exhibit 15–9 analyzes total benefits costs of the enterprise and of the survey group with the external comparison figures provided by the Chamber of Commerce totals and the industry figures for the Chamber of Commerce chemical group.

Note, for example, that Brucell's average of $647 (consisting mainly of $110 for the thrift plan and $420 for the Christmans bonus) places this unit way ahead of the Chamber's $163 and the Chamber subgroup's $205, but only slightly ahead of the Brucell survey group's $522. Investigation would show that the survey group's figures are due largely to profit-sharing (average $498–80 percent of total) and because of the higher average payroll figures used to generate benefit costs.

This kind of analysis provides the kind of approach that is desirable for making top management and personnel decisions that will be cost oriented as well as strategic. It involves examination of the total benefits package, and encourages comparison of the program within the industry and in the economy.

BENEFITS AND SERVICES DECISION MAKING

When top managers make benefit and services decisions such as the cost decision discussed above, they must consider the following facts:

At present, there is little evidence that benefits and services really motivate performance. Nor do they necessarily increase satisfaction.

The costs are escalating dramatically.

As regards mandated programs, managers have no choice but to offer them.

As regards voluntary programs, unions, competitors, and industry trends put pressures on the manager to provide or increase benefits.

Generally, two options are open to top managers. One is to try to increase the effectiveness of the present programs. This can be done by:

• Better communication of the programs (see the section on communications below).

EXHIBIT 15–9
Summary analysis of Chamber of Commerce data and enterprise data for Brucell Company

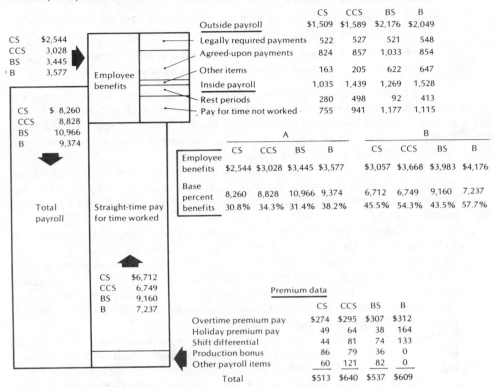

	CS	CCS	BS	B
Outside payroll	$1,509	$1,589	$2,176	$2,049
Legally required payments	522	527	521	548
Agreed-upon payments	824	857	1,033	854
Other items	163	205	622	647
Inside payroll	1,035	1,439	1,269	1,528
Rest periods	280	498	92	413
Pay for time not worked	755	941	1,177	1,115

Employee benefits
CS $2,544
CCS 3,028
BS 3,445
B 3,577

CS $ 8,260
CCS 8,828
BS 10,966
B 9,374

Total payroll   Straight-time pay for time worked

CS $6,712
CCS 6,749
BS 9,160
B 7,237

	A				B			
	CS	CCS	BS	B	CS	CCS	BS	B
Employee benefits	$2,544	$3,028	$3,445	$3,577	$3,057	$3,668	$3,983	$4,176
Base	8,260	8,828	10,966	9,374	6,712	6,749	9,160	7,237
percent benefits	30.8%	34.3%	31.4%	38.2%	45.5%	54.3%	43.5%	57.7%

Premium data

	CS	CCS	BS	B
Overtime premium pay	$274	$295	$307	$312
Holiday premium pay	49	64	38	164
Shift differential	44	81	74	133
Production bonus	86	79	36	0
Other payroll items	60	121	82	0
Total	$513	$640	$537	$609

CS = Chamber of Commerce survey.
CCS = Chemical group in Chamber.
BS = Brucell survey group.
B = Brucell data.
Source: Bruce Ellig, "Determining the Competitiveness of Employee Benefits Systems," *Compensation Review,* 1st quarter, 1974.

- Involving the participants in the choice of benefits and services to be provided.
- Administering the programs better.
- Buying the programs more efficiently.
- Planning the total program better.

The second option the top manager has in this area is to consider future additions to benefits and services programs carefully, trying to offer the less costly ones or to reduce the list of present benefits and services, especially those that are not strongly desired by employees.

Involving participants in benefits decisions

In most enterprises, top managers do their best to judge which benefits the employees prefer, but the research on benefit preferences reported in

Exhibit 15–2 indicates wide differences in preferences. Without getting some participant input, it is impossible to make these decisions intelligently. It is similar to a marketing manager trying to decide on consumer preferences with no market research input.

Therefore it is wise to permit (and encourage) employee participation in benefits and services decision making. When employees share in benefits decisions, they show more interest in them. One way for employees to participate in the decision is to poll them with attitude surveys and similar instruments. Another is to set up employee benefits advisory committees.

Will these devices work? Many believe so, but others think employees are not well enough informed to be of much help.[67] Others oppose asking employees about benefits because this might raise their expectations so that they will expect more. Instead, supervisors and union leaders might be asked about workers' preferences; most research shows they are good predictors,[68] though research in New Zealand found managers and union officials were the opposite.[69] Perhaps these managers were too far from the shop floor and did not know the employees well.

A more direct way of allowing employee participation in benefit decisions and dealing with the problem of major preference differences is called the cafeteria approach to benefits, introduced above. Each employee is told how much money the employer has set aside for benefits plans, after provision for mandated programs and minimal health insurance. Then the employee can choose to receive the funds in cash in lieu of benefits, or decide which benefits are wanted. This approach lets employees know how much the employer is spending on the programs. Because they pick the benefits they want for themselves, their performance and satisfaction are more likely to be affected favorably.

Many experts advocate the cafeteria approach,[70] but though it sounds like an excellent idea, in fact it has rarely been used. Some unions oppose it as unfair; the Internal Revenue Service has questions about it; and it could be costlier to administer. How often employees would make these decisions is a difficult problem, research has shown that a person's preferences change considerably over a relatively short time,[71] and many experts claim the choices are too time-consuming and too technical for most employees. Robert Goode, for example, has shown that many state of California employees using the cafeteria plan passed up the most useful benefit choices and chose to receive more of some benefits which already were amply covered.[72] But until the cafeteria approach is tried more or more research is done on it, it will have to remain as an interesting approach that could help with benefit decisions.

Decisions in management of benefits

Any program takes time and effort to administer; benefits and services are no exception. Special care must be taken to avoid inconsistent applications of benefit policies, which can result in grievances. From an administration viewpoint, it is probably a good rule to have as few benefits and services as possible. The number should be reduced in order to concentrate on a few.[73]

One answer to more effective administration is for enterprises providing many benefits to handle as much of the administration as possible on the computer. Robin Williams suggests a number of ways the computer can make benefits administration more efficient and effective.[74] They include:

Production of periodic reports. As a result of putting the benefits data on payroll, all kinds of regular reports can be provided on the current status of pensions, sick leaves, and vacations. Current and potential costs of benefits can be reported for management, and individualized reports of the value of each benefit to each employee can be computerized and communicated to employees.

Special reporting systems. In addition to regular reports, the computer can prepare cost estimates of several modifications of the benefit package, and it can perform statistical analyses of the program.

Special studies. Computer modeling can be used to simulate possible future benefit packages and costs. The computer can also be used to administer cafeteria benefit plans where this is almost impossible manually.

Williams fails to mention the obvious point that computer processing greatly simplifies the numerous computations necessary and thus makes benefit plans more efficient. Another issue of great future importance is to ensure that when benefit plans are combined in mergers, employees do not get shortchanged.[75]

In addition to these routine decisions, certain important cost-oriented decisions must be made. As indicated above, these include purchasing the program components more effectively and at less cost and planning the program totally rather than one benefit at a time. A number of experts provide good advice on how to control costs of programs.[76] Information on cost comparisons as a basis for cost/benefit analysis was given in the preceding section.

Benefits communications

Another method for improving the effectiveness of benefits and services, as pointed out above, is to develop an effective communication program. How can benefits and services affect the satisfaction and performance of employees if they do not know about the benefits or understand them? Yet most studies of employees [77] and executives [78] indicate they are unaware of the benefits or significantly undervalue their cost and usefulness.

It has always been desirable to improve benefit communications for this reason. But now there is another reason. ERISA requires employers in the United States to communicate with employees by sending them an annual report on the pension plan and basic information on their pensions in language they can understand.[79]

Of course, many communication media can be used: employee handbooks;

EXHIBIT 15–10
Summary page from a typical benefit-audit statement

YOUR TOTAL PAY PACKAGE

	Your yearly contributions	Estimated cost if you bought it all
Basic and major medical	$138	$1,101
Salary continuation and disability insurance	none	2,261
Life and accident insurance	none	535
Pension plan	none	3,021
Social security	632	1,264
Total	$770	$8,182
Net value of benefits		$ 7,412
Annual salary		$35,000
Total pay package value		$42,412

This report tells you what your company-provided benefits can mean to you and your family at retirement or in case of illness, disability, or death. There is no way of knowing how many dollars you will actually receive. The table above, however, shows your yearly contributions and the estimated cost in annual individual insurance and benefit policy premiums if you were to buy this protection and income yourself. The company pays the full cost of your basic and major medical insurance, salary continuation, long-term coverage, and your pension. You and the company together share the cost of social security and the medical insurance program.

company newspapers, magazines, or newsletters; booklets; bulletin boards; annual reports; payroll stuffers; and employee reports. Other communication methods include filmstrips, cassettes, open houses, and meetings with supervisors and personnel.[80] A typical employee report is Exhibit 15–10, which spells out the value of the benefits to each employee. How much the employee would need to save to provide this coverage himself should be stressed. Another direct means of communication is to send employees copies of bills paid by the company for medical expenses on their behalf.

The problem (as most learning psychologists would tell you) is retention of the message and learning it in its entirety. Most effective enterprises handle these problems by using multiple media and sending the message many times. For example, when the First National Bank of Chicago changed its benefits package, it told about the plan with a range of communications.[81] These included, from first to last, the following:

A letter from the president was sent to each employee's home to explain the purpose and general nature of the changes. This letter was tested out on 15 "typical" employees for readability prior to sending it.

The company newsletter carried several articles per week for weeks after.

Employee handouts were distributed to explain the plan.

Meetings of 40 employees each were held.

Each employee was exposed to easy-to-read loose-leaf binders explaining the benefits.

EXHIBIT 15–11
Preferred benefit communications methods (ranked in order of popularity)

U.S. companies	Canadian companies
1. Employee publications	1. Handbooks or booklets
2. Annual reports	2. Individual annual statements
3. Intermittent employee meetings	3. Employee publication articles
4. Letters to employees' homes	4. Intermittent employee meetings
5. Benefits manuals	5. Letters to employees' homes
6. Booklets and brochures	6. Pay envelope stuffers
7. Slide presentations	7. Slide presentations
8. Pay envelope stuffers	8. Posters
9. Regularly scheduled employee meetings	9. Reports (other than annual)
	10. Regular training meetings
10. Reports (other than annual)	11. Filmstrips
11. Posters	12. Motion pictures and videotape
12. Filmstrip presentations	
13. Motion pictures	
14. Commercial television or radio	

Source: Joyce Gildea, "What's Happening in Employee Benefit Communications?" *Pension and Welfare News,* March 1972.

Finally, employees received their individual annual benefits reports explaining what the benefits meant to them.

Johnson and Johnson Ltd. used a similar multimedia, multiimpression campaign, except that it used some elaborate audiovisual aids at an employee meeting. These included a four-projector system using two dissolve units and a Spendler Saupe program unit.[82]

One study surveyed 430 U.S. and 100 large Canadian organizations to determine how they tried to communicate with their employees on benefits and what it cost them to do so.[83] Exhibit 15–11 lists the media favored, and Exhibit 15–12 gives the costs of this communication per employee. Many organizations surveyed could not compute these costs accurately.

Another study of 202 large firms found that the two most frequently used communication methods are articles in company newspapers or magazines and personalized annual reports.[84] Several studies have found that most communication efforts fail. The ineffectiveness of many benefit programs, however, is often blamed on poor communication when this may not be the real cause.

Employees who are satisfied with their benefits are satisfied with their

EXHIBIT 15–12
Benefit communications expenditures, per employee

U.S. companies	Canadian companies
53%—No response	55%—No response
23 —$5 or less	21 —$5 or less
12 —$6–$10	11 —$6–$10
7 —$11–$15	7 —$11–$15
5 —$15 or more	6 —$15 or more
100%	100%

Source: Joyce Gildea, "What's Happening in Employee Benefit Communications?" *Pension and Welfare News,* March 1972.

jobs; this lowers absenteeism and turnover and increases quality, according to one survey.[85] The cost of the benefits was not related to employee satisfaction! This study found satisfaction was improved with increased communication frequency and varied with the type of media used (verbal and written). Thus when employees knew more about the benefits, they could be more satisfied!

In sum, enterprises are spending billions on benefits and very little on benefit communications. To make these billions pay off, they need to increase the quantity and quality of their communications about the benefits they represent.

SUMMARY, CONCLUSIONS, AND RECOMMENDATIONS

Chapter 15 has described benefits and services as part of the rewards which reinforce loyal service to the employer. Some benefits are described in other chapters: pensions in Chapter 16, workers' compensation in Chapter 17, and profit sharing in Chapter 13.

The cost and variety of benefits have been increasing rapidly in the United States and Canada. Several benefits are mandated by government. The economy also affects benefits, as proposition 15.1 indicates:

> *Proposition 15.1.* The more labor intensive the industry, the lower will be the affordable per-person expenditure on benefits and services.

The chapter described mandated and voluntary employee benefits in the United States and Canada and discussed some critical benefits decisions, such as communications, administration, and employee participation. Top management's strategy on benefits and services probably should be to offer most benefits in the preferred categories (such as health insurance) and minimize the others, both to reduce costs and to make the benefit communication program easier and more effective. Three propositions in this area include:

> *Proposition 15.2.* To make benefits and services more effective, employers must communicate more effectively with their employees about employee benefits.
>
> *Proposition 15.3* To increase the usefulness of employee benefits and services, employee participation in choice of the benefits should be encouraged.
>
> *Proposition 15.4* To avoid administrative nightmares, employers should concentrate on fewer benefit plans, those preferred by most employees.

The benefit plans recommended for the model organizations are given in Exhibit 15–13. All organizations must by law participate in workers' compensation, social security, and unemployment compensation programs. Time off with pay should be minimized. There is no evidence of any payback on this, so the employer should remain competitive and perhaps design a plan to encourage the foregoing of some vacation time. Group life plans should also be minimized because few studies show much employee prefer-

EXHIBIT 15–13
Recommendations on benefit and service programs for model organizations

Type of organization	Benefits						
	Legally required benefits	Vacation plans	Paid holi-days	Group life insur-ance	Hospital-medical insur-ance	Accident-disability insurance	Services
1. Large size, low complexity, high stability	X	*	*	*	X	X	*
2. Medium size, low complexity, high stability	X	*	*	*	X	X	*
3. Small size, low complexity, high stability	X	*	*	*	X	X	*
4. Medium size, moderate complex-ity, moderate stability	X	*	*	*	X	X	*
5. Large size, high complexity, low stability	X	*	*	*	X	X	*
6. Medium size, high complexity, low stability	X	*	*	*	X	X	*
7. Small size, high complexity, low stability	X	*	*	*	X	X	*

* Minimized.

ence for them. Most services should be minimized, although a few are recommended for some organizations. Enterprises might experiment with a plan to offer employees more pay for fewer benefits and services and determine its effect on satisfaction and performance.

Benefits is one personnel area where there are *significant* differences between full-time and part-time employees. One study of four geographic areas found that part-time workers typically did not receive insurance, pensions, holidays, vacations, or, frankly, *any* benefits at all.[86] Other studies indicate that the *major* dissatisfaction of part-time or temporary employees concerns lack of benefits, and few part-timers are paid more to offset loss of benefits.[87] This is a clear case where employers save in total compensation costs by employing part-timers or temporary help.

For the benefits and services program to be effective, the operating manager and personnel manager must work together. The operating manager helps the personnel manager know what the employees prefer in benefits and asks for help in explaining the benefits and getting administrative problems cleared up. The personnel manager helps the operating manager communicate the benefits to employees and administer the program.

Chapter 16 completes the discussion of compensation with an analysis of pensions and retirement systems.

QUESTIONS

1. What are employee benefits and services?
2. Why do employers have benefit and service programs?

3. What are the most significant of the diagnostic factors for benefits and services?

4. Which benefits and services do employees prefer? Which do you prefer? Why are these preferences significant?

5. Describe government-mandated benefits and services. Should these programs exist? How can they be improved?

6. What is a typical time-off-with-pay benefit program?

7. What is a typical voluntary insurance program?

8. What is a typical service program?

9. How will you try to assess benefits and services the next time you look for a job?

10. If you could compare just two or three benefits and services between two potential employers, which would these be? Why?

11. Which of the benefits and services are the most costly?

12. How can managers make better benefits decisions?

13. How can managers communicate about benefits better?

14. What are the most significant propositions in Chapter 15?

15. What are the most significant recommendations in Chapter 15?

NOTES AND REFERENCES

1. Annual surveys by U.S. Chamber of Commerce on Fringe Benefits, *Nation's Business;* U.S. Department of Labor statistics; Stanely Babson, Jr., *Fringe Benefits* (New York: Wiley Interscience, 1974); Ralph L. Harris, "Let's Take the Fringe Out of Fringe Benefits," *Personnel Journal,* February 1975, pp. 86–89; Douglas Hyer, "Employee Benefits: No Longer on the Fringe," *Pension World,* September 1975; Mitchell Meyer and Harland Fox, *Profile of Employee Benefits* (New York: Conference Board, 1974). For reduction of benefits items see "Dwindling Benefits Fuel a UMW Strike Threat," *Business Week,* July 25, 1977, pp. 120–21; "Legislature May Reduce State Holidays," *Atlanta Journal Constitution,* October 30, 1977, pp. 1, 9.

2. Robert Ashall, and John Child, "Employee Services: People, Profits, or Parkinson?" *Personnel Management,* Fall 1972, pp. 18–22.

3. Frederick Herzberg, Bernard Mausner, and Barbara Snyderman, *The Motivation to Work* (New York: John Wiley & Sons, 1959).

4. *The Personnel Executive's Job* (Englewood Cliffs, N.J.: Prentice-Hall/ASPA, 1977).

5. Ashall and Child, "Employee Services."

6. Arthur Ross, "Fringe Benefits Today and Tomorrow," *Labor Law Journal,* August 1957, pp. 467–82.

7. Donna Allen, *Fringe Benefits: Wages or Social Obligation* (Ithaca: New York State School of Industrial and Labor Relations, 1969).

8. Lee Modjeska, "Eligibility Clauses in Benefit Plans under the LMRA," *Labor Law Journal,* February 1973, pp. 67–80.

9. See, for example, Bruce Ellig, "Determining the Competitiveness of Employee Benefits Systems," *Compensation Review,* first quarter, 1974, pp. 8–34; Joseph Feldmeir and William Groenekamp, "The Profile-Ranking Method of Evaluating Fringe Benefits," *Personnel,* January–February 1965, pp. 35–39.

10. Peter Brosnan, "The Ability to Predict Workers' Preferences," *Human Relations* 28, 6 (1975), pp. 519–41; Peter Brosnan, "Predicting Workers' Preferences," *British Journal of Industrial Relations* (1973), pp. 291–97; Brad Chapman and Robert Otteman, "Employee Preference

for Various Compensation and Benefit Options," *The Personnel Administrator,* November, 1975, pp. 31–36; Peter Drucker, "What We Can Learn From Japanese Management," *Harvard Business Review,* March–April 1971, pp. 110–22; Jerry Geisler and William Glueck, "Employee Benefit Preferences and Employee Satisfaction," University of Georgia, mimeographed, 1977; Ury Gluskinos, and Bruce Kestelman, "Management and Labor Leader's Perception of Worker Needs as Compared with Self-Reported Needs," *Personnel Psychology* 24 (1971), pp. 239–46; Robert V. Goode, "Complications at the Cafeteria Checkout Lines," *Personnel,* November–December 1974, pp. 45–49; J. M. Howells and Peter Brosnan, "The Ability to Predict Workers' Preferences," *Human Relations* 25, 3 (1972), pp. 265–281; J. M. Howells and A. E. Woodfield, "The Ability of Managers and Trade Union Officers to Predict Workers' Preferences," *British Journal of Industrial Relations* 8, 2 (1970), pp. 237–51; Douglas Hyer, "Employee Benefits: No Longer on the Fringe," *Pension World,* September 1975; Harish Jain and Edward Janzen, "Employee Pay and Benefit Preferences," *Industrial Relations Industrielles* 29, 1 (1974), pp. 99–109; Edward Lawler, "The Mythology of Management Compensation," *California Management Review,* Fall 1966, pp. 11–22; Edward Lawler and Edward Levin, "Union Officers' Perception of Members' Pay Preferences" *Industrial and Labor Relations Review* 21, 4 (1968), pp. 509–17. Also Stanley Nealey, "Pay and Benefit Preference," *Industrial Relations,* October 1963, pp. 17–28; Stanley Nealey, "Determining Worker Preferences among Employee Benefit Programs," *Journal of Applied Psychology* 48, 1 (1964), p. 7–12; Stanley Nealey and James Goodale, "Worker Preferences among Time-Off Benefits and Pay," *Journal of Applied Psychology* 51, 4 (1967), pp. 357–61; Thomas Paine, "Flexible Compensation Can Work," *Financial Executive,* February 1974; Jay Schuster, "Another Look at Compensation Preferences," *Industrial Management Review,* Spring 1969, pp. 1–18; Ludwig Wagner and Theodore Bakerman, "Wage Earner's Opinions of Insurance Fringe Benefits," *Journal of Insurance,* June 1960, pp. 17–28; William Werther, "Variable Benefits: A New Approach to Fringe Benefits," *Arizona Business,* November 1975, pp 18–22; E. S. Willis, "Problems in Selecting Employee Benefits," *Monthly Labor Review,* April 1969, pp. 61–63.

11. George Milkovich and Michael Delaney, "A Note on Cafeteria Pay Plans," *Industrial Relations,* February 1975, pp. 112–116.

12. Richard Lester, "Benefits as Preferred Form of Compensation," *Southern Economic Journal,* April 1967, pp. 488–95; Lloyd Reynolds, *The Structure of the Labor Market* (New York: Harper, 1951), p. 94.

13. Colin Campbell and Rosemary Campbell, *A Comparative Study of the Fiscal Systems of New Hampshire and Vermont, 1940–1947,* cited in *The Wall Street Journal,* July 7, 1976. To keep up on these costs, check references like Joseph Hickey, "Unemployment Insurance: State Changes in 1975," *Monthly Labor Review,* January 1976, pp. 37–41.

14. "The Hidden Crises in Jobless Pay," *Business Week,* January 24, 1977, pp. 20–21; U.S. Department of Labor, *The Unemployment Insurance System: Past, Present, and Future* 1976 Employment and Training Report to the President (Washington, D.C., 1976); Byron Klapper, "States May Force Federal Bailout of Jobless Funds," *The Wall Street Journal,* March 28, 1977; "Jobless Pay Funds Go Deeper in Debt," *Business Week,* February 21, 1977, p. 30; "Cheating on Unemployment," *Time,* September 13, 1976, pp. 48–50; "Labor Letter," *The Wall Street Journal,* March 8, 1977.

15. Robert Gray, "Will Your Jobless Taxes Double?" *Nations Business,* May 1975 pp. 30–33.

16. Economic Council in Canada, *People and Jobs* (Ottawa: Information Canada, 1976); Peter Cook et al., *Economic Impact of Selected Programs Directed toward the Labour Market* (Ottawa: Economic Council in Canada, 1976); Christopher Greene and Jean Cousineau, *Unemployment in Canada: The Impact of Unemployment Insurance* (Ottawa: Economic Council in Canada, 1976).

17. Shirley Won, "Canada's Unemployment Insurance Program," *The Labour Gazette,* November 1975, pp. 826–30.

18. Ronald Ehrenberg and Ronald Oaxaca, "Do Benefits Cause Unemployed to Hold Out

for Better Jobs?" *Monthly Labor Review,* March 1976, pp. 37–39; Martin Feldstein, Unemployment Compensation: Its Effect on Unemployment," *Monthly Labor Review,* March 1976, pp. 39–41; Arlene Holen and Stanley Horowitz, "Partial Unemployment Insurance Benefits and the Extent of Partial Unemployment," *Journal of Human Resources,* Summer 1974, pp. 420–22; Raymond Munts and Irwin Garfinkel, *The Work Disincentive Effects of Unemployment Insurance* (Kalamazoo, Mich.: Upjohn Institute, 1974).

19. Paul Burgess and Jerry Kingston, "The Impact of Unemployment Insurance Benefits on Reemployment Success," *Industrial and Labor Relations Review,* October 1976, pp. 25–31.

20. David Edgell and Stephen Wandner, "Unemployment Insurance: Its Economic Performance," *Monthly Labor Review,* April 1974, pp. 33–40.

21. Geisler and Glueck, "Employee Benefit Preferences and Employee Satisfaction."

22. Douglas Sease, "Bo Grier, Aristocrat of the Streets," *The Wall Street Journal,* January 31, 1977; Harry Anderson, "Layoffs and Jobless Benefits," *The Wall Street Journal,* February 11, 1977.

23. For ways to cut UI costs, see Stewart Bailenson, *How to Control the Cost of Unemployment Compensation Claims and Taxes on Your Business* (Homewood, Ill.: Dow Jones–Irwin, 1976); Allan Janoff, "You Can Reduce your Unemployment Taxes," *The Personnel Administrator,* January 1976, pp. 27–30; Phillip Kaplan, "Unemployment Taxes Are Variable, Controllable Expenses Which Employers Must Recognize as a Growing Profit Drain," *Personnel Journal,* April 1976, pp. 170–72; Thomas Wahrobe, *Aggressive Benefits Management* (New York: Amacom, 1976).

24. Herbert Gutman, *Work, Culture, and Society in Industrialing America* (New York: Alfred A. Knopf, 1975).

25. John Emshwiller, "Key Auto Issue," *The Wall Street Journal,* July 15, 1976; L. Bruce Fryberger, "Maternity Leave Policies under Title VII," *Labor Law Journal,* March 1975.

26. Linda Kistler and Carol McDonough, "Paid Maternity Leave Benefits May Justify the Cost," *Labor Law Journal,* December 1975; Margaret Sysser, "Maternity Leave: Judicial and Arbitral Interpretation, 1970–1972," *Labor Law Journal,* March 1973.

27. Bureau of National Affairs, *Paid Leave and Leave of Absence Policies,* Personnel Policies Form Survey 111 (Washington, D.C., November 1975).

28. U.S. Bureau of Labor Statistics, *Employee Compensation in the Non-Farm Economy* (Washington, D.C.: U.S. Government Printing Office, 1976).

29. Mitchell Meyer and Harland Fox, *Profile of Employee Benefits;* Bureau of National Affairs, *Basic Patterns in Union Contracts* (Washington, D.C., 1975).

30. Meyer and Fox, *Profile of Employee Benefits.*

31. Gregor Caldwell, "Future Trends in Employee Benefits in Canada," *The Canadian Business Review,* Summer 1974, pp. 22–23.

32. John Shea, "The Rise and Fall of Extended Vacation Plans," *Personnel,* January–February 1967, pp. 38–43; John Shea, "Holidays, Vacations, Accidents, Sickness, Long-Term Disability, and Other Time Off the Job," in *Handbook of Modern Personnel Administration,* ed. Joseph Famularo, chap. 36 (New York: McGraw-Hill Book Co., 1972); See also, Wilbur Cross, "How to Take a Mini Sabbatical," *Nation's Business,* November 1974, pp. 54–55.

33. BNA, *Basic Patterns in Union Contracts.*

34. Meyer and Fox, *Profile of Employee Benefits,* ch. 2, 3; Bureau of National Affairs, *Employee Health and Welfare Benefits,* Personnel Policies Forum Survey 107 (Washington, D.C., 1974).

35. "500,000 Railroad Employees Get Dental Coverage," *Employee Benefit Plan Review,* June 1976; Jerold Frankel, "Prepaid Dental Care: Pulling for Growth," *Pension World,* October 1975, 40–44, 62; Keith Mark, "Dental Insurance Growing in Canada," *Canadian Personnel and*

Industrial Relations, March 1973, pp. 26–28; Thomas Patten, and Phillip Dutton, "Employee Dental Insurance Plans for Today and Tomorrow," *MSU Business Topics,* Autumn, 1976, pp. 13–25; BNA, *Employee Health and Welfare Benefits.*

36. BNA, *Employee Health and Welfare Benefits;* Meyer and Fox, *Profile of Employee Benefits,* ch. 8; Dorothy Kittner, "Changes in Health and Insurance Plans for Salaried Employees," *Monthly Labor Review,* February 1970, pp. 32–39.

37. BNA, *Employee Health and Welfare Benefits.*

38. Theodore Marmor et al., "National Health Insurance: Some Lessons from the Canadian Experience," *Policy Sciences* 6, 4 (1975), pp. 447–66; Amanda Bennett, "Canada's National Health Plan," *The Wall Street Journal,* December 13, 1976; Lee Soderstrom, "Health Insurance and Collective Bargaining in Quebec," *Labor Law Journal,* July 1975, pp. 497–507.

39. Keith Mark, "Dental Insurance Growing in Canada," *Canadian Personnel and Industrial Relations Journal,* March 1973, pp. 26–28.

40. Bureau of National Affairs, *"Services for Employees,"* Personnel Policies Forum Survey 105 (Washington, D.C., 1974); Bureau of National Affairs, *Social, Recreational, and Holiday Program* Personnel Policies Forum Survey 109, (Washington, D.C., 1975); also see, for example, "Commuter Vans Catch on at Corporations," *Business Week,* February 28, 1977.

41. Eli Goldston, "Executive Sabbaticals: About to Take Off?" *Harvard Business Review,* September–October 1973, pp. 57–68; National Industrial Conference Board, *Tuition Aid Plans for Employees,* Studies in Personnel Policy 151 (New York, 1956); J. Roger O'Meara, *Company Sponsored Scholarship and Student Loan Plans,* Studies in Personnel Policy 192 (New York: National Industrial Conference Board, 1964); Charles Watson and Alexis Grzybowski, "What Your Company Should Know about Tuition and Plans," *Business Horizons,* October 1975, pp. 75–80.

42. Alexander Smith, "Employee-Assisted Education," *The Personnel Administrator* September–October 1973, pp. 23–28.

43. Administrative Management Society, "Going Back Means Moving Up," *Administrative Management,* May 1971, pp. 61–62.

44. NICB, *Tuition Aid Plans for Employees.*

45. Muriel Merkel, "Financial, Educational and Other Aids to Employees," in *Handbook of Modern Personnel Administration,* ed. Joseph Famularo ch. 47. New York: McGraw-Hill Book Co., 1972; Bernard Mandel, "Profit Sharing, Bonuses, Stock Purchase, Stock Option, Savings and Thrift Plans," in *Handbook of Modern Personnel Administration* ed. Joseph Famularo ch. 39. (New York: McGraw-Hill Book Co., 1972); Harland Fox and Mitchell Meyer, *Employee Savings Plans in the United States,* Studies in Personnel Policy 184 (New York: National Industrial Conference Board, 1962).

46. BNA, *Employee Health and Welfare Benefits.*

47. Fox and Meyer, "Employee Savings Plans in the United States."

48. Donald Lewis, "Financial Counseling for Corporate Executives," *The Canadian Business Review,* Summer 1975, pp. 46–47.

49. "Operations Outdoors," *Time,* December 16, 1974; Arthur Conrad, "Industrial Recreation Comes of Age," *The Personnel Administrator,* March–April 1974, pp. 51–55.

50. BNA, *Basic Patterns in Union Contracts.*

51. Robert Bauer, "Recreation Programs, in *Handbook of Modern Personnel Administration,* ed. Joseph Famularo, ch. 46 (New York: McGraw-Hill Book Co., 1972).

52. BNA, *Employee Health and Welfare Benefits.*

53. Shirley Chisholm, "The Day Care Dilemma," *The Wall Street Journal.* April 26, 1976.

54. George Milkovich and Luis Gomez, "Day Care and Selected Employee Work Behaviors," *Academy of Management Journal* 19, 1 (March 1976) 111–115; see also, Bruce Briggs, "Getting a Handle on Day Care," *The Wall Street Journal,* September 27, 1976.

55. "Labor Letter," *The Wall Street Journal,* September 9, 1976; Sheldon Sandler, "Negotiated Prepaid Legal Services," *Labor Law Journal,* May 1976, pp. 301–4.

56. Vernon Louviere, "How Pastors' Aid Raises Job Performance," *Nation's Business,* March 1976, pp. 55–56.

57. "Labor Letter," *The Wall Street Journal,* June 12, 1977.

58. T. J. Gordon and R. E. LeBleu, "Employee Benefits: 1970–1985," *Harvard Business Review,* January–February 1970, pp. 93–107; Robert Paul, *Employee Benefits Factbook* (New York: Martin Segal Co., 1976); John Sullivan, "Indirect Compensation: The Years Ahead" *California Management Review,* Winter 1972, pp. 65–76; R. O. Moore, "Fringe Benefits and Perquisites," *The Canadian Business Review,* Spring 1976, pp. 29–32.

59. Paul, *Employee Benefits Factbook.*

60. Gordon and LeBleu, "Employee Benefits: 1970–1985", Copyright © 1969 by the President and Fellows of Harvard College, all rights reserved; For references on prepaid legal insurance see, "Labor Letter," *The Wall Street Journal,* July 17, 1977; Roy Harris, "Labor's Next Goal," *The Wall Street Journal,* July 29, 1977.

61. Syed Hameed, "Employment Impact of Fringe Benefits in the Canadian Manufacturing Sector 1957–1965," *Relations Industrielles,* 28, 2 (1973), p. 380.

62. A. Ross, "Do We Have New Industrial Feudalism?" *American Economic Review,* 48 (1958), pp. 903–20.

63. For a comparison with British benefits costs, see Jane Moonman, *The Effectiveness of Fringe Benefits in Industry* (Epping, Essex: Gomes Press, 1973).

64. Ahsall and Child, "Employee Services."

65. J. H. Foegen, "The Fringe Benefit Spiral," *Human Resource Management,* Fall 1974, pp. 23–26; "The Skyrocketing Costs of Health Care," *Business Week,* May 17, 1976.

66. Ellig, "Determining the Competitiveness of Employee Benefit Costs."

67. Willis, "Problems in Selecting Employee Benefits."

68. Geisler and Glueck, "Employee Benefit Preferences and Employee Satisfaction"; Lawler and Levin, "Union Officers' Perception of Members' Pay Preferences."

69. Brosnan, "Ability to Predict Workers' Preferences"; Brosnan, "Predicting Workers' Preferences"; J. M. Howells, and A. E. Woodfield, "Ability of Managers and Trade Union Officials to Predict"; Howells and Brosnan, "Ability to Predict Workers' Preferences."

70. Drucker, "What We Can Learn from Japanese Management"; Hyer, "Employee Benefits"; Schuster, "Another Look at Compensation Preferences." Werther, "Variable Benefits"; Jay Schuster, et al., "Epic: New Cafeteria Compensation Plan," *Datamation,* February 1, 1971, pp. 28–30; William Werther, "A New Direction in Rethinking Fringe Benefits," *MSU Business Topics,* Winter 1974, pp. 35–40; Howard Risher and Colin Mill, "Cafeteria Compensation: Present Status and Future Potential," *Canadian Personnel and Industrial Relations Journal,* March 1974, pp. 35–39; Thomas Paine, "Flexible Compensation Can Work," *Financial Executive* 42, 2 (1974), pp. 56–66; David Oates, "A Cafeteria Approach to Compensation," *International Management* 28, 7 (1973), pp. 14–17.

71. Milkovich and Delaney, "Note on Cafeteria Pay Plans."

72. Goode, "Complications at the Cafeteria Checkout Line."

73. David McLaughlin, "Bringing Order Out of Chaos in the Benefits Program," *Personnel,* January–February 1965, pp. 27–34.

74. Robin Williams, "Use of Computer in Benefits Administration," *Canadian Personnel and Industrial Relations Journal,* March 1972, pp. 15–21.

75. Richard Wambold, "Merging of Employee Benefits," in *Handbook of Modern Personnel Administration,* ed. Joseph Famularo ch. 60 (New York: McGraw-Hill Book Co., 1972).

76. See, for example, Brock Macdonald, "The Design of Fringe Benefit Costing Program," *Relationes Industrielles* 28, 4 (1973), pp. 779–807.

77. Jerry Geisler and William Glueck, "Benefit Communication and Employee Satisfaction," 1977, mimeographed. Matthew W. Jewett, "Employee Benefits: The Need to Know," *Personnel Journal,* January 1976, pp. 18–22; Rudolph Kagerer, "Do Employees Understand Your Benefits Program?" *The Personnel Administrator,* October 1975, pp. 29–31; James Sheard, "The Relationship between Attitudes and Knowledge in Employee Benefit Orientation," *Personnel Journal,* November 1966; Arthur Sloane and Edward Hodges, "What Workers Don't Know About Employee Benefits," *Personnel,* November–December 1968, pp. 27–34; W. R. Shaw, "Benefit Communication: Problem and Opportunity," *Canadian Personnel and Industrial Relations Journal,* January 1976, pp. 32–39.

78. George Hettenhouse et al., "Communicating the Compensation Package," *Personnel,* November–December 1975, pp. 19–30.

79. Kagerer, "Do Employees Understand Your Benefits Program?"; Kathleen Gill, "Employee Communications in ERISA," *The Personnel Administrator,* May 1975, pp. 23–26; Albert Scholachtmeyer, "How to Communicate Benefits in ERISA Reports," *Personnel,* September–October 1976, pp. 31–36.

80. Hettenhouse et al., "Communicating the Compensation Package"; William Holley, Jr. and Earl Ingram II, "Communicating Fringe Benefits," *Personnel Administrator,* March–April 1973, pp. 21–22; Richard Henderson, *Compensation Management* (Reston, Va.: Reston Press, 1976), pp. 409–425; Richard Coffin and Michael Shaw, *Effective Communication of Employee Benefits* (New York: American Management Association, 1971).

81. Gerald Shott and Richard Schulz, "A Communication Road Map," *The Personnel Administrator,* May–June 1972, pp. 18–20.

82. John Davis, "J & J Tests Effectiveness of Benefit Communications Program," *Canadian Personnel and Industrial Relations Journal,* January 1976, pp. 40–42.

83. Joyce Gildea, "What's Happening in Employee Benefit Communications?" *Pension and Welfare News,* March 1972, pp. 31–35.

84. Coffin and Shaw, *Effective Communication of Employees Benefits.*

85. Geisler and Glueck, "Employee Benefit Preferences and Employee Satisfaction."

86. Robert Daski, "Area Wage Survey Test Focuses on Part Timers," *Monthly Labor Review,* April 1974, pp. 60–63.

87. Martin Gannon, "A Profile of the Temporary Help Industry and Its Workers," *Monthly Labor Review,* May 1974, pp. 44–49; Martin Gannon, "The Management of Peripheral Employees," *Personnel Journal,* September 1975, pp. 482–86.

Pensions and retirement

CHAPTER OBJECTIVES

■ To show what pensions are and how pension plans are funded and regulated.

■ To investigate the significant problems with Social Security and public pensions.

■ To discuss preretirement, early retirement, and retirement policies and programs.

■ To suggest future trends in pensions.

CHAPTER OUTLINE

Chapter 16 completes the four chapters in Part Five on compensation and benefits. The diagnostic factors discussed in Chapter 15 apply to pensions too, except that the government regulations are different. Pensions are now so important they deserve separate treatment. A few years ago, personnel managers rated pensions as a duty that was about fourth or so in importance. In the recent Prentice-Hall/ASPA survey of 1,400 personnel managers, pensions were named as one of the three fastest growing challenges they face.[1] (The others were safety, Chapter 17, and equal employment opportunities, Chapter 18.)

In addition to personnel managers' perceptions, these facts about pensions and retirement have significance for you:

Private pension funds were worth about $350 billion 1977. If their rate of growth continues as at present, they will equal $700 billion in 1985. That's more than the value of the total stock market in 1977.

Many experts believe that social security is bankrupt or seriously underfunded, and pensions for military and government employees are leading to a tax system like the one in Sweden, which recently taxed an author 102 percent of her royalties. To fund social security, your take-home pay will likely be reduced.

Many experts believe that New York City, which is almost bankrupt, will have to increase taxes to keep up payments out of its pension plans to former employees. New Yorkers will be paying more taxes as a result.

Some experts believe that because of shifts in age distribution, pensions everywhere will cost the enterprise much more to maintain payments.[2] Therefore pensions will increase the cost of goods and services, and again your payroll deductions will increase.

Inflation is so great that many people on retirement can't make it financially. Your parents may have to move in with you, and eventually you might have to move in with your children.

The ERISA law (a new U.S. pension regulation) has caused so much paper work that the operating or personnel manager must take time from regular duties to fill out forms such as EBS–l, which seem to change every year.[3]

What do these facts and pension situations mean to operating, personnel, and top managers? Everyone who gets older and stops working needs money to survive. Since many people live 10–20 years in retirement, this takes a great deal of money. Enterprises set up pension plans as a form of deferred compensation to help finance the retirement years.

The strategic decisions top managers must make about pensions and retirement include:

Besides the mandated pension plans, should the enterprise offer a pension plan?

What kind of pension plan should the enterprise adopt if it chooses to have one?

Should there be preretirement programs to aid employees in the transition to retirement?

Should employees be required to retire at a specific age, such as 65?

Pensions is an area in which most of the technical work is done by personnel experts. Operating managers help by referring pension problems of their employees to personnel and providing feed-back on pensions from employees.

PENSIONS, RETIREMENT, AND EMPLOYEE PREFERENCES

In the United States, Canada, and most of the developed world, a specific period in life can be described as the work period. It begins after full-time schooling is completed and ends when full-time working ceases. The period following the work period is called retirement.

Some words and constructs evoke positive or negative responses in almost everyone: love, hate; friends, enemies. Others bring forth significantly different responses from various individuals. Retirement is such a construct. Some look forward to retirement for years as a wonderful period during which many good experiences can take place: One can sleep late, vacation, visit friends, develop hobbies, and so on. It is seen as a release from burdens. To others, retirement evokes negative feelings; to them it is a period of uselessness, filled with empty make-work projects. This may be because many relate the concepts of retirement and death closely. This is frequently the response of professional and managerial personnel, to whom work and life are almost synonymous. To still others, retirement has both negative and positive aspects. Although the employee is free, he is also close to the end of life and therefore death.

George Katona conducted interviews with 5,000 households to examine attitudes toward retirement. He found that, overall, about 60 percent had positive attitudes, although the oldest age groups were less positive. The more financially well off the potential retiree perceived himself to be, the more positive he was towards retirement.[4] A more recent study by Mary Hopkins and Marcia Wood examined the retirement attitudes of 163 Hawaiians close to retirement (53 percent had five years to go) and found that about two thirds accepted it rather willingly. The third which did not accept it tended to enjoy work more, saw new things happening at work all the time, earned more, did not worry about health, and were better educated. Almost one half of the unwilling had made *no* plans for retirement.[5] This study supports Katona and adds new dimensions to his findings.

Retirement can mean a period in which the individual's energies can be devoted to interests other than work. It also means a period in which the paycheck stops. Some employers provide income in the form of deferred wages and salaries called pensions. Retired persons may receive their incomes from this source of income, their savings, and government pensions. In the

United States, the pension is called social security; in Canada, it is known as the Canada Pension Plan.

The purposes of pensions

One reason enterprises support pension plans is that they provide a means by which less productive workers can be retired. They also hope pensions will keep their most productive employees working for them, and employees will be motivated by knowing pension funds will be available. As is true of other employee benefits, however, there is little evidence that employees are motivated to work harder or better by pension plans. For one thing, most plans are only remotely tied to individual productivity, and if pensions are paid equally, based on salary clauses, the pension does not reward merit directly. Further, the payoff, especially for the under-45 worker, is far in the future.

The studies cited in Exhibit 15–2 (Chapter 15) showed that workers studied preferred pensions at an average level. The preferences increase as age increases and are quite low in the younger years. Studies indicate that pensions do not affect mobility or turnover of employees.[6]

There is little evidence that employees even know much about their pensions, much less are motivated by them. In a study of the employees of one company, Ronald West found that percentage of correct answers to questions on pensions varied from a low of 20% for the youngest to 75% for age 55–60 employees. Their knowledge increased with age except just before retirement, where it dropped off. West theorized that the older employees *did not want to think about retiring.* He also found patterns of interest by age groups. Younger employees are interested in long-range planning in the financial area, and they want to know how the pension program fits with their future some 40 years later. Between ages 25 and 45, employees gain most of their general knowledge (and, it may be assumed, most of their misconceptions) about the pension program. Therefore, whatever general information the company wants employees to have should be given out before age 50. Employees near retirement want individual attention—they are interested in the specifics of the pension plan as they apply to them.[7]

West suggested that programs designed to communicate with employees about pensions should keep their differential interests in mind. Employers should realize they have a communication problem (see the section on benefits communication in Chapter 15) if they hope to get any motivation effect from pensions.

INCOME IN RETIREMENT

Retired employees receive their income from three principal sources: (1) savings and investments and part-time work, (2) a government pension program, (3) private pension plans provided by employers. The first two are discussed in this section; private pensions are the topic of the next two sections; and public pensions provided by government are discussed separately.

Retirement income from savings and work

One source of income for retirees is postretirement work and savings. In Katona's study of 5,000 families, he found that 52 percent of persons expected to earn money by part-time employment after retirement. The percentage who expected to work declined somewhat as current income increased. Most who intended to work expected to earn about 20 percent of their current salaries in this way.[8]

Another source of income is from savings. Katona found that persons save more (percentagewise and absolutely), the higher their income, and those with private pensions are more likely to save money for retirement than those without them. Alicia Munnell studied whether, after social security went into effect, people continued to save for retirement. Her conclusion was that up until the mid–1970s, little change in savings took place because two strong forces offset each other. As people were forced to pay social security taxes, their private savings for retirement tended to decline. But social security does not allow much work after retirement, and people are living longer, thanks to medical science. So they saw the need to save more during their working years and they began to do so. Munnell believes more persons will have to work to supplement social security payments in view of inflation, but if social security benefits increase, people will save less during their work years.[9]

The U.S. government has encouraged people without private pensions to save for retirement. The Keogh plan allows a self-employed person to set aside up to $7,500 yearly for retirement, tax free. People working for others can set up tax-free independent retirement accounts (IRA), and a 1976 law allows workers to include their spouses in these plans. Under proposed legislation, employees are allowed to set aside $1,500 yearly for their spouse-homemakers.

Social security[10]

In 1935, the pension portion of the social security system was established under the Old-Age, Survivors and Disability Insurance (OASDI) program (see Chapter 17 for disability and other provisions). The goal of the pension portion was to provide some income to retired persons to *supplement* savings, private pensions, and part-time work. It was created at a time when the wealthy continued to live alone, the average person moved in with relatives, and the poor with no one to help them were put in a "poor house," or government-supported retirement home.

The basic concept was that the employee and employer were to pay taxes that would cover the retirement payments each employee would later receive; in a self-funding insurance program. Initially, two goals were sought: adequate payments for all, and individual equity, which means that each employee was to receive what he or she and the employer put in to the fund. In the past 15 years, however, individual equity has lost out.

The program has a worthwhile objective. No one wants older people to live out their last years in crushing poverty and with little or no dignity. Anyone who has seen the Italian movie *Umberto D* understands the goal. Umberto, a dignified retired civil servant, cannot live on his pension. He contemplates suicide, begging, and cheating the health system simply to survive. Anyone whose grandparents had to live with their children because they could not survive any other way (as both my grandmothers did) knows how hard this can be on everyone involved.

Until recently, the system worked pretty well. The Social Security Administration is a rather efficient government agency which has provided innovative administrative procedures such as direct deposit of checks in banks. At present, one person in seven is receiving a social security pension check monthly, and between a third and a half of the working population gets a check from social security (under the disability and medical programs, as well as pensions). The average pension check is $205 per month, adjusted for inflation.

Social security taxes are paid by *both* employers and employees. Both pay a percentage of the employee's pay to the government. The percentage, the maximum income the percentage is paid on, and maximum tax to be paid are as follows: 1978: 6.05 percent, $17,700, $1,071; 1979: 6.13 percent, $22,900, $1,404; and 1980: 6.13 percent, $25,000, $1,588. The percentage will continue to rise to 7.65 percent for employee and employer in 1990. The maximum tax will rise to $3,046 in 1987 for an employee earning $42,600. How much is paid by employee and employer is calculated on the average monthly wage (weighted toward the later years).

Those receiving social security pensions can work part-time, up to a maximum amount which is increased each year to reflect inflation. The maximum a person aged 65 to 70 can earn before loss of social security benefits is: 1978, $4,000; 1979, $4,500; 1980, $5,000; rising to $6,000 in 1982 and thereafter. Just about all employees except civilian federal government employees are eligible for social security coverage. Self-employed persons can join the system. They pay 8.1 percent in 1978, rising to 10.75 percent in 1990, a tax of $4,579 for a person earning $42,600.

Employees become eligible to receive full benefits at age 65, or for lower benefits at age 62. If an employee dies, a family with children under 18 receives survivor benefits, regardless of the employee's age. If the employee become totally disabled before age 65, he becomes eligible to receive insurance benefits. Under Medicare provisions of the social security system, eligible individuals 65 and older receive payments for doctor and hospital bills as well as other related benefits and services.

The reason the system stopped working well a few years ago, as noted above, is that the trust fund set up to pay the pensions is being rapidly depleted. Depending on whose figures you accept, the fund will be gone in 1980 or shortly thereafter. A series of events, most of them political, has threatened the viability of the system.

First, the payments employers and employees make are based on a very low inflation rate. In recent years inflation has raised the cost of living so high the taxes cannot raise enough to accommodate them, especially since in 1972, Congress passed a law granting an inflation escalator clause that increases the pension payout *more than* the rate of inflation in the preceding year. One of the causes of inflation, in fact, is the dramatic increase in the payroll taxes employers must pay, including those for social security. Inflation pressure is applied when employers increase prices to cover these tax costs. Thus, increases in social security taxes designed to help pensioners fight inflation in fact contribute to the inflation problem. For example, in 1970, employers paid $426 per employee per year for social security and unemployment compensation. In 1976, the cost was $1,021 per employee. A Senate study argues that these increases cause both inflation and more unemployment.

Second, the taxes are based on incorrect assumptions of population growth. With the birth rate cut in half between 1957 and 1976, and with people living longer, there will be fewer employees to pay the taxes as the number of pensioners receiving checks increases. Let me put it this way. In 1940, when Ida Fuller received the first social security check, 150 workers were paying in taxes for each pensioner receiving benefits. In 1950, the rate was 14 to 1; in 1960, 5 to 1; and in 1976, 3 to 1. Soon it will be 2 to 1. You don't have to be a math major to figure out how much of a tax increase on employers and employees is necessary when these ratios shift from 150 to 1 to 2 to 1.

Third, the taxes paid also assumed an improved productivity rate per employee which appears unrealistic today. The system assumes payments will tend to stabilize as gains are made in productivity. But as the economy continues to shift away from goods and services, as environmental protection costs increase, as the costs of raw materials and other resources grow, as unemployment rates go higher, the productivity assumption tends to be overrated. The result is more pressure for higher taxes.

Fourth, Congress has continued to allow more people to receive checks who did not pay in the full amount over the years. These include survivors and dependents, persons over 72 who did not pay into the system, the disabled, and Medicare for all those over 65. Coverage for wives who never worked themselves is now being advocated. Where is all the money to come from?

Fifth, potential taxpayers to the system are withdrawing; specifically employees of state and local governments, who have the option of taking part. The National Conference of State Legislatures reports that 401 state and local government units (with 52,100 workers) have dropped social security, and another 301 (representing 500,000 employees) have filed notice of possi-

bly opting out within two years. Some recent dropouts are the city of San
Jose; county of Los Angeles, metropolitan Washington, D.C.; state of Alaska;
Santa Cruz, Santa Maria, Sacramento, and San Mateo counties (California);
and Fairfax County, Virginia. Many states (like Illinois) never belonged.
This increases the burden on the private sector, which is *not* allowed legally
to drop the program.

Sixth, many people continue to believe that social security is not a supplement but should provide full support in retirement, at almost the same
standard of living as when they were working. "Gray power" voters reward
congressmen and senators who vote their way. This goal simply cannot
be reached without a dramatic increase in taxes. Yet politicians promise
the system can deliver such support. How can social security be put back
on a sound basis? There are few options:

1. *Raise taxes.* The Social Security Financing Act (1977) raised taxes by
   $277 billion for 1977–1987. It tripled the taxes for the highest paid
   employees. Tax increases like this are likely to mean fewer dollars
   for employees to spend, and fewer for employers to increase wages
   or invest in job-creating activities like new product design. This is
   likely to mean lower employee motivation, more inflation, and fewer
   jobs. For example, by 1987 these taxes will dictate that for a person
   earning just over $20,000, out of every dollar received as a pay increase,
   more than 50 percent will go to federal income and social security
   taxes. Employee motivation is likely to decrease. Employers are likely
   to replace people with machines. Result: more inflation, less employment, fewer dollars for private pensions. But will it be enough to
   save social security?

2. *Lower payout.* This can be done several ways:
   a. Stop adding to the recipient list.
   b. Reduce the excess wage indexing formula. The 1977 Social Secu-
      rity Financing Act did readjust the formula to reduce this outflow.
   c. Increase the age limit before benefits can be paid. Instead of partial
      benefits at 62 and full benefits at 65, one proposal is to pay partial
      benefits at 65 and full benefits at 67, 68, or 70.
   d. Increase the amount a pensioner can earn at part-time work.
   e. Eliminate multiple public pension payouts. Some individuals are
      drawing military pensions; federal, state, or local pensions; and
      social security. As in workers compensation and disability pro-
      grams, a limitation on total payments from nonprivate funds should
      be considered. In the Railroad Retirement System, parallel to social
      security, Congress recently approved elimination of some pensions
      of 130,000 former railroad employees who were drawing both social
      security and railroad retirement payments.

Probably the most significant necessity to save social security is to create
a significant *communication* program to tell people the facts about retirement
and social security. Everyone must understand these facts and comprehend
their applicability to their own situations:

Social security is a *supplement.* You cannot live on it alone. And if population trends for the foreseeable future prevail, the country will be unwilling to tax wage earners enough so that social security could cover all expenses.

You must expect to save during your lifetime to supplement social security payments in retirement.

If possible, you should try to get a job with a private pension to supplement social security.

You probably will have to lower your standard of living when you retire in order to pay your expenses, even if you have savings, social security, and a private pension. You may have to work part-time in retirement or even live with relatives to make ends meet.

Canada Pension Plan[11]

The government pension plan is the Canada Pension Plan (Quebec Pension Plan in Quebec). The CPC/QPC is a nationwide, mandatory, portable, contributory plan for all employees and self-employed persons, except for federal government employees. It began in 1967 and has been in full operation since January 1976.

CPC/QPC pays retirement pensions, disability pensions, pensions for survivors' spouses, orphans' benefits, benefits for children of disabled contributors, and a lump-sum death benefit to eligible applicants. No longer are there differences between male and female contributions, nor is there an earnings test. At present, employees and employers each pay 1.8 percent of earnings; self-employed persons pay 3.6 percent. There are residence requirements to receive a pension: 40 years of residence in Canada if the person is 65 or over, or 10 years' residence, including the last year prior to retirement.

In 1975, the pension paid was $120 per person per month. For those who must survive on this pension alone, it can be supplemented by an guaranteed income supplement of $84 for a single person or $75 for both married person and spouse. This is adjusted yearly according to the consumer price index.

In 1974, about 325,000 persons received pensions, 75,000 widows' pensions, 60,000 orphans' benefits, and 32,000 disability pensions. Funding for the plan has presented problems similar to those of Social Security's. Inflation has made it difficult to keep the value of the pensions stable. But taxing to fund the plan with increasing inflation has been a serious problem.

PRIVATE PENSIONS

As we shall see shortly, ERISA requires that all persons participating in pensions must be notified about them in writing and in language *they can understand.* The U.S. Department of Labor set out a six-page notification form in "laymen's language" which employers could use to notify retirees about their pensions. Yet when one firm sent this report, littered with pension terms like "vested benefits" and "fiduciary," to its retirees, "The reaction of retired employees who received the letters was near hysteria," according to Mr. Donnelly, personnel director at Vulcan, and the company's pension-plan administrator. "Nearly half of them called the company, desperate to learn whether the gobbledygook meant their pensions were going to be raised or cut."[12] We will translate the gobbledygook into "pension terms" to help follow the rest of the chapter.

Vesting. This is the right to participate in a pension plan. Pension plans state how long a person must be employed before he has a right to a pension or a portion of it should he terminate his employment. When the employee has completed the minimum time after which he has a right to a pension, he is said to be vested in the pension.

Portability. This means the right to transfer pension credits accrued from one employer to another. It becomes possible when several employers pool their pensions through reciprocal agreements.[13]

Contributory or noncontributory. Some pension plans require employees to pay some of the costs of the pensions during employment (contributory). Other employers pay all the pension costs (noncontributory).

Funded or nonfunded. Some pension plans finance future payments by setting money aside in special funds. These are called funded pension plans. Nonfunded or pay-as-you-go plans make pension payments out of current funds.

Insured or uninsured. Funded plans can be administered by insurance companies. Under the insured method, the payments made for each employee buy him an annuity for the retirement years. An uninsured or trustee plan is usually administered by a bank or trust company. In these cases, the administrators invest the pension funds in securities, real estate, and so on, from which pension payments are generated.

Pension payments. Pensions can be paid in one of two ways: a flat or defined dollar payment, or an annuity. The defined benefit approach uses a benefit formula, as described below. In an annuity, the payments vary according to the value of the investment trust used to pay the pensions. If the value increases, the payment increases, and *the reverse* is also true. In the stock market decline of the mid–1970s, some pensioners learned that valuable annuities vary downward as well as upward.

Fiduciary. Fiduciaries are persons responsible for pension trust funds, such as pension trustees, officers or directors of the company, controlling shareholders, and attorneys.

Benefit formula. A benefit formula is used to calculate the size of a pension payment. It expresses the relationship between wages and salaries earned while employed and the pension paid.

The first step in determining the formula is to indicate which earning figure should be used as a base in this computation. Some experts have noted a trend toward using the average of the final several years of employment as the base earnings figure.[14] An earlier approach was to average career earnings, but this is not useful in an inflationary period.

Once average earnings are determined, by whichever formula approach is used, the actual pension benefit is determined by multiplying the average earnings times the number of years of service times the stipulated percentage, generally between 1 and 3 percent. Some firms offset this figure to some degree by social security benefits. This approach is generally designed to yield a monthly benefit, including social security, that is approximately 50 percent of the individual's projected salary during the final year of employment.[15]

Criticisms of private pensions

In the late 1960s and early 1970s, there was much criticism of the private pension system. The major criticism was that they were a hoax; many people who thought they were covered were not because of complicated rules, insufficient funding, irresponsible financial management, and employer bankruptcies.[16] Some pension funds, including both employer-managed and union-managed funds, were accused of mismanagement, and others required what the critics considered unusually long vesting periods. Over the years, therefore, pension regulation laws were regularly debated.[17] ERISA was passed in 1974 to respond to these kinds of criticisms.

Status of private pensions (U.S.)

If you have not been worrying about a pension because you thought social security would take care of you, you may begin to look more closely at them now. Unfortunately, few people consider seriously the *tax-sheltered value* of a pension before they take a job. More often than not, the difference in job offers are bigger between benefit and pension programs than in pay, especially in view of their tax-free aspects.

> DEFINITION
>
> A pension is a fixed amount paid by an employer or its representatives at regular intervals to a former employee or the employee's surviving dependents, for past services performed.

About half the nonagricultural employees in the United States (about 30,000,000 people) expect a private pension. Like many other benefits, private pensions are relatively new; the private pension plans in existence prior to 1950 covered less than one sixth of the nonagricultural work force. In the decade of the fifties many new plans were introduced and coverage doubled, so that by 1960 about 15 million workers were covered. Coverage during the sixties remained rather stable, and the percentage participating has also stabilized. Studies have found that the kinds of employees covered vary greatly.[18] Certain industries (mining; manufacturing, especially nondurable goods; construction; transportation; communication; and public utilities) are more likely to provide pensions than others (retailing and services). Larger firms are more likely than smaller firms to have pensions. And the higher the employee's income, the more likely it is that a pension exists. Unionized employees are more likely to be covered than nonunion employees. And everyone working for employers with pension plans is not covered by them; the Treasury Department estimates that 35 to 45 percent of employees of companies with pension plans are not covered. Part-time employees, for example, are rarely included in pension plans.[19]

Status of private pensions (Canada)

In 1977, about 3,000,000 Canadians were covered by about 16,500 private plans. Exhibit 16–1 presents some data on private pension plans in 1971–73.

Given inflation and investment conditions, similar problems of funding private pensions exist in Canada. Private pensions in Canada are governed by the Pension Benefits Act, which regulates solvency and funding.

Major criticisms of Canadian private pensions concern limited coverage (only 40 percent of Canadian employees), lengthy and complicated vesting requirements, lack of indexing of the plans, the solvency of the plans, and other problems.[20]

U. S. GOVERNMENT REGULATION OF PRIVATE PENSIONS   *ERISA*

The law regulating private pensions in the United States is the Employee Retirement Income Security Act of 1974. As noted above, ERISA was designed to cover practically all employee benefit plans of private employers, including multiemployer plans. Basically, the legislation was developed to ensure that employees covered under pension plans would receive the benefits promised.

Existing regulations were tightened in ERISA, but the major impact of the law is in the minimum standards established which all plans are required to meet. ERISA *does not require an employer to have a private pension plan;* indeed, many existing private pension plans were terminated rather than meet ERISA's requirements. The major provisions of the law are as follows.[21]

Eligibility requirements

Enterprises were prohibited from establishing requirements of more than one year of service, or an age greater than 25, whichever is later. An employee hired before the age of 22 who continues unbroken service must at age 25 be given at least three years' service credit for vesting purposes. An exception

EXHIBIT 16–1

Trusteed pension funds, income, expenditures and assets, 1971–73 (in millions of dollars)

Item	1971	1972	1973
Trust arrangements (number)			
Corporate trustees	2,966	2,857	2,952
Individual trustees	888	813	789
Combinations of (a) and (b)	64	80	90
Pension fund societies	28	28	28
Total trusteed funds	3,946	3,778	3,859
Income			
Total contributions	$ 1,260	$ 1,469	$ 1,763
Employer	798	944	1,168
Employee	462	525	595
Investment income	631	736	883
Net profit on sale of securities	34	117	114
Other	21	18	20
Total income	$ 1,946	$ 2,340	$ 2,780
Expenditures			
Pension payments out of funds	$ 482	$ 557	$ 640
Cost of pension purchased	21	17	50
Cash withdrawals	115	160	202
Administration costs	15	18	20
Net loss on sale of securities	60	38	39
Other expenditures	57	13	6
Total expenditures	$ 750	$ 803	$ 957
Assets (book value)			
Investment in pooled funds	$ 894	$ 978	$ 1,063
Investment in mutual funds	51	55	49
Investment in segregated funds of insurance companies			146
Bonds	6,386	6,982	7,704
Bonds of or guaranteed by Government of Canada	424	393	356
Bonds of or guaranteed by provincial governments	3,324	3,707	4,132
Bonds of Canadian municipal governments, school boards, etc	749	736	761
Other Canadian	1,878	2,132	2,432
Non-Canadian	11	14	23
Stocks	3,214	3,901	4,421
Canadian, common	2,531	3,200	3,717
Canadian, preferred	79	92	93
Non-Canadian, common	596	603	599
Non-Canadian, preferred	8	6	12
Mortgages	1,170	1,296	1,551
Insured residential (NHA)	641	700	898
Conventional	529	536	653
Real estate and lease-backs	47	46	51
Miscellaneous			
Cash on hand and in chartered banks	136	163	161
Guaranteed investment certificates	96	95	164
Short-term investments	247	261	554
Accrued interest and dividends receivable	104	125	143
Accounts receivable	113	145	162
Other assets	3	3	2
Total assets	$12,461	$14,050	$16,171

Source: *Canada Year Book.* (Ottawa, Ontario: Publishing Centre, Supply and Services Canada, 1975), p. 338. Reproduced by permission of the Ministry of Supply and Services Canada.

is allowed employers who provide immediate 100 percent vesting in that they may require a three-year eligibility period.

Vesting practices

The employer may choose from three vesting alternatives: (1) the 10-year service rule, whereby the employee receives 100 percent vesting after ten years of service; (2) the graded 15-year service rule, whereby the employee receives 25 percent vesting after five years of service, graded up to 100 percent after 15 years; and (3) the rule of 45, which provides 50 percent vesting when age and service equal 45 (if the employee has at least five years of service), graded up to 100 percent vesting five years later.

The new vesting standards appear to provide a major advantage to employees. Previously, those who changed employment after 10 or 15 years of service did not receive benefits; now they will. Although small, the benefits received will increase the total income at retirement.

Portability practices

From the employee's point of view, it is desirable for pensions to be transferable or portable. Employers, however, find portability an expensive provision. Under ERISA, portability becomes a voluntary option of the employee and his employer. If the employer agrees, a vested employee leaving a company is permitted to transfer (tax free) the assets attributable to his vested pension benefits or his vested profit-sharing or savings plan funds to an individual retirement account (IRA). The benefit to employees is in the opportunity to defer the payment of taxes on the funds.

Funding

Many employers have been funding their pension plans at a rate equivalent to or faster than that required under ERISA. Those who have not must accelerate funding of pension costs. The funding provision has two sections: (1) the employer operating a new plan is required to pay annually the full cost of current benefit accruals *and* amortize past service liabilities over 30 years; and (2) plans in existence as of January 1, 1976, must make the annual payments but are allowed 40 years to amortize costs.

Fiduciary responsibility

Because of the need to provide more effective safeguards for pension funds, the law imposes new standards for fiduciaries and parties-in-interest, such as trustees, officers or directors of the company, controlling shareholders, or attorneys. The "prudent man" rule is established as the standard for handling and investing pension plan funds.

A fiduciary is prohibited from engaging in certain activities. He may not:

(1) deal with the fund for his own account; (2) receive personal consideration from any party dealing with the fund in connection with a transaction involving the fund; (3) make loans between the fund and a party-in-interest; and (4) invest more than 10 percent of the assets of the pension plan in securities of the employer. These prohibitions have caused a great deal of concern, and it is expected that Congress will amend the standards.

Other provisions

ERISA provides for plan termination insurance to ensure vested pension benefits (similar to FDIC provisions at banks). The Pension Benefit Guaranty Corporation currently is paying a total of $225,000 a month to 1,700 retired workers formerly covered by 15 terminated pension plans.

Reporting and disclosure provisions of the law require the employer to provide employees with a comprehensive booklet describing major plan provisions, and to report annually to the Secretary of Labor detailed information concerning the operation and financing of the plan. The act also imposes limits on contributions and benefits and changes the tax rules related to lump-sum distributions to employees. As discussed in Chapter 14, ERISA and other laws created the conditions for setting up ESOPs.

What about those who have no employer-sponsored pension plan or who are self-employed? Persons having an employer but without a pension plan can set aside 15 percent of their compensation or $1,500, whichever is less, and pay no taxes on this income until they are 70.5 years old. IRAs (individual retirement accounts) are managed by banks and other financial institutions. ERISA limits the investment of these funds to specific choices: savings accounts, certificates of deposit, retirement annuities, endowment or retirement income policies, mutual funds, trust accounts, individual retirement bonds, and others. The money cannot be withdrawn before age 59.5 without tax penalty. Firms without pension plans can set up IRAs for their employees. Self-employed persons can set up IRAs or Keogh plans. Legislation allows a self-employed person to set aside up to 15 percent (or $7,500) in tax-deferred trusts. There is more flexibility for investment of Keogh funds than IRA funds, and the withdrawal provisions are the same. About $2.5 billion is invested in about 7,000,000 Keogh plans.[22]

THE IMPACT OF ERISA

What has ERISA done since 1974? Are American employees better off? Are American employers? It is a mixed blessing; evaluation depends on which set of facts you accept. In general, it appears to involve a lot of government regulations for very little added protection. To review what has happened in pensions as a consequence of ERISA's passage in 1974, consider the following developments:

A flood of employees and employers have been to Washington to complain about the law and its administration.[23] More than 5,000 pension plans had to be rewritten to meet the legal requirements. The Internal Revenue Service is enforcing the letter of the law. The Securities and Exchange Commission may get involved in enforcement too. With this many government agencies involved, conflict over enforcement was almost inevitable. In mid–1976, IRS and the Department of Labor were working at cross-purposes in enforcing ERISA, and interagency coordination broke down.[24] The 1975 budget requests of Department of Labor included $5,000,000 *more* for policing pensions. This does not count Internal Revenue, SEC, or Pension Benefit Guarantee Corporation costs.

In the first full year of operation 5,035 pension plans were terminated by employers: four times the number expected by the bill's sponsors. In 1976, 8,000 were terminated. Some say the terminations were due to costly and complicated regulations; others contend that the economy was bad, or cite other reasons.[25] Many experts believed few new plans would be created until the regulations were clarified. When they were finally issued, on December 28, 1976, in the *Federal Register,* the regulations took up 300 typewritten pages. Key provisions included how employers determine the number of hours an employee has worked: One year of credit is given for 1,000 hours or more yearly. A number of methods can be used to count those 1,000 hours. Other regulations concern how employees accrue benefits and how conglomerates transfering persons across divisions are to handle these credits.

Pension plan consultant fees tripled. CPAs required firms to tell stockholders in annual reports ERISA's cost to the firm.

The law limited per-person pensions a year to $75,000, to cut the level of executive pensions. Companies have reacted by designing deferred bonuses and other forms of alternative compensation.

Lower corporate profits were expected because of funding requirements of ERISA; one expert predicted $3 to 7 billion more per year would be necessary.[26] Trust fund costs by banks went up 90 percent. Others contended the costs would not be as high.[27]

Some experts claim the new law will cause older workers who are laid off or let go to be permanently unemployed.[28] Only time will tell on this charge.

Since pension managers or firms are liable for losses, many are now having to buy $1 million liability insurance policies. The law's requirement that pension fund managers be "prudent men" has had a major impact on their investment decisions and on the securities markets. Many experts believe that the managers are buying more bonds and fewer stocks to be adjudged "prudent." Some ERISA experts contend that all *collectively bargained* pension funds are covered by the plan termination insurance provisions of the act. If this were so, the employer could be *required* to reimburse the Pension Benefit Guarantee Corporation for any shortfall of plan assets in case of termination of the plan, up to 30 percent of the net worth of the company. (See discussion below.) It is possible that multiemployer plans may not be covered; the courts have not definitely ruled on all these points yet.[29]

Paper work is a real problem. Partly this is a consequence of the law being administered by several federal agencies (Department of Labor and Treasury), as well as IRS and SEC influence. In 1975, the Department of Labor required completion of Form EBS–1 (12 pages plus attachments); then it changed its mind and told employers to complete only the first and last pages. In 1976, the EBS–1 form was redesigned to six pages, all to be completed. In addition, the 5500 annual reporting forms were created, and Internal Revenue came up with two reports. One part of the 5500 form required CPA work which cost $1,000 at a minimum. Now a 5500–C form is being

EXHIBIT 16–2
ERISA information requirements

Item	Benefit plans affected	Deadline	Related information
1. Communications Required for All Employees			
Summary plan description	All welfare and pension plans	August 31, 1975 (except for pension plans using alternate)	EBS-1 Form may be substituted
Announcement of material modifications	All welfare and pension plans	120 days after end of plan year in which changes were made	Except for pension plans using alternate, modifications will be included in the Summary Plan Descriptions this year; when future changes are made, they will be reported separately
Summary annual report	All plans with funds controlled by a bank, insurance carrier, or similar institution; certain plans with under 100 participants are exempt	Calendar year plans: July 28, 1976; Noncalendar year plans: 210 days after 1975 plan year ends	Includes assets and liabilities; receipts and disbursements; other information necessary for an accurate summary
Interim summary plan description	Pension plans using alternate	August 31, 1975	Existing booklet or other description with a supplement of new information required, such as names and addresses of administrator and trustees
Updated summary plan description	Pension plans using alternate	120 days after end of plan year	New plan description of amended pension plan and incorporating information required, such as names and addresses of administrator and trustees
2. Information Available for Examination			
Plan document	All welfare and pension plans	January 1, 1975	Clearly identified copies must exist at each geographic location of employer at reasonal times for viewing
Annual report	(Same as summary annual report above)	(Same as summary annual report above)	(Same as plan document above)
3. Information to be Furnished on Request			
Annual report	(Same as summary annual report above)	(Same as summary annual report above)	Employee may be charged up to 20 cents per page
Plan document	All welfare and pension plans	January 1, 1975	Employee may be charged up to 20 cents per page
Vesting statement	Pension plans	January 1, 1975	Employee may request one statement during each 12-month period

Source: Sandra Fleming, "Getting Your Money's Worth from ERISA," *Personnel*, May–June 1975.

sent out. The same paper work is required of the 72 percent of plans with 51 or less employees as the 1.5 percent with 5,000 employees. In 1976 IRS decided that the reports had to be completed only once a year instead of twice.

The reports also have proved to be a real problem for the 15 permanent and 15 temporary file clerks hired by the Department of Labor; 600,000 annual pension plan reports are arriving each year. Many are in cardboard boxes, some are microfilmed. Many are unfiled; the question is, if they ever do get filed, will they ever be used?[30]

On the positive side, ERISA's disclosure requirements have focused needed attention on benefits communications. Several experts provide good advice on pension communications under ERISA.[31] The items which must be disclosed to employees about the pension plan are listed in Exhibit 16–2. Sandra Felmming makes the point that in the process of fulfilling the law's disclosure requirements, employers can improve benefits communications in general, and this is useful.[32]

Another positive aspect is that the Pension Benefit Guarantee Corporation began paying out $225,000 *per month* to 1,700 people whose pensions collapsed in 1975. The total assets of the PBGC at the time were $28 million, but by mid–1977 it had taken over 102 pension plans covering 12,653 employees and was paying out $558,000 monthly. At the time of writing, the fund is $45 million *underfunded* to cover *its present* liability, and 200 additional pension plans are known to have insufficient funds but have not been taken over yet. In 1977, the House passed a bill raising the per-employee payment from $1 to $2.25. The Senate bill raises it to $2.60 and at the time of this writing, the two bills must be reconciled and signed by the President.[33] Of course, the 12,653 former employees receiving pensions are glad there is ERISA and PBGC.

Another positive result is that ERISA has focused the attention of managers on the unfunded pension liabilities of their companies. It is difficult to determine the actual size of these liabilities because accountants have not developed uniform accounting rules for them yet. But a survey in 1977 by Standard and Poor's estimated that these liabilities were huge. ERISA allows the government to take over up to 30 percent of the net worth of a company's assets if the pension plan is underfunded. Samples of unfunded vested benefits as a percent of net worth are the following: Lockheed 166 percent; LTV 108 percent; Uniroyal 89 percent; Pan American Airways 59 percent; Bethlehem Steel 48 percent.[34]

In sum, the results of ERISA are mixed so far. Some employees are getting pensions that would have been lost without the Pension Benefit Guarantee Corporation. But employers are unhappy with administration and costs, and many more than expected are terminating plans.

PUBLIC PENSIONS

Employees in the public sector also receive pensions. The Tax Foundation estimates that pensions are now almost universally available at the state

EXHIBIT 16–3
Private versus public pensions at a glance

	Private sector	*Public sector*
Number of plans	Over 32,000 (excluding 10,000 profit-sharing plans)	2,100 state and local
Covered participants	30 million	9.5 million
Retired beneficiaries	6 million	1.4 million
Retirement payments ..... annually	$10 billion	$4 billion
Asset value (book)	$133 billion	$93 billion
Contributions	1972—$14 billion (with $1.2 billion contributed by employees)	$9.6 billion in 1973 (with $3.5 billion contributed by employees)

Source: John Sweeney, "More Like the Private System Every Day," *Pension World,* August 1975.

and local levels. Federal employees are covered by civilian or military pension plans, and about two thirds of state and local government employees are also covered by social security. Typically, public pensions are contributory. The bulk of the costs is paid by the government and investment income.[35] The employee usually contributes about 7 percent of wages or salary.

Exhibit 16–3 compares private to public pensions. When Robert Tilove, who studied public pensions for the 20th Century Fund, compared private and public pensions, he found that the benefit levels of the latter are approximately *twice* the level of those in private industry.[36] Even adjusting for the portion paid for by the employees themselves, public pensions are still one third larger than industry's. The plans are not coordinated with social security. Since public pension and social security payments have been rising dramatically, a number of public servants now retire at *greater* net income than they had when working. Needless to say, this is a strong inducement to retire and has helped lead to the crisis in public pensions.

The crisis is this: As public pensions rose (often because politicians gave public employees greater pensions than wage increases and left the bill for their successors to pay), funding did not. All the studies show a consistent pattern: a rising spread between funds and pay outs,[37] and Exhibit 16–4 illustrates how as benefits rose, contributions did not. There are only two ways to take care of this: raise taxes dramatically, or lower pensions checks. In one year recently, Arthur Andersen and Co. (the CPA firm) calculated that federal pensions systems promised $20 billion more than was paid in. *Duns* estimated that pension payments for federal civilian pensions will rise 1,000 percent between 1970 and 1980 because of the increased number of retirees and the forces of inflation. The General Accounting Office estimated that in 1977 the federal pension system had promised $280 billion more in pensions than is allowed for in their budgets. The costs of these pensions was already $15.7 billion in 1976. With easy vesting, easy entrance, early retirement (1 in 4 military persons retire in their thirties, to draw lifetime pensions), generous benefit formulas, and after-retirement cost-of-living adjustments, the costs of public pensions are skyrocketing, and they are not

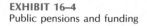

EXHIBIT 16–4
Public pensions and funding

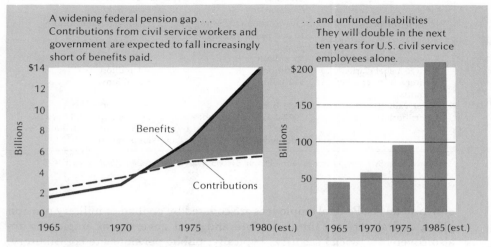

Source: John Perham, "The Mess in Public Pensions," *Duns*, March 1976.

adequately funded. At all levels, the plans are paying out more than they take in. The precarious status of local and state government pensions will deteriorate further if the IRS's current push to gather federal taxes on the investment income of state and local government pension funds is successful.

One answer is to place the public plans under ERISA.[38] A better solution is to reform the public pensions so that benefit payouts are coordinated with social security and total no more than private industry's payout of say 55 percent of final salary. The length of service required to receive full pensions should be more like that in private industry, too. Taxes must rise or benefits must fall, or the total government budget could be going to pensions. Citizens have a responsibility to be heard on this issue.

PRERETIREMENT AND RETIREMENT

Retirement has mixed meanings for people: some look forward to it, others dread it. Various policies affect the way people will live in retirement: compulsory or flexible retirement policies, early retirement policies, and employer preretirement programs.

Compulsory or flexible retirement

A major issue regarding retirement is whether it should be compulsory or flexible. Fred Slavick, in a study of over 1,000 employment locations, defined six company policies as regards retirement.[39] These are:

Type 1.   Compulsory retirement at normal retirement age (usually age 65).

Type 2.   Flexible retirement with no upper age limit.

Type 3.   Compulsory at an age later than normal retirement age.

Type 4.   Type 2 for some employees, type 1 for others.

Type 5.   Type 1 for some employees, type 3 for others.

Type 6.   Type 2 for some employees, type 3 for others.

Slavick found that most companies in his sample (42 percent) had a type 1 policy. Next most frequent was Type 2 (25 percent); the least popular policy was type 6 (about 1½ percent). Types 4 and 5 were also not found too often (about 7 percent). Type 3 was found in about 11 percent of the companies studied. In analyzing which companies followed which policies, Slavick concluded that there was no relationship between types of retirement policy and the presence of a union. There was a relationship between the size of retirement benefits (social security plus pension) and compulsory retirement; the greater the benfits, the more likely the type 1 policy was to be followed. In 1966 dollars, if the retirement benefits exceeded $3,000 yearly (for those earning $5,000–8,000 per year), the organization was likely to have compulsory retirement.

Slavick also found that the larger the company, the more likely there was to be some element of compulsion to retirement. He concluded that about 45 percent of companies permitted some exceptions to type 1 policy, but they were less likely to do so in periods of high unemployment or bad times for the company. Unions tended to encourage strict compliance with compulsory policies to avoid employer favoritism.

Another study of 700 large manufacturing firms and 300 large nonmanufacturing firms also found a direct relationship between the size of the firm and compulsory retirement policies. They found, too, that nonmanufacturing firms (utilities, banks, insurance companies) were more likely to have compulsory retirement policies than were manufacturing firms.[40]

There are advantages to both of these policies. Flexible retirement policies take account of individual differences but can cause difficulty in administration, especially as regards favoritism. Compulsory retirement assures a predictable turnover of older employees, opening up positions for younger ones, and equality of treatment for all employees. When new job openings came up, EEO requirements can be fulfilled more easily, too. Those closest to retirement age favor flexible retirement policies, not compulsory ones.[41]

A number of older employees contend that mandatory retirement regulations or laws violate the equal protection clause of the U.S. Constitution. Thus far, the courts have ruled that it is legal. Some of the cases include *McElvaine* v. *Pennsylvania State Police; Weisbrod* v. *Lynn; Cleveland Board of Education* v. *La Fleur,* and a large number of state court decisions.[42] In a very significant case (*Massachusetts Board of Retirement* v. *Murgia,* 12 EPD), the Supreme Court reversed a state appeals court decision and ruled mandatory retirement to be legal. Twelve states have already passed laws which prohibit mandatory retirement provisions earlier than age 70. In 1977 the House passed a bill to extend the protected age period of the Age Discrimination Act of 1967 to 40–70 years. The Senate was debating this bill and considering allowing mandatory retirement at age 65 for college professors and highly paid executives. In 1977 mandatory retirement is legal in the United States. If mandatory retirement were eliminated legislatively, it would have a significant impact on pension funding, since present pensions are built on those actuarial assumptions. It could also have major impact on unemployment and many other factors.

Early retirement

One form of flexible retirement is early retirement. Some prefer not to work up until normal retirement age. In recent years, more than 90 percent of pension plans studied have made provision for early retirement.[43]

Typically, the minimum age for early retirement is 55; others call for a minimum age of 60. Most early retirement plans require a minimum number of years of work (typically 10 or 15 years) before the employee is eligible for early retirement. As far as benefits are concerned, all plans will pay the actuarial equivalent of the normal retirement benefits, but 30 percent of the plans pay more than that. One study found that in a typical year an average of 10 percent of those eligible retire early, but this is related to the benefits paid. Only 5 percent of those with nonliberalized payments retire early, whereas 30 percent of those eligible for early retirement with liberalized benefits do so.[44] The U.S. Census Bureau found that more men retire early than women.

Paul Jackson examined early retirement plans, which first appeared in the 1950s and early 1960s. In the typical plan of that time, the early retirement age was 60; later it was changed to 55. Initially, minimum employment service requirements were 20 years, then 15, now 10. Jackson points out that early retirement plans appeared earlier in public service and that public service plans are more generous than private plans. The U.S. military retirement plan, for example, pays benefits after 20 years' service and is computed as 2½ percent per year of service time, 80 percent base pay, and all allowances. In civil service, it is 2 percent per year, times the number of years, times final pay.[45] Lately, early retirement pensions have become 50 percent of final average pay after 20 years of service *regardless of age,* and unions are pressing for 75 to 100 percent after 30 years, regardless of age. The automobile manufacturing unions negotiated a "30 and out" early retirement plan whereby the worker could retire with a benefit of $500 per month after 30 years' service, regardless of age. The pension would be the same as the normal pension after age 65.

Jackson describes how many employers have used liberalized early retirement to reduce the size of their labor force when necessary. Employers sometimes also guarantee the right to be reemployed later if the employee takes early retirement; a few plans restrict this right. Enterprises must be careful not to violate the Age Discrimination Act of 1967 in "encouraging" people to retire early.

Several studies have examined which employees take early retirement. The U.S. Department of Labor found that black men have a lower propensity to retire early than white men. Their study also found that the employee is more likely to retire early the higher the pension benefits, the smaller the number of dependents, the higher the assets, and the poorer the health. Blue-collar workers are more likely to retire early than white-collar workers.[46] Executives are especially averse to early retirement.[47] Government workers retire early more frequently than private-sector employees. These findings are confirmed by other studies.[48] People are reluctant to retire early in times of raging inflation; one expert argues that at those times, management must take positive steps to make early retirement more attractive.[49] Finally, although some experts expected ERISA to encourage early retirement, one analysis indicates that ERISA is likely to have little or no effect on early retirement.[50]

Employer preretirement programs

An impending "retirement revolution" in the United States is foreseen by one expert.[51] In the early 1970s there were over 20 million retirees. By 1980 there will be 25 million, and 50 million people will be over 50. What have American employers done to smooth the way for these potential retirees?

In the 1960s, an *Administrative Management* study found 86 percent of 200 companies studied did nothing.[52] Another study indicates that few of 100 American companies did anything significant about preretirement,[53] and a third indicates that little is done in Britain, either.[54] But that appears to be changing in the 1970s.[55] This may be partly because of ERISA's communication requirement. But enterprises must be careful that the information regarding pension options is accurate or the company can be sued by the retiree.

One expert believes at least six hours of intensive counseling is desirable.[56] O'Connell describes a comprehensive preretirement program that includes six sessions.[57] They are:

First meeting: Developing a healthy attitude for a happy retirement. This session emphasizes the positive steps society has taken to ease the financial burdens on senior citizens by reducing the costs of recreation, housing, and taxes. The potential retirees are encouraged to keep mentally and physically active, and programs designed to help, such as adult education, are discussed.

Second meeting: Leisure time converted to happiness. Potential retirees are acquainted with the variety of leisuretime activities, and they are encouraged to choose specific goals and to take steps to develop plans that will bring them to fruition.

Third meeting: Is working in retirement for me?   Retirees are given lectures on service projects and part-time job experiences that may provide variety in the retirement period.

Fourth meeting: Money matters.   This session discusses the sources of funds available to retirees: social security, pensions, and supplementary jobs. Personal budgeting is developed for each retiree to help him adjust to his new income level more smoothly.

Fifth meeting: Relocation in retirement.   The advantages and disadvantages of living in retirement communities, staying in present quarters (if possible), or moving in with children are discussed.

Sixth meeting: Other subjects.   Rights under Medicare are discussed. Retirement publications such as *Harvest Years* and *Modern Maturity* are analyzed. The preparation of wills is encouraged. Social and marital adjustment problems during retirement are covered.

O'Connell also feels that such a preretirement program is a good investment in employee relations. It costs little, and it helps the employees a great deal. In a survey of 112 Pittsburgh firms, Pellicano found that of the 95 which engaged in preretirement counseling, most counseled on pension options, group insurance conversion, medicare and its supplements, and social security. Few covered more than these items. The great majority of firms did the counseling when the employee was 64 or 65 years old. About a third counseled employees between ages of 60 to 65. Very few did so prior to age 60. Still we are not sure employees really want the counseling. For the Chrysler UAW preretirement program, of the 41,780 eligible between 1965 and 1975, only 6,267 actually participated.[58]

Many organizations also keep in contact with retired former employees. General Electric sends a four-page monthly newsletter to its 50,000 retirees. Some companies, such as IBM and Pacific Telephone, provide personnel consultants to aid retirees in such things as tax counseling. Texas Instruments provides a retiree medical insurance plan. These programs round out a full personnel program for loyal employees.

Once in retirement, of course, people do a variety of things. Some move away, others stay put.[59] Some work part time.[60] It is important to keep busy because of the slowdown problem many career-oriented people face.[61] Gerontology is providing help in understanding the challenges and problems of retirement.[62]

SUMMARY, CONCLUSIONS, AND RECOMMENDATIONS

Several summary propositions can be stated to emphasize some of the main points of this chapter.

Proposition 16.1.   The larger the employer, the more likely it is to have a compulsory retirement plan.

Proposition 16.2.   The larger the employer, the more likely it is to have a pension and retirement program for its employees.

Proposition 16.3   The more liberal the early retirement pension, the larger
will be the percentage of employees who retire early.

Exhibit 16–5 lists the recommendations on pensions for the model organizations described in Exhibit 1–14, chapter 1. Preretirement programs are
inexpensive, especially compared to pension costs. Smaller employers should
be encouraged to join multiple-employer programs and pensions.

EXHIBIT 16–5
Recommendations on retirement and pension programs for model organizations

Type of organization	*Joint employer pre-retire-ment program*	*Em-ployer pre-retire-ment program*	*Post-retire-ment program*	*Joint employer pension*	*Employer pension program*
1. Large size, low complexity, high stability		X	X		X
2. Medium size, low complexity, high stability	X				X
3. Small size, low complexity, high stability				X	
4. Medium size, moderate complex-ity, moderate stability	X				X
5. Large size, high complexity, low stability		X	X		X
6. Medium size, high complexity, low stability	X				X
7. Small size, high complexity, low stability				X	

It would seem that retirement programs and pensions have been thrust
upon many employers. They may try to minimize the costs by restrictive
vesting requirements, using computers to lower administrative costs, and
effective investing programs to reduce the flows to pension funds.

The benefits to society are large: more older persons who are self-sufficient.
Benefits to employers may be hard to calculate directly. Perhaps better employees do remain with employers who pay better pensions. But, as discussed
in Chapter 15, employers have done a very poor job of communicating to
employees about benefits, including pensions. Imagine how well an employer
could merchandise a 13.85 percent raise to his employees. Yet a 5.85 percent
social security contribution and an 8 percent (on average) cost of pensions
are seldom mentioned, though they could remind employees about the nontaxable benefits they are receiving.

There is no doubt that some of the criticism about pension abuse and
"trickery" is correct. It is to be hoped that current legislation will remedy
the abuses to help protect the incomes of older citizens, in spite of all the
bureaucracy.

Pensions is another factor which differentiates full-time from part-time employees. Normally less than a fourth of part-timers are entitled to pensions. This reduces the costs of employment, but it leaves part-timers dependent on social security.[63] ERISA may require that part-timers who work more than 20 hours per week must be brought into pension plans.[64]

In the beginning of this chapter, it was pointed out that personnel needs the guidance of top managers about pensions and retirement. Top managers must make a series of strategic decisions on retirement and pensions such as enterprise policies on: mandatory retirement, whether to have a private pension plan, and whether to provide preretirement programs.

One factor in the decisions is cost.[65] It is obvious that if the plan is set up, it must be efficiently managed. But top managers must decide whether they can afford a plan, given the high cost of pensions and the weak evidence that pensions affect employee satisfaction or performance. Often a pension is offered because, even though it is costly and an analysis of cost/benefits of it would not be positive, top managers believe it is the socially responsible decision.

Chapter 17 is on health and safety, one of the fastest growing personnel activities.

QUESTIONS

1. What are the strategic questions on pensions and retirement that top managers must decide?
2. Why do enterprises have pensions and retirement plans?
3. Are people's attraction toward retirement positive or negative? Why?
4. How do retired people support themselves?
5. What is social security? Is it a viable program? How does it work? How can it be improved?
6. What is the Canada Pension Plan? Compare and contrast it with social security.
7. What is meant by vesting, portability, contributory, funded, insured, fiduciary, and benefit formula in reference to pensions?
8. What are the criticisms of private pensions that led to ERISA? Are these criticisms more or less severe than those of social security and the Canada Pension Plan?
9. How many people are covered by private pensions in the United States and Canada?
10. What are the major provisions of ERISA regarding vesting, funding, fiduciary, responsibility, and portability?
11. What has been the major impact of ERISA? Have they been negative or positive?
12. Are public pensions sound? How do they compare to Social Security? The Canada Pension Plan? Private pensions?
13. Should there be mandatory retirement? At what age? Why?
14. Are early retirement programs a good idea? Have they been successful?
15. Describe a successful preretirement and postretirement program.

NOTES AND REFERENCES

1. *The Personnel Executive's Job* (Englewood Cliffs, N.J.: Prentice-Hall/ASPA, 1977).

2. Robert Paul, "Can Private Pensions Deliver?" *Harvard Business Review,* September–October 1974, pp. 22–32; 164–166 ff.

3. David Ignatius, "Paper Weight," *The Wall Street Journal,* July 16, 1976.

4. George Katona, *Private Pensions and Individual Savings,* Monograph 40 (Ann Arbor: Survey Research Center, University of Michigan, 1965).

5. Mary Hopkins and Marcia Wood, "Who Wants to Retire?" *The Personnel Administrator,* October 1976, pp. 38–41. Also see Gordon Streib and Clement Schneider, *Retirement in American Society* (Ithaca, N.Y.: Cornell Press, 1971); Arthur Ross, "Do We Have a New Industrial Feudalism?" *American Economic Review,* December 1958, pp. 904–20.

6. D. J. Wynne, "Employee Mobility: Relationship to Pensions," *Public Personnel Review* 32 (1971), pp. 219–22.

7. Ronald G. West, "Interest in Pensions: A Company Quizzes Its Employees," *Personnel,* September–October 1970, pp. 54–58.

8. Katona, *Private Pensions and Individual Savings.*

9. Alicia Munnell, *The Effect of Social Security on Personal Savings* (Cambridge, Mass.: Ballinger Publishing Company, 1974).

10. The social security section of this chapter is based on a number of sources, including: "Propping Up Social Security," *Business Week,* July 19, 1976, pp. 34–38, 43; Wilbur Cohen and Milton Friedman, *Social Security: Universal or Selective?* (Washington, D.C.: American Enterprise Institute on Public Policy, 1972); "Is Social Security Going Broke?" *The Economist,* March 15, 1975, pp. 67–68; James Hyatt, "Railroad Pension Fund, Rescued by Congress in 1974, May Need $2 Billion More in Aid," *The Wall Street Journal,* March 18, 1977; Robert Myers, *Social Security* (Homewood Ill.: Richard D. Irwin, Inc., 1975); "Will The Social Security Bubble Burst?" *Nation's Business,* November 1974, pp. 28–32; "Is it True What They Say About Social Security?" *Nation's Business,* June 1973, pp. 53–55; Railroad Retirement Board, *Railroad Retirement and Survivor Benefits* (Chicago, Ill., 1976); Railroad Retirement Board, "Statement on Inactive Employees Not Eligible for Windfall Benefits," Chicago, 1976, mimeographed; "Dual Benefit Financing: The Financial Interchange," *Actuarial Notes* (Chicago: Railroad Retirement Board, April 1977); A. Haeworth Robertson, "The Cost of Social Security: 1975 to 2050," *The Personnel Administrator,* May 1976, pp. 28–31; J. W. Van Gorkom, *Social Security: The Long Term Deficit* (Washington: American Enterprise Institute for Public Policy Research, 1976); "Social Security in Review," *Social Security Bulletin,* January 1976; Jonathan Spivak, "Ebbing Resources: Social Security Is on Its Way to Going Broke, Analysts Warn," *The Wall Street Journal,* May 23, 1976; Jonathan Spivak, "New Social Security Estimates Will Show A 50% Widening of Long Range Deficits," *The Wall Street Journal,* May 24, 1976.

11. This section is based on a number of sources including: Donald Coxe, "Pensions: Up to Government or Business?" *The Canadian Business Review,* Spring 1973, pp. 36–40; Donald Neelands, "Twin Threats to Pensions Funds," *The Canadian Business Review,* Summer 1974, pp. 43–45; Roy LaBerge, "Canadian Retirement Policies," *The Labour Gazette,* June 1976, pp. 316–319.

12. Ignatius, "Paper Weight."

13. Susan Phillips and Linda Fletcher, "The Future of the Portable Pension Concept," *Industrial and Labor Relations Review,* January 1977, pp. 197–204.

14. Daniel F. McGinn, "The 1970 Survey of Industrial Pension Plans," *Pension and Welfare News,* May 1971, pp. 22–27; Carolyn Winkler and Charles Selinske, "The 1970 Study of Industrial Retirement Plans," *Pension and Welfare News,* March 1971, pp. 29–34.

15. Stanley Babson, *Fringe Benefits* (New York: Wiley Interscience, 1974), pp. 13–44; Joseph Melone and Everett Allen, Jr., *Pension Planning* (Homewood, Ill.: Richard D. Irwin Inc., 1972), ch. 1, 2, 10.

16. Ralph Nader and Kate Blackwell, *You and Your Pension* (New York: Grossman Publishers, 1972).

17. John Dent, "Inside View of Pension Plan Reform," *Labor Law Journal,* November 1973, pp. 715–17; Peter Henle and Raymond Schmidt, "Pension Reform: The Long Hard Road to Enactment," *Monthly Labor Review,* November 1974, pp. 3–12; Harrison Williams, "Development of the New Pension Reform Laws," *Labor Law Journal,* March 1975, pp. 123–26.

18. William Bailey and Albert Schwenk, "Employer Expenditures for Private Retirement and Insurance Plans," *Monthly Labor Review,* July 1972, pp. 15–20; Katona, *Private Pensions and Individual Savings;* Emerson Beier, "Incidence of Private Retirement Plans," *Monthly Labor Review,* July 1971, pp. 37–43.

19. Donald Bell, "Prevalence of Private Retirement Plans," *Monthly Labor Review,* October 1975, pp. 17–20; Harry E. Davis and Arnold Strasser, "Private Pension Plans, 1960–1969—An Overview," *Monthly Labor Review,* July 1970, pp. 45–56; Harlan Fox, "Top Executive Pensions," *The Conference Board Record,* February 1975, pp. 36–39; Mitchell Meyer and Harlan Fox, *Profile of Employee Benefits* (New York: The Conference Board, 1974), ch. 6; "Pension and Retirement Plans: A Review," *Pension Facts,* 1975, pp. 1–12.

20. Arthur Smith, "Key Compensation Issues: Some Economic Perspectives," *The Canadian Business Review,* Summer 1975, pp. 38–42; Coxe, "Pensions"; J. Douglas Gibson, "Inflation and Private Pension Funds," *The Canadian Business Review,* Winter 1975, pp. 22–25; George Arber, "Trends in Fringe Benefits," *The Canadian Business Review,* Spring 1974, pp. 26–28.

21. Based on Donald Carlson, "Responding to the Pension Reform Law," *Harvard Business Review,* November–December 1974, pp. 133–44.

22. For more information on ERISA, see John Erlenborn, "Problems in Pension Plan Regulation," *Labor Law Journal,* April 1976, pp. 195–200; Donald Stout, "New Pension Option for High Level Managers," *Harvard Business Review,* September–October 1976, pp. 128–32; Powell Niland, "Reforming Private Pension Plan Administration," *Business Horizons,* February 1976; *Individual Retirement Accounts* (Washington, D.C., Pension Benefit Guarantee Corp. 1976); Jacob Javits, "Future Dimensions in Pension Legislation," *Labor Law Journal,* July 1975, pp. 391–95; Larry Kreiser, "Flow Charts of ERISA," *Journal of Accountancy,* April 1976, pp. 74–79.

23. Frank Kleiner, "House Oversight Committee Hears Complaints about ERISA; Its Administration," *Employee Benefit Plan Review,* June 1975; "Bankers Trust Releases Pension Provision Survey," *Employment Benefit Plan Review,* May 1975, pp. 38–39.

24. Bruce Agnew, "Washington Outlook," *Business Week,* August 9, 1976.

25. Roy Harris, "Uneasy Truce," *The Wall Street Journal,* January 12, 1977; "ERISA Won't Alter Pension Plan Costs, Accountants Say," *Employment Benefit Plan Review,* July 1975, pp. 16–18, 63; "Economy, Not ERISA, Spurs Plan Terminations," *Employment Benefit Plan Review,* August 1975, pp. 8–9; 59; October 1975, pp. 16–20; 44–48.

26. Edmund Faltermayer, "A Steeper Climb Up Pension Mountain," *Fortune,* January 1975, pp. 78–81, 157–65.

27. Charles Stabler, "A Closer Look," *The Wall Street Journal,* October 1, 1974; William Buppert, "ERISA: Compliance May Be Easier Than You Expect and Pay Unexpected Dividends," *Personnel Journal,* April 1976, pp. 179–80; 184.

28. Harry Davis, "Pension Provisions Affecting the Employment of Older Workers," *Monthly Labor Review,* April 1973, pp. 41–45.

29. Wayne Jett, "Employer Contingent Liabilities under Union Pension Plans," *Labor Law Journal,* June 1976, pp. 361–69.

30. "Labor Letter," *The Wall Street Journal,* May 31, 1977.

31. Paul Fasser, "The Disclosure Requirements of ERISA," *Personnel,* January–February 1975, pp. 11–17; Sandra Fleming, "Getting Your Money's Worth from ERISA," *Personnel,* May–June 1975, pp. 32–33.

32. Fleming, "Getting Your Money's Worth."

33. James Hyatt, "U.S. PBGC Weighing Higher Employee's Premiums per Employee," *The Wall Street Journal,* May 16, 1977; Pension Benefit Guarantee Corporation, *Annual Report to the President and Congress,* Washington, D.C., June 30, 1976.

34. "Unfunded Pension Liabilities," *Business Week,* July 18, 1977, pp. 86–88; "Accounting for Pensions," *Business Week,* July 18, 1977, p. 96.

35. Leslie Wohlman, "Second Annual Survey of State Retirement Plan Investment Portfolios," *Pension World,* August 1975, pp. 26–32; 63–66; Leslie Wohlman, "Crisis for City Employees—or False Alarm?" *Pension World,* September 1975, pp. 34–42.

36. Robert Tilove, *Public Employee Pension Funds,* Twentieth-Century Fund Report (New York: Columbia University Press, 1976).

37. Ibid.; Frank Keiler, "Congress Studies State and Municipal Pension Plans," *Employee Benefit Plan Review,* November 1975, pp. 8–9; 48–49; John Perham, "The Mess in Public Pensions," *Duns,* March 1976, pp. 48–50.

38. Hugh Gillespie, "Should They be under ERISA?" *Pension World,* August 1975, pp. 33–36. John Sweeny, "More Like the Private System Every Day," *Pension World,* August 1975, p. 23.

39. Fred Slavick, *Compulsory and Flexible Retirement in the American Economy* (Ithaca: New York State School of Industrial and Labor Relations, 1966).

40. Harland Fox and Miriam Kerpen, *Corporate Retirement Policy and Practices,* Studies in Personnel Policy 190 (New York: National Industrial Conference Board, 1964).

41. G. Mathiasen, *Flexible Retirement* (New York: Putnam, 1975).

42. Norman Wood, "The Challenge to Mandatory Retirement, *Labor Law Journal,* July 1976, pp 437–40.

43. Mitchell Meyer and Harland Fox, *Early Retirement Programs* (New York: National Industrial Conference Board, 1971); James Walker, "The New Appeal of Early Retirement," *Business Horizons,* June 1975, pp. 43–48.

44. Meyer and Fox, *Early Retirement Programs.*

45. Paul Jackson, "Early Retirement," *Pension and Welfare News,* September 1972; October 1972.

46. U.S. Department of Labor, *The Preretirement Years,* Manpower Research Monograph 15, ch. 6. (Washington, D.C.: U.S. Government Printing Office, 1970).

47. "Hanging in There After 65," *Business Week,* January 17, 1977.

48. Lowell Gallaway, *The Retirement Decision,* Research Report 9, Social Security Administration (Washington, D.C.: U.S. Government Printing Office, 1965).

49. Walker, "New Appeal of Early Retirement"; James Walker, "Will Early Retirement Retire Early?" *Personnel,* January–February 1976, pp. 33–39.

50. Robert Frank and Vladimir Stoikov, "Changes in Pension Benefits and the Timing of Retirement," International Institute of Management, 1976, mimeographed; Other references for this section include: Richard Barfield and James Morgan, *Early Retirement* (Ann Arbor: Institute of Social Research, University of Michigan, 1969); Dan Jacobson, "Rejection of the Retiree Role," *Human Relations* 27, 5 (1974) pp. 477–492; Katona, *Private Pensions and Individual Savings;* Robert Kinzel, "Resolving Executive Early Retirement Problems," *Personnel,* May–June 1974, pp. 55–63; Wheelock Whitney and William Damroth, "Don't Call It Early Retirement," *Harvard Business Review,* September–October 1975, pp. 103–18.

51. Blake Newton, "Preretirement Planning," *Pension and Welfare News,* March 1972.

52. "Most Firms Neglect Retirement Counseling," *Administrative Management,* October 1971, pp. 44–45.

53. H. C. Pyron, "Preparing Employees for Retirement," *Personnel Journal,* September 1969, pp. 722–27.

54. Alastair Heron, "Preparation for Retirement," *Occupational Psychology* 36 (1962), pp. 1–9.

55. William Holley and Hubert Field, "The Design of a Retirement Preparation Program," *Personnel Journal,* July 1974, pp. 527–30; Don Pellicano, "Retirement Counseling," *Personnel Journal,* July 1973, pp. 614–18; Richard Prentis, "Who Helps the Retiree Retire?" *Pension World,* December 1975, pp. 52–56; Douglas Bartlett, "Retirement Counseling," *Personnel,* November–December 1974, pp. 26–36; Peter Giovannini and Vito Soranno, "Retirement Planning: Choice or Chance," *Training and Development Journal,* September 1974, pp. 40–42; Mark Staley, "Preretirement Planning: Primer," *The Personnel Administrator,* September 1975, pp. 44–46; Charles Ullmann, "Preretirement Planning: Does It Prevent Postretirement Shock?" *Personnel Guidance Journal,* November 1976, pp. 115–18; V. Vincent Manion, "Preretirement Counseling: The Need for a New Approach," *Personnel Guidance Journal,* November 1976, pp. 119–20.

56. Pyron, "Preparing Employee for Retirement."

57. Chester O'Connell, "Long Service and Retiring Employees," in *Handbook of Modern Personnel Administration,* ed. Joseph Famularo, ch. 71 (New York: McGraw-Hill Book Co., 1972).

58. Don Pellicano, "Overview of Corporate Preretirement Counseling," *Personnel Journal,* May 1977, pp. 235–37, 255 ff.

59. Robert Prinsky, "Economic Refugees," *The Wall Street Journal,* February 25, 1977.

60. Vernon Louviere, "What a Salesman Can Do After 65," *Nation's Business,* September 1975, pp. 77–78; "Top Managers Try Venturing," *Business Week,* May 9, 1977, pp. 101–2.

61. Bradley Hitchins, "Personal Business," *Business Week,* March 28, 1977; "How to be a Success in Retirement," *Nation's Business,* December 1973, pp. 52–57.

62. Beverly Watkins, "Gerontology Comes of Age as an Academic Field," *Chronicle of Higher Education,* March 21, 1977, p. 10.

63. Robert Daski, "Area Wage Survey Test Focuses on Part Timers," *Monthly Labor Review,* April 1974, pp. 60–62.

64. Winthrop Thies, "New Participation and Eligibility Tests under the Pension Reform Legislation," *Journal of Taxation,* November 1974, pp. 268–69.

65. S. Travis Pritchett, "Cost Conscious Design and Management of Defined Benefit Pensions," *Personnel,* October–November 1975, pp. 51–59.

Safety, equal employment opportunity, and labor relations

Part Six is comprised of chapters that focus on three of the most significant personnel activities. All are closely regulated by the government, and all directly affect most employees today.

Chapter 17 describes safety and health programs. These programs, operated by personnel departments, are designed to minimize, if not eliminate, the accidents, occupational illnesses, and work-related deaths that threaten the physical security of most employees.

Chapter 18 focuses on equal employment opportunity programs (in the United States) and human rights programs (in Canada). These programs are designed to assure all employees, regardless of sex, race, ethnic background, religion, and, in some cases, age, a fair chance to be hired and to have worthwhile careers.

Chapter 19 discusses formal and informal mechanics for processing employee grievances. It also describes how some employees join unions and associations and how these unions negotiate and help administer contracts for their members.

Employee safety and health

CHAPTER OBJECTIVES

■ To demonstrate why enterprises and the government have safety and health programs.

■ To show how enterprises have tried to create healthy and safe workplaces for their employees.

■ To discuss government requirements and programs designed to assure the health and safety of employees.

CHAPTER OUTLINE

Joe George works on a construction site for a large building in the downtown area of a major city. Tuesday, one of Joe's best friends, Herb Straws, fell off a scaffold he was working from and was severely injured. Herb may not work again for a long time—in fact, he may be disabled for life.

Herb's case is not a rarity. On the average, one employee in ten is killed or injured at work *each year*.[1] But some occupations (such as dock workers) have many more injuries per year than others (e.g., file clerks), so the odds for some workers are worse than 1 in 10 each year.

An unsafe or unhealthy work environment can affect an employee's ability and motivation to work. As noted in Chapter 2, security is one of the most fundamental needs people have. Poor safety and health conditions are likely to endanger fulfillment of the security needs of employees.

Until recently, the typical response to concern about health and safety was to compensate the victims of job-related accidents with worker's compensation and similar insurance schemes. This chapter will discuss both the compensation approaches and the programs designed to prevent accidents, health hazards, and deaths at work.

Who is responsible for the health and safety of employees? First, top management must be responsible enough to make the health and safety of the employees a major enterprise objective. Operating managers also are responsible, since accidents and injuries will take place, and health hazards will exist, in the work unit. They must be aware of health and safety considerations and cooperate with the specialists who can help them reduce accidents and occupational illnesses.

The third group responsible for health and safety is the personnel department. In larger enterprises, personnel has a separate health and safety department. In 1977, Prentice-Hall ASPA released results of a survey of 1,400 personnel executives in which health and safety was labeled as one of the three fastest-growing personnel activities. This evaluation has led to an increase in the safety staffs enterprises have hired, particularly since passage of the Occupational Safety and Health Act of 1970, as indicated in Exhibit 17–1. Exhibit 17–2 indicates, however, that a number of different specialists and supervisors are responsible for and involved in safety programs.

It is the job of health and safety specialists in personnel to do accident research and apply the procedures developed by scientists and engineers to reducing or eliminating accidents or illnesses caused by conditions at work. Both operating management and safety specialists benefit from the research and training of such groups as the National Safety Council, Industrial Medical Association, and Industrial Hygiene Foundation. These associations also develop reporting systems used for accidents and injuries. Yet the fact is, the major burden of providing safe conditions at work falls on the operating supervisor and line manager. The personnel specialist helps the supervisors, but the latter are at the job site, where they can encourage safe behavior on the part of employees, control safety violations, and help investigate accidents and injuries. The health section of the personnel department treats those who become ill at work and provides preventive medicine for employees.

EXHIBIT 17–1
Staffs hired to handle OSHA compliance

Industry	Companies reporting full-time safety officers	Companies reporting hiring new employees for OSHA duties since 1972
Manufacturing (under 500 employees)	21.9%	16.0%
Manufacturing (500–999)	31.6	22.4
Manufacturing (1,000–4,999)	64.1	38.8
Manufacturing (over 5,000)	68.0	56.0
Research and development	26.7	6.7
Public utilities	80.0	41.4
Hospitals	21.7	13.0
Retail stores	26.1	13.0
Banks	3.9	3.0
Insurance companies	13.1	7.4
Transportation and distribution	66.7	25.0
Government agencies	39.0	26.3
Education	38.2	25.0
Nonprofit organizations	10.7	7.4
Other	26.3	15.5

Source: *The Personnel Executive's Job* (Englewood Cliffs, N.J.: Prentice-Hall/ASPA, 1977).

Many organizations use health and safety committees to improve involvement in this personnel activity. (These will be discussed in more length later in the chapter.) Top managers, operating managers, and personnel must work together to make the workplace safe and healthy.

Employee health and safety is a mature personnel function—Stage IV, as described in Exhibit 1–13 (Chapter 1). Many studies have been made of it, especially by engineers and psychologists.

EXHIBIT 17–2
Responsibility for compliance with OSHA

Function	Person assigned responsibility			
	Safety specialist	Medical staffer	Personnel generalist	First-line supervisors
Self-inspection for OSHA compliance	43.1%	1.4%	27.9%	28.9%
Recordkeeping and posting notices	25.6	9.6	61.9	6.8
Monitoring working environment	37.9	4.8	35.6	37.7
Safety training	38.7	3.3	36.6	30.8
First aid	14.4	35.9	26.0	25.5
Periodic medical testing	8.4	37.1	21.0	3.7
Communicating and enforcing safety and health rules	31.5	7.5	52.6	41.4

Source: *The Personnel Executive's Job* (Englewood Cliffs, N.J.: Prentice-Hall/ASPA, 1977).

A DIAGNOSTIC APPROACH TO SAFETY AND HEALTH

The environmental factors important to health and safety are highlighted in Exhibit 17–3. Probably the most crucial one is the nature of the task, especially as it is affected by the technology and working conditions of the organizational environment. Health and safety problems are a lot more

EXHIBIT 17–3
Factors affecting health and safety and organizational effectiveness

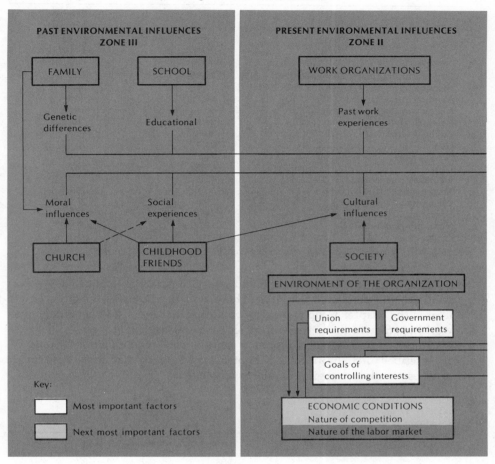

serious for coal miners, whose working conditions entail coal dust in the air, than for typists in the Social Security Administration. An X-ray technician has a much greater chance of getting cancer as a result of working conditions than does an elementary school teacher.

A second vital factor is employee attitudes toward health and safety; they can vary from concern for safety and cooperation regarding safety programs, to apathy. If employees are apathetic about it, the best employer safety program and the most stringent safety inspection by the government or the safety specialists in the personnel department will not be successful in improving safety and health conditions.

A third factor affecting health and safety on the job is government. Federal, state, and provincial governments have attempted to legislate conditions

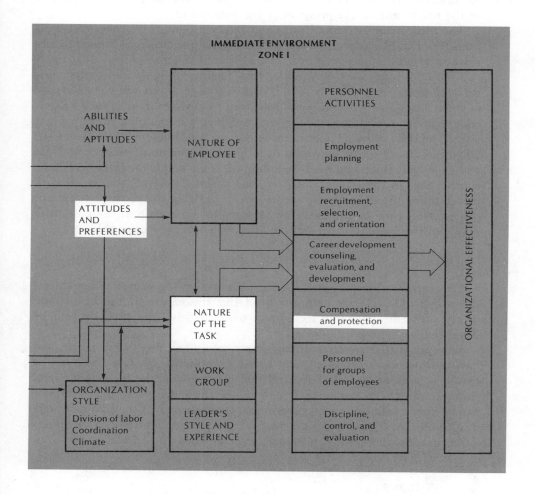

to improve safety and health for some years. The government programs currently in operation will be discussed later.

A fourth factor is the trade unions. Many unions have been very concerned about the safety and health of their employees and have pressured employers for better programs. They also have used their political power to get legislation passed to improve the safety and health of members.

The fifth factor is management's goals. Some socially responsible managers and owners had active safety programs long before the laws required them. They made safety and health an important strategic goal and implemented it with significant safety considerations designed into the enterprises layout and program that included safety statistics, contests, and training programs. Other managers, not so safety conscious, did little other than what was required by law. Thus managerial attitudes play a large part in the significance of the health and safety program of the enterprise.

The final factor affecting health and safety programs is economic conditions. We would accept the worst possible assumptions about human nature if we believed that any employer *knowingly* would choose to provide dangerous working conditions or would refuse to provide reasonable safeguards for employees. But there is a lack of knowledge about the consequences of some dangerous working conditions, and even when there is such knowledge, economic conditions can prevent employers from doing all they might wish. The risks of being a uranium miner are well known: 10 to 11 percent will die of cancer within ten years. As long as there are no alternative methods and as long as there is a need for uranium, some employees will be risking shorter lives in these jobs. Engineers and scientists are constantly at work to determine the dangers and to prevent or mitigate the consequences. But the costs of some of the prevention programs are such that the enterprise may find them prohibitive, and the work economically infeasible.

THE NATURE OF SAFETY AND HEALTH PROGRAMS

This section of the chapter and the next section (on causes of work accidents and illnesses) are designed to clarify the nature of the health and safety problem. Then the techniques used to solve the problem will be discussed.

Enterprises that are large enough have safety and health specialists, and smaller enterprises use safety and health consultants, because there can be many hazards at a workplace, and the effects of employee accidents and illnesses can be far-reaching. If employees are endangered, the enterprise can be fined or shut down by government agencies such as the administrative arm of OSHA. If employees are hurt or are killed, the enterprise's worker's compensation and similar insurance coverage goes up as well.

DEFINITIONS

Safety hazards are those aspects of the work environment which have the potential of immediate and sometimes violent harm to an employee. Examples are loss of hearing, eyesight, or body parts; cuts, sprains, bruises, broken bones; burns and electric shock.

Health hazards are those aspects of the work environment which slowly and cumulatively (and often irreversibly) lead to deterioration of an employee's health. Examples are cancer, poisoning, and respiratory diseases. Typical causes include physical and biological hazards, toxic and cancer-causing dusts and chemicals, and stressful working conditions.

Statistics on safety and health hazards are debated. The official statistics indicate that about 400,000 persons per year contract an occupational disease.

But Nicholas Ashford cites data to indicate this figure is too low and argues that many occupationally contracted diseases are not reported as being caused by work.[2]

The official U.S. statistic for death from occupational diseases is 100,000 per year. The National Safety Council reports about 15,000 accidental deaths at work in a recent year (and about 6,000,000 reported accidents); OSHA places work-related deaths at about 9,000 per year. All agencies do not report the same figures. Note the use of the verb "reported"; a number of studies indicate that perhaps as few as half of all occupational accidents are reported.

Accidents and illnesses are not evenly distributed among employers in the United States. Employees facing serious health and safety dangers include fire fighters, miners, construction and transportation workers, roofing and sheet metal workers, recreational vehicle manufacturers, lumber and wood workers, and blue-collar and first-line supervisors in manufacturing and agriculture. A few white-collar jobs are relatively dangerous: dentists and hospital operating room personnel, beauticians, and X-ray technicians.[3]

The Canadian statistics are equally grim. About 1,500 Canadians are killed at work per year; in 1974, for example, 1,441 men and 24 women were killed at work. And about 1 million Canadians are injured each year at work. The most dangerous occupations and industries in Canada are forestry and mining; others are construction and transportation.[4]

All accidents and diseases are tragic to the employees involved, of course. There is pain at the time of the accident, and there can be psychological problems later.[5] In addition to pain, suffering, and death, there are also direct measurable costs to both employee and employer. About 30,000,000 work days were lost in the United States because of health-related absenteeism in a recent year; this may mean direct costs of workers' compensation and indirect costs of lost productivity for the enterprise. The average company's workers' compensation for disability payments is 1 percent of payroll, and the indirect costs are estimated to be five times greater. These indirect costs include cost of wages paid the injured employee, damage to plant and equipment, costs of replacement employees, and time costs for supervisors and personnel people investigating and reporting the accident or illness. Both because of the humanitarian desire of management to reduce suffering and because of the huge direct and indirect costs of accidents, deaths, and illnesses, the effective enterprise tries hard to create safe and healthy conditions at work.[6]

Unions are also very concerned with workers' safety and health. The Teamsters Union recently hired a nationally known occupational health expert to investigate unexplained illnesses at the Robert Shaw Controls Company plant in Ohio, for example.[7] The Oil, Chemical and Atomic Workers Union has been subsidizing medical student interns and residents to help study occupational health conditions in plants where their members work.[8] And the Canadian Labour Congress is sponsoring regular health and safety conferences to increase awareness of health and safety problems at work.[9]

CAUSES OF WORK ACCIDENTS AND WORK–RELATED ILLNESSES

Work accidents and work-related illnesses have many causes.[10] The causes for accidents in the home diagrammed in Exhibit 17–4 are the same factors that are responsible for work accidents and work-related illnesses.

The major causes of occupational accidents, are the task to be done, the working conditions, and the employee. Some examples of causes in the task and working conditions area include poorly designed or inadequately repaired machines, lack of protective equipment, and the presence of dangerous chemicals or gases.[11] Other working conditions that contribute to accidents include excessive work hours leading to employee fatigue, noise, lack of proper lighting, boredom, and horseplay and fighting at work. The new National Institute for Occupational Safety and Health should find out more amout the causes of accidents.[12]

There are data to indicate that some employees have more accidents than the average. Such a person is said to be accident prone. These studies indicate that employees who (1) are under 30 years of age,[13] (2) who lack psychomotor and perceptual skills,[14] (3) are impulsive[15] and (4) are easily bored[16] are more likely to have accidents than others. Although some believe accident proneness can be measured by a set of attitude or motivationial instruments,[17] most experts who have examined the data carefully do not believe that attitudinal-motivational "causes" of accidents are a significant influence on accident rates.[18] We need to know much more about accident proneness before such serious actions as attempting to screen out the "accident prone" person.

The rest of the chapter will describe what organizations and governments have done and are doing to decrease work-related accidents and illnesses.

ORGANIZATIONAL RESPONSES TO HEALTH AND SAFETY CHALLENGES

Some enterprises have responded to the environmental problems which can increase accidents, deaths, and disabilities by placing the responsibility for employee health and safety with the chief executive officer of the organization: the hospital administrator, the agency administrator, the company president. This is the approach taken by most smaller organizations that have health and safety threats, or middle-sized organizations with few health or safety threats.

Other enterprises create a safety department; this is usually done in organizations with 2,000 employees or more. Safety departments are frequently part of the personnel administration team. For organizations under 2,000 employees, safety is the responsibility of the personnel or operations departments.[19]

EXHIBIT 17-4

The dynamics of home accidents

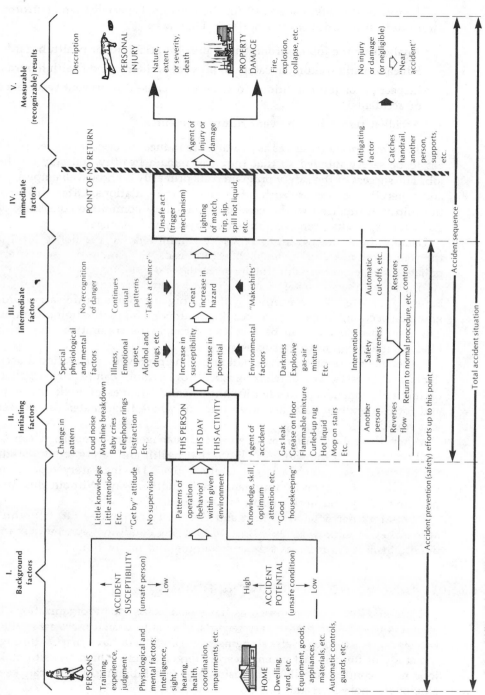

Source: William Johnson, "Sequences in Accident Causation," *Journal of Safety Research*, June 1973, pp. 54–59.

The role of the safety specialist (or the personnel specialist who performs safety duties) includes several duties.[20] They are:

- Analysis of the job environment to prevent accidents or health hazards.
- Education and training in safety to prevent accidents and health hazards.
- Inspection of job conditions to determine causes to prevent recurrence of accidents.
- Accident research to prevent future accidents.

The safety specialist serves as a catalyst to induce supervisors and employees to be safety minded so that they can remain healthy and stay on the job. The success of the safety program rests primarily on how well employees and supervisors cooperate with safety rules and regulations. Often this relationship is formalized in the creation of a safety committee consisting of the safety specialist, representative employees, and managers.

Usually there are two levels of safety committees. At the policy level is the committee made up of major division heads; this committee sets safety policy and rules, investigates major hazards, and has budget responsibility. At the departmental level, both supervisors and managers are members. Safety committees are concerned with the organization's entire safety program: inspection, design, record keeping, training, and motivation programs. The more people who can be involved through the committees, the more likely is the program to be successful.[21]

Other members of the organization can help prevent occupational accidents and illnesses. The purchasing agent, for example, can require suppliers of industrial chemicals to identify the chemical names of toxic materials and furnish toxicity data, and keep track of where toxic materials are used and stored.

When the safety program receives top management support, it can be really effective.[22] One way to indicate that health and safety are important to the enterprise is with a larger safety budget. Having safety reports reviewed and acted upon by top managers is another way. Without this support, the safety and health effort is hampered.

The safety department or unit and the safety committee can take three approaches to improving the safety of working conditions: prevention and design, inspection and research, and training and motivation.

Safety design and preventive approaches

Numerous preventive measures have been adopted by organizations in attempts to improve their safety records. One is to design more safety into the workplace through safety engineering. Engineers have helped through the study of human-factors engineering (ergonomics), which seeks to make jobs more comfortable, less confusing and less fatiguing.[23] This can keep employees more alert and less open to accidents.

Safety engineers design safety into the workplace with analytical design.[24]

This total design approach analyzes all factors around the job, including speed of the assembly line, stresses in the work, and job design.[25] On the basis of this analysis, steps are taken to inprove safety precautions. Protective guards are designed for machinery and equipment, and color coding warns of dangerous areas. Standard safety colors, which should be taught in safety classes, include gray for machinery and red where the area presents danger of fire. Other dangers are highlighted by orange paint.

Protective clothing and devices are also supplied for employees working in hazardous job situations. As proposed by James Gardner, this is designed to protect various parts of the body.[26] They provide:

- Head protection, principally with helmets.
- Eye and face protection, with goggles, face shields, and spectacles.
- Hearing protection, with muffs and inserts.
- Respiratory protection, with air-purifying devices such as filter respirators and gas masks, and air-supplying devices.
- Hand protection, with gloves.
- Foot and leg protection, with safety shoes, boots, guards, and leggings.
- Body protection, with garments such as suits, aprons, jackets, and coveralls.

One more item of safety equipment should be added—belts and lifelines to prevent falls or reduce their results for persons working in high places.

Tenneco's Newport News Shipbuilding Company became so alarmed by safety and disability costs that it took safety into the home. The company sent to each of its 23,000 employees' homes a packet which described the more stringent safety rules. These included requirements for special foot coverings and eyeglasses with special frames and mesh side shields. Reimbursing the employees for these and other protective equipment cost Tenneco $210,000 in 1976 alone.[27]

The few studies on the effectiveness of these preventive design measures indicate they do reduce accidents.[28]

Well-designed rest periods increase safety and productivity, as do clearly understood rules and regulations, which are developed from analyses of equipment and conditions such as flammability. No smoking areas and hard hat areas where safety helmets are required for all employees and visitors are examples. Effective selection and placement of employees can also improve safety. It makes sense, for example, to assign the physically handicapped where their handicaps cannot add to the possibility of accidents.

Inspection, reporting, and accident research

A second activity of safety departments or specialists is to inspect the workplace with the goal of reducing accidents and illnesses. The safety specialist is looking for a number of things, including:

Are safety rules being observed?

Are safety guards, protective equipment, and so on being used?

Are there potential hazards in the workplace that safety redesign could improve?

Are there potential occupational health hazards?

A related activity is to investigate accidents or "close calls" to determine the facts for insurance purposes and, more important, the preventive measures that should be taken in the future. Following an accident requiring more than first aid treatment, the safety specialist, personnel specialist, or manager *investigates* and must report the facts to the government and insurance companies. These data are also used to analyze the causes of accidents with a view to preventing possible recurrences.

Reporting of accidents and occupational illnesses is an important part of the safety specialists' job. Usually, the report is filled out by the injured employee's supervisor and checked by the safety specialist. The supervisor compiles the report because he or she usually is present when the accident occurs, and doing so requires the supervisor to think about safety in the unit and what can be done to prevent similar accidents.

Exhibit 17–5 is an example of an accident report. The form is generally

EXHIBIT 17–5
Accident report form

ACCIDENT REPORT

Date/time of alleged accident _____

Place _____

Description of the incident _____

Accident type _____

Unsafe act _____ Unsafe personal factor _____

Agency or related conditions _____

Unsafe condition of agency _____

Unsafe act _____

Unsafe personal conditions _____

Nature and extent of injury _____

Attending physician (if any) _____

Days lost _____ Recommendations to prevent similar incidents _____

Employee _____ Address _____

Age _____ Sex _____ Job title _____

Job unit _____ Compensation _____

Prepared by _____

Name   Title

Date _____

self-explanatory. It usually refers to an "alleged" accident for legal-insurance reasons. "Agency" refers to the probable cause of the accident, such as machinery, chemicals, or noise, and accident type refers to how the accident happened—a fall, toxic chemicals, and so on. Note that the supervisor is asked what can be done to prevent future accidents of this type.

At regular intervals during the work year, safety and personnel specialists carry out *accident research*, that is, systematic evaluation of the evidence concerning accidents and health hazards. Data for this research should be gathered from both external and internal sources. Safety and health journals point out recent findings which should stimulate the safety specialist to look for hazardous conditions at the workplace. In the United States, reports from the National Institute of Occupational Safety and Health, a research organization created by OSHA legislation, also provide important data inputs for research. Data developed at the workplace will include accident reports, inspection reports by government and the organization's safety specialists, and recommendations of the safety committees.

Accident research often involves computation of organizational accident rates. These are compared to industry and national figures to determine the organization's relative safety performance. Several statistics are computed. Accident frequency rate is computed as follows:

$$\text{Frequency rate} = \frac{\text{Number of accidents} \times 1{,}000{,}000}{\text{Number of work hours in the period}}.$$

The accidents used in this computation are those causing the worker to lose work time.

The second statistic is the accident severity rate. This is computed as follows:

$$\text{Accident severity rate} = \frac{\text{Number of work days lost} \times 1{,}000{,}000}{\text{Number of work hours in the period}}.$$

OSHA suggests reporting accidents as number of injuries per 100 full-time employees per year, as a simpler approach. The formula is.

$$\frac{\text{Number of illnesses and injuries}}{\text{Total hours worked by all employees for the year}} \times \text{Base}.$$

The base equals the number of workers employed (full-time equivalent) working full time (for example 40 hours per week and for 49 weeks if vacation is three weeks.)

The enterprise's statistics should be compared with the industry's statistics and government statistics (in the United States, from the Department of Labor, and OSHA; in Canada, from the Department of Labour).

Most studies find that although effective accident research would be very complex,[29] in reality it is unsophisticated and unscientific.[30]

Safety training and motivation programs

The third approach organizations take to safety is training and motivation programs. Safety training usually is part of the orientation program, it also takes place during the employee's career. This training is usually voluntary, but some is required by government agencies.[31]

The techniques used vary (Chapter 11 described most of them). Studies of the effectiveness of such training are mixed.[32] Some studies indicate that some methods (for example, JIT[33] and accident simulations[34]) are more effective than others. Others contend that the employees' perception that management really believes in safety training accounts for its success.[35] Negative studies find that the programs make the employee more *aware* of safety, but not necessarily more safe in their behavior.[36] Effectively developed safety training programs can help provide a safer environment for all employees.

Safety specialists have also tried to improve safety conditions and accident statistics by various motivation devices such as contests and communication programs. These are intended to reinforce safety training. One device is to place posters around the workplace with slogans such as "A Safe Worker is a Happy Worker." Posters are available from the National Safety Council or can be printed for the enterprise. Communication programs also include items in the company publication and safety booklets, and billboards at the plant entrance with something like the following notice:

Welcome to Mattell Toy Company
A Good Place to Work
A Safe Place to Work
We have had no accidents for _____ days

Sometimes safety communications are tied into a safety contest. If lower accidents result over a period, an award is given. The little research that has been done on safety communications and contests is mixed. Some believe they are useful.[37] Others contend they have no effect or produce undesirable side effects, such as failure to report accidents or a large number of accidents once the contest is over or lost.[38] In general, too little is known scientifically at this point to recommend use or reduction of safety motivation programs. One example of the needed research is a study which examined the conditions under which safety motivation and education programs were effective in a shelving manufacturing company.[39] It found that:

There are safety-conscious people and others who are unaware of safety. The safety-conscious people were influenced by safety posters.

Safety booklets were influential to the safety-conscious employees when their work group was also safety-conscious.

Five-minute safety talks by supervisors were effective when the work group was safety-conscious and when the supervisor was safety-conscious.

Safety training was effective on the safety-conscious employee when the supervisor and top management were safety-conscious.

Safety inspections were effective when the work group and supervisor were safety-conscious.

Auditing safety programs

It is all very well to design organization safety programs. But to assure that the program is put into effect, most enterprises need to audit the program while it is underway. One expert suggests an audit committee composed of the safety professional, the supervisor, and his superior.[40] Others propose nonaccident measures to be used to supplement accident measures as standards for the audits.[41]

Organizational safety programs and the manager

What do all these programs mean to the personnel specialist or operating manager? Organizational safety and health programs can have a much greater impact on employees' safety and health than government inspections can. The manager is there every day; the government might inspect once in 77 years, or about as often as Halley's comet appears, according to the rate at which inspections are made. Health and safety can be improved at the workplace by:

Encouraging the design and engineering of preventive safety methods. Requiring safety equipment to be used. Studying employee fatigue and using rest periods to provide a safe and productive environment.

Making conscientious inspections to find unsafe conditions, and then making changes to prevent accidents.

Encouraging occupational health research to reduce occupational disease.

Examining safety and accident records as clues to safety hazards and taking steps to reduce these hazards.

Being enthusiastic about safety training and motivation programs. Research evidence, although skimpy, suggests that if managers are enthusiastic and involve employees in these programs, safety statistics will improve.

In sum, the manager can make a much greater impact on health and safety at work than the government ever will. For the responsible, safety-

conscious manager, no cost/benefit ratio will ever have the impact of knowing accidents, deaths, and illnesses have been prevented by his or her safety
efforts.

Health programs for employees

Some larger enterprises maintain their own medical and health facilities.[42]
Bernard Burbank notes that these facilities provide various kinds of services
for employees and employers.[43] Their responsibilities can include:

Treating accidents and medical emergencies at work.

Performing physical examinations in conjunction with the selection of
employees.

Evaluating possible health hazards involved in transfers of employees
to different regions or countries.

Advising management on health hazards associated with the use of materials, chemicals in manufacture, or consumer usage of products. Today,
larger enterprises such as Shell, Goodrich, and Dupont maintain extensive health laboratories to detect and prevent occupational diseases
on their premises.

Advising management on health-related problems of employees, such
as drug addiction, alcoholism, and emotional problems.

Undertaking preventive medicine through periodic examinations and im-
munization and group surveys for diabetes, cancer, TB, and heart
disease.

Many of these functions are more important now than in the past because
of government regulations (to be discussed shortly). To the list of activities
Burbank provides, two more can be added which have received more emphasis recently:

Supervising physical fitness programs for executives and other
employees.[44]

Supervising mental health counseling and stress-reduction programs.[45]

The type of programs available is a function of two crucial variables:
organization size and degree of health hazards on the job. The larger the
company and the more hazardous the jobs, the more likely it is that on-
site health programs will be available. Burbank maintains that small (under
500 employees), nonhazardous organizations near medical facilities do not
need their own health programs. Organizations from 500 to 1,500 employees
should have a nurse, physician on retainer, and health facilities consisting
of several rooms. Larger enterprises (with more than 1,500 employees) will
need two nurses and one additional nurse per thousand employees; a full-
time physician should be hired by one with 2,500 employees.[46]

There are differences of opinion on whether enterprises should employ
physicians, use them on a contract basis, or join together to form a health
maintenance organization. The argument basically is over costs for and best

use of the physician, plus possible professional and ethical problems for physicians employed by an enterprise.[47]

Health programs are much less widespread than safety programs, and there are wide differences between industries and enterprises on their use.

GOVERNMENT RESPONSES TO HEALTH AND SAFETY PROBLEMS

Although many enterprises have done a good job of safeguarding the safety and health of their employees with little or no supervision from government sources, others have not. This has led governments to become involved in holding the enterprise responsible for prevention of accidents, disabilities, illnesses, and deaths related to the tasks workers perform and the conditions under which they work.

Prior to passage of the Occupational Safety and Health Act (OSHA) in 1970, the feeling was that private enterprise had not done enough to assure safe and healthy working conditions. The federal law in effect, the Walsh-Healy Act, was thought to be too weak or inadequately enforced, and state programs were incomplete, diverse, and lacked authority.

Lobbying by unions and employees led to the passage of several federal laws related to specific occupations, such as the Coal Mine Health and Safety Act of 1969 and the related Black Lung Benefits Act of 1972. The movement for federal supervision of health and safety programs culminated in passage of the Occupational Safety and Health Act. Benjamin Brown provides an interesting analysis of how OSHA became law.[48]

OSHA, the product of three years of bitter legislative lobbying, was designed to remedy safety problems on the job. The compromise law that was enacted initially received wide support. Its purpose was to provide employment "free from recognized hazards" to employees. OSHA provisions originally applied to 4.1 million businesses and 57 million employees in almost every enterprise engaged in interstate commerce.

If OSHA and the employer fail to provide safe working conditions, employees as individuals or their unions can seek injunctions against the employer to provide safe working conditions.[49] OSHA has many requirements, but the three that most directly affect most employers are:

- Meeting safety standards set by OSHA.
- Submiting to OSHA inspections.
- Keeping records and reporting accidents and illnesses.

OSHA safety standards

OSHA has established safety standards, defined as those "practices, means, operations, or processes, reasonably necessary to provide safe . . . employment." The standards can affect any aspect of the workplace; new standards were established or proposed, for example, for such factors as lead, mercury, silica, epichlorohydrin, talc dust, cotton dust, noise, and general health hazards.[50] The standards may be industrywide or apply only to a specific enterprise.

The Secretary of Labor revises, modifies, or revokes existing standards or creates new ones on his own initiative or on the basis of petitions from interested parties (employees or unions). The National Institute of Occupational Safety and Health in the Department of Health, Education, and Welfare is responsible for doing research from which standards are developed and for training those involved to implement them. OSHA, an agency of the Department of Labor, administers the act. Federal or national consensus standards (such as those of the National Fire Protection Association) have also become OSHA standards. And temporary emergency standards can be created for imminent danger. Employers may be granted temporary variances by showing inability to comply with a standard within the time allowed, if they have a plan to protect employees against the hazard.

The employer is responsible for knowing what these standards are and abiding by them, and this is not easy.[51] The *initial* standards were published in *The Federal Register* in 350 pages of small print,[52] and interpretations of the standards are issued yearly *by volume;* one recent annual volume was 780 pages long! OSHA officers work with compliance operations manuals two inches thick.[53] Even the *checklist* which summarizes the general industry standards is 11 pages long and lists 80 items.[54] An excerpt of the standards for guarding portable power tools is given in Exhibit 17–6. The responsible manager is subject to thousands of pages of such standards and can be fined, shut down, or jailed for not meeting them.

OSHA inspections

To make sure the law is obeyed, OSHA inspectors visit places of employment, on their own schedule or on the invitation of an employer, union, or employee. An employee who requests an inspection need not be identified to the employer. If the employer is found guilty of a violation, the penalties include (1) willful or repeated violations, $10,000 per violation; (2) citation for serious violation, $1,000 each; (3) citation for less serious violation, up to $1,000 discretionary; (4) failure to correct cited violation, $1,000 per day; (5) willful violation causing death, up to $10,000 or up to six months in jail; (6) falsification of statements or records, up to $10,000 and/or six months in jail. In 1977, OSHA fined Dawes Laboratories a record $34,100 for allegedly unsafe conditions.

If you think this is bad, France has started jailing its plant managers for safety violations. American and Canadian managers ought to be pleased they don't have to comply with Hammurabi's safety code, which was quite severe.

OSHA inspectors examine the premises for compliance and the records for accuracy. They categorize a violation as imminent danger (in which case they can close the place down), serious (which calls for a major fine),

EXHIBIT 17–6
OSHA standards for the guarding of portable power tools (excerpt)

§ 1910.243 Guarding of portable powered tools.

(a) *Portable powered tools.*—(1) *Portable circular saws.*—(i) All portable, power-driven circular saws having a blade diameter greater than 2 in shall be equipped with guards above and below the base plate or shoe. The upper guard shall cover the saw to the depth of the teeth, except for the minimum arc required to permit the base to be tilted for bevel cuts. The lower guard shall cover the saw to the depth of the teeth, except for the minimum arc required to allow proper retraction and contact with the work. When the tool is withdrawn from the work, the lower guard shall automatically and instantly return to covering position.

(ii) Paragraph (a)(1)(i) of this section does not apply to circular saws used in the meat industry for meat cutting purposes.

(2) *Switches and controls.*—(i) All hand-held powered circular saws having a blade diameter greater than 2 inches, electric, hydraulic or pneumatic chain saws, and percussion tools without positive accessory holding means shall be equipped with a constant pressure switch or control that will shut of the power when the pressure is released. All hand-held gasoline powered chain saws shall be equipped with a constant pressure throttle control that will shut off the power to the saw chain when the pressure is released.

(ii) All hand-held powered drills, tappers, fastener drivers, horizontal, vertical, and angle grinders with wheels greater than 2 inches in diameter, disc sanders with discs greater than 2 inches in diameter, belt sanders, reciprocating saws, saber, scroll, and jig saws with blade shanks greater than a nominal one-fourth inch, and other similarly operating powered tools shall be equipped with a constant pressure switch or control, and may have a lock-on control provided that turnoff can be accomplished by a single motion of the same finger or fingers that turn it on.

(iii) (*a*) All other hand-held powered tools, such as, but not limited to, platen sanders, grinders with wheels 2 inches in diameter or less, disc sanders with discs 2 inches in diameter or less, routers, planers, laminate trimmers, nibblers, shears, saber, scroll, and jig saws with blade shanks a nominal one-fourth of an inch wide or less, may be equipped with either a positive "on-off" control, or other controls as described by paragraph (a) (2) (i) and (ii) of this section.

(*b*) Saber, scroll, and jig saws with nonstandard blade holders may use blades with shanks which are nonuniform in width, provided the narrowest portion of the blade shank is an integral part in mounting the blade.

(*c*) Blade shank width shall be measured at the narrowest portion of the blade shank when saber, scroll, and jig saws have nonstandard blade holders.

(*d*) "Nominal" in this subparagraph means ±0.05 inch.

(iv) The operating control on hand-held power tools shall be so located as to minimize the possibility of its accidental operation, if such accidental operation would constitute a hazard to employees.

(v) This subparagraph does not apply to concrete vibrators, concrete breakers, powered tampers, jack hammers, rock drills, garden appliances, household and kitchen appliances, personal care appliances, medical or dental equipment, or to fixed machinery.

(3) *Portable belt sanding machines.* Belt sanding machines shall be provided with guards at each nip point where the sanding belt runs onto a pulley. These guards shall effectively prevent the hands or fingers of the operator from coming in contact

EXHIBIT 17–6 *(continued)*

with the nip points. The unused run of the sanding belt shall be guarded against accidental contact.

(4) *Cracked saws.* All cracked saws shall be removed from service.

(5) *Grounding.*—Portable electric powered tools shall meet the electrical requirements of subpart S of this part.

(b) *Pneumatic powered tools and hose*—(1) *Tool retainer.*—A tool retainer shall be installed on each piece of utilization equipment which, without such a retainer, may eject the tool.

(2) *Airhose.*—Hose and hose connections used for conducting compressed air to utilization equipment shall be designed for the pressure and service to which they are subjected.

(c) *Portable abrasive wheels.*—(1) *General requirements.*—Abrasive wheels shall be used only on machine provided with safety guards as defined in paragraph (c) (1) through (4) of this section.

(i) *Exceptions.*—The requirements of this subparagraph (1) shall not apply to the following classes of wheels and conditions:

(*a*) Wheels used for internal work while within the work being ground;

(*b*) Mounted wheels used in portable operations 2 inches and smaller in diameter; (see definition § 1910.241 (b)(1)); and

(*c*) Types 16, 17, 18, 18R, and 19 cones, and plugs, and threaded hole pot balls where the work offers protection.

(ii)(*a*) A safety guard shall cover the spindle end, nut and flange projections. The safety guard shall be mounted so as to maintain proper alignment with the wheel, and the strength of the fastenings shall exceed the strength of the guard.

(*b*) *Exception.*—Safety guards on all operations where the work provides a suitable measure of protection to the operator may be so constructed that the spindle end, nut and outer flange are exposed. Where the nature of the work is such as to entirely cover the side of the wheel, the side covers of the guard may be omitted.

(*c*) *Exception.*—The spindle end, nut, and outer flange may be exposed on portable machines designed for, and used with, type 6, 11, 27, and 28 abrasive wheels, cutting off wheels, and tuck-pointing wheels.

(2) *Cup wheels.* Cup wheels (Types and 11) shall be protected by:

(i) Safety guards as specified in subparagraph (1) of this paragraph; or,

(ii) Special "revolving cup guards" which mount behind the wheel and turn with it. They shall be made of steel or other material with adequate strength and shall enclose the wheel sides upward from the back for one-third of the wheel thickness. The mounting features shall conform with all regulations. (See subparagraph (5) of this paragraph.) It is necessary to maintain clearance between the wheel side and the guard. The clearance shall not exceed one-sixteenth inch or,

(iii) Some other form of guard that will insure as good protection as that which would be provided by the guards specified in subdivision (i) or (ii) of this subparagraph.

(3) *Vertical portable grinders.* Safety guards used on machines known as right angle head or vertical portable grinders shall have a maximum exposure angle of 180°, and the guard shall be so located so as to be between the operator and the wheel during use. Adjustment of guard shall be such that pieces of an accidentally broken wheel will be deflected away from the operator. (See Figure P-4.)

(4) *Other portable grinders.* The maximum angular exposure of the grinding wheel periphery and sides for safety guards used on other portable grinding machines

EXHIBIT 17–6 *(concluded)*

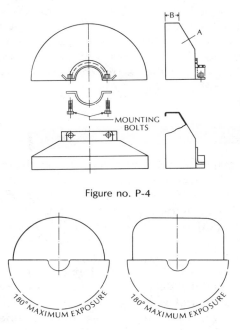

MOUNTING
BOLTS

Figure no. P-4

180° MAXIMUM EXPOSURE   180° MAXIMUM EXPOSURE

Figure no. P-5   Figure no. P-6

shall not exceed 180° and the top half of the wheel shall be enclosed at all times. (See Figures P-5 and P-6.)

(5) *Mounting and inspection of abrasive wheels.* (i) Immediately before mounting, all wheels shall be closely inspected and sounded by the user (ring test, see Subpart O, § 1910.215(d)(1) to make sure they have not been damaged in transit, storage, or otherwise. The spindle speed of the machine shall be checked before mounting of the wheel to be certain that it does not exceed the maximum operating speed marked on the wheel.

(ii) Grinding wheels shall fit freely on the spindle and remain free under all grinding conditions. A controlled clearance between the wheel hole and the machine spindle (or wheel sleeves or adaptors) is essential to avoid excessive pressure from mounting and spindle expansion. To accomplish this, the machine spindle shall be made to nominal (standard) size plus zero minus .002 inch, and the wheel hole shall be made suitably oversize to assure safety clearance under the conditions of operating heat and pressure.

(iii) All contact surfaces of wheels, blotters, and flangers shall be flat and free of foreign matter.

---

nonserious (fine up to $1,000), or de minimus (small—a notification is given, but no fine.)[55] In 1977, Atlas Roofing (Georgia) and Frank Irey (Pennsylvania) argued that fining without court action violated the Seventh Amendment, but the Supreme Court supported OSHA unanimously.[56]

The employer has the right to appeal fines or citations within OSHA (up to the level of the OSHA Review Commission) or in the courts. OSHA tries to portray their inspectors as helpful to employee and employers, but employers seldom see it that way. Judges in Texas, Idaho, and elsewhere have recently ruled that inspectors need search warrants. The Supreme Court has agreed to rule on whether unscheduled inspections are violations of the Constitution.[57]

OSHA record keeping and reporting

The third major OSHA requirement is that the employer keep standardized records of illnesses and injuries and calculate accident ratios. These must be sent to OSHA annually and shown to OSHA inspectors who ask to see them. The form used is shown in Exhibit 17–7. Accidents and illnesses that must be reported are those that result in deaths, disabilities that cause the employee to miss work, and medical-care injuries that require treatment by a physician.

An OSHA guide to when to report and record an illness, injury, or death is shown in Exhibit 17–8. Injuries or illnesses that require only first aid and involve no loss of work time need not be reported. Employers go to great lengths to categorize incidents as "minor injuries," trying to treat them through first aid and keeping the employee on the job (even a make-work job), to avoid reporting them. To do so might lead to an OSHA inspection or raise their workers' compensation insurance rates. The employer must also report accident frequency and severity rates.

OSHA and state safety laws

OSHA can be enforced by federal inspectors or in partnership with state safety and health agencies. OSHA encourages the states to assume responsibility for developing and administering occupational and health laws and carrying out their own statistical programs. Before being granted full authority for its programs, a state must go through three steps. First, the state plan must have the preliminary approval of OSHA. Second, the state promises to take "developmental steps" to do certain things at certain times, such as adjusting legislation, hiring inspectors, and providing for an industrial hygiene laboratory. OSHA monitors the state plan for three years, and if the state fulfills these obligations, the third step is a trial period at full enforcement levels for at least a year. At the end of this intensive evaluation period, a final decision is made by OSHA on the qualifications of the state program.

The first state to complete its three-year developmental period was South Carolina, in November 1975, followed by Oregon, Utah, Washington, North Carolina, and California. During 1975, four states—Illinois, New Jersey, Mis-

EXHIBIT 17–7
OSHA onjury and illness reporting form

VIII. Injury and Illness Summary (covering calendar year 1977)

Instructions:
- This section may be completed by copying data from OSHA Form No. 102 "Summary, Occupational Injuries and Illnesses," which you are required to complete and post in your establishment.
- Leave Section VIII blank if there were no recordable injuries or illnesses during 1977.
- Code 30 — Add all occupational illnesses (Code 21 + 22 + 23 + 24 + 25 + 26 + 29) and enter on this line for each column (3) through (8).
- Code 31 — Add occupational injuries (Code 10) and the sum of all occupational illnesses (Code 30) and enter on this line for each column (3) through (8).

		Fatalities (deaths)	Lost workday cases			Nonfatal cases without lost workdays*	
			Number of cases	Number of cases involving permanent transfer to another job or termination of employment	Number of lost workdays	Number of cases	Number of cases involving transfer to another job or termination of employment
Code (1)	Category (2)	(3)	(4)	(5)	(6)	(7)	(8)
10	Occupational injuries						
21	Occupational skin diseases or disorders						
22	Dust diseases of the lungs (pneumoconioses)						
23	Respiratory conditions due to toxic agents						
24	Poisoning (systemic effects of toxic materials)						
25	Disorders due to physical agents (other than toxic materials)						
26	Disorders due to repeated trauma						
29	All other occupational illnesses						
30	Sum of all occupational illnesses (Add Codes 21 through 29)						
31	Total of all occupational injuries and illnesses (Add Codes 10 + 30)						

*Nonfatal cases without lost workdays—Cases resulting in: Medical treatment beyond first aid, diagnosis of occupational illness, loss of consciousness, restriction of work or motion, or transfer to another job (without lost workdays).

Comments: _____

_____

IX. Report prepared by: _____ Date: _____

Title: _____ Area code and phone: _____

souri, and New York—dropped their state plans, largely because of state costs for the program. Other states are at varying stages in developing state plans. There are several reasons why a state might want its own program, but the main reason is that the state thinks it can provide a better program than the federal government because it has particular labor and industry characteristics. A state has to go through a long, hard process to assume control of its program and must put up substantial money. Unless a state has a real commitment, it will probably drop its program.[58]

Many unions prefer the federal-based OSHA programs because state programs have not been as strong as they liked.[59] But lately, federal enforcement has been less stringent than that in some states, making it difficult for unions to decide which approach to support.[60]

EXHIBIT 17–8
Guide for reporting and recording accidents, illnesses, and deaths

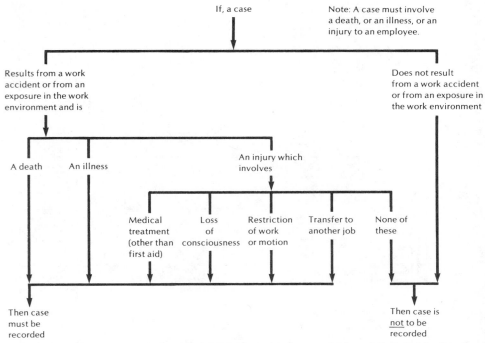

Source: U.S. Department of Labor, Bureau of Labor Statistics, *Occupational Safety and Health Statistics: Concepts and Methods,* BLS Report 438 (Washington, D.C., 1975).

Some consequences of OSHA

Since OSHA opened for business in 1971, it has had one of the rockiest histories of new government agencies. There were three changes in the top administrative job in the first five years, for example. It had trouble hiring good people, partly because of its relatively low salary structure. *Business Week* ran a critical article (typical of OSHA's press) entitled "Why Nobody Wants to Listen to OSHA: The World's Worst Startup Made Everyone Mad."[61] The agency got into a position where organized labor said it was too soft on industry, and management groups said it was too hard. In 1976, President Gerald Ford appointed a White House Task Force to review and revise OSHA. The agency fought back but was damaged by the existence of the Task Force.

When Jimmy Carter took office as President, he appointed Eula Bingham as head of OSHA and charged her to make the agency more effective. One fairly early step was to require OSHA officials to hold regional forums to hear complaints and do something about them. However, regional forums are not necessary to air complaints. The criticisms are well known.

Safety standards six years later.   The general conclusion of most experts is that the agency's standards are unreadable, arbitrary, overly specific, too oriented toward trivia, too costly to implement, and unworkable.[62] As an example of the trivia in the OSHA standards in circulation, in a publication on ranch safety it suggested to ranchers that "since dangerous gases come from manure pits, you should be careful not to fall into manure pits." I don't suppose many ranchers willingly fell into them, with or without dangerous gases. Exhibit 17–9 is an example of the kind of critical material that is being circulated.

A more critical condition than the poor quality of the standards is the fact that many of them originally were not in written form. In the first five years, only three new sets of standards were written; many others are still in the process. OSHA has difficulty writing standards for existing technology, but it *really* has problems with new technologies where no standards exist. It is very difficult to adjust old standards to new technologies.

OSHA is under attack from many directions and is giving way on some standards; for example, it is not going to enforce the standards for small

EXHIBIT 17–9
OSHA standards critiqued

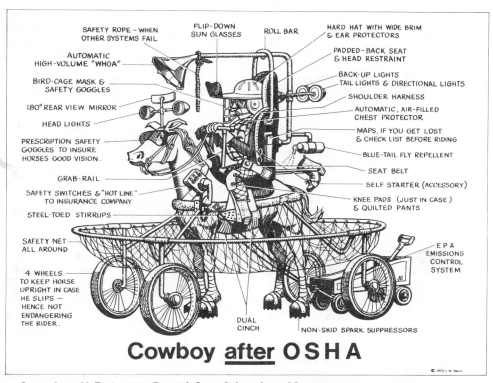

Cowboy **after** OSHA

Source: James N. Devin, 11906 East 37th Street, Independence, Missouri 64052.

businesses. It is trying to get rid of some of its more ridiculous requirements, such as placing field toilets within five minutes' walk of all agricultural workers. OSHA is also trying to rewrite its standards to make them more readable.[63] And it has been required by the courts to justify some of its standards, as in *AFL–CIO* v. *Brennan.*

What is needed is a whole new strategy for standard setting and enforcement.[64] In the same way OSHA did not try to inspect all industries equally but created priorities based upon known hazardous occupations, all standards should not have equal emphasis. In the standards already set, the readability should be improved. More importantly, the agency should categorize the subparts of the standards into categories based on likelihood of accident or illness. These might be:

Most important.   To be enforced at once and fully.

Of average importance.   To be enforced later and in the spirit, not the letter, of the regulation.

Desirable.   To be enforced when the most important standards and those of average importance are in full compliance.

If the standards were publicized to highlight these weights, employers could live with OSHA a bit more easily.

In 1977, OSHA responded to criticisms of its standards. It revoked or said it would minimally enforce 10 percent of the 1977 standards and would try to eliminate more which are trivial and/or outdated. Further progress like this will be appreciated by most enterprises.

Consequences of inspections.   To enforce the law, on-site inspections are required. The records of the first several years of enforcement show:

1970–71 . . . . 29,255 locations inspected; 45 percent penalized.
1972 . . . . 36,100 inspections, with 125,400 violations and fines of $3,121,000.
1970–73 . . . . 95 percent of all sites *not* inspected.
1973 . . . . 98 percent of violations were nonserious; average fine $18.
1974 . . . . 150,000 inspections by state officials; 54,461 federal inspections.
1975 . . . . From January to August; 42,791 citations issued, with fines of $6,121,638, an average of $743.

OSHA does not inspect each industry with equal frequency. Initially, they set up five target industries to be inspected often because of their high rates of accidents: longshoring; roof and sheet metal work; meat packing; miscellaneous transportation (mobile homes), and lumber and wood products. Later foundries and casting and metal-stamping industries were added to the target industries list. Target health hazard industries are those involving asbestos, carbon monoxide, cotton dust, lead, and silica. The ten areas where violations were found most frequently are given in Exhibit 17–10.

An employer who wishes to appeal a violation citation can do so within OSHA, through the Occupational Safety and Health Review Commission,[65]

EXHIBIT 17–10
OSHA's terrible 10

Area of violation	Violations in fiscal year 1975	Penalties levied (in thousands)
National Electrical Code requirements (from loose wires to ungrounded equipment)	37,273	$493.3
Safety of abrasive wheel machinery	6,662	37.1
Construction and placement of compressed gas containers	6,196	59.0
Marking of exits	6,121	14.1
Safety of pulleys in mechanical power-transmission gear	6,037	75.6
Maintaining portable fire extinguishers	5,965	29.6
Safety of drives in mechanical power-transmission gear	5,431	53.2
Guarding floor and wall openings, platforms, and runways	5,321	140.2
General housekeeping requirements (from unmopped puddles to flammable rubbish piles)	5,204	74.8
Effectiveness of machinery guards	4,779	157.3

Data: OSHA
Source: "Why Nobody Wants to Listen to OSHA," *Business Week,* June 14, 1976, p. 67.

or through the federal courts. The Commission is a three-member body (one each from government, labor, and business) and is designed to be independent. About 95 percent of the citations are accepted without appeal to the Commission or the court.

Generally speaking, neither management nor labor has been happy with the inspections, one side claiming too few, the other too many.[66] If the cases now in court (such as *Barlow's* v. *Usery*) and past cases such as *Camara* v. *Municipal Court of Chicago, Colonnade Catering* v. *U.S.,* and *U.S.* v. *Biswell* are upheld, the present inspection system will fall apart.

Because of a shortage of inspectors and these court cases, and because OSHA recognizes that it cannot enforce the law without the employers' help, the agency has begun to emphasize voluntary compliance.[67] This consists of educational programs and "dry run" inspections in which the employer is advised of hazards but is given a chance to correct them before a citation is issued. Current OSHA administration would like to shift to a service or advisory approach rather than fines and citations. Congress appears ready to approve a program in which OSHA will advise employers if a visit is desired and will not issue citations on that visit.

The inspection process also is being abused by some employees. The *Business Week* article cited above reports a number of instances in which employees threatened employers with notifying OSHA that a safety inspection was needed unless they received special treatment. To the extent that this happens, inspectors are misallocated from more needed locations.

There are serious problems with OSHA's inspection system, and developing a helpful, voluntary compliance system makes a great deal of sense. The target-industry strategy should be continued, with the industry list revised with changing statistics. Employers should try to abide by the standards, cooperate with the inspectors, and if unfairly treated, take the case through OSHA channels, the courts, and their congressmen.

Consequences of recordkeeping and reporting. Few people would quarrel with the need to keep adequate records on accidents and health and to calculate accident ratios. It seems reasonable for them to be recorded and reported in a standardized way, for ease in summarizing. But OSHA has been severely criticized for the amount of paper work required and the frequent changes in it.

The Commission on Federal Paperwork was especially critical of OSHA in 1976, when it issued a complex study of job-safety paperwork which made 26 separate recommendations to the Secretary of Labor. The commission suggested that employers with fewer than 100 workers be exempt from keeping logs of injuries and illnesses, that the government assume the cost of monitoring the medical condition of workers in hazardous plants, and that certain duplicate reports required of companies and state governments be dropped.

David Ignatius reports on the trials and tribulations of the Vulcan Corporation, which he considers to be typical of most medium-sized firms today. He found that a typical plant-level personnel manager's workload allocated 20 percent of the time to OSHA paper work. This takes the personnel executive away from more fruitful work, including safety training. Ignatius reports on another typical paper work bungle. He says:

> The government's inability to handle its own paperwork may be the surest sign that the problem has gotten out of hand. After a lengthy OSHA inspection of Vulcan's Cook County, Illinois foundry last October, Vulcan awaited a formal record of the citations, promised by the inspectors within four weeks. The company was still waiting last May when a second pair of OSHA inspectors showed up for an inspection. "We told them fine, but that we'd never received our first set of citations," Mr. Suprock recalls. After a hurried phone call back to headquarters, the embarrassed inspectors departed. Several days later the first citations, somehow misplaced for over six months, arrived at the plant.[68]

Overall evaluation of OSHA

How can we evaluate a program which in 1975 cost enterprises $3.2 billion to implement, not counting the costs of wages and salaries? So far, there is only impressionistic evidence on the "It's doing a great job" versus "It's a failure" issue. Ashford, who had great hopes for OSHA, concluded his Ford Foundation report in 1976 by saying "The OSHA Act has failed thus far to live up to its potential for reducing job injury and disease."[69] And John Ahern, director of safety for General Motors, pointed out that although GM was spending $15 per car to implement OSHA, and although up to 1975 GM had been inspected 614 times, received 258 citations, and spent $29,000,000 to fulfill the requirements (and 11,000,000 *man-years* to get in compliance) "there was no correlation between meeting OSHA's regulations and reduction of accidents."[70]

On the positive side, one study reported a 30 percent drop in meat-packing accidents (one of OSHA's target industries) since the agency came into being and attributes this to OSHA regulations.[71] Another study reports decreased accidents in utilities since OSHA regulations took effect.[72] OSHA claims that in 1975 injuries were down 16 percent and deaths down 10 percent from 1974. How much of this was due to unemployment and non–OSHA causes is not known.[73] One expert says workers like OSHA three times better than the state plans,[74] and in general, OSHA does seem to be making progress in research through the National Institute of Occupational Safety and Health, which it has reorganized into seven divisions and three administrative groups. It has begun to build a strategy for safety research and a systematic way to set target-industry strategies.[75]

Ultimately, whether OSHA succeeds or fails depends on a decrease in the number and severity of accidents and the incidence of occupational disease in the working population. OSHA's annual reports are phrased in bureaucratic "success" terms such as increases in numbers of inspections, pamphlets printed, and dollars of research spent. Until it can show that the *costs* of enforcement are exceeded by *benefits* in terms of reduced accidents and fewer disease victims, we shall have to wait and see whether the program should be called a success or a bureaucratic nightmare.[76]

Surely, some of the changes discussed above must be implemented before OSHA will receive the support it needs from industry and the public.[77] And OSHA can become more effective if the unions and workers involve themselves more in safety. There is evidence that safety is becoming an important union goal in collective bargaining, and this should reinforce the OSHA thrust.[78]

Still management feels that an important factor is not presently covered in OSHA's approach: the worker's responsibility for his or her own health and safety. All the responsibility is placed on *management.* For example, if employees wish to skip medical tests to determine if they are developing an occupational disease, OSHA has ruled they can. If an employee refuses to cooperate in safety matters and an OSHA inspector finds a violation, the *company* is held responsible. For example, there are many instances of employees refusing to wear the safety equipment required by OSHA. If the inspector sees this, he *fines the company.* All the company can do is discipline the employee or possibly fire him.

What can the operating manager or personnel specialist do to help keep the enterprise in compliance with OSHA? The personnel specialist should know the standards that apply to the enterprise and check to see that they are being met. Personnel is also responsible for keeping OSHA records up to date and filing them on time. The operating manager must know the standards that apply to her or his unit or department and see that the unit meets the standards.

As citizens, all managers should see to it that OSHA is effective at the enterprise. But they can also write their representatives to improve it so that:

- Standards are understandable and focus on important items.
- Advisory inspections are permitted.
- Records and reports are minimized and efficient.

Together, managers and OSHA can make safety and health at work a reality.

EMPLOYEE SAFETY AND HEALTH IN CANADA

The need for management to provide safe conditions at work, collect accident and fatality statistics, investigate accidents, and so on is the same in Canada as in the United States. The Canadian federal service has a health and safety program,[79] but this section will focus on the activity in the private and third sectors.

Part IV of the Canada Labour Code (Safety of Employees) incorporates the provisions of the Canada Labour Safety Code of 1968. Part IV provides for the elements of an industrial safety program, authorizes regulations to deal with occupational safety problems, and complements other federal laws and provincial legislation. Advisory committees and special task forces to assist in developing the program, with continuous consultation among federal and provincial government departments, industry, and organized labour was authorized, and research into causes and prevention of accidents for an extended safety education program is provided for.

As of January 1975, regulations existed governing coal mine safety, elevating devices, first aid, machine guarding, noise control, hand tools, fire safety, temporary work structures, confined spaces, lighting, boilers and pressure vessels, building safety, dangerous substances, electrical safety, materials handling, protective clothing and equipment, sanitation, hours of service in the motor transport industry, and accident investigation and reporting.

The provincial legislatures have the power to enact laws and regulations concerning the protection of workers against industrial accidents or diseases. Legal standards designed to ensure the safety, health, and welfare of persons employed in industrial and commercial establishments, in mines and quarries, and in other work places exist in all provinces. The authorities responsible for the administration of such standards are, in the main, the Departments of Labour, Health and Mines, and the Workers' Compensation Boards.

Safety inspection is provided for in all provinces. An inspector has the power to implement any matter regulated by the legislation. Penalties exist if an employer contravenes any provision of an occupational safety act or regulation or neglects to comply with a direction made by a safety inspector.

The regulations change regularly, and the effective personnel manager keeps up with them as reported in the literature.[80]

As regards safety and health regulations, it appears that Canada is where the United States was prior to passage of OSHA in 1970. Canadians have the opportunity to develop a system which is less antagonistic and troublesome than OSHA if they will learn from our mistakes.

WORKERS' COMPENSATION AND DISABILITY PROGRAMS

Disability programs are designed to help workers who are ill or injured and cannot work. These programs were mentioned in Chapters 15 (Exhibit 15–2 indicated employees showed little preference for them) and Chapter 16.

There are three programs in the United States for private- and third-sector employees. One is federal; the social security system is called OASDI, and the "DI" stands for disability insurance. A person who is totally disabled and unable to work can receive a small payment, perhaps $60 a week, from social security until age 65. As with other social security programs, this is financed by employer and employee payroll contributions.

The second program is the state-run workers' compensation,[81] financed by employer payments, which pay for permanent partial, total partial, or total disability arising out of the employment situation.[82] Requirements, payments, and procedures vary somewhat from state to state. Workers' compensation systems are compulsory in most states.[83] For federal government employees, the Federal Employees Compensation Act of 1949 (last amended in 1974) provides for payments for accidents and injuries paralleling workers' compensation.

The compensation comes in two forms: monetary reimbursement, and payment of medical expenses. The amount of compensation is based on fixed schedules of minimum and maximum payments. Disability payments are often based on formulas of the employee's earnings, modified by economic conditions such as the number of dependents. There is usually a week's waiting period prior to the payment of the compensation and fixed compensation for permanent losses (such as $200 for loss of a finger).

The employee receives workers' compensation no matter whose fault an accident is. Payment is made for physical impairments and for neuroses which may result from a physical loss. The employer must also pay compensation for diseases which result from occupations (such as black lung disease in mining) and for the results of undue stress laid on employees, such as hernias resulting from lifting heavy materials. Both workers' compensation laws and OSHA require the employer to keep detailed accident and death records.

The employer pays the entire cost of workers' compensation, usually by participating in private insurance plans or state-run schemes. The improvement of safety conditions at the work site can lead to lower insurance costs if accidents decline as a result.

The cost of workers' compensation varies by industry and type of work. For example, in a recent year, all of the private sector paid less than 1 percent of its total compensation for workers' compensation. This varied from 1.5 percent for nonoffice, nonmanufacturing jobs to a low of 0.03 percent for office employees. The total cost of workers' compensation has almost doubled in the past ten years, however.[84]

In some states, if the employee will receive social security disability payments, workers' compensation is adjusted so that a joint maximum (for example $80 per week) is not exceeded. Usually workers' compensation begins to be paid after a loss of a week's work.

Criticism of workers' compensation programs centers on the fact that the system was designed to prevent hardship but not to discourage return to work or rehabilitation of the injured worker.[85] The National Commission on State Workers' Compensation was very critical of state workers' compensation plans in effect in 1972, considering the benefits to be too low, and finding that too many employers had inadequate accident prevention programs. The Commission made 80 specific recommendations to the states which, if not actuated, should be legislated by the Congress.[86] Researchers have found substantial movement toward these standards since, [87] but some managers are opposed.[88] One reason may be that the funds are close to bankruptcy, perhaps because of fraud as well as increased benefits.[89]

One final comment. When the OSHA legislation was passed, many felt it was not needed, since an industry incentive for safety could be provided by substantially increasing the workers' compensation payments required of firms whose accident rates were too high. Further, employers could receive the safety advice they needed from the state. Perhaps this would have worked better.

The third program under which employees receive workers' compensation is private disability insurance provided by employers. One study found that about two thirds of the companies surveyed provide accident and sickness insurance to their employees (usually for blue-collar workers).[90] A variation for white-collar workers is sick pay—salary continuance insurance; 85 percent of the companies had this. These plans pay wages or salaries to employees with short-term disabilities; generally they supplement workers' compensation. Long-term disability pay or pensions for employees was also being offered by 74 percent of companies for managers, 62 percent for white-collar employees, and 28 percent for blue-collar workers. This insurance is designed to supplement government programs and bring total compensation up to a more livable level.

Workers' compensation and disability programs in Canada

Workers' compensation in Canada is similar to the program in the United States, but the workers' compensation laws are all at the provincial and territorial levels. In the provinces compensation is provided for workers in most types of industries, for personal injuries in the course of employment, unless the disablement is for less than a stated number of days or is attributable *solely* to the worker's serious and willful misconduct and does not result in death or serious disablement. Compensation is also payable for specified industrial diseases. The laws change, and regular updates such as Michel Gauvin's reports, are helpful in keeping the managers up to date.[91]

Benefits for disability are based on a percentage of average weekly earnings, subject to an annual ceiling. Persons having a permanent or temporary total disability are presumed not to be able to work at all and receive 75 percent of their average weekly earnings for as long as the disability lasts. Partial disablement entitles a worker to proportionate compensation.

The funds for workers' compensation are paid in by employers, with the rate of payment varying with the hazards in the industry. They are fixed by the workers' compensation board. In the midsixties, about $500 million was paid yearly in workers' compensation to disabled Canadians.

EVALUATION OF SAFETY AND HEALTH PROGRAMS

Health and (especially) safety programs have begun to receive more attention in recent years. The consequences of inadequate programs are measurable: increased workers' compensation payments, larger insurance costs, fines from OSHA, and union pressures.

George Odiorne indicates how a safety management program can be developed.[92] The steps include:

- Establishment of indicator systems (for example, accident statistics).
- Development of effective reporting systems.
- Development of rules and procedures.
- Rewarding supervisors for effective management of the safety function.

An effective safety system is diagrammed in Exhibit 17–11. Management support is needed, and proper design of jobs and man-machine interactions is necessary, but probably the key is participation by employees. The exhibit gives the factors likely to affect employee participation and the positive effects on the organization of such a participative safety program.

A health and safety program can be evaluated fairly directly in a cost/benefits sense. The costs of safety specialists, new safety devices, and other measures can be calculated. Reductions in accidents, lowered insurance costs, and lowered fines can be weighed against these costs. In one good study evaluating safety and health programs, Rollin Simonds has shown that safety is cost effective.[93]

In a very sophisticated study, Foster Rinefort interviewed 54 respondents and received questionnaires from 86 more in the chemical, paper, and wood-product industries in Texas. Rinefort found that the most cost-effective safety programs were *not* the most expensive ones. Rather they were programs which combined a number of safety approaches: safety rules, off-the-job

EXHIBIT 17–11

Scheme for development of an interaction influence system through participation in plant safety programs

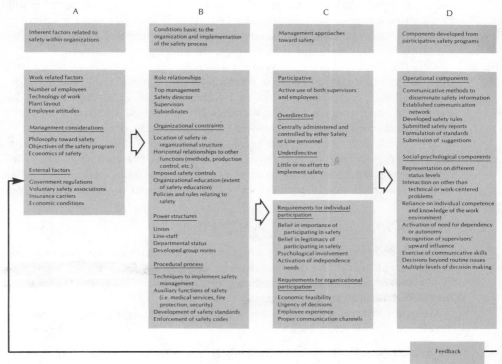

Source: Roderick Forsgren, "A Model of Supportive Work Conditions through Safety Management," *Personnel Journal*, May 1969, pp. 351–58.

safety, safety training, safety orientation, safety meetings, medical facilities and staff, and strong top management participation and support of the safety program.[94] Engineering and nonengineering approaches were used, but the emphasis was on the engineering aspects of safety. Thus cost/benefits studies for health and safety programs can be very helpful in analyzing and improving them.

SUMMARY, CONCLUSIONS, AND RECOMMENDATIONS

Effective safety and health programs can exist in all enterprises. The nature of the safety program varies, as the diagnostic approach emphasizes. Some clues to this are given in the propositions below:

Proposition 17.1. The more pressure from government and unions is exerted, the more emphasis will be given to health and safety programs by employers.

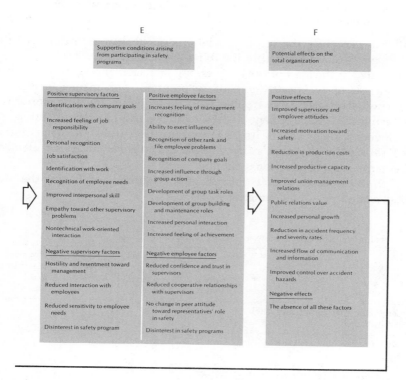

E

Supportive conditions arising from participating in safety programs

F

Potential effects on the total organization

Positive supervisory factors

Identification with company goals

Increased feeling of job responsibility

Personal recognition

Job satisfaction

Identification with work

Recognition of employee needs

Improved interpersonal skill

Empathy toward other supervisory problems

Nontechnical work-oriented interaction

Negative supervisory factors

Hostility and resentment toward management

Reduced interaction with employees

Reduced sensitivity to employee needs

Disinterest in safety program

Positive employee factors

Increases feeling of management recognition

Ability to exert influence

Recognition of other rank and file employee problems

Recognition of company goals

Increased influence through group action

Development of group task roles

Development of group building and maintenance roles

Increased personal interaction

Increased feeling of achievement

Negative employee factors

Reduced confidence and trust in supervisors

Reduced cooperative relationships with supervisors

No change in peer attitude toward representatives' role in safety

Disinterest in safety programs

Positive effects

Improved supervisory and employee attitudes

Increased motivation toward safety

Reduction in production costs

Increased productive capacity

Improved union-management relations

Public relations value

Increased personal growth

Reduction in accident frequency and severity rates

Increased flow of communication and information

Improved control over accident hazards

Negative effects

The absence of all these factors

Proposition 17.2. The more emphasis on health and safety, the more will organizations create safety departments and health facilities.

Proposition 17.3. The larger the organization, the more likely it is to have a health facility.

Proposition 17.4. The greater the health hazards in the workplace, the more likely the organization is to have a health facility.

Proposition 17.5. The larger the organization, the more likely it is to have a safety department.

Proposition 17.6. The more hazards there are in the workplace, the more likely is the employer to have a safety department.

Proposition 17.7. The more employees participate in the design of safety programs and training, the more effective will the program be in reducing accidents.

Proposition 17.8. The more support top management and union gives to health and safety, the more effective will the program be.

Proposition 17.9. The more approaches the organization uses to its safety and health program (such as inspections, training, motivation), the more effective will the program be.

Exhibit 17–12 gives the recommendations on health and safety for the model organizations described in Exhibit 1–14, Chapter 1.

As indicated at the start of the chapter, top management support is crucial for the success of the health and safety program. Top management does not want to be fined or have trouble with the government. But more than that, effective top management desires to make the health and safety of the employees a major goal of its personnel function and strategic planning. This will satisfy the employee's safety needs and create an important element in the enterprise's organizational climate.

Chapter 18 discusses EEO/Human Rights programs and begins the unit on group related personnel functions.

EXHIBIT 17–12
Recommendations on health and safety for model organizations

Type of organization	Formal safety department	Safety as duty of personnel specialist	Formal health department	Arrange-ment with health team
1. Large size, low complexity, high stability	X		X	
2. Medium size, low complexity, high stability	X			X
3. Small size, low complexity, high stability		X		X
4. Medium size, moderate complexity, moderate stability	X			X
5. Large size, high complexity, low stability	X		X	
6. Medium size, high complexity, low stability	X			X
7. Small size, high complexity, low stability				X

QUESTIONS

1. How do top managers, operating executives, employees, union officials, safety committees, and safety specialists interact to make the workplace healthy and safe?
2. What diagnostic factors are most important in health and safety?
3. Why do enterprises set up safety and health programs?
4. What are safety hazards? Health hazards?

5. How dangerous is it to work in the United States and Canada? Which places are the most risky?

6. What causes accidents and work-related illnesses?

7. Describe the programs enterprises have to prevent accidents and illnesses. Which are most effective? Least effective?

8. Why did the U.S. government legislate in the occupational safety and health area? What are the major laws affecting work safety?

9. What legal requirements must an enterprise follow in the health and safety area?

10. Evaluate the relative success or failure of OSHA, the U.S. health and safety agency. What can be done to improve its future operations?

11. Compare and contrast Canadian with U.S. agencies and regulations on safety and health.

12. What is workers' compensation? Why does it exist? What does it do?

13. Compare and contrast U.S. and Canadian workers' compensating programs.

14. Describe a cost/benefit study of health and safety.

15. What are the most significant propositions for Chapter 17? The most significant recommendations for the model organizations?

NOTES AND REFERENCES

1. *Accident Facts,* National Safety Council, 1976 edition; Nicholas Ashford, *Crisis in the Workplace: Occupational Disease and Injury: A Report to the Ford Foundation* (Cambridge, Mass.: MIT Press, 1976) ch. 1, 3; International Labour Office, *Yearbook of Labour Statistics* (Geneva, Switzerland, 1976), ch. 8; U.S. Department of Labor, *Occupational Safety and Health Statistics of the Federal Government* (Washington, D.C.; Occupational Safety and Health Administration, 1976); U.S. Department of Labor, *Injury Rates by Industry,* 1975 (Washington, D.C.: Bureau of Labor Statistics, 1976).

2. Ashford, *Crisis in the Workplace.*

3. Statistics in this section are from sources given in Note 1.

4. Roy LaBerge, "On-the-Job Health Hazards Abound," *The Labour Gazette,* June 1976, pp. 308–9; "Unions Seek Safer Working Conditions," *The Labour Gazette,* November 1975, pp. 816–21; "Employment Fatalities in Canada," *The Labour Gazette,* June 1976, pp. 323–27.

5. Jules Asher and Janet Asher, "Psychological Consequences of On-the-Job Injury," *Job Safety and Health,* March 1976, pp. 5–11.

6. Ashford, *Crisis in the Workplace;* Paul Burgess and Jerry Kingston, "The Effect of Health on Duration of Unemployment," *Monthly Labor Review,* April 1974, pp. 53–54; *The Personnel Executive's Job* (Englewood Cliffs, N.J.: Prentice-Hall/ASPA, 1977).

7. "Labor Letter," *The Wall Street Journal,* November 21, 1976.

8. "Labor Letter," *The Wall Street Journal,* December 21, 1976.

9. "Unions Seek Safer Working Conditions," *The Labour Gazette.*

10. William Johnson, "Sequences in Accident Causation," *Journal of Safety Research,* June 1973, pp. 54–59; William Johnson, "MORT: The Management Oversight and Risk Tree," *Journal of Safety Research,* March 1975, pp. 4–15; Norman Maier, *Psychology in Industrial Organizations* (Englewood Cliffs, N.J.: Prentice-Hall, Inc., 1974), pp. 479–539; Jerry Ramsey, "Identification of Contributory Factors in Occupational Injury," *Journal of Safety Research,* December 1973, pp. 260–67.

11. LeBerge, "On-the-Job Health Hazards Abound."

12. Herbert Hohn, "Occupational Safety and Health Research: New Challenges," *Journal of Safety Research,* June 1972, pp. 53–59.

13. R. M. Harano et al., "The Prediction of Accident Liability through Biographical Data and Psychometric Tests," *Journal of Safety Research,* March 1975, pp. 16–52; J. B. Gordon et al., *Industrial Accident Statistics: A Re-examination* (New York: Frederick A. Praeger, Inc., 1971).

14. G. V. Barrett and C. L. Thornton, "Relationship between Perceptual Style and Driver Reaction to an Emergency Situation," *Journal of Applied Psychology,* 52, 2 (1968), pp. 169–76.

15. P. Barbarik, "Automobile Accidents and Driver Reaction Pattern," *Journal of Applied Psychology,* 52 (1968), pp. 49–54; C. A. Drake, "Accident-Proneness: A Hypothesis," *Character and Personality,* 8 (1940), pp. 335–41; J. T. Kunce, "Vocational Interests and Accident Proneness," *Journal of Applied Psychology,* 51 (1967), pp. 223–25.

16. W. N. McBain, "Arousal, Monotony, and Accidents in Line Driving," *Journal of Applied Psychology,* 54 (1970), pp. 509–19.

17. H. M. Schroder, "Safety Performance Measurement," *Journal of Safety Research,* September 1970, pp. 188–95; Paul Schugsta, "The Theory of Accident Proneness and the Role of the Poisson Distribution," *ASSE Journal,* November 1973, pp. 24–28.

18. Maier, Psychology in Industrial Organizations; Joseph Tiffin and Ernest McCormick, *Industrial Psychology* (Englewood Cliffs, N.J.: Prentice-Hall, Inc., 1974).

19. James Gardner, "Employee Safety," in *Handbook of Modern Personnel Administration,* ed. Joseph Famularo (New York: McGraw-Hill Book Co., 1972), ch. 48; James Gardner, *Safety Training for the Supervisor* (Reading, Mass.: Addison-Wesley Publishing Co., 1969).

20. Leon Schenkelbach, *The Safety Management Primer* (Homewood, Ill.: Dow Jones–Irwin, Inc., 1975).

21. Doris Baldwin, "Industry's Secret Weapon: The Safety Committee," *Job Safety and Health,* July 1974, pp. 14–19; G. R. Carnahan, "Using Safety Committees Effectively," *The Personnel Administrator,* 19, 2 (1974), pp. 46–49; J. M. Lyons, "Safety: The Company, the Committee and the Committed," *Personnel Journal,* 51 (1972), pp. 95–98, 137; Albert Mims, "Are Safety Committees Useful?" *Job Safety and Health,* March 1974, pp. 22–23; G. R. Atherley et al. "Workers' Involvement in Occupational Health and Safety in Britain," *International Labor Review,* June 1975, pp. 469–82.

22. Rollin Simonds, "OSHA Compliance: Safety Is Good Business," *Personnel,* July–August, 1973, pp. 30–38; Charles Walters, "Management of the Safety and Health Function to Help Attain Productivity Objectives," *ASSE Journal,* September, 1974, pp. 39–43.

23. Virginia Reinhart, "Ergonomic Studies Improving Life on the Job," *Job Safety and Health,* December, 1975, pp. 16–21.

24. "System Safety Spreads into Industry," *Business Week,* July 17, 1971.

25. "How Fast The Assembly Line," *ASSE Journal,* November 1973, pp. 17–19; Maier, *Psychology in Industrial Organizations,* pp. 449–56; Tiffin and McCormick, *Industrial Psychology,* pp. 479–88; 533–34.

26. Gardner, "Employee Safety."

27. "Costly Hazards Prompt One Company to Take Safety into Workers' Homes," *The Wall Street Journal,* November 16, 1976.

28. See, for example, Michael Heschel, "Hazards Reduction Improves Safety," *Industrial Engineering,* March 1974, pp. 8–11; Maier, *Psychology in Industrial Psychology.*

29. Murray Blumenthal, "An Alternative Approach to Measurement of Industrial Safety Performance," *Journal of Safety Research,* September 1970, pp. 123–30; C. West Churchman,

"Suggestive, Predictive, Decisive and Systematic Measurement," *Journal of Safety Research,* September 1970, pp. 131–36; Herbert Jacobs, "Towards More Effective Safety Measurement Systems," *Journal of Safety Research,* September 1970, pp. 160–75; Thomas Rockwell and Vivek Bhise, "Two Approaches to a Nonaccident Measure for Continuous Assessment of Safety Performance," *Journal of Safety Research,* September 1970, pp. 176–87.

30. John Grimaldi, "The Measurement of Safety Engineering Performance," *Journal of Safety Research,* September 1970, pp. 137–58; William Haddon, *Accident Research Methods and Approaches* (New York: Harper & Row, 1964).

31. C. Richard Anderson, *OSHA and Accident Control through Training* (New York: Industrial Press, 1975).

32. See, for example, Lee Ellis, "A Review of Research on Efforts to Promote Occupational Safety," *Journal of Safety Research,* December 1975, pp. 180–89; Gary Mitler and Neil Agnew, "First Aid Training and Safety," *Occupational Psychology* 47 (1973), pp. 209–18.

33. Gardner, *Safety Training for the Supervisor;* L. Smith, "Let's Wed J.I.T. and J.S.A.," *National Safety News,* January 1970.

34. S. Rubinsky and N. Smith, "Safety Training by Accident Simulation," *Journal of Applied Psychology,* 57 (1973), pp. 68–73.

35. Roger Dunbar, "Manager's Influence on Subordinates' Thinking about Safety," *Academy of Management Journal,* June 1975, pp. 364–69; Dan Peterson, "The Effectiveness of Safety Programs," *ASSE Journal,* August 1973, pp. 22–26; Lawrence Schlesinger, "Are You Getting Your People Involved in Your Safety Communications?" *ASSE Journal,* January 1973, pp. 25–27.

36. Russell DeReamer, *Modern Safety Practices* (New York: John Wiley & Sons, 1958); F. G. Lippert, "Role Conflict and Ambiguity in Enforcing Safe Work Practice," *Journal of American Society of Safety Engineers,* No. 5 (1968), pp. 12–14.

37. See, for example, Andrew Czernek and George Clark, "Incentives for Safety," *Job Safety and Health,* October 1973, pp. 7–11; Robert McKelvey et al., "Performance Efficiency and Injury Avoidance as a Function of Positive and Negative Incentives," *Journal of Safety Research,* June 1973, pp. 90–96.

38. See, for example, Ann Stresan, "Do Safety Award Plans Pay Off?" *Journal of the American Society of Safety Engineers,* March 1969; David Hampton, "Contests Have Side Effects, Too," *California Management Review,* 12, 4 (1970), pp. 86–94.

39. Dan Peterson, "The Future of Safety Management," *Professional Safety,* January 1976, pp. 19–26.

40. D. W. Jones, "Implementing a Safety Audit," *ASSE Journal,* November 1973, pp. 20–23.

41. Rockwell and Bhisi, "Two Approaches to a Nonaccident Measure of Safety Performance."

42. Bureau of National Affairs, *Services for Employees,* Personnel Policies Forum Survey 105 (Washington, D.C.: March 1974); David Graulich, "Doctor's Dilemma," *The Wall Street Journal,* October 8, 1975; Patricia O'Brien, "Health, Safety and the Corporate Balance Sheet," *Personnel Journal,* August 1973, pp. 725–29.

43. Bernard Burbank, "Employee Health," in *Handbook of Modern Personnel Administration,* ed. Joseph Famularo (New York: McGraw-Hill Book Co., 1972), ch. 49.

44. P. M. Yarvote et al., "Organization and Evaluation of a Physical Fitness Program in Industry," *Journal of Occupational Medicine,* 16 (1974), pp. 589–98.

45. R. B. Buzzard, "A Practical Look at Industrial Stress," *Occupational Psychology* 47 (1973), pp. 51–61; Lawrence Loban, "Mental Health and Company Progress," *Management Review,* December 1966; Frank Uhlmann, "Put the Supervisor on the Couch, Not the Employee," *Public Personnel Review,* April 1971, pp. 110–12.

46. Burbank, "Employee Health."

47. H. T. Ludlow, "Becoming the Boss's Patient," *Conference Board Record* 9, 7 (1974), pp. 37–41; S. Lusterman, *Industry Roles in Health Care* (New York: Conference Board, 1974); H. W. Richmond, "Health Care Delivery in Cummins Engine Company," *Archives of Environmental Health*, 29 (1974), pp. 328–35.

48. Benjamin Brown, "A Law Is Made," *Labor Law Journal*, October 1974, pp. 595–606.

49. Alfred Blumrosen et al., "Injunctions against Occupational Hazards: The Right to Work under Safe Conditions," *Industrial Relations Law Journal* 1 (1976), pp. 25–38.

50. Doris Baldwin, "Caution: Office Zone," *Job Safety and Health*, February 1976, pp. 4–12; OSHA, "OSHA Proposes New Health Standards," *Job Safety and Health*, December 1975, pp. 10–15; "U.S. Issues Voluntary Guides to Protect Worker from Lead, Mercury, and Silica," *The Wall Street Journal*, July 27, 1976; Gail Bronson, "Exposure of Workers to Epichlorohydrin Should Be Slashed, Federal Scientists Say," *The Wall Street Journal*, September 30, 1976; Gail Bronson, "Confrontation of Dupont, Health Agency Is Sparked by Employee's Cancer Worries," *The Wall Street Journal*, February 11, 1977; "Lower Exposure to Cotton Dust Seen for Workers," *The Wall Street Journal*, December 24, 1976; "Labor Agency Cancels Its Safety Exemption on Industrial Talcs," *The Wall Street Journal*, February 3, 1977; James Hyatt, "U.S. Plan to Cut Worker Exposure to Lead Raises Economic, Legal, Moral Questions," *The Wall Street Journal*, March 16, 1971; Joachim Wohemill et al., "Behavioral Effects of a Noisy Environment," *Journal of Applied Psychology*, February 1976, pp. 67–74; Neil Weinstein, "Noise, Intellectual Performance," *Journal of Applied Psychology* 62, 1 (1977), pp. 104–10.

51. J. Wade Mitler, "OSHA: The Big Reach," *Personnel*, September–October 1976, pp. 45–53.

52. "Occupational Safety and Health Standards," *Federal Register*, June 27, 1974.

53. OSHA, *Compliance Operations Manual*, January 1976; OSHA, *General Industry Standards and Interpretations*, yearly volumes.

54. OSHA, "General Industry Safety and Health Checklist," *Job Safety and Health*, September 1974.

55. OSHA, "OSHA Inspections," *Job Safety and Health*, July 1975, pp. 17–21; Jon Sargent, "Other People's Business Is Their Business," *Occupational Outlook Quarterly*, Spring 1973, pp. 2–14; Ralph Wirfs, "New Man on the Beat," *Job Safety and Health*, October 1973, pp. 16–20; Ralph Wirfs, "An Industrial Hygienist Inspects a Plant," *Job Safety and Health*, April 1973, pp. 2–8.

56. "Justices Uphold Right of Job Safety Unit to Set Penalties without Going to Court," *The Wall Street Journal*, March 24, 1977.

57. "Justices to Hear Test of Job Unit's Safety Checks," *The Wall Street Journal*, April 19, 1977, p. 14.

58. Barry Brown, "OSHA and the States," *Job Safety and Health*, October 1974, pp. 25–27; OSHA, *How States Plan for Job Safety and Health* (Washington, D.C., 1976); Sally Seymour, "The Federal Role in Job Safety and Health: Forging a Partnership with the States," *Monthly Labor Review*, August 1973, pp. 28–34; John Sheehan, "OSHA and State Job Safety Plans," *Monthly Labor Review*, April 1974, pp. 44–46; John Stender, "OSHA; The States and Safety Professional," *ASSE Journal*, December 1973, pp. 10–12; Barry White, "What the States Have to Match," *Job Safety and Health*, July 1975, pp. 24–29.

59. Blumrosen et al., "Injunctions Against Occupational Hazards"; Norman Wood, "Environmental Law and Occupational Health," *Labor Law Journal*, March 1976, pp. 152–62.

60. "Labor Letter: Reluctant State Plan to Copy Weakened Federal Job Safety Rules," *The Wall Street Journal*, October 12, 1976; "Labor Letter," *The Wall Street Journal*, October 19, 1976.

61. *Business Week,* June 14, 1976.

62. Ibid.; Robert Moran, "Are Job Safety Standards Understandable?" *The Personnel Administrator,* March–April 1974, pp. 22–25; Robert Moran, "Our Job Safety Law Should Say What It Means," *Nation's Business,* April 1974, pp. 23–26; "Putting Trivia Ahead of Safety," *Time,* May 3, 1976, pp. 65–66.

63. Chuck Beek, "Getting Through to OSHA," *Job Safety and Health,* May 1975, pp. 17–21; Richard Berman, "Making the Act Workable," *Job Safety and Health,* January 1976, pp. 27–31; Morton Corn, "A New Posture for OSHA," *Labor Law Journal,* May 1976, pp. 259–64.

64. Fred Foulkes, "Learning to Live with OSHA," *Harvard Business Review,* November–December 1973, pp. 57–67.

65. Robert Moran, "How to Obtain Job Safety Justice," *Labor Law Journal,* July 1973, pp. 387–404; John Tavela, "If a Citation Is Appealed," *Monthly Labor Review,* August 1973, pp. 43–47; Frank Sartwell, "When OSHA Faces the Judge," *Job Safety and Health,* February 1974, pp. 11–15; Timothy Clearly, "Pleading and Practice before OSHA Review Commission," *Labor Law Journal,* December 1973, pp. 779–87; Timothy Cleary, "A Court of Conscience," *Job Safety and Health,* October 1975, pp. 26–30.

66. John Zalusky, "The Worker Views the Enforcement of Safety Laws," *Labor Law Journal,* March 1975, pp. 224–35.

67. Ralph Wirfs, "Voluntary Compliance," *Job Safety and Health,* June 1975, pp. 11–14; *OSHA, A Guide to Voluntary Compliance,* OSHA 2222 (Washington, D.C., 1975); Dominick Daniels, "The Tip of the Iceberg," *Job Safety and Health,* February 1976, pp. 28–32; James Foster, "OSHA Launches Voluntary Compliance Course," *Job Safety and Health,* January 1973, pp. 15–24; Darold Barnum, and John Gleason, "A Penalty System to Discourage OSHA Violations," *Monthly Labor Review,* April 1976, pp. 30–31.

68. David Ignatius, "Paper Weight," *The Wall Street Journal,* July 16, 1976.

69. Ashford, *Crisis in the Workplace.*

70. "Why Nobody Wants to Listen to OSHA," *Business Week,* June 14, 1976.

71. Lawrence Ettkin and J. Brad Chapman, "Is OSHA Effective in Reducing Industrial Injuries?" *Labor Law Journal,* July 1975, pp. 236–49.

72. Joseph Yaney et al., "Environmental Changes in the Workplace," *Proceedings,* Midwest Academy of Management, 1974, pp. 235–46.

73. "Job Related Injuries; Illnesses and Deaths Fell Substantially in 1975, Agency Says," *The Wall Street Journal,* December 9, 1976.

74. Zalusky, "Worker Views Enforcement."

75. Herbert Hohn, "Research to Determine What's Dangerous," *Monthly Labor Review,* August 1973, pp. 48–52; John Inzana, "A New Survey of Occupational Injuries and Illnesses," *Monthly Labor Review,* August 1973, pp. 53–55; Frank Sartwell, "Statistics Can Save Lives," *Job Safety and Health,* October 1973, pp. 3–11; Lyle Schauer and Thomas Ryder, "New Approach to Occupational Safety and Health Statistics," *Monthly Labor Review,* March 1972, pp. 14–19.

76. OSHA, *Annual Report to the President,* yearly; Phyllis Lehmann, "Two Years of OSHA," *Job Safety and Health,* June 1973, pp. 2–7; William Steiger, "OSHA: Four Years Later," *Labor Law Journal,* December 1974, pp. 723–28; John Stender, "An OSHA Perspective and Prospective," *Labor Law Journal,* February 1975, pp. 71–78.

77. "Government Intervention," *Business Week,* April 4, 1977, pp. 42–56.

78. Bureau of National Affairs, *OSHA and the Unions* (Washington, D.C., 1973); Frank Ferris, "Resolving Safety Disputes: Work or Walk," *Labor Law Journal,* November 1975, pp. 695–

709; John Irving, "The Inter-Relationships between CMRA and Policy Considerations Covering Industrial Safety," *ASSE Journal,* January 1973, pp. 25–31; George Koons, "Negotiation Experience and Future Anticipated Trends in the Areas of Job Safety and Health," *ASSE Journal,* January 1973, pp. 32–34; Walter Mossberg, "Jobs and Safety," *The Wall Street Journal,* August 19, 1974; Donald Peterson, "Management Perception of Changes in Union Management Relations Due to OSHA," *Industrial Management,* November 1973, pp. 11–15; Sheldon Samuels, "A Greater Voice for the Worker," *Job Safety and Health,* February 1974, pp. 23–26; Jack Sheehan, "You Can't Bargain about A Safe Environment," *Job Safety and Health,* September 1974, pp. 29–31; Joseph Summer, "Criteria for Health and Safety Arbitration," *Labor Law Journal,* June 1975, pp. 366–74; Winston Tillery, "Safety and Health Provisions before and after OSHA," *Monthly Labor Review,* September 1975, pp. 40–43; Leonard Woodcock, "Occupational Safety: Promise and Opportunity," *Professional Safety,* January 1976, pp. 31–32.

79. *Occupational Health and Safety* (Ottawa: Treasury Board, Information Canada, 1974).

80. See, for example, Michel Gauvin, "Labour Legislation in 1975: Part 3, Industrial Safety and Health," *Labour Gazette,* May 1976, pp. 270–72.

81. Formerly called workmen's compensation.

82. For details on workers' compensation, see Ann Davis, "Workmen's Compensation," in *Handbook of Modern Personnel Administration,* ed. Joseph Famularo, ch. 51 (New York: McGraw-Hill Book Co., 1972).

83. States where the program is voluntary are Montana, Colorado, New Mexico, Texas, Kansas, Missouri, Louisiana, Alabama, Georgia, South Carolina, North Carolina, Tennessee, Kentucky, Indiana, Pennsylvania, West Virginia, Vermont, and Maine.

84. U.S. Department of Labor, Bureau of Labor Statistics, *Employee Compensation in the Non-Farm Economy* (Washington, D.C.: U.S. Government Printing Office, 1976).

85. William Johnson and Edward Murphy, "The Response of Low Income Households to Income Losses from Disability," *Industrial and Labor Relations Review,* 1975–1976, pp. 85–96.

86. Robert Paul, "Workers' Compensation: An Adequate Employee Benefit?" *Academy of Management Review* 2 (1977); John Burton, "Workers' Compensation Reform," *Labor Law Journal,* July 1976, pp. 399–406.

87. Amy Hribal and G. M. Minor, "Workers' Compensation—1975 Enactments," *Monthly Labor Review,* January 1976, pp. 30–36; Jonathan Laing, "Better Benefits," *The Wall Street Journal,* Febraury 25, 1974.

88. "Another Costly Headache for the Employer," *Nation's Business,* June 1974, pp. 36–38.

89. "Scandals: Get Mine," *Time,* August 23, 1976, pp. 54–55; "Labor Letter: Worries Grow About the Health of the Social Security Disability Fund," *The Wall Street Journal,* October 5, 1976.

90. Meyer and Fox, Chapter 16, 1st edition; *Early Retirement Programs* (New York: National Industrial Conference Board, 1971).

91. These are updated yearly. A recent one is Michel Gauvin, "Labour Legislation in Canada 1975: Part V: Workers' Compensation," *The Labour Gazette,* September 1976, pp. 495–97.

92. Odiorne, George, *Personnel Administration by Objectives* (Homewood, Ill.: Richard D. Irwin, Inc., 1971), ch. 14.

93. Simonds, "OSHA Compliance."

94. Foster Rinefort, *A Study of Some Costs and Benefits Related to Occupational Safety and Health in Selected Texas Industries,* unpublished Ph.D. thesis, Texas A & M University, 1976; Foster Rinefort, "A New Look at Occupational Safety," *Personnel Administrator,* November 1977, pp. 29–36.

Equal employment opportunity programs

CHAPTER OBJECTIVES

■ To demonstrate what equal employment opportunity is and why it is important.

■ To discuss how to run an effective EEO program.

■ To describe how to meet the legal requirements for equal employment opportunity.

CHAPTER OUTLINE

INTRODUCTION

The world has changed a great deal in the past 15 years or so. If you had read a personnel book in the first half of the sixties you would have found the term "equal employment opportunity" barely mentioned. Certainly, an entire chapter would not have been devoted to it. Moreover, if you had examined prevailing employment practices, you would have found these conditions present in many enterprises:

> Women were employed only as low-level clerical personnel, and they were paid less than men doing comparable work and seldom promoted. Generally, it was believed women worked only until they got married or to supplement their husbands' incomes.

> Blacks, Hispanics, Japanese, Chinese, Filipinos and American Indians were employed only in the lowest level blue-collar and service jobs.

> Older employees were laid off when managers felt they could replace them with more energetic, younger employees demanding lower compensation

> Employees of certain religious groups (especially Jews and Catholics) were excluded from all but the lowest level jobs in certain banks and large firms.

Before you conclude that the world of work in the early sixties was a horrible one for minorities, you should realize that these attitudes and conditions were not universal. Many employers participated in voluntary programs to increase the hiring of minorities and others who are now protected against discrimination in employment. They cooperated with Goodwill Industries to hire the handicapped or had ties to the black community through the Urban League or pastors who referred likely prospects for employment. Some unions made a genuine effort to accept minority apprentices or journeymen. A sense of social responsibility induced some employers to run their own equal employment opportunity (EEO) programs, with little or no profit or other monetary rewards in return. Still, discrimination existed—in business, government, hospitals—in all employment sectors.

Today, unprecedented changes in employers' attitudes and hiring practices have led to conditions such as these:

> Minorities and women are getting jobs that in the past were considered exclusively white male occupations, such as underground mining; in 1976 the first woman miner was killed on the job. The first woman commercial pilot was Emily Howell, for Frontier Airlines.

> Firms in the service industries are being sued for employment discrimination. Some recent cases include Dean Witter and Merrill Lynch (stock brokerage), Fireman's Fund (insurance), Chase Manhattan (banking), United Airlines, and NBC (television).

Note: This chapter was co-authored by James Ledvinka of the University of Georgia.

Manufacturing firms also are enduring costly lawsuits alleging discrimination in employment opportunities. Examples include UniRoyal (tires), Allyn & Bacon and Addison-Wesley (publishers), General Electric, and Gulf Oil.

Even the government has been named a defendant in discrimination cases. Recently the City of Chicago, the U.S. Army, and ex-President Ford were sued.

Similar accusations are being directed toward universities and other not-for-profit enterprises like hospitals, as well as toward professional groups such as the law firm of Crevath, Sevaine, and Moore (New York).

DEFINITION

Equal employment opportunity programs are operated by employers to prevent employment discrimination in the workplace or to take remedial action to offset past employment discrimination.

Equal employment opportunities is one of the most significant activities in the personnel function today. In the recent Prentice-Hall/ASPA survey of 1,400 personnel executives, the respondents labeled it as one of the big three of such activities.[1] Personnel managers and specialists are spending 14.2 percent of their time on EEO: not just compliance, but full EEO implementation. This is expensive; typical yearly amounts devoted to the activity as reported in the survey were:

$1,000, $5,000, $6,000, $7,200 (small manufacturers).

$3,000, $10,000, $20,000, $30,000 (medium-sized manufacturers).

$30,000, $45,000 (public utilities).

$2,500, $5,000, $10,000, $12,000, $34,000 (hospitals).

$1,000, $8,000 (retail stores).

$5,000, $13,000, $20,000, $25,000, $110,000 (government agencies).

Of the 1,400 company representatives surveyed, 18 percent reported they had established full-time EEO offices, and 15 percent had hired new employees to handle EEO. Exhibit 18–1 shows in which industries EEO officers and new executives were hired most frequently.

EEO cuts across a number of personnel activities, and various personnel officials and others are involved, as Exhibit 18–2 indicates. Top managers must also get involved in EEO/human rights issues and programs to make sure that the enterprise is in compliance with the law, to avoid fines, and to establish a discrimination-free workplace.

EEO is in an early stage of development, probably between Stage II and Stage III as defined in Exhibit 1–13 in Chapter 1. The effectiveness of EEO

EXHIBIT 18–1
Staffs to handle Title VII (EEO) compliance

Industry	Companies reporting full-time EEO officers	Companies reported hiring new employees for EEO duties
Manufacturing (under 500 employees)	8.7%	7.0%
Manufacturing (500–999)	9.8	4.7
Manufacturing (1,000–4,999)	20.1	16.3
Manufacturing (over 5,000)	68.0	60.9
Research and development	23.1	20.0
Public utilities	35.7	25.0
Hospitals	4.8	7.8
Retail stores	8.7	7.0
Banks	18.6	16.3
Insurance companies	18.5	15.5
Transportation and distribution	13.0	17.4
Government agencies	55.0	47.5
Education	53.1	46.7
Nonprofit organizations	3.8	22.2
Other	20.4	15.7

Source: *The Personnel Executive's Job* (Englewood Cliffs, N.J.: Prentice-Hall/ASPA, 1977).

depends on the strength of top management's commitment to it. This can be either reinforced or countered by the influence of the unions.

EEO affects all aspects of the personnel function, as noted in preceding chapters. For example, the ingredients of an EEO program for women might be:

- A new focus in employment planning.
- A more sophisticated position evaluation system.
- Increased recruiting, selection, and orientation of women.
- Reassessment of compensation and benefits provided women.
- Awareness of evaluation of women.
- More training and development of women.

EXHIBIT 18–2
Responsibility for compliance with Title VII (EEO)

Function	Person assigned responsibility*				
	EEO specialist	Recruiter	Personnel generalist	Psychologist or specialist	Line supervisors
Testing.........................	4.1%	9.6%	46.7%	6.5%	1.9%
Validation	5.4	3.2	39.2	8.9	0.8
Recruiting	4.6	23.6	64.4	0.4	4.4
Recordkeeping and reporting	12.5	6.1	77.0	0.5	2.1
Affirmative action program	18.3	3.7	68.9	0.5	5.8
Community relations; outreach programs	12.0	5.5	63.4	0.2	3.7

* These do not total 100 percent because at some companies Title VII tasks are shared, while at others some tasks are not performed at all.

Source: *The Personnel Executive's Job* (Englewood Cliffs, N.J.: Prentice-Hall/ASPA, 1977).

A DIAGNOSTIC APPROACH TO EQUAL EMPLOYMENT OPPORTUNITIES

Exhibit 18–3 highlights the key factors in the diagnostic model of the personnel function which affect the provision of equal employment opportunities. Some of these were noted in the introduction above: union requirements, goals of controlling interests, and personnel activities involved. Others are discussed below: societal values, attitudes and preferences of workers as reflected in economic status of minorities and women, and government regulations. Knowledge of these factors can contribute to an understanding of why EEO developed and how it operates.

HOW EEO EMERGED

The three main influences on the development of EEO were: (1) changes in societal values, (2) the economic status of women and minorities, and (3) the emerging role of government regulation. The first two are discussed below; information on the third factor is so detailed it is considered in a separate section.

Societal values and EEO

For over 2,000 years, Western society has accepted the principle that people should be rewarded according to the worth of their contributions. When the United States became a nation, that principle was embodied in the American dream: the idea that any individual, through hard work, could advance from the most humble origins to the highest station, according to the worth of her or his contributions. In America, success did not depend on being born into a privileged family; equal opportunity was everyone's birthright. To this day, the American dream, with its emphasis on merit rather than privilege, is widely accepted by the American public.[2]

Another value that has encouraged equal opportunity is the profit motive: Nondiscrimination makes good business sense. If a company limits opportunities to white males, it cuts itself off from the vast reservoir of human talent comprised of women and minorities. Moreover, it adds to such societal problems as poverty, crime, high taxes, and civic disorder, which also hurt the business community.

Up to the early sixties it was not unusual for people, while believing in the American dream of rewards based on merit, to also believe that blacks (and other minorities) had their "place"—a place largely cut off from the rewards that the majority received. This apparent contradiction in beliefs was the American dilemma observed by the distinguished Swedish economist Gunnar Myrdal in his studies of American race relations for the Carnegie

EXHIBIT 18–3
Factors affecting equal employment opportunities and organizational effectiveness

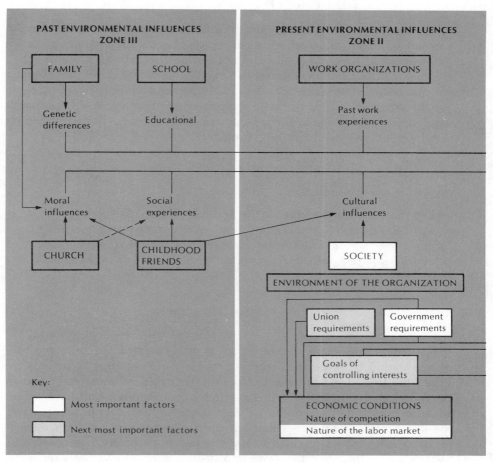

Corporation.[3] Blacks were often excluded from schools, public accommodations, jobs, and voting, and economic realities for blacks belied the ideals of the American dream.

The disparity between American ideals and American realities lent special significance to the civil rights conflict of the 1960s. The conflict began in Montgomery, Alabama, on December 1, 1955, when Mrs. Rosa Parks, a black department store worker in her fifties, was arrested for refusing to give up her bus seat to a white man. Out of that single act of protest emerged a previously unthinkable act—a bus boycott by blacks. At the center of the boycott was a loosely knit group called the Montgomery Improvement Association, which chose as its leader a new young minister in town, Dr. Martin Luther King, Jr.

Then came years of demonstrations, marches, and battles with the police

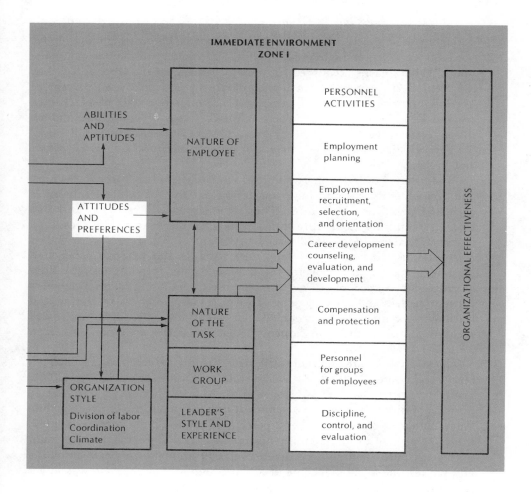

which captured headlines throughout most of the early 1960s. Television accounts included scenes of civil rights demonstrators being attacked with cattle prods, dogs, and fire hoses. These events shocked the public into recognition that civil rights was the most critical social problem of the time in the United States. Gradually, overt discrimination declined and recognition of the problems faced by minorities grew. The business community shared in this attitude change, voluntarily supporting such EEO-related efforts as the National Alliance of Businessmen.[4]

As the U.S. Congress turned its attention to civil rights, laws were passed prohibiting discrimination in education, voting, public accommodations, and the administration of federal programs, as well as discrimination in employment. The civil rights movement was instrumental in raising congressional concern and stimulating the passage of this legislation.

Economic status of women and minorities

Undeniable economic inequality helped focus national attention on employment as a specific area of discrimination. Unemployment figures for blacks were twice as high as for whites, and higher still among nonwhite youth. While blacks accounted for only 10 percent of the labor force, they represented 20 percent of total unemployment and nearly 30 percent of *long-term* unemployment. Moreover, in 1961, only one half of black men worked steadily at full-time jobs, while two thirds of white men did so. Blacks were three times as likely as whites to work less than full time.[5] Similar statistical differences existed for other minorities, such as Hispanics and Indians.

When they did find work, minorities were relegated to lower status jobs, and consequently their income was far below that of whites. Minorities such as blacks were over three times as likely as whites to be unskilled laborers; whites were over three times as likely as blacks to be in professional or managerial positions. While only 9 percent of black men were skilled craftsworkers, 20 percent of white men were. In the tobacco, paper, and trucking industries, blacks were ordinarily segregated into less desirable lines of progression or sections of the company. In the building trades, they were concentrated in the lower paying "trowel trades," such as plastering and bricklaying. Some unions excluded blacks entirely, and others organized separate locals for them. In carpentry, blacks actually *lost* ground between 1910 and 1969.[6]

The inequalities are especially striking in the income comparisons between blacks and whites. In 1962, the average family income for blacks was $3,000, compared with nearly $6,000 for whites. More importantly, the relative position of blacks had been worsening during the preceding ten years; while black family income was only 52 percent of white family income in 1962, it was 57 percent of white family income in 1952.[7] These inequalities could not be attributed entirely to differences in educational level between blacks and whites: the average income of a black high school graduate was lower than the average income of a white elementary school graduate.[8]

Facts and events such as these led to the passage of laws designed to bring about economic equality. Recent evidence that things have not improved much since then is prompting Congress, the courts, and the presidency to strengthen those laws.[9]

A related influence is the changing aspirations of women and minorities. One of the biggest changes has been the increasing need and desire of women to be fully employed. Often two incomes are needed, and many young women today seek to free themselves from the kinds of family ties that interfere with outside work, and may choose not to have children or not to marry. The number of family units with two workers or more (normally male and female adults) grew from 36 to 49 percent of the total, from 1970 to 1975.[10] Moreover, large numbers of unmarried women are now heads of families with children. And, as societal attitudes have changed, larger numbers of blacks, Hispanics and other minorities are attempting to enter the labor force, while older Americans are seeking to reenter it. All these persons trying more actively to find work constitute another pressure on the EEO effort.

GOVERNMENT REGULATION OF EEO PROGRAMS

In the United States, there are many laws and executive orders prohibiting employment discrimination. Exhibit 18–4 gives a brief summary of the more important ones. Since it would be impossible to discuss all of them in a single chapter, this chapter will consider Title VII of the 1964 Civil Rights Act and Executive Order 11246. Considerable understanding of the entire legal framework can be gained by considering how these operate.

Title VII of the 1964 Civil Rights Act

Employers, unions, employment agencies, and joint labor-management committees controlling apprenticeship or training programs are prohibited from discriminating on the basis of race, color, religion, sex, or national origin by Title VII of the 1964 Civil Rights Act. Other laws protect the aged, the handicapped, and special classes of veterans. Title VII prohibits discrimination with regard to any employment condition, including hiring, firing, promotion, transfer, compensation, and admission to training programs. The Equal Employment Opportunity Act of 1972 amended Title VII by strengthening its enforcement and expanding its coverage to include employees of state and local governments and of educational institutions, as well as private employment of more than 15 persons. However, Indian tribes and private membership clubs are not covered, and religious corporations may discriminate on the basis of religion in some cases. Federal government employees are also covered by Title VII, but enforcement is carried out by the Civil Service Commission with procedures that are unique to federal employees.

The EEO coverage of government employees is noteworthy. While discrimination has been illegal in government employment since the end of the spoils system and the advent of open competitive examinations in the public service, race and sex inequalities have persisted in the public service. The "merit system" in government employment has had a mixed record— some of its features have held back minorities over the years. Now, with the 1972 amendments to Title VII, public administrators are finding themselves subject to the same sorts of EEO burdens that managers in private enterprise have shouldered since the passage of Title VII in 1964.[11]

One clause of Title VII permits employers to discriminate based on sex, religion, or national origin if these attributes are a "bona fide occupational qualification." This seems like a loophole, but it is a small one indeed. For instance, courts have said that the clause does not allow an employer to discriminate against women simply because they feel that the work is "inap-

EXHIBIT 18–4
Antidiscrimination laws and orders, United States

Federal law	Type of employment discrimination prohibited	Employers covered
U.S. Constitution, 1st and 5th Amendment	Deprivation of employment rights without due process of law	Federal government
U.S. Constitution, 14th Amendment	Deprivation of employment rights without due process of law	State and local governments
Civil Rights Acts of 1866 and 1870 (based on 13th Amendment)	Race discrimination in hiring, placement, and continuation of employment	Private employers, unions, employment agencies
Civil Rights Act of 1871 (based on 14th Amendment)	Deprivation of equal employment rights under cover of state law	State and local governments (private employers if conspiracy is involved)
National Labor Relations Act	Unfair representation by unions, or interference with employee rights, that discriminates on the basis of race, color, religion, sex, or national origin	Private employers and unions
Equal Pay Act of 1963	Sex differences in pay for substantially equal work	Private employers (state and local governments uncertain)
Executive Order 11141 (1964)	Age discrimination	Federal contractors and subcontractors
Title VI, 1964 Civil Rights Act	Discrimination based on race, color, or national origin	Employers receiving federal financial assistance
Title VII, 1964 Civil Rights Act (as amended in 1972 by the Equal Employment Act of 1972	Discrimination or segregation based on race, color, religion, sex, or national origin	Private employers with 15 or more employees; federal, state, and local governments; unions and apprenticeship committees; employment agencies.
Executive Orders 11246 and 11375 (1965)	Discrimination based on race, color, religion, sex, or national origin (affirmative action required)	Federal contractors and subcontractors
Age Discrimination in Employment Act of 1967	Age discrimination against those between the ages of 40 and 65	Private employers with 20 or more employees, unions with 25 or more members, employment agencies, apprenticeship and training programs (state and local governments uncertain)
Title I, 1968 Civil Rights Act	Interference with a person's exercise of rights with respect to race, religion, color, or national origin	Persons generally
Executive Order 11478 (1969)	Discrimination based on race, color, religion, sex, national origin, political affiliation, marital status, or physical handicap	Federal government
Revenue Sharing Act of 1972	Discrimination based on race, color, national origin, or sex	State and local governments receiving revenue-sharing funds
Education Amendments of 1972	Sex discrimination	Educational institutions receiving federal financial assistance
Rehabilitation Act of 1973; Executive Order no. 11914 (1974)	Discrimination based on physical or mental handicap (affirmative action required)	Federal contractors, federal government
Vietnam Era Veterans Readjustment Act of 1974	Discrimination against disabled veterans and Vietnam era veterans (affirmative action required)	Federal contractors, federal government
Age Discrimination Act of 1975	Age discrimination	Employers receiving federal financial assistance
State laws State fair employment practices laws	Similar to Title VII and Equal Employment Act of 1972	Varies by state; passed in about 85% of states

propriate" for them, or because customers might object. The most celebrated example of this reasoning was the decision in *Diaz* v. *Pan American Airways* that an airline could not limit its employment of flight attendants to women.[12] At the time, the idea of a male flight attendant was unheard of, but that was not a legal justification for Pan American's refusal to hire Diaz in that position.

When is sex a bona fide occupational qualification? One obvious but unusual situation is when one sex is by definition unequipped to do the work—as in the case of a wet nurse. Another is when the position demands one sex for aesthetic authenticity—as in the case of a fashion model. A third instance is when one sex is required for a position in order to satisfy basic social mores about modesty—as in the case of a locker room attendant. And that is about all. Clearly, the bona fide occupational qualification clause is virtually useless as a defense against charges of discrimination for most employers.

Executive Orders 11246 and 11375 were issued by President Lyndon B. Johnson in 1965, superseding President John F. Kennedy's Executive Order 10925. Employment discrimination by federal government contractors, subcontractors, and federally assisted construction contracts is prohibited. While Executive Order 11246 prohibits the same actions as Title VII does, it carried the additional requirement that contractors must develop a written plan of affirmative action and establish numerical integration goals and timetables to achieve equal opportunity. The affirmative action planning requirement is discussed in greater detail later in this chapter.

Virtually every state also has some form of equal employment law; 41 states, plus the District of Columbia and Puerto Rico, have comprehensive state "fair employment" laws similar in operation to Title VII. In fact, some of these state laws antedate Title VII. If a state's law is strong enough, charges of discrimination brought under Title VII are turned over by the federal government to the state fair employment practices agency, which has the first chance at investigating it.[13]

Another recent legal development is the proposed Equal Rights Amendment to the Constitution. At the time of this writing, almost all the legislatures necessary for a constitutional amendment have passed it, but several have rescinded their votes, and the legality of this move is not clear. Even if ERA were passed it would probably have little effect on employment. Title VII appears to be stronger legal medicine than ERA, and it covers most all the employment settings ERA does. The biggest exception is the military, which Title VII does not cover—and we can only speculate on the effects of ERA there.

Discrimination: A legal definition

All the laws discussed above are designed to eliminate discrimination. Would you believe the laws never defined it? It's true; the courts have had to do this when they interpret the laws. The courts arrive at definitions by looking at the history behind a statute, examining the *Congressional Record* to gain insight into the social problems Congress hoped it would solve. Then they define terms like "discrimination" in a way to help solve these problems. For Title VII, the history of the civil rights conflict clearly identifies the problems: economic inequality and the denial of employment opportunities to blacks and other minorities.

The courts have defined discrimination in three different ways since the first days of federal involvement in employment practices.[14] Initially, during World War II, discrimination was defined as *prejudiced treatment:* harmful actions motivated by personal animosity toward the group of which the target person was a member. However, that definition was ineffective as a means of solving the problem of economic inequality because it is difficult to prove harmful motives, and that made it difficult to take action against many employment practices that perpetuated inequality.

Then the courts redefined discrimination to mean *unequal treatment.* Under this definition, a practice was unlawful if it applied different standards or different treatment to different groups of employees or applicants. This definition outlawed the practice of keeping minorities in less desirable departments (different treatment), and it also outlawed the practice of rejecting women applicants with preschool-aged children (different standards). The employer was allowed to impose any requirements, so long as they were imposed *on all groups alike.*

Yet even though many of the most common job requirements, such as education and testing, were imposed on all groups equally, they had an adverse effect on blacks. Usually, blacks were less able to meet educational requirements and less likely to attain a passing score on employment tests. The problem with the unequal-treatment definition of employment discrimination, then, was that it allowed employers to impose requirements that minorities were less likely than whites to pass—even when those requirements had no relationship to the job in question. This threatened to leave blacks and other minorities in the same disadvantaged status that prevailed prior to Title VII.

To enable Title VII to solve the social problems that Congress wanted it to, the U.S. Supreme Court arrived at the third definition of employment discrimination: *unequal impact.* In the case of *Griggs* v. *Duke Power Co.,*[15] the Court struck down employment tests and educational requirements that screened out a greater proportion of blacks than whites. These practices were prohibited because they had the consequence of excluding blacks disproportionately, *and* because they were not *related* to the jobs in question. The practices were apparently not motivated by prejudice against blacks, and they certainly were applied equally: both whites and blacks had to pass the requirements. But they did have an adverse impact on blacks.

The unequal-impact definition is important to managers, because many traditional personnel practices have a built-in unequal impact on race, sex, religion, or national origin groups. Examples are numerous: The minimum height and weight requirements of many police departments have unequal impact because they tend to screen out women, Orientals, and Hispanics disproportionately. Such requirements have been struck down by the courts.[16] The policy of discharging employees for getting their wages attached or garnished to pay off debts, which tends to fall heavily on minorities, has also been struck down.[17] The same is true of automatically rejecting job applicants with arrest records[18] or even criminal records.[19]

The only defense for employment practices that have an unequal impact on employer is that the practices are job-related or otherwise necessary to the safe and efficient operation of the enterprise. It may sound easy for a company to show that its practices are job-related and necessary; if they were not, why would the company continue to use them? But in fact employers have had a difficult time defending their practices in court. The reason is that the courts have held employers to a very demanding standard of job-relatedness or business necessity. The U.S. Supreme Court has said that employers wishing to defend tests that have unequal impact must follow the guidelines issued by the Equal Employment Opportunity Commission.[20] These guidelines require extensive research to determine the job-relatedness of the test. Because of the stringent demands, many employers have given up their tests.[21]

Nevertheless, if an employment practice that has an adverse impact serves a *legitimate need,* and if there is *no alternative* that has less of an adverse impact, it is usually worthwhile for the organization to try to defend that practice. Sometimes it can be defended without extensive research or data collection. For instance, United Airlines defended their experience requirements for pilot trainees largely by appealing to the Court's common sense.[22] The requirements tended to exclude black trainees disproportionately, but United had carefully and critically considered its requirements and decided they were necessary. Then they collected some basic statistics showing that pilots with more experience were more successful in training. The Court accepted United's argument, but this is not to say that all courts would have been persuaded, or that all practices are so easy to defend. It does argue against abandoning practices that demonstrably serve a business need.

A two-question criterion. By way of a summary, the criterion for EEO and affirmative action compliance or noncompliance can theoretically be reduced to two questions:

Does an employment practice have unequal impact on the groups covered by the law? (race, sex, religious or national origin groups).

Is that practice job-related or otherwise necessary to the organization?

The practice is prohibited *only* if the answers to *both* questions are unfavorable. Even practices that are unnecessary and irrelevant to the job are legal if they have equal impact on the groups covered by the law. This means that employers do not have to validate tests or follow the employee selection regulations if their tests do not exclude one group disproportionately.

This two-question approach does have some exceptions, and getting a straight answer to the second question is especially difficult because of the stringent guidelines that employers must follow. Nevertheless, the two questions are a good place to begin in understanding EEO and affirmative action.

Some believe that, because new cases are constantly being decided and guidelines are undergoing important changes, EEO programs are in a period of total uncertainty. Nevertheless these two basic questions remain as underlying principles through all the changes.

Enforcement agencies and regulations

Most employment discrimination laws provide for enforcement agencies, which issue the regulations that affect personnel administrators most directly. Exhibit 18–5 provides an overview of the complex agency scene, showing some of the principal laws, the agencies that enforce them, and the guidelines issued by these agencies. The units of government *most* responsible for enforc-

EXHIBIT 18–5
Partial summary of major employment discrimination laws and orders, enforcement agencies, and regulations

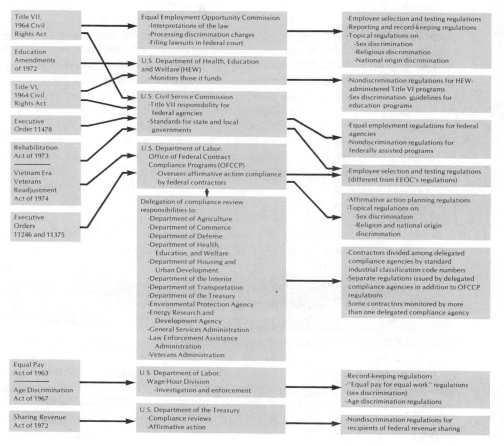

ing the regulations considered here are the U.S. Equal Employment Opportunity Commission (EEOC) and the federal courts, which enforce Title VII; and the Office of Federal Contract Compliance Programs (OFCCP), which enforces Executive Order 11246.

Equal Employment Opportunity Commission. Title VII originally gave EEOC the rather limited powers of resolving charges of discrimination and interpreting the meaning of Title VII. Later, in 1972, Congress gave EEOC the power to bring lawsuits against employers in the federal courts, but the agency still does not have the power to issue directly enforceable orders, as many other federal agencies have. Thus EEOC cannot order an employer to discontinue a discriminatory practice, nor can it direct an employer to give back pay to victims of discrimination. However, EEOC has won these things in out-of-court settlements, and it has made effective use of the limited powers it does have. It has won considerable respect from the legal community for its interpretations of the law, not to mention an understandable deference from employers who wish to avoid problems.[23]

One EEO requirement is the reporting of employment statistics. All employers of 100 or more employees subject to Title VII (as amended) and the executive orders must submit form EEO–1 or a similar form provided for that purpose. This form reports employment by sex, race, and other protected categories by broad job classifications (for example, managerial). Multiple-establishment enterprises must file a report for each establishment of 25 or more employers.

EEOC combines these data and reports the aggregate patterns in *Job Patterns for Minorities and Women in Private Industry.* This information makes it possible to analyze patterns by industry, job category, metropolitan area, and in many other ways.

EEOC's major activity is the processing of discrimination charges brought by those who believe themselves to be the victims of discrimination. The preinvestigation division of EEOC's charge-processing operation interviews each complainant to determine whether the complaint falls within the coverage of Title VII. If it does, then the charge is turned over to the state or local fair employment practice agency. But if there is no agency with adequate powers in the state, the preinvestigation division notifies the employer that a charge has been made, phrases the complaint in a legally correct way, and passes it on to an investigation division.

The investigation division attempts to interview the parties concerned with the alleged discrimination and to collect facts that might have a bearing on the charge. Ordinarily, the inspection division's staff are the first EEOC personnel with whom the employer comes into contact. EEOC inspectors have the power to obtain many types of information from the employer, even information that is difficult or costly to assembly, or that seems irrelevant to the charge being made. Thus, for example, in the course of investigating a charge by a black female that she has been discharged unfairly, the inspector might ask the employer for a complete census of each job classification by race and sex and a list of all disciplinary actions that had been taken over a certain long period of time. Chances are that the request for information will include many other pieces of information too. If the employer resists, EEOC can often back up its requests for information with a court order.

When the investigation indicates that the charge of discrimination was unfounded, the matter ends there, as far as EEOC is concerned. But if there appears to be some basis for the charge, EEOC will attempt to bring about an agreement between the employer and the charging party. This process is called *conciliation*. A conciliation agreement is more or less an out-of-court settlement. It may be a stringent settlement, with considerable back pay and numerical hiring ratios. If the employer accepts the settlement, then the matter ends there.

But if conciliation efforts fail, EEOC may decide to file suit in federal district court and pursue the matter further. More frequently, however, EEOC will choose not to file suit. Still, the complainant can file suit on his or her own. Court enforcement of Title VII is discussed in a later section of this chapter.

Is the EEOC effective? One way to find out is to review EEOC's annual report.[24] The 11th annual report, appearing in January 1978, reports on data that are two years old at the time of publication. In 1976, EEOC filed 414 lawsuits—up about 100 from 1975. One year later, it had a backlog of over 150,000 cases. When EEOC sought to clear away some of the backlog, its employee union complained this was a speed-up and forced employees to violate the law in processing the cases too hastily. Each year, the agency tries to deal with the backlog by requesting sharp increases in its budget. As a result of the backlog, charges take years to be investigated. During that time, records get lost and memories fade, making it hard for investigators to determine how justifiable the original charge was. Besides that problem, critics claim that investigations are often not conducted competently enough to uncover all the information that is available. This leads to selective enforcement of the law.

The result of these problems is that only a very small percentage of charges ever get resolved by EEOC or the courts. Consequently civil rights advocates are not happy with the agency, and of course, many employers are less than enthusiastic about it (or any regulatory agency, for that matter).

On top of all this, internal audits of the agency led to charges of fraud, illegal use of federal property, failure to submit contracts to competitive bidding, and chaos in the accounting system. The FBI investigated, as did congressional committees. This led to proposals for restructuring of the federal governments EEO work.[25]

In spite of this, EEOC has made legal history, and its combativeness has probably helped to exact favorable settlements from employers. The agency has done much to fulfill the objectives Congress set for it, but it may have to change drastically in order to survive.

Office of federal contract compliance programs. This office was originally established to enforce Executive Order 11246. Now it also enforces laws covering employment of veterans and the handicapped. OFCCP has the power to remove a federal contractor's privileges of doing business with the government, but it seldom exercises that power. OFCCP regulations require that all contractors with over $50,000 in contracts and over 50 employees have a written affirmative action plan on file.

The preparation of the affirmative action plan is governed by an OFCCP regulation commonly known as Revised Order No. 4.[26] This order calls on the employer to survey the external labor market to determine the availability of women and minority group members as potential employees. Then the employer is required to determine the jobs in which women and minorities are underrepresented in the organization. The employer is also called upon to set numerical integration goals and timetables for removing that underrepresentation, and to indicate how employment practices are to be changed in order to attain those goals.

There are numerous problems in complying with Revised Order No. 4. For instance, it is difficult to determine the "availability" of women and minorities for various jobs, because it is virtually impossible to find the statistics listing individuals with the requisite skills who are willing to accept the jobs. Also there is little specific guidance on how to set numerical integration goals, and it is difficult to know whether any given goal is a realistic one. As a result, while some affirmative action plans are effective guides for helping management to bring about equality of opportunity, others turn out to be little more than "boilerplate"—words copied from some "model" affirmative action plan in an effort to satisfy agency officials.

The government can audit or review an affirmative action plan whenever it wishes. Sometimes the reviews are infrequent—usually no more than once every two years.[27] The review is supposed to follow an established pattern that is written into the federal guidelines and is publicly available.[28] This pattern includes seeking out a wide range of information on company operations and reviewing the company's numerical integration goals.

If the investigator decides that the contractor is not in compliance with Executive Order 11246, he may have a "show cause" order issued against the contractor. This triggers a lengthy sequence of administrative decisions and appeals, which can culminate in the contractor being debarred from government contract work. But contractors are disbarred so seldom that critics claim that the threat is ineffectual.[29] Yet managers often treat OFCCP reviews with the same deference that they treat EEOC investigations.

Is the OFCCP effective?   Most studies have found that OFCCP is administratively inept, and a cost/benefit analysis would show submarginal yields for the agency's efforts.[30] Some data have indicated small positive effects on employment gains for black males, a smaller gain for white males, zero or negative effect for other minorities and women, and zero effects on wage and occupational gains on all minority groups.[31] Some experts doubt that OFCCP can alter employment distributions of minorities.[32]

One reason for the ineffectiveness can be seen in Exhibit 18–5 above: OFCCP delegates its compliance review authority to 13 other agencies. It should come as no surprise, then, that contractors complain of conflicting agency regulations.[33] Moreover, the 13 agencies are principally in business for some reason other than equal employment. For instance, the Department of Defense's EEO operation is housed in the bureau that is principally responsible for making sure that defense contracting is carried out well, with the right goods and services delivered at the right time. Undue concern with EEO, however, can impede contract fulfillment. Thus EEO is not an overriding concern in some delegate agencies.[34]

Glen Cain suggests that all the OFCCP does is shift government contracts to firms who employed a large number of minorities before OFCCP existed.[35] Nathan Glazer argues persuasively that OFCCP cannot do the job.[36] And George Johnson and Finis Welch maintain that even if they could,[37] it would have some surprising results:

A significant proportion of skilled minority workers would not be employed.

If reverse discrimination comes into being, whites will be paid substantially less than minorities, and the unemployment rates of whites will increase dramatically.

The incentives for minorities to become highly skilled would be reduced, and the incentive for whites to become highly skilled would be increased.

These are hardly the purposes of OFCCP. But government programs often have quite different results from those they set out to achieve.

Other agencies.   Besides EEOC and OFCCP, other agencies such as the Civil Rights Commission, Civil Service Commission, Treasury Department, Department of Health, Education, and Welfare and others are involved in EEO matters. The conflicts among them have led *Business Week* to call this the "EEO Maze"[38] and *The Wall Street Journal* to ask: "Which federal agency do you obey?"[39] The government's attempt to deal with this diversity is to set up an EEO Coordinating Council to create uniform guidelines—with disappointing results.[40]

The courts

Besides the agencies (federal and state), the courts are constantly interpreting the laws, and these rulings can conflict. Appellate courts then reconcile any conflicts.

All the employment discrimination laws provide for court enforcement, often as a last resort if agency enforcement fails. With regard to Title VII, the federal courts are frequently involved in two ways: settling disputes between EEOC and employers over such things as access to company records, and deciding the merits of discrimination charges when out-of-court conciliation efforts fail.

The legal maneuvering often makes the court enforcement picture confusing, largely because every step of the process is appealable. And with three parties involved—EEOC, the charging party, and the employer—appeals are commonplace. Suppose one party appeals the conclusions made by the first court in the judicial chain, which is a federal district court. The appeal is generally heard by a three-judge panel of a federal court of appeals, which can affirm the district court's opinion, change it, or send it back for the district court to consider more evidence. Sometimes the decision of the three-judge panel is further appealed to a larger group of appeals court judges for the circuit, and that group can also affirm, change, or send the case back. Finally, the appeals court decision can always be appealed to the U.S. Supreme Court, and, if the Supreme Court agrees to hear the case, it too can affirm, change, or send it back. The appeal possibilities are increased further when there is a state or local fair employment practices law, for then the state courts can enter the picture as well.

All these possibilities for trial, appeal, retrial, and even appeal of the retrial can cause several years' delay before the issue is settled. When that delay is added to EEOC's charge-processing delay, the result is discouraging to anyone who wants to see justice served.

A good example is the Georgia Power case.[41] Georgia Power employees first filed discrimination charges with EEOC in 1966. When conciliation efforts failed, the charging parties brought suit in 1968. As time passed, the case expanded into a class action suit, with back pay and jobs sought for a broadly defined group of black employees and job applicants. The subsequent legal maneuvers resulted in at least nine published court opinions and probably several unpublished court opinions, with the case finally resolved in *1974*. During such lengthy delays, two things usually happen: (1) people in the group seeking back pay and jobs give up, take other jobs, move away, or otherwise disappear; and (2) the employer's liability for back pay increases year by year.

Once a final court decision is reached in a Title VII case, it can provide for drastic remedies: back pay, hiring quotas, reinstatement of employees, immediate promotion of employees, abolition of testing programs, creation of special recruitment or training programs, and others. In the Georgia Power case, the court ordered the company to set aside $1.75 million for back pay, and another $388,925 for other purposes. Moreover, the court imposed numerical goals and timetables for black employment in various job classes. If Georgia Power failed to meet the goals, then the court order provided for mandatory hiring ratios: one black for each white was to be hired until the goal percentages were reached. Other courts have ordered companies to give employees seniority credit for the time they have been discriminatorily denied employment.[42]

However, many court orders are not so drastic. Much depends, of course, on the facts surrounding the case. One important factor is whether the employer is making any voluntary efforts to comply with employment discrimination laws. If the company shows evidence of successfully pursuing an affirmative action plan, the court may decide to impose less stringent measures. This is discussed further in the section on costs and benefits of affirmative action plans, later in this chapter.

HUMAN RIGHTS LEGISLATION IN CANADA

There have been similar major changes in societal attitudes toward the equal employment of women and minorities in Canada, where EEO is called human rights. The focal minority in Canada is the French-speaking person; there are also such minorities as Indians and similar native Canadians, women, and immigrants. The contention that they have been discriminated against is supported by statistics,[43] and they have made their case to the Canadian people. Labor force shifts as in the United States also have supported the trend.

A substantial minority of Canadians are of French origin. France was one of two colonizers and ruled a major part of Canada until the eighteenth century. Canada is officially a bilingual country, but many experts contend that French-speaking Canadians were discriminated against in employment, even in Quebec where they are a majority. Recently a party was elected to rule Quebec that included as one of its goals the separation of Quebec from Canada. This government (and its predecessor) passed Bills 25 and 101 which require that only the French language be used in advertisements, outdoor signs, and other communications. Public education in French is now required in most of Quebec's schools. These happenings point up the significance of human rights for Canadians of all ancestries.

The federal and provincial-territorial governments have responded to these complaints with legislation. At the federal level, Part 1 of the Canada Labour Code (Fair Employment Practices), as amended in 1977 by the Canadian Human Rights Act, prohibits discrimination in employment on the basis of age, sex, race, color, religion, national origin, ancestry, place of origin, and marital status. It also protects the physically handicapped and pardoned ex-convicts. Equal pay legislation also exists, and Canada Bill of Rights (1960) touches on discrimination. Up until now, the Bill of Rights has been ignored by the Canadian courts with regard to discrimination.

Human rights is a joint responsibility of Ottawa and the provinces and territories, all of which have passed human rights acts and have commissions to enforce them. Ontario's ombudsmen may also get involved in discrimination cases. There are some differences, but most provincial laws prohibit discrimination to protected categories of people, as in the federal law. Some jurisdictions also prohibit discrimination based on political opinion and physical handicaps.

The human rights commissions (which are appointed) administer the human rights acts in all provinces. In most cases, they investigate complaints of discrimination. Alberta, Nova Scotia, Ontario, and Manitoba have some powers to initiate investigations on their own. The provincial laws prohibit reprisals against those filing complaints to human rights commissions.[44]

EXHIBIT 18–6
Fines for violation of human rights acts in Canada

Individuals	Others	Jurisdiction
$ 100	$ 500	Federal, Newfoundland, Northwest Territories, Yukon
200	1,000	Alberta
500	1,000	Nova Scotia
500	2,000	New Brunswick
1,000	5,000	Ontario, British Columbia
Minimum–Maximum		
$100–1,000	$500–5,000	Manitoba
$100– 500	$200–2,000	Prince Edward Island
$100– 500	$400–2,000	Saskatchewan

Source: "Fines for Violation of Human Rights Acts," Supply and Services Canada, Ottawa, Canada, 1975. Reproduced by permission of the Minister of Supply and Services Canada.

The commissions try first to settle the complaints by conciliation and persuasion. If this fails, the complaint is typically referred to a board or an inquiries commission which investigates and hears evidence and then issues an order requiring compliance. Violation of the act or failure to comply is an offense and can lead to a fine, according to the schedule given in Exhibit 18–6. One major difference between Canadian and U.S. citizens' actions about discrimination is that in Canada, the complainant cannot sue his or her employer over alleged discrimination.

EEO PROGRAMS: A PREVENTIVE APPROACH

Many employers face the legal enforcement of EEO regulations with a mixture of resignation and despair, feeling little can be done to minimize the threat of legal action. To some, the agencies and their regulations seem arbitrary, punitive, and chaotic—more susceptible to the artistry of an attorney than to the problem-solving skill of a personnel administrator. They fear that the only thing the personnel administrator can do is pick up the pieces.

Yet a preventive strategy is possible which can reduce the likelihood of employment discrimination charges and assure equal employment opportunities for applicants and employees. EEO compliance is required of virtually all government contractors, but a preventive approach for enterprises involves using it as a means to bring about change in employment practices before discrimination charges can arise.

Ideally, the preventive approach should be embodied in the affirmative action program required by Executive Order 11246 and monitored by the OFCCP. These legal sanctions are not the only reason for establishing such a program, however. At least as important is the fact that a well-designed affirmative action program can remove some of the conditions that might lead employees and applicants to file discrimination charges with the EEOC.

Many journal articles explore various ways of carrying out an affirmative action program.[45] The manager can even buy kits or how-to-do-it guides that purport to simplify the task.[46] Perhaps the best way to gain an initial understanding of such a program, however, is to consider an example: AT&T's program for women in outside crafts.

AT&T's program for women outside-crafts workers

Of all employers in the United States, probably none has received more attention for its affirmative action program than the American Telephone and Telegraph Company. AT&T was involved in the largest back-pay settlement in the history of equal employment.[47] As part of that settlement, the company was required to make significant strides in increasing employment opportunities for women and minorities. The program that resulted from that settlement exemplifies some of the more advanced EEO efforts in American industry.

The scope of AT&T's affirmative action program is so vast that it is impractical to focus on more than a small segment here. One particularly interesting segment of AT&T's program is its provisions for increasing the employment of women in outside-crafts positions: the various lineworkers, telephone installers, and repair workers whose work is mostly done outdoors.

In examining AT&T's program for women in outside crafts, it is useful to divide the EEO program into three parts:

1. Determining the jobs in which any group is underrepresented and appraising the availability of that group in the labor market.
2. Setting numerical integration goals for increasing the representation of that group in those jobs.
3. Specifying how those goals are to be attained.

These components are an integral part of affirmative action for any job at any company.

Step 1: Analyzing underrepresentation and availability. AT&T found a problem simply by examining the sex composition of their job classes: There were almost no women in outside-crafts positions. But how great was the extent of underrepresentation? Many enterprises find the answer to this question in the statistics compiled for affirmative action plans by state labor departments in every state,[48] which show the number of women and minorities in each of 10 or 20 broad occupational groups. Others use the overall population figures compiled by the U.S. Census. Both sets of data are readily available from the appropriate government agencies.

However, both state labor department statistics and the overall population statistics distort the picture for women outside-crafts workers. Most state departments of labor give one set of figures for all skilled trades combined but do not subdivide skilled trades further. This combined figure overestimates the percentage of women in outside crafts, where they are less well represented than in either the skilled trades generally or in the total population.

When AT&T attempted to determine the number of women actually working in outside crafts, it found that the statistics could not be compiled without the kind of digging that most companies could not afford. But AT&T did the digging, and some of the resulting statistics showed that the availability of women for those positions was quite low indeed. If women were not available for the jobs, AT&T was not the serious offender that the statistics on women in the skilled trades suggested.

There is a problem with all of this, however. Statistics on the number of women actually working in outside crafts would not be very good estimates of the *availability* of women *if* employers tended to discriminate against women for those positions. Suppose that managers felt it was not a woman's place to perform manual labor out of doors, and the supervisors of outdoor work crews resented the invasion of their crews by women. That would tend to keep women out or drive them away, and then the statistics that AT&T worked so hard to collect would be biased indicators: more women would be "available" than the statistics would suggest.

Unfortunately, there is no easy solution to this problem. All availability statistics are open to justifiable criticism. Still, many employers strive to collect those that put them in the best light.[49] While some may argue that such a strategy is manipulative, it often does succeed in reducing enforcement pressures. Employers are likely to continue using it until such time as there emerges a generally accepted statistical definition of availability.

Step 2: Goal setting. One additional reason employers have for seeking out the "best" availability statistics is that they are ordinarily viewed by the government as a source of information about the "ideal" distribution of women and minorities in the organization's work force. If whatever availability statistics are on hand indicate that 50 percent of the available skilled craftsworkers are female, then the organization is expected to strive for 50 percent representation of women in its skilled-crafts positions. Consequently, if the enterprise can persuade the agency to accept availability statistics that are closer to the actual distribution of women in the company's skilled-crafts positions, it will not have as far to go in striving to meet affirmative action goals.

The enterprise also faces a related problem: If it sets the numerical integration goals for women and minorities too high, it may not be able to attain them without discriminating against white males. But if the company were to favor women and minorities, it would be vulnerable to charges of discrimination by white males. This is discussed in more detail later in this chapter.

In AT&T's case, a federal court approved the numerical goals for women, which were formulated before the company had collected data documenting the low availability of women for outside-crafts positions. Predictably, AT&T found it very difficult to meet those goals (this was one of the reasons it went to the trouble of finding out the actual number of women working in outside-crafts positions in a given labor market area). Eventually the company succeeded in using its statistics to persuade the court to lower the goals for employment of women in outside crafts.

In short, EEO goals must be realistic, and they must be attainable without discriminating against those in the majority. Nevertheless, while good availability statistics help make goals realistic, there is no way to be sure that goals will not discriminate in reverse unless the means by which the company seeks to attain them are carefully planned.

Step 3: Specifying how goals are to be attained. If the means to goal attainment are to be nondiscriminatory against white males, management should find out the causes of underrepresentation of women and minorities in the company's work force. Otherwise, it will not know what discriminatory employment practices must be changed in order to increase representation without preferential treatment of women and minorities. For example, the underrepresentation of women in a certain job class may be caused by a company's reputation for being rough on women, or by a policy that unnecessarily schedules work shifts so that women workers cannot get home in time to meet their children coming back from school. If management knows the cause, it can attempt to increase the representation of women by working on its public image and by exploring the possibility of retiming the shifts. But if management doesn't know it, it may attempt to increase the representation of women by lowering the requirements for women applying from the outside, or by granting transfers to women employees while refusing to grant them to more qualified men employees. This would not only increase the risk of discrimination charges from white males, it would also contribute to morale problems and foster resentment against women in the company.

Identifying discriminatory employment practices calls for a full-scale audit of personnel administration in the organization.[50] This audit reviews each step of the personnel function, from recruitment to retirement. Ideally, it also examines supervisory practices that might have an unfavorable impact on women or minority employees. If the audit uncovers barriers to the employment of women or minorities, action could be taken to reduce or remove those barriers.

In AT&T's case, a careful examination of the company's practices and its position in the labor market led to several actions. To combat the image of telephone crafts work as being an exclusively male domain, the company began using advertisements that portrayed females performing such work. The company also replaced male pronouns and other male references in company literature and documents with substitutes that were appropriate to either sex. Subsidiary telephone company offices made public relations efforts too; for instance, they began to take Girl Scout troop tours through predominantly male maintenance operations as well as such predominantly female departments as the operators' stations. They also stressed to high school guidance counselors that outside-crafts work was a perfectly acceptable occupation for girls and held seminars to encourage women employed elsewhere in AT&T to apply for such work. All these approaches were designed to foster an image of AT&T as welcoming women into traditionally male telephone company jobs.

AT&T also carried out research on ways to redesign the outside-craft jobs so that women could perform them more readily. This research found problems with an extension ladder that was hard for women to handle and a safety harness used by workers in climbing telephone poles. Also, a particularly grueling training program was redesigned by spreading out the hard physical labor over a longer period of time—to the benefit of the men as well as the women.[51]

As this example from AT&T makes abundantly clear, EEO programs can entail a substantial change in the way a company manages its personnel program. But not every employer needs to undertake as thorough a program as AT&T's; many employers could never afford to. Still, the barriers to full employment for women and minorities can be deeply ingrained in the organization's practices, and it may take a substantial expenditure of both time and money to identify and eliminate them.

Other examples of EEO programs

As indicated earlier in the chapter, EEO permeates the personnel process. It can require changes in employment planning, recruiting, selecting, evaluation, career planning, training, and other functions. Rather than discuss each personnel function, we will focus on some special features of EEO programs for various groups.

Women.   In many companies, affirmative action for women is more a matter of career design than job design. Women often find themselves locked into their positions with no career path upward; this is especially true of clerical positions. Typists and secretaries usually have little likelihood of promotion to supervisory or managerial positions.

Sometimes the solution to that problem involves training or job rotation for clerical workers. Management training can give them the specific skills they need to assume higher level positions, and job rotation can give them the breadth of experience they need to become effective managers. In other cases, the problem is that the employees of the enterprise, women included, are unaware of the promotion and transfer opportunities it offers. Larger companies often establish very thorough and elaborate systems to inform employees of job openings in the company. Among other things, these systems may include individual career counseling for employees, which helps identify promising talent at the same time it keeps employees informed.

A second problem area is management attitudes. Ten years ago, resistance to placing blacks in management positions was widespread. Today that resistance seems to have dissipated somewhat, but resistance to women in management positions remains. A man in a management position may doubt that a woman could survive in the world of management, or he may be reluctant to have an especially competent woman in his group because he is afraid that the company will promote her ahead of him to satisfy affirmative action goals. In an atmosphere like that, it does not help much to give women better training and job rotation opportunities. The attitude problem must be taken into account.

Solutions to the attitude problem have changed over the past decade. It used to be that these problems were attacked by a combination of training and exhortation. Some managers were sent through various forms of sensitivity or awareness training to make them more accepting of EEO and more understanding of the special problems faced by women and minorities. More recently, however, there seems to have been a growing recognition that attitudes seldom are changed readily unless the person holding them is motivated to do so. One way to motivate managers in this respect is to give them EEO responsibilities. Accordingly, operating managers are being given increasing responsibility for the conduct of EEO programs. They are being included in goal setting as well as deciding what steps should be taken to attain them. Having participated in these processes, an otherwise reluctant manager is more likely to develop favorable attitudes toward them, especially if he or she is held accountable for goal attainment. Another approach is to reward managers for achieving EEO goals, as described below.

A third problem area for women is policies that single them out for unfavorable treatment. For instance, married women may be denied opportunities because the company fears they will leave if their husbands change jobs. This can become a self-fulfilling prophecy. What is the incentive for a couple to remain in an area for the sake of the wife's career if the wife's employer denies her career opportunities?[52]

Employee benefit programs also may treat men and women unequally in retirement plans, hospitalization insurance provisions, and disability income programs. Many, but not all, of these inequalities are prohibited by Title VII. One which is not is the policy of excluding pregnancy-related disabilities from disability insurance coverage; the Supreme Court has said that such a policy is legal.[53] Legal or not, such a policy is no help to a company that is trying to attract women employees.

In sum, to prevent EEO problems with women employees, the employer must examine the total personnel program to see that personnel policies encourage equal employment opportunity and do not restrict the employment potential of females.

Older employees.   The Age Discrimination in Employment Act protects workers between the ages of 40 and 64 against job discrimination. In the past, the enforcement agencies did not press too hard on discrimination against older persons, but recent actions suggest this will no longer be true. Employers being sued for this kind of discrimination include American Motors, Standard Oil of California, Kimberly Clark, and Chessie Systems. In Chessie's case, the company is being sued for $20 million. In 1976, one enforcement agency filed three times the number of age discrimination lawsuits as in the preceding year.[54] While age requirements are illegal in most jobs, the law does not cover all of them. For example, a bus company was allowed to refuse bus driver jobs to applicants over age 35 with the justification that aging brings on slower reaction times, which can adversely affect safety.[55] The law prevents employers from replacing their staffs with younger workers, whether the purpose be to give the company a more youthful image or to save money in the pension program.[56]

A number of barriers face older workers in many enterprises. Some are a matter of company economics, others a matter of management attitudes. The economic reasons include the added expense of funding pensions for older workers and the increased premiums necessary for health and life insurance benefit plans. The attitude problems are more difficult to pin down. Sometimes managers feel that older workers lose their faculties, making them less effective on the job. Yet there is evidence that the intelligence levels of many older employees increase as they near retirement age.[57] Besides, there are other advantages to hiring older workers: lower turnover, greater consciousness of safety matters, and longer work experience.[58]

When an enterprise determines it has an EEO problem with older employees, it should follow a pattern similar to the three-step approach described above for AT&T.

Racial and ethnic minorities. The laws prohibit discrimination against a person because of race, color, and national origin. The specific protected minorities are blacks, Hispanics, American Indians, Asian–Pacific Islanders, and Alaskan natives, groups which historically have had higher unemployment and underemployment and have held the lowest level jobs.[59]

While every ethnic and racial minority is unique, one problem facing them all is adverse personnel policies. Examples of such practices are numerous. The height and weight requirements, which have an adverse impact on Asian Americans and Hispanic Americans, were until recently commonplace among police departments in the United States. Seniority and experience requirements based on time in a department, which are still typical, tend to lock in blacks who move out of segregated departments; they find themselves at the bottom of the seniority lists in their new departments even though they have had many years with the company.[60] Vague, subjective performance evaluations by supervisors are so subject to bias that many minority group members find they cannot attain high enough ratings to get promotions or merit pay increases.[61] All these practices, along with others, are prime targets for change in the EEO program.

Some barriers are more difficult to change, even though they have an adverse impact on minorities. College degree requirements are common for some jobs, although one study found that 65 percent of the jobs reserved for college graduates could be performed by workers with no more than a high school education.[62] Employers should examine their own job specifications to see if educational requirements can be reduced without sacrificing job performance. Where the requirements cannot be reduced, the organization might consider redesigning or breaking down the job so that people with less education could perform them satisfactorily. While job redesign is usually a big step, the resulting increase in opportunities for minorities may make it worthwhile for the enterprise.

Another barrier is that racial and ethnic minorities are often reluctant to complain to a largely white company management when they are dissatisfied about something. This problem is even more difficult when the company has no formal grievance system or other acceptable procedure for making complaints known to management. The result is often low morale and a high turnover rate among minorities.

One solution by the R. R. Donnelly Publishing Company takes a twofold approach: encouraging minority workers to use the company grievance system, and a communications program called Let's Hear It. Let's Hear It offered employees the opportunity to address written, anonymous gripes to a special management group separate from the chain of command.[63] That way, employees could speak their minds without fear of retaliation. While there are risks in such an approach, the company can find out about discrimination problems before they turn into court cases.

Employers need to go through the three-part program designed by AT&T to improve equal employment opportunity for minorities, too. There are many examples of successful minority programs.[64]

Religious minorities. The EEO–type laws prohibit discrimination in employment based on religious preference, but there have been few cases thus far charging that employers have discriminated against religious groups in employment and promotion.[65] This is surprising, given the reality that certain employers have had a policy of limited or no hiring of persons who are Jewish, Orthodox Christian, or Roman Catholic, at least for the managerial class. Catholics, for example, are seriously underrepresented in managerial and professional groups in the United States.

The focus of religious discrimination cases has been on hours of work and working conditions. The cases largely concern employers telling employees to work on days or times that conflict with their religious beliefs—at regular times or on overtime. For example, employees who are Orthodox Jews, Seventh-Day Adventists, or Worldwide Church of God members cannot work from sunset Friday through sundown Saturday. Many devout Christians will not work on Sunday, and others feel they must attend Wednesday evening services. If the employer changes work schedules or schedules overtime at times that employees feel they must practice their religion, a confrontation develops.

A series of court cases and EEOC decisions have established a reasonable procedure for dealing with the hours-of-work issue. EEOC tells employers they must take steps to accommodate the reasonable religious needs of employees when this can be done without interfering with the conduct of the business. The employer must treat all religions substantially the same in accommodation of their requirements.

EEOC will ask employers the following types of questions to determine if the employer tried to accommodate the employee's seriously held religious practices:

> Can the employer find a substitute for the worker unable to work a particular shift because of his religious beliefs? Alternatively, where the problem is a continuing one, can the religious employee trade shifts with another worker whose schedule does not require Sabbath day work?

Is it possible for the individual to make up lost production time on another date? This might be ordered in white-collar jobs where one person's performance is not dependent on others.

Where these arrangements cannot be implemented and the job has to be performed, a conflict between the employee's religious beliefs and the employer's production needs could be avoided by transferring the worker to another installation or department where work on the Sabbath is not necessary. This is similar to policies of transferring personnel who cannot perform work in one department to another rather than discharging the worker for substandard performance.[66]

Again, the enterprise can take the steps AT&T did to make sure it is not discriminating against the employment rights of particular religious groups. It must do all it can in accommodating the working hours and days of its employees to avoid charges of religious discrimination. Although the law and enforcement agencies are consistent in their interpretation, for some reason, some arbitrators are not in concert. They are still finding primarily for the employer, if the contract gives the employer the right to set working hours.[67] But the provisions of Title VII take precedence over the provisions of a collective bargaining agreement, and an employer would be well advised to reappraise questionable working hours, even if the union has agreed to them.

Veterans.   The Vietnam Era Veterans Readjustment Act of 1972 requires federal contractors to take affirmative action for the employment of disabled veterans and veterans of the Vietnam era. This act imposes fewer obligations than the other employment discrimination laws. No numerical goals are required, but the enterprise must show it makes special efforts to recruit them. In determining a veteran's qualifications, the employer cannot consider any part of the military record that is not directly relevant to the specific qualifications of the job in question. In 1977, the Carter administration proposed the focusing of veterans preferences to help Vietnam vets. This proposal received mixed reactions.[68]

Physically and mentally handicapped workers.   Section 503 of the Vocational Rehabilitation Act of 1973, which is enforced by OFCCP, requires that all employers with government contracts of $2,500 or more must set up affirmative action programs for the handicapped. At present these programs require no numerical goals but they do call for special efforts in recruiting handicapped persons, such as outreach programs; communication of the obligation to hire and promote the handicapped; the development of procedures to seek out and promote handicapped persons presently on the payroll; and making physical changes which allow the handicapped to be employed (e.g., ramps).[69] Those who are really dedicated to improving the handicapped's chances also will set up training programs and partially redesign jobs so the handicapped can perform them effectively.[70]

The biggest hurdle that handicapped persons must face is not their physical (or mental) handicap, but myths and negative attitudes on their ability to do the job. It has been demonstrated that they are myths, and the handicapped can do the job.[71] So affirmative action may help give them the chance to use their abilities too.

Other minorities. Two other groups not presently covered by EEO or "fairness" programs may be covered in the future. One is ex-convicts,[72] which Canada's program presently covers. The other group seeking EEO-type coverage is homosexuals. At present, some employers prohibit discrimination against homosexuals if their behavior does not affect their fitness for the job; examples include the Civil Service Commission for federal employees and AT&T. EEO ordinances protecting homosexuals have been passed in many cities, including Ann Arbor, Berkeley, Columbus, Detroit, Minneapolis, San Francisco, Toronto, Seattle, and Washington.[73] While the defeat of the Miami gay rights ordinance may precipitate a reconsideration of these statutes, it seems unlikely that homosexuals will reduce their demands for equal treatment.

White males. If you are a white male, you probably are thinking about now: This is great, that women and minorities are getting a better chance for employment and promotion than they used to, but what does this do to me? Will I get a job? Will I get promoted to a better job? Or is *reverse discrimination* likely in my future?

This concern is natural. Whether or not it is justified, white males are filing charges of discrimination against employers—and they are making the charges stick. Title VII prohibits discrimination based on race and sex, *and that includes* discrimination against white males as well as discrimination that favors them. The laws that were originally passed to give better opportunities to women and minorities are now being interpreted as protecting the rights of the majority as well.[74]

The obligations of the enterprise to white males are the same as its obligations to other groups: It must not discriminate for or against any race, sex, religion, or minority group. This presents a problem to employers with numerical affirmative action goals. How are goals to be attained without favoring the disadvantaged groups? The answer is to seek *other* means of satisfying goals which do not in turn discriminate against the advantaged groups. For example, employers could undertake more intensive recruiting efforts for women and minorities, as well as eliminating those employment practices that inhibit their hiring and promotion.

Employers should never set numerical goals so high that they can be attained *only* through reverse discrimination. If the goals are already too high, action should be taken to lower them. The courts are increasingly saying that employers cannot use their numerical affirmative action goals as an excuse to discriminate against white males.[75]

At present there appear to be problems in interpreting these rulings. Recently the New York Bell division of AT&T promoted a woman rather than a white male who had greater seniority and better performance evaluation ratings. The judge ruled that the company should have promoted the woman to meet its EEO goals, but the male was discriminated against. The judge ordered the promotion to go through but also ordered the company to pay the white male $100,000 in damages.

The courts themselves may still impose goals that discriminate against white males. But federal agencies may not impose such goals on employers, and employers may not impose them on themselves.

The conclusion that emerges is that employment discrimination laws are primarily for the benefit of those groups that have historically been the victims of discrimination. Nevertheless, these laws do not allow the employer to bestow such benefits voluntarily by depriving white males of their rights.

Canadian human rights programs. Canada's Human Rights programs in general have followed the lead of EEO programs in the United States. Federal and provincial governments have come to them later, and the statutes are only now beginning to be enforced.

The results of Canadian human rights programs so far have been modest relative to the results of EEOC and OFCC in the United States. Some of the human rights commissions in various jurisdictions have set up training programs and so on designed to improve the positions of minorities (especially in Manitoba, Nova Scotia, New Brunswick, Ontario, British Columbia, the Northwest Territories, and, to a lesser extent, Quebec). There have been some attempts to aid minorities and the disadvantaged,[76] and the government and some businesses, such as Canadian National Railways, Bell Canada, and the Royal Bank, have set up programs for women.[77] But many observers feel that the effort thus far has been too small.[78] Employers may see the situation quite differently. Nevertheless, Canadian employers might do well to follow the preventive approach that has been adopted in the United States in order to avoid future mandated programs.

MANDATED ACTIONS IN EEO–AFFIRMATIVE ACTION PROGRAMS

We have reviewed EEO programs as a "preventive" approach aimed at ensuring equality of employment opportunity and avoiding charges of discrimination. What happens if charges are made anyway? What requirements are likely to be imposed on an employer if the charging party wins?

Actually, many of the "preventive" approaches we have been discussing are in fact a compromise resulting from discrimination charges. The sophisticated AT&T program was part of a settlement which the company agreed to rather than face a court battle. It was hammered out in negotiations between AT&T and several EEO compliance agencies. In a very real sense, AT&T's program is an example of a required program.

Most cases do not proceed further than an EEOC investigation. When EEOC investigates a charge of discrimination, all it can force the employer to do is provide information. But this power is more threatening to employers than one might guess, for EEOC's request for information almost inevitably goes beyond the facts and incidents surrounding the original charge. It involves a very extensive investigation into the company's employment practices in an effort to uncover evidence of more systematic discrimination. The idea is that this evidence might support a more ambitious lawsuit, possibly a class action suit involving a large group of employees or applicants.

As a consequence of EEOC's demand for extensive information, companies that are the subject of discrimination charges often face demands for information that require hundreds of hours of staff time to assemble. Imagine, for instance, a demand that the employer produce information on every applicant interviewed, including the reasons for accepting or rejecting each applicant! And this may be but one of dozens of items requested.

In the legal steps beyond investigation, the employer may also be faced with mandates that are part of the settlement of the charges. In the first step beyond investigation, which is conciliation, EEOC will attempt to gain a voluntary settlement of any charge that the agencys' investigation has corroborated. If a voluntary settlement is not forthcoming and the case goes to court, a settlement will come either through mutual agreement among the parties to the suit, or through the judgment of the court if the parties cannot agree.

At a minimum, the employer in these settlements will usually be required to eliminate any practice that evidence indicates is discriminatory. For example, the company could be required to give up its testing program, revise its seniority system, stop using subjective supervisory evaluations as a basis for promotions, or cease doing whatever else is deemed to be illegal. Also, the employer may be required to give back pay or other monetary compensation. If the back pay is awarded to a *class* of people (such as all black employees in certain labor grades during a certain period), it can get expensive—as in the cases of AT&T and Georgia Power discussed above. A third ingredient of some settlements is mandatory hiring ratios. The logic is that since discrimination operates against a group (e.g., blacks), the relief should be given in a way that restores the group to where it would be if the discrimination had not occurred. While employers cannot adopt a quota system of hiring blacks and whites as a method for satisfying affirmative action plans, a court can order a company to do so. Usually courts do not do this unless they have reason to believe that an employer will not increase the employment of underutilized groups voluntarily. Nevertheless, the fact is that quotas have become commonplace in court orders—and this fuels the fires of resentment by white males over what they regard as widespread "reverse discrimination."

COSTS/BENEFIT ANALYSIS OF EEO–AFFIRMATIVE ACTION PROGRAMS

The costs of an affirmative action plan can be calculated for an employer. They include the added expense of recruitment, special training programs, test validation, job-posting systems, equipment redesign, and whatever other programs the organization includes in its plan. An added cost is for the preparation of reports and other red tape.[79] The personnel manager or specialist may have to compute these costs and justify the expense to higher management by citing the benefits to be derived.

Unfortunately, the benefits are difficult to compute. Even if they are computed, they may not outweigh the costs in the short run. Consequently, some top managers may tend to view EEO as a necessary evil, something that must be done because the government requires it, not because of any benefits to be derived by the organization. This can do much to destroy the personnel manager's position as the person responsible for the plan because top management attitudes are contagious: if higher management does not provide the necessary support and resources, then lower levels of management may be reluctant to cooperate.

Therefore, it is important to be aware of the benefits of EEO programs, even if they are long-range ones that are difficult to quantify.[80] One immediate benefit is that affirmative action increases the likelihood that the company will stay eligible for government contracts. Another benefit, perhaps a longer range one, is an increase in the pool of eligible workers that results from providing opportunities to women and minorities. Then there is the obvious benefit of better public relations and increased goodwill among employees that comes from a properly administered EEO program.

One benefit that affirmative action does not provide is insulation from liability in discrimination court cases. While a good EEO plan may make employees more satisfied and less likely to file charges of discrimination, it provides no presumption of innocence if an employee does take a charge to court. For instance, one General Motors plant had a commendable record of hiring minorities, but that did not keep a court from finding that it was guilty of discrimination in promoting them.[81] And the Detroit Edison Company had a commendable record of promoting blacks, but that did not keep a court from ordering back pay to those few blacks that it felt were kept out of higher positions unfairly.[82]

Still, EEO programs can help an employer in court. Some courts have been less stringent when companies seem to be making progress with their affirmative action plans. One court used this reasoning in deciding not to issue an injunction against Southwestern Bell Telephone Company, and another used it to postpone legal action on a discrimination claim against a bank in Texas.[83] The important thing to remember is that, while affirmative action may be irrelevant in determining a verdict of guilty or not guilty, it is very relevant in determining what will be done to the employer if the verdict does turn out to be guilty. It is very unlikely, for example, that a court will impose a mandatory hiring quota if it believes that the employer is successfully implementing an affirmative action program.[84] The prospect of avoiding such an intrusion into management prerogative might be enough alone to motivate EEO efforts.

SUMMARY, CONCLUSIONS AND RECOMMENDATIONS

EEO programs cannot succeed if operating managers do not understand the concept. They are the ones who hire, discipline, promote, assign work to, and terminate employees in most organizations, and they can spell the difference between success and failure in meeting the company's numerical affirmative action goals. Yet EEO is an emotion-laden topic subject to distortion which endangers the success of the company's EEO efforts.

There are no magical cures for these problems, but one proposition that does seem to go a long way is *involvement.* Too often, EEO is treated as the exclusive province of the personnel department. If this can be changed by involving operating managers in planning and goal setting, it is likely that their acceptance of EEO will grow.

To make EEO programs work, top management must not only communicate its desires but must build EEO effectiveness into the reward system for managers. The goal is to make the EEO program "courtproof," as well as ethical and workable.[85]

General Electric requires its managers to report their progress in achieving EEO goals. Their degree of goal achievement in EEO affects their progress in their compensation as would their progress in cost control.[86] This has helped GE meet its EEO goals, and this kind of communication and control system is more likely to achieve courtproof EEO systems than hortatory memos or other such means.

In sum, top managers must get involved in EEO and human rights programs to make sure that the enterprise is in fact an equal employment opportunity employer and that the EEO–affirmative action program meets the letter as well as the spirit of the law.

This chapter has focused on EEO programs in the United States and Canada designed to eliminate bias in personnel programs. In 1976, Library of Congress researchers attempted to estimate the cost to the United States of job discrimination. Their conclusions are that, assuming the nation could absorb the additional workers without job discrimination, 638,000 minority employees would have jobs and millions more would have better skills and earnings. The nation would gain $55.8 billion (3.7 percent) in gross national product, reflecting $22.3 billion in increased wages and salaries. With this kind of potential achievement for the minorities and the nation, a better understanding of the EEO–human rights legislation and programs in the United States and Canada is well worthwhile.

The chapter concludes with some summary propositions and recommendations. First there are several propositions regarding the extent of EEO programs at present and their future thrust.

> *Proposition 18.1.* The larger the organization, the more likely it is to emphasize EEO programs.
>
> *Proposition 18.2.* The more socially responsible the top managers of the organization perceive themselves to be, the more likely is it that the organization will have successful EEO programs.

EXHIBIT 18–7
EEO programs for model organizations

Type of organization	Staff responsibility for EEO program			Recruiting methods for EEO program			Training and facilitating			
	Separate department	Separate program director	Part of manager's job	State employment service	Liaison with community groups	Separate offices, etc.	Longer training	Buddy system	Transportation	Financial counseling
1. Large size, low complexity, high stability	X			X	X	X	X	X	X	X
2. Medium size, low complexity, high stability		X		X	X	X	X	X		X
3. Small size, low complexity, high stability			X	X	X		X	X		
4. Medium size, moderate complexity, moderate stability		X		X	X		X	X		X
5. Large size, high complexity, low stability	X			X	X	X	X	X	X	X
6. Medium size, high complexity, low stability		X		X	X		X	X		X
7. Small size, high complexity, low stability			X	X			X	X		

Proposition 18.3. The greater the dependence of the organization on the federal government, the more likely is it to have an EEO program.

Proposition 18.4. Although minority employees were the major focus of EEO programs in the past, the major emphasis of these programs is shifting to female employees.

Proposition 18.5. Protection of older employees and reemployment of older employees who have lost their jobs through no fault of their own will continue to gain emphasis in EEO programs.

Next, several propositions about effective EEO programs are:

Proposition 18.6. Other things being equal, the preventive approach to EEO programs is more effective than mandatory programs.

Proposition 18.7. Effective EEO programs require an analysis of underrepresentation and availability of minorities prior to goal setting for hiring and promotion of minorities.

Proposition 18.8. Once the EEO goals are set, the effective EEO program specifies how the goals are to be attained.

Finally, for EEO to be effective, the total personnel program needs to be examined to determine that present practices do not inhibit attainment of EEO goals. A few propositions describing this process include:

Proposition 18.9. To develop an effective EEO program, innovative recruiting programs are a necessity.

Proposition 18.10. If EEO programs for hiring and retention of disadvantaged employees are to be effective, stronger orientation and facilitative programs will have to be developed.

Proposition 18.11. To make EEO programs for retention most effective, supervisors and co-workers should be involved in the process of integrating minorities into the organization.

Exhibit 18–7 lists some recommendations for effective EEO programs, including the staff responsibility for EEO programs and some recruiting and training suggestions.

Chapter 19 discusses how enterprises deal with another group of employees: the unionized employee group.

QUESTIONS

1. What are the crucial factors in the diagnostic model affecting EEO and human rights programs?
2. How did societal values affect EEO efforts?
3. Are women and minorities better off now than in the 1920s?
4. What are the major laws affecting EEO in the United States? Human rights in Canada?
5. What is discrimination?
6. What government agencies enforce the EEO laws? The human rights laws?

7. Are the enforcement agencies effective?

8. What can the agencies and courts do if an enterprise violates EEO regulations?

9. Describe a preventive-approach EEO program.

10. Compare and contrast the present position of women, minorities, and other protected categories in our society. Who is better off? Worse off?

11. Outline a program for cost/benefit analysis of an EEO program.

12. Discuss the most significant propositions in this chapter.

13. What are the most important EEO recommendations for the model organizations?

NOTES AND REFERENCES

1. *The Personnel Executive's Job* (Englewood Cliffs, N.J.: Prentice-Hall/ASPA, 1977).

2. *Work in America,* (Cambridge, Mass.: MIT Press, 1974).

3. Gunnar Myrdal, *An American Dilemma: The Negro Problem and American Democracy* (New York: Harper & Row, 1944).

4. National Alliance of Businessmen, Inc., *Annual Report,* June 30, 1975.

5. Charles Silberman, *Crisis in Black and White* (New York: Random House, 1964), p. 237.

6. George Simpson and J. Milton Yinger, *Racial and Cultural Minorities,* 3rd ed. (New York: Harper & Row, 1965), pp. 268–89, 274–75.

7. Ibid.

8. St. Clair Drake, "The Social and Economic Status of the Negro in the United States," in *The Negro American,* ed. Talcott Parsons and Kenneth B. Clark (Boston: Houghton Mifflin Co., 1966), pp. 3–46.

9. U.S. Commission on Civil Rights, *The Federal Civil Rights Enforcement Effort—1974,* vol. 5, *To Eliminate Employment Discrimination* (Washington, D.C., July 1975).

10. Liz Gallese, "Going It Alone," *The Wall Street Journal,* July 27, 1976; Howard Hayghe, "Families and the Rise of Working Wives: An Overview," *Monthly Labor Review,* May 1976, pp. 12–19.

11. David H. Rosenbloom and Carole Cassler Obuchowski,"Public Personnel Examinations and the Constitution—Emergent Trends," *Public Administration Review,* January–February 1977, pp. 9–18.

12. *Diaz v. Pan American Airways,* 442 F.2d 385.

13. *Employment Practices Guide,* vol. 3 (Chicago: Commerce Clearing House).

14. Alfred Blumrosen "Strangers in Paradise: Griggs v. Duke Power Co. and the Concept of Employment Discrimination," *Michigan Law Review,* November 1972, pp. 59–110.

15. *Griggs v. Duke Power Co.,* 401 U.S. 424, 1971.

16. *Smith v. City of East Cleveland,* 520 F.2d 492, 1975.

17. *Wallace v. Debron Corp,* 494 F.2d 674, 8th Cir, 1974.

18. *Gregory v.Litton Systems,* 472 F.2d 631, 9th Cir., 1972.

19. *Green v. Missouri-Pacific R.R. Co.,* 523 F.2d 1290, 8th Cir., 1975.

20. *Albermarle Paper Co. v. Moody,* 422 U.S. 407, 1975; EEOC, "Guidelines on Employment Selection Procedures," 29 C.F.R., Sec. 1607.

21. Prentice-Hall, Inc. "P-H/ASPA Survey: Employee Testing Procedures—Where Are They Headed?" *Personnel Management: Policies and Practices,* April 22, 1975.

22. *Spurlock* v. *United Airlines,* Inc., 475 F.2d 215, 10th Cir., 1972.

23. Blumrosen, "Strangers in Paradise."

24. EEOC, *Annual Report,* (Washington, D.C.: Superintendent of Documents, U.S. Government Printing Office, annually).

25. James Ledvinka, and Hugh Watson, "Processing of Discrimination Charges by EEOC," *Journal of Business Research* 3, 2 (1975), pp. 149–56; Delbert Spurlock, Jr., "EEOC's Compliance Process: The Problems of Selective Enforcement," *Labor Law Journal,* July 1975, pp. 369–409; "EEOC's Chairman Says He Never Read Internal Reports Charging Corruption," *The Wall Street Journal,* May 13, 1976; Walter Mossberg, "Wary Watchdogs," *The Wall Street Journal,* August 26, 1977.

26. 41 C.F. R. Sec. 60–2.

27. U.S. Commission on Civil Rights, *Federal Civil Rights Enforcement Effort.*

28. Revised Order no. 14, 41 C.F.R., Sec. 60–60.

29. U.S. Commission on Civil Rights, *Federal Civil Rights Enformement Effort.*

30. Robert Flanagan, "Actual v. Potential Impact of Government Antidiscrimination Programs," *Industrial and Labor Relations Review,* 1975–76, pp. 486–507; Morris Goldstein and Robert Smith, "The Estimated Impact of Anti-Discrimination Program Aimed at Federal Contractors," *Industrial and Labor Relations Review,* 1975–76, pp. 523–43; James Jones, "Comment," *Industrial and Labor Relations Review,* 1975–76, pp. 581–84; Gregory Ahart, "A Process Evaluation of the Contract Compliance Program in Non-Construction Industry," *Industrial and Labor Relations Review,* 1975–1976, pp. 565–71.

31. Glen Cain, "Comment," *Industrial and Labor Relations Review,* 1975–76, pp. 572–76.

32. James Heckman and Kenneth Wolpin, "Does the Contract Compliance Program Work? An Analysis of Chicago Data," *Industrial and Labor Relations Review,* 1975–76, pp. 544–64; George Johnson and Finis Welch, "The Labor Market Implications of an Economywide Affirmative Action Program," *Industrial and Labor Relations Review,* 1975–76, pp. 508–22.

33. U.S. Commission on Civil Rights, *Federal Civil Rights Enforcement Effort.*

34. "Developments in the Law: Employment Discrimination and Title VII of the Civil Rights Act of 1964," *Harvard Law Review* 84 (1971), pp. 1109–316.

35. Cain, "Comment."

36. Nathan Glazer, *Affirmative Discrimination* (New York: Basic Books, 1976).

37. Johnson and Welch, "Labor Market Implications."

38. "Washington Outlook," *Business Week,* August 2, 1976.

39. "Which Federal Agency Do You Obey?" *The Wall Street Journal,* March 4, 1976.

40. American Society for Personnel Administration, "Comment on July 9, 1976 Proposal for Uniform Guidelines on Employee Selection Procedures," Berea, Ohio, August 18, 1976; U.S. Commission on Civil Rights, *Federal Civil Rights Enforcement Effort.*

41. For case citations, see the case table in Commerce Clearing House's *Employment Practices Guide,* vol. 1, under *U.S.* v. *Georgia Power Co., King* v. *Georgia Power Co.,* and *Moreman* v. *Georgia Power Co.*

42. *Franks v. Bowman Transportation Co.,* 423 U.S. 814, U.S. Supreme Ct., 1975.

43. Jane Burton, "Studies on the Status of Canadian Women," *The Labour Gazette,* July 1976, pp. 377–80; Sharleen Bannon, "Women in the Workplace," *The Labour Gazette,* February 1976, pp. 69–74; Ray Traversy, "FEP Legislation," *The Labour Gazette,* Anniversary issue, 1975, pp. 625–28.

44. Department of Labour. See also, Harish Jain, "Race and Sex Discrimination in North America and Britain: Some Lessons for Canada," Working paper, Faculty of Business,

McMaster University, Hamilton, Ontario; and Naresh Agarwal and Harish Jain, "Pay Discrimination Against Females in Canada: Issues and Policies," Working paper, Faculty of Business, McMaster University, Hamilton, Ontario.

45. For example, see Antonia Chayes, "Make Your Equal Employment Opportunity Program Court Proof," *Harvard Business Review,* September–October 1974, pp. 81–89; N. Churchill and J. Shank, "Affirmative Action and Guilt-Edged Goals," *Harvard Business Review* 54, no. 2 (1976), pp. 111–16; J. Higgins, "The Complicated Process of Establishing Goals for Equal Employment," Personnel Journal, vol. 54 (1975), pp. 631–37; James Ledvinka, R. L. LaForge, and T. G. Corbett, "Test of an Affirmative Action Goal-Setting Model," *The Personnel Administrator,* November 1976; K. Marimont, P. Maize, and E. Harley, "Using FAIR to Set Numerical EEO Goals," *Public Personnel Management* 5 (1976), pp. 191–98; and J. Nisberg, "A Response to Affirmative Action Planning," *The Personnel Administrator,* January 1975, pp. 27–31; Howard Lockwood, "Equal Employment Opportunities," in Dale Yoder *Personnel and Industrial Relations Handbook,* ed. Dale Yoder and Herbert Heneman, Jr. (Berea, Ohio: American Society for Personnel Administration, 1976); James Long, "Employment Discrimination in the Federal Sector," *Journal of Human Resources,* 1976, pp. 86–97.

46. For example, see the *Affirmative Action Book* (Reading, Mass: Addison-Wesley Publishing Co., 1976).

47. "Equal Employment Opportunity Agreement between American Telephone and Telegraph Co. and Equal Employment Opportunity Commission and U.S. Department of Labor, January 18, 1973," *Commerce Clearing House Labor Law Reports,* Issue no. 373, 1973.

48. See Commerce Clearing House, *Employment Practices Guide,* no. 1488.

49. *Legal Aid Society of Alameda County* v. *Brennan,* 381 F. Supp. 125; U.S. Dist. Ct., Calif, 1974.

50. William Byham and Morton Spitzer, *The Law and Personnel Testing* (New York: American Management Association, 1971).

51. Richard Campbell, "The Movement of Women into Jobs Requiring Heavy Physical Activity," paper presented at Academy of Management meeting, Kansas City, Mo., May 1976.

52. Benson Rosen, and Thomas Jerdee, "On-the-Job Sex Bias: Increasing Mangerial Awareness," *The Personnel Administrator,* January 1977, pp. 15–18.

53. *Gilbert* v. *General Electric Co.,* U.S. 12 CCH *Employment Practices Decisions,* ¶ 11,240, U.S. Supreme Court, 1976.

54. Donald Shire, "Age Discrimination in Employment," *The Personnel Administrator,* June 1975, pp. 28–30; 54–55ff.; U.S. Department of Labor, *Age Discrimination in Employment Act of 1967: A Report Covering Activities under the Act During 1977* (Washington, D.C.: U.S. Government Printing Office).

55. *Hodgson* v. *Greyhound Lines, Inc.,* 499 F.2d 859, 7th Cir., 1974.

56. *Schultz* v. *Hickok Manufacturing Co., Inc.,* 358 F. Supp. 1208; U.S. Dist. Ct., Ga., 1973.

57. Glen Elder, "Age Differentiations and the Life Course," in *Annual Review of Sociology* (Palo Alto, Cal.: Annual Reviews, 1975), pp. 165–90; James Kelly, "Women, the Handicapped, and Older Workers," in *Handbook of Modern Personnel Administration,* ed. Joseph Famularo, ch. 70. (New York: McGraw-Hill Book Co., 1972); "Aging and the IQ: The Myth of the Twilight Years," *Psychology Today,* March 1974, pp. 35–40.

58. Robert Fjerstad, "Is It Economical to Hire the Over Forty-Five Worker?" *Personnel Administration,* March–April 1965, pp. 22–32.

59. Lois Gray, "The Jobs Puerto Ricans Hold in New York City," *Monthly Labor Review,* October 1975, pp. 12–16; Daniel Jaco and George Wilbur, "Asian Americans in the Labor Market," *Monthly Labor Review,* July 1975, pp. 33–38; Paul Ryscavage and Earl Mellor, "The Economic Situation of Spanish Surnames," *Monthly Labor Review,* April 1973, pp. 3–9; U.S. Commission on Civil Rights, *The Navajo Nation: An American Colony* (Washington, D.C.: U.S. Government Printing Office, 1975).

60. The Supreme Court decided in May 1977 that such a system was legal if it was not adopted for discriminatory purposes (*Teamsters* v. *U.S.*). See also, *Local 189, Papermakers and Paperworkers* v. *U.S.*, 416 F.2d 980, 5th Cir., 1969; *U.S.* v. *T.I.M.E.—D.C.*, 517 F.2d 299, 5th Cir., 1975.

61. William Holley, and Hubert Feild, "Performance Appraisal and the Law: A Review," *Labor Law Journal*, July 1975, pp. 423–30.

62. Virginia Herwegh, "Compliance in the Real World of Business," presentation at the Equal Employment Opportunity Seminar of the American Society for Personnel Administration, June 29, 1976; Ivar Berg, *Education and Jobs: The Great Training Robbery* (New York: Frederick A. Praeger, Inc.,1970).

63. Herwegh, "Compliance in the Real World of Business."

64. Elmer Burack et al.,"An Organizational Analysis of Manpower Issues in Employing the Disadvantaged," *Academy of Management Journal* 15 (1972), pp. 255–71; John Garrity, "Red Ink in Ghetto Industries," *Harvard Business Review*, May–June 1968, pp. 4–16; Lee Gassler, "Minorities and the Disadvantaged," *Handbook of Modern Personnel Administration*, ed. Joseph Famularo, ch. 69, New York: McGraw-Hill Book Co., 1972; Brian Morgan et al., "Employee Attitudes toward a Hard Core Hiring Program," *Journal of Applied Psychology*, December 1970, pp. 473–78; Gloria Shaw, et al., "How Employers Screen Disadvantaged Job Applicants," *Monthly Labor Review*, September 1972, pp. 14–21.

65. The principal law on religious discrimination is Title VII of the 1964 Civil Rights Act, Sec. 701 (j), as amended by the 1972 law. Some relevant court cases are: *Avco v. Lycoming Div.*, 52 La. 707, 708, 1969; *Dewey v. Reynolds Metal* 300 F. Supp. 709, W.D.Michigan, 1969; *Jackson* v. *Veri Fresh Poultry* 304 F. Supp 1276, E.D. La, 1969. *Riley* v. *Bendix Corp* 330 F. Supp. M.D. Fla, 1971; *Reid* v. *Memphis Publishing Co.*, 486 F.2d 346, 6th Cir., 1972, *Claybaugh* v. *Pacific Northwest Bell*, 355 F. Supp. 1, Dist. Ct. Ore., 1973; *Shaffield* v. *Northrup Worldwide*, 373 F. Supp. 937, M.D. Ala., 1974. Among the Principal EEOC–written decisions are:70–716 (1970), 71–463 (1970), 71–779 (1971), 72–0606 (1971), 72–114 (1972), 72–1301 (1972).

66. EEOC, "Guidelines on Religious Discrimination," 1977; Benjamin Wolkinson, "Title VII and the Religious Employee: The Neglected Duty of Accommodation," *Arbitration Journal*, June 1975, pp. 89–113.

67. The Supreme Court recently supported collectively-bargained seniority systems by denying an employee's claims that the seniority system violated his religious rights by assigning him to work on Saturday, his Sabbath day (*Trans-World Airlines* v. *Hardison*).

68. See Commerce Clearing House, *Employment Practices Guide*, 1463; "Labor Agency Seeks to Ensure Veterans Get Jobs, Promotions," *The Wall Street Journal*, October 23, 1975, p. 28.

69. Louis Decker and Daniel Peed, "Affirmative Action for the Handicapped," *Personnel*, May–June 1976, pp. 64–69.

70. Frederick Dyer and Chris Ford, "Training the Handicapped: Now Its Their Turn for Affirmative Action," *Personnel Journal*, April 1976, pp. 181–83; Robert Gortner, "I.E.'s Help Handicapped Workers Raise Productivity," *Industrial Engineering*, April 1973, pp, pp. 10–15; Joan Lublin, "Lowering Barriers: Pressured Companies Decide the Disabled Can Handle More Jobs," *The Wall Street Journal*, January 27, 1976.

71. Bernard DeLury, "Equal Job Opportunity for the Handicapped Means Positive Thinking and Positive Action," *Labor Law Journal*, November 1975, pp. 679–85; Sandra Kalenik, "Myths about Hiring the Physically Handicapped," *Job Safety and Health* 2, 9 (1974), pp. 9–12; Margaret Lyth, "Employer's Attitudes to the Employment of the Disabled," *Occupational Psychology* 47 (1973), pp. 67–70; Richard Shaffer, "Learning to Cope," *The Wall Street Journal*, June 2, 1976; Jeffrey Tannenbaum, "New Crusaders: Angry Blind Militants, Seeking 'Equal Rights' Try Tougher Tactics," *The Wall Street Journal*, July 10, 1975.

72. Sol Chanels, "Project Second Chance: A Job Program for Ex-Convicts That Works," *Psychology Today*, March 1975, pp. 41–46.

73. Mike Thorp, "Last Minority? With Little Fanfare, More Firms Accept Homosexual Employees," *The Wall Street Journal*, July 1, 1974.

74. *McDonald* v. *Sante Fe Trail Transportation Co.*, 423 U.S. 923, U.S. Supreme Ct., 1976.

75. *Weber* v. *Kaiser Aluminum & Chemical Corp*, 415 F. Supp. 761, 12 CCH *Employment Practices Decisions* ¶ 11,115, U.S. Dist, Ct., La., 1976; *Brunetti* v. *City of Berkeley*, 11 CCH *Employment Practices Decisions*, ¶ 10,804, U.S. Dist. Ct., Calif., 1976.

76. David Murray, "Integration of the Disadvantaged," *Canadian Personnel and Industrial Relations Journal*, May 1976, pp. 30–31.

77. Kay Eastham, "Women on the Move," *The Canadian Business Review*, Spring 1976, pp. 34–35; "Equal Opportunity: A Need to Update," *Canadian Personnel and Industrial Relations Journal*, October 1976, pp. 50–52; W. Earle McLaughlin, "Women in Business: Policies of Three Canadian Corporations," *The Canadian Business Review*, Summer 1976, pp. 8–10; Joy Moore and Frank Laverty, "Positive Action for Integrating Women into Management," *CanadianPersonnel and Industrial Relations Journal*, March 1975, pp. 15–21.

78. Kay Eastham, "How Affirmative Should Affirmative Action Be?" *Canadian Personnel and Industrial Relations Journal*, November 1976, pp. 23–26; Joy Moore and Frank Laverty, "Affirmative Action: A Sadly Passive Event," *The Business Quarterly*, Autumn 1976, pp. 22–26; Bette Pié, "Affirmative Action: Can the Voluntary Approach Work?" *The Business Quarterly*, Spring, 1976, pp. 15–19; Phillip Seams, "Canada's Female Academies Wary of Affirmative Action," *Chronicle of Higher Education*, November 10, 1975, p. 3; Traversy, "FEP Legislation."

79. "A Bid to Recoup Compliance Expense," *Chronicle of Higher Education*, January 10, 1977; Cheryl Fields, "Analyzing Campus Costs of Federal Programs," *Chronicle of Higher Education*, November 3, 1975; James Hyatt, "Sex and The Federal Contractor," *The Wall Street Journal*, April 4, 1974; James Hyatt, "Strangling in Red Tape," *The Wall Street Journal*, October 13, 1975.

80. Commerce Clearing House, *Employment Practices Guide*, no. 1360.

81. *Rowe* v. *General Motors Corp*, 457 F.2d 348, 5th Cir., 1972.

82. *EEOC* v. *Detroit Edison Co.*, 515 F.2d 301, 6th Cir., 1975.

83. *Parham* v. *Southwestern Bell Telephone Co.*, 433 F.2d 421, 8th Cir., 1970; *EEOC* v. *Garland Bank & Trust Co.*, 9 CCH *Employment Practices Decisions* ¶ 9875, U.S. Dist. Ct., Tex., 1974.

84. "Employment Discrimination: Statistics and Preference under Title VII," *Virginia Law Review, 59 (1973), pp. 463–91.*

85. Chayes, "Make Your Equal Opportunity Program Court Proof."

86. Theodore Purcell, "How G.E. Measures in Fair Employment," *Harvard Business Review*, November–December 1974, pp. 99–104.

Labor relations and group representation

- ■ To describe the labor relations process.
- ■ To show you how to become an effective manager of the labor relations process at the unit and division levels.
- ■ To demonstrate why grievances arise and how to manage them effectively.

CHAPTER OUTLINE

CHAPTER OUTLINE, CONTINUED

In a nonunionized enterprise, management has flexibility in paying and promoting people, establishing work rules, handling disciplinary situations, administering benefits, and other personnel matters. This can change when the employees join a union. Then, the union and the enterprise draw up a contract which spells out how things will be done. Strikes, slowdowns, secondary boycotts, and other pressures to accept the union's proposals may face the enterprise.

This chapter examines how operating and personnel managers proceed to manage labor relations.[1] It also discusses the employee grievance process in unionized and nonunionized enterprises.

DEFINITION

Labor relations is a continuous relationship between a defined group of employees (represented by a union or association) and an employer. The relationship includes the negotiation of a written contract concerning wages, hours, and other conditions of employment and the interpretation and administration of this contract over its period of coverage.

Labor relations is an emotionally charged personnel activity; few employers or employees get as emotionally involved over recruiting methods or career development plans, for example, as they do over this aspect of the personnel function. The reason is that collective bargaining goes to the heart of employee relations problems: power. Whoever has the power to fire an employee has power over whether that employee and his family can survive. Whoever has the power to discipline an employee in performance evaluation has the power to affect significant human needs negatively, as noted in Chapter 2. Underlying the concept of leadership in management is the need for power, as David McClelland describes it.[2] People thirst for the power to affect others' destinies, if only for eight hours a day.

Most employers have used their power fairly. They have hired employees, given them reasonable jobs, compensated them well, respected their dignity, and retired them after rewarding careers. Others have not dealt with their employees as well. They have exploited them economically and dealt many a blow to their human dignity.

When employers have behaved inequitably toward their employees, some employees have reacted by entering the political process. In extreme circumstances, revolutions are mounted and labor and socialist governments, pledged to protect employee rights and dignity, are elected. Employees also have sought and received the blessing of organized religions for their cause.

In the United States, conditions considered unfair or exploitative have led to the development of the collective bargaining process. Employees have joined together so that, as individuals, they did not have to stand alone against the power of a General Electric, or a Department of Defense or a

Wayne State University, or the Barnes Hospital. In general, successful American and Canadian unions have not tried to form a labor party or to change the political structure significantly.

In considering collective bargaining, one focus is the big picture: national and international unions all locked in major struggles with industry or in Congress.[3] As interesting as this is, the focus of this chapter is primarily on the effects of labor relations activities on the personnel function of the employer. National contracts, and especially national contracts for a multi-unit enterprise, are the business of a few top managers, a few top union officials, some staff lawyers and support persons, and a few government officials. Very few individuals are involved in these interactions. This chapter is concerned with how the collective bargaining process affects the *day-to-day operations* of an employer and its employees.

Both personnel and operating managers are involved in labor relations. Personnel managers or specialists are of necessity technical experts on labor relations who train and advise operating managers on the contract provisions. They also bargain with the union on the contract and serve as a step in the grievance process. But operating managers are the persons who make the contract work. They advise personnel on problem areas in the contract so they can try to improve them during the next negotiations, and they face grievances first. An overall vital influence in labor relations is exerted by top management. Top managers' attitudes toward unions strongly influence the attitudes of personnel and operating managers and help determine whether union-management relations will be amiable or combative. Top managers also strongly influence the negotiating process. The bargaining philosophy and strategy they assume at the time of negotiations will help determine whether a contract will be signed, and how soon, or whether impasses such as strikes, lockouts, and arbitration will occur.

Labor relations is a stage III personnel activity as outlined in Exhibit 1–13 in Chapter 1. Studies about unions have conflicting results, and, as noted above, labor relations elicits a more emotional response than perhaps any other considered in this text.

A DIAGNOSTIC APPROACH TO LABOR RELATIONS AND COLLECTIVE BARGAINING

Exhibit 19–1 highlights the diagnostic factors important in labor relations. The attitudes of employees toward unions influence whether they will join or support a union in the workplace. Managerial attitudes toward unions in general and the union officials they deal with in particular also affect labor relations.

The goals of the controlling interests influence managerial attitudes and behavior toward labor relations. If management is very antiunion, the negotiation and administration process will not proceed smoothly. The union is the other focal organization in effective collective bargaining relationships. Union officials face management daily and at contract time. Union and managerial attitudes toward each other affect the degree of peace and effectiveness that can exist in labor management relations.

Two other environmental factors influence the nature of collective bargaining. Labor market conditions influence both sides in their relationships. If the labor market is tight and demand for goods is strong, the union can hurt management by striking. If the demand for goods is soft and the labor market has a surplus, management has an advantage: It can sustain a strike, and perhaps even benefit economically from one.[4] The government creates the legal environment within which labor relations take place. Government boards adjudicate legal differences in the system, and government mediators and conciliators often help settle disputes.

Labor relations varies by the sector in which the enterprise operates. As will be described shortly, unions relate to managers in the business world (private sector), in government settings (public sector), and in other settings such as health, education, and voluntary organizations (third sector). Differing labor relations among the sectors are due to institutional and legal differences.

This chapter discusses how each of these factors inpacts on labor-management relationships and affects how the labor relations process, including collective bargaining works.

CONCEPTUAL FRAMEWORKS FOR LABOR RELATIONS

There have been several approaches to conceptualizing labor relations. The best known was conceived by John Dunlop, who calls his approach industrial relations systems.[5] Dunlop sees labor relations as an interaction of the union, the hierarchy of managers, and the government agencies involved. Three environmental factors influence these relationships: the power relations in the larger community, market or budgetary constraints, and the technology. The web of rules that regulate the workplace is comprised of these three factors. Although it has been criticized, Dunlop's approach is a useful one, as S. J. Wood et al. have demonstrated.[6]

A second well-known framework is the one proposed by Richard Walton and Robert McKersie, who view labor relations as one of several social negotiations.[7] Social negotiations are deliberate interactions of two groups to help define or redefine the terms of their interdependence. Walton and McKersie's four types of bargaining used in these negotiations will be discussed later in the chapter.

A third framework is that of Gerald Somers, who sees labor relations as an interaction of workers and managers in an exchange relationship.[8] External-oriented fields (such as law, politics, and economics) and internal-oriented fields (such as psychology and sociology) are important to understanding this exchange, Somers argues.

A developing subdivision of organizational theory called interorganizational analysis is a current emphasis which may provide another framework for analyzing labor relations.[9]

EXHIBIT 19–1
Factors affecting collective bargaining and organizational effectiveness

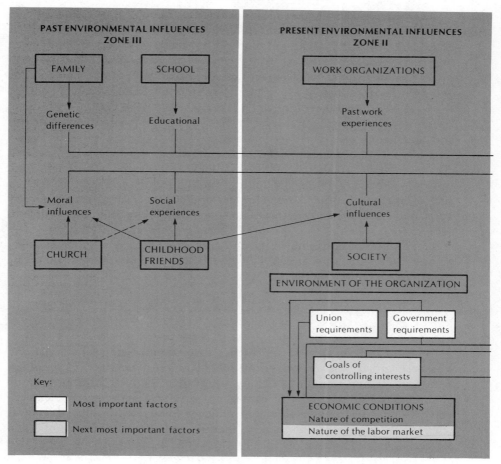

THE PSYCHOLOGY OF LABOR–MANAGEMENT RELATIONS

Managers sometimes have trouble comprehending how unions work, They might say, "How can you understand people? I gave my employees the best of everything, and what did they do? They joined a union." "That crazy union, do you know what they did now?"

To understand labor-management relations, specifically collective bargaining, it must first be understood that people act; organizations respond to people's decisions. Unions do not do this and corporations do that; rather, spokesmen and role occupiers make decisions and attempt to mobilize their organizations to action. The people and groups of people involved in collective bargaining are, to a greater or less extent unionized employees, union

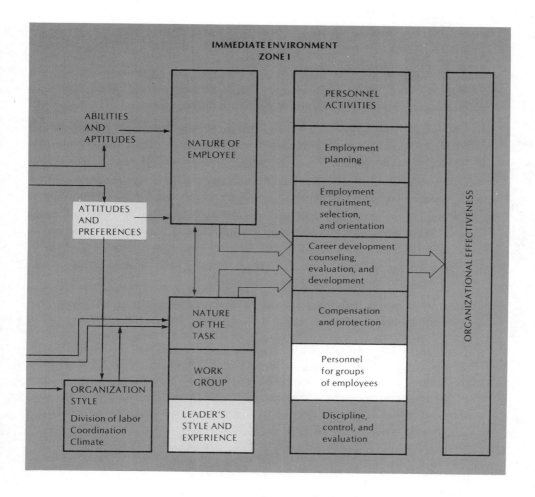

officials, employers and employers' officials, government officials, cutsomers
and clients, and the general public. The motivations and perceptions of
these persons are the most important factors in the collective bargaining
process. This section will help you understand the actions a little better.

Unionized employees

One of the first sets of individuals to be understood in order to comprehend the collective bargaining process is those who join unions, and perhaps
the most crucial factor is why they do so. Various theorists and researchers
have tried to explain this process. One group argues that employees join
unions because they are in conflict with management over the class struggle
of the haves and the have-nots.[10] Others contend that employees join unions

to achieve security in a world of competitive pressures and big employers.[11] And some theorists argue that people join unions to relieve their psychological frustrations and feelings of anomie in the workplace.[12]

Several analysts have tried to integrate the thinking of many of these global theorists by listing the multiple reasons persons join unions. This makes sense, since few decisions of this type are likely to be made for a single reason. Derek Bok and John Dunlop, for example, say people have certain perceptions about unions.[13] They believe unions have:

Increased the wages of their members. When this happens, employers raise the wages of nonunion workers as well. Thus unions increase all workers' wages.

Bargained for and achieved benefits such as pensions, insurance, vacations, and rest periods which have also improved the lot of the employee.

Provided formal rules and procedures for discipline, promotion, wage differentials, and other important job-related factors. This has led to greater justice and less arbitrary treatment of employees by employers.

Become the lobbyists for the common man and have made his voice heard in Congress and state legislatures.

Another expert lists these reasons why employees join unions: they provide better communication with management, better job conditions, improved supervision, more democracy in the workplace, greater employee unity, and higher morale.[14] Other experts emphasize the ability of associations such as unions to release job-related frustrations, ensure job security, and build employee self-confidence.[15]

Others have argued that people join unions for the same reasons they join fraternal groups: to belong to a group of persons with whom they can share experiences and have good fellowship. Like other social groups, some unions are beginning to offer other benefits, such as group auto insurance rates, group medical and dental care, and union-owned vacation facilities. Some people, of course, join unions because the employment contract requires union membership to keep a job.

It is probable that most people join unions as much for protection, security, and self-respect as to increase their economic status. Better wages obviously is one of the reasons, but the employer who thinks it is the only one will not be able to understand the collective bargaining process well. There is evidence that noneconomic reasons are more important, at least at some times.[16]

A recent study of public-sector employees concluded they joined unions for economic reasons (increased pay and benefits), to ensure protection of their rights and get better treatment, because they believed in unions, and because unions allowed them to participate in decisions affecting them. They did *not* join unions because of social pressures from current members.[17]

To whom does the unionized employee feel loyal? One study indicates that although some employees feel primarily tied to either union or employer, most feel a dual allegiance to both. They feel positively toward both and want to see both prosper. This is quite different from the situation in certain other countries, where the workers are antagonistic toward employers and may even wish to destroy them as a class or to destroy the present organization of society.[18]

Although many have argued that blue-collar employees are more likely to be attracted to unions than white-collar, professional, technical, and managerial employees, this seems to be changing. Recent evidence indicates a shift whereby these groups are now more positively inclined toward unions than in the past.[19]

One area of research that has been neglected is why union members will vote to drop the union. In 1976, 28,000 U.S. employees voted to throw unions out. In 1977 of the decertifying elections conducted by the National Labor Relations Board, the unions lost 628 of 811.

Employees not presently unionized

All employees have not accepted the rationale for unions. Attitudes develop out of the individuals' experience and the experiences of others. Thus new workers in heavily unionized areas such as the East, Midwest, and Far West are more likely to know about and accept the rationale and operations of unions than rural workers in the Southeast. Many of the reasons employees have for joining unions could be modified if the employer provided the benefits voluntarily, as some do. They may provide company-run camps and county clubs, try to maintain good jobs supervised by well-trained managers, and communicate with workers often and effectively.

Generally there are three reasons people do *not* join unions.

1. *They identify with management.* Those who work with or are close to management tend to identify with it and consider the union as an adversary. If they experience job dissatisfaction, however, they will lose this identification and consider joining a union.[20]

2. *They do not agree with the goals of unions.* Other employees may disagree with the objectives of unions politically and organizationally. For example, they may prefer merit to seniority rules, may fear union social or political power, may resent dues paying, and may feel unions interfere in free enterprise and individual initiative.[21]

3. *They see themselves as professionals and unions as inappropriate for professionals.* For years, many employees such as engineers, nurses, teachers, and others saw themselves as independent professionals working for an organization.[22] The concepts of union member and independent professional were viewed as opposites. These perceptions may be breaking down, as noted above.

Union officials and labor relations executives

The people most directly involved in collective bargaining are the parties sitting across the table from each other: union leaders and employers (or labor relations managers). Their job is to come to an agreement on future conditions of work at contract time or interpretation of the contract between contracts. Most such agreements require the two parties to assess the data involved in the decision and decide the set of conditions with which they can live.

The role of labor relations manager is a very important one on the personnel team. In the recent Prentice-Hall/ASPA study of 1,400 personnel executives, labor relations were rated as the most important issue to be faced in unionized firms.[23]

The facts and opinions considered in collective bargaining and their interpretation are filtered by the attitudes and motivations of labor relations managers and union officials. There have been a number of studies of the attitudes of these two groups toward one another in the private sector which show the unflattering, dysfunctional stereotypes they have developed of one another.[24] These stereotypes can disort the data presented during the collective bargaining process. The typical union official's stereotype of a labor relations manager is a pretty boy, snobbish, country-club type, fawning over his boss, who could not find his way to the bathroom without a map and never worked a real day's work in his life. His job is only to cheat honest workers out of a few cents an hour to get a big bonus. The labor relations manager, on the other hand, may stereotype the union official as a loud-mouth, uneducated goon who probably is stealing pension funds and no doubt beats up uncooperative workers. He will ruin the company because he does not understand the dog-eat-dog marketplace it must compete in.

Studies have shown that these stereotypes go back to at least college days for the managerial group.[25] Other research indicates that managers and union leaders have almost opposite opinions on the evaluative meaning of the words (like *strike*) used in labor relations.[26]

Although most of the research on the topic has been done in the private sector, studies in the public and third sectors indicate the perceptions of managerial and union officials are as unflattering as they are in the private sector.[27] These feelings about each other may cause each participant in collective bargaining to view the other side and the facts it presents suspiciously.

These differences have developed the same way all differences do: from differences in past experiences, education, social position, and so on. After examining perceptual differences between union and business managers, Ross Stagner and Hjalmar Rosen drew several implications for the collective bargaining process. First, differences in perceived reality between these two groups may precipitate disputes; the facts look different to different participants. Second, the cumulative effect of the various sources of uniformity in perceiving will operate to exaggerate the differences between managers and workers. These groups, on the average, differ in socioeconomic backgrounds, education, social roles, and emotional identification. It has become rare indeed that an ordinary worker rises to a high executive level.[28] Although these stereotypes and antagonisms appear to be the typical pattern, there are many examples where the two groups are compatible and get along well. This is because they have worked at it (for example, the steel industry) or one side has corrupted the other.

Bok and Dunlop reinforce these observations about union leaders. Unlike managers, who are hired as officials, almost all union leaders rise from the rank of the workers. Very few have professional backgrounds or much education beyond high school. They come from a working-class background. This is less true in smaller or professional unions, but in the main the background of the union leader is different from the manager's.[29]

As important as socioeconomic and educational background are the differences in the nature of their organizations, which can strongly affect the perception, motivation, and behavior of these two groups in collective bargaining. Most employer organizations are hierarchically organized. The personnel specialist representing the employer is responsible to a boss. He enters negotiations knowing how far he can go and what his boss expects. If he achieves these expectations, he will keep his job and be rewarded. Another study by Stagner indicates that labor relations managers in business are primarily concerned about vertical relations with their superiors. He suggests that these officials would have successfully identified with their fathers. The union organization is quite different, as are union officials. Stagner found them much more horizontally oriented, toward peers, and suggests that they identified with peer groups and brothers rather than fathers in their past.[30] This is functional because often unions are less hierarchical and follow a more democratic or liberal model. Even a cursory analysis of unions would find some more democratic than others, of course. But unlike the official representing the employer, the union official must submit the contract he has negotiated to a vote of the members. They can and do reject contracts. If they are dissatisfied with his behavior, they can and do remove the official by voting him out.

To a much larger extent, union leaders are politicians. They must persuade their members that they have done a good job in the negotiations, that they got the best contract they could, and that the distribution of the compensation, work rules, benefits, and other elements of the contract is fair. This is not always easy to do, especially when the union is composed of a varied membership, with younger workers generally desiring more wages and older workers opting for more pensions and "welfare" benefits.

Thus many of the difficulties that arise in collective bargaining stem from differences in the persons involved in the process. Labor relations managers are hierarchically oriented. They may be younger and are likely to be better educated. They are not knowledgeable of workers' true desires and aspirations, do not know union officials socially, and do not understand the union world. Union officials are older, have come up from the ranks, and are less well educated. They are subject to political pressure from their members and live in a different world from their counterparts.

A managers' union?

A managers' union may seem to be a contradiction in terms. However, a series of recent analyses indicates that supervisors and middle managers could unionize if they become alienated from top managers.[31] The identification of supervisors and middle managers with the attitudes and interests of top managers could end if management does not satisfy their needs and unions promise to do so. All the research indicates that junior managers may unionize as professionals have done if top management does not take steps to prevent it. Managerial unionism is not likely soon, however, and it is likely to be reactive to specific situations rather than a national trend. At present, the law does not encourage or support management unions, but laws have a way of changing to meet people's needs.

Government officials and others

The major actors and actresses in labor relations are the employees, labor relations executives, and unions and union officers. But others do have an impact.

Customers and clients of the enterprise may mobilize to move the negotiation process along faster. Customers who need goods or services may exert pressure on the employer directly to settle or lose the business. They also do this indirectly by buying elsewhere and letting the home office know it.

The general public tends to be neutral or uninterested in most collective bargaining incidents. Both sides try to mobilize support through the media, however, because if the public is denied service it can bring political or other pressures to bear on its settlement. This normally happens when the public is severely affected by loss of the goods or services.

One other group is involved in labor relations and collective bargaining: the government regulatory bodies that administer the labor laws. In the United States, the National Labor Relations Board (NLRB) administers the laws and regulations in the private and third sectors. Many states also have state boards to administer state labor laws.

In Canada, the federal labor law is administered by the Canada Labour Relations Board for the private and third sectors. The public-sector body is the Public Service Staff Relations Board. The provinces and territories have Labour Relations Boards composed of representatives of management, the unions, and the public to administer these legislation passed in these jurisdictions.

Labor relations administrators have two major duties:

- To supervise representation elections and certify unions as bargaining agents.
- To hear appeals of alleged violations of the laws.

Most experts believe the boards do a satisfactory job with elections, but some contend they are too slow in processing violations appeals.[32] However, they receive a large number of complaints, and it is not an easy job. In the month of March 1977, 5,273 new cases were filed with the NLRB. Some who favor the union side contend that these delays benefit management, and management deliberately takes its time and regularly appeals violation decisions. For example, cases where management is charged with firing prounion employees might take two years (with appeals and delays) to decide. By then the fired employees have other jobs or are tired of the process. Management disputes this, and the NLRB and other boards have attempted to expedite these cases. In 1977 the House passed a bill amending the Wagner Act and attempting to deal with these problems. It increases the National Labor Relations Board from five to seven members. It authorizes two-member panels to hear routine appeals alleging unfair labor practices. The NLRB is also given the power to seek court injunctions to enforce its rulings unless one side appeals within 30 days. The NLRB can also cause "willful violators" of the law or its rulings to lose government contracts for three years. Additional powers also include the authority to halt wildcat strikes and prohibit picketing of enterprises already unionized. The NLRB also receives greater power to determine the bargaining units. Since the Carter administration supports the bill, it is expected to become law early in 1978.

UNIONS IN THE UNITED STATES

About 21 million belong to trade unions and employee organizations in 1977. This is about 33 percent of the *eligible nonagricultural* civilian labor force. Essentially, union membership has been stable in the private sector. The union leadership is not happy with the stagnant growth of membership and is trying to reverse the trend. Union membership is growing rapidly in the public sector; membership in public unions grew from approximately 1.5 million to 5.5 million from 1964 to 1974. The goal of this section is to help you understand unions as organizations and why their officials behave the way they do.[33]

To become a union member, a person joins one of the 70,000 or so local unions. The local is a subunit of one of the 173 national unions, of which 110 belong to the American Federation of Labor–Congress of Industrial Organizations (AFL–CIO). This federation represents 80 percent of unionized employees and is organized as shown in Exhibit 19–2. The AFL-CIO does for unions what the chamber of commerce does for business: it provides research, education, lobbying, and public relations services.

The AFL–CIO's chief governing body is the biennial convention, which sets policy. Between conventions, the executive officers, assisted by the executive council and the general board, run the AFL–CIO. Executive officers are the president, who interprets the constitution between meetings of the executive council and heads the union staff, and the secretary-treasurer, who is responsible for financial affairs. The executive council also has 33

EXHIBIT 19–2
Structural organization of the American Federation of Labor and Congress of Industrial Organizations

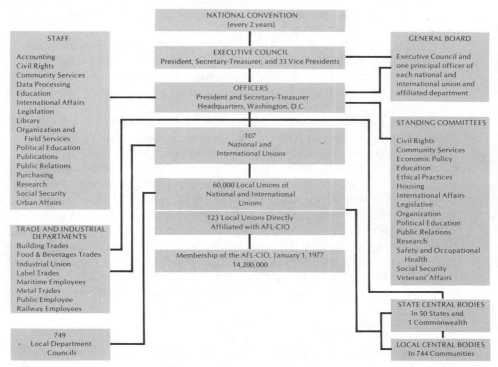

vice presidents. It meets three times a year and sets policy between conventions. The general board consists of the executive council and the head of each affiliated national union and department.

National headquarters provides many services to subsidiary union bodies: training for regional and local union leaders, organizing help, strike funds, and data to be used in negotiating contracts. Specialists available for consultation include lawyers, public relations specialists, and research personnel. Under the national union are regional groups of local unions which may provide office space and facilities for local unions.

The 173 national unions are a varied group. A number of the larger unions are independent of the AFL–CIO: the teamsters, auto workers, and mine workers. Very large unions which are members of the AFL–CIO are steel workers, electrical workers, carpenters, machinists, and hotel and restaurant workers. The smallest national union, a unit in the printing trade, has 18 members.

The fastest growing unions from 1964 to 1974 were all in the public sector: teachers (+344 percent), state, county, and municipal workers (+176 percent), and the American Federation of Government Employees (+116 percent). Some of the more innovative unions are the National Farm Workers and the major league baseball players group.

In addition to major moves into public sector, unions have also been active in the third sector. College professors are now unionized at 300 colleges and universities. Other major unionization moves have come in health organizations and in the arts.

The keystone of the trade union movement is the 70,000 local unions, representing all the union members in a geographic area for a craft union (e.g., all carpenters in San Francisco) or in a plant for an industrial union (e.g., UAW members at the Lansing, Michigan, Oldsmobile plant). Our major focus is on the local level.

The local union and labor relations

In general, the local union is a branch of the national union and has little legal autonomy. The national can charter or disband a local as well as suspend it or put it under national trusteeship. In many unions, the local must get permission from the national union before it can strike.

Just as there is great variety in the size and power of nationals, so there is great variety in locals. They vary in size from eight or so members up to the 40,000 or so members in Local 32–B (New York City) of the Service Employees International Union. The local union elects officials such as president, secretary-treasurer, business representative, and committee chairmen. If the local is large enough, the business representative and secretary-treasurer are full-time employees. The business representative plays a crucial role in contract negotiations and grievances. He usually administers the local office and handles such duties as public relations. The president and other officials, such as committee chairmen, hold full-time jobs in the trade or industry. Typically, they get some released time for union duties and are paid several hundred dollars a year in expenses.[34]

Another local unit personality is the shop steward or job steward. The steward has a position equivalent to foreman. He represents the union on the job site and is charged with handling grievances and disciplinary matters. Normally the steward is elected by members in the unit for a one-year term. In fact, the effectiveness of the local is usually judged in terms of effective grievance handling.[35]

Union leaders, especially local union leaders, have much less power than their managerial equivalents. They are always subject to reelection, and the contracts they negotiate must be ratified by union members. Members can also keep union leaders in line by voting their union out or by engaging in wildcat strikes. But the union member is typically apathetic about union affairs except in times of crisis, such as the decision to strike. Usually only 10 to 15 percent of the members attend an ordinary union meeting. This gives more freedom and power to the union leader during "normal" times.

In theory, unions are democratic; their members are supposed to influence their policies and decisions.[36] However, as one study found, some union leaders question the value of member participation and try to discourage it.[37] Various governmental hearings have discovered that there are unions in which the members have no say. As another study has shown, in the typical union an oligarchy has developed; a small percentage of members run it, and the higher the salaries of the union officials, the more this is so.[38]

The union leader often has a strong personality and can mobilize the members against the "enemy"—the employer.[39] The effective union leader realizes, however, that the demands made by the union must not put the employer out of business. Good union leaders help employers by policing the contract and keeping maverick members in line. Leonard Sayles shows how union leaders' personalities vary by the type of work done. More highly skilled workers choose quiet, competent, senior leaders. Semiskilled workers choose aggressive, vocal leaders.[40] Union leaders are as different as managers are. Some of the difficulties in collective bargaining arise because management and union leaders' personalities conflict.

Despite union leaders' control efforts, union members have a lot to say; as George Taylor says, the union leader's job should be "to discern, reconcile, and then represent the diverse and often conflicting demands and interests of the membership."[41] This is a significant point—the membership is frequently divided on what it wants. Managers usually exaggerate the power of the local union leader and overlook the pressures members and union subordinates can apply.[42]

In addition to internal pressures, unions compete with each other for members.[43] Unions have trouble deciding what personnel functions they should provide, whether they should allow their own employees to unionize (most do not allow this), and when to be militant or amenable.[44]

In sum, one of the challenges of labor relations is that on the union side of the bargaining table the representatives have more conflicts and usually less power than those on the employer's side. There are conflicts within the management side, too, but usually there is an official, such as a president, who can "settle" these conflicts by a decision. This is not so on the union side.

UNIONS AND LABOR RELATIONS IN CANADA

About 2,750,000 Canadians belong to unions (about 30 percent of the civilian labor force and 36 percent of the agricultural civilian labor force). Of these members, 71.2 percent belong to unions affiliated with the Canadian Labour Congress (CLC), 6.3 percent belong to unions in the Confederation of National Trade Unions (CNTU), and 20.2 percent are members of unaffiliated national and international unions or independent local unions. The rest belong to two small national union groups. Over half (55 percent) of the members belong to international unions, the largest being CLC (AFL–CIO) groups.

There are 21 larger unions (30,000 members or more). The five largest are United Steel Workers, 173,700; Canadian Union of Public Employees,

167,500; Public Service Alliance of Canada, 133,500; UAW International, 107,300; and Quebec Teachers Corporation, 87,500.

From 1953 to 1973 union membership in Canada more than doubled, from 1,220,000 to 2,610,000. This growth has been significant for the past 60 years.[45]

One concern some Canadian labor specialists have is that many of their major unions are linked to unions in the United States. In the same way some Canadians fear that "control" of Canadian industry by U.S. capital might not be in Canada's best interest, they express a similar concern for U.S. influence on unions. It has been shown, however, that although there are some disadvantages, in some circumstances this link can be a strength for the Canadian labor movement.[46]

The local union—lodge, branch, syndicate—is the basic labor unit in Canada. Each has its own constitution, and members participate, pay dues, and elect officers in the local, which does most of the negotiating. Exhibit 19–3 shows the place of the local union in a federation; there are also independent locals, as noted above.

The local often participates in joint efforts with other locals, in such groups as the local labor council for joint, citywide union efforts; the allied trades federation, which are mostly craft union locals coordinating with each other, often over jurisdictional disputes; and district councils. The feder-

EXHIBIT 19–3
Organization of Canadian unions

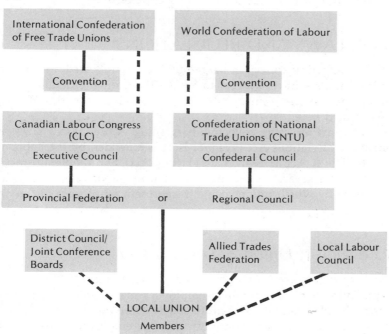

ations have regional or provincial offices to guard their interests, particularly in legislation.

The ultimate power of the Canadian Labour Congress is in the convention. Between conventions, the Executive Council meets quarterly to set policy. In CNTU, the Confederal Council meets quarterly also.[47]

The nature of labor relations is influenced by the relative strength of unions and employers and by the values and ideology of the union members and the managers.

There are several attitude sets on unionization in Canada. One is codetermination, or a sharing of authority.[48] Another is the traditional industrial relations model,[49] which assumes two separate groups, opposed to each other on the major issues. The third position is an in-between one—less than codetermination, but not two opposing forces either. This is the professional—white–collar model.[50] These attitudes no doubt affect the extent of unionization in Canada as compared to the greater degree of unionization in Europe.[51]

Management's view of unionization is another crucial factor affecting labor relations. Mark Thompson and Larry Moore contrasted these attitudes in the United States and Canada and found that English Canadian and U.S. managers' attitudes toward unions and labor relations are patterned differently; Canadians seemed to accept the institution of unions and collective bargaining more than American managers did but were more dissatisfied with the bargaining itself.[52] This difference bears out the finding that Canada has a different strike pattern than the United States does and that Canadian labor unions follow different political action patterns.[53]

U.S. LABOR LAWS AND REGULATIONS

The laws affecting collective bargaining are complicated, and most employers and unions have lawyers to advise them on the details. The laws change all the time, it seems. Only the general characteristics of the laws will be outlined here.

The major law affecting collective bargaining in the United States is the National Labor Relations Act (Wagner Act) as amended by the Labor-Management Relations Act of 1947 (Taft-Hartley Act), and the Landrum-Griffin Act of 1959. These acts cover many aspects of labor relations, including the procedure by which unions come to represent employees in the private sector.[54]

The private sector: Union organizing law

Union organizing goes through several phases to reach fruition. The first is the preliminary phase, in which employees invite union representatives to come to the place of employment to solicit union membership. Less often, unions on their own initiative seek to unionize employees. The law allows organizers to solicit employees for membership as long as this does not endanger the safety or performance of the employee. It can take place at lunch, at break time, and even during work time *if* the employer has allowed other groups such as United Appeal to solicit contributions during work time. If the employer has not allowed solicitations of any kind, it can refuse to allow union organizers on the property (including parking lots) and will usually refuse the union a list of employees.[55] Thus it is in the employer's interest to prohibit soliciting at work and in the parking lot.

Union organizers try to get the employees to sign authorization cards for that union to represent them in collective bargaining; 30 percent of the employees must sign them before the union can call for a representation election. It is illegal for employers to interfere with, threaten, or do violence to organizers or to install listening or similar surveillance devices to stop unionization, although management may observe what is going on in person. It is also illegal to discharge employees for prounion activity, and management must be careful to document discharges for inadequate performance during organizing efforts. It is illegal for either employers or union organizers to threaten employees during the unionization campaign. Unions can picket the organization if the employees are not already unionized, if a petition for election procedures was filed within 30 days to the National Labor Relations Board (NLRB), and if there has *not* been a recognition election in the preceding 12 months. As a result of the *Gissell Packing Company* decision by the Supreme Court,[56] if the union gets 50 percent plus one employee to sign the cards and can prove the employer committed a serious unfair labor practice, the NLRB will often declare the union the bargaining agent *without* an election. The employer cannot even challenge the conditions under which the cards were signed.

After the preliminary unionization period, the NLRB gets involved in a hearing stage. When the union or employer files NLRB form 502, the regional director of NLRB sends a hearing officer to investigate the situation. The examiner sends the union and management a notice of representation hearing (NLRB form 852), stating place and time of hearing. The examiner examines the situation to decide if there is enough evidence to hold an election (if 30 percent or more of the employees signed the authorization cards, for example). The examiner must also decide what the bargaining unit will be: the organization (exclusive of managerial personnel) or a series of subunits. If there appears to be enough evidence and if the examiner's decision to schedule an election is approved by superiors at NLRB, the employees are notified of the election and the employer of its rights (NLRB form 666).

There are two types of elections: consent elections and stipulation for certification upon consent election. The latter is preferable to management, since it allows appeals. Within 30 to 60 days, an election is held by the NLRB, which provides secret ballots and ballot boxes, counts the votes, and certifies the election. The union becomes the employees' representative if it wins the election. A number of sources are available to both sides summarizing what can and cannot be done during the organizing effort; one of the best is by Stephen Cabot and Douglas Linn.[57]

The NLRB and equivalent governing boards go to great lengths to enforce the law at organizing time. Many of the cases it accepts arise over alleged "illegal" practices during the campaign. Yet a landmark study of the campaigns and elections drew the conclusion that this was misplaced effort. Julius Getman et al. studied 31 elections and found that the Board's implicit assumptions were incorrect.[58]

Specifically the Board assumes that the employees' precampaign intent to vote one way or the other is tenuous and the campaign is likely to change their intent. In fact, the researchers found that the employees' intent was strong; 81 percent had made up their minds before the campaign and voted that way. The typical prounion voter was dissatisfied with current working conditions (though not necessarily with the work itself) and had favorable attitudes toward unions. The signing of an authorization card is a good predictor of a prounion position and normally is done before employers can get their position across.

Because the Board assumes voters are attentive to the campaign, it has clean-campaign rules. Yet the average voter remembered only 10 percent of the company's campaign issues and 7 percent of the union's. No issues and no campaign tactics or communication techniques were successful across the 31 elections. The Board enforces the regulations on unlawful tactics because it assumes they could coerce voters. Yet in the campaigns found to be using unlawful tactics, the percentage voting against unions did *not* increase, nor did employees appear to be threatened by employer interrogation about their sympathies.

Because the Board's assumptions were found incorrect in this study, Getman and his associates suggest it should stop enforcing its speech rules and similar campaign regulations. This would release about 25 percent of the Board's time, which it could use to enforce more significant violations of the law. The Board should also develop and enforce regulations for real threats such as the firings of prounion employees at organizing time, the authors conclude.

Several provisions designed to speed up organizing campaigns and toughen penalties for violations of the law are present in the House bill referred to earlier (expected to become law in 1978). These are: if the petition for an election is signed by a majority of the employees, the election must be held with 25 days; if between 30 and 50 percent sign, it must be held within 50 days; and only in special circumstances can the election be held as late as 75 days after the petition. Research by Greer and Martin indicates that it is in the employer's interest to lengthen the organizing periods.[59] The NLRB was given additional power to get court injunctions to force employers to rehire employees fired for pro-union activity. The bill also requires employers to allow unions to campaign at the workplace if the employer attempts to influence employees about the union at the workplace. Employers are given the right to campaign against the union at union headquarters.

Other private-sector labor relations laws

The specific rights of the parties involved in collective bargaining have been defined by law. The Wagner Act protects "employee rights" by prohibiting employers:

To interfere with, restrain, or coerce employees in the exercise of their rights to join unions and bargain collectively.

To dominate or interfere with the formation or administration of any labor organization or contribute financial or other support to it.

To encourage or discourage membership in any labor organization, by discrimination in regard to hire or tenure or any term or condition of employment. Section 8(3), however, included a proviso removing union security agreements from the general prohibition of encouragement or discouragement of labor organizations.

To discharge or otherwise discriminate against an employee for filing charges or giving testimony under the act.

To refuse to bargain collectively with the representatives of the employees.

The Taft-Hartley Act prohibits unions from engaging in six specific unfair labor practices:

To coerce employees in the exercise of their rights or to coerce employers in the selection of their representatives for purposes of collective bargaining or adjustment of grievances.

To cause an employer under a union shop agreement to discriminate against employees denied admission to the union or expelled from the unions for reasons other than nonpayment of dues and initiation fees.

To refuse to bargain collectively.

To engage in a jurisdictional strike or secondary boycott.

To charge excessive or discriminatory initiation fees to employees covered by a union shop agreement.

To cause an employer "in the nature of an exaction" to pay for services not performed.

The Taft-Hartley Law also includes the controversial Section 14.b, which allowed states to pass right-to-work laws which prohibit union shops and other union security agreements.

The third sector

In rulings in 1970 and 1974, the National Labor Relations Board and the courts ruled that third-sector enterprises were subject to private-sector labor relations laws.[60] Although the laws are the same, there are differences in how labor relations takes place in the third sector. There is a good deal of labor relations action in this sector today—in health care,[61] universities and colleges,[62] and the performing arts.[63] Essentially, however, the structure and legal environment are similar to those in the private sector.

The public sector

The second largest group of unionized employees is in the public sector. One third of all unionized public employees work for the federal government, and the rest are employed primarily by local government.

There are major differences between labor law and regulations in the private and public sectors.[64] In the private sector, the law tries to get management and labor to the table as equals. In the public sector, the government defines itself as the superior through the use of the sovereignty doctrine. Public managers in the past opposed collective bargaining for public employees, who were encouraged to seek improvements from the legislatures. In addition, responsibility for negotiating with employees is complicated by the separation-of-powers doctrine. Some managerial responsibility lies with the executive branch, others with the legislative.

Public-sector collective bargaining is relatively new in the United States and has not been developed definitively. There is more clarity for federal employees than others, although the system is not as well developed legally as it is in Canada.

Unlike the private sector, where labor relations regulations must be changed by laws passed by Congress and signed by the President, in the public sector federal labor relations are regulated by executive orders issued by the President alone, and each new order rescinds previous orders on the same topic. In 1962, President John F. Kennedy issued Executive Order 10988 designed to parallel federal bargaining to private bargaining, with the exception of inclusion of a strong management-rights clause and the banning of strikes and the union shop.

Executive Order 11491, issued by President Richard Nixon to update 10988, was designed to bring public bargaining even closer to that in the private sector. The order continued to list unfair labor practices by management and labor, as in the private sector, but under this order, the Secretary of Labor has the authority to determine bargaining units, to supervise procedures for union recognition, and to examine standards for and rule on unfair labor practices.

Order 11491 also created the Federal Labor Relations Council (FLRC), which reviews decisions of the Department of Labor and interprets the executive order implementation. It is composed of the Secretary of Labor, chairman of the Civil Service Commission, and director of the Office of Management and Budget. The FLRC supervises the Federal Service Impasse Panel, comprised of seven neutral members appointed by the President from outside the federal service to settle labor disputes in that sector.

Executive Order 11491 also required a simple majority of employees to choose an exclusive representative union and stipulated criteria for determining the bargaining unit. Cases and studies since then have helped clarify its meaning.[65]

Executive Order 11838, issued by President Gerald Ford in 1975, required federal agencies to bargain with their employees on all issues unless the agency could show *compelling need* not to negotiate. All personnel policies became subject to negotiation, and the FLRC was appointed the final arbitrator on these issues and what constituted compelling need. Subjects for grievances were also broadened. But this order still bans union-agency shops and requires a strong management-rights clause.

Labor relations regulations for public employees at state and local levels are diverse and complicated.[66] For example, 12 states have no applicable labor law at all for public employees; 20 states have such laws, and the other 18 have laws that cover certain aspects of labor relations for these employees.

For a time it was thought the answer to this confusion might be a federal law applicable to state and local employees. But in *AFSCME* v. *Woodward* (406F, 2D 137, 1969) and *National League of Cities* v. *Usery* (1976), the Supreme Court and other federal courts have made it clear that the federal government cannot interfere with state and local employees. These rulings have also said that these government employers do not have to bargain with their employees. So the degree of public bargaining practiced and the methods used vary from state to state and city to city.[67]

State labor relations laws

In addition to federal law, the states have passed labor laws affecting certain aspects of labor relations, as shown in Exhibit 19–4.

LABOR RELATIONS LAW IN CANADA

In Canada, all jurisdictions have laws regulating labor relations. The federal law is the Canada Labour Code (Part V: Industrial Relations, 1973). Each province has a similar law, such as Ontario's Labour Relations Act. The federal act applies only to industries under federal coverage, such as shipping and interprovincial railroads; provincial and territorial laws cover others.

All these laws recognize the right of employees to organize, and they require an employer and a certified trade union to conclude a contract on wages and other terms of employment. Except in Quebec, a representative labor relations board is responsible for the certification of a trade union as the exclusive bargaining agent for a unit of employees. In Quebec, certification functions are performed by special officers of the Department of Labour and Manpower. There is provision for appeals to the Labour Court. Unfair-practice provisions limit interference of employers and employees and their unions with each other's rights.

A collective agreement is binding on the parties covered. While it is in

EXHIBIT 19–4
State labor laws

State	State labor relations acts	Public employees: Collective bargaining	Right-to-work laws	Strikes	Picketing, boycotts
Alabama		X	X	X	X
Alaska		X		X	
Arizona		X	X	X	X
Arkansas			X	X	X
California		X		X	X
Colorado	X	X		X	X
Connecticut	X	X		X	X
Delaware		X		X	X
District of Columbia				X	X
Florida		X	X	X	X
Georgia			X	X	X
Hawaii	X	X		X	X
Idaho		X		X	X
Illinois				X	X
Indiana		X		X	X
Iowa			X	X	
Kansas	X	X	X	X	X
Kentucky				X	X
Louisiana		X	X	X	X
Maine		X		X	X
Maryland		X		X	X
Massachusetts	X	X		X	X
Michigan	X	X		X	X
Minnesota	X	X		X	X
Mississippi			X		X
Missouri		X		X	X
Montana		X		X	X
Nebraska		X	X	X	X
Nevada		X	X	X	
New Hampshire		X		X	X
New Jersey		X		X	X
New Mexico				X	X
New York	X	X		X	
North Carolina			X		X
North Dakota	X	X	X	X	X
Ohio				X	X
Oklahoma		X		X	X
Oregon	X	X		X	X
Pennsylvania	X	X		X	X
Puerto Rico	X			X	X
Rhode Island	X	X		X	X
South Carolina			X	X	X
South Dakota	X	X	X	X	X
Tennessee			X	X	X
Texas			X	X	X
Utah	X		X	X	X
Vermont	X	X		X	X
Virginia			X	X	X
Washington		X		X	X
West Virginia	X			X	X
Wisconsin	X	X		X	X
Wyoming		X	X	X	X

Source: Bureau of National Affairs, *Labor Relations* (Washington, D.C., 1976).

force, strikes are prohibited and disputes must be settled through a grievance procedure and, if necessary, arbitration. Under all the acts, government conciliation services are available to assist the parties to reach an agreement; a strike or lockout is forbidden while such conciliation is in progress.[68]

The laws are amended regularly, and the effective personnel manager will consult updates such as William Langford provides.[69] The laws vary by provinces. For example, in late 1977, Quebec was in the process of passing a bill to require dues checkoffs and to prevent employers from hiring strikebreakers. All provinces have legislation similar in principle to Part V of the Canada Labour Code, designed to establish harmonious relations between employers and employees and to facilitate the settlement of industrial disputes. These laws guarantee the right to organize, establish machinery (labor relations boards or other administrative systems) for the certification of a union as the exclusive bargaining agent of an appropriate unit of employees, and require an employer to bargain with the certified union representing its employees.

The labor relations boards are composed of representatives of management and labor and an independent chairman and vice chairman.[70] In 1975, the Department of Labour (Ottawa) set up a Canada Labour Relations Council. It includes representatives of labor, management, and the government, and its purpose is to promote labor peace at the federal level.[71]

In the past 25 years, Ottawa has passed 11 emergency labor legislation bills requiring key groups of employees whose labor negotiations have broken down to remain at work. Examples of these groups have been railways, longshoring, grain handling, and ferry services.[72] The provinces have passed similar laws within their jurisdictions.

In the public sector, federal employees' labor relations are governed by the Public Service Staff Relations Act of 1967. This law allows all federal employees (except managers) to join unions and bargaining collectively. The law also created the Public Service Staff Relations Board.[73] In most provinces civil servants have collective bargaining rights, and the right to negotiate is being extended to members of various professional groups. In some provinces, certain classes of employees engaged in essential services, such as firemen, police officers, or hospital employees, are forbidden to strike and must submit any unsettled contract disputes to binding arbitration. Both ad hoc and continuing laws have been adopted in a number of jurisdictions to end strikes that are deemed to endanger the public interest. The laws do change, and Marchand updates them regularly.[74]

H. W. Arthurs has described four models of collective bargaining by public employees: the federal model; public-sector model (e.g., the police in Ontario); informal public-sector model (public service in Ontario), and professional model (Ontario schools).[75] Most public-sector agreements require employees to choose ahead of time whether they will submit to binding arbitration or strike. Canadian union leaders criticize public-sector employers for this provision and other shortcomings just as strongly as private sector employers.[76]

UNION ORGANIZING

When employees are not represented by a union, three groups can initiate unionization: the employees themselves, a union, or management (the latter rarely does so). In some cases, when employees are quite dissatisfied, they can take the initiative and invite a union in to begin the organizing of an employer. There is little or no empirical evidence on the frequency of employee initiative.

The ability of a union to organize the workers in an enterprise, or an industry depends first on its own financial support for the initial organizing of employees. This varies by union and from time to time. Generally speaking, better financed unions attempt to organize employees more frequently. Organizing is also a function of the unions' motivation to organize. Some unions organize because they wish to grow larger—growth motivation is present in unions as it is in businesses. Or they may wish to unionize an enterprise if similar enterprises are union affiliated because nonunionized enterprises could harm the success of the unionized enterprises. Some unions will selectively organize those employees who have strategic market or technological positions.

The organizing campaign

Whether the employees or the union take the initiative, next comes a time of high drama: the organizing campaign itself. From the union's point of view, the object is to get 30 percent of the employees to sign authorization cards and then to get a majority vote in the election. Some research has been done on these campaigns.[77]

In general, the union tries to keep the initial stages secret so it can get up momentum before management can mount a counteroffensive. One study claims that the union might even use scare tactics to get the cards signed.[78] During the organizing period, unions and management pursue campaigns to affect employee attitudes toward unionization. Typically the union stresses how it can improve the workers' lot in terms of compensation, benefits, and employee protection. Management mounts a countercampaign stressing how well off the employees are already and the costs of union membership in dollars and "loss of freedom." As noted above, it is illegal for either side, in mass meetings, literature, or individual meetings, to threaten employees with discharge or violence. Both sides must be truthful, or the procedure can be set aside. It is probably unlawful for management to interrogate employees individually about their feelings toward unions, but secret polls are allowed.

Who wins these elections? Why do people sign these cards? They sign when they are dissatisfied with working conditions and feel the union can satisfy their needs.[79] Unions are also likely to win when the work unit is large.[80]

Analyses of the results of NLRB elections since 1936 indicate that about

80 percent of employees vote in the elections. Prounion votes are registered by about 60 percent of those who vote yearly. But each year, about 12,000 employees vote to throw the union out in a decertification election.

Some studies of management successes in representation elections have found that when management communicates with employees early in the process and consistently during it, management wins.[81] In the most successful campaigns management holds meetings with employees and distributes letters and memorandums stating its case. Some employers send their managers outside the firm to be trained in these techniques.[82] However, it has been found that issues and communication techniques do not win elections by themselves.

NEGOTIATING CONTRACTS WITH UNIONS

Once a union is recognized as the bargaining representative for a group of employees, its officials are authorized to negotiate an employment contract. There are usually three phases to this: preparation for negotiations, negotiation, and settlement. The negotiations often are very businesslike. Sometimes they are exciting, with strikes and publicity involved, but this is a rarity.

Preparations for contract negotiations

Prior to the actual negotiations, management and the union prepare for them. There are major differences in the degree of preparations, with smaller unions and employers understandably preparing less thoroughly or more informally than larger ones.

Preparation for contracts is an area in which little research has been done. One study of how 40 large companies prepared for contracts found that personnel people are mainly responsible for preparations for contract negotiations, but operating people often participate. And the more complex the bargaining, *the further ahead* preparations begin. Typical time requirements are three to four months of preparation prior to negotiations for a small firm that bargains through employer bargaining associations, and nine months for large, multiplant firms.[83]

The preparation process consists of five steps.

1. The beginning part of the preparation concerns problems in contract administration and changes in contract language. Both offensive and defensive strategies regarding contract changes are prepared. If management or the union wishes to make changes in a contract, it must notify the other party in writing of desire to terminate or modify the contract at least 60 days before the contract expires. This notification also should include an offer to meet the other side to discuss the issue.

Probably since the signing of the last contract, both sides have been compiling a list of issues to be brought up the next time. Management has asked its supervisors how they would like the contract modified to avoid problem areas. The personnel department has been studying patterns in grievances to see where problems to be remedied lie. The contract has been examined to identify undesirable sections, especially those that management feels restrict its rights.

2. Statistical information is gathered next, and visual displays and bargaining books are prepared. For example, management seeks information on economic conditions affecting the job (e.g., wage rates, productivity) from its staff, industry data, and published sources. One study points out the usefulness of work measurement in preparations for bargaining, and another describes how Canadian employers can receive up-to-date data on wage settlements made in recent negotiations from a computerized listing of daily settlements.[84]

An attempt is made to determine the cost of each likely union demand.[85] Often computer simulation can help here, but this is easier in wage offers than in the elimination of a compulsory overtime rule, for example. Preliminary tradeoffs are thought through. The union tends to ask for more than it knows it can get, so management tries to calculate the best strategy.

3. Detailed studies of the union leadership and membership personalities are prepared to help develop the bargaining strategy.

4. If the organizing effort is industrywide, intercompany preparation begins next. Enterprises in the industry exchange information at many levels.

5. A few enterprises next meet with the union to try to narrow the bargaining scope and get a feel of each other's priorities.

Often there are differences within management groups over bargaining objectives.[86] A common complaint is: "I'm having more trouble with my company than I am with the union." If these management differences are worked out before the negotiations start, the bargaining process will be more effective. One expert points out that an employer who negotiates with more than one union must prepare carefully, for what it negotiates with one union will be brought up by the other.[87] Typically a careful balance of wage, benefit, and status differentials must be maintained among unions. Careful preparations will help maintain that balance.

The union also prepares for negotiations by preparing lists of problems with the contract. It too gathers statistical information, studies the opponent closely, and coordinates with other unions involved. Unions may also have internal differences, usually over what the bargaining objectives are; for example, younger workers may want a pay increase, older workers better pensions. An example of how a union sets bargaining objectives was reported prior to the 1976 United Auto Workers negotiations.[88] Increasingly, unions poll their members on their preferred objectives for negotiation.

Very few studies have been done of how unions set their priorities. It is probable that members' expectations are formalized by the union leadership, which compares past trends and extrapolates them to the present situation. If a 3 percent raise was secured two contracts back and 4 percent last time, they may shoot for 5 percent this time. Or the leadership compares recent settlements of unions like their own and sets these as their goals; steelworkers, for example, may compare the results of a recent automakers' settlement. The latter approach seems more likely, if case study research is accurate.[89]

Contract issues

Any labor contract can have a large number of clauses, and there are numerous issues over which the two parties can bargain. One study shows how the number of items an employer must bargain over has increased from less than 5 in 1940 to almost 70 in the 1970s.[90] They can be categorized into the five groups named below.

1. *Compensation and working conditions.*   All contracts stipulate compensation and working conditions, such as direct compensation rates, benefits, and hours of work. Issues concern whether overtime should be voluntary, cost-of-living adjustments, and newer benefits such as dental care. Unions bargain about not only payments for pensions but also the details of early retirement provisions, for example. Two examples of compensation and working conditions being negotiated in the late 1970s are shorter work weeks and less rigorous work rules.[91]

2. *Employee security.*   Seniority is a special concern in this bargaining category. Unions feel that seniority should be the determining factor in promotions, layoffs, and recalls. Management contends that it is its right to make these decisions on the basis of job performance, or efficiency will suffer. The clause many contracts have stipulates that in cases of promotion and layoff, when efficiency and ability are substantially equal, the most senior employee shall be favored. (Seniority is continuous service in a work unit, plant, or organization.) In the late 1970s unions are negotiating for lifetime job security, especially in steel and higher education.[92]

3. *Union security.*   To have as much influence over members as possible, the union tries to write a requirement for a union shop into the contract. A union shop is an employment location at which all employees must join the union after a brief introductory period. Failing this, the union tries to get a modified union shop: all employees except a few exempted groups must join the union. If the union shop clause cannot be won, an agency shop may be acceptable to the union. In this, those who do not join the union must pay the equivalent of union dues to the union.

4. *Management rights.*   This issue usually presents an especially difficult set of problems. Management lists certain areas or decisions as management rights or prerogatives which are thus excluded from bargaining. Management tries to make these lists long, and unions have chipped away at them. Recently the United Auto Workers argued that handling health and safety problems should be a joint union-management area. This union also disputes a foreman's right to suspend a worker without pay over issues other than violence, drunkenness, and illegal refusal to work.

5. *Contract duration.*   This issue is of special concern to the enterprise. Com-

EXHIBIT 19–5
Collective bargaining by objectives—a guide for data preparation, strategy, and evaluation of bargaining results (blank form)

Bargaining* items	Priorities†	Range of bargaining objectives			Initial ‡ bargaining position	Evaluation results		
		Pessimistic	Realistic	Optimistic		P	R	O

*Classify items in two groups: financial and nonfinancial.
† Relative priority of each bargaining item to all bargaining items.
‡ Actual visible position taken by parties at opening of negotiation (union initial proposal or company response or counteroffer).
Source: Reed Richardson, "Positive Collective Bargaining," in *Employee and Labor Relations,* vol. 3, ed. H. Heneman, Jr., and D. Yoder (Washington, D.C.: Bureau of National Affairs, 1976), pp. 7-111–7-143.

panies tend to prefer longer contracts to avoid the turmoil of frequent negotiation. Over 90 percent of U.S. contracts now cover two- or three-year periods.

To increase the effectiveness of the bargaining process, one suggestion is for both sides to make a list of the bargaining items and rank order them, as shown in Exhibit 19–5.

The structure of negotiations

How the 150,000 or so labor contracts are negotiated yearly in the United States (and many others in Canada) varies a great deal, depending on the size and importance of the agreement. There are several possible structures for the negotiations:

A single union negotiates with a single employer (type A).

A single union negotiates with more than one employer (type B).

Several unions negotiate simultaneously with a single employer (type C).

Several unions negotiate simultaneously with several employers (type D).

Most contract negotiations are type A bargaining structures. Multiple-employer bargaining (type B) allows all the employers to get the same wage rates and prevents some employers from settling for higher wages and becoming uncompetitive. Multiple-employer bargaining is common in construction, retailing, local trucking, and service industries such as hotels.[93]

Coordinated bargaining (type C) takes place when several unions coordinate their contract demands and strategies. It appears to be increasing in the private and public sectors,[94] although some experts doubt its long-run viability.[95] There are few examples of type D bargaining at present. In Canada, 75 percent of contracts are type A; 17 percent are type B.[96]

These bargaining structures develop as a consequence of the changing ways enterprises do business; that is, as the technology and markets change, their structures change. Unions adjust the bargaining structure accordingly.[97] One study shows that unions also adapt their bargaining structures in higher education to the structure of the universities (for example, single-campus or multiple-campus bargaining).[98]

David Greenberg examined characteristics of the structure of collective bargaining as evidenced by 52 U.S. industries.[99] He found several combinations of structures besides single employer or multiple employer; for example, single-employer bargaining can be subdivided into company subunit bargaining (single establishments or regional groupings of establishments). Greenberg's classification of industry bargaining structures is shown in Exhibit 19–6; his five types, A–E, are different from the four types named above.

Greenberg found that the greater the seller concentration in an industry (monopoly, oligopoly), the more pattern there is to bargaining in the industry. One company settles; the others follow suit with the same terms. He also found that the greater the seller concentration, the less likely there was to be multiple-employer bargaining. Company size also was an important factor; the smaller the company, the more likely it was to try multiple-employer bargaining. This approach has cost savings and gives the smaller firm more power in the negotiations. Multiple-employer bargaining is also fostered if it is a labor-intensive industry, the firms are closely located spatially, and the union hires and recruits the workers for the employers.

Once the preparations for negotiations are ready and the structure of the bargaining is clarified, both sides begin to muster support. The union holds membership meetings and gets publicity in the press. The employer communicates his position through the public press and company publications. Both are seeking employee support and the support of the community as well.

Much of this process is ritualistic for some contracts. The union leaders make speeches about fat capitalists with enormous profit margins cheating the workers. Management implies that ignorant or malicious union leaders have led good workers astray and encouraged others to become lazy and will force the employer into bankruptcy. Other negotiations, particularly for larger numbers of employees, are more businesslike. The sides exchange offers and demands which are close to final terms and quietly settle the contract.

Negotiating and bargaining approaches

Various theorists have described the different approaches to bargaining negotiations. Traditional economic theory describes negotiating as a basically rational process in which each side seeks to advance its own interests.[100]

EXHIBIT 19–6
Extent of unionization and type of negotiating unit

Relations between bargaining units	Multiemployer			Individual-employer		
					Pure individual-employer	
	Pure multiemployer — A	Significant single employer — B	Multiemployer significant — C	Companywide — D	Company subunit — E
I. Industrywide	Wallpaper Men's suits and coats Anthracite coal Railroads* Pineapple Auto sprinkler			Postal Service	Oil refining Cement
II. Strong pattern	Elevator construction Glass containers* Fur Bituminous coal Trucking	Basic steel	Meat packing	Aluminum Cigarettes Tin cans Tires and tubes Flat glass* Motor vehicles and parts Farm implements	Nonferrous metals Aerospace Telephone
III. Middle pattern	Millinery		Shoes Pressed and blown glassware	Airlines Rugs and carpets* Fabricated rubber Woolen and worsted textiles	
IV. Strongly linked regional pattern	Offshore maritime* Stevedoring	Ladies' garments		Cotton and rayon textiles	
V. Weak pattern	Great Lakes Maritime* Lithographic*	Caps and cloth hats	Inland waterways	Electrical machinery Hats*	
VI. Regional pattern		Supermarkets	Shipbuilding		Pulp and paper†
VII. No pattern (or local pattern)	Hotels*	Malt liquor		Local transit Electric and gas utilities Primary and secondary education	Chemicals

* At least 5 percent of the unionized employees in multiemployer industry are in single-employer bargaining units or vice versa.

† Significant multiemployer bargaining exists in industry.

Source: David Greenberg, "The Structure of Collective Bargaining and Some of Its Determinants," *Proceedings*, Industrial Relations Research Association, December 1966 (Albany, N.Y., 1966).

Other economists still describe the process as "economically rational" but recognize the emotional factors in it.[101] More recently, formal attempts to integrate economic and rational with other factors have led to several behavioral models, the best known of which was formulated by Walton and McKersie.[102] Walton and McKersie describe two opposing negotiating strategies: distributive and integrative.

The predominant negotiating pattern appears to be distributive bargaining. This involves the assumption of a win-lose relationship; if the employers give up something to the union, or vice versa, they lose. To minimize the losses, horse trading takes place until some sort of equilibrium is found.

An alternative to this strategy is integrative bargaining. In this approach, continued attempts to improve relationships between management and union take place while the contract is on. Mutual studies of problem areas could lead to acceptable solutions for both.

Both these approaches are supplemented by attitude structuring and intraorganizational bargaining. Attitude change and bargaining within the union and within management are also going on during collective bargaining.

In general, most writings about these approaches are prescriptive or descriptive. One study examines the Walton and McKersie hypothesis that integrative bargaining is more effective. Richard Peterson and L. N. Tracy formalized Walton and McKersie's assumptions and hypothesized that success in problem solving (integrative bargaining) is more likely when six sets of conditions exist (H1.0–H6.0) (see Exhibit 19–7). They tested the model using questionnaires completed by 37 management and 28 union chief negotiators involved in 60 negotiations and found the model generally useful, except for professional orientation of negotiators and length of bargaining relationships. Peterson and Tracy subsequently added economic and power subvariables and proposed the revised model shown in Exhibit 19–8, as an attempt to test for effective approaches to negotiations.

Another expert who describes bargaining approaches is Benjamin Selekman.[103] He contends that nine types of bargaining postures can be taken. A few are rather *rarely* found. These include:

Racketeering.   Corrupt union leaders have relationships with "cooperating" managements.

Ideological.   The bargaining process is viewed as part of a class struggle, to reach ends other than just short-run improvement in working conditions.

Collusion.   Management and labor combine to get an advantage over the public or competitors by illegal or quasi-illegal means.

Deal.   Management and labor negotiate secretly, with little involvement of employees.

I have ranked five of Selekman's postures along Walton and McKersie's dimensions from most distributive to most integrative. They are:

EXHIBIT 19–7

Model of factors affecting successful nondistributive bargaining (problem-solving) behavior in collective bargaining

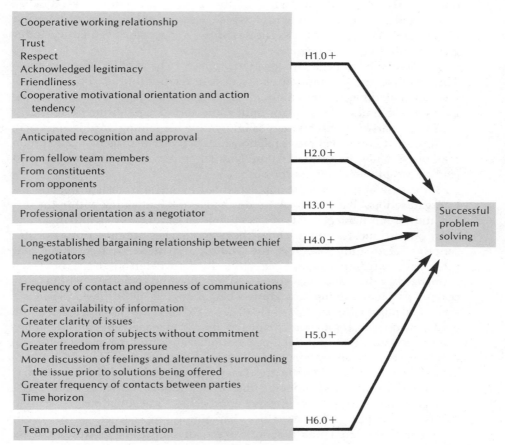

Source: Richard Peterson and L. N. Tracy, "A Behavioural Model of Problem Solving in Labor Negotiations," *British Journal of Industrial Relations,* 14, 2 (1976), pp. 159–73.

Containment-aggression. The union aggressively tries to take over management rights, and management aggressively tries to keep the union down (most distributive).

Conflict. The employer tries hard to get rid of a union, and the union resists.

Power. Union and management try to get all possible advantages from each other.

Accommodation. Both sides live and let live.

Cooperation. Both sides are concerned about the total work environment and try hard to improve bargaining and the work environment (most integrative).

EXHIBIT 19–8

Revised model of factors affecting successful nondistributive bargaining (problem-solving) behavior in collective bargaining

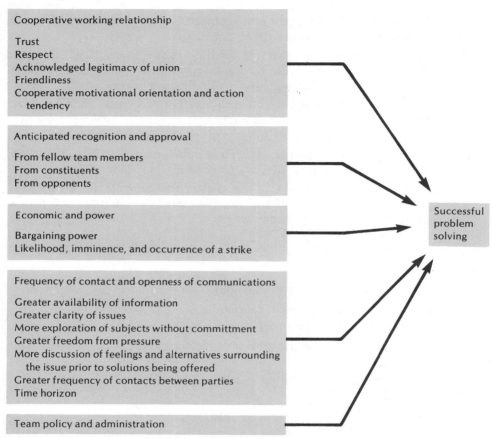

Source: Richard Peterson and L. N. Tracy, "A Behavioural Model of Problem Solving in Labor Negotiations," *British Journal of Industrial Relations,* 14, 2 (1976), pp. 159–73.

Over time, the two parties might move from postures of containment-aggression to cooperation. Others may move back and forth, partially as a result of changing leadership and economic conditions. Some sectors have had relatively more labor peace than others.

J. Stacey Adams has summarized some experimental research on the behavior of persons who operate at the "boundary" between the enterprise and other interests, such as negotiators.[104] He believes that the bargaining behavior adopted depends on a series of variables. Some of these are:

Visibility. If the negotiations are open and the actions of the negotiators are known, the behavior will be less flexible. Thus the union may be willing to give in less if all its actions become known to the public.

If only the outcome is public, it can claim "this is the best we could do."

Mutual perceptions of strategies. If the negotiator perceives the opponent as exploitative, she'll bargain more competitively and demandingly, even if the verbal offers appear to be conciliatory.

Expectations of future negotiations. If the negotiators know they will meet the other side again in the future, they will be willing to compromise. If it is a one-time bargain, they will bargain harder.

Consensus on issues. If the negotiators perceive consensus on both sides, they can get down to business and bargain cooperatively. If they perceive differences in either side's position, the maneuvering begins.

Time pressure to achieve an agreement. Time influences the process; the direction of the outcome is not easy to predict.

Control over negotiators' rewards. The greater the control over negotiators rewards (pay, prestige, and so on), the more the negotiator will follow instructions to negotiate one way.

Reed Richardson recommends procedures to make negotiations effective.[105] They include:

Keep your real objectives confidential.

Don't hurry; when in doubt, caucus.

Be flexible and remember bargaining is by nature compromise.

Try to understand why the other side is taking its position. Respect their need for face-saving.

Build a reputation of firm but fair negotiation.

Control your emotions.

Measure each move against your objectives.

Remember, the impact of present concessions affects the future.

Negotiations at the local union and single-operation level usually take place between two teams of negotiators. The union team is larger; typically it has about seven members, including local officers, several stewards and committeemen, and a representative from the regional or national union. Management fields a team of three or four from personnel and line management. They usually operate within guidelines set by their top management officers.

Bargaining stages. Typically, distributive bargaining follows several stages of development.

1. *Each side presents its demands.* Usually the two parties are far apart on some issues.

2. *Reduction of demands.* After the postures have been taken, each side trades off some of the demands they were not too serious about. These demands were included for trading purposes. Pressure is received from the

public, customers, union members, and others regarding the bargaining terms.

3. *Subcommittee studies.*   Getting down to business, the two parties form joint subcommittees which try to work out reasonable alternatives.

4. *Informal settlement.*   The two sides go back to their reference groups. The management team determines if top management will accept the terms, and union leaders take soundings of the memberships to see their reaction. If management is agreeable, the process develops into the formal settlement stage.

One final stage has appeared recently. Peter Henle calls it *reverse collective bargaining,* or it could be called renegotiations. This is his discription for cases where, in the middle of a contract, the union asks to reopen negotiations to increase wages in a time of inflation. This is less likely if cost-of-living allowances are included in wage contracts. But Henle also describes 12 cases in 1971–72 where contracts were renegotiated to *lower* wages or fringe benefits. These occurred when larger multiplant corporations announced that because wages were too high, they would have to close a plant or greatly scale down employment. The unions agreed to lower wages in these cases to save jobs, because the companies could demonstrate the wage disparities. Henle argues they also did so because the two parties had a history of mutual trust and confidence in bargaining.[106]

Ann Douglas gives one of the best descriptions of negotiations ever written. To experience the reality of negotiations, see her book, *Industrial Peacemaking.*[107]

Agreeing upon, ratifying, and formalizing the contract

An agreement comes about when both sides feel they have produced the best contract they can. Their perceptions are influenced by the negotiations, the relative power of the two at the time, and other factors. Power factors such as a weak union or a strong employer are very important in the settlement of the contract. If the economy is slack, the union may be under more pressure to settle than in times of full employment. If the employer's business has certain crucial times (e.g., new-model time for autos, harvesttime for food, Christmastime for the post office), the union may choose that time for negotiation to give it an advantage. If the government is committed to few strikes, it may intervene. All of these external factors and more enter the bargaining process.

Labor relations has lacked an empirical research emphasis. Recently a few researchers have tried to determine the conditions under which one side or the other wins, loses, or compromises. This trend is promising, but much needs to be done in the area.[108]

After the two sides have tentatively agreed, the union leadership must receive the membership's support. The members must believe the contract is the best the union could get. At one time membership ratification was mostly a rubber stamp, but union locals may now refuse to ratify contracts.

EXHIBIT 19–9
Standard labor contract format

Section no.	Subject
1	Purpose of the parties (union and management)
2	Management rights
3	Union security and dues checkoff
4	Grievance procedures
5	Arbitration of grievances
6	Disciplinary procedures
7	Compensation rates
8	Hours of work and overtime
9	Benefits: Vacations
	Holidays
	Insurance
	Pensions
10	Health and safety provisions
11	Employee security-seniority provisions
12	Contract expiration date

In one year in the mid seventies, for example, 12.3 percent were rejected by members. Some experts believe this trend is not serious, because the statistics used are not weighted properly;[109] others dispute this.[110] In any case, the statistics on rejections have been increasing. If the membership refuses ratification, the union negotiating team must try to achieve more concessions from management.

To create a formal settlement, a memorandum of agreement is prepared for the negotiating committee's assent. Both sides sign this memorandum. In most unions, the contract does not become official until the union membership ratifies it.

The agreement or contract sets out the rules of the job for the contract period. It restricts some behavior and requires other behavior. Proper wording of the agreement can prevent future difficulties in interpretation. Both sides should thoroughly discuss the meaning of each clause to prevent misunderstanding, if possible. A typical format for the sections normally covered in the contract or agreement is given in Exhibit 19–9.

Even if the contract is accepted at one level, it may require adjustments at other levels. For example, when Ford signs a contract with the UAW at the national level, local plants must then settle disputes on work rules and other issues at each plant. Only when these are settled is the contract negotiation process over for a while.[111]

IMPASSES IN COLLECTIVE BARGAINING

The description of contract negotiation above suggests a smooth flow, from presentation of demands to settlement. This flow is not always so smooth and impasses may develop at which one or both sides cannot keep the process moving. Three things can happen when an impasse develops: conciliation or mediation, a strike or lockout, or arbitration. The tempers can be rising at such times, and brutally long hours are put in by the negotiators.

Conciliation and mediation

> **DEFINITION**
> Conciliation or mediation is the process by which a professional, neutral
> third party is invited in by both parties to help remove an impasse to
> the negotiations.

All experts agree that it is better for the two parties to negotiate alone.
When it appears this process has broken down, however, a mediator, usually
a government mediator such as those provided by the Federal Mediation
and Conciliation Service (FMCS), can be invited in. Some states and provinces
also offer mediation services to both sides. The 250 men and women of
FMCS offer such services as developing factual data if the two sides disagree,
setting up joint study committees on difficult points, or trying to help the
two sides find common grounds for further bilateral negotiations. Instead
of waiting until an impasse, the FMCS also offers preventative mediation—
when the two parties anticipate serious problems prior to deadlines for
strikes, and so on.

By U.S. federal law, both parties must notify FMCS of unresolved disputes
not later than 30 days before the contract expires. One of the most frequent
uses of mediation and conciliation is in public-sector disputes, where strikes
are prohibited.[112]

Are fact-finding, mediation, and conciliation helpful in breaking impasses?
In general, the evidence is that conciliation required by law is not effective.
Some research finds the evidence mixed: sometimes it helps, sometimes not.
Too little evidence is available to specify the conditions when it is effective.[113]

Strikes and lockouts

If an impasse in negotiations is quite serious, a strike or a lockout can
take place. Confronted with the costs and inconveniences of strikes, many
employers and employees might like to outlaw them and use compulsory
arbitration as a substitute, but just about all experts in the field oppose
this alternative. During World War II, a system similar to compulsory arbitration was used. It was the *unanimous opinion* of the arbitrators that the best
thing that happened to the United States was the return to free collective
bargaining, strikes and all.

> **DEFINITIONS**
> A strike is a refusal by employees to work.
> A lockout is a refusal by management to allow employees to work.

Strikes can be categorized by the objectives they seek. A *contract* strike occurs when management and the union cannot agree on terms of a new contract. More than 90 percent of strikes are contract strikes.

A *grievance* strike occurs when the union disagrees on how management is interpreting the contract or handling day-to-day problems such as discipline. Strikes over grievances are prohibited in about 95 percent of contracts, but they occur fairly frequently in mining, transportation, and construction industries.

A *jurisdictional* strike takes place when two or more unions disagree on which jobs should be organized by each union. About 2.5 percent of strikers are involved in these strikes, although the Taft-Hartley law gives the NLRB the power to settle these issues, and unions also have internal methods for settling them.

About 1 percent of strikes are *recognition* strikes. These occur as a strategy to force an employer to accept the union. *Political* strikes take place to influence government policy and are extremely rare in the United States.

Strikes differ too in the percentage of employees who refuse to work. A *total* strike takes place when all unionized employees walk out; if only a percentage of the workers does so, the result may be a partial strike, semi-strike, or slowdown. In a *slowdown,* all employees come to work but they do little work; the union insists on all work rules being followed to the letter, with the result that output slows down. In England, they call this "working to rule." In a *partial strike,* many employees strike but others come to work. This type is especially prevalent in the public sector so essential services can be continued. In Canada, for example essential services are defined for each government unit, and workers rotate to do them. Some researchers suggest that a partial strike is a solution to no-strike provisions in public employment; all employees could do some work and withhold some services. Both employers and employees would be hurt and thus pressured to settle, but the public's essential interest would be preserved. Other researchers suggest a graduated partial strike as a solution. If an impasse exists, the workers would reduce services two hours per week and get three fourths of their regular pay for hours not worked. The next week, they would work four hours less but get only five-eighths regular pay for hours not worked, and so on.[114] This idea puts financial pressures on both sides, but it is less costly than a total strike.

In Europe, a much more destructive type of partial strike is used—the ratchet strike. Employees deliberately slow down, or what appears to be random absenteeism and sick calls take place. The ratchet or rotating type of strike has been used very effectively in Italy. Workers 1, 3, 5, 7, 9, etc., on an assembly line call in sick for the morning. Workers 2, 4, 6, 8, etc., become sick for the afternoon. This causes havoc for production and cuts the cost to the strikers from loss of pay. This method also was apparently used by striking Canadian rail workers in 1973.

Anatomy of a strike.   For a strike to take place, three actors must make decisions. Management must decide it can afford to "take a strike"; that is, it has built its inventories up, has sufficient financial resources, feels it will not lose too many customers during a strike, and believes it can win. The union must believe it will win more than it loses, that the enterprise will not go out of business, and that management will not replace the union employees with strikebreakers. The union members must be willing to live with hardships and worries about no paychecks and be willing to give the union a strike vote. When members give the union the authority to strike, its bargaining hand is strengthened, and it can time the strike to occur when it will hurt management the most.

During the strike, the union sets up the legally allowed number of pickets at the plants. Union headquarters becomes strike headquarters, and the union tries to mobilize support among allies in other unions and the public. It also might try to get them not to use the enterprise's goods and services. A strike is a very emotional experience, and violence can occur if management tries to bring in strikebreakers. Union officials build the morale of the strikers, especially on the picket line. One account describes how a union leader played his role during the long 1976 rubber strike.[115]

What does management do if there is a strike? Lockouts are rarely used. In general, it tries to encourage the workers to return to work by advertising circulars, phone calls, and so on. The longer the strike, the harder it is on the strikers. If the union has only limited strike funds and workers' savings run out, a back-to-work movement can cause the strike to collapse, which is what management wants. In recent years, management has tended to play a defensive "wait them out" game and to keep the enterprise operating during a strike. Nonunionized employees such as white-collar workers and managers may try to keep things going, and if management goes on the offensive, it can hire strikebreakers or threaten to close the plant. It is difficult to calculate when to operate and when to close down, and there are many imponderables and unknowns in the conditions. The advantages of continued operations include teaching the union a lesson, continuance of vital services, and an improved bargaining position. The disadvantages include increased bitterness during and after the strike, property damage and violence, and public relations defeats.[116] A strike ends when both sides return to the bargaining table, or the weaker side gives in.

Strikes in the public sector. In Canada, partial public employee strikes are allowed, and some total strikes have taken place, but in general few strikes have materialized in the public sector. Several postal strikes are the best known. In Canada, where the employees can elect either binding arbitration or strikes, the majority choose arbitration. In the United States, most states have antistrike laws, but they are generally ineffective.[117] One study of these laws found that after no-strike laws were passed in eight states, in one (New York) the number of strikes *increased*, in three they decreased, and in four they stayed the same.

Strikes in the public sector are shorter than in the private sector and involve fewer employees. The public employees most likely to strike are sanitation employees, utility and transportation workers, and teachers. However, strikes in the public sector are increasing. Researchers are beginning to turn their attention to the conditions under which public strikes are likely, but the research is in its infancy.[118]

Strikes in the private sector. The Bureau of Labor Statistics estimates that fewer than 4 percent of contract negotiations result in strikes, and less than 0.4 percent of working time was lost to strikes in recent years. It is instructive to examine the trends of these and similar data. According to the International Labour Office, in the decade 1965–74 the number of strikes increased from 3,963 to 6,074; the number of workers involved in strikes increased from 1,550,000 to 2,778,000; and the number of work days lost from strikes increased from 23,300,000 to 48,044,660.[119] In all cases the figures about doubled during the period. U.S. statistics are better on this than those in most of the developed world.

The actual strike figures and trends are important, of course, but perhaps more interesting are the attempts to explain why some enterprises and industries have more strikes than others. A number of theories have been advanced, but no single explanation has been sufficiently supported. It has been contended that strikes take place when there is uncertainty about the other side's position, and thus poor chances for advantageous collective bargaining. Strikes also are more likely when management expectations are too low and union members' are too high; in this case, a strike may take place to adjust expectations.[120] And they occur when the bargaining power of one side is substantially higher than the other's.[121] Studies have shown strikes occur more often when the work group size is very large,[122] in middle-sized plants,[123] and when the work group is composed of male workers with low employee security combined with low efficiency and poor employee relations.[124]

One study of strike incidents in a number of countries concluded that two factors are crucial to the propensity for workers to strike. If the physical location of the work is isolated and the workers are homogeneous, the environment encourages strikes and a feeling of solidarity—"us against the world." And if the work is difficult, unpleasant, or seasonal, strike-prone workers are encouraged.[125]

In some industries, such as mining and longshore work, the probability of strikes is high; in others, such as agriculture and trade, it is low. The Committee of Industrial Peace tried to find conditions where strikes were not likely.[126] A recent reanalysis of these data, however, found that they were less applicable today than 25 years ago.[127] Two other studies examined more rigorously whether union structure, internal control, or location of the facility increases strike propensity.[128] Thus far, none of these theories is an adequate explanation of strike incidence.

Strikes or the threat of strikes do put added pressures on both sides to settle their differences. Most strikes do not seriously affect the public welfare, but if it appears this is the case, the Taft-Hartley Act allows the President to appoint a board of inquiry and issue an injunction for an 80-day cooling-off period. During this period, the employees are polled by secret ballot to see if they will accept the employer's latest offer.

Arbitration

> ## DEFINITION
> Arbitration is the process by which two parties to a dispute agree in advance of the hearing to abide by the decision of an independent quasi-judge called an arbitrator. Arbitration can be used to settle issues at contract time or to settle grievance issues during the contract's period.

Exhibit 19–10 indicates which types of issues are dealt with by arbitration. In such situations, arbitration is quicker and cheaper than court action would be, and the law and courts have virtually guaranteed that the "loser" cannot win an appeal from an arbitration award.[129] The Taft-Hartley Act and such

EXHIBIT 19–10
Issues in cases in which arbitrators selected from FMCS panels made awards, fiscal year 1972

Issue*	Frequency of occurrence
General issues	
New or reopened contract terms	29
Contract interpretation or application	2,586
Specific issues	
Discharge and disciplinary actions	1,226
Incentive rates or standards	77
Job evaluation	387
Seniority†	646
Overtime‡	363
Union officers—superseniority and union business	21
Strike or lockout issues	18
Vacations and vacation pay	132
Holidays and holiday pay	101
Scheduling of work	182
Reporting, call-in, and call-back pay	77
Health and welfare	51
Pensions	21
Other fringe benefits	92
Scope of agreement§	211
Working conditions, including safety	48
Arbitrability of grievance‖	261
Miscellaneous	237

  * Compilations based on the number of arbitration awards for which data were available; that is, 3,414 of the 3,432 awards. Some awards involved more than one issue.
  † Includes promotion and upgrading (137), layoff, bumping, recall (327), transfer (96), and other matters (86).
  ‡ Includes pay (172), distribution of overtime (172), and compulsory overtime (19).
  § Includes subcontracting (92), jurisdictional disputes (17), foreman, supervision, and so on (61), mergers, consolidations, accretion, other plants (11).
  ‖ Includes procedural (141), substantive (68), procedural/substantive (32), and other issues (20).
  Source: James Power, "Improving Arbitration: Roles of Parties and Agencies," *Monthly Labor Review*, November 1972, pp. 15–22.

legal cases as *Textile Workers Union* v. *Lincoln Mills* (353 U.S. 488), *United Steel Workers* v. *Warrior and Gulf Navigation* (363 U.S. 574), and others have generally assured the legality of the arbitration process.

A more detailed overview of arbitration than can be given here can be found in numerous books.[130] Many feel that arbitration is, however, an indication of the failure of free collective bargaining to reach a settlement.

The first step in arbitration is to select an arbitrator. Some unions and managements have an arbitrator they call on regularly. Others receive lists of the names of arbitrators from the American Arbitration Association or the FMCS. The arbitrator, who must be acceptable to both sides, ideally will have experience in the sector and be fair in making judgments. Persons with varying backgrounds serve in these posts, but most arbitrators are lawyers or professors. Typically they are paid $150–225 a day plus expenses for their services.[131] Some enterprises and unions choose an arbitrator based on computer printouts of arbitrators' backgrounds, and so on, but this can be an unreliable way to make the choice because the cases are too different.

Once the arbitrator (or board of arbitrators) is chosen, the arbitration hearings are held. The subject of the hearing is stipulated in the submission agreement, which also states that the arbitrator has final authority to settle the issue. Both sides prepare their cases carefully in advance. Although precedences need not hold, they are accumulated. Both sides develop the evidence, reduce witnesses to a minimum by getting stipulations to facts, and use documents instead of witnesses where possible for efficiency purposes. The case presentation begins with an opening statement. The hearings vary in formality from sessions similar to those in court, with the swearing in of witnesses and so forth, to quite informal hearings. The arbitrator seeks to assure a fair hearing to both sides. He can admit relevant hearsay evidence, question witnesses, and ask for more information from one or both parties. The arbitrator wishes to have all the facts available before the decision is made.

Most arbitrators stipulate that the burden of proof is on the party who filed the grievance or disciplined the employee in these types of cases. In arbitrating contracts, both sides must present their evidence. In arbitrating grievances or deciding disciplinary cases, the arbitrator tries to see if there is guilt beyond a reasonable doubt, something like in criminal court cases. In grievance cases, he examines the contract and precedents in the case as well as how long the precedents have been in existence.

How do arbitrators decide cases? Harold Davey researched the question and found it was easier to say how arbitrators did *not* decide than how they did. They do not flip coins, decide on the basis of the power issue, ignore the record, or decide on personalities rather than the record.[132] The process used varies from informal to formal. Some write up the facts, and in the process the decision comes. Others research the issues further after the case presentation is completed.[133]

Once the arbitrator has heard all the evidence and the hearing is adjourned, he proceeds to write the arbitration award, which is binding on both parties. The award normally reviews the facts in the case prior to stating the decision and usually is presented within 30 days of the hearing. The arbitrator writes the award in language that is understandable to all parties concerned, including the employee involved in a grievance. It should attempt to clarify the problem situation so as to prevent future problems from arising. The arbitrator will usually look over previous arbitration awards in similar cases but need not be bound by them.

What about compulsory arbitration as an alternative to a strike? Is it effective? The evidence is mixed. Some positive results have been found for use of a variation of compulsory arbitration called final-offer arbitration[134] and compulsory arbitration itself.[135] But most of the evidence is negative,[136] and some question its constitutionality.[137] In general, compulsory arbitration is used in the public sector. In the most extensive usage so far—in Australia, where 90 percent of the work force is covered—the number of days lost due to strikes has *increased* under arbitration, not decreased.

Improving arbitration. Essentially there are three criticisms of arbitration as a system of dispute settlement; it takes too long, it costs too much, and it is getting too formal.[138] Some data on costs and length of time required to arbitrate a case are given in Exhibits 19–11 and 19–12. Between 1971 and 1972, the time it took to settle an arbitration case actually decreased, from 251 to 241 days, while costs increased about 15 percent. Some of the time needed to arbitrate is due to an increase in the number of cases submitted to arbitration. Delays are caused when the parties take too long to select an arbitrator or submit to any posthearing briefs. The FMCS has engaged in training sessions to increase the number of arbitrators and has computerized requests for arbitration with the ARBIT system.

An examination of time patterns of grievance arbitration from 1942 to 1972 found that the time from grievance date to award date lengthened 65 percent over those 30 years; from grievance date to hearing date, the time lengthened 70 percent; and from hearing date to award date, 200 percent.[139]

EXHIBIT 19–11
Changes in average costs and average time charged in arbitration cases, 1968–72

Cost items and time charged	Fiscal year				
	1968	1969	1970	1971	1972
Total charges (dollars)	$513.12	$511.06	$539.88	$566.59	$590.12
Rate per day	141.45	145.09	156.83	163.88	172.53
Fee charged	441.87	435.03	457.97	480.88	510.52
Expenses charged	71.25	76.03	81.91	85.71	79.60
Total time charged (days)	3.07	3.03	2.93	2.96	2.96
Hearing time charged	1.00	.95	.92	.92	.91
Travel time charged	.32	.38	.35	.38	.36
Study time charged	1.75	1.70	1.66	1.65	1.69
Number of cases sampled	600	643	722	719	850

James Power, "Improving Arbitration: Roles of Parties and Agencies," *Monthly Labor Review*, November 1972, pp. 15–22.

EXHIBIT 19–12
Average number of days required to complete arbitration cases, 1968–72

	Fiscal year				
Events in the span	1968	1969	1970	1971	1972
Time between filing of grievance and request for panel	77.9	77.6	81.3	83.3	75.1
Time between request and sending of list	8.1	9.2	7.8	11.1	15.1
Time between date list is sent and appointment	40.7	39.9	44.3	46.0	43.8
Time between appointment and hearing	61.2	63.7	63.1	63.4	61.1
Time between hearing and award	47.4	50.3	49.0	47.7	46.4
Total time between request for panel and arbitration award	157.5	163.1	164.2	168.2	166.4
Total time between filing of grievance and arbitration award	235.4	240.4	245.6	251.5	241.5
Number of cases sampled	600	643	722	719	850

James Power, "Improving Arbitration: Roles of Parties and Agencies," *Monthly Labor Review*, November 1972, pp. 15–22.

Industry, particularly steel, has tried several systems for speeding up the arbitration process. These experiments try to speed up selection of arbitrators by having lists of acceptable arbitrators approved ahead of time and by streamlining the hearings. In general, they have been successful.[140]

GROUP REPRESENTATION AND GRIEVANCES

The final topic to be considered in this chapter is the grievance process, an integral part of labor relations.

> **DEFINITION**
> A grievance is a formal dispute between an employee and management on the conditions of employment.

Grievances arise because of (1) differing interpretations of the contract by employees, stewards, and management; (2) a violation of a contract provision; (3) violation of law; (4) a violation of work procedures or other precedents; or (5) perceived unfair treatment of an employee by management. The rate of grievances may increase when employees are dissatisfied or frustrated on their jobs or they resent the supervisory style, or because the union is using grievances as a tactic against management. Grievances may also be due to unclear contractual language or employees with personal problems or who are otherwise "difficult."

The U.S. Department of Labor has found that the most frequent incidents to lead to the filing of a grievance are employee discipline, seniority decisions at promotion or layoff time, work assignment, management rights, and compensation and benefits. As will be discussed in Chapter 21, some enterprises use grievance and complaint statistics as a measure of the personnel department's effectiveness.

The grievance-processing system

The employee grievance process involves a systematic set of steps for handling an employee complaint. Most union contracts provide the channels and mechanisms for processing these grievances.

The grievance process has at least three purposes and consequences. First, by settling smaller problems early, it may prevent larger problems (like strikes) from occurring in the future. Second, properly analyzed, grievances serve as a source of data to focus the attention of the two parties on ambiguities in the contract for negotiation at a future date. Finally, the grievance process is an effective communication channel from employees to management.

The method by which formal grievances are processed varies with the labor contract. Exhibit 19–13 diagrams the grievance process, and the steps in the following description apply to many, if not most, smaller enterprises.

1. *Initiation of the formal grievance.*   When an employee feels that he or she has been mistreated or that some action or application of policy violates his rights in the contract, he files a grievance with his supervisor. He can do this in writing or (at least initially) orally. If he wishes, he can formulate the grievance with the help and support of the union steward. By far most of the grievances are settled by this level between the steward, the employee, and the supervisor.

The supervisor may let the employee blow off steam and cool down before attempting to deal with the grievance but must take it seriously and attempt to determine accurately the reason for it. The grievance should be attended to as soon as possible after making sure the facts are accurate. The effective approach is to try to solve the problem, not to assess blame or find excuses. The supervisor should consider what the contract says as modified by the employer's policies and past precedents in such cases. If the supervisor has a good working relationship with the steward, they can work together to settle the problem at that level. Supervisors should be trained in how to handle grievances using effective counseling techniques.

2. *Department head or unit manager.*   If the steward, supervisor, and employee together cannot solve the grievance, it goes to the next level in the hierarchy. At this point, the grievance must be presented in writing, and both sides must document their cases. What this level consists of depends on the size of the organization. In small organizations, it could be the head of the local

EXHIBIT 19–13
Processing a grievance

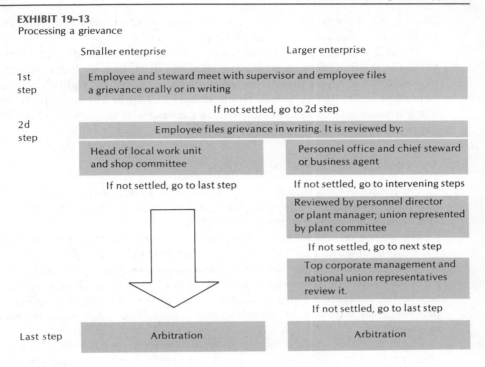

employment unit—general manager, or administrator. The union may be represented by a shop committee. In larger enterprises, there may be an intermediate level, such as a department head. In the largest enterprises, the personnel department and union business agent may be the second step, followed by a third step of unit manager and local union president. Most other grievances are settled at this step.

3. *Arbitration.* If the grievance cannot be settled at this intervening step (or steps), an independent arbitrator may be called in to settle the issue.

In larger enterprises, one or possibly two steps can be inserted between steps 2 and 3, as shown on the right side of Exhibit 19–13.

Most studies of grievances show that more than 75 percent are settled at the first step and another 20 percent are settled at the second. Only about 1 percent go to arbitration. The rest, primarily in larger enterprises, are taken care of in the intervening steps. Relatively few studies have been done on grievances. Studies of the personal characteristics of those who have filed grievances as contrasted with those who have not revealed some differences; in general, those who filed grievances were younger, were hired earlier, had more formal education, and got more wage increases.[141]

Ken Jennings made a rather comprehensive study of how supervisors perceive the grievance process in ten unionized plants.[142] He found that supervisors perceive that top management views grievances as a very important part of their job, but the supervisors themselves did not see grievances as very important and did not believe they were rewarded for doing a good job with them. Nor did they believe that loss of a grievance would reflect badly on them. A substantial porportion of the supervisors surveyed (47 percent) did not even think they had the responsibility for processing grievances. A large majority of the supervisors consulted the personnel department *before* they gave a grievant an answer and were pleased with the help personnel gave them. Nevertheless, they considered the biggest problems in the grievance procedures to be that some personnel staff members were not well trained, and the contract did not consider the differing characteristics of each supervisor's job. The supervisors Jennings surveyed reported that shop stewards did not often bypass them in processing a grievance and knew how to process a grievance better than some supervisors did, and their relations with shop stewards on grievances were generally good. Finally, supervisors were kept well informed on the progress of grievances which went beyond step 1.

Grievances in the public and third sectors

Executive Order 11491 set the grievance process for federal employees. The first two steps are as in the private sector, then conciliation and mediation are tried. If no solution is found, the grievance goes to the Federal Service Impasses Panel and finally to arbitration. The incidence of grievance systems for state and local government employees is also increasing. In one study 90 percent of the contracts examined provided for grievance processes similar to those in the private sector, and in 55 percent of them binding arbitration was the basis for settlement.[143] Other studies found that instructions in grievance handling for federal executives made the process much more effective, and grievance procedures are developing rapidly in unionized community colleges.[144]

Grievances in nonunionized enterprises

As described in more detail in Chapter 20, nonunionized enterprises offer alternatives to the grievance system to give employees justice. Approaches used include counseling; the open-door policy, whereby the grievant can go over the supervisor's head; and use of an ombudsman, or a quasi-grievance process in which the personnel specialist or a third party represents the employee.[145]

Reducing grievances and improving the process

Various approaches have been suggested for reducing grievances. One is to reduce the causes of the grievances such as bad working conditions or a less employer-oriented supervisory style.[146] Educating managers on contract provisions and effective human relations—oriented grievance processing helps, and quick and efficient processing will ultimately reduce the grievance rates.[147] It is also suggested that supervisors should consult personnel and other supervisors before processing grievances to get the best advice and improve effectiveness in the grievance process.

SUMMARY, CONCLUSIONS, AND RECOMMENDATIONS

This chapter has discussed the mechanisms used in collective bargaining and group negotiations. In general, since less than 1 percent of work days is lost due to work stoppages such as strikes, the system seems to work reasonably well.[148] Most contracts are administered cooperatively and most stewards, supervisors, and employees make the system work most of the time. When there are difficulties, the grievance system provides an outlet to handle them.

Top managers make major labor decisions on such matters as bargaining structure and bargaining approach. They also have the ultimate authority in deciding issues such as how much the enterprise can afford to offer in negotiations. Thus labor relations require the participation of top managers.

Collective bargaining is a technical area requiring experience and legal knowledge; usually, it is the subject of an entire course. These few pages are intended to familiarize you with the system enough to know how local contracts are negotiated and how to operate within the contract to deal with grievances and similar problems. No propositions or recommendations for model organizations will be given in this chapter because more detailed data would be required to do so.

Chapter 20 discusses the employee disciplinary process in unionized and nonunionized enterprises.

QUESTIONS

1. What is labor relations?
2. What are the significant diagnostic factors affecting labor relations?
3. Discuss the major conceptual frameworks that help explain labor relations.
4. Why do people join unions?
5. How do union officials and labor relations experts perceive each other? Why?
6. What role does the government play in labor relations?
7. Describe the major unions in the United States and Canada. How are they organized?
8. Are unions democratically run?
9. Are unions growing in strength?
10. Describe the major provisions of the most important labor laws and regulations.
11. How do labor relations differ among the public, private, and third sectors?
12. Describe what a union organizing campaign is like. What are managers allowed to do? What should managers do if they wish to prevent unionization?
13. Describe how contracts are negotiated.
14. How do bargaining structures differ?

15. How do bargaining approaches differ? Which would you use?

16. When are mediators helpful to negotiations?

17. When do strikes take place?

18. Under what conditions would you use arbitrators in labor relations?

19. What is a grievance? How do enterprises process them?

NOTES AND REFERENCES

1. A number of references on labor relations will be cited throughout the chapter. General ones are Reed Richardson, *Collective Bargaining by Objectives* (Englewood Cliffs, N.J.: Prentice-Hall, Inc., 1977); Arthur Sloane, and Fred Whitney, *Labor Relations* (Englewood Cliffs, N.J.: Prentice-Hall, Inc., 3rd ed., 1977). The area of labor relations has not received its fair share of empirical research. See James D. Workin and Angelo De Nisi, "Empirical Research on Labor Relations Law: A Review, Some Problems, and Some Directions for Future Research," *Labor Law Journal,* September 1977, pp. 563–71.

2. David McClelland, *Power* (New York: 1977).

3. On the international dimension, see, for example, Roy Adams, "Canada–U.S. Labor Link Under Stress," *Industrial Relations,* October 1976, pp. 295–312; Richard Rowan and Herbert Northrup, "Multinational Bargaining in Metals and Electrical Industries," *Journal of Industrial Relations,* March 1975, pp. 1–29; Sterling Slappey, "Will Unions Win International Bargaining?" *Nation's Business,* June 1975, pp. 36–40; William Dodge, "Labour and the Multinational Corporations," *Canadian Business Review,* Winter 1974, pp. 35–37; Herbert Northrup and Richard Rowan, "Multinational Collective Bargaining Activity," *Columbus Journal of World Business,* Spring 1974, pp. 112–24; Paul Heise, "The Multinational Corporation and Industrial Relations," *Relationes Industrelles* 28, 1 (1973), pp. 34–55; John James, "Multinational Trade Unions Muscle Their Strength," *European Business,* Autumn 1973, pp. 36–45.

4. Michael Moskow, "Collective Bargaining Strategies in the Context of Unemployment and Inflation: The Economic Context," *Labor Law Journal,* August 1976, pp. 461–66; also comments by John O'Connell, "A Management View," pp. 467–71; Richard Liebes, "A Labor View," pp. 471–75; and Paul Yager, "A Mediator's View," pp. 475–79.

5. John Dunlop, *Industrial Relations Systems* (New York: Holt, Rinehart & Winston, 1958); updated in Derek Bok and John Dunlop, *Collective Bargaining in the United States: An Overview* (New York: Simon & Schuster 1970).

6. S. J. Wood et al., "The Industrial Relations System Concept as a Basis for Theory in Industrial Relations," *British Journal of Industrial Relations,* November 1975, pp. 291–308.

7. Richard E. Walton and Robert McKersie, *A Behavioral Theory of Labor Negotiations* (New York: McGraw-Hill Book Co., 1967).

8. Gerald Somers (ed.), "Bargaining Power and Industrial Relations Theory," in *Essays in Industrial Relations Theory* (Ames: Iowa State University Press, 1969), pp. 39–53.

9. D. Quinn Mills, "Managing Human Relationships among Organizations," *Organizational Dynamics,* Spring 1975, pp. 35–50.

10. Karl Marx, *Capital: A Critique of Political Economy* (New York: International Publishers, 1967); John A. Commons, *The Economics of Collective Action* (New York: Macmillan, Inc., 1950); Sidney Webb and Beatrice Webb, *Industrial Democracy* (New York: Longmont, Green and Company, 1902); Clark Kerr et al., *Industrialism and the Industrial Man* (Cambridge, Mass.: Harvard University, 1960).

11. Marx, *Capital;* Selig Perlman, A Theory of the Labor Movement (New York: A. M. Kelly, 1949); Commons, *The Economics of Collective Action;* Webb and Webb, *Industrialism and the Industrial Man.*

12. Carlton Parker, *The Casual Laborer and Other Essays* (New York: Harcourt Brace and Howe, 1920); Frank Tannenbaum, *A Philosophy of Labor* (New York: Alfred E. Knopf, Inc., 1951).

13. Bok and Dunlop, *Collective Bargaining in the United States.*

14. V. Clayton Sherman, "Unionism and the Non-Union Company," *Personnel Journal,* June 1969, pp. 413–22.

15. Ross Stagner and Hjalmar Rosen, *Psychology of Union-Management Relations* (Belmont, Cal.: Wadsworth Publishing Co., 1965).

16. Joel Seidman et al., "Why Workers Join Unions," *Annals of American Academy of Political and Social Sciences,* March 1951.

17. Louis Imundo, "Why Federal Government Employees Join Unions," *Public Personnel Management,* January–February 1973, pp. 23–28.

18. Cited in Stagner and Rosen, *Psychology of Union-Management Relations.*

19. Russell Lansbury, "Career Orientations and Unionization among Technical Specialists," *The Journal of Industrial Relations,* March 1976, pp. 1–16; Dennis Charmot, "Professional Employees Turn to Unions" *Harvard Business Review,* May–June 1976, pp. 119–27; Bernard Bass and Charles Mitchell, "Influences on the Felt Need for Collective Bargaining by Business and Science Professionals," *Journal of Applied Psychology* 61, 6 (1976), pp. 770–73; "Collective Action of IE's," *Industrial Engineering,* January 1973, pp. 46–47.

20. Bagar Husaini and James Geschwender, "Some Correlates of Attitudes toward and Membership in White Collar Unions," *Southwestern Social Science Quarterly,* March 1967, pp. 595–601; Peter Feville and James Blandin, "Faculty Job Satisfaction and Bargaining Sentiments," *Academy of Management Journal,* December 1974, pp. 678–92; Everett Ladd and Seymour Lysset, "Faculty Members Note Both Positive and Negative Aspects of Campus Unions," *Chronicle of Higher Education,* February 23, 1976; Alfred Vogel, "Your Clerical Workers Are Ripe for Unionism," *Harvard Business Review,* March–April 1971, pp. 48–54.

21. Louis Imundo, "Attitudes of Non-Union White Collar Federal Government Employees toward Unions," *Public Personnel Management,* January–February 1974, pp. 87–92.

22. Frances Bairstow, "Professionalism and Unionism: Are They Compatible," *Industrial Engineering,* April 1974, pp. 40–42; Archie Kleingartner, "Professionalism and Engineering Unionism," *Industrial Relations,* May 1969, pp. 224–35.

23. *The Personnel Executive's Job* (Englewood Cliffs, N.J.: Prentice-Hall/ASPA, 1977).

24. Kenneth Walker, "Executives and Union Leaders' Perceptions of Each Other's Attitudes in Industrial Relations," *Human Relations,* August 1962, pp. 183–96; Mason Haire, "Role Perceptions in Labor Management Relations," *Industrial and Labor Relations Review* 8 (1955), pp. 204–16. One piece of research that questions these negative stereotypes is A. Ranger Curran and Donald Hovey, "Role Perceptions in Labor Management Relations: A Stereotype Revisited," *Proceedings, Academy of Management,* 1977.

25. Charles Holloman and Jerald Robinson, "Student Perceptions of Management and Union Leaders, *Proceedings,* Southern Management Association, 1972, pp. 192–208; Charles Holloman, and Jerald Robinson, "Stereotypes of Management and Union Leaders among College Students," *Journal of Industrial Relations,* September 1973, pp. 315–23.

26. M. M. Schwartz et al., "Responses of Union and Management Leaders to Emotionally Toned Industrial Relations Terms," *Personnel Psychology* 23 (1973), pp. 361–67; M. M. Schwartz et al., "The Perception by Two Industrial Membership Groups to Each Other's Affective Reactions to Industrial Relations Terms," *Personnel Psychology,* Summer 1972, pp. 283–92.

27. H. George Frederickson, "Role Occupancy and Attitudes toward Labor Relations in Government," *Administrative Science Quarterly,* December 1969, pp. 595–606; Charles Odewahn

and Allan Spritzer, "Administrators' Attitudes toward Faculty Unionism," *Industrial Relations*, May 1976, pp. 206–15.

28. Stagner and Rosen, *Psychology of Union-Management Relations*.

29. Bok and Dunlop, *Collective Bargaining in the United States*.

30. Ross Stagner, *Psychology of Industrial Conflict* (New York: John Wiley & Sons, 1956).

31. Heinz Hartman, "Managerial Employees: New Participant in Industrial Relations," *British Journal of Industrial Relations*, July 1974, pp. 268–81; Arch Patton, "The Boom in Executive Self-Interest," *Business Week*, May 24, 1976; Gabriel Rosica, "Organized Professions?" *Business Horizons*, June 1972, pp. 59–65; David Weir, "Radical Managerialism: Middle Managers' Perceptions of Collective Bargaining," *British Journal of Industrial Relations* 14, 3 (1976), pp. 324–38.

32. John Fanning, "We Are Forty: Where Do We Go?" *Labor Law Journal*, January 1976, pp. 3–10; Frank Thompson and Daniel Pollett, "Oversight Hearings of the NLRB," *Labor Law Journal*, September 1976, pp. 539–47; "The Chairman Looks at the NLRB," *The Personnel Administrator*, May 1976, pp. 22–26; "What NLRB Madam Chairman Has in Mind For the Future," *Nation's Business*, August 1975, pp. 36–40; "Labor Law Task Force Urges NLRB to Speed Its Handling of Cases," *The Wall Street Journal*, November 8, 1976; Kenneth Simon-Rose, "Deferral Under *Collyer* by the NLRB of Section 8(a)(3) Cases," *Labor Law Journal*, April 1976, pp. 201–16; Jon Pettibone, "Section 10J Bargaining Order in *Gissell* Type Cases," *Labor Law Journal*, October 1976, pp. 648–61.

33. This section is based on Arvid Anderson and Seymour Kaye, "The United States," in *International Manual on Collective Bargaining for Public Employees* ed. Seymour Kaye and Arthur Marsh (New York: Frederick A. Praeger, Inc., 1973); Richard Billings and John Greenya, *Power to the Public Worker*, (Washington, D.C.: Robert B. Luce, Inc., 1974); Marten Estey, *The Unions* (New York: Harcourt Brace, 1967); Michael Moskow and Robert Doherty, "The United States," in *Teacher Unions and Associations*, ed. Albert Blum (Urbana: University Of Illinois Press, 1969); Malcolm Warner, "Unions as Complex Organizations," *Relationes Industrelles* 30, 1 (1975), pp. 43–55; Arie Shirom, "Union Use of Staff Experts: The Case of the Histadrut," *Industrial and Labor Relations Review*, 1975–76, pp. 107–120; Soloman Barkin, "Diversity in Industrial Relations Patterns," *Labor Law Journal*, November 1976, pp. 678–85; N. F. Dufty, "Trade Unions and Their Operations," *Journal of Industrial Relations*, November 1976, pp. 203–19; Sloane and Whitney, *Labor Relations*, ch. 4.; Peter Drucker, "The Decline in Unionization," *The Wall Street Journal*, October 5, 1977; "Labor Tries to Revitalize Itself," *Business Week*, September 12, 1977, pp. 37–39.

34. Ronald Ehrenberg and Steve Goldberg, "Officer Performance and Compensation in Local Building Trade Unions," *Industrial and Labor Relations Review*, 1976, pp. 188–96.

35. B. E. Partridge, "The Role of the Steward," University of Aston Management Centre, 1975, mimeographed.

36. Seymour Lipset et al., *Union Democracy* (Glencoe, Ill.: Free Press, 1956).

37. Raymond Miles and J. B. Ritchie, "Leadership Attitudes among Union Officials," *Industrial Relations*, October 1968.

38. Leon Applebaum and Harry Blaine, "The 'Iron Law' Revisited: Oligarchy in Trade Union Locals," *Labor Law Journal*, July 1975.

39. Al Nash, "Local 1199," *Human Relations* 27 (1974), pp. 547–66.

40. Leonard Sayles, *Behavior of Industrial Work Groups* (New York: McGraw-Hill Book Co., 1958).

41. George Taylor, "The Role of Unions in a Democratic Society," in *Government Regulation of Internal Union Affairs Affecting the Rights of Members* (Washington, D.C.: U.S. Government Printing Office, 1958), p. 19.

42. Derek Bok and John Dunlop, "How Trade Union Policy Is Made," *Monthly Labor Review,* February 1970, pp. 17–20.

43. Gary Chaison, "The Frequency and Outcomes of Union Raids," *Industrial Relations,* February 1976, pp. 107–10; Gary Chaison and William Rock, "Competition between Local Independent and National Unions," *Labor Law Journal,* May 1974, pp. 293–97; Gary Chaison, "Federation Expulsions and Union Mergers in the United States," *Relations Industrelles* 28, 2 (1973), pp. 343–61; Herbert Northrup and Richard Rowan, "The ICF–IFPCW Conflict," *Columbia Journal of World Business,* Winter 1974, pp. 109–20; Harriet Berger and Edward Blomstedt, "Clerk vs. Mail Handler: Jurisdictional Disputes in the Postal Service," *Labor Law Journal,* October 1976, pp. 641–47.

44. John Flagler and William Schroeder, "Unions and Worker Participation in PAIR Management," in *Employee and Labor Relations,* vol. 3, ed. H. Heneman, Jr., and D. Yoder (Washington, D.C.: Bureau of National Affairs, 1976), pp. 2-4, 7-17; David Shair, "Labor Organizations as Employers; Unions within Unions," *The Journal of Business,* July 1970, pp. 296–316; Irwin Ross, "How to Tell When the Unions Will Be Tough," *Fortune* (July 1975) pp. 100–103; 151–156 ff; William Fox and Michael Wince, "The Structure and Determinants of Occupational Militancy Among Public School Teachers," *Industrial and Labor Relations Review,* October 1976, pp. 47–58.

45. Arthur Kruger, "The Direction of Unionism in Canada," *Canadian Labour in Transition* ed. Miller and Isbester (Scarborough, Ont.: Prentice-Hall, 1971); R. Swidinsky, "Trade Union Growth in Canada: 1911–1970," *Relations Industrielles* 29, 3 (1974), pp. 435–49; J. K. Eaton, "The Growth of the Canadian Labour Movement," *The Labour Gazette,* Anniversary Issue, 1975, pp. 643–49.

46. John Crispo, *The Role of International Unionism in Canada* (Montreal: Canadian-American Committee, 1967); Bogdan Kipling, "Is Canadian-American Labour Solidarity Forever?," *The Labour Gazette,* March 1974, pp. 184–90.

47. Francis McKendy, "The Structure of the Union Movement in Canada," in *Canadian Labour and Industrial Relations,* ed. H. C. Jain (Toronto: McGraw-Hill Ryerson, 1975); Malcolm Warner, "Unions as Complex Organizations," *Industrial Relations* 30, 1 (1974), p. 43–59.

48. Charles Connaghan, "Co-determination—A Partial Answer to Good Labour Relations," *The Labour Gazette,* August 1976, pp. 405–7; Jean Pascal, "Would West German 'Co-determination' Work Here?", *The Labour Gazette,* August 1976, pp. 408–14; Gilbert Levine, "Industrial Democracy Is Workers' Control," *The Labour Gazette,* August 1976, p. 436; R. Kent Rowley, "A Skeptical View of the West German Model," *The Labour Gazette,* August 1976, pp. 435–45; Donald Rumball, "Worker Participation in Canada?" *The Labour Gazette,* August 1976, pp. 429–35; Friedrich Furstenberg, "Workers' Participation—The European Experience," *The Labour Gazette,* August 1976, pp. 424–28; Paul Malles, "Co-determination in Canada: What Forms Could It Take?" *The Labour Gazette,* August 1976, pp. 415–23.

49. Roy Adams, "Solidarity, Self-Interest and the Unionization Differential between Europe and North America," *Relations Industrielles* 29, 3 (1974), pp. 497–512.

50. Frances Bairstow, "Professionalism and Unionism: Are They Compatible?," *Industrial Engineering,* April 1974, pp. 40–42.

51. Roy J. Adams, "Conflict and the Nature of the Industrial Relations System," *The Labour Gazette,* April 1975, pp. 220–24.

52. Mark Thompson and Larry F. Moore, "Managerial Attitudes toward Industrial Relations," *Relations Industrielles* 30, 3, (1975), pp. 331–40.

53. John Vanderkamp, "Economic Activity and Strikes in Canada," *Industrial Relations,* February 1970, pp. 215–30; Jean Boivin, "L'Action Politique du CTC et de la FAT–COI, une comparison depuis 1956," *Relations Industrielles,* August 1971, pp. 541–574.

54. This section is based on Edwin Beal et al., *The Practice of Collective Bargaining* (Homewood, Ill.: Richard D. Irwin, Inc., 1976), ch. 5; Lawrence Doppelt, "Employee Interests in Labor Law: The Supreme Court Swings Back the Pendulum," *Industrial Relations Law Journal* 1, 2 (1976), pp. 323–45; Benjamin Taylor and Fred Whitney, *Labor Relations Law* (Englewood Cliffs, N.J.: Prentice-Hall, 1975), ch. 2–11; W. J. Usery, "The Impact of Legislation on Collective Bargaining," *Labor Law Journal,* July 1974, pp. 428–31; Ronald Miller, "Right to Work Laws and Compulsory Union Membership in the United States," *British Journal of Industrial Relations,* 14, 2 (1976), pp. 186–93.

55. Max Zimny, "Access of Union Organizers to Private Property," *Labor Law Journal,* October 1974, pp. 618–24.

56. Robert Lewis, "The Law and Strategy of Dealing with Union Organizing Campaigns," *Labor Law Journal,* January 1974, pp. 42–47; Pettibone, "Section 10J Bargaining Order."

57. Stephen Cabot and Douglas Linn, "What Management Can Do during a Union Organization Campaign," *The Practical Lawyer,* March 1, 1976, pp. 13–28.

58. Julius Getman et al., *Union Representation Elections: Law and Reality* (New York: Russell Sage Foundation, 1976).

59. Charles Greer and Stanley Martin, "Unfair Labor Practices during Union Organizing Campaigns Calculative Decisions," *Proceedings,* Academy of Management, 1977, pp. 235–39.

60. Taylor and Whitney, *Labor Relations Law,* pp. 558–69; Robert Woodworth and Richard Peterson (eds.), *Collective Negotiation for Public and Professional Employees* (Chicago: Scott Foresman & Co., 1969).

61. Frank Cassell, "The Direction of Labour Relations in the U.S. Health Sector," *British Journal of Industrial Relations,* March 1976, pp. 18–25; William Terrence, "Health Services and Collective Bargaining," *Training and Development Journal,* August 1974, pp. 36–39; Walter Gershenfeld, "Hospitals," in *Emerging Sectors of Collective Bargaining,* ed. S. Wolfbein (Braintree, Mass.: D. H. Mark, 1970), pp. 173–218; William Werther and Carol Lockhart, *Labor Relations in the Health Professions* (Boston: Little, Brown & Co., 1975).

62. Carl Schramm, "Union Organizing at Private Colleges and Universities," *Labor Law Journal,* November 1975; Herman Dok and Stanley Johnson, "Collective Bargaining—SUNY," *Journal of College and University Personnel Association,* April 1974, pp. 55–73; Joseph Garabino, "State Patterns of Faculty Bargaining," *Industrial Relations,* May 1976, pp. 191–205; Raymond Hogler, "Collective Bargaining in Education and the Student," *Labor Law Journal,* November 1976, pp. 712–20; Mario Bognanno and Edward Suntrup, "Graduate Assistants' Response to Unionization: The Minnesota Experience," *Labor Law Journal,* January 1976, pp. 32–37; Mario Bognanno and Edward Suntrup, "Occupational Inclusions in Faculty Bargaining Units," *Industrial Relations,* October 1975, pp. 358–63; Daniel Pollitt and Frank Thompson, "Collective Bargaining on the Campus: A Survey Five Years after Cornell," *Industrial Relations Law Journal,* Summer 1976, pp. 191–248; Virginia Lussier, "Academic Collective Bargaining: Panacea or Palliative for Women and Minorities?" *Labor Law Journal,* September 1976, pp. 565–72.

63. Edward Arian, "Some Problems of Collective Bargaining in Symphony Orchestras," *Labor Law Journal,* November 1974, pp. 666–72; Michael Moskow, "The Performing Arts," in *Emerging Sectors of Collective Bargaining,* ed. Wolfbein, pp. 51–94.

64. Louis Imundo, "Some Comparisons between Public Sector and Private Sector Collective Bargaining," *Labor Law Journal,* December 1973, pp. 810–17.

65. Marvin Levine, "The Mechanics of Securing National Exclusive Recognitions in the Federal Service," *Public Personnel Management,* January–February 1974, pp. 44–52; Raymond Palombo, "The Agency Shop in a Public Service Merit System," *Labor Law Journal,* July 1975, pp. 409–16; Darold Barnum, "National Public Labor Relations Legislation," *Labor Law Journal,* March 1976, pp. 168–76; Paul Staudohar, "Rights and Limitations of Picketing by Public

Employees," *Labor Law Journal,* October 1974, pp. 632–42; Nels Nelson, "Union Security in the Public Sector," *Labor Law Journal,* June 1976, pp. 334–42; Charles Redenius, "Public Employees: A Survey of Some Critical Problems on the Frontier of Collective Bargaining," *Labor Law Journal,* September 1976, pp. 588–99; David Lewin, "Collective Bargaining Impacts on Personnel Administration in the American Public Sector," *Labor Law Journal,* July 1976, pp. 426–36; James Martin, "Union Management Consultation in the Federal Government: Problems and Promise," *Labor Law Journal,* January 1976, pp. 11–17.

66. Jay Erstling, "Federal Regulation of Non-Federal Public Employment," *Labor Law Journal,* November 1973, pp. 739–54.

67. I. B. Helburn, "Public Employee Labor Relations in Texas: The Widening Gap," *Labor Law Journal,* February 1976, pp. 107–22; Thomas Kochan and Hoyt Wheeler, "Municipal Collective Bargaining: A Mode and Analysis of Bargaining Outcomes," *Industrial and Labor Relations Journal,* 21, 1 (1975), pp. 46–66.

68. Stuart Jamison, *Industrial Relations in Canada* (Toronto: Macmillan & Company of Canada Ltd., 1973); *Labour Relations Law* (Kingston, Ont.: Industrial Relations Centre, Queens University, 1970); *Canadian Labour Relations Boards Reports* (Scarborough, Ont.: Butterworth & Co., 1976); *The Labour Relations Act,* The Queen's Printer and Publisher, May 1973.

69. For example, see William H. Langford, "Labour Legislation in Canada, 1975," *The Labour Gazette,* January 1976, pp. 35–38.

70. William H. Langford, "The Composition of Labour Relations Boards in Canada," *The Labour Gazette,* Anniversary Issue, 1975, pp. 657–59.

71. "Canada Labour Relations Council," *The Labour Gazette,* Anniversary Issue, 1975, p. 617; Leslie W. C. S. Barnes, "The National Joint Council: Consultation and Advice," *The Canadian Business Review,* Summer 1976, pp. 32–34.

72. Nicole Marchand, "Labour Legislation in Canada, 1975, Part 1B—Emergency Legislation," *The Labour Gazette,* February 1976, pp. 95–96; Nicole Marchand, "Labour Legislation in Canada in 1974, Part 1B—Special Groups, Emergency Legislation," *The Labour Gazette,* April 1975, pp. 247–49.

73. L. B. Pearson, "The Introduction of Collective Bargaining in the Federal Public Service," in Williams and Kernaghan, *op cit;* Brian Huggins, "Observations on the Public Service Staff Relations Act," *The Labour Gazette,* October 1975, pp. 725–28; A. G. Gillespie, "The Public Service Staff Relations Board," *Relations Industrielles* 30, 4 (1975), pp. 628–40.

74. See, for example, Nicole Marchand, "Labour Legislation in Canada, 1975 Part 1C—Public Sector," *The Labour Gazette,* March 1976, pp. 152–54.

75. H. W. Arthurs, *Collective Bargaining by Public Employees in Canada* (Ann Arbor: Institute of Labor and Industrial Relations, 1971).

76. William Doherty, "The Government as Employer," *The Labour Gazette,* October 1975, pp. 711–15; John Clarke, "Labour-Government Relations in B.C.," *The Labour Gazette,* February 1976, pp. 75–80.

77. Irving Brotslaw, "Attitude of Retail Workers toward Trade Union Organizations," *Labor Law Journal* 18, 3 (1967), pp. 149–71; William Kirchner, "Yardstick for More Effective Organizing," *American Federationist* 76, 3 (1969), pp. 21–23; Edwin Rogers, "The Need for a More Intensive Analysis of Union Organizing Campaigns: Comment," *Academy of Management Journal,* June 1973, pp. 340–43; William Whyte, *Organizational Behavior: Theory and Application* (Homewood, Ill.: Dorsey Press, 1969), ch. 19; Getman et al., *Union Representation Elections.*

78. Lewis, "Union Organizing Campaigns."

79. David Messick, "To Join or Not to Join," *Organizational Behavior and Human Performance* 10 (1973), pp. 145–56; Getman et al., *Union Representation Elections;* Robert Dubin, "Attachment to Work and Union Militancy," *Industrial Relations,* February 1973, pp. 51–64; Feville and Blandin, "Faculty Job Satisfaction and Bargaining Sentiments"; Woodruff Imberman,

"How Expensive Is a NLRB Election?", *MSU Business Topics*, Summer 1975, pp. 13–18; Jeanne Herman, "Are Situational Contingencies Limiting Job Attitude–Job Performance Relationships?", *Organizational Behavior and Human Performance* 10 (1973), pp. 208–24.

80. Gary Chaison, "Unit Size and Union Success in Representation Elections," *Monthly Labor Review*, February 1973, pp. 51–52; Getman et al., *Union Representation Elections*.

81. Lewis, "Union Organizing Campaigns"; Edward Curtin, *White Collar Unionization*, Studies in Personnel Policy 220 (New York: National Industrial Conference Board, 1970); Matthew Goodfellow, "How to Lose an NLRB Election," *The Personnel Administrator*, September 1976, pp. 40–45; Robert Hershey, "Predicting Outcomes of Union Representation Election," *The Personnel Administrator*, January 1976, pp. 42–46; Richard Anthony, "When There's a Union at the Gate," *Personnel*, November–December 1976, pp. 47–52; Bureau of National Affairs, "Bulletin to Management: Faculty Organizing: Special Report," Washington, D.C., March 25, 1976.

82. James Hyatt, "Firms Learn Art of Keeping Unions Out," *The Wall Street Journal*, April 19, 1977.

83. Meyer Ryder et al., *Management Preparation for Collective Bargaining* (Homewood, Ill.: Dow Jones–Irwin, 1966).

84. Richard Shell and Charles Jung, "The Role of Work Measurement in the Bargaining Process," *Industrial Management*, December 1975, pp. 1–7; Gordon Cooper, "Complete Wage Data Streamlines Collective Bargaining," *Industrial Engineering*, April 1971, pp. 13–18.

85. Michael Granof, *How to Cost Your Labor Contract* (Washington, D.C.: Bureau of National Affairs, 1973); Robert Penfield, "A Guide to the Computation and Evaluation of Direct Labor Costs," *Personnel Journal*, June 1976, pp. 285–87.

86. Thomas Kochan, "City Government Bargaining," *Industrial Relations*, February 1975, pp. 90–101; Thomas Kochan et al., "Determinants of Intraorganizational Conflict in Collective Bargaining in the Public Sector," *Administrative Science Quarterly*, March 1975, pp. 10–22; Ryder et al., *Management Preparation for Collective Bargaining*.

87. Joel Seidman, "Bargaining Structure: Some Problems of Complexity and Dislocation," *Labor Law Journal*, June 1973, pp. 340–50.

88. Charles Camp, "As UAW Begins Pre-Bargaining Parley, Job Security Tops List of Issues This Year," *The Wall Street Journal*, January 21, 1976.

89. Richard Cyert and James March, *A Behavioral Theory of the Firm* (Englewood Cliffs, N.J.: Prentice-Hall, Inc., ed. 1964).

90. Reed Richardson, "Positive Collective Bargaining," in *Employee and Labor Relations*, ed. Heneman and Yoder, pp. 7-111–7-143.

91. "The Leading Edge of a Shorter Work Week," *Business Week*, October 4, 1976; "The UAW's Small Step to a Shorter Work Week," *Business Week*, October 18, 1976; "Construction Workers to Loosen the Rules," *Business Week*, March 21, 1977.

92. "Steel Models the 1977 Pattern," *Business Week*, February 28, 1977; "Union to Demand Job Security Provisions in AT&T Pact to Spread Available Work," *The Wall Street Journal*, February 16, 1977; Walter Mossberg and Byron Colame, "Unions to Stress Job Security Issues," *The Wall Street Journal*, December 16, 1976; Phillip Semas, "Faculty Unions Focusing on Job Security," *Chronicle of Higher Education*, November 1, 1976.

93. Abraham Cohen, "Coordinated Bargaining and Structures of Collective Bargaining," *Labor Law Journal*, June 1975, pp. 375–85.

94. Arthur Leonard, "Coordinated Bargaining with Multinational Firms by American Labor Unions," *Labor Law Journal*, December 1974, pp. 746–59; Joseph Lowenberg, "Multilateral Bargaining: Variation on a Theme," *Labor Law Journal*, February 1975, pp. 107–18; Roger Mansfield, "The advent of Public Sector Multiemployer Bargaining," *Personnel Journal*, May

1975, pp. 290–94; Abraham Cohen, "Union Rationale and Objectives of Coordinated Bargaining," *Labor Law Journal*, February 1976, pp. 75–83; John Burton, "Local Government Bargaining and Management Structure," *Industrial Relations*, May 1972, pp. 123–39; Hy Kornbluh, "Public Schools: Multi-Unit Common Bargaining Agents: A Next Phase in Teacher–School Board Bargaining in Michigan," *Labor Law Journal*, August 1976, pp. 520–30.

95. George Hildebrand, "Cloudy Future for Coalition Bargaining," *Harvard Business Review*, November–December 1968, pp. 114–28.

96. Alton Craig and Harry Waisglass, "Collective Bargaining Perspective," *Relations Industrielles* 23, 4 (1968); *Decisions Information* (Ottawa: Canada Labour Relations Board, 1976 and later).

97. Kenneth Alexander, "Union Structure and Bargaining Structure," *Labor Law Journal*, March 1973, pp. 164–72.

98. William Weinberg, "Structural Realities of Collective Bargaining in Public Higher Education," *Journal of College and University Personnel Association*, April 1974, pp. 4–11.

99. David Greenberg, "The Structure of Collective Bargaining and Some of Its Determinants," *Proceedings*, Industrial Relations Research Association (December 1966) pp. 343–53. Albany, N.Y., 1966.

100. See, for example, A. C. Pigou, *Principles and Methods of Industrial Peace* (London: Macmillan & Co., 1905); J. F. Nash, "The Bargaining Problem," *Econometrica*, April 1950, pp. 155–62.

101. J. Pen, "A General Theory of Bargaining," *American Economic Review*, March 1952, pp. 24–42; J. G. Cross, *The Economics of Bargaining* (New York: Basic Books, 1969).

102. Walton and McKersie, *Behavioral Theory of Labor Negotiations;* see also C. M. Stevens, *Strategy and Collective Negotiation* (New York: McGraw-Hill Book Co., 1963); C. L. Karrass, *The Negotiating Game* (New York: World Publishing Co., 1970).

103. Richard Peterson and L. N. Tracy, "A Behavioural Model of Problem Solving in Labor Negotiations," *British Journal of Industrial Relations* 14, 2 (1976), pp. 159–73. For another variation of a behavioral model, see Benjamin Selekman, "Varieties of Labor Relations," *Harvard Business Review*, March 1949, pp. 177–85.

104. J. Stacey Adams, "The Structure and Dynamics of Behavior in Organizational Boundary Roles," in *Handbook of Industrial and Organizational Psychology*, ed. Marvin Dunnette (Chicago: Rand McNally & Co., 1975), pp. 1175–99.

105. Richardson, "Positive Collective Bargaining."

106. Peter Henle, "Reverse Collective Bargaining? A Look at Some Union Concession Situations," *Industrial and Labor Relations Review*, January 1973, pp. 956–68.

107. Ann Douglas, *Industrial Peacemaking* (New York: Columbia University Press, 1962).

108. Kochan and Wheeler, "Municipal Collective Bargaining"; Paul Gerhardt, "Determinants of Bargaining Outcomes in Local Government Labor Negotiations," *Industrial and Labor Relations Review*, 1975–76, pp. 331–51; Paul Brinker and Benjamin Taylor, "Secondary Boycott Analysis by Industry," *Labor Law Journal*, October 1973, pp. 671–83; Daniel Hanersmesh, "Who Wins in Wage Bargaining?" *Industrial and Labor Relations Review*, April 1973, pp. 1146–49; Kochan, "City Government Bargaining"; P. F. Lynch, "The Dynamics of Negotiating," *The Personnel Administrator*, September–October 1973, pp. 48–52.

109. Donald Burke and Lester Rubin, "Is Contract Rejection a Major Collective Bargaining Problem?" *Industrial and Labor Relations Review*, January 1973, pp. 820–33.

110. Charles Odewahn and Joseph Kroslov, "Is Contract Rejection a Major Collective Bargaining Problem?: Comment and Reply," *Industrial and Labor Relations Review*, April 1975, pp. 439–43.

111. John Emshwiller, "Long Road Ahead," *The Wall Street Journal*, October 8, 1976; "The Local Issues That Threaten Steel," *Business Week*, March 28, 1977; "Why the Tires Won't Be Bouncing Out of Akron," *Business Week*, August 30, 1976.

112. George Bennett, "New Horizons for Mediation," *Personnel*, January–February 1974, pp. 43–52; Anthony Sinicropi and Thomas Gilroy, "The Legal Framework of Public Sector Dispute Resolution," *Arbitration Journal*, March 1973, pp. 1–19; Herbert Fishgold, "Dispute Resolution in the Public Sector: The Role of FMCS," *Labor Law Journal*, December 1976, pp. 731–37; Jerome Ross, "Federal Mediation in the Public Sector," *Monthly Labor Review*, February 1976, pp. 41–45.

113. Peter Veglahn, "Education by Third Party Neutrals: Functions, Methods, and Extent," *Labor Law Journal*, January 1977, pp. 20–28; James Scearce and Lucretia Tanner, "Health Care Bargaining: The FMCS Experience," *Labor Law Journal*, July 1976, pp. 387–98; Jean McKelvey, "Fact Finding in Public Employment Disputes: Promise or Illusion," *Industrial and Labor Relations Review*, 1968, pp. 528–43; "U.S. Mediators Try a New Role," *Business Week*, April 21, 1975; Harold Davey, "Third Parties in Labor Relations," in *Employee and Labor Relations*, ed. Yoder and Heneman; Barbara Doering, "Impasse Issues in Teacher Disputes Submitted to Fact Finding in New York," *Arbitration Journal* 27, 1 (1972), pp. 1–17; John Drotning and David Lipsky, "The Outcome of Impasse Procedures in New York Schools under the Taylor Law," *Arbitration Journal*, June 1971, pp. 87–103; N. F. Drifty, "Compulsory Conciliation—The Albertan Experience," *Journal of Industrial Relations*, March 1972, pp. 29–46; Lucian Gatewood, "Factfinding in Teacher Disputes: The Wisconsin Experience," *Monthly Labor Review*, October 1974, pp. 47–51; J. F. B. Goodman and Joseph Krislov, "Conciliation in Industrial Disputes in Great Britain," *British Journal of Industrial Relations*, November 1974, pp. 327–51; Eileen Hoffman, "Resolving Labor Management Disputes: A Nine Country Comparison," *Arbitration Journal*, September 1974, pp. 185–204; John Logan, "The Effect of Compulsory Conciliation in Canada on Strikes," 1967, mimeographed.

114. Michael Brookshire and Fred Holly, "Resolving Bargaining Impasses through Gradual Pressure Strikes," *Labor Law Journal*, October 1973, pp. 662–70.

115. Phillip Revzin, "On the Line," *The Wall Street Journal*, July 8, 1976.

116. John Hutchinson, *Management Under Strike Conditions* (New York: Holt Rinehart & Winston, 1966).

117. Sami Kassem and Marcia Mitterer, "A Critique of Public Policy toward Teacher Strikes and Some Alternatives," *Public Personnel Review*, April 1971, pp. 82–86.

118. Two studies appear to be a good beginning. See John Burton, and Charles Krider, "The Incidence of Strikes in Public Employment," in *Labor in the Public and Non Profit Sector*, ed. Daniel Hamermesh (Princeton: Princeton University Press, 1975); Fox and Wince, "Occupational Militancy Among Public School Teachers." For an analysis of the issues of local government studies, see William Torrence, "City Public Employee Work Stoppages," *Labor Law Journal*, March 1976, p. 177–183.

119. *Yearbook of Labour Statistics* (Geneva: International Labour Office, 1975).

120. J. R. Hicks, *The Theory of Wages* (New York: Macmillan, Inc., 1964).

121. A. Ashenfelter and G. Johnson, "Bargaining Theory, Trade Unions, and Industrial Strike Activity," *American Economic Review*, March 1969, pp. 35–49; C. Krider, "The Pattern and Determinants of Public-Sector Strikes," unpublished manuscript, University of Chicago Graduate School of Business, 1971.

122. John Shorey, "The Size of the Work Unit and Strike Incidence," *Journal of Industrial Economics*, March 1975, pp. 175–88.

123. C. F. Eisele, "Plant Size and Frequency of Strikes," *Labor Law Journal* 21 (1970), pp. 779–86.

124. C. Northcote Parkinson (ed.). *Industrial Disruption* (London: Leviathan, 1973).

125. Clark Kerr and A. Siegel, "The Interindustry Propensity to Strike," in *Industrial Conflict* ed. Arnold Kornhauser et al. (New York: McGraw-Hill Book Co., 1954), pp. 189–212.

126. National Planning Association, *Fundamentals of Labor Peace: A Final Report* (Washington, D.C., 1953).

127. Herbert Northrup and Harvey Young, "The Causes of Industrial Peace Revisited," *Industrial and Labor Relations Review* 22, 1 (1968), pp. 31–47.

128. Myron Roomkin, "Union Structure, Internal Control, and Strike Activity," *Industrial and Labor Relations Review*, 1975–76, pp. 198–217; Robert Stern, "Intermetropolitan Patterns of Strike Frequency," *Industrial and Labor Relations Review*, 1975–76, pp. 218–35.

129. Robert Bonn, "Arbitration: An Alternative System for Handling Contract-Related Disputes," *Administrative Science Quarterly*, June 1972, pp. 254–64.

130. Walter Baer, *The Labor Arbitration Guide* (Homewood, Ill.: Dow Jones–Irwin, 1974); Frank Elkouri and Edna Elkouri, *How Arbitration Works* (Washington, D.C.: Bureau of National Affairs, 1973); Paul Prasov and Edward Peters, *Arbitration and Collective Bargaining* (New York: McGraw-Hill Book Co., 1970); Maurice Trotta, *Arbitration of Labor Management Disputes* (New York: Avacon, 1974).

131. Walter Primeaux and Dalton Brannen, "Why Few Arbitrators are Deemed Acceptable," *Monthly Labor Review*, September 1975, pp. 27–30.

132. Harold Davey, "How Arbitrators Decide Cases," *Labor Law Journal*, April 1974, pp. 200–209.

133. James Gross, "Value Judgments in the Decision of Labor Arbitrators," *Industrial and Labor Relations Review*, 1967, pp. 55–72.

134. David Ross, "The Arbitrater of Public Employee Wage Disputes," *Industrial and Labor Relations Review*, October 1969, pp. 3–14; William Kilberg, et al., "Grievance and Arbitration Patterns in the Federal Service," *Monthly Labor Review*, November 1972, pp. 23–30.

135. Lawrence Holden, "Final Offer Arbitration in Massachusetts," *The Arbitration Journal* 31, 1 (1976), pp. 26–33; Paul Staudohar, "Results of Final Offer Arbitration of Bargaining Disputes," *California Management Review*, Fall 1975, pp. 57–61; James Stern, "Final Offer Arbitration: Initial Experience in Wisconsin," *Monthly Labor Review*, September 1974, pp. 39–43; Fred Whitney, "Final Offer Arbitration: The Indianapolis Experience," *Monthly Labor Review*, May 1973, pp. 20–25; Gary Long and Peter Feville, "Final Offer Arbitration: Sudden Death in Eugene," *Industrial and Labor Relations Review* 27, 2 (January 1974), pp. 186–203; James Stern et al., *Final Author Arbitration* (Lexington, Mass.: Lexington Books, 1975).

136. Karl Van Asselt, "Binding Arbitration: A Recent Experience," *Monthly Labor Review*, May 1973, pp. 20–25; Peter Seitz, "Mandatory Contract Arbitration," *Industrial and Labor Relations Review*, April 1973, pp. 1009–12; Gerald Caiden, *Public Employment and Compulsory Arbitration in Australia* (Ann Arbor: Institute of Labor and Industrial Relations, University of Michigan—Wayne State University, 1971); Kingsley Laffer, "Compulsory Arbitration: The Australian Experience," *Monthly Labor Review*, May 1972, pp. 45–59; Sally Bochner, "Grievance Arbitration on Trial," *Canadian Personnel and Industrial Relations Journal*, January 1975.

137. Paul Staudohar, "Constitutionality of Compulsory Arbitration: Statutes in Public Employment," *Labor Law Journal*, November 1976, pp. 670–77.

138. James Power, "Improving Arbitration: Roles of Parties and Agencies," *Monthly Labor Review*, November 1972, pp. 15–22; W. J. Usery, "Some Attempts to Reduce Arbitration Costs and Delays," *Monthly Labor Review*, November 1972, pp. 3–7.

139. P. Davis and A. C. Pati, "Elapsed Time Patterns in Labor Grievance Arbitration—1942–1972," *Arbitration Journal* 29, 1 (1974), pp. 15–27.

140. Hyman Cohen, "The Search for Innovative Procedures in Labor Arbitration," *Arbitration Journal*, June 1974, pp. 104–14; Sam Kagel and John Kagel, "Using Two New Arbitration Techniques," *Monthly Labor Review*, November 1972, pp. 11–14; Ben Fischer, "Arbitration: The Steel Experience," *Monthly Labor Review*, November 1972, pp. 7–10; Ben Fischer, "The Steel Industry's Expedited Arbitration," *Arbitration Journal*, December 1973, pp. 185–91.

141. Phillip Ash, "The Parties to the Grievance," *Personnel Psychology* 23 (1970), pp. 13–37; John Price et al., "Three Studies of Grievances," *Personnel Journal*, January 1976, pp. 33–37; H. Sulkin and R. Pranis, "Comparison of Grievants in a Heavy Machinery Company," *Personnel Psychology* 20, 2 (1967), pp. 111–19.

142. Ken Jennings, "Foremen's Views of Their Involvement with Other Management Officials in the Grievance Process," *Labor Law Journal*, May 1974, pp. 305–16; Ken Jennings, "Foremen's Views of Their Involvement with the Union Steward in the Grievance Process," *Labor Law Journal*, September 1974, pp. 541–49.

143. James Begin, "The Private Grievance Model in the Public Sector," *Industrial Relations*, February 1971.

144. Julius Draznin, "A New Approach to Grievance Handling in the Federal Sector," *Personnel Journal*, November 1974, pp. 822–24; Thomas Mannix, "Community College Grievance Procedures," *Journal of College and University Personnel Association*, April 1974, pp. 23–40.

145. Wiley Beavers, "Employee Relations without a Union," in *Employee and Labor Relations*, ed. Yoder and Heneman.

146. Edward Fleishman and E. F. Harris, "Patterns of Leadership Behavior Related to Employee Grievances and Turnover," *Personnel Psychology*, Spring, 1962, pp. 45–53.

147. Julius Draznin, "A New Approach to Grievance Handling in the Public Sector."

148. Tim Bornstein, "Unions, Critics, and Collective Bargaining," *Labor Law Journal*, October 1976, pp. 614–22; Alexander Holmes, "Effects of Union Activity on Teachers' Earnings," *Industrial Relations*, October 1976, pp. 328–32.

Discipline, control, and evaluation

Efforts to control and evaluate the human resource in the enterprise take various forms. Chapter 20 discusses the symptoms indicating that an employee is difficult to deal with and the systems available to attempt to modify his or her behavior. In Chapter 21 the emphasis is not on the individual employee but on methods used to evaluate and measure the overall effectiveness of the human resources and personnel function of an enterprise.

PART SEVEN

Discipline and the difficult employee

CHAPTER OBJECTIVES

■ To show why disciplinary systems are necessary in enterprises.

■ To examine the characteristics of different types of employees.

■ To discuss the variety of disciplinary philosophies, methods, and systems available for use in managing difficult employees.

CHAPTER OUTLINE

Managers supervise a variety of types of employees as part of their work. Most employees perform effectively most of the time. But any management development session eventually comes around to a discussion of employees like Al, Susan, Joyce, or Tom.

Al is the salesman who had the largest sales increases of any of the sales force just after he was hired. Later, his sales dropped off. When his supervisor checked, Al was found to be making just enough sales calls to reach his quota.

Susan is often a good worker. Then there are days when all the forms she types at the state employment bureau have serious errors on them. These are the days Susan is on drugs or drinking.

Joyce seems to do good work. She is courteous to the customers. She puts the stock up quickly and marks the prices accurately. But Joyce takes more than her paycheck home from Kmart every week.

Tom is a pretty good employee. But John, his supervisor, is driven up the wall by him. Tom just can't seem to follow the company rules. And when John tries to talk to him about it, Tom gives him a hard time and may even seem to threaten him if he tries to do anything about the problem.

These examples illustrate a time-consuming and worrisome aspect of the personnel job: dealing fairly with the difficult employee. The seriousness of the problem is shown by the fact that the largest number of cases going to arbitration involves disciplinary matters. Unionized organizations have ways of dealing with these incidents, but most employees do not work in a unionized situation.

This chapter is concerned with the characteristics of difficult employees and some of the reasons they are the way they are. It also considers systems of discipline and appropriate means for rehabilitating difficult employees. Too often discipline has been oriented toward punishment for past misdeeds. This is required in Joyce's case, but more important for the others is behavioral change to improve employee productivity.

The emphasis of the chapter will be on *on-the-job behavior.* Enterprises such as the military and the church have tried to control the total behavior of the employee; the military often will court-martial and punish soldiers for civilian offenses such as speeding, whether or not civilian authorities prosecute. The work organization, however, should be concerned with off-the-job behavior only when it affects work behavior. Thus if Susan "shoots up" before work so that she cannot do her job, this is of concern to her employer. If Sally has a few drinks after work and this in no way affects her job, it is none of her employer's business, even if the boss happens to be a teetotaler.

Generally, the operating supervisor is the person primarily involved in disciplining employees. Personnel specialists may be involved as advisers if they are asked to do so by the operating manager. Sometimes the personnel manager serves as a second step in investigation and appeal of a disciplinary case. Or, when the union is involved, the personnel manager may advise the operating manager on contract interpretation for a specific case.

Discipline is a Stage III personnel activity as defined in Exhibit 1–13 (Chapter 1). Some studies have been performed on the topic, but there is a wide divergence in the disciplinary practices applied in various enterprises.

A DIAGNOSTIC APPROACH TO DISCIPLINE

Exhibit 20–1 highlights the factors affecting the discipline process in an enterprise. The employee is the crucial factor, especially insofar as his or her attitude toward work. Discipline problems are not as likely with work-oriented people as with instrumental employees (see Chapter 2). These work attitudes probably were developed from the employee's past work experiences and cultural heritage.

The kind of discipline system used is normally related to the enterprise; it will be more formal in larger enterprises, especially those that are unionized. It is quite informal in smaller enterprises.

How strict discipline is depends on the nature of the prevailing labor market; in times of high unemployment, for example, it can be quite strict. It also is related to the supportiveness of the work group (if the work group "covers" for the employee and feels the issue is unimportant, management's ability to discipline will be limited), and to the nature of the leader or supervisor (a liberal leader's approach to discipline will be quite different from a conservative leader's). The government and the legal system may provide support for employer or employee.

The effective operating or personnel manager will try to diagnose each of these factors in the discipline situation. For example, the supervisor may try to diagnose the difficult employee's motivation with a view toward improving performance. This is not always easy to do, and, if the manager does not know the employee well because there are many employees or for other reasons, it may be virtually impossible. Discipline is one of the most challenging areas in the personnel function, and the diagnostic approach rather than the "give her a fair trial before you hang her" approach is especially helpful in dealing with the difficult employee.

CATEGORIES OF DIFFICULT EMPLOYEES

This chapter will focus on discipline and behavior modification of four kinds of employees whose behavior can be described as difficult.

Category 1. Those whose quality or quantity of work is unsatisfactory due to lack of abilities, training, or job motivation. (Al is an example.)

Category 2. Those whose personal problems off the job begin to affect job productivity. These problems can include alcoholism, drugs, or family relationships. (Susan is an example.)

Category 3. Those who violate laws while on the job by such behavior as stealing from the organization or its employees or physical abuse of employees or property. (Joyce is an example.)

EXHIBIT 20–1
Factors affecting discipline and organizational effectiveness

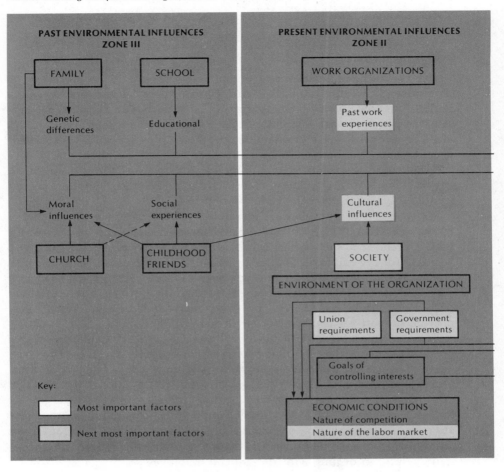

Category 4., Those who consistently break company rules and do not respond to superviory reactions. (Tom is an example.)

The difficulty of determining the causes of any human behavior pattern
was noted in Chapter 2. It is especially difficult to assess the causes of
undesired behavior, but John Miner has devised a scheme for analyzing
deficient behavior which provides a checklist of possible causes.[1] Exhibit
20–2 is based on this list.

Many of these causes can influence deficient behavior, which can result
from behavior of the employee alone, behavior of the employer alone, or
interaction of the employee and the employer. Al's behavior (category 1),
which is directly related to the work situation, could be caused by Miner's
factors II, III, and VII, while Susan could take drugs (category 2) because
of Miner's factors II, IV, V, and others; the primary cause of her behavior

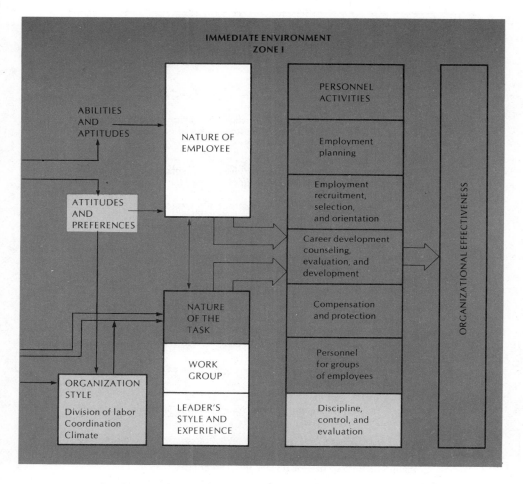

is outside the control of the employer. Or she could take drugs because of Miner's factor VII, which the employer could remedy. Frequently, difficult behavior is caused by personal and employment conditions which feed one another. Joyce's behavior—theft and other illegal activities (category 3)—is normally dealt with by security departments and usually results in termination and possibly prosecution of the employee. Tom's behavior (category 4) is often caused by Miner's factors III, VII, VIII, and IX.

Category 1: The ineffective employee

Employees who are performing ineffectively may do so because of factors which are directly related to the work situation and are theoretically the easiest to work with and to adjust. Robert Mager and Peter Pipe have system-

EXHIBIT 20–2
Possible causes of difficult job behavior

  I. Problems of Intelligence and Job Knowledge**
     A. Insufficient verbal ability
     B. Insufficient special ability
     C. Insufficient job knowledge
     D. Defects of judgment or memory

 II. Emotional Problems***
     A. Frequent disruptive emotion (anxiety, depression, anger, excitement, shame, guilt, jealousy)
     B. Neurosis (with anxiety, depression, anger, and so on, predominating)
     C. Psychosis (with anxiety, depression, anger, and so on, predominating)
     D. Alcohol and drug problems

III. Motivational Problems***
     A. Strong motives frustrated at work (pleasure in success, fear of failure, avoidance motives, dominance, desire to be popular, social motivation, need for attention, and so on)
     B. Unintegrated means used to satisfy strong motives
     C. Excessively low personal work standards
     D. Generalized low work motivation

 IV. Physical Problems*
     A. Physical illness or handicap, including brain disorders
     B. Physical disorders of emotional origin
     C. Inappropriate physical characteristics
     D. Insufficient muscular or sensory ability or skill

  V. Family-Related Problems*
     A. Family crises (divorce, death, severe illness, and the like)
     B. Separation from the family and isolation
     C. Predominance of family considerations over work demands

 VI. Problems Caused in the Work Group**
     A. Negative consequences associated with group cohesion
     B. Ineffective management
     C. Inappropriate managerial standards or criteria

VII. Problems Originating in Company Policies and Higher Level Decisions***
     A. Insufficient organizational action
     B. Placement error
     C. Organizational overpermissiveness
     D. Excessive spans of control
     E. Inappropriate organizational standards and criteria

VIII. Problems Stemming from Society and Its Values*
     A. Application of legal sanctions
     B. Enforcement of societal values by means other than the law (including the use of value-based inappropriate criteria)
     C. Conflict between job demands and cultural values (equity, freedom, moral and religious values, and so on)

 IX. Problems Growing Out of the Work Context and the Work Itself**
     A. Negative consequences of economic forces
     B. Negative consequences of geographic location
     C. Detrimental conditions in the work setting
     D. Excessive danger
     E. Problems in the work itself

* Highly significant causes of undesirable employee behavior.
** Very significant causes.
*** Significant causes.
   Source: Based on John Miner, *The Challenge of Managing* (Philadelphia: W. B. Saunders Co., 1975), pp. 330–31.

atized this pattern of undesirable behavior and have designed a conceptual model of questions by which management can deal with it.[2] Their model is presented as flow diagram in Exhibit 20–3.

Mager and Pipe indicate that there are four key issues with which managers must cope. The first (I on the diagram) is: The employee is not performing well; the manager thinks there is a training problem. They suggest three general questions and follow-up questions to analyze the problem:

1. *What is the performance discrepancy?* Why do I think there is a training problem? What is the difference between what is being done and what is supposed to be done? What is the event that causes me to say that things aren't right? Why am I dissatisfied?

2. *Is it important?* Why is the discrepancy important? What would happen if I left the discrepancy alone? Could doing something to resolve the discrepancy have any worthwhile result?

3. *Is it a skill deficiency?* Could he do it if he really had to? Could he do it if his life depended on it? Are his present skills adequate for the desired performance?

Question 3 leads to II on the diagram. Key issue I is solved: Yes, it is a skill deficiency. To check this further, Mager and Pipe suggest general questions 4–7:

4. *Could he do it in the past?* Did he once know how to perform as desired? Has he forgotten how to do what I want him to do?

5. *Is the skill used often?* How often is the skill or performance used? Does he get regular feedback about how well he performs? Exactly how does he find out how well he is doing?

6. *Is there a simpler solution?* Can I change the job by providing some kind of job aid? Can I store the needed information some way (written instructions, checklists) other than in someone's head? Can I show rather than train? Would informal (i.e., on-the-job) training be sufficient?

7. *Does he have what it takes?* Could he learn the job? Does he have the physical and mental potential to perform as desired? Is he overqualified for the job?

At this point it might appear that the conclusion to II was not correct, or the question may have been answered no in the first place. In this case the key issue would be: It is not a skill deficiency; he could do it if he wanted to. At III; general questions 8–11 apply:

8. *Is desired performance punishing?* What is the consequence of performing as desired? Is it punishing to perform as expected? Does he perceive desired performance as being geared to penalties? Would his world become a little dimmer (to him) if he performed as desired?

9. *Is nonperformance rewarding?* What is the result of doing it his way instead of my way? What does he get out of his present performance in the way of reward, prestige, status, jollies? Does he get more attention for misbehaving than for behaving? What event in the world supports (rewards) his present way of doing things? (Are you inadvertently rewarding irrelevant behavior while overlooking the crucial behaviors?) Is he "mentally inadequate," so that

EXHIBIT 20–3
Analyzing undesirable employee behavior

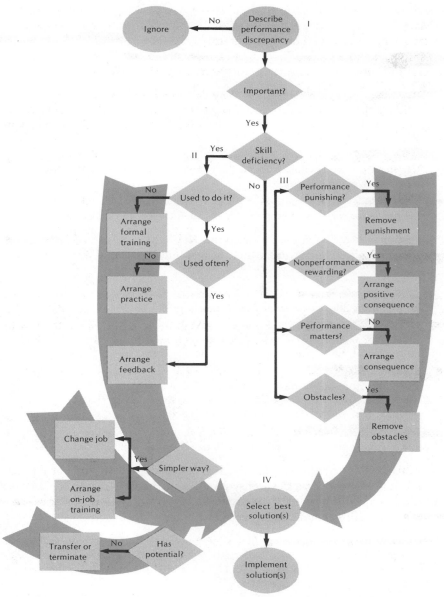

Source: Robert Mager and Peter Pipe, *Analyzing Performance Problems* (Palo Alto, Calif.: Fearon Publishers, 1970).

the less he does the less he has to worry about? Is he physically inadequate, so that he gets less tired if he does less?

10. *Does performing really matter?*   Does performing as desired matter to the performer? Is there a favorable outcome for performing? Is there an undesirable outcome for not performing? Is there a source of satisfaction for performing? Is he able to take pride in his performance, as an individual or as a member of a group? Does he get satisfaction of his needs from the job?

11. *Are there obstacles to performing?*   What prevents him from performing? Does he know what is expected of him? Does he know when to do what is expected of him? Are there conflicting demands on his time? Does he lack the authority? . . . the time? . . . the tools? Is he restricted by policies or by a "right way of doing it" or "way we've always done it" that ought to be changed? Can I reduce interference by improving lighting? . . . changing colors? . . . increasing comfort? . . . modifying the work position? . . . reducing visual or auditory distractions? Can I reduce "competition from the job"—phone calls, "brush fires," demands of less important but more immediate problems?

Finally, we arrive at IV, the key issue: Which solution is best? Mager and Pipe suggest these questions to analyze that problem:

Are any solutions inappropriate or impossible to implement? Are any solutions plainly beyond our resources? What would it "cost" to go ahead with the solution? What would be the added "value" if I did? Is it worth doing? Which remedy is likely to give us the most result for the least effort? Which are we best equipped to try? Which remedy interests us most? (Or, on the other side of the coin, which remedy is most visible to those who must be pleased?)

This is a useful approach to dealing with a category 1 employee.

Category 2: Alcoholic and addicted employees

Abuse of alcoholic consumption which affects an employee's job performance is an international problem. In surveys on this over a ten-year period, the National Industrial Conference Board found companies much more concerned about the problem in the second survey than the first.[3] More and more, alcoholism is being viewed by the courts and by therapists as an illness, a *treatable* illness.

Estimates of the number of alcoholics employed in America vary, but the National Council on Alcoholism estimates that about 10 percent of the labor force are alcoholics and another 10 percent are borderline alcoholics. The greatest incidence of alcoholism is in people aged 35–55 who have been employed at the same enterprise 14–20 years. The direct cost to industry alone is estimated at $8 billion a year in lost productivity and allied expenses. This estimate may be low because alcoholics often are sent home as "sick" rather than as drunk.

Of course, alcoholic consumption does not affect all employees the same at work, nor does it affect performance of tasks equally. Studies indicate that alcoholic intake tends to reduce some ability performance levels (for example cognitive and perceptual-sensory skills) more than others (psycho-motor skills). For many persons, it takes about an hour for the alcohol to affect performance negatively.[4]

One expert contends that there are three predisposing factors to alcoholism: hereditary sensitivity, personality disorders, and the widespread practice of social drinking.[5] Co-workers and supervisors often overlook drinking behavior even on the job if the overall performance is not too far from standard, but alcoholism is not a disease that will go away on its own, like chicken pox. The same expert reported that in 1966 over a third of America's largest employers had set up alcoholism control programs. Many medical plans now cover the costs of treatment for alcoholism if the employee will take it, and if they refuse, many companies fire them.

Generally the successful program for alcoholics includes a conference between supervisor and employee.[6] These points are covered:

The supervisor documents the effects at work of the employee's alcoholism to the employee.

The supervisor offers to help.

The supervisor *requires* the employee to participate in a rehabilitation program such as Alcoholics Anonymous (which was evaluated as by far the best program).

The supervisor notifies the employee that the consequence of not participating in rehabilitation is loss of the job.

Many unions are now participating in joint employer-union programs designed to deal with alcoholism.

A number of success stories following these programs have been reported recently.[7] Enterprises with successful alcoholism programs include Oldsmobile, the New York City Police Department, Illinois Bell Telephone, Kennecott Copper, DuPont, Consolidated Edison, Bell of Canada, Honeywell, Caterpillar, Eastman Kodak, and United California Bank.

In larger enterprises, the health department helps alcoholics. In medium-sized and smaller enterprises, personnel refers them to consultants and to treatment programs. Personnel and the supervisor cooperate to help the employee to become well again or, alternatively, to be terminated. If the decision is to terminate, personnel and operating managers need documentation to support their decision, in arbitration hearings if necessary.

The addicted employee. Employers also are finding more employees addicted to drugs such as cocaine and heroin and are becoming more aware of this problem area. Drug addiction manifests itself in ways similar to alcoholism. The problem may be less well known to employers because of laws against possession and use of drugs, which causes employees to hide their habit.

How many drug addicts there are in the employment situation is not known precisely. In one study, employers in New York state estimated that about 12 percent of their employees had used marijuana at one time or another, and about 7 percent of employees had used marijuana in the past six months, 2 percent *on the job.* Less than 2 percent of employees had used heroin, about 1 percent in the past six months, and 0.33 percent had used it *on the job.* Somewhat similar or lesser percentages of employees were found to be using LSD and speed. Barbituates were more widely used; 19 percent of employees had used them, 7 percent in the past six months and about 2 percent on the job. Drug usage varies by occupation and location to some degree.[8]

In another study of 231 companies by the American Management Association in 1971, more than half of the companies surveyed said they had dealt with problems of employee drug abuse during the preceding year. The drugs involved were marijuana (29 percent), amphetamines (18 percent), heroin (17 percent), cocaine (2 percent), and other (10 percent).[9] A third researcher estimates that about 10 percent of the people use hard drugs and 50 percent have used or use marijuana.[10]

Companies believe that absenteeism, turnover, accidents, and lower productivity are caused by drug addiction, and some thievery is due to the need for addicts to support their habit. What have they done about it? One survey of 108 companies on employees' use of drugs found that 81 percent tried to find out if the employee had used drugs prior to hiring, and 51 percent have company policies against drug use by employees.[11] Their responses to the problem include detection methods to determine the extent of the problem, more careful recruitment and selection, educational programs for supervisors, policy statements, and counseling programs which refer addicts to rehabilitation programs.[12]

The U.S. military used random urine tests to determine drug use but dropped the program because of its costs. In 1975 the Air Force tested 195,000 employees and turned up 604 drug users, at an average cost of $3,710 each.

Drug users could be screened out better in the selection process if knowledge of factors likely to lead to drug usage were available. A recent literature search found numerous factors likely to predispose a person to drug usage.[13] These include:

- Disruption of normal parent/child relationships.
- Lack of involvement in organized groups.
- Few effective peer relationships.
- Involvement with drug-using peers.
- Positive experiences with drugs.
- Nontraditional upbringing and socialization.
- Permissive attitudes toward drugs by parents.

Companies follow similar control programs for drugs as they do for alcohol, although treatment methods vary more in the drug area.[14] Drug usage is illegal, and public attitudes are much more negative on drugs than on alcohol. In industry, the company health department can try to rehabilitate drug users.[15] Often, however, the ultimate decision is discharge and discipline, although this may lead to arbitration. A summary of arbitration rulings on the subject and a survey of members of the National Academy of Arbitrators by Edward Levin and Tia Denenberg found that because of the legal implications and the difficulty drug users would have in getting future jobs, arbitrators demand full and complete proof of drug usage. This is sometimes difficult for employers to provide. Employers can help protect themselves by asking the employee to certify previous drug experiences. If it can be shown this record is falsified, arbitrators view this as grounds for discharge or discipline. If company policy is to discipline or discharge employees who use drugs, company rules and employment controls should be explicit about this prohibition. Evidence must also be given that these prohibitions were communicated clearly to all employees.

Arbitrators have discharged drug-using employees if their habit ruined a firm's reputation or lost it business. They are more likely to uphold discharges for drug usage after conviction than after arrest alone, and they discipline drug pushers more severely than drug users. In general, according to Levin and Denenberg, arbitrators tend to urge employers to give drug-using employees a second chance if they agree to rehabilitation programs.[16]

Category 3: Participants in theft, crime, and illegal acts

Employers have to deal with employees who engage in various illegal acts: they may steal (remember Joyce), misuse company facilities or property, disclose trade secrets, embezzle, or kidnap executives for terrorist purposes. They may sabotage products and use company telephones and credit cards for personal purposes or company materials or labor to repair their homes. *The Wall Street Journal* estimates that 75 percent of stolen goods is taken by employees and suppliers.[17] Yet some arbitrators have recently ruled that employee property (such as their cars in the parking lot) cannot be searched without a warrant. The enterprise must also be concerned with thefts and similar crimes by visitors and guests.

Enterprises try to deal with employee theft and similar problems in a number of ways. One is to try to screen out likely thieves; Richard Rosenbaum has developed a weighted application blank to help with this.[18]

Other enterprises try to prevent thefts by training and preventative measures. Mark Lipman suggests ten steps to be taken to prevent thefts.[19] They are:

1. The employee should be made to feel that the job is worth keeping and it would not be easy to earn more elsewhere.
2. Normal good housekeeping practices—no piles of rubbish or rejects or boxes, no disused machines with tarpaulins on them, and no unlocked, empty drawers—will help assure that there are no places where stolen goods can be hidden. The first act of the thief is to divert merchandise from the normal traffic flow.

3. Paperwork must be carefully examined and checked at all stages so invoices cannot be stolen or altered.

4. Employees' cars should not be parked close to their places of work. There should be no usable cover between the plant doors and the cars.

5. Women employees must not be allowed to keep their handbags next to them at work. Lockers that lock must be provided for handbags. Merchandise has a way of disappearing into a handbag, and once the bag is closed a search warrant is needed to get it open again.

6. Whether the plant is open or closed at night, bright lights should blaze all around the perimeter so no one can enter or leave without being seen.

7. There should be adequate measures to control issuance of keys. There have been cases where a manager or supervisor would come back at night for a tryst with a girlfriend and would give her an armload of merchandise to take home with her. Key control is very important.

8. As far as possible, everyone entering or leaving should have an identification card.

9. Unneeded doors should be kept locked. If only two must be open to handle the normal flow of traffic, the rest should be bolted.

10. Everything of value that thieves could possibly remove, not just obvious items, must be safeguarded.

Many of these steps suggest that enterprises can deal with these problems by setting up a security department or program. Often this responsibility is assigned to the personnel department. The protection program typically is called industrial security and includes security education, employment screening, physical security, theft and fraud control, and fire prevention. Some of the more common of these security measures are listed in Exhibit 20–4. Most companies engage in at least minimal industrial security operations such as identification or "badge" systems, prior employment screening, special safeguards and destruction of sensitive documents, and escort services for visitors.

Jerry Wall believes an enterprise is of sufficient size to have a security program when it has about 100 employees. It can approach this in two ways, by hiring a technically skilled person to serve at least part time as a security manager, or by leasing this service from a local security agency. In many cases, these agencies will provide both security consulting services and a guard force. Wall found that the larger the enterprise, the greater the likelihood that security measures would be used. Most enterprises also attempt at least some industrial security planning in selecting sites and designs for remodeling or construction of facilities. Security vulnerabilities are assessed and structural barriers such as fences, lighting, and the building itself are designed to reduce security hazards. Wall's 1974 study of 1,200 enterprises found them much more security conscious than ten years ago.[20]

Operating and personnel managers may both be involved in disciplinary

EXHIBIT 20–4
Use of various security measures

	Extent of usage		
Measure	Never	Occasionally	Often
Locker searches	76%	23%	1%
Package checks	54	36	10
Counterintelligence "sweeps" for hidden microphones (bugs)	87	12	1
Guard dogs	91	7	3
Escort service for visitors	27	27	46
Undercover operatives for in-house checking on embezzlement, stealing, and so on	61	33	6
Electronic surveillance of high-risk areas	62	21	17
Document marking for sensitive documents	40	28	32
Special computer and/or computer equipment —i.e., "software" safeguards	41	29	30
Special safeguards for sensitive documents	15	30	55
Special destruction of sensitive waste	29	31	40
Personality tests—i.e., tests that measure characteristics, not abilities	47	35	17
Identification badges or cards for access control for:			
All employees	49	11	41
Special employee groups	49	13	38
Visitors	39	13	48
Controlled access to workplace by:			
Receptionist	16	12	72
Guards	39	14	47
Electronic surveillance	60	19	21
Lie detector tests for employees in positions of trust:			
Before employment	93	5	2
After employment	90	9	1
Investigation of job applicants by:			
Prior employment check	4	18	78
Police arrest record check	25	36	39
Credit check	22	38	40
Drug abuse detection check	51	33	16
Handwriting analysis	90	9	1

Source: Jerry L. Wall, "What The Competition Is Doing: Your Need To Know," *Harvard Business Review,* November–December 1974, p. 38, copyright © 1974 by the President and Fellows of Harvard College, all rights reserved.

matters involving category 3 employees. Often firings are considered as well as legal action. Visitors involved in illegal acts may also face the law.

Category 4: The rule violators

The fourth category of difficult employees consistently violate company rules, such as those prohibiting sleeping on the job, having weapons at work, fighting at work, coming in late, or abusing the supervisor. One researcher sees the rule violator as a special kind of person: very vigorous, irresponsible, unstable, and with a "devil may care attitude."[21]

An especially difficult issue is verbal and physical abuse of supervisors.

Those who abuse high school teachers are likely to take the same attitude toward work supervisors. It is useful (though not necessary) for the enterprise to have an established rule prohibiting verbal and physical abuse. Disputes charging abuse often go to arbitration, and Ken Jennings has reviewed the decisions of arbitrators in such cases.[22] In general, arbitrators take the position that the decisions of supervisors deserve respect. Their rulings have been influenced by several facets of the cases:

> *The nature of the verbal abuse.* If the shop talk is usually obscene, unless the employee personally applies the obscenities to the supervisor ("God damn you"), arbitrators are not likely to uphold disciplinary measures for use of obscene words.
>
> *The nature of the threat.* Discipline will be upheld if an employee *personally* threatens a supervisor, not if the employee talks vaguely about threats.
>
> *The facts in physical abuse cases.* If the employee directly attacks the supervisor personally or indirectly (e.g., abusive phone calls) *and if* the employee was not provoked, the disciplinary decision will be upheld by arbitrators.

Jennings found that arbitrators frequently reduce disciplinary penalties (in 54 percent of the cases). They take into account mitigating circumstances like prior excellent work records and how fairly the management has treated the employee prior to and at the time of the incident. They also check to make sure that management has consistently disciplined other employees in similar cases and that the disciplinary decisions were consistent. Arbitrators have treated altercations between supervisors and union stewards differently from those between supervisors and other employees; they view the supervisor and steward as equal and feel the steward need not be as "respectful" as other employees.

It is more difficult to establish rules about other infractions. Many enterprises prohibit gambling on company grounds, to avoid lowering productivity and losing time from fights over gambling losses, yet few want to prohibit nickel-dime poker at lunch.

Enterprises usually have rules prohibiting employees from making decisions when there is a conflict of interest (such as a purchasing agent who has an interest in a supplier) or when they are indebted to others. Many enterprises prohibit their employees from accepting gifts over some nominal value or lavish entertaining. Conflict-of-interest dealings are usually specifically prohibited.

The enterprise probably should have a rule prohibiting sexual harassment, but it may be difficult to investigate or enforce.[23] Women who have had to submit to sexual relations with the boss (or clients) to hold a job are turning to the EEOC and the courts to resolve this issue. This is a difficult problem for management; not too long ago, it was criticized for rules prohibiting fraternization between employees as constituting an invasion of privacy.

The problem of the ex-convict as an employee is a long-standing one. Many can become excellent employees, others will not. Personnel must be especially careful in the supervision and discipline of ex-convicts if they are to be developed as good employees.[24]

Are certain types of employees likely to be difficult?

Various experts have tried to identify the personality characteristics of the difficult employee.[25] This search may be as illusive as trying to find the personality characteristics of good leaders.

One who has tried to isolate these characteristics is Claire Anderson, who studied 1,635 hourly workers in two plants of a manufacturing company in the eastern United States. She was searching for the "marginal worker"— the one who consistently and frequently is difficult, as measured by more frequent absences, turnover, firings, discipline cases, grievances, and accidents. She reviewed the literature *thoroughly* prior to testing hypotheses and found that the marginal worker was most likely to be one of a *few* employees who caused the most problems. Characteristically, this type of employee was a production worker in a large production department, working on a late shift and receiving high overtime or incentive pay rather than the day rate. The marginal worker was also most likely to be young, male, U.S.– born, and black.[26]

Anderson's study is carefully qualified—it is a one-company study in the East, and so on. But the probability is that some of these characteristics are likely to be universal, in view of many collaborating studies on age, sex, type of job, shift, and pay. Whether the race and native-born factors would hold up in studies of locales such as El Paso, Chicago, or Los Angeles needs further testing. It is possible that socioeconomic class rather than race is the deciding variable.

In any event, it is possible, from Anderson's and similar studies,[27] to identify a group of marginal employees and carefully watch this group. Whether all marginal employees would have the same characteristics as those described above is yet to be determined.

THE DISCIPLINE PROCESS

Exhibit 20–5 is a model of the discipline process. The employer establishes goals and rules and communicates them to employees. Employee behavior is then assessed, and modification may be found desirable. This process is an attempt to prevent difficulties and is positive: it is designed to help employees succeed.

The first element in the process is the establishment of *work and behavior rules.* Work goals and standards were discussed as part of performance evaluation (Chapters 10). Through whatever method is used (time and motion study, examination of past performance or performances by others, management by objectives) a set of minimally acceptable work goals is established. Behavior rules cover many facets of on-the-job behavior. They can be categorized as concerning behavior that is directly or indirectly related to work

EXHIBIT 20–5
Elements in a disciplinary system

productivity. Both types are often negatively described as prohibited behavior. Exhibit 20–6 lists some examples of employee behavior rules.

The second important element in the disciplinary process is the *communication* of the rules to all employees. Unless employees are aware of the rules, they can hardly be expected to follow them. Closely related is a willingness to accept the rules and their enforceability. If employees or their representatives participate in the formation of the rules, their cooperation is more likely to be assured. Employees must be convinced that the rule is *fair and related to job effectiveness.* For example, up until a little over a year ago, a college tried to enforce a dress code which prohibited pants suits or

EXHIBIT 20–6
Examples of employee behavior rules

I.   Rules directly related to productivity
    A.   Time rules
        1.   Starting and late times
        2.   Quitting times
        3.   Maximum break and lunch times
        4.   Maximum absenteeism
    B.   Prohibited-behavior rules
        1.   No sleeping on the job
        2.   No leaving workplace without permission
        3.   No drinking on the job
        4.   No drug taking on the job
        5.   Limited nonemployer activities during work hours
    C.   Insubordination rules
        1.   Penalties for refusal to obey supervisors
        2.   Rules against slowdowns and sit-downs
    D.   Rules emphasizing laws
        1.   Theft rules
        2.   Falsification rules
    E.   Safety rules
        1.   No-smoking rules
        2.   Safety regulations
        3.   Sanitation requirements
        4.   Rules prohibiting fighting
        5.   Rules prohibiting dangerous weapons
II.   Rules indirectly related to productivity
    A.   Prevention of moonlighting
    B.   Prohibition of gambling
    C.   Prohibition of selling or soliciting at work
    D.   Clothing and uniform regulations
    E.   Rules about fraternization with other employees at work or off the job

slacks for women. When some of the employees started ignoring this rule, the dean's secretary tried to enforce it. A group of the employees went to the dean demanding the rule be dropped. He appointed an employee committee to redesign the dress code, and the rule was dropped.

It is useful for management to seek employee advice on periodic revision of rules. The objective is to reduce the number of rules to the minimum and enforce those that are important. Customs and conditions change. Rules, like laws, need regular updating to achieve the respect and acceptance necessary for order in the workplace.

The third element of the disciplinary process is an *assessment mechanism.* In most organizations, performance evaluation is the mechanism for assessing work behavior deficiency. Rule-breaking behavior usually comes to the attention of management when it is observed or when difficulties arise and investigation reveals certain behavior as the cause.

Finally, the disciplinary process consists of a system of *administering punishment or attempting to motivate change.* This varies from supervisory administration of discipline to formal systems somewhat like courts or grievance procedures.

PHILOSOPHIES OF DISCIPLINE

For most employees most of the time, if the enterprise establishes rules and goals and communicates them this is enough to induce productivity and satisfaction. But there are the category 1, 2, 3, and 4 employees. How does the enterprise deal with them?

Lawrence Steinmetz suggests four ways to handle the marginal or unsatisfactory performer.[28] In order of precedence; these are:

The preventive approach. This approach emphasizes analysis to make sure that the match between job and employee is right.

The therapeutic technique. When the preventive approach does not apply, counseling employees to let them know they are ineffective and to suggest how they might improve is in order. Many employees respond to this approach.

The self-improvement program. A variation of the therapeutic technique is for the supervisor to first document their ineffectiveness to employees and then encourage them to design a self-improvement program. This puts the emphasis where it belongs: on employees improving their performance with the supervisor's counsel and help.

The punitive approach. When none of these methods work, corrective discipline is the last resort. These methods vary from "chewing out" the employee to termination.

Steinmetz's description of the four ways to handle the marginal worker and upgrade performance has not always been accepted by managers. George Odiorne contrasts the punitive approach, which he calls discipline by tradition, to discipline by objectives.[29] The traditional discipline process is to list the crimes, attach punishments to each, promulgate the list, and apply punishment to each act. According to Odiorne, discipline by tradition (punitive, punishment-oriented behavior) has certain characteristics:

Discipline is what superiors apply to subordinates, never the reverse.

The past is the arbiter of present and future actions.

Discipline is punishment for forbidden actions, and punishment should be directly proportional to the severity of the offense.

The effect of punishment is to deter others from performing these acts.

If the forbidden behavior is continuing or accelerating, increasing the severity of punishment to the next offenders is in order.

If the guilty individual cannot be isolated, the whole group should be punished.

Absolute consistency in punishment must be maintained at all times in all cases.

The severity of the punishment for the second offense should always be more severe than for the first identical offense.

Punishment should be given maximum publicity to deter future misbehavior.

Odiorne contrasts this philosophy with discipline by objectives—a more modern approach, he feels. He proposes these characteristics of an effective disciplinary program:

Discipline at work is for the most part voluntarily accepted (by the employees), and if not voluntarily accepted is not legitimate.

Discipline is not a punishment system but a behavior modifier.

The past provides useful experience in defining and changing behavior but is not an infallible guide to right and wrong.

Contribution to objectives is a reasonable guide as to when to depart from rules and regulations. By this Odiorne means at times all may need to break an unimportant rule to achieve organizational objectives.

Rules and regulations should be reviewed periodically against organizational objectives to see if they are still productive.

Individual discipline by objectives makes each individual responsible for his or her own output, and the individual differences are explainable in individual results.

Which approach predominates, discipline by tradition or by objectives? One study has found that about half the arbitrators follow each one.[30] There is little research on this subject, but the traditional approach seems to predominate at present.[31]

DISCIPLINARY METHODS

Whether following the traditional or discipline by objectives method, when an employee has violated a behavior rule or is not meeting performance objectives, the manager can apply a series of sanctions to improve future performance or behavior. These vary from the brief fatherly or motherly chat to locking up the violator, as the military does on occasion.

The first technique the manager can use is counseling; this is the most frequent method of disciplinary action. The supervisor determines if in fact a violation took place, explains to the employee why the violation significantly affects productivity, and suggests that it should not happen again. Sometimes the supervisor pushes counseling to the "chewing out" stage. This approach works for most violations. Counseling will probably be more effective if the supervisor applies the behavior modeling–interaction management technique (see Chapter 12).

If a second or more serious violation takes place, the supervisor again counsels the employee, this time noting that the incident will be entered in the employees' personnel file. If the violation was sufficiently serious, the employee may also be given an oral or written warning of the consequences of a future recurrence.

If the incident concerns ineffective productivity, the employee may request transfer or be asked to transfer to another job. The employee may have been placed in the wrong job, there may be a personality conflict between the employee and the supervisor, or more training might help. In some rare cases, demotions or downward transfers are used.

If counseling and warnings do not result in changed behavior, and if a transfer is not appropriate, the next step is normally a disciplinary layoff. If damage resulted from the deviant behavior, the deductions may be made from employee's pay over a period of time to pay for the damage. Most disciplinary action will not require this severe a step. The layoff is usually of short duration, perhaps a few days up to a week.

The next most severe form of punishment is what Steinmetz calls dehiring,[32] and most people call getting an employee to quit. Getting the unsatisfactory employee to quit has many advantages over termination, for both employee and employer. Both save face. The employee finds another job and then quits, telling the peer group how much better off he is at the new location. The employer is happy because he has rid himself of an ineffective employee without having to fire him or her.

In order to dehire an employee, the employer normally sends clues that his services are no longer desired. The supervisor starts giving the employee less desirable duties with fewer rewards, is cold in mutual discussions, and, if necessary, tells him point-blank that it would be better if he sought employment elsewhere. In universities, deans and department chairmen begin by giving the professor they wish to be rid of onerous and unrewarding duties like registering students, dull committee work, and early morning and late afternoon and Saturday classes. Then smaller, less comfortable offices are assigned but graduate students are not. The professor receives no raises but does receive larger teaching loads. The longer this process takes and the more moves that are taken, the more obvious it becomes that it is a firing, not a dehiring.[33]

Dehiring is not a forthright approach to discipline. Many supervisors find it unethical. It should be used only if the supervisor prefers it to the next step: discharge.

The ultimate punishment is discharge.[34] To many inexperienced managers, discharge is the solution to any problem with a difficult employee. Often discharge is not possible, because of seniority rules, union rules, too few replacements in the labor market, or a number of other reasons. In Europe, laws and union regulations are such that terminations are almost prohibited. This may be the case in the United States and Canada before too long. Discharge has many costs, both direct and indirect. Directly, a discharge leads to a loss of all the personnel investments already made, for recruiting, selection, evaluation, and training; many organizations also pay severance pay. Then these same personnel investments must be made again for the replacement, and frequently there is a period during which the new employee is not as productive as the former employee was. The indirect costs are the effect on other employees of firing one of their numbers. If it is a blatant case of severe inability or deviant behavior, there is not too much problem with peer group resentment. But too often, the facts are not clear, and other employees may feel the employer acted arbitrarily. Some employees may seek employment elsewhere to prevent an arbitrary action happening to them. Others may reduce productivity in protest.

Thus discharge is the *last alternative* to be tried—when all else fails or in very serious cases, such as discovery of fraud or massive theft. One final, subtle reason restrains many supervisors from suggesting discharges. If the supervisor has had the employee a long time, management may begin to ask: "If this employee is so bad, why wasn't he downgraded sooner? Why didn't he get rid of him sooner? Why did he hire him in the first place? Do you think he's a good judge of employees? Is he supervisory timber?"

Actual discharges, or separation of an employee from the employer's service against his will, are rare. A study by Steinmetz of 80 companies' practices on discharge of managers found that only 13 had discharged a manager over the previous five years, and then it was a rare occurrence—about one over the five-year period.[35] Little research has been done on the effectiveness of discharge for the employer and employee, partly because discharges are so rare. Steinmetz interviewed 17 discharged managers and contends that the discharges were good for them because they liked their new jobs better, salaries were better, and so forth. This could be true, of course. But Steinmetz accepted what they said at face value. Cognitive dissonance theory and common sense would predict that most people would try to forget unpleasant experiences. Other researchers who studied the behavior of 53 employees who had been discharged and were reinstated later by an arbitrator concluded:

In the majority of cases, it was found that subsequent performance of the reinstated employees was good or satisfactory; few were discharged a second time. However, employees whose job performance was poor prior to discharge were unlikely to show improvement after reinstatement . . . Overall, the findings of this investigation support the principle of corrective discipline.[36]

Terminations were also considered as part of a critical incidents study by Jay Heizer. He found that terminations were some of the most effective managerial acts and their least effective decisions were not to terminate someone who should have been. He also found most supervisors and personnel specialists very reluctant to terminate employees.[37]

There is little empirical evidence on how discharge should take place. The following guidelines were synthesized from a much longer list Steinmetz provided in the study cited above.

A discharge should always take place only after the facts have been verified and with the advice and counsel of other supervisors and managers involved.

Discharge should be made shortly after the crisis or last-straw action has taken place. Dismissals should not be made when the supervisor is emotionally charged or angry.

Discharges should be made at the end of a day or week when other employees are gone, to avoid embarrassment to both the supervisor and the employee.

The employee should be told straightforwardly about the discharge and discharge date, and the severance arrangements (such as pay) should be stated.

Reasons to support the decision should be prepared, but the supervisor should not get into an argument, much less a physical encounter, with the employee.

A memo for the employee's personnel file of what took place at the termination conference should be prepared.

These or similar steps are essential to preserve equity at work and to prevent reversals by arbitrators. It is vital that the contract requirements be closely followed or (in nonunionized enterprises) that employees are treated fairly and receive due process. Otherwise, if the case goes to arbitration, the difficult employee may be back.[38] Results of a study of what arbitrators decided in discharge cases from 1971 to 1974 are given in Exhibit 20–7. These researchers found that compared to periods in the 1950s and 1960s, management's discharges were less likely to be sustained by arbitrators in the 1970s.[39]

One researcher found that employers who have a severance-pay policy tend to use the following rules of thumb: If the length of service is less than one year, the severance pay is one day's pay for each month. If it is one year and over, the pay is one week's pay for each six months of service. The pay is usually based on the basic salary plus commission or equivalent but not including bonuses or overtime. Some employers limit the maximum of severance pay to 26 or 52 weeks' pay, which may do a disservice to senior employees.[40]

EXHIBIT 20–7
Percentage of cases in which arbitrators sustained discharge of an employee

Violation of plant rules that led to discharge	*Percentage of discharges sustained by arbitrators*
Altercations	43%
Dishonesty, theft, and disloyalty	45
Gambling	22
Intoxication	22
Loafing, leaving post, and sleeping on the job	25
Insubordination	46

Source: Ken Jennings and Roger Wolters, "Discharge Cases Reconsidered," *The Arbitration Journal,* November, 1976, p. 167.

Most employers pay severance allowances to all discharged employees except to those in category 3. They differ on whether severance pay should be offered to category 1 employees and the most blatant cases of laziness and so forth in category 4 employees.

ADMINISTRATION OF DISCIPLINE

Another important issue in discipline is how it is accomplished so as to protect employees' rights. In unionized organizations, the employee has a formalized procedure which provides adequate protection: the grievance procedure discussed in chapter 19. In nonunionized situations, the hierarchical system is the most prevalent.

Hierarchical discipline systems

Discipline is administered to most nonunion employees by the supervisor, who also evaluates the employee.[41] When the employee is found to be ineffective, the superivisor decides what needs to be done. In this hierarchical system, the conditions allow a supervisor who might be arbitrary, wrong, or ineffective himself to be policeman, judge, and jury over the employee.

A person accused of a crime such as speeding in many of our courts can have counsel, the judge is not the arresting officer, and the penalty may be a $50 fine. In the employment situation, where the employee has none of these safeguards, the penalty for an infraction of work rules may be his job and salary. Even if the employee is convicted of speeding, he can appeal to a higher court. What can the employee do if he is unfairly fired by his supervisor? There is, of course, the open-door policy: he could appeal to the supervisor's superior. But, as Lee Taylor comments, this is usually no help at all. The whole value system of the hierarchy is based on support of the supervisors to build a good management team.[42] Of course, the informal open-door policy can lead to a quasi-legal form of justice such as that developed by IBM, in which the employee's case is recorded and systematically reviewed at several levels.[43] A feeling of helplessness and lack of due process on the part of employees can become a *powerful* force leading to the unionization of enterprises.[44]

A strictly hierarchical justice system is more prevalent in businesses than in other work organizations. To work at all, hierarchical systems must be considered fair by employees, and there must be adequate proof of the deviance. Employees will support discipline only if they feel that the disciplined employee was treated fairly and consistently compared to other past offenders and that mitigating circumstances were considered if disciplinary procedures were taken. One expert suggests that the minimal safeguard to prevent serious injustice in the hierarchical system is the mandated right to job transfer in disputes with less than overwhelming evidence against the employee.[45]

If hierarchical systems are to be effective and fair, operating and personnel managers must administer discipline equitably. There have been a few studies of the extent to which this is so. One study gave 250 managers of five utility companies eight case studies of discipline problems that included mostly deviances outside category 2.[46] These cases were as follows:

1. Meter repairman reports to work in intoxicated condition despite two prior instances of intoxication on job.
2. Truck driver with no prior record drives off with ladder extended, resulting in ladder breaking.
3. Crewman having previous discipline record refuses to climb pole, feeling it to be unsafe. Foreman disagrees.
4. Worker with record of insubordination refuses to leave truck cab which is in garage due to rain, though ordered out of it.
5. Worker with good record develops repeated tardiness due to driving wife to work.
6. Worker permitted to take leftover wire by foreman but apprehended taking it by higher management.
7. Lineman with good record removes safety gloves on way down the pole. This results in a serious injury.
8. Equipment lineman borrowed is stolen from his car. Borrowing equipment is common practice.

Managers were asked to rate the severity of the problem and what discipline they would apply. The consequences *varied from no action to dismissal.* The authors found that the higher in the company the executives were, the more severely they would have applied punishment. The lowest level managers (such as foremen) were more lenient and more willing to consider individual circumstances. Problems rated as the most severe by all managers were in the safety area. Foremen and lower executives did not regard case 2 as severe. In addition to statistically significant different interpretations between levels of managers, the analysis also differed significantly between companies.

The conclusion from this study is that an employee could be punished severely in one company and not punished in another for a similar infraction, or within a company, the employee could receive a wide variety of responses from no punishment to severe punishment. This was so even though the companies had well-developed sets of work rules.

Other studies found similar variations in discipline, which can be compounded by prejudices. One study found that supervisors used more punitive discipline methods on blacks and union members than on whites and nonunion members.[47] The data on differences in degree of discipline provide reasons for having systems of appeal besides the open-door policy to supplement or supplant the hierarchical approach.

Other discipline and appeal systems

Although the hierarchical discipline and grievance system is *by far* the most used in industry, other employing organizations use different models more often. A few business organizations have also taken steps to design systems which may protect the employee from arbitrary supervisory action more effectively than the hierarchical model does. The alternatives to the hierarchical model are considered below.

Peer disciplinary systems.   Peer systems rely on independent or related peers to assess deviance and recommend behavior modification. They can be implemented in several ways. A jury of peers to adjudicate is, of course, the method used in professional discipline situations such as disbarment of a lawyer or removal of a physician's license.[48] Another is the use of student disciplinary boards as judges of discipline in colleges and universities.

Quasi-judicial systems.   These systems involve independent *outside* persons to adjudicate cases. Isidore Silver advocates the use of a corporate ombudsman—a person who is independent and somewhat aware of the law and can provide a fact-finding mechanism and exercise independent judgment of all the rights covered in disputes. He is similar to an arbitrator in unionized situations.[49] *Business Week* reports ombudsmen systems work well at such enterprises as Xerox, General Electric, and Boeing.[50] One variation of the ombudsman is a board of neutral observers from the community who can provide independent judgments in important disputes.[51]

Modified hierarchical systems.   Regular appeals channels *inside* the organization, but including someone other than the supervisor's superior, are used in the modified hierarchical discipline systems. One mechanism is to have all disputed dismissals or behavior modification plans submitted to specified personnel specialists for conciliation and assessment. Another is to have a top management executive or executives far removed from the scene hear the facts and judge whether proper action was taken. There has been little research into the effectiveness of the modified hierarchical approaches.

Examples of a cross between a modified hierarchical and a peer system were suggested by Clayton Sherman.[52] These include:

A formal shop committee.   A group selected by employees to adjudicate grievances.

A floating committee. Management members from personnel department and hierarchy at least two levels above the incident and employees selected by each department on a rotating basis adjudicate disputes.

A company grievance committee. Department members, management members selected by top management, and a management member selected by the grievant adjudicate disputes.

All these mechanisms must be used in good faith by management. The system could be corrupted (and employees would recognize it quickly) if management stacked the deck or influenced the employee members on the boards.

The reality of nonhierarchical systems. The extent to which nonhierarchical systems exist in the world of work has been researched most thoroughly by William G. Scott.[53] He has studied the presence of nonhierarchical systems or modified hierarchical systems in many employment spheres: the government, the military, unions, and nonwork situations such as voluntary organizations.

Scott describes how members of such unions as the UAW can initiate a complaint against a union leader to the membership of the local. If they do not agree with his complaint, he can appeal to the international executive board, then to the UAW convention or the Public Review Board. In cases of corruption, he can bypass the local membership.

For employees of the U.S. government, if the employee is dissatisfied with the judgment of his superior, he can appeal to the Civil Service Commission, which has regular appeals channels up to the Board of Appeals and Review. The Civil Service Commission serves as a sort of super personnel department for the federal government. There are several levels of appeal, including local, regional, and national appeals examining offices, culminating in the Board of Appeals and Review. But there are limits to the appeal. The Supreme Court recently ruled that the public employee does not have the right to a hearing before being fired unless the contract says the right exists.

The American military has also set up a nonhierarchical appeals channel. It has an ombudsman for each unit called an inspector general. The ombudsman is required to visit each unit at least once a year, and appeals may be directed to him at other times. These inspectors have special authority to investigate and report their findings and take action to redress grievances.

The sector with the fewest nonhierarchical justice systems is industry. Scott surveyed justice and discipline systems in 1,800 companies in the midsixties; 793 replied. Of these, 518 said they had no policy, formal or informal, for handling employee complaints. Of those who claimed they had a method of handling employee grievances about justice, most cited the open-door policy. Some said they made their personnel department available to listen to such grievances. Scott found the use of grievance committees and boards of review to be very rare. Even those few that had nonhierarchical systems applied them to nonexempt employees. Scott found only one firm that had a system of appeal for managerial, professional, or technical employees.

It must be noted that there is little or no empirical evidence that providing nonhierarchical systems necessarily provides fairer treatment of employees. A study of the history of justice under various systems in the public domain would indicate justice is much more likely under systems that provide for independent assessment of evidence and judgments than one in which the superior is prosecutor, judge, and jury.

SUMMARY , CONCLUSIONS, AND RECOMMENDATIONS

Some of the most difficult human and personnel problems involve handling the difficult or ineffective employee. A guideline for assessing the causes of this behavior can be stated in proposition form.

> *Proposition 20.1.* Most deviant or difficult employees' problems probably have multiple causes. Employers should concentrate on trying to modify the effects and advise rehabilitation and counseling for such problems as alcoholism and drug addiction.

Organizations use many approaches to discipline. They can try to prevent problems by reasonable rules and goals, as Proposition 20.2 suggests:

> *Proposition 20.2.* Rules are more likely to be obeyed if employees participate in their formulation and regular reformulation and updating.

Once deficiences are apparent, supervisors can use a variety of disciplinary approaches. In increasing order of punitiveness, they are: counseling, warnings, transfers, demotions and layoffs, dehiring, and termination. Proposition 20.3 applies:

> *Proposition 20.3.* The best methods of discipline are those that are relatively positive and less punitive. Only when all else fails should such measures as termination be used.

Finally, organizations create systems to administer discipline. Most use supervisory or hierarchically oriented systems, too but often these do not provide safeguards for employee rights if the employee has an arbitrary or ineffective supervisor. Exhibit 20.8 gives recommendations for the use of different kinds of justice systems in the model organizations defined in Exhibit 1–14, Chapter 1. Proposition 20.4 applies:

> *Proposition 20.4.* The larger the organization, the more likely it is to need to supplement the hierarchial justice system with other methods.

For discipline systems to be effective, the disciplinary review must take place as soon after the action as possible. Discipline must be applied consistently and impersonally. Nothing can ruin a discipline system more than for the supervisor to treat friends differently than other employees.

No doubt the computer will be used more often in the future to try to detect trouble spots needing discipline. Just as the police have analyzed

EXHIBIT 20–8
Recommendations for model organizations on difficult employees and discipline

Type of organization	Hierarchical justice systems	Reinforce hierarchical justice systems with:		
		Peer committees	Ombudsmen	Outside committees
1. Large size, low complexity, high stability	X		X	X
2. Medium size, low complexity, high stability	X		X	
3. Small size, low complexity, high stability	X	X		
4. Medium size, moderate complexity, moderate stability	X		X	
5. Large size, high complexity, low stability	X		X	X
6. Medium size, high complexity, low stability	X			
7. Small size, high complexity, low stability	X	X		

past crime records to predict where and when to place extra police support, so work organizations can analyze troubled departments and troubled times. They then can make special counseling and supervisory efforts to try to prevent problems, or at least to handle them speedily when they occur.

Discipline is an area in which help is needed from many sources. The supervisor is the primary actor or actress in the drama. Personnel can advise the supervisor and serve as a type of ombudsman. The work group can help productivity if it reinforces the norms of playing by the rules, as can the union. When differences appear, arbitrators are called into investigate and decide where justice lies. Top management's position in the discipline process is to determine its philosophy and set up the discipline process. Top managers must decide such questions as what kind of appeal system, if any, is to be used in the enterprise. These are crucial decisions that will help determine the effectiveness of the discipline process.

Chapter 21 concludes the book with a discussion of evaluation and research of the personnel function.

QUESTIONS

1. What is discipline?
2. What are the four categories of difficult employees?
3. Which diagnostic factors are significant to the effectiveness of the discipline process?

4. What are the major causes of difficult job behavior?

5. Describe the ineffective employee. How do Mager and Pipe suggest analyzing undesirable behavior?

6. How serious a problem is the alcoholic employee at work? How should the alcoholic be handled?

7. How serious a problem is the addicted employee? How should the addict be dealt with?

8. How serious is the employee who violates laws? How should this employee be dealt with?

9. How serious a problem is the rule violator? How should this kind of employee be dealt with?

10. Describe the discipline process.

11. Contract various discipline philosophies. Which one do you accept?

12. Describe the disciplinary methods available and when you would use each.

13. Contrast hierarchical disciplinary systems with other discipline and appeal systems. Which are the best systems? Under what conditions?

14. What are the major propositions of this chapter?

15. What are the major recommendations for the model organizations?

NOTES AND REFERENCES

1. John Miner, *The Challenge of Managing* (Philadelphia: W. B. Saunders Co., 1975), pp. 330–31. Also see John Miner and Frank Brewer, "The Management of Ineffective Performance," in *Handbook of Industrial and Organizational Psychology,* ed. Marvin Dunnette (Chicago: Rand McNalley & Co., 1976).

2. Robert Mager and Peter Pipe, *Analyzing Performance Problems* (Palo Alto, Ca.: Fearon Publishers, 1970).

3. Stephen Habbe, *Company Controls for Drinking Problems,* Studies in Personnel Policy 218 (New York: National Industrial Conference Board, 1969); National Industrial Conference Board, *Company Controls of Alcoholism,* Studies in Personnel Policy 167 (New York, 1959).

4. See, for example, Jerrold Levine, et al., "Effects of Alcohol on Human Performance," *Journal of Applied Psychology* 60, 3 (1975), pp. 285–93.

5. C. Sternhagen, "Absenteeism and Tardiness," in *Handbook of Modern Personnel Administration,* ed. Joseph Famularo, 61 (New York: McGraw-Hill Book Co., 1972).

6. Habbe, *Company Controls for Drinking Problems.*

7. Marion Sadler and James Horst, "Company/Union Programs for Alcoholics," *Harvard Business Review,* September–October 1972b, pp. 22–30, 34, 152–56; Ross Alander and Campbell Thomas, "An Evaluation Study of an Alcohol and Drug Recovery Program: A Case Study of the Oldsmobile Experience," *Human Resource Management,* Spring 1975, pp. 14–18; Richard Williams and Gene Moffat (eds.), *Occupational Alcoholism Programs* (Springfield, Ill.: Charles C Thomas, Publisher, 1975); Joseph Follmann, *Alcoholics and Business* (New York: Amacon, 1976); Harrison Trice and Paul Roman, *Spirits and Demons at Work* (Ithaca, N.Y.: State School of Industrial and Labor Relations, 1972); Charles Hemphill and Thomas Hemphill, *The Secure Company* (Homewood, Ill.: Dow Jones–Irwin, 1975), ch. 3.

8. Carl Chambers and Richard Heckman, *Employee Drug Abuse* (Boston: Cahners Books, 1972).

9. Susan Halpern, *Drug Abuse and Your Company.* New York: American Management Association, 1972.

10. H. Wackenhut, cited in Hemphill and Hemphill, *The Secure Company,* ch. 2.

11. Chambers and Heckman, *Employee Drug Abuse.*

12. Charles Langdon, "Experiences with and Policies concerning Employees Using Drugs of Twenty Large New Orleans Area Firms," *Proceedings,* Southern Management Association, 1973, pp. 21–31.

13. Richard Gorsuch and Mark Butler, "Initial Drug Abuse: A Review of Predisposing Social Psychological Factors," *Psychological Bulletin* 83 (1976), pp. 120–37.

14. Rolf Rogers, "Drug Abuse and Organizational Response," *Personnel Journal,* May 1975, p. 266; Dale Callner, "Behavioral Treatment Approaches to Drug Abuse," *Psychological Bulletin,* 82, 2 (1975), pp. 143–64; Doris Baldwin, "The Trouble with Drugs," *Job Safety and Health,* February 1975, pp. 4–10.

15. Pasquale Carone and Leonard Krinsky, *Drug Abuse in Industry* (Springfield, Ill.: Charles C Thomas, Publisher, 1973). See especially chapters by Jessup, Brill, and Meiselas.

16. Edward Levin and Tia Denenberg, "How Arbitrators View Drug Abuse," *The Arbitration Journal,* 31, 2 (1976), pp. 97–108.

17. "Employees, Suppliers Account for 75% of Stolen Merchandise," *The Wall Street Journal,* November 21, 1973.

18. Richard Rosenbaum, "Predictability of Employees' Theft Using Weighted Application Blanks," *Journal of Applied Psychology,* February 1976, pp. 46–98.

19. Mark Lipman, "What You Can Do About Employee Theft," *Nation's Business,* May 1976, pp. 63–65. Also see Hemphill and Hemphill, *The Secure Company,* ch. 5, 8, 11; Charles Hemphill, Jr., *Management's Role in Loss Prevention* (New York: Amacom, 1976); Priscilla Meyers, "Sabotage on the Rise at Construction Sites in New York City," *The Wall Street Journal,* January 20, 1976; Donald Morgenson, "White Collar Crime and the Violation of Trust," *Personnel Journal,* March 1975, pp. 154–55; 176–78 ff.

20. Jerry L. Wall, *Industrial Espionage in American Firms,* unpublished Ph.D. thesis, University of Missouri—Columbia, 1974, pp. 56–71; Jerry L. Wall, "What the Competition Is Doing: Your Need to Know," *Harvard Business Review,* November–December 1974, p. 34.

21. F. Mulder, "Characteristics of Violators of Formal Company Rules," *Journal of Applied Psychology,* 55 (1971), pp. 500–502.

22. Ken Jennings, "Verbal and Physical Abuse toward Supervision," *Arbitration Journal,* December 1974, pp. 258–71.

23. Mary Bralove, "Cold Shoulder," *The Wall Street Journal,* January 29, 1976.

24. Timothy Larkin, "Removing the Ex-Offenders Catch 22," *Journal of Employment Counseling,* September 1975, pp. 126–31. For material on category 4 in general, see Hemphill and Hemphill, *The Secure Company,* ch. 4, 5, 7, 10, 13.

25. See, for example, Mulder, "Violators of Formal Company Rules."

26. Claire Anderson, *The Marginal Worker: A Search for Correlates,* unpublished Ph.D. thesis, University of Massachusetts, 1976.

27. See, for example, Leonard Sayles, *The Behavior of Industrial Work Groups* (New York: McGraw-Hill Book Co., 1964).

28. Lawrence Steinmetz, *Managing the Marginal and Unsatisfactory Performer* (Reading, Mass.: Addison-Wesley Publishing Co., 1969).

29. George Odiorne, *Personnel Administration by Objectives,* ch. 18. Homewood, Ill.: Richard D. Irwin, Inc., 1971.

30. Hoyt Wheeler, "Punishment Theory and Industrial Discipline," *Industrial Relations,* May 1976, pp. 235–43.

31. Fremont Shull and L. L. Cummings, "Enforcing the Rules: How Do Managers Differ?"

Personnel, 43 (1966), pp. 33–39; Wallace Wohlking, "Effective Discipline in Employee Relations," *Personnel Journal,* September 1975, pp. 489–93; 500–501 ff. One study that provides some data on this subject is *Employee Performance: Evaluation and Control,* Study #108, Bureau of National Affairs, Washington, D.C., February, 1975.

32. Steinmetz, *Managing the Marginal Performer.*

33. Deborah Meyers and Lee Abrahamson, "Firing with Finesse," *Personnel Journal,* August 1975, pp. 432–37.

34. See Aurora Parisi, "Employee Terminations," in *Handbook of Modern Personnel Administration,* ed. Joseph Famularo, ch. 65 (New York: McGraw-Hill Book Co., 1972). See also ᒐᙢ · 5 above, on terminations as an action decision.

35. Steinmetz, *Managing the Marginal Performer.*

36. T. McDermott and T. Newhams, "Discharge Reinstatement: What Happens Thereafter," *Industrial and Labor Relations Review,* 24 (1971), pp. 526–40.

37. Jay Heizer, "Transfer and Terminations as Staffing Options," *Academy of Management Journal,* March 1976, pp. 115–20.

38. Walter Baer, *Discipline and Discharge under the Labor Agreement* (New York: American Management Association, 1972); Maurice Benewitz, "Discharge, Arbitration and the Quantitative Proof," *Arbitration Journal,* June 1973, pp. 95–104; Robert Fisher, "When Workers are Discharged: An Overview," *Monthly Labor Review,* June 1973, pp. 4–17; James O'Reilly, "Job Related Discrimination and Discharge Under Federal Safety Statistics," *Labor Law Journal,* November 1973, pp. 718–22; Edwin Stanton, "The Discharged Employee and the EEO Laws," *Personnel Journal,* March 1976, pp. 128–29; 133 ff.

39. Ken Jennings and Roger Wolters, "Discharge Cases Reconsidered," *The Arbitration Journal,* November, 1976, pp. 164–86.

40. Parisi, "Employee Terminations."

41. See William G. Scott and Terrence R. Mitchell, *Organization Theory: A Structural and Behavioral Analysis,* 3rd ed. (Homewood, Ill.: Richard D. Irwin, Inc., 1976), ch. 20.

42. Lee Taylor, *Occupational Sociology,* ch. 13 (New York: Oxford University Press, 1968).

43. William G. Scott, "Organization Government: The Prospects for a Truly Participative System," *Public Administration Review,* January–February 1969.

44. V. Clayton Sherman, "Unionism and the Non-Union Company," *Personnel Journal,* June 1969, pp. 413–22.

45. William Evan, "Organization Man and Due Process of Law," *American Sociological Review* 26 (1961), pp. 540–47.

46. Phillip Shaak and Milton Schwartz, "Uniformity of Policy Interpretation among Managers in American Industry," *Academy of Management Journal,* March 1973, pp. 77–83.

47. David Kipnis et al., "Effects of Emotional Arousal on the Use of Supervised Coercion with Black and Union Employees," *Journal of Applied Psychology* 57, 1 (1973), pp. 38–43; also see Benson Rosen and Thomas Jerdee, "Factors Influencing Disciplinary Judgments," *Journal of Applied Psychology* 59, 3 (1974), pp. 327–31.

48. Mark Abrahamson, *The Professional in the Organization* (Chicago: Rand McNally & Co., 1967).

49. Isidore Silver, "The Corporate Ombudsman," *Harvard Business Review,* May–June 1967, pp. 77–87.

50. "Where Ombudsmen Work Out," *Business Week,* May 3, 1976, pp. 114–16.

51. Sherman, "Unionism and the Non-Union Company."

52. Ibid.

53. William G. Scott, *The Management of Conflict: Appeal Systems in Organizations* (Homewood, Ill.: Richard D. Irwin, Inc., 1965).

Evaluation of the personnel function and personnel's future

CHAPTER OBJECTIVES

- ■ To demonstrate what evaluation of the personnel function is and why it is done.
- ■ To discuss the methods used to evaluate the personnel function.
- ■ To consider what the future is likely to be for the personnel function and the personnel manager.

CHAPTER OUTLINE

The setting is a massive conference room. The top managers of a large bank are participating in the annual planning meeting. Each functional vice president presents the department's budget for next year after a review of the past year's accomplishments.

Martha Renstrom, vice president for marketing, has just completed her budget request and had her advertising budget cut for the next year. Last year, profits were down at the bank.

Andrew Major, vice president for personnel and organization planning, speaks next.

Andrew: Well, folks, I'm not going to take much of your time. It's been a long day. You know what we do for the bank. We hire, train, and pay the employees, provide benefits, counsel, help with discipline, EEO, and so on. Personnel is not asking for any major increases. My budget is simply enough last year's budget adjusted upward 7 percent for inflation. Any questions?

Martha: Wait a minute, Andy. My budget just got cut. Here you come asking for 7 percent more than last year. I suppose we have to have a personnel department. But why shouldn't my advertising budget be increased and your budget cut? After all, advertising brings customers into the bank and helps us make money. What *specifically* does personnel do for this bank's profit and loss statement? How *specifically* does personnel help us reach our goals of growth and profitability?

Martha has pointed out to Andy what the personnel audit is for. If Andy had been systematically evaluating his personnel department, he would have some answers ready. And it looks like he will need some good ones, or personnel's budget and activities could well be cut.

DEFINITION

Evaluation of the personnel function (the personnel audit) is a systematic, formal experience designed to measure the costs and benefits of the total personnel program and to compare its efficiency and effectiveness with the enterprise's past performance, the performance of comparable effective enterprises, and the enterprise's objectives.

Evaluation of personnel is performed:

- To justify personnel's existence and budget.
- To improve the personnel function by providing a means to decide when to drop activities and when to add them.
- To provide feedback from employees and operating managers on personnel's effectiveness.
- To help personnel do its part to achieve the enterprise's objectives.[1]

Top management's part in the personnel audit is to insist that all aspects of the enterprise be evaluated and to establish the general philosophy of evaluation. Personnel's job is to design the audit. In part the data for the audit arise from the cost benefit studies of the personnel activities as described in Chapters 4–20. The operating manager's role is to help gather the data and to help evaluate the personnel function in the same way it evaluates other functions and uses of resources in the enterprise.

Evaluation of the personnel function is a Stage II activity—many researchers have advocated its implementation, but only a few good empirical studies of effective and ineffective ways of evaluating or auditing the activity have been done. Nevertheless, personnel evaluation is gaining in usage, and informal programs are being replaced by formal programs. The results of a recent BNA survey on the extent of evaluation and the general methods used are shown in Exhibit 21–1. BNA found that more than 80 percent of the companies surveyed formally evaluate the personnel function.[2]

EXHIBIT 21–1
Personnel evaluation methods used

	All companies	Larger	Smaller
Evaluating departmental results against goals	33% *	37%	23%
Periodic audit of policies, procedures	25	25	26
Surveys, meetings, discussions, and interviews	20	19	23
Analysis of turnover figures	16	15	19
Analysis of grievances	8	9	10
Analysis of cost of performing various personnel functions	6	7	5
Analysis of training effectiveness	5	5	5
Analysis of accident frequency	5	6	4
Feedback from managers	5	5	5

* Includes 7 percent of companies specifying an MBO program for the personnel department.
Source: *Labor Policy and Practice—Personnel Management* (Washington, D.C.: Bureau of National Affairs, 1975).

A DIAGNOSTIC APPROACH TO EVALUATION

Exhibit 21–2 shows the factors in the diagnostic model which affect evaluation of the personnel function in an enterprise. The major factors in determining whether evaluation takes place are the orientation or attitudes of the controlling interests toward evaluation and the organization's style.

Some managers feel formal evaluations of the function are very useful; others do not favor them. Formal evaluation programs of functions are more likely to be conducted in some types of enterprises than others. Larger organizations that are labor intensive and geographically dispersed probably have some type of evaluation for most functional departments, including personnel. Such programs are also more likely when economic conditions are bad, particularly for economically oriented organizations, because they can establish the cost effectiveness of such functions.

PERSONNEL REPORTS AND RECORDS

Organizations keep personnel records for many practical reasons. They are necessary for legal enforcement reasons and also can be used for personnel

EXHIBIT 21–2
Factors affecting evaluation of the personnel process.

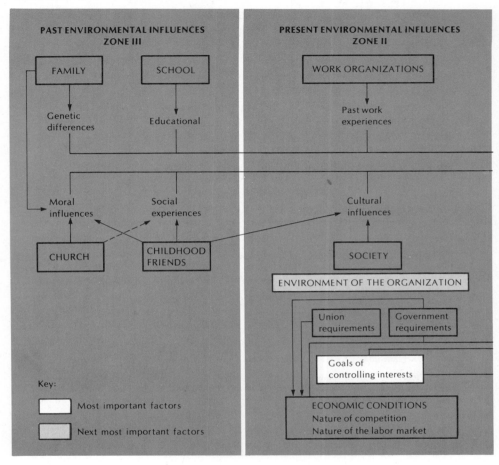

research, problem solving in personnel, and as a basis for personnel evaluation.

Data for these records are gathered in many ways. For the smaller organization, they are usually compiled on forms and kept in personnel files. Personnel data are alphabetized by employee and filed chronologically, with the latest information and changes in data at the front. Larger and more sophisticated organizations convert these data to a form suitable for use on the computer, although some researchers have found that most business and government enterprises they studied were not making effective use of computerized personnel data banks.[3]

Personnel records must be kept up to date, and less frequently used or older records should be filed in the most efficient manner: warehousing the data cheaply, or turning it over to data storage and retrieval firms. For larger units, this may mean reducing the data to microfilm form.[4] The Associ-

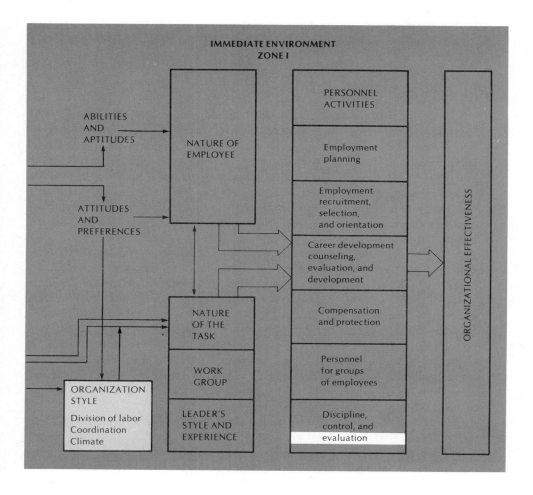

ation of Records Executives and Administrators has suggested that the following data be carefully stored for a work organization: payroll registers, personnel records, wage rates, workers' compensation data, benefit plan details, and labor contracts.

Many personnel records are required to be kept by law. The number of employees by sex, race, national origin, and age must be available for EEOC. OSHA requires employers to keep records of occupational illnesses and injuries for five years and to provide a summary of accident data. Unemployment compensation laws require the employer to file reports on turnover of employees for tax computation reasons. Records must be kept for the number hired, laid off, and discharged, as well as those who quit, die, or retire for the period. Other records that arise from performance of personnel are promotion lists, records of attendance and absenteeism, grievances filed, and details of benefits administration, such as payments on retirement plans.

When these records are properly filed and stored, useful analyses can be made to evaluate the personnel function. When it is possible to determine where personnel problems are the most severe, the department can follow up with personnel research which will help the employer solve personnel problems.

PERSONNEL RESEARCH

The purposes of personnel research are to find solutions for personnel problems for the employer, to aid in evaluation of the personnel function, and to extend the knowledge of personnel to all those concerned. This activity is performed by universities, consultants, independent research institutes, and a few employers.[5] The 150 or so employers who perform their own personnel research are invariably large, such as AT&T.[6] One expert estimates that as few as 15 corporations actually use their research fully.[7] These studies also indicate that personnel research does not have a significant impact on top management.[8]

John Hinrichs studied some of the characteristics of personnel research staff. He found the best departments were staffed by persons with Ph.D.'s, mainly in psychology or personnel, and that sometimes personnel research was attached to units other than personnel departments, such as research and development groups. Hinrichs also asked personnel researchers to estimate how they spent their time; they reported that they spent 20 percent consulting with line managers, 15 percent running their department, 9 percent on self-development, and 55 percent on research. Of this, 13 percent was spent analyzing personnel statistics, 15 percent studying improved means of employment, 16 percent on improving the organization climate, and 11 percent studying training and development.[9]

Much of the research the personnel department does is descriptive. One study found that most used surveys, historical studies, and case studies.[10] Few tried experimenting with various approaches to personnel.

One researcher who surveyed personnel research departments to see which aspects of personnel were studied in personnel research found that most followed the problems emphasized in industrial psychology: 98 percent studied selection and placement, 75 percent ran attitude and communication studies, and 30 percent studied training and development. About 20 percent studied evaluation methods and motivation; 16 percent, overall effectiveness. Less than 10 percent spent any time on supervisory style, accident prevention, stress, managerial obsolescence, counseling, recruitment, or any basic research that did not directly affect the employer at the time.[11]

APPROACHES TO EVALUATION OF THE PERSONNEL PROCESS

Once it has been decided that it is useful to evaluate the effectiveness of the personnel function and the organization's use of human resources, the next issue is how it should be done and what measures or criteria of effectiveness should be used.[12] The criteria can be grouped as follows:

1. Performance measures.
   a. Overall personnel performance; for example, the unit labor costs per unit of output.
   b. Personnel department costs and performance—the cost per employee of personnel programs.
2. Employee satisfaction measures.
   a. Employees' satisfaction with their jobs.
   b. Employees' satisfaction with personnel activities such as training, pay, benefits, and career development.
3. Indirect measures of personnel performance.
   a. Employee turnover—Rate of quits as a percentage of the labor force and by units over time.
   b. Absenteeism: Rate of voluntary absences of the labor force and by units over time.
   c. Scrap rates.
   d. Other measures of quality.
   e. Rates of employee request for transfer.
   f. Number of grievances per unit and in total labor force over time.
   g. Safety and accident rates (see Chapter 17).
   h. Number of improvement suggestions per employee over time.

Each of these measures or some combinations of them measures the efficiency and/or effectiveness of the personnel effort.

George Odiorne has suggested five principal methods of evaluation.[13]

The first is to *copy* successful companies' personnel programs. This can be done in several ways; the most likely is to prepare a checklist of what the esteemed organization does.

A second approach is to have the organization evaluated by an *outside authority,* such as a consultant. Many of these consultants operate similar to the copying approach. If they do not know the organization well, they tend to compare it against some "ideal" checklist.

A third approach is measurement against averages, or the *statistical approach.* Analysts compute a series of ratios (to be discussed shortly) and compare the organization's ratios with averages. The key is which averages are used. It makes little sense to throw all organizations into a hat and get an average; anyone who has had a statistics course recognizes the fallacy. To the extent that reasonable groupings of homogeneous organizations have been used as the base for computing the ratios, the approach can be useful.

A fourth approach is the *compliance* method. In this case, the personnel department is viewed as a lawgiver, and the evaluation assesses the extent to which personnel policies, procedures, and rules are being used. This makes the department a policeman. The audit approach has its place insofar as compliance with legal requirements such as EEOC, OSHA, and similar programs are concerned. Many personnel activities, however, cannot operate effectively with this approach.

The evaluation method recommended by Odiorne is the *management by objectives* approach. This method suggests that all duties and goals of any work group can be divided into three categories: routine chores, problem-solving objectives, and innovative goals. Once this is done, the employees concerned create qualitative and quantitative goals for each activity and work unit. These become the standards for the next evaluation.

EVALUATION BY CHECKLIST OR COPYING

The approach of copying other enterprises' practices is usually implemented by developing a checklist of the model enterprises' personnel activities. Checklists are also used by consultants to analyze an enterprise's personnel function.

In the checklist approach to evaluation, the personnel department or a consultant prepares a list of important personnel activities to be performed. The checklist usually requires the analyst to check yes or no columns beside the listed activity. The checklist may also include items designed to determine if existing personnel policies are being followed. The items on the checklist are usually grouped by personnel activity area, such as employment planning or safety and health.

Although a checklist is better than a totally informal approach, it still is a rather simple approach to evaluation. And even though checklists provide a format that is relatively easy to record and prepare, scoring interpretation is quite difficult. Three nos in one group of items may not equal three others. Some of the policies are more important than others. Ignoring EEOC or OSHA rules is a lot more negative than the absence of a Christmas party, for example. One study found about 20 percent of enterprises with formal audits use the checklist approach.[14]

STATISTICAL APPROACHES TO EVALUATION

The most frequently used formal evaluation methods are those which examine the work organization's employment statistics and analyze them. The statistical approach can be much more sophisticated than checklists. The statistics gathered are compared to the unit's own past performance or to some other yardstick of measurement. Of course, quantitative factors alone never explain or evaluate anything by themselves. The *reasons* for the statistics are the important thing; statistics only indicate where to begin to look for evaluation problems.

The raw data of such reports are interesting themselves, and they can provide some input to evaluation. Most organizations that perform evaluation, however, analyze these data by the use of ratios and similar comparative methods. Exhibit 21–3 provides a list of such ratios and similar analytical

EXHIBIT 21–3
Personnel evaluation ratios[15]

Effectiveness ratios
    Ratio of number of employees to total output—in general.
    Sales in dollars per employee for the whole company or by organizational unit (business).
    Output in units per employee hour worked for the entire enterprise or organizational unit.
    Scrap loss per unit of the enterprise.
    Payroll costs by unit per employee grade.

Accident ratios
    Frequency of accident rate for the enterprise as a whole or by organizational unit.
    Number of lost-time accidents
    Compensation paid per 1,000 hours worked for accidents.
    Accidents by type.
    Accidents classified by type of injury to each part of the body.
    Average cost of accident by part of the body involved.

Organizational health ratios
    Number of grievances filed.
    Number of arbitration awards lost.

Turnover and absenteeism ratios
    Attendance, tardiness, and overtime comparisons by organizational unit as a measure of how well an operation is handling manpower loading.
    Employee turnover by unit and for the organization.

Employment ratios
    Vacations granted as a percentage of employees eligible.
    Sick-leave days granted as a percentage of man-days worked.
    Military leaves granted per 100 employees.
    Jury duty leaves granted per 100 employees.
    Maternity leaves granted per 100 employees.
    Educational leaves granted per 100 employees.
    Personal leaves granted per 100 employees.
    Employment distribution by chronological age.
    Employment distribution by length of service with organization.
    Employment distribution by sex, race, national origin, religion.
    Managerial manpower distribution by chronological age, sex, race, national origin, religion.
    Average age of work force.
    Average age of managerial work force.

---

methods. Once these and similar ratios are computed for an organization, they can be compared to similar organizations' ratios.

    The statistical approaches used most frequently consider turnover, absenteeism, grievances, attitude surveys and other measures of effectiveness, and statistical analysis of the personnel department itself.

Evaluation of turnover

    Turnover is the net result of the exit of some employees and entrance of others to the work organization. Turnover can be quite costly to an employer; one estimate is that it costs American industry $11 billion a year.[16] The costs of turnover include: increased costs for social security and unemployment compensation; terminal vacations; severance pay; underutilized facilities until the replacement is hired; employment costs, such as recruiting ads and expenses, interview time, test costs, computer record costs, and moving expenses; and administration costs of notification and payroll changes.[17] Obviously there is also a loss of productivity until the new employee reaches the performance level of the one who left the job.

All turnover is not a net loss, however. Employees who are not contibuting to organizational effectiveness should be retrained or dehired. And the employer has no control over some turnover: A student's wife, for example, works as a typist until he graduates and they move away.

There are several quantitative methods for computing turnover. Some of the traditional formulations are:

(1) $$\text{Separation rate} = \frac{\text{Number of separations during the month}}{\text{Total number of employees at midmonth}} \times 100$$

(2) $$\text{Quit rate} = \frac{\text{Total quits}}{\text{Average working force}} \times 100$$

(3) $$\text{Avoidable turnover} = \frac{\text{Total separations} - \text{unavoidables}}{\text{Average work force}} \times 100$$

Formula 1 is the most general and is the one recommended by the Department of Labor. Formula 2 tries to isolate a difficult type of turnover, and formula 3 is the most refined. It eliminates quits by those groups that can be expected to leave: part-timers and women leaving for maternity reasons. These data can be refined further by computing turnover per 100 employees by length of employment, by job classification, by job category, and by each organizational unit.

In a BNA study of absenteeism and turnover in 136 companies, it was found that 53 percent used formula 1 and most others used slight variations of this if they calculated turnover rates.[18] Usually the variations used as the divisor either total number of employees at the beginning (or end) of the month or average number of employees for the month.

In the BNA study, about two thirds of companies reported computing turnover; 73 percent of new businesses calculated it, and more large businesses than small ones did so. Almost 70 percent computed the rate monthly, and most of the others calculated it annually.

The BNA study also found that 57 percent of the enterprises surveyed computed the data in such a way as to analyze turnover by department or division. This is more likely to be done in large businesses and nonmanufacturing firms than in other types of enterprises. Enterprises which include all employees in the calculation (67 percent) could calculate the differences in turnover by employee groups. In one recent year, the average turnover was 4.2 percent but the range was as high as 38 percent.

One way employers analyze the turnover rate is to compare the enterprise's turnover rate with those of other enterprises. Various sources publish average turnover rates quarterly or yearly. These include agencies such as the government labor departments, the Administrative Management Society, and BNA's quarterly reports on turnover and absenteeism.[19] Another approach is to analyze the enterprise's turnover by comparing the differences in rates by employee classifications or departments.

Most theories of turnover maintain that employees leave their jobs when their needs are not being satisfied at their present place of work *and* an alternative job becomes available which the employees believe will satisfy more of their needs. These theories have not received a great deal of support but they seem plausible.[20]

Hundreds of studies have been done on turnover. In a review and analysis by Lyman Porter and Richard Steers, job satisfaction was defined as the degree to which an employee's expectations about the job were met at four levels in the organization. The study found that for a person to be satisfied, all four levels of expectations must be met. At the organization level, these include factors like pay and promotion policies. At the work-group level, the size of the work group, supervisory style, and relations with co-workers affect satisfaction. The nature of the job requirements must be satisfying. Somewhat less support was found for the idea that satisfaction increases if the job requirements are clear and if the employee receives feedback recognition for performance. Porter and Steers concluded that turnover occurs when an employee's overall job satisfaction decreases to a low enough level. They also found that satisfaction is related to the employee's age and tenure.[21]

Analysis of a large number of studies examining the interrelationships between turnover and absenteeism show that, in general, they are intercorrelated; that is, if turnover is high, the absenteeism is also likely to be high. These studies also found that both were caused by the same factors and that, in general, employees first exhibited high absenteeism and this led to high turnover. Thus absenteeism and turnover are not alternative methods of showing dissatisfaction; rather, high absenteeism is a sign that high turnover is likely in the future.[22]

Overall, enterprises try to reduce turnover by a number of methods: better employee selection, orientation, communication, supervisor training, incentive awards, and data analyses.[23] In addition, many enterprises have tried to determine why their turnover takes place. One method is to interview employees just before they leave the enterprise to try to determine why they are leaving—an exit interview. Some find exit interviews unreliable and not useful; [24] others contend that, properly done, they are reliable enough for these purposes.[25] Problems can arise when exiting employees give partial reasons for leaving because they need references from the employer or might want to be reemployed at a future date.

Other methods which have been tried to reduce turnover, besides exit interviews, include telephone or in-person interviews a few weeks after termination. These would seem to have the same flaws as exit interviews, but little data are available on the reliability of these methods. Another approach being tried is to give employees a questionnaire as they are exiting and ask them to complete it and mail it back a month or so later. This gives the employee some protection and would appear to be a much better approach than the others. Organizations using this method find a rather low percentage of employees complete them, however. No reliability data appear to be available on these questionnaires.

Evaluation of absenteeism

A second measure used to evaluate the personnel function is absenteeism rates.

> **DEFINITIONS**
> Absenteeism is the failure of employees to report for work when they are scheduled to work.
> Tardiness is partial absenteeism in that employees report late to work.

Absenteeism is undesirable because of its costs and the operating problems it causes. A study of absenteeism which identified its cost to the enterprise noted that costs of benefits continue even when workers are absent, so benefit costs are higher per unit of output; overtime pay may be necessary for the worker who is doing the job for the missing worker. Facilities may be underutilized and productivity may drop because of reduced output due to understaffing. There also may be increased break-in costs for replacements, substandard production, the need for more help from supervisors and peers, and increased inspection costs.[26]

How is absenteeism computed? According to a BNA study,[27] the standard formula recommended by government bodies and used by over 70 percent of those who compute absenteeism is:

$$\frac{\text{Number of employee days lost through job absence in the period}}{\text{Average number of employees} \times \text{Number of work days}} \times 100.$$

Most others use a variation of this formula, such as

$$\frac{\text{Total hours of absence}}{\text{Total hours worked (or scheduled)}} \times 100.$$

Of the 136 enterprises surveyed by BNA, about 40 percent calculated absenteeism rates, usually for all employees, and most often monthly (54 percent) or annually (40 percent). Of those calculating absenteeism 70 percent did so by department or division. Most also separated out long-term absences from short-term ones.

One longitudinal study based on census data found that absenteeism has increased significantly from the 1960s to the 1970s. About 4.3 percent of the full-time work force is absent part of the week and 2.3 percent of the full-time work force is gone an entire week. The study demonstrated that at least part of this increase in absenteeism is due to the wider availability of paid sick leave. It found absenteeism higher in government and manufacturing; lower in service industries and finance and banking; higher among blue-collar employees and service workers than white-collar and managerial employees; higher among younger workers (especially absences of less than a week) and women; lower for married men than single men and higher for married women (especially with children) than single women.[28]

The BNA study cited above found the average absenteeism rate per month to be 4 percent. Other studies have found that absenteeism is higher on some days (Monday and Friday, day after payday) than others and at some times (November, December) and around regional holidays (like deer-hunting season or Mardi Gras in New Orleans).

The literature has advanced a number of causes of absenteeism: job dissatisfaction, alcoholism, sickness and injury, repetitive or unenriched jobs, lack of group cohesiveness, problems at home, transportation problems, and so on. Most studies of absenteeism tend to analyze it as a phenomenon with a single cause. After a thorough analysis of the literature, Nigel Nicholson et al. point out that absenteeism can be caused and constrained by a series of factors related to people (absence proneness), the workplace, and the outside world. They conclude that before much can be said about the causes of absenteeism systematic comparisons of absence-prone and absence-free individuals, longitudinally studied and taking into account community factors and absenteeism at both the individual and work-group levels, are needed.[29] Some studies of this type have begun to appear.

One excellent example of the person factors or absence-proneness emphasis is the six-year study of a General Motors parts plant in Scotland by Hilde Behrend and Stuart Pocock.[30] They examined the absence records of over 1,200 men each year and systematically compared the absence records of 610 men who were continuously employed over the six-year period from 1969 to 1974. One of the major conclusions of this study was that overall absence ratios, although of some use, are open to serious misinterpretation. For example, the "average" employee in their study experienced three absences per year, totaling about 18 days. But the range was from employees who were not absent one day in six years to several who were absent 600 days over the six-year period. The authors convincingly demonstrate that it makes much more sense to classify employees into categories of absence proneness, as in Exhibit 21–4. When this approach is used, management can focus on workers with higher absence rates and take remedial action in health terms (if the cause appears to be illness) or by counseling, discipline, and so on if health is not a factor.

The authors found a statistically significant group of employees who were absence prone over the six-year period. This finding indicates likely future absences can be predicted on the basis of past behavior patterns. They also found that absences were especially high among new employees and those who were about to quit. The high new-recruit absences in GM (as compared to earlier studies) may be due to a more generous sick pay scheme at GM. The Behrend and Pocock study cited is an example of the

EXHIBIT 21–4
Classification of individual absence records for the six-year period, 1969–1974

	Absences		
*Work force distribution**	*Days lost*	*Total spells*	*One-day spells†*
Lower decile	16	5	2
Lower quartile	40	9	5
Median	79	18	10
Upper quartile	151	28	17
Upper decile	228	40	24

* Lower decile, lower quartile, etc., denote the amount of absence exceeded or equalled by 90, 75, 50, 25, and 10 percent of employees, respectively.
† Absence periods—one-day or longer than one-day spells.
Source: Hilde Behrend and Stuart Pocock, "Absence and the Individual: A Six-Year Study in One Organization," *International Labour Review*, November–December 1976, pp. 311–327.

kind necessary to help managers understand and manage absence behavior better. At present, more can be reported on the patterns of absenteeism than the causes. Various studies have found, for example, that absenteeism is correlated with turnover, increases as work group size increases, is higher for blue-collar workers than others, and tends to be higher when the job is repetitive and lacks autonomy and responsibility.[31]

One of the traditional beliefs of managers and those in personnel work is that when an employee is dissatisfied, he or she expresses it by absenteeism. In fact, this is one of the rationales for using absence behavior to evaluate the personnel function. Nicholson's study and review of the literature (cited above) questions this relationship. More research needs to be done to determine if they are related; perhaps absenteeism is not as good a criterion for personnel evaluation as is presently thought.

To attempt to control absences, the BNA study reports employers use data analysis, discipline, counseling, and reward methods. Data analysis can be used in the way prescribed by Behrend and Pocock (Exhibit 21–4). After the non-health-related absence-prone person is identified, the traditional approach to controlling absences is to use a combination of discipline and counseling (see Chapter 9 and 20). Others have suggested the use of behavior modification or variations of expectancy motivation theory to influence the absence-prone employee.[32] This is satisfactory, Lillie Morgan and Jeanne Herman report, as a negative influence on the absence prone, but their study of the absence behavior of 60 blue-collar workers found that such methods alone were inadequate. Because the absence-prone employee receives positive rewards from absence even when the most powerful sanctions (loss of pay and benefits) apply, they suggest positive incentives for attendance. Specifically, since the absence prone listed as their strongest reason for absence a desire for more free time, they suggest rewarding good attendance with scheduled free time.[33] Another approach suggested for the management of absence behavior is for the enterprise to have a standby force of employees to be used for the absent workers and to prevent losses in productivity.[34]

The preceding discussion raises questions about the use of absence rates, certainly aggregate measures of absenteeism, to evaluate the personnel function. Some observers suggest abandoning the measure.[35] It appears that it is more useful to pursue research designed to identify absence-prone persons, work groups, working conditions, and communities with a view to designing strategies to reduce absenteeism.

Evaluation of complaints and grievances

> **DEFINITIONS**
> A complaint is a statement (in writen or oral form) of dissatisfaction or criticism by an employee to a manager.
> A grievance is a complaint which has been presented formally and in writing to a management or union official.

Chapter 19 discussed what grievances are and how they are processed. The complaint-grievance rate and the severity of the grievances is another way to evaluate the personnel function. Of course, not all complaints or grievances relate to personnel issues; they can be about equipment, machinery, and other matters, too. And the grievance rate can be related to the militancy of the union or the imminence to contract negotiations. Nevertheless, an increase in the rate and severity of complaints and grievances can indicate dissatisfaction, which in turn might lead to increases in absenteeism and turnover. Both factors indicate how successful the personnel department is in securing productivity and satisfaction for the employee.

Statistical analyses of complaints and grievances have not been done as scientifically as for turnover and absenteeism. Some research indicates the grievance rate is higher from younger, more educated, active union members[36] and lower when the contract administration process is more effective.[37] Analyses of grievance rates might provide clues of failures in personnel programs. Longitudinally analyzed, they might provide additional data for evaluation of personnel. More research is needed in this area before much more can be said about this indicator, however.

Evaluation of other indicators

Turnover, absenteeism, and grievances appear to be frequent measures of the effectiveness of the personnel function. Other quantitative measures include accident and health ratios, which are listed in Exhibit 21–3 and are explained more fully in Chapter 17. Less frequently used indicators include the employment and effectiveness ratios, also described briefly in Exhibit 21–3. These ratios appear to be used less frequently than the other indicators described in more detail in this chapter.

Evaluation using attitude and opinion surveys

Another indicator of employee and managerial evaluation of the personnel program is obtained through the use of attitude or opinion surveys.[38]

DEFINITION

An attitude or opinion survey is a set of written instruments completed by employees (usually anonymously) expressing their reactions to employer policies and practices.

Effective attitude surveys are designed with precise goals in mind. The questions and items used are designed professionally and are tested on a sample of employees for reliability and validity prior to administration. Several other administrative factors may affect the validity; one is whether the employees feel that the employer is sincerely interested in knowing the truth and will act wherever possible to follow up on their suggestions.

The survey may include many personnel activities, job satisfaction,[39] and other aspects of the enterprise's operations. Usually, after the results of the survey are in they are analyzed and fed back to the employee units.[40] One study found that about a third of the large employers surveyed used attitude surveys to help evaluate the effectiveness of the total personnel program or parts of it, such as pay, benefits, or training.[41]

Statistical analyses of personnel department operations

The methods of evaluation and audit discussed thus far are aimed at discovering the effectiveness of the personnel department with all of the enterprise's employees. A different approach is to study what the personnel department does and how well it performs compared to other personnel departments. This approach is sometimes called work analysis. Stephen Carroll describes how work analysis is done using the work-sampling technique, in which "observations are made at random intervals of what the employee is doing with the purpose of providing a basis for inferences about the various elements that comprise his total work activity."[42] Exhibits 21–5 and 21–6 report some of Carroll's findings. Exhibit 21–5 shows that persons who enter personnel to work with people may be partially satisfied. These personnel specialists spent 38 percent of their time conversing with others in person and on the telephone. Almost as much time was spent preparing and examining reports. Exhibit 21–6 provides data from Carroll's work analyses that can be used to indicate if proper emphasis has been placed on various personnel activities in a certain period. In the example in Exhibit 21–6, if the objectives of the department included emphasis on benefits and services and staffing functions, the goals were achieved, since 50 percent

EXHIBIT 21–5

Percentage of total work time spent on various work activities by personnel department members

Type of work activity	Five clerical workers		Four personnel department managers		Total staff in department	
	No. of observations	Percentage of total work time	No. of observations	Percentage of total work time	No. of observations	Percentage of total work time
Conversing with others in person	105	09%	578	60%	683	33%
Conversing on telephone	58	05	50	05	108	05
Preparing and writing reports, letters, etc	492	43	143	16	645	31
Examining reports, letters, etc	54	05	53	06	107	05
Inspecting products, procedures, etc	0	00	6	01	6	00
Mathematical computation	24	02	3	00	27	01
Operating equipment of all types	67	06	2	00	69	03
Thinking and reflection	0	00	0	00	0	00
Minor clerical jobs (filing, delivering, etc)	161	14	52	05	213	10
Personal activities	43	04	61	06	104	05
Marking, recording, or sorting	134	12	0	00	134	06
Insufficient data	5	00	0	00	5	00
Total	1,143	100%	958	99%	2,101	99%

Source: Stephen J. Carroll, Jr., "Measuring the Work of a Personnel Department," *Personnel*, July–August 1960, p. 51.

EXHIBIT 21-6
Percentage of total work time spent on various employee relations functions by personnel department members

Type of function	Five clerical workers		Four personnel department managers		Total staff in department	
	No. of observations	Percentage of total work time	No. of observations	Percentage of total work time	No. of observations	Percentage of total work time
Administration of the department	60	05%	214	22%	274	13%
Staffing	88	08	196	20	284	14
Training	0	00	5	01	5	00
Labor relations	72	06	122	13	194	09
Wage and salary administration	117	10	46	05	163	08
Benefits and services	490	43	257	27	747	36
Research, audit, and review	76	07	35	04	111	05
Personal activities	43	04	61	06	104	05
Insufficient data*	197	17	22	02	219	10
Total	1,143	100%	958	100%	2,101	100%

* These observations could not be classified because two participants failed to explain adequately the purpose of some of their activities.
Source: Stephen J. Carroll, Jr., "Measuring the Work of a Personnel Department." Reprinted by permission of the publisher from *Personnel*, July–August 1960, p. 55. Copyright © 1960 by the American Management Association, Inc.

of the time was spent on these. If the goal was to emphasize training, it's back to the old drawing board.

One use of attitude survey methods to evaluate personnel activities is to give an opinion survey form to job applicants *and* employees and ask them directly about personnel's operations. This method was used to evaluate the personnel department for King County, Washington.[43]

Donald Peterson and Robert Malone propose another such evaluation which uses a personnel effectiveness grid (PEG). They assume that effective personnel departments have the support of top management and other operating managers in trying to achieve success in their performance of service, counseling, stabilization of policies, and research. The four conditions on their grid vary from full partnership (support by operating managers on all four personnel roles) to routine service (little support). Items to assign personnel departments to this audit condition were developed.[44]

COMPLIANCE METHODS OF EVALUATION

In the compliance approach to evaluation of the personnel function, the main concern is the extent to which personnel procedures reflecting the law or company policy are being followed in the enterprise. Attempts are then made to determine where changes are needed.

EXHIBIT 21–7
Personnel compliance audit process at Citibank

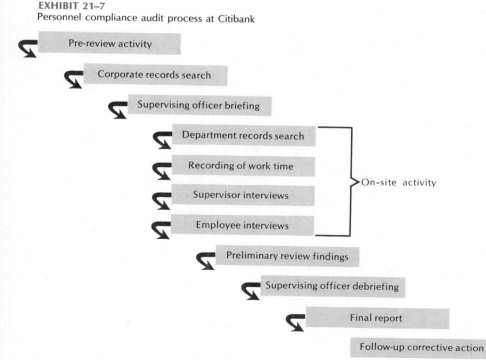

Source: Paul Sheibar, "Personnel Practices Review: A Personnel Audit Activity," *Personnel Journal,* March 1974, p. 213.

One study describes how First National City Bank (New York), one of America's largest banks, performs this audit. The first step is to identify 18 crucial personnel areas it wishes to audit. Then the bank randomly chooses branch banks (eliminating recently reorganized banks) to be studied.[45] The audit procedure followed is diagrammed in Exhibit 21–7. The review is conducted by the Personnel Practices Review Unit (six personnel reviewers, an operations manager, and clerical support), which reviews all branches every other year. The bank believes that this audit has substantially improved its personnel effectiveness. Another study describes a similar program of the California State University and Colleges System.[46]

Evaluation of personnel using management by objectives

Management by objectives is the system recommended by George Odiorne in the list of methods cited above. Without systematic goals or objectives, the personnel department may fall into the trap of being activity instead of objectives oriented. Thus it may list as progress the running of 12 training programs as compared with 10 the year before, forgetting that the criteria of effectiveness are productivity and satisfaction, not activities alone. MBO was described in Chapter 10. It is not known how many enterprises follow the MBO approach, but it is probably not a large number at present.

SUMMARY, CONCLUSIONS, AND RECOMMENDATIONS

Any function as important as the effective use of human resources needs to be evaluated. The difficulty in evaluating the results of the personnel function is that effectiveness has multiple causes. For example, plant employees could be more effective as a result of a good personnel program or of clean, comfortable facilities with the latest equipment. It is quite difficult to separate out how much of the effectiveness results from each cause. This chapter has presented some of the ways this can be done.

Exhibit 21–8 provides recommendations for the model organizations on personnel audits and evaluation and research. Some propositions which serve as a summary of the major points in the chapter include the following on the nature of the organization:

Proposition 21.1 The larger the organization the more likely it is to evaluate its personnel program formally.

Proposition 21.2 The more labor intensive the organization, the more likely it is to evaluate its personnel program formally.

Proposition 21.3 The more geographically dispersed the organization's units, the more likely it is to evaluate its personnel program formally.

Proposition 21.4 The worse the economic conditions in the environ-

EXHIBIT 21–8
Recommendations for model organizations on personnel research and evaluation of the personnel functions

Type of organization	Performed by							
	Checklist	Statistical	Compliance	MBO	Organization	Consultant	Organization and consultant	Personnel research department
1. Large size, low complexity, high stability			X	X	X			X
2. Medium size, low complexity, high stability		X	X				X	
3. Small size, low complexity, high stability	X					X		
4. Medium size, moderate complexity, moderate stability		X	X				X	
5. Large size, high complexity, low stability			X	X	X			X
6. Medium size, high complexity, low stability	X						X	
7. Small size, high complexity, low stability								

ment, the more likely the organization is to evaluate its personnel program formally.

Proposition 21.5. The more economically oriented the goals of the organization, the more likely it is to evaluate its personnel program formally.

The rationale for Proposition 21.2 is that the larger the percentage of total costs attributed to the cost of human resources, the greater is the economic pressure to assess how well these resources are used. This pressure is intensified in bad times. Even the nonprofit sector faces budgetary strains which accentuate the pressure for personnel audits.

The following propositions can be stated with regard to personnel research:

Proposition 21.6. The larger the organization the more likely it is to have a personnel research function.

Proposition 21.7. The more the research section studies problems that management considers important, the more influence the unit is likely to have on behavior.

With regard to employee absenteeism, it appears that:

Proposition 21.8. As work-unit size increases, absenteeism increases for blue-collar workers.

Proposition 21.9. As the task gets more repetitive, absenteeism has a tendency to rise.

Proposition 21.10. If the task lacks autonomy or responsibility, absenteeism tends to be high.

Propositions about turnover include:

Proposition 21.11. If employees are dissatisfied with pay and promotion policies, turnover will increase.

Proposition 21.12. The larger the work-group size, the higher the turnover rate.

Proposition 21.13. The more satisfied the employees are with supervisory style, the lower the turnover.

Proposition 21.14. The more satisfied employees are with their co-workers, the lower the turnover.

The chapter concludes with a brief summary of the book and a glimpse of the future of the personnel function.

THE NEW PERSONNEL MANAGER AND PERSONNEL'S FUTURE

This book has been designed to help you develop as a successful manager of the personnel function, either as a personnel professional or as an operating manager with people to manage. The book used a series of mechanisms to advance the necessary knowledge:

The diagnostic approach. It was shown that the effective new personnel manager is a diagnostician who observes the various aspects of the organization's environment. She or he considers the size, structure, goals, and style of the organization, and the nature of the employee, the task, the work group, and the leader. The manager realizes that the personnel policies of the enterprise must be congruent with all these factors, and others, if personnel is to do its part to contribute to enterprise effectiveness.

Model organizations. This mechanism was used to focus attention specifically on how personnel activities are performed differently in different types of organizations. This is certainly true of the many different kinds of enterprises in the private, public, and third sectors and the differences between Canadian and U.S. enterprises.

The role of the top manager and operating manager. Top managers and operating managers have important parts to play in the personnel process. Successful personnel managers know how to relate to these persons and to present personnel programs to them in the language and thought processes of operating and top managers. How is this done?

The new personnel manager manages by objectives and shows how personnel has helped achieve enterprise goals. Few enterprises exist to hire and develop people. They exist to reach goals such as producing goods to satisfy customers while achieving a profit, or curing patients at reasonable cost, or improving the education of teen-age children in a community.

The new personnel manager can show how, through the careful performance evaluation of employees, their satisfaction will be increased, absenteeism and turnover will be decreased, and their performance will be improved. Thus both quality and quantity of output improves and enterprise goals are achieved. This requires a cost benefits comparison emphasis.

The new personnel manager is part of the team that makes the key decisions, the strategic decisions such as: Are we going to grow? In what direction are we going to grow? Are we going to merge with another enterprise? What's the future going to be if our plans work out?

Each of these strategic decisions has important implications for personnel, and the personnel department can provide important counsel about the human resources affecting these decisions. Personnel can only have the impact it should have if its leadership is well trained to do the job and if it can convey to top management a goal-oriented attitude when seeking additional funds to do its job.

The new personnel manager who is part of the top management team will be reporting what programs have been phased out, with appropriate savings, and what programs have been kept, and the savings and improvements resulting from them. Specific budget justifications will be made for proposed additions and specific measurable results that will help the enterprise reach its goals will be proposed. Further, the personnel manager will be able to show how to achieve these results. Managers who are used to making decisions this way will know that this executive team makes the *real* decisions that affect personnel.

In the smaller enterprise, the new executive responsible for personnel and other functions should begin to consider personnel decisions in the same hardnosed way he or she does other decisions. Resources are scarce, and human resources are the most precious to conserve and develop.

The new personnel manager must do her or his part to help top management face some future threats and opportunities. Some of these may include:

Shortage of resources. Consider the impact of the lack of energy on work schedules in 1977, for example.

Declining population of younger employees.

Outdated manufacturing facilities in many industries.

Fewer manufacturing jobs, more service jobs.

Low-growth strategies for some industries.

The possibility of more employees working at home some of the time.[47]

New privacy legislation affecting many aspects of personnel.[48]

But, better training and new attitudes will equip the new personnel executive to handle all the challenges the environment and the enterprise can present— EEOC, OFCCP, OSHA, and others we don't even know about yet.

If the book has provided the data to improve decision making and has made clear these attitudinal emphases, in short, if it has helped develop the new personnel manager, it has satisfied my own goals.

QUESTIONS

1. What is evaluation of personnel?
2. Why do we evaluate personnel activities and functions?
3. Compare and contrast the checklist, compliance, and MBO evaluation methods. Which is best?
4. Compare and contrast the statement indicators of personnel evaluation. Which are the best indicators? How are they measured?
5. What are the most significant propositions for this chapter? The most significant recommendations?
6. What significant future events are likely to affect personnel practices?
7. How will the new personnel executive help achieve enterprise goals? Personnel's goals?

NOTES AND REFERENCES

1. E. H. Caplan,"A Behavioral View of Performance and Evaluation," *Management Accounty and Behavioral Science* (Reading, Mass.: Addison-Wesley Publishing Co., 1971).

2. Bureau of National Affairs, *Labor Policy and Practice: Personnel Management* (Washington, D.C., 1975).

3.   Edward Tomeski and Harold Lazarus, "Computerized Information Services in Personnel," *Academy of Management Journal,* March 1974, pp. 162–72.

4.   Frank Wolling and John Bercen, "Essential Personnel Records and Reports," in *Handbook of Modern Personnel Administration,* ed. Joseph Famularo, ch. 77 (New York: McGraw-Hill Book Co., 1972).

5.   Dean Berry, *The Politics of Personnel Research* (Ann Arbor: University of Michigan, Bureau of Industrial Relations, 1967); W. Byham, *The Uses of Personnel Research,* AMA Research Study 91 (New York: American Management Association, 1968); Cecil Goode, *Personnel Research Frontiers* (Chicago: Public Personnel Association, 1958); Robert Paul, "Constructing Personnel Research Programs," ed. Joseph Famularo, *Handbook of Modern Personnel Administration,* ch. 81 (New York: McGraw-Hill Book Co., 1972).

6.   Harold Flanders, "The AT&T Company Manpower Laboratory, Circa 1971," *Proceedings, Academy of Management,* 1971, pp. 203–6.

7.   Byham, *Uses of Personnel Research.*

8.   For other information on personnel research, see Wilmer Bernthal, "Research Foundations for Modern Personnel Administration: A Review and Appraisal, *"The Personnel Administrator,* May–June 1965; Herbert Heneman, Jr., "Contributions of Industrial Relations Research," *Manpower and Applied Psychology* 2, 2 (1970), pp. 5–16; H. Meltzer, "Review of Reviews in Industrial Psychology, 1950–1969," *Personnel Psychology* 25 (1972), pp. 201–22.

9.   John Hinnrichs, "Characteristics of the Personnel Research Functions," *Personnel Journal* August 1969, pp. 597–604.

10.   Max Wortman, Jr., "Corporated Industrial Relations Research: Dream or Reality?" *Academy of Management Journal,* June 1966, pp. 127–35.

11.   Byham, *Uses of Personnel Research.*

12.   W. Rabe, "Yardsticks for Measuring Personnel Department Effectiveness," *Personnel,* January–February 1967, pp. 56–62.

13.   George Odiorne, "Evaluating the Personnel Program," in *Handbook of Modern Personnel Administration,* ed. Joseph Famularo, ch. 8 (New York: McGraw-Hill Book Co., 1972).

14.   Geneva Seybold, *Personnel Audits and Reports to Top Management,* Studies in Personnel Policy 191 (New York: National Industrial Conference Board, 1964).

15.   This list combines the items suggested by Thomas L. Luck, *Personnel Audit and Appraisal* (New York: McGraw-Hill Book Co., 1955); Rabe, "Yardstick for Measuring Personnel Department Effectiveness"; Seybold, *Personnel Audits and Reports.*

16.   Joseph Augustine, "Personnel Turnover," in *Handbook of Modern Personnel Administration,* ed. Joseph Famularo, ch. 62, New York: McGraw-Hill Book Co., 1972.

17.   Thomas Jeswald, "The Cost of Absenteeism and Turnover in a Large Organization," in *Contemporary Problems in Personnel,* ed. Clay Hamner and Frank Schmidt, Chicago: St. Clair, 1974, pp. 352–57.

18.   Bureau of National Affairs, *Employee Absenteeism and Turnover,* Personnel Policies Forum 106 (Washington, D.C., May 1974).

19.   Bureau of National Affairs, *Bulletin to Management,* Personnel Policies Forum (Washington, D.C., November 1977).

20.   Christopher Forrest et al., "Turnover Theory and Research," *Proceedings, Academy of Management,* 1973, pp. 338–43; Donald Schwab and Lee Dyer, "Turnover as a Function of Perceived Ease and Desirability," February 1974, mimeographed, University of Wisconsin, Madison; John Newman, "Predicting Absenteeism and Turnover," *Journal of Applied Psychology* 59 (1974), pp. 610–15.

21. Lyman Porter and Richard Steers, "Organizational, Work, and Personal Factors in Employee Turnover and Absenteeism," *Psychological Bulletin* 80, 2 (1973), pp. 151–76.

22. Thomas Lyons, "Turnover and Absenteeism: A Review of Relationships and Shared Correlates," *Personnel Psychology*, June 1972, pp. 271–81; Barrie Pettman (ed.); *Labour Turnover and Retention* (New York: John Wiley & Sons, 1976); Vincent Flowers, and Charles Hughes, "Why Employees Stay," *Harvard Business Review*, July–August 1973, pp. 49–60; D. L. Howell and G. T. Stewart, "Labor Turnover in Hospitals," *Personnel Journal*, December 1975, pp. 624–37.

23. BNA, *Employee Absenteeism and Turnover.*

24. Joel Lefkowitz and Myron Katz, "Validity of Exit Interviews," *Personnel Psychology* 22 (1969), pp. 445–55; John Hinrichs, "Measurement of Reasons for Resignation of Professionals: Questionnaire versus Company and Consultant Exit Interviews," *Journal of Applied Psychology* 60, 4 (1975), pp. 530–32.

25. James Laniff, "The Exit Interview: Antiquated or Underrated?" *The Personnel Administrator*, May 1976, pp. 55–60.

26. Jeswald, "Cost of Absenteeism and Turnover."

27. BNA, *Employee Absenteeism and Turnover.*

28. Janice Hedges, "Absence from Work: A Look at Some National Data," *Monthly Labor Review*, July 1973, pp. 24–30.

29. Nigel Nicholson et al., "Absence from Work and Job Satisfaction," *Journal of Applied Psychology* 61, 6 (1976), pp. 728–37.

30. Hilde Behrend and Stuart Pocock, "Absence and the Individual: A Six-Year Study in One Organization," *International Labour Review*, November–December 1976, pp. 311–27.

31. Lyons, "Turnover and Absenteeism"; J. K. Chadwick-Jones et al., "A Type and B Type Absence: Empirical Trends for Women Employees," *Occupational Psychology* 47 (1973), pp. 75–80; Oliver R. Gibson, "Toward a Conceptualization of Absence Behavior of Personnel in Organizations," *Administrative Science Quarterly*, June 1966, pp. 107–33; Newman, "Predicting Absenteeism and Turnover"; Porter and Steers, "Employee Turnover and Absenteeism"; Harvey Shore, "Absenteeism," *Supervisory Management* 20, 9 (1975), pp. 9–18 ff.

32. Walter Nord, "Improving Attendance through Rewards," *Personnel Administration*, November–December 1970, pp. 37–41; Ed Pedalino and Victor Gamboa, "Behavior Modification and Absenteeism," *Journal of Applied Psychology* 59 (1974), pp. 694–98; Fred Luthans and Mark Martinko, "An Organizational Behavior Modification Analysis of Absenteeism," *Human Resource Management*, Fall 1976, pp. 11–18.

33. Lillie Morgan and Jeanne Herman, "Perceived Consequences of Absenteeism," *Journal of Applied Psychology* 61, 6 (1976), pp. 738–42.

34. Paul Berger and James Monahan, "A Planning Model to Cope with Absenteeism," *Journal of Business* 47 (1974), pp. 512–17.

35. Ronald Johnson and Tim Peterson, "Absenteeism or Attendance: Which Is Industry's Problem?" *Personnel Journal*, November 1975, pp. 568–72; Gary Latham and Elliott Pursell, "Measuring Absenteeism from the Opposite Side of the Coin," *Journal of Applied Psychology* 60, 3 (1975), pp. 369–71.

36. Howard Sulkin and Robert Pranis, "Comparison of Grievants with Non-Grievants in a Heavy Machinery Company," *Personnel Psychology* 20, 2 (1967), pp. 111–19.

37. William Werther, "Reducing Grievances through Effective Contract Administration," *Labor Law Journal* 25, 4 (1974), pp. 211–16.

38. Robert Goode, "How to Get Better Results from Attitude Surveys," *Personnel Journal*, March 1973, pp. 187–92; Elizabeth Howe, "Opinion Surveys: Taking the Task Force Approach,"

Personnel, September–October 1974, pp. 16–23; Richard Morano, "Opinion Surveys: The How To's of Design and Application," *Personnel* (September–October, 1974), pp. 8–15.

39.   Edwin Locke, "The Nature and Causes of Job Satisfaction," in *Handbook of Industrial and Organizational Psychology,* ed. Marvin Dunnettle (Chicago: Rand McNally & Co., 1976).

40.   Stuart Klein et al., "Employee Reactions to Attitude Survey Feedback," *Administrative Science Quarterly* 16 (1971), pp. 497–514; David Sirota, "Opinion Surveys: The Results Are In: What De We Do With Them?" *Personnel,* September–October, 1974, pp. 24–31.

41.   Stephen Habbe, *Following Up Attitude Survey Findings,* Studies in Personnel Policy 181 (New York: National Industrial Conference Board, 1961); Seybold, *Personnel Audits and Reports.*

42.   Stephen J. Carroll Jr., "Measuring the Work of a Personnel Department," *Personnel,* July–August 1960, pp. 49–56.

43.   J. L. Stone, "The Use of an Applicant Service Questionnaire," *Public Personnel Management,* March–April 1974, pp. 155–58.

44.   Donald Peterson, and Robert Malone, "The Personnel Effectiveness Grid PEG," *Human Resource Management,* Winter 1975, pp. 10–21.

45.   Paul Sheibar, "Personnel Practices Review: A Personnel Audit Activity," *Personnel Journal,* March 1974, pp. 211–17.

46.   C. Mansel Keene, "Personnel Management Reviews in a Multicampus State University," *Public Personnel Management,* March–April, 1976, pp. 120–31.

47.   Christopher Evans, "A Way to Improve the Office's Efficiency: Just Stay at Home," *Wall Street Journal,* December 14, 1976.

48.   Jim Montgomery, "Listening In," *The Wall Street Journal,* March 21, 1974; Mordechai Mironi, "The Confidentiality of Personnel Records: A Legal and Ethical View," *Labor Law Journal,* May 1974, pp. 270–91; Allen Otten, "Privacy Pioneers," *The Wall Street Journal,* October 2, 1975; Kenneth Walters, "Employee Freedom of Speech," *Industrial Relations,* February 1976, pp. 26–43; Frank Cary, "IBM's Guidelines to Employee Privacy," *Harvard Business Review,* September–October 1976, pp. 82–90; Pierre Juvigny, "Data Handling and the Protection of Workers' Rights," *International Labour Review,* 2 November–December 1976, pp. 247–60; Kenneth Kovach, "A Retrospective Look at the Privacy and Freedom of Information Acts," *Labor Law Journal,* September 1976, pp. 548–64; David Palmer, "Free Speech and Arbitration: Implications for the Future," *Labor Law Journal,* May 1976, pp. 287–300.

Cases and exercises

I. CASES

1. FLINT MEMORIAL HOSPITAL*

Flint Memorial is a large, proprietary hospital. It is located in a growing, progressive city. Originally built about 20 years ago, it is now in the midst of a large expansion program. Soon the original 250-bed capacity will have been enlarged to accommodate about 800 beds. The hospital has enjoyed increasingly good public relations recently because of good patient service and a fine school of nursing.

Many changes have taken place in the administrative staff during the past two years. A new, well-qualified hospital administrator was employed. About the time he arrived, several members of the staff left. Anne Jones, the director of nursing, was employed to replace the former director. This position involved both nursing service and nursing education. An experienced nursing administrator, Miss Jones held an MS degree in nursing from a well-known university.

The morale of the nursing staff and faculty had been affected adversely by years of inadequate leadership. Henry Collins, the new administrator, was anxious to do something about this morale problem. When he told Miss Jones that she had been employed to meet the growing needs of the hospital and that he expected changes to be made, Miss Jones replied that she intended to make haste slowly. Each agreed that too much change might be even more detrimental to morale during this period of adjustment. Collins delegated responsibility readily. Conditions seemed to improve gradually.

Miss Jones surveyed her staff and concluded that it was above average. The members of the staff with whom she had held discussions seemed friendly and willing to cooperate. The supervisors and faculty members seemed to accept her readily. In reviewing the personnel policies that affected her employees she realized that no policy changes had been made in years; she was anxious to begin making some necessary revisions. Soon she began holding meetings with the staff to find areas of weakness and of strength.

New problems arose daily, now in nursing service, now in nursing education. Miss Jones and the faculty reviewed the rules and regulations for the student nurses and revised these in the light of present-day democratic principles. Revision was time-consuming and left little time to work on the problems of the staff of nursing service; this was the most pressing need of the moment.

John Terrell, the personnel manager, had been employed about four months after Miss Jones, to head a newly established personnel department. Miss Jones worked cooperatively with the personnel department, transferring

---

* Note: This case is from Richard P. Calhoun, CASES IN PERSONNEL MANAGEMENT AND SUPERVISION, © 1966, pp. 17–20. Reprinted by permission of Prentice-Hall, Inc., Englewood Cliffs, New Jersey.

EXHIBIT 1
Organization chart: Flint Memorial Hospital

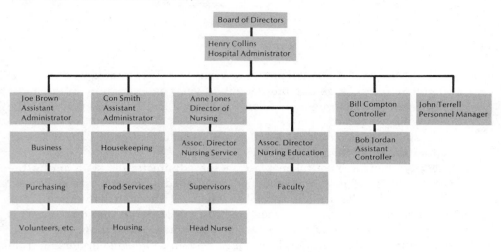

records, putting in job requisitions, and exchanging information. The associate director of nursing service and Miss Jones's secretary were less willing to delegate responsibility to the new personnel department, but after some persuasion they began to realize that this would lighten their work load.

Mr. Terrell had previously been employed as an administrative assistant in a small hospital. Because he was apparently insecure at first, Miss Jones tried to cooperate and support him in his efforts. She had several years' experience in hospital personnel management and made available to him the literature and information she had.

Several times Joe Brown, an assistant administrator, remarked about Mr. Terrell's practice of reporting every trivial incident to Mr. Collins; Miss Jones felt Mr. Terrell might just be following directions.

Mr. Terrell and Miss Jones had discussed several times the need to revise and implement the personnel policies. After six months on the job, Mr. Terrell told Miss Jones he was revising the policies and would like her to read them over before he presented them to his committee on personnel policies. She indicated that she was very interested and wished to see them even though reorganization and the daily stress of the many disciplines and personalities in the hospital organization kept her busy.

One Tuesday morning Mr. Terrell called Miss Jones to ask when he could see her to discuss the new personnel policies. Consulting her desk calendar, she suggested Friday morning.

> **Mr. Terrell:** But that's too late! My meeting is Thursday afternoon at 5 P.M.
>
> **Miss Jones:** In that case bring them down and I'll go over them at home—I certainly want to see them.

Mr. Terrell's secretary brought the suggested policies to Miss Jones's office later that morning. Tuesday evening and Wednesday evening she read the new policy changes; she fumed inwardly. She could see the results of her efforts toward morale and cooperation evaporating. She wrote notes and recommended changes on the margin; she suggested additional policies. On Thursday morning Miss Jones called on Mr. Terrell in his office.

Miss Jones: Terrell, you can't take things away from people and expect a satisfied staff. One of your policies reduces some of the supervisors' vacation period by a week. I have 450 employees in my department. I can see nothing but hostility arising from many of these changes. Here are *my* suggestions—in writing!

Mr. Terrell: I'll look over them before the meeting this afternoon.

Miss Jones: I've been around hospitals too long to be sensitive, and as I've said, most of the employees in this institution are under Nursing. I intend to be at your meeting this afternoon, invited or not.

Miss Jones then angrily left Mr. Terrell's office.

That afternoon she attended the Personnel Policy Committee meeting. Copies of the suggested policies were passed out. Miss Jones asked for the copy on which she had noted her suggestions. Mr. Terrell, looking pained, said he had made her suggested changes. On glancing through her copy, she realized he had. Miss Jones was appeased.

Matters went along smoothly for a while after that; the combination of new-old policies was approved. One of the new personnel policies stated: "Those employees who have been employed over five years and are no longer receiving periodic increment salary raises will have their records reviewed on the anniversary of employment date; merit raises will be given consistent with performance appraisal by the supervisor."

Bob Jordan, one of the assistants to the controller, called Miss Jones about a month after the policy had gone into effect and asked if he could see her for a minute.

Mr. Jordan: This guy Terrell is getting into everyone's hair. I thought you might be interested in these.

Mr. Jordan had two authorization slips for merit raises for two of Miss Jones's supervisors. She had signed these herself, and they had been countersigned by Mr. Brown, the assistant administrator. Mr. Terrell had cancelled the authorization.

Miss Jones took the authorization slips and went to Mr. Brown's office. After he read them, the two of them appeared at Mr. Collins's office and requested a short conference.

Discussion questions

1. What is happening here?
2. Whose responsibility is it that this situation exists?
3. Could Miss Jones have helped Mr. Terrell?

4. Should this matter of merit raises have been taken up with Mr. Terrell—or had it gone too far?

5. How should Miss Jones approach Mr. Collins?

6. How should Mr. Collins handle the interview with Miss Jones and Mr. Brown?

7. What should Mr. Collins do in his subsequent interview with Mr. Terrell?

2.   TYLER MANUFACTURING COMPANY

Tyler Manufacturing Company is a medium-sized firm producing parts for the auto industry. The firm fabricates major metal subassemblies for autos and sells its products on contract to such firms as General Motors, Ford, and Chrysler. Tyler's main plant is located in the Detroit, Michigan, area, but it has a branch plant in California and another in the East.

Tyler has always had good employee relations. Their wages and benefits have always exceeded the industry's. Tyler has a company union. Recently the union leadership asked to see the Vice President—Vance Henry. The union leader, Peter Vuychich, said: "Mr. Henry, at our most recent get-together, some of the boys brought up the subject of the four-day week. As you know, the *Detroit Free Press* carried an article on this and the TV has played it up some. Some of the men have boats and others like to hunt. This appeals to them since they could take longer breaks that way. We'd like to give it a try."

Vance said: "Well, Peter, it's a big step. Let me give it some thought." After checking around with other personnel men and reading up on the topic, Vance decided to experiment with it, but in the Detroit plant alone. He asked Peter to come in again. After a brief discussion of the Lions game the previous weekend, he said: "Look, Peter, about your request on the four-day week. You know we've always gone along with what the boys want. I'm willing to try it and the president, Archibald Seeley, says he is too, if the men want it. Take a mail poll of the men and let me know how it comes out."

The union polled the men and 85 percent favored the move. The new arrangement called for work on Monday through Thursday, 7:00 A.M. to 6:00 P.M., with a half hour for lunch and a 15-minute break midmorning and midafternoon.

About a month after the experiment started, a rush order came in from General Motors. This required some overtime work. There was a lot of grumbling about Friday and Saturday work among the men. A typical comment was found in the suggestion box: "You'll kill us with this pace— six-day 60-hour weeks—leaves us no time for our families and no energy left for our wives.

Vance and Richard Peterson, operations manager at the plant, looked over the productivity figures. They found that quality had dropped (reject

EXHIBIT 2
Productivity data for Tyler Manufacturing: Four-day week and overtime week compared to previous five-day week figures

	Monday	Tuesday	Wednes-day	Thurs-day	Friday	Saturday
Week 1						
Morning	Same	Same	−1%	−2%		
Afternoon	Same	Same	−1%	−2%		
Week 2						
Morning	+2%	+1%	Same	Same	−1%	−2%
Afternoon	Same	Same	−1%	−2%	−2%	−3%
Week 3						
Morning	+2%	+1%	Same	−2%		
Afternoon	Same	Same	−1%	−2%		

rates went up 10 percent from inspectors) and output rate had dropped 5 percent. This upset them both a great deal. Richard said: "You know, Vance, this is all due to your damn experiment. You never asked me about it before you started, but I knew it would never work. I'll bet those last couple of hours per day are killing us. I'll get some data on productivity per half day and check it out."

Three weeks later, Richard returned with the data. During these weeks, two weeks had had no overtime, one had overtime. The productivity data were worked up to compare an "average" week before the change with these weeks (see Exhibit 2).

Richard said, "Vance, as you can see, this experiment is a disaster. We talked to the men about the productivity drop, emphasizing that if they wanted to keep the experiment going, they'd have to get production up. As you see, on some of the days, they did. But the later in the week it got, the worse things were. And quality figures parallel these quantity figures. The work is just too heavy for these hours."

Vance agreed something had to be done. He called Peter in, explained the situation, and said: "I'm thinking of dropping the four-day week. My bet is that the men have lost some of their enthusiasm too. Let's see."

The poll results came in. 65 percent of the men said they'd like to continue the experiment, 35 percent wanted to revert back. Vance is wondering how to handle the situation now.

Discussion questions

1. You are Vance. How do you handle the situation?

2. What do the statistics prove about the productivity or unproductivity of the employees?

3. What part should the union play in the decision?

3.   CONSOLIDATED DEFENSE MANUFACTURING

CDM is a large firm producing devices primarily purchased by the Department of Defense of the United States. It does sell some of the devices to foreign governments (with the approval of the U.S. government) such as Iran, the Federal Republic of Germany, and Australia.

CDM is considering bidding on a new contract to make an improved version of its product for the U.S. Army. This would be a large contract and would require additional hiring of several hundred skilled workers to produce the devices.

These workers (tool and die workers, machinists, etc.) are thought to be in short supply. Before CDM bids on the contract, top management has asked for the advice of its management as to feasibility of the project. Thus the financial people are working with production people on minimum bid. The production people are rejecting their needs for plant and equipment.

Discussion question

1.   You have been asked to recommend whether the personnel are available and at what cost. Several production sites are feasible: Hartford, Connecticut, Milwaukee, Wisconsin, and Birmingham, Alabama. Your recommended site, projected personnel availability, and costs are expected in 30 days. Where do you begin?

4.   GIGANTIC AIRCRAFT COMPANY

Gigantic Aircraft Company is a large firm with a plant near Santa Barbara, California. The personnel manager has called in Boyce Piersol, a management consultant specializing in personnel, for advice on selection policies. Bill Fabris invited Piersol to come in the first thing in the morning. When Piersol arrive, Fabris said: "Boyce, I'm glad you're here. I've been having a lot of trouble in selection recently. My long suit has always been collective bargaining. I'm a lawyer by training, and I think I need help. Briefly, let me outline how we handle selection here now."

Blue-collar employees—Screening interview to separate out the misfits; then a test battery—mostly abilities tests—and then interview the best of the lot. For crucial jobs, either security-wise, or if the job involves expensive equipment, get two letters of reference from prior employers.

White-collar employees—Clerical, and so forth—same as blue-collar procedures except references always are checked out.

Managerial employees—Multiple interviews, intelligence test, personality tests, and references.

Fabris added: "I've also been making a list of what's happened in selection in the last six months since I've been in this job."

1. Our best managerial candidate was lost because he refused to take the personality test we use, The Minnesota Multiphasic Personality Inventory. He said it was an invasion of his privacy.

2. For employees who handle expensive supplies, we use a polygraph test, too. We've had a few refuse to take it. Our thefts are high. We wonder if it's any good! My boss feels the polygraph is essential.

3. One man we hired is doing a good job. We accidentally found out he has a prison record. His supervisor wants to know how we missed that and wants to let him go. We have no policy on this, but I feel he's proved himself in three months on the job.

4. We're having a lot of trouble on the reference letters. When we ask people to rate the applicants on the basis of all factors, including references, we find the supervisors read different things into these letters.

5. Our turnover has been high. My boss thinks it's because we aren't matching the best people to the right jobs. I need your help.

Discussion question

1. You are Boyce Piersol. Make a list of additional information necessary to help Gigantic. How would you go about acquiring the information? Based on what you know now, what are the biggest problems, and what would you do about them?

---

5. BLOCK DRUG COMPANY

Block Drug Company is a large firm located near Boston. It employs several thousand persons.

One subunit of the firm is the research division. Research employs a number of scientists such as chemists and pharmacological scientists, assisted by laboratory technicians. The latter require training in the same fields but not as much as the scientists themselves.

Although much of the technicians' work is routine, to free the scientists for more creative work, many of the technicians are quite competent. These are given more challenging work. Often, teams of several scientists and a half dozen technicians work on the same research project. Synergy develops: All members of the team come up with new ideas and procedures.

Most of the technicians are women, and many of them are women helping "put hubby through" college or graduate school at one of Boston's many colleges and universities—M.I.T., Boston College, Northeastern, Boston University, or Harvard. As a result, frequently a technician leaves a project in the middle, when her husband finishes or drops out of a program.

Dr. Lawrence Pyrbomba, director of research for Block, has requested that the personnel department make recommendations to improve this situation and help develop a career pattern for lab technicians. Because of budgetary constraints, he is not able to increase their salary much above its current level, but fringe benefits such as insurance and pensions are very generous.

Discussion questions

1. Would it be feasible for the personnel department to develop a career pattern for the lab technicians? What benefits may be derived for the company?
2. How else can the company recognize employee performance other than pay increases?
3. What action might the company take to reduce turnover among the women technicians?

---

6.   SHALL BEATRICE BE RETAINED?*

State Agency was a state-administered unit located in an industrialized city that worked in conjunction with the Social Security Administration to determine eligibility for social security disability benefits. State Agency was a section of the larger State Department of Education's Division of Vocational Rehabilitation.

The relationship between the state and federal agencies was essentially one where local social security district offices handled the initial data gathering procedures and the financial side of the determination procedure, while State Agency developed the medical and vocational aspects. The activities of both were reviewed and coordinated by the Bureau of Disability Insurance in Baltimore, Maryland.

Due to the increasing numbers of people applying for existing social security disability benefit programs and to the overwhelming number of cases expected in a few months with the takeover by the Social Security Administration of the state-administered welfare programs of old-age assistance, aid to the blind, and aid to the permanently and totally disabled, State Agency was faced with a shortage of both professional and clerical personnel.

State Agency's staff was structured at the time in such a way that it had on its professional staff mostly people who had been there for five years or more. The professional staff consisted of two supervisors (one of whom was Bob Fields, who managed the agency), four consulting physicians, one quality assurance specialist, two continuing disability specialists, and six disability claims examiners.

---

* Note: This case was prepared by Danny L. Worrell and Leon C. Megginson of Louisiana State University as a basis for classroom discussion and not to illustrate either effective or ineffective handling of an administrative situation. Distributed by the Intercollegiate Case Clearing House, Soldiers Field, Boston, Massachusetts, 02163.

All names are disguised.

Bob Fields was 42 years old and had "worked his way up through the ranks." He had started out with the State Department of Education over 14 years previously and had been with State Agency ever since. He had 25 semester hours above a Master's degree in Education and had completed two semesters of law school. He was "a very easy-going man and he allowed his professional staff pretty much freedom so long as they did their job."

"Disability Claims Examiner" was the entry position for professional employees, and it required a college degree and the passing of the appropriate civil service test. Competition was keen for the job, as the salary was good and State Agency was in a desirable location.

State Agency's clerical staff was sufficient for each disability examiner, each continuing disability specialist, and each supervisor to have his or her own secretary. Each of the above professional employees was the direct supervisor over his or her secretary and was responsible for such things as signing leave forms and seeing to it that work was performed satisfactorily. The physicians and quality assurance specialists were assumed not to need their own secretarial help.

Mr. Field's secretary, Jennifer Hamilton, supervised the clerical staff. She was "young, attractive, and very efficient." A few of the other girls, however, occasionally resented her because they felt she was sometimes too harsh in her manner with them.

This, then, was the situation in State Agency some ten months ago when Sue Garrison was hired as a disability claims examiner and Beatrice Brown was hired as her secretary a month later.

Sue Garrison was 24 years old and had graduated from State University about a year and a half earlier in the top fourth of her class in personnel management. She thought of herself as being very "human-relations" oriented, and had in fact worked for a year as a social worker. She "adapted to the new job at State Agency quickly, made friends with other young examiners who had been recruited at the same time, and got along well with members of the older staff." All in all, she was "very pleased with her job and was performing quite satisfactorily."

Beatrice Brown, however, was another story. It seemed as though she just couldn't quite "cut the mustard." She had worked once before as a telephone operator, but this was her first clerical job. Beatrice received her secretarial training from Manpower Training which was also a program under the direction of the State Department of Education. Its focus was on training the underprivileged by providing basic skills which were taught in trade school environments.

Mr. Fields had actually "passed over" Beatrice several times on the clerical employment register before he decided to hire her. Her appearance "usually was rather unkempt" and she "was not well endowed with physical attributes." It was obvious from her appearance and her vocabulary that she came from a lower socioeconomic background. Also, as mentioned above, she had not worked in a clerical position before, and she had made a low score on her typing test. It was only because the demand for clerical workers was so unusually high at the time of her employment that her score was good enough to be considered under the civil service regulations. Ordinarily, her score would not have been high enough.

Mr. Fields, however, finally decided to hire Beatrice in spite of her obvious limitations. State Agency was rapidly expanding, needed clerical help immediately, and it was highly uncertain as to how long it would be before more qualified employees would be placed on the register. Mr. Fields also felt that since both State Agency and Manpower Training were under the direction of the Department of Education that he had somewhat of an obligation to "hire his own."

The main reason Mr. Fields hired Beatrice, however, was because he felt that "someone should give her a chance and because he felt sorry for her." In addition to the difficulties mentioned earlier, Beatrice had four children ranging in age from 14 months to six years and she had "an unemployed, unskilled, construction worker husband." Beatrice in sum "projected a very pathetic image."

As expected, Beatrice had difficulties on the job from the start. She often misunderstood Sue's requests, frequently left vital information off of determinations, often neglected to follow up on diaried information, and repeatedly misspelled short everyday words, not to mention the more complex medical terminology which was essential to this type of work.

Sue had to proofread all of Beatrice's work and she would pencil in the easier corrections, but Beatrice had to retype the more involved mistakes. This all took up valuable time, but Sue attempted always to point out the mistakes (even the smaller ones which she penciled in) to Beatrice. This resulted in a somewhat better performance, but a lot was still left to be desired.

Sue decided to talk the problem over with Mr. Fields. It was decided that Jennifer would devote extra time to training Beatrice and also get a couple of the other more experienced secretaries to help Beatrice when they were not too busy, or if Beatrice had emergencies.

For the next few months time passed slowly, but Beatrice's performance began steadily to improve. She was "not a lazy person and she really seemed to be trying hard." However, her performance was still not up to that of the other women, and she frequently required their help and continued to make more errors than they did. She also had a tendency to be absent or spend too much time on the phone because of her family difficulties. Whenever she was cautioned about these activities, though, her performance always seemed to pick up right away.

One day Mr. Fields called Sue into his office and stated that he wanted to discuss the approaching expiration of Beatrice's six months' probationary period. He told Sue some facts that the latter did not know about Beatrice's background and said that since it was Sue who would have "to live with" Beatrice if she were retained, he was therefore going to leave the decision of Beatrice's future with State Agency largely up to Sue.

Sue was somewhat unfamiliar with the options available to her under the civil service regulations, so she asked Mr. Fields to clarify the choices of action. Mr. Fields said that there were three. Beatrice could be fired, placed on permanent status, or her probation could be extended for another three months. Mr. Fields also stated that once an employee is placed on permanent status, it becomes much more difficult to terminate employment. Many thoughts darted through Sue's mind as she sat across the desk from Mr. Fields:

Will Beatrice continue to improve or will she always be substandard?

Does State Agency owe Beatrice extra consideration since her limitations were known at the time of her employment?

How much longer can State Agency keep asking the other girls to help Beatrice, since a landslide of cases is expected in the very near future?

Can, and should, State Agency do anything to try to improve Beatrice's home situation?

Finally, Sue wondered, "Do I have enough expertise in this area to make a valid decision which will greatly affect the lives of not only Beatrice but of the other five people that depend upon her for their support?"

Discussion questions

1. You are Sue. What action do you recommend regarding Beatrice? Justify.
2. Does the agency have the responsibility to hire and retain substandard employees because they were trained by the Manpower training program under the Department of Education? Why?
3. What effect could Beatrice have on the performance of the other secretaries in the office if she is retained?

7. AFFIRMATIVE ACTION?*

Belville Hospital is a large fully integrated hospital in Memphis, Tennessee. The hospital has 450 beds and presently is planning an expansion to 650 beds. The hospital has never experienced many personnel problems. However, recent actions taken by certain state and federal agencies have caused uneasiness among many of the employees.

Many organizations over the last few years have been approached by the Equal Employment Opportunity Commission regarding alleged discrimination in their hiring and promotion practices. In 1970, EEOC charged that certain hiring and promotion practices in the Belville Hospital were discrimi-

* Note: This case was prepared by Donald D. White, University of Arkansas, and H. William Vroman, Tennessee Tech University, as members of the SCRA. The case is to be used for teaching purposes and is not meant to reflect correct or incorrect practices.

Presented at a Case Workshop and distributed by the Intercollegiate Case Clearing House, Soldiers Field, Boston, Massachusetts 02163.

natory. After nearly two years of hearings and periodic negotiations, an agreement to resolve most EEOC issues was signed and judicially endorsed in a consent degree by a U.S. District Court. As a result, the EEOC moved to dismiss its charges against the hospital.

In a memorandum issued by the EEOC, the commission stated that the progress of Belville Hospital in fulfilling commitments that the consent decree set forth would be closely monitored for the next six years. Violations of the consent decree would make Belville liable to citation for contempt of court, and inadequate hiring of blacks, women, and other minorities for management-level positions.

The effect of the memorandum was quickly evident in hospital communications. For example, the following directive was issued to all persons responsible for acquiring personnel for nonentry level jobs:

In filling vacancies for nonentry level jobs (both inside and outside), Belville Hospital will continue to fill vacancies on the basis of best qualified and seniority. But if the hospital is unable to meet intermediate targets on this basis, a woman or minority member with less seniority and basic qualifications may be selected to permit a department to make satisfactory progress in meeting an intermediate target. Should there be no employees with appropriate basic skills who are available for selection, the company will hire, if necessary [sic] in order to make satisfactory progress in meeting an intermediate target.

The impact of this new program was felt throughout the organization. Such an example took place in the business office.

A case in point

The function of the assignment office was to assign new patients to appropriate rooms and floors, to maintain the patient records, and to communicate by phone with nursing stations when problems were encountered or specific information was necessary. The office was part of the Business Office (see Exhibit 1) and consisted of five records clerks (classified as semiskilled), three patient-contact assignors (classified as skilled), and an office manager. The procedures of this office were relatively complicated. Therefore, it was generally conceded that a period of approximately 12 months was required to learn all of the various procedures thoroughly.

The office had been managed by Ellen Nash for the last five years. Mrs. Nash had been with Belville for 17 years. She worked in the Processing Department for five years and as an assignment clerk in the Assignment Office for seven years. She had spent the last five years as the Assignment Office Manager. Mrs. Nash was a high school graduate. She was competent and well liked. Most of the employees recognized her as the "old pro" in the office. When difficult problems in the office arose, they usually found their way to her desk because of her experience.

The Processing Office was located in the room adjacent to the Assignment Office and had many interrelated activities with Assignment. There was a sequential interdependence between the two offices. Processing handled all patients upon termination of their stay at Belville and maintained continuous records on all out-patients required to take multiple treatments over a period of time. Therefore, the Processing Office depended upon records forwarded to them by the Assignment Office. The manager of the Processing Office was Mr. Dave Randle. Mr. Randle was a business college graduate and had been manager of the Processing Department for about nine months. As a result of his inexperience, he too depended upon Mrs. Nash to help him with difficult problems.

Ed Crosby, the Hospital Administrator Manager, was aware of Ellen Nash's ability and competence. He also was under pressure to meet his assigned targets for placing a certain percentage of women and minorities in various levels of management within his department. Crosby saw in the Assignment and Processing organizations an opportunity to give Ellen the responsibility for both offices. For all practical purposes, she already was informally administering both offices, anyway. In addition, he thought that the change would open up another position which in turn could be filled by another woman or a black. Ed was convinced that the reorganization would be in the best interest of Ellen and the company. Shortly thereafter, he met with Ellen and discussed his proposed action. Ellen's new role was explained to her:

Ed Crosby: This is a completely new position, Ellen. Your job will be to provide general supervision to the two offices and to help the two office managers maintain current efficiency levels. You really will be serving as an advisor, since I still want the day-to-day decisions to be made by the office managers. By the way, Dave Randle will remain in his present position and we should have a new assignment manager on the job in a week or so. Does everything sound ok to you?

Ellen was pleased with Mr. Crosby's decision. She said that she would do her best to help maintain the good work that currently was being done in the offices. She said that she really had no questions other than who would replace her as Assignment Manager. Mr. Crosby indicated that no decision had been made yet.

The replacement

As Mr. Crosby had suggested, it was not long before someone was hired to replace Ellen as Assignment Office Manager. His name was John Matthews. John was a graduate of Grambling University, a predominantly black school, where he majored in business administration.

He had taken a special course in hospital administration while in school and had worked for about three months in a business office of a large urban hospital. There, he had worked with customer billing and assisted the business manager more or less as a trouble shooter.

John also received limited training for an assignment-office management

EXHIBIT 1
Original hospital organization

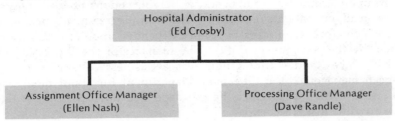

position. Upon joining the Belville organization, John was given the position that Ellen previously held. (See Exhibits 1 and 2)

John had been in his new position for four weeks, during which several problems had arisen in the Assignment Office. The problems had caused some dissension among the employees and had markedly decreased the office's efficiency. Errors in assignments had caused numerous complaints from patients. Ed Crosby informed Ellen of one such incident and asked her to look into it. Ellen examined the records of John's office and determined that a mistake in posting had been made by a newly-hired girl. Ellen asked the girl responsible for the error about what she had done. The girl told Ellen that she had asked Mr. Matthews what to do regarding the assignment and that he had told her he simply did not know. Since Ellen was not available to the girl at the time she used her own judgment on the matter, and her decision turned out to be wrong.

After hearing the girl's explanation, Ellen decided to confront John about the problem. She did so the same afternoon as he was preparing to leave the office. She told him he should know better ". . . then to leave the girls in a situation like this," and that he should call her if any other cases similar to this one arose. John was obviously upset by the nature and openness of the discussion. He thought for a moment and then replied, "This

EXHIBIT 2
Reorganized hospital

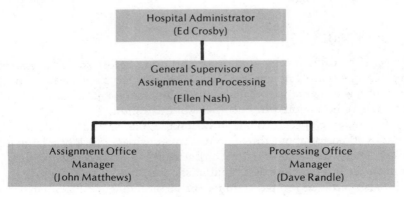

is my office, and I can take care of it. Anyway, you weren't here when the girl needed the help." After his remark, he turned and left the room. The next day he told one of the girls in the office (the only black Assignment Clerk), I'm not about to ask a woman who only has a high school diploma how to run my job." A few minor complaints continued to be registered against the assignment office. However, no further altercations took place between Ellen and John for some time.

New problems

Approximately one month later, an incident arose that was related to an employee practice formerly condoned by Ellen when she held the position of Assignment Manager. Several of the women in the office had received permission from Ellen to take off work on occasion for appointments with their beauticians. Ellen and the women had come to an agreement that anyone taking off work for such an appointment would make up the time by either coming in early, working through lunch, or working late. John had noticed the practice during the first few weeks he was on the job but had said nothing. Finally, he issued a memo to the women which stated that they would have to make their appointments on their own time, and that they would no longer be allowed to do so during working hours.

One evening one of the older clerks asked John if she could leave an hour early so that she could be on time for an appointment with her beautician. John responded by pulling out and waving the memo. He reaffirmed his position on the request, and the woman walked away. When the time came for the appointment, the woman got up and walked toward the door. John stepped before her and told her, "you can go if you want to, but if you do, don't come back tomorrow." The woman left and came back the next day. John did not mention the incident to her. None of the other women left work for similar appointments after the incident. However, John overheard them threatening to do so.

Eventually, this incident and others were passed on to Ellen. She confided in one of the girls, "sometimes I think this job is just a lot of headaches." She decided that she must have a meeting about these problems and her own future with the company with Ed Crosby. As she was about to enter Mr. Crosby's office, Dave Randle walked out. He looked sheepishly at Ellen and then quickly walked away.

Ed Crosby looked up and addressed Ellen.

Crosby: Good morning, Ellen; I was just about to give you a call. You look disturbed. What's the matter?

Ellen: I guess I am just not sure about this job anymore, Mr. Crosby. I've told you about some of the problems that have been occurring in the Assignment Office, and they don't seem to be getting any better. Frankly, I don't think John Matthews cares enough about the girls that we have working in the office. I have been hearing more complaints about the way he treats them. Also, some of the girls think that he is giving special treatment to the new black girl that we just hired. I just don't know what I am going to do.

Crosby: Ellen, perhaps you are getting too involved with the personal problems of the girls in the offices. You know, that's Randle's and Matthews' jobs.

Ellen: Too close to them! Why, in my new position, I don't even have a chance to get involved with the day-to-day operations of the offices, anymore. I have so much paper work to do and so many meetings to go to that I can't see to it that the offices are being run properly.

Crosby: You're right, Ellen, we do have a problem. The efficiency rating of the Assignment Office and the Processing Office are both lower than before all of these changes were made. I have talked to John Matthews about this matter, and he feels that you have not given him enough help. He also thinks that the girls who work around him favor you. Dave Randle also is having some problems. Since he now reports to you rather than directly to me, he has the feeling that he has been demoted.

Ellen: I get that feeling, myself. He seems to resent it whenever I offer him a suggestion. In fact, he hardly ever comes to me any more for advice.

To tell you the truth, Mr. Crosby, I am not as sure about this job now as I was before. If these problems aren't straightened out pretty soon, I think I'd rather have my old job back.

Mr. Crosby assured Ellen that he would do what he could to help her restore the harmonious and productive atmosphere that had existed before the personnel changes. When Ellen left the room, Ed Crosby called in his secretary. "Get me the personnel folders on Matthews, Randle, and Nash."

Discussion questions

1. What factors contributed to Ellen's dislike for her present job?
2. Why is John having trouble managing the once smoothly operating department?
3. What might have prevented the present situation? If you were Mr. Crosby, what action would you take to rectify the problem as it now exists?

8. PENNSYLVANIA OIL COMPANY

Jane Barbour is employed as a clerk-typist at Pennsylvania Oil Company, a medium-sized firm in Pittsburgh. She has been there for two years and her evaluations have been good. She is a good worker, as Dale Bunting, her supervisor, has told her repeatedly.

Jane supports her invalid mother and needs all the wages she can get. Recently she received an offer from Meyer Construction which would increase her wages about 75 cents an hour.

Jane likes her work at PO because it is easy to get to from her apartment, the hours are good, she likes her boss, and the benefits, especially the health benefits, are adequate. The new job with Meyer Construction would be harder to get to, and she doesn't know if she'd like the boss as well.

Jane went to Dale and said: "Mr. Bunting, I like it here at Pennsylvania Oil, but my wages aren't the best. I have an offer of $30 a week more. Do you think you could do something for me?"

Dale replied, "Jane, you are one of the best girls we have. You know many companies will offer you more to leave than to stay. I'm not sure I can get you the whole $30, but it'll be close."

Jane thanked Dale. She phoned Meyer Construction and declined the job. She told the details to her best friend, Mary Castalini, who worked in payroll at PO. Mary said: "Oh, I'm so glad for you, Jane. You are so underpaid and I want you to stay."

When Dale went to Joseph Stutz, his boss, in Jane's behalf, he got a shock. "Sorry, Dale," Joe said. "We're in a profit squeeze this quarter. I've been told to approve no increases for anyone. Just got the word."

"But Joe," Dale protested, "I promised Jane and she turned the other job down."

"OK Dale, tell you what I'll do," said Joe. "Let's give her 20 cents an hour now, and I'll try to up it later when we get out of the slump."

Jane was sick for a few days. When she returned, the whole office was in an uproar. Mary had told everyone about the "insult" that management had given Jane by awarding her "that stingy 20-cent raise."

Discussion questions

1. What problems are likely to result from Mary's gossip about Jane's raise?
2. The situation with Jane's salary may be an indicator of other problems with the company's compensation policies. What are they?
3. How can the company prevent similar situations from occurring?

9.   STATE GOVERNMENT

Harley Fleenor is responsible for personnel for a state in the western United States. An official in the state government has a problem.

State Senator Roger McAreavy, a Republican, has just made a fiery speech on the floor of the Senate. He was attacking inefficient and ineffective government. In his speech, which was widely covered throughout the state, he said:

I suppose that a simple businessman like myself just can't comprehend really complex matters like state government. But I'll tell you that any business which had the record this administration does would be bankrupt by now. If Republicans were running the state, it would be run on a businesslike basis. Instead, we have the wholesale incompetence and waste of this Shaw administration which I'm sure when the people wake up will be thrown unceremoniously out the front door of the statehouse and the governor's mansion. Until that happy day, I guess the people will have to swallow hard and pay higher taxes for the incompetence in Capital City.

Even the TV picked it up. Rarely does the electronic media give much play to state government administration.

The facts the esteemed senator cited were excerpted from the recently published report by the Good Government League. Normally, these reports are filed in libraries and sent to women's clubs without much comment. But this is an election year—three months from the primaries and six months from the election. Governor Shaw has announced that he will run for reelection. Senator McAreavy is running unapposed in the Republican primary.

The Good Government League's report covered many aspects of the state administration. The part that the senator cited was on page 10. It criticized the state administration for having the worst employee turnover in the area. The report showed that this state had a higher turnover than the other nine western states. It compared the state to *overall* turnover and in each category of employment as well. The report said:

It is distressing to learn that our beloved state finishes absolute last in every category of employment turnover. Turnover is important because it is expensive and leads to gross ineffectiveness. It is expensive because every time an employee leaves, the state must incur recruiting costs, selection costs, and training costs. It is ineffective because everyone knows that there is a period during which all new employees have not reached their peak effectiveness. During that time, the employee makes mistakes. He also slows down the wheels of justice or the hospital. Something *must* be done to stop this waste of the taxpayer's money!

About an hour after the speech was on TV, the governor's office called, and the governor's administrative assistant requested that Fleenor be in the governor's office at 7:30 A.M. tomorrow to brief the governor prior to his regular Wednesday press conference. Governor Shaw knows he will get a question about McAreavy's speech, and he wants to be ready.

That's why Fleenor is still at his desk at 10 P.M. Tuesday trying to prepare a briefing for the governor.

The trouble is that the figures are true. The state has had terrible turnover. Why? Well, the pay the state government offers has been poor for years. Often, what happens is that the government winds up with those employees who cannot get employment elsewhere. This may be so because they had a bad work record or because they are not adequately trained. Once they are trained, they leave for better jobs. Or the less desirable employees get fired.

One supervisor in the conservation department has characterized his plight this way. "They send us people who come into my office and say 'Oh! What is that machine there?' I reply that it is a typewriter. As soon as they are adequately trained for clerk typists, they go cross-town to the mining company or the lumber company at a 33⅓ percent raise."

The state has always had this problem, but it has gotten worse in the last few years. For one thing, more industry has come into Capital City. Second, the older industry has expanded. Since the population hasn't increased that much, the salary structure of private industry has risen to attract the people. The legislature was made aware of this, but in the spirit of "economy in government" did not raise the salary scale enough.

What the state does have is a very generous benefit plan. Most of the items in the plan are nontaxable income. In fact, the state's plan is more generous than most of the industry in the area. Too often, state employees have left for a raise in industry but fewer benefits, so that they are really behind after taxes. But that is a hard message to get across to large numbers of employees.

Fleenor has run a series of articles about the matter in the house organ, *The Stater*, but readership studies of the magazine are depressing. Most people don't read it. He has encouraged supervisors to discuss this, but his followup studies find that most supervisors don't do it. Their excuse is that the benefits are complicated it's hard to explain to employees, many of whom are not interested.

Fleenor wonders what to tell Governor Shaw in the morning.

Discussion question

1. You are Harley Fleenor. Prepare the brief for Governor Shaw. Prepare a program to improve the turnover situation. Assume for plan 1 that the legislature refuses to increase wages; for plan 2, that it raises them one half of the difference between the present salaries.

10.   CHICAGO MANUFACTURING, INC. (A)

Chicago Manufacturing is a small manufacturer of heavy equipment. It is located in an older section of Chicago. The plant building was constructed in 1897.

CM employs 278 blue-collar workers. Charles Reinke, president, had always run a tight ship. He has tried to keep managerial and staff employment to a minimum. Recently he has been noting more references in his trade magazines to the perils of the Occupational Safety and Health Act. Case studies of suits and similar proceedings by these interfering government inspectors worried him.

Reinke believed he ran a safe plant, but at times in the past he had "finessed" safety inspectors on a few minor points of violation. Tickets to the Bears games, a good dinner with a few drinks, and a nice Christmas present had done it. He wondered if the new safety emphasis the politicians were pushing would be different.

Reinke called in his personnel man, Ed Barner, to talk about it. "How likely are we to get hung by these new OSHA regulations, Ed? When is the government going to stay out of business? All they want is a big contribution to their campaign fund, anyway."

"Chuck, I really don't know how we'd come out on this one. You know, we've never pushed safety here. Oh, we mention it once in a while and put up those posters the safety group sends out, but other than that. . . . Our accident rate is up, though."

"What should we do to find out, Ed?"

"At a recent meeting of our personnel group, Harlan Bentzen, a safety specialist, spoke. He's a consultant, but probably for a couple of hundred bucks we could find out where we stand."

"OK Ed, hire him and let's get this over with." The consultant was hired. His report to Reinke was as follows:

To: Charles Reinke
From: Harlan Bentzen
Subject: OSHA Prevention Report

I have analyzed your safety records and note that you are running 10% higher than your industry on major accidents and 22% higher on minor accidents. Some of this can be attributed to the fact that new workers are not given safety orientation. About 20% turnover each year means you get 40 new ones yearly. You have no safety program reminders for experienced workers, either.

Because your records are not accurately kept, it was arbitrary to classify accidents as major or minor. Your insurance company for workers' compensation provides no safety services. No follow-up on accident reports has been made, nor is there even a safety committee at your plant.

Much of your equipment is antiquated. The unsafe areas are not carefully marked or painted. In short, I feel an OSHA inspection would cause you real trouble.

I recommend the development of a safety program at once. I could do this for you. I estimate it would involve 10 days of my time at $275 per day.

Sincerely,
Harlan Bentzen

Reinke was discussing the report with Barner. "This is just a snow job to get himself almost three big ones for 10 days 'work.' I think I'm going to file it in the circular file."

"I don't know, Chuck," Barner replied. "I received notice that OSHA inspectors will make a scheduled inspection in six weeks."

Discussion question

1. You are Ed Barner. How do you induce Reinke to do something, if you feel it should be done?

11. CHICAGO MANUFACTURING, INC. (B)

Two weeks after Bentzen's report, Harry Conners was severely hurt in a machine accident. His work group, with whom he was popular, was very angry and complained bitterly. Then they walked out in protest. They demanded a meeting of their union, a unit of the Machinists Union. As one of the group, Sam Tender, said to the steward, Chip Flanders, "Chip, when are you going to do your job? Accidents are increasing every day in this place. You know they don't care anything about us. Do we all have to lose an arm before you act? The government is supposed to watch out for things like this, but where have the government inspectors been?"

Another worker, Dave Pendleton, said: "Listen, my wife is really carrying on to me about this. Sally Conners is about to have a nervous breakdown. We want action. There was some kind of safety guy snooping around a couple of weeks ago. You find out what happened on his report. How about us getting the government in here? Or how about a strike? Workers' compensation can never pay you back the pain an accident can cause."

Flanders had rarely seen the employees so mad. The next morning, he went to see Ed Barner. He told Barner what had happened at the meeting. Then he said: "Look, Ed, I want to look over the report of that safety consultant to see what he recommended and what you've done about it."

Barner replied, "That report's confidential, Chip."

Flanders yelled. "Don't give me that nonsense about it being confidential! I'm serious. We'll have the government in here or you'll have a strike on!"

Barner was really worried now. He went to see Charles Reinke and told him all that had happened. Reinke sat and listened impatiently. Then he said, "You are too upset, Barner. This'll all blow over. You wait and see."

Discussion question

1. You are Ed Barner. What do you do now?

12.   DEEP SOUTH UNIVERSITY*

Dr. Peter Scott, still somewhat in a state of shock, sat back in his chair and wondered how his ten years' teaching experience, scholarly research, and activities in the professional zoological societies could possibly prepare him to face the problem with which he was now confronted. Yet, only six months earlier when his appointment to academic vice president was announced, he and the rest of the university community had no question regarding his qualifications for the position. Dr. Charles Johnson, vice president for community and public relations in the university administration, had just left Dr. Scott to ponder the developing situation and decide upon a course of action after reviewing all of the pertinent facts at his disposal.

Dr. Scott's involvement with this problem had begun only three hours before with the ring of his office telephone. Dr. James Durand, the chairman of the history department, had called to request an appointment with Dr. Scott. When questioned regarding the reason for the appointment, Dr. Durand had been quite evasive, saying only that a serious problem was developing in his department and it was not the sort of problem which should be discussed over the telephone. The date was August 23, five days before registration, and Dr. Scott was puzzled by the intrigue as he waited for Dr. Durand to come across campus. An appointment request at this time was particularly unusual as the campus was practically deserted, with professors and students alike resting up from the summer session just concluded and preparing for the new semester about to begin.

Dr. Durand entered the office rather flushed and breathless, seated himself, and began with no words wasted on idle chatter: "You've met Charles Bottcher, who teaches several freshman history courses for us, haven't you?"

After thinking a moment, Dr. Scott replied that he couldn't recall having met the individual, but he was vaguely familiar with his record and knew Mr. Bottcher had been with the university for about four years. Dr. Durand replied:

Well, you're quite correct there, but I'd better tell you a little more about this person. He came to us highly recommended from a state university in the Midwest where he had just completed work on his MA. He was hired as an instructor of history to teach both parts of a two-semester American history course, 113–114. He was 23 years old when he began teaching at DSU and has recently turned 27. None of us in the department got to know him very well, as he is a rather shy, studious individual. However, he has always seemed to get along quite well with his colleagues in the department and our secretary, Mrs. Moore. He also seems to have been quite effective in his classroom duties. I have been hoping that he will decide to pursue doctoral work some day and eventually return to our faculty with

* Note: This case was prepared by Associate Professor Ernest B. Gurman and Assistant Professor Roland B. Cousins, both of the University of Southwestern Louisiana. This case is intended to be a basis for classroom discussion and not to illustrate either effective or ineffective handling of an administrative situation.

Distributed by the Intercollegiate Case Clearing House, Soldiers Field, Boston, Mass. 02163. All rights reserved to the contributors.

a Ph.D. Even though he has shown no such inclination yet, I had just about decided to extend tenure to him, since his rapport with students is quite good in the counseling situation and on the student evaluations he has been rather consistently rated near the top of my faculty. As you well know, we have to make tenure decision this year, and I never like to wait until the last moment to discuss it with my faculty.

Mr. Bottcher was not employed this summer and I haven't seen him since May, but today I got the shock of my life. Mrs. Moore, our secretary, told me that she ran into Mr. Bottcher at the supermarket last evening. She said that she saw this person standing directly in front of her in the check-out line, thought it a vaguely familiar figure, but didn't pay much attention. As the two got to the counter, the person in front smiled to Mrs. Moore, and addressed her by name with a warm greeting. It was then she realized that here was Mr. Bottcher appearing as a well-dressed, attractive young lady. Mrs. Moore was speechless, as I imagine I would have been too, and merely mumbled an embarrassed hello. Mr. Bottcher waited until Mrs. Moore's groceries had been bagged and walked with her to her car. He said that he was sorry that he had caused her embarrassment, but that he was glad to have met her when he did. He had just returned to town and said that he had not known how to break his news to his colleagues in the department and the university administration. Now, since he had seen Mrs. Moore, he thought that the situation would be less awkward if she would discuss his position with me.

He then proceeded to confide in her regarding his background and the decision upon which he had finally acted this summer. The gist of what he told her was that he for many years had felt that he should have been created a woman. Somehow a tragic error had been made and he had been born and grown up as a female in a male's body. Apparently, the obstacles were tremendous and he had tried to identify with the male sex in every way conceivable until he came to the realization that it was impossible to do so. After passing rigorous screening designed to distinguish between true transsexuals and others merely temporarily dissatisfied with, or unclear of, their sexual identities, he was accepted this summer for a sex change operation by a large eastern hospital. Surgery was performed early in June, and he is now living totally as a woman. He has already legally changed his name from Charles Andrew Bottcher to Charlene Ann Bottcher, and is now in the process of having all other records changed. Charlene told Mrs. Moore to tell me that she will be there as expected on August 27 for the first faculty meeting and she is anxious to begin the new semester. She said she feels better than she can ever remember feeling and that it's nice to be at peace with one's self. Mrs. Moore did also mention that Charlene had investigated her civil rights and she was sure that the university would not choose to violate them. Honestly, Dr. Scott, I don't know what to do about this situation.

Dr. Scott's initial reaction was one of amazement, but he remembered telling Dr. Durand just to sit tight and see what developed. He also told Dr. Durand that he would talk to him later, after he discussed the situation with others in the administration.

Shortly after Dr. Durand left, Dr. Scott met with Dr. Johnson, another rather recent appointment to the administration, and informed him of Bottcher's new status. As vice president for community and public relations, Johnson's immediate reaction to this development was that of concern over public reaction. DSU is located in a quite conservative area of the country by most standards, and the town of Centerville, in which the campus is located, is in one of the most conservative areas of the state. Dr. Johnson could readily imagine state legislators outraged, local community leaders appalled, and irate parents of students calling and demanding that all perverts be removed from the staff. Possible student reaction was also discussed at length, as obviously Ms. Bottcher was going to be a topic of conversation on campus. Dr. Scott and Dr. Johnson were both wondering if this would affect Ms. Bottcher's effectiveness in the classroom.

Dr. Johnson and Dr. Scott parted with the understanding that they would each consider the various alternative courses of action open to the University and the implications of those courses of action, and would decide on the best approach for the university to adopt. They would meet tomorrow morning to make a decision regarding Ms. Bottcher's future at DSU, for they felt that a decision should be reached before the opening of the fall semester.

Later that same day, Dr. Johnson called Dr. Scott back and said,

It looks like our alternatives for action may be narrowing. The president of the Bulldog Booster Club just called the president of the university and demanded to know what was going to be done about this homosexual that was now on the faculty. Further, he didn't see how he could continue to support an institution that would allow our youth to placed in contact with deviates of this type.

Discussion questions

1. You are Dr. Scott. What action will you take?
2. Could Dr. Scott justify not granting Ms. Bottcher tenure without reference to the recent operation and concern for public reaction?
3. What rights does Ms. Bottcher have regarding her employment with the university?

13. LEESBURG POLICE DEPARTMENT: UNFAIR LABOR PRACTICES*

From 1951 to 1973, the police of the Town of Leesburg were represented by the Leesburg Police Relief Association as their bargaining agent. During this period, the association had some limited success in obtaining wage increases and fringe benefits.

By 1973, many younger officers who had been union members in their previous jobs had joined the Leesburg force. These younger officers began to influence the association. Under the supervision of the state labor board

* Note: This case was prepared by Richard M. Ayres, FBI Academy, and Thomas L. Wheelen, McIntire School of Commerce, University of Virginia, as the basis for class discussion. Copyright © 1975 by Thomas L. Wheelen and Richard M. Ayres.

Presented at a case workshop and distributed by Intercollegiate Case Clearing House, Soldiers Field, Boston, Mass. 02163. All rights reserved to the contributors.

an election was held to select a new union to represent the policemen. The International Public Employees Association (IPEA) was chosen to represent all officers up to the rank of lieutenant.

At approximately the same time, the city engaged a well-known labor attorney and also created a position of manpower director for the city. The man chosen for this position was a former local industrial union president.

The first contract obtained by the IPEA provided the policemen with a wage increase of approximately $1,000 over an 18-month period. In addition, they negotiated for a four-and-two schedule, that is, four days on and two days off, and incentive pay for college credits.

On January 1, 1975, the new mayor took office, following a campaign pledging fiscal austerity. This had been his mode of operation in two previous terms as mayor.

The police contract had expired on December 31, 1974, at which time the outgoing mayor, who had lost the election, declined to start new negotiations. The new mayor stalled negotiations until the city budget had been adopted.

A few token meetings between police and the city took place, but no settlement was reached. All negotiations finally terminated in late April, with the city taking the position that no part of the previous contract was binding. The chief then initiated rotating shifts for the department, which would commence on June 8, 1975. The union interpreted his action as a means by the city to force the IPEA back to the negotiating table. At the first meeting the city agreed to settle the wage issue but refused to negotiate on the rotating shifts.

The IPEA then sought a court injunction to enjoin the chief of police from initiating the rotating shifts on the date planned, June 8, 1975. The chief had wanted rotating shift because he felt it would increase the efficiency of his department, and it would afford the younger men opportunities to experience all phases of police work on all three shifts. The IPEA argument was that his system did not recognize seniority.

At the same time, the IPEA members and their wives, children, and friends began to picket city hall during working hours. Both young and older members of the force joined the picket line. This lasted for one month. During this time, the mayor and the chief received many telephoned threats, and their homes were subject to acts of vandalism. The issue of picketing and vandalism received a great deal of local media coverage.

The police then devised a new picketing technique, that of asking the public to "honk" their car horn to show support for their police as they drove past City Hall. The picketers carried signs asking the public to participate in this program. Many complaints began to pour in from merchants, employees in the city hall, and adjoining buildings. Also, the city had an anti-noise law which outlawed "honking" horns unless emergency conditions existed.

The mayor also happened to be a farmer, and several of the picketers' placards read, "Send the ass back to the farm."

Many acts of vandalism continued and resulted in further damage to city property. At this point, the city filed an unfair labor practice against the IPEA before the state labor board. The court turned down the IPEA's request to enjoin the chief on the rotating shift issue.

The union's next move was to place advertisements in the local paper to solicit support from the local merchants to force the mayor back to the bargaining table. This campaign was unsuccessful, and the IPEA then announced a citywide boycott of all local merchants. Police officers and their wives were put on buses and taken to the next city to do their shopping. Pictures of this action were in the local paper, and local merchants were enraged.

Picket lines began to thin after Memorial Day. There was a great deal of dissatisfaction within the union and its leadership. It was the younger members who developed the strike tactics. The sick list began to grow, and many of the policemen eligible for retirement applied for it, rather than go on the rotating shifts. On June 9, the mayor fired five probationary police officers for violations of department rules and regulations. The probationary period for these five officers expired on June 20, 1975. The IPEA quickly claimed that these officers were fired because of their union involvement, and filed an unfair labor practice claim against the city.

The vandalism and phone threats continued. On June 19, two local male adults were arrested, tried, and convicted in the district court for vandalism and sentenced with orders to make restitution. The two individuals declined to implicate any members of the police department. The city again initiated an unfair labor action against the IPEA.

Discussion questions

1. Where there any unfair labor practices committed by either the city of Leesburg or the IPEA?
2. Did the IPEA evaluate the negative impact the tactic of boycotting the local merchants might have on their objectives?
3. Does the union have a responsibility to prevent acts of vandalism or to take appropriate action to deter future incidents?
4. How did the relationship between the IPEA and the city management contribute to the labor conflict?

A. INCIDENT CASES

In incident cases, only the basic data are printed in the book. After analyzing the data presented, questions should be formulated for the instructor, who has additional data available if the right questions are asked.

14. BOWEN CANDY COMPANY

Bowen Candy Company is a large candy and snack manufacturing enterprise with headquarters in Toronto, Ontario. The firm has a plant in Moncton, New Brunswick. Ray Munneke, the personnel manager, has been interviewing candidates for a supervisory position at this plant.

One candidate is John Neighbor. The plant manager, Paul Leib, sent him to Munneke. Neighbor is 22, seems like a nice chap, but doesn't measure up to the other choices. He is from Toronto. He has no experience, took some courses in commerce at the University of Toronto, where he received average grades. He did not receive a degree. A nice chap, but he is not impressive. His test scores were average.

Another candidate is George Fetter. Fetter has a degree from McGill in business and has worked summers in plants. His personality is strong and likeable. He scored the highest on the tests.

The third candidate is Henry Anthony. Anthony did well at the University of Vermont. He worked his way through college and had the second highest scores on the test. He seems to have good management potential.

At a recent lunch, Leib asked Munneke how the supervisor decision was coming.

Munneke: It's coming along fine. I have all the information, now that the test scores are in. I can't make up my mind between Anthony and Fetter.

Leib: I thought I sent you John Neighbor. Why isn't he in the running?

Munneke: Oh, he's a nice chap. I really like him. But on test scores, grades, interviews, everything, he comes out last. Sorry.

Leib: Look Ray, I guess you didn't follow me. Hire Neighbor!

15. PERFORMANCE EVALUATION

This situation occurred in a large service organization in a medium-sized midwestern city in the United States. The individuals involved are the departmental supervisor, Nancy Smith, and Joe Adams, a member of the professional staff reporting directly to Smith. Both are in their early thirties.

Adams worked for the organization for about three months. During this time his performance was marginal. His work was sloppy. He lacked initiative and had to be told exactly what to do; even with intense supervision, he often failed to carry through with assignments properly.

Smith submitted a three-month performance rating on Adams, a standard procedure with new employees. Given his marginal performance, Adams received a poor rating. Company policy also required that anyone who received a poor evaluation had to have a number of counseling sessions with his or her immediate supervisor. The purpose of these sessions was to point out the worker's strong and weak points and to try to help the worker bring his or her performance up to standard.

Smith called Adams into her office for one of these sessions. During the conference, Smith suggested tactfully that perhaps Adams would be happier and do better in some other line of work. At this point, Adams put his head down on the desk. Finally, he groaned and said "I can't take this," and lay down on the floor. Smith immediately summoned medical assistance. By the time attendants arrived with the wheelchair, Adams had recovered enough to protest that he did not need their help. Smith insisted that he be taken in the wheelchair to the company physician's office, which was in the same building. Adams returned to his desk shortly thereafter.

When she asked the medical personnel what had happened when Adams arrived at their office, Smith learned that Adams had not told the doctor about lying down on the floor. He merely asked for treatment for his sinuses.

The following morning Smith arranged with the personnel department to have another counseling session in the personnel office, in the presence of a representative of the personnel department, Tom Long. The discussion took the same general pattern as the one the previous afternoon. At about the same point in the conversation, Adams again sprawled on the floor. After remaining on the floor for several minutes, Adams said, "Go on." Long replied, "That's all right, we can wait until you are ready." Finally, Adams returned to his chair, and the discussion proceeded.

Adams subsequently admitted to having had psychiatric counseling; however, he was never institutionalized. One disconcerting feature of this situation was Adams's frank statement on a number of occasions that his use of marijuana helped to clear his sinuses; there is speculation whether this had anything to do with his erratic behavior.

Smith is in a quandary. She wonders whether she should have handled the counseling differently. She wonders what one should do when an apparently healthy person behaves in this manner.

16. TELEVISION SALES

KYYY is a television station broadcasting from Sante Fe, New Mexico. In the TV sales division, Dick Eastman is the boss. One of his salesmen is Nick Dipietro. Dipietro has been employed by KYYY for a year and a half. He graduated with an associate of arts in business administration from a nearby junior college. He tried several jobs, but at age 24 he took the job at KYYY. About that time he got married; he and his wife Consuela have a son, Nick, Jr.

Dipietro likes his job. Like many other people, he worries about money. TV stations do not necessarily pay very well. Many people view TV work as a "glamour" job and are willing to work for less.

Eastman has regular performance appraisals with his salesmen. Later, he discusses future compensation with the salesmen. He does this yearly.

Dipietro knew he was about due for a compensation session with Eastman. He and his wife were all excited about getting a raise. They felt they needed the money now that there was a new baby. Finally, Eastman told Dipietro he would like to have lunch with him. After they had returned to the office, their conversation came to the point.

Eastman: Nick, I asked you in because it's about time to talk raise with you. You've done a good job, especially since you are so new. The company has not been very profitable this year, and we have a lid on raises to some degree. However, I'm very pleased to tell you that starting now your pay envelope will be $20 a month thicker than last month. One final thing, I always warn my men not to discuss their compensation with others at the office . . .

Dipietro: (interrupting): Don't worry, boss, I won't discuss it. I'm just as ashamed of it as you are!

At this, Dipietro made an excuse about a sales call he had to make and thanked Eastman for his time.

17. UNION OFFICE

At a large local of the United Auto Workers in a major eastern U.S. city, the business agent has a problem. Actually, he has two problems— Polly Rea and Rhonda Hart.

These women work in the office doing routine clerical work, such as typing, stenography, and filing. They always seem to be bickering with each other over who does the most work. They don't seem to like each other and have even begun to curse each other at work. This disturbs the others. Ed Dhanani, the business agent, has called them to come to his office in two hours to get this straightened out. He is sitting there wondering how he'll handle this.

B. ROLE-PLAYING EXERCISES

18. EGLOFF PLASTICS

Egloff Plastics Company (EPC) is a medium-sized manufacturer of industrial plastics. The company's main location is in the Bronx, a part of New York City.

Recently, Richard Hutcheon, head of the bookkeeping department, had a chat with Ernesto Munoz. Munoz is one of the younger bookkeepers in Hutcheon's department.

About a month ago, an opening for a senior bookkeeper had developed. Munoz had indicated an interest in the job. Hutcheon had not taken this very seriously, for Munoz was having a hard job doing his present job well. His supervisor, Mervyn Eastman, told Hutcheon that Munoz made more errors than anyone in the department.

> **Eastman:** Really, he isn't qualified to do what he's doing now. We only hired him because he's Puerto Rican. We thought we'd give him a chance. He's had twice the training our other bookkeepers received. I spend three times as much time with him as I do with others, training him and correcting his work. He seems to be a slow learner.

Later, Munoz stopped in to see Hutcheon.

> **Munoz:** I didn't get that promotion. I know the reason. Eastman is prejudiced against Puerto Ricans. I think I'll file a complaint with the EEOC. There are no Puerto Ricans here in jobs other than the lowest ones, even though New York has a large percentage of Puerto Ricans.

Hutcheon pointed out that Samuel Rubinowitz, who had gotten the job, had several years of bookkeeping classes and three more years' experience than Munoz. This didn't impress Munoz, who walked out mentioning a visit to EEOC.

Hutcheon is 42 years old, a graduate of NYU's accounting program. He's had 15 years' experience with EPC, mostly in accounting. He likes his job, and the company and feels it has not discriminated against Munoz.

Munoz is 24 years old, a high school graduate. He took one course in bookkeeping in his junior year of high school. He had a hard time getting a good job. He believes that it was because he was a Puerto Rican. He has had two years' bookkeeping experience, one at EPC. Before that, he worked in a restaurant, a gas station, and served in the army.

19. TROY HARLOW

Troy Harlow is a salesman for the Wheeler Cement Company (WCC). This company has headquarters in Seattle and plants around the northwestern United States and western Canada. Harlow lives in Missoula, Montana, and is assigned a territory.

Harlow's boss is Jack Currie. He is explaining the situation to the sales manager, R. E. Stick.

Currie: Troy has the capabilities for being a great salesman for WCC. He is capable, knowledgeable, and can do a good job. When I work the territory with him, we make a lot of calls and a lot of sales. When I go on to another territory, his sales fall off. I have 12 salesmen to supervise. I can't work with him all the time. My territory is a large one. How do you motivate a guy to do the job you know he can do?

Stick: I really don't know much about him. Tell me about him.

Currie: Troy is 36, married, two children. He and his wife married very early—she was 14, he was 16. They have children 20 and 18 years of age. The boy is in the army. The girl just got married. Troy has a lot of interests. He hunts, fishes, and raises hunting dogs. He belongs to several service clubs and is active in his church. His wife works for the University of Montana as an administrative assistant to the department chairman of a large department. Troy is quiet and easy going. His friends call him a "good old boy."

Stick: As I see it, you can't let this get you. Get him straightened out. Don't lose a good man with 12 years with the company unless you have to.

Currie is 33 and very ambitious. He worked his way through the University of Washington's business school as an accounting major. He tried public accounting and didn't like it. He joined Wheeler's accounting department and asked to switch functions. He made a record for himself as the saleman responsible for sales in British Columbia. He was made sales manager six months ago. A bachelor, he enjoys a good time. But he has no serious outside interests. His career is his hobby.

Currie has just flown to Missoula and is met at the plane by Harlow.

---

20. AMERICAN STEEL WORKS

The American Steel Works (ASW) is a large firm which manufactures a wide variety of steel products. One of its plants is located in Richmond, Indiana.

As with many firms, American Steel has negotiated an affirmative action program with the Equal Employment Opportunity Commission (EEOC). Managers throughout the company have had it impressed upon them that they should hire and promote as many minority persons and females as possible.

Angelo Pieruccini is the office manager at ASW's Richmond plant. He recently hired a black woman named Jessie Mae Brown. She is a graduate of Richmond High School in its vocational program. She is a clerk-typist.

Her supervisor, Debbie Braker, has recently reported to Pieruccini that she is having trouble with Brown. According to Braker, Brown comes in late consistently. She is also absent from work about once a week.

> **Braker:** I've talked to Jessie Mae several times now. I told her that her work was good and that we missed her when she wasn't here. She never calls in when she's absent, by the way. I even gave her a raise and praised her work as often as possible. She just doesn't respond.

Debbie also related how the other girls are complaining that they have to do Brown's work. They also complained when they heard she got a raise, saying this was reverse discrimination.

> **Pieruccini:** What kind of excuses, if any, does she give for being late or absent?
>
> **Braker:** Oh, she's got a hundred stories! Each one is different. Monday morning, she arrived an hour late. I asked her why. Believe it or not, she said: "There was a terrible wind storm near where I live. So I had to stop by the graveyard to see if the wind had blown the family headstone over." I'm about at the end of my rope!

This is Brown's first job. She's had it for six months. She lives with several girl friends in an apartment. This is her first time living away from the family. She feels Braker is too bossy, and she really doesn't pay much attention to her.

Braker has been working since she left high school. She is 39 years old. She has worked all these years, except for six months when her daughter was born. Her husband was killed in Korea, and she is the sole support of her daughter. She gets a small military pension from the government.

She worked 16 years before she became a supervisor. She took a series of clerk-typist jobs, trying to find the best paying job each time. She takes her supervisory job seriously and she has recommended termination in several other cases less serious than Brown's.

Pieruccini is 53 years old. He was born in Italy, and he has worked his way up the hard way. He is married and has six children. It is hard for him to understand anyone who isn't willing to take advantage of the opportunities available in America. He works hard and expects to see others do likewise. He's been with ASW for 26 years and has been office manager the past 6. At one point in his discussion with Braker he said, "Everyone seems scared to death of the EEOC. Not me. If she doesn't cut it, she goes. I don't care about her color!"

21. CONFLICT IN PERSONALITY

Turner Plumbing Equipment Company is a medium-sized manufacturing firm with headquarters in St. Joseph, Missouri. Recently, Lynn Zimet, a regional sales manager, was told by Cameron Kulp, the sales manager, to terminate Anthony Burkey, a salesman who operates out of Sheridan, Wyoming, in Zimet's territory.

Kulp had observed Burkey at sales meetings and similar occasions and immediately disliked him. Burkey did nothing special to upset Kulp. Their personalities were not compatible.

Burkey's sales record was fine. Zimet had ten salesmen. He would rate Burkey as his third or fourth best salesmen, but he'd only been in the territory a year. Burkey's territory was a tough one for Turner. Turner had never been strong there. Besides, the potential for his territory wasn't that great.

Zimet had made this case with Kulp, but Kulp said: "Look, his sales record is below average. Besides he's not the kind of salesman with a future here. We're doing him a favor to move him into a situation elsewhere where he can do better, don't you see?"

Zimet felt he'd hurt his own future some by standing up for Burkey. He felt he had little choice but to terminate Burkey. At age 57, Zimet was not exactly in great demand elsewhere. He needed the money, too. He was going to try to stay on to age 70, if he lived that long.

Burkey is 26 years old. He had two years of junior college at Fort Hayes State in Kansas. He'd been in the Air Force for four years. He feels he's worked hard for Turner. Times are rough now and there aren't a lot of jobs around. Burkey is quiet and idealistic. Burkey has a wife and three children, one of whom is a spastic child.

Zimet is scheduled to work the territory with Burkey next week.

22.   GIBSON PETROLEUM, LTD.

Gibson Petroleum (GP) is a moderate-sized oil exploration firm. Its head-quarters are located in Red Deer, Alberta. The firm explores for oil in Alberta, British Columbia, Northwest Territory, and the Yukon.

Gibson presently employs about 600 persons. This number has gone as high as 800 and as low as 200. The number of employees varies by the amount of business Gibson can sustain at any one time.

Gibson's personnel manager, John Sorenson, is to retire in nine months. He has recommended that the firm hire a professionally trained personnel man with at least ten years' experience. Instead, J. W. F. Gibson, the firm's president, has decided to appoint Harry VonTwistern to this position.

VonTwistern has given 15 years' service to GP. His wife wants him to stay home more of the time instead of going off to the exploration sites as he has for 15 years. VonTwistern is 50 years old. He was graduated in petroleum engineering from MIT 25 years ago.

VonTwistern went to see Sorenson.

EXHIBIT 1
Gibson Petroleum organization chart

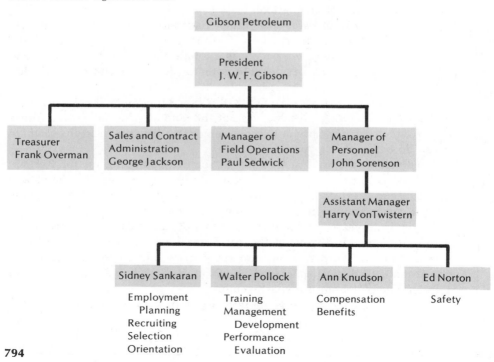

VonTwistern: John, I'm your replacement, I guess. I am really excited at the prospect of starting out on this new career. But, all I know is oil exploration. I've never spent any time in the office. I know everything there is to know about the field, but I am a complete novice about personnel work. Where do I start?

Exhibit 1 is an organization chart of GP's personnel department. The four-person department also has clerical help, employee consultants, and extra trainers, as needed.

Sidney Sankaran is 27 years old, a graduate of the University of Calgary in personnel several years ago. He has worked at GP for two years. Walter Pollock is 32 years old and has a degree in secondary education. He has worked at GP for six years. Ann Knudson is 37 years old, a graduate of the University of British Columbia in economics. She has worked at GP for 15 years. Ed Norton is 42 years old, an engineer and a graduate of the University of Washington. He has worked at GP for 12 years.

Discussion question

1. You are John Sorenson. Design a program to develop VonTwistern into a top-knotch personnel executive.

23. MOTOR CYCLES, LTD.

Motor Cycles (MCL), a British firm, has a large division in Kitchener, Ontario. The firm manufactures high-quality, high-performance motorcycles for the Canadian and U.S. markets.

Motorcycles have been increasing in popularity for some years. There has been a great deal of good publicity about bikes on television and in other media. No longer is it assumed that if you ride a bike you are part of a gang or of lower-class origins. Many people see them as fun, adventure, and an answer to the energy crisis.

MCL's plant has 500 employees at present. Because of new machinery, better job design, low turnover, and good training, the labor productivity rate has been increasing. For example, the rate was 4 percent ten years

TABLE 1
Labor productivity level per employee and value added as percent of sales revenue

	Labor productivity level per employee	Value added as percent of sales revenue		
		48%	50%	52%
Time		$3.80m	$3.96m	$4.12m
Three years ago	$6,740	564	588	611
Two years ago	$8,010	475	495	514
One year ago	$8,240	462	481	500

ago, 6 percent five years ago, and has risen to the level of 8 percent at present.

Employment turnover has been dropping. It was 11 percent per year ten years ago, 6 percent five years ago, and in the last five years has been 6½ percent, 6 percent, 7 percent, 5½ percent, and last year 5 percent.

Recently, the personnel department was asked to prepare some data on labor productivity for the last three years. Table 1 is the result.

Discussion question

1. Top management wishes you to prepare an employment forecast based on these data for the next several years. No new technological changes are anticipated during this period. Sales forecast is for $10,925,000.

24. WATER POLLUTION AGENCY

The Water Pollution Agency of a large state government in the eastern United States recently decided to investigate the effectiveness of various recruiting methods it had been using. Because of recent increases in emphasis

TABLE 1
Write-in applicants at Water Pollution Agency

Year	Number of positions open	Number of letters received	Number selected from write-ins
1964	10	54	1
1965	15	60	2
1966	20	59	1
1967	15	54	1
1968	20	52	2
1969	25	72	3
1970	27	85	2
1971	25	97	1
1972	30	86	2
1973	35	110	1

Note: The agency did not hire its full quota each year. So the total selected does not always equal the number of positions open.

TABLE 2
Walk-in applicants at Water Pollution Agency

Year	Number of positions open	Number of walk-ins received	Number selected from walk-in's
1964	10	6	1
1965	15	8	0
1966	20	10	2
1967	15	12	1
1968	20	10	3
1969	25	14	0
1970	27	12	1
1971	25	16	2
1972	30	13	0
1973	35	17	3

Note: The agency did not hire its full quota each year. So the total selected does not always equal the number of positions open.

TABLE 3
Advertising and recruiting at Water Pollution Agency

Year	New York Times				Wall Street Journal			Los Angeles Times			Professional journal (1)			Professional journal (2)		
	Number of positions open	Number of letters received	Number selected	Cost	Number of letters received	Number selected	Cost	Number of letters received	Number selected	Cost	Number of letters received	Number selected	Cost	Number of letters received	Number selected	Cost
1964	10	10	1	$100	3	0	$ 75	5	0	$ 75	12	2	$100	16	2	$ 75
1965	15	8	3	120	4	1	75	4	1	85	10	3	100	15	2	75
1966	20	11	3	140	2	0	85	6	2	100	7	4	100	12	3	100
1967	15	6	1	140	4	2	85	5	1	100	6	2	150	4	2	100
1968	20	5	2	140	4	1	85	4	3	100	6	3	150	7	3	100
1969	25	7	2	150	4	2	100	12	2	125	10	5	150	17	4	125
1970	27	9	3	150	5	1	100	15	2	125	18	5	150	18	5	125
1971	25	12	4	150	9	2	100	18	3	125	15	4	175	20	4	150
1972	30	7	2	150	8	2	100	12	3	125	20	5	175	26	6	150
1973	35	6	3	150	6	3	120	10	4	125	18	7	175	23	5	150

Note: The agency did not hire its full quota each year. So the total selected does not always equal the number of positions open.

TABLE 4
Employee referrals at Water Pollution Agency

Year	Number of positions open	Number of applicants	Number selected
1964	10	7	2
1965	15	9	3
1966	20	10	4
1967	15	13	4
1968	20	16	3
1969	25	18	5
1970	27	21	6
1971	25	19	5
1972	30	23	8
1973	35	24	9

Note: The agency did not hire its full quota each year. So the total selected does not always equal the number of positions open.

in the area of pollution, the agency was planning to increase substantially its recruiting efforts.

The first source of recruits is from unsolicited letters requesting information and sometimes including resumés and so forth. Table 1 summarizes data on this source for recent years. The cost of processing each of these letters was calculated as follows: clerical time, $10, and managerial time, $12. These estimates do not include costs of applicants who are given serious consideration and who receive many interviews, a site visit, and so forth. Such costs are the same for all methods.

A second source of recruits is walk-ins—candidates who arrive to be interviewed, normally after a call to arrange an interview. Table 2 presents the data on these candidates. The cost of walk-ins was calculated as follows per employee: clerical time, $5, and managerial time, $36.

A third source is advertising. The agency runs ads in the *New York Times, The Wall Street Journal, The Los Angeles Times,* and two professional journals.

Table 3 presents the data on this method. The costs, in addition to the ad costs, were the same as for write-ins: clerical time, $10, and managerial time, $12.

Finally, the agency encourages referrals by present employees. Table 4 presents the data on this source. The costs per referral were about the same as for walk-ins.

1. Discussion question

1. Evaluate the effectiveness of each recruiting method presently used. Which would you increase or decrease? Consider the following additions—private employment agencies and college recruiting by the agency. Project the estimated costs and benefits of each of these. Finally, prepare a recommendation to the agency head for implementation to recruit 45 persons in 1974, 55 in 1975, 65 in 1976, 75 in 1976.

25. EASTERN SCHOOL DISTRICT

Eastern School District is a medium-sized district in the eastern part of the country. The district has 883 employees distributed as follows:

Administrators
  Principals and district administrators 49
Primary teachers 312
Secondary teachers 316
Clerical 87
Operative
  Custodians, maintenance, and so forth 119

The district operates one special education facility, one vocational education high school, 26 primary schools, six junior high schools, and four high schools.

Eastern is located near a state university. Many of the younger teachers stay a relatively short time, since they are primarily supporting their spouses through graduate or professional school. The turnover ratio for each category of employment is given in Table 1.

Dr. John Fleming, superintendent of schools, attributes the decline in turnover to several factors. He was able to get an increase in the wages of clerical and operative employees approved by the school board. He feels that the decline in teacher turnover is due to the attractiveness of the district and the steady increase in the number of career teachers. Many teachers, especially the women, now return to the classroom when their own families enter school. In the past, many women taught a few years and left the profession when they started their families.

Although there has been a decline in turnover. Superintendent Fleming wishes to reduce it further. He believes turnover is expensive in training costs, disrupts the system, and lowers morale. He asked Jane Cutler, professor of educational administration at the nearby state university, to develop an orientation program for the district. He is not sure whether or not the same program should be given to teachers as to other employees. To assure that

TABLE 1
Turnover at Eastern schools

	1964	1965	1966	1967	1968
Administrators	3%	3½ %	4%	3½ %	3%
Primary school teachers	31	28	27	29	23
Secondary school teachers	19	16	15	15	14
Clerical employees	20	22	21	16	17
Operative employees	33	31	28	27	26
	1969	1970	1971	1972	1973
Administrators	2%	1%	0%	2%	3%
Primary school teachers	20	19	20	22	24
Secondary school teachers	12	13	11	9	7
Clerical employees	15	10	13	14	12
Operative employees	23	21	17	16	18

the schools in the district cooperate, Dr. Fleming would like a control system set up to be monitored by the school district office.

At present, the relevant material that might be covered includes (1) salary scales, (2) summer school teaching, (3) extracurricular activities policies, (4) promotion opportunities, (5) adult education policies, (6) benefits (insurance–health, life, and accident; credit union; pension plan; cafeterias; vacations and rest periods; and social security and workers' compensation), and (7) working conditions (hours of work, punctuality, fire protection, clothing to be worn, proper attitude, and the P.T.A.).

There might be other factors which should be covered. Professor Cutler thought that she might begin her orientation by outlining a good program and a reasonable follow-up system. Then she might sample teacher and other employee responses to her ideas.

Discussion question

1. You are Professor Cutler. Design an orientation program or programs for the district. Prepare a strategy for follow-up control. Describe how you would test the system for acceptance prior to introducing it into Eastern School District.

26. STOESS YARN, INC.

Stoess Yarn Company has a plant located in Charlestown, South Carolina. The jobs in the plant are relatively simple and require only a small amount of training. The intelligence and mechanical ability necessary to do the job effectively are minimal.

Recently the Equal Employment Opportunity Commission had a complaint about the Charlestown plant. It investigated and required the firm to file an affirmative action program. It noted:

Although Charlestown area has a black population of at least 40 percent the distribution of blacks at the plant is as follows: top management—none; middle management and staff—none; supervisory management—1 percent; and employees management—6 percent.

We require that Stoess hire and retain two black top managers and staff, five black middle managers, nine black supervisors, and 150 black nonsupervisory employees.

We also note that although the employees are 74 percent women, there are only three female supervisors, and there are no female middle or top managers.

We require that Stoess hire and retain five female top managers, 11 female middle managers, and 16 female supervisors.

The sales trend for Stoess has been downward. The marketing department is projecting no sales increase next year. In fact, Stoess had furloughed 15 employees each month prior to the EEOC visit.

TABLE 1
Seniority distribution of Stoess employees

Seniority	Years (in percent)					
	<5	6–10	11–15	16–20	21–25	>25
Top managers	0	0	7	32	28	33
Middle managers	0	5	13	29	29	23
Supervisory managers	2	16	20	27	23	12
Nonsupervisory employees	20	29	26	18	6	1

The seniority distribution of the present Stoess employees is given in Table 1. The number of employees involved in the study was top management, 15; middle management and staff, 35; supervisory management, 50; and nonsupervisory employees, 175.

Discussion question

1. You are Charles Tedrowe, personnel manager of Stoess. Draw up your plan to meet with the EEOC and develop an implementation plan that would reach the EEOC goals.

Indexes

Name index

Subject index

This book has been set in 10 and 9 point Compano, leaded 2 points. Part numbers and titles, and chapter titles are 20 point Roma. Chapter numbers are 48 point Roma.